Less managing. More teaching. Greater learning.

 INSTRUCTORS...

Would you like your **students** to show up for class **more prepared**?
(Let's face it, class is much more fun if everyone is engaged and prepared...)

Want an **easy way to assign** homework online and track student **progress**?
(Less time grading means more time teaching...)

Want an **instant view** of student or class performance relative to learning objectives? *(No more wondering if students understand...)*

Need to **collect data and generate reports** required for administration or accreditation? *(Say goodbye to manually tracking student learning outcomes...)*

Want to **record and post your lectures** for students to view online?

 With **McGraw-Hill's *Connect*™ *Plus Business Statistics*,**

INSTRUCTORS GET:

- Simple **assignment management**, allowing you to spend more time teaching.
- **Auto-graded** assignments, quizzes, and tests.
- **Detailed Visual Reporting** where student and section results can be viewed and analyzed.
- Sophisticated **online testing** capability.
- A **filtering and reporting** function that allows you to easily select Excel-based homework problems as well as assign and report on materials that are correlated to accreditation standards, learning outcomes, and Bloom's taxonomy.
- An easy-to-use **lecture capture** tool.
- The option to **upload course documents** for student access.

Want an online, **searchable version** of your textbook?

Wish your textbook could be **available online** while you're doing your assignments?

 ### *Connect™ Plus Business Statistics* eBook

If you choose to use *Connect™ Plus Business Statistics*, you have an affordable and searchable online version of your book integrated with your other online tools.

Connect™ Plus Business Statistics eBook offers features like:

- Topic search
- Direct links from assignments
- Adjustable text size
- Jump to page number
- Print by section

 Want to get more **value** from your textbook purchase?

Think learning business statistics should be a bit more **interesting**?

 ### Check out the STUDENT RESOURCES section under the *Connect™* Library tab.

Here you'll find a wealth of resources designed to help you achieve your goals in the course. You'll find things like **quizzes, PowerPoints, and Internet activities** to help you study. Every student has different needs, so explore the STUDENT RESOURCES to find the materials best suited to you.

Bruce L. Bowerman
Miami University

Richard T. O'Connell
Miami University

Emily S. Murphree
Miami University

J. B. Orris
Butler University

Essentials of Business Statistics

FOURTH EDITION

with major contributions by

Steven C. Huchendorf
University of Minnesota

Dawn C. Porter
University of Southern California

Patrick J. Schur
Miami University

McGraw-Hill
Irwin

ESSENTIALS OF BUSINESS STATISTICS

Published by McGraw-Hill/Irwin, a business unit of The McGraw-Hill Companies, Inc., 1221 Avenue of the Americas, New York, NY, 10020. Copyright © 2012, 2010, 2008, 2004 by The McGraw-Hill Companies, Inc. All rights reserved. No part of this publication may be reproduced or distributed in any form or by any means, or stored in a database or retrieval system, without the prior written consent of The McGraw-Hill Companies, Inc., including, but not limited to, in any network or other electronic storage or transmission, or broadcast for distance learning.

Some ancillaries, including electronic and print components, may not be available to customers outside the United States.

This book is printed on acid-free paper.

2 3 4 5 6 7 8 9 0 DOW/DOW 1 0 9 8 7 6 5 4 3 2 1

ISBN   978-0-07-340182-9
MHID 0-07-340182-X

Vice president and editor-in-chief: *Brent Gordon*
Editorial director: *Stewart Mattson*
Publisher: *Tim Vertovec*
Executive editor: *Steve Schuetz*
Senior developmental editor: *Wanda J. Zeman*
Marketing manager: *Kathleen White*
Lead project manager: *Harvey Yep*
Senior buyer: *Michael R. McCormick*
Lead designer: *Matthew Baldwin*
Senior photo research coordinator: *Keri Johnson*
Photo researcher: *PoYee Oster*
Senior media project manager: *Jennifer Lohn*
Cover designer: *Laurie Entringer*
Cover image: *© Getty Images*
Typeface: *10/12 Times New Roman*
Compositor: *MPS Limited, a Macmillan Company*
Printer: *RR Donnelley, Willard*

Library of Congress Cataloging-in-Publication Data

Essentials of business statistics / Bruce L. Bowerman ... [et al.].—4th ed.
     p. cm.
   Includes bibliographical references and indexes.
   ISBN-13: 978-0-07-340182-9 (alk. paper)
   ISBN-10: 0-07-340182-X (alk. paper)
   1. Commercial statistics. I. Bowerman, Bruce L.
HF1017.B6554 2012
519.5—dc22
                                                  2010046179

About the Authors

Bruce L. Bowerman Bruce L. Bowerman is professor emeritus of decision sciences at Miami University in Oxford, Ohio. He received his Ph.D. degree in statistics from Iowa State University in 1974, and he has over 41 years of experience teaching basic statistics, regression analysis, time series forecasting, survey sampling, and design of experiments to both un-

dergraduate and graduate students. In 1987 Professor Bowerman received an Outstanding Teaching award from the Miami University senior class, and in 1992 he received an Effective Educator award from the Richard T. Farmer School of Business Administration. Together with Richard T. O'Connell, Professor Bowerman has written 17 textbooks. In his spare time, Professor Bowerman enjoys watching movies and sports, playing tennis, and designing houses.

Richard T. O'Connell Richard T. O'Connell is associate professor of decision sciences at Miami University in Oxford, Ohio. He has more than 36 years of experience teaching basic statistics, statistical quality control and process improvement, regression analysis, time series forecasting, and design of experiments to both undergraduate and graduate business students.

He also has extensive consulting experience and has taught workshops dealing with statistical process control and process improvement for a variety of companies in the Midwest. In 2000 Professor O'Connell received an Effective Educator award from the Richard T. Farmer School of Business Administration. Together with Bruce L. Bowerman, he has written 17 textbooks. In his spare time, Professor O'Connell enjoys fishing, collecting 1950s and 1960s rock music, and following the Green Bay Packers and Purdue University sports.

Emily S. Murphree Emily S. Murphree is Associate Professor of Statistics in the Department of Mathematics and Statistics at Miami University in Oxford, Ohio. She received her Ph.D. degree in statistics from the University of North Carolina and does research in applied probability. Professor Murphree received Miami's College of Arts and Science Distin-

guished Educator Award in 1998. In 1996, she was named one of Oxford's Citizens of the Year for her work with Habitat for Humanity and for organizing annual Sonia Kovalevsky Mathematical Sciences Days for area high school girls. Her enthusiasm for hiking in wilderness areas of the West motivated her current research on estimating animal population sizes.

James Burdeane "Deane" Orris J. B. Orris is a professor of management science at Butler University in Indianapolis, Indiana. He received his Ph.D. from the University of Illinois in 1971, and in the late 1970s with the advent of personal computers, he combined his interest in statistics and computers to write one of the first personal computer statistics

packages—MICROSTAT. Over the past 20 years, MICROSTAT has evolved into MegaStat which is an Excel add-in statistics program. He wrote an Excel book, *Essentials: Excel 2000 Advanced,* in 1999 and *Basic Statistics Using Excel and MegaStat* in 2006. He has taught statistics and computer courses in the College of Business Administration of Butler University since 1971. He is a member of the American Statistical Association and is past president of the Central Indiana Chapter. In his spare time, Professor Orris enjoys reading, working out, and working in his woodworking shop.

In *Essentials of Business Statistics, Fourth Edition,* we provide a modern, practical, and unique framework for teaching the first course in business statistics. As in previous editions, this edition uses real or realistic examples, continuing case studies, and a business improvement theme to teach business statistics. Moreover, we believe this fourth edition features significantly simplified explanations, an improved topic flow, and a judicious use of the best, most interesting examples. We now discuss the attributes and new features that we think make this book an effective learning tool. Specifically, the book includes:

- **Continuing case studies that tie together different statistical topics.** These continuing case studies span not only individual chapters but also groups of chapters. Students tell us that when new statistical topics are developed using familiar data from previous examples, their "fear factor" is reduced. Of course, to keep the examples from becoming tired and overused, we introduce new case studies throughout the book.

- **Business improvement conclusions that explicitly show how statistical results lead to practical business decisions.** When appropriate, we conclude examples and case studies with a practical business improvement conclusion. To emphasize the text's theme of business improvement, icons **BI** are placed in the page margins to identify when statistical analysis has led to an important business conclusion. Each conclusion is also highlighted in yellow for additional clarity.

- **New chapter introductions that list learning objectives and preview the case study analysis to be carried out in each chapter.**

- **A shorter and more intuitive introduction to business statistics in Chapter 1.** Chapter 1 introduces data (using a new home sales example that illustrates the value of data), discusses data sources, and gives an intuitive presentation of sampling. The technical discussion of how to select random and other types of samples has been moved to Chapter 7 (Sampling and Sampling Distributions), but the reader has the option of reading the sampling discussion in Chapter 7 immediately after completing Chapter 1.

- **A streamlined discussion of the graphical and numerical methods of descriptive statistics in Chapters 2 and 3.** The streamlining has been accomplished by rewriting some explanations, using fewer examples, and focusing on the best, most interesting examples.

- **A simplified and improved discussion of probability and probability distributions.** We have removed the somewhat complex AccuRatings case from Chapter 4 (Probability) and replaced it with some simpler examples, including the song rating case. We have also moved counting rules (formerly in an appendix) to an optional section in Chapter 4, and we have moved the hypergeometric distribution (formerly in an appendix) to an optional section in Chapter 5 (Discrete Random Variables). In addition, we have introduced continuous probability distributions using a more intuitive approach, and improved the explanation of the exponential distribution.

- **A simplified, unique, and more inferentially oriented approach to sampling distributions.** In previous editions, we have introduced sampling distributions by using the game show and stock return cases. Although many reviewers liked this approach, others preferred the introduction to sampling distributions to be more oriented toward statistical inference. In this new edition, we begin with a unique and realistic example of estimating the mean mileage of a population of six preproduction cars. Because four of the six cars will be taken to auto shows and not be subjected to testing (which could harm their appearance), the true population mean mileage is not known and must be estimated by using a random sample of two cars that will not be taken to auto shows. Expanding from this small example, we generalize the discussion and show the sampling distribution of the sample mean when we select a random sample of five cars from the first year's production of cars. The effect of sample size on the sampling distribution is then considered, as is the Central Limit Theorem.

AUTHORS

- **A simpler discussion of confidence intervals employing a more graphical approach.**
  We have completely rewritten and shortened the introduction to confidence intervals, using a simpler, more graphical approach. We have also added other new graphics throughout the chapter to help students more easily construct and interpret confidence intervals.

- **A simpler and more streamlined discussion of hypothesis testing.** This discussion includes an improved explanation of how to formulate null and alternative hypotheses, a shorter, five-step hypothesis testing procedure, and greatly improved hypothesis testing summary boxes that feature innovative graphics showing students how to use critical values and p-values.

- **Simpler and improved discussions of comparing means, proportions, and variances.** In Chapter 10 (Statistical Inferences Based on Two Samples) we only briefly mention the unrealistic variance-known approach to comparing two population means and move directly to the realistic variance-unknown case. We have also improved the discussion of comparing two population variances. In Chapter 11 (Experimental Design and Analysis of Variance) we have simplified and clarified the discussions of the F-tests and multiple comparisons for one-way ANOVA and the randomized block design. We have also added a short section on two-way ANOVA.

- **A new and better flowing discussion of simple and multiple regression analysis.** Previous editions intertwined two case studies through the basic discussion of simple regression and intertwined two case studies through the basic discussion of multiple regression. The book now employs a single new case, The Tasty Sub Shop Case, throughout the basic explanation of each technique. Based partly on how the real Quiznos restaurant chain suggests that business entrepreneurs evaluate potential sites for Quiznos restaurants, the Tasty Sub Shop case considers an entrepreneur who is evaluating potential sites for a Tasty Sub Shop restaurant. In the simple regression chapter, the entrepreneur predicts Tasty Sub Shop revenue by using population in the area. In the multiple regression and model building chapter, the entrepreneur predicts Tasty Sub Shop revenue by using population and business activity in the area. After the basic explanations of simple regression and multiple regression are completed, a further example illustrating each technique is presented. (The fuel consumption case of previous editions is now an exercise.) All discussions have been simplified and improved, and we have included a new short section on using squared and interaction variables, as well as slightly expanded discussions of model building and residual analysis in multiple regression.

- **Increased emphasis on Excel (and to some extent, MINITAB) throughout the text.** Previous editions included approximately equal proportions of Excel, MINITAB, and MegaStat (an Excel add-in) outputs throughout the main text. Because three different types of output might seem overwhelming, we now include approximately equal proportions of Excel and MINITAB outputs throughout the main text. (MegaStat outputs appear in the main text only in advanced chapters where there is no viable way to use Excel.) There are now many more Excel outputs (which often replace the former MegaStat outputs) in the main text, and there are also more MINITAB outputs. The end-of-chapter appendices still show how to use all three software packages, and there are MegaStat outputs included in the end-of-chapter appendices that illustrate how to use MegaStat.

Bruce L. Bowerman
Richard T. O'Connell
Emily S. Murphree
J. B. Orris

Chapter Introductions

Each chapter begins with a list of the section topics that are covered in the chapter, along with chapter learning objectives and a preview of the case study analysis to be carried out in the chapter.

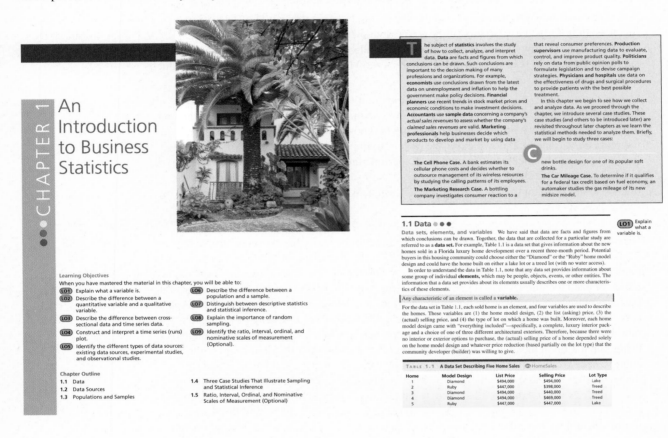

Continuing Case Studies and Business Improvement Conclusions

The main chapter discussions feature real or realistic examples, continuing case studies, and a business improvement theme. The continuing case studies span not only individual chapters but also groups of chapters and tie together different statistical topics. To emphasize the text's theme of business improvement, icons 🅱 are placed in the page margins to identify when statistical analysis has led to an important business improvement conclusion. Each conclusion is also highlighted in yellow for additional clarity. For example, in Chapters 1 and 3 we consider **The Cell Phone Case:**

TABLE 1.4   A Sample of Cellular Usages (in minutes) for 100 Randomly Selected Employees
DS CellUse

75	485	37	547	753	93	897	694	797	477
654	578	504	670	490	225	509	247	597	173
496	553	0	198	507	157	672	296	774	479
0	822	705	814	20	513	546	801	721	273
879	433	420	521	648	41	528	359	367	948
511	704	535	585	341	530	216	512	491	0
542	562	49	505	461	496	241	624	885	259
571	338	503	529	737	444	372	555	290	830
719	120	468	730	853	18	479	144	24	513
482	683	212	418	399	376	323	173	669	611

EXAMPLE 3.5 The Cell Phone Case

Remember that if the cellular cost per minute for the random sample of 100 bank employees is over 18 cents per minute, the bank will benefit from automated cellular management of its calling plans. Last month's cellular usages for the 100 randomly selected employees are given in Table 1.4 (page 9), and a dot plot of these usages is given in the page margin. If we add together the usages, we find that the 100 employees used a total of 46,625 minutes. Furthermore, the total cellular cost incurred by the 100 employees is found to be $9,317 (this total includes base costs, overage costs, long distance, and roaming). This works out to an average of $9,317/46,625 = $.1998, or 19.98 cents per minute. Because this average cellular cost per minute exceeds 18 cents per minute, the bank will hire the cellular management service to manage its calling plans.

🅱

TEXT'S FEATURES

Figures and Tables

Throughout the text, charts, graphs, tables, and Excel and MINITAB outputs are used to illustrate statistical concepts. For example:

- In Chapter 3 (**Descriptive Statistics: Numerical Methods**), the following figures are used to help explain the **Empirical Rule**. Moreover, in **The Car Mileage Case** an automaker uses the Empirical Rule to find estimates of the "typical," "lowest," and "highest" mileage that a new midsize car should be expected to get in combined city and highway driving. In actual practice, real automakers provide similar information broken down into separate estimates for city and highway driving—see the Buick LaCrosse new car sticker in Figure 3.14.

- In chapter 7 (**Sampling and Sampling Distributions**), the following figures (and others) are used to help explain the **sampling distribution of the sample mean** and the **Central Limit Theorem**. In addition, the figures describe different applications of random sampling in **The Car Mileage Case**, and thus this case is used as an integrative tool to help students understand sampling distributions.

- In Chapter 8 (**Confidence Intervals**), the following figure (and others) are used to help explain the meaning of a **95 percent confidence interval** for the population mean. Furthermore, in **The Car Mileage Case** an automaker uses a confidence interval procedure specified by the Environmental Protection Agency (EPA) to find the EPA estimate of a new midsize model's true mean mileage.

FIGURE 8.2   Three 95 Percent Confidence Intervals for μ

- In Chapter 9 (**Hypothesis Testing**), a five-step hypothesis testing procedure, **new graphical hypothesis testing summary boxes**, and many graphics are used to show how to carry out hypothesis tests.

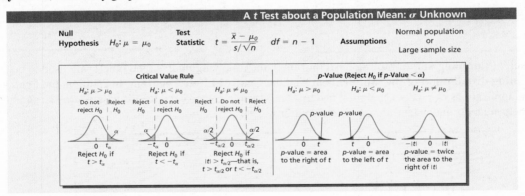

A t Test about a Population Mean: σ Unknown

Null Hypothesis $H_0: \mu = \mu_0$ Test Statistic $t = \dfrac{\bar{x} - \mu_0}{s/\sqrt{n}}$ $df = n - 1$ Assumptions   Normal population or Large sample size

The Five Steps of Hypothesis Testing

1. State the null hypothesis H_0 and the alternative hypothesis H_a.
2. Specify the level of significance α.
3. Select the test statistic.

Using a critical value rule:

4. Determine the critical value rule for deciding whether to reject H_0.
5. Collect the sample data, compute the value of the test statistic, and decide whether to reject H_0. Interpret the statistical results.

Using a p-value:

4. Collect the sample data, compute the value of the test statistic, and compute the p-value.
5. Reject H_0 at level of significance α if the p-value is less than α. Interpret the statistical results.

FIGURE 9.5   Testing $H_0: \mu = 1.5$ versus $H_a: \mu < 1.5$ by Using a Critical Value and the p-Value

- In Chapters 13 and 14 (**Simple Linear and Multiple Regression**), a substantial number of data plots, Excel and MINITAB outputs, and other graphics are used to teach simple and multiple regression analysis. For example, in **The Tasty Sub Shop Case** a business entrepreneur uses data plotted in Figures 14.1 and 14.2 and the Excel and MINITAB outputs in Figure 14.4 to predict the yearly revenue of a potential Tasty Sub Shop restaurant site on the basis of the population and business activity near the site. Using the **95 percent prediction interval** on the MINITAB output and projected restaurant operating costs, the entrepreneur decides whether to purchase a Tasty Sub Shop franchise for the potential restaurant site.

FIGURE 14.1 Plot of *y* (Yearly Revenue) versus x_1 (Population Size)

FIGURE 14.2 Plot of *y* (Yearly Revenue) versus x_2 (Business Rating)

FIGURE 14.4 Excel and MINITAB Outputs of a Regression Analysis of the Tasty Sub Shop Revenue Data in Table 14.1 Using the Model $y = \beta_0 + \beta_1 x_1 + \beta_2 x_2 + \varepsilon$

(a) The Excel output

Regression Statistics

Multiple R	0.9905
R Square	0.9810 [8]
Adjusted R Square	0.9756 [9]
Standard Error	36.6856 [7]
Observations	10

ANOVA

	df	SS	MS	F	Significance F
Regression	2	486355.7 [10]	243177.8	180.689 [13]	9.46E-07 [14]
Residual	7	9420.8 [11]	1345.835		
Total	9	495776.5 [12]			

	Coefficients	Standard Error [4]	t Stat [5]	P-value [6]	Lower 95%	Upper 95% [19]
Intercept	125.289 [1]	40.9333	3.06	0.0183	28.4969	222.0807
population	14.1996 [2]	0.9100	15.60	1.07E-06	12.0478	16.3517
bus_rating	22.8107 [3]	5.7692	3.95	0.0055	9.1686	36.4527

(b) The MINITAB output

```
The regression equation is
revenue = 125 + 14.2 population + 22.8 bus_rating

Predictor      Coef      SE Coef [4]      T [5]      P [6]
Constant     125.29 [1]   40.93            3.06       0.018
population   14.1996 [2]   0.91            15.6        0.000
bus_rating   22.811 [3]   5.769            3.95       0.006

S = 36.6856 [7]       R-Sq = 98.10% [8]       R-Sq(adj) = 97.6% [9]

Analysis of Variance

Source          DF       SS           MS           F            P
Regression       2   486356 [10]   243178       180.69 [13]   0.000 [14]
Residual Error   7     9421 [11]     1346
Total            9   495777 [12]

Predicted Values for New Observations
New Obs   Fit [15]    SE Fit [16]        95% CI [17]              95% PI [18]
   1       956.6         15          (921.0, 992.2)          (862.8, 1050.4)

Values of Predictors for New Observations
New Obs    population     bus_rating
   1          47.3            7
```

[1] b_0	[2] b_1	[3] b_2	[4] s_{b_j} = standard error of the estimate b_j	[5] t statistics	[6] p-values for t statistics	[7] s = standard error
[8] R^2	[9] Adjusted R^2	[10] Explained variation	[11] SSE = Unexplained variation	[12] Total variation	[13] F(model) statistic	
[14] p-value for F(model)	[15] $\hat{y}$ = point prediction when x_1 = 47.3 and x_2 = 7		[16] $s_{\hat{y}}$ = standard error of the estimate $\hat{y}$			
[17] 95% confidence interval when x_1 = 47.3 and x_2 = 7		[18] 95% prediction interval when x_1 = 47.3 and x_2 = 7		[19] 95%-confidence interval for β_j		

Exercises

Many of the exercises in the text use real data. Data sets are identified by an icon in the text and are included on the Online Learning Center (OLC): www.mhhe.com/bowermaness4e. Exercises in each section are broken into two parts—"Concepts" and "Methods and Applications"—and there are supplementary and Internet exercises at the end of each chapter.

2.7 Below we give pizza restaurant preferences for 25 randomly selected college students.
DS PizzaPizza

Godfather's	Little Caesar's	Papa John's	Pizza Hut	Domino's	Papa John's
Papa John's	Papa John's	Pizza Hut	Pizza Hut	Papa John's	Domino's
Little Caesar's	Domino's	Domino's	Godfather's	Pizza Hut	Papa John's
Pizza Hut	Pizza Hut	Papa John's	Papa John's	Godfather's	Papa John's
Domino's					

a Find the frequency distribution and relative frequency distribution for these data.
b Construct a percentage bar chart for these data.
c Construct a percentage pie chart for these data.
d Which restaurant is most popular with these students? Least popular?

Chapter Ending Material and Excel/MINITAB/MegaStat® Tutorials

The end-of-chapter material includes a chapter summary, a glossary of terms, important formula references, and comprehensive appendices that show students how to use Excel, MINITAB, and MegaStat.

Chapter Summary

We began this chapter by presenting and comparing several measures of **central tendency**. We defined the **population mean** and we saw how to estimate the population mean by using a **sample mean**. We also defined the **median** and **mode**, and we compared the mean, median, and mode for symmetrical distributions and for distributions that are skewed to the right or left. We then studied measures of **variation** (or *spread*). We defined the **range**, **variance**, and **standard deviation**, and we saw how to estimate a population variance and standard deviation by using a sample. We learned that a good way to interpret the standard deviation when a population is (approximately) normally distributed is to use the **Empirical Rule**, and we studied **Chebyshev's Theorem**, which gives us intervals containing reasonably large fractions of

the population units no matter what the population's shape might be. We also saw that, when a data set is highly skewed, it is best to use **percentiles** and **quartiles** to measure variation, and we learned how to construct a **box-and-whiskers plot** by using the quartiles.

After learning how to measure and depict central tendency and variability, we presented several optional topics. First, we discussed several numerical measures of the relationship between two variables. These included the **covariance**, the **correlation coefficient**, and the **least squares line**. We then introduced the concept of a **weighted mean** and also explained how to compute descriptive statistics for **grouped data**. Finally, we showed how to calculate the **geometric mean** and demonstrated its interpretation.

Construct a scatter plot of sales volume versus advertising expenditure as in Figure 2.24 on page 67 (data file: SalesPlot.xlsx).

- Enter the advertising and sales data in Table 2.20 on page 67 into columns A and B—advertising expenditures in column A with label "Ad Exp" and sales values in column B with label "Sales Vol." **Note: The variable to be graphed on the horizontal axis must be in the first column (that is, the left-most column) and the variable to be graphed on the vertical axis must be in the second column (that is, the rightmost column).**
- Click in the range of data to be graphed, or select the entire range of the data to be graphed.
- Select Insert : Scatter : Scatter with only Markers
- The scatter plot will be displayed in a graphics window. Move the plot to a chart sheet and edit appropriately.

Glossary of Terms

box-and-whiskers display (box plot): A graphical portrayal of a data set that depicts both the central tendency and variability of the data. It is constructed using Q_1, M_d, and Q_3. (pages 123, 124)
central tendency: A term referring to the middle of a population or sample of measurements. (page 101)

normal curve: A bell-shaped, symmetrical relative frequency curve. We will present the exact equation that gives this curve in Chapter 6. (page 113)
outer fences (in a box-and-whiskers display): Points located $3 \times IQR$ below Q_1 and $3 \times IQR$ above Q_3. (page 124)

WHAT TECHNOLOGY CONNECTS

McGraw-Hill Connect™ Business Statistics

Less Managing. More Teaching. Greater Learning. McGraw-Hill *Connect Business Statistics* is an online assignment and assessment solution that connects students with the tools and resources they'll need to achieve success. McGraw-Hill *Connect Business Statistics* helps prepare students for their future by enabling faster learning, more efficient studying, and higher retention of knowledge.

Features. *Connect Business Statistics* offers a number of powerful tools and features to make managing assignments easier, so faculty can spend more time teaching. With *Connect Business Statistics,* students can engage with their coursework anytime and anywhere, making the learning process more accessible and efficient. *Connect Business Statistics* offers you the features described below.

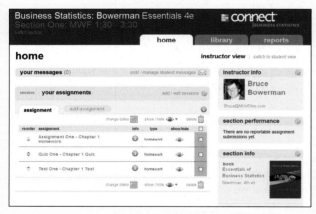

Simple Assignment Management. With *Connect Business Statistics,* creating assignments is easier than ever, so you can spend more time teaching and less time managing. The assignment management function enables you to:

- Create and deliver assignments easily with selectable end-of-chapter questions and test bank items.
- Streamline lesson planning, student progress reporting, and assignment grading to make classroom management more efficient than ever.
- Go paperless with the eBook and online submission and grading of student assignments.

Smart Grading. When it comes to studying, time is precious. *Connect Business Statistics* helps students learn more efficiently by providing feedback and practice material when they need it, where they need it. When it comes to teaching, your time also is precious. The grading function enables you to:

- Have assignments scored automatically, giving students immediate feedback on their work and side-by-side comparisons with correct answers.
- Access and review each response; manually change grades or leave comments for students to review.
- Reinforce classroom concepts with practice tests and instant quizzes.

Integration of Excel Data Sets. A convenient feature is the inclusion of an Excel data file link in many

problems using data sets in their calculation. This allows students to easily launch into Excel, work the problem, and return to Connect to key in the answer.

Instructor Library. The *Connect Business Statistics* Instructor Library is your repository for additional resources to improve student engagement in and out of class. You can select and use any asset that enhances your lecture. The *Connect Business Statistics* Instructor Library includes:

- eBook
- PowerPoint presentations
- Test Bank
- Solutions Manual
- Digital Image Library

Student Study Center. The *Connect Business Statistics* Student Study Center is the place for students to access additional resources. The Student Study Center:

- Offers students quick access to lectures, practice materials, eBooks, and more.
- Provides instant practice material and study questions, easily accessible on-the-go.

Student Progress Tracking. Connect Business Statistics keeps instructors informed about how each student, section, and class is performing, allowing for more productive use of lecture and office hours. The progress-tracking function enables you to:

- View scored work immediately and track individual or group performance with assignment and grade reports.
- Access an instant view of student or class performance relative to learning objectives.
- Collect data and generate reports required by many accreditation organizations, such as AACSB.

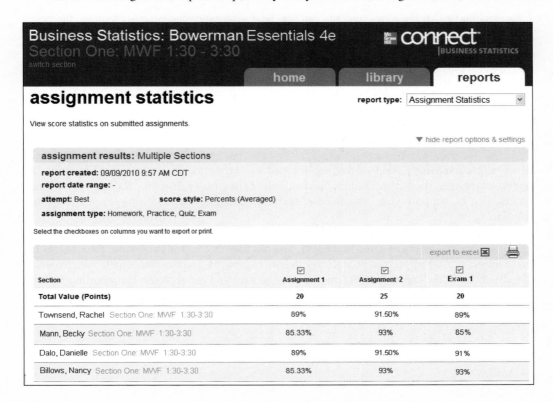

Section	Assignment 1	Assignment 2	Exam 1
Total Value (Points)	20	25	20
Townsend, Rachel Section One: MWF 1:30-3:30	89%	91.50%	89%
Mann, Becky Section One: MWF 1:30-3:30	85.33%	93%	85%
Dalo, Danielle Section One: MWF 1:30-3:30	89%	91.50%	91%
Billows, Nancy Section One: MWF 1:30-3:30	85.33%	93%	93%

McGraw-Hill Connect Plus Business Statistics. McGraw-Hill reinvents the textbook learning experience for the modern student with *Connect Plus Business Statistics.* A seamless integration of an eBook and *Connect Business Statistics, Connect Plus Business Statistics* provides all of the *Connect Business Statistics* features plus the following:

- An integrated eBook, allowing for anytime, anywhere access to the textbook.
- Dynamic links between the problems or questions you assign to your students and the location in the eBook where that problem or question is covered.
- A powerful search function to pinpoint and connect key concepts in a snap.

In short, *Connect Business Statistics* offers you and your students powerful tools and features that optimize your time and energy, enabling you to focus on course content, teaching, and student learning. *Connect Business Statistics* also offers a wealth of content resources for both instructors and students. This state-of-the-art, thoroughly tested system supports you in preparing students for the world that awaits. For more information about Connect, go to www.mcgrawhillconnect.com, or contact your local McGraw-Hill sales representative.

Tegrity Campus: Lectures 24/7

Tegrity Campus is a service that makes class time available 24/7 by automatically capturing every lecture in a searchable format for students to review when they study and complete assignments. With a simple one-click start-and-stop process, you capture all computer screens and corresponding audio. Students can replay any part of any class with easy-to-use browser-based viewing on a PC or Mac.

Educators know that the more students can see, hear, and experience class resources, the better they learn. In fact, studies prove it. With Tegrity Campus, students quickly recall key moments by using Tegrity Campus's unique search feature. This search helps students efficiently find what they need, when they need it, across an entire semester of class recordings. Help turn all your students' study time into learning moments immediately supported by your lecture.

To learn more about Tegrity, watch a 2-minute Flash demo at http://tegritycampus.mhhe.com.

Assurance-of-Learning Ready

Many educational institutions today are focused on the notion of *assurance of learning,* an important element of some accreditation standards. *Essentials of Business Statistics* is designed specifically to support your assurance-of-learning initiatives with a simple, yet powerful, solution.

Each test bank question for *Essentials of Business Statistics* maps to a specific chapter learning outcome/objective listed in the text. You can use our test bank software, EZ Test and EZ Test Online, or *Connect Business Statistics* to easily query for learning outcomes/objectives that directly relate to the learning objectives for your course. You can then use the reporting features of EZ Test to aggregate student results in similar fashion, making the collection and presentation of assurance-of-learning data simple and easy.

AACSB Statement

The McGraw-Hill Companies is a proud corporate member of AACSB International. Understanding the importance and value of AACSB accreditation, *Essentials of Business Statistics* recognizes the curricula guidelines detailed in the AACSB standards for business accreditation by connecting selected questions in the text and the test bank to the six general knowledge and skill guidelines in the AACSB standards.

The statements contained in *Essentials of Business Statistics* are provided only as a guide for the users of this textbook. The AACSB leaves content coverage and assessment within the purview of individual schools, the mission of the school, and the faculty. While *Essentials of Business Statistics* and the teaching package make no claim of any specific AACSB qualification or evaluation, we have labeled within *Essentials of Business Statistics* selected questions according to the six general knowledge and skills areas.

category analysis: Multiple Sections

• Bowerman, Bruce: Section One: MWF 1:30-3:30   • Bowerman, Bruce: Section Two: TTh 2:00-5:00

report created: 09/09/2010 4:45PM CDT

report date range: 01/01/2010 - 09/09/2010

Assignment 1

Click a subcategory to view **section** details

expand all | collapse all   export to excel ☒   🖶

Difficulty	# questions	# times submitted	# students submitted	category score
▶ Difficulty: Easy	20	60	1/2	17.36%
▶ Difficulty: Hard	16	43	1/2	3.85%
▶ Difficulty: Medium	12	21	1/2	0.7%

Learning Objective	# questions	# times submitted	# students submitted	category score
▶ Learning Objective: 01-1	4	12	1/2	0.5%
▶ Learning Objective: 01-2	8	24	1/2	26.04%
▶ Learning Objective: 01-4	8	24	1/2	17.17%
▶ Learning Objective: 01-5	2	6	1/2	1.17%
▶ Learning Objective: 01-6	8	24	1/2	8.33%

McGraw-Hill Customer Care Information

At McGraw-Hill, we understand that getting the most from new technology can be challenging. That's why our services don't stop after you purchase our products. You can e-mail our Product Specialists 24 hours a day to get product-training online. Or you can search our knowledge bank of Frequently Asked Questions on our support website. For Customer Support, call **800-331-5094**, e-mail hmsupport@mcgraw-hill.com, or visit www.mhhe.com/support. One of our Technical Support Analysts will be able to assist you in a timely fashion.

WHAT RESOURCES ARE AVAILABLE FOR INSTRUCTORS

ALEKS®

ALEKS is an assessment and learning program that provides individualized instruction in Business Statistics, Business Math, and Accounting. Available online in partnership with McGraw-Hill/Irwin, ALEKS interacts with students much like a skilled human tutor, with the ability to assess precisely a student's knowledge and provide instruction on the exact topics the student is most ready to learn. By providing topics to meet individual students' needs, allowing students to move between explanation and practice, correcting and analyzing errors, and defining terms, ALEKS helps students to master course content quickly and easily.

ALEKS also includes an Instructor Module with powerful, assignment-driven features and extensive content flexibility. ALEKS simplifies course management and allows instructors to spend less time with administrative tasks and more time directing student learning.

To learn more about ALEKS, visit www.aleks.com/highered/business. ALEKS is a registered trademark of ALEKS Corporation.

Online Learning Center: www.mhhe.com/bowermaness4e

The Online Learning Center (OLC) is the text website with online content for both students and instructors. It provides the instructor with a complete Instructor's Manual in Word format, the complete Test Bank in both Word files and computerized EZ Test format, Instructor PowerPoint slides, text art files, an introduction to ALEKS®, an introduction to McGraw-Hill *Connect Business Statistics*™, access to the eBook, and more.

 TEST

All test bank questions are available in an EZ Test electronic format. Included are a number of multiple-choice, true/false, and short-answer questions and problems. The answers to all questions are given, along with a rating of the level of difficulty, Bloom's taxonomy question type, and AACSB knowledge category.

Visual Statistics

www.mhhe.com/bowermaness4e

Visual Statistics 2.2 by Doane, Mathieson, and Tracy is a software program for teaching and learning statistics concepts. It is unique in that it allows students to learn the concepts through interactive experimentation and visualization. The software and worktext promote active learning through competency-building exercises, individual and team projects, and built-in databases. Over 400 data sets from business settings are included within the package as well as a worktext in electronic format. This software is available on the Online Learning Center (OLC) for Bowerman 4e.

WebCT/Blackboard/eCollege

All of the material in the Online Learning Center is also available in portable WebCT, Blackboard, or e-College content "cartridges" provided free to adopters of this text.

WHAT RESOURCES ARE AVAILABLE FOR STUDENTS

CourseSmart

CourseSmart is a new way to find and buy eTextbooks. CourseSmart has the largest selection of eTextbooks available anywhere, offering thousands of the most commonly adopted textbooks from a wide variety of higher education publishers. CourseSmart eTextbooks are available in one standard online reader with full text search, notes and highlighting, and e-mail tools for sharing notes between classmates. Visit www.CourseSmart.com for more information on ordering.

Online Learning Center: www.mhhe.com/bowermaness4e

The Online Learning Center (OLC) provides students with the following content:

- Quizzes
- Data sets
- PowerPoint
*• PowerPoint (narrated)
*• ScreenCam Tutorials
*• Visual Statistics

- Chapter 15
- Appendixes

*Premium content

Business Statistics Center (BSC): www.mhhe.com/bstat/

The BSC contains links to statistical publications and resources, software downloads, learning aids, statistical websites and databases, and McGraw-Hill/Irwin product websites and online courses.

WHAT SOFTWARE IS AVAILABLE

MegaStat® for Excel (ISBN: 0077395131)

MegaStat is a full-featured Excel add-in by J. B. Orris of Butler University that is available with this text. It performs statistical analyses within an Excel workbook. It does basic functions such as descriptive statistics, frequency distributions, and probability calculations, as well as hypothesis testing, ANOVA, and regression.

MegaStat output is carefully formatted. Ease-of-use features include Auto Expand for quick data selection and Auto Label detect. Since MegaStat is easy to use, students can focus on learning statistics without being distracted by the software. MegaStat is always available from Excel's main menu. Selecting a menu item pops up a dialog box. MegaStat works with all recent versions of Excel, including Excel 2010.

MINITAB®/SPSS®/JMP®

Minitab® Student Version 14, SPSS® Student Version 18.0, and JMP 8 Student Edition are software tools that are available to help students solve the business statistics exercises in the text. Each is available in the student version and can be packaged with any McGraw-Hill business statistics text.

ACKNOWLEDGMENTS

We wish to thank many people who have helped to make this book a reality. We thank Drena Bowerman, who spent many hours cutting and taping and making trips to the copy shop, so that we could complete the manuscript on time. As indicated on the title page, we thank Professor Steven C. Huchendorf, University of Minnesota; Dawn C. Porter, University of Southern California; and Patrick J. Schur, Miami University; for major contributions to this book. We also thank Susan Cramer of Miami University for helpful advice on writing this book.

We also wish to thank the people at McGraw-Hill/Irwin for their dedication to this book. These people include executive editor Steve Schuetz, who is an extremely helpful resource to the authors; executive editor Dick Hercher, who persuaded us initially to publish with McGraw-Hill/Irwin and who continues to offer sound advice and support; senior developmental editor Wanda Zeman, who has shown great dedication to the improvement of this book; and lead project manager Harvey Yep, who has very capably and diligently guided this book through its production and who has been a tremendous help to the authors. We also thank our former executive editor, Scott Isenberg, for the tremendous help he has given us in developing all of our McGraw-Hill business statistics books.

Many reviewers have contributed to this book, and we are grateful to all of them. They include

Lawrence Acker, Harris-Stowe State University
Ajay K. Aggarwal, Millsaps College
Mohammad Ahmadi, University of Tennessee–Chattanooga
Sung K. Ahn, Washington State University
Eugene Allevato, Woodbury University
Mostafa S. Aminzadeh, Towson University
Henry Ander, Arizona State University–Tempe
Randy J. Anderson, California State University–Fresno
Mohammad Bajwa, Northampton Community College
Ron Barnes, University of Houston–Downtown
John D. Barrett, University of North Alabama
Mary Jo Boehms, Jackson State Community College
Pamela A. Boger, Ohio University–Athens
Dave Bregenzer, Utah State University
Philip E. Burian, Colorado Technical University–Sioux Falls
Giorgio Canarella, California State University–Los Angeles
Margaret Capen, East Carolina University
Priscilla Chaffe-Stengel, California State University–Fresno
Ali A. Choudhry, Florida International University
Richard Cleary, Bentley College
Bruce Cooil, Vanderbilt University
Sam Cousley, University of Mississippi
Teresa A Dalton, University of Denver
Nit Dasgupta, University of Wisconsin–Eau Claire
Linda Dawson, University of Washington–Tacoma
Jay Devore, California Polytechnic State University
Joan Donohue, University of South Carolina
Anne Drougas, Dominican University
Mark Eakin, University of Texas–Arlington
Hammou Elbarmi, Baruch College
Soheila Fardanesh, Towson University
Nicholas R. Farnum, California State University–Fullerton
James Flynn, Cleveland State University
Lillian Fok, University of New Orleans
Tom Fox, Cleveland State Community College
Charles A. Gates Jr., Olivet Nazarene University
Linda S. Ghent, Eastern Illinois University
Allen Gibson, Seton Hall University
Scott D. Gilbert, Southern Illinois University
Nicholas Gorgievski, Nichols College
TeWhan Hahn, University of Idaho

Clifford B. Hawley, West Virginia University
Rhonda L. Hensley, North Carolina A&T State University
Eric Howington, Valdosta State University
Zhimin Huang, Adelphi University
C. Thomas Innis, University of Cincinnati
Jeffrey Jarrett, University of Rhode Island
Craig Johnson, Brighan Young University
Nancy K. Keith, Missouri State University
Thomas Kratzer, Malone University
Alan Kreger, University of Maryland
Michael Kulansky, University of Maryland
Risa Kumazawa, Georgia Southern University
David A. Larson, University of South Alabama
John Lawrence, California State University–Fullerton
Lee Lawton, University of St. Thomas
John D. Levendis, Loyola University–New Orleans
Barbara Libby, Walden University
Carel Ligeon, Auburn University–Montgomery
Kenneth Linna, Auburn University–Montgomery
David W. Little, High Point University
Donald MacRitchie, Framingham State College
Edward Markowski, Old Dominion University
Mamata Marme, Augustana College
Jerrold H. May, University of Pittsburgh
Brad McDonald, Northern Illinois University
Richard A. McGowan, Boston College
Christy McLendon, University of New Orleans
John M. Miller, Sam Houston State University
Robert Mogull, California State University–Sacramento
Jason Molitierno, Sacred Heart University
Daniel Monchuck, University of Southern Mississippi
Tariq Mughal, University of Utah
Patricia Mullins, University of Wisconsin–Madison
Thomas Naugler, Johns Hopkins University
Quinton J. Nottingham, Virginia Tech University
Ceyhun Ozgur, Valparaiso University
Linda M. Penas, University of California–Riverside
Cathy Poliak, University of Wisconsin–Milwaukee
Michael D. Polomsky, Cleveland State University
Robert S. Pred, Temple University
Sunil Ramlall, University of St. Thomas

ACKNOWLEDGMENTS

Steven Rein, California Polytechnic State University
Donna Retzlaff-Roberts, University of South Alabama
Peter Royce, University of New Hampshire
Fatollah Salimian, Salisbury University
Yvonne Sandoval, Pima Community College
Sunil Sapra, California State University–Los Angeles
Patrick J. Schur, Miami University
William L. Seaver, University of Tennessee
Kevin Shanahan, University of Texas–Tyler
Arkudy Shemyakin, University of St. Thomas
Charlie Shi, Daiblo Valley College
Joyce Shotick, Bradley University
Plamen Simeonov, University of Houston Downtown
Bob Smidt, California Polytechnic State University
Rafael Solis, California State University–Fresno
Toni M. Somers, Wayne State University
Ronald L. Spicer, Colorado Technical University–Sioux Falls
Mitchell Spiegel, Johns Hopkins University

Timothy Staley, Keller Graduate School of Management
David Stoffer, University of Pittsburgh
Cliff Stone, Ball State University
Courtney Sykes, Colorado State University
Bedassa Tadesse, University of Minnesota–Duluth
Stanley Taylor, California State University–Sacramento
Patrick Thompson, University of Florida
Emmanuelle Vaast, Long Island University–Brooklyn
Ed Wallace, Malcolm X College
Bin Wang, Saint Edwards University
Allen Webster, Bradley University
Blake Whitten, University of Iowa
Susan Wolcott-Hanes, Binghamton University
Mustafa Yilmaz, Northeastern University
Gary Yoshimoto, Saint Cloud State University
William F. Younkin, Miami University
Xiaowei Zhu, University of Wisconsin–Milwaukee

We also wish to thank the error checkers, Lou Patille, Colorado Heights University, and Peter Royce, University of New Hampshire, who were very helpful. Most importantly, we wish to thank our families for their acceptance, unconditional love, and support.

DEDICATION

Bruce L. Bowerman
To my wife, children, sister, and
other family members:
Drena
Michael, Jinda, Benjamin, and Lex
Asa, Nicole, and Laine
Susan
Barney, Fiona, and Radeesa
Daphne, Chloe, and Edgar
Gwyneth and Tony
Callie, Bobby, Marmalade, Randy,
and Penney
Clarence, Quincy, and Teddy

Richard T. O'Connell
To my children:
Christopher and Bradley

J. B. Orris
To my children:
Amy and Bradley

Emily S. Murphree
To Kevin and the Math Ladies

Chapter-by-Chapter Revisions for 4/e

Chapter 1

- Chapter is totally rewritten.
- New example involving home sales illustrating the value of data.
- 7 new or rewritten exercises.

Chapter 2

- Rewritten/reorganized example describing Jeep purchasing patterns.
- Additional discussion of histograms.
- Revised instructions for creating bar charts and pie charts in Excel.

Chapter 3

- Slightly shortened discussions of central tendency and variation.

Chapter 4

- AccuRatings case removed and replaced with simpler examples, including the song rating case.
- Optional section on counting rules added to the chapter.
- 11 new exercises added.

Chapter 5

- Optional section on the Hypergeometric distribution added to the chapter.
- 7 new exercises added.

Chapter 6

- Rewritten introduction to continuous probability distributions.
- Rewritten explanation of the exponential distribution.

Chapter 7

- New discussion of random sampling.
- Rewritten discussion of the sampling distribution of the sample mean.
- New example of the sampling distribution of the sample mean employing the car mileage case.
- New optional section on stratified random, cluster, and systematic sampling.
- New optional section about surveys and errors in survey sampling.
- 20 new exercises—5 involving the game show case

Chapter 8

- Rewritten discussion of z-based confidence intervals for a population mean when sigma is known (including a step-by-step approach and two revised illustrative figures).
- 8 new marginal figures that supplement examples of calculating confidence intervals.
- 4 new exercises.

Chapter 9

- Revised explanation of the null and alternative hypotheses.
- Revised step-by-step procedure for performing a hypothesis test.
- New hypothesis-testing summary boxes using innovative graphics.
- New debt-to-equity ratio case.
- Revised electronic article surveillance case.
- 15 new/revised exercises.

Chapter 10

- Proceeds directly to comparing two population means for the variance-unknown case.
- 10 new marginal figures that supplement examples demonstrating two sample confidence intervals and hypothesis tests.

Chapter 11

- Revised and shortened discussions of one-way ANOVA and the randomized block design.
- New section on two-way ANOVA.
- Substantial number of new Excel and MINITAB outputs.
- 4 new exercises.

Chapter 12

- No significant changes.

Chapter 13

- Tasty Sub Shop case replaces the fuel consumption case as the primary example.
- Explanation of the simple linear regression model completely rewritten in the context of the Tasty Sub Shop case.
- Chapter substantially rewritten in the context of the Tasty Sub Shop case.
- Durbin–Watson test added.
- 9 new exercises (7 of these in the context of the fuel consumption case).

Chapter 14

- Tasty Sub Shop case replaces the fuel consumption case as the primary example.
- Explanation of the multiple regression model substantially rewritten in the context of the Tasty Sub Shop case.
- Chapter substantially rewritten in the context of the Tasty Sub Shop case.
- New section on using squared and interaction variables.
- Discussions of model building slightly expanded (stepwise regression and partial F-test added.)
- Discussion of residual analysis slightly expanded (outlier analysis added).
- 8 new exercises (4 of these in the context of the fuel consumption case).

Additions to website:

Appendix B:	Properties of the Mean and the Variance of a Random Variable, and the Covariance
Appendix C:	Derivations of the Mean and Variance of $\bar{x}$ and $\hat{p}$
Appendix D:	Confidence Intervals for Parameters of Finite Populations
Appendix E:	Logistic Regression

Brief Table of Contents

Chapter 1   2
An Introduction to Business Statistics

Chapter 2   34
Descriptive Statistics: Tabular and Graphical
Methods

Chapter 3   100
Descriptive Statistics: Numerical Methods

Chapter 4   154
Probability

Chapter 5   190
Discrete Random Variables

Chapter 6   228
Continuous Random Variables

Chapter 7   270
Sampling and Sampling Distributions

Chapter 8   304
Confidence Intervals

Chapter 9   342
Hypothesis Testing

Chapter 10   386
Statistical Inferences Based on Two Samples

Chapter 11   428
Experimental Design and Analysis
of Variance

Chapter 12   462
Chi-Square Tests

Chapter 13   490
Simple Linear Regression Analysis

Chapter 14   558
Multiple Regression and Model Building

Appendix A   630
Statistical Tables

**Answers to Most Odd-Numbered
Exercises**   651

References   657

Photo Credits   659

Index   660

Chapter 15   On Website
Process Improvement Using Control Charts

Appendix B   On Website
Properties of the Mean and the Variance
of a Random Variable, and the Covariance

Appendix C   On Website
Derivations of the Mean and Variance of
$\bar{x}$ and $\hat{p}$

Appendix D   On Website
Confidence Intervals for Parameters
of Finite Populations

Appendix E   On Website
Logistic Regression

Table of Contents

Chapter 1
An Introduction to Business Statistics
1.1 ▦ Data   3
1.2 ▦ Data Sources   5
1.3 ▦ Populations and Samples   7
1.4 ▦ Three Case Studies That Illustrate Sampling and Statistical Inference   8
1.5 ▦ Ratio, Interval, Ordinal, and Nominative Scales of Measurement (Optional)   14
App 1.1 ▦ Getting Started with Excel   18
App 1.2 ▦ Getting Started with MegaStat   23
App 1.3 ▦ Getting Started with MINITAB   27

Chapter 2
Descriptive Statistics: Tabular and Graphical Methods
2.1 ▦ Graphically Summarizing Qualitative Data   35
2.2 ▦ Graphically Summarizing Quantitative Data   42
2.3 ▦ Dot Plots   54
2.4 ▦ Stem-and-Leaf Displays   56
2.5 ▦ Cross-tabulation Tables (Optional)   61
2.6 ▦ Scatter Plots (Optional)   67
2.7 ▦ Misleading Graphs and Charts (Optional)   70
App 2.1 ▦ Tabular and Graphical Methods Using Excel   80
App 2.2 ▦ Tabular and Graphical Methods Using MegaStat   88
App 2.3 ▦ Tabular and Graphical Methods Using MINITAB   92

Chapter 3
Descriptive Statistics: Numerical Methods
3.1 ▦ Describing Central Tendency   101
3.2 ▦ Measures of Variation   110
3.3 ▦ Percentiles, Quartiles, and Box-and-Whiskers Displays   120
3.4 ▦ Covariance, Correlation, and the Least Squares Line (Optional)   129
3.5 ▦ Weighted Means and Grouped Data (Optional)   134

3.6 ▦ The Geometric Mean (Optional)   139
App 3.1 ▦ Numerical Descriptive Statistics Using Excel   146
App 3.2 ▦ Numerical Descriptive Statistics Using MegaStat   149
App 3.3 ▦ Numerical Descriptive Statistics Using MINITAB   151

Chapter 4
Probability
4.1 ▦ The Concept of Probability   155
4.2 ▦ Sample Spaces and Events   157
4.3 ▦ Some Elementary Probability Rules   163
4.4 ▦ Conditional Probability and Independence   169
4.5 ▦ Bayes' Theorem (Optional)   178
4.6 ▦ Counting Rules (Optional)   182

Chapter 5
Discrete Random Variables
5.1 ▦ Two Types of Random Variables   191
5.2 ▦ Discrete Probability Distributions   192
5.3 ▦ The Binomial Distribution   203
5.4 ▦ The Poisson Distribution (Optional)   213
5.5 ▦ The Hypergeometric Distribution (Optional)   219
App 5.1 ▦ Binomial, Poisson, and Hypergeometric Probabilities Using Excel   224
App 5.2 ▦ Binomial, Poisson, and Hypergeometric Probabilities Using MegaStat   226
App 5.3 ▦ Binomial, Poisson, and Hypergeometric Probabilities Using MINITAB   227

Chapter 6
Continuous Random Variables
6.1 ▦ Continuous Probability Distributions   229
6.2 ▦ The Uniform Distribution   231
6.3 ▦ The Normal Probability Distribution   234
6.4 ▦ Approximating the Binomial Distribution by Using the Normal Distribution (Optional)   252
6.5 ▦ The Exponential Distribution (Optional)   256
6.6 ▦ The Normal Probability Plot (Optional)   259

App 6.1 ▦ Normal Distribution Using Excel 266

App 6.2 ▦ Normal Distribution Using MegaStat 267

App 6.3 ▦ Normal Distribution Using MINITAB 268

Chapter 7
Sampling and Sampling Distributions

7.1 ▦ Random Sampling 271

7.2 ▦ The Sampling Distribution of the Sample Mean 275

7.3 ▦ The Sampling Distribution of the Sample Proportion 288

7.4 ▦ Stratified Random, Cluster, and Systematic Sampling (Optional) 291

7.5 ▦ More about Surveys and Errors in Survey Sampling (Optional) 293

App 7.1 ▦ Generating Random Numbers Using Excel 301

App 7.2 ▦ Generating Random Numbers Using MegaStat 302

App 7.3 ▦ Generating Random Numbers and Simulating Sampling Distributions Using MINITAB 302

Chapter 8
Confidence Intervals

8.1 ▦ z-Based Confidence Intervals for a Population Mean: σ Known 305

8.2 ▦ t-Based Confidence Intervals for a Population Mean: σ Unknown 314

8.3 ▦ Sample Size Determination 321

8.4 ▦ Confidence Intervals for a Population Proportion 325

8.5 ▦ A Comparison of Confidence Intervals and Tolerance Intervals (Optional) 332

App 8.1 ▦ Confidence Intervals Using Excel 338

App 8.2 ▦ Confidence Intervals Using MegaStat 339

App 8.3 ▦ Confidence Intervals Using MINITAB 340

Chapter 9
Hypothesis Testing

9.1 ▦ The Null and Alternative Hypotheses and Errors in Hypothesis Testing 343

9.2 ▦ z Tests about a Population Mean: σ Known 349

9.3 ▦ t Tests about a Population Mean: σ Unknown 359

9.4 ▦ z Tests about a Population Proportion 363

9.5 ▦ Type II Error Probabilities and Sample Size Determination (Optional) 368

9.6 ▦ The Chi-Square Distribution (Optional) 374

9.7 ▦ Statistical Inference for a Population Variance (Optional) 375

App 9.1 ▦ One-Sample Hypothesis Testing Using Excel 382

App 9.2 ▦ One-Sample Hypothesis Testing Using MegaStat 383

App 9.3 ▦ One-Sample Hypothesis Testing Using MINITAB 384

Chapter 10
Statistical Inferences Based on Two Samples

10.1 ▦ Comparing Two Population Means by Using Independent Samples 387

10.2 ▦ Paired Difference Experiments 397

10.3 ▦ Comparing Two Population Proportions by Using Large, Independent Samples 405

10.4 ▦ Comparing Two Population Variances by Using Independent Samples 411

App 10.1 ▦ Two-Sample Hypothesis Testing Using Excel 422

App 10.2 ▦ Two-Sample Hypothesis Testing Using MegaStat 423

App 10.3 ▦ Two-Sample Hypothesis Testing Using MINITAB 425

Chapter 11
Experimental Design and Analysis of Variance

11.1 ▦ Basic Concepts of Experimental Design 429

11.2 ▦ One-Way Analysis of Variance 431

11.3 ▦ The Randomized Block Design 441

11.4 ▦ Two-Way Analysis of Variance 447

App 11.1 ▦ Experimental Design and Analysis of Variance Using Excel 457

App 11.2 ▦ Experimental Design and Analysis of Variance Using MegaStat 458

App 11.3 ▦ Experimental Design and Analysis of Variance Using MINITAB 460

Chapter 12
Chi-Square Tests

12.1 ▦ Chi-Square Goodness-of-Fit Tests 463

12.2 ▦ A Chi-Square Test for Independence 472

App 12.1 ▦ Chi-Square Tests Using Excel 483

App 12.2 ▦ Chi-Square Tests Using MegaStat 485

App 12.3 ▦ Chi-Square Tests Using MINITAB 487

Chapter 13
Simple Linear Regression Analysis

13.1 ▦ The Simple Linear Regression Model and the Least Squares Point Estimates 491

13.2 ■ Model Assumptions and the Standard Error 504

13.3 ■ Testing the Significance of the Slope and y-Intercept 507

13.4 ■ Confidence and Prediction Intervals 514

13.5 ■ Simple Coefficients of Determination and Correlation 520

13.6 ■ Testing the Significance of the Population Correlation Coefficient 525

13.7 ■ An F Test for the Model 526

13.8 ■ The QHIC Case 529

13.9 ■ Residual Analysis 531

13.10 ■ Some Shortcut Formulas (Optional) 546

App 13.1 ■ Simple Linear Regression Analysis Using Excel 552

App 13.2 ■ Simple Linear Regression Analysis Using MegaStat 554

App 13.3 ■ Simple Linear Regression Analysis Using MINITAB 556

Chapter 14
Multiple Regression and Model Building

14.1 ■ The Multiple Regression Model and the Least Squares Point Estimates 559

14.2 ■ Model Assumptions and the Standard Error 569

14.3 ■ R^2 and Adjusted R^2 571

14.4 ■ The Overall F Test 573

14.5 ■ Testing the Significance of an Independent Variable 575

14.6 ■ Confidence and Prediction Intervals 579

14.7 ■ The Sales Territory Performance Case 582

14.8 ■ Using Dummy Variables to Model Qualitative Independent Variables 584

14.9 ■ Using Squared and Interaction Variables 596

14.10 ■ Model Building and the Effects of Multicollinearity 601

14.11 ■ Residual Analysis in Multiple Regression 610

App 14.1 ■ Multiple Regression Analysis Using Excel 620

App 14.2 ■ Multiple Regression Analysis Using MegaStat 623

App 14.3 ■ Multiple Regression Analysis Using MINITAB 626

Appendix A
Statistical Tables 630

Answers to Most Odd-Numbered Exercises **651**

References **657**

Photo Credits **659**

Index **660**

Chapter 15 **On Website**
Process Improvement Using Control Charts

Appendix B **On Website**
Properties of the Mean and the Variance of a Random Variable, and the Covariance

Appendix C **On Website**
Derivations of the Mean and Variance of $\bar{x}$ and $\hat{p}$

Appendix D **On Website**
Confidence Intervals for Parameters of Finite Populations

Appendix E **On Website**
Logistic Regression

Essentials of Business Statistics

FOURTH EDITION

CHAPTER 1

An Introduction to Business Statistics

Learning Objectives

When you have mastered the material in this chapter, you will be able to:

LO1 Explain what a variable is.

LO2 Describe the difference between a quantitative variable and a qualitative variable.

LO3 Describe the difference between cross-sectional data and time series data.

LO4 Construct and interpret a time series (runs) plot.

LO5 Identify the different types of data sources: existing data sources, experimental studies, and observational studies.

LO6 Describe the difference between a population and a sample.

LO7 Distinguish between descriptive statistics and statistical inference.

LO8 Explain the importance of random sampling.

LO9 Identify the ratio, interval, ordinal, and nominative scales of measurement (Optional).

Chapter Outline

1.1 Data

1.2 Data Sources

1.3 Populations and Samples

1.4 Three Case Studies That Illustrate Sampling and Statistical Inference

1.5 Ratio, Interval, Ordinal, and Nominative Scales of Measurement (Optional)

he subject of **statistics** involves the study of how to collect, analyze, and interpret data. **Data** are facts and figures from which conclusions can be drawn. Such conclusions are important to the decision making of many professions and organizations. For example, **economists** use conclusions drawn from the latest data on unemployment and inflation to help the government make policy decisions. **Financial planners** use recent trends in stock market prices and economic conditions to make investment decisions. **Accountants** use **sample data** concerning a company's *actual sales revenues* to assess whether the company's *claimed sales revenues* are valid. **Marketing professionals** help businesses decide which products to develop and market by using data that reveal consumer preferences. **Production supervisors** use manufacturing data to evaluate, control, and improve product quality. **Politicians** rely on data from public opinion polls to formulate legislation and to devise campaign strategies. **Physicians and hospitals** use data on the effectiveness of drugs and surgical procedures to provide patients with the best possible treatment.

In this chapter we begin to see how we collect and analyze data. As we proceed through the chapter, we introduce several case studies. These case studies (and others to be introduced later) are revisited throughout later chapters as we learn the statistical methods needed to analyze them. Briefly, we will begin to study three cases:

The Cell Phone Case. A bank estimates its cellular phone costs and decides whether to outsource management of its wireless resources by studying the calling patterns of its employees.

The Marketing Research Case. A bottling company investigates consumer reaction to a new bottle design for one of its popular soft drinks.

The Car Mileage Case. To determine if it qualifies for a federal tax credit based on fuel economy, an automaker studies the gas mileage of its new midsize model.

1.1 Data ● ● ●

LO1 Explain what a variable is.

Data sets, elements, and variables   We have said that data are facts and figures from which conclusions can be drawn. Together, the data that are collected for a particular study are referred to as a **data set.** For example, Table 1.1 is a data set that gives information about the new homes sold in a Florida luxury home development over a recent three-month period. Potential buyers in this housing community could choose either the "Diamond" or the "Ruby" home model design and could have the home built on either a lake lot or a treed lot (with no water access).

In order to understand the data in Table 1.1, note that any data set provides information about some group of individual **elements,** which may be people, objects, events, or other entities. The information that a data set provides about its elements usually describes one or more characteristics of these elements.

Any characteristic of an element is called a **variable.**

For the data set in Table 1.1, each sold home is an element, and four variables are used to describe the homes. These variables are (1) the home model design, (2) the list (asking) price, (3) the (actual) selling price, and (4) the type of lot on which a home was built. Moreover, each home model design came with "everything included"—specifically, a complete, luxury interior package and a choice of one of three different architectural exteriors. Therefore, because there were no interior or exterior options to purchase, the (actual) selling price of a home depended solely on the home model design and whatever price reduction (based partially on the lot type) that the community developer (builder) was willing to give.

TABLE 1.1   A Data Set Describing Five Home Sales   ⦿ HomeSales

Home	Model Design	List Price	Selling Price	Lot Type
1	Diamond	$494,000	$494,000	Lake
2	Ruby	$447,000	$398,000	Treed
3	Diamond	$494,000	$440,000	Treed
4	Diamond	$494,000	$469,000	Treed
5	Ruby	$447,000	$447,000	Lake

The data in Table 1.1 are real (with some minor modifications to protect privacy) and were provided by a business executive—a friend of the authors—who recently received a promotion and needed to move to central Florida. While searching for a new home, the executive and his family visited the luxury home community and decided they wanted to purchase a Diamond model on a treed lot. The list price of this home was $494,000, but the developer offered to sell it for an "incentive" price of $469,000. Intuitively, the incentive price's $25,000 savings off list price seemed like a good deal. However, the executive resisted making an immediate decision. Instead, he decided to collect data on the selling prices of new homes recently sold in the community and use the data to assess whether the developer might be amenable to a lower offer. In order to collect "relevant data," the executive talked to local real estate professionals and learned that new homes sold in the community during the previous three months were a good indicator of current home value. Using real estate sales records, the executive also learned that five of the community's new homes had sold in the previous three months. The data given in Table 1.1 are the data that the executive collected about these five homes.

LO2 Describe the difference between a quantitative variable and a qualitative variable.

In order to understand the conclusions the business executive reached using the data in Table 1.1, we need to further discuss variables. For any variable describing an element in a data set, we carry out a **measurement** to assign a value of the variable to the element. For example, in the real estate example, real estate sales records gave the actual selling price of each home to the nearest dollar. In another example, a credit card company might measure the time it takes for a cardholder's bill to be paid to the nearest day. Or, in a third example, an automaker might measure the gasoline mileage obtained by a car in city driving to the nearest one-tenth of a mile per gallon by conducting a mileage test on a driving course prescribed by the Environmental Protection Agency (EPA). If the possible measurements of the values of a variable are numbers that represent quantities (that is, "how much" or "how many"), then the variable is said to be **quantitative.** For example, the actual selling price of a home, the payment time of a bill, and the gasoline mileage of a car are all quantitative. However, if we simply record into which of several categories an element falls, then the variable is said to be **qualitative** or **categorical.** Examples of categorical variables include (1) a person's gender, (2) the make of an automobile, (3) whether a person who purchases a product is satisfied with the product, and (4) the type of lot on which a home is built.[1]

Of the four variables in Table 1.1, two variables—list price and selling price—are quantitative, and two variables—model design and lot type—are qualitative. Furthermore, when the business executive examined Table 1.1, he noted that homes on lake lots had sold at their list price, but homes on treed lots had not. Because the executive and his family wished to purchase a Diamond model on a treed lot, the executive also noted that two Diamond models on treed lots had sold in the previous three months. One of these Diamond models had sold for the incentive price of $469,000, but the other had sold for a lower price of $440,000. Hoping to pay the lower price for his family's new home, the executive offered $440,000 for the Diamond model on the treed lot. Initially, the home builder turned down this offer, but two days later the builder called back and accepted the offer. The executive had used data to buy the new home for $54,000 less than the list price and $29,000 less than the incentive price!

LO3 Describe the difference between cross-sectional data and time series data.

LO4 Construct and interpret a time series (runs) plot.

Cross-sectional and time series data   Some statistical techniques are used to analyze *cross-sectional data,* while others are used to analyze *time series data.* **Cross-sectional data** are data collected at the same or approximately the same point in time. For example, suppose that a bank wishes to analyze last month's cell phone bills for its employees. Then, because the cell phone costs given by these bills are for different employees in the same month, the cell phone costs are cross-sectional data. **Time series data** are data collected over different time periods. For example, Table 1.2 presents the average basic cable television rate in the United States for each of the years 1995 to 2005. Figure 1.1 is a **time series plot**—also called a **runs plot**—of these data. Here we plot each television rate on the vertical scale versus its corresponding time index on the horizontal scale. For instance, the first cable rate ($23.07) is plotted versus 1995, the second cable rate (24.41) is plotted versus 1996, and so forth. Examining the time series plot, we see that the cable rates increased substantially from 1995 to 2005. Finally, because the five homes in Table 1.1 were sold over a three-month period that represented a relatively stable real estate market, we can consider the data in Table 1.1 to essentially be cross-sectional data.

---

[1]Optional Section 1.5 discusses two types of quantitative variables (ratio and interval) and two types of qualitative variables (ordinal and nominative).

Year	Average Basic Cable Rate
1995	$ 23.07
1996	24.41
1997	26.48
1998	27.81
1999	28.92
2000	30.37
2001	32.87
2002	34.71
2003	36.59
2004	38.14
2005	39.63

TABLE 1.2 The Average Basic Cable Rates in the U.S. from 1995 to 2005
DS BasicCable

Source: Kagan Research, LLC. From the Broadband Cable Financial Databook 2004, 2005 (copyright). Cable Program Investor, Dec. 16, 2004, March 30, 2006, and other publications, http://www.census.gov/compendia/statab/information_communications/

FIGURE 1.1 Time Series Plot of the Average Basic Cable Rates in the U.S. from 1995 to 2005
DS BasicCable

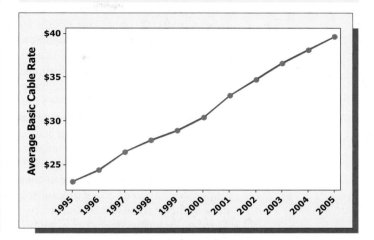

1.2 Data Sources ● ● ●

LO5 Identify the different types of data sources: existing data sources, experimental studies, and observational studies.

Data can be obtained from *existing sources* or from **experimental and observational studies.**

Existing sources Sometimes we can use data *already gathered* by public or private sources. The Internet is an obvious place to search for electronic versions of government publications, company reports, and business journals, but there is also a wealth of information available in the reference section of a good library or in county courthouse records.

If a business needs information about incomes in the Northeastern states, a natural source is the US Census Bureau's website at http://www.census.gov. By following various links posted on the homepage, you can find income and demographic data for specific regions of the country. Other useful websites for economic and financial data are listed in Table 1.3. All of these are trustworthy sources.

TABLE 1.3 Examples of Public Economic and Financial Data Sites

Title	Website	Data Type
Global Financial Data	http://www.globalfindata.com/	Annual data on stock markets, inflation rates, interest rates, exchange rates, etc.
National Bureau of Economic Research Macrohistory Database	http://www.nber.org/databases/macrohistory/contents/index.html	Historic data on production, construction, employment, money, prices, asset market transactions, foreign trade, and government activity
Federal Reserve Economic Data	http://www.stls.frb.org/fred/	Historical U.S. economic and financial data, including daily U.S. interest rates, monetary and business indicators, exchange rate, balance of payments, and regional economic data
Bureau of Labor Statistics	http://stats.bls.gov/	Data concerning employment, inflation, consumer spending, productivity, safety, labor demographics, and the like.
WebEc Economics Data	http://netec.wustl.edu/WebEc/	One of the best complete economics data links including both international and domestic data categorized by area and country
Economic Statistics Briefing Room	http://www.whitehouse.gov/fsbr/esbr.html	Links to the most current available values of federal economic indicators on 8 categories

Source: Prepared by Lan Ma and Jeffrey S. Simonoff. The authors provide no warranty as to the accuracy of the information provided.

However, given the ease with which anyone can post documents, pictures, weblogs, and video on the World Wide Web, not all sites are equally reliable. If we were to use a search engine from Google, Netscape, Yahoo, Ask.com, or AltaVista (just to name a few) to find information about the price of a two-bedroom apartment in Manhattan, we would be inundated by millions of "hits." (In fact, a recent search on Google using the keywords "price 2 bedroom apartments Manhattan" yielded 1,040,000 sites.) Some of the sources will be more useful, exhaustive, and error-free than others. Fortunately, the search engines prioritize the lists and provide the most relevant and highly used sites first.

Obviously, performing such web searches costs next to nothing and takes relatively little time, but the tradeoff is that we are also limited in terms of the type of information we are able to find. Another option may be to use a private data source. Most companies keep employee records, for example, and retail establishments retain information about their customers, products, and advertising results. Manufacturing companies may collect information about their processes and defect propagation in order to monitor quality. If we have no affiliation with these companies, however, these data may be more difficult to obtain.

Another alternative would be to contact a data collection agency, which typically incurs some kind of cost. You can either buy subscriptions or purchase individual company financial reports from agencies like Dun & Bradstreet, Bloomberg, Dow Jones & Company, Travel Industry of America, Graduate Management Admission Council, and the Educational Testing Service. If you need to collect specific information, some companies, such as ACNielsen and Information Resources, Inc., can be hired to collect the information for a fee.

Experimental and observational studies   There are many instances when the data we need are not readily available from a public or private source. The data might not have been collected at all or they may have been collected in a statistically unsound manner. In cases like these, we need to collect the data ourselves. Suppose we work for a soft drink producer and want to assess consumer reactions to a new bottled water. Since the water has not been marketed yet, we may choose to conduct taste tests, focus groups, or some other market research. Projecting political election results also requires information that is not readily available. In this case, exit polls and telephone surveys are commonly used to obtain the information needed to predict voting trends. New drugs for fighting disease are tested by collecting data under carefully controlled and monitored experimental conditions. In many marketing, political, and medical situations of these sorts, companies hire outside consultants or statisticians to help them obtain appropriate data. Regardless of whether newly minted data are gathered in-house or by paid outsiders, this type of data collection requires much more time, effort, and expense than are needed when data can be found from public or private sources.

When initiating a study, we first define our variable of interest, or **response variable.** Other variables, typically called **factors,** that may be related to the response variable of interest will also be measured. When we are able to set or manipulate the values of these factors, we have an **experimental study.** For example, a pharmaceutical company might wish to determine the most appropriate daily dose of a cholesterol-lowering drug for patients having cholesterol levels over 240 mg/dL, a level associated with a high risk of coronary disease. (http://www.americanheart.org/presenter.jhtml?identifier=4500) The company can perform an experiment in which one sample of patients receives a placebo; a second sample receives some low dose; a third a higher dose; and so forth. This is an experiment because the company controls the amount of drug each group receives. The optimal daily dose can be determined by analyzing the patients' responses to the different dosage levels given.

When analysts are unable to control the factors of interest, the study is **observational.** In studies of diet and cholesterol, patients' diets are not under the analyst's control. Patients are often unwilling or unable to follow prescribed diets; doctors might simply ask patients what they eat and then look for associations between the factor *diet* and the response variable *cholesterol.*

Asking people what they eat is an example of performing a **survey.** In general, people in a survey are asked questions about their behaviors, opinions, beliefs, and other characteristics. For instance, shoppers at a mall might be asked to fill out a short questionnaire which seeks their opinions about a new bottled water. In other observational studies, we might simply observe the behavior of people. For example, we might observe the behavior of shoppers as they look at a store display, or we might observe the interactions between students and teachers.

Exercises for Sections 1.1 and 1.2

CONCEPTS

connect

1.1 Define what we mean by a *variable,* and explain the difference between a quantitative variable and a qualitative (categorical) variable.

1.2 Below we list several variables. Which of these variables are quantitative and which are qualitative? Explain.

    a The dollar amount on an accounts receivable invoice.

    b The net profit for a company in 2009.

    c The stock exchange on which a company's stock is traded.

    d The national debt of the United States in 2009.

    e The advertising medium (radio, television, or print) used to promote a product.

1.3 Discuss the difference between cross-sectional data and time series data. If we record the total number of cars sold in 2009 by each of 10 car salespeople, are the data cross-sectional or time series data? If we record the total number of cars sold by a particular car salesperson in each of the years 2005, 2006, 2007, 2008, and 2009, are the data cross-sectional or time series data?

1.4 Consider a medical study that is being performed to test the effect of smoking on lung cancer. Two groups of subjects are identified; one group has lung cancer and the other one doesn't. Both are asked to fill out a questionnaire containing questions about their age, sex, occupation, and number of cigarettes smoked per day. What is the response variable? Which are the factors? What type of study is this (experimental or observational)?

METHODS AND APPLICATIONS

1.5 Consider the five homes in Table 1.1 (page 3). What do you think you would have to pay for a Ruby model on a treed lot?

1.6 Consider the five homes in Table 1.1 (page 3). What do you think you would have to pay for a Diamond model on a lake lot? For a Ruby model on a lake lot?

1.7 The number of Bismark X-12 electronic calculators sold at Smith's Department Stores over the past 24 months have been: 197, 211, 203, 247, 239, 269, 308, 262, 258, 256, 261, 288, 296, 276, 305, 308, 356, 393, 363, 386, 443, 308, 358, and 384. Make a time series plot of these data. That is, plot 197 versus month 1, 211 versus month 2, and so forth. What does the time series plot tell you?

1.3 Populations and Samples ● ● ●

We often collect data in order to study a population.

LO6 Describe the difference between a population and a sample.

> A **population** is the set of all elements about which we wish to draw conclusions.

Examples of populations include (1) all of last year's graduates of Dartmouth College's Master of Business Administration program, (2) all current MasterCard cardholders, and (3) all Buick LaCrosses that have been or will be produced this year.

We usually focus on studying one or more variables describing the population elements. If we carry out a measurement to assign a value of a variable to each and every population element, we have a *population of measurements* (sometimes called *observations*). If the population is small, it is reasonable to do this. For instance, if 150 students graduated last year from the Dartmouth College MBA program, it might be feasible to survey the graduates and to record all of their starting salaries. In general:

> If we examine all of the population measurements, we say that we are conducting a **census** of the population.

Often the population that we wish to study is very large, and it is too time-consuming or costly to conduct a census. In such a situation, we select and analyze a subset (or portion) of the population elements.

> A **sample** is a subset of the elements of a population.

For example, suppose that 8,742 students graduated last year from a large state university. It would probably be too time-consuming to take a census of the population of all of their starting salaries. Therefore, we would select a sample of graduates, and we would obtain and record their starting salaries. When we measure a characteristic of the elements in a sample, we have a **sample of measurements.**

We often wish to describe a population or sample.

LO7 Distinguish between descriptive statistics and statistical inference.

> **Descriptive statistics** is the science of describing the important aspects of a set of measurements.

As an example, if we are studying a set of starting salaries, we might wish to describe (1) how large or small they tend to be, (2) what a typical salary might be, and (3) how much the salaries differ from each other.

When the population of interest is small and we can conduct a census of the population, we will be able to directly describe the important aspects of the population measurements. However, if the population is large and we need to select a sample from it, then we use what we call **statistical inference.**

> **Statistical inference** is the science of using a sample of measurements to make generalizations about the important aspects of a population of measurements.

For instance, we might use a sample of starting salaries to **estimate** the important aspects of a population of starting salaries. In the next section, we begin to look at how statistical inference is carried out.

LO8 Explain the importance of random sampling.

1.4 Three Case Studies That Illustrate Sampling and Statistical Inference ● ● ●

When we select a sample from a population, we hope that the information contained in the sample reflects what is true about the population. One of the best ways to achieve this goal is to select a *random sample.* In Section 7.1 we will define exactly what a random sample is.[2] For now, it suffices to know that a random sample is selected in such a way that every element in the population has the *same chance* of being included in the sample. Most procedures for selecting a random sample from a population begin by making or obtaining a list of the population elements and assigning a unique number to each population element in the list. We then *randomly select* population elements from the numbered list. One intuitive way to do this would be to place numbered slips of paper representing the population elements in a suitable container. We would thoroughly mix the slips of paper and (blind folded) choose slips of paper from the container. The numbers on the chosen slips of paper would identify the randomly selected population elements that make up the random sample. Of course, numbering a large number of slips of paper can be very time consuming. Therefore, in Section 7.1 we will discuss the more practical method of using a *random number table* or *computer generated random numbers* to select a random sample. We will also see that, although in many situations it is not possible to make or obtain a list of all of the population elements, we can sometimes select an "approximately" random sample of these elements.

We now introduce three case studies that illustrate the need for a random (or approximately random) sample and the use of such a sample in making statistical inferences. After studying these cases, the reader has the option of studying Section 7.1 (see page 271) and learning practical ways to select random and approximately random samples.

EXAMPLE 1.1 The Cell Phone Case: Estimating Cell Phone Costs

Part 1: The cost of company cell phone use   Rising cell phone costs have forced companies having large numbers of cellular users to hire services to manage their cellular and other wireless resources. These cellular management services use sophisticated software and mathematical models to choose cost efficient cell phone plans for their clients. One such firm, MobileSense Inc. of Westlake Village, California, specializes in automated wireless cost management. According to Doug L. Stevens, Vice President of Sales and Marketing at MobileSense, cell phone carriers count on *overage*—using more minutes than one's plan allows—and *underage*—using fewer minutes than those already paid for—to deliver almost half of their revenues. As a result, a company's typical cost of cell phone use can easily exceed 25 cents per minute. However, Mr. Stevens explains that by using MobileSense automated cost management to select calling plans, this cost can be reduced to 12 cents per minute or less.

---

[2]Actually, there are several different kinds of random samples. The type we will define is sometimes called a *simple random sample.* For brevity's sake, however, we will use the term *random sample.*

TABLE 1.4	A Sample of Cellular Usages (in minutes) for 100 Randomly Selected Employees								
	DS CellUse								
75	485	37	547	753	93	897	694	797	477
654	578	504	670	490	225	509	247	597	173
496	553	0	198	507	157	672	296	774	479
0	822	705	814	20	513	546	801	721	273
879	433	420	521	648	41	528	359	367	948
511	704	535	585	341	530	216	512	491	0
542	562	49	505	461	496	241	624	885	259
571	338	503	529	737	444	372	555	290	830
719	120	468	730	853	18	479	144	24	513
482	683	212	418	399	376	323	173	669	611

In this case we consider a bank that wishes to decide whether to hire a cellular management service to choose its employees' calling plans. While the bank has over 10,000 employees on many different types of calling plans, the cellular management service suggests that by studying the calling patterns of cellular users on 500-minute-per-month plans, the bank can accurately assess whether its cell phone costs can be substantially reduced.

The bank has 2,136 employees on a variety of 500-minute-per-month plans with different basic monthly rates, different overage charges, and different additional charges for long distance and roaming. It would be extremely time consuming to analyze in detail the cell phone bills of all 2,136 employees. Therefore, the bank will estimate its cellular costs for the 500-minute plans by analyzing last month's cell phone bills for a *random sample* of 100 employees on these plans. According to the cellular management service, if the cellular cost per minute for the random sample of 100 employees is over 18 cents per minute, the bank should benefit from automated cellular management of its calling plans.[3]

Part 2: A random sample   Because the bank can list and number the 2,136 employees on the 500-minute plans, the bank can select a random sample of 100 of these employees. A practical way to do this is discussed in Section 7.1. When the random sample of 100 employees is chosen, the number of cellular minutes used by each sampled employee during last month (the employee's *cellular usage*) is found and recorded. The 100 cellular-usage figures are given in Table 1.4. Looking at this table, we can see that there is substantial overage and underage—many employees used far more than 500 minutes, while many others failed to use all of the 500 minutes allowed by their plan. In Chapter 3 we will use these 100 usage figures to estimate the cellular cost per minute for 500-minute plans.

EXAMPLE 1.2 The Marketing Research Case: Rating a New Bottle Design[4]

Part 1: The importance of a bottle design   The design of a package or bottle can have an important effect on a company's bottom line. For example, in September of 2004 Coca-Cola reported substantial customer dissatisfaction with the size and shape of a new, contoured 1.5 liter bottle for Coke products. This dissatisfaction was playing a major role in Coca-Cola's projected failure to meet third-quarter earnings forecasts in 2004.[5]

In this case a brand group is studying whether changes should be made in the bottle design for a popular soft drink. To research consumer reaction to a new design, the brand group will use the "mall intercept method"[6] in which shoppers at a large metropolitan shopping mall are intercepted as they walk by and asked to participate in a consumer survey. Each shopper will be exposed to the

---

[3]In Chapter 8 we will discuss how to plan the *sample size*—the number of elements (for example, 100) that should be included in a sample. Throughout this book we will take large enough samples to allow us to make reasonably accurate statistical inferences.

[4]This case was motivated by an example in the book *Essentials of Marketing Research* by W. R. Dillon, T. J. Madden, and N. H. Firtle (Burr Ridge, IL: Richard D. Irwin, 1993). The authors also wish to thank Professor L. Unger of the Department of Marketing at Miami University for helpful discussions concerning how this type of marketing study would be carried out.

[5]Theresa Howard, "Coke Says Earnings Will Come up Short," *USA Today,* September 16, 2004, p. 801.

[6]This is a commonly used research design. For example, see the Burke Marketing Research website at http://burke.com/about/inc_background.htm, Burke Marketing Research, March 26, 2005.

FIGURE 1.2   **The Bottle Design Survey Instrument**

Please circle the response that most accurately describes whether you agree or disagree with each statement about the bottle you have examined.

Statement	Strongly Disagree						Strongly Agree
The size of this bottle is convenient.	1	2	3	4	5	6	7
The contoured shape of this bottle is easy to handle.	1	2	3	4	5	6	7
The label on this bottle is easy to read.	1	2	3	4	5	6	7
This bottle is easy to open.	1	2	3	4	5	6	7
Based on its overall appeal, I like this bottle design.	1	2	3	4	5	6	7

TABLE 1.5   **A Sample of Bottle Design Ratings (Composite Scores for a Systematic Sample of 60 Shoppers)**
DS Design

34	33	33	29	26	33	28	25	32	33
32	25	27	33	22	27	32	33	32	29
24	30	20	34	31	32	30	35	33	31
32	28	30	31	31	33	29	27	34	31
31	28	33	31	32	28	26	29	32	34
32	30	34	32	30	30	32	31	29	33

new bottle design and asked to rate the bottle image. Bottle image will be measured by combining consumers' responses to five items, with each response measured using a 7-point "Likert scale." The five items and the scale of possible responses are shown in Figure 1.2. Here, since we describe the least favorable response and the most favorable response (and we do not describe the responses between them), we say that the scale is "anchored" at its ends. Responses to the five items will be summed to obtain a composite score for each respondent. It follows that the minimum composite score possible is 5 and the maximum composite score possible is 35. Furthermore, experience has shown that the smallest acceptable composite score for a successful bottle design is 25.

Part 2: An approximately random sample   Suppose that the brand group has decided to use the mall intercept method to interview a sample of 60 shoppers at the shopping mall on a particular Saturday. Because it is not possible to list and number all of the shoppers who will be at the mall on this Saturday, the brand group cannot obtain a random sample of these shoppers. However, in Section 7.1 we will learn that the brand group can intercept shoppers in such a way that it obtains an approximately random sample of these shoppers. When each shopper is chosen, he or she is asked to rate the bottle design by responding to the five items in Figure 1.2, and a composite score is calculated for the shopper. The 60 composite scores obtained are given in Table 1.5. Since these scores vary from a minimum of 20 to a maximum of 35, we might infer that *most* of the shoppers at the mall on the Saturday of the study would rate the new bottle design between 20 and 35. Furthermore, since 57 of the 60 composite scores are at least 25, we might estimate that the proportion of all shoppers at the mall on the Saturday of the study who would give the bottle design a composite score of at least 25 is $57/60 = .95$. That is, we estimate that 95 percent of the shoppers would give the bottle design a composite score of at least 25. In future chapters we will further analyze the composite scores.

In some situations, we need to decide whether a sample taken from one population can be employed to make statistical inferences about another, related population. Often logical reasoning is used to do this. For instance, we might reason that the bottle design ratings given by shoppers at the mall on the Saturday of the research study would be representative of the ratings given by (1) shoppers at the same mall at other times, (2) shoppers at other malls, and (3) consumers in general. However, if we have no data or other information to back up this reasoning, making such generalizations is dangerous. In practice, marketing research firms choose locations and sampling times that data and experience indicate will produce a representative cross-section of consumers. To simplify our presentation, we will assume that this has been done in the bottle design case. Therefore, we will suppose that it is reasonable to use the 60 bottle design ratings in Table 1.5 to make statistical inferences about *all consumers.*

Before presenting the next case, note that sometimes we are interested in studying the population of all of the elements that will be or could potentially be produced by a *process.*

> A **process** is a sequence of operations that takes inputs (labor, materials, methods, machines, and so on) and turns them into outputs (products, services, and the like).

Processes produce output *over time.* For example, this year's Buick LaCrosse manufacturing process produces LaCrosses over time. Early in the model year, General Motors might wish to study the population of the city driving mileages of all Buick LaCrosses that will be produced during the model year. Or, even more hypothetically, General Motors might wish to study the population of the city driving mileages of all LaCrosses that could *potentially* be produced by this model year's manufacturing process. The first population is called a **finite population** because only a finite number of cars will be produced during the year. The second population is called an **infinite population** because the manufacturing process that produces this year's model could in theory always be used to build "one more car." That is, theoretically there is no limit to the number of cars that could be produced by this year's process. There are a multitude of other examples of finite or infinite hypothetical populations. For instance, we might study the population of all waiting times that will or could potentially be experienced by patients of a hospital emergency room. Or we might study the population of all the amounts of grape jelly that will be or could potentially be dispensed into 16-ounce jars by an automated filling machine. To study a population of potential process observations, we sample the process—often at equally spaced time points—over time. This is illustrated in the following case.

EXAMPLE 1.3   The Car Mileage Case: Estimating Mileage   C

Part 1: The importance of auto fuel economy   Personal budgets, national energy security, and the global environment are all affected by our gasoline consumption. Filling up our car eats away at our disposable income and shifts the trade balance in favor of petroleum-exporting nations. Furthermore, even if a reliable, affordable supply of petroleum were not an issue, burning fossil fuels such as gasoline and diesel adds greenhouse gases, mostly carbon dioxide, to the earth's atmosphere. Large-scale increases in greenhouse gases in the Earth's atmosphere can lead to global warming.[7] A car creates 20 pounds of carbon dioxide per gallon of gasoline it consumes. However, the U.S. Department of Energy estimates that by choosing a car that gets an additional 5 miles per gallon, a person can prevent the release of about 17 tons of greenhouse gases over the lifetime of his or her car.[8]

Hybrid and electric cars will be a vital part of a long-term strategy to reduce our nation's gasoline consumption. However, these cars are still being developed, and the projected costs of electric cars must be reduced before they will have a practical impact on reducing gasoline consumption.[9] Moreover, because gasoline powered cars will probably remain on the road into the foreseeable future, many experts believe that an important way to increase fuel economy is to improve existing gasoline engines. In the short term, "that will give you the biggest bang for your buck," says David Friedman, research director of the Union of Concerned Scientists' Clean Vehicle Program.[10]

In this case study we consider a tax credit offered by the federal government to automakers for improving the fuel economy of gasoline powered midsize cars. According to *The Fuel Economy Guide—2009 Model Year,* virtually every gasoline powered midsize car equipped with an automatic transmission has an EPA combined city and highway mileage estimate of 26 miles per gallon (mpg) or less.[11] Furthermore, the EPA has concluded that a 5 mpg increase in fuel economy is significant and feasible.[12] Therefore, suppose that the government has decided to offer the tax credit to any automaker selling a midsize model with an automatic transmission that achieves an EPA combined city and highway mileage estimate of at least 31 mpg.

[7, 8]World Wide Web, http://www.fueleconomy.gov
[9, 10]Bryan Walsh, "Plugged In," *Time,* September 29, 2008 (see page 56).
[11]The "26 miles per gallon (mpg) or less" figure relates to midsize cars with an automatic transmission *and* at least a 4 cylinder, 2.4 liter engine (such cars are the most popular midsize models). Therefore, when we refer to a midsize car with an automatic transmission in future discussions, we are assuming that the midsize car also has at least a 4 cylinder, 2.4 liter engine.
[12]The authors wish to thank Jeff Alson of the EPA for this information.

TABLE 1.6	A Sample of 50 Mileages				DS GasMiles
30.8	30.8	32.1	32.3	32.7	Note: **Time**
31.7	30.4	31.4	32.7	31.4	**order is given**
30.1	32.5	30.8	31.2	31.8	**by reading**
31.6	30.3	32.8	30.7	31.9	**down the**
32.1	31.3	31.9	31.7	33.0	**columns from**
33.3	32.1	31.4	31.4	31.5	**left to right.**
31.3	32.5	32.4	32.2	31.6	
31.0	31.8	31.0	31.5	30.6	
32.0	30.5	29.8	31.7	32.3	
32.4	30.5	31.1	30.7	31.4	

FIGURE 1.3   A Runs Plot of the 50 Mileages

Part 2: An approximately random sample   Consider an automaker that has recently introduced a new midsize model with an automatic transmission and wishes to demonstrate that this new model qualifies for the tax credit. In order to study the population of all cars of this type that will or could potentially be produced, the automaker will choose a sample of 50 of these cars. Furthermore, because the midsize cars are produced over time on consecutive production shifts (with 100 cars being produced on each shift), the automaker will choose the sample of 50 cars from different production shifts. No cars will be chosen from the model year's initial production shifts so that any production start-up problems can be identified and corrected. When the midsize car manufacturing process is operating consistently over time, the automaker will choose the sample of 50 cars by randomly selecting one car from the 100 cars produced on each of 50 consecutive production shifts. How such random selections can be made will be discussed in Section 7.1. Once selected, each car is to be subjected to an EPA test that determines the EPA combined city and highway mileage of the car. This mileage is obtained by testing the car on a device similar to a giant treadmill. The device is used to simulate a 7.5-mile city driving trip and a 10-mile highway driving trip, and the resulting city and highway mileages are used to calculate the EPA combined mileage for the car.[13]

Suppose that when the 50 cars are selected and tested, the sample of 50 EPA combined mileages shown in Table 1.6 is obtained. A runs plot of the mileages is given in Figure 1.3. Examining this plot, we see that, although the mileages vary over time, they do not seem to vary in any unusual way. For example, the mileages do not tend to either decrease or increase (as did the basic cable rates in Figure 1.1) over time. This intuitively verifies that the midsize car manufacturing process is producing consistent car mileages over time, and thus we can regard the 50 mileages as an approximately random sample that can be used to make statistical inferences about the population of all possible midsize car mileages. Therefore, since the 50 mileages vary from a minimum of 29.8 mpg to a maximum of 33.3 mpg, we might conclude that most midsize cars produced by the manufacturing process will obtain between 29.8 mpg and 33.3 mpg. Moreover, because 38 out of the 50 mileages—or 76 percent of the mileages—are greater than or equal to the tax credit standard of 31 mpg, we have some evidence that the "typical car" produced by the process will meet or exceed the tax credit standard. We will further evaluate this evidence in later chapters.

Exercises for Sections 1.3 and 1.4

CONCEPTS

1.8   Define a *population*. Give an example of a population.

1.9   Explain the difference between a census and a sample.

1.10   Explain the term *descriptive statistics*. Explain the term *statistical inference*.

1.11   Explain what a process is.

connect™

---

[13]Since the EPA estimates that 55 percent of all driving is city driving, it calculates combined mileage by adding 55 percent of the city mileage test result to 45 percent of the highway mileage test result.

METHODS AND APPLICATIONS

1.12 THE VIDEO GAME SATISFACTION RATING CASE ⑤ VideoGame

A company that produces and markets video game systems wishes to assess its customer's level of satisfaction with a relatively new model, the XYZ-Box. In the six months since the introduction of the model, the company has received 73,219 warranty registrations from purchasers. The company will select a random sample of 65 of these registrations and will conduct telephone interviews with the purchasers. Specifically, each purchaser will be asked to state his or her level of agreement with each of the seven statements listed on the survey instrument given in Figure 1.4. Here, the level of agreement for each statement is measured on a 7-point Likert scale. Purchaser satisfaction will be measured by adding the purchaser's responses to the seven statements. It follows that for each consumer the minimum composite score possible is 7 and the maximum is 49. Furthermore, experience has shown that a purchaser of a video game system is "very satisfied" if his or her composite score is at least 42. Suppose that when the 65 customers are interviewed, their composite scores are as given in Table 1.7. Using the data, estimate limits between which most of the 73,219 composite scores would fall. Also, estimate the proportion of the 73,219 composite scores that would be at least 42.

1.13 THE BANK CUSTOMER WAITING TIME CASE ⑤ WaitTime

A bank manager has developed a new system to reduce the time customers spend waiting to be served by tellers during peak business hours. Typical waiting times during peak business hours under the current system are roughly 9 to 10 minutes. The bank manager hopes that the new system will lower typical waiting times to less than six minutes and wishes to evaluate the new system. When the new system is operating consistently over time, the bank manager decides to select a sample of 100 customers that need teller service during peak business hours. Specifically, for each of 100 peak business hours, the first customer that starts waiting for teller service at or after a randomly selected time during the hour will be chosen. In Exercise 7.5 (see page 275) we will discuss how to obtain a randomly selected time during an hour. When each customer is chosen, the number of minutes the customer spends waiting for teller service is recorded. The 100 waiting times that are observed are given in Table 1.8. Using the data, estimate limits

FIGURE 1.4 The Video Game Satisfaction Survey Instrument

Statement	Strongly Disagree						Strongly Agree
The game console of the XYZ-Box is well designed.	1	2	3	4	5	6	7
The game controller of the XYZ-Box is easy to handle.	1	2	3	4	5	6	7
The XYZ-Box has high quality graphics capabilities.	1	2	3	4	5	6	7
The XYZ-Box has high quality audio capabilities.	1	2	3	4	5	6	7
The XYZ-Box serves as a complete entertainment center.	1	2	3	4	5	6	7
There is a large selection of XYZ-Box games to choose from.	1	2	3	4	5	6	7
I am totally satisfied with my XYZ-Box game system.	1	2	3	4	5	6	7

TABLE 1.7 Composite Scores for the Video Game Satisfaction Rating Case ⑤ VideoGame

39	44	46	44	44
45	42	45	44	42
38	46	45	45	47
42	40	46	44	43
42	47	43	46	45
41	44	47	48	
38	43	43	44	
42	45	41	41	
46	45	40	45	
44	40	43	44	
40	46	44	44	
39	41	41	44	
40	43	38	46	
42	39	43	39	
45	43	36	41	

TABLE 1.8 Waiting Times (in Minutes) for the Bank Customer Waiting Time Case ⑤ WaitTime

1.6	6.2	3.2	5.6	7.9	6.1	7.2
6.6	5.4	6.5	4.4	1.1	3.8	7.3
5.6	4.9	2.3	4.5	7.2	10.7	4.1
5.1	5.4	8.7	6.7	2.9	7.5	6.7
3.9	.8	4.7	8.1	9.1	7.0	3.5
4.6	2.5	3.6	4.3	7.7	5.3	6.3
6.5	8.3	2.7	2.2	4.0	4.5	4.3
6.4	6.1	3.7	5.8	1.4	4.5	3.8
8.6	6.3	.4	8.6	7.8	1.8	5.1
4.2	6.8	10.2	2.0	5.2	3.7	5.5
5.8	9.8	2.8	8.0	8.4	4.0	
3.4	2.9	11.6	9.5	6.3	5.7	
9.3	10.9	4.3	1.3	4.4	2.4	
7.4	4.7	3.1	4.8	5.2	9.2	
1.8	3.9	5.8	9.9	7.4	5.0	

TABLE 1.9

Trash Bag Breaking Strengths DS TrashBag

48.5	50.7
52.3	48.2
53.5	51.5
50.5	49.0
50.3	51.7
49.6	53.2
51.0	51.1
48.3	52.6
50.6	51.2
50.2	49.5
52.5	49.4
47.5	51.9
50.9	52.0
49.8	48.8
50.0	46.8
50.8	51.3
53.0	49.3
50.9	54.0
49.9	49.2
50.1	51.4

LO9 Identify the ratio, interval, ordinal, and nominative scales of measurement (Optional).

between which the waiting times of most of the customers arriving during peak business hours would be. Also, estimate the proportion of waiting times of customers arriving during peak business hours that are less than six minutes.

1.14   THE TRASH BAG CASE[14] DS TrashBag

A company that produces and markets trash bags has developed an improved 30-gallon bag. The new bag is produced using a specially formulated plastic that is both stronger and more biodegradable than previously used plastics, and the company wishes to evaluate the strength of this bag. The *breaking strength* of a trash bag is considered to be the amount (in pounds) of a representative trash mix that when loaded into a bag suspended in the air will cause the bag to sustain significant damage (such as ripping or tearing). The company has decided to select a sample of 40 of the new trash bags. For each of 40 consecutive hours, the first trash bag produced at or after a randomly selected time during the hour is chosen. The bag is then subjected to a *breaking strength test*. The 40 breaking strengths obtained are given in Table 1.9. Estimate limits between which the breaking strengths of most trash bags would fall. Assume that the trash bag manufacturing process is operating consistently over time.

1.5 Ratio, Interval, Ordinal, and Nominative Scales of Measurement (Optional) ● ● ●

In Section 1.1 we said that a variable is **quantitative** if its possible values are *numbers that represent quantities* (that is, "how much" or "how many"). In general, a quantitative variable is measured on a scale having a *fixed unit of measurement* between its possible values. For example, if we measure employees' salaries to the nearest dollar, then one dollar is the fixed unit of measurement between different employees' salaries. There are two types of quantitative variables: **ratio** and **interval.** A **ratio variable** is a quantitative variable measured on a scale such that ratios of its values are meaningful and there is an inherently defined zero value. Variables such as salary, height, weight, time, and distance are ratio variables. For example, a distance of zero miles is "no distance at all," and a town that is 30 miles away is "twice as far" as a town that is 15 miles away.

An **interval variable** is a quantitative variable where ratios of its values are not meaningful and there is not an inherently defined zero value. Temperature (on the Fahrenheit scale) is an interval variable. For example, zero degrees Fahrenheit does not represent "no heat at all," just that it is very cold. Thus, there is no inherently defined zero value. Furthermore, ratios of temperatures are not meaningful. For example, it makes no sense to say that 60° is twice as warm as 30°. In practice, there are very few interval variables other than temperature. Almost all quantitative variables are ratio variables.

In Section 1.1 we also said that if we simply record into which of several categories a population (or sample) unit falls, then the variable is **qualitative** (or **categorical**). There are two types of qualitative variables: **ordinal** and **nominative.** An **ordinal variable** is a qualitative variable for which there is a meaningful *ordering,* or *ranking,* of the categories. The measurements of an ordinal variable may be nonnumerical or numerical. For example, a student may be asked to rate the teaching effectiveness of a college professor as excellent, good, average, poor, or unsatisfactory. Here, one category is higher than the next one; that is, "excellent" is a higher rating than "good," "good" is a higher rating than "average," and so on. Therefore, teaching effectiveness is an ordinal variable having nonnumerical measurements. On the other hand, if (as is often done) we substitute the numbers 4, 3, 2, 1, and 0 for the ratings excellent through unsatisfactory, then teaching effectiveness is an ordinal variable having numerical measurements.

In practice, both numbers and associated words are often presented to respondents asked to rate a person or item. When numbers are used, statisticians debate whether the ordinal variable is "somewhat quantitative." For example, statisticians who claim that teaching effectiveness rated as 4, 3, 2, 1, or 0 is *not* somewhat quantitative argue that the difference between 4 (excellent) and 3 (good) may not be the same as the difference between 3 (good) and 2 (average). Other statisticians argue that as soon as respondents (students) see equally spaced numbers (even though the numbers are described by words), their responses are affected enough to make the variable (teaching effectiveness) somewhat quantitative. Generally speaking, the specific words associated with the numbers

---

[14]This case is based on conversations by the authors with several employees working for a leading producer of trash bags. For purposes of confidentiality, we have withheld the company's name.

probably substantially affect whether an ordinal variable may be considered somewhat quantitative. It is important to note, however, that in practice numerical ordinal ratings are often analyzed as though they are quantitative. Specifically, various arithmetic operations (as discussed in Chapters 2 through 14) are often performed on numerical ordinal ratings. For example, a professor's teaching effectiveness average and a student's grade point average are calculated.

To conclude this section, we consider the second type of qualitative variable. A **nominative variable** is a qualitative variable for which there is no meaningful ordering, or ranking, of the categories. A person's gender, the color of a car, and an employee's state of residence are nominative variables.

Exercises for Section 1.5

CONCEPTS

1.15 Discuss the difference between a ratio variable and an interval variable.

1.16 Discuss the difference between an ordinal variable and a nominative variable.

connect

METHODS AND APPLICATIONS

1.17 Classify each of the following qualitative variables as ordinal or nominative. Explain your answers.

Qualitative Variable	Categories
Statistics course letter grade	A B C D F
Door choice on *Let's Make A Deal*	Door #1 Door #2
Television show classifications	TV-G TV-PG TV-14 TV-MA
Personal computer ownership	Yes No
Restaurant rating	***** **** *** ** *
Income tax filing status	Married filing jointly Married filing separately Single Head of household Qualifying widow(er)

1.18 Classify each of the following qualitative variables as ordinal or nominative. Explain your answers.

Qualitative Variable	Categories
Personal computer operating system	DOS Windows XP Windows Vista Windows 7
Motion picture classifications	G PG PG-13 R NC-17 X
Level of education	Elementary Middle school High school College Graduate school
Rankings of the top 10 college football teams	1 2 3 4 5 6 7 8 9 10
Exchange on which a stock is traded	AMEX NYSE NASDAQ Other
Zip code	45056 90015 etc.

Chapter Summary

We began this chapter by discussing **data.** We learned that the data that are collected for a particular study are referred to as a **data set,** and we learned that **elements** are the entities described by a data set. In order to determine what information we need about a group of elements, we define important **variables,** or characteristics, describing the elements. **Quantitative variables** are variables that use numbers to measure quantities (that is, "how much" or "how many") and **qualitative, or categorical, variables** simply record into which of several categories an element falls.

We next discussed the difference between cross-sectional data and time series data. **Cross-sectional data** are data collected at the same or approximately the same point in time. **Time series data** are data collected over different time periods. There are various **sources of data.** Specifically, we can obtain data from **existing sources** or from **experimental or observational studies** done in-house or by paid outsiders.

We often collect data to study a **population,** which is the set of all elements about which we wish to draw conclusions. We saw

that, since many populations are too large to examine in their entirety, we frequently study a population by selecting a **sample,** which is a subset of the population elements. Next we learned that, if the information contained in a sample is to accurately represent the population, then the sample should be **randomly selected** from the population.

We concluded this chapter with optional Section 1.5, which considered different types of quantitative and qualitative variables. We learned that there are two types of **quantitative variables— ratio variables,** which are measured on a scale such that ratios of its values are meaningful and there is an inherently defined zero value, and **interval variables,** for which ratios are not meaningful and there is no inherently defined zero value. We also saw that there are two types of **qualitative variables—ordinal variables,** for which there is a meaningful ordering of the categories, and **nominative variables,** for which there is no meaningful ordering of the categories.

Glossary of Terms

categorical (qualitative) variable: A variable having values that indicate into which of several categories a population element belongs. (pages 4, 14)

census: An examination of all the elements in a population. (page 7)

cross-sectional data: Data collected at the same or approximately the same point in time. (page 4)

data: Facts and figures from which conclusions can be drawn. (page 3)

data set: Facts and figures, taken together, that are collected for a statistical study. (page 3)

descriptive statistics: The science of describing the important aspects of a set of measurements. (page 8)

element: A person, object, or other entity about which we wish to draw a conclusion. (page 3)

experimental study: A statistical study in which the analyst is able to set or manipulate the values of the factors. (page 6)

factor: A variable that may be related to the response variable. (page 6)

finite population: A population that contains a finite number of elements. (page 11)

infinite population: A population that is defined so that there is no limit to the number of elements that could potentially belong to the population. (page 11)

interval variable: A quantitative variable such that ratios of its values are not meaningful and for which there is not an inherently defined zero value. (page 14)

measurement: The process of assigning a value of a variable to each of the elements in a population or sample. (page 4)

nominative variable: A qualitative variable for which there is no meaningful ordering, or ranking, of the categories. (page 15)

observational study: A statistical study in which the analyst is not able to control the values of the factors. (page 6)

ordinal variable: A qualitative variable for which there is a meaningful ordering or ranking of the categories. (page 14)

population: The set of all elements about which we wish to draw conclusions. (page 7)

process: A sequence of operations that takes inputs and turns them into outputs. (page 11)

qualitative (categorical) variable: A variable having values that indicate into which of several categories a population element belongs. (pages 4, 14)

quantitative variable: A variable having values that are numbers representing quantities. (pages 4, 14)

ratio variable: A quantitative variable such that ratios of its values are meaningful and for which there is an inherently defined zero value. (page 14)

response variable: A variable of interest that we wish to study. (page 6)

sample: A subset of the elements in a population. (page 7)

statistical inference: The science of using a sample of measurements to make generalizations about the important aspects of a population. (page 8)

survey: An instrument employed to collect data. (page 6)

time series data: Data collected over different time periods. (page 4)

time series plot (runs plot): A plot of time series data versus time. (page 4)

variable: A characteristic of a population element. (page 3)

Supplementary Exercises

1.19   THE COFFEE TEMPERATURE CASE   DS Coffee

According to the website of the Association of Trial Lawyers of America,[15] Stella Liebeck of Albuquerque, New Mexico, was severely burned by McDonald's coffee in February 1992. Liebeck, who received third-degree burns over 6 percent of her body, was awarded $160,000 in compensatory damages and $480,000 in punitive damages. A postverdict investigation revealed that the coffee temperature at the local Albuquerque McDonald's had dropped from about 185°F before the trial to about 158° after the trial.

This case concerns coffee temperatures at a fast-food restaurant. Because of the possibility of future litigation and to possibly improve the coffee's taste, the restaurant wishes to study the temperature of the coffee it serves. To do this, the restaurant personnel measure the temperature of the coffee being dispensed (in degrees Fahrenheit) at a randomly selected time during each of the 24 half-hour periods from 8 A.M. to 7:30 P.M. on a given day. The coffee temperatures given in Table 1.10 are observed. Make a runs plot of the coffee temperatures, and assuming process consistency, estimate limits between which most of the coffee temperatures at the restaurant would fall.

1.20   In the article "Accelerating Improvement" published in *Quality Progress,* Gaudard, Coates, and Freeman describe a restaurant that caters to business travelers and has a self-service breakfast buffet. Interested in customer satisfaction, the manager conducts a survey over a three-week period and finds that the main customer complaint is having to wait too long to be seated. On each day from September 11 to October 1, a problem-solving team records the percentage of patrons who must wait more than one minute to be seated. A runs plot of the daily percentages is shown in Figure 1.5.[16] What does the runs plot tell us about how to improve the waiting time situation?

---

[15]http://www.atla.org, Association of Trial Lawyers of America, June 16, 2006.

[16]The source of Figure 1.5 is M. Gaudard, R. Coates, and L. Freeman, "Accelerating Improvement," *Quality Progress,* October 1991, pp. 81–88. © 1991 American Society for Quality Control. Used with permission.

TABLE 1.10	The Coffee Temperatures for Exercise 1.19 DS Coffee	
163°F	159	158
169	154	170
156	167	155
152	161	162
165	152	156
158	165	167
157	161	155
162	154	164

Note: **Time order is given by reading down the columns from left to right.**

FIGURE 1.5 **Runs Plot of Daily Percentages of Customers Waiting More Than One Minute to Be Seated (for Exercise 1.20)**

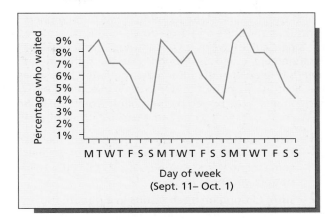

1.21 Internet Exercise

The website maintained by the U.S. Census Bureau provides a multitude of social, economic, and government data. In particular, this website houses selected data from the most recent *Statistical Abstract of the United States* (http://www.census.gov/compendia/statab/). Among these selected features are "Frequently Requested Tables" that can be accessed simply by clicking on the label. Go to the U.S. Census Bureau website and open the "Frequently requested tables" from the *Statistical Abstract*. Find the table of "Consumer Price Indexes by Major Groups." Construct runs plots of (1) the price index for all items over time (years), (2) the price index for food over time, (3) the price index for fuel oil over time, and (4) the price index for electricity over time. For each runs plot, describe apparent trends in the price index.

Excel, MegaStat, and MINITAB for Statistics

In this book we use three types of software to carry out statistical analysis—Excel 2007, MegaStat, and MINITAB 15. Excel is, of course, a general purpose electronic spreadsheet program and analytical tool. The analysis Tool-Pak in Excel includes many procedures for performing various kinds of basic statistical analyses. MegaStat is an add-in package that is specifically designed for performing statistical analysis in the Excel spreadsheet environment. MINITAB is a computer package designed expressly for conducting statistical analysis. It is widely used at many colleges and universities, and in a large number of business organizations. The principal advantage of Excel is that, because of its broad acceptance among students and professionals as a multipurpose analytical tool, it is both well known and widely available. The advantage of a special-purpose statistical software package like MINITAB is that it provides a far wider range of statistical procedures and it offers the experienced analyst a range of options to better control the analysis. The advantages of MegaStat include (1) its ability to perform a number of statistical calculations that are not automatically done by the procedures in the Excel ToolPak, and (2) features that make it easier to use than Excel for a wide variety of statistical analyses. In addition, the output obtained by using MegaStat is automatically placed in a standard Excel spreadsheet and can be edited by using any of the features in Excel. MegaStat can be copied from the book's website. Excel, MegaStat, and MINITAB through built-in functions, programming languages, and macros, offer almost limitless power. Here, we will limit our attention to procedures that are easily accessible via menus without resort to any special programming or advanced features.

Commonly used features of Excel 2007, MegaStat, and MINITAB 15 are presented in this chapter along with an initial application—the construction of a time series plot of the gas mileages in Table 1.6. You will find that the limited instructions included here, along with the built-in help features of all three software packages, will serve as a starting point from which you can discover a variety of other procedures and options. Much more detailed descriptions of MINITAB 15 can be found in other sources, in particular in the manual *Meet MINITAB 15 for Windows*. This manual is available in print and as a .pdf file, viewable using Adobe Acrobat Reader, on the MINITAB Inc. website (http://www.minitab.com/support/docs/rel15/MeetMinitab.pdf). Note that the MINITAB 15 instructions given in this book are also valid for MINITAB 16. Similarly, there are a number of alternative reference materials for Microsoft Excel 2007. Of course, an understanding of the related statistical concepts is essential to the effective use of any statistical software package.

Appendix 1.1 ■ Getting Started with Excel

Because Excel 2007 may be new to some readers, and because the Excel 2007 window looks quite different from previous versions of Excel, we will begin by describing some characteristics of the Excel 2007 window. Previous versions of Excel employed many drop-down menus. This meant that many features were "hidden" from the user, which resulted in a steep learning curve for beginners. In Excel 2007, Microsoft tried to reduce the number of features that are hidden in drop-down menus. Therefore, Excel 2007 displays all of the applicable commands needed for a particular type of task at the top of the Excel window. These commands are represented by a tab-and-group arrangement called the **ribbon**—see the right side of the illustration of an Excel 2007 window below. The commands displayed in the ribbon are regulated by a series of **tabs** located near the top of the ribbon. For example, in the illustration below, the **Home tab** is selected. If we selected a different tab, say, for example, the **Page Layout tab,** the commands displayed by the ribbon would be different.

We now briefly describe some basic features of the Excel 2007 window:

1 **Office button:** By clicking on this button, the user obtains a menu of often used commands—for example, Open, Save, Print, and so forth. This is very similar to the "File menu" in older versions of Excel. However, some menu items are unique to Excel 2007. This menu also provides access to a large number of Excel options settings.

2 **Tabs:** Clicking on a tab results in a ribbon display of features, commands, and options related to a particular type of task. For example, when the *Home tab* is selected (as in the figure below), the features, commands, and options displayed by the ribbon are all related to making entries into the Excel worksheet. As another example, if the *Formula tab* is selected, all of the features, commands, and options displayed in the ribbon relate to using formulas in the Excel worksheet.

3 **Quick access toolbar:** This toolbar displays buttons that provide shortcuts to often used commands. Initially, this toolbar displays Save, Undo, and Redo buttons. The user can customize this toolbar by adding shortcut buttons for other commands (such as, New, Open, Quick Print, and so forth). This can be done by clicking on the arrow button directly to the right of the Quick access toolbar and by making selections from the "Customize" drop-down menu that appears.

4   **Title bar:** This bar shows the name of the currently active workbook and contains the Quick Access Toolbar as well as the Maximize, Minimize, and Close buttons.

5   **Ribbon:** A grouping of toolbars, tabs, commands, and features related to performing a particular kind of task—for example, making entries into the Excel spreadsheet. The particular features displayed in the ribbon are controlled by selecting a *Tab*. If the user is working in the spreadsheet workspace and wishes to reduce the number of features displayed by the ribbon, this can be done by right-clicking on the ribbon and by selecting "Minimize the Ribbon." We will often Minimize the Ribbon in the Excel appendices of this book in order to focus attention on operations being performed and results being displayed in the Excel spreadsheet.

6   **Sheet tabs:** These tabs show the name of each sheet in the Excel workbook. When the user clicks a sheet tab, the selected sheet becomes active and is displayed in the Excel spreadsheet. The name of a sheet can be changed by double-clicking on the appropriate sheet tab and by entering the new name.

7   **Formula bar:** When a worksheet cell is selected, the formula bar displays the current content of the cell. If the cell content is defined by a formula, the defining formula is displayed in the formula bar.

8   **Tab group:** This is a labeled grouping of commands and features related to performing a particular type of task.

9   **Launcher button:** Some of the tab groups have a launcher button—for example, the Clipboard, Font, Alignment, and Number tab groups each has such a button. Clicking on the launcher button opens a dialog box or task pane related to performing operations in the tab group.

10   **Zoom slider:** By moving this slider right and left, the cells in the Excel spreadsheet can be enlarged or reduced in size.

We now a look at some features of Excel that are common to many analyses. When the instructions call for a sequence of selections, the sequence will be presented in the following form:

Select Home : Format : Row Height

This notation indicates that we first select the Home tab on the ribbon, then we select Format from the Cells Group on the ribbon, and finally we select Row Height from the Format drop-down menu.

For many of the statistical and graphical procedures in Excel, it is necessary to provide a range of cells to specify the location of data in the spreadsheet. Generally, the range may be specified either by typing the cell locations directly into a dialog box or by dragging the selected range with the mouse. Though, for the experienced user, it is usually easier to use the mouse to select a range, the instructions that follow will, for precision and clarity, specify ranges by typing in cell locations. The selected range may include column or variable labels—labels at the tops of columns that serve to identify variables. When the selected range includes such labels, it is important to select the "Labels check box" in the analysis dialog box.

Starting Excel   Procedures for starting Excel may vary from one installation to the next. If you are using a public computing laboratory, you may wish to consult local documentation. For typical Excel installations, you will generally be able to start Excel with a sequence of selections from the Microsoft Windows start menu something like the following:

Start : Microsoft Office XP : Microsoft Office Excel 2007

You can also start Excel with a previously saved Excel spreadsheet (like GasMiles.xlsx or one of the other data files that can be downloaded from this book's website) by double-clicking on the spreadsheet file's icon in the Windows Explorer.

After starting Excel, the display will generally show a blank Excel workbook.

Help resources Like most Windows programs, Excel includes on-line help via a Help Menu that includes search capability as well as a table of contents. To display the Help Menu, click on the "Question Mark" button in the upper-right corner of the ribbon.

Entering data (entering the gas mileages in Table 1.6 on page 12) from the keyboard (data file: GasMiles.xlsx):

- In a new Excel workbook, click on cell A1 in Sheet1 and type a label—that is, a variable name—say, Mileage, for the gasoline mileages.
- Beginning in cell A2 (directly under the column label Mileage) type the mileages from Table 1.6 on page 12 down the column, pressing the Enter key following each entry.

Saving data (saving the gasoline mileage data):

- To begin, click on the **Office** button.
- Select **Save As : Excel Workbook**
- In the "Save As" dialog box, use the "Save in" drop-down menu to select the destination drive and folder. Here we have selected a folder called Data Files on the Local C drive.
- Enter the desired file name in the "File name" box. Here we have chosen the name GasMiles. Excel will automatically add the extension .xlsx.
- Click the Save button in the "Save As" dialog box.

Retrieving an Excel spreadsheet containing the gasoline mileages in Table 1.6 on page 12 (data file: GasMiles.xlsx):

- Select **Office : Open**
  That is, click on the Office button and then select Open.

- In the Open dialog box, use the "Look in" drop-down menu to select the source drive and folder. Here we have selected a folder called Data Files on the Local C drive.

- Enter the desired file name in the "File name" box. Here we have chosen the Excel spreadsheet GasMiles.xlsx.

- Click the Open button in the Open dialog box.

Creating a runs (time series) plot similar to Figure 1.3 on page 12 (data file: GasMiles.xlsx):

- Enter the gasoline mileage data into column A of the worksheet with label Mileage in cell A1.

- Click on any cell in the column of mileages, or select the range of the data to be charted by dragging with the mouse. Selecting the range of the data is good practice because—if this is not done—Excel will sometimes try to construct a chart using all of the data in your worksheet. The result of such a chart is often nonsensical. Here, of course, we only have one column of data—so there would be no problem. But, in general, it is a good idea to select the data before constructing a graph.

- Select **Insert : Line : 2-D Line : Line with Markers**
  Here select the Insert tab and then select Line from the Charts group. When Line is selected, a gallery of line charts will be displayed. From the gallery, select the desired chart—in this case a 2-D Line chart with markers. The proper chart can be selected by looking at the sample pictures. As an alternative, if the cursor is held over a picture, a descriptive "tool tip" of the chart type will be displayed. In this case, the "Line with Markers" tool tip was obtained by holding the cursor over the highlighted picture.

- When you click on the "2-D Line with Markers" icon, the chart will appear in a graphics window and the Chart Tools ribbon will be displayed.

- To prepare the chart for editing, it is best to move the chart to a new worksheet called a "chart sheet". To do this, click on the **Design** tab and select **Move Chart.**

- In the Move Chart dialog box, select the "New sheet" option, enter a name for the new sheet— here, "Runs Plot"—into the "New sheet" window, and click OK.

- The Chart Tools ribbon will be displayed and the chart will be placed in a chart sheet in a larger format that is more convenient for editing.

- In order to edit the chart, select the **Layout** tab from the Chart Tools ribbon. By making selections from the ribbon, many chart attributes can be edited. For instance, when you click on Axes as shown, various options for formatting the horizontal and vertical axes can be selected.

- A chart can also be edited by right-clicking on the portion of the chart that we wish to revise. For instance, in the screen shown, we have right-clicked on one of the plotted data points. When this is done, we obtain a menu as shown. If we select "Format Data Series", we obtain a dialog box that provides many options for editing the data series (the plotted points and their connecting lines). For example, if (as shown) we select

Line Color : Solid Line

and then click on the Color arrow button, we obtain a drop-down menu that allows us to select a desired color for the connecting lines between the plotted points. We can edit other portions of the chart in the same way.

- Here we show an edited runs plot. This revised chart was constructed from the original runs plot created by Excel using various options like those illustrated above. This chart can be copied directly from the worksheet (simply right click on the graph and select Copy from the pop-up menu) and can then be pasted into a word processing document.

The chart can be printed from this worksheet as follows:

- Select **Office : Print**
  That is, click on the Office button and then select Print.

- Select the desired printer in the Printer Name window and click OK in the Print dialog box.

There are many print options available in Excel for printing—a selected range, selected sheets, or an entire workbook—making it possible to build and print fairly sophisticated reports directly from Excel.

Printing a spreadsheet with an embedded graph:

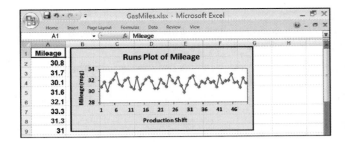

- Click outside the graph to print both the work-sheet contents (here the mileage data) and the graph. Click on the graph to print only the graph.
- Select **Office : Print**
  That is, click on the Office button and then select Print.
- Select the desired printer in the Printer Name window and click OK in the Print dialog box.

Including Excel output in reports   The preceding example showed how to print selected analysis results from Excel. Printing is a useful way to capture a quick hard-copy record of an analysis result, and Excel offers a variety of options for building sophisticated reports. However, you may at times prefer to collect selected analysis results and arrange them with related narrative in a word processing document that can be saved and printed as a unit. You can simply copy Excel results—selected spreadsheet ranges and graphs—to the Windows clipboard. Then paste them into an open word processing document. Once copied to a word processing document, Excel results can be documented, edited, resized, and rearranged as desired into a cohesive record of your analysis. The cut and paste process is quite similar to the MINITAB examples at the end of Appendix 1.3.

Appendix 1.2 ■ Getting Started with MegaStat

MegaStat, which was developed by Professor J. B. Orris of Butler University, is an Excel add-in that performs statistical analyses within an Excel workbook. Instructions for installing MegaStat can be found on this book's website.

- After installation, you can access MegaStat by clicking on the Add-Ins tab (on the ribbon) and by then selecting MegaStat from the Add-Ins group of Menu Commands. When you select MegaStat, the MegaStat menu appears as shown in the screen. Most of the menu options display sub-menus. If a menu item is followed by an ellipsis (...) clicking it will display a dialog box for that option.

- A dialog box allows you to specify the data to be used and other inputs and options. A typical dialog box is shown in the screen.

- After you have selected the needed data and options, you click OK. The dialog box then disappears and MegaStat performs the analysis.

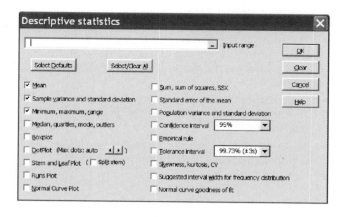

Before we look at specific dialog boxes, we will describe some features that are common to all of the options. MegaStat use is intuitive and very much like other Excel operations; however, there are some features unique to MegaStat.

Data selection   Most MegaStat dialog boxes have fields where you select input ranges that contain the data to be used. Such a field is shown in the dialog box illustrated above—it is the long horizontal window with the label "Input range" to its right. Input ranges can be selected using four methods:

1 Pointing and dragging with the mouse. Simply select the desired data by pointing to the data, by left-clicking on the first data item, and dragging the cursor to select the rest of the data as illustrated below.

Since the dialog box "pops-up" on the screen, it may block some of your data. You can move a dialog box around on the screen by placing the mouse pointer over the title bar (colored area at the top), and by then clicking and holding the left mouse button while dragging the dialog box to a new location. You can even drag it partially off the screen.

You will also notice that when you start selecting data by dragging the mouse pointer, the dialog box will collapse to a smaller size to help you see the underlying data. It will automatically return to full size when you release the mouse button. You can also collapse and uncollapse the dialog box manually by clicking the collapse (-) button at the right end of the field. Clicking the button again will un-collapse the dialog box. (Never use the X button to try to collapse or uncollapse a dialog box.)

2 Using MegaStat's AutoExpand feature. Pointing and dragging to select data can be tedious if you have a lot of data. When you drag the mouse down it is easy to overshoot the selection and then you have to drag the mouse back until you get the area correctly selected. AutoExpand allows rapid data selection without having to drag through the entire column of data. Here's how it works:

- Make sure the input box has the focus (that is, click in it to make the input box active). An input box has the focus when the insertion pointer is blinking in it.

- Click in one cell of the column you want. If more than one column is being selected, drag the mouse across the columns.

- Right-click over the input field or left-click the label "Input Range" to the right of the input box. The data range will expand to include all of the rows in the region where you selected one row.

This procedure is illustrated below. In the left screen, we have left-clicked on one cell in the column of data labeled Mileage. In the right screen, we see the result after we right-click over the input field or left-click on the label "Input range." Notice that the entire column of data has been selected in the right screen. This can be seen by examining the input field or by looking at the column of data.

With a little practice you will find this is a very efficient way to select data. The only time you cannot use it is when you want to use a partial column of data. You should also be aware that the autoexpand stops when it finds a blank cell; thus any summations or other calculations at the bottom of a column would be selected.

Note: When using the above methods of data selection you may select variables in an alternating sequence by holding the CTRL key while making multiple selections.

3 **Typing the name of a named range.** If you have previously identified a range of cells using Excel's name box, you may use that name to specify a data range in a MegaStat dialog box. This method can be very useful if you are using the same data for several different statistical procedures.

4 **Typing a range address.** You may type any valid Excel range address, for example, $A$1:$A$101, into the input field. This is the most cumbersome way to specify data ranges, but it certainly works.

Data labels   For most procedures, the first cell in each input range can be a label. If the first cell in a range is text, it is considered a label; if the first cell is a numeric value, it is considered data. If you want to use numbers as variable labels, you must enter the numbers as text by preceding them with a single quote mark—for instance, '2. Even though Excel stores times and dates as numbers, MegaStat will recognize them as labels if they are formatted as time/date values. If data labels are not part of the input range, the program automatically uses the cell immediately above the data range as a label if it contains a text value. If an option can consider the entire first row (or column) of an input range as labels, any numeric value in the row will cause the entire row to be treated as data. Finally, if the program detects sequential integers (1,2,3...) in a location where you might want labels, it will display a warning message. Otherwise, the rule is: **text cells are labels, numeric cells are data.**

Output   When you click OK on a MegaStat dialog box, it performs some statistical analysis and needs a place to put its output. It looks for a worksheet named Output. If it finds one, it goes to the end of it and appends its output; if it doesn't find an Output worksheet, it creates one. MegaStat will never make any changes to the user's worksheets; it only sends output to its Output sheet.

MegaStat makes a good attempt at formatting the output, but **it is important to remember that the Output sheet is just a standard Excel worksheet and can be modified in any way by the user.** You can adjust column widths and change any formatting that you think needs improvement. You can insert, delete, and modify cells. You can copy all or part of the output to another worksheet or to another application such as a word processor.

When the program generates output, it adjusts column widths for the current output. If you have previous output from a different option already in the Output sheet, the column widths for the previous output may be altered. You can attempt to fix this by manually adjusting the column widths. Alternatively, you can make it a practice to always start a new output sheet. The **Utilities menu** has options for **deleting the Output sheet, for making a copy of it, and for starting a new one.**

An example   We now give an example of using MegaStat to carry out statistical analysis. When the instructions call for a sequence of selections, the sequence will be presented in the following form:

Add-Ins : MegaStat : Probability : Counting Rules

This notation says that **Add-Ins** is the first selection (from the ribbon), **MegaStat** is the second selection from the Add-Ins group of Menu Commands; next **Probability** is selected from the MegaStat drop-down menu; and finally **Counting Rules** is selected from the Probability submenu.

Creating a runs plot of gasoline mileages similar to Figure 1.3 on page 12 (data file: GasMiles.xlsx):

- Enter the mileage data in Table 1.6 on page 12 into column A with the label Mileage in cell A1 and with the 50 mileages in cells A2 through A51.

- Select **Add-Ins : MegaStat : Descriptive Statistics**

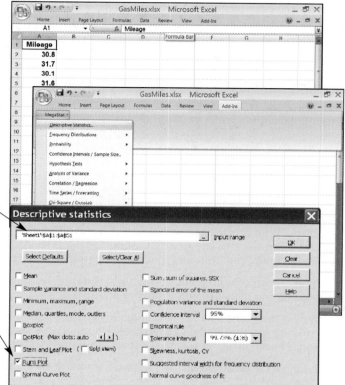

- In the Descriptive Statistics dialog box, enter the range $A$1:$A$51 into the Input range box. The easiest way to do this is to use the MegaStat autoExpand feature. Simply select one cell in column A (say, cell A4, for instance) by clicking on the cell. Then, either right-click in the Input range box or left-click on the label "Input range" to the right of the Input range box.

- Place a checkmark in the Runs Plot checkbox.

- Click OK in the Descriptive Statistics dialog box.

MegaStat places the resulting analysis (in this case the runs plot) in an output worksheet. This is a standard Excel worksheet, which can be edited using any of the usual Excel features. For instance, by right-clicking on various portions of the runs plot graphic, the plot can be edited in many ways. Here we have right-clicked on the plot area. By selecting **Format Plot Area**, we are able to edit the graphic in a variety of ways.

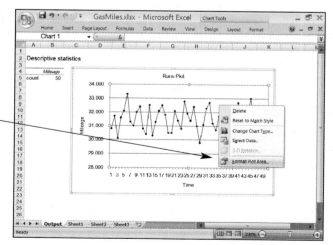

In the Format Plot Area dialog box, we can add color to the runs plot and edit the plot in many other ways.

Alternatively, we can edit the runs plot by selecting

Chart Tools : Layout

By making selections from the Labels, Axes, and Background groups, the plot can be edited in a variety of ways. For example, in the screen shown we have selected the Plot Area button in the Background group. This gives us many options for editing the plot area of the graphic.

Appendix 1.3 ■ Getting Started with MINITAB

We begin with a look at some features of MINITAB that are common to most analyses. When the instructions call for a sequence of selections from a series of menus, the sequence will be presented in the following form:

Stat : Basic Statistics : Descriptive Statistics

This notation indicates that Stat is the first selection from the Minitab menu bar, next Basic Statistics is selected from the Stat pull-down menu, and finally Descriptive Statistics is selected from the Basic Statistics pull-down menu.

Starting MINITAB Procedures for starting MINITAB may vary from one installation to the next. If you are using a public computing laboratory, you may have to consult local documentation. For typical MINITAB installations, you will generally be able to start MINITAB with a sequence of selections from the Microsoft Windows Start menu something like the following:

- Select **Start : Programs : Minitab : Minitab 15 Statistical Software English**

You can also start MINITAB with a previously saved MINITAB worksheet (like GasMiles.MTW or one of the many other data files that can be downloaded from this book's website) by double-clicking on the worksheet's icon in the Windows Explorer.

After you start MINITAB, the display is partitioned into two working windows. These windows serve the following functions:

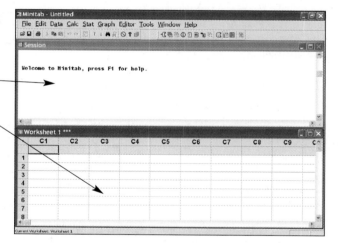

- The "Session window" is the area where MINITAB commands and basic output are displayed.
- The "Data window" is an Excel-like worksheet where data can be entered and edited.

Help resources Like most Windows programs, MINITAB includes on-line help via a Help Menu. The Help feature includes standard Contents and Search entries as well as Tutorials that introduce MINITAB concepts and walk through some typical MINITAB sessions. Also included is a StatGuide that provides guidance for interpreting statistical tables and graphs in a practical, easy-to-understand way.

Entering data (entering the gasoline mileage data in Table 1.6 on page 12) from the keyboard:

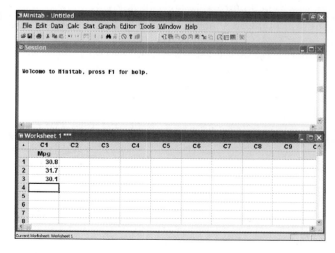

- In the Data window, click on the cell directly below C1 and type a name for the variable—say, Mpg—and press the Enter key.
- Starting in row 1 under column C1, type the values for the variable (gasoline mileages from Table 1.6 on page 12) down the column, pressing the Enter key after each number is typed.

Saving data (saving the gasoline mileage data):

- Select **File : Save Current Worksheet As**

- In the "Save Worksheet As" dialog box, use the "Save in" drop-down menu to select the destination drive and folder. (Here we have selected a folder named Data Files on the Local C drive.)

- Enter the desired file name in the File name box. Here we have chosen the name GasMiles. MINITAB will automatically add the extension .MTW.

- Click the Save button in the "Save Worksheet As" dialog box.

Retrieving a MINITAB worksheet containing the gasoline mileage data in Table 1.6 (data file: GasMiles .MTW):

- Select **File : Open Worksheet**

- In the Open Worksheet dialog box, use the "Look in" drop-down menu to select the source drive and folder. (Here we have selected a folder named Data Files on the Local C drive.)

- Enter the desired file name in the File name box. (Here we have chosen the MINITAB worksheet GasMiles.MTW.)

- Click the Open button in the Open Worksheet dialog box.

- MINITAB may display a dialog box with the message, "A copy of the content of this file will be added to the current project." If so, click OK.

Creating a runs (or time series) plot similar to Figure 1.3 on page 12 (data file: GasMiles.MTW):

- Select **Graph : Time Series Plot**

- In the Time Series Plots dialog box, select Simple, which produces a time series plot of data that is stored in a single column, and click OK.

- In the "Time Series Plot—Simple" dialog box, enter the name of the variable, Mpg, into the Series window. Do this either (1) by typing its name, or (2) by double-clicking on its name in the list of variables on the left side of the dialog box. Here, this list consists of the single variable Mpg in column C1.

- Click OK in the "Time Series Plot—Simple" dialog box.

- **The runs (or time series) plot** will appear in a graphics window.

- **The graph can be edited** by right-clicking on the portion you wish to edit. For instance, here we have right-clicked on the data region.
- Selecting "Edit Data Region" from the pop-up window gives a dialog box that allows you to edit this region. The x and y scales, x and y axis labels, title, plot symbols, connecting lines, data region, figure region, and so forth can all be edited by right-clicking on that particular portion of the graph

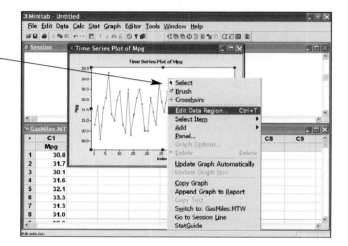

- For instance, after right-clicking on the data region and then selecting "Edit Data Region" from the pop-up menu, the Edit Data Region dialog box allows us to edit various attributes of this region. As shown, selecting Custom and clicking on the Background Color arrow allows us to change the background color of the data region.

Printing a high-resolution graph similar to Figure 1.3 on page 12 (data file: GasMiles.MTW):

- Click in the graphics window to select it as the active window.
- Select **File : Print Graph** to print the graph.
- Select the appropriate printer and click OK in the Print dialog box.

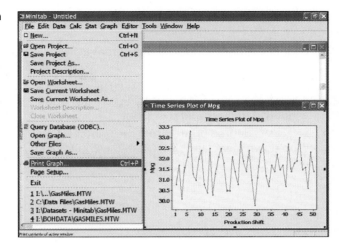

Saving the high-resolution graph:

- Click on the graph to make the graphics window the active window.
- Select **File : Save Graph As**
- In the "Save Graph As" dialog box, use the "Save in" drop-down menu to select the destination drive and folder (here we have selected the DVD/CD-RW drive).
- Enter the desired file name in the File name box (here we have chosen the name MileagePlot). MINITAB will automatically add the file extension .MGF.
- Click the Save button in the "Save Graph As" dialog box.

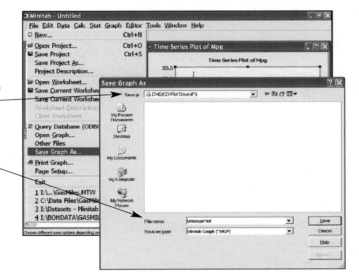

Printing data from the Session window (shown) or Data window (data file: GasMiles.MTW):
To print selected output from the Session window:

- Use the mouse to select the desired output or text (selected output will be reverse-highlighted in black).
- Select **File : Print Session Window**
- In the Print dialog box, the Print range will be the "Selection" option. To print the entire session window, select the Print range to be "All."
- Select the desired printer from the Printer Name drop-down menu.
- Click OK in Print dialog box.

To print the contents of the Data window (that is, to print the MINITAB worksheet):

- Click in the Data window to select it as active.
- Select **File : Print Worksheet**
- Make selections as desired in the Data Window Print Options dialog box, add a title in the Title window if desired, and click OK.
- Select the desired printer from the Printer Name drop-down menu and click OK in the Print dialog box.

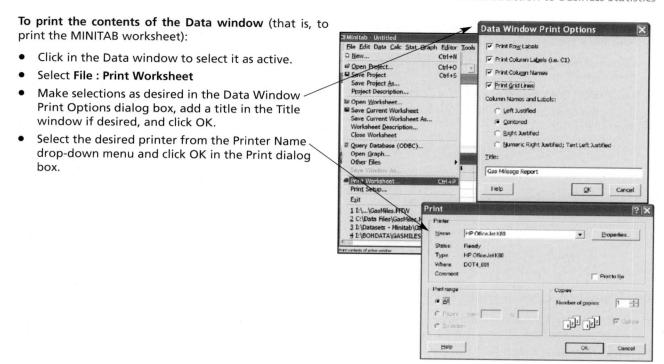

Including MINITAB output in reports The immediately preceding examples show how to print various types of output directly from MINITAB. Printing is a useful way to capture a quick hard-copy record of an analysis result. However, you may prefer at times to collect selected analysis results and arrange them with related narrative documentation in a report that can be saved and printed as a unit. This is easily accomplished by copying selected MINITAB results to the Windows clipboard and by pasting them into your favorite word processor. Once copied to a word processor document, MINITAB results can be documented, edited, resized, and rearranged as desired into a cohesive record of your analysis. The following sequence of examples illustrates the process of copying MINITAB output into a Microsoft Word document.

Copying session window output to a word processing document:

- Be sure to have a word processing document open to receive the results.
- Use the scroll bar on the right side of the Session window to locate the results to be copied and drag the mouse to select the desired output (selected output will be reverse-highlighted in black).
- Copy the selected output to the Windows clipboard by clicking the Copy icon on the MINITAB toolbar or by right-clicking on the selected text and then selecting Copy from the pop-up menu.
- Switch to your word processing document by clicking the button on the Windows task bar (here labeled MS Word Report.doc).
- Click in your word processing document to position the cursor at the desired insertion point.
- Click the Paste button on the word processing power bar or right-click at the insertion point and select Paste from the pop-up menu.
- Return to your MINITAB session by clicking the MINITAB button on the Windows task bar.

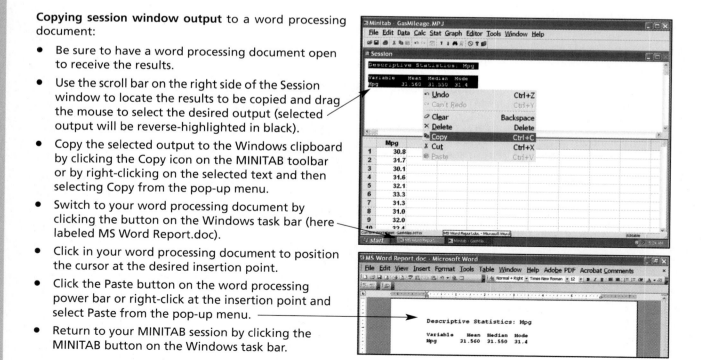

Copying high-resolution graphics output to a word processing document:

- Be sure to have a word processing document open to receive the results.

- Copy the selected contents of the high-resolution graphics window to the Windows clipboard by right-clicking in the graphics window and by then clicking Copy Graph on the pop-up menu.

- Switch to your word processing document by clicking the button on the Windows task bar (here labeled MS Word Report.doc).

- Click in your word processing document to position the cursor at the desired insertion point.

- Click the Paste button on the word processor power bar or right-click at the insertion point and select Paste from the pop-up menu.

- Return to your MINITAB session by clicking the MINITAB button on the Windows task bar.

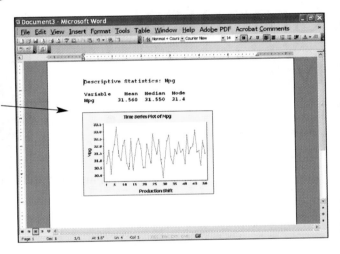

Results   Here is how the copied results might appear in Microsoft Word. These results can be edited, resized, repositioned, and combined with your own additional documentation to create a cohesive record of your analysis.

TABLE 2.1 **2006 Sales at a Greater Cincinnati Jeep Dealership** ⓓⓢ JeepSales

W	L	L	W	G	C	C	L	C	L	G	W	C
L	L	G	L	C	C	G	C	C	G	C	L	W
G	L	G	C	C	C	C	C	G	G	L	G	G
L	G	L	L	G	L	C	W	G	L	G	L	G
G	L	C	L	C	L	L	L	C	G	L	C	L
C	G	C	C	C	C	C	C	C	G	C	C	W
L	L	C	G	L	C	C	L	L	G	G	L	L
G	G	G	L	C	L	L	G	L	C	C	L	G
C	L	L	G	G	L	W	W	L	C	C	C	G
G	W	L	L	C	G	C	C	W	C	L	L	L
L	L	C	C	G	L	L	W	C	G	G	C	L
W	G	G	W	G	C	W	W	G	L	L	G	
L	L	L	C	C	G	C	L	G	G	G	L	
G	G	C	G	W	G	L	L	L	C	C	L	
W	L	W	G	W	C	W	C	W	C	L	C	
G	C	G	L	L	C	L	L	G	G	G	L	
L	C	G	L	C	L	W	L	L	C	G	C	
W	W	W	C	C	C	G	G	L	G	C	G	
W	C	C	W	L	G	W	L	L	L	G	G	
G	G	W	L	L	C	L	G	G	W	G	G	

TABLE 2.2 **A Frequency Distribution of Jeeps Sold at a Greater Cincinnati Dealer in 2006** ⓓⓢ JeepTable

Jeep Model	Frequency
Commander	71
Grand Cherokee	70
Liberty	80
Wrangler	30
	251

TABLE 2.3 **Relative Frequency and Percent Frequency Distributions for the 2006 Jeep Sales Data** ⓓⓢ JeepPercents

Jeep Model	Relative Frequency	Percent Frequency
Commander	71/251 = .2829	28.29%
Grand Cherokee	.2789	27.89%
Liberty	.3187	31.87%
Wrangler	.1195	11.95%
	1.0	100%

When we wish to summarize the proportion (or fraction) of items in each class, we employ the **relative frequency** for each class. If the data set consists of n observations, we define the relative frequency of a class as follows:

$$\textbf{Relative frequency of a class} = \frac{\text{frequency of the class}}{n}$$

This quantity is simply the fraction of items in the class. Further, we can obtain the **percent frequency** of a class by multiplying the relative frequency by 100.

Table 2.3 gives a relative frequency distribution and a percent frequency distribution of the Jeep sales data. A **relative frequency distribution** is a table that lists the relative frequency for each class, and a **percent frequency distribution** lists the percent frequency for each class. Looking at Table 2.3, we see that the relative frequency for Jeep Commander is $71/251 = .2829$ (rounded to four decimal places) and that (from the percent frequency distribution) 28.29% of the Jeeps sold were Commanders. Similarly, the relative frequency for Jeep Wrangler is $30/251 = .1195$ and 11.95% of the Jeeps sold were Wranglers. Finally, the sum of the relative frequencies in the relative frequency distribution equals 1.0, and the sum of the percent frequencies in the percent frequency distribution equals 100%. These facts will be true for any relative frequency and percent frequency distribution.

Part 2: Studying 2006 sales by using bar charts and pie charts   A bar chart is a graphic that depicts a frequency, relative frequency, or percent frequency distribution. For example, Figure 2.1 gives an Excel bar chart of the Jeep sales data. On the horizontal axis we have placed a label for each class (Jeep model), while the vertical axis measures frequencies. To construct the bar chart, Excel draws a bar (of fixed width) corresponding to each class label. Each bar is drawn so that its height equals the frequency corresponding to its label. Because the height of each bar is a frequency, we refer to Figure 2.1 as a **frequency bar chart.** Notice that the bars have gaps

FIGURE **2.1**   **Excel Bar Chart of the 2006 Jeep Sales Data**

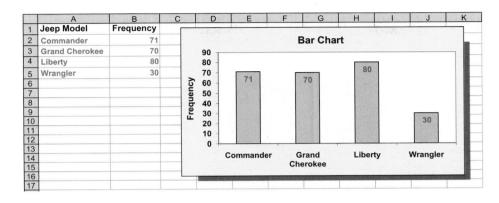

FIGURE **2.2**   **MINITAB Percent Bar Chart of the 2006 Jeep Sales Data**

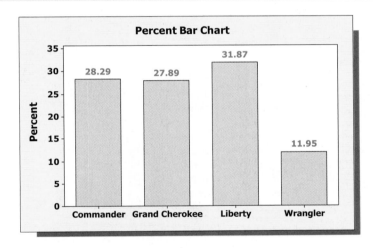

between them. When data are qualitative, the bars should always be separated by gaps in order to indicate that each class is separate from the others. The bar chart in Figure 2.1 clearly illustrates that, for example, the dealer sold more Jeep Libertys than any other model and that the dealer sold far fewer Wranglers than any other model.

If desired, the bar heights can represent relative frequencies or percent frequencies. For instance, Figure 2.2 is a MINITAB **percent bar chart** for the Jeep sales data. Here the heights of the bars are the percentages given in the percent frequency distribution of Table 2.3. Lastly, the bars in Figures 2.1 and 2.2 have been positioned vertically. Because of this, these bar charts are called **vertical bar charts.** However, sometimes bar charts are constructed with horizontal bars and are called **horizontal bar charts.**

A **pie chart** is another graphic that can be used to depict a frequency distribution. When constructing a pie chart, we first draw a circle to represent the entire data set. We then divide the circle into sectors or "pie slices" based on the relative frequencies of the classes. For example, remembering that a circle consists of 360 degrees, the Jeep Liberty (which has relative frequency .3187) is assigned a pie slice that consists of .3187(360) = 115 degrees (rounded to the nearest degree for convenience). Similarly, the Jeep Wrangler (with relative frequency .1195) is assigned a pie slice having .1195(360) = 43 degrees. Similarly, the Jeep Commander is assigned a pie slice having 102 degrees and Jeep Grand Cherokee is assigned a pie slice having 100 degrees. The resulting pie chart (constructed using Excel) is shown in Figure 2.3. Here we have labeled the pie slices using the percent frequencies. The pie slices can also be labeled using frequencies or relative frequencies.

A Frequency Distribution of Jeeps Sold at a Greater Cincinnati Dealer in 2010

Jeep Model	Frequency
Commander	10
Grand Cherokee	20
Liberty	24
Wrangler (2 door)	20
Wrangler (4 door)	40
Patriot	31
Compass	33
	178

Part 3: Comparing 2006 and 2010 sales   To make this comparison, the sales manager constructs the frequency distribution of 2010 sales shown in the page margin (raw data not shown).

FIGURE 2.3   **Excel Pie Chart of the 2006 Jeep Sales Data**

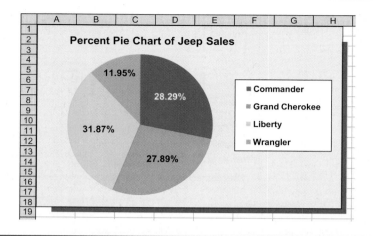

FIGURE 2.4   **Excel Frequency Table and Pareto Chart of Labeling Defects**   Labels

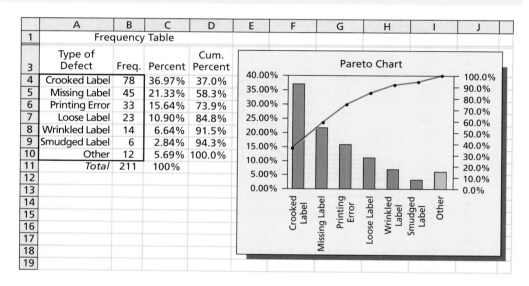

Notice that the three models introduced in 2007 (the Wrangler 4-door, Patriot, and Compass) outsold the older models. Also, sales of the Commander—the least fuel efficient model—decreased substantially from 2006 to 2010. Finally, overall sales decreased almost 30 percent (from 251 to 178). This decrease was probably due to the downturn in the U.S. economy.

LO2 Construct and interpret Pareto charts (Optional).

The Pareto chart (optional)   **Pareto charts** are used to help identify important quality problems and opportunities for process improvement. By using these charts we can prioritize problem-solving activities. The Pareto chart is named for Vilfredo Pareto (1848–1923), an Italian economist. Pareto suggested that, in many economies, most of the wealth is held by a small minority of the population. It has been found that the **"Pareto principle"** often applies to defects. That is, only a few defect types account for most of a product's quality problems.

To illustrate the use of Pareto charts, suppose that a jelly producer wishes to evaluate the labels being placed on 16-ounce jars of grape jelly. Every day for two weeks, all defective labels found on inspection are classified by type of defect. If a label has more than one defect, the type of defect that is most noticeable is recorded. The Excel output in Figure 2.4 presents the frequencies and percentages of the types of defects observed over the two-week period.

In general, the first step in setting up a **Pareto chart** summarizing data concerning types of defects (or categories) is to construct a frequency table like the one in Figure 2.4. Defects or categories should be listed at the left of the table in *decreasing order by frequencies*—the defect with the highest frequency will be at the top of the table, the defect with the second-highest frequency below the first, and so forth. If an "other" category is employed, it should be placed at the bottom of the table. The "other" category should not make up 50 percent or more of the total of the frequencies, and the frequency for the "other" category should not exceed the frequency for the defect at the top of the table. If the frequency for the "other" category is too high, data should be collected so that the "other" category can be broken down into new categories. Once the frequency and the percentage for each category are determined, a cumulative percentage for each category is computed. As illustrated in Figure 2.4, the cumulative percentage for a particular category is the sum of the percentages corresponding to the particular category and the categories that are above that category in the table.

A Pareto chart is simply a bar chart having the different kinds of defects or problems listed on the horizontal scale. The heights of the bars on the vertical scale typically represent the frequency of occurrence (or the percentage of occurrence) for each defect or problem. The bars are arranged in decreasing height from left to right. Thus, the most frequent defect will be at the far left, the next most frequent defect to its right, and so forth. If an "other" category is employed, its bar is placed at the far right. The Pareto chart for the labeling defects data is given in Figure 2.4. Here the heights of the bars represent the percentages of occurrences for the different labeling defects, and the vertical scale on the far left corresponds to these percentages. The chart graphically illustrates that crooked labels, missing labels, and printing errors are the most frequent labeling defects.

As is also illustrated in Figure 2.4, a Pareto chart is sometimes augmented by plotting a **cumulative percentage point** for each bar in the Pareto chart. The vertical coordinate of this cumulative percentage point equals the cumulative percentage in the frequency table corresponding to the bar. The cumulative percentage points corresponding to the different bars are connected by line segments, and a vertical scale corresponding to the cumulative percentages is placed on the far right. Examining the cumulative percentage points in Figure 2.4, we see that crooked and missing labels make up 58.3 percent of the labeling defects and that crooked labels, missing labels, and printing errors make up 73.9 percent of the labeling defects.

Technical note   The Pareto chart in Figure 2.4 illustrates using an "other" category which combines defect types having low frequencies into a single class. In general, when we employ a frequency distribution, a bar chart, or a pie chart and we encounter classes having small class frequencies, it is common practice to combine the classes into a single "other" category. Classes having frequencies of 5 percent or less are usually handled this way.

Exercises for Section 2.1

CONCEPTS

2.1   Explain the purpose behind constructing a frequency or relative frequency distribution.

2.2   Explain how to compute the relative frequency and percent frequency for each class if you are given a frequency distribution.

2.3   Find an example of a pie chart or bar chart in a newspaper or magazine. Copy it, and hand it in with a written analysis of the information conveyed by the chart.

METHODS AND APPLICATIONS

2.4   A multiple choice question on an exam has four possible responses—(a), (b), (c), and (d). When 250 students take the exam, 100 give response (a), 25 give response (b), 75 give response (c), and 50 give response (d).
   a   Write out the frequency distribution, relative frequency distribution, and percent frequency distribution for these responses.
   b   Construct a bar chart for these data using frequencies.

2.5   Consider constructing a pie chart for the exam question responses in Exercise 2.4.
   a   How many degrees (out of 360) would be assigned to the "pie slice" for the response (a)?
   b   How many degrees would be assigned to the "pie slice" for response (b)?
   c   Construct the pie chart for the exam question responses.

2.6   Consider the partial relative frequency distribution of consumer preferences for four products—W, X, Y, and Z—that is shown in the page margin.
   a   Find the relative frequency for product X.
   b   If 500 consumers were surveyed, give the frequency distribution for these data.
   c   Construct a percent frequency bar chart for these data.
   d   If we wish to depict these data using a pie chart, find how many degrees (out of 360) should be assigned to each of products W, X, Y, and Z. Then construct the pie chart.

Product	Relative Frequency
W	.15
X	—
Y	.36
Z	.28

connect

2.7   Below we give pizza restaurant preferences for 25 randomly selected college students.
DS PizzaPizza

Godfather's	Little Caesar's	Papa John's	Pizza Hut	Domino's	Papa John's
Papa John's	Papa John's	Pizza Hut	Pizza Hut	Papa John's	Domino's
Little Caesar's	Domino's	Domino's	Godfather's	Pizza Hut	Papa John's
Pizza Hut	Pizza Hut	Papa John's	Papa John's	Godfather's	Papa John's
Domino's					

   a   Find the frequency distribution and relative frequency distribution for these data.
   b   Construct a percentage bar chart for these data.
   c   Construct a percentage pie chart for these data.
   d   Which restaurant is most popular with these students? Least popular?

2.8   Fifty randomly selected adults who follow professional sports were asked to name their favorite
professional sports league. The results are as follows where MLB = Major League Baseball,
MLS = Major League Soccer, NBA = National Basketball Association, NFL = National Football
League, and NHL = National Hockey League.   **DS** ProfSports

NFL	NBA	NFL	MLB	MLB	NHL	NFL	NFL	MLS	MLB
MLB	NFL	MLB	NBA	NBA	NFL	NFL	NFL	NHL	NBA
NBA	NFL	NHL	NFL	MLS	NFL	MLB	NFL	MLB	NFL
NHL	MLB	NHL	NFL	NFL	NFL	MLB	NFL	NBA	NFL
MLS	NFL	MLB	NBA	NFL	NFL	MLB	NBA	NFL	NFL

   a   Find the frequency distribution, relative frequency distribution, and percent frequency
distribution for these data.
   b   Construct a frequency bar chart for these data.
   c   Construct a pie chart for these data.
   d   Which professional sports league is most popular with these 50 adults? Which is least popular?

2.9   **a**   On March 11, 2005, the Gallup Organization released the results of a CNN/USA Today/Gallup
national poll regarding Internet usage in the United States. Each of 1,008 randomly selected
adults was asked to respond to the following question:

> As you may know, there are Web sites known as "blogs" or "Web logs," where people
> sometimes post their thoughts. How familiar are you with "blogs"—very familiar, some-
> what familiar, not too familiar, or not at all familiar?

The poll's results were as follows: Very familiar (7%); Somewhat familiar (19%); Not too
familiar (18%); Not at all familiar (56%).[1] Use these data to construct a bar chart and a pie chart.
   b   On February 15, 2005, the Gallup Organization released the results of a Gallup UK poll
regarding Internet usage in Great Britain. Each of 1,009 randomly selected UK adults was
asked to respond to the following question:

> How much time, if at all, do you personally spend using the Internet—more than an hour
> a day, up to one hour a day, a few times a week, a few times a month or less, or never?

The poll's results were as follows: More than an hour a day (22%); Up to an hour a day (14%);
A few times a week (15%); A few times a month or less (10%); Never (39%).[2] Use these data
to construct a bar chart and a pie chart.

2.10   The National Automobile Dealers Association (NADA) publishes *AutoExec* magazine, which
annually reports on new vehicle sales and market shares by manufacturer. As given on the
AutoExec magazine website in May 2006, new vehicle market shares in the United States
for 2005 were as follows[3]: Daimler-Chrysler 13.6%, Ford 18.3%, GM 26.3%, Japanese
(Toyota/Honda/Nissan) 28.3%, other imports 13.5%.   **DS** AutoShares05
   a   Construct a percent frequency bar chart and a percentage pie chart for the 2005 auto market shares.
   b   Figure 2.5 gives a percentage bar chart of new vehicle market shares in the U.S. for 1997. Use
this bar chart and your results from part (a) to write an analysis explaining how new vehicle
market shares in the United States have changed from 1997 to 2005.   **DS** AutoShares97

2.11   On January 11, 2005, the Gallup Organization released the results of a poll investigating how
many Americans have private health insurance. The results showed that among Americans making
less than $30,000 per year, 33% had private insurance, 50% were covered by Medicare/Medicaid,
and 17% had no health insurance, while among Americans making $75,000 or more per year,

---

[1]Source: Copyright © 2005 Gallup Inc. used with permission, http://gallup.com/poll/content/default.aspx?ci=15217
[2]Source: Copyright © 2005 Gallup Inc. used with permission, http://gallup.com/poll/content/default.aspx?ci=14947
[3]Source: www.autoexecmag.com, May 15, 2006.

FIGURE 2.5 **An Excel Bar Chart of U.S. Automobile Sales in 1997 (for Exercise 2.10)**
DS AutoShares97

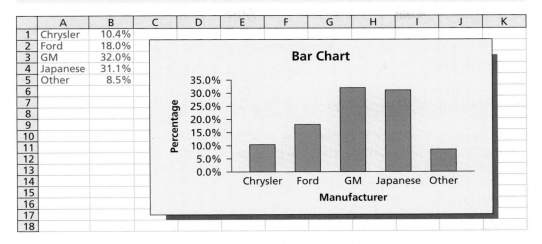

	A	B	C	D	E	F	G	H	I	J	K
1	Chrysler	10.4%									
2	Ford	18.0%									
3	GM	32.0%									
4	Japanese	31.1%									
5	Other	8.5%									
6											
7											
8											
9											
10											
11											
12											
13											
14											
15											
16											
17											
18											

FIGURE 2.6 **A Pareto Chart for Incomplete Customer Calls (for Exercise 2.12)**

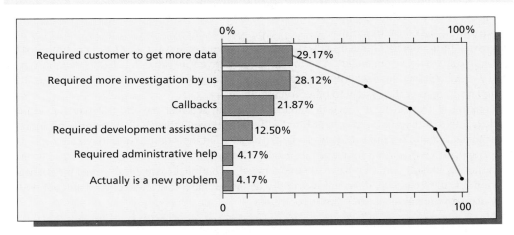

Source: B. A. Cleary, "Company Cares about Customers' Calls," *Quality Progress* (November 1993), pp. 60–73. Copyright © 1993 American Society for Quality Control. Used with permission.

87% had private insurance, 9% were covered by Medicare/Medicaid, and 4% had no health insurance.[4] Use bar and pie charts to compare health coverage of the two income groups.

2.12 In an article in *Quality Progress,* Barbara A. Cleary reports on improvements made in a software supplier's responses to customer calls. In this article, the author states:

> In an effort to improve its response time for these important customer-support calls, an inbound telephone inquiry team was formed at PQ Systems, Inc., a software and training organization in Dayton, Ohio. The team found that 88 percent of the customers' calls were already being answered immediately by the technical support group, but those who had to be called back had to wait an average of 56.6 minutes. No customer complaints had been registered, but the team believed that this response rate could be improved.

As part of its improvement process, the company studied the disposition of complete and incomplete calls to its technical support analysts. A call is considered complete if the customer's problem has been resolved; otherwise the call is incomplete. Figure 2.6 shows a Pareto chart analysis for the incomplete customer calls.

a What percentage of incomplete calls required "more investigation" by the analyst or "administrative help"?

b What percentage of incomplete calls actually presented a "new problem"?

c In light of your answers to *a* and *b,* can you make a suggestion?

[4]Source: http://gallup.com/poll/content/default.aspx?ci=14581

LO3 Summarize quantitative data by using frequency distributions, histograms, frequency polygons, and ogives.

2.2 Graphically Summarizing Quantitative Data ● ● ●

Frequency distributions and histograms   We often need to summarize and describe the shape of the distribution of a population or sample of **measurements**. Such data are often summarized by grouping the measurements into the classes of a frequency distribution and by displaying the data in the form of a **histogram.** We explain how to construct a histogram in the following example.

EXAMPLE 2.2 The Payment Time Case: Reducing Payment Times[5]

Major consulting firms such as Accenture, Ernst & Young Consulting, and Deloitte & Touche Consulting employ statistical analysis to assess the effectiveness of the systems they design for their customers. In this case a consulting firm has developed an electronic billing system for a Hamilton, Ohio, trucking company. The system sends invoices electronically to each customer's computer and allows customers to easily check and correct errors. It is hoped that the new billing system will substantially reduce the amount of time it takes customers to make payments. Typical payment times—measured from the date on an invoice to the date payment is received—using the trucking company's old billing system had been 39 days or more. This exceeded the industry standard payment time of 30 days.

The new billing system does not automatically compute the payment time for each invoice because there is no continuing need for this information. Therefore, in order to assess the system's effectiveness, the consulting firm selects a random sample of 65 invoices from the 7,823 invoices processed during the first three months of the new system's operation. The payment times for the 65 sample invoices are manually determined and are given in Table 2.4. If this sample can be used to establish that the new billing system substantially reduces payment times, the consulting firm plans to market the system to other trucking firms.

Looking at the payment times in Table 2.4, we can see that the shortest payment time is 10 days and that the longest payment time is 29 days. Beyond that, it is pretty difficult to interpret the data in any meaningful way. To better understand the sample of 65 payment times, the consulting firm will form a frequency distribution of the data and will graph the distribution by constructing a histogram. Similar to the frequency distributions for qualitative data we studied in Section 2.1, the frequency distribution will divide the payment times into classes and will tell us how many of the payment times are in each class.

Step 1: Find the number of classes   One rule for finding an appropriate number of classes says that the number of classes should be the smallest whole number K that makes the quantity 2^K greater than the number of measurements in the data set. For the payment time data we have 65 measurements. Because $2^6 = 64$ is less than 65 and $2^7 = 128$ is greater than 65, we should use $K = 7$ classes. Table 2.5 gives the appropriate number of classes (determined by the 2^K rule) to use for data sets of various sizes.

Step 2: Find the class length   We find the length of each class by computing

$$\text{approximate class length} = \frac{\text{largest measurement} - \text{smallest measurement}}{\text{number of classes}}$$

TABLE 2.4   **A Sample of Payment Times (in Days) for 65 Randomly Selected Invoices**   Ⓟ PayTime

22	29	16	15	18	17	12	13	17	16	15
19	17	10	21	15	14	17	18	12	20	14
16	15	16	20	22	14	25	19	23	15	19
18	23	22	16	16	19	13	18	24	24	26
13	18	17	15	24	15	17	14	18	17	21
16	21	25	19	20	27	16	17	16	21	

---

[5]This case is based on a real problem encountered by a company that employs one of our former students. For purposes of confidentiality, we have withheld the company's name.

TABLE 2.5	Recommended Number of Classes for Data Sets of *n* Measurements*
Number of Classes	**Size, *n*, of the Data Set**
2	$1 \leq n < 4$
3	$4 \leq n < 8$
4	$8 \leq n < 16$
5	$16 \leq n < 32$
6	$32 \leq n < 64$
7	$64 \leq n < 128$
8	$128 \leq n < 256$
9	$256 \leq n < 528$
10	$528 \leq n < 1056$

*For completeness sake we have included all values of $n \geq 1$ in this table. However, we do not recommend constructing a histogram with fewer than 16 measurements.

TABLE 2.6	Seven Nonoverlapping Classes for a Frequency Distribution of the 65 Payment Times
Class 1	10 days and less than 13 days
Class 2	13 days and less than 16 days
Class 3	16 days and less than 19 days
Class 4	19 days and less than 22 days
Class 5	22 days and less than 25 days
Class 6	25 days and less than 28 days
Class 7	28 days and less than 31 days

Because the largest and smallest payment times in Table 2.4 are 29 days and 10 days, the approximate class length is $(29 - 10)/7 = 2.7143$. To obtain an easier to read final class length, we round this value. Commonly, the approximate class length is rounded up to the precision of the data measurements (that is, increased to the next number that has the same number of decimal places as the data measurements). For instance, because the payment times are measured to the nearest day, we round 2.7143 days up to 3 days.

Step 3: Form nonoverlapping classes of equal width   We can form the classes of the frequency distribution by defining the **boundaries** of the classes. To find the first class boundary, we find the smallest payment time in Table 2.4, which is 10 days. This value is the lower boundary of the first class. Adding the class length of 3 to this lower boundary, we obtain $10 + 3 = 13$, which is the upper boundary of the first class and the lower boundary of the second class. Similarly, the upper boundary of the second class and the lower boundary of the third class equals $13 + 3 = 16$. Continuing in this fashion, the lower boundaries of the remaining classes are 19, 22, 25, and 28. Adding the class length 3 to the lower boundary of the last class gives us the upper boundary of the last class, 31. These boundaries define seven nonoverlapping classes for the frequency distribution. We summarize these classes in Table 2.6. For instance, the first class—10 days and less than 13 days—includes the payment times 10, 11, and 12 days; the second class—13 days and less than 16 days—includes the payment times 13, 14, and 15 days; and so forth. Notice that the largest *observed* payment time—29 days—is contained in the last class. In cases where the largest measurement is not contained in the last class, we simply add another class. Generally speaking, the guidelines we have given for forming classes are not inflexible rules. Rather, they are intended to help us find reasonable classes. Finally, the method we have used for forming classes results in classes of equal length. Generally, forming classes of equal length will make it easier to appropriately interpret the frequency distribution.

Step 4: Tally and count the number of measurements in each class   Having formed the classes, we now count the number of measurements that fall into each class. To do this, it is convenient to tally the measurements. We simply list the classes, examine the payment times in Table 2.4 one at a time, and record a tally mark corresponding to a particular class each time we encounter a measurement that falls in that class. For example, since the first four payment times in Table 2.4 are 22, 19, 16, and 18, the first four tally marks are shown below. Here, for brevity, we express the class "10 days and less than 13 days" as "$10 < 13$" and use similar notation for the other classes.

Class	First 4 Tally Marks	All 65 Tally Marks	Frequency
$10 < 13$		///	3
$13 < 16$		7HL 7HL ////	14
$16 < 19$	//	7HL 7HL 7HL 7HL ///	23
$19 < 22$	/	7HL 7HL //	12
$22 < 25$	/	7HL ///	8
$25 < 28$		////	4
$28 < 31$		/	1

TABLE 2.7   Frequency Distributions of the 65 Payment Times

Class	Frequency	Relative Frequency	Percent Frequency
10 < 13	3	3/65 = .0462	4.62%
13 < 16	14	14/65 = .2154	21.54
16 < 19	23	.3538	35.38
19 < 22	12	.1846	18.46
22 < 25	8	.1231	12.31
25 < 28	4	.0615	6.15
28 < 31	1	.0154	1.54

FIGURE 2.7   A Frequency Histogram of the 65 Payment Times

After examining all 65 payment times, we have recorded 65 tally marks—see the bottom of page 43. We find the **frequency** for each class by counting the number of tally marks recorded for the class. For instance, counting the number of tally marks for the class "13 < 16", we obtain the frequency 14 for this class. The frequencies for all seven classes are summarized in Table 2.7. This summary is the **frequency distribution** for the 65 payment times. Table 2.7 also gives the *relative frequency* and the *percent frequency* for each of the seven classes. The **relative frequency** of a class is the proportion (fraction) of the total number of measurements that are in the class. For example, there are 14 payment times in the second class, so its relative frequency is 14/65 = .2154. This says that the proportion of the 65 payment times that are in the second class is .2154, or, equivalently, that 100(.2154)% = 21.54% of the payment times are in the second class. A list of all of the classes—along with each class relative frequency—is called a **relative frequency distribution.** A list of all of the classes—along with each class percent frequency—is called a **percent frequency distribution.**

Step 5: Graph the histogram   We can graphically portray the distribution of payment times by drawing a **histogram.** The histogram can be constructed using the frequency, relative frequency, or percent frequency distribution. To set up the histogram, we draw rectangles that correspond to the classes. The base of the rectangle corresponding to a class represents the payment times in the class. The height of the rectangle can represent the class frequency, relative frequency, or percent frequency.

We have drawn a **frequency histogram** of the 65 payment times in Figure 2.7. The first (left-most) rectangle, or "bar," of the histogram represents the payment times 10, 11, and 12. Looking at Figure 2.7, we see that the base of this rectangle is drawn from the lower boundary (10) of the first class in the frequency distribution of payment times to the lower boundary (13) of the second class. The height of this rectangle tells us that the frequency of the first class is 3. The second histogram rectangle represents payment times 13, 14, and 15. Its base is drawn from the lower boundary (13) of the second class to the lower boundary (16) of the third class, and its height tells us that the frequency of the second class is 14. The other histogram bars are constructed similarly. Notice that there are no gaps between the adjacent rectangles in the histogram. Here, although the payment times have been recorded to the nearest whole day, the fact that the histogram bars touch each other emphasizes that a payment time could (in theory) be any number on the horizontal axis. In general, histograms are drawn so that adjacent bars touch each other.

Looking at the frequency distribution in Table 2.7 and the frequency histogram in Figure 2.7, we can describe the payment times:

1   None of the payment times exceeds the industry standard of 30 days. (Actually, all of the payment times are less than 30—remember the largest payment time is 29 days.)

2   The payment times are concentrated between 13 and 24 days (57 of the 65, or (57/65) × 100 = 87.69%, of the payment times are in this range).

3   More payment times are in the class "16 < 19" than are in any other class (23 payment times are in this class).

FIGURE 2.8   A Percent Frequency Histogram of the 65 Payment Times

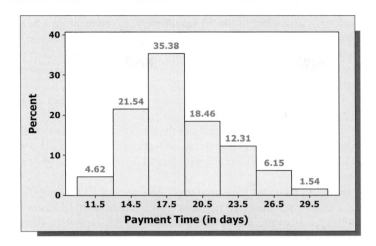

Notice that the frequency distribution and histogram allow us to make some helpful conclusions about the payment times, whereas looking at the raw data (the payment times in Table 2.4) did not.

A **relative frequency histogram** and a **percent frequency histogram** of the payment times would both be drawn like Figure 2.7 except that the heights of the rectangles represent, respectively, the relative frequencies and the percent frequencies in Table 2.7. For example, Figure 2.8 gives a percent frequency histogram of the payment times. This histogram also illustrates that we sometimes label the classes on the horizontal axis using the **class midpoints.** Each class midpoint is exactly halfway between the boundaries of its class. For instance, the midpoint of the first class, 11.5, is halfway between the class boundaries 10 and 13. The midpoint of the second class, 14.5, is halfway between the class boundaries 13 and 16. The other class midpoints are found similarly. The percent frequency distribution of Figure 2.8 tells us that 21.54% of the payment times are in the second class (which has midpoint 14.5 and represents the payment times 13, 14, and 15).

In the following box we summarize the steps needed to set up a frequency distribution and histogram:

Constructing Frequency Distributions and Histograms

1 Find the number of classes. Generally, the number of classes K should equal the smallest whole number that makes the quantity 2^K greater than the total number of measurements n (see Table 2.5 on page 43).

2 Compute the approximate **class length:**

$$\frac{\text{largest measurement} - \text{smallest measurement}}{K}$$

Often the final class length is obtained by rounding this value up to the same level of precision as the data.

3 Form nonoverlapping classes of equal length. Form the classes by finding the **class boundaries.** The lower boundary of the first class is the smallest measurement in the data set. Add the class length to this boundary to obtain the next boundary. Successive boundaries are found by repeatedly adding the class length until the upper boundary of the last (Kth) class is found.

4 Tally and count the number of measurements in each class. The **frequency** for each class is the count of the number of measurements in the class. The **relative frequency** for each class is the fraction of measurements in the class. The **percent frequency** for each class is its relative frequency multiplied by 100%.

5 Graph the histogram. To draw a **frequency histogram,** plot each frequency as the height of a rectangle positioned over its corresponding class. Use the class boundaries to separate adjacent rectangles. A **relative frequency histogram** and a **percent histogram** are graphed in the same way except that the heights of the rectangles are, respectively, the relative frequencies and the percent frequencies.

The procedure in the above box is not the only way to construct a histogram. Often, histograms are constructed more informally. For instance, it is not necessary to set the lower boundary of the first (leftmost) class equal to the smallest measurement in the data. As an example, suppose that we wish to form a histogram of the 50 gas mileages given in Table 1.6 (page 12). Examining the mileages, we see that the smallest mileage is 29.8 mpg and that the largest mileage is 33.3 mpg. Therefore, it would be convenient to begin the first (leftmost) class at 29.5 mpg and end the last (rightmost) class at 33.5 mpg. Further, it would be reasonable to use classes that are .5 mpg in length. We would then use 8 classes: 29.5 < 30, 30 < 30.5, 30.5 < 31, 31 < 31.5, 31.5 < 32, 32 < 32.5, 32.5 < 33, and 33 < 33.5. A histogram of the gas mileages employing these classes is shown in Figure 2.9.

Sometimes it is desirable to let the nature of the problem determine the histogram classes. For example, to construct a histogram describing the ages of the residents in a city, it might be reasonable to use classes having 10-year lengths (that is, under 10 years, 10–19 years, 20–29 years, 30–39 years, and so on).

Notice that in our examples we have used classes having equal class lengths. In general, it is best to use equal class lengths whenever the raw data (that is, all the actual measurements) are available. However, sometimes histograms are formed with unequal class lengths—particularly when we are using published data as a source. Economic data and data in the social sciences are often published in the form of frequency distributions having unequal class lengths. Dealing with this kind of data is discussed in Exercise 2.85. Also discussed in this exercise is how to deal with **open-ended** classes. For example, if we are constructing a histogram describing the yearly incomes of U.S. households, an open-ended class could be households earning over $500,000 per year.

As an alternative to constructing a frequency distribution and histogram by hand, we can use software packages such as Excel and MINITAB. Each of these packages will automatically define histogram classes for the user. However, these automatically defined classes will not necessarily be the same as those that would be obtained using the manual method we have previously described. Furthermore, the packages define classes by using different methods. (Descriptions of how the classes are defined can often be found in help menus.) For example, Figure 2.10 gives a MINITAB frequency histogram of the payment times in Table 2.4. Here, MINITAB has defined 11 classes and has labeled five of the classes on the horizontal axis using midpoints (12, 16, 20, 24, 28). It is easy to see that the midpoints of the unlabeled classes are 10, 14, 18, 22, 26, and 30. Moreover, the boundaries of the first class are 9 and 11, the boundaries of the second class are 11 and 13, and so forth. MINITAB counts frequencies as we have previously described. For instance, one payment time is at least 9 and less than 11, two payment times are at least 11 and less than 13, seven payment times are at least 13 and less than 15, and so forth.

| FIGURE 2.9 | A Percent Frequency Histogram of the Gas Mileages: The Gas Mileage Distribution Is Symmetrical and Mound Shaped |

| FIGURE 2.10 | A MINITAB Frequency Histogram of the Payment Times with Automatic Classes: The Payment Time Distribution Is Skewed to the Right |

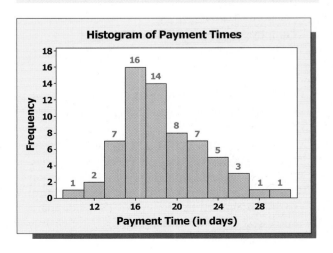

FIGURE 2.11   **An Excel Frequency Histogram of the Bottle Design Ratings: The Distribution of Ratings Is Skewed to the Left**

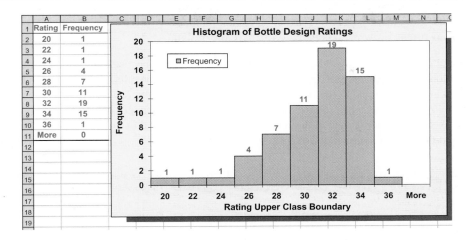

Figure 2.11 gives an Excel frequency distribution and histogram of the bottle design ratings in Table 1.5. Excel labels histogram classes using their upper class boundaries. For example, the first class has an upper class boundary equal to the smallest rating of 20 and contains only this smallest rating. The boundaries of the second class are 20 and 22, the boundaries of the third class are 22 and 24, and so forth. The last class corresponds to ratings more than 36. Excel's method for counting frequencies differs from that of MINITAB (and, therefore, also differs from the way we counted frequencies by hand in Example 2.2). Excel assigns a frequency to a particular class by counting the number of measurements that are greater than the lower boundary of the class and less than or equal to the upper boundary of the class. For example, one bottle design rating is greater than 20 and less than or equal to (that is, at most) 22. Similarly, 15 bottle design ratings are greater than 32 and at most 34.

In Figure 2.10 we have used MINITAB to automatically form histogram classes. It is also possible to use software packages to form histogram classes that are defined by the user. We explain how to do this in the appendices at the end of this chapter. Because Excel does not always automatically define acceptable classes, the classes in Figure 2.11 are a modification of Excel's automatic classes. We also explain this modification in the appendices at the end of this chapter.

Some common distribution shapes   We often graph a frequency distribution in the form of a histogram in order to visualize the *shape* of the distribution. If we look at the histogram of payment times in Figure 2.10, we see that the right tail of the histogram is longer than the left tail. When a histogram has this general shape, we say that the distribution is **skewed to the right.** Here the long right tail tells us that a few of the payment times are somewhat longer than the rest. If we look at the histogram of bottle design ratings in Figure 2.11, we see that the left tail of the histogram is much longer than the right tail. When a histogram has this general shape, we say that the distribution is **skewed to the left.** Here the long tail to the left tells us that, while most of the bottle design ratings are concentrated above 25 or so, a few of the ratings are lower than the rest. Finally, looking at the histogram of gas mileages in Figure 2.9, we see that the right and left tails of the histogram appear to be mirror images of each other. When a histogram has this general shape, we say that the distribution is **symmetrical.** Moreover, the distribution of gas mileages appears to be piled up in the middle or **mound shaped.**

Mound-shaped, symmetrical distributions as well as distributions that are skewed to the right or left are commonly found in practice. For example, distributions of scores on standardized tests such as the SAT and ACT tend to be mound shaped and symmetrical, whereas distributions of scores on tests in college statistics courses might be skewed to the left—a few students don't study and get scores much lower than the rest. On the other hand, economic data such as income data are often skewed to the right—a few people have incomes much higher than most others.

Many other distribution shapes are possible. For example, some distributions have two or more peaks—we will give an example of this distribution shape later in this section. It is often very useful to know the shape of a distribution. For example, knowing that the distribution of bottle design ratings is skewed to the left suggests that a few consumers may have noticed a problem with design that others didn't see. Further investigation into why these consumers gave the design low ratings might allow the company to improve the design.

Frequency polygons Another graphical display that can be used to depict a frequency distribution is a **frequency polygon.** To construct this graphic, we plot a point above each class midpoint at a height equal to the frequency of the class—the height can also be the class relative frequency or class percent frequency if so desired. Then we connect the points with line segments. As we will demonstrate in the following example, this kind of graphic can be particularly useful when we wish to compare two or more distributions.

EXAMPLE 2.3 Comparing the Grade Distributions for Two Statistics Exams

Table 2.8 lists (in increasing order) the scores earned on the first exam by the 40 students in a business statistics course taught by one of the authors several semesters ago. Figure 2.12 gives a percent frequency polygon for these exam scores. Because exam scores are often reported by using 10-point grade ranges (for instance, 80 to 90 percent), we have defined the following classes: $30 < 40, 40 < 50, 50 < 60, 60 < 70, 70 < 80, 80 < 90$, and $90 < 100$. This is an example of letting the situation determine the classes of a frequency distribution, which is common practice when the situation naturally defines classes. The points that form the polygon have been plotted corresponding to the midpoints of the classes (35, 45, 55, 65, 75, 85, 95). Each point is plotted at a height that equals the percentage of exam scores in its class. For instance, because 10 of the 40 scores are at least 90 and less than 100, the plot point corresponding to the class midpoint 95 is plotted at a height of 25 percent.

Looking at Figure 2.12, we see that there is a concentration of scores in the 85 to 95 range and another concentration of scores around 65. In addition, the distribution of scores is somewhat skewed to the left—a few students had scores (in the 30s and 40s) that were quite a bit lower than the rest.

This is an example of a distribution having two peaks. When a distribution has multiple peaks, finding the reason for the different peaks often provides useful information. The reason for the two-peaked distribution of exam scores was that some students were not attending class regularly. Students who received scores in the 60s and below admitted that they were cutting class, whereas students who received higher scores were attending class on a regular basis.

After identifying the reason for the concentration of lower scores, the instructor established an attendance policy that forced students to attend every class—any student who missed a class was

TABLE 2.8	Exam Scores for the First Exam Given in a Statistics Class ⒹⓈ FirstExam			
32	63	69	85	91
45	64	69	86	92
50	64	72	87	92
56	65	76	87	93
58	66	78	88	93
60	67	81	89	94
61	67	83	90	96
61	68	83	90	98

FIGURE 2.12   A Percent Frequency Polygon of the Exam Scores

TABLE 2.9	Exam Scores for the Second Statistics Exam—after a New Attendance Policy ⑤ SecondExam			
55	74	80	87	93
62	74	82	88	94
63	74	83	89	94
66	75	84	90	95
67	76	85	91	97
67	77	86	91	99
71	77	86	92	
73	78	87	93	

FIGURE 2.13 Percent Frequency Polygons of the Scores on the First Two Exams in a Statistics Course

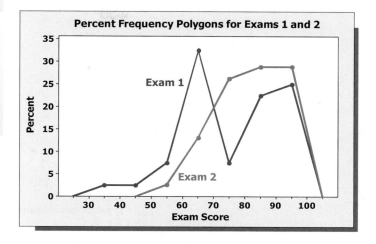

to be dropped from the course. Table 2.9 presents the scores on the second exam—after the new attendance policy. Figure 2.13 presents (and allows us to compare) the percent frequency polygons for both exams. We see that the polygon for the second exam is single peaked—the attendance policy[6] eliminated the concentration of scores in the 60s, although the scores are still somewhat skewed to the left.

Cumulative distributions and ogives   Another way to summarize a distribution is to construct a cumulative distribution. To do this, we use the same number of classes, the same class lengths, and the same class boundaries that we have used for the frequency distribution of a data set. However, in order to construct a **cumulative frequency distribution,** we record for each class *the number of measurements that are less than the upper boundary of the class.* To illustrate this idea, Table 2.10 gives the cumulative frequency distribution of the payment time distribution summarized in Table 2.7 (page 44). Columns (1) and (2) in this table give the frequency distribution of the payment times. Column (3) gives the **cumulative frequency** for each class. To see how these values are obtained, the cumulative frequency for the class $10 < 13$ is the number of payment times less than 13. This is obviously the frequency for the class $10 < 13$, which is 3. The cumulative frequency for the class $13 < 16$ is the number of payment times less than 16, which is obtained by adding the frequencies for the first two classes—that is, $3 + 14 = 17$. The cumulative frequency for the class $16 < 19$ is the number of payment times less than 19— that is, $3 + 14 + 23 = 40$. We see that, in general, a cumulative frequency is obtained by summing the frequencies of all classes representing values less than the upper boundary of the class.

TABLE 2.10	A Frequency Distribution, Cumulative Frequency Distribution, Cumulative Relative Frequency Distribution, and Cumulative Percent Frequency Distribution for the Payment Time Data			
(1) Class	(2) Frequency	(3) Cumulative Frequency	(4) Cumulative Relative Frequency	(5) Cumulative Percent Frequency
$10 < 13$	3	3	$3/65 = .0462$	4.62%
$13 < 16$	14	17	$17/65 = .2615$	26.15
$16 < 19$	23	40	.6154	61.54
$19 < 22$	12	52	.8000	80.00
$22 < 25$	8	60	.9231	92.31
$25 < 28$	4	64	.9846	98.46
$28 < 31$	1	65	1.0000	100.00

[6]Other explanations are possible. For instance, all of the students who did poorly on the first exam might have studied harder for the second exam. However, the instructor's 30 years of teaching experience suggest that attendance was the critical factor.

FIGURE 2.14   **A Percent Frequency Ogive of the Payment Times**

Column (4) gives the **cumulative relative frequency** for each class, which is obtained by summing the relative frequencies of all classes representing values less than the upper boundary of the class. Or, more simply, this value can be found by dividing the cumulative frequency for the class by the total number of measurements in the data set. For instance, the cumulative relative frequency for the class $19 < 22$ is $52/65 = .8$. Column (5) gives the **cumulative percent frequency** for each class, which is obtained by summing the percent frequencies of all classes representing values less than the upper boundary of the class. More simply, this value can be found by multiplying the cumulative relative frequency of a class by 100. For instance, the cumulative percent frequency for the class $19 < 22$ is $.8 (100) = 80$ percent.

As an example of interpreting Table 2.10, 60 of the 65 payment times are 24 days or less, or, equivalently, 92.31 percent of the payment times (or a fraction of .9231 of the payment times) are 24 days or less. Also, notice that the last entry in the cumulative frequency distribution is the total number measurements (here, 65 payment times). In addition, the last entry in the cumulative relative frequency distribution is 1.0 and the last entry in the cumulative percent frequency distribution is 100%. In general, for any data set, these last entries will be, respectively, the total number of measurements, 1.0, and 100%.

An **ogive** (pronounced "oh-jive") is a graph of a cumulative distribution. To construct a frequency ogive, we plot a point above each upper class boundary at a height equal to the cumulative frequency of the class. We then connect the plotted points with line segments. A similar graph can be drawn using the cumulative relative frequencies or the cumulative percent frequencies. As an example, Figure 2.14 gives a percent frequency ogive of the payment times. Looking at this figure, we see that, for instance, a little more than 25 percent (actually, 26.15 percent according to Table 2.10) of the payment times are less than 16 days, while 80 percent of the payment times are less than 22 days. Also notice that we have completed the ogive by plotting an additional point at the lower boundary of the first (leftmost) class at a height equal to zero. This depicts the fact that none of the payment times is less than 10 days. Finally, the ogive graphically shows that all (100 percent) of the payment times are less than 31 days.

Exercises for Section 2.2

CONCEPTS

connect

2.13   Explain
   a   Why we construct a frequency distribution and a histogram for a data set.
   b   The difference between a frequency histogram and a frequency polygon.
   c   The difference between a frequency polygon and a frequency ogive.

2.14   Explain how to find
   a   The frequency for a class
   b   The relative frequency for a class
   c   The percent frequency for a class

2.15 Explain what each of the following distribution shapes looks like. Then draw a picture that illustrates each shape.

  a Symmetrical and mound shaped
  b Double peaked
  c Skewed to the right
  d Skewed to the left

METHODS AND APPLICATIONS

2.16 Consider the following data: ⑤ HistoData

36	39	36	35	36	20	19
46	40	42	34	41	36	42
40	38	33	37	22	33	28
38	38	34	37	17	25	38

  a Find the number of classes needed to construct a histogram.
  b Find the class length.
  c Define nonoverlapping classes for a frequency distribution.
  d Tally the number of values in each class and develop a frequency distribution.
  e Draw a histogram for these data.
  f Develop a percent frequency distribution.

2.17 Consider the frequency distribution of exam scores given below.

Class	Frequency
90 < 100	12
80 < 90	17
70 < 80	14
60 < 70	5
50 < 60	2

  a Develop a relative frequency distribution and a percent frequency distribution.
  b Develop a cumulative frequency distribution and a cumulative percent frequency distribution.
  c Draw a frequency polygon.
  d Draw a frequency ogive.

THE MARKETING RESEARCH CASE ⑤ Design

Recall that 60 randomly selected shoppers have rated a new bottle design for a popular soft drink. The data are given below.

34	33	33	29	26	33	28	25	32	33
32	25	27	33	22	27	32	33	32	29
24	30	20	34	31	32	30	35	33	31
32	28	30	31	31	33	29	27	34	31
31	28	33	31	32	28	26	29	32	34
32	30	34	32	30	30	32	31	29	33

Use these data to work exercises 2.18 and 2.19.

2.18 a Find the number of classes that should be used to construct a frequency distribution and histogram for the bottle design ratings.
  b If we round up to the nearest whole rating point, show that we should employ a class length equal to 3.
  c Define the nonoverlapping classes for a frequency distribution.
  d Tally the number of ratings in each class and develop a frequency distribution.
  e Draw the frequency histogram for the ratings data, and describe the distribution shape. ⑤ Design

2.19 a Construct a relative frequency distribution and a percent frequency distribution for the bottle design ratings.
  b Construct a cumulative frequency distribution and a cumulative percent frequency distribution.
  c Draw a frequency ogive for the bottle design ratings. ⑤ Design

2.20 Table 2.11 gives the 25 most powerful celebrities and their annual pay as ranked by the editors of *Forbes* magazine and as listed on the Forbes.com website on February 25, 2007. ⑤ PowerCeleb
  a Develop a frequency distribution for the celebrity pay data and draw a histogram.
  b Develop a cumulative frequency distribution and a cumulative percent frequency distribution for the celebrity pay data.
  c Draw a percent frequency ogive for the celebrity pay data.

TABLE 2.11   The 25 Most Powerful Celebrities as Rated by *Forbes* Magazine   DS PowerCeleb

Power Ranking	Celebrity Name	Pay ($mil)	Power Ranking	Celebrity Name	Pay ($mil)
1	Tom Cruise	67	14	Paul McCartney	40
2	Rolling Stones	90	15	George Lucas	235
3	Oprah Winfrey	225	16	Elton John	34
4	U2	110	17	David Letterman	40
5	Tiger Woods	90	18	Phil Mickelson	47
6	Steven Spielberg	332	19	J.K. Rowling	75
7	Howard Stern	302	20	Brad Pitt	25
8	50 Cent	41	21	Peter Jackson	39
9	Cast of The Sopranos	52	22	Dr. Phil McGraw	45
10	Dan Brown	88	23	Jay Leno	32
11	Bruce Springsteen	55	24	Celine Dion	40
12	Donald Trump	44	25	Kobe Bryant	31
13	Muhammad Ali	55			

Source: http://www.forbes.com/2006/06/12/06celebrities_money-power-celebrities-list_land.html (accessed February 25, 2007).

FIGURE 2.15   Excel Frequency Histogram of the 65 Satisfaction Ratings (for Exercise 2.21)

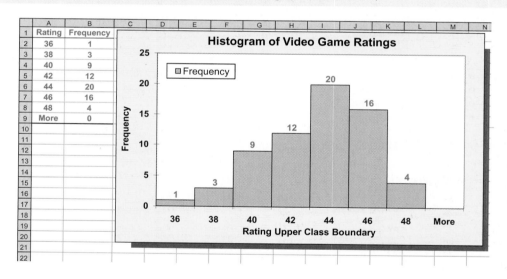

2.21   THE VIDEO GAME SATISFACTION RATING CASE   DS VideoGame

Recall that Table 1.7 (page 13) presents the satisfaction ratings for the XYZ-Box video game system that have been given by 65 randomly selected purchasers. Figure 2.15 gives the Excel output of a histogram of these satisfaction ratings.
a Describe where the satisfaction ratings seem to be concentrated.
b Describe and interpret the shape of the distribution of ratings.
c Write out the eight classes used to construct this histogram.
d Construct a cumulative frequency distribution of the satisfaction ratings using the histogram classes.

2.22   THE BANK CUSTOMER WAITING TIME CASE   DS WaitTime

Recall that Table 1.8 (page 13) presents the waiting times for teller service during peak business hours of 100 randomly selected bank customers. Figure 2.16 gives the MINITAB output of a histogram of these waiting times that has been constructed using automatic classes.
a Describe where the waiting times seem to be concentrated.
b Describe and interpret the shape of the distribution of waiting times.
c What is the class length that has been automatically defined by MINITAB?
d Write out the automatically defined classes and construct a cumulative percent frequency distribution of the waiting times using these classes.

FIGURE 2.16   **MINITAB Frequency Histogram of the 100 Waiting Times Using Automatic Classes (for Exercise 2.22)**

FIGURE 2.17   **Percent Frequency Histogram of the 40 Breaking Strengths (for Exercise 2.23)**

2.23   THE TRASH BAG CASE   DS TrashBag

Recall that Table 1.9 (page 14) presents the breaking strengths of 40 trash bags selected during a 40-hour pilot production run. Figure 2.17 gives a percent frequency histogram of these breaking strengths.
a   Describe where the breaking strengths seem to be concentrated.
b   Describe and interpret the shape of the distribution of breaking strengths.
c   What is the class length?
d   Write out the classes and construct a percent frequency ogive for the breaking strengths using these classes.

2.24   Table 2.12 gives the franchise value and 2006 revenues for each of the 30 teams in Major League Baseball as reported by *Forbes* magazine and as listed on the Forbes.com website on February 25, 2007.   DS MLBTeams
a   Develop a frequency distribution and a frequency histogram for the 30 team values. Then describe the distribution of team values.
b   Develop a percent frequency distribution and a percent frequency histogram for the 30 team revenues. Then describe the distribution of team revenues.
c   Draw a percent frequency polygon for the 30 team values.

TABLE 2.12   **Major League Baseball Team Valuations and Revenues as Given on the Forbes.com Website on February 25, 2007 (for Exercise 2.24)**   DS MLBTeams

Rank	Team	Value ($mil)	Revenues ($mil)	Rank	Team	Value ($mil)	Revenues ($mil)
1	New York Yankees	1026	277	16	Texas Rangers	353	153
2	Boston Red Sox	617	206	17	Cleveland Indians	352	150
3	New York Mets	604	195	18	Chicago White Sox	315	157
4	Los Angeles Dodgers	482	189	19	Arizona Diamondbacks	305	145
5	Chicago Cubs	448	179	20	Colorado Rockies	298	145
6	Washington Nationals	440	145	21	Detroit Tigers	292	146
7	St Louis Cardinals	429	165	22	Toronto Blue Jays	286	136
8	Seattle Mariners	428	179	23	Cincinnati Reds	274	137
9	Philadelphia Phillies	424	176	24	Pittsburgh Pirates	250	125
10	Houston Astros	416	173	25	Kansas City Royals	239	117
11	San Francisco Giants	410	171	26	Milwaukee Brewers	235	131
12	Atlanta Braves	405	172	27	Oakland Athletics	234	134
13	Los Angeles Angels @ Anaheim	368	167	28	Florida Marlins	226	119
14	Baltimore Orioles	359	156	29	Minnesota Twins	216	114
15	San Diego Padres	354	158	30	Tampa Bay Devil Rays	209	116

Source: http://www.forbes.com/lists/2006/33/Rank_1.html (accessed February 25, 2007).

TABLE 2.13   **The Best Performing Retailers from the *Forbes* List of "The 400 Best Big Companies" as Listed on the Forbes.com Website on February 27, 2007**   DS ForbesBest

Company	5-Year Total Return (%)	Sales ($bil)	Net Income ($mil)	Company	5-Year Total Return (%)	Sales ($bil)	Net Income ($mil)
Aaron Rents	31.2	1.3	74	Fastenal	20.2	1.7	193
Abercrombie & Fitch	24.1	3.1	389	Lowe's Cos	7.1	47.3	3,180
Advance Auto Parts	21.5	4.6	235	MarineMax	26.9	1.2	39
Aeropostale	10.5	1.3	85	Nordstrom	39.6	8.2	636
Amer Eagle Outfitters	29.6	2.6	345	O'Reilly Automotive	14.4	2.2	177
AnnTaylor Stores	22.6	2.3	149	Office Depot	19.7	14.9	487
Bed Bath & Beyond	3.3	6.1	579	Petsmart	27.8	4.1	179
Best Buy	12.4	32.6	1,246	Pool	30.6	1.9	100
CarMax	18.2	6.9	178	Ross Stores	16.7	5.4	220
Charming Shoppes	22.0	3.0	103	Staples	17.0	17.3	927
Children's Place	13.1	1.8	73	Target	9.2	56.7	2,607
Claire's Stores	36.0	1.4	171	TJX Cos	8.5	17.1	821
CVS	16.2	41.5	1,358	United Auto Group	23.5	11.1	125
Dick's Sporting Goods	66.2	2.9	99	Walgreen	3.8	47.4	1,751
Dress Barn	29.3	1.3	86				

Source: http://www.forbes.com/lists/2007/88/biz_07platinum_The-400-Best-Big-Companies-Retailing_7Company.html (accessed February 27, 2007).

2.25   *Forbes* magazine publishes a list of "The 400 Best Big Companies" as selected by the magazine's writers and editors. Table 2.13 gives the best companies in the retailing industry as given by this list on the Forbes.com website on February 27, 2007.   DS ForbesBest

    a   Develop a frequency distribution and a frequency histogram for the five-year total return percentages. Describe the distribution of these percentages.

    b   Develop a percent frequency histogram for the sales values and then describe this distribution.

    c   Develop a relative frequency ogive for the net incomes.

LO4   Construct and interpret dot plots.

2.3 Dot Plots ● ● ●

A very simple graph that can be used to summarize a data set is called a **dot plot.** To make a dot plot we draw a horizontal axis that spans the range of the measurements in the data set. We then place dots above the horizontal axis to represent the measurements. As an example, Figure 2.18(a) shows a dot plot of the exam scores in Table 2.8. Remember, these are the scores for the first

FIGURE 2.18   Comparing Exam Scores Using Dot Plots

(a) Dot Plot of Scores on Exam 1: Before Attendance Policy

(b) Dot Plot of Scores on Exam 2: After Attendance Policy

exam given before implementing a strict attendance policy. The horizontal axis spans exam scores from 30 to 100. Each dot above the axis represents an exam score. For instance, the two dots above the score of 90 tell us that two students received a 90 on the exam. The dot plot shows us that there are two concentrations of scores—those in the 80s and 90s and those in the 60s. Figure 2.18(b) gives a dot plot of the scores on the second exam (which was given after imposing the attendance policy). As did the percent frequency polygon for Exam 2 in Figure 2.13, this second dot plot shows that the attendance policy eliminated the concentration of scores in the 60s.

Dot plots are useful for detecting **outliers,** which are unusually large or small observations that are well separated from the remaining observations. For example, the dot plot for exam 1 indicates that the score 32 seems unusually low. How we handle an outlier depends on its cause. If the outlier results from a measurement error or an error in recording or processing the data, it should be corrected. If such an outlier cannot be corrected, it should be discarded. If an outlier is not the result of an error in measuring or recording the data, its cause may reveal important information. For example, the outlying exam score of 32 convinced the author that the student needed a tutor. After working with a tutor, the student showed considerable improvement on Exam 2. A more precise way to detect outliers is presented in Section 3.3.

Exercises for Section 2.3

CONCEPTS

2.26   When we construct a dot plot, what does the horizontal axis represent? What does each dot represent?

2.27   If a data set consists of 1,000 measurements, would you summarize the data set using a histogram or a dot plot? Explain.

METHODS AND APPLICATIONS

2.28   The following data consist of the number of students who were absent in a professor's statistics class each day during the last month.   DS AbsenceData

2	0	3	1	2	5	8	0	1	4
1	10	6	2	2	0	3	6	0	1

Construct a dot plot of these data, and then describe the distribution of absences.

2.29   The following are the revenue growth rates for the 30 fastest-growing companies as listed March 16, 2005, on the *Fortune* magazine website.   DS RevGrowth

93%	43%	91%	49%	70%	44%	71%	70%	52%	59%
33%	40%	60%	35%	51%	48%	39%	61%	25%	87%
87%	46%	38%	30%	33%	43%	29%	38%	60%	32%

Source: Fortune.com (accessed March 16, 2005)

Develop a dot plot for these data and describe the distribution of revenue growth rates.

2.30 The yearly home run totals for Babe Ruth during his career as a New York Yankee are as follows (the totals are arranged in increasing order): 22, 25, 34, 35, 41, 41, 46, 46, 46, 47, 49, 54, 54, 59, 60. Construct a dot plot for these data and then describe the distribution of home run totals.
Ⓓ RuthsHomers

LO5 Construct and interpret stem-and-leaf displays.

2.4 Stem-and-Leaf Displays ● ● ●

Another simple graph that can be used to quickly summarize a data set is called a **stem-and-leaf display.** This kind of graph places the measurements in order from smallest to largest, and allows the analyst to simultaneously see all of the measurements in the data set and see the shape of the data set's distribution.

EXAMPLE 2.4 The Car Mileage Case

Table 2.14 presents the sample of 50 gas mileages for the new midsize model previously introduced in Chapter 1. To develop a stem-and-leaf display, we note that the sample mileages range from 29.8 to 33.3 and we place the leading digits of these mileages—the whole numbers 29, 30, 31, 32, and 33—in a column on the left side of a vertical line as follows.

```
29 |
30 |
31 |
32 |
33 |
```

This vertical arrangement of leading digits forms the **stem** of the display. Next, we pass through the mileages in Table 2.14 one at a time and place each last digit (the tenths place) to the right of the vertical line in the row corresponding to its leading digits. For instance, the first three mileages—30.8, 31.7, and 30.1—are arranged as follows:

```
29 |
30 | 8 1
31 | 7
32 |
33 |
```

We form the **leaves** of the display by continuing this procedure as we pass through all 50 mileages. After recording the last digit for each of the mileages, we sort the digits in each row from smallest to largest and obtain the stem-and-leaf display that follows:

```
29 | 8
30 | 1 3 4 5 5 6 7 7 8 8 8
31 | 0 0 1 2 3 3 4 4 4 4 5 5 6 6 7 7 7 8 8 9 9
32 | 0 1 1 1 2 3 3 4 4 5 5 7 7 8
33 | 0 3
```

As we have said, the numbers to the left of the vertical line form the stem of the display. Each number to the right of the vertical line is a leaf. Each combination of a stem value and a leaf value

TABLE 2.14   A Sample of 50 Mileages for a New Midsize Model Ⓓ GasMiles

30.8	30.8	32.1	32.3	32.7
31.7	30.4	31.4	32.7	31.4
30.1	32.5	30.8	31.2	31.8
31.6	30.3	32.8	30.7	31.9
32.1	31.3	31.9	31.7	33.0
33.3	32.1	31.4	31.4	31.5
31.3	32.5	32.4	32.2	31.6
31.0	31.8	31.0	31.5	30.6
32.0	30.5	29.8	31.7	32.3
32.4	30.5	31.1	30.7	31.4

represents a measurement in the data set. For instance, the first row in the display

$$29 \mid 8$$

tells us that the first two digits are 29 and that the last (tenth place) digit is 8—that is, this combination represents the mileage 29.8 mpg. Similarly, the last row

$$33 \mid 0\ 3$$

represents the mileages 33.0 mpg and 33.3 mpg.

The entire stem-and-leaf display portrays the overall distribution of the sample mileages. It groups the mileages into classes, and it graphically illustrates how many mileages are in each class, as well as how the mileages are distributed within each class. The first class corresponds to the stem 29 and consists of the mileages from 29.0 to 29.9. There is one mileage—29.8—in this class. The second class corresponds to the stem 30 and consists of the mileages from 30.0 to 30.9. There are 11 mileages in this class. Similarly, the third, fourth, and fifth classes correspond to the stems 31, 32, and 33 and contain, respectively, 22 mileages, 14 mileages, and 2 mileages. Moreover, the stem-and-leaf display shows that the distribution of mileages is quite symmetrical. To see this, imagine turning the stem-and-leaf display on its side so that the vertical line becomes a horizontal number line. We see that the display now resembles a symmetrically shaped histogram. However, *the stem-and-leaf display is advantageous because it allows us to actually see the measurements in the data set* in addition to the distribution's shape.

When constructing a stem-and-leaf display, there are no rules that dictate the number of stem values (rows) that should be used. If we feel that the display has collapsed the mileages too closely together, we can stretch the display by assigning each set of leading digits to two or more rows. This is called *splitting the stems*. For example, in the following stem-and-leaf display of the mileages the first (uppermost) stem value of 30 is used to represent mileages between 30.0 and 30.4. The second stem value of 30 is used to represent mileages between 30.5 and 30.9.

```
29 |  8
30 |  1 3 4
30 |  5 5 6 7 7 8 8 8
31 |  0 0 1 2 3 3 4 4 4 4 4
31 |  5 5 6 6 7 7 7 8 8 9 9
32 |  0 1 1 1 2 3 3 4 4
32 |  5 5 7 7 8
33 |  0 3
```

Notice that, in this particular case, splitting the stems produces a display that seems to more clearly reveal the symmetrical shape of the distribution of mileages.

Most statistical software packages can be used to construct stem-and-leaf displays. Figure 2.19 gives a MINITAB stem-and-leaf display of the 50 sample mileages. This output has been obtained by splitting the stems—MINITAB produced this display automatically. MINITAB also provides

FIGURE 2.19   **MINITAB Stem-and-Leaf Display of the 50 Mileages**

```
Stem-and-Leaf Display: Mpg
Stem-and-leaf of Mpg N = 50
Leaf unit = 0.10

   1     29   8
   4     30   134
  12     30   55677888
  23     31   00123344444
 (11)    31   55667778899
  16     32   011123344
   7     32   55778
   2     33   03
```

an additional column of numbers (on the left) that provides information about how many mileages are in the various rows. For example, if we look at the MINITAB output, the 11 (in parentheses) tells us that there are 11 mileages between 31.5 mpg and 31.9 mpg. The 12 (no parentheses) tells us that a total of 12 mileages are at or below 30.9 mpg, while the 7 tells us that a total of 7 mileages are at or above 32.5 mpg.

It is possible to construct a stem-and-leaf display from measurements containing any number of digits. To see how this can be done, consider the following data which consists of the number of DVD players sold by an electronics manufacturer for each of the last 12 months.

| 13,502 | 15,932 | 14,739 | 15,249 | 14,312 | 17,111 | DS DVDPlayers |
| 19,010 | 16,121 | 16,708 | 17,886 | 15,665 | 16,475 | |

To construct a stem-and-leaf display, we will use only the first three digits of each sales value and we will define leaf values consisting of one digit. The stem will consist of the values 13, 14, 15, 16, 17, 18, and 19 (which represent thousands of units sold). Each leaf will represent the remaining three digits rounded to the nearest 100 units sold. For example, 13,502 will be represented by placing the leaf value 5 in the row corresponding to 13. To express the fact that the leaf 5 represents 500, we say that the **leaf unit** is 100. Using this procedure, we obtain the following stem-and-leaf display:

$$\text{Leaf unit} = 100$$

$$
\begin{array}{r|l}
13 & 5 \\
14 & 3\ 7 \\
15 & 2\ 7\ 9 \\
16 & 1\ 5\ 7 \\
17 & 1\ 9 \\
18 & \\
19 & 0 \\
\end{array}
$$

The standard practice of always using a single digit for each leaf allows us to construct a stem-and-leaf display for measurements having any number of digits as long as we appropriately define a leaf unit. However, it is not possible to recover the original measurements from such a display. If we do not have the original measurements, the best we can do is to approximate them by multiplying the digits in the display by the leaf unit. For instance, the measurements in the row corresponding to the stem value 17 can be approximated to be $171 \times (100) = 17{,}100$ and $179 \times (100) = 17{,}900$. In general, leaf units can be any power of 10 such as 0.1, 1, 10, 100, 1000, and so on. If no leaf unit is given for a stem-and-leaf display, we assume its value is 1.0.

We summarize how to set up a stem-and-leaf display in the following box:

Constructing a Stem-and-Leaf Display

1 Decide what units will be used for the stems and the leaves. Each leaf must be a single digit and the stem values will consist of appropriate leading digits. As a general rule, there should be between 5 and 20 stem values.

2 Place the stem values in a column to the left of a vertical line with the smallest value at the top of the column and the largest value at the bottom.

3 To the right of the vertical line, enter the leaf for each measurement into the row corresponding to the proper stem value. Each leaf should be a single digit—these can be rounded values that were originally more than one digit if we are using an appropriately defined leaf unit.

4 Rearrange the leaves so that they are in increasing order from left to right.

If we wish to compare two distributions, it is convenient to construct a **back-to-back stem-and-leaf display.** Figure 2.20 presents a back-to-back stem-and-leaf display for the previously discussed exam scores. The left side of the display summarizes the scores for the first exam. Remember, this exam was given before implementing a strict attendance policy. The right side of the display summarizes the scores for the second exam (which was given after imposing the attendance policy). Looking at the left side of the display, we see that for the first exam there are two concentrations of scores—those in the 80s and 90s and those in the 60s. The right side of the

FIGURE 2.20   **A Back-to-Back Stem-and-Leaf Display of the Exam Scores**

Exam 1		Exam 2
2	3	
	3	
	4	
5	4	
0	5	
8 6	5	5
4 4 3 1 1 0	6	2 3
9 9 8 7 7 6 5	6	6 7 7
2	7	1 3 4 4 4
8 6	7	5 6 7 7 8
3 3 1	8	0 2 3 4
9 8 7 7 6 5	8	5 6 6 7 7 8 9
4 3 3 2 2 1 0 0	9	0 1 1 2 3 3 4 4
8 6	9	5 7 9

display shows that the attendance policy eliminated the concentration of scores in the 60s and illustrates that the scores on exam 2 are almost single peaked and somewhat skewed to the left.

Stem-and-leaf displays are useful for detecting **outliers,** which are unusually large or small observations that are well separated from the remaining observations. For example, the stem-and-leaf display for exam 1 indicates that the score 32 seems unusually low. How we handle an outlier depends on its cause. If the outlier results from a measurement error or an error in recording or processing the data, it should be corrected. If such an outlier cannot be corrected, it should be discarded. If an outlier is not the result of an error in measuring or recording the data, its cause may reveal important information. For example, the outlying exam score of 32 convinced the author that the student needed a tutor. After working with a tutor, the student showed considerable improvement on Exam 2. A more precise way to detect outliers is presented in Section 3.3.

Exercises for Section 2.4

CONCEPTS

connect

2.31   Explain the difference between a histogram and a stem-and-leaf display.

2.32   What are the advantages of using a stem-and-leaf display?

2.33   If a data set consists of 1,000 measurements, would you summarize the data set by using a stem-and-leaf display or a histogram? Explain.

METHODS AND APPLICATIONS

2.34   The following data consist of the 2007 revenue growth rates (in percent) for a group of 20 firms. Construct a stem-and-leaf display for these data.   DS RevGrow2007

36	59	42	65	91	32	56	28	49	51
30	55	33	63	70	44	42	83	53	43

2.35   The following data consist of the 2007 profit margins (in percent) for a group of 20 firms. Construct a stem-and-leaf display for these data.   DS ProfitMar2007

25.2	16.1	22.2	15.2	14.1	15.2	14.4	15.9	10.4	14.0
16.4	13.9	10.4	13.8	14.9	16.1	15.8	13.2	16.8	12.6

2.36   The following data consist of the 2007 sales figures (in millions of dollars) for a group of 20 firms. Construct a stem-and-leaf display for these data. Use a leaf unit equal to 100.   DS Sales2007

6835	1973	2820	5358	1233	3291	2707	3291	2675	3707
3517	1449	2384	1376	1725	6047	7903	4616	1541	4189

2.37   Figure 2.21 gives a stem-and-leaf display of the revenue growth rates (in percent) for the 30 fastest-growing companies as listed on March 16, 2005, on the *Fortune* magazine website.

    a   Use the stem-and-leaf display to describe the distribution of revenue growth rates.

    b   Write out the 30 observed revenue growth rates. That is, write out the original data.

people are asked whether they drink wine and whether they watch tennis. The following results are obtained: DS WineCons

	Watch Tennis	Do Not Watch Tennis	Total
Drink Wine	16	24	40
Do Not Drink Wine	4	56	60
Total	20	80	100

a   What percentage of those surveyed both watch tennis and drink wine? What percentage of those surveyed do neither?
b   Using the survey data, construct a table of row percentages.
c   Using the survey data, construct a table of column percentages.
d   What kind of relationship, if any, seems to exist between whether or not a person watches tennis and whether or not a person drinks wine?
e   Illustrate your conclusion of part (d) by plotting bar charts of appropriate column percentages for people who watch tennis and for people who do not watch tennis.

2.49   In a survey of 1,000 randomly selected U.S. citizens aged 21 years or older, 721 believed that the amount of violent television programming had increased over the past 10 years, 454 believed that the overall quality of television programming had gotten worse over the past 10 years, and 362 believed both.

a   Use this information to fill in the cross-tabulation table below.

	TV Violence Increased	TV Violence Not Increased	Total
TV Quality Worse			
TV Quality Not Worse			
Total			

b   Using the completed cross-tabulation table, construct a table of row percentages.
c   Using the completed cross-tabulation table, construct a table of column percentages.
d   What kind of relationship, if any, seems to exist between whether a person believed that TV violence had increased over the past ten years and whether a person believed that the overall quality of TV programming had gotten worse over the past ten years?
e   Illustrate your answer to part (d) by constructing bar charts of appropriate row percentages.

In Exercises 2.50 and 2.51 we consider the results of a Gallup Lifestyle Poll about restaurant tipping habits as reported by the Gallup News Service on January 8, 2007. The poll asked Americans to recommend the percentage of a restaurant bill that should be left as a tip. As reported on galluppoll.com, Americans gave an overall (average) recommendation of 16.2 percent.

2.50   As part of its study, Gallup investigated a possible relationship between tipping attitudes and income. Using the poll results, the following row percentages can be obtained for three income ranges—less than $30,000; $30,000 through $74,999; and $75,000 or more.   DS RowPercents

	Appropriate Tip Percent[*]				
Income	**Less than 15%**	**15%**	**16–19%**	**20% or more**	**Total**
Less than $30,000	28.41%	42.04%	1.14%	28.41%	100%
$30,000 through $74,999	15.31%	42.86%	6.12%	35.71%	100%
$75,000 or more	8.16%	32.66%	9.18%	50.00%	100%

[*]Among those surveyed having an opinion.

a   Construct a percentage bar chart of recommended tip percentage for each of the three income ranges.
b   Using the bar charts, describe the relationship between recommended tip percentage and income level.

2.51   Gallup also asked survey participants if they have ever eaten at a restaurant and left no tip at all because of poor service. Almost half (46 percent) of those surveyed said they have done so. Because it seems that whether or not a person has left a restaurant without tipping might be related to a person's generosity in terms of recommended tip percentage, the survey investigated this possible relationship. Using the poll results, the column percentages at the top of page 67 can be obtained for each of the categories "Yes, have left without tipping" and "No, have not left without tipping."   DS ColPercents

	Tip less than 15%	Tip 15% through 19%	Tip 20% or more
Yes, have left without tipping	64%	50%	35%
No, have not left without tipping	36%	50%	65%
Total	100%	100%	100%

a   Construct a percentage bar chart of the categories "Yes, have left without tipping" and "No, have not left without tipping" for each of the tip categories "less than 15%," "15% through 19%," and "20% or more."

b   Using the bar charts, describe the relationship between whether or not a person has left without tipping and tipping generosity.

2.6 Scatter Plots (Optional) ● ● ●

LO7   Examine the relationships between variables by using scatter plots (Optional).

We often study relationships between variables by using graphical methods. A simple graph that can be used to study the relationship between two variables is called a **scatter plot.** As an example, suppose that a marketing manager wishes to investigate the relationship between the sales volume (in thousands of units) of a product and the amount spent (in units of $10,000) on advertising the product. To do this, the marketing manager randomly selects 10 sales regions having equal sales potential. The manager assigns a different level of advertising expenditure for January 2011 to each sales region as shown in Table 2.20. At the end of the month, the sales volume for each region is recorded as also shown in Table 2.20.

A scatter plot of these data is given in Figure 2.24. To construct this plot, we place the variable advertising expenditure (denoted x) on the horizontal axis and we place the variable sales volume (denoted y) on the vertical axis. For the first sales region, advertising expenditure equals 5 and sales volume equals 89. We plot the point with coordinates $x = 5$ and $y = 89$ on the scatter plot to represent this sales region. Points for the other sales regions are plotted similarly. The scatter plot shows that there is a positive relationship between advertising expenditure and sales volume—that is, higher values of sales volume are associated with higher levels of advertising expenditure.

We have drawn a straight line through the plotted points of the scatter plot to represent the relationship between advertising expenditure and sales volume. We often do this when the relationship between two variables appears to be a **straight line, or linear.** Of course, the relationship between x and y in Figure 2.24 is not perfectly linear—not all of the points in the scatter plot are exactly on the line. Nevertheless, because the relationship between x and y appears to be approximately linear, it seems reasonable to represent the general relationship between these variables using a straight line. In future chapters we will explain ways to quantify such a relationship—that is, describe such a relationship numerically. We will show that we can statistically express the strength of a linear relationship and that we can calculate the equation of the line that best fits the points of a scatter plot.

TABLE 2.20	Values of Advertising Expenditure (in $10,000s) and Sales Volume (in 1000s) for Ten Sales Regions DS SalesPlot	
Sales Region	Advertising Expenditure, x	Sales Volume, y
1	5	89
2	6	87
3	7	98
4	8	110
5	9	103
6	10	114
7	11	116
8	12	110
9	13	126
10	14	130

FIGURE 2.24   A Scatter Plot of Sales Volume versus Advertising Expenditure

FIGURE 2.25   A Positive Linear Relationship

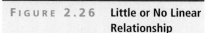

FIGURE 2.26   Little or No Linear Relationship

FIGURE 2.27   A Negative Linear Relationship

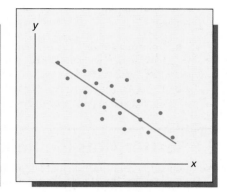

A scatter plot can reveal various kinds of relationships. For instance, Figures 2.25, 2.26, and 2.27 show several possible relationships between two variables x and y. Figure 2.25 shows a relationship similar to that of our advertising expenditure–sales volume example—here y has a tendency to increase as x increases. Figure 2.26 illustrates a situation in which x and y do not appear to have any linear relationship. Figure 2.27 illustrates a negative linear relationship—here y has a tendency to decrease as x increases. Finally, not all relationships are linear. In Chapter 14 we will consider how to represent and quantify curved relationships.

To conclude this section, recall from Chapter 1 that a runs plot—also called a **time series plot**—is a plot of individual process measurements versus time. This implies that a runs plot is a scatter plot, where values of a process variable are plotted on the vertical axis versus corresponding values of time on the horizontal axis.

Exercises for Section 2.6

CONCEPTS

2.52 Explain the purpose for constructing a scatter plot of y versus x.

2.53 Draw a scatter plot of y versus x in which y increases in a linear fashion as x increases.

2.54 Draw a scatter plot of y versus x in which y decreases in a linear fashion as x increases.

2.55 Draw a scatter plot of y versus x in which there is little or no linear relationship between y and x.

2.56 Discuss the relationship between a scatter plot and a runs plot.

METHODS AND APPLICATIONS

2.57 **THE REAL ESTATE SALES PRICE CASE**   ⒹⓈ RealEst

A real estate agency collects data concerning y = the sales price of a house (in thousands of dollars), and x = the home size (in hundreds of square feet). The data are given in Table 2.21. Construct a scatter plot of y versus x and interpret what the plot says.

2.58 **THE FUEL CONSUMPTION CASE**   ⒹⓈ FuelCon1

Table 2.22 gives the average hourly outdoor temperature (x) in a city during a week and the city's natural gas consumption (y) during the week for each of the previous eight weeks (the temperature readings are expressed in degrees Fahrenheit and the natural gas consumptions are expressed in millions of cubic feet of natural gas). The MINITAB output in Figure 2.28 gives a scatter plot of y versus x. Discuss the nature of the relationship between y and x.

connect

TABLE 2.21
Real Estate Sales Price Data
ⒹⓈ RealEst

Sales Price (y)	Home Size (x)
180	23
98.1	11
173.1	20
136.5	17
141	15
165.9	21
193.5	24
127.8	13
163.5	19
172.5	25

TABLE 2.22	**The Fuel Consumption Data** ⒹⓈ FuelCon1							
Week	**1**	**2**	**3**	**4**	**5**	**6**	**7**	**8**
Temperature, x	28.0	28.0	32.5	39.0	45.9	57.8	58.1	62.5
Natural Gas Consumption, y	12.4	11.7	12.4	10.8	9.4	9.5	8.0	7.5

FIGURE 2.28 **MINITAB Scatter Plot of the Fuel Consumption Data (for Exercise 2.58)**

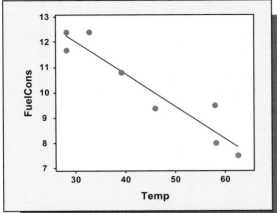

FIGURE 2.29 **Runs Plots for Exercise 2.59**
DS PayTVRates

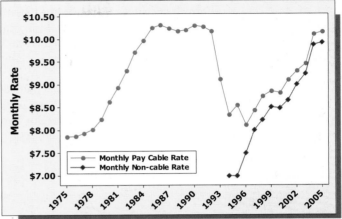

FIGURE 2.30 **A Scatter Plot of Units Sold versus Shelf Space (for Exercise 2.60)**

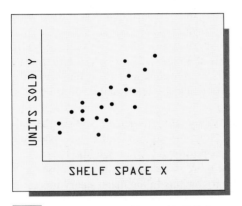

Source: W. R. Dillon, T. J. Madden, and N. H. Firtle, *Essentials of Marketing Research* (Burr Ridge, IL: Richard D. Irwin, Inc., 1993), p. 452. Copyright © 1993. Reprinted by permission of McGraw-Hill Companies, Inc.

FIGURE 2.31 **Excel Output of the Mean Restaurant Ratings and a Scatter Plot of Mean Preference versus Mean Taste (for Exercise 2.61)** **DS** FastFood

	A	B	C	D	E	F
1	Restaurant	Meantaste	Meanconv	Meanfam	Meanprice	Meanpref
2	Borden Burger	3.5659	2.7005	2.5282	2.9372	4.2552
3	Hardee's	3.329	3.3483	2.7345	2.7513	4.0911
4	Burger King	2.4231	2.7377	2.3368	3.0761	3.0052
5	McDonald's	2.0895	1.938	1.4619	2.4884	2.2429
6	Wendy's	1.9661	2.892	2.3376	4.0814	2.5351
7	White Castle	3.8061	3.7242	2.6515	1.708	4.7812
8						
9						
10						
11						
12						
13						
14						
15						
16						
17						
18						
19						
20						
21						
22						

Source: The Ohio State University.

2.59 Figure 2.29 gives a runs plot of the average U.S. monthly pay cable TV rate (for premium services) for each year from 1975 to 2005. Figure 2.29 also gives a runs plot of the average monthly non-cable (mostly satellite) TV rate (for premium services) for each year from 1994 to 2005.[7] Satellite TV became a serious competitor to cable TV in the early 1990s. Does it appear that the emergence of satellite TV had an influence on cable TV rates? What happened after satellite TV became more established in the marketplace? **DS** PayTVRates

2.60 Figure 2.30 gives a scatter plot of the number of units sold, *y*, of 20 varieties of a canned soup versus the amount of shelf space, *x*, allocated to each variety. Do you think that sales are affected by the amount of allocated shelf space, or vice versa?

2.61 **THE FAST-FOOD RESTAURANT RATING CASE** **DS** FastFood

Figure 2.31 presents the ratings given by 406 randomly selected individuals of six fast food restaurants on the basis of taste, convenience, familiarity, and price. The data were collected by researchers at The Ohio State University in the early 1990s. Here, 1 is the best rating and 6 the worst. In addition, each individual ranked the restaurants from 1 through 6 on the basis of overall preference. Interpret the Excel scatter plot, and construct and interpret other relevant scatter plots.

[7]The time series data for this exercise are on the website for this book.

2.7 Misleading Graphs and Charts (Optional) ● ● ●

The statistical analyst's goal should be to present the most accurate and truthful portrayal of a data set that is possible. Such a presentation allows managers using the analysis to make informed decisions. However, it is possible to construct statistical summaries that are misleading. Although we do not advocate using misleading statistics, you should be aware of some of the ways statistical graphs and charts can be manipulated in order to distort the truth. By knowing what to look for, you can avoid being misled by a (we hope) small number of unscrupulous practitioners.

As an example, suppose that the faculty at a major university will soon vote on a proposal to join a union. Both the union organizers and the university administration plan to distribute recent salary statistics to the entire faculty. Suppose that the mean faculty salary at the university and the mean salary increase at the university (expressed as a percentage) for each of the years 2004 through 2007 are as follows:

Year	Mean Salary (All Ranks)	Mean Salary Increase (Percent)
2004	$60,000	3.0%
2005	61,600	4.0
2006	63,500	4.5
2007	66,100	6.0

The university administration does not want the faculty to unionize and, therefore, hopes to convince the faculty that substantial progress has been made to increase salaries without a union. On the other hand, the union organizers wish to portray the salary increases as minimal so that the faculty will feel the need to unionize.

Figure 2.32 gives two bar charts of the mean salaries at the university for each year from 2004 to 2007. Notice that in Figure 2.32(a) the administration has started the vertical scale of the bar chart at a salary of $58,000 by using a *scale break* (⌇). Alternatively, the chart could be set up without the scale break by simply starting the vertical scale at $58,000. Starting the vertical scale at a value far above zero makes the salary increases look more dramatic. Notice that when the union organizers present the bar chart in Figure 2.32(b), which has a vertical scale starting at zero, the salary increases look far less impressive.

Figure 2.33 presents two bar charts of the mean salary increases (in percentages) at the university for each year from 2004 to 2007. In Figure 2.33(a), the administration has made the widths of the bars representing the percentage increases proportional to their heights. This makes the upward movement in the mean salary increases look more dramatic because the observer's eye tends to compare the areas of the bars, while the improvements in the mean salary increases are really only proportional to the heights of the bars. When the union organizers present the bar chart of Figure 2.33(b), the improvements in the mean salary increases look less impressive because each bar has the same width.

FIGURE 2.32 **Two Bar Charts of the Mean Salaries at a Major University from 2004 to 2007**

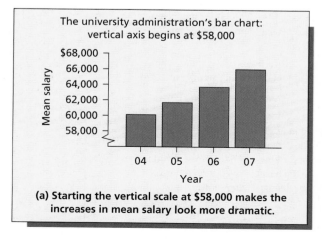

(a) Starting the vertical scale at $58,000 makes the increases in mean salary look more dramatic.

(b) When the vertical scale starts at zero, the increases in mean salary look less impressive.

FIGURE 2.33   **Two Bar Charts of the Mean Salary Increases at a Major University from 2004 to 2007**

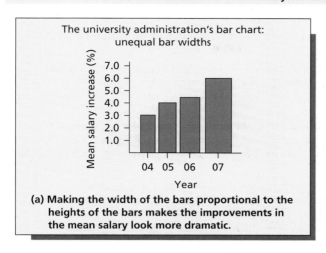

(a) Making the width of the bars proportional to the heights of the bars makes the improvements in the mean salary look more dramatic.

(b) The improvements in the mean salary increases look less impressive when the widths of the bars are the same.

FIGURE 2.34   **Two Time Series Plots of the Mean Salary Increases at a Major University from 2004 to 2007**

(a) The stretched vertical axis makes the upward trend look steep.

(b) The compressed vertical axis makes the upward trend look very gradual.

Figure 2.34 gives two time series plots of the mean salary increases at the university from 2004 to 2007. In Figure 2.34(a) the administration has stretched the vertical axis of the graph. That is, the vertical axis is set up so that the distances between the percentages are large. This makes the upward trend of the mean salary increases appear to be steep. In Figure 2.34(b) the union organizers have compressed the vertical axis (that is, the distances between the percentages are small). This makes the upward trend of the mean salary increases appear to be gradual. As we will see in the exercises, stretching and compressing the horizontal axis in a time series plot can also greatly affect the impression given by the plot.

It is also possible to create totally different interpretations of the same statistical summary by simply using different labeling or captions. For example, consider the bar chart of mean salary increases in Figure 2.33(b). To create a favorable interpretation, the university administration might use the caption "Salary Increase Is Higher for the Fourth Year in a Row." On the other hand, the union organizers might create a negative impression by using the caption "Salary Increase Fails to Reach 10% for Fourth Straight Year."

In summary, we do not approve of using statistics to mislead and distort reality. Statistics should be used to present the most truthful and informative summary of the data that is possible. However, it is important to carefully study any statistical summary so that you will not be misled. Look for manipulations such as stretched or compressed axes on graphs, axes that do not begin at zero, and bar charts with bars of varying widths. Also, carefully think about assumptions, and make your own conclusions about the meaning of any statistical summary rather than relying on captions written by others. Doing these things will help you to see the truth and to make well-informed decisions.

Exercises for Section 2.7

CONCEPTS

connect

2.62   When we construct a bar chart or graph, what is the effect of starting the vertical axis at a value that is far above zero? Explain.

2.63   Find an example of a misleading use of statistics in a newspaper, magazine, corporate annual report, or other source. Then explain why your example is misleading.

METHODS AND APPLICATIONS

2.64   Figure 2.35 gives two more time series plots of the previously discussed salary increases. In Figure 2.35(a) the administration has compressed the horizontal axis. In Figure 2.35(b) the union organizers have stretched the horizontal axis. Discuss the different impressions given by the two time series plots.

2.65   In the article "How to Display Data Badly" in the May 1984 issue of *The American Statistician,* Howard Wainer presents a *stacked bar chart* of the number of public and private elementary schools (1929–1970). This bar chart is given in Figure 2.36. Wainer also gives a line graph of the number of private elementary schools (1930–1970). This graph is shown in Figure 2.37.

FIGURE 2.35   **Two Time Series Plots of the Mean Salary Increases at a Major University from 2004 to 2007 (for Exercise 2.64)**

(a) The administration's plot: compressed horizontal axis

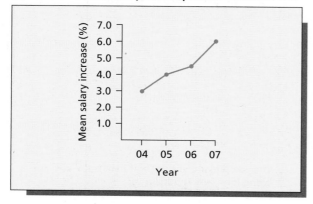

(b) The union organizer's plot: stretched horizontal axis

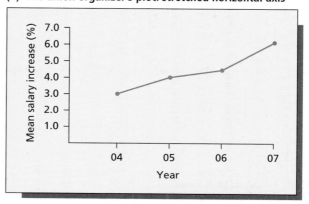

FIGURE 2.36   **Wainer's Stacked Bar Chart (for Exercise 2.65)**

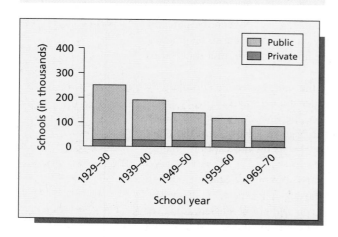

FIGURE 2.37   **Wainer's Line Graph (for Exercise 2.65)**

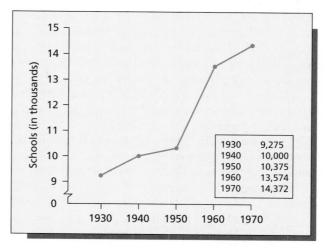

a Looking at the bar chart of Figure 2.36, does there appear to be an increasing trend in the number of private elementary schools from 1930 to 1970?

b Looking at the line graph of Figure 2.37, does there appear to be an increasing trend in the number of private elementary schools from 1930 to 1970?

c Which portrayal of the data do you think is more appropriate? Explain why.

d Is either portrayal of the data entirely appropriate? Explain.

Chapter Summary

We began this chapter by explaining how to summarize qualitative data. We learned that we often summarize this type of data in a table that is called a **frequency distribution.** Such a table gives the **frequency, relative frequency,** or **percent frequency** of items that are contained in each of several nonoverlapping classes or categories. We also learned that we can summarize qualitative data in graphical form by using **bar charts** and **pie charts** and that qualitative quality data are often summarized using a special bar chart called a **Pareto chart.** We continued in Section 2.2 by discussing how to graphically portray quantitative data. In particular, we explained how to summarize such data by using frequency distributions and histograms. We saw that a **histogram** can be constructed using frequencies, relative frequencies, or percentages, and that we often construct histograms using statistical software such as MINITAB or the analysis toolpak in Excel. We used histograms to describe the shape of a distribution and we saw that distributions are sometimes **mound shaped and symmetrical,** but that a distribution can also be **skewed** (**to the right** or **to the left**). We also learned that a frequency distribution can

be graphed by using a **frequency polygon** and that a graph of a **cumulative frequency distribution** is called an **ogive.** In Sections 2.3 and 2.4 we showed how to summarize relatively small data sets by using **dot plots** and **stem-and-leaf displays.** These graphics allow us to see all of the measurements in a data set and to (simultaneously) see the shape of the data set's distribution. Next, we learned about how to describe the relationship between two variables. First, in optional Section 2.5 we explained how to construct and interpret a **cross-tabulation table,** which classifies data on two dimensions using a table that consists of rows and columns. Then, in optional Section 2.6 we showed how to construct a **scatter plot.** Here, we plot numerical values of one variable on a horizontal axis versus numerical values of another variable on a vertical axis. We saw that we often use such a plot to look at possible straight-line relationships between the variables. Finally, in optional Section 2.7 we learned about misleading graphs and charts. In particular, we pointed out several graphical tricks to watch for. By careful analysis of a graph or chart, one can avoid being misled.

Glossary of Terms

bar chart: A graphical display of data in categories made up of vertical or horizontal bars. Each bar gives the frequency, relative frequency, or percentage frequency of items in its corresponding category. (page 36)

class midpoint: The point in a class that is halfway between the lower and upper class boundaries. (page 45)

cross-tabulation table: A table consisting of rows and columns that is used to classify data on two dimensions. (page 61)

cumulative frequency distribution: A table that summarizes the number of measurements that are less than the upper class boundary of each class. (page 49)

cumulative percent frequency distribution: A table that summarizes the percentage of measurements that are less than the upper class boundary of each class. (page 50)

cumulative relative frequency distribution: A table that summarizes the fraction of measurements that are less than the upper class boundary of each class. (page 50)

dot plot: A graphical portrayal of a data set that shows the data set's distribution by plotting individual measurements above a horizontal axis. (page 54)

frequency distribution: A table that summarizes the number of items (or measurements) in each of several nonoverlapping classes. (pages 35, 44)

frequency polygon: A graphical display in which we plot points representing each class frequency (or relative frequency or percent

frequency) above their corresponding class midpoints and connect the points with line segments. (page 48)

histogram: A graphical display of a frequency distribution, relative frequency distribution, or percentage frequency distribution. It divides measurements into classes and graphs the frequency, relative frequency, or percentage frequency for each class. (pages 42, 44)

ogive: A graph of a cumulative distribution (frequencies, relative frequencies, or percent frequencies may be used). (page 50)

outlier: An unusually large or small observation that is well separated from the remaining observations. (page 55)

Pareto chart: A bar chart of the frequencies or percentages for various types of defects. These are used to identify opportunities for improvement. (page 38)

percent frequency distribution: A table that summarizes the percentage of items (or measurements) in each of several nonoverlapping classes. (pages 36, 44)

pie chart: A graphical display of data in categories made up of "pie slices." Each pie slice represents the frequency, relative frequency, or percentage frequency of items in its corresponding category. (page 37)

relative frequency distribution: A table that summarizes the fraction of items (or measurements) in each of several nonoverlapping classes. (pages 36, 44)

scatter plot: A graph that is used to study the possible relationship between two variables y and x. The observed values of y are plotted on the vertical axis versus corresponding observed values of x on the horizontal axis. (page 67)

skewed to the left: A distribution shape having a long tail to the left. (page 47)

skewed to the right: A distribution shape having a long tail to the right. (page 47)

stem-and-leaf display: A graphical portrayal of a data set that shows the data set's distribution by using stems consisting of leading digits and leaves consisting of trailing digits. (page 56)

symmetrical distribution: A distribution shape having right and left sides that are "mirror images" of each other. (page 47)

Important Formulas and Graphics

Frequency distribution: page 45

Relative frequency: page 36

Percent frequency: page 36

Bar chart: page 37

Pie chart: page 37

Pareto chart: page 38

Histogram: page 45

Frequency polygon: page 48

Cumulative distribution: page 49

Ogive: page 50

Dot plot: page 54

Stem-and-leaf display: page 58

Cross-tabulation table: page 61

Scatter plot: page 67

Time series plot: page 68

Supplementary Exercises

connect™

2.66 A manufacturer produces a bulk chemical product. Customer requirements state that this product must have a specified viscosity when melted at a temperature of 300°F (viscosity measures how thick and gooey the product is when melted). Chemical XB-135 is used in the production of this chemical product, and the company's chemists feel that the amount of chemical XB-135 may be related to viscosity. In order to verify and quantify this relationship, 24 batches of the product are produced. The amount (x) of chemical XB-135 (in pounds) is varied from batch to batch and the viscosity (y) obtained for each batch is measured. Table 2.23 gives (in time order) the values of x and the corresponding values of y obtained for the 24 batches. **DS** Viscosity

a Construct a scatter plot of viscosity (y) versus the amount (x) of chemical XB-135.

b Describe any apparent relationship between y and x.

c It might be tempting to conclude that changes in the amount of chemical XB-135 cause changes in viscosity. Under what circumstances might such a conclusion be reasonable?

TABLE 2.23   **Viscosity Data for 24 Batches of a Chemical Product Produced on August 1, 2010** **DS** Viscosity

Batch	Pounds of Chemical XB-135 (x)	Viscosity (y)	Batch	Pounds of Chemical XB-135 (x)	Viscosity (y)
1	10.0	31.76	13	11.2	32.93
2	10.0	31.91	14	11.2	33.19
3	10.2	32.02	15	11.4	33.35
4	10.2	31.85	16	11.4	32.76
5	10.4	32.17	17	11.6	33.33
6	10.4	32.30	18	11.6	33.19
7	10.6	32.60	19	11.8	33.28
8	10.6	32.15	20	11.8	33.57
9	10.8	32.52	21	12.0	33.60
10	10.8	32.46	22	12.0	33.43
11	11.0	32.41	23	12.2	33.91
12	11.0	32.77	24	12.2	33.76

Exercises 2.67 through 2.74 are based on the data in Table 2.24. This table gives the results of the J.D. Power initial quality study of 2006 automobiles. Each model is rated on overall manufacturing quality and overall design quality on a scale from "among the best" to "the rest"—see the scoring legend at the bottom of the table. **DS** JDPower

TABLE 2.24　Results of the J. D. Power Initial Quality Study of 2006 Automobiles　DS JDPower

Company	Country of Origin	Overall Quality Manufacturing	Overall Quality Design	Company	Country of Origin	Overall Quality Manufacturing	Overall Quality Design
Acura	Japan	●●●	●●●	Lexus	Japan	●●●●●	●●●●
Audi	Germany	●●●	●●●	Lincoln	United States	●●●	●●●
BMW	Germany	●●●●	●●	Mazda	Japan	●●	●●
Buick	United States	●●●●	●●	Mercedes-Benz	Germany	●●●	●●
Cadillac	United States	●●●●	●●●	Mercury	United States	●●●	●●●
Chevrolet	United States	●●●●	●●●	MINI	Great Britain	●●●	●●
Chrysler	United States	●●●●	●●●	Mitsubishi	Japan	●●	●●●●
Dodge	United States	●●●	●●●	Nissan	Japan	●●●	●●●●
Ford	United States	●●●	●●●	Pontiac	United States	●●●	●●●
GMC	United States	●●●	●●●●	Porsche	Germany	●●●●	●●●●●
Honda	Japan	●●●	●●●●	Saab	Sweden	●●	●●●
HUMMER	United States	●●	●●	Saturn	United States	●●●	●●●
Hyundai	Korea	●●●●	●●●●	Scion	Japan	●●●	●●●
Infiniti	Japan	●●●	●●●	Subaru	Japan	●●●	●●
Isuzu	Japan	●●	●●	Suzuki	Japan	●●	●●
Jaguar	Great Britain	●●●	●●●●	Toyota	Japan	●●●●	●●●
Jeep	United States	●●	●●●	Volkswagen	Germany	●●	●●
Kia	Korea	●●●	●●●	Volvo	Sweden	●●●	●●●
Land Rover	Great Britain	●●	●●				

Scoring Legend

●●●●● Among the best　　●●● About average
●●●● Better than most　　●● The rest

Source: http://www.jdpower.com/autos/brand-ratings/

2.67 Develop a frequency distribution of the overall manufacturing quality ratings. Describe the distribution.　DS JDPower

2.68 Develop a relative frequency distribution of the overall design quality ratings. Describe the distribution.　DS JDPower

2.69 Construct a percentage bar chart of the overall manufacturing quality ratings for each of the following: automobiles of United States origin; automobiles of Pacific Rim origin (Japan/Korea); and automobiles of European origin (Germany/Great Britain/Sweden). Compare the three distributions in a written report.　DS JDPower

2.70 Construct a percentage pie chart of the overall design quality ratings for each of the following: automobiles of United States origin; automobiles of Pacific Rim origin (Japan/Korea); and automobiles of European origin (Germany/Great Britain/Sweden). Compare the three distributions in a written report.　DS JDPower

2.71 Construct a crosstabulation table of automobile origin versus overall manufacturing quality rating. Set up rows corresponding to the United States, the Pacific Rim (Japan/Korea), and Europe (Germany/Great Britain/Sweden), and set up columns corresponding to the ratings "among the best" through "the rest." Describe any apparent relationship between origin and overall manufacturing quality rating.　DS JDPower

2.72 Develop a table of row percentages for the crosstabulation table you set up in Exercise 2.71. Using these row percentages, construct a percentage frequency distribution of overall manufacturing quality rating for each of the United States, the Pacific Rim, and Europe. Illustrate these three frequency distributions using percent bar charts and compare the distributions in a written report.　DS JDPower

2.73 Construct a crosstabulation table of automobile origin versus overall design quality rating. Set up rows corresponding to the United States, the Pacific Rim (Japan/Korea), and Europe (Germany/Great Britain/Sweden), and set up columns corresponding to the ratings "among the best" through "the rest." Describe any apparent relationship between origin and overall design quality.　DS JDPower

2.74 Develop a table of row percentages for the crosstabulation table you set up in Exercise 2.73. Using these row percentages, construct a percentage frequency distribution of overall design quality rating for each of the United States, the Pacific Rim, and Europe. Illustrate these three frequency distributions using percentage pie charts and compare the distributions in a written report.　DS JDPower

a Go to the Gallup Organization website and access several of the articles presenting recent poll results. ... paragraph describing why you think the summary or graphic is misleading.

78   Chapter 2   Descriptive Statistics: Tabular and Graphical Methods

ISO 9000   construct a histogram. An example is provided by data concerning the benefits of ISO 9000 regis-

Appendix 2.2 ■ Tabular and Graphical Methods Using MegaStat

The instructions in this section begin by describing the entry of data into an Excel worksheet. Alternatively, the data may be downloaded from this book's website. The appropriate data file name is given at the top of each instruction block. Please refer to Appendix 1.1 for further information about entering data, saving data, and printing results in Excel. Please refer to Appendix 1.2 for more information about MegaStat basics.

Construct a frequency distribution and bar chart of Jeep sales as in Table 2.2 on page 36 and Figure 2.2 on page 37 (data file: JeepSales.xlsx):

- Enter the Jeep sales data in Table 2.1 on page 36 (C = Commander; G = Grand Cherokee; L = Liberty; W = Wrangler) into column A with label Jeep Model in cell A1.

- Enter the categories for the qualitative variable (C, G, L, W) into the worksheet. Here we have placed them in cells B2 through B5—the location is arbitrary.

- Select **Add-Ins : MegaStat : Frequency Distributions : Qualitative**

- In the "Frequency Distributions—Qualitative" dialog box, use the autoexpand feature to enter the range A1.A252 of the Jeep sales data into the Input Range window.

- Enter the cell range B2.B5 of the categories (C, G, L, W) into the "specification range" window.

- Place a checkmark in the "histogram" checkbox to obtain a bar chart.

- Click OK in the "Frequency Distributions— Qualitative" dialog box.

- The frequency distribution and bar chart will be placed in a new output sheet.

- The output can be edited in the output sheet. Alternatively, the bar chart can be moved to a chart sheet (see Appendix 1.2) for more convenient editing.

Construct a frequency distribution and percent frequency histogram of the gas mileages as in Figure 2.9 on page 46 (data file: GasMiles.xlsx):

- Enter the gasoline mileage data in Table 1.6 on page 12 into column A with the label Mpg in cell A1 and with the 50 gas mileages in cells A2 to A51.

- Select **Add-Ins : MegaStat : Frequency Distributions : Quantitative**

- In the "Frequency Distributions—Quantitative" dialog box, use the autoexpand feature to enter the range A1.A51 of the gas mileages into the Input Range window.

- To obtain **automatic classes** for the histogram, leave the "interval width" and "lower boundary of first interval" windows blank.

- Place a checkmark in the Histogram checkbox.

- Click OK in the "Frequency Distributions— Quantitative" dialog box.

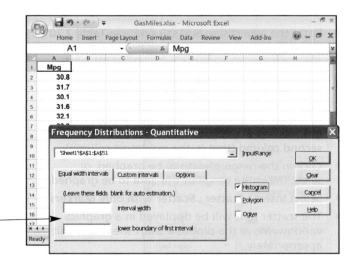

- The frequency distribution and histogram will be placed in a new output worksheet.
- The chart can be edited in the Output worksheet or you can move the chart to a chart sheet for editing.
- To obtain **data labels** (the numbers on the tops of the bars that indicate the bar heights), right click on one of the histogram bars and select "Add data labels" from the pop-up menu.

To construct a **frequency polygon and a percent frequency ogive,** simply place checkmarks in the Polygon and Ogive checkboxes in the "Frequency Distributions—Quantitative" dialog box.

Construct a percent frequency histogram of the bottle design ratings similar to Figure 2.11 on page 47 with **user specified classes** (data file: Design.xlsx):

- Enter the 60 bottle design ratings in Table 1.5 on page 10 into Column A with label Rating in cell A1.
- Select **Add-Ins : MegaStat : Frequency Distributions : Quantitative**
- In the "Frequency Distributions—Quantitative" dialog box, use the autoexpand feature to enter the input range A1.A61 of the bottle design ratings into the Input Range window.
- Enter the class width (in this case equal to 2) into the "interval width" window.
- Enter the lower boundary of the first—that is, leftmost—interval of the histogram (in this case equal to 20) into the "lower boundary of first interval" window.
- Make sure that the Histogram checkbox is checked.
- Click OK in the "Frequency Distributions—Quantitative" dialog box.
- We obtain a histogram with class boundaries 20, 22, 24, 26, 28, 30, 32, 34, and 36. Note that the appearance of this histogram is not exactly the same as that of the Excel histogram in Figure 2.11 on page 47 because we recall that MegaStat and Excel count frequencies differently.
- The histogram can be moved to a chart sheet for editing purposes.

Construct a dot plot (as in Figure 2.18 on page 55) **and a stem-and-leaf display** (as in Figure 2.20 on page 59) of the scores on the first statistics exam as discussed in Example 2.3 on page 48 (data file: FirstExam.xlsx):

- Enter the 40 scores for exam 1 in Table 2.8 on page 48 into column A with label "Exam 1" in cell A1.
- Select **Add-Ins : MegaStat : Descriptive Statistics.**
- In the "Descriptive Statistics" dialog box, use the autoexpand feature to enter the range A1.A41 of the exam scores into the "Input range" window.
- Place a checkmark in the DotPlot checkbox to obtain a dot plot.
- Place a checkmark in the "Stem and Leaf Plot" checkbox to obtain a stem-and-leaf display.
- Place a checkmark in the "Split Stem" checkbox. (In general, whether or not this should be done depends on how you want the output to appear. You may wish to construct two plots—one with the Split Stem option and one without—and then choose the output you like best.) In the exam score situation, the Split Stem option is needed to obtain a display that looks like the one in Figure 2.20.
- Click OK in the "Descriptive Statistics" dialog box.
- The dot plot and stem-and-leaf display will be placed in an output sheet. Here, the stem-and-leaf display we have obtained for exam 1 is the "mirror image" of the plot shown in Figure 2.20 (because we have constructed a single display for exam 1, while Figure 2.20 shows back-to-back displays for both exams 1 and 2).
- The dot plot can be moved to a chart sheet for editing.

Construct a cross-tabulation table of fund type versus level of client satisfaction as in Table 2.17 on page 62 (data file: Invest.xlsx):

- Enter the customer satisfaction data in Table 2.16 on page 62—fund types in column A with label FundType and satisfaction ratings in column B with label SRating.
- Enter the three labels (BOND; STOCK; TAXDEF) for the qualitative variable FundType into cells C2, C3, and C4 as shown in the screen.
- Enter the three labels (HIGH; MED; LOW) for the qualitative variable SRating into cells C6, C7, and C8 as shown in the screen.
- Select **Add-Ins : MegaStat : Chi-Square/CrossTab : Crosstabulation**
- In the Crosstabulation dialog box, use the autoexpand feature to enter the range A1.A101 of the row variable FundType into the "Row variable Data range" window.
- Enter the range C2.C4 of the labels of the qualitative variable FundType into the "Row variable Specification range window."
- Use the autoexpand feature to enter the range B1.B101 of the column variable SRating into the "Column variable Data range" window.
- Enter the range C6.C8 of the labels of the qualitative variable SRating into the "Column variable Specification range window."

- Uncheck the "chi-square" checkbox.
- Click OK in the Crosstabulation dialog box.
- The cross-tabulation table will be displayed in an Output worksheet.
- **Row percentages and column percentages** can be obtained by simply placing checkmarks in the "% of row" and "% of column" checkboxes.

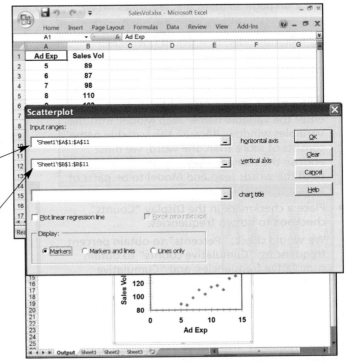

Construct a scatter plot of sales volume versus advertising expenditure as in Figure 2.24 on page 67 (data file: SalesPlot.xlsx):

- Enter the advertising and sales data in Table 2.20 on page 67 into columns A and B—advertising expenditures in column A with label "Ad Exp" and sales values in column B with label "Sales Vol."
- Select **Add-Ins : MegaStat : Correlation/Regression : Scatterplot**
- In the Scatterplot dialog box, use the autoexpand feature to enter the range A1.A11 of the advertising expenditures into the "horizontal axis" window.
- Use the autoexpand feature to enter the range B1.B11 of the sales volumes into the "vertical axis" window.
- Uncheck the "Plot linear regression line" checkbox.
- Under Display options, select Markers.
- Click OK in the Scatterplot dialog box.
- The scatterplot is displayed in an Output worksheet and can be moved to a chart sheet for editing.

Construct a pie chart of Jeep sales percentages similar to that shown in Figure 2.3 on page 38.

- Enter the Jeep sales data in Table 2.1 on page 36 (C = Commander; G = Grand Cherokee; L = Liberty; W = Wrangler) into column C1 with label (variable name) Jeep Model.

- Select **Graph : Pie Chart**

- In the Pie Chart dialog box, select "Chart counts of unique values".

- Enter the variable name 'Jeep Model' into the "Categorical variables" window. Be sure to remember the single quotes around the name Jeep Model.

- In the Pie Chart dialog box, click on the Labels... button.

- In the "Pie Chart—Labels" dialog box, click on the Slice Labels tab.

- Place checkmarks in the Category name, Percent, and "Draw a line from label to slice" checkboxes.

  To obtain a frequency pie chart, select Frequency rather than Percent in this dialog box. Or, both Percent and Frequency can be selected.

- Click OK in the "Pie Chart—Labels" dialog box.

- Click OK in the Pie Chart dialog box.

- The pie chart will appear in a graphics window.

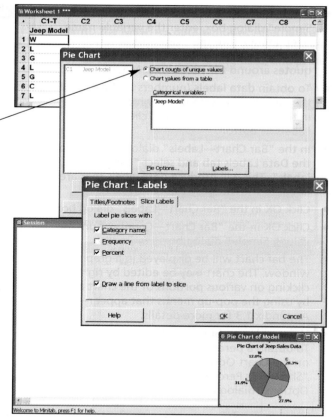

Construct a pie chart from the tabular percent frequency distribution of Jeep sales in Table 2.3 on page 36 (data file: JeepPercents.MTW):

- Enter the Jeep sales percent frequency distribution from Table 2.3 as shown in the screen with the four models in column C1 (with variable name Jeep Model) and with the associated percent frequencies in column C2 (with variable name Percent Freq).

- Select **Graph : Pie Chart**

- In the Pie Chart dialog box, select "Chart values from a table."

- Enter the variable name 'Jeep Model' into the "Categorical variable" window. Be sure to remember the single quotes around the name Jeep Model.

- Enter the variable name 'Percent Freq' into the "Summary variables" window. Be sure to remember the single quotes around the name Percent Freq.

- Continue by following the directions directly above for adding data labels and generating the pie chart.

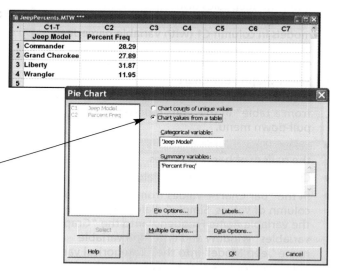

Construct a frequency histogram of the payment times in Figure 2.10 on page 46 (data file: PayTime .MTW):

- Enter the payment time data from Table 2.4 on page 42 into column C1 with variable name PayTime.
- Select **Graph : Histogram**
- In the Histograms dialog box, select Simple from the gallery of histogram types and click OK.
- In the "Histogram—Simple" dialog box, enter the variable name PayTime into the Graph Variables window and click on the Scale button.

- In the "Histogram—Scale" dialog box, click on the "Y- Scale Type" tab and select **Frequency** to obtain a frequency histogram. We would select **Percent** to request a percent frequency histogram. Then click OK in the "Histogram— Scale" dialog box.
- **Data labels** are requested in the same way as we have demonstrated for bar charts. Click on the Labels… button in the "Histogram— Simple" dialog box. In the "Histogram— Labels" dialog box, click on the Data Labels tab and select "Use y-value labels." Then click OK in the "Histogram—Labels" dialog box.

- To create the histogram, click OK in the "Histogram—Simple" dialog box.
- The histogram will appear in a graphics window and can be edited as described in Appendix 1.3.
- The histogram can be selected for printing or can be copied and pasted into a word processing document. (See Appendix 1.3.)

- Notice that MINITAB **automatically** defines classes for the histogram bars, and auto-matically provides labeled tick marks (here 12, 16, 20, 24 and 28) on the *x*-scale of the histogram. These automatic classes are not the same as those we formed in Example 2.2, summarized in Table 2.7, and illustrated in Figure 2.7 on page 44. However, we can edit the automatically constructed histogram to produce the histogram classes of Figure 2.7. This is sometimes called **"binning."**

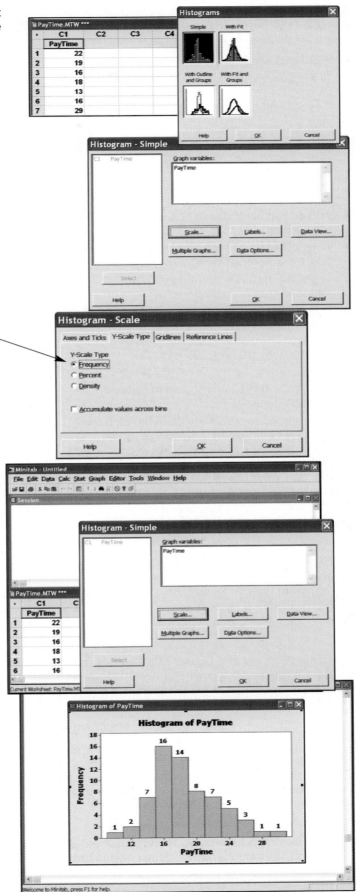

To obtain user specified histogram classes—for example, the payment time histogram classes of Figure 2.7 on page 44 (data file: PayTime.MTW):

- Right click inside any of the histogram bars.
- In the pop-up menu, select "Edit bars."

- In the "Edit Bars" dialog box, select the Binning tab.
- To label the x-scale by using class boundaries, select the "Interval Type" to be Cutpoint.
- Select the "Interval Definition" to be Midpoint/Cutpoint positions.
- In the Midpoint/Cutpoint positions window, enter the class boundaries (or cutpoints)

    10   13   16   19   22   25   28   31

    as given in Table 2.7 or shown in Figure 2.7 (both on page 44).
- If we wished to label the x-scale by using class midpoints as in Figure 2.8 on page 45, we would select the "Interval Type" to be Midpoint and we would enter the midpoints of Figure 2.8 (11.5, 14.5, 17.5, and so forth) into the Midpoint/Cutpoint positions window.
- Click OK in the Edit Bars dialog box.

- The histogram in the graphics window will be edited to produce the class boundaries, histogram bars, and x-axis labels shown in Figure 2.7.

Frequency Polygons and Ogives: MINITAB does not have automatic procedures for constructing frequency polygons and ogives. However, these graphics can be constructed quite easily by using the MINITAB Graph Annotation Tools. To access these tools and have them placed on the MINITAB toolbar, select

Tools : Toolbars : Graph Annotation Tools

- **To construct a frequency polygon,** follow the preceding instructions for constructing a histogram. In addition, however, click on the Data View button, select the Data Display tab, place a checkmark in the Symbols checkbox (also uncheck the Bars checkbox). This will result in plotted points above the histogram classes—rather than bars. Now select the polygon tool

from the Graph Annotation Tools toolbar and draw connecting lines to form the polygon. Instructions for using the polygon tool can be found in the MINITAB help resources listed under "To create a polygon."

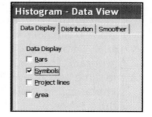

- **To construct an ogive,** follow the above instructions for constructing a frequency polygon. In addition, however, click on the Scale button, select the "Y-Scale Type" tab, and place a checkmark in the "Accumulate values across bins" checkbox. This will result in a plot of cumulative frequencies—rather than histogram bars. Now select the polyline tool

from the Graph Annotation Tools toolbar and draw connecting lines to form the ogive. Instructions for using the polyline tool can be found in the MINITAB help resources listed under "To create a polyline."

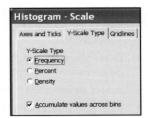

Construct a dot plot of the exam scores as in Figure 2.18(a) on page 55 (data file: FirstExam.MTW):

- Enter the scores for exam 1 in Table 2.8 on page 48 into column C1 with variable name 'Score on Exam 1'.

- Select **Graph : Dot Plot**

- In the Dotplots dialog box, select "One Y Simple" from the gallery of dot plots.

- Click OK in the Dotplots dialog box.

- In the "Dotplot—One Y, Simple" dialog box, enter the variable name 'Score on Exam 1' into the "Graph variables" window. Be sure to include the single quotes.

- Click OK in the "Dotplot—One Y, Simple" dialog box.

- The dotplot will be displayed in a graphics window.

- To change the x-axis labels (or, **ticks**), right-click on any one of the existing labels (say, the 45, for instance) and select "Edit X Scale..." from the popup menu.

- In the Edit Scale dialog box, select the Scale tab and select "Position of Ticks" as the "Major Tick Positions" setting.

- Enter the desired ticks (30 40 50 60 70 80 90 100) into the "Position of ticks" window and click OK in the Edit Scale dialog box.

- The x-axis labels (ticks) will be changed and the new dot plot will be displayed in the graphics window.

Construct a stem-and-leaf display of the gasoline mileages as in Figure 2.19 on page 57 (data file: GasMiles.MTW):

- Enter the mileage data from Table 2.14 on page 56 into column C1 with variable name Mpg.
- Select **Graph : Stem-and-Leaf**
- In the Stem-and-Leaf dialog box, enter the variable name Mpg into the "Graph Variables" window.
- Click OK in the Stem-and-Leaf dialog box.
- The stem-and-leaf display appears in the Session window and can be selected for printing or copied and pasted into a word processing document. (See Appendix 1.3.)

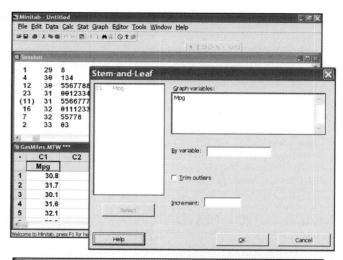

Construct a cross-tabulation table of fund type versus level of client satisfaction as in Table 2.17 on page 62 (data file: Invest.MTW):

- Enter the client satisfaction data from Table 2.16 on page 62 with client number in column C1 having variable name Client, and with fund type and satisfaction rating in columns C2 and C3, respectively, having variable names 'Fund Type' and 'Satisfaction Level'.

The default ordering for the different levels of each categorical variable in the cross-tabulation table will be alphabetical—that is, BOND, STOCK, TAXDEF for 'Fund Type' and HIGH, LOW, MED for 'Satisfaction Rating'. **To change the ordering to HIGH, MED, LOW** for 'Satisfaction Rating':

- Click on any cell in column C3 (Satisfaction Rating).
- Select **Editor : Column : Value order**
- In the "Value Order for C3 (Satisfaction Level)" dialog box, select the "User-specified order" option.
- In the "Define an order (one value per line)" window, specify the order HIGH, MED, LOW.
- Click OK in the "Value Order for C3 (Satisfaction Level)" dialog box.

To construct the cross-tabulation table:

- Select **Stat : Tables : Cross Tabulation and Chi-Square**
- In the "Cross Tabulation and Chi-Square" dialog box, enter the variable name 'Fund Type' (including the single quotes) into the "Categorical variables: For rows" window.
- Enter the variable name 'Satisfaction Rating' (including the single quotes) into the "Categorical variables: For columns" window.
- Place a checkmark in the "Display Counts" checkbox. We would check "Display Row percents" to produce a table of row percentages and we would check "Display Column percents" to produce a table of column percentages.
- Click OK in the "Cross Tabulation and Chi-Square" dialog box to obtain results in the Session window.

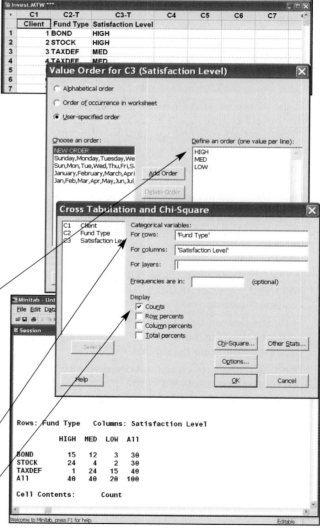

Construct a scatter plot of sales volume versus advertising expenditure as in Figure 2.24 on page 67 (data file: SalesPlot.MWT).

- Enter the sales and advertising data in Table 2.20 (on page 67)—sales region in column C1 (with variable name 'Sales Region'), advertising expenditure in column C2 (with variable name 'Adv Exp'), and sales volume in column C3 (with variable name 'Sales Vol').

- Select **Graph : Scatterplot**

- In the Scatterplots dialog box, select "With Regression" from the gallery of scatterplots in order to produce a scatterplot with a "best line" fitted to the data (see Chapter 13 for discussion of this "best line"). Select "Simple" if a fitted line is not desired.

- Click OK in the Scatterplots dialog box.

- In the "Scatterplot—With Regression" dialog box, enter the variable name 'Sales Vol' (including the single quotes) into row 1 of the "Y variables" window and enter the variable name 'Adv Exp' (including the single quotes) into row 1 of the "X variables" window.

- Click OK in the "Scatterplot—With Regression" dialog box.

- The scatterplot and fitted line will be displayed in a graphics window.

- Additional plots can be obtained by placing appropriate variable names in other rows in the "Y variables" and "X variables" windows.

> A **sample statistic** is a number calculated using the sample measurements that describes some aspect of the sample. That is, a sample statistic is a descriptive measure of the sample.

The sample statistic that we use to estimate the population mean is the **sample mean,** which is denoted as $\bar{x}$ (pronounced *x bar*) and is the average of the sample measurements.

In order to write a formula for the sample mean, we employ the letter n to represent the number of sample measurements, and we refer to n as the **sample size.** Furthermore, we denote the sample measurements as $x_1, x_2, \ldots, x_n$. Here x_1 is the first sample measurement, x_2 is the second sample measurement, and so forth. We denote the last sample measurement as x_n. Moreover, when we write formulas we often use *summation notation* for convenience. For instance, we write the sum of the sample measurements

$$x_1 + x_2 + \cdots + x_n$$

as $\sum_{i=1}^{n} x_i$. Here the symbol Σ simply tells us to add the terms that follow the symbol. The term x_i is a generic (or representative) observation in our data set, and the $i = 1$ and the n indicate where to start and stop summing. Thus

$$\sum_{i=1}^{n} x_i = x_1 + x_2 + \cdots + x_n$$

We define the sample mean as follows:

> The **sample mean** $\bar{x}$ is defined to be
>
> $$\bar{x} = \frac{\sum_{i=1}^{n} x_i}{n} = \frac{x_1 + x_2 + \cdots + x_n}{n}$$
>
> and is the **point estimate of the population mean** μ.

EXAMPLE 3.1 The Car Mileage Case

In order to offer its tax credit, the federal government has decided to define the "typical" EPA combined city and highway mileage for a car model as the mean μ of the population of EPA combined mileages that would be obtained by all cars of this type. Here, using the mean to represent a typical value is probably reasonable. We know that some individual cars will get mileages that are lower than the mean and some will get mileages that are above it. However, because there will be many thousands of these cars on the road, the mean mileage obtained by these cars is probably a reasonable way to represent the model's overall fuel economy. Therefore, the government will offer its tax credit to any automaker selling a midsize model equipped with an automatic transmission that achieves a mean EPA combined mileage of at least 31 mpg.

To demonstrate that its new midsize model qualifies for the tax credit, the automaker in this case study wishes to use the sample of 50 mileages in Table 3.1 to estimate μ, the model's mean mileage. Before calculating the mean of the entire sample of 50 mileages, we will illustrate the formulas involved by calculating the mean of the first five of these mileages. Table 3.1 tells us that $x_1 = 30.8$, $x_2 = 31.7$, $x_3 = 30.1$, $x_4 = 31.6$, and $x_5 = 32.1$, so the sum of the first five mileages is

$$\sum_{i=1}^{5} x_i = x_1 + x_2 + x_3 + x_4 + x_5$$

$$= 30.8 + 31.7 + 30.1 + 31.6 + 32.1 = 156.3$$

Therefore, the mean of the first five mileages is

$$\bar{x} = \frac{\sum_{i=1}^{5} x_i}{5} = \frac{156.3}{5} = 31.26$$

TABLE 3.1	A Sample of 50 Mileages	DS GasMiles		
30.8	30.8	32.1	32.3	32.7
31.7	30.4	31.4	32.7	31.4
30.1	32.5	30.8	31.2	31.8
31.6	30.3	32.8	30.7	31.9
32.1	31.3	31.9	31.7	33.0
33.3	32.1	31.4	31.4	31.5
31.3	32.5	32.4	32.2	31.6
31.0	31.8	31.0	31.5	30.6
32.0	30.5	29.8	31.7	32.3
32.4	30.5	31.1	30.7	31.4

Of course, intuitively, we are likely to obtain a more accurate point estimate of the population mean by using all of the available sample information. The sum of all 50 mileages can be verified to be

$$\sum_{i=1}^{50} x_i = x_1 + x_2 + \cdots + x_{50} = 30.8 + 31.7 + \cdots + 31.4 = 1578$$

Therefore, the mean of the sample of 50 mileages is

$$\bar{x} = \frac{\sum_{i=1}^{50} x_i}{50} = \frac{1578}{50} = 31.56$$

This point estimate says we estimate that the mean mileage that would be obtained by all of the new midsize cars that will or could potentially be produced this year is 31.56 mpg. Unless we are extremely lucky, however, there will be **sampling error.** That is, the point estimate $\bar{x} = 31.56$ mpg, which is the average of the sample of fifty randomly selected mileages, will probably not exactly equal the population mean μ, which is the average mileage that would be obtained by all cars. Therefore, although $\bar{x} = 31.56$ provides some evidence that μ is at least 31 and thus that the automaker should get the tax credit, it does not provide definitive evidence. In later chapters, we discuss how to assess the *reliability* of the sample mean and how to use a measure of reliability to decide whether sample information provides definitive evidence.

Another descriptive measure of the central tendency of a population or a sample of measurements is the **median.** Intuitively, the median divides a population or sample into two roughly equal parts. We calculate the median, which is denoted M_d, as follows:

Consider a population or a sample of measurements, and arrange the measurements in increasing order. The **median, M_d,** is found as follows:

1 If the number of measurements is odd, the median is the middlemost measurement in the ordering.

2 If the number of measurements is even, the median is the average of the two middlemost measurements in the ordering.

For example, recall that Chris's five classes have sizes 60, 41, 15, 30, and 34. To find the median of the population of class sizes, we arrange the class sizes in increasing order as follows:

$$15 \quad 30 \quad \textcircled{34} \quad 41 \quad 60$$

Because the number of class sizes is odd, the median of the population of class sizes is the middlemost class size in the ordering. Therefore, the median is 34 students (it is circled).

As another example, suppose that in the middle of the semester Chris decides to take an additional class—a sprint class in individual exercise. If the individual exercise class has 30 students, then the sizes of Chris's six classes are (arranged in increasing order):

$$15 \quad 30 \quad \textcircled{30} \quad \textcircled{34} \quad 41 \quad 60$$

Because the number of classes is even, the median of the population of class sizes is the average of the two middlemost class sizes, which are circled. Therefore, the median is $(30 + 34)/2 = 32$ students. Note that, although two of Chris's classes have the same size, 30 students, each observation is listed separately (that is, 30 is listed twice) when we arrange the observations in increasing order.

As a third example, if we arrange the sample of 50 mileages in Table 3.1 in increasing order, we find that the two middlemost mileages—the 25th and 26th mileages—are 31.5 and 31.6. It follows that the median of the sample is 31.55. Therefore, we estimate that the median mileage that would be obtained by all of the new midsize cars that will or could potentially be produced this year is 31.55 mpg. The Excel output in Figure 3.1 shows this median mileage, as well as the previously calculated mean mileage of 31.56 mpg. Other quantities given on the output will be discussed later in this chapter.

A third measure of the central tendency of a population or sample is the **mode,** which is denoted M_o.

> The **mode,** M_o, of a population or sample of measurements is the measurement that occurs most frequently.

For example, the mode of Chris's six class sizes is 30. This is because more classes (two) have a size of 30 than any other size. Sometimes the highest frequency occurs at more than one measurement. When this happens, two or more modes exist. When exactly two modes exist, we say the data are *bimodal*. When more than two modes exist, we say the data are *multimodal*. If data are presented in classes (such as in a frequency or percent histogram), the class having the highest frequency or percent is called the *modal class*. For example, Figure 3.2 shows a histogram of the car mileages that has two modal classes—the class from 31.0 mpg to 31.5 mpg and the class from 31.5 mpg to 32.0 mpg. Since the mileage 31.5 is in the middle of the modal classes, we might estimate that the population mode for the new midsize model is 31.5 mpg. Or, alternatively, because the Excel output in Figure 3.1 tells us that the mode of the sample of 50 mileages is 31.4 mpg (it can be verified that this mileage occurs five times in Table 3.1), we might estimate that the population mode is 31.4 mpg. Obviously, these two estimates are somewhat contradictory. In general, it can be difficult to define a reliable method for estimating the population mode. Therefore, although it can be informative to report the modal class or classes in a frequency or percent histogram, the mean or median is used more often than the mode when we wish to describe a data set's central tendency by using a single number. Finally, the mode is a useful descriptor of qualitative data. For example, we have seen in Chapter 2 that the most frequently sold 2006 Jeep model at the Cincinnati Jeep dealership was the Jeep Liberty, which accounted for 31.87 percent of Jeep sales.

Comparing the mean, median, and mode   Often we construct a histogram for a sample to make inferences about the shape of the sampled population. When we do this, it can be useful to "smooth out" the histogram and use the resulting *relative frequency curve* to describe the shape

FIGURE 3.1	Excel Output of Statistics Describing the 50 Mileages

Mileage

Mean	31.56
Standard Error	0.1128
Median	31.55
Mode	31.4
Standard Deviation	0.7977
Sample Variance	0.6363
Kurtosis	−0.5112
Skewness	−0.0342
Range	3.5
Minimum	29.8
Maximum	33.3
Sum	1578
Count	50

FIGURE 3.2	A Percent Histogram Describing the 50 Mileages

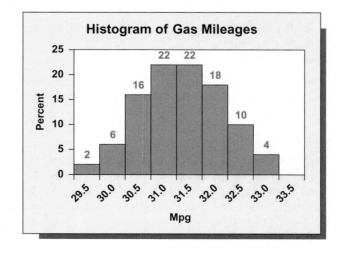

FIGURE 3.3 **Typical Relationships among the Mean μ, the Median M_d, and the Mode M_o**

(a) A symmetrical curve   (b) A curve skewed to the right   (c) A curve skewed to the left

of the population. Relative frequency curves can have many shapes. Three common shapes are illustrated in Figure 3.3. Part (a) of this figure depicts a population described by a symmetrical relative frequency curve. For such a population, the mean (μ), median (M_d), and mode (M_o) are all equal. Note that in this case all three of these quantities are located under the highest point of the curve. It follows that when the frequency distribution of a sample of measurements is approximately symmetrical, then the sample mean, median, and mode will be nearly the same. For instance, consider the sample of 50 mileages in Table 3.1. Because the histogram of these mileages in Figure 3.2 is approximately symmetrical, the mean—31.56—and the median—31.55—of the mileages are approximately equal to each other.

Figure 3.3(b) depicts a population that is skewed to the right. Here the population mean is larger than the population median, and the population median is larger than the population mode (the mode is located under the highest point of the relative frequency curve). In this case the population mean *averages in* the large values in the upper tail of the distribution. Thus the population mean is more affected by these large values than is the population median. To understand this, we consider the following example.

EXAMPLE 3.2 The Household Income Case

An economist wishes to study the distribution of household incomes in a midwestern city. To do this, the economist randomly selects a sample of $n = 12$ households from the city and determines last year's income for each household.[1] The resulting sample of 12 household incomes—arranged in increasing order—is as follows (the incomes are expressed in dollars):

    7,524   11,070   18,211   26,817   36,551   (41,286)

    (49,312)   57,283   72,814   90,416   135,540   190,250

DS Incomes

Because the number of incomes is even, the median of the incomes is the average of the two middlemost incomes, which are enclosed in ovals. Therefore, the median is $(41,286 + 49,312)/2 =$ \$45,299. The mean of the incomes is the sum of the incomes, 737,076, divided by 12, or \$61,423. Here, the mean has been affected by averaging in the large incomes \$135,540 and \$190,250 and thus is larger than the median. The median is said to be *resistant* to these large incomes because the value of the median is affected only by the position of these large incomes in the ordered list of incomes, not by the *exact sizes* of the incomes. For example, if the largest income were smaller—say \$150,000—the median would remain the same but the mean would decrease. If the largest income were larger—say \$300,000—the median would also remain the same but the mean would increase. Therefore, the median is resistant to large values but the mean is not. Similarly, the median is resistant to values that are much smaller than most of the measurements. In general, we say that **the median is resistant to extreme values.**

Figure 3.3(c) depicts a population that is skewed to the left. Here the population mean is smaller than the population median, and the population median is smaller than the population mode. In this case the population mean *averages in* the small values in the lower tail of the distribution, and the

[1]Note that, realistically, an economist would sample many more than 12 incomes from a city. We have made the sample size in this case small so that we can simply illustrate various ideas throughout this chapter.

mean is more affected by these small values than is the median. For instance, in a survey several years ago of 20 Decision Sciences graduates at Miami University, 18 of the graduates had obtained employment in business consulting that paid a mean salary of about $43,000. One of the graduates had become a Christian missionary and listed his salary as $8,500, and another graduate was working for his hometown bank and listed his salary as $10,500. The two lower salaries decreased the overall mean salary to about $39,650, which was below the median salary of about $43,000.

When a population is skewed to the right or left with a very long tail, the population mean can be substantially affected by the extreme population values in the tail of the distribution. In such a case, the population median might be better than the population mean as a measure of central tendency. For example, the yearly incomes of all people in the United States are skewed to the right with a very long tail. Furthermore, the very large incomes in this tail cause the mean yearly income to be inflated above the typical income earned by most Americans. Because of this, the median income is more representative of a typical U.S. income.

When a population is symmetrical or not highly skewed, then the population mean and the population median are either equal or roughly equal, and both provide a good measure of the population central tendency. In this situation, we usually make inferences about the population mean because much of statistical theory is based on the mean rather than the median.

EXAMPLE 3.3 The Marketing Research Case

The Excel output in Figure 3.4 tells us that the mean and the median of the sample of 60 bottle design ratings are 30.35 and 31, respectively. Because the histogram of the bottle design ratings in Figure 3.5 is not highly skewed to the left, the sample mean is not much less than the sample median. Therefore, using the mean as our measure of central tendency, we estimate that the mean rating of the new bottle design that would be given by all consumers is 30.35. This is considerably higher than the minimum standard of 25 for a successful bottle design.

EXAMPLE 3.4 The Payment Time Case

The MINITAB output in Figure 3.6 gives a histogram of the 65 payment times, and the MINITAB output in Figure 3.7 tells us that the mean and the median of the payment times are 18.108 days and 17 days, respectively. Because the histogram is not highly skewed to the right, the sample mean is not much greater than the sample median. Therefore, using the mean as our measure of central tendency, we estimate that the mean payment time of all bills using the new billing system is 18.108 days. This is substantially less than the typical payment time of 39 days that had been experienced using the old billing system.

FIGURE 3.4   Excel Output of Statistics Describing the 60 Bottle Design Ratings

STATISTICS	
Mean	30.35
Standard Error	0.401146
Median	31
Mode	32
Standard Deviation	3.107263
Sample Variance	9.655085
Kurtosis	1.423397
Skewness	−1.17688
Range	15
Minimum	20
Maximum	35
Sum	1821
Count	60

FIGURE 3.5   Excel Frequency Histogram of the 60 Bottle Design Ratings

FIGURE 3.6   MINITAB Frequency Histogram of the 65 Payment Times

FIGURE 3.7   MINITAB Output of Statistics Describing the 65 Payment Times

Variable	Count	Mean	StDev	Variance
PayTime	65	18.108	3.961	15.691

Variable	Minimum	Q1	Median	Q3	Maximum	Range
PayTime	10.000	15.000	17.000	21.000	29.000	19.000

EXAMPLE 3.5 The Cell Phone Case

Remember that if the cellular cost per minute for the random sample of 100 bank employees is over 18 cents per minute, the bank will benefit from automated cellular management of its calling plans. Last month's cellular usages for the 100 randomly selected employees are given in Table 1.4 (page 9), and a dot plot of these usages is given in the page margin. If we add together the usages, we find that the 100 employees used a total of 46,625 minutes. Furthermore, the total cellular cost incurred by the 100 employees is found to be $9,317 (this total includes base costs, overage costs, long distance, and roaming). This works out to an average of $9,317/46,625 = $.1998, or 19.98 cents per minute. Because this average cellular cost per minute exceeds 18 cents per minute, the bank will hire the cellular management service to manage its calling plans.

To conclude this section, note that the mean and the median convey useful information about a population having a relative frequency curve with a sufficiently regular shape. For instance, the mean and median would be useful in describing the mound-shaped, or single-peaked, distributions in Figure 3.3. However, these measures of central tendency do not adequately describe a double-peaked distribution. For example, the mean and the median of the exam scores in the double-peaked distribution of Figure 2.12 (page 48) are 75.225 and 77. Looking at the distribution, neither the mean nor the median represents a *typical* exam score. This is because the exam scores really have *no central value*. In this case the most important message conveyed by the double-peaked distribution is that the exam scores fall into two distinct groups.

Exercises for Section 3.1

CONCEPTS

3.1   Explain the difference between each of the following:

    a   A population parameter and its point estimate.

    b   A population mean and a corresponding sample mean.

connect

3.2   Explain how the population mean, median, and mode compare when the population's relative frequency curve is

    a   Symmetrical.

    b   Skewed with a tail to the left.

    c   Skewed with a tail to the right.

METHODS AND APPLICATIONS

3.3   Calculate the mean, median, and mode of each of the following populations of numbers:

    a   9, 8, 10, 10, 12, 6, 11, 10, 12, 8

    b   110, 120, 70, 90, 90, 100, 80, 130, 140

3.4   Calculate the mean, median, and mode for each of the following populations of numbers:

    a   17, 23, 19, 20, 25, 18, 22, 15, 21, 20

    b   505, 497, 501, 500, 507, 510, 501

3.5   **THE VIDEO GAME SATISFACTION RATING CASE**   DS VideoGame

Recall that Table 1.7 (page 13) presents the satisfaction ratings for the XYZ-Box game system that have been given by 65 randomly selected purchasers. Figures 3.8 and 3.11(a) give the MINITAB and Excel outputs of statistics describing the 65 satisfaction ratings.

    a   Find the sample mean on the outputs. Does the sample mean provide some evidence that the mean of the population of all possible customer satisfaction ratings for the XYZ-Box is at least 42? (Recall that a "very satisfied" customer gives a rating that is at least 42.) Explain your answer.

    b   Find the sample median on the outputs. How do the mean and median compare? What does the histogram in Figure 2.15 (page 52) tell you about why they compare this way?

3.6   **THE BANK CUSTOMER WAITING TIME CASE**   DS WaitTime

Recall that Table 1.8 (page 13) presents the waiting times for teller service during peak business hours of 100 randomly selected bank customers. Figures 3.9 and 3.11(b) give the MINITAB and Excel outputs of statistics describing the 100 waiting times.

    a   Find the sample mean on the outputs. Does the sample mean provide some evidence that the mean of the population of all possible customer waiting times during peak business hours is less than six minutes (as is desired by the bank manager)? Explain your answer.

    b   Find the sample median on the outputs. How do the mean and median compare? What does the histogram in Figure 2.16 (page 53) tell you about why they compare this way?

3.7   **THE TRASH BAG CASE**   DS TrashBag

Consider the trash bag problem. Suppose that an independent laboratory has tested 30-gallon trash bags and has found that none of the 30-gallon bags currently on the market has a mean breaking strength of 50 pounds or more. On the basis of these results, the producer of the new, improved trash bag feels sure that its 30-gallon bag will be the strongest such bag on the market if the new trash bag's mean breaking strength can be shown to be at least 50 pounds. Recall that Table 1.9 (page 14) presents the breaking strengths of 40 trash bags of the new type that were selected during

---

FIGURE 3.8   **MINITAB Output of Statistics Describing the 65 Satisfaction Ratings (for Exercise 3.5)**

Variable	Count	Mean	StDev	Variance
Ratings	65	42.954	2.642	6.982

Variable	Minimum	Q1	Median	Q3	Maximum	Range
Ratings	36.000	41.000	43.000	45.000	48.000	12.000

FIGURE 3.9   **MINITAB Output of Statistics Describing the 100 Waiting Times (for Exercise 3.6)**

Variable	Count	Mean	StDev	Variance
WaitTime	100	5.460	2.475	6.128

Variable	Minimum	Q1	Median	Q3	Maximum	Range
WaitTime	0.400	3.800	5.250	7.200	11.600	11.200

FIGURE 3.10 MINITAB Output of Statistics Describing the 40 Breaking Strengths (for Exercise 3.7)

Variable	Count	Mean	StDev	Variance		
Strength	40	50.575	1.644	2.702		

Variable	Minimum	Q1	Median	Q3	Maximum	Range
Strength	46.800	49.425	50.650	51.650	54.000	7.200

FIGURE 3.11 Excel Outputs of Statistics Describing Three Data Sets (for Exercises 3.5, 3.6, and 3.7)

(a) Satisfaction rating statistics

Ratings	
Mean	42.9538
Standard Error	0.3277
Median	43
Mode	44
Standard Deviation	2.6424
Sample Variance	6.9822
Kurtosis	−0.3922
Skewness	−0.4466
Range	12
Minimum	36
Maximum	48
Sum	2792
Count	65

(b) Waiting time statistics

WaitTime	
Mean	5.46
Standard Error	0.2475
Median	5.25
Mode	5.8
Standard Deviation	2.4755
Sample Variance	6.1279
Kurtosis	−0.4050
Skewness	0.2504
Range	11.2
Minimum	0.4
Maximum	11.6
Sum	546
Count	100

(c) Breaking strength statistics

Strength	
Mean	50.575
Standard Error	0.2599
Median	50.65
Mode	50.9
Standard Deviation	1.6438
Sample Variance	2.7019
Kurtosis	−0.2151
Skewness	−0.0549
Range	7.2
Minimum	46.8
Maximum	54
Sum	2023
Count	40

a 40-hour pilot production run. Figures 3.10 and 3.11(c) give the MINITAB and Excel outputs of statistics describing the 40 breaking strengths.

a Find the sample mean on the outputs. Does the sample mean provide some evidence that the mean of the population of all possible trash bag breaking strengths is at least 50 pounds? Explain your answer.

b Find the sample median on the outputs. How do the mean and median compare? What does the histogram in Figure 2.17 (page 53) tell you about why they compare this way?

3.8 Lauren is a college sophomore majoring in business. This semester Lauren is taking courses in accounting, economics, management information systems, public speaking, and statistics. The sizes of these classes are, respectively, 350, 45, 35, 25, and 40. Find the mean and the median of the class sizes. What is a better measure of Lauren's "typical class size"—the mean or the median?

Exercises 3.9 through 3.13 refer to information in Table 3.2, which gives data concerning lifestyles in the United States and eight other countries. In each exercise (a) compute the appropriate mean and median; (b) compare the mean and median and explain what they say about skewness; (c) construct a dot plot and discuss what the dot plot says about skewness and whether this agrees with how the mean and median compare; (d) discuss how the United States compares to the mean and median. DS LifeStyle

3.9 Analyze the data concerning voters in Table 3.2 as described above. DS LifeStyle

3.10 Analyze the data concerning income tax rates in Table 3.2 as described above. DS LifeStyle

3.11 Analyze the data concerning video rentals in Table 3.2 as described above. DS LifeStyle

3.12 Analyze the data concerning PCs in Table 3.2 as described above. DS LifeStyle

3.13 Analyze the data concerning religion in Table 3.2 as described above. DS LifeStyle

3.14 Table 3.3 gives the number of unique visitors during December 2006 to the top 10 websites as rated by comScore Media Metrix, a division of comScore Networks, Inc. Compute the mean and median for the website data and compare them. What do they say about skewness? DS WebVisit

3.15 In 1998 the National Basketball Association (NBA) experienced a labor dispute that canceled almost half of the professional basketball season. The NBA owners, who were worried about escalating salaries because several star players had recently signed huge contracts, locked out the

TABLE 3.2   **Data Comparing Lifestyles in the U.S. and Eight Other Countries**
DS LifeStyle

	Voters Percentage Who Voted in Last National Election	Income Tax Highest Personal National Rate	Video Rentals Per Capita per Year	PCs Per 100 People	Religion Percentage of Households Who Attend Services Regularly
U.S.	49.1%	40%	13.8	35.0	51.6%
Germany	82.2	56	2.1	17.0	20.0
France	68.9	54	0.9	16.0	N.A.
Britain	71.5	40	3.3	20.0	23.6
Netherlands	78.3	60	1.8	20.0	28.9
Sweden	78.6	55	2.1	18.0	10.0
Italy	85.0	46	0.7	11.5	55.8
Japan	58.8	50	7.5	14.0	N.A.
South Korea	63.9	44	N.A.	N.A.	N.A.

N.A. = Not available.

Source: "America vs. The New Europe: By The Numbers," *Fortune*, December 21, 1998, p. 156. Reprinted from the December 21, 1998, issue of *Fortune*, copyright 1998 Time, Inc. All rights reserved.

TABLE 3.3
Top 10 Websites in December 2006 as Rated by comScore Media Metrix DS WebVisit

	Unique Visitors (Millions)
Yahoo! sites	131
Time Warner Network	121
Microsoft sites	117
Google sites	113
eBay	84
Fox Interactive Media	73
Amazon sites	57
Ask Network	56
Wal-Mart	44
Viacom Digital	40

Source: Courtesy of ComScore Networks. Copyright © 2007. All rights reserved.

FIGURE 3.12
1997–98 NBA Salaries

Source: Reprinted courtesy of ESPN.

LO2   Compute and interpret the range, variance, and standard deviation.

players and demanded that a salary cap be established. This led to discussion in the media about excessive player salaries. On October 30, 1998, an article titled "What does average salary really mean in the NBA?" by Jonathan Sills appeared in his *Behind the Numbers* column on the ESPN.com website. The article discussed the validity of some media claims about NBA player salaries. Figure 3.12 shows a frequency distribution of NBA salaries as presented in the Sills article. Use the frequency distribution to do the following:

a Compare the mean, median, and mode of the salaries and explain the relationship. Note that the minimum NBA salary at the time of the lockout was $272,500.

b Noting that 411 NBA players were under contract, estimate the percentage of players who earned more than the mean salary; more than the median salary.

c Below we give three quotes from news stories cited by Sills in his article. Comment on the validity of each statement.

> "Last year, the NBA middle class made an average of $2.6 million. On that scale, I'd take the NBA lower class."—*Houston Chronicle*

> "The players make an obscene amount of money—the median salary is well over $2 million!"—*St. Louis Post Dispatch*

> "The players want us to believe they literally can't 'survive' on $2.6 million a year, the average salary in the NBA."—*Washington Post*

3.2 Measures of Variation ● ● ●

Range, variance, and standard deviation   In addition to estimating a population's central tendency, it is important to estimate the **variation** of the population's individual values. For example, Figure 3.13 shows two histograms. Each portrays the distribution of 20 repair times (in days) for personal computers at a major service center. Because the mean (and median and mode) of each distribution equals four days, the measures of central tendency do not indicate any difference between the American and National Service Centers. However, the repair times for the American Service Center are clustered quite closely together, whereas the repair times for the National Service Center are spread farther apart (the repair time might be as little as one day, but could also be as long as seven days). Therefore, we need measures of variation to express how the two distributions differ.

One way to measure the variation of a set of measurements is to calculate the *range*.

> Consider a population or a sample of measurements. The **range** of the measurements is the largest measurement minus the smallest measurement.

In Figure 3.13, the smallest and largest repair times for the American Service Center are three days and five days; therefore, the range is $5 - 3 = 2$ days. On the other hand, the range for the

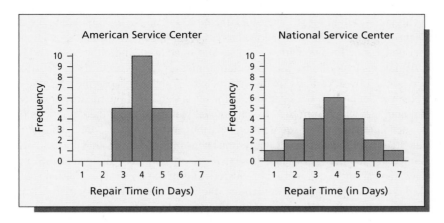

FIGURE 3.13   Repair Times for Personal Computers at Two Service Centers

National Service Center is $7 - 1 = 6$ days. The National Service Center's larger range indicates that this service center's repair times exhibit more variation.

In general, the range is not the best measure of a data set's variation. One reason is that it is based on only the smallest and largest measurements in the data set and therefore may reflect an extreme measurement that is not entirely representative of the data set's variation. For example, in the marketing research case, the smallest and largest ratings in the sample of 60 bottle design ratings are 20 and 35. However, to simply estimate that most bottle design ratings are between 20 and 35 misses the fact that 57, or 95 percent, of the 60 ratings are at least as large as the minimum rating of 25 for a successful bottle design. In general, to fully describe a population's variation, it is useful to estimate intervals that contain *different percentages* (for example, 70 percent, 95 percent, or almost 100 percent) of the individual population values. To estimate such intervals, we use the **population variance** and the **population standard deviation.**

The Population Variance and Standard Deviation

The **population variance** σ^2 (pronounced *sigma squared*) is the average of the squared deviations of the individual population measurements from the population mean μ.

The **population standard deviation** σ (pronounced *sigma*) is the positive square root of the population variance.

For example, consider again the population of Chris's class sizes this semester. These class sizes are 60, 41, 15, 30, and 34. To calculate the variance and standard deviation of these class sizes, we first calculate the population mean to be

$$\mu = \frac{60 + 41 + 15 + 30 + 34}{5} = \frac{180}{5} = 36$$

Next, we calculate the deviations of the individual population measurements from the population mean $\mu = 36$ as follows:

$(60 - 36) = 24$ $(41 - 36) = 5$ $(15 - 36) = -21$ $(30 - 36) = -6$ $(34 - 36) = -2$

Then we compute the sum of the squares of these deviations:

$$(24)^2 + (5)^2 + (-21)^2 + (-6)^2 + (-2)^2 = 576 + 25 + 441 + 36 + 4 = 1082$$

Finally, we calculate the population variance σ^2, the average of the squared deviations, by dividing the sum of the squared deviations, 1,082, by the number of squared deviations, 5. That is, σ^2 equals $1,082/5 = 216.4$. Furthermore, this implies that the population standard deviation σ (the positive square root of σ^2) is $\sqrt{216.4} = 14.71$.

To see that the variance and standard deviation measure the variation, or spread, of the individual population measurements, suppose that the measurements are spread far apart. Then, many measurements will be far from the mean μ, many of the squared deviations from the mean will be large, and the sum of squared deviations will be large. It follows that the average of the squared deviations—the population variance—will be relatively large. On the other hand, if the population measurements are clustered close together, many measurements will be close to μ, many of the squared deviations from the mean will be small, and the average of the squared deviations—the population variance—will be small. Therefore, the more spread out the population measurements, the larger is the population variance, and the larger is the population standard deviation.

To further understand the population variance and standard deviation, note that one reason we square the deviations of the individual population measurements from the population mean is that the sum of the raw deviations themselves is zero. This is because the negative deviations cancel the positive deviations. For example, in the class size situation, the raw deviations are 24, 5, −21, −6, and −2, which sum to zero. Of course, we could make the deviations positive by finding their absolute values. We square the deviations instead because the resulting population variance and standard deviation have many important interpretations that we study throughout this book. Since the population variance is an average of squared deviations of the original population values, the variance is expressed in squared units of the original population values. On the other hand, the population standard deviation—the square root of the population variance—is expressed in the same units as the original population values. For example, the previously discussed class sizes are expressed in numbers of students. Therefore, the variance of these class sizes is $\sigma^2 = 216.4$ (students)^2, whereas the standard deviation is $\sigma = 14.71$ students. Since the population standard deviation is expressed in the same units as the population values, it is more often used to make practical interpretations about the variation of these values.

When a population is too large to measure all the population units, we estimate the population variance and the population standard deviation by the **sample variance** and the **sample standard deviation.** We calculate the sample variance by dividing the sum of the squared deviations of the sample measurements from the sample mean by $n - 1$, the sample size minus one. Although we might intuitively think that we should divide by n rather than $n - 1$, it can be shown that dividing by n tends to produce an estimate of the population variance that is too small. On the other hand, dividing by $n - 1$ tends to produce a larger estimate that we will show in Chapter 7 is more appropriate. Therefore, we obtain:

The Sample Variance and the Sample Standard Deviation

The **sample variance** s^2 (pronounced s *squared*) is defined to be

$$s^2 = \frac{\sum\limits_{i=1}^{n} (x_i - \bar{x})^2}{n - 1} = \frac{(x_1 - \bar{x})^2 + (x_2 - \bar{x})^2 + \cdots + (x_n - \bar{x})^2}{n - 1}$$

and is the **point estimate of the population variance** σ^2.

The **sample standard deviation** $s = \sqrt{s^2}$ is the positive square root of the sample variance and is the **point estimate of the population standard deviation** σ.

EXAMPLE 3.6 The Car Mileage Case   C

To illustrate the calculation of the sample variance and standard deviation, we begin by considering the first five mileages in Table 3.1 (page 103): $x_1 = 30.8$, $x_2 = 31.7$, $x_3 = 30.1$, $x_4 = 31.6$, and $x_5 = 32.1$. Since the mean of these five mileages is $\bar{x} = 31.26$, it follows that

$$\sum_{i=1}^{5} (x_i - \bar{x})^2 = (x_1 - \bar{x})^2 + (x_2 - \bar{x})^2 + (x_3 - \bar{x})^2 + (x_4 - \bar{x})^2 + (x_5 - \bar{x})^2$$

$$= (30.8 - 31.26)^2 + (31.7 - 31.26)^2 + (30.1 - 31.26)^2$$
$$+ (31.6 - 31.26)^2 + (32.1 - 31.26)^2$$

$$= (-.46)^2 + (.44)^2 + (-1.16)^2 + (.34)^2 + (.84)^2$$

$$= 2.572$$

Therefore, the variance and the standard deviation of the sample of the first five mileages are

$$s^2 = \frac{2.572}{5 - 1} = .643 \qquad \text{and} \qquad s = \sqrt{.643} = .8019$$

Of course, intuitively, we are likely to obtain more accurate point estimates of the population variance and standard deviation by using all the available sample information. Recall that the mean of all 50 mileages is $\bar{x} = 31.56$. Using this sample mean, it can be verified that

$$\sum_{i=1}^{50}(x_i - \bar{x})^2 = (x_1 - \bar{x})^2 + (x_2 - \bar{x})^2 + \cdots + (x_{50} - \bar{x})^2$$

$$= (30.8 - 31.56)^2 + (31.7 - 31.56)^2 + \cdots + (31.4 - 31.56)^2$$

$$= (-.76)^2 + (.14)^2 + \cdots + (-.16)^2$$

$$= 31.18$$

Therefore, the variance and the standard deviation of the sample of 50 mileages are

$$s^2 = \frac{31.18}{50 - 1} = .6363 \qquad \text{and} \qquad s = \sqrt{.6363} = .7977.$$

Notice that the Excel output in Figure 3.1 (page 104) gives these quantities. Here $s^2 = .6363$ and $s = .7977$ are the point estimates of the variance, σ^2, and the standard deviation, σ, of the population of the mileages of all the cars that will be or could potentially be produced. Furthermore, the sample standard deviation is expressed in the same units (that is, miles per gallon) as the sample values. Therefore $s = .7977$ mpg.

Before explaining how we can use s^2 and s in a practical way, we present a formula that makes it easier to compute s^2. This formula is useful when we are using a handheld calculator that is not equipped with a statistics mode to compute s^2.

The **sample variance** can be calculated using the *computational formula*

$$s^2 = \frac{1}{n-1}\left[\sum_{i=1}^{n}x_i^2 - \frac{\left(\sum_{i=1}^{n}x_i\right)^2}{n}\right]$$

EXAMPLE 3.7 The Payment Time Case

Consider the sample of 65 payment times in Table 2.4 (page 42). Using these data, it can be verified that

$$\sum_{i=1}^{65}x_i = x_1 + x_2 + \cdots + x_{65} = 22 + 19 + \cdots + 21 = 1{,}177 \quad \text{and}$$

$$\sum_{i=1}^{65}x_i^2 = x_1^2 + x_2^2 + \cdots + x_{65}^2 = (22)^2 + (19)^2 + \cdots + (21)^2 = 22{,}317$$

Therefore,

$$s^2 = \frac{1}{(65-1)}\left[22{,}317 - \frac{(1{,}177)^2}{65}\right] = \frac{1{,}004.2464}{64} = 15.69135$$

and $s = \sqrt{s^2} = \sqrt{15.69135} = 3.9612$ days (see the MINITAB output in Figure 3.7 on page 107).

A practical interpretation of the standard deviation: The Empirical Rule   One type of relative frequency curve describing a population is the **normal curve,** which is discussed in Chapter 6. The normal curve is a symmetrical, bell-shaped curve and is illustrated in Figure 3.14(a). If a population is described by a normal curve, we say that the population is normally distributed, and the following result can be shown to hold.

LO3 Use the Empirical Rule and Chebyshev's Theorem to describe variation.

FIGURE 3.14   The Empirical Rule and Tolerance Intervals

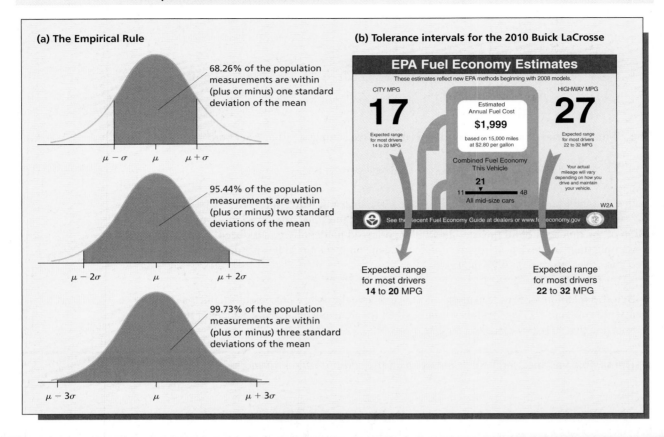

The Empirical Rule for a Normally Distributed Population

If a population has **mean μ** and **standard deviation σ** and is **described by a normal curve,** then, as illustrated in Figure 3.14(a),

1 68.26 percent of the population measurements are within (plus or minus) one standard deviation of the mean and thus lie in the interval $[\mu - \sigma, \mu + \sigma] = [\mu \pm \sigma]$

2 95.44 percent of the population measurements are within (plus or minus) two standard devi-ations of the mean and thus lie in the interval $[\mu - 2\sigma, \mu + 2\sigma] = [\mu \pm 2\sigma]$

3 99.73 percent of the population measurements are within (plus or minus) three standard devi-ations of the mean and thus lie in the interval $[\mu - 3\sigma, \mu + 3\sigma] = [\mu \pm 3\sigma]$

In general, an interval that contains a specified percentage of the individual measurements in a population is called a **tolerance interval.** It follows that the one, two, and three standard deviation intervals around μ given in (1), (2), and (3) are tolerance intervals containing, respec-tively, 68.26 percent, 95.44 percent, and 99.73 percent of the measurements in a normally distrib-uted population. Often we interpret the *three-sigma interval* $[\mu \pm 3\sigma]$ to be a tolerance interval that contains *almost all* of the measurements in a normally distributed population. Of course, we usually do not know the true values of μ and σ. Therefore, we must estimate the tolerance inter-vals by replacing μ and σ in these intervals by the mean $\bar{x}$ and standard deviation s of a sample that has been randomly selected from the normally distributed population.

EXAMPLE 3.8 The Car Mileage Case

Again consider the sample of 50 mileages. We have seen that $\bar{x} = 31.56$ and $s = .7977$ for this sample are the point estimates of the mean μ and the standard deviation σ of the population of all mileages. Furthermore, the histogram of the 50 mileages in Figure 3.15 suggests that the

F I G U R E   3 . 1 5   **Estimated Tolerance Intervals in the Car Mileage Case**

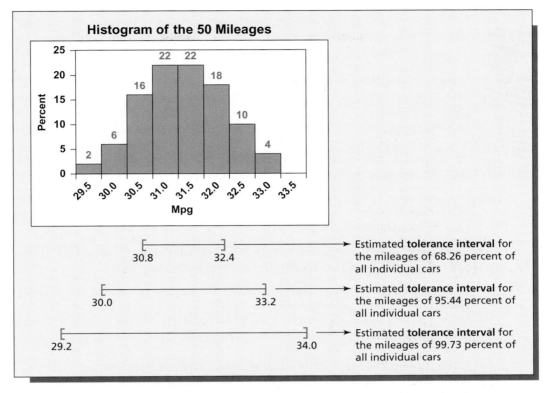

population of all mileages is normally distributed. To more simply illustrate the Empirical Rule, we will round $\bar{x}$ to 31.6 and s to .8. It follows that, using the interval

1   $[\bar{x} \pm s] = [31.6 \pm .8] = [31.6 - .8, 31.6 + .8] = [30.8, 32.4]$, we estimate that 68.26 percent of all individual cars will obtain mileages between 30.8 mpg and 32.4 mpg.

2   $[\bar{x} \pm 2s] = [31.6 \pm 2(.8)] = [31.6 \pm 1.6] = [30.0, 33.2]$, we estimate that 95.44 percent of all individual cars will obtain mileages between 30.0 mpg and 33.2 mpg.

3   $[\bar{x} \pm 3s] = [31.6 \pm 3(.8)] = [31.6 \pm 2.4] = [29.2, 34.0]$, we estimate that 99.73 percent of all individual cars will obtain mileages between 29.2 mpg and 34.0 mpg.

Figure 3.15 depicts these estimated tolerance intervals, which are shown below the histogram. Since the difference between the upper and lower limits of each estimated tolerance interval is fairly small, we might conclude that the variability of the individual car mileages around the estimated mean mileage of 31.6 mpg is fairly small. Furthermore, the interval $[\bar{x} \pm 3s] = [29.2, 34.0]$ implies that almost any individual car that a customer might purchase this year will obtain a mileage between 29.2 mpg and 34.0 mpg.

   Before continuing, recall that we have rounded $\bar{x}$ and s to one decimal point accuracy in order to simplify our initial example of the Empirical Rule. If, instead, we calculate the Empirical Rule intervals by using $\bar{x} = 31.56$ and $s = .7977$ and then round the interval endpoints to one decimal place accuracy at the end of the calculations, we obtain the same intervals as obtained above. In general, however, rounding intermediate calculated results can lead to inaccurate final results. Because of this, throughout this book we will avoid greatly rounding intermediate results.

   We next note that if we actually count the number of the 50 mileages in Table 3.1 that are contained in each of the intervals $[\bar{x} \pm s] = [30.8, 32.4]$, $[\bar{x} \pm 2s] = [30.0, 33.2]$, and $[\bar{x} \pm 3s] = [29.2, 34.0]$, we find that these intervals contain, respectively, 34, 48, and 50 of the 50 mileages. The corresponding sample percentages—68 percent, 96 percent, and 100 percent—are close to the theoretical percentages—68.26 percent, 95.44 percent, and 99.73 percent—that apply to a normally distributed population. This is further evidence that the population of all mileages is (approximately) normally distributed and thus that the Empirical Rule holds for this population.

To conclude this example, we note that the automaker has studied the combined city and highway mileages of the new model because the federal tax credit is based on these combined mileages. When reporting fuel economy estimates for a particular car model to the public, however, the EPA realizes that the proportions of city and highway driving vary from purchaser to purchaser. Therefore, the EPA reports both a combined mileage estimate and separate city and highway mileage estimates to the public. Figure 3.14(b) presents a window sticker that summarizes these estimates for the 2010 Buick LaCrosse equipped with a six-cylinder engine and an automatic transmission. The city mpg of 17 and the highway mpg of 27 given at the top of the sticker are point estimates of, respectively, the mean city mileage and the mean highway mileage that would be obtained by all such 2010 LaCrosses. The expected city range of 14 to 20 mpg says that most LaCrosses will get between 14 mpg and 20 mpg in city driving. The expected highway range of 22 to 32 mpg says that most LaCrosses will get between 22 mpg and 32 mpg in highway driving. The combined city and highway mileage estimate for the LaCrosse is 21 mpg.

Skewness and the Empirical Rule   The Empirical Rule holds for normally distributed populations. In addition:

> The Empirical Rule also approximately holds for populations having **mound-shaped (single-peaked) distributions that are not very skewed to the right or left.**

In some situations, the skewness of a mound-shaped distribution can make it tricky to know whether to use the Empirical Rule. This will be investigated in the end-of-section exercises. When a distribution seems to be too skewed for the Empirical Rule to hold, it is probably best to describe the distribution's variation by using **percentiles,** which are discussed in the next section.

Chebyshev's Theorem   If we fear that the Empirical Rule does not hold for a particular population, we can consider using **Chebyshev's Theorem** to find an interval that contains a specified percentage of the individual measurements in the population. Although Chebyshev's Theorem technically applies to any population, we will see that it is not as practically useful as we might hope.

Chebyshev's Theorem

Consider any population that has mean μ and standard deviation σ. Then, for any value of k greater than 1, at least $100(1 - 1/k^2)\%$ of the population measurements lie in the interval $[\mu \pm k\sigma]$.

For example, if we choose k equal to 2, then at least $100(1 - 1/2^2)\% = 100(3/4)\% = 75\%$ of the population measurements lie in the interval $[\mu \pm 2\sigma]$. As another example, if we choose k equal to 3, then at least $100(1 - 1/3^2)\% = 100(8/9)\% = 88.89\%$ of the population measurements lie in the interval $[\mu \pm 3\sigma]$. As yet a third example, suppose that we wish to find an interval containing at least 99.73 percent of all population measurements. Here we would set $100(1 - 1/k^2)\%$ equal to 99.73%, which implies that $(1 - 1/k^2) = .9973$. If we solve for k, we find that $k = 19.25$. This says that at least 99.73 percent of all population measurements lie in the interval $[\mu \pm 19.25\sigma]$. Unless σ is extremely small, this interval will be so long that it will tell us very little about where the population measurements lie. We conclude that Chebyshev's Theorem can help us find an interval that contains a reasonably high percentage (such as 75 percent or 88.89 percent) of all population measurements. However, unless σ is extremely small, Chebyshev's Theorem will not provide a useful interval that contains almost all (say, 99.73 percent) of the population measurements.

Although Chebyshev's Theorem technically applies to any population, it is only of practical use when analyzing a **non-mound-shaped** (for example, a double-peaked) **population that is not *very* skewed to the right or left.** Why is this? First, **we would not use Chebyshev's Theorem to describe a mound-shaped population that is not very skewed because we can use the Empirical Rule** to do this. In fact, the Empirical Rule is better for such a population because it gives us a shorter interval that will contain a given percentage of measurements. For example, if the Empirical Rule can be used to describe a population, the interval $[\mu \pm 3\sigma]$ will contain

99.73 percent of all measurements. On the other hand, if we use Chebyshev's Theorem, the interval $[\mu \pm 19.25\sigma]$ is needed. As another example, the Empirical Rule tells us that 95.44 percent of all measurements lie in the interval $[\mu \pm 2\sigma]$, whereas Chebyshev's Theorem tells us only that at least 75 percent of all measurements lie in this interval.

It is also not appropriate to use Chebyshev's Theorem—or any other result making use of the population standard deviation σ—to describe a population that is very skewed. This is because, if a population is very skewed, the measurements in the long tail to the left or right will inflate σ. This implies that tolerance intervals calculated using σ will be so long that they are of little use. In this case, it is best to measure variation by using **percentiles,** which are discussed in the next section.

z-scores   We can determine the relative location of any value in a population or sample by using the mean and standard deviation to compute the value's z-score. For any value x in a population or sample, the **z-score** corresponding to x is defined as follows:

---

z-score:

$$z = \frac{x - \text{mean}}{\text{standard deviation}}$$

The z-score, which is also called the *standardized value,* is the number of standard deviations that x is from the mean. A positive z-score says that x is above (greater than) the mean, while a negative z-score says that x is below (less than) the mean. For instance, a z-score equal to 2.3 says that x is 2.3 standard deviations above the mean. Similarly, a z-score equal to -1.68 says that x is 1.68 standard deviations below the mean. A z-score equal to zero says that x equals the mean.

A z-score indicates the relative location of a value within a population or sample. For example, below we calculate the z-scores for each of the profit margins for five of the best big companies in America as rated by *Forbes* magazine on its website on March 25, 2005.[2] For these five companies, the mean profit margin is 10% and the standard deviation is 3.406%.

Company	Profit margin, x	x − mean	z-score
Black & Decker	8%	$8 - 10 = -2$	$-2/3.406 = -.59$
Washington Post	10	$10 - 10 = 0$	$0/3.406 = 0$
Texas Instruments	15	$15 - 10 = 5$	$5/3.406 = 1.47$
Clorox	12	$12 - 10 = 2$	$2/3.406 = .59$
Foot Locker	5	$5 - 10 = -5$	$-5/3.406 = -1.47$

These z-scores tell us that the profit margin for Texas Instruments is the farthest above the mean. More specifically, this profit margin is 1.47 standard deviations above the mean. The profit margin for Foot Locker is the farthest below the mean—it is 1.47 standard deviations below the mean. Since the z-score for the Washington Post equals zero, its profit margin equals the mean.

Values in two different populations or samples having the same z-score are the same number of standard deviations from their respective means and, therefore, have the same relative locations. For example, suppose that the mean score on the midterm exam for students in Section A of a statistics course is 65 and the standard deviation of the scores is 10. Meanwhile, the mean score on the same exam for students in Section B is 80 and the standard deviation is 5. A student in Section A who scores an 85 and a student in Section B who scores a 90 have the same relative locations within their respective sections because their z-scores, $(85 - 65)/10 = 2$ and $(90 - 80)/5 = 2$, are equal.

The coefficient of variation   Sometimes we need to measure the size of the standard deviation of a population or sample relative to the size of the population or sample mean. The **coefficient of variation,** which makes this comparison, is defined for a population or sample as follows:

$$\text{coefficient of variation} = \frac{\text{standard deviation}}{\text{mean}} \times 100$$

---

[2]Source: *Forbes*, March 16, 2005. © 2005 Forbes, Inc. Reprinted with permission.

The coefficient of variation compares populations or samples having different means and different standard deviations. For example, Morningstar.com[3] gives the mean and standard deviation[4] of the returns for each of the Morningstar Top 25 Large Growth Funds. As given on the Morningstar website, the mean return for the Strong Advisor Select A fund is 10.39 percent with a standard deviation of 16.18 percent, while the mean return for the Nations Marisco 21st Century fund is 17.7 percent with a standard deviation of 15.81 percent. It follows that the coefficient of variation for the Strong Advisor fund is $(16.18/10.39) \times 100 = 155.73$, and that the coefficient of variation for the Nations Marisco fund is $(15.81/17.7) \times 100 = 89.32$. This tells us that, for the Strong Advisor fund, the standard deviation is 155.73 percent of the value of its mean return. For the Nations Marisco fund, the standard deviation is 89.32 percent of the value of its mean return.

In the context of situations like the stock fund comparison, the coefficient of variation is often used as a measure of *risk* because it measures the variation of the returns (the standard deviation) relative to the size of the mean return. For instance, although the Strong Advisor fund and the Nations Marisco fund have comparable standard deviations (16.18 percent versus 15.81 percent), the Strong Advisor fund has a higher coefficient of variation than does the Nations Marisco fund (155.73 versus 89.32). This says that, *relative to the mean return,* the variation in returns for the Strong Advisor fund is higher. That is, we would conclude that investing in the Strong Advisor fund is riskier than investing in the Nations Marisco fund.

Exercises for Section 3.2

connect

CONCEPTS

3.16 Define the range, variance, and standard deviation for a population.

3.17 Discuss how the variance and the standard deviation measure variation.

3.18 The Empirical Rule for a normally distributed population and Chebyshev's Theorem have the same basic purpose. In your own words, explain what this purpose is.

METHODS AND APPLICATIONS

3.19 Consider the following population of five numbers: 5, 8, 10, 12, 15. Calculate the range, variance, and standard deviation of this population.

3.20 Table 3.4 (at the top of the next page) gives the percentage of homes sold during the fourth quarter of 2006 that a median income household could afford to purchase at the prevailing mortgage interest rate for six Texas metropolitan areas. The data were compiled by the National Association of Home Builders. Calculate the range, variance, and standard deviation of this population of affordability percentages.   DS HouseAff

3.21 Table 3.5 (at the top of the next page) gives data concerning the top 10 U.S. airlines (ranked by revenue) as listed on the *Fortune* magazine website on April 27, 2007.   DS AirRev
  a Calculate the population range, variance, and standard deviation of the 10 revenues and of the 10 profits (note that negative values are losses rather than profits).
  b Using the population of profits, compute and interpret the z-score for each airline.

3.22 In order to control costs, a company wishes to study the amount of money its sales force spends entertaining clients. The following is a random sample of six entertainment expenses (dinner costs for four people) from expense reports submitted by members of the sales force.   DS DinnerCost

$$\$157 \qquad \$132 \qquad \$109 \qquad \$145 \qquad \$125 \qquad \$139$$

  a Calculate $\bar{x}$, s^2, and s for the expense data. In addition, show that the two different formulas for calculating s^2 give the same result.
  b Assuming that the distribution of entertainment expenses is approximately normally distributed, calculate estimates of tolerance intervals containing 68.26 percent, 95.44 percent, and 99.73 percent of all entertainment expenses by the sales force.
  c If a member of the sales force submits an entertainment expense (dinner cost for four) of $190, should this expense be considered unusually high (and possibly worthy of investigation by the company)? Explain your answer.
  d Compute and interpret the z-score for each of the six entertainment expenses.

---
[3]Source: http://poweredby.morningstar.com/Selectors/AolTop25/AolTop25List.html, March 17, 2005.
[4]Annualized return based on the last 36 monthly returns.

TABLE 3.4	Housing Affordability in Texas (for Exercise 3.20) DS HouseAff
Metro Area	**Percentage**
Austin-Round Rock	57.5
Dallas-Plano-Irving*	61.7
El Paso	32.5
Fort Worth-Arlington*	67.4
Houston-Sugar Land-Baytown	55.7
San Antonio	49.2

* Indicate Metropolitan Divisions. All others are Metropolitan Statistical Areas.

Data compiled by National Association of Home Builders
http//www.nabb.org/

TABLE 3.5 The Top 10 Airlines (Ranked by Revenue) in 2006 (for Exercise 3.21) DS AirRev

Airline	Revenue ($ billions)	Profits ($ millions)
American Airlines	22.6	231
United Airlines	19.3	22,876
Delta Air Lines	17.2	−6,203
Continental Airlines	13.1	343
Northwest Airlines	12.6	−2,835
US Airways Group	11.6	304
Southwest Airlines	9.1	499
Alaska Air Group	3.3	−53
SkyWest	3.1	146
Jetblue Airways	2.4	−1

Source: Fortune 500, April 27, 2007,
http://money.cnn.com/magazines/fortune500/2007/industries/Airlines/1.html.

3.23 THE TRASH BAG CASE DS TrashBag

The mean and the standard deviation of the sample of 40 trash bag breaking strengths are $\bar{x} = 50.575$ and $s = 1.6438$.

a What does the histogram in Figure 2.17 (page 53) say about whether the Empirical Rule should be used to describe the trash bag breaking strengths?

b Use the Empirical Rule to calculate estimates of tolerance intervals containing 68.26 percent, 95.44 percent, and 99.73 percent of all possible trash bag breaking strengths.

c Does the estimate of a tolerance interval containing 99.73 percent of all breaking strengths provide evidence that almost any bag a customer might purchase will have a breaking strength that exceeds 45 pounds? Explain your answer.

d How do the percentages of the 40 breaking strengths in Table 1.9 (page 14) that actually fall into the intervals $[\bar{x} \pm s]$, $[\bar{x} \pm 2s]$, and $[\bar{x} \pm 3s]$ compare to those given by the Empirical Rule? Do these comparisons indicate that the statistical inferences you made in parts b and c are reasonably valid?

3.24 THE BANK CUSTOMER WAITING TIME CASE DS WaitTime

The mean and the standard deviation of the sample of 100 bank customer waiting times are $\bar{x} = 5.46$ and $s = 2.475$.

a What does the histogram in Figure 2.16 (page 53) say about whether the Empirical Rule should be used to describe the bank customer waiting times?

b Use the Empirical Rule to calculate estimates of tolerance intervals containing 68.26 percent, 95.44 percent, and 99.73 percent of all possible bank customer waiting times.

c Does the estimate of a tolerance interval containing 68.26 percent of all waiting times provide evidence that at least two-thirds of all customers will have to wait less than eight minutes for service? Explain your answer.

d How do the percentages of the 100 waiting times in Table 1.8 (page 13) that actually fall into the intervals $[\bar{x} \pm s]$, $[\bar{x} \pm 2s]$, and $[\bar{x} \pm 3s]$ compare to those given by the Empirical Rule? Do these comparisons indicate that the statistical inferences you made in parts b and c are reasonably valid?

3.25 THE VIDEO GAME SATISFACTION RATING CASE DS VideoGame

The mean and the standard deviation of the sample of 65 customer satisfaction ratings are $\bar{x} = 42.95$ and $s = 2.6424$.

a What does the histogram in Figure 2.15 (page 52) say about whether the Empirical Rule should be used to describe the satisfaction ratings?

b Use the Empirical Rule to calculate estimates of tolerance intervals containing 68.26 percent, 95.44 percent, and 99.73 percent of all possible satisfaction ratings.

c Does the estimate of a tolerance interval containing 99.73 percent of all satisfaction ratings provide evidence that 99.73 percent of all customers will give a satisfaction rating for the XYZ-Box game system that is at least 35 (the minimal rating of a "satisfied" customer)? Explain your answer.

d How do the percentages of the 65 customer satisfaction ratings in Table 1.7 (page 13) that actually fall into the intervals $[\bar{x} \pm s]$, $[\bar{x} \pm 2s]$, and $[\bar{x} \pm 3s]$ compare to those given by the Empirical Rule? Do these comparisons indicate that the statistical inferences you made in parts b and c are reasonably valid?

TABLE 3.6   ATM Transaction Times (in Seconds) for 63 Withdrawals   🗐 ATMTime

Transaction	Time	Transaction	Time	Transaction	Time
1	32	22	34	43	37
2	32	23	32	44	32
3	41	24	34	45	33
4	51	25	35	46	33
5	42	26	33	47	40
6	39	27	42	48	35
7	33	28	46	49	33
8	43	29	52	50	39
9	35	30	36	51	34
10	33	31	37	52	34
11	33	32	32	53	33
12	32	33	39	54	38
13	42	34	36	55	41
14	34	35	41	56	34
15	37	36	32	57	35
16	37	37	33	58	35
17	33	38	34	59	37
18	35	39	38	60	39
19	40	40	32	61	44
20	36	41	35	62	40
21	32	42	33	63	39

3.26   Consider the 63 automatic teller machine (ATM) transaction times given in Table 3.6 above.
   a   Construct a histogram (or a stem-and-leaf display) for the 63 ATM transaction times. Describe the shape of the distribution of transaction times.   🗐 ATMTime
   b   When we compute the sample mean and sample standard deviation for the transaction times, we find that $\bar{x} = 36.56$ and $s = 4.475$. Compute each of the intervals $[\bar{x} \pm s]$, $[\bar{x} \pm 2s]$, and $[\bar{x} \pm 3s]$. Then count the number of transaction times that actually fall into each interval and find the percentage of transaction times that actually fall into each interval.
   c   How do the percentages of transaction times that fall into the intervals $[\bar{x} \pm s]$, $[\bar{x} \pm 2s]$, and $[\bar{x} \pm 3s]$ compare to those given by the Empirical Rule? How do the percentages of transaction times that fall into the intervals $[\bar{x} \pm 2s]$ and $[\bar{x} \pm 3s]$ compare to those given by Chebyshev's Theorem?
   d   Explain why the Empirical Rule does not describe the transaction times extremely well.

3.27   The Morningstar Top Fund lists at the Morningstar.com website give the mean yearly return and the standard deviation of the returns for each of the listed funds. As given by Morningstar.com on March 17, 2005, the RS Internet Age Fund has a mean yearly return of 10.93 percent with a standard deviation of 41.96 percent; the Franklin Income A fund has a mean yearly return of 13 percent with a standard deviation of 9.36 percent; the Jacob Internet fund has a mean yearly return of 34.45 percent with a standard deviation of 41.16 percent.
   a   For each mutual fund, find an interval in which you would expect 95.44 percent of all yearly returns to fall. Assume returns are normally distributed.
   b   Using the intervals you computed in part *a*, compare the three mutual funds with respect to average yearly returns and with respect to variability of returns.
   c   Calculate the coefficient of variation for each mutual fund, and use your results to compare the funds with respect to risk. Which fund is riskier?

LO4 Compute and interpret percentiles, quartiles, and box-and-whiskers displays.

3.3 Percentiles, Quartiles, and Box-and-Whiskers Displays ● ● ●

Percentiles, quartiles, and five-number displays   In this section we consider **percentiles** and their applications. We begin by defining the *p*th percentile.

For a set of measurements arranged in increasing order, the **pth percentile** is a value such that *p* percent of the measurements fall at or below the value, and $(100 - p)$ percent of the measurements fall at or above the value.

There are various procedures for calculating percentiles. **One procedure for calculating the pth percentile for a set of n measurements uses the following three steps:**

Step 1: Arrange the measurements in increasing order.
Step 2: Calculate the index

$$i = \left(\frac{p}{100}\right)n$$

Step 3: (a) If i is not an integer, round up to obtain the next integer greater than i. This integer denotes the position of the pth percentile in the ordered arrangement.
   (b) If i is an integer, the pth percentile is the average of the measurements in positions i and $i + 1$ in the ordered arrangement.

To illustrate the calculation and interpretation of percentiles, recall in the household income case that an economist has randomly selected a sample of $n = 12$ households from a Midwestern city and has determined last year's income for each household. In order to assess the variation of the population of household incomes in the city, we will calculate various percentiles for the sample of incomes. Specifically, we will calculate the 10th, 25th, 50th, 75th, and 90th percentiles of these incomes. The first step is to arrange the incomes in increasing order as follows:

7,524	11,070	18,211	26,817	36,551	41,286
49,312	57,283	72,814	90,416	135,540	190,250

To find the 10th percentile, we calculate (in step 2) the index

$$i = \left(\frac{p}{100}\right)n = \left(\frac{10}{100}\right)12 = 1.2$$

Because $i = 1.2$ is not an integer, step 3(a) says to round $i = 1.2$ up to 2. It follows that the 10th percentile is the income in position 2 in the ordered arrangement—that is, 11,070. To find the 25th percentile, we calculate the index

$$i = \left(\frac{p}{100}\right)n = \left(\frac{25}{100}\right)12 = 3$$

Because $i = 3$ is an integer, step 3(b) says that the 25th percentile is the average of the incomes in positions 3 and 4 in the ordered arrangement—that is, $(18{,}211 + 26{,}817)/2 = 22{,}514$. To find the 50th percentile, we calculate the index

$$i = \left(\frac{p}{100}\right)n = \left(\frac{50}{100}\right)12 = 6$$

Because $i = 6$ is an integer, step 3(b) says that the 50th percentile is the average of the incomes in positions 6 and 7 in the ordered arrangement—that is, $(41{,}286 + 49{,}312)/2 = 45{,}299$. To find the 75th percentile, we calculate the index

$$i = \left(\frac{p}{100}\right)n = \left(\frac{75}{100}\right)12 = 9$$

Because $i = 9$ is an integer, step 3(b) says that the 75th percentile is the average of the incomes in positions 9 and 10 in the ordered arrangement—that is, $(72{,}814 + 90{,}416)/2 = 81{,}615$. To find the 90th percentile, we calculate the index

$$i = \left(\frac{p}{100}\right)n = \left(\frac{90}{100}\right)12 = 10.8$$

Because $i = 10.8$ is not an integer, step 3(a) says to round $i = 10.8$ up to 11. It follows that the 90th percentile is the income in position 11 in the ordered arrangement—that is, 135,540.

One appealing way to describe the variation of a set of measurements is to divide the data into four parts, each containing approximately 25 percent of the measurements. This can be done by defining the *first, second,* and *third quartiles* as follows:

The **first quartile,** denoted Q_1, is the **25th percentile.**
The **second quartile** (or **median**), denoted M_d, is the **50th percentile.**
The **third quartile,** denoted Q_3, is the **75th percentile.**

Note that the second quartile is simply another name for the median. Furthermore, the procedure we have described here that is used to find the 50th percentile (second quartile) will always give the same result as the previously described procedure (see Section 3.1) for finding the median. To illustrate how the quartiles divide a set of measurements into four parts, consider the following display of the sampled incomes, which shows the first quartile (the 25th percentile), $Q_1 = 22,514$, the median (the 50th percentile), $M_d = 45,299$, and the third quartile (the 75th percentile), $Q_3 = 81,615$:

$$7,524 \quad 11,070 \quad 18,211 \quad \bigg| \quad 26,817 \quad 36,511 \quad 41,286 \quad \bigg|$$
$$Q_1 = 22,514 \qquad\qquad\qquad\qquad M_d = 45,299$$
$$49,312 \quad 57,283 \quad 72,814 \quad \bigg| \quad 90,416 \quad 135,540 \quad 190,250$$
$$Q_3 = 81,615$$

Using the quartiles, we estimate that for the household incomes in the Midwestern city: (1) 25 percent of the incomes are less than or equal to $22,514, (2) 25 percent of the incomes are between $22,514 and $45,299, (3) 25 percent of the incomes are between $45,299 and $81,615, and (4) 25 percent of the incomes are greater than or equal to $81,615. In addition, to assess some of the lowest and highest incomes, the 10th percentile estimates than 10 percent of the incomes are less than or equal to $11,070, and the 90th percentile estimates that 10 percent of the incomes are greater than or equal to $135,540.

In general, unless percentiles correspond to very high or very low percentages, they are resistant (like the median) to extreme values. For example, the 75th percentile of the household incomes would remain $81,615 even if the largest income—$190,250—were, instead, $7,000,000. On the other hand, the standard deviation in this situation would increase. In general, if a population is highly skewed to the right or left, the standard deviation is so large that using it to describe variation does not provide much useful information. For example, the standard deviation of the 12 household incomes is inflated by the large incomes $135,540 and $190,250 and can be calculated to be $54,567. Because the mean of the 12 incomes is $61,423, Chebyshev's Theorem says that we estimate that at least 75 percent of all household incomes in the city are in the interval $[\bar{x} \pm 2s] = [61,423 \pm 2(54,567)] = [-47,711, 170,557]$—that is, are $170,557 or less. This is much less informative than using the 75th percentile, which estimates that 75 percent of all household incomes are less than or equal to $81,615. In general, if a population is highly skewed to the right or left, it can be best to describe the variation of the population by using various percentiles. This is what we did when we estimated the variation of the household incomes in the city by using the 10th, 25th, 50th, 75th, and 90th percentiles of the 12 sampled incomes. Using other percentiles can also be informative. For example, the Bureau of the Census sometimes assesses the variation of all household incomes in the United States by using the 20th, 40th, 60th, and 80th percentiles of these incomes.

We sometimes describe a set of measurements by using a **five-number summary.** The summary consists of (1) the smallest measurement; (2) the first quartile, Q_1; (3) the median, M_d; (4) the third quartile, Q_3; and (5) the largest measurement. It is easy to graphically depict a five-number summary. For example, the MINITAB output in Figure 3.16 below tells us that for the 65 payment times, the smallest payment time is 10, $Q_1 = 15$, $M_d = 17$, $Q_3 = 21$, and the largest payment time is 29. It follows that a graphical depiction of this five-number summary is as shown in the page margin. Notice that we have drawn a vertical line extending from the smallest payment time to the largest payment time. In addition, a rectangle is drawn that extends from Q_1 to Q_3, and a horizontal line is drawn to indicate the location of the median. The summary divides the payment

Payment Time Five-Number Summary

FIGURE 3.16   **MINITAB Output of Statistics Describing the 65 Payment Times**

Variable	Count	Mean	StDev	Variance		
PayTime	65	18.108	3.961	15.691		

Variable	Minimum	Q1	Median	Q3	Maximum	Range
PayTime	10.000	15.000	17.000	21.000	29.000	19.000

times into four parts, with the middle 50 percent of the payment times depicted by the rectangle. The summary indicates that the largest 25 percent of the payment times is more spread out than the smallest 25 percent of the payment times, and that the second-largest 25 percent of the payment times is more spread out than the second-smallest 25 percent of the payment times. Overall, the summary indicates that the payment times are somewhat skewed to the right.

As another example, it can be shown that for the 60 bottle design ratings, the smallest rating is 20, $Q_1 = 29$, $M_d = 31$, $Q_3 = 33$, and the largest rating is 35. It follows that a graphical depiction of this five-number summary is also as shown in the page margin. The summary shows that the smallest 25 percent of the ratings is more spread out than any of the other quarters of the ratings, and that the other three quarters are equally spread out. Overall, the summary shows that the bottle design ratings are skewed to the left. In addition, it can be verified that the 5th percentile of the ratings is 25. This says that we estimate that 95 percent of all consumers would give the new bottle design ratings that are at least as large as the minimum rating of 25 for a successful bottle design.

Using the first and third quartiles, we define the **interquartile range** to be $IQR = Q_3 - Q_1$. This quantity can be interpreted as the length of the interval that contains the *middle 50 percent* of the measurements. For instance, the interquartile range of the 65 payment times is $Q_3 - Q_1 = 21 - 15 = 6$. This says that we estimate that the middle 50 percent of all payment times fall within a range that is six days long.

The procedure we have presented for calculating the first and third quartiles is not the only procedure for computing these quantities. In fact, several procedures exist, and, for example, different statistical computer packages use several somewhat different methods for computing the quartiles. These different procedures sometimes obtain different results, but the overall objective is always to divide the data into four equal parts.

Box-and-whiskers displays (box plots)   A more sophisticated modification of the graphical five-number summary is called a **box-and-whiskers display** (sometimes called a **box plot**). Such a display is constructed by using Q_1, M_d, Q_3, and the interquartile range. As an example, suppose that 20 randomly selected customers give the following satisfaction ratings (on a scale of 1 to 10) for a DVD recorder:

1   3   5   5   7   8   8   8   8   8   9   9   9   9   9   10   10   10   10

It can be shown that for these ratings $Q_1 = 7.5$, $M_d = 8$, $Q_3 = 9$, and $IQR = Q_3 - Q_1 = 9 - 7.5 = 1.5$. To construct a box-and-whiskers display, we first draw a box that extends from Q_1 to Q_3. As shown in Figure 3.17(a) on the next page, for the satisfaction ratings data this box extends from $Q_1 = 7.5$ to $Q_3 = 9$. The box contains the middle 50 percent of the data set. Next a vertical line is drawn through the box at the value of the median M_d (sometimes a plus sign ($+$) is plotted at the median instead of a vertical line). This line divides the data set into two roughly equal parts. We next define what we call **inner** and **outer fences.** The **inner fences** are located $1.5 \times IQR$ below Q_1 and $1.5 \times IQR$ above Q_3. For the satisfaction ratings data, the inner fences are

$$Q_1 - 1.5(IQR) = 7.5 - 1.5(1.5) = 5.25 \qquad \text{and} \qquad Q_3 + 1.5(IQR) = 9 + 1.5(1.5) = 11.25$$

(again see Figure 3.17(a)). The **outer fences** are located $3 \times IQR$ below Q_1 and $3 \times IQR$ above Q_3. For the satisfaction ratings data, the outer fences are

$$Q_1 - 3(IQR) = 7.5 - 3(1.5) = 3.0 \qquad \text{and} \qquad Q_3 + 3(IQR) = 9 + 3(1.5) = 13.5$$

(these are also shown in Figure 3.17(a)). The inner and outer fences help us to draw the plot's **whiskers:** dashed lines extending below Q_1 and above Q_3 (as in Figure 3.17(a)). One whisker is drawn from Q_1 to the smallest measurement between the inner fences. For the satisfaction ratings data, this whisker extends from $Q_1 = 7.5$ down to 7, because 7 is the smallest rating between the inner fences 5.25 and 11.25. The other whisker is drawn from Q_3 to the largest measurement between the inner fences. For the satisfaction ratings data, this whisker extends from $Q_3 = 9$ up to 10, because 10 is the largest rating between the inner fences 5.25 and 11.25. The inner and outer fences are also used to identify **outliers.** An **outlier** is a measurement that is separated from (that is, different from) most of the other measurements in the data set. Measurements that are located between the inner and outer fences are considered to be **mild outliers,** whereas measurements that are located outside the outer fences are considered to be **extreme outliers.** We indicate the locations of mild outliers by plotting these measurements with the symbol ∗, and we indicate the locations of extreme outliers by plotting these measurements with the symbol o. For the satisfaction

Bottle Design Rating Five-Number Summary

ⒹⓈ DVDSat

FIGURE 3.17   A Box-and-Whiskers Display of the Satisfaction Ratings

(a) Constructing the display

(b) MINITAB output

ratings data, the ratings 3 and 5 are mild outliers ($*$) because these ratings are between the inner fence of 5.25 and the outer fence of 3.0. The rating 1 is an extreme outlier (o) because this rating is outside the outer fence 3.0. These outliers are plotted in Figure 3.17(a). Part (b) of Figure 3.17 gives a MINITAB output of a box-and-whiskers plot. Note that MINITAB computes the quartiles by using a method that is different from what we describe. Therefore, MINITAB obtains a different box-and-whiskers display and identifies two outliers—1 and 3—using asterisks.

We now summarize how to construct a box-and-whiskers plot.

Constructing a Box-and-Whiskers Display (Box Plot)

1 Draw a **box** that extends from the first quartile Q_1 to the third quartile Q_3. Also draw a vertical line through the box located at the median M_d.

2 Determine the values of the **inner fences** and **outer fences**. The inner fences are located $1.5 \times IQR$ below Q_1 and $1.5 \times IQR$ above Q_3. That is, **the inner fences are**

$$Q_1 - 1.5(IQR) \quad \text{and} \quad Q_3 + 1.5(IQR)$$

The outer fences are located $3 \times IQR$ below Q_1 and $3 \times IQR$ above Q_3. That is, **the outer fences are**

$$Q_1 - 3(IQR) \quad \text{and} \quad Q_3 + 3(IQR)$$

3 Draw **whiskers** as dashed lines that extend below Q_1 and above Q_3. Draw one whisker from Q_1 to the *smallest* measurement that is between the inner fences. Draw the other whisker from Q_3 to the *largest* measurement that is between the inner fences.

4 Measurements that are located between the inner and outer fences are called **mild outliers**. Plot these measurements using the symbol $*$.

5 Measurements that are located outside the outer fences are called **extreme outliers**. Plot these measurements using the symbol o.

When interpreting a box-and-whiskers display, keep several points in mind. First, the box (between Q_1 and Q_3) contains the middle 50 percent of the data. Second, the median (which is inside

FIGURE 3.18   **A Stem-and-Leaf Display and Box Plot of the Exam Scores**

Stem and Leaf Plot for ExamScore
Stem unit = 10
Leaf unit = 1

Frequency	Stem	Leaf
1	3	2
0	3	
0	4	
1	4	5
1	5	0
2	5	68
6	6	011344
7	6	5677899
1	7	2
2	7	68
3	8	133
6	8	567789
8	9	00122334
2	9	68
40		

the box) divides the data into two roughly equal parts. Third, if one of the whiskers is longer than the other, the data set is probably skewed in the direction of the longer whisker. Last, observations designated as outliers should be investigated. Understanding the root causes behind the outlying observations will often provide useful information. For instance, understanding why several of the satisfaction ratings in the box plot of Figure 3.17 are substantially lower than the great majority of the ratings may suggest actions that can improve the DVD recorder manufacturer's product and/or service. Outliers can also be caused by inaccurate measuring, reporting, or plotting of the data. Such possibilities should be investigated, and incorrect data should be adjusted or eliminated.

     Generally, a box plot clearly depicts the central tendency, variability, and overall range of a set of measurements. A box plot also portrays whether the measurements are symmetrically distributed. However, the exact shape of the distribution is better portrayed by a stem-and-leaf display and/or a histogram. For instance, Figure 3.18 shows a stem-and-leaf display and box plot of the scores on the 100-point statistics exam of Table 2.8 (page 48) that was given before an attendance policy was begun. We see that, although the box plot in Figure 3.18 tells us that the exam scores are somewhat skewed with a tail to the left, it does not reveal the double-peaked nature of the exam score distribution. On the other hand, the stem-and-leaf display clearly shows that this distribution is double-peaked.

     Graphical five-number summaries and box-and-whiskers displays are perhaps best used to compare different sets of measurements. We demonstrate this use of such displays in the following example.

EXAMPLE 3.9 The VALIC Case

In July of 1993, the Variable Annuity Life Insurance Company (VALIC) sent its investors an analysis of the performance of its variable account mutual fund options relative to other variable annuity fund options in various categories (stock index, money market, and so forth). VALIC used the graphical five-number summaries in Figure 3.19 on the next page to summarize and compare performances. The dot within each five-number summary represents the return of the VALIC mutual fund option for that category. In explaining the plots, VALIC said

> The data show that all of VALIC's mutual fund options ranked at or above their respective category median return for the three-month period ending March 31, 1993. Also, eight of VALIC's mutual fund options ranked above their respective category median return for the 12-month period ending March 31, 1993.

Notice that the lengths of the graphical five-number summaries indicate performance variability for the various funds. For example, while the median three-month returns for Midcap Index funds and Small Cap Index funds are similar, the returns for Small Cap funds are more variable. Also, in general, three-month returns for funds of all types are more variable than 12-month returns.

class. When we do this, we are really assuming that the average of the measurements in each class equals the class midpoint. Letting M_i denote the midpoint of class i, and letting f_i denote the frequency of class i, we compute the mean by calculating a weighted mean of the class midpoints using the class frequencies as the weights. The logic here is that if f_i measurements are included in class i, then the midpoint of class i should count f_i times in the weighted mean. In this case, the sum of the weights equals the sum of the class frequencies, which equals the sample size. Therefore, we obtain the following equation for the sample mean of grouped data:

Sample Mean for Grouped Data

$$\bar{x} = \frac{\sum f_i M_i}{\sum f_i} = \frac{\sum f_i M_i}{n}$$

where
  f_i = the frequency for class i
  M_i = the midpoint for class i
  $n = \sum f_i$ = the sample size

Table 3.8 summarizes the calculation of the mean satisfaction rating for the previously given frequency distribution of satisfaction ratings. Note that in this table each midpoint is halfway between its corresponding class limits. For example, for the first class $M_1 = (36 + 38)/2 = 37$. We find that the sample mean satisfaction rating is 43.

We can also compute an approximation of the sample variance for grouped data. Recall that when we compute the sample variance using individual measurements, we compute the squared deviation from the sample mean $(x_i - \bar{x})^2$ for each individual measurement x_i and then sum the squared deviations. For grouped data, we do not know each of the x_i values. Because of this, we again let the class midpoint M_i represent each measurement in class i. It follows that we compute the squared deviation $(M_i - \bar{x})^2$ for each class and then sum these squares, weighting each squared deviation by its corresponding class frequency f_i. That is, we approximate $\sum (x_i - \bar{x})^2$ by using $\sum f_i(M_i - \bar{x})^2$. Finally, we obtain the sample variance for the grouped data by dividing this quantity by the sample size minus 1. We summarize this calculation in the following box:

Sample Variance for Grouped Data

$$s^2 = \frac{\sum f_i(M_i - \bar{x})^2}{n - 1}$$

where $\bar{x}$ is the sample mean for the grouped data.

Table 3.9 illustrates calculating the sample variance of the previously given frequency distribution of satisfaction ratings. We find that the sample variance is $s^2 = 8.15625$ and, therefore, that the sample standard deviation is $s = \sqrt{8.15625} = 2.8559$.

TABLE 3.8   **Calculating the Sample Mean Satisfaction Rating**

Satisfaction Rating	Frequency (f_i)	Class Midpoint (M_i)	$f_i M_i$
36–38	4	37	4(37) = 148
39–41	15	40	15(40) = 600
42–44	25	43	25(43) = 1,075
45–47	19	46	19(46) = 874
48–50	2	49	2(49) = 98
	$n = 65$		2,795

$$\bar{x} = \frac{\sum f_i M_i}{n} = \frac{2,795}{65} = 43$$

TABLE 3.9   Calculating the Sample Variance of the Satisfaction Ratings

Satisfaction Rating	Frequency f_i	Class Midpoint M_i	Deviation $(M_i - \bar{x})$	Squared Deviation $(M_i - \bar{x})^2$	$f_i(M_i - \bar{x})^2$
36–38	4	37	$37 - 43 = -6$	36	$4(36) = 144$
39–41	15	40	$40 - 43 = -3$	9	$15(9) = 135$
42–44	25	43	$43 - 43 = 0$	0	$25(0) = 0$
45–47	19	46	$46 - 43 = 3$	9	$19(9) = 171$
48–50	2	49	$49 - 43 = 6$	36	$2(36) = 72$
	65				$\sum f_i(M_i - \bar{x})^2 = 522$

$$s^2 = \text{sample variance} = \frac{\sum f_i(M_i - \bar{x})^2}{n - 1} = \frac{522}{65 - 1} = 8.15625$$

Finally, although we have illustrated calculating the mean and variance for grouped data in the context of a sample, similar calculations can be done for a population of measurements. If we let N be the size of the population, the grouped data formulas for the population mean and variance are given in the following box:

Population Mean for Grouped Data

$$\mu = \frac{\sum f_i M_i}{N}$$

Population Variance for Grouped Data

$$\sigma^2 = \frac{\sum f_i(M_i - \mu)^2}{N}$$

Exercises for Section 3.5

CONCEPTS

connect

3.40 Consider calculating a student's grade point average using a scale where 4.0 represents an A and 0.0 represents an F. Explain why the grade point average is a weighted mean. What are the x_i values? What are the weights?

3.41 When we perform grouped data calculations, we represent the measurements in a class by using the midpoint of the class. Explain the assumption that is being made when we do this.

3.42 When we compute the mean, variance, and standard deviation using grouped data, the results obtained are approximations of the population (or sample) mean, variance, and standard deviation. Explain why this is true.

METHODS AND APPLICATIONS

3.43 According to the Morningstar.com website, the 2004 total return percentages for several popular funds were as follows: ⒹⓈ FundReturns

Fund	2004 Total Return %
Vanguard 500 Index	10.7
Wasatch Core Growth	21.7
Fidelity Stock Selector	9.9
Fidelity Dividend Growth	5.8
Janus Worldwide	5.5

Source: http://quicktake.morningstar.com/Fund/TotalReturns.asp (accessed March 17, 2005).

Suppose that an investor had $100,000 invested in the Vanguard 500 Index fund, $500,000 invested in the Wasatch Core Growth fund, $500,000 invested in the Fidelity Stock Selector fund, $200,000 invested in the Fidelity Dividend Growth fund, and $50,000 invested in the Janus Worldwide fund.

a Compute a weighted mean that measures the 2004 average total return for the investor's portfolio.

b Compare your weighted mean with the unweighted mean of the five total return percentages. Explain why they differ.

3.44 The following are the January 2005 unemployment rates and civilian labor force sizes for five states in the Midwest. ⒹⓈ UnEmpStates

State	Size of Civilian Labor Force (Millions)	Unemployment Rate (%)
Iowa	1.62	5.1
Michigan	5.09	7.1
Illinois	6.45	5.6
Indiana	3.18	5.4
Wisconsin	3.08	4.8

Source: United States Bureau of Labor Statistics, http://stats.bls.gov/ (accessed March 17, 2005).

a Using a weighted mean, compute an average unemployment rate for the five-state region.

b Calculate the unweighted mean for the five unemployment rates. Explain why the weighted and unweighted means differ.

3.45 The following frequency distribution summarizes the weights of 195 fish caught by anglers participating in a professional bass fishing tournament. ⒹⓈ BassWeights

Weight (Pounds)	Frequency
1–3	53
4–6	118
7–9	21
10–12	3

a Calculate the (approximate) sample mean for these data.

b Calculate the (approximate) sample variance for these data.

3.46 The following is a frequency distribution summarizing earnings per share (EPS) growth data for the 30 fastest-growing firms as given on *Fortune* magazine's website on March 16, 2005. ⒹⓈ EPSGrowth

EPS Growth (Percent)	Frequency
0–49	1
50–99	17
100–149	5
150–199	4
200–249	1
250–299	2

Source: http://www.fortune.com (accessed March 16, 2005).

Calculate the (approximate) population mean, variance, and standard deviation for these data.

3.47 The Data and Story Library website (a website devoted to applications of statistics) gives a histogram of the ages of a sample of 60 CEOs taken in 1993. We present the data in the form of a frequency distribution below. ⒹⓈ CEOAges

Age (Years)	Frequency
28–32	1
33–37	3
38–42	3
43–47	13
48–52	14
53–57	12
58–62	9
63–67	1
68–72	3
73–77	1

Source: http://lib.stat.cmu.edu/DASL/Stories/ceo.html (accessed April 15, 2005).

Calculate the (approximate) sample mean, variance, and standard deviation of these data.

3.6 The Geometric Mean (Optional) ● ● ●

In Section 3.1 we defined the mean to be the average of a set of population or sample measure-ments. This mean is sometimes referred to as the arithmetic mean. While very useful, the arithmetic mean is not a good measure of the rate of change exhibited by a variable over time. To see this, con-sider the rate at which the value of an investment changes—its rate of return. Suppose that an ini-tial investment of \$10,000 increases in value to \$20,000 at the end of one year and then decreases in value to its original \$10,000 value after two years. The rate of return for the first year, R_1, is

$$R_1 = \left(\frac{20{,}000 - 10{,}000}{10{,}000}\right) \times 100\% = 100\%$$

and the rate of return for the second year, R_2, is

$$R_2 = \left(\frac{10{,}000 - 20{,}000}{20{,}000}\right) \times 100\% = -50\%$$

Although the value of the investment at the beginning and end of the two-year period is the same, the arithmetic mean of the yearly rates of return is $(R_1 + R_2)/2 = (100\% + (-50\%))/2 = 25\%$. This arithmetic mean does not communicate the fact that the value of the investment is un-changed at the end of the two years.

To remedy this situation, we define the **geometric mean** of the returns to be **the constant return R_g, that yields the same wealth at the end of the investment period as do the actual returns.** In our example, this says that if we express R_g, R_1, and R_2 as decimal fractions (here $R_1 = 1$ and $R_2 = -.5$),

$$(1 + R_g)^2 \times 10{,}000 = (1 + R_1)(1 + R_2) \times 10{,}000$$

or

$$R_g = \sqrt{(1 + R_1)(1 + R_2)} - 1$$
$$= \sqrt{(1 + 1)(1 + (-.5))} - 1$$
$$= \sqrt{1} - 1 = 0$$

Therefore, the geometric mean R_g expresses the fact that the value of the investment is un-changed after two years.

In general, if $R_1, R_2, \ldots, R_n$ are returns (expressed in decimal form) over n time periods:

The **geometric mean** of the returns $R_1, R_2, \ldots, R_n$ is

$$R_g = \sqrt[n]{(1 + R_1)(1 + R_2) \cdots (1 + R_n)} - 1$$

and the ending value of an initial investment I experiencing returns $R_1, R_2, \ldots, R_n$ is $I(1 + R_g)^n$.

As another example, suppose that in year 3 our investment's value increases to \$25,000, which says that the rate of return for year 3 (expressed as a percentage) is

$$R_3 = \left(\frac{25{,}000 - 10{,}000}{10{,}000}\right) \times 100\%$$
$$= 150\%$$

Since (expressed as decimals) $R_1 = 1$, $R_2 = -.5$, and $R_3 = 1.5$, the geometric mean return at the end of year 3 is

$$R_g = \sqrt[3]{(1 + 1)(1 + (-.5))(1 + 1.5)} - 1$$
$$= 1.3572 - 1$$
$$= .3572$$

and the value of the investment after 3 years is

$$10{,}000 \, (1 + .3572)^3 = \$25{,}000$$

Exercises for Section 3.6

connect

CONCEPTS

3.48 In words, explain the interpretation of the geometric mean return for an investment.

3.49 If we know the initial value of an investment and its geometric mean return over a period of years, can we compute the ending value of the investment? If so, how?

METHODS AND APPLICATIONS

3.50 Suppose that a company's sales were $5,000,000 three years ago. Since that time sales have grown at annual rates of 10 percent, −10 percent, and 25 percent.
   a Find the geometric mean growth rate of sales over this three-year period.
   b Find the ending value of sales after this three-year period.

3.51 Suppose that a company's sales were $1,000,000 four years ago and are $4,000,000 at the end of the four years. Find the geometric mean growth rate of sales.

3.52 The Standard & Poor's 500 stock index is a commonly used measure of stock market performance in the United States. In the table below, we give the value of the S&P 500 index on the first day of market trading for each year from 2000 to 2005. ▣S S&P500

Year	S&P 500 Index
2000	1,455.22
2001	1,283.27
2002	1,154.67
2003	909.03
2004	1,108.48
2005	1,211.92

Source: http://table.finance.yahoo.com.

   a Show that the percentage changes (rates of return) for the S&P 500 index for the years from 2000 to 2001 and from 2001 to 2002 are, respectively, −11.8 percent and −10.0 percent (that is, −.118 and −.100 expressed as decimal fractions).
   b Find the rates of return for the S&P 500 index for each of the years: from 2002 to 2003; from 2003 to 2004; from 2004 to 2005.
   c Calculate the geometric mean return for the S&P 500 index over the period from 2000 to 2005.
   d Suppose that an investment of $1,000,000 is made in 2000 and that the portfolio performs with returns equal to those of the S&P 500 index. What is the investment portfolio worth in 2005?

3.53 According to the USA Statistics in Brief summary of U.S. census data, the amount of consumer credit outstanding (in billions of dollars) is as follows:[6]

   1990: $789   1995: $1,096   2000: $1,534

   a Find the geometric mean five-year rate of increase in consumer credit outstanding.
   b Use the geometric mean rate of increase to project the amount of consumer credit outstanding in 2005.

Chapter Summary

We began this chapter by presenting and comparing several measures of **central tendency.** We defined the **population mean** and we saw how to estimate the population mean by using a **sample mean.** We also defined the **median** and **mode,** and we compared the mean, median, and mode for symmetrical distributions and for distributions that are skewed to the right or left. We then studied measures of **variation** (or *spread*). We defined the **range, variance,** and **standard deviation,** and we saw how to estimate a population variance and standard deviation by using a sample. We learned that a good way to interpret the standard deviation when a population is (approximately) normally distributed is to use the **Empirical Rule,** and we studied **Chebyshev's Theorem,** which gives us intervals containing reasonably large fractions of

the population units no matter what the population's shape might be. We also saw that, when a data set is highly skewed, it is best to use **percentiles** and **quartiles** to measure variation, and we learned how to construct a **box-and-whiskers plot** by using the quartiles.

After learning how to measure and depict central tendency and variability, we presented several optional topics. First, we discussed several numerical measures of the relationship between two variables. These included the **covariance,** the **correlation coefficient,** and the **least squares line.** We then introduced the concept of a **weighted mean** and also explained how to compute descriptive statistics for **grouped data.** Finally, we showed how to calculate the **geometric mean** and demonstrated its interpretation.

[6]Source: http://www.census.gov/statlab/www/part5.html.

Glossary of Terms

box-and-whiskers display (box plot): A graphical portrayal of a data set that depicts both the central tendency and variability of the data. It is constructed using Q_1, M_d, and Q_3. (pages 123, 124)

central tendency: A term referring to the middle of a population or sample of measurements. (page 101)

Chebyshev's Theorem: A theorem that (for any population) allows us to find an interval that contains a specified percentage of the individual measurements in the population. (page 116)

coefficient of variation: A quantity that measures the variation of a population or sample relative to its mean. (page 117)

correlation coefficient: A numerical measure of the linear relationship between two variables that is between -1 and 1. (page 131)

covariance: A numerical measure of the linear relationship between two variables that depends upon the units in which the variables are measured. (page 129)

Empirical Rule: For a normally distributed population, this rule tells us that 68.26 percent, 95.44 percent, and 99.73 percent, respectively, of the population measurements are within one, two, and three standard deviations of the population mean. (page 114)

extreme outlier (in a box-and-whiskers display): Measurements located outside the outer fences. (page 124)

first quartile (denoted Q_1): A value below which approximately 25 percent of the measurements lie; the 25th percentile. (page 121)

geometric mean: The constant return (or rate of change) that yields the same wealth at the end of several time periods as do actual returns. (page 139)

grouped data: Data presented in the form of a frequency distribution or a histogram. (page 135)

inner fences (in a box-and-whiskers display): Points located $1.5 \times IQR$ below Q_1 and $1.5 \times IQR$ above Q_3. (page 124)

interquartile range (denoted IQR): The difference between the third quartile and the first quartile (that is, $Q_3 - Q_1$). (page 123)

least squares line: The line that minimizes the sum of the squared vertical differences between points on a scatter plot and the line. (page 132)

measure of variation: A descriptive measure of the spread of the values in a population or sample. (page 110)

median (denoted M_d): A measure of central tendency that divides a population or sample into two roughly equal parts. (page 103)

mild outlier (in a box-and-whiskers display): Measurements located between the inner and outer fences. (page 124)

mode (denoted M_o): The measurement in a sample or a population that occurs most frequently. (page 104)

mound-shaped: Description of a relative frequency curve that is "piled up in the middle." (page 116)

normal curve: A bell-shaped, symmetrical relative frequency curve. We will present the exact equation that gives this curve in Chapter 6. (page 113)

outer fences (in a box-and-whiskers display): Points located $3 \times IQR$ below Q_1 and $3 \times IQR$ above Q_3. (page 124)

percentile: The value such that a specified percentage of the measurements in a population or sample fall at or below it. (page 120)

point estimate: A one-number estimate for the value of a population parameter. (page 101)

population mean (denoted μ): The average of a population of measurements. (page 101)

population parameter: A descriptive measure of a population. It is calculated using the population measurements. (page 101)

population standard deviation (denoted σ): The positive square root of the population variance. It is a measure of the variation of the population measurements. (page 111)

population variance (denoted σ^2): The average of the squared deviations of the individual population measurements from the population mean. It is a measure of the variation of the population measurements. (page 111)

range: The difference between the largest and smallest measurements in a population or sample. It is a simple measure of variation. (page 110)

sample mean (denoted $\bar{x}$): The average of the measurements in a sample. It is the point estimate of the population mean. (page 102)

sample size (denoted n): The number of measurements in a sample. (page 102)

sample standard deviation (denoted s): The positive square root of the sample variance. It is the point estimate of the population standard deviation. (page 112)

sample statistic: A descriptive measure of a sample. It is calculated from the measurements in the sample. (page 102)

sample variance (denoted s^2): A measure of the variation of the sample measurements. It is the point estimate of the population variance. (page 112)

third quartile (denoted Q_3): A value below which approximately 75 percent of the measurements lie; the 75th percentile. (page 121)

tolerance interval: An interval of numbers that contains a specified percentage of the individual measurements in a population. (page 114)

weighted mean: A mean where different measurements are given different weights based on their importance. (page 134)

z-score (of a measurement): The number of standard deviations that a measurement is from the mean. This quantity indicates the relative location of a measurement within its distribution. (page 117)

Important Formulas

The population mean, μ: page 101

The sample mean, $\bar{x}$: page 102

The median: page 103

The mode: page 104

The population range: page 110

The population variance, σ^2: page 111

The population standard deviation, σ: page 111

The sample variance, s^2: pages 112 and 113

The sample standard deviation, s: page 112

Computational formula for s^2: page 113

The Empirical Rule: page 114

Chebyshev's Theorem: page 116

z-score: page 117

The coefficient of variation: page 117

The *p*th percentile: pages 120, 121

The quartiles: page 121

The sample covariance: page 129

The sample correlation coefficient: page 131

The least squares line: page 132

The weighted mean: page 134

Sample mean for grouped data: page 136

Sample variance for grouped data: page 136

Population mean for grouped data: page 137

Population variance for grouped data: page 137

The geometric mean: page 139

Supplementary Exercises

connect

3.54   In the book *Modern Statistical Quality Control and Improvement,* Nicholas R. Farnum presents data concerning the elapsed times from the completion of medical lab tests until the results are recorded on patients' charts. Table 3.10 gives the times it took (in hours) to deliver and chart the results of 84 lab tests over one week. Use the techniques of this and the previous chapter to determine if there are some deliveries with excessively long waiting times. Which deliveries might be investigated in order to discover reasons behind unusually long delays? ⦾ LabTest

3.55   Figure 3.25 depicts data for a study of 80 software projects at NASA's Goddard Space Center. The figure shows the number of bugs per 1,000 lines of code from 1976 to 1990. Write a short paragraph describing how the reliability of the software has improved. Explain how the data indicate improvement.

3.56   **THE INVESTMENT CASE** ⦾ InvestRet

The Fall 1995 issue of *Investment Digest,* a publication of The Variable Annuity Life Insurance Company of Houston, Texas, discusses the importance of portfolio diversification for long-term investors. The article states:

> While it is true that investment experts generally advise long-term investors to invest in variable investments, they also agree that the key to any sound investment portfolio is diversification. That is, investing in a variety of investments with differing levels of historical return and risk.
>
> Investment risk is often measured in terms of the volatility of an investment over time. When volatility, sometimes referred to as *standard deviation,* increases, so too does the level of return. Conversely, as risk (standard deviation) declines, so too do returns.

TABLE 3.10	Elapsed Time (in Hours) for Completing and Delivering Medical Lab Tests ⦾ LabTest		
6.1	8.7	1.1	4.0
2.1	3.9	2.2	5.0
2.1	7.1	4.3	8.8
3.5	1.2	3.2	1.3
1.3	9.3	4.2	7.3
5.7	6.5	4.4	16.2
1.3	1.3	3.0	2.7
15.7	4.9	2.0	5.2
3.9	13.9	1.8	2.2
8.4	5.2	11.9	3.0
24.0	24.5	24.8	24.0
1.7	4.4	2.5	16.2
17.8	2.9	4.0	6.7
5.3	8.3	2.8	5.2
17.5	1.1	3.0	8.3
1.2	1.1	4.5	4.4
5.0	2.6	12.7	5.7
4.7	5.1	2.6	1.6
3.4	8.1	2.4	16.7
4.8	1.7	1.9	12.1
9.1	5.6	13.0	6.4

Source: N. R. Farnum, *Modern Statistical Quality Control and Improvement,* p. 55. Reprinted by permission of Brooks/Cole, an imprint of the Wadsworth Group, a division of Thompson Learning. Fax 800-730-2215.

FIGURE 3.25   **Software Performance at NASA's Goddard Space Center, 1976–1990 (for Exercise 3.55)**

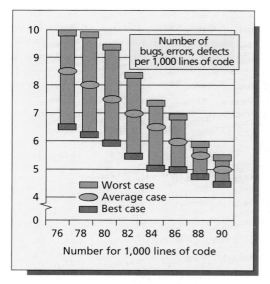

Source: Reprinted from the January 15, 1992, issue of *BusinessWeek* by special permission. Copyright © 1992 by The McGraw-Hill Companies.

FIGURE 3.26   The Risk/Return Trade-Off
                (for Exercise 3.56)

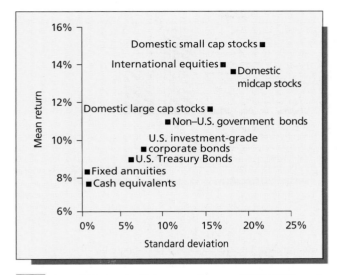

TABLE 3.11   Mean Return and Standard
               Deviation for Nine Investment
               Classes   DS InvestRet

Investment Class	Mean Return	Standard Deviation
Fixed annuities	8.31%	.54%
Cash equivalents	7.73	.81
U.S. Treasury bonds	8.80	5.98
U.S. investment-grade corporate bonds	9.33	7.92
Non–U.S. government bonds	10.95	10.47
Domestic large cap stocks	11.71	15.30
International equities	14.02	17.16
Domestic midcap stocks	13.64	18.19
Domestic small cap stocks	14.93	21.82

Source: The Variable Annuity Life Insurance Company, VALIC 9 (1995), no. 3.

In order to explain the relationship between the return on an investment and its risk, *Investment Digest* presents a graph of mean return versus standard deviation (risk) for nine investment classes over the period from 1970 to 1994. This graph, which *Investment Digest* calls the "risk/return trade-off," is shown in Figure 3.26. The article says that this graph

> . . . illustrates the historical risk/return trade-off for a variety of investment classes over the 24-year period between 1970 and 1994.
>
> In the chart, cash equivalents and fixed annuities, for instance, had a standard deviation of 0.81% and 0.54% respectively, while posting returns of just over 7.73% and 8.31%. At the other end of the spectrum, domestic small-company stocks were quite volatile—with a standard deviation of 21.82%—but compensated for that increased volatility with a return of 14.93%.
>
> The answer seems to lie in asset allocation. Investment experts know the importance of asset allocation. In a nutshell, asset allocation is a method of creating a diversified portfolio of investments that minimize historical risk and maximize potential returns to help you meet your retirement goals and needs.

Suppose that, by reading off the graph of Figure 3.26, we obtain the mean return and standard deviation combinations for the various investment classes as shown in Table 3.11.

Further suppose that future returns in each investment class will behave as they have from 1970 to 1994. That is, for each investment class, regard the mean return and standard deviation in Table 3.11 as the population mean and the population standard deviation of all possible future returns. Then do the following:

a Assuming that future returns for the various investment classes are mound-shaped, for each investment class compute intervals that will contain approximately 68.26 percent and 99.73 percent of all future returns.

b Making no assumptions about the population shapes of future returns, for each investment class compute intervals that will contain at least 75 percent and 88.89 percent of all future returns.

c Assuming that future returns are mound-shaped, find

   (1) An estimate of the maximum return that might be realized for each investment class.

   (2) An estimate of the minimum return (or maximum loss) that might be realized for each investment class.

d Assuming that future returns are mound-shaped, which two investment classes have the highest estimated maximum returns? What are the estimated minimum returns (maximum losses) for these investment classes?

e Assuming that future returns are mound-shaped, which two investment classes have the smallest estimated maximum returns? What are the estimated minimum returns for these investment classes?

FIGURE 3.27   1993 Insurance Expenditures of Households in the United Kingdom (for Exercise 3.57)

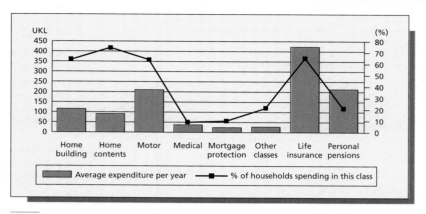

Source: CSO family expenditure survey.

f   Calculate the coefficient of variation for each investment class and compare the investment classes with respect to risk. Which class is riskiest? Least risky?

3.57   THE UNITED KINGDOM INSURANCE CASE

Figure 3.27 summarizes information concerning insurance expenditures of households in the United Kingdom in 1993.

a   Approximately what percentage of households spent money to buy life insurance?

b   What is the approximate average expenditure (in UKL) per household on life insurance? Note: the averages given in Figure 3.27 are for households that spend in the class.

3.58   THE INTERNATIONAL BUSINESS TRAVEL EXPENSE CASE

Suppose that a large international corporation wishes to obtain its own "benchmark" for one-day travel expenses in Moscow. To do this, it records the one-day travel expenses for a random sample of 35 executives visiting Moscow. The mean and the standard deviation of these expenses are calculated to be $\bar{x} = \$538$ and $s = \$41$. Furthermore, a histogram shows that the expenses are approximately normally distributed.

a   Find an interval that we estimate contains 99.73 percent of all one-day travel expenses in Moscow.

b   If an executive submits an expense of $720 for a one-day stay in Moscow, should this expense be considered unusually high? Why or why not?

3.59   THE FLORIDA POOL HOME CASE   ⑤ PoolHome

In Florida, real estate agents refer to homes having a swimming pool as *pool homes.* In this case, Sunshine Pools Inc. markets and installs pools throughout the state of Florida. The company wishes to estimate the percentage of a pool's cost that can be recouped by a buyer when he or she sells the home. For instance, if a homeowner buys a pool for which the current purchase price is $30,000 and then sells the home in the current real estate market for $20,000 more than the homeowner would get if the home did not have a pool, the homeowner has recouped $(20,000/30,000) \times 100\% = 66.67\%$ of the pool's cost. To make this estimate, the company randomly selects 80 homes from all of the homes sold in a Florida city (over the last six months) having a size between 2,000 and 3,500 square feet. For each sampled home, the following data are collected: selling price (in thousands of dollars); square footage; the number of bathrooms; a niceness rating (expressed as an integer from 1 to 7 and assigned by a real estate agent); and whether or not the home has a pool (1 = yes, 0 = no). The data are given in Table 3.12. Figure 3.28 gives descriptive statistics for the 43 homes having a pool and for the 37 homes that do not have a pool.

a   Using Figure 3.28, compare the mean selling prices of the homes having a pool and the homes that do not have a pool. Using this data, and assuming that the average current purchase price of the pools in the sample is $32,500, estimate the percentage of a pool's cost that can be recouped when the home is sold.

b   The comparison you made in part (a) could be misleading. Noting that different homes have different square footages, numbers of bathrooms, and niceness ratings, explain why.

TABLE 3.12 The Florida Pool Home Data 🖸 PoolHome

Home	Price ($1000s)	Size (Sq Feet)	Number of Bathrooms	Niceness Rating	Pool? yes=1; no=0	Home	Price ($1000s)	Size (Sq Feet)	Number of Bathrooms	Niceness Rating	Pool? yes=1; no=0
1	260.9	2666	2 1/2	7	0	41	285.6	2761	3	6	1
2	337.3	3418	3 1/2	6	1	42	216.1	2880	2 1/2	2	0
3	268.4	2945	2	5	1	43	261.3	3426	3	1	1
4	242.2	2942	2 1/2	3	1	44	236.4	2895	2 1/2	2	1
5	255.2	2798	3	3	1	45	267.5	2726	3	7	0
6	205.7	2210	2 1/2	2	0	46	220.2	2930	2 1/2	2	0
7	249.5	2209	2	7	0	47	300.1	3013	2 1/2	6	1
8	193.6	2465	2 1/2	1	0	48	260.0	2675	2	6	0
9	242.7	2955	2	4	1	49	277.5	2874	3 1/2	6	1
10	244.5	2722	2 1/2	5	0	50	274.9	2765	2 1/2	4	1
11	184.2	2590	2 1/2	1	0	51	259.8	3020	3 1/2	2	1
12	325.7	3138	3 1/2	7	1	52	235.0	2887	2 1/2	1	1
13	266.1	2713	2	7	0	53	191.4	2032	2	3	0
14	166.0	2284	2 1/2	2	0	54	228.5	2698	2 1/2	4	0
15	330.7	3140	3 1/2	6	1	55	266.6	2847	3	2	1
16	289.1	3205	2 1/2	3	1	56	233.0	2639	3	3	0
17	268.8	2721	2 1/2	6	1	57	343.4	3431	4	5	1
18	276.7	3245	2 1/2	2	1	58	334.0	3485	3 1/2	5	1
19	222.4	2464	3	3	1	59	289.7	2991	2 1/2	6	1
20	241.5	2993	2 1/2	1	0	60	228.4	2482	2 1/2	2	0
21	307.9	2647	3 1/2	6	1	61	233.4	2712	2 1/2	1	1
22	223.5	2670	2 1/2	4	0	62	275.7	3103	2 1/2	2	1
23	231.1	2895	2 1/2	3	0	63	290.8	3124	2 1/2	3	1
24	216.5	2643	2 1/2	3	0	64	230.8	2906	2 1/2	2	0
25	205.5	2915	2	1	0	65	310.1	3398	4	4	1
26	258.3	2800	3 1/2	2	1	66	247.9	3028	3	4	0
27	227.6	2557	2 1/2	3	1	67	249.9	2761	2	5	0
28	255.4	2805	2	3	1	68	220.5	2842	3	3	0
29	235.7	2878	2 1/2	4	0	69	226.2	2666	2 1/2	6	0
30	285.1	2795	3	7	1	70	313.7	2744	2 1/2	7	1
31	284.8	2748	2 1/2	7	1	71	210.1	2508	2 1/2	4	0
32	193.7	2256	2 1/2	2	0	72	244.9	2480	2 1/2	5	0
33	247.5	2659	2 1/2	2	1	73	235.8	2986	2 1/2	4	0
34	274.8	3241	3 1/2	4	1	74	263.2	2753	2 1/2	7	0
35	264.4	3166	3	3	1	75	280.2	2522	2 1/2	6	1
36	204.1	2466	2	4	0	76	290.8	2808	2 1/2	7	1
37	273.9	2945	2 1/2	5	1	77	235.4	2616	2 1/2	3	0
38	238.5	2727	3	1	1	78	190.3	2603	2 1/2	2	0
39	274.4	3141	4	4	1	79	234.4	2804	2 1/2	4	0
40	259.6	2552	2	7	1	80	238.7	2851	2 1/2	5	0

FIGURE 3.28 Descriptive Statistics for Homes With and Without Pools (for Exercise 3.59)

Descriptive Statistics (Homes with Pools)	Price	Descriptive Statistics (Homes without Pools)	Price
count	43	count	37
mean	276.056	mean	226.900
sample variance	937.821	sample variance	609.902
sample standard deviation	30.624	sample standard deviation	24.696
minimum	222.4	minimum	166
maximum	343.4	maximum	267.5
range	121	range	101.5

3.60 Internet Exercise

The Data and Story Library (DASL) houses a rich collection of data sets useful for teaching and learning statistics, from a variety of sources, contributed primarily by university faculty members. DASL can be reached through the BSC by clicking on the Data Bases button in the BSC home screen and by then clicking on the Data and Story Library link. The DASL can also be reached directly using the url http://lib.stat.cmu.edu/DASL/. The objective of this exercise is to retrieve a data set of chief executive officer salaries and to construct selected graphical and numerical statistical summaries of the data.

a From the McGraw-Hill/Irwin Business Statistics Center Data Bases page, go to the DASL website and select "List all topics." From the Stories by Topic page, select Economics, then CEO Salaries to reach the CEO Salaries story. From the CEO Salaries story page, select the Datafile Name: CEO Salaries to reach the data set page. The data set includes the ages and salaries (save for a single missing observation) for a sample of 60 CEOs. Capture these observations and copy them into an Excel or MINITAB worksheet. This data capture can be accomplished in a number of ways. One simple approach is to use simple copy and paste procedures from the DASL data set to Excel or MINITAB (data sets CEOSal.xlsx, CEOSal.MTW).

b Use your choice of statistical software to create graphical and numerical summaries of the CEO Salaries data and use these summaries to describe the data. In Excel, create a histogram of salaries and generate descriptive statistics. In MINITAB, create a histogram, stem-and-leaf display, box plot, and descriptive statistics. Offer your observations about typical salary level, the variation in salaries, and the shape of the distribution of CEO salaries.

Appendix 3.1 ■ Numerical Descriptive Statistics Using Excel

The instructions in this section begin by describing the entry of data into an Excel worksheet. Alternatively, the data may be downloaded from this book's website. The appropriate data file name is given at the top of each instruction block. Please refer to Appendix 1.1 for further information about entering data, saving data, and printing results when using Excel.

Numerical descriptive statistics for the bottle design ratings in Figure 3.4 on page 106 (data file: Design.xlsx):

- Enter the bottle design ratings data into column A with the label Rating in cell A1 and with the 60 design ratings from Table 1.5 on page 10 in cells A2 to A61.

- Select **Data : Data Analysis : Descriptive Statistics.**

- Click OK in the Data Analysis dialog box.

- In the Descriptive Statistics dialog box, enter the range for the data, A1:A61, into the "Input Range" box.

- Check the "Labels in First Row" checkbox.

- Click in the "Output Range" window and enter the desired cell location for the upper left corner of the output, say cell C1.

- Check the "Summary Statistics" checkbox.

- Click OK in the Descriptive Statistics dialog box.

- The descriptive statistics summary will appear in cells C1:D15. Drag the column C border to reveal complete labels for all statistics.

Least squares line, correlation, and covariance for the sales volume data in Figure 3.22(a) on page 130 (data file: SalesPlot.xlsx):

To **compute the equation of the least squares line**:

- Follow the directions in Appendix 2.1 for constructing a scatter plot of sales volume versus advertising expenditure.

- When the scatter plot is displayed in a graphics window, move the plot to a chart sheet.

- In the new chart sheet, right-click on any of the plotted points in the scatter plot (Excel refers to the plotted points as the **data series**) and select Add Trendline from the pop-up menu.

- In the Format Trendline dialog box, select Trendline Options.

- In the Trendline Options task pane, select Linear for the "Trend/Regression Type".

- Place a checkmark in the "Display Equation on chart" checkbox.

- Click the Close button in the Format Trendline dialog box.

- The Trendline equation will be displayed in the scatter plot and the chart can be edited appropriately.

To compute the sample covariance between sales volume and advertising expenditure:

- Enter the advertising and sales data in Figure 3.22(a) on page 130 into columns A and B—advertising expenditures in column A with label "Ad Exp" and sales values in column B with label "Sales Vol".

- Select **Data : Data Analysis : Covariance**

- Click OK in the Data Analysis dialog box.

- In the Covariance dialog box, enter the range of the data, A1:B11 into the Input Range window.

- Select "Grouped By: Columns" if this is not already the selection.

- Place a checkmark in the "Labels in first row" checkbox.

- Under "Output options", select Output Range and enter the cell location for the upper left corner of the output, say A14, in the Output Range window.

- Click OK in the Covariance dialog box.

The Excel ToolPak Covariance routine calculates the population covariance. This quantity is the value in cell B16 (=36.55). To compute the sample covariance from this value, we multiply by $n/(n-1)$ where n is the sample size. In this situation, the sample size is 10. Therefore, we compute the sample covariance as follows:

- Type the label "Sample Covariance" in cell E15.

- In cell E16 write the cell formula =(10/9)*B16 and type enter.

- The sample covariance (=40.61111) is the result in cell E16.

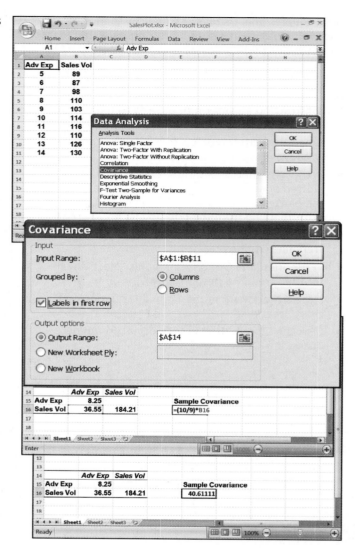

To compute the sample correlation coefficient between sales volume and advertising expenditure:

- Select **Data : Data Analysis : Correlation**
- In the correlation dialog box, enter the range of the data, A1:B11 into the Input Range window.
- Select "Grouped By: Columns" if this is not already the selection.
- Place a checkmark in the "Labels in first row" checkbox.
- Under output options, select "New Worksheet Ply" to have the output placed in a new worksheet and enter the name Output for the new worksheet.
- Click OK in the Correlation dialog box.
- The sample correlation coefficient (=0.93757) is displayed in the Output worksheet.

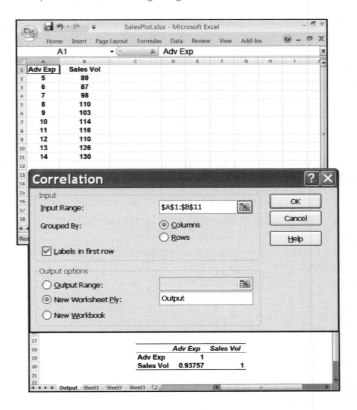

Appendix 3.2 ■ Numerical Descriptive Statistics Using MegaStat

The instructions in this section begin by describing the entry of data into an Excel worksheet. Alternatively, the data may be downloaded from this book's website. The appropriate data file name is given at the top of each instruction block. Please refer to Appendix 1.1 for further information about entering data, saving data, and printing results in Excel. Please refer to Appendix 1.2 for more information about using MegaStat.

To analyze the gas mileage data in Table 3.1 on page 103 (data file: GasMiles.xlsx):

- Enter the mileage data from Table 3.1 into column A with the label Mpg in cell A1 and with the 50 gas mileages in cells A2 through A51.

In order to compute **descriptive statistics** similar to those given in Figure 3.1 on page 104:

- Select **Add-Ins : MegaStat : Descriptive Statistics**
- In the "Descriptive Statistics" dialog box, use the autoexpand feature to enter the range A1:A51 into the Input Range box.
- Place checkmarks in the checkboxes that correspond to the desired statistics. If tolerance intervals based on the Empirical Rule are desired, check the "Empirical Rule" checkbox.
- Click OK in the "Descriptive Statistics" dialog box.
- The output will be placed in an Output worksheet.

To construct a **boxplot** of satisfaction ratings (data file: DVDSat.xlsx):

- Enter the satisfaction rating data on page 123 into column A with the label Ratings in cell A1 and with the 20 satisfaction ratings in cells A2 to A21.

- Select **Add-Ins : MegaStat : Descriptive Statistics**

- In the "Descriptive Statistics" dialog box, use the autoexpand feature to enter the input range A1:A21 into the Input Range box.

- Place a checkmark in the Boxplot checkbox.

- Click OK in the "Descriptive Statistics" dialog box.

- The boxplot output will be placed in an output worksheet.

- Move the boxplot to a chart sheet and edit as desired.

Least squares line and correlation for the sales volume data in Figure 3.22(a) on page 130 (data file: SalesPlot.xlsx):

To **compute the equation of the least squares line**:

- Enter the advertising and sales data in Figure 3.22(a) on page 130 into columns A and B— advertising expenditures in column A with label "Ad Exp" and sales values in column B with label "Sales Vol".

- Select **Add-Ins : MegaStat : Correlation / Regression : Scatterplot**

- In the Scatterplot dialog box, use the autoexpand feature to enter the range of the values of advertising expenditure (x), A1:A11, into the "horizontal axis" window.

- Enter the range of the values of sales volume (y), B1:B11, into the "vertical axis" window.

- Place a checkmark in the "Plot linear regression line" checkbox.

- Select Markers as the Display option.

- Click OK in the Scatterplot dialog box.

- The equation of the least squares line is displayed in the scatterplot.

- Move the scatterplot to a chart sheet and edit the plot as desired.

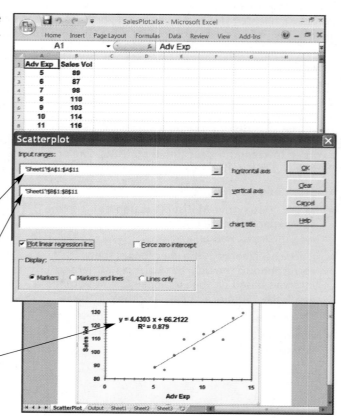

To compute the sample correlation coefficient between sales volume (y) and advertising expenditure (x):

- Select **Add-Ins : MegaStat : Correlation / Regression : Correlation Matrix**

- In the Correlation Matrix dialog box, use the mouse to select the range of the data A1:B11 into the Input window.

- Click OK in the Correlation Matrix dialog box.

- The sample correlation coefficient between advertising expenditure and sales volume is displayed in an output sheet.

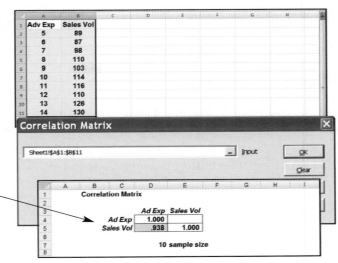

Appendix 3.3 ■ Numerical Descriptive Statistics Using MINITAB

The instructions in this section begin by describing the entry of data into the MINITAB data window. Alternatively, the data may be downloaded from this book's website. The appropriate data file name is given at the top of each instruction block. Please refer to Appendix 1.3 for further information about entering data, saving data, and printing results when using MINITAB.

Numerical descriptive statistics in Figure 3.7 on page 107 (data file: PayTime.MTW):

- Enter the payment time data from Table 2.4 (page 42) into column C1 with variable name PayTime.

- Select **Stat : Basic Statistics : Display Descriptive Statistics.**

- In the Display Descriptive Statistics dialog box, select the variable Paytime into the Variables window.

- In the Display Descriptive Statistics dialog box, click on the Statistics button.

- In the "Descriptive Statistics—Statistics" dialog box, enter checkmarks in the checkboxes corresponding to the desired descriptive statistics. Here we have checked the mean, standard deviation, variance, first quartile, median, third quartile, minimum, maximum, range, and N total checkboxes.

- Click OK in the "Descriptive Statistics—Statistics" dialog box.

- Click OK in the Display Descriptive Statistics dialog box.

- The requested descriptive statistics are displayed in the session window.

Box plot similar to Figure 3.17(b) on page 124 (data file DVDSat.MTW):

- Enter the satisfaction rating data from page 123 into column C1 with variable name Ratings.

- Select **Graph : Boxplot**

- In the Boxplots dialog box, select "One Y, Simple" and click OK.

- In the "Boxplot—One Y, Simple" dialog box, select Ratings into the "Graph variables" window.

- Click on the Scale button, select the Axes and Ticks tab, check "Transpose value and category scales" and click OK.

- Click OK in the "Boxplot—One Y, Simple" dialog box.

- The boxplot is displayed in a graphics window.

- Note that the boxplot produced by MINITAB is constructed using methods somewhat different from those presented in Section 3.3 of this book. Consult the MINITAB help menu for a precise description of the boxplot construction method used. A boxplot that is constructed using the methods of Section 3.3 can be displayed in the Session window—rather than in a graphics window. Instructions for constructing such a boxplot—called a **character boxplot**—can be found in the MINITAB help menu (see "Character graphs").

Least squares line, correlation, and covariance for the sales volume data in Section 3.4 (data file: SalesPlot.MTW):

To **compute the equation of the least squares line**:

- Enter the sales and advertising data in Figure 3.22(a) on page 130—advertising expenditure in column C1 with variable name 'Adv Exp', and sales volume in column C2 with variable name 'Sales Vol'.

- Select **Stat : Regression : Fitted Line Plot**

- In the Fitted Line Plot dialog box, enter the variable name 'Sales Vol' (including the single quotes) into the "Response (Y)" window.

- Enter the variable name 'Adv Exp' (including the single quotes) into the "Predictor (X)" window.

- Select Linear for the "Type of Regression Model".

- Click OK in the Fitted Line Plot dialog box.

- A scatter plot of sales volume versus advertising expenditure that includes the equation of the least squares line will be displayed in a graphics window.

To compute the sample correlation coefficient:

- Select **Stat : Basic Statistics : Correlation**

- In the Correlation dialog box, enter the variable names 'Adv Exp' and 'Sales Vol' (including the single quotes) into the Variables window.

- Remove the checkmark from the "Display p-values" checkbox—or keep this checked as desired (we will learn about *p*-values in later chapters).

- Click OK in the Correlation dialog box.

- The correlation coefficient will be displayed in the session window.

To compute the sample covariance:

- Select **Stat : Basic Statistics : Covariance**

- In the Covariance dialog box, enter the variable names 'Adv Exp' and 'Sales Vol' (including the single quotes) into the Variables window.

- Click OK in the Covariance dialog box.

- The covariance will be displayed in the session window.

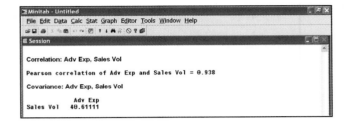

Here, there are *two* equally likely experimental outcomes—head (H) and tail (T). Therefore, logic suggests that the probability of observing a head, denoted $P(H)$, is $1/2 = .5$, and that the probability of observing a tail, denoted $P(T)$, is also $1/2 = .5$. Notice that each probability is between 0 and 1. Furthermore, because H and T are all of the experimental outcomes, $P(H) + P(T) = 1$.

Probability is often interpreted to be a **long-run relative frequency.** As an example, consider repeatedly tossing a coin. If we get 6 heads in the first 10 tosses, then the relative frequency, or fraction, of heads is $6/10 = .6$. If we get 47 heads in the first 100 tosses, the relative frequency of heads is $47/100 = .47$. If we get 5,067 heads in the first 10,000 tosses, the relative frequency of heads is $5,067/10,000 = .5067$.[1] Since the relative frequency of heads is approaching (that is, getting closer to) .5, we might estimate that the probability of obtaining a head when tossing the coin is .5. When we say this, we mean that, if we tossed the coin an indefinitely large number of times (that is, a number of times *approaching infinity*), the relative frequency of heads obtained would approach .5. Of course, in actuality it is impossible to toss a coin (or perform any experiment) an indefinitely large number of times. Therefore, a relative frequency interpretation of probability is a mathematical idealization. To summarize, suppose that E is an experimental outcome that might occur when a particular experiment is performed. Then the probability that E will occur, $P(E)$, can be interpreted to be the number that would be approached by the relative frequency of E if we performed the experiment an indefinitely large number of times. It follows that we often think of a probability in terms of the percentage of the time the experimental outcome would occur in many repetitions of the experiment. For instance, when we say that the probability of obtaining a head when we toss a coin is .5, we are saying that, when we repeatedly toss the coin an indefinitely large number of times, we will obtain a head on 50 percent of the repetitions.

Sometimes it is either difficult or impossible to use the classical method to assign probabilities. Since we can often make a relative frequency interpretation of probability, we can estimate a probability by performing the experiment in which an outcome might occur many times. Then, we estimate the probability of the experimental outcome to be the proportion of the time that the outcome occurs during the many repetitions of the experiment. For example, to estimate the probability that a randomly selected consumer prefers Coca-Cola to all other soft drinks, we perform an experiment in which we ask a randomly selected consumer for his or her preference. There are two possible experimental outcomes: "prefers Coca-Cola" and "does not prefer Coca-Cola." However, we have no reason to believe that these experimental outcomes are equally likely, so we cannot use the classical method. We might perform the experiment, say, 1,000 times by surveying 1,000 randomly selected consumers. Then, if 140 of those surveyed said that they prefer Coca-Cola, we would estimate the probability that a randomly selected consumer prefers Coca-Cola to all other soft drinks to be $140/1,000 = .14$. This is called the *relative frequency method* for assigning probability.

If we cannot perform the experiment many times, we might estimate the probability by using our previous experience with similar situations, intuition, or special expertise that we may possess. For example, a company president might estimate the probability of success for a one-time business venture to be .7. Here, on the basis of knowledge of the success of previous similar ventures, the opinions of company personnel, and other pertinent information, the president believes that there is a 70 percent chance the venture will be successful.

When we use experience, intuitive judgement, or expertise to assess a probability, we call this a **subjective probability.** Such a probability may or may not have a relative frequency interpretation. For instance, when the company president estimates that the probability of a successful business venture is .7, this may mean that, if business conditions similar to those that are about to be encountered could be repeated many times, then the business venture would be successful in 70 percent of the repetitions. Or the president may not be thinking in relative frequency terms but rather may consider the venture a "one-shot" proposition. We will discuss some other subjective probabilities later. However, the interpretations of statistical inferences we will explain in later chapters are based on the relative frequency interpretation of probability. For this reason, we will concentrate on this interpretation.

---

[1] The South African mathematician John Kerrich actually obtained this result when he tossed a coin 10,000 times while imprisoned by the Germans during World War II.

4.2 Sample Spaces and Events ● ● ●

LO2 List the outcomes in a sample space and use the list to compute probabilities.

In order to calculate probabilities by using the classical method, it is important to understand and use the idea of a *sample space*.

The **sample space** of an experiment is the set of all possible experimental outcomes. The experimental outcomes in the sample space are often called **sample space outcomes.**

EXAMPLE 4.1

A company is choosing a new chief executive officer (CEO). It has narrowed the list of candidates to four finalists (identified by last name only)—Adams, Chung, Hill, and Rankin. If we consider our experiment to be making a final choice of the company's CEO, then the experiment's sample space consists of the four possible experimental outcomes:

$A \equiv$ Adams is chosen as CEO.

$C \equiv$ Chung is chosen as CEO.

$H \equiv$ Hill is chosen as CEO.

$R \equiv$ Rankin is chosen as CEO.

Each of these outcomes is a sample space outcome, and the set of these sample space outcomes is the sample space.

Next, suppose that industry analysts feel (subjectively) that the probabilities that Adams, Chung, Hill, and Rankin will be chosen as CEO are .1, .2, .5, and .2, respectively. That is, in probability notation

$$P(A) = .1 \qquad P(C) = .2 \qquad P(H) = .5 \qquad \text{and} \qquad P(R) = .2$$

Notice that each probability assigned to a sample space outcome is between 0 and 1 and that the sum of the probabilities equals 1.

EXAMPLE 4.2

A newly married couple plans to have two children. Naturally, they are curious about whether their children will be boys or girls. Therefore, we consider the experiment of having two children. In order to find the sample space of this experiment, we let B denote that a child is a boy and G denote that a child is a girl. Then, it is useful to construct the tree diagram shown in Figure 4.1. This diagram pictures the experiment as a two-step process—having the first child, which could be either a boy or a girl (B or G), and then having the second child, which could also be either a boy or a girl (B or G). Each branch of the tree leads to a sample space outcome. These outcomes are listed at the right ends of the branches. We see that there are four sample space outcomes. Therefore, the sample space (that is, the set of all the sample space outcomes) is

$$BB \qquad BG \qquad GB \qquad GG$$

In order to consider the probabilities of these outcomes, suppose that boys and girls are equally likely each time a child is born. Intuitively, this says that each of the sample space outcomes is equally likely. That is, this implies that

$$P(BB) = P(BG) = P(GB) = P(GG) = \frac{1}{4}$$

This says that there is a 25 percent chance that each of these outcomes will occur. Again, notice that these probabilities sum to 1.

FIGURE 4.1   **A Tree Diagram of the Genders of Two Children**

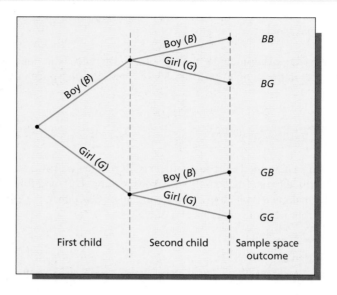

EXAMPLE 4.3

A student takes a pop quiz that consists of three true–false questions. If we consider our experiment to be answering the three questions, each question can be answered correctly or incorrectly. We will let *C* denote answering a question correctly and *I* denote answering a question incorrectly. Then, Figure 4.2 depicts a tree diagram of the sample space outcomes for the experiment. The diagram portrays the experiment as a three-step process—answering the first question (correctly or incorrectly, that is, *C* or *I*), answering the second question, and answering the third question. The tree diagram has eight different branches, and the eight sample space outcomes are listed at the ends of the branches. We see that the sample space is

$$
\begin{array}{cccc}
CCC & CCI & CIC & CII \\
ICC & ICI & IIC & III
\end{array}
$$

Next, suppose that the student was totally unprepared for the quiz and had to blindly guess the answer to each question. That is, the student had a 50–50 chance (or .5 probability) of correctly answering each question. Intuitively, this would say that each of the eight sample space outcomes is equally likely to occur. That is,

$$
P(CCC) = P(CCI) = \cdots = P(III) = \frac{1}{8}
$$

Here, as in Examples 4.1 and 4.2, the sum of the probabilities of the sample space outcomes is equal to 1.

Events and finding probabilities by using sample spaces   At the beginning of this chapter, we informally talked about events. We now give the formal definition of an event.

An **event** is a set of one or more sample space outcomes.

For instance, if we consider the couple planning to have two children, the event "the couple will have at least one girl" consists of the sample space outcomes *BG*, *GB*, and *GG*. That is, the event "the couple will have at least one girl" will occur if and only if one of the sample

FIGURE 4.2   A Tree Diagram of Answering Three True–False Questions

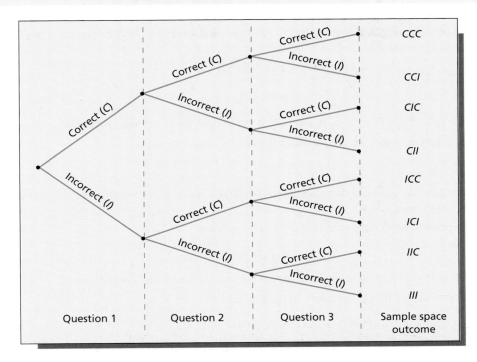

space outcomes *BG*, *GB*, or *GG* occurs. As another example, in the pop quiz situation, the event "the student will answer at least two out of three questions correctly" consists of the sample space outcomes *CCC*, *CCI*, *CIC*, and *ICC*, while the event "the student will answer all three questions correctly" consists of the sample space outcome *CCC*. In general, we see that the word description of an event determines the sample space outcomes that correspond to the event.

Suppose that we wish to find the probability that an event will occur. We can find such a probability as follows:

The **probability of an event** is the **sum of the probabilities of the sample space outcomes** that correspond to the event.

As an example, in the CEO situation, suppose only Adams and Hill are internal candidates (they already work for the company). Letting *INT* denote the event that "an internal candidate is selected for the CEO position," then *INT* consists of the sample space outcomes *A* and *H* (that is, *INT* will occur if and only if either of the sample space outcomes *A* or *H* occurs). It follows that $P(INT) = P(A) + P(H) = .1 + .5 = .6$. This says that the probability that an internal candidate will be chosen to be CEO is .6.

In general, we have seen that the probability of any sample space outcome (experimental outcome) is a number between 0 and 1, and we have also seen that the probabilities of all the sample space outcomes sum to 1. It follows that **the probability of an event** (that is, the probability of a set of sample space outcomes) **is a number between 0 and 1.** That is,

If *A* is an event, then $0 \leq P(A) \leq 1$.
   Moreover:

1   If an event never occurs, then the probability of this event equals 0.

2   If an event is certain to occur, then the probability of this event equals 1.

EXAMPLE 4.4

Consider the couple that is planning to have two children, and suppose that each child is equally likely to be a boy or girl. Recalling that in this case each sample space outcome has a probability equal to 1/4, we see that:

1   The probability that the couple will have two boys is

$$P(BB) = \frac{1}{4}$$

since two boys will be born if and only if the sample space outcome *BB* occurs.

2   The probability that the couple will have one boy and one girl is

$$P(BG) + P(GB) = \frac{1}{4} + \frac{1}{4} = \frac{1}{2}$$

since one boy and one girl will be born if and only if one of the sample space outcomes *BG* or *GB* occurs.

3   The probability that the couple will have two girls is

$$P(GG) = \frac{1}{4}$$

since two girls will be born if and only if the sample space outcome *GG* occurs.

4   The probability that the couple will have at least one girl is

$$P(BG) + P(GB) + P(GG) = \frac{1}{4} + \frac{1}{4} + \frac{1}{4} = \frac{3}{4}$$

since at least one girl will be born if and only if one of the sample space outcomes *BG*, *GB*, or *GG* occurs.

EXAMPLE 4.5

Again consider the pop quiz consisting of three true–false questions, and suppose that the student blindly guesses the answers. Remembering that in this case each sample space outcome has a probability equal to 1/8, then:

1   The probability that the student will get all three questions correct is

$$P(CCC) = \frac{1}{8}$$

2   The probability that the student will get exactly two questions correct is

$$P(CCI) + P(CIC) + P(ICC) = \frac{1}{8} + \frac{1}{8} + \frac{1}{8} = \frac{3}{8}$$

since two questions will be answered correctly if and only if one of the sample space outcomes *CCI*, *CIC*, or *ICC* occurs.

3   The probability that the student will get exactly one question correct is

$$P(CII) + P(ICI) + P(IIC) = \frac{1}{8} + \frac{1}{8} + \frac{1}{8} = \frac{3}{8}$$

since one question will be answered correctly if and only if one of the sample space outcomes *CII*, *ICI*, or *IIC* occurs.

4   The probability that the student will get all three questions incorrect is

$$P(III) = \frac{1}{8}$$

5   The probability that the student will get at least two questions correct is

$$P(CCC) + P(CCI) + P(CIC) + P(ICC) = \frac{1}{8} + \frac{1}{8} + \frac{1}{8} + \frac{1}{8} = \frac{1}{2}$$

since the student will get at least two questions correct if and only if one of the sample space outcomes *CCC*, *CCI*, *CIC*, or *ICC* occurs.

Notice that in the true–false question situation we find that, for instance, the probability that the student will get exactly two questions correct equals the ratio

$$\frac{\text{the number of sample space outcomes resulting in two correct answers}}{\text{the total number of sample space outcomes}} = \frac{3}{8}$$

In general, when a sample space is finite we can use the following method for computing the probability of an event.

If all of the sample space outcomes are equally likely, then the probability that an event will occur is equal to the ratio

$$\frac{\text{the number of sample space outcomes that correspond to the event}}{\text{the total number of sample space outcomes}}$$

When we use this rule, we are using the *classical method* for computing probabilities. Furthermore, it is important to emphasize that we can use this rule only when all of the sample space outcomes are equally likely (as they are in the true–false question situation). For example, if we were to use this rule in the CEO situation, we would find that the probability of choosing an internal candidate as CEO is

$$P(INT) = \frac{\text{the number of internal candidates}}{\text{the total number of candidates}} = \frac{2}{4} = .5$$

This result is not equal to the correct value of $P(INT)$, which we previously found to be equal to .6. Here, this rule does not give us the correct answer because the sample space outcomes $A, C, H,$ and R are not equally likely—recall that $P(A) = .1$, $P(C) = .2$, $P(H) = .5$, and $P(R) = .2$.

EXAMPLE 4.6

Suppose that 650,000 of the 1,000,000 households in an eastern U.S. city subscribe to a newspaper called the *Atlantic Journal,* and consider randomly selecting one of the households in this city. That is, consider selecting one household by giving each and every household in the city the same chance of being selected. Let A be the event that the randomly selected household subscribes to the *Atlantic Journal.* Then, because the sample space of this experiment consists of 1,000,000 equally likely sample space outcomes (households), it follows that

$$P(A) = \frac{\text{the number of households that subscribe to the } Atlantic\ Journal}{\text{the total number of households in the city}}$$

$$= \frac{650,000}{1,000,000}$$

$$= .65$$

This says that the probability that the randomly selected household subscribes to the *Atlantic Journal* is .65.

To conclude this section, we note that in optional Section 4.6 we discuss several *counting rules* that can be used to count the number of sample space outcomes in an experiment. These rules are particularly useful when there are many sample space outcomes and thus these outcomes are difficult to list.

CONCEPTS

connect

4.1 Define the following terms: *experiment, event, probability, sample space.*

4.2 Explain the properties that must be satisfied by a probability.

METHODS AND APPLICATIONS

4.3 Two randomly selected grocery store patrons are each asked to take a blind taste test and to then state which of three diet colas (marked as *A*, *B*, or *C*) he or she prefers.
  a Draw a tree diagram depicting the sample space outcomes for the test results.
  b List the sample space outcomes that correspond to each of the following events:
    (1) Both patrons prefer diet cola *A*.
    (2) The two patrons prefer the same diet cola.
    (3) The two patrons prefer different diet colas.
    (4) Diet cola *A* is preferred by at least one of the two patrons.
    (5) Neither of the patrons prefers diet cola *C*.
  c Assuming that all sample space outcomes are equally likely, find the probability of each of the events given in part *b*.

4.4 Suppose that a couple will have three children. Letting *B* denote a boy and *G* denote a girl:
  a Draw a tree diagram depicting the sample space outcomes for this experiment.
  b List the sample space outcomes that correspond to each of the following events:
    (1) All three children will have the same gender.
    (2) Exactly two of the three children will be girls.
    (3) Exactly one of the three children will be a girl.
    (4) None of the three children will be a girl.
  c Assuming that all sample space outcomes are equally likely, find the probability of each of the events given in part *b*.

4.5 Four people will enter an automobile showroom, and each will either purchase a car (*P*) or not purchase a car (*N*).
  a Draw a tree diagram depicting the sample space of all possible purchase decisions that could potentially be made by the four people.
  b List the sample space outcomes that correspond to each of the following events:
    (1) Exactly three people will purchase a car.
    (2) Two or fewer people will purchase a car.
    (3) One or more people will purchase a car.
    (4) All four people will make the same purchase decision.
  c Assuming that all sample space outcomes are equally likely, find the probability of each of the events given in part *b*.

4.6 The U.S. Census Bureau compiles data on family income and summarizes its findings in *Current Population Reports*. The below table is a frequency distribution of the annual incomes of U.S. families. Find the probability that a randomly selected U.S. family has an income between $60,000 and $199,999.

Income	Frequency (in thousands)
Under $20,000	11,470
$20,000–$39,999	17,572
$40,000–$59,999	14,534
$60,000–$79,999	11,410
$80,000–$99,999	7,535
$100,000–$199,999	11,197
$200,000 and above	2,280
	75,998

4.7 Let *A*, *B*, *C*, *D*, and *E* be sample space outcomes forming a sample space. Suppose that $P(A) = .2$, $P(B) = .15$, $P(C) = .3$, and $P(D) = .2$. What is $P(E)$? Explain how you got your answer.

4.3 Some Elementary Probability Rules ● ● ●

LO3   Use elementary probability rules to compute probabilities.

We can often calculate probabilities by using formulas called **probability rules.** We will begin by presenting the simplest probability rule: the *rule of complements.* To start, we define the complement of an event:

> Given an event A, the **complement of A** is the event consisting of all sample space outcomes that do not correspond to the occurrence of A. The complement of A is denoted $\overline{A}$. Furthermore, $P(\overline{A})$ denotes **the probability that A will not occur.**

FIGURE 4.3

The Complement of an Event (the Shaded Region Is $\overline{A}$, the Complement of A)

Figure 4.3 is a **Venn diagram** depicting the complement $\overline{A}$ of an event A. In any probability situation, either an event A or its complement $\overline{A}$ must occur. Therefore, we have

$$P(A) + P(\overline{A}) = 1$$

This implies the following result:

> **The Rule of Complements**
>
> Consider an event A. Then, **the probability that A will not occur** is
>
> $$P(\overline{A}) = 1 - P(A)$$

EXAMPLE 4.7

Recall from Example 4.6 that the probability that a randomly selected household in an eastern U.S. city subscribes to the *Atlantic Journal* is .65. It follows that the probability of the complement of this event (that is, the probability that a randomly selected household in the eastern U.S. city does not subscribe to the *Atlantic Journal*) is $1 - .65 = .35$.

EXAMPLE 4.8

Consider Example 4.6, and recall that 650,000 of the 1,000,000 households in an eastern U.S. city subscribe to the *Atlantic Journal.* Also, suppose that 500,000 households in the city subscribe to a competing newspaper, the *Beacon News,* and further suppose that 250,000 households subscribe to both the *Atlantic Journal* and the *Beacon News.* As in Example 4.6, we consider randomly selecting one household in the city, and we define the following events.

    $A \equiv$ the randomly selected household subscribes to the *Atlantic Journal.*
    $\overline{A} \equiv$ the randomly selected household does not subscribe to the *Atlantic Journal.*
    $B \equiv$ the randomly selected household subscribes to the *Beacon News.*
    $\overline{B} \equiv$ the randomly selected household does not subscribe to the *Beacon News.*

Using the notation $A \cap B$ to denote *both A and B,* we also define

    $A \cap B \equiv$ the randomly selected household subscribes to both the *Atlantic Journal* and the *Beacon News.*

Since 650,000 of the 1,000,000 households subscribe to the *Atlantic Journal* (that is, correspond to the event A occurring), then 350,000 households do not subscribe to the *Atlantic Journal* (that is, correspond to the event $\overline{A}$ occurring). Similarly, 500,000 households subscribe to the *Beacon News* (B), so 500,000 households do not subscribe to the *Beacon News* ($\overline{B}$). We summarize this information, as well as the 250,000 households that correspond to the event $A \cap B$ occurring, in Table 4.1.

TABLE 4.1	A Summary of the Number of Households Corresponding to the Events A, $\overline{A}$, B, $\overline{B}$, and $A \cap B$

Events	Subscribes to Beacon News, B	Does Not Subscribe to Beacon News, $\overline{B}$	Total
Subscribes to Atlantic Journal, A	250,000		650,000
Does Not Subscribe to Atlantic Journal, $\overline{A}$			350,000
Total	500,000	500,000	1,000,000

Next, consider the events

$A \cap \overline{B} \equiv$ the randomly selected household subscribes to the *Atlantic Journal* and does not subscribe to the *Beacon News*.

$\overline{A} \cap B \equiv$ the randomly selected household does not subscribe to the *Atlantic Journal* and does subscribe to the *Beacon News*.

$\overline{A} \cap \overline{B} \equiv$ the randomly selected household does not subscribe to the *Atlantic Journal* and does not subscribe to the *Beacon News*.

Because 650,000 households subscribe to the *Atlantic Journal* (A) and 250,000 households subscribe to both the *Atlantic Journal* and the *Beacon News* ($A \cap B$), it follows that 650,000 − 250,000 = 400,000 households subscribe to the *Atlantic Journal* but do not subscribe to the *Beacon News* ($A \cap \overline{B}$). This subtraction is illustrated in Table 4.2(a). By similar logic, it also follows that:

1   As illustrated in Table 4.2(b), 500,000 − 250,000 = 250,000 households do not subscribe to the *Atlantic Journal* but do subscribe to the *Beacon News* ($\overline{A} \cap B$).

2   As illustrated in Table 4.2(c), 350,000 − 250,000 = 100,000 households do not subscribe to the *Atlantic Journal* and do not subscribe to the *Beacon News* ($\overline{A} \cap \overline{B}$).

TABLE 4.2	Subtracting to Find the Number of Households Corresponding to the Events $A \cap \overline{B}$, $\overline{A} \cap B$, and $\overline{A} \cap \overline{B}$

(a) The Number of Households Corresponding to (A and $\overline{B}$)

Events	Subscribes to Beacon News, B	Does Not Subscribe to Beacon News, $\overline{B}$	Total
Subscribes to Atlantic Journal, A	250,000	650,000 − 250,000 = 400,000	650,000
Does Not Subscribe to Atlantic Journal, $\overline{A}$			350,000
Total	500,000	500,000	1,000,000

(b) The Number of Households Corresponding to ($\overline{A}$ and B)

Events	Subscribes to Beacon News, B	Does Not Subscribe to Beacon News, $\overline{B}$	Total
Subscribes to Atlantic Journal, A	250,000	650,000 − 250,000 = 400,000	650,000
Does Not Subscribe to Atlantic Journal, $\overline{A}$	500,000 − 250,000 = 250,000		350,000
Total	500,000	500,000	1,000,000

TABLE 4.2 (*continued*)

(c) The Number of Households Corresponding to ($\overline{A}$ and $\overline{B}$)

Events	Subscribes to Beacon News, B	Does Not Subscribe to Beacon News, $\overline{B}$	Total
Subscribes to *Atlantic Journal, A*	250,000	650,000 − 250,000 = 400,000	650,000
Does Not Subscribe to *Atlantic Journal, $\overline{A}$*	500,000 − 250,000 = 250,000	350,000 − 250,000 = 100,000	350,000
Total	500,000	500,000	1,000,000

TABLE 4.3 A Contingency Table Summarizing Subscription Data for the *Atlantic Journal* and the *Beacon News*

Events	Subscribes to Beacon News, B	Does Not Subscribe to Beacon News, $\overline{B}$	Total
Subscribes to *Atlantic Journal, A*	250,000	400,000	650,000
Does Not Subscribe to *Atlantic Journal, $\overline{A}$*	250,000	100,000	350,000
Total	500,000	500,000	1,000,000

We summarize all of these results in Table 4.3, which is called a **contingency table.** Because we will randomly select one household (making all of the households equally likely to be chosen), the probability of any of the previously defined events is the ratio of the number of households corresponding to the event's occurrence to the total number of households in the city. Therefore, for example,

$$P(A) = \frac{650,000}{1,000,000} = .65 \qquad\qquad P(B) = \frac{500,000}{1,000,000} = .5$$

$$P(A \cap B) = \frac{250,000}{1,000,000} = .25$$

This last probability says that the probability that the randomly selected household subscribes to both the *Atlantic Journal* and the *Beacon News* is .25.

Next, letting $A \cup B$ denote A or B (or both), we consider finding the probability of the event

$A \cup B \equiv$ the randomly selected household subscribes to the *Atlantic Journal* or the *Beacon News* (or both)—that is, subscribes to at least one of the two newspapers.

Looking at Table 4.3, we see that the households subscribing to the *Atlantic Journal* or the *Beacon News* are (1) the 400,000 households that subscribe to only the *Atlantic Journal*, $A \cap \overline{B}$, (2) the 250,000 households that subscribe to only the *Beacon News*, $\overline{A} \cap B$, and (3) the 250,000 households that subscribe to both the *Atlantic Journal* and the *Beacon News*, $A \cap B$. Therefore, since a total of 900,000 households subscribe to the *Atlantic Journal* or the *Beacon News*, it follows that

$$P(A \cup B) = \frac{900,000}{1,000,000} = .9$$

This says that the probability that the randomly selected household subscribes to the *Atlantic Journal* or the *Beacon News* is .90. That is, 90 percent of the households in the city subscribe to the *Atlantic Journal* or the *Beacon News*. Notice that $P(A \cup B) = .90$ does not equal

$$P(A) + P(B) = .65 + .5 = 1.15$$

Logically, the reason for this is that both $P(A) = .65$ and $P(B) = .5$ count the 25 percent of the households that subscribe to both newspapers. Therefore, the sum of $P(A)$ and $P(B)$ counts this

25 percent of the households once too often. It follows that if we subtract $P(A \cap B) = .25$ from the sum of $P(A)$ and $P(B)$, then we will obtain $P(A \cup B)$. That is,

$$P(A \cup B) = P(A) + P(B) - P(A \cap B)$$
$$= .65 + .5 - .25 = .90$$

In order to generalize the ideas in the previous example, we make the following definitions:

The Intersection and Union of Two Events

Given two events A and B,

1   The **intersection of A and B** is the event consisting of the sample space outcomes belonging to both A and B. The intersection is denoted by $A \cap B$. Furthermore, $P(A \cap B)$ denotes **the probability that _both A and B will simultaneously occur._**

2   The **union of A and B** is the event consisting of the sample space outcomes belonging to A or B (or both). The union is denoted $A \cup B$. Furthermore, $P(A \cup B)$ denotes **the probability that _A or B (or both) will occur._**

Noting that Figure 4.4 shows **Venn diagrams** depicting the events A, B, $A \cap B$, and $A \cup B$, we have the following general result:

The Addition Rule

Let A and B be events. Then, **the probability that _A or B (or both) will occur_** is

$$P(A \cup B) = P(A) + P(B) - P(A \cap B)$$

The reasoning behind this result has been illustrated at the end of Example 4.8. Similarly, the Venn diagrams in Figure 4.4 show that when we compute $P(A) + P(B)$, we are counting each of the sample space outcomes in $A \cap B$ twice. We correct for this by subtracting $P(A \cap B)$.

We next define the idea of _mutually exclusive events:_

Mutually Exclusive Events

Two events A and B are **mutually exclusive** if they have no sample space outcomes in common. In this case, the events A and B cannot occur simultaneously, and thus

$$P(A \cap B) = 0$$

Noting that Figure 4.5 is a Venn diagram depicting two mutually exclusive events, we consider the following example.

EXAMPLE 4.9

Consider randomly selecting a card from a standard deck of 52 playing cards. We define the following events:

$J \equiv$ the randomly selected card is a jack.

$Q \equiv$ the randomly selected card is a queen.

$R \equiv$ the randomly selected card is a red card (that is, a diamond or a heart).

Because there is no card that is both a jack and a queen, the events J and Q are mutually exclusive. On the other hand, there are two cards that are both jacks and red cards—the jack of diamonds and the jack of hearts—so the events J and R are not mutually exclusive.

FIGURE 4.4   Venn Diagrams Depicting the Events A, B, $A \cap B$, and $A \cup B$

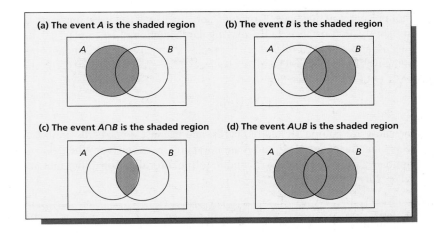

(a) The event A is the shaded region

(b) The event B is the shaded region

(c) The event $A \cap B$ is the shaded region

(d) The event $A \cup B$ is the shaded region

FIGURE 4.5
Two Mutually
Exclusive Events

We have seen that for any two events A and B, the probability that A or B (or both) will occur is

$$P(A \cup B) = P(A) + P(B) - P(A \cap B)$$

Therefore, when calculating $P(A \cup B)$, we should always subtract $P(A \cap B)$ from the sum of $P(A)$ and $P(B)$. However, when A and B are mutually exclusive, $P(A \cap B)$ equals 0. Therefore, in this case—and only in this case—we have the following:

The Addition Rule for Two Mutually Exclusive Events

Let A and B be **mutually exclusive** events. Then, **the probability that A or B will occur** is

$$P(A \cup B) = P(A) + P(B)$$

EXAMPLE 4.10

Again consider randomly selecting a card from a standard deck of 52 playing cards, and define the events

   $J \equiv$ the randomly selected card is a jack.

   $Q \equiv$ the randomly selected card is a queen.

   $R \equiv$ the randomly selected card is a red card (a diamond or a heart).

Because there are four jacks, four queens, and 26 red cards, we have $P(J) = \frac{4}{52}$, $P(Q) = \frac{4}{52}$, and $P(R) = \frac{26}{52}$. Furthermore, since there is no card that is both a jack and a queen, the events J and Q are mutually exclusive and thus $P(J \cap Q) = 0$. It follows that the probability that the randomly selected card is a jack or a queen is

$$P(J \cup Q) = P(J) + P(Q)$$
$$= \frac{4}{52} + \frac{4}{52} = \frac{8}{52} = \frac{2}{13}$$

Because there are two cards that are both jacks and red cards—the jack of diamonds and the jack of hearts—the events J and R are not mutually exclusive. Therefore, the probability that the randomly selected card is a jack or a red card is

$$P(J \cup R) = P(J) + P(R) - P(J \cap R)$$
$$= \frac{4}{52} + \frac{26}{52} - \frac{2}{52} = \frac{28}{52} = \frac{7}{13}$$

We now consider an arbitrary group of events—$A_1, A_2, \ldots, A_N$. We will denote the probability that A_1 or A_2 or $\cdots$ or A_N occurs (that is, the probability that at least one of the events occurs) as $P(A_1 \cup A_2 \cup \cdots \cup A_N)$. Although there is a formula for this probability, it is quite complicated and we will not present it in this book. However, sometimes we can use sample spaces to reason out such a probability. For instance, in the playing card situation of Example 4.10, there are four jacks, four queens, and 22 red cards that are not jacks or queens (the 26 red cards minus the two red jacks and the two red queens). Therefore, because there are a total of 30 cards corresponding to the event $J \cup Q \cup R$, it follows that

$$P(J \cup Q \cup R) = \frac{30}{52} = \frac{15}{26}$$

Because some cards are both jacks and red cards, and because some cards are both queens and red cards, we say that the events J, Q, and R are not mutually exclusive. When, however, a group of events is mutually exclusive, there is a simple formula for the probability that at least one of the events will occur:

The Addition Rule for N Mutually Exclusive Events

The events $A_1, A_2, \ldots, A_N$ are mutually exclusive if no two of the events have any sample space outcomes in common. In this case, no two of the events can occur simultaneously, and

$$P(A_1 \cup A_2 \cup \cdots \cup A_N) = P(A_1) + P(A_2) + \cdots + P(A_N)$$

As an example of using this formula, again consider the playing card situation and the events J and Q. If we define the event

$$K \equiv \text{the randomly selected card is a king}$$

then the events J, Q, and K are mutually exclusive. Therefore,

$$P(J \cup Q \cup K) = P(J) + P(Q) + P(K)$$
$$= \frac{4}{52} + \frac{4}{52} + \frac{4}{52} = \frac{12}{52} = \frac{3}{13}$$

Exercises for Section 4.3

CONCEPTS

connect

4.8 Explain what it means for two events to be mutually exclusive; for N events.

4.9 If A and B are events, define $\overline{A}$, $A \cup B$, $A \cap B$, and $\overline{A} \cap \overline{B}$.

METHODS AND APPLICATIONS

4.10 Consider a standard deck of 52 playing cards, a randomly selected card from the deck, and the following events:

$$R = \text{red} \quad B = \text{black} \quad A = \text{ace} \quad N = \text{nine} \quad D = \text{diamond} \quad C = \text{club}$$

   a Describe the sample space outcomes that correspond to each of these events.

   b For each of the following pairs of events, indicate whether the events are mutually exclusive. In each case, if you think the events are mutually exclusive, explain why the events have no common sample space outcomes. If you think the events are not mutually exclusive, list the sample space outcomes that are common to both events.

   (1) R and A (3) A and N (5) D and C
   (2) R and C (4) N and C

4.11 Of 10,000 students at a college, 2,500 have a Mastercard (M), 4,000 have a VISA (V), and 1,000 have both.

   a Find the probability that a randomly selected student

   (1) Has a Mastercard.
   (2) Has a VISA.
   (3) Has both credit cards.

TABLE 4.4	Results of a Concept Study for a New Wine Cooler		DS WineCooler				
			Gender			**Age Group**	
Rating	**Total**	**Male**	**Female**	**21–24**	**25–34**	**35–49**	
Extremely appealing (5)	151	68	83	48	66	37	
(4)	91	51	40	36	36	19	
(3)	36	21	15	9	12	15	
(2)	13	7	6	4	6	3	
Not at all appealing (1)	9	3	6	4	3	2	

Source: W. R. Dillon, T. J. Madden, and N. H. Firtle, *Essentials of Marketing Research* (Burr Ridge, IL: Richard D. Irwin, Inc., 1993), p. 390.

b Construct and fill in a contingency table summarizing the credit card data. Employ the following pairs of events: M and $\overline{M}$, V and $\overline{V}$.

c Use the contingency table to find the probability that a randomly selected student
  (1) Has a Mastercard or a VISA.
  (2) Has neither credit card.
  (3) Has exactly one of the two credit cards.

4.12 The card game of Euchre employs a deck that consists of all four of each of the aces, kings, queens, jacks, tens, and nines (one of each suit—clubs, diamonds, spades, and hearts). Find the probability that a randomly selected card from a Euchre deck is a jack (J), a spade (S), a jack or an ace (A), a jack or a spade. Are the events J and A mutually exclusive? J and S? Why or why not?

4.13 Each month a brokerage house studies various companies and rates each company's stock as being either "low risk" or "moderate to high risk." In a recent report, the brokerage house summarized its findings about 15 aerospace companies and 25 food retailers in the following table:

Company Type	Low Risk	Moderate to High Risk
Aerospace company	6	9
Food retailer	15	10

If we randomly select one of the total of 40 companies, find
a The probability that the company is a food retailer.
b The probability that the company's stock is "low risk."
c The probability that the company's stock is "moderate to high risk."
d The probability that the company is a food retailer and has a stock that is "low risk."
e The probability that the company is a food retailer or has a stock that is "low risk."

4.14 In the book *Essentials of Marketing Research,* William R. Dillon, Thomas J. Madden, and Neil H. Firtle present the results of a concept study for a new wine cooler. Three hundred consumers between 21 and 49 years old were randomly selected. After sampling the new beverage, each was asked to rate the appeal of the phrase

> Not sweet like wine coolers, not filling like beer, and more refreshing than wine or mixed drinks

as it relates to the new wine cooler. The rating was made on a scale from 1 to 5, with 5 representing "extremely appealing" and with 1 representing "not at all appealing." The results obtained are given in Table 4.4. Estimate the probability that a randomly selected 21- to 49-year-old consumer
a Would give the phrase a rating of 5.
b Would give the phrase a rating of 3 or higher.
c Is in the 21–24 age group; the 25–34 age group; the 35–49 age group.
d Is a male who gives the phrase a rating of 4.
e Is a 35- to 49-year-old who gives the phrase a rating of 1.

4.15 In Exercise 4.14 estimate the probability that a randomly selected 21- to 49-year-old consumer is a 25- to 49-year-old who gives the phrase a rating of 5.

4.4 Conditional Probability and Independence ● ● ●

LO4 Compute conditional probabilities and assess independence.

Conditional probability   In Table 4.5 we repeat the contingency table summarizing the subscription data for the *Atlantic Journal* and the *Beacon News.* Suppose that we randomly select a household, and that the chosen household reports that it subscribes to the *Beacon News.* Given this new information, we wish to find the probability that the household subscribes to the *Atlantic*

TABLE 4.5	A Contingency Table Summarizing Subscription Data for the *Atlantic Journal* and the *Beacon News*

Events	Subscribes to Beacon News, B	Does Not Subscribe to Beacon News, $\overline{B}$	Total
Subscribes to *Atlantic Journal, A*	250,000	400,000	650,000
Does Not Subscribe to *Atlantic Journal, $\overline{A}$*	250,000	100,000	350,000
Total	500,000	500,000	1,000,000

Journal. This new probability is called a **conditional probability.**

The **probability of the event *A*, given the condition that the event *B* has occurred,** is written as **$P(A|B)$**—pronounced "the probability of *A* given *B*." We often refer to such a probability as the **conditional probability of *A* given *B*.**

In order to find the conditional probability that a household subscribes to the *Atlantic Journal,* given that it subscribes to the *Beacon News,* notice that if we know that the randomly selected household subscribes to the *Beacon News,* we know that we are considering one of 500,000 households (see Table 4.5). That is, we are now considering what we might call a **reduced sample space** of 500,000 households. Since 250,000 of these 500,000 *Beacon News* subscribers also subscribe to the *Atlantic Journal,* we have

$$P(A|B) = \frac{250,000}{500,000} = .5$$

This says that the probability that the randomly selected household subscribes to the *Atlantic Journal,* given that the household subscribes to the *Beacon News,* is .5. That is, 50 percent of the *Beacon News* subscribers also subscribe to the *Atlantic Journal.*

Next, suppose that we randomly select another household from the community of 1,000,000 households, and suppose that this newly chosen household reports that it subscribes to the *Atlantic Journal.* We now wish to find the probability that this household subscribes to the *Beacon News.* We write this new probability as $P(B|A)$. If we know that the randomly selected household subscribes to the *Atlantic Journal,* we know that we are considering a reduced sample space of 650,000 households (see Table 4.5). Since 250,000 of these 650,000 *Atlantic Journal* subscribers also subscribe to the *Beacon News,* we have

$$P(B|A) = \frac{250,000}{650,000} = .3846$$

This says that the probability that the randomly selected household subscribes to the *Beacon News,* given that the household subscribes to the *Atlantic Journal,* is .3846. That is, 38.46 percent of the *Atlantic Journal* subscribers also subscribe to the *Beacon News.*

If we divide both the numerator and denominator of each of the conditional probabilities $P(A|B)$ and $P(B|A)$ by 1,000,000, we obtain

$$P(A|B) = \frac{250,000}{500,000} = \frac{250,000/1,000,000}{500,000/1,000,000} = \frac{P(A \cap B)}{P(B)}$$

$$P(B|A) = \frac{250,000}{650,000} = \frac{250,000/1,000,000}{650,000/1,000,000} = \frac{P(A \cap B)}{P(A)}$$

We express these conditional probabilities in terms of $P(A)$, $P(B)$, and $P(A \cap B)$ in order to obtain a more general formula for a conditional probability. We need a more general formula because, although we can use the reduced sample space approach we have demonstrated to find conditional probabilities when all of the sample space outcomes are equally likely, this approach may not give correct results when the sample space outcomes are *not* equally likely. We now give expressions for conditional probability that are valid for any sample space.

Conditional Probability

1 The **conditional probability that *A* will occur given that *B* will occur** is written **$P(A\,|\,B)$** and is defined to be

$$P(A\,|\,B) = \frac{P(A \cap B)}{P(B)}$$

Here we assume that $P(B)$ is greater than 0.

2 The **conditional probability that *B* will occur given that *A* will occur** is written **$P(B\,|\,A)$** and is defined to be

$$P(B\,|\,A) = \frac{P(A \cap B)}{P(A)}$$

Here we assume that $P(A)$ is greater than 0.

If we multiply both sides of the equation

$$P(A\,|\,B) = \frac{P(A \cap B)}{P(B)}$$

by $P(B)$, we obtain the equation

$$P(A \cap B) = P(B)P(A\,|\,B)$$

Similarly, if we multiply both sides of the equation

$$P(B\,|\,A) = \frac{P(A \cap B)}{P(A)}$$

by $P(A)$, we obtain the equation

$$P(A \cap B) = P(A)P(B\,|\,A)$$

In summary, we now have two equations that can be used to calculate $P(A \cap B)$. These equations are often referred to as the **general multiplication rule** for probabilities.

The General Multiplication Rule—Two Ways to Calculate $P(A \cap B)$

Given any two events A and B,

$$P(A \cap B) = P(A)P(B\,|\,A)$$
$$= P(B)P(A\,|\,B)$$

EXAMPLE 4.11   Ⓒ

Jim and Mary are married. The probability that Jim watches *The Tonight Show* on Monday evening is .6. The probability that Mary watches *The Tonight Show* on Monday evening is .5. The probability that Jim watches *The Tonight Show* on Monday evening, given that Mary does, is .8. What is the probability that both Jim and Mary watch *The Tonight Show* on Monday evening? Also, what is the probability that Mary watches *The Tonight Show* on Monday evening, given that Jim does? Finally, what is the probability that either Jim or Mary watches *The Tonight Show* on Monday evening?

To answer the above questions, let J denote the event that Jim watches *The Tonight Show* on Monday evening, and let M denote the event that Mary watches *The Tonight Show* on Monday evening. Then, we know that $P(J) = .6$, $P(M) = .5$, and $P(J\,|\,M) = .8$. To find $P(J \cap M)$, note that the general multiplication rule says that

$$P(J \cap M) = P(J)P(M\,|\,J) = P(M)P(J\,|\,M)$$

Although we know that $P(J) = .6$, we do not know $P(M \mid J)$. Therefore, we cannot calculate $P(J \cap M)$ as $P(J)P(M \mid J)$. However, because we know that $P(M) = .5$ and that $P(J \mid M) = .8$, we can calculate

$$P(J \cap M) = P(M)P(J \mid M) = (.5)(.8) = .40$$

This says that the probability that both Jim and Mary watch *The Tonight Show* on Monday evening is .40. Moreover, the probability that Mary watches *The Tonight Show* on Monday evening, given that Jim does, is

$$P(M \mid J) = \frac{P(J \cap M)}{P(J)} = \frac{.40}{.60} = .67$$

Finally, the probability that either Jim or Mary watches *The Tonight Show* on Monday evening is

$$P(J \cup M) = P(J) + P(M) - P(J \cap M) = .6 + .5 - .40 = .7$$

EXAMPLE 4.12

In a soft drink taste test, each of 1,000 consumers chose between two colas—Cola 1 and Cola 2—and stated whether they preferred their cola drinks *sweet* or *very sweet.* Unfortunately, some of the survey information was lost. The following information remains:

1   68.3 percent of the consumers (that is, 683 consumers) preferred Cola 1 to Cola 2.

2   62 percent of the consumers (that is, 620 consumers) preferred their cola *sweet* (rather than *very sweet*).

3   85 percent of the consumers who said that they liked their cola *sweet* preferred Cola 1 to Cola 2.

To recover all of the lost survey information, consider randomly selecting one of the 1,000 survey participants, and define the following events:

$C1 \equiv$ the randomly selected consumer prefers Cola 1.

$C2 \equiv$ the randomly selected consumer prefers Cola 2.

$S \equiv$ the randomly selected consumer prefers *sweet* cola drinks.

$V \equiv$ the randomly selected consumer prefers *very sweet* cola drinks.

From the survey information that remains, (1) says that $P(C1) = .683$, (2) says that $P(S) = .62$, and (3) says that $P(C1 \mid S) = .85$.

We will see that we can recover all of the lost survey information if we can find $P(C1 \cap S)$. Because we know that $P(S) = .62$ and that $P(C1 \mid S) = .85$, we can calculate

$$P(C1 \cap S) = P(S)P(C1 \mid S) = (.62)(.85) = .527$$

This implies that 527 consumers preferred Cola 1 and preferred their cola *sweet.* Since 683 consumers preferred Cola 1, and 620 consumers preferred *sweet* cola drinks, we can summarize the numbers of consumers corresponding to the events $C1$, $C2$, S, V, and $C1 \cap S$ as shown in Table 4.6. Furthermore, by performing subtractions as shown in Table 4.7, the numbers of consumers corresponding to the events $C1 \cap V$, $C2 \cap S$, and $C2 \cap V$ can be obtained. We summarize all of our results in Table 4.8. We will use these results in the next subsection to investigate the relationship between cola preference and sweetness preference.

Independence   We have seen in Example 4.12 that $P(C1) = .683$, while $P(C1 \mid S) = .85$. Because $P(C1 \mid S)$ is greater than $P(C1)$, the probability that a randomly selected consumer will prefer Cola 1 is higher if we know that the person prefers *sweet* cola than it is if we have no knowledge of the person's sweetness preference. Another way to see this is to use Table 4.8 to

TABLE 4.6	A Summary of the Number of Consumers Corresponding to the Events C1, C2, S, V, and C1 ∩ S		
Events	S (Sweet)	V (Very Sweet)	Total
C1 (Cola 1)	527		683
C2 (Cola 2)			317
Total	620	380	1,000

TABLE 4.7	Subtractions to Obtain the Number of Consumers Corresponding to the Events C1 ∩ V, C2 ∩ S, and C2 ∩ V		
Events	S (Sweet)	V (Very Sweet)	Total
C1 (Cola 1)	527	683 − 527 = 156	683
C2 (Cola 2)	620 − 527 = 93	380 − 156 = 224	317
Total	620	380	1,000

TABLE 4.8	A Contingency Table Summarizing the Cola Brand and Sweetness Preferences		
Events	S (Sweet)	V (Very Sweet)	Total
C1 (Cola 1)	527	156	683
C2 (Cola 2)	93	224	317
Total	620	380	1,000

calculate

$$P(C1 \mid V) = \frac{P(C1 \cap V)}{P(V)} = \frac{156/1,000}{380/1,000} = .4105$$

Since $P(C1 \mid S) = .85$ is greater than $P(C1 \mid V) = .4105$, the probability that a randomly selected consumer will prefer Cola 1 is higher if the consumer prefers *sweet* colas than it is if the consumer prefers *very sweet* colas. Since the probability of the event $C1$ is influenced by whether the event S occurs, we say that the events $C1$ and S are **dependent.** If $P(C1 \mid S)$ were equal to $P(C1)$, then the probability of the event $C1$ would not be influenced by whether S occurs. In this case we would say that the events $C1$ and S are **independent.** This leads to the following definition of **independence:**

Independent Events

Two events A and B are **independent** if and only if

1 $P(A \mid B) = P(A)$ or, equivalently,

2 $P(B \mid A) = P(B)$

Here we assume that $P(A)$ and $P(B)$ are greater than 0.

When we say that conditions (1) and (2) are equivalent, we mean that condition (1) holds if and only if condition (2) holds. Although we will not prove this, we can demonstrate it in the soft drink taste test example. Specifically, we have seen that $P(C1 \mid S) = .85$ does not equal $P(C1) = .683$. This implies that $P(S \mid C1)$ does not equal $P(S)$. To demonstrate this, note from Table 4.8 that

$$P(S \mid C1) = \frac{P(C1 \cap S)}{P(C1)} = \frac{527/1,000}{683/1,000} = .7716$$

This probability is larger than $P(S) = 620/1,000 = .62$. In summary:

1   A comparison of $P(C1 \mid S) = .85$ and $P(C1) = .683$ says that a consumer is more likely to prefer Cola 1 if the consumer prefers *sweet* colas.

2   A comparison of $P(S \mid C1) = .7716$ and $P(S) = .62$ says that a consumer is more likely to prefer *sweet* colas if the consumer prefers Cola 1.

This suggests, but does not prove, that one reason Cola 1 is preferred to Cola 2 is that Cola 1 is *sweet* (as opposed to *very sweet*).

If the occurrences of the events A and B have nothing to do with each other, then we know that A and B are independent events. This implies that $P(A \mid B)$ equals $P(A)$ and that $P(B \mid A)$ equals $P(B)$. Recall that the general multiplication rule tells us that, for any two events A and B, we can say that

$$P(A \cap B) = P(A)P(B \mid A)$$

Therefore, if $P(B \mid A)$ equals $P(B)$, it follows that

$$P(A \cap B) = P(A)P(B)$$

which is called the **multiplication rule for independent events.** To summarize:

The Multiplication Rule for Two Independent Events

If A and B are **independent events,** then

$$P(A \cap B) = P(A)P(B)$$

As a simple example, define the events C and P as follows:

$C \equiv$ your favorite college football team wins its first game next season.

$P \equiv$ your favorite professional football team wins its first game next season.

Suppose you believe that for next season $P(C) = .6$ and $P(P) = .6$. Then, because the outcomes of a college football game and a professional football game would probably have nothing to do with each other, it is reasonable to assume that C and P are independent events. It follows that

$$P(C \cap P) = P(C)P(P) = (.6)(.6) = .36$$

This probability might be surprisingly low. That is, since you believe that each of your teams has a 60 percent chance of winning, you might feel reasonably confident that both your college and professional teams will win their first game. Yet, the chance of this happening is really only .36!

Next, consider a group of events $A_1, A_2, \ldots, A_N$. Intuitively, the events $A_1, A_2, \ldots, A_N$ are independent if the occurrences of these events have nothing to do with each other. Denoting the probability that A_1 and A_2 and $\cdots$ and A_N will simultaneously occur as $P(A_1 \cap A_2 \cap \cdots \cap A_N)$, we have the following:

The Multiplication Rule for N Independent Events

If $A_1, A_2, \ldots, A_N$ are independent events, then

$$P(A_1 \cap A_2 \cap \cdots \cap A_N) = P(A_1)P(A_2) \cdots P(A_N)$$

This says that the multiplication rule for two independent events can be extended to any number of independent events.

EXAMPLE 4.13

This example is based on a real situation encountered by a major producer and marketer of consumer products. The company assessed the service it provides by surveying the attitudes of its customers regarding 10 different aspects of customer service—order filled correctly, billing amount on invoice correct, delivery made on time, and so forth. When the survey results were analyzed, the company was dismayed to learn that only 59 percent of the survey participants indicated that they were satisfied with all 10 aspects of the company's service. Upon investigation, each of the 10 departments responsible for the aspects of service considered in the study insisted that it satisfied its customers 95 percent of the time. That is, each department claimed that its error rate was only 5 percent. Company executives were confused and felt that there was a substantial discrepancy between the survey results and the claims of the departments providing the services. However, a company statistician pointed out that there was no discrepancy. To understand this, consider randomly selecting a customer from among the survey participants, and define 10 events (corresponding to the 10 aspects of service studied):

$A_1 \equiv$ the customer is satisfied that the order is filled correctly (aspect 1).

$A_2 \equiv$ the customer is satisfied that the billing amount on the invoice is correct (aspect 2).

$\vdots$

$A_{10} \equiv$ the customer is satisfied that the delivery is made on time (aspect 10).

Also, define the event

$S \equiv$ the customer is satisfied with all 10 aspects of customer service.

Since 10 different departments are responsible for the 10 aspects of service being studied, it is reasonable to assume that all 10 aspects of service are independent of each other. For instance, billing amounts would be independent of delivery times. Therefore, $A_1, A_2, \ldots, A_{10}$ are independent events, and

$$P(S) = P(A_1 \cap A_2 \cap \cdots \cap A_{10})$$
$$= P(A_1)P(A_2) \cdots P(A_{10})$$

If, as the departments claim, each department satisfies its customers 95 percent of the time, then the probability that the customer is satisfied with all 10 aspects is

$$P(S) = (.95)(.95) \cdots (.95) = (.95)^{10} = .5987$$

This result is almost identical to the 59 percent satisfaction rate reported by the survey participants.

If the company wants to increase the percentage of its customers who are satisfied with all 10 aspects of service, it must improve the quality of service provided by the 10 departments. For example, to satisfy 95 percent of its customers with all 10 aspects of service, the company must require each department to raise the fraction of the time it satisfies its customers to x, where x is such that $(x)^{10} = .95$. It follows that

$$x = (.95)^{\frac{1}{10}} = .9949$$

and that each department must satisfy its customers 99.49 percent of the time (rather than the current 95 percent of the time).

EXAMPLE 4.14 The Song Rating Case

There are many song rating services in the United States. In order to rate a particular song, these services survey listeners and ask them to rate the song on a 1 to 5 rating scale, with 1 being the lowest possible rating and 5 being the highest. Figure 4.6 gives a bar chart of the ratings of *Poker Face* by Lady GaGa obtained by a song rating service; notice that *UNFAM* indicates that the listener was not familiar with this particular song. The percentages above the bars of the histogram give the percentages of listeners rating the song 5, 4, 3, 2, 1, and *UNFAM*, respectively. If we let the symbol denoting a particular rating also denote the event that a randomly selected listener would give the song the rating, it follows that we estimate that

$$P(5) = .38 \qquad P(4) = .19 \qquad P(3) = .20$$
$$P(2) = .06 \qquad P(1) = .06 \qquad P(UNFAM) = .11$$

The two boxes on the left of Figure 4.6 give *recognition* and *popularity* indexes for the song being analyzed. Letting *FAM* denote the event that a randomly selected listener is familiar with the song, it follows that $P(FAM) = 1 - P(UNFAM) = 1 - .11 = .89$. This probability is expressed as the *recognition* index of 89 percent in Figure 4.6. The *popularity* index is an estimate of an *average rating* for the song. This average rating is obtained by combining the ratings 5, 4, 3, 2, and 1 with the estimated *conditional probabilities* of these ratings, given that a randomly selected listener is familiar with the song. How the combining is done will be discussed in Chapter 5. For now, we find the appropriate conditional probabilities. To do this, first note that the event $5 \cap FAM$ is equivalent to the event 5, because the only way a listener can give the song a rating of 5 (or any other rating from 1 to 4) is to be familiar with the song. Therefore, we estimate that the probability

FIGURE 4.6   A Portion of a Song Rating Analysis for *Poker Face* by Lady GaGa.

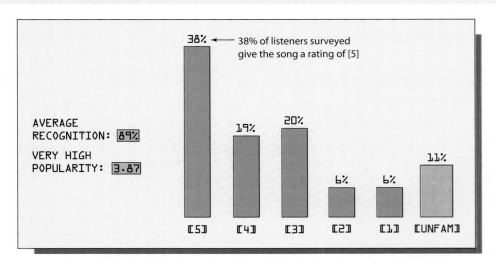

that a randomly selected listener would give the song a rating of 5, given that the listener is famil-iar with the song, is

$$P(5 \mid FAM) = \frac{P(5 \cap FAM)}{P(FAM)} = \frac{P(5)}{P(FAM)} = \frac{.38}{.89} = .43$$

Generalizing this, we conclude that the conditional probability of a particular rating, given familiarity, is the probability of the rating divided by the probability of familiarity. Therefore, be-cause we estimate that $P(4) = .19, P(3) = .20, P(2) = .06, P(1) = .06$, and $P(FAM) = .89$, we es-timate that $P(4 \mid FAM) = .19/.89 = .21, P(3 \mid FAM) = .20/.89 = .22, P(2 \mid FAM) = .06/.89 = .07$, and $P(1 \mid FAM) = .06/.89 = .07$. These conditional probabilities will be used in Chapter 5 to help find the popularity index of 3.87 in Figure 4.6.

Exercises for Section 4.4

CONCEPTS

connect

4.16   Give an example of a conditional probability that would be of interest to you.

4.17   Explain what it means for two events to be independent.

METHODS AND APPLICATIONS

4.18   Recall from Exercise 4.11 (page 168) that of 10,000 students at a college, 2,500 have a Mastercard (*M*), 4,000 have a VISA (*V*), and 1,000 have both. Find
   a   The proportion of Mastercard holders who have VISA cards. Interpret and write this proportion as a conditional probability.
   b   The proportion of VISA cardholders who have Mastercards. Interpret and write this proportion as a conditional probability.
   c   Are the events *having a Mastercard* and *having a VISA* independent? Justify your answer.

4.19   Recall from Exercise 4.13 (page 169) that each month a brokerage house studies various compa-nies and rates each company's stock as being either "low risk" or "moderate to high risk." In a recent report, the brokerage house summarized its findings about 15 aerospace companies and 25 food retailers in the following table:

Company Type	Low Risk	Moderate to High Risk
Aerospace company	6	9
Food retailer	15	10

If we randomly select one of the total of 40 companies, find

 a The probability that the company's stock is moderate to high risk given that the firm is an aerospace company.

 b The probability that the company's stock is moderate to high risk given that the firm is a food retailer.

 c Determine if the *company type* is independent of the *level of risk* of the firm's stock.

4.20 John and Jane are married. The probability that John watches a certain television show is .4. The probability that Jane watches the show is .5. The probability that John watches the show, given that Jane does, is .7.

 a Find the probability that both John and Jane watch the show.

 b Find the probability that Jane watches the show, given that John does.

 c Do John and Jane watch the show independently of each other? Justify your answer.

4.21 In Exercise 4.20, find the probability that either John or Jane watches the show.

4.22 In the July 29, 2001, issue of the *Journal News* (Hamilton, Ohio), Lynn Elber of the Associated Press reported that "while 40 percent of American families own a television set with a V-chip installed to block designated programs with sex and violence, only 17 percent of those parents use the device."[2]

 a Use the report's results to find an estimate of the probability that a randomly selected American family has used a V-chip to block programs containing sex and violence.

 b According to the report, more than 50 percent of parents have used the TV rating system (TV-14, etc.) to control their children's TV viewing. How does this compare to the percentage using the V-chip?

4.23 According to the Associated Press report (in Exercise 4.22), 47 percent of parents who have purchased TV sets after V-chips became standard equipment in January 2000 are aware that their sets have V-chips, and of those who are aware of the option, 36 percent have programmed their V-chips. Using these results, find an estimate of the probability that a randomly selected parent who has bought a TV set since January 2000 has programmed the V-chip.

4.24 Fifteen percent of the employees in a company have managerial positions, and 25 percent of the employees in the company have MBA degrees. Also, 60 percent of the managers have MBA degrees. Using the probability formulas,

 a Find the proportion of employees who are managers and have MBA degrees.

 b Find the proportion of MBAs who are managers.

 c Are the events *being a manager* and *having an MBA* independent? Justify your answer.

4.25 In Exercise 4.24, find the proportion of employees who either have MBAs or are managers.

4.26 Consider Exercise 4.14 (page 169). Using the results in Table 4.4 (page 169), estimate the probability that a randomly selected 21- to 49-year-old consumer would

 a Give the phrase a rating of 4 or 5 given that the consumer is male; give the phrase a rating of 4 or 5 given that the consumer is female. Based on these results, is the appeal of the phrase among males much different from the appeal of the phrase among females? Explain.

 b Give the phrase a rating of 4 or 5, given that the consumer is in the 21–24 age group; given that the consumer is in the 25–34 age group; given that the consumer is in the 35–49 age group. Based on these results, which age group finds the phrase most appealing? Least appealing?

4.27 In a survey of 100 insurance claims, 40 are fire claims (*FIRE*), 16 of which are fraudulent (*FRAUD*). Also, there are a total of 40 fraudulent claims.

 a Construct a contingency table summarizing the claims data. Use the pairs of events *FIRE* and $\overline{FIRE}$, *FRAUD* and $\overline{FRAUD}$.

 b What proportion of the fire claims are fraudulent?

 c Are the events *a claim is fraudulent* and *a claim is a fire claim* independent? Use your probability of part *b* to prove your answer.

4.28 Recall from Exercise 4.3 (page 162) that two randomly selected customers are each asked to take a blind taste test and then to state which of three diet colas (marked as *A*, *B*, or *C*) he or she prefers. Suppose that cola *A*'s distributor claims that 80 percent of all people prefer cola *A* and that only 10 percent prefer each of colas *B* and *C*.

 a Assuming that the distributor's claim is true and that the two taste test participants make independent cola preference decisions, find the probability of each sample space outcome.

 b Find the probability that neither taste test participant will prefer cola *A*.

 c If, when the taste test is carried out, neither participant prefers cola *A*, use the probability you computed in part *b* to decide whether the distributor's claim seems valid. Explain.

---

[2]Source: *Journal News* (Hamilton, Ohio), July 29, 2001, p. C5.

4.29   A sprinkler system inside an office building has two types of activation devices, *D*1 and *D*2, which operate independently. When there is a fire, if either device operates correctly, the sprinkler system is turned on. In case of fire, the probability that *D*1 operates correctly is .95, and the probability that *D*2 operates correctly is .92. Find the probability that

    a   Both *D*1 and *D*2 will operate correctly.

    b   The sprinkler system will come on.

    c   The sprinkler system will fail.

4.30   A product is assembled using 10 different components, each of which must meet specifications for five different quality characteristics. Suppose that there is a .9973 probability that each individual specification will be met. Assuming that all 50 specifications are met independently, find the probability that the product meets all 50 specifications.

4.31   In Exercise 4.30, suppose that we wish to have a 99.73 percent chance that all 50 specifications will be met. If each specification will have the same chance of being met, how large must we make the probability of meeting each individual specification?

4.32   **THE SONG RATING CASE**

Suppose that the percentage of sampled listeners giving *Used To Love U* by John Legend the ratings 5, 4, 3, 2, 1, and *UNFAM* are, respectively, 18 percent, 27 percent, 28 percent, 8 percent, 10 percent, and 9 percent. Find an estimate of the percentage of all listeners who are familiar (*FAM*) with the song. Also, find estimates of $P(5 \mid FAM)$, $P(4 \mid FAM)$, $P(3 \mid FAM)$, $P(2 \mid FAM)$, and $P(1 \mid FAM)$.

4.33   In a murder trial in Los Angeles, the prosecution claims that the defendant was cut on the left middle finger at the murder scene, but the defendant claims the cut occurred in Chicago, the day after the murders had been committed. Because the defendant is a sports celebrity, many people noticed him before he reached Chicago. Twenty-two people saw him casually, one person on the plane to Chicago carefully studied his hands looking for a championship ring, and another person stood with him as he signed autographs and drove him from the airport to the hotel. None of these 24 people saw a cut on the defendant's finger. If in fact he was not cut at all, it would be extremely unlikely that he left blood at the murder scene.

    a   Since a person casually meeting the defendant would not be looking for a cut, assume that the probability is .9 that such a person would not have seen the cut, even if it was there. Furthermore, assume that the person who carefully looked at the defendant's hands had a .5 probability of not seeing the cut even if it was there and that the person who drove the defendant from the airport to the hotel had a .6 probability of not seeing the cut even if it was there. Given these assumptions, and also assuming that all 24 people looked at the defendant independently of each other, what is the probability that all 24 people would not have seen the cut, even if it was there?

    b   What is the probability that at least one of the 24 people would have seen the cut if it was there?

    c   Given the result of part *b* and given the fact that none of the 24 people saw a cut, do you think the defendant had a cut on his hand before he reached Chicago?

    d   How might we estimate what the assumed probabilities in *a* would actually be? (Note: This would not be easy.)

 Use Bayes' Theorem to update prior probabilities to posterior probabilities (Optional).

4.5 Bayes' Theorem (Optional) ● ● ●

Sometimes we have an initial or **prior probability** that an event will occur. Then, based on new information, we revise the prior probability to what is called a **posterior probability.** This revision can be done by using a theorem called **Bayes' theorem.**

EXAMPLE 4.15

HIV (Human Immunodeficiency Virus) is the virus that causes AIDS. Although many have proposed mandatory testing for HIV, statisticians have frequently spoken against such proposals. In this example, we use Bayes' theorem to see why.

Let HIV represent the event that a randomly selected American has the HIV virus, and let $\overline{HIV}$ represent the event that a randomly selected American does not have this virus. Since it is estimated that .6 percent of the American population has the HIV virus, $P(HIV) = .006$ and $P(\overline{HIV}) = .994$. A diagnostic test is used to attempt to detect whether a person has HIV. According to historical data, 99.9 percent of people with HIV receive a positive (*POS*) result when this test is administered, while 1 percent of people who do not have HIV receive a positive result. That is, $P(POS \mid HIV) = .999$ and $P(POS \mid \overline{HIV}) = .01$. If we administer the test to a randomly selected American (who may or may not have HIV) and the person receives a positive test result, what is the probability that the person actually has HIV? This probability is

$$P(HIV \mid POS) = \frac{P(HIV \cap POS)}{P(POS)}$$

The idea behind Bayes' theorem is that we can find $P(HIV \mid POS)$ by thinking as follows. A person will receive a positive result (POS) if the person receives a positive result and actually has HIV—that is, ($HIV \cap POS$)—or if the person receives a positive result and actually does not have HIV—that is, ($\overline{HIV} \cap POS$). Therefore,

$$P(POS) = P(HIV \cap POS) + P(\overline{HIV} \cap POS)$$

This implies that

$$
\begin{aligned}
P(HIV \mid POS) &= \frac{P(HIV \cap POS)}{P(POS)} \\
&= \frac{P(HIV \cap POS)}{P(HIV \cap POS) + P(\overline{HIV} \cap POS)} \\
&= \frac{P(HIV)P(POS \mid HIV)}{P(HIV)P(POS \mid HIV) + P(\overline{HIV})P(POS \mid \overline{HIV})} \\
&= \frac{.006(.999)}{.006(.999) + (.994)(.01)} = .38
\end{aligned}
$$

This probability says that, if all Americans were given a test for HIV, only 38 percent of the people who get a positive result would actually have HIV. That is, 62 percent of Americans identified as having HIV would actually be free of the virus! The reason for this rather surprising result is that, because so few people actually have HIV, the majority of people who test positive are people who are free of HIV and, therefore, erroneously test positive. This is why statisticians have spoken against proposals for mandatory HIV testing.

In the preceding example, there were two *states of nature*—HIV and $\overline{HIV}$—and two outcomes of the diagnostic test—POS and $\overline{POS}$. In general, there might be any number of states of nature and any number of experimental outcomes. This leads to a general statement of Bayes' theorem.

Bayes' Theorem

Let $S_1, S_2, \ldots, S_k$ be k mutually exclusive states of nature, one of which must be true, and suppose that $P(S_1)$, $P(S_2), \ldots, P(S_k)$ are the prior probabilities of these states of nature. Also, let E be a particular outcome of an experiment designed to help determine which state of nature is really true. Then, the **posterior probability** of a particular state of nature, say S_i, given the experimental outcome E, is

$$P(S_i \mid E) = \frac{P(S_i \cap E)}{P(E)} = \frac{P(S_i)P(E \mid S_i)}{P(E)}$$

where

$$P(E) = P(S_1 \cap E) + P(S_2 \cap E) + \cdots + P(S_k \cap E)$$

$$= P(S_1)P(E \mid S_1) + P(S_2)P(E \mid S_2) + \cdots + P(S_k)P(E \mid S_k)$$

Specifically, if there are two mutually exclusive states of nature, S_1 and S_2, one of which must be true, then

$$P(S_i \mid E) = \frac{P(S_i)P(E \mid S_i)}{P(S_1)P(E \mid S_1) + P(S_2)P(E \mid S_2)}$$

We have illustrated Bayes' theorem when there are two states of nature in Example 4.15. In the next example, we consider three states of nature.

EXAMPLE 4.16 The Oil Drilling Case

An oil company is attempting to decide whether to drill for oil on a particular site. There are three possible states of nature:

1   No oil (state of nature S_1, which we will denote as *none*)

2   Some oil (state of nature S_2, which we will denote as *some*)

3   Much oil (state of nature S_3, which we will denote as *much*)

Based on experience and knowledge concerning the site's geological characteristics, the oil company feels that the prior probabilities of these states of nature are as follows:

$$P(S_1 \equiv \text{none}) = .7 \qquad P(S_2 \equiv \text{some}) = .2 \qquad P(S_3 \equiv \text{much}) = .1$$

In order to obtain more information about the potential drilling site, the oil company can perform a seismic experiment, which has three readings—low, medium, and high. Moreover, information exists concerning the accuracy of the seismic experiment. The company's historical records tell us that

1   Of 100 past sites that were drilled and produced no oil, 4 sites gave a high reading. Therefore,

$$P(\text{high} \mid \text{none}) = \frac{4}{100} = .04$$

2   Of 400 past sites that were drilled and produced some oil, 8 sites gave a high reading. Therefore,

$$P(\text{high} \mid \text{some}) = \frac{8}{400} = .02$$

3   Of 300 past sites that were drilled and produced much oil, 288 sites gave a high reading. Therefore,

$$P(\text{high} \mid \text{much}) = \frac{288}{300} = .96$$

Intuitively, these conditional probabilities tell us that sites that produce no oil or some oil seldom give a high reading, while sites that produce much oil often give a high reading.

Now, suppose that when the company performs the seismic experiment on the site in question, it obtains a high reading. The previously given conditional probabilities suggest that, given this new information, the company might feel that the likelihood of much oil is higher than its prior probability $P(\text{much}) = .1$, and that the likelihoods of some oil and no oil are lower than the prior probabilities $P(\text{some}) = .2$ and $P(\text{none}) = .7$. To be more specific, we wish to *revise the prior probabilities* of no, some, and much oil to what we call *posterior probabilities*. We can do this by using Bayes' theorem as follows.

If we wish to compute $P(\text{none} \mid \text{high})$, we first calculate

$$P(\text{high}) = P(\text{none} \cap \text{high}) + P(\text{some} \cap \text{high}) + P(\text{much} \cap \text{high})$$
$$= P(\text{none})P(\text{high} \mid \text{none}) + P(\text{some})P(\text{high} \mid \text{some}) + P(\text{much})P(\text{high} \mid \text{much})$$
$$= (.7)(.04) + (.2)(.02) + (.1)(.96) = .128$$

Then Bayes' theorem says that

$$P(\text{none} \mid \text{high}) = \frac{P(\text{none} \cap \text{high})}{P(\text{high})} = \frac{P(\text{none})P(\text{high} \mid \text{none})}{P(\text{high})} = \frac{.7(.04)}{.128} = .21875$$

Similarly, we can compute $P(\text{some} \mid \text{high})$ and $P(\text{much} \mid \text{high})$ as follows.

$$P(\text{some} \mid \text{high}) = \frac{P(\text{some} \cap \text{high})}{P(\text{high})} = \frac{P(\text{some})P(\text{high} \mid \text{some})}{P(\text{high})} = \frac{.2(.02)}{.128} = .03125$$

$$P(\text{much} \mid \text{high}) = \frac{P(\text{much} \cap \text{high})}{P(\text{high})} = \frac{P(\text{much})P(\text{high} \mid \text{much})}{P(\text{high})} = \frac{.1(.96)}{.128} = .75$$

These revised probabilities tell us that, given that the seismic experiment gives a high reading, the revised probabilities of no, some, and much oil are .21875, .03125, and .75, respectively.

Since the posterior probability of much oil is .75, we might conclude that we should drill on the oil site. However, this decision should also be based on economic considerations. The science of **decision theory** provides various criteria for making such a decision. An introduction to decision theory can be found in Bowerman, O'Connell, and Murphree (2011).

In this section we have only introduced Bayes' theorem. There is an entire subject called **Bayesian statistics,** which uses Bayes' theorem to update prior belief about a probability or population parameter to posterior belief. The use of Bayesian statistics is controversial in the case where the prior belief is largely based on subjective considerations, because many statisticians do not believe that we should base decisions on subjective considerations. Realistically, however, we all do this in our daily lives. For example, how each of us viewed the evidence in the O. J. Simpson murder trial had a great deal to do with our prior beliefs about both O. J. Simpson and the police.

Exercises for Section 4.5

CONCEPTS

4.34 What is a prior probability? What is a posterior probability?

4.35 Explain the purpose behind using Bayes' theorem.

connect

METHODS AND APPLICATIONS

4.36 Suppose that A_1, A_2, and B are events where A_1 and A_2 are mutually exclusive and

$$P(A_1) = .8 \qquad P(B|A_1) = .1$$
$$P(A_2) = .2 \qquad P(B|A_2) = .3$$

Use this information to find $P(A_1|B)$ and $P(A_2|B)$.

4.37 Suppose that A_1, A_2, A_3, and B are events where A_1, A_2, and A_3 are mutually exclusive and

$$P(A_1) = .2 \qquad P(A_2) = .5 \qquad P(A_3) = .3$$
$$P(B|A_1) = .02 \qquad P(B|A_2) = .05 \qquad P(B|A_3) = .04$$

Use this information to find $P(A_1|B)$, $P(A_2|B)$ and $P(A_3|B)$.

4.38 Again consider the diagnostic test for HIV discussed in Example 4.15 (page 178) and recall that $P(POS|HIV) = .999$ and $P(POS|\overline{HIV}) = .01$, where POS denotes a positive test result. Assuming that the percentage of people who have HIV is 1 percent, recalculate the probability that a randomly selected person has HIV, given that his or her test result is positive.

4.39 A department store is considering a new credit policy to try to reduce the number of customers defaulting on payments. A suggestion is made to discontinue credit to any customer who has been one week or more late with his/her payment at least twice. Past records show 95 percent of defaults were late at least twice. Also, 3 percent of all customers default, and 30 percent of those who have not defaulted have had at least two late payments.

  a Find the probability that a customer with at least two late payments will default.

  b Based on part *a*, should the policy be adopted? Explain.

4.40 A company administers an "aptitude test for managers" to aid in selecting new management trainees. Prior experience suggests that 60 percent of all applicants for management trainee positions would be successful if they were hired. Furthermore, past experience with the aptitude test indicates that 85 percent of applicants who turn out to be successful managers pass the test and 90 percent of applicants who turn out not to be successful managers fail the test.

  a If an applicant passes the "aptitude test for managers," what is the probability that the applicant will succeed in a management position?

  b Based on your answer to part *a*, do you think that the "aptitude test for managers" is a valuable way to screen applicants for management trainee positions? Explain.

4.41 **THE OIL DRILLING CASE**

    Recall that the prior probabilities of no oil (*none*), some oil (*some*), and much oil (*much*) are:

$$P(\text{none}) = .7 \qquad P(\text{some}) = .2 \qquad P(\text{much}) = .1$$

Because each sample is specified only with respect to which returns are contained in the sample, and therefore not with respect to the different orders in which the returns can be randomly selected, each sample is called a **combination of $n = 3$ stock returns selected from $N = 6$ stock returns.** In general, the following result can be proven:

A Counting Rule for Combinations

The number of combinations of n items that can be selected from N items is

$$\binom{N}{n} = \frac{N!}{n!\,(N - n)!}$$

where

$$N! = N(N - 1)(N - 2) \cdots 1$$
$$n! = n(n - 1)(n - 2) \cdots 1$$

Note: 0! is defined to be 1.

For example, the number of combinations of $n = 3$ stock returns that can be selected from the six previously discussed stock returns is

$$\binom{6}{3} = \frac{6!}{3!(6 - 3)!} = \frac{6!}{3!\,3!} = \frac{6 \cdot 5 \cdot 4\,(3 \cdot 2 \cdot 1)}{(3 \cdot 2 \cdot 1)\,(3 \cdot 2 \cdot 1)} = 20$$

The 20 combinations are listed above. As another example, the Ohio lottery system uses the random selection of 6 numbers from a group of 47 numbers to determine each week's lottery winner. There are

$$\binom{47}{6} = \frac{47!}{6!\,(47 - 6)!} = \frac{47 \cdot 46 \cdot 45 \cdot 44 \cdot 43 \cdot 42\,(41!)}{6 \cdot 5 \cdot 4 \cdot 3 \cdot 2 \cdot 1\,(41!)} = 10{,}737{,}573$$

combinations of 6 numbers that can be selected from 47 numbers. Therefore, if you buy a lottery ticket and pick six numbers, the probability that this ticket will win the lottery is $1/10{,}737{,}573$.

Exercises for Section 4.6

CONCEPTS

connect

4.45 Explain why counting rules are useful.

4.46 Explain when it is appropriate to use the counting rule for multiple-step experiments.

4.47 Explain when it is appropriate to use the counting rule for combinations.

METHODS AND APPLICATIONS

4.48 A credit union has two branches; each branch has two departments, and each department has four employees. How many total people does the credit union employ? If you work for the credit union, and one employee is randomly selected to go to a convention, what is the probability that you will be chosen?

4.49 Construct a tree diagram (like Figure 4.7) for the situation described in Exercise 4.48.

4.50 How many combinations of two high-risk stocks could you randomly select from eight high-risk stocks? If you did this, what is the probability that you would obtain the two highest-returning stocks?

4.51 A pop quiz consists of three true–false questions and three multiple choice questions. Each multiple choice question has five possible answers. If a student blindly guesses the answer to every question, what is the probability that the student will correctly answer all six questions?

4.52 A company employs eight people and plans to select a group of three of these employees to receive advanced training. How many ways can the group of three employees be selected?

4.53 The company of Exercise 4.52 employs Mr. Withrow, Mr. Church, Ms. David, Ms. Henry, Mr. Fielding, Mr. Smithson, Ms. Penny, and Mr. Butler. If the three employees who will receive advanced training are selected at random, what is the probability that Mr. Church, Ms. Henry, and Mr. Butler will be selected for advanced training?

Chapter Summary

In this chapter we studied **probability.** We began by defining an **event** to be an experimental outcome that may or may not occur and by defining the **probability of an event** to be a number that measures the likelihood that the event will occur. We learned that a probability is often interpreted as a **long-run relative frequency,** and we saw that probabilities can be found by examining **sample spaces** and by using **probability rules.** We learned several important probability rules—**addition rules, multiplication rules,** and **the rule of complements.** We also studied a special kind of probability called a **conditional probability,** which is the probability that one event will occur given that another event occurs, and we used probabilities to define **independent events.** We concluded this chapter by studying two optional topics. The first of these was **Bayes' theorem,** which can be used to update a **prior** probability to a **posterior** probability based on receiving new information. Second, we studied **counting rules** that are helpful when we wish to count sample space outcomes.

Glossary of Terms

Bayes' theorem: A theorem (formula) that is used to compute posterior probabilities by revising prior probabilities. (page 179)

Bayesian statistics: An area of statistics that uses Bayes' Theorem to update prior belief about a probability or population parameter to posterior belief. (page 181)

complement (of an event): If A is an event, the complement of A is the event that A will not occur. (page 163)

conditional probability: The probability that one event will occur given that we know that another event occurs. (page 170)

decision theory: An approach that helps decision makers to make intelligent choices. (page 181)

dependent events: When the probability of one event is influenced by whether another event occurs, the events are said to be dependent. (page 173)

event: A set of one or more sample space outcomes. (page 158)

experiment: A process of observation that has an uncertain outcome. (page 155)

independent events: When the probability of one event is not influenced by whether another event occurs, the events are said to be independent. (page 173)

mutually exclusive events: Events that have no sample space outcomes in common, and, therefore, cannot occur simultaneously. (page 166)

prior probability: The initial probability that an event will occur. (page 178)

probability (of an event): A number that measures the chance, or likelihood, that an event will occur when an experiment is carried out. (page 155)

posterior probability: A revised probability obtained by updating a prior probability after receiving new information. (page 178)

sample space: The set of all possible experimental outcomes (sample space outcomes). (page 157)

sample space outcome: A distinct outcome of an experiment (that is, an element in the sample space). (page 157)

subjective probability: A probability assessment that is based on experience, intuitive judgment, or expertise. (page 156)

Important Formulas

Probabilities when all sample space outcomes are equally likely: page 161

The rule of complements: page 163

The addition rule for two events: page 166

The addition rule for two mutually exclusive events: page 167

The addition rule for N mutually exclusive events: page 168

Conditional probability: page 171

The general multiplication rule: page 171

Independence: page 173

The multiplication rule for two independent events: page 174

The multiplication rule for N independent events: page 174

Bayes' theorem: page 179

Counting rule for multiple-step experiments: page 182

Counting rule for combinations: page 184

Supplementary Exercises

Exercises 4.54 through 4.57 are based on the following situation: An investor holds two stocks, each of which can rise (R), remain unchanged (U), or decline (D) on any particular day.

4.54 Construct a tree diagram showing all possible combined movements for both stocks on a particular day (for instance, RR, RD, and so on, where the first letter denotes the movement of the first stock, and the second letter denotes the movement of the second stock).

4.55 If all outcomes are equally likely, find the probability that both stocks rise; that both stocks decline; that exactly one stock declines.

4.56 Find the probabilities you found in Exercise 4.55 by assuming that for each stock $P(R) = .6$, $P(U) = .1$, and $P(D) = .3$, and assuming that the two stocks move independently.

4.57 Assume that for the first stock (on a particular day)

$$P(R) = .4, \quad P(U) = .2, \quad P(D) = .4$$

and that for the second stock (on a particular day)

$$P(R) = .8, \quad P(U) = .1, \quad P(D) = .1$$

Assuming that these stocks move independently, find the probability that both stocks decline; the probability that exactly one stock rises; the probability that exactly one stock is unchanged; the probability that both stocks rise.

The Bureau of Labor Statistics reports on a variety of employment statistics. "College Enrollment and Work Activity of 2004 High School Graduates" provides information on high school graduates by gender, by race, and by labor force participation as of October 2004.[3] (All numbers are in thousands.) The following two tables provide information on the "Labor force status of persons 16 to 24 years old by educational attainment and gender, October 2004." Using the information contained in the tables, do Exercises 4.58 through 4.62. **DS** LabForce

Women, Age 16 to 24	Civilian Labor Force Employed	Civilian Labor Force Unemployed	Not in Labor Force	Row Total
< High School	662	205	759	1,626
HS degree	2,050	334	881	3,265
Some college	1,352	126	321	1,799
Bachelors degree or more	921	55	105	1,081
Column Total	4,985	720	2,066	7,771

Men, Age 16 to 24	Civilian Labor Force Employed	Civilian Labor Force Unemployed	Not in Labor Force	Row Total
< High School	1,334	334	472	2,140
HS degree	3,110	429	438	3,977
Some college	1,425	106	126	1,657
Bachelors degree or more	708	37	38	783
Column Total	6,577	906	1,074	8,557

4.58 Find the probability that a randomly selected female aged 16 to 24 is in the civilian labor force, if she has a high school degree. **DS** LabForce

4.59 Find the probability that a randomly selected female aged 16 to 24 is in the civilian labor force, if she has a bachelor's degree or more. **DS** LabForce

4.60 Find the probability that a randomly selected female aged 16 to 24 is employed, if she is in the civilian labor force and has a high school degree. **DS** LabForce

4.61 Find the probability that a randomly selected female aged 16 to 24 is employed, if she is in the civilian labor force and has a bachelors degree or more. **DS** LabForce

4.62 Repeat Exercises 4.58 through 4.61 for a randomly selected male aged 16 to 24. In general, do the tables imply that labor force status and employment status depend upon educational attainment? Explain your answer. **DS** LabForce

Suppose that in a survey of 1,000 U.S. residents, 721 residents believed that the amount of violent television programming had increased over the past 10 years, 454 residents believed that the overall quality of television programming had decreased over the past 10 years, and 362 residents believed both. Use this information to do Exercises 4.63 through 4.69.

4.63 What proportion of the 1,000 U.S. residents believed that the amount of violent programming had increased over the past 10 years?

[3]Source: *College Enrollment and Work Activity of 2004 High School Graduates*, Table 2, "Labor force status of persons 16 to 24 years old by school enrollment, educational attainment, sex, race, and Hispanic or Latino ethnicity, October 2004," www.bls.gov.

4.64 What proportion of the 1,000 U.S. residents believed that the overall quality of programming had decreased over the past 10 years?

4.65 What proportion of the 1,000 U.S. residents believed that both the amount of violent programming had increased and the overall quality of programming had decreased over the past 10 years?

4.66 What proportion of the 1,000 U.S. residents believed that either the amount of violent programming had increased or the overall quality of programming had decreased over the past 10 years?

4.67 What proportion of the U.S. residents who believed that the amount of violent programming had increased believed that the overall quality of programming had decreased?

4.68 What proportion of the U.S. residents who believed that the overall quality of programming had decreased believed that the amount of violent programming had increased?

4.69 What sort of dependence seems to exist between whether U.S. residents believed that the amount of violent programming had increased and whether U.S. residents believed that the overall quality of programming had decreased? Explain your answer.

4.70 Enterprise Industries has been running a television advertisement for Fresh liquid laundry detergent. When a survey was conducted, .21 of the individuals surveyed had purchased Fresh, .41 of the individuals surveyed had recalled seeing the advertisement, and .13 of the individuals surveyed had purchased Fresh and recalled seeing the advertisement.
  a What proportion of the individuals surveyed who recalled seeing the advertisement had purchased Fresh?
  b Based on your answer to part a, does the advertisement seem to have been effective? Explain.

4.71 A company employs 400 salespeople. Of these, 83 received a bonus last year, 100 attended a special sales training program at the beginning of last year, and 42 both attended the special sales training program and received a bonus. (Note: the bonus was based totally on sales performance.)
  a What proportion of the 400 salespeople received a bonus last year?
  b What proportion of the 400 salespeople attended the special sales training program at the beginning of last year?
  c What proportion of the 400 salespeople both attended the special sales training program and received a bonus?
  d What proportion of the salespeople who attended the special sales training program received a bonus?
  e Based on your answers to parts a and d, does the special sales training program seem to have been effective? Explain your answer.

4.72 Suppose that A and B are events and that $P(A)$ and $P(B)$ are both positive.
  a If A and B are mutually exclusive, what is $P(A \cap B)$?
  b If A and B are independent events, explain why $P(A \cap B)$ is positive.
  c Can two mutually exclusive events, each having a positive probability of occurrence, also be independent? Prove your answer using your answers to parts a and b.

4.73 On any given day, the probability that the Ohio River at Cincinnati is polluted by a carbon tetrachloride spill is .10. Each day, a test is conducted to determine whether the river is polluted by carbon tetrachloride. This test has proved correct 80 percent of the time. Suppose that on a particular day the test indicates carbon tetrachloride pollution. What is the probability that such pollution actually exists?

4.74 A marketing major will interview for an internship with a major consumer products manufacturer/distributor. Before the interview, the marketing major feels that the chances of being offered an internship are 40 percent. Suppose that of the students who have been offered internships with this company, 90 percent had good interviews, and that of the students who have not been offered internships, 50 percent had good interviews. If the marketing major has a good interview, what is the probability that he or she will be offered an internship?

4.75 In the book *Making Hard Decisions: An Introduction to Decision Analysis,* Robert T. Clemen presents an example in which he discusses the 1982 John Hinckley trial. In describing the case, Clemen says:

> In 1982 John Hinckley was on trial, accused of having attempted to kill President Reagan. During Hinckley's trial, Dr. Daniel R. Weinberger told the court that when individuals diagnosed as schizophrenics were given computerized axial tomography (CAT) scans, the scans showed brain atrophy in 30% of the cases compared with only 2% of the scans done on normal people. Hinckley's defense attorney wanted to introduce as evidence Hinckley's CAT scan, which showed brain atrophy. The defense argued that the presence of atrophy strengthened the case that Hinckley suffered from mental illness.

a   Approximately 1.5 percent of the people in the United States suffer from schizophrenia. If we consider the prior probability of schizophrenia to be .015, use the information given to find the probability that a person has schizophrenia given that a person's CAT scan shows brain atrophy.

b   John Hinckley's CAT scan showed brain atrophy. Discuss whether your answer to part *a* helps or hurts the case that Hinckley suffered from mental illness.

c   It can be argued that .015 is not a reasonable prior probability of schizophrenia. This is because .015 is the probability that a randomly selected U.S. citizen has schizophrenia. However, John Hinckley was not a randomly selected U.S. citizen. Rather, he was accused of attempting to assassinate the president. Therefore, it might be reasonable to assess a higher prior probability of schizophrenia. Suppose you are a juror who believes there is only a 10 percent chance that Hinckley suffers from schizophrenia. Using .10 as the prior probability of schizophrenia, find the probability that a person has schizophrenia given that a person's CAT scan shows brain atrophy.

d   If you are a juror with a prior probability of .10 that John Hinckley suffers from schizophrenia and given your answer to part *c*, does the fact that Hinckley's CAT scan showed brain atrophy help the case that Hinckley suffered from mental illness?

e   If you are a juror with a prior probability of .25 that Hinckley suffers from schizophrenia, find the probability of schizophrenia given that Hinckley's CAT scan showed brain atrophy. In this situation, how strong is the case that Hinckley suffered from mental illness?

4.76   Below we give two contingency tables of data from reports submitted by airlines to the U.S. Department of Transportation. The data concern the numbers of on-time and delayed flights for Alaska Airlines and America West Airlines at five major airports.   **DS** AirDelays

Alaska Airlines	On Time	Delayed	Total		America West	On Time	Delayed	Total
Los Angeles	497	62	559		Los Angeles	694	117	811
Phoenix	221	12	233		Phoenix	4,840	415	5,255
San Diego	212	20	232		San Diego	383	65	448
San Francisco	503	102	605		San Francisco	320	129	449
Seattle	1,841	305	2,146		Seattle	201	61	262
Total	3,274	501	3,775		Total	6,438	787	7,225

a   What percentage of all Alaska Airlines flights were delayed? That is, use the data to estimate the probability that an Alaska Airlines flight will be delayed. Do the same for America West Airlines. Which airline does best overall?

b   For Alaska Airlines find the percentage of delayed flights at each airport. That is, use the data to estimate each of the probabilities $P(\text{delayed} \mid \text{Los Angeles})$, $P(\text{delayed} \mid \text{Phoenix})$, and so on. Then do the same for America West Airlines. Which airline does best at each individual airport?

c   We find that America West Airlines does worse at every airport, yet America West does best overall. This seems impossible, but it is true! By looking carefully at the data, explain how this can happen. Hint: Consider the weather in Phoenix and Seattle. (This exercise is an example of what is called *Simpson's paradox*.)

4.77 Internet Exercise

What is the age, gender, and ethnic composition of U.S. college students? As background for its 1995 study of college students and their risk behaviors, the Centers for Disease Control and Prevention collected selected demographic data—age, gender, and ethnicity—about college students. A report on the 1995 National Health Risk Behavior Survey can be found at the CDC website by going directly to http://www.cdc.gov/mmwr/preview/mmwrhtml/00049859.htm. This report includes a large number of tables, the first of which summarizes the demographic information for the sample of $n = 4609$ college students. An excerpt of Table 1 is given on the right.

Using conditional probabilities, discuss (a) the dependence between age and gender and (b) the dependence between age and ethnicity for U.S. college students.

DS CDCData

TABLE 1. Demographic Characteristics of Undergraduate College Students Aged >=18 Years, by Age Group — United States, National College Health Risk Behavior Survey, 1995

Category	Total (%)	Age Group (%) 18-24 Years	>=25 Years
Total	--	63.6	36.4
Sex			
Female	55.5	52.0	61.8
Male	44.5	48.0	38.2
Race/ethnicity			
White*	72.8	70.9	76.1
Black*	10.3	10.5	9.6
Hispanic	7.1	6.9	7.4
Other	9.9	11.7	6.9

at, perhaps, 26 mpg) to an interval of numbers on the real line. We cannot count or list the numbers in such an interval because they are infinitesimally close together. That is, given any two numbers in an interval on the real line, there is always another number between them. To understand this, try listing the mileages starting with 26 mpg. Would the next mileage be 26.1 mpg? No, because we could obtain a mileage of 26.05 mpg. Would 26.05 mpg be the next mileage? No, because we could obtain a mileage of 26.025 mpg. We could continue this line of reasoning indefinitely. That is, whatever value we would try to list as the *next mileage,* there would always be another mileage between this *next mileage* and 26 mpg.

Some other examples of continuous random variables are

1   The temperature (in degrees Fahrenheit) of a cup of coffee served at a McDonald's restaurant.

2   The weight (in ounces) of strawberry preserves dispensed by an automatic filling machine into a 16-ounce jar.

3   The time (in minutes) that a customer in a store must wait to receive a credit card authorization.

4   The interest rate (in percent) charged for mortgage loans at a bank.

Exercises for Section 5.1

CONCEPTS

5.1   Explain the concept of a random variable.

5.2   Explain how the values of a discrete random variable differ from the values of a continuous random variable.

5.3   Classify each of the following random variables as discrete or continuous:
   a x = the number of girls born to a couple who will have three children.
   b x = the number of defects found on an automobile at final inspection.
   c x = the weight (in ounces) of the sandwich meat placed on a submarine sandwich.
   d x = the number of incorrect lab procedures conducted at a hospital during a particular week.
   e x = the number of customers served during a given day at a drive-through window.
   f x = the time needed by a clerk to complete a task.
   g x = the temperature of a pizza oven at a particular time.

LO2 Find a discrete probability distribution and compute its mean and standard deviation.

5.2 Discrete Probability Distributions ◐ ● ●

The value assumed by a discrete random variable depends on the outcome of an experiment. Because the outcome of the experiment will be uncertain, the value assumed by the random variable will also be uncertain. However, it is often useful to know the probabilities that are associated with the different values that the random variable can take on. That is, we often wish to know the random variable's **probability distribution.**

> The **probability distribution** of a discrete random variable is a table, graph, or formula that gives the probability associated with each possible value that the random variable can assume.

We denote the probability distribution of the discrete random variable x as $p(x)$. As will be demonstrated in the following example, we can sometimes use the sample space of an experiment and probability rules to find the probability distribution of a random variable.

EXAMPLE 5.2

Consider the pop quiz consisting of three true–false questions. Remember that the sample space when a student takes such a quiz consists of the outcomes

$$CCC \quad CCI \quad CIC \quad ICC$$
$$CII \quad ICI \quad IIC \quad III$$

We now define the random variable x to be the number of questions that the student answers correctly. Here x can assume the values 0, 1, 2, or 3. That is, the student could answer anywhere between 0 and 3 questions correctly. In Examples 4.3 and 4.5 we assumed that the

TABLE 5.1 Finding the Probability Distribution of $x =$ the Number of Questions Answered Correctly When the Student Studies and Has a 90 Percent Chance of Answering Each Question Correctly

Value of $x =$ the Number of Correct Answers	Sample Space Outcomes Corresponding to Value of x	Probability of Sample Space Outcome	$p(x) =$ Probability of the Value of x
$x = 0$ (no correct answers)	III	$(.1)(.1)(.1) = .001$	$p(0) = .001$
$x = 1$ (one correct answer)	CII	$(.9)(.1)(.1) = .009$	$p(1) = .009 + .009 + .009 = .027$
	ICI	$(.1)(.9)(.1) = .009$	
	IIC	$(.1)(.1)(.9) = .009$	
$x = 2$ (two correct answers)	CCI	$(.9)(.9)(.1) = .081$	$p(2) = .081 + .081 + .081 = .243$
	CIC	$(.9)(.1)(.9) = .081$	
	ICC	$(.1)(.9)(.9) = .081$	
$x = 3$ (three correct answers)	CCC	$(.9)(.9)(.9) = .729$	$p(3) = .729$

student is totally unprepared for the quiz and thus has only a .5 probability of answering each question correctly. We now assume that the student studies and has a .9 probability of answering each question correctly. Table 5.1 summarizes finding the probabilities associated with each of the values of x (0, 1, 2, and 3). As an example of the calculations, consider finding the probability that x equals 2. Two questions will be answered correctly if and only if we obtain one of the sample space outcomes

$$CCI \quad CIC \quad ICC$$

Assuming that the three questions will be answered independently, these sample space outcomes have probabilities

$$P(CCI) = (.9)(.9)(.1) = .081$$
$$P(CIC) = (.9)(.1)(.9) = .081$$
$$P(ICC) = (.1)(.9)(.9) = .081$$

Therefore,

$$P(x = 2) = P(CCI) + P(CIC) + P(ICC)$$
$$= .081 + .081 + .081$$
$$= .243$$

Similarly, we can obtain probabilities associated with $x = 0$, $x = 1$, and $x = 3$. The probability distribution of x is summarized as follows:

x, Number of Questions Answered Correctly	$p(x)$, Probability of x
0	$p(0) = P(x = 0) = .001$
1	$p(1) = P(x = 1) = .027$
2	$p(2) = P(x = 2) = .243$
3	$p(3) = P(x = 3) = .729$

Notice that the probabilities in this probability distribution sum to $.001 + .027 + .243 + .729 = 1$.

To show the advantage of studying, note that the above probability distribution says that if the student has a .9 probability of answering each question correctly, then the probability that the student will answer all three questions correctly is .729. Furthermore, the probability that the student will answer *at least* two out of three questions correctly is (since the events $x = 2$ and $x = 3$ are mutually exclusive)

$$P(x \geq 2) = P(x = 2 \text{ or } x = 3)$$
$$= P(x = 2) + P(x = 3)$$
$$= .243 + .729$$
$$= .972$$

By contrast, we saw in Example 4.5 that if the student is totally unprepared and has only a .5 probability of answering each question correctly, then the probabilities that the student will answer zero, one, two, and three questions correctly are, respectively, 1/8, 3/8, 3/8, and 1/8. Therefore, the probability that the unprepared student will answer all three questions correctly is only 1/8, and the probability that this student will answer at least two out of three questions correctly is only $(3/8 + 1/8) = .5$.

In general, a discrete probability distribution $p(x)$ must satisfy two conditions:

Properties of a Discrete Probability Distribution $p(x)$

A **discrete probability distribution $p(x)$** must be such that

1 $p(x) \geq 0$ for each value of x

2 $\sum_{\text{All } x} p(x) = 1$

The first of these conditions says that each probability in a probability distribution must be zero or positive. The second condition says that the probabilities in a probability distribution must sum to 1. Looking at the probability distribution illustrated in Example 5.2, we can see that these properties are satisfied.

Often it is not possible to examine the entire sample space of an experiment. In such a case we sometimes collect data that will allow us to estimate the probabilities in a probability distribution.

EXAMPLE 5.3

Recall that Sound City sells the TrueSound-XL car radio, and define the random variable x to be the number of such radios sold in a particular week. In order to know the true probabilities of the various values of x, we would have to observe sales during all of the (potentially infinite number of) weeks in which the TrueSound-XL radio could be sold. That is, if we consider an experiment in which we randomly select a week and observe sales of the TrueSound-XL, the sample space would consist of a potentially infinite number of equally likely weeks. Obviously, it is not possible to examine this entire sample space.

Suppose, however, that Sound City has kept historical records of TrueSound-XL sales during the last 100 weeks. These records tell us that

1 No radios have been sold in 3 (that is, $3/100 = .03$) of the weeks.

2 One radio has been sold in 20 (that is, .20) of the weeks.

3 Two radios have been sold in 50 (that is, .50) of the weeks.

4 Three radios have been sold in 20 (that is, .20) of the weeks.

5 Four radios have been sold in 5 (that is, .05) of the weeks.

6 Five radios have been sold in 2 (that is, .02) of the weeks.

7 No more than five radios were sold in any of the past 100 weeks.

It follows that we might *estimate* that the probability distribution of x, the number of TrueSound-XL radios sold during a particular week at Sound City, is as shown in Table 5.2. A graph of this distribution is shown in Figure 5.1.

TABLE 5.2   An Estimate (Based on 100 Weeks of Historical Data) of the Probability Distribution of x, the Number of TrueSound-XL Radios Sold at Sound City in a Week

x, Number of Radios Sold	$p(x)$, the Probability of x
0	$p(0) = P(x = 0) = 3/100 = .03$
1	$p(1) = P(x = 1) = 20/100 = .20$
2	$p(2) = P(x = 2) = 50/100 = .50$
3	$p(3) = P(x = 3) = 20/100 = .20$
4	$p(4) = P(x = 4) = 5/100 = .05$
5	$p(5) = P(x = 5) = 2/100 = .02$

FIGURE 5.1   **A Graph of the Probability Distribution of *x*, the Number of TrueSound-XL Radios Sold at Sound City in a Week**

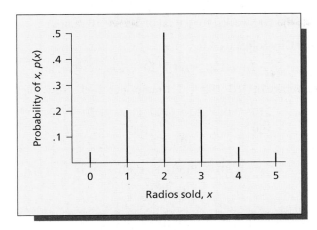

Finally, it is reasonable to use the historical sales data from the past 100 weeks to estimate the true probabilities associated with the various numbers of radios sold if the sales process remains stable over time and is not seasonal (that is, if radio sales are not higher at one time of the year than at others).

Suppose that the experiment described by a random variable *x* is repeated an indefinitely large number of times. If the values of the random variable *x* observed on the repetitions are recorded, we would obtain the population of all possible observed values of the random variable *x*. This population has a mean, which we denote as μ_x and which we sometimes call the **expected value of *x*.** In order to calculate μ_x, we multiply each value of *x* by its probability $p(x)$ and then sum the resulting products over all possible values of *x*.

The Mean, or Expected Value, of a Discrete Random Variable

The **mean**, or **expected value**, of a discrete random variable *x* is

$$\mu_x = \sum_{\text{All }x} xp(x)$$

In the next example we illustrate how to calculate μ_x, and we reason that the calculation really does give the mean of all possible observed values of the random variable *x*.

EXAMPLE 5.4

Remember that Table 5.2 gives the probability distribution of *x*, the number of TrueSound-XL radios sold in a week at Sound City. Using this distribution, it follows that

$$
\begin{aligned}
\mu_x &= \sum_{\text{All }x} xp(x) \\
&= 0p(0) + 1p(1) + 2p(2) + 3p(3) + 4p(4) + 5p(5) \\
&= 0(.03) + 1(.20) + 2(.50) + 3(.20) + 4(.05) + 5(.02) \\
&= 2.1
\end{aligned}
$$

To see that such a calculation gives the mean of all possible observed values of *x*, recall from Example 5.3 that the probability distribution in Table 5.2 was estimated from historical records of TrueSound-XL sales during the last 100 weeks. Also recall that these historical records tell us that during the last 100 weeks Sound City sold

1   Zero radios in 3 of the 100 weeks, for a total of 0(3) = 0 radios

2   One radio in 20 of the 100 weeks, for a total of 1(20) = 20 radios

3   Two radios in 50 of the 100 weeks, for a total of 2(50) = 100 radios

4   Three radios in 20 of the 100 weeks, for a total of 3(20) = 60 radios

5   Four radios in 5 of the 100 weeks, for a total of 4(5) = 20 radios

6   Five radios in 2 of the 100 weeks, for a total of 5(2) = 10 radios

In other words, Sound City sold a total of

$$0 + 20 + 100 + 60 + 20 + 10 = 210 \text{ radios}$$

in 100 weeks, or an average of 210/100 = 2.1 radios per week. Now, the average

$$\frac{210}{100} = \frac{0 + 20 + 100 + 60 + 20 + 10}{100}$$

can be written as

$$\frac{0(3) + 1(20) + 2(50) + 3(20) + 4(5) + 5(2)}{100}$$

which can be rewritten as

$$0\left(\frac{3}{100}\right) + 1\left(\frac{20}{100}\right) + 2\left(\frac{50}{100}\right) + 3\left(\frac{20}{100}\right) + 4\left(\frac{5}{100}\right) + 5\left(\frac{2}{100}\right)$$
$$= 0(.03) + 1(.20) + 2(.50) + 3(.20) + 4(.05) + 5(.02)$$

which equals $\mu_x = 2.1$. That is, if observed sales values occur with relative frequencies equal to those specified by the probability distribution in Table 5.2, then the average number of radios sold per week is equal to the expected value of x.

Of course, if we observe radio sales for another 100 weeks, the relative frequencies of the observed sales values would not (unless we are very lucky) be exactly as specified by the estimated probabilities in Table 5.2. Rather, the observed relative frequencies would differ somewhat from the estimated probabilities in Table 5.2, and the average number of radios sold per week would not exactly equal $\mu_x = 2.1$ (although the average would likely be close). However, the point is this: If the probability distribution in Table 5.2 were the true probability distribution of weekly radio sales, and if we were to observe radio sales for an indefinitely large number of weeks, then we would observe sales values with relative frequencies that are exactly equal to those specified by the probabilities in Table 5.2. In this case, when we calculate the expected value of x to be $\mu_x = 2.1$, we are saying that *in the long run* (that is, over an indefinitely large number of weeks) Sound City would average selling 2.1 TrueSound-XL radios per week.

As another example, again consider Example 5.2, and let the random variable x denote the number of the three true–false questions that the student who studies answers correctly. Using the probability distribution shown in Table 5.1, the expected value of x is

$$\mu_x = 0(.001) + 1(.027) + 2(.243) + 3(.729)$$
$$= 2.7$$

This expected value says that if a student takes a large number of three-question true–false quizzes and has a .9 probability of answering any single question correctly, then the student will average approximately 2.7 correct answers per quiz.

EXAMPLE 5.5 The Song Rating Case

In this example we will compute the *popularity* index for the song *Poker Face* by Lady GaGa. Recall from Example 4.14 (pages 175–176) that the song rating service had listeners rate this song as a 5, 4, 3, 2, 1, or *UNFAM*. Also recall that we estimated the proportions of listeners *familiar with the song* who would give the song ratings of 5, 4, 3, 2, and 1 to be, respectively, .43, .21, .22, .07, and .07. Now, it is reasonable to assign the numerical values 1 through 5 to the ratings 1 through 5 (this sort of thing is done when colleges assign the numerical values 4 through 0 to the grades A through F). Therefore, we can regard x, the song's rating by a

TABLE 5.3 **An Estimate of the Probability Distribution of x, the Rating of *Poker Face* by Lady GaGa by a Randomly Selected Listener Who Is Familiar with This Song**

x, Rating	$p(x)$, Probability of x
1	$p(1) = .07$
2	$p(2) = .07$
3	$p(3) = .22$
4	$p(4) = .21$
5	$p(5) = .43$

randomly selected listener who is familiar with the song, to be a discrete random variable having the estimated probability distribution shown in Table 5.3. It follows that the expected value of this estimated probability distribution is

$$\mu_x = 1(.07) + 2(.07) + 3(.22) + 4(.21) + 5(.43)$$
$$= 3.86$$

This estimated expected value is reported as the *popularity* index for *Poker Face* in Figure 4.6 (page 176) (the difference between the 3.86 calculated here and the 3.87 in Figure 4.6 is due to rounding). It says that the song rating service estimates that the mean rating of the song that would be given by all listeners who are familiar with the song is 3.86. As indicated in Figure 4.6, the song rating service reports that *Poker Face* has a "very high popularity" index.

EXAMPLE 5.6

An insurance company sells a $20,000 whole life insurance policy for an annual premium of $300. Actuarial tables show that a person who would be sold such a policy with this premium has a .001 probability of death during a year. Let x be a random variable representing the insurance company's profit made on one of these policies during a year. The probability distribution of x is

x, Profit	$p(x)$, Probability of x
$300 (if the policyholder lives)	.999
$300 − $20,000 = −$19,700 (a $19,700 loss if the policyholder dies)	.001

The expected value of x (expected profit per year) is

$$\mu_x = \$300(.999) + (-\$19,700)(.001)$$
$$= \$280$$

This says that if the insurance company sells a very large number of these policies, it will average a profit of $280 per policy per year. Since insurance companies actually do sell large numbers of policies, it is reasonable for these companies to make profitability decisions based on expected values.

Next, suppose that we wish to find the premium that the insurance company must charge for a $20,000 policy if the company wishes the average profit per policy per year to be greater than $0. If we let *prem* denote the premium the company will charge, then the probability distribution of the company's yearly profit x is

x, Profit	$p(x)$, Probability of x
prem (if policyholder lives)	.999
prem − $20,000 (if policyholder dies)	.001

The expected value of x (expected profit per year) is

$$\mu_x = prem(.999) + (prem - 20,000)(.001)$$
$$= prem - 20$$

To summarize, the standard deviation σ_x of a discrete random variable measures the spread of the population of all possible observed values of x. When the probability distribution of x can be approximated by a normal curve, this spread can be characterized by the Empirical Rule. When this is not possible, we can use Chebyshev's Theorem to characterize the spread of x.

To conclude this section, note that in Appendix B—on the book's website—we discuss various theoretical properties of the means and variances of random variables. In this appendix we also discuss the idea of the **covariance** between two random variables.

Exercises for Section 5.2

CONCEPTS

connect

5.4 What is a discrete probability distribution? Explain in your own words.

5.5 What conditions must be satisfied by the probabilities in a discrete probability distribution? Explain what these conditions mean.

5.6 Describe how to compute the mean (or expected value) of a discrete random variable, and interpret what this quantity tells us about the observed values of the random variable.

5.7 Describe how to compute the standard deviation of a discrete random variable, and interpret what this quantity tells us about the observed values of the random variable.

METHODS AND APPLICATIONS

5.8 Explain whether each of the following is a valid probability distribution. If the probability distribution is valid, show why. Otherwise, show which condition(s) of a probability distribution are not satisfied.

a	x	$p(x)$	b	x	$p(x)$	c	x	$p(x)$	d	x	$p(x)$
	-1	.2		1/2	-1		2	.25		.1	2/7
	0	.6		3/4	0		4	.35		.7	4/7
	1	.2		1	2		6	.3		.9	1/7

5.9 Consider each of the following probability distributions.

a	x	$p(x)$	b	x	$p(x)$	c	x	$p(x)$
	0	.2		0	.25		-2	.1
	1	.8		1	.45		0	.3
				2	.2		2	.4
				3	.1		5	.2

Calculate μ_x and σ_x for each distribution. Then explain, using the probabilities, why μ_x is the mean of all possible observed values of x.

5.10 For each of the following, write out and graph the probability distribution of x. That is, list all the possible values of x and also list the corresponding probabilities. Then graph the distribution.
a Refer to Exercise 4.3 (page 162), and let x equal the number of patrons who prefer diet cola A.
b Refer to Exercise 4.4 (page 162), and let x equal the number of girls born to the couple.
c Refer to Exercise 4.5 (page 162), and let x equal the number of people who will purchase a car.

5.11 For each of the following, find μ_x, σ_x^2, and σ_x. Then interpret in words the meaning of μ_x, and employ Chebyshev's rule to find intervals that contain at least 3/4 and 8/9 of the observed values of x.
a $x =$ the number of patrons who prefer diet cola A as defined in Exercise 5.10a.
b $x =$ the number of girls born to the couple as defined in Exercise 5.10b.
c $x =$ the number of people who will purchase a car as defined in Exercise 5.10c.

5.12 Suppose that the probability distribution of a random variable x can be described by the formula

$$p(x) = \frac{x}{15}$$

for each of the values $x = 1$, 2, 3, 4, and 5. For example, then, $P(x = 2) = p(2) = 2/15$.
a Write out the probability distribution of x.
b Show that the probability distribution of x satisfies the properties of a discrete probability distribution.
c Calculate the mean of x.
d Calculate the variance, σ_x^2, and the standard deviation, σ_x.

5.13   The following table summarizes investment outcomes and corresponding probabilities for a particular oil well:

x = the outcome in \$	$p(x)$
−\$40,000 (no oil)	.25
10,000 (some oil)	.7
70,000 (much oil)	.05

a   Graph $p(x)$; that is, graph the probability distribution of x.
b   Find the expected monetary outcome. Mark this value on your graph of part a. Then interpret this value.

5.14   In the book *Foundations of Financial Management* (7th ed.), Stanley B. Block and Geoffrey A. Hirt discuss risk measurement for investments. Block and Hirt present an investment with the possible outcomes and associated probabilities given in Table 5.4. The authors go on to say that the probabilities

> may be based on past experience, industry ratios and trends, interviews with company executives, and sophisticated simulation techniques. The probability values may be easy to determine for the introduction of a mechanical stamping process in which the manufacturer has 10 years of past data, but difficult to assess for a new product in a foreign market.   ⑤ OutcomeDist

a   Use the probability distribution in Table 5.4 to calculate the expected value (mean) and the standard deviation of the investment outcomes. Interpret the expected value.
b   Block and Hirt interpret the standard deviation of the investment outcomes as follows: "Generally, the larger the standard deviation (or spread of outcomes), the greater is the risk." Explain why this makes sense. Use Chebyshev's Theorem to illustrate your point.
c   Block and Hirt compare three investments having the following means and standard deviations of the investment outcomes:

Investment 1	Investment 2	Investment 3
$\mu = \$600$	$\mu = \$600$	$\mu = \$600$
$\sigma = \$20$	$\sigma = \$190$	$\sigma = \$300$

Which of these investments involves the most risk? The least risk? Explain why by using Chebyshev's Theorem to compute an interval for each investment that will contain at least 8/9 of the investment outcomes.
d   Block and Hirt continue by comparing two more investments:

Investment A	Investment B
$\mu = \$6,000$	$\mu = \$600$
$\sigma = \$600$	$\sigma = \$190$

The authors explain that Investment A

> appears to have a high standard deviation, but not when related to the expected value of the distribution. A standard deviation of \$600 on an investment with an expected value of \$6,000 may indicate less risk than a standard deviation of \$190 on an investment with an expected value of only \$600.
>
> We can eliminate the size difficulty by developing a third measure, the **coefficient of variation** (V). This term calls for nothing more difficult than dividing the standard deviation of an investment by the expected value. Generally, the larger the coefficient of variation, the greater is the risk.

$$\text{Coefficient of variation } (V) = \frac{\sigma}{\mu}$$

TABLE 5.4   **Probability Distribution of Outcomes for an Investment**   ⑤ OutcomeDist

Outcome	Probability of Outcome	Assumptions
\$300	.2	Pessimistic
600	.6	Moderately successful
900	.2	Optimistic

Source: S. B. Block and G. A. Hirt, *Foundations of Financial Management*, 7th ed., p. 378. Copyright © 1994. Reprinted by permission of McGraw-Hill Companies, Inc.

Calculate the coefficient of variation for investments A and B. Which investment carries the greater risk?

e Calculate the coefficient of variation for investments 1, 2, and 3 in part c. Based on the coefficient of variation, which investment involves the most risk? The least risk? Do we obtain the same results as we did by comparing standard deviations (in part c)? Why?

5.15 An insurance company will insure a $50,000 diamond for its full value against theft at a premium of $400 per year. Suppose that the probability that the diamond will be stolen is .005, and let x denote the insurance company's profit.

a Set up the probability distribution of the random variable x.

b Calculate the insurance company's expected profit.

c Find the premium that the insurance company should charge if it wants its expected profit to be $1,000.

5.16 In the book *Foundations of Financial Management* (7th ed.), Stanley B. Block and Geoffrey A. Hirt discuss a semiconductor firm that is considering two choices: (1) expanding the production of semiconductors for sale to end users or (2) entering the highly competitive home computer market. The cost of both projects is $60 million, but the net present value of the cash flows from sales and the risks are different.

Figure 5.3 gives a tree diagram of the project choices. The tree diagram gives a probability distribution of expected sales for each project. It also gives the present value of cash flows from sales and the net present value (NPV = present value of cash flow from sales minus initial cost) corresponding to each sales alternative. Note that figures in parentheses denote losses.

a For each project choice, calculate the expected net present value.

b For each project choice, calculate the variance and standard deviation of the net present value.

c Calculate the coefficient of variation for each project choice. See Exercise 5.14d for a discussion of the coefficient of variation.

d Which project has the higher expected net present value?

e Which project carries the least risk? Explain.

f In your opinion, which project should be undertaken? Justify your answer.

5.17 Five thousand raffle tickets are to be sold at $10 each to benefit a local community group. The prizes, the number of each prize to be given away, and the dollar value of winnings for each prize are as follows: **DS** Raffle

Prize	Number to Be Given Away	Dollar Value
Automobile	1	$20,000
Entertainment center	2	3,000 each
DVD recorder	5	400 each
Gift certificate	50	20 each

FIGURE 5.3 **A Tree Diagram of Two Project Choices**

	(1) Sales	(2) Probability	(3) Present Value of Cash Flow from Sales ($ millions)	(4) Initial Cost ($ millions)	(5) Net Present Value, NPV = (3) − (4) ($ millions)
Expand semiconductor capacity	High	.50	$100	$60	$40
	Moderate	.25	75	60	15
	Low	.25	40	60	(20)
A Start B					
Enter home computer market	High	.20	$200	$60	$140
	Moderate	.50	75	60	15
	Low	.30	25	60	(35)

Source: S. B. Block and G. A. Hirt, *Foundations of Financial Management*, 7th ed., p. 387. Copyright © 1994. Reprinted by permission of McGraw-Hill Companies, Inc.

TABLE 5.5   Return Distributions for Companies *A*, *B*, and *C* and for Two Possible Acquisitions   📀 AcqDistributions

Economic Condition	Probability	Company *A* Returns	Company *B* Returns	Company *C* Returns	Company *A* + *B* Returns	Company *A* + *C* Returns
1	.2	17%	19%	13%	18%	15%
2	.2	15	17	11	16	13
3	.2	13	15	15	14	14
4	.2	11	13	17	12	14
5	.2	9	11	19	10	14

If you buy one ticket, calculate your expected winnings. (Form the probability distribution of x = your dollar winnings, and remember to subtract the cost of your ticket.)

5.18   Company *A* is considering the acquisition of two separate but large companies, Company *B* and Company *C*, having sales and assets equal to its own. Table 5.5 gives the probabilities of returns for each of the three companies under various economic conditions. The table also gives the probabilities of returns for each possible combination: Company *A* plus Company *B*, and Company *A* plus Company *C*.   📀 AcqDistributions

   a   For each of Companies *A*, *B*, and *C* find the mean return and the standard deviation of returns.

   b   Find the mean return and the standard deviation of returns for the combination of Company *A* plus Company *B*.

   c   Find the mean return and the standard deviation of returns for the combination of Company *A* plus Company *C*.

   d   Compare the mean returns for each of the two possible combinations—Company *A* plus Company *B* and Company *A* plus Company *C*. Is either mean higher? How do they compare to Company *A*'s mean return?

   e   Compare the standard deviations of the returns for each of the two possible combinations—Company *A* plus Company *B* and Company *A* plus Company *C*. Which standard deviation is smaller? Which possible combination involves less risk? How does the risk carried by this combination compare to the risk carried by Company *A* alone?

   f   Which acquisition would you recommend—Company *A* plus Company *B* or Company *A* plus Company *C*?

5.19   THE SONG RATING CASE

Again consider Exercise 4.32 (page 178) and recall that we estimated the proportions of listeners *familiar with Used To Love U* by John Legend who would give the song ratings of 5, 4, 3, 2, and 1 to be, respectively, .1978, .2967, .3077, .0879, and .1099. Assign the numerical values 1 through 5 to the ratings 1 through 5.

   a   Find an estimate of the probability distribution of x = this song's rating by a randomly selected listener who is familiar with the song.

   b   Find the *popularity* index for *Used To Love U*. That is, find an estimate of the mean rating of this song that would be given by all listeners who are familiar with this song.

5.3 The Binomial Distribution ● ● ●

In this section we discuss what is perhaps the most important discrete probability distribution—the binomial distribution. We begin with an example.

LO3   Use the binomial distribution to compute probabilities.

EXAMPLE 5.8

Suppose that historical sales records indicate that 40 percent of all customers who enter a discount department store make a purchase. What is the probability that two of the next three customers will make a purchase?

In order to find this probability, we first note that the experiment of observing three customers making a purchase decision has several distinguishing characteristics:

1   The experiment consists of three identical *trials;* each trial consists of a customer making a purchase decision.

Noting that we sometimes refer to the formula for $p(x)$ as the **binomial formula,** we illustrate the use of this formula in the following example.

EXAMPLE 5.9

Consider the discount department store situation discussed in Example 5.8. In order to find the probability that three of the next five customers make purchases, we calculate

$$p(3) = \frac{5!}{3!\,(5-3)!}\,(.4)^3(.6)^{5-3} = \frac{5!}{3!\,2!}\,(.4)^3(.6)^2$$

$$= \frac{5 \cdot 4 \cdot 3 \cdot 2 \cdot 1}{(3 \cdot 2 \cdot 1)(2 \cdot 1)}\,(.4)^3(.6)^2$$

$$= 10(.064)(.36)$$

$$= .2304$$

Here we see that

1   $\frac{5!}{3!\,(5-3)!} = 10$ is the number of ways to arrange three successes among five trials. For instance, two ways to do this are described by the sample space outcomes *SSSFF* and *SFSSF.* There are eight other ways.

2   $(.4)^3(.6)^2$ is the probability of any sample space outcome consisting of three successes and two failures.

Thus far we have shown how to calculate binomial probabilities. We next give several examples that illustrate some practical applications of the binomial distribution. As we demonstrate in the first example, the term *success* does not necessarily refer to a *desirable* experimental outcome. Rather, it refers to an outcome that we wish to investigate.

EXAMPLE 5.10

Antibiotics occasionally cause nausea as a side effect. A major drug company has developed a new antibiotic called Phe-Mycin. The company claims that, at most, 10 percent of all patients treated with Phe-Mycin would experience nausea as a side effect of taking the drug. Suppose that we randomly select $n = 4$ patients and treat them with Phe-Mycin. Each patient will either experience nausea (which we arbitrarily call a success) or will not experience nausea (a failure). We will assume that p, the true probability that a patient will experience nausea as a side effect, is .10, the maximum value of p claimed by the drug company. Furthermore, it is reasonable to assume that patients' reactions to the drug would be independent of each other. Let x denote the number of patients among the four who will experience nausea as a side effect. It follows that x is a binomial random variable, which can take on any of the potential values 0, 1, 2, 3, or 4. That is, anywhere between none of the patients and all four of the patients could potentially experience nausea as a side effect. Furthermore, we can calculate the probability associated with each possible value of x as shown in Table 5.6. For instance, the probability that none of the four randomly selected patients experiences nausea is

$$p(0) = P(x = 0) = \frac{4!}{0!\,(4-0)!}\,(.1)^0(.9)^{4-0}$$

$$= \frac{4!}{0!\,4!}\,(.1)^0(.9)^4$$

$$= \frac{4!}{(1)(4!)}\,(1)(.9)^4$$

$$= (.9)^4 = .6561$$

Because Table 5.6 lists each possible value of x and also gives the probability of each value, we say that this table gives the **binomial probability distribution of x.**

TABLE 5.6 **The Binomial Probability Distribution of x, the Number of Four Randomly Selected Patients Who Will Experience Nausea as a Side Effect of Being Treated with Phe-Mycin**

x (Number Who Experience Nausea)	$p(x) = \dfrac{n!}{x!\,(n-x)!}\,p^x(1-p)^{n-x}$
0	$p(0) = P(x = 0) = \dfrac{4!}{0!\,(4-0)!}\,(.1)^0(.9)^{4-0} = .6561$
1	$p(1) = P(x = 1) = \dfrac{4!}{1!\,(4-1)!}\,(.1)^1(.9)^{4-1} = .2916$
2	$p(2) = P(x = 2) = \dfrac{4!}{2!\,(4-2)!}\,(.1)^2(.9)^{4-2} = .0486$
3	$p(3) = P(x = 3) = \dfrac{4!}{3!\,(4-3)!}\,(.1)^3(.9)^{4-3} = .0036$
4	$p(4) = P(x = 4) = \dfrac{4!}{4!\,(4-4)!}\,(.1)^4(.9)^{4-4} = .0001$

FIGURE 5.4 **The Binomial Probability Distribution with $p = .10$ and $n = 4$**

(a) Excel output of the binomial distribution

Binomial distribution with n = 4 and p = 0.10

x	P(X = x)
0	0.6561
1	0.2916
2	0.0486
3	0.0036
4	0.0001

(b) A graph of the distribution

The binomial probabilities given in Table 5.6 need not be hand calculated. Excel and MINITAB can be used to calculate binomial probabilities. For instance, Figure 5.4(a) gives the Excel output of the binomial probability distribution listed in Table 5.6.[1] Figure 5.4(b) shows a graph of this distribution.

In order to interpret these binomial probabilities, consider administering the antibiotic Phe-Mycin to all possible samples of four randomly selected patients. Then, for example,

$$P(x = 0) = 0.6561$$

says that none of the four sampled patients would experience nausea in 65.61 percent of all possible samples. Furthermore, as another example,

$$P(x = 3) = 0.0036$$

says that three out of the four sampled patients would experience nausea in only .36 percent of all possible samples.

Another way to avoid hand calculating binomial probabilities is to use **binomial tables,** which have been constructed to give the probability of x successes in n trials. A table of binomial

[1]As we will see in this chapter's appendixes, we can use MINITAB to obtain output of the binomial distribution that is essentially identical to the output given by Excel.

TABLE 5.7   A Portion of a Binomial Probability Table

(a) A Table for n = 4 Trials

↓	.05	.10	.15	.20	.25	.30	.35	.40	.45	.50	
0	.8145	.6561	.5220	.4096	.3164	.2401	.1785	.1296	.0915	.0625	4
1	.1715	.2916	.3685	.4096	.4219	.4116	.3845	.3456	.2995	.2500	3
2	.0135	.0486	.0975	.1536	.2109	.2646	.3105	.3456	.3675	.3750	2
3	.0005	.0036	.0115	.0256	.0469	.0756	.1115	.1536	.2005	.2500	1
4	.0000	.0001	.0005	.0016	.0039	.0081	.0150	.0256	.0410	.0625	0
	.95	.90	.85	.80	.75	.70	.65	.60	.55	.50	↑

Values of p (.05 to .50) (top); Values of p (.50 to .95) (bottom). Number of Successes on left; Number of Successes on right.

(b) A Table for n = 8 trials

↓	.05	.10	.15	.20	.25	.30	.35	.40	.45	.50	
0	.6634	.4305	.2725	.1678	.1001	.0576	.0319	.0168	.0084	.0039	8
1	.2793	.3826	.3847	.3355	.2670	.1977	.1373	.0896	.0548	.0313	7
2	.0515	.1488	.2376	.2936	.3115	.2965	.2587	.2090	.1569	.1094	6
3	.0054	.0331	.0839	.1468	.2076	.2541	.2786	.2787	.2568	.2188	5
4	.0004	.0046	.0185	.0459	.0865	.1361	.1875	.2322	.2627	.2734	4
5	.0000	.0004	.0026	.0092	.0231	.0467	.0808	.1239	.1719	.2188	3
6	.0000	.0000	.0002	.0011	.0038	.0100	.0217	.0413	.0703	.1094	2
7	.0000	.0000	.0000	.0001	.0004	.0012	.0033	.0079	.0164	.0313	1
8	.0000	.0000	.0000	.0000	.0000	.0001	.0002	.0007	.0017	.0039	0
	.95	.90	.85	.80	.75	.70	.65	.60	.55	.50	↑

Values of p (.05 to .50) (top); Values of p (.50 to .95) (bottom). Number of Successes on left; Number of Successes on right.

probabilities is given in Table A.1 (page 631). A portion of this table is reproduced in Table 5.7(a) and (b). Part (a) of this table gives binomial probabilities corresponding to $n = 4$ trials. Values of p, the probability of success, are listed across the top of the table (ranging from $p = .05$ to $p = .50$ in steps of .05), and more values of p (ranging from $p = .50$ to $p = .95$ in steps of .05) are listed across the bottom of the table. When the value of p being considered is one of those across the top of the table, values of x (the number of successes in four trials) are listed down the left side of the table. For instance, to find the probabilities that we have computed in Table 5.6, we look in part (a) of Table 5.7 ($n = 4$) and read down the column labeled .10. Remembering that the values of x are on the left side of the table because $p = .10$ is on top of the table, we find the probabilities in Table 5.6 (they are shaded). For example, the probability that none of four patients experiences nausea is $p(0) = .6561$, the probability that one of the four patients experiences nausea is $p(1) = .2916$, and so forth. If the value of p is across the bottom of the table, then we read the values of x from the right side of the table. As an example, if p equals .60, then the probability of two successes in four trials is $p(2) = .3456$ (we have shaded this probability).

EXAMPLE 5.11

Suppose that we wish to investigate whether p, the probability that a patient will experience nausea as a side effect of taking Phe-Mycin, is greater than .10, the maximum value of p claimed by the drug company. This assessment will be made by assuming, for the sake of argument, that p equals .10, and by using sample information to weigh the evidence against this assumption and in favor of the conclusion that p is greater than .10. Suppose that when a sample of $n = 4$ randomly selected patients is treated with Phe-Mycin, three of the four patients experience nausea. Because the fraction of patients in the sample that experience nausea is $3/4 = .75$, which is far greater than .10, we have some evidence contradicting the assumption that p equals .10. To evaluate the strength of this evidence, we calculate the probability that at least 3 out of 4 randomly selected patients would experience nausea as a side effect if, in fact, p equals .10. Using the binomial probabilities in Table 5.7(a), and realizing that the events $x = 3$ and $x = 4$ are mutually exclusive, we have

$$
\begin{aligned}
P(x \geq 3) &= P(x = 3 \text{ or } x = 4) \\
&= P(x = 3) + P(x = 4) \\
&= .0036 + .0001 \\
&= .0037
\end{aligned}
$$

This probability says that, if p equals .10, then in only .37 percent of all possible samples of four randomly selected patients would at least three of the four patients experience nausea as a side effect. This implies that, if we are to believe that p equals .10, then we must believe that we have observed a sample result that is so rare that it can be described as a 37 in 10,000 chance. Because observing such a result is very unlikely, we have very strong evidence that p does not equal .10 and is, in fact, greater than .10.

Next, suppose that we consider what our conclusion would have been if only one of the four randomly selected patients had experienced nausea. Because the sample fraction of patients who experienced nausea is $1/4 = .25$, which is greater than .10, we would have some evidence to contradict the assumption that p equals .10. To evaluate the strength of this evidence, we calculate the probability that at least one out of four randomly selected patients would experience nausea as a side effect of being treated with Phe-Mycin if, in fact, p equals .10. Using the binomial probabilities in Table 5.7(a), we have

$$
\begin{aligned}
P(x \geq 1) &= P(x = 1 \text{ or } x = 2 \text{ or } x = 3 \text{ or } x = 4) \\
&= P(x = 1) + P(x = 2) + P(x = 3) + P(x = 4) \\
&= .2916 + .0486 + .0036 + .0001 \\
&= .3439
\end{aligned}
$$

This probability says that, if p equals .10, then in 34.39 percent of all possible samples of four randomly selected patients, at least one of the four patients would experience nausea. Since it is not particularly difficult to believe that a 34.39 percent chance has occurred, we would not have much evidence against the claim that p equals .10.

Example 5.11 illustrates what is sometimes called the **rare event approach to making a statistical inference.** The idea of this approach is that if the probability of an observed sample result under a given assumption is *small,* then we have *strong evidence* that the assumption is false. Although there are no strict rules, many statisticians judge the probability of an observed sample result to be small if it is less than .05. The logic behind this will be explained more fully in Chapter 9.

EXAMPLE 5.12

The manufacturer of the ColorSmart-5000 television set claims that 95 percent of its sets last at least five years without requiring a single repair. Suppose that we contact $n = 8$ randomly selected ColorSmart-5000 purchasers five years after they purchased their sets. Each purchaser's set will have needed no repairs (a success) or will have been repaired at least once (a failure). We will assume that p, the true probability that a purchaser's television set will require no repairs within five years, is .95, as claimed by the manufacturer. Furthermore, it is reasonable to believe that the repair records of the purchasers' sets are independent of each other. Let x denote the number of the $n = 8$ randomly selected sets that have lasted at least five years without a single repair. Then x is a binomial random variable that can take on any of the potential values 0, 1, 2, 3, 4, 5, 6, 7, or 8. The binomial distribution of x is listed in Table 5.8. Here we have obtained these probabilities from Table 5.7(b). To use the table, we look at the column corresponding to $p = .95$. Because $p = .95$ is listed at the bottom of the table, we read the values of x and their

TABLE 5.8 The Binomial Distribution of x, the Number of Eight ColorSmart-5000 Television Sets That Have Lasted at Least Five Years Without Needing a Single Repair, When $p = .95$

x, Number of Sets That Require No Repairs	$p(x) = \dfrac{8!}{x!\,(8 - x)!}(.95)^x(.05)^{8-x}$
0	$p(0) = .0000$
1	$p(1) = .0000$
2	$p(2) = .0000$
3	$p(3) = .0000$
4	$p(4) = .0004$
5	$p(5) = .0054$
6	$p(6) = .0515$
7	$p(7) = .2793$
8	$p(8) = .6634$

FIGURE 5.5 The Binomial Probability Distribution with $p = .95$ and $n = 8$

(a) MINITAB output of the binomial distribution

```
Binomial with n = 8 and p = 0.95

       x          P( X = x )
       3             0.0000
       4             0.0004
       5             0.0054
       6             0.0515
       7             0.2793
       8             0.6634
```

(b) A graph of the distribution

corresponding probabilities from bottom to top (we have shaded the probabilities). Notice that the values of x are listed on the right side of the table.

Figure 5.5(a) gives the MINITAB output of the binomial distribution with $p = .95$ and $n = 8$ (that is, the binomial distribution of Table 5.8). This binomial distribution is graphed in Figure 5.5(b). Now, suppose that when we actually contact eight randomly selected purchasers, we find that five out of the eight television sets owned by these purchasers have lasted at least five years without a single repair. Because the sample fraction, $5/8 = .625$, of television sets needing no repairs is less than .95, we have some evidence contradicting the manufacturer's claim that p equals .95. To evaluate the strength of this evidence, we will calculate the probability that five or fewer of the eight randomly selected televisions would last five years without a single repair if, in fact, p equals .95. Using the binomial probabilities in Table 5.8, we have

$$
\begin{aligned}
P(x \leq 5) &= P(x = 5 \text{ or } x = 4 \text{ or } x = 3 \text{ or } x = 2 \text{ or } x = 1 \text{ or } x = 0) \\
&= P(x = 5) + P(x = 4) + P(x = 3) + P(x = 2) + P(x = 1) + P(x = 0) \\
&= .0054 + .0004 + .0000 + .0000 + .0000 + .0000 \\
&= .0058
\end{aligned}
$$

This probability says that, if p equals .95, then in only .58 percent of all possible samples of eight randomly selected ColorSmart-5000 televisions would five or fewer of the eight televisions last five years without a single repair. Therefore, if we are to believe that p equals .95, we must believe that a 58 in 10,000 chance has occurred. Since it is difficult to believe that such a small chance has occurred, we have strong evidence that p does not equal .95, and is, in fact, less than .95.

FIGURE 5.6   **Several Binomial Distributions**

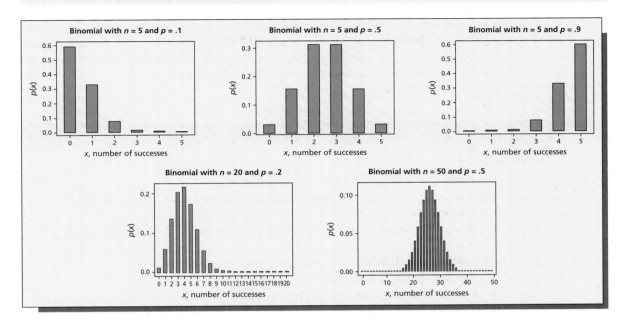

In Examples 5.10 and 5.12 we have illustrated binomial distributions with different values of n and p. The values of n and p are often called the **parameters** of the binomial distribution. Figure 5.6 shows several different binomial distributions. We see that, depending on the parameters, a binomial distribution can be skewed to the right, skewed to the left, or symmetrical.

We next consider calculating the mean, variance, and standard deviation of a binomial random variable. If we place the binomial probability formula into the expressions (given in Section 5.2) for the mean and variance of a discrete random variable, we can derive formulas that allow us to easily compute μ_x, σ_x^2, and σ_x for a binomial random variable. Omitting the details of the derivation, we have the following results:

The Mean, Variance, and Standard Deviation of a Binomial Random Variable

If x is a binomial random variable, then

$$\mu_x = np \qquad \sigma_x^2 = npq \qquad \sigma_x = \sqrt{npq}$$

where n is the number of trials, p is the probability of success on each trial, and $q = 1 - p$ is the probability of failure on each trial.

As a simple example, again consider the television manufacturer, and recall that x is the number of eight randomly selected ColorSmart-5000 televisions that last five years without a single repair. If the manufacturer's claim that p equals .95 is true (which implies that q equals $1 - p = 1 - .95 = .05$), it follows that

$$\mu_x = np = 8(.95) = 7.6$$
$$\sigma_x^2 = npq = 8(.95)(.05) = .38$$
$$\sigma_x = \sqrt{npq} = \sqrt{.38} = .6164$$

In order to interpret $\mu_x = 7.6$, suppose that we were to randomly select all possible samples of eight ColorSmart-5000 televisions and record the number of sets in each sample that last five years without a repair. If we averaged all of our results, we would find that the average number of sets per sample that last five years without a repair is equal to 7.6.

To conclude this section, note that in optional Section 5.5, we discuss the **hypergeometric distribution.** This distribution is related to the binomial distribution. The main difference between the two distributions is that in the case of the hypergeometric distribution, the trials are not independent and the probabilities of success and failure change from trial to trial. This occurs when we sample without replacement from a finite population. However, when the finite population is large compared to the sample, the binomial distribution can be used to approximate the hypergeometric distribution. The details are explained in Section 5.5.

Exercises for Section 5.3

CONCEPTS

connect

5.20   List the four characteristics of a binomial experiment.

5.21   Suppose that x is a binomial random variable. Explain what the values of x represent. That is, how are the values of x defined?

5.22   Explain the logic behind the rare event approach to making statistical inferences.

METHODS AND APPLICATIONS

5.23   Suppose that x is a binomial random variable with $n = 5$, $p = .3$, and $q = .7$.
  a   Write the binomial formula for this situation and list the possible values of x.
  b   For each value of x, calculate $p(x)$, and graph the binomial distribution.
  c   Find $P(x = 3)$.
  d   Find $P(x \leq 3)$.
  e   Find $P(x < 3)$.
  f   Find $P(x \geq 4)$.
  g   Find $P(x > 2)$.
  h   Use the probabilities you computed in part b to calculate the mean, μ_x, the variance, σ_x^2, and the standard deviation, σ_x, of this binomial distribution. Show that the formulas for μ_x, σ_x^2, and σ_x given in this section give the same results.
  i   Calculate the interval $[\mu_x \pm 2\sigma_x]$. Use the probabilities of part b to find the probability that x will be in this interval.

5.24   Thirty percent of all customers who enter a store will make a purchase. Suppose that six customers enter the store and that these customers make independent purchase decisions.
  a   Let $x =$ the number of the six customers who will make a purchase. Write the binomial formula for this situation.
  b   Use the binomial formula to calculate
    (1)   The probability that exactly five customers make a purchase.
    (2)   The probability that at least three customers make a purchase.
    (3)   The probability that two or fewer customers make a purchase.
    (4)   The probability that at least one customer makes a purchase.

5.25   The customer service department for a wholesale electronics outlet claims that 90 percent of all customer complaints are resolved to the satisfaction of the customer. In order to test this claim, a random sample of 15 customers who have filed complaints is selected.
  a   Let $x =$ the number of sampled customers whose complaints were resolved to the customer's satisfaction. Assuming the claim is true, write the binomial formula for this situation.
  b   Use the binomial tables (see Table A.1, page 631) to find each of the following if we assume that the claim is true:
    (1) $P(x \leq 13)$.
    (2) $P(x > 10)$.
    (3) $P(x \geq 14)$.
    (4) $P(9 \leq x \leq 12)$.
    (5) $P(x \leq 9)$.
  c   Suppose that of the 15 customers selected, 9 have had their complaints resolved satisfactorily. Using part b, do you believe the claim of 90 percent satisfaction? Explain.

5.26   The United States Golf Association requires that the weight of a golf ball must not exceed 1.62 oz. The association periodically checks golf balls sold in the United States by sampling specific brands stocked by pro shops. Suppose that a manufacturer claims that no more than 1 percent of its brand of golf balls exceed 1.62 oz. in weight. Suppose that 24 of this manufacturer's golf balls are randomly selected, and let x denote the number of the 24 randomly selected golf balls that exceed 1.62 oz. Figure 5.7 gives part of an Excel output of the binomial distribution with $n = 24$, $p = .01$, and $q = .99$. (Note that, since $P(X = x) = .0000$ for values of x from 6 to 24, we omit these probabilities.) Use this output to

a Find $P(x = 0)$, that is, find the probability that none of the randomly selected golf balls exceeds 1.62 oz. in weight.

b Find the probability that at least one of the randomly selected golf balls exceeds 1.62 oz. in weight.

c Find $P(x \leq 3)$.

d Find $P(x \geq 2)$.

e Suppose that 2 of the 24 randomly selected golf balls are found to exceed 1.62 oz. Using your result from part d, do you believe the claim that no more than 1 percent of this brand of golf balls exceed 1.62 oz. in weight?

FIGURE 5.7

Excel Output of the Binomial Distribution with $n = 24$, $p = .01$, and $q = .99$

Binomial distribution with n = 24 and p = 0.01

x	P (X = x)
0	0.7857
1	0.1905
2	0.0221
3	0.0016
4	0.0001
5	0.0000

5.27 An industry representative claims that 50 percent of all satellite dish owners subscribe to at least one premium movie channel. In an attempt to justify this claim, the representative will poll a randomly selected sample of dish owners.

a Suppose that the representative's claim is true, and suppose that a sample of four dish owners is randomly selected. Assuming independence, use an appropriate formula to compute

(1) The probability that none of the dish owners in the sample subscribes to at least one premium movie channel.

(2) The probability that more than two dish owners in the sample subscribe to at least one premium movie channel.

b Suppose that the representative's claim is true, and suppose that a sample of 20 dish owners is randomly selected. Assuming independence, what is the probability that

(1) Nine or fewer dish owners in the sample subscribe to at least one premium movie channel?

(2) More than 11 dish owners in the sample subscribe to at least one premium movie channel?

(3) Fewer than five dish owners in the sample subscribe to at least one premium movie channel?

c Suppose that, when we survey 20 randomly selected dish owners, we find that 4 of the dish owners actually subscribe to at least one premium movie channel. Using a probability you found in this exercise as the basis for your answer, do you believe the industry representative's claim? Explain.

5.28 For each of the following, calculate μ_x, σ_x^2, and σ_x by using the formulas given in this section. Then (1) interpret the meaning of μ_x, and (2) find the probability that x falls in the interval $[\mu_x \pm 2\sigma_x]$.

a The situation of Exercise 5.24, where $x =$ the number of the six customers who will make a purchase.

b The situation of Exercise 5.25, where $x =$ the number of 15 sampled customers whose complaints were resolved to the customer's satisfaction.

c The situation of Exercise 5.26, where $x =$ the number of the 24 randomly selected golf balls that exceed 1.62 oz. in weight.

5.29 The January 1986 mission of the Space Shuttle *Challenger* was the 25th such shuttle mission. It was unsuccessful due to an explosion caused by an O-ring seal failure.

a According to NASA, the probability of such a failure in a single mission was 1/60,000. Using this value of p and assuming all missions are independent, calculate the probability of no mission failures in 25 attempts. Then calculate the probability of at least one mission failure in 25 attempts.

b According to a study conducted for the Air Force, the probability of such a failure in a single mission was 1/35. Recalculate the probability of no mission failures in 25 attempts and the probability of at least one mission failure in 25 attempts.

c Based on your answers to parts a and b, which value of p seems more likely to be true? Explain.

d How small must p be made in order to ensure that the probability of no mission failures in 25 attempts is .999?

5.4 The Poisson Distribution (Optional) ● ● ●

LO4 Use the Poisson distribution to compute probabilities (Optional).

We now discuss a discrete random variable that describes the number of occurrences of an event over a specified interval of time or space. For instance, we might wish to describe (1) the number of customers who arrive at the checkout counters of a grocery store in one hour, or (2) the number of major fires in a city during the next two months, or (3) the number of dirt specks found in one square yard of plastic wrap.

Such a random variable can often be described by a **Poisson distribution.** We describe this distribution and give two assumptions needed for its use in the following box:

The Poisson Distribution

Consider the number of times an event occurs over an interval of time or space, and assume that

1 The probability of the event's occurrence is the same for any two intervals of equal length, and

2 Whether the event occurs in any interval is independent of whether the event occurs in any other nonoverlapping interval.

Then, the probability that the event will occur x times in a *specified interval* is

$$p(x) = \frac{e^{-\mu}\mu^x}{x!}$$

Here μ is the mean (or expected) number of occurrences of the event in the *specified interval,* and $e = 2.71828\ldots$ is the base of Napierian logarithms.

In theory, there is no limit to how large x might be. That is, theoretically speaking, the event under consideration could occur an indefinitely large number of times during any specified interval. This says that a **Poisson random variable** might take on any of the values 0, 1, 2, 3, . . . and so forth. We will now look at an example.

EXAMPLE 5.13

In an article in the August 15, 1998, edition of the *Journal News* (Hamilton, Ohio),[2] the Associated Press reported that the Cleveland Air Route Traffic Control Center, the busiest in the nation for guiding planes on cross-country routes, had experienced an unusually high number of errors since the end of July. An error occurs when controllers direct flights either within five miles of each other horizontally, or within 2,000 feet vertically at a height of 18,000 feet or more (the standard is 1,000 feet vertically at heights less than 18,000 feet). The controllers' union blamed the errors on a staff shortage, whereas the Federal Aviation Administration (FAA) claimed that the cause was improved error reporting and an unusual number of thunderstorms.

Suppose that an air traffic control center has been averaging 20.8 errors per year and that the center experiences 3 errors in a week. The FAA must decide whether this occurrence is unusual enough to warrant an investigation as to the causes of the (possible) increase in errors. To investigate this possibility, we will find the probability distribution of x, the number of errors in a week, when we assume that the center is still averaging 20.8 errors per year.

Arbitrarily choosing a time unit of one week, the average (or expected) number of errors per week is $20.8/52 = .4$. Therefore, we can use the Poisson formula (note that the Poisson assumptions are probably satisfied) to calculate the probability of no errors in a week to be

$$p(0) = P(x = 0) = \frac{e^{-\mu}\mu^0}{0!} = \frac{e^{-.4}(.4)^0}{1} = .6703$$

Similarly, the probability of three errors in a week is

$$p(3) = P(x = 3) = \frac{e^{-.4}(.4)^3}{3!} = \frac{e^{-.4}(.4)^3}{3 \cdot 2 \cdot 1} = .0072$$

As with the binomial distribution, tables have been constructed that give Poisson probabilities. A table of these probabilities is given in Table A.2 (page 635). A portion of this table is reproduced

---

[2]F. J. Frommer, "Errors on the Rise at Traffic Control Center in Ohio," *Journal News,* August 15, 1998.

TABLE 5.9   A Portion of a Poisson Probability Table

μ, Mean Number of Occurrences

x, Number of Occurrences	.1	.2	.3	.4	.5	.6	.7	.8	.9	1.0
0	.9048	.8187	.7408	.6703	.6065	.5488	.4966	.4493	.4066	.3679
1	.0905	.1637	.2222	.2681	.3033	.3293	.3476	.3595	.3659	.3679
2	.0045	.0164	.0333	.0536	.0758	.0988	.1217	.1438	.1647	.1839
3	.0002	.0011	.0033	.0072	.0126	.0198	.0284	.0383	.0494	.0613
4	.0000	.0001	.0003	.0007	.0016	.0030	.0050	.0077	.0111	.0153
5	.0000	.0000	.0000	.0001	.0002	.0004	.0007	.0012	.0020	.0031
6	.0000	.0000	.0000	.0000	.0000	.0000	.0001	.0002	.0003	.0005

μ, Mean Number of Occurrences

x, Number of Occurrences	1.1	1.2	1.3	1.4	1.5	1.6	1.7	1.8	1.9	2.0
0	.3329	.3012	.2725	.2466	.2231	.2019	.1827	.1653	.1496	.1353
1	.3662	.3614	.3543	.3452	.3347	.3230	.3106	.2975	.2842	.2707
2	.2014	.2169	.2303	.2417	.2510	.2584	.2640	.2678	.2700	.2707
3	.0738	.0867	.0998	.1128	.1255	.1378	.1496	.1607	.1710	.1804
4	.0203	.0260	.0324	.0395	.0471	.0551	.0636	.0723	.0812	.0902
5	.0045	.0062	.0084	.0111	.0141	.0176	.0216	.0260	.0309	.0361
6	.0008	.0012	.0018	.0026	.0035	.0047	.0061	.0078	.0098	.0120
7	.0001	.0002	.0003	.0005	.0008	.0011	.0015	.0020	.0027	.0034
8	.0000	.0000	.0001	.0001	.0001	.0002	.0003	.0005	.0006	.0009

Source: From Brooks/Cole © 1991.

TABLE 5.10   The Poisson Distribution of x, the Number of Errors at an Air Traffic Control Center in a Week, When $\mu = .4$

x, the Number of Errors in a Week	$p(x) = \dfrac{e^{-\mu}\mu^x}{x!}$
0	$p(0) = \dfrac{e^{-.4}(.4)^0}{0!} = .6703$
1	$p(1) = \dfrac{e^{-.4}(.4)^1}{1!} = .2681$
2	$p(2) = \dfrac{e^{-.4}(.4)^2}{2!} = .0536$
3	$p(3) = \dfrac{e^{-.4}(.4)^3}{3!} = .0072$
4	$p(4) = \dfrac{e^{-.4}(.4)^4}{4!} = .0007$
5	$p(5) = \dfrac{e^{-.4}(.4)^5}{5!} = .0001$
6	$p(6) = \dfrac{e^{-.4}(.4)^6}{6!} = .0000$

in Table 5.9. In this table, values of the mean number of occurrences, μ, are listed across the top of the table, and values of x (the number of occurrences) are listed down the left side of the table. In order to use the table in the traffic control situation, we look at the column in Table 5.9 corresponding to .4, and we find the probabilities of 0, 1, 2, 3, 4, 5, and 6 errors (we have shaded these probabilities). For instance, the probability of one error in a week is .2681. Also, note that the probability of any number of errors greater than 6 is so small that it is not listed in the table. Table 5.10 summarizes the Poisson distribution of x, the number of errors in a week. This table also shows how the probabilities associated with the different values of x are calculated.

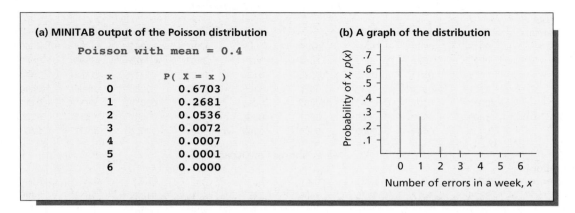

FIGURE 5.8 The Poisson Probability Distribution with $\mu = .4$

Poisson probabilities can also be calculated by using MINITAB and Excel. For instance, Figure 5.8(a) gives the MINITAB output of the Poisson distribution presented in Table 5.10.[3] This Poisson distribution is graphed in Figure 5.8(b).

Next, recall that there have been three errors at the air traffic control center in the last week. This is considerably more errors than .4, the expected number of errors assuming the center is still averaging 20.8 errors per year. Therefore, we have some evidence to contradict this assumption. To evaluate the strength of this evidence, we calculate the probability that at least three errors will occur in a week if, in fact, μ equals .4. Using the Poisson probabilities in Table 5.10 (for $\mu = .4$), we obtain

$$P(x \geq 3) = p(3) + p(4) + p(5) + p(6) = .0072 + .0007 + .0001 + .0000 = .008$$

This probability says that, if the center is averaging 20.8 errors per year, then there would be three or more errors in a week in only .8 percent of all weeks. That is, if we are to believe that the control center is averaging 20.8 errors per year, then we must believe that an 8 in 1,000 chance has occurred. Since it is very difficult to believe that such a rare event has occurred, we have strong evidence that the average number of errors per week has increased. Therefore, an investigation by the FAA into the reasons for such an increase is probably justified.

EXAMPLE 5.14

In the book *Modern Statistical Quality Control and Improvement,* Nicholas R. Farnum (1994) presents an example dealing with the quality of computer software. In the example, Farnum measures software quality by monitoring the number of errors per 1,000 lines of computer code.

Suppose that the number of errors per 1,000 lines of computer code is described by a Poisson distribution with a mean of four errors per 1,000 lines of code. If we wish to find the probability of obtaining eight errors in 2,500 lines of computer code, we must adjust the mean of the Poisson distribution. To do this, we arbitrarily choose a *space unit* of one line of code, and we note that a mean of four errors per 1,000 lines of code is equivalent to $4/1,000$ of an error per line of code. Therefore, the mean number of errors per 2,500 lines of code is $(4/1,000)(2,500) = 10$. It follows that

$$p(8) = \frac{e^{-\mu}\mu^8}{8!} = \frac{e^{-10}10^8}{8!} = .1126$$

---

[3]As we will show in the appendixes to this chapter, we can use Excel and MegaStat to obtain output of the Poisson distribution that is essentially identical to the output given by MINITAB.

FIGURE 5.9   **Several Poisson Distributions**

The mean, μ, is often called the *parameter* of the Poisson distribution. Figure 5.9 shows several Poisson distributions. We see that, depending on its parameter (mean), a Poisson distribution can be very skewed to the right or can be quite symmetrical.

Finally, if we place the Poisson probability formula into the general expressions (of Section 5.2) for μ_x, σ_x^2, and σ_x, we can derive formulas for calculating the mean, variance, and standard deviation of a Poisson distribution:

The Mean, Variance, and Standard Deviation of a Poisson Random Variable

Suppose that x is a **Poisson random variable**. If μ is the average number of occurrences of an event over the specified interval of time or space of interest, then

$$\mu_x = \mu \qquad \sigma_x^2 = \mu \qquad \sigma_x = \sqrt{\mu}$$

Here we see that both the mean and the variance of a Poisson random variable equal the average number of occurrences μ of the event of interest over the specified interval of time or space. For example, in the air traffic control situation, the Poisson distribution of x, the number of errors at the air traffic control center in a week, has a mean of $\mu_x = .4$ and a standard deviation of $\sigma_x = \sqrt{.4} = .6325$.

Exercises for Section 5.4

CONCEPTS

5.30   The values of a Poisson random variable are $x = 0, 1, 2, 3, \ldots$ Explain what these values represent.

5.31   Explain the assumptions that must be satisfied when a Poisson distribution adequately describes a random variable x.

connect

METHODS AND APPLICATIONS

5.32   Suppose that x has a Poisson distribution with $\mu = 2$.
    a   Write the Poisson formula and describe the possible values of x.
    b   Starting with the smallest possible value of x, calculate $p(x)$ for each value of x until $p(x)$ becomes smaller than .001.
    c   Graph the Poisson distribution using your results of b.
    d   Find $P(x = 2)$.   **e**   Find $P(x \leq 4)$.   **f**   Find $P(x < 4)$.
    g   Find $P(x \geq 1)$ and $P(x > 2)$.   **h**   Find $P(1 \leq x \leq 4)$.
    i   Find $P(2 < x < 5)$.   **j**   Find $P(2 \leq x < 6)$.

5.33   Suppose that x has a Poisson distribution with $\mu = 2$.
    a   Use the formulas given in this section to compute the mean, μ_x, variance, σ_x^2, and standard deviation, σ_x.
    b   Calculate the intervals $[\mu_x \pm 2\sigma_x]$ and $[\mu_x \pm 3\sigma_x]$. Then use the probabilities you calculated in Exercise 5.32 to find the probability that x will be inside each of these intervals.

5.34   A bank manager wishes to provide prompt service for customers at the bank's drive-up window. The bank currently can serve up to 10 customers per 15-minute period without significant delay. The average arrival rate is 7 customers per 15-minute period. Let x denote the number of customers arriving per 15-minute period. Assuming x has a Poisson distribution:

   a   Find the probability that 10 customers will arrive in a particular 15-minute period.

   b   Find the probability that 10 or fewer customers will arrive in a particular 15-minute period.

   c   Find the probability that there will be a significant delay at the drive-up window. That is, find the probability that more than 10 customers will arrive during a particular 15-minute period.

5.35   A telephone company's goal is to have no more than five monthly line failures on any 100 miles of line. The company currently experiences an average of two monthly line failures per 50 miles of line. Let x denote the number of monthly line failures per 100 miles of line. Assuming x has a Poisson distribution:

   a   Find the probability that the company will meet its goal on a particular 100 miles of line.

   b   Find the probability that the company will not meet its goal on a particular 100 miles of line.

   c   Find the probability that the company will have no more than five monthly failures on a particular 200 miles of line.

   d   Find the probability that the company will have more than 12 monthly failures on a particular 150 miles of line.

5.36   A local law enforcement agency claims that the number of times that a patrol car passes through a particular neighborhood follows a Poisson process with a mean of three times per nightly shift. Let x denote the number of times that a patrol car passes through the neighborhood during a nightly shift.

   a   Calculate the probability that no patrol cars pass through the neighborhood during a nightly shift.

   b   Suppose that during a randomly selected night shift no patrol cars pass through the neighborhood. Based on your answer in part a, do you believe the agency's claim? Explain.

   c   Assuming that nightly shifts are independent and assuming that the agency's claim is correct, find the probability that exactly one patrol car will pass through the neighborhood on each of four consecutive nights.

5.37   When the number of trials, n, is large, binomial probability tables may not be available. Furthermore, if a computer is not available, hand calculations will be tedious. As an alternative, the Poisson distribution can be used to approximate the binomial distribution when n is large and p is small. Here the mean of the Poisson distribution is taken to be $\mu = np$. That is, when n is large and p is small, we can use the Poisson formula with $\mu = np$ to calculate binomial probabilities; we will obtain results close to those we would obtain by using the binomial formula. A common rule is to use this approximation when $n/p \geq 500$.

   To illustrate this approximation, in the movie *Coma,* a young female intern at a Boston hospital was very upset when her friend, a young nurse, went into a coma during routine anesthesia at the hospital. Upon investigation, she found that 10 of the last 30,000 healthy patients at the hospital had gone into comas during routine anesthesias. When she confronted the hospital administrator with this fact and the fact that the national average was 6 out of 100,000 healthy patients going into comas during routine anesthesias, the administrator replied that 10 out of 30,000 was still quite small and thus not that unusual.

   a   Use the Poisson distribution to approximate the probability that 10 or more of 30,000 healthy patients would slip into comas during routine anesthesia, if in fact the true average at the hospital was 6 in 100,000. Hint: $\mu = np = 30,000(6/100,000) = 1.8$.

   b   Given the hospital's record and part a, what conclusion would you draw about the hospital's medical practices regarding anesthesia?

   (Note: It turned out that the hospital administrator was part of a conspiracy to sell body parts and was purposely putting healthy adults into comas during routine anesthesias. If the intern had taken a statistics course, she could have avoided a great deal of danger.)

5.38   Suppose that an automobile parts wholesaler claims that .5 percent of the car batteries in a shipment are defective. A random sample of 200 batteries is taken, and four are found to be defective.

   a   Use the Poisson approximation discussed in Exercise 5.37 to find the probability that four or more car batteries in a random sample of 200 such batteries would be found to be defective, if we assume that the wholesaler's claim is true.

   b   Based on your answer to part a, do you believe the claim? Explain.

5.5 The Hypergeometric Distribution (Optional) ● ● ●

The Hypergeometric Distribution

Suppose that a population consists of N items and that r of these items are *successes* and $(N - r)$ of these items are *failures*. If we randomly select n of the N items **without replacement**, it can be shown that the probability that x of the n randomly selected items will be successes is given by the **hypergeometric probability formula**

$$p(x) = \frac{\binom{r}{x}\binom{N - r}{n - x}}{\binom{N}{n}}$$

Here $\binom{r}{x}$ is the number of ways x successes can be selected from the total of r successes in the population, $\binom{N - r}{n - x}$ is the number of ways $n - x$ failures can be selected from the total of $N - r$ failures in the pupulation, and $\binom{N}{n}$ is the number of ways a sample of size n can be selected from a population of size N.

LO5 Use the hypergeometric distribution to compute probabilities (Optional).

To demonstrate the calculations, suppose that a population of $N = 6$ stocks consists of $r = 4$ stocks having positive returns (that is, there are $r = 4$ *successes*) and $N - r = 6 - 4 = 2$ stocks having negative returns (that is, there are $N - r = 2$ *failures*). Also suppose that we randomly select $n = 3$ of the six stocks in the population without replacement and that we define x to be the number of the three randomly selected stocks that give a positive return. Then, for example, the probability that $x = 2$ is

$$p(x = 2) = \frac{\binom{r}{x}\binom{N - r}{n - x}}{\binom{N}{n}} = \frac{\binom{4}{2}\binom{2}{1}}{\binom{6}{3}} = \frac{(6)(2)}{20} = .6$$

Similarly, the probability that $x = 3$ is

$$p(x = 3) = \frac{\binom{4}{3}\binom{2}{0}}{\binom{6}{3}} = \frac{(4)(1)}{20} = .2$$

It follows that the probability that at least two of the three randomly selected stocks will give a positive return is $p(x = 2) + p(x = 3) = .6 + .2 = .8$.

If we place the hypergeometric probability formula into the general expressions (of Section 5.2) for μ_x and σ_x^2, we can derive formulas for the mean and variance of the hypergeometric distribution.

The Mean and Variance of a Hypergeometric Random Variable

Suppose that x is a hypergeometric random variable. Then

$$\mu_x = n\left(\frac{r}{N}\right) \qquad \text{and} \qquad \sigma_x^2 = n\left(\frac{r}{N}\right)\left(1 - \frac{r}{N}\right)\left(\frac{N - n}{N - 1}\right)$$

In the previous example, we have $N = 6$, $r = 4$, and $n = 3$. It follows that

$$\mu_x = n\left(\frac{r}{N}\right) = 3\left(\frac{4}{6}\right) = 2, \qquad \text{and}$$

$$\sigma_x^2 = n\left(\frac{r}{N}\right)\left(1 - \frac{r}{N}\right)\left(\frac{N - n}{N - 1}\right) = 3\left(\frac{4}{6}\right)\left(1 - \frac{4}{6}\right)\left(\frac{6 - 3}{6 - 1}\right) = .4$$

and that the standard deviation $\sigma_x = \sqrt{.4} = .6325$.

To conclude this section, note that, on the first random selection from the population of N items, the probability of a success is r/N. Since we are making selections **without replacement,** the probability of a success changes as we continue to make selections. However, if the population size N is "much larger" than the sample size n (say, at least 20 times as large), then making the selections will not substantially change the probability of a success. In this case, we can assume that the probability of a success stays essentially constant from selection to selection, and the different selections are essentially independent of each other. Therefore, we can approximate the hypergeometric distribution by the binomial distribution. That is, we can compute probabilities about the hypergeometric random variable x by using the easier binomial probability formula

$$p(x) = \frac{n!}{x!\,(n-x)!}\, p^x (1-p)^{n-x} = \frac{n!}{x!\,(n-x)!} \left(\frac{r}{N}\right)^x \left(1 - \frac{r}{N}\right)^{n-x}$$

where the binomial probability of success equals r/N. The reader will use this approximation in Exercise 5.45.

Exercises for Section 5.5

CONCEPTS

connect

5.39   In the context of the hypergeometric distribution, explain the meanings of N, r, and n.

5.40   When can a hypergeometric distribution be approximated by a binomial distribution? Explain carefully what this means.

METHODS AND APPLICATIONS

5.41   Suppose that x has a hypergeometric distribution with $N = 8$, $r = 5$, and $n = 4$. Find:
   a $P(x = 0)$ **e** $P(x = 4)$
   b $P(x = 1)$ **f** $P(x \geq 2)$
   c $P(x = 2)$ **g** $P(x < 3)$
   d $P(x = 3)$ **h** $P(x > 1)$

5.42   Suppose that x has a hypergeometric distribution with $N = 10$, $r = 4$, and $n = 3$.
   a Write out the probability distribution of x.
   b Find the mean μ_x, variance σ_x^2, and standard deviation σ_x of this distribution.

5.43   Among 12 metal parts produced in a machine shop, 3 are defective. If a random sample of three of these metal parts is selected, find:
   a The probability that this sample will contain at least two defectives.
   b The probability that this sample will contain at most one defective.

5.44   Suppose that you purchase (randomly select) 3 TV sets from a production run of 10 TV sets. Of the 10 TV sets, 9 are destined to last at least five years without needing a single repair. What is the probability that all three of your TV sets will last at least five years without needing a single repair?

5.45   Suppose that you own an electronics store and purchase (randomly select) 15 TV sets from a production run of 500 TV sets. Of the 500 TV sets, 450 are destined to last at least five years without needing a single repair. Set up an expression using the hypergeometric distribution for the probability that at least 14 of your 15 TV sets will last at least five years without needing a single repair. Then, using the binomial tables (see Table A.1, page 631), approximate this probability by using the binomial distribution. What justifies the approximation? Hint: $p = r/N = 450/500 = .9$.

Chapter Summary

In this chapter we began our study of **random variables.** We learned that **a random variable represents an uncertain numerical outcome.** We also learned that a random variable whose values can be listed is called a **discrete random variable,** while the values of a **continuous random variable** correspond to one or more intervals on the real number line. We saw that a **probability distribution** of a discrete random variable is a table, graph, or formula that gives the probability associated with each of the random variable's possible values. We also discussed several descriptive measures of a discrete random variable—its **mean** (or **expected value**), its **variance,** and its **standard deviation.** We continued this chapter by studying two important, commonly used discrete probability distributions—the **binomial distribution** and the **Poisson distribution**—and we demonstrated how these distributions can be used to make statistical inferences. Finally, we studied a third important discrete probability distribution, the **hypergeometric distribution.**

Glossary of Terms

binomial distribution: The probability distribution that describes a binomial random variable. (page 205)

binomial experiment: An experiment that consists of n independent, identical trials, each of which results in either a success or a failure and is such that the probability of success on any trial is the same. (page 205)

binomial random variable: A random variable that is defined to be the total number of successes in n trials of a binomial experiment. (page 205)

binomial tables: Tables in which we can look up binomial probabilities. (page 208)

continuous random variable: A random variable whose values correspond to one or more intervals of numbers on the real number line. (page 191)

discrete random variable: A random variable whose values can be counted or listed. (page 191)

expected value (of a random variable): The mean of the population of all possible observed values of a random variable. That is, the long-run average value obtained if values of a random variable are observed a (theoretically) infinite number of times. (page 195)

hypergeometric distribution: The probability distribution that describes a hypergeometric random variable. (page 219)

hypergeometric random variable: A random variable that is defined to be the number of successes obtained in a random sample selected without replacement from a finite population of N elements that contains r successes and $N - r$ failures. (page 219)

Poisson distribution: The probability distribution that describes a Poisson random variable. (page 214)

Poisson random variable: A discrete random variable that can often be used to describe the number of occurrences of an event over a specified interval of time or space. (page 214)

probability distribution (of a discrete random variable): A table, graph, or formula that gives the probability associated with each of the random variable's values. (page 192)

random variable: A variable that assumes numerical values that are determined by the outcome of an experiment. That is, a variable that represents an uncertain numerical outcome. (page 191)

standard deviation (of a random variable): The standard deviation of the population of all possible observed values of a random variable. It measures the spread of the population of all possible observed values of the random variable. (page 198)

variance (of a random variable): The variance of the population of all possible observed values of a random variable. It measures the spread of the population of all possible observed values of the random variable. (page 198)

Important Formulas

Properties of a discrete probability distribution: page 194

The mean (expected value) of a discrete random variable: page 195

Variance and standard deviation of a discrete random variable: page 198

Binomial probability formula: page 205

Mean, variance, and standard deviation of a binomial random variable: page 211

Poisson probability formula: page 214

Mean, variance, and standard deviation of a Poisson random variable: page 217

Hypergeometric probability formula: page 219

Mean and variance of a hypergeometric random variable: page 219

Supplementary Exercises

5.46 An investor holds two stocks, each of which can rise (R), remain unchanged (U), or decline (D) on any particular day. Let x equal the number of stocks that rise on a particular day.
  a Write the probability distribution of x assuming that all outcomes are equally likely.
  b Write the probability distribution of x assuming that for each stock $P(R) = .6$, $P(U) = .1$, and $P(D) = .3$ and assuming that movements of the two stocks are independent.
  c Write the probability distribution of x assuming that for the first stock

$$P(R) = .4, \quad P(U) = .2, \quad P(D) = .4$$

and that for the second stock

$$P(R) = .8, \quad P(U) = .1, \quad P(D) = .1$$

and assuming that movements of the two stocks are independent.

5.47 Repeat Exercise 5.46, letting x equal the number of stocks that decline on the particular day.

5.48 Consider Exercise 5.46, and let x equal the number of stocks that rise on the particular day. Find μ_x and σ_x for
  a The probability distribution of x in Exercise 5.46a.
  b The probability distribution of x in Exercise 5.46b.
  c The probability distribution of x in Exercise 5.46c.
  d In which case is μ_x the largest? Interpret what this means in words.
  e In which case is σ_x the largest? Interpret what this means in words.

5.49   Suppose that the probability distribution of a random variable x can be described by the formula

$$p(x) = \frac{(x - 3)^2}{55}$$

for each of the values $x = -2, -1, 0, 1,$ and 2.
a   Write the probability distribution of x.
b   Show that the probability distribution of x satisfies the properties of a discrete probability distribution.
c   Calculate the mean of x.
d   Calculate the variance and standard deviation of x.

5.50   A rock concert promoter has scheduled an outdoor concert on July 4th. If it does not rain, the promoter will make \$30,000. If it does rain, the promoter will lose \$15,000 in guarantees made to the band and other expenses. The probability of rain on the 4th is .4.
a   What is the promoter's expected profit? Is the expected profit a reasonable decision criterion? Explain.
b   How much should an insurance company charge to insure the promoter's full losses? Explain your answer.

5.51   The demand (in number of copies per day) for a city newspaper is listed below with corresponding probabilities:

x = Demand	$p(x)$
50,000	.1
70,000	.25
90,000	.4
110,000	.2
130,000	.05

a   Graph the probability distribution of x.
b   Find the expected demand. Interpret this value, and label it on the graph of part a.
c   Using Chebyshev's Theorem, find the minimum percentage of all possible daily demand values that will fall in the interval $[\mu_x \pm 2\sigma_x]$.
d   Calculate the interval $[\mu_x \pm 2\sigma_x]$. Illustrate this interval on the graph of part a. According to the probability distribution of demand x previously given, what percentage of all possible daily demand values fall in the interval $[\mu_x \pm 2\sigma_x]$?

5.52   United Medicine, Inc., claims that a drug, Viro, significantly relieves the symptoms of a certain viral infection for 80 percent of all patients. Suppose that this drug is given to eight randomly selected patients who have been diagnosed with the viral infection.
a   Let x equal the number of the eight randomly selected patients whose symptoms are significantly relieved. What distribution describes the random variable x? Explain.
b   Assuming that the company's claim is correct, find $P(x \leq 3)$.
c   Suppose that of the eight randomly selected patients, three have had their symptoms significantly relieved by Viro. Based on the probability in part b, would you believe the claim of United Medicine, Inc.? Explain.

5.53   A consumer advocate claims that 80 percent of cable television subscribers are not satisfied with their cable service. In an attempt to justify this claim, a randomly selected sample of cable subscribers will be polled on this issue.
a   Suppose that the advocate's claim is true, and suppose that a random sample of five cable subscribers is selected. Assuming independence, use an appropriate formula to compute the probability that four or more subscribers in the sample are not satisfied with their service.
b   Suppose that the advocate's claim is true, and suppose that a random sample of 25 cable subscribers is selected. Assuming independence, find
   (1)   The probability that 15 or fewer subscribers in the sample are not satisfied with their service.
   (2)   The probability that more than 20 subscribers in the sample are not satisfied with their service.
   (3)   The probability that between 20 and 24 (inclusive) subscribers in the sample are not satisfied with their service.
   (4)   The probability that exactly 24 subscribers in the sample are not satisfied with their service.
c   Suppose that when we survey 25 randomly selected cable television subscribers, we find that 15 are actually not satisfied with their service. Using a probability you found in this exercise as the basis for your answer, do you believe the consumer advocate's claim? Explain.

5.54 A retail store has implemented procedures aimed at reducing the number of bad checks cashed by its cashiers. The store's goal is to cash no more than eight bad checks per week. The average number of bad checks cashed is three per week. Let x denote the number of bad checks cashed per week. Assuming that x has a Poisson distribution:

  a Find the probability that the store's cashiers will not cash any bad checks in a particular week.
  b Find the probability that the store will meet its goal during a particular week.
  c Find the probability that the store will not meet its goal during a particular week.
  d Find the probability that the store's cashiers will cash no more than 10 bad checks per two-week period.
  e Find the probability that the store's cashiers will cash no more than five bad checks per three-week period.

5.55 Suppose that the number of accidents occurring in an industrial plant is described by a Poisson process with an average of 1.5 accidents every three months. During the last three months, four accidents occurred.

  a Find the probability that no accidents will occur during the current three-month period.
  b Find the probability that fewer accidents will occur during the current three-month period than occurred during the last three-month period.
  c Find the probability that no more than 12 accidents will occur during a particular year.
  d Find the probability that no accidents will occur during a particular year.

5.56 A high-security government installation has installed four security systems to detect attempted break-ins. The four security systems operate independently of each other, and each has a .85 probability of detecting an attempted break-in. Assume an attempted break-in occurs. Use the binomial distribution to find the probability that at least one of the four security systems will detect it.

5.57 A new stain removal product claims to completely remove the stains on 90 percent of all stained garments. Assume that the product will be tested on 20 randomly selected stained garments, and let x denote the number of these garments from which the stains will be completely removed. Use the binomial distribution to find $P(x \leq 13)$ if the stain removal product's claim is correct. If x actually turns out to be 13, what do you think of the claim?

5.58 Consider Exercise 5.57, and find $P(x \leq 17)$ if the stain removal product's claim is correct. If x actually turns out to be 17, what do you think of the claim?

5.59 A state has averaged one small business failure per week over the past several years. Let x denote the number of small business failures in the next eight weeks. Use the Poisson distribution to find $P(x \geq 17)$ if the mean number of small business failures remains what it has been. If x actually turns out to be 17, what does this imply?

5.60 A candy company claims that its new chocolate almond bar averages 10 almonds per bar. Let x denote the number of almonds in the next bar that you buy. Use the Poisson distribution to find $P(x \leq 4)$ if the candy company's claim is correct. If x actually turns out to be 4, what do you think of the claim?

5.61 Consider Exercise 5.60, and find $P(x \leq 8)$ if the candy company's claim is true. If x actually turns out to be 8, what do you think of the claim?

Appendix 5.1 ■ Binomial, Poisson, and Hypergeometric Probabilities Using Excel

Binomial probabilities in Figure 5.4(a) on page 207:

- Enter the title, "Binomial with n = 4 and p = 0.10," in the location in which you wish to place the binomial results. Here we have placed the title beginning in cell A15 (any other choice will do).

- In cell A16, enter the heading, x.

- Enter the values 0 through 4 in cells A17 through A21.

- In cell B16, enter the heading P(X = x).

- Click in cell B17 (this is where the first binomial probability will be placed). Click on the Insert Function button f_x on the Excel toolbar.

- In the Insert Function dialog box, select Statistical from the "Or select a category:" menu, select BINOMDIST from the "Select a function:" menu, and click OK.

- In the BINOMDIST Function Arguments dialog box, enter the cell location A17 (this cell contains the value for which the first binomial probability will be calculated) in the "Number_s" box.

- Enter the value 4 in the Trials box.

- Enter the value 0.10 in the "Probability_s" box.

- Enter the value 0 in the Cumulative box.

- Click OK in the BINOMDIST Function Arguments dialog box.

- When you click OK, the calculated result (0.6561) will appear in cell B17. Double-click the drag handle (in the lower right corner) of cell B17 to automatically extend the cell formula to cells B18 through B21.

- The remaining probabilities will be placed in cells B18 through B21.

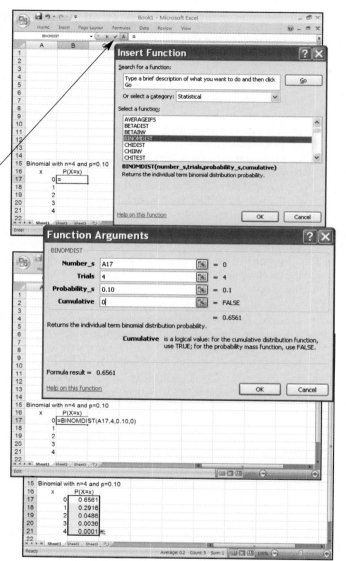

To obtain **hypergeometric probabilities:**
Enter data as above, click the Insert Function button, and select HYPGEOMDIST from the "Select a function" menu. Then in the Function Arguments dialog box:

- Enter the location of the initial number of successes in the Sample_s window.

- Enter the size of the sample in the Number_sample window.

- Enter the number of successes in the population in the Population_s window.

- Enter the size of the population in the Number_pop window.

Then click OK and proceed as above to compute the probabilities.

Poisson probabilities similar to Figure 5.8(a) on page 216:

- Enter the title "Poisson with mean = 0.40" in the location in which you wish to place the Poisson results. Here we have placed the title beginning in cell A13 (any other choice will do).

- In cell A14, enter the heading, x.

- Enter the values 0 through 6 in cells A15 through A21.

- In cell B14, enter the heading, P(X = x).

- Click in cell B15 (this is where the first Poisson probability will be placed). Click on the Insert Function button f_x on the Excel toolbar.

- In the Insert Function dialog box, select Statistical from the "Or select a category" menu, select POISSON from the "Select a function" menu, and click OK.

- In the POISSON Function Arguments dialog box, enter the cell location A15 (this cell contains the value for which the first Poisson probability will be calculated) in the "X" box.

- Enter the value 0.40 in the Mean box.

- Enter the value 0 in the Cumulative box.

- Click OK in the POISSON Function Arguments dialog box.

- The calculated result for the probability of 0 events will appear in cell B15.

- Click on cell B15 and select **Home : Format : Format Cells.**

- In the Format Cells dialog box, click on the Number tab, select Number from the Category menu, enter 4 in the Decimal places box, and click OK.

- Double-click the drag handle (in the lower right corner) of cell B15 to automatically extend the cell formula to cells B16 through B21.

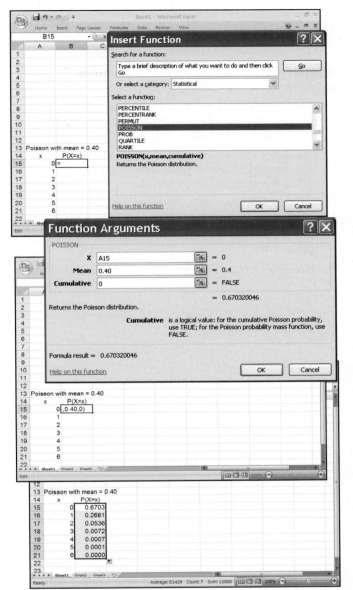

Appendix 5.2 ■ Binomial, Poisson, and Hypergeometric Probabilities Using MegaStat

Binomial probabilities similar to those in Figure 5.7 on page 213:

- Select **Add-Ins : MegaStat : Probability : Discrete Probability Distributions.**
- In the "Discrete Probability Distributions" dialog box, enter the number of trials (here equal to 24) and the probability of success p (here equal to .01) in the appropriate windows.
- Click the Display Graph checkbox if a plot of the distribution is desired.
- Click OK in the "Discrete Probability Distributions" dialog box.

The binomial output is placed in an output worksheet.

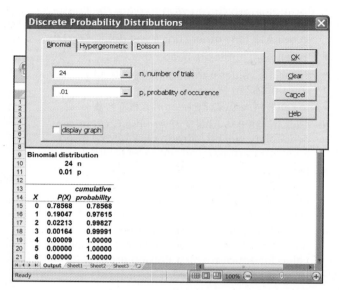

To calculate **Poisson probabilities**, click on the Poisson tab and enter the mean of the Poisson distribution. Then click OK.

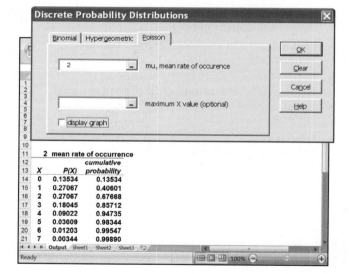

To calculate **Hypergeometric probabilities,** click on the Hypergeometric tab. Then enter the population size, the number of successes in the population, and the sample size in the appropriate windows and click OK.

Appendix 5.3 ■ Binomial, Poisson, and Hypergeometric Probabilities Using MINITAB

Binomial probabilities similar to Figure 5.4(a) on page 207:

- In the data window, enter the values 0 through 4 into column C1 and name the column x.
- Select **Calc : Probability Distributions : Binomial.**
- In the Binomial Distribution dialog box, select the Probability option by clicking.
- In the "Number of trials" window, enter 4 for the value of n.
- In the "Event Probability" window, enter 0.1 for the value of p.
- Select the "Input column" option and enter the variable name x into the "Input column" window.
- Click OK in the Binomial Distribution dialog box.
- The binomial probabilities will be displayed in the Session window.

To compute **hypergeometric probabilities:**

- Enter data as above.
- Select **Calc : Probability Distributions : Hypergeometric.**
- In the Hypergeometric Distribution dialog box: Enter the "Population size," "Event count (number of successes) in population," "Sample Size," and enter x as the "Input column" option.
- Click OK to obtain the probabilities in the Session Window.

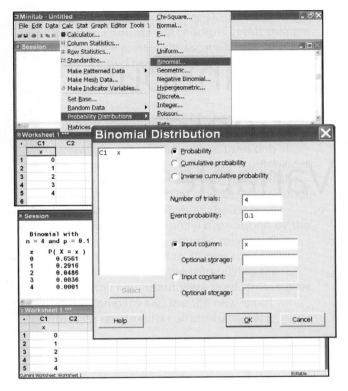

Poisson probabilities in Figure 5.8(a) on page 216:

- In the data window, enter the values 0 through 6 into column C1 and name the column x.
- Select **Calc : Probability Distributions : Poisson.**
- In the Poisson Distribution dialog box, select the Probability option by clicking.
- In the Mean window, enter 0.4.
- Select the "Input column" option and enter the variable name x into the "Input column" window.
- Click OK in the Poisson Distribution dialog box.
- The Poisson probabilities will be displayed in the Session window.

FIGURE 6.1   An Example of a Continuous Probability Distribution $f(x)$

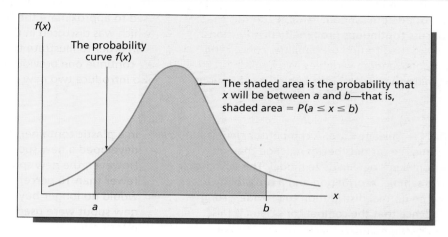

An *area* under a continuous probability distribution (or probability curve) is a *probability*. For instance, consider the range of values on the number line from the number a to the number b—that is, the interval of numbers from a to b. If the continuous random variable x is described by the probability curve $f(x)$, then the area under $f(x)$ corresponding to the interval from a to b is the probability that x will attain a value between a and b. Such a probability is illustrated as the shaded area in Figure 6.1. We write this probability as $P(a \leq x \leq b)$. For example, suppose that the continuous probability curve $f(x)$ in Figure 6.1 describes the random variable x = the temperature of a randomly selected cup of coffee at the fast-food restaurant. It then follows that $P(153 \leq x \leq 167)$— the probability that the temperature of a randomly selected cup of coffee at the fast-food restaurant will be between 153° and 167°—is the area under the curve $f(x)$ between 153 and 167.

We know that any probability is 0 or positive, and we also know that the probability assigned to all possible values of x must be 1. It follows that, similar to the conditions required for a discrete probability distribution, a probability curve must satisfy the following properties:

Properties of a Continuous Probability Distribution

The **continuous probability distribution** (or **probability curve**) $f(x)$ of a random variable x must satisfy the following two conditions:

1 $f(x) \geq 0$ for any value of x.

2   The total area under the curve $f(x)$ is equal to 1.

Any continuous curve $f(x)$ that satisfies these conditions is a valid continuous probability distribution. Such probability curves can have a variety of shapes—bell-shaped and symmetrical, skewed to the right, skewed to the left, or any other shape. In a practical problem, the shape of a probability curve would be estimated by looking at a frequency (or relative frequency) histogram of observed data (as we have done in Chapter 2). Later in this chapter, we study probability curves having several different shapes. For example, in the next section we introduce the *uniform distribution*, which has a rectangular shape.

We have seen that to calculate a probability concerning a continuous random variable, we must compute an appropriate area under the curve $f(x)$. In theory, such areas are calculated by calculus methods and/or numerical techniques. Because these methods are difficult, needed areas under commonly used probability curves have been compiled in statistical tables. As we need them, we show how to use the required statistical tables. Also, note that since there is no area under a continuous curve at a single point, the probability that a continuous random variable x will attain a single value is always equal to 0. It follows that in Figure 6.1 we have $P(x = a) = 0$ and $P(x = b) = 0$. Therefore, $P(a \leq x \leq b)$ equals $P(a < x < b)$ because each of the interval endpoints a and b has a probability that is equal to 0.

6.2 The Uniform Distribution ● ● ●

Suppose that over a period of several days the manager of a large hotel has recorded the waiting times of 1,000 people waiting for an elevator in the lobby at dinnertime (5:00 P.M. to 7:00 P.M.). The observed waiting times range from zero to four minutes. Furthermore, when the waiting times are arranged into a histogram, the bars making up the histogram have approximately equal heights, giving the histogram a rectangular appearance. This implies that the relative frequencies of all waiting times from zero to four minutes are about the same. Therefore, it is reasonable to use the *uniform distribution* to describe the random variable x, the amount of time a randomly selected hotel patron spends waiting for the elevator. In general, the equation that describes the uniform distribution is given in the following box, and this equation is graphed in Figure 6.2(a).

The Uniform Distribution

If c and d are numbers on the real line, the probability curve describing the **uniform distribution** is

$$f(x) = \begin{cases} \dfrac{1}{d - c} & \text{for } c \le x \le d \\ 0 & \text{otherwise} \end{cases}$$

Furthermore, the mean and the standard deviation of the population of all possible observed values of a random variable x that has a uniform distribution are

$$\mu_x = \frac{c + d}{2} \quad \text{and} \quad \sigma_x = \frac{d - c}{\sqrt{12}}$$

FIGURE 6.2   The Uniform Distribution

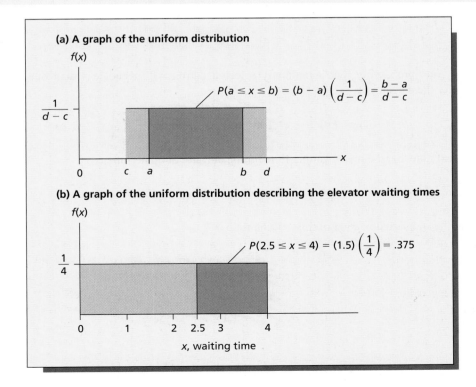

(a) A graph of the uniform distribution

$$P(a \le x \le b) = (b - a)\left(\frac{1}{d - c}\right) = \frac{b - a}{d - c}$$

(b) A graph of the uniform distribution describing the elevator waiting times

$$P(2.5 \le x \le 4) = (1.5)\left(\frac{1}{4}\right) = .375$$

x, waiting time

Notice that the total area under the uniform distribution is the area of a rectangle having a base equal to $(d - c)$ and a height equal to $1/(d - c)$. Therefore, the probability curve's total area is

$$\text{base} \times \text{height} = (d - c)\left(\frac{1}{d - c}\right) = 1$$

(remember that the total area under any continuous probability curve must equal 1). Furthermore, if a and b are numbers that are as illustrated in Figure 6.2(a), then the probability that x will be between a and b is the area of a rectangle with base $(b - a)$ and height $1/(d - c)$. That is,

$$P(a \leq x \leq b) = \text{base} \times \text{height}$$

$$= (b - a)\left(\frac{1}{d - c}\right)$$

$$= \frac{b - a}{d - c}$$

EXAMPLE 6.1

In the introduction to this section we have said that the amount of time, x, that a randomly selected hotel patron spends waiting for the elevator at dinnertime is uniformly distributed between zero and four minutes. In this case, $c = 0$ and $d = 4$. Therefore,

$$f(x) = \begin{cases} \dfrac{1}{d - c} = \dfrac{1}{4 - 0} = \dfrac{1}{4} & \text{for } 0 \leq x \leq 4 \\ \\ 0 & \text{otherwise} \end{cases}$$

Noting that this equation is graphed in Figure 6.2(b), suppose that the hotel manager wishes to find the probability that a randomly selected patron will spend at least 2.5 minutes waiting for the elevator. This probability is the area under the curve $f(x)$ that corresponds to the interval [2.5, 4]. As shown in Figure 6.2(b), this probability is the area of a rectangle having a base equal to $4 - 2.5 = 1.5$ and a height equal to $1/4$. That is,

$$P(x \geq 2.5) = P(2.5 \leq x \leq 4) = \text{base} \times \text{height} = 1.5 \times \frac{1}{4} = .375$$

Similarly, the probability that a randomly selected patron will spend less than one minute waiting for the elevator is

$$P(x < 1) = P(0 \leq x \leq 1) = \text{base} \times \text{height} = 1 \times \frac{1}{4} = .25$$

We next note that the mean waiting time for the elevator at dinnertime is

$$\mu_x = \frac{c + d}{2} = \frac{0 + 4}{2} = 2 \text{ (minutes)}$$

and that the standard deviation of this waiting time is

$$\sigma_x = \frac{d - c}{\sqrt{12}} = \frac{4 - 0}{\sqrt{12}} = 1.1547 \text{ (minutes)}$$

Therefore, because

$$\mu_x - \sigma_x = 2 - 1.1547 = .8453$$

and

$$\mu_x + \sigma_x = 2 + 1.1547 = 3.1547$$

the probability that the waiting time of a randomly selected patron will be within (plus or minus) one standard deviation of the mean waiting time is

$$P(.8453 \leq x \leq 3.1547) = (3.1547 - .8453) \times \frac{1}{4}$$

$$= .57735$$

Exercises for Sections 6.1 and 6.2

CONCEPTS

6.1 A discrete probability distribution assigns probabilities to individual values. To what are probabilities assigned by a continuous probability distribution?

6.2 How do we use the continuous probability distribution (or probability curve) of a random variable x to find probabilities? Explain.

6.3 What two properties must be satisfied by a continuous probability distribution (or probability curve)?

6.4 Is the height of a probability curve over a given point a probability? Explain.

6.5 When is it appropriate to use the uniform distribution to describe a random variable x?

METHODS AND APPLICATIONS

6.6 Suppose that the random variable x has a uniform distribution with $c = 2$ and $d = 8$.
  a Write the formula for the probability curve of x, and write an interval that gives the possible values of x.
  b Graph the probability curve of x.
  c Find $P(3 \leq x \leq 5)$.
  d Find $P(1.5 \leq x \leq 6.5)$.
  e Calculate the mean μ_x, variance σ_x^2, and standard deviation σ_x.
  f Calculate the interval $[\mu_x \pm 2\sigma_x]$. What is the probability that x will be in this interval?

6.7 Consider the figure given in the margin. Find the value h that makes the function $f(x)$ a valid continuous probability distribution.

6.8 Assume that the waiting time x for an elevator is uniformly distributed between zero and six minutes.
  a Write the formula for the probability curve of x.
  b Graph the probability curve of x.
  c Find $P(2 \leq x \leq 4)$.
  d Find $P(3 \leq x \leq 6)$.
  e Find $P(\{0 \leq x \leq 2\}$ or $\{5 \leq x \leq 6\})$.

6.9 Refer to Exercise 6.8.
  a Calculate the mean, μ_x, the variance, σ_x^2, and the standard deviation, σ_x.
  b Find the probability that the waiting time of a randomly selected patron will be within one standard deviation of the mean.

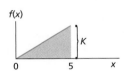

6.10 Consider the figure given in the margin. Find the value k that makes the function $f(x)$ a valid continuous probability distribution.

6.11 Suppose that an airline quotes a flight time of 2 hours, 10 minutes between two cities. Furthermore, suppose that historical flight records indicate that the actual flight time between the two cities, x, is uniformly distributed between 2 hours and 2 hours, 20 minutes. Letting the time unit be one minute,
  a Write the formula for the probability curve of x.
  b Graph the probability curve of x.
  c Find $P(125 \leq x \leq 135)$.
  d Find the probability that a randomly selected flight between the two cities will be at least five minutes late.

6.12 Refer to Exercise 6.11.
  a Calculate the mean flight time and the standard deviation of the flight time.
  b Find the probability that the flight time will be within one standard deviation of the mean.

6.13 Consider the figure given in the margin. Find the value c that makes the function $f(x)$ a valid continuous probability distribution.

6.14 A weather forecaster predicts that the May rainfall in a local area will be between three and six inches but has no idea where within the interval the amount will be. Let x be the amount of May rainfall in the local area, and assume that x is uniformly distributed over the interval three to six inches.

a Write the formula for the probability curve of x.

b Graph the probability curve of x.

c What is the probability that May rainfall will be at least four inches? At least five inches? At most 4.5 inches?

6.15 Refer to Exercise 6.14.

a Calculate the expected May rainfall.

b What is the probability that the observed May rainfall will fall within two standard deviations of the mean? Within one standard deviation of the mean?

 Describe the properties of the normal distribution and use a cumulative normal table.

6.3 The Normal Probability Distribution ● ● ●

The normal curve The bell-shaped appearance of the normal probability distribution is illustrated in Figure 6.3. The equation that defines this normal curve is given in the following box:

The Normal Probability Distribution

The **normal probability distribution** is defined by the equation

$$f(x) = \frac{1}{\sigma\sqrt{2\pi}}\, e^{-\frac{1}{2}\left(\frac{x-\mu}{\sigma}\right)^2} \quad \text{for all values of } x \text{ on the real line}$$

Here μ and σ are the mean and standard deviation of the population of all possible observed values of the random variable x under consideration. Furthermore, $\pi = 3.14159\ldots$, and $e = 2.71828\ldots$ is the base of Napierian logarithms.

FIGURE 6.3

The Normal Probability Curve

The normal curve is symmetrical around μ, and the total area under the curve equals 1.

The normal probability distribution has several important properties:

1 There is an entire family of normal probability distributions; the specific shape of each normal distribution is determined by its mean μ and its standard deviation σ.

2 The highest point on the normal curve is located at the mean, which is also the median and the mode of the distribution.

3 The normal distribution is symmetrical: The curve's shape to the left of the mean is the mirror image of its shape to the right of the mean.

4 The tails of the normal curve extend to infinity in both directions and never touch the horizontal axis. However, the tails get close enough to the horizontal axis quickly enough to ensure that the total area under the normal curve equals 1.

5 Since the normal curve is symmetrical, the area under the normal curve to the right of the mean (μ) equals the area under the normal curve to the left of the mean, and each of these areas equals .5 (see Figure 6.3).

Intuitively, the mean μ positions the normal curve on the real line. This is illustrated in Figure 6.4(a). This figure shows two normal curves with different means μ_1 and μ_2 (where μ_1 is greater than μ_2) and with equal standard deviations. We see that the normal curve with mean μ_1 is centered farther to the right.

The variance σ^2 (and the standard deviation σ) measure the spread of the normal curve. This is illustrated in Figure 6.4(b), which shows two normal curves with the same mean and two different standard deviations σ_1 and σ_2. Because σ_1 is greater than σ_2, the normal curve with standard deviation σ_1 is more spread out (flatter) than the normal curve with standard deviation σ_2. In general, larger standard deviations result in normal curves that are flatter and more spread out, while smaller standard deviations result in normal curves that have higher peaks and are less spread out.

Suppose that a random variable x is normally distributed with mean μ and standard deviation σ. If a and b are numbers on the real line, we consider the probability that x will attain a value

F I G U R E 6 . 4   **How the Mean μ and Standard Deviation σ Affect the Position and Shape of a Normal Probability Curve**

(a) Two normal curves with different means and equal standard deviations. If μ_1 is greater than μ_2, the normal curve with mean μ_1 is centered farther to the right.

(b) Two normal curves with the same mean and different standard deviations. If σ_1 is greater than σ_2, the normal curve with standard deviation σ_1 is flatter and more spread out.

F I G U R E 6 . 5   **An Area under a Normal Curve Corresponding to the Interval [a, b]**

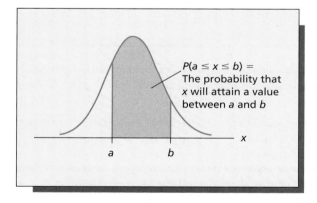

$P(a \leq x \leq b) =$ The probability that x will attain a value between a and b

F I G U R E 6 . 6   **Three Important Percentages Concerning a Normally Distributed Random Variable x with Mean μ and Standard Deviation σ**

between a and b. That is, we consider

$$P(a \leq x \leq b)$$

which equals the area under the normal curve with mean μ and standard deviation σ corresponding to the interval $[a, b]$. Such an area is depicted in Figure 6.5. We soon explain how to find such areas using a statistical table called a **normal table.** For now, we emphasize three important areas under a normal curve. These areas form the basis for the **Empirical Rule** for a normally distributed population. Specifically, if x is normally distributed with mean μ and standard deviation σ, it can be shown (using a normal table) that, as illustrated in Figure 6.6:

Three Important Areas under the Normal Curve

1 $P(\mu - \sigma \leq x \leq \mu + \sigma) = .6826$

This means that 68.26 percent of all possible observed values of x are within (plus or minus) one standard deviation of μ.

2 $P(\mu - 2\sigma \leq x \leq \mu + 2\sigma) = .9544$

This means that 95.44 percent of all possible

observed values of x are within (plus or minus) two standard deviations of μ.

3 $P(\mu - 3\sigma \leq x \leq \mu + 3\sigma) = .9973$

This means that 99.73 percent of all possible observed values of x are within (plus or minus) three standard deviations of μ.

Finding normal curve areas   There is a unique normal curve for every combination of μ and σ. Since there are many (theoretically, an unlimited number of) such combinations, we would like to have one table of normal curve areas that applies to all normal curves. There is such a table, and we can use it by thinking in terms of how many standard deviations a value of interest is from the mean. Specifically, consider a random variable x that is normally distributed with mean μ and standard deviation σ. Then the random variable

$$z = \frac{x - \mu}{\sigma}$$

expresses the number of standard deviations that x is from the mean μ. To understand this idea, notice that if x equals μ (that is, x is zero standard deviations from μ), then $z = (\mu - \mu)/\sigma = 0$. However, if x is one standard deviation above the mean (that is, if x equals $\mu + \sigma$), then $x - \mu = \sigma$ and $z = \sigma/\sigma = 1$. Similarly, if x is two standard deviations below the mean (that is, if x equals $\mu - 2\sigma$), then $x - \mu = -2\sigma$ and $z = -2\sigma/\sigma = -2$. Figure 6.7 illustrates that for values of x of, respectively, $\mu - 3\sigma$, $\mu - 2\sigma$, $\mu - \sigma$, μ, $\mu + \sigma$, $\mu + 2\sigma$, and $\mu + 3\sigma$, the corresponding values of z are $-3, -2, -1, 0, 1, 2$, and 3. This figure also illustrates the following general result:

The Standard Normal Distribution

If a random variable x (or, equivalently, the population of all possible observed values of x) is normally distributed with mean μ and standard deviation σ, then the random variable

$$z = \frac{x - \mu}{\sigma}$$

(or, equivalently, the population of all possible observed values of z) is normally distributed with mean 0 and standard deviation 1. A normal distribution (or curve) with mean 0 and standard deviation 1 is called a **standard normal distribution** (or **curve**).

Table A.3 (on pages 638 and 639) is a table of *cumulative* areas under the standard normal curve. This table is called a *cumulative normal table*, and it is reproduced as Table 6.1 (on pages 237 and 238). Specifically,

The **cumulative normal table** gives, for many different values of z, the area under the standard normal curve to the left of z.

FIGURE 6.7   **If x Is Normally Distributed with Mean μ and Standard Deviation σ, Then $z = \dfrac{x - \mu}{\sigma}$ Is Normally Distributed with Mean 0 and Standard Deviation 1**

Two such areas are shown next to Table 6.1—one with a negative z value and one with a positive z value. The values of z in the cumulative normal table range from -3.99 to 3.99 in increments of .01. As can be seen from Table 6.1, values of z accurate to the nearest tenth are given in the far left column (headed z) of the table. Further graduations to the nearest hundredth (.00, .01, .02, . . . , .09) are given across the top of the table. The areas under the normal curve are given in the body of the table, accurate to four (or sometimes five) decimal places.

TABLE 6.1   **Cumulative Areas under the Standard Normal Curve**

z	0.00	0.01	0.02	0.03	0.04	0.05	0.06	0.07	0.08	0.09
−3.9	0.00005	0.00005	0.00004	0.00004	0.00004	0.00004	0.00004	0.00004	0.00003	0.00003
−3.8	0.00007	0.00007	0.00007	0.00006	0.00006	0.00006	0.00006	0.00005	0.00005	0.00005
−3.7	0.00011	0.00010	0.00010	0.00010	0.00009	0.00009	0.00008	0.00008	0.00008	0.00008
−3.6	0.00016	0.00015	0.00015	0.00014	0.00014	0.00013	0.00013	0.00012	0.00012	0.00011
−3.5	0.00023	0.00022	0.00022	0.00021	0.00020	0.00019	0.00019	0.00018	0.00017	0.00017
−3.4	0.00034	0.00032	0.00031	0.00030	0.00029	0.00028	0.00027	0.00026	0.00025	0.00024
−3.3	0.00048	0.00047	0.00045	0.00043	0.00042	0.00040	0.00039	0.00038	0.00036	0.00035
−3.2	0.00069	0.00066	0.00064	0.00062	0.00060	0.00058	0.00056	0.00054	0.00052	0.00050
−3.1	0.00097	0.00094	0.00090	0.00087	0.00084	0.00082	0.00079	0.00076	0.00074	0.00071
−3.0	0.00135	0.00131	0.00126	0.00122	0.00118	0.00114	0.00111	0.00107	0.00103	0.00100
−2.9	0.0019	0.0018	0.0018	0.0017	0.0016	0.0016	0.0015	0.0015	0.0014	0.0014
−2.8	0.0026	0.0025	0.0024	0.0023	0.0023	0.0022	0.0021	0.0021	0.0020	0.0019
−2.7	0.0035	0.0034	0.0033	0.0032	0.0031	0.0030	0.0029	0.0028	0.0027	0.0026
−2.6	0.0047	0.0045	0.0044	0.0043	0.0041	0.0040	0.0039	0.0038	0.0037	0.0036
−2.5	0.0062	0.0060	0.0059	0.0057	0.0055	0.0054	0.0052	0.0051	0.0049	0.0048
−2.4	0.0082	0.0080	0.0078	0.0075	0.0073	0.0071	0.0069	0.0068	0.0066	0.0064
−2.3	0.0107	0.0104	0.0102	0.0099	0.0096	0.0094	0.0091	0.0089	0.0087	0.0084
−2.2	0.0139	0.0136	0.0132	0.0129	0.0125	0.0122	0.0119	0.0116	0.0113	0.0110
−2.1	0.0179	0.0174	0.0170	0.0166	0.0162	0.0158	0.0154	0.0150	0.0146	0.0143
−2.0	0.0228	0.0222	0.0217	0.0212	0.0207	0.0202	0.0197	0.0192	0.0188	0.0183
−1.9	0.0287	0.0281	0.0274	0.0268	0.0262	0.0256	0.0250	0.0244	0.0239	0.0233
−1.8	0.0359	0.0351	0.0344	0.0336	0.0329	0.0322	0.0314	0.0307	0.0301	0.0294
−1.7	0.0446	0.0436	0.0427	0.0418	0.0409	0.0401	0.0392	0.0384	0.0375	0.0367
−1.6	0.0548	0.0537	0.0526	0.0516	0.0505	0.0495	0.0485	0.0475	0.0465	0.0455
−1.5	0.0668	0.0655	0.0643	0.0630	0.0618	0.0606	0.0594	0.0582	0.0571	0.0559
−1.4	0.0808	0.0793	0.0778	0.0764	0.0749	0.0735	0.0721	0.0708	0.0694	0.0681
−1.3	0.0968	0.0951	0.0934	0.0918	0.0901	0.0885	0.0869	0.0853	0.0838	0.0823
−1.2	0.1151	0.1131	0.1112	0.1093	0.1075	0.1056	0.1038	0.1020	0.1003	0.0985
−1.1	0.1357	0.1335	0.1314	0.1292	0.1271	0.1251	0.1230	0.1210	0.1190	0.1170
−1.0	0.1587	0.1562	0.1539	0.1515	0.1492	0.1469	0.1446	0.1423	0.1401	0.1379
−0.9	0.1841	0.1814	0.1788	0.1762	0.1736	0.1711	0.1685	0.1660	0.1635	0.1611
−0.8	0.2119	0.2090	0.2061	0.2033	0.2005	0.1977	0.1949	0.1922	0.1894	0.1867
−0.7	0.2420	0.2389	0.2358	0.2327	0.2296	0.2266	0.2236	0.2206	0.2177	0.2148
−0.6	0.2743	0.2709	0.2676	0.2643	0.2611	0.2578	0.2546	0.2514	0.2482	0.2451
−0.5	0.3085	0.3050	0.3015	0.2981	0.2946	0.2912	0.2877	0.2843	0.2810	0.2776
−0.4	0.3446	0.3409	0.3372	0.3336	0.3300	0.3264	0.3228	0.3192	0.3156	0.3121
−0.3	0.3821	0.3783	0.3745	0.3707	0.3669	0.3632	0.3594	0.3557	0.3520	0.3483
−0.2	0.4207	0.4168	0.4129	0.4090	0.4052	0.4013	0.3974	0.3936	0.3897	0.3859
−0.1	0.4602	0.4562	0.4522	0.4483	0.4443	0.4404	0.4364	0.4325	0.4286	0.4247
−0.0	0.5000	0.4960	0.4920	0.4880	0.4840	0.4801	0.4761	0.4721	0.4681	0.4641
0.0	0.5000	0.5040	0.5080	0.5120	0.5160	0.5199	0.5239	0.5279	0.5319	0.5359
0.1	0.5398	0.5438	0.5478	0.5517	0.5557	0.5596	0.5636	0.5675	0.5714	0.5753
0.2	0.5793	0.5832	0.5871	0.5910	0.5948	0.5987	0.6026	0.6064	0.6103	0.6141
0.3	0.6179	0.6217	0.6255	0.6293	0.6331	0.6368	0.6406	0.6443	0.6480	0.6517
0.4	0.6554	0.6591	0.6628	0.6664	0.6700	0.6736	0.6772	0.6808	0.6844	0.6879
0.5	0.6915	0.6950	0.6985	0.7019	0.7054	0.7088	0.7123	0.7157	0.7190	0.7224
0.6	0.7257	0.7291	0.7324	0.7357	0.7389	0.7422	0.7454	0.7486	0.7518	0.7549
0.7	0.7580	0.7611	0.7642	0.7673	0.7704	0.7734	0.7764	0.7794	0.7823	0.7852
0.8	0.7881	0.7910	0.7939	0.7967	0.7995	0.8023	0.8051	0.8078	0.8106	0.8133
0.9	0.8159	0.8186	0.8212	0.8238	0.8264	0.8289	0.8315	0.8340	0.8365	0.8389

(Table Continues)

T A B L E 6 . 1   **Cumulative Areas under the Standard Normal Curve (*Continued*)**

z	0.00	0.01	0.02	0.03	0.04	0.05	0.06	0.07	0.08	0.09
1.0	0.8413	0.8438	0.8461	0.8485	0.8508	0.8531	0.8554	0.8577	0.8599	0.8621
1.1	0.8643	0.8665	0.8686	0.8708	0.8729	0.8749	0.8770	0.8790	0.8810	0.8830
1.2	0.8849	0.8869	0.8888	0.8907	0.8925	0.8944	0.8962	0.8980	0.8997	0.9015
1.3	0.9032	0.9049	0.9066	0.9082	0.9099	0.9115	0.9131	0.9147	0.9162	0.9177
1.4	0.9192	0.9207	0.9222	0.9236	0.9251	0.9265	0.9279	0.9292	0.9306	0.9319
1.5	0.9332	0.9345	0.9357	0.9370	0.9382	0.9394	0.9406	0.9418	0.9429	0.9441
1.6	0.9452	0.9463	0.9474	0.9484	0.9495	0.9505	0.9515	0.9525	0.9535	0.9545
1.7	0.9554	0.9564	0.9573	0.9582	0.9591	0.9599	0.9608	0.9616	0.9625	0.9633
1.8	0.9641	0.9649	0.9656	0.9664	0.9671	0.9678	0.9686	0.9693	0.9699	0.9706
1.9	0.9713	0.9719	0.9726	0.9732	0.9738	0.9744	0.9750	0.9756	0.9761	0.9767
2.0	0.9772	0.9778	0.9783	0.9788	0.9793	0.9798	0.9803	0.9808	0.9812	0.9817
2.1	0.9821	0.9826	0.9830	0.9834	0.9838	0.9842	0.9846	0.9850	0.9854	0.9857
2.2	0.9861	0.9864	0.9868	0.9871	0.9875	0.9878	0.9881	0.9884	0.9887	0.9890
2.3	0.9893	0.9896	0.9898	0.9901	0.9904	0.9906	0.9909	0.9911	0.9913	0.9916
2.4	0.9918	0.9920	0.9922	0.9925	0.9927	0.9929	0.9931	0.9932	0.9934	0.9936
2.5	0.9938	0.9940	0.9941	0.9943	0.9945	0.9946	0.9948	0.9949	0.9951	0.9952
2.6	0.9953	0.9955	0.9956	0.9957	0.9959	0.9960	0.9961	0.9962	0.9963	0.9964
2.7	0.9965	0.9966	0.9967	0.9968	0.9969	0.9970	0.9971	0.9972	0.9973	0.9974
2.8	0.9974	0.9975	0.9976	0.9977	0.9977	0.9978	0.9979	0.9979	0.9980	0.9981
2.9	0.9981	0.9982	0.9982	0.9983	0.9984	0.9984	0.9985	0.9985	0.9986	0.9986
3.0	0.99865	0.99869	0.99874	0.99878	0.99882	0.99886	0.99889	0.99893	0.99897	0.99900
3.1	0.99903	0.99906	0.99910	0.99913	0.99916	0.99918	0.99921	0.99924	0.99926	0.99929
3.2	0.99931	0.99934	0.99936	0.99938	0.99940	0.99942	0.99944	0.99946	0.99948	0.99950
3.3	0.99952	0.99953	0.99955	0.99957	0.99958	0.99960	0.99961	0.99962	0.99964	0.99965
3.4	0.99966	0.99968	0.99969	0.99970	0.99971	0.99972	0.99973	0.99974	0.99975	0.99976
3.5	0.99977	0.99978	0.99978	0.99979	0.99980	0.99981	0.99981	0.99982	0.99983	0.99983
3.6	0.99984	0.99985	0.99985	0.99986	0.99986	0.99987	0.99987	0.99988	0.99988	0.99989
3.7	0.99989	0.99990	0.99990	0.99990	0.99991	0.99991	0.99992	0.99992	0.99992	0.99992
3.8	0.99993	0.99993	0.99993	0.99994	0.99994	0.99994	0.99994	0.99995	0.99995	0.99995
3.9	0.99995	0.99995	0.99996	0.99996	0.99996	0.99996	0.99996	0.99996	0.99997	0.99997

As an example, suppose that we wish to find the area under the standard normal curve to the left of a z value of 2.00. This area is illustrated in Figure 6.8. To find this area, we start at the top of the leftmost column in Table 6.1 (previous page) and scan down the column past the negative z values. We then scan through the positive z values (which continue on the top of this page) until we find the z value 2.0—see the red arrow above. We now scan across the row in the table corresponding to the z value 2.0 until we find the column corresponding to the heading .00. The desired area (which we have shaded blue) is in the row corresponding to the z value 2.0 and in the column headed .00. This area, which equals .9772, is the probability that the random variable z will be less than or equal to 2.00. That is, we have found that $P(z \leq 2) = .9772$. Note that, because there is no area under the normal curve at a single value of z, there is no difference between $P(z \leq 2)$ and $P(z < 2)$. As another example, the area under the standard normal curve to the left of the z value 1.25 is found in the row corresponding to 1.2 and in the column corresponding to .05. We find that this area (also shaded blue) is .8944. That is, $P(z \leq 1.25) = .8944$ (see Figure 6.9).

We now show how to use the cumulative normal table to find several other kinds of normal curve areas. First, suppose that we wish to find the area under the standard normal curve to the right of a z value of 2—that is, we wish to find $P(z \geq 2)$. This area is illustrated in Figure 6.10 and is called a **right-hand tail area.** Since the total area under the normal curve equals 1, the area under the curve to the right of 2 equals 1 minus the area under the curve to the left of 2. Because Table 6.1 tells us that the area under the standard normal curve to the left of 2 is .9772, the area under the standard normal curve to the right of 2 is $1 - .9772 = .0228$. Said in an equivalent fashion, because $P(z \leq 2) = .9772$, it follows that $P(z \geq 2) = 1 - P(z \leq 2) = 1 - .9772 = .0228$.

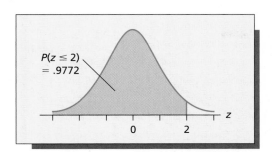

FIGURE 6.8   Finding $P(z \le 2)$

$P(z \le 2)$
$= .9772$

0   2   z

FIGURE 6.9   Finding $P(z \le 1.25)$

$P(z \le 1.25)$
$= .8944$

0   1.25   z

FIGURE 6.10   Finding $P(z \ge 2)$

.9772

$P(z \ge 2)$
$= 1 - .9772$
$= .0228$

0   2   z

FIGURE 6.11   Finding $P(z \le -2)$

$P(z \le -2)$
$= .0228$

-2   0   z

Next, suppose that we wish to find the area under the standard normal curve to the left of a z value of -2. That is, we wish to find $P(z \le -2)$. This area is illustrated in Figure 6.11 and is called a **left-hand tail area.** The needed area is found in the row of the cumulative normal table corresponding to -2.0 (on page 237) and in the column headed by .00. We find that $P(z \le -2) = .0228$. Notice that the area under the standard normal curve to the left of -2 is equal to the area under this curve to the right of 2. This is true because of the symmetry of the normal curve.

Figure 6.12 illustrates how to find the area under the standard normal curve to the right of -2. Since the total area under the normal curve equals 1, the area under the curve to the right of -2 equals 1 minus the area under the curve to the left of -2. Because Table 6.1 tells us that the area under the standard normal curve to the left of -2 is .0228, the area under the standard normal curve to the right of -2 is $1 - .0228 = .9772$. That is, because $P(z \le -2) = .0228$, it follows that $P(z \ge -2) = 1 - P(z \le -2) = 1 - .0228 = .9772$.

The smallest z value in Table 6.1 is -3.99, and the table tells us that the area under the standard normal curve to the left of -3.99 is .00003 (see Figure 6.13). Therefore, if we wish to find the area under the standard normal curve to the left of any z value less than -3.99, the most we can say (without using a computer) is that this area is less than .00003. Similarly, the area under

FIGURE 6.12   Finding $P(z \ge -2)$

.0228

$P(z \ge -2)$
$= 1 - .0228$
$= .9772$

-2   0   z

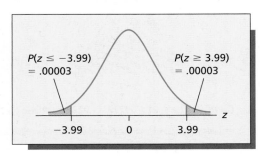

FIGURE 6.13   Finding $P(z \le -3.99)$

$P(z \le -3.99)$
$= .00003$

$P(z \ge 3.99)$
$= .00003$

-3.99   0   3.99   z

FIGURE 6.14   Calculating $P(1 \leq z \leq 2)$

the standard normal curve to the right of any z value greater than 3.99 is also less than .00003 (see Figure 6.13).

Figure 6.14 illustrates how to find the area under the standard normal curve between 1 and 2. This area equals the area under the curve to the left of 2, which the normal table tells us is .9772, minus the area under the curve to the left of 1, which the normal table tells us is .8413. Therefore, $P(1 \leq z \leq 2) = .9772 - .8413 = .1359$.

To conclude our introduction to using the normal table, we will use this table to justify the empirical rule. Figure 6.15(a) illustrates the area under the standard normal curve between -1 and 1. This area equals the area under the curve to the left of 1, which the normal table tells us is .8413, minus the area under the curve to the left of -1, which the normal table tells us is .1587. Therefore, $P(-1 \leq z \leq 1) = .8413 - .1587 = .6826$. Now, suppose that a random variable x is normally distributed with mean μ and standard deviation σ, and remember that z is the number of standard deviations σ that x is from μ. It follows that when we say that $P(-1 \leq z \leq 1)$ equals .6826, we are saying that 68.26 percent of all possible observed values of x are between a point that is one standard deviation below μ (where z equals -1) and a point that is one standard deviation

FIGURE 6.15   Some Areas under the Standard Normal Curve

(a) $P(-1 \leq z \leq 1) = .8413 - .1587 = .6826$ (c) $P(-3 \leq z \leq 3) = .99865 - .00135 = .9973$

(b) $P(-2 \leq z \leq 2) = .9772 - .0228 = .9544$ (d) $P(-1.96 \leq z \leq 1.96) = .9750 - .0250 = .9500$

above μ (where z equals 1). That is, 68.26 percent of all possible observed values of x are within (plus or minus) one standard deviation of the mean μ.

Figure 6.15(b) illustrates the area under the standard normal curve between -2 and 2. This area equals the area under the curve to the left of 2, which the normal table tells us is .9772, minus the area under the curve to the left of -2, which the normal table tells us is .0228. Therefore, $P(-2 \leq z \leq 2) = .9772 - .0228 = .9544$. That is, 95.44 percent of all possible observed values of x are within (plus or minus) two standard deviations of the mean μ.

Figure 6.15(c) illustrates the area under the standard normal curve between -3 and 3. This area equals the area under the curve to the left of 3, which the normal table tells us is .99865, minus the area under the curve to the left of -3, which the normal table tells us is .00135. Therefore, $P(-3 \leq z \leq 3) = .99865 - .00135 = .9973$. That is, 99.73 percent of all possible observed values of x are within (plus or minus) three standard deviations of the mean μ.

Although the empirical rule gives the percentages of all possible values of a normally distributed random variable x that are within one, two, and three standard deviations of the mean μ, we can use the normal table to find the percentage of all possible values of x that are within any particular number of standard deviations of μ. For example, in later chapters we will need to know the percentage of all possible values of x that are within plus or minus 1.96 standard deviations of μ. Figure 6.15(d) illustrates the area under the standard normal curve between -1.96 and 1.96. This area equals the area under the curve to the left of 1.96, which the normal table tells us is .9750, minus the area under the curve to the left of -1.96, which the table tells us is .0250. Therefore, $P(-1.96 \leq z \leq 1.96) = .9750 - .0250 = .9500$. That is, 95 percent of all possible values of x are within plus or minus 1.96 standard deviations of the mean μ.

Some practical applications   We have seen how to use z values and the normal table to find areas under the standard normal curve. However, most practical problems are not stated in such terms. We now consider an example in which we must restate the problem in terms of the standard normal random variable z before using the normal table.

LO4 Use the normal distribution to compute probabilities.

EXAMPLE 6.2 The Car Mileage Case

Recall from previous chapters that an automaker has recently introduced a new midsize model and that we have used the sample of 50 mileages to estimate that the population of mileages of all cars of this type is normally distributed with a mean mileage equal to 31.56 mpg and a standard deviation equal to .798 mpg. Suppose that a competing automaker produces a midsize model that is somewhat smaller and less powerful than the new midsize model. The competitor claims, however, that its midsize model gets better mileages. Specifically, the competitor claims that the mileages of all its midsize cars are normally distributed with a mean mileage μ equal to 33 mpg and a standard deviation σ equal to .7 mpg. In the next example we consider one way to investigate the validity of this claim. In this example we assume that the claim is true, and we calculate the probability that the mileage, x, of a randomly selected competing midsize car will be between 32 mpg and 35 mpg. That is, we wish to find $P(32 \leq x \leq 35)$. As illustrated in Figure 6.16 on the next page, this probability is the area between 32 and 35 under the normal curve having mean $\mu = 33$ and standard deviation $\sigma = .7$. In order to use the normal table, we must restate the problem in terms of the standard normal random variable z. The z value corresponding to 32 is

$$z = \frac{x - \mu}{\sigma} = \frac{32 - 33}{.7} = \frac{-1}{.7} = -1.43$$

which says that the mileage 32 is 1.43 standard deviations below the mean $\mu = 33$. The z value corresponding to 35 is

$$z = \frac{x - \mu}{\sigma} = \frac{35 - 33}{.7} = \frac{2}{.7} = 2.86$$

FIGURE 6.16   Finding $P(32 \leq x \leq 35)$ When $\mu = 33$ and $\sigma = .7$ by Using a Normal Table

which says that the mileage 35 is 2.86 standard deviations above the mean $\mu = 33$. Looking at Figure 6.16, we see that the area between 32 and 35 under the normal curve having mean $\mu = 33$ and standard deviation $\sigma = .7$ equals the area between -1.43 and 2.86 under the standard normal curve. This equals the area under the standard normal curve to the left of 2.86, which the normal table tells us is .9979, minus the area under the standard normal curve to the left of -1.43, which the normal table tells us is .0764. We summarize this result as follows:

$$P(32 \leq x \leq 35) = P\left(\frac{32 - 33}{.7} \leq \frac{x - \mu}{\sigma} \leq \frac{35 - 33}{.7}\right)$$

$$= P(-1.43 \leq z \leq 2.86) = .9979 - .0764 = .9215$$

This probability says that, if the competing automaker's claim is valid, then 92.15 percent of all of its midsize cars will get mileages between 32 mpg and 35 mpg.

Example 6.2 illustrates the general procedure for finding a probability about a normally distributed random variable x. We summarize this procedure in the following box:

Finding Normal Probabilities

1 Formulate the problem in terms of the random variable x.

2 Calculate relevant z values and restate the problem in terms of the standard normal random variable

$$z = \frac{x - \mu}{\sigma}$$

3 Find the required area under the standard normal curve by using the normal table.

4 Note that it is always useful to draw a picture illustrating the needed area before using the normal table.

EXAMPLE 6.3 The Car Mileage Case   C

Recall from Example 6.2 that the competing automaker claims that the population of mileages of all its midsize cars is normally distributed with mean $\mu = 33$ and standard deviation $\sigma = .7$. Suppose that an independent testing agency randomly selects one of these cars and finds that it gets a mileage of 31.2 mpg when tested as prescribed by the EPA. Because the sample mileage of 31.2 mpg is *less than* the claimed mean $\mu = 33$, we have some evidence that contradicts the competing automaker's claim. To evaluate the strength of this evidence, we will calculate the probability that the mileage, x, of a randomly selected midsize car would be *less than or equal to* 31.2 if, in fact, the competing automaker's claim is true. To calculate $P(x \leq 31.2)$ under the assumption that the claim is true, we find the area to the left of 31.2 under the normal curve with mean $\mu = 33$ and standard deviation $\sigma = .7$ (see Figure 6.17). In order to use the normal table, we must find the z value corresponding to 31.2. This z value is

$$z = \frac{x - \mu}{\sigma} = \frac{31.2 - 33}{.7} = -2.57$$

which says that the mileage 31.2 is 2.57 standard deviations below the mean mileage $\mu = 33$. Looking at Figure 6.17, we see that the area to the left of 31.2 under the normal curve having mean $\mu = 33$ and standard deviation $\sigma = .7$ equals the area to the left of -2.57 under the standard normal curve. The normal table tells us that the area under the standard normal curve to the left of -2.57 is .0051, as shown in Figure 6.17. It follows that we can summarize our calculations as follows:

$$P(x \leq 31.2) = P\left(\frac{x - \mu}{\sigma} \leq \frac{31.2 - 33}{.7}\right)$$

$$= P(z \leq -2.57) = .0051$$

This probability says that, if the competing automaker's claim is valid, then only 51 in 10,000 cars would obtain a mileage of less than or equal to 31.2 mpg. Since it is very difficult to believe that a 51 in 10,000 chance has occurred, we have very strong evidence against the competing automaker's claim. It is probably true that μ is less than 33 and/or σ is greater than .7 and/or the population of all mileages is not normally distributed.

FIGURE 6.17   Finding $P(x \leq 31.2)$ When $\mu = 33$ and $\sigma = .7$ by Using a Normal Table

EXAMPLE 6.4 The Coffee Temperature Case

Marketing research done by a fast-food restaurant indicates that coffee tastes best if its temperature is between 153°(F) and 167°(F). The restaurant samples the coffee it serves and observes 24 temperature readings over a day. The temperature readings have a mean $\bar{x} = 160.0833$ and a standard deviation $s = 5.3724$ and are described by a bell-shaped histogram. Using $\bar{x}$ and s as point estimates of the mean μ and the standard deviation σ of the population of all possible coffee temperatures, we wish to calculate the probability that x, the temperature of a randomly selected cup of coffee, is outside the customer requirements for best testing coffee (that is, less than 153° or greater than 167°). In order to compute the probability $P(x < 153 \text{ or } x > 167)$ we compute the z values

$$z = \frac{153 - 160.0833}{5.3724} = -1.32 \quad \text{and} \quad z = \frac{167 - 160.0833}{5.3724} = 1.29$$

Because the events $\{x < 153\}$ and $\{x > 167\}$ are mutually exclusive, we have

$$P(x < 153 \text{ or } x > 167) = P(x < 153) + P(x > 167)$$
$$= P(z < -1.32) + P(z > 1.29)$$
$$= .0934 + .0985 = .1919$$

This calculation is illustrated in Figure 6.18. The probability of .1919 says that 19.19 percent of the coffee temperatures do not meet customer requirements. Therefore, if management believes that meeting this requirement is important, the coffee-making process must be improved.

LO5 Find population values that correspond to specified normal distribution probabilities.

Finding a point on the horizontal axis under a normal curve   In order to use many of the formulas given in later chapters, we must be able to find the z value so that the tail area to the right of z under the standard normal curve is a particular value. For instance, we might need to find the z value so that the tail area to the right of z under the standard normal curve is .025. This z value is denoted $z_{.025}$, and we illustrate $z_{.025}$ in Figure 6.19(a). We refer to $z_{.025}$ as **the point on the horizontal axis under the standard normal curve that gives a right-hand tail area equal to .025.** It is easy to use the cumulative normal table to find such a point. For instance, in order to find $z_{.025}$, we note from Figure 6.19(b) that the area under the standard normal curve to the left of $z_{.025}$ equals .975. Remembering that areas under the standard normal curve to the left of z are

FIGURE 6.18   Finding $P(x < 153 \text{ or } x > 167)$ in the Coffee Temperature Case

FIGURE 6.19   The Point $z_{.025} = 1.96$

(a) $z_{.025}$ is the point on the horizontal axis under the standard normal curve that gives a right-hand tail area equal to .025

(b) Finding $z_{.025}$

the four-digit (or five-digit) numbers given in the body of Table 6.1, we scan the body of the table and find the area .9750. We have shaded this area in Table 6.1 on page 238, and we note that the area .9750 is in the row corresponding to a z of 1.9 and in the column headed by .06. It follows that the z value corresponding to .9750 is 1.96. Because the z value 1.96 gives an area under the standard normal curve to its left that equals .975, it also gives a right-hand tail area equal to .025. Therefore, $z_{.025} = 1.96$.

In general, **we let z_α denote the point on the horizontal axis under the standard normal curve that gives a right-hand tail area equal to α.** With this definition in mind, we consider the following example.

EXAMPLE 6.5

A large discount store sells 50 packs of HX-150 blank DVDs and receives a shipment every Monday. Historical sales records indicate that the weekly demand, x, for HX-150 DVD 50 packs is normally distributed with a mean of $\mu = 100$ and a standard deviation of $\sigma = 10$. How many 50 packs should be stocked at the beginning of a week so that there is only a 5 percent chance that the store will run short during the week?

If we let st equal the number of 50 packs that will be stocked, then st must be chosen to allow only a .05 probability that weekly demand, x, will exceed st. That is, st must be chosen so that

$$P(x > st) = .05$$

Figure 6.20(a) on the next page shows that the number stocked, st, is located under the right-hand tail of the normal curve having mean $\mu = 100$ and standard deviation $\sigma = 10$. In order to find st, we need to determine how many standard deviations st must be above the mean in order to give a right-hand tail area that is equal to .05.

The z value corresponding to st is

$$z = \frac{st - \mu}{\sigma} = \frac{st - 100}{10}$$

and this z value is the number of standard deviations that st is from μ. This z value is illustrated in Figure 6.20(b), and it is the point on the horizontal axis under the standard normal curve that gives a right-hand tail area equal to .05. That is, the z value corresponding to st is $z_{.05}$. Since the area under the standard normal curve to the left of $z_{.05}$ is $1 - .05 = .95$—see Figure 6.20(b)—we look for .95 in the body of the normal table. In Table 6.1, we see that the areas closest to .95 are .9495, which has a corresponding z value of 1.64, and .9505, which has a corresponding z value of 1.65. Although it

FIGURE 6.20   **Finding the Number of 50 Packs of DVDs Stocked, *st*, so That $P(x > st) = .05$ When $\mu = 100$ and $\sigma = 10$**

(a) The number stocked, *st*, must be chosen so that there is a .05 probability that the demand, *x*, will exceed *st*

(b) Finding $z_{.05}$, the *z* value corresponding to *st*

would probably be sufficient to use either of these z values, we will (because it is easy to do so) interpolate halfway between them and assume that $z_{.05}$ equals 1.645. To find *st*, we solve the equation

$$\frac{st - 100}{10} = 1.645$$

for *st*. Doing this yields

$$st - 100 = 1.645(10)$$

or

$$st = 100 + 1.645(10) = 116.45$$

This last equation says that *st* is 1.645 standard deviations ($\sigma = 10$) above the mean ($\mu = 100$). Rounding $st = 116.45$ up so that the store's chances of running short will be *no more* than 5 percent, the store should stock 117 of the 50 packs at the beginning of each week.

Sometimes we need to find the point on the horizontal axis under the standard normal curve that gives a particular **left-hand tail area** (say, for instance, an area of .025). Looking at Figure 6.21, it is easy to see that, if, for instance, we want a left-hand tail area of .025, the needed z value is $-z_{.025}$, where $z_{.025}$ gives a right-hand tail area equal to .025. To find $-z_{.025}$, we look for .025 in the body of the normal table and find that the z value corresponding to .025 is -1.96. Therefore, $-z_{.025} = -1.96$. In general, $-z_{\alpha}$ **is the point on the horizontal axis under the standard normal curve that gives a left-hand tail area equal to α.**

FIGURE 6.21   **The *z* Value $-z_{.025} = -1.96$ Gives a Left-Hand Tail Area of .025 under the Standard Normal Curve**

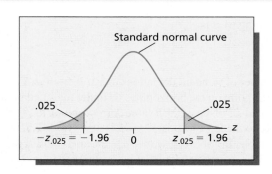

EXAMPLE 6.6

Extensive testing indicates that the lifetime of the Everlast automobile battery is normally distributed with a mean of $\mu = 60$ months and a standard deviation of $\sigma = 6$ months. The Everlast's manufacturer has decided to offer a free replacement battery to any purchaser whose Everlast battery does not last at least as long as the minimum lifetime specified in its guarantee. How can the manufacturer establish the guarantee period so that only 1 percent of the batteries will need to be replaced free of charge?

If the battery will be guaranteed to last l months, l must be chosen to allow only a .01 probability that the lifetime, x, of an Everlast battery will be less than l. That is, we must choose l so that

$$P(x < l) = .01$$

Figure 6.22(a) shows that the guarantee period, l, is located under the left-hand tail of the normal curve having mean $\mu = 60$ and standard deviation $\sigma = 6$. In order to find l, we need to determine how many standard deviations l must be below the mean in order to give a left-hand tail area that equals .01. The z value corresponding to l is

$$z = \frac{l - \mu}{\sigma} = \frac{l - 60}{6}$$

and this z value is the number of standard deviations that l is from μ. This z value is illustrated in Figure 6.22(b), and it is the point on the horizontal axis under the standard normal curve that gives a left-hand tail area equal to .01. That is, the z value corresponding to l is $-z_{.01}$. To find $-z_{.01}$, we look for .01 in the body of the normal table. Doing this, we see that the area closest to .01 is .0099, which has a corresponding z value of -2.33. Therefore, $-z_{.01}$ is (roughly) -2.33. To find l, we solve the equation

$$\frac{l - 60}{6} = -2.33$$

for l. Doing this yields

$$l - 60 = -2.33(6)$$

or

$$l = 60 - 2.33(6) = 46.02$$

Note that this last equation says that l is 2.33 standard deviations ($\sigma = 6$) below the mean ($\mu = 60$). Rounding $l = 46.02$ down so that *no more* than 1 percent of the batteries will need to be replaced free of charge, it seems reasonable to guarantee the Everlast battery to last 46 months.

FIGURE 6.22   **Finding the Guarantee Period, l, so That $P(x < l) = .01$ When $\mu = 60$ and $\sigma = 6$**

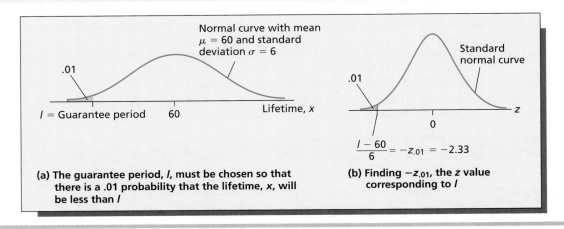

(a) The guarantee period, l, must be chosen so that there is a .01 probability that the lifetime, x, will be less than l

(b) Finding $-z_{.01}$, the z value corresponding to l

F I G U R E   6 . 2 3   **Finding a Tolerance Interval $[\mu \pm k\sigma]$ That Contains 99 Percent of the Measurements in a Normally Distributed Population**

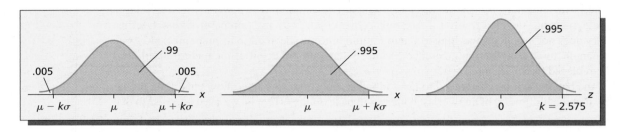

Earlier in this section we saw that the intervals $[\mu \pm \sigma]$, $[\mu \pm 2\sigma]$, and $[\mu \pm 3\sigma]$ are **tolerance intervals** containing, respectively, 68.26 percent, 95.44 percent, and 99.73 percent of the measurements in a normally distributed population having mean μ and standard deviation σ. In the following example we demonstrate how to use the normal table to find the value k so that the interval $[\mu \pm k\sigma]$ contains any desired percentage of the measurements in a normally distributed population.

EXAMPLE 6.7

Consider computing a tolerance interval $[\mu \pm k\sigma]$ that contains 99 percent of the measurements in a normally distributed population having mean μ and standard deviation σ. As illustrated in Figure 6.23, we must find the value k so that the area under the normal curve having mean μ and standard deviation σ between $(\mu - k\sigma)$ and $(\mu + k\sigma)$ is .99. Because the total area under this normal curve is 1, the area under the normal curve that is not between $(\mu - k\sigma)$ and $(\mu + k\sigma)$ is $1 - .99 = .01$. This implies, as illustrated in Figure 6.23, that the area under the normal curve to the left of $(\mu - k\sigma)$ is $.01/2 = .005$, and the area under the normal curve to the right of $(\mu + k\sigma)$ is also $.01/2 = .005$. This further implies, as illustrated in Figure 6.23, that the area under the normal curve to the left of $(\mu + k\sigma)$ is .995. Because the z value corresponding to a value of x tells us how many standard deviations x is from μ, the z value corresponding to $(\mu + k\sigma)$ is obviously k. It follows that k is the point on the horizontal axis under the standard normal curve so that the area to the left of k is .995. Looking up .995 in the body of the normal table, we find that the values closest to .995 are .9949, which has a corresponding z value of 2.57, and .9951, which has a corresponding z value of 2.58. Although it would be sufficient to use either of these z values, we will interpolate halfway between them, and we will assume that k equals 2.575. It follows that the interval $[\mu \pm 2.575\sigma]$ contains 99 percent of the measurements in a normally distributed population having mean μ and standard deviation σ. For example, recall that the histogram of the sample of 50 midsize car mileages in Figure 3.15 (page 115) suggests that the population of all midsize car mileages is normally distributed. Because the sample mean and the sample standard deviation are $\bar{x} = 31.56$ and $s = .7977$, we estimate that 99 percent of the new midsize cars will obtain mileages in the interval $[\bar{x} \pm 2.575s] = [31.56 \pm 2.575(.7977)] = [29.5, 33.6]$—that is, between 29.5 mpg and 33.6 mpg.

Whenever we use a normal table to find a z point corresponding to a particular normal curve area, we will use the *halfway interpolation* procedure illustrated in Examples 6.5 and 6.7 if the area we are looking for is exactly halfway between two areas in the table. Otherwise, as illustrated in Example 6.6, we will use the z value corresponding to the area in the table that is closest to the desired area.

Exercises for Section 6.3

CONCEPTS

connect

6.16   List five important properties of the normal probability curve.

6.17   Explain what the mean, μ, tells us about a normal curve, and explain what the standard deviation, σ, tells us about a normal curve.

6.18 If the random variable x is normally distributed, what percentage of all possible observed values of x will be
   a Within one standard deviation of the mean?
   b Within two standard deviations of the mean?
   c Within three standard deviations of the mean?

6.19 Explain how to compute the z value corresponding to a value of a normally distributed random variable. What does the z value tell us about the value of the random variable?

6.20 Explain how x relates to the mean μ if the z value corresponding to x
   a Equals zero.
   b Is positive.
   c Is negative.

6.21 Why do we compute z values when using the normal table? Explain.

METHODS AND APPLICATIONS

6.22 In each case, sketch the two specified normal curves on the same set of axes:
   a A normal curve with $\mu = 20$ and $\sigma = 3$, and a normal curve with $\mu = 20$ and $\sigma = 6$.
   b A normal curve with $\mu = 20$ and $\sigma = 3$, and a normal curve with $\mu = 30$ and $\sigma = 3$.
   c A normal curve with $\mu = 100$ and $\sigma = 10$, and a normal curve with $\mu = 200$ and $\sigma = 20$.

6.23 Let x be a normally distributed random variable having mean $\mu = 30$ and standard deviation $\sigma = 5$. Find the z value for each of the following observed values of x:
   a $x = 25$ **d** $x = 40$
   b $x = 15$ **e** $x = 50$
   c $x = 30$
   In each case, explain what the z value tells us about how the observed value of x compares to the mean, μ.

6.24 If the random variable z has a standard normal distribution, sketch and find each of the following probabilities:
   a $P(0 \le z \le 1.5)$ **d** $P(z \ge -1)$ **g** $P(-2.5 \le z \le .5)$
   b $P(z \ge 2)$ **e** $P(z \le -3)$ **h** $P(1.5 \le z \le 2)$
   c $P(z \le 1.5)$ **f** $P(-1 \le z \le 1)$ **i** $P(-2 \le z \le -.5)$

6.25 Suppose that the random variable z has a standard normal distribution. Sketch each of the following z points, and use the normal table to find each z point.
   a $z_{.01}$ **d** $-z_{.01}$
   b $z_{.05}$ **e** $-z_{.05}$
   c $z_{.02}$ **f** $-z_{.10}$

6.26 Suppose that the random variable x is normally distributed with mean $\mu = 1{,}000$ and standard deviation $\sigma = 100$. Sketch and find each of the following probabilities:
   a $P(1{,}000 \le x \le 1{,}200)$ **e** $P(x \le 700)$
   b $P(x > 1{,}257)$ **f** $P(812 \le x \le 913)$
   c $P(x < 1{,}035)$ **g** $P(x > 891)$
   d $P(857 \le x \le 1{,}183)$ **h** $P(1{,}050 \le x \le 1{,}250)$

6.27 Suppose that the random variable x is normally distributed with mean $\mu = 500$ and standard deviation $\sigma = 100$. For each of the following, use the normal table to find the needed value k. In each case, draw a sketch.
   a $P(x \ge k) = .025$ **d** $P(x \le k) = .015$ **g** $P(x \le k) = .975$
   b $P(x \ge k) = .05$ **e** $P(x < k) = .985$ **h** $P(x \ge k) = .0228$
   c $P(x < k) = .025$ **f** $P(x > k) = .95$ **i** $P(x > k) = .9772$

6.28 Stanford–Binet IQ Test scores are normally distributed with a mean score of 100 and a standard deviation of 16.
   a Sketch the distribution of Stanford–Binet IQ test scores.
   b Write the equation that gives the z score corresponding to a Stanford–Binet IQ test score. Sketch the distribution of such z scores.
   c Find the probability that a randomly selected person has an IQ test score
      (1) Over 140.
      (2) Under 88.
      (3) Between 72 and 128.
      (4) Within 1.5 standard deviations of the mean.
   d Suppose you take the Stanford–Binet IQ Test and receive a score of 136. What percentage of people would receive a score higher than yours?

6.29   Weekly demand at a grocery store for a brand of breakfast cereal is normally distributed with a mean of 800 boxes and a standard deviation of 75 boxes.
   a   What is the probability that weekly demand is
       (1) 959 boxes or less?
       (2) More than 1,004 boxes?
       (3) Less than 650 boxes or greater than 950 boxes?
   b   The store orders cereal from a distributor weekly. How many boxes should the store order for a week to have only a 2.5 percent chance of running short of this brand of cereal during the week?

6.30   The lifetimes of a particular brand of DVD player are normally distributed with a mean of eight years and a standard deviation of six months. Find each of the following probabilities where x denotes the lifetime in years. In each case, sketch the probability.
   a $P(7 \leq x \leq 9)$ **e** $P(x \leq 7)$
   b $P(8.5 \leq x \leq 9.5)$ **f** $P(x \geq 7)$
   c $P(6.5 \leq x \leq 7.5)$ **g** $P(x \leq 10)$
   d $P(x \geq 8)$ **h** $P(x > 10)$

6.31   United Motors claims that one of its cars, the Starbird 300, gets city driving mileages that are normally distributed with a mean of 30 mpg and a standard deviation of 1 mpg. Let x denote the city driving mileage of a randomly selected Starbird 300.
   a   Assuming that United Motors' claim is correct, find $P(x \leq 27)$.
   b   If you purchase (randomly select) a Starbird 300 and your car gets 27 mpg in city driving, what do you think of United Motors' claim? Explain your answer.

6.32   An investment broker reports that the yearly returns on common stocks are approximately normally distributed with a mean return of 12.4 percent and a standard deviation of 20.6 percent. On the other hand, the firm reports that the yearly returns on tax-free municipal bonds are approximately normally distributed with a mean return of 5.2 percent and a standard deviation of 8.6 percent. Find the probability that a randomly selected
   a   Common stock will give a positive yearly return.
   b   Tax-free municipal bond will give a positive yearly return.
   c   Common stock will give more than a 10 percent return.
   d   Tax-free municipal bond will give more than a 10 percent return.
   e   Common stock will give a loss of at least 10 percent.
   f   Tax-free municipal bond will give a loss of at least 10 percent.

6.33   A filling process is supposed to fill jars with 16 ounces of grape jelly. Specifications state that each jar must contain between 15.95 ounces and 16.05 ounces. A jar is selected from the process every half hour until a sample of 100 jars is obtained. When the fills of the jars are measured, it is found that $\bar{x} = 16.0024$ and $s = .02454$. Using $\bar{x}$ and s as point estimates of μ and σ, estimate the probability that a randomly selected jar will have a fill, x, that is out of specification. Assume that the process is in control and that the population of all jar fills is normally distributed.

6.34   A tire company has developed a new type of steel-belted radial tire. Extensive testing indicates the population of mileages obtained by all tires of this new type is normally distributed with a mean of 40,000 miles and a standard deviation of 4,000 miles. The company wishes to offer a guarantee providing a discount on a new set of tires if the original tires purchased do not exceed the mileage stated in the guarantee. What should the guaranteed mileage be if the tire company desires that no more than 2 percent of the tires will fail to meet the guaranteed mileage?

6.35   Recall from Exercise 6.32 that yearly returns on common stocks are normally distributed with a mean of 12.4 percent and a standard deviation of 20.6 percent.
   a   What percentage of yearly returns are at or below the 10th percentile of the distribution of yearly returns? What percentage are at or above the 10th percentile? Find the 10th percentile of the distribution of yearly returns.
   b   Find the first quartile, Q_1, and the third quartile, Q_3, of the distribution of yearly returns.

6.36   Two students take a college entrance exam known to have a normal distribution of scores. The students receive raw scores of 63 and 93, which correspond to z scores (often called the standardized scores) of -1 and 1.5, respectively. Find the mean and standard deviation of the distribution of raw exam scores.

6.37   **THE TRASH BAG CASE**   ⒹⓈ TrashBag

   Suppose that a population of measurements is normally distributed with mean μ and standard deviation σ.
   a   Write an expression (involving μ and σ) for a tolerance interval containing 98 percent of all the population measurements.

b Estimate a tolerance interval containing 98 percent of all the trash bag breaking strengths by using the fact that a random sample of 40 breaking strengths has a mean of $\bar{x} = 50.575$ and a standard deviation of $s = 1.6438$.

6.38 Consider the situation of Exercise 6.32.

    a Use the investment broker's report to estimate the maximum yearly return that might be obtained by investing in tax-free municipal bonds.

    b Find the probability that the yearly return obtained by investing in common stocks will be higher than the maximum yearly return that might be obtained by investing in tax-free municipal bonds.

6.39 In the book *Advanced Managerial Accounting*, Robert P. Magee discusses monitoring cost variances. A *cost variance* is the difference between a budgeted cost and an actual cost. Magee describes the following situation:

> Michael Bitner has responsibility for control of two manufacturing processes. Every week he receives a cost variance report for each of the two processes, broken down by labor costs, materials costs, and so on. One of the two processes, which we'll call process A, involves a stable, easily controlled production process with a little fluctuation in variances. Process B involves more random events: the equipment is more sensitive and prone to breakdown, the raw material prices fluctuate more, and so on.
>
> "It seems like I'm spending more of my time with process B than with process A," says Michael Bitner. "Yet I know that the probability of an inefficiency developing and the expected costs of inefficiencies are the same for the two processes. It's just the magnitude of random fluctuations that differs between the two, as you can see in the information below.
>
> "At present, I investigate variances if they exceed $2,500, regardless of whether it was process A or B. I suspect that such a policy is not the most efficient. I should probably set a higher limit for process B."

The means and standard deviations of the cost variances of processes A and B, when these processes are in control, are as follows:

	Process A	Process B
Mean cost variance (in control)	$ 0	$ 0
Standard deviation of cost variance (in control)	$5,000	$10,000

Furthermore, the means and standard deviations of the cost variances of processes A and B, when these processes are out of control, are as follows:

	Process A	Process B
Mean cost variance (out of control)	$7,500	$ 7,500
Standard deviation of cost variance (out of control)	$5,000	$10,000

    a Recall that the current policy is to investigate a cost variance if it exceeds $2,500 for either process. Assume that cost variances are normally distributed and that both Process A and Process B cost variances are in control. Find the probability that a cost variance for Process A will be investigated. Find the probability that a cost variance for Process B will be investigated. Which in-control process will be investigated more often?

    b Assume that cost variances are normally distributed and that both Process A and Process B cost variances are out of control. Find the probability that a cost variance for Process A will be investigated. Find the probability that a cost variance for Process B will be investigated. Which out-of-control process will be investigated more often?

    c If both Processes A and B are almost always in control, which process will be investigated more often?

    d Suppose that we wish to reduce the probability that Process B will be investigated (when it is in control) to .3085. What cost variance investigation policy should be used? That is, how large a cost variance should trigger an investigation? Using this new policy, what is the probability that an out-of-control cost variance for Process B will be investigated?

6.40 Suppose that yearly health care expenses for a family of four are normally distributed with a mean expense equal to $3,000 and a standard deviation of $500. An insurance company has decided to offer a health insurance premium reduction if a policyholder's health care expenses do not exceed a specified dollar amount. What dollar amount should be established if the insurance company wants families having the lowest 33 percent of yearly health care expenses to be eligible for the premium reduction?

6.41 Suppose that the 33rd percentile of a normal distribution is equal to 656 and that the 97.5th percentile of this normal distribution is 896. Find the mean μ and the standard deviation σ of the normal distribution. Hint: Sketch these percentiles.

LO6 Use the normal distribution to approximate binomial probabilities (Optional).

6.4 Approximating the Binomial Distribution by Using the Normal Distribution (Optional) ● ● ●

Figure 6.24 illustrates several binomial distributions. In general, we can see that as n gets larger and as p gets closer to .5, the graph of a binomial distribution tends to have the symmetrical, bell-shaped appearance of a normal curve. It follows that, under conditions given in the following box, we can approximate the binomial distribution by using a normal distribution.

The Normal Approximation of the Binomial Distribution

Consider a binomial random variable x, where n is the number of trials performed and p is the probability of success on each trial. If n and p have values so that $np \geq 5$ and $n(1 - p) \geq 5$, then x is approximately normally distributed with mean $\mu = np$ and standard deviation $\sigma = \sqrt{npq}$, where $q = 1 - p$.

This approximation is often useful because binomial tables for large values of n are often unavailable. The conditions $np \geq 5$ and $n(1 - p) \geq 5$ must be met in order for the approximation to be appropriate. Note that if p is near 0 or near 1, then n must be larger for a good approximation, while if p is near .5, then n need not be as large.[1]

When we say that we can approximate the binomial distribution by using a normal distribution, we are saying that we can compute binomial probabilities by finding corresponding areas under a normal curve (rather than by using the binomial formula). We illustrate how to do this in the following example.

FIGURE 6.24   **Several Binomial Distributions**

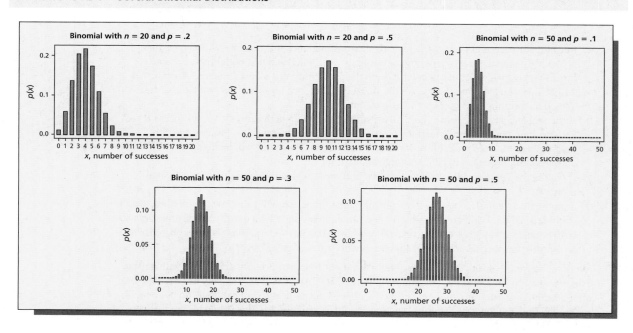

---

[1]As an alternative to the rule that both np and $n(1 - p)$ must be at least 5, some statisticians suggest using the more conservative rule that both np and $n(1 - p)$ must be at least 10.

FIGURE 6.25   **Approximating the Binomial Probability $P(x = 23)$ by Using the Normal Curve When $\mu = np = 25$ and $\sigma = \sqrt{npq} = 3.5355$**

EXAMPLE 6.8

Consider the binomial random variable x with $n = 50$ trials and probability of success $p = .5$. This binomial distribution is one of those illustrated in Figure 6.24. Suppose we want to use the normal approximation to this binomial distribution to compute the probability of 23 successes in the 50 trials. That is, we wish to compute $P(x = 23)$. Because $np = (50)(.5) = 25$ is at least 5, and $n(1 - p) = 50(1 - .5) = 25$ is also at least 5, we can appropriately use the approximation. Moreover, we can approximate the binomial distribution of x by using a normal distribution with mean $\mu = np = 50(.5) = 25$ and standard deviation $\sigma = \sqrt{npq} = \sqrt{50(.5)(1 - .5)} = 3.5355$.

In order to compute the needed probability, we must make a **continuity correction.** This is because a discrete distribution (the binomial) is being approximated by a continuous distribution (the normal). Because there is no area under a normal curve at the single point $x = 23$, we must assign an area under the normal curve to the binomial outcome $x = 23$. It is logical to assign the area corresponding to the interval from 22.5 to 23.5 to the integer outcome $x = 23$. That is, the area under the normal curve corresponding to all values within .5 unit of the integer outcome $x = 23$ is assigned to the value $x = 23$. So we approximate the binomial probability $P(x = 23)$ by calculating the normal curve area $P(22.5 \leq x \leq 23.5)$. This area is illustrated in Figure 6.25. Calculating the z values

$$z = \frac{22.5 - 25}{3.5355} = -.71 \qquad \text{and} \qquad z = \frac{23.5 - 25}{3.5355} = -.42$$

we find that $P(22.5 \leq x \leq 23.5) = P(-.71 \leq z \leq -.42) = .3372 - .2389 = .0983$. Therefore, we estimate that the binomial probability $P(x = 23)$ is .0983.

Making the proper continuity correction can sometimes be tricky. A good way to approach this is to list the numbers of successes that are included in the event for which the binomial probability is being calculated. Then assign the appropriate area under the normal curve to each number of successes in the list. Putting these areas together gives the normal curve area that must be calculated. For example, again consider the binomial random variable x with $n = 50$ and $p = .5$. If we wish to find $P(27 \leq x \leq 29)$, then the event $27 \leq x \leq 29$ includes 27, 28, and 29 successes. Because we assign the areas under the normal curve corresponding to the intervals [26.5, 27.5], [27.5, 28.5], and [28.5, 29.5] to the values 27, 28, and 29, respectively, then the area to be found under the normal curve is $P(26.5 \leq x \leq 29.5)$. Table 6.2 on the next page gives several other examples.

TABLE 6.2   Several Examples of the Continuity Correction ($n = 50$)

Binomial Probability	Numbers of Successes Included in Event	Normal Curve Area (with Continuity Correction)
$P(25 < x \leq 30)$	26, 27, 28, 29, 30	$P(25.5 \leq x \leq 30.5)$
$P(x \leq 27)$	0, 1, 2, . . . , 26, 27	$P(x \leq 27.5)$
$P(x > 30)$	31, 32, 33, . . . , 50	$P(x \geq 30.5)$
$P(27 < x < 31)$	28, 29, 30	$P(27.5 \leq x \leq 30.5)$

EXAMPLE 6.9 The Cheese Spread Case

A food processing company markets a soft cheese spread that is sold in a plastic container with an "easy pour" spout. Although this spout works extremely well and is popular with consumers, it is expensive to produce. Because of the spout's high cost, the company has developed a new, less expensive spout. While the new, cheaper spout may alienate some purchasers, a company study shows that its introduction will increase profits if fewer than 10 percent of the cheese spread's current purchasers are lost. That is, if we let p be the true proportion of all current purchasers who would stop buying the cheese spread if the new spout were used, profits will increase as long as p is less than .10.

Suppose that (after trying the new spout) 63 of 1,000 randomly selected purchasers say that they would stop buying the cheese spread if the new spout were used. To assess whether p is less than .10, we will assume for the sake of argument that p equals .10, and we will use the sample information to weigh the evidence against this assumption and in favor of the conclusion that p is less than .10. Let the random variable x represent the number of the 1,000 purchasers who say they would stop buying the cheese spread. Assuming that p equals .10, then x is a binomial random variable with $n = 1,000$ and $p = .10$. Since the sample result of 63 is less than $\mu = np = 1,000(.1) = 100$, the expected value of x when p equals .10, we have some evidence to contradict the assumption that p equals .10. To evaluate the strength of this evidence, we calculate the probability that *63 or fewer* of the 1,000 randomly selected purchasers would say that they would stop buying the cheese spread if the new spout were used if, in fact, p equals .10.

Since both $np = 1,000(.10) = 100$ and $n(1 - p) = 1,000(1 - .10) = 900$ are at least 5, we can use the normal approximation to the binomial distribution to compute the needed probability. The appropriate normal curve has mean $\mu = np = 1,000(.10) = 100$ and standard deviation $\sigma = \sqrt{npq} = \sqrt{1,000(.10)(1 - .10)} = 9.4868$. In order to make the continuity correction, we note that the discrete value $x = 63$ is assigned the area under the normal curve corresponding to the interval from 62.5 to 63.5. It follows that the binomial probability $P(x \leq 63)$ is approximated by the normal probability $P(x \leq 63.5)$. This is illustrated in Figure 6.26. Calculating the z value for 63.5 to be

$$z = \frac{63.5 - 100}{9.4868} = -3.85$$

FIGURE 6.26   Approximating the Binomial Probability $P(x \leq 63)$ by Using the Normal Curve When $\mu = np = 100$ and $\sigma = \sqrt{npq} = 9.4868$

we find that

$$P(x \leq 63.5) = P(z \leq -3.85)$$

Using the normal table, we find that the area under the standard normal curve to the left of -3.85 is .00006. This says that, if p equals .10, then in only 6 in 100,000 of all possible random samples of 1,000 purchasers would 63 or fewer say they would stop buying the cheese spread if the new spout were used. Since it is very difficult to believe that such a small chance (a .00006 chance) has occurred, we have very strong evidence that p does not equal .10 and is, in fact, less than .10. Therefore, it seems that using the new spout will be profitable.

Exercises for Section 6.4

CONCEPTS

6.42 Explain why it might be convenient to approximate binomial probabilities by using areas under an appropriate normal curve.

6.43 Under what condition may we use the normal approximation to the binomial distribution?

6.44 Explain how we make a continuity correction. Why is a continuity correction needed when we approximate a binomial distribution by a normal distribution?

METHODS AND APPLICATIONS

6.45 Suppose that x has a binomial distribution with $n = 200$ and $p = .4$.
   a Show that the normal approximation to the binomial can appropriately be used to calculate probabilities about x.
   b Make continuity corrections for each of the following, and then use the normal approximation to the binomial to find each probability:
   (1) $P(x = 80)$
   (2) $P(x \leq 95)$
   (3) $P(x < 65)$
   (4) $P(x \geq 100)$
   (5) $P(x > 100)$

6.46 Repeat Exercise 6.45 with $n = 200$ and $p = .5$.

6.47 An advertising agency conducted an ad campaign aimed at making consumers in an Eastern state aware of a new product. Upon completion of the campaign, the agency claimed that 20 percent of consumers in the state had become aware of the product. The product's distributor surveyed 1,000 consumers in the state and found that 150 were aware of the product.
   a Assuming that the ad agency's claim is true:
   (1) Verify that we may use the normal approximation to the binomial.
   (2) Calculate the mean, μ, and the standard deviation, σ, we should use in the normal approximation.
   (3) Find the probability that 150 or fewer consumers in a random sample of 1,000 consumers would be aware of the product.
   b Should the distributor believe the ad agency's claim? Explain.

6.48 In order to gain additional information about respondents, some marketing researchers have used ultraviolet ink to precode questionnaires that promise confidentiality to respondents. Of 205 randomly selected marketing researchers who participated in an actual survey, 117 said that they disapprove of this practice. Suppose that, before the survey was taken, a marketing manager claimed that at least 65 percent of all marketing researchers would disapprove of the practice.
   a Assuming that the manager's claim is correct, calculate the probability that 117 or fewer of 205 randomly selected marketing researchers would disapprove of the practice. Use the normal approximation to the binomial.
   b Based on your result of part a, do you believe the marketing manager's claim? Explain.

6.49 When a store uses electronic article surveillance (EAS) to combat shoplifting, it places a small sensor on each item of merchandise. When an item is legitimately purchased, the sales clerk is supposed to remove the sensor to prevent an alarm from sounding as the customer exits the store. In an actual survey of 250 consumers, 40 said that if they were to set off an EAS alarm because store personnel (mistakenly) failed to deactivate merchandise leaving the store, then they would never shop at that store again. A company marketing the alarm system claimed that no more than 5 percent of all consumers would say that they would never shop at that store again if they were subjected to a false alarm.

a Assuming that the company's claim is valid, use the normal approximation to the binomial to calculate the probability that at least 40 of the 250 randomly selected consumers would say that they would never shop at that store again if they were subjected to a false alarm.

b Do you believe the company's claim based on your answer to part *a*? Explain.

6.50 A department store will place a sale item in a special display for a one-day sale. Previous experience suggests that 20 percent of all customers who pass such a special display will purchase the item. If 2,000 customers will pass the display on the day of the sale, and if a one-item-per-customer limit is placed on the sale item, how many units of the sale item should the store stock in order to have at most a 1 percent chance of running short of the item on the day of the sale? Assume here that customers make independent purchase decisions.

LO7 Use the exponential distribution to compute probabilities (Optional).

6.5 The Exponential Distribution (Optional) ● ● ●

In Example 5.13 (pages 214–216), we considered an air traffic control center where controllers occasionally misdirect pilots onto flight paths dangerously close to those of other aircraft. We found that the number of these controller errors in a given time period has a Poisson distribution and that the control center is averaging 20.8 errors per year. However, rather than focusing on the number of errors occurring in a given time period, we could study the time elapsing between successive errors. If we let x denote the number of weeks elapsing between successive errors, then x is a continuous random variable that is described by what is called the *exponential distribution*. Moreover, because the control center is averaging 20.8 errors per year, the center is averaging a mean, denoted λ, of $20.8/52 = .4$ error per week and thus a mean of $52/20.8 = 2.5$ (that is, $1/\lambda = 1/.4 = 2.5$) weeks between successive errors.

In general, if the number of events occurring per unit of time or space (for example, the number of controller errors per week or the number of imperfections per square yard of cloth) has a Poisson distribution with mean λ, then the number of units, x, of time or space between successive events has an *exponential distribution* with mean $1/\lambda$. The equation of the probability curve describing the exponential distribution is given in the following formula box.

The Exponential Distribution

If x is described by an exponential distribution with mean $1/\lambda$, then the equation of the probability curve describing x is

$$f(x) = \begin{cases} \lambda e^{-\lambda x} & \text{for } x \geq 0 \\ 0 & \text{otherwise} \end{cases}$$

Using this probability curve, it can be shown that:

$$P(a \leq x \leq b) = e^{-\lambda a} - e^{-\lambda b}$$

In particular, since $e^0 = 1$ and $e^{-\infty} = 0$, this implies that

$$P(x \leq b) = 1 - e^{-\lambda b} \quad \text{and} \quad P(x \geq a) = e^{-\lambda a}$$

Furthermore, both the mean and the standard deviation of the population of all possible observed values of a random variable x that has an exponential distribution are equal to $1/\lambda$. That is, $\mu_x = \sigma_x = 1/\lambda$.

The graph of the equation describing the exponential distribution and the probability $P(a \leq x \leq b)$ where x is described by this exponential distribution are illustrated in Figure 6.27.

FIGURE 6.27   A Graph of the Exponential Distribution $f(x) = \lambda e^{-\lambda x}$

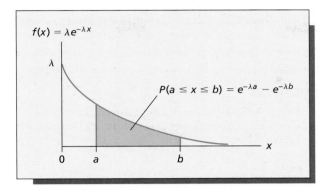

We illustrate the use of the exponential distribution in the following examples.

EXAMPLE 6.10

We have seen in the air traffic control example that the control center is averaging $\lambda = .4$ error per week and $1/\lambda = 1/.4 = 2.5$ weeks between successive errors. It follows that the equation of the exponential distribution describing x is $f(x) = \lambda e^{-\lambda x} = .4e^{-.4x}$. For example, the probability that the time between successive errors will be between 1 and 2 weeks is

$$P(1 \leq x \leq 2) = e^{-\lambda a} - e^{-\lambda b} = e^{-\lambda(1)} - e^{-\lambda(2)}$$
$$= e^{-.4(1)} - e^{-.4(2)} = e^{-.4} - e^{-.8}$$
$$= .6703 - .4493 = .221$$

EXAMPLE 6.11

Suppose that the number of people who arrive at a hospital emergency room during a given time period has a Poisson distribution. It follows that the time, x, between successive arrivals of people to the emergency room has an exponential distribution. Furthermore, historical records indicate that the mean time between successive arrivals of people to the emergency room is seven minutes. Therefore, $\mu_x = 1/\lambda = 7$, which implies that $\lambda = 1/7 = .14286$. Noting that $\sigma_x = 1/\lambda = 7$, it follows that

$$\mu_x - \sigma_x = 7 - 7 = 0 \qquad \text{and} \qquad \mu_x + \sigma_x = 7 + 7 = 14$$

Therefore, the probability that the time between successive arrivals of people to the emergency room will be within (plus or minus) one standard deviation of the mean interarrival time is

$$P(0 \leq x \leq 14) = e^{-\lambda a} - e^{-\lambda b}$$
$$= e^{-(.14286)(0)} - e^{-(.14286)(14)}$$
$$= 1 - .1353$$
$$= .8647$$

To conclude this section we note that the exponential and related Poisson distributions are useful in analyzing waiting lines, or **queues.** In general, **queueing theory** attempts to determine the number of servers (for example, doctors in an emergency room) that strikes an optimal balance between the time customers wait for service and the cost of providing service. The reader is referred to any textbook on management science or operations research for a discussion of queueing theory.

Exercises for Section 6.5

CONCEPTS

connect

6.51 Give two examples of situations in which the exponential distribution might be used appropriately. In each case, define the random variable having an exponential distribution.

6.52 State the formula for the exponential probability curve. Define each symbol in the formula.

6.53 Explain the relationship between the Poisson and exponential distributions.

METHODS AND APPLICATIONS

6.54 Suppose that the random variable x has an exponential distribution with $\lambda = 2$.
  a Write the formula for the exponential probability curve of x. What are the possible values of x?
  b Sketch the probability curve.
  c Find $P(x \le 1)$.
  d Find $P(.25 \le x \le 1)$.
  e Find $P(x \ge 2)$.
  f Calculate the mean, μ_x, the variance, σ_x^2, and the standard deviation, σ_x, of the exponential distribution of x.
  g Find the probability that x will be in the interval $[\mu_x \pm 2\sigma_x]$.

6.55 Repeat Exercise 6.54 with $\lambda = 3$.

6.56 Recall in Exercise 5.34 (page 218) that the number of customer arrivals at a bank's drive-up window in a 15-minute period is Poisson distributed with a mean of seven customer arrivals per 15-minute period. Define the random variable x to be the time (in minutes) between successive customer arrivals at the bank's drive-up window.
  a Write the formula for the exponential probability curve of x.
  b Sketch the probability curve of x.
  c Find the probability that the time between arrivals is
    (1) Between one and two minutes.
    (2) Less than one minute.
    (3) More than three minutes.
    (4) Between $1/2$ and $3^1/_2$ minutes.
  d Calculate μ_x, σ_x^2, and σ_x.
  e Find the probability that the time between arrivals falls within one standard deviation of the mean; within two standard deviations of the mean.

6.57 The length of a particular telemarketing phone call, x, has an exponential distribution with mean equal to 1.5 minutes.
  a Write the formula for the exponential probability curve of x.
  b Sketch the probability curve of x.
  c Find the probability that the length of a randomly selected call will be
    (1) No more than three minutes.
    (2) Between one and two minutes.
    (3) More than four minutes.
    (4) Less than 30 seconds.

6.58 The maintenance department in a factory claims that the number of breakdowns of a particular machine follows a Poisson distribution with a mean of two breakdowns every 500 hours. Let x denote the time (in hours) between successive breakdowns.
  a Find λ and μ_x.
  b Write the formula for the exponential probability curve of x.
  c Sketch the probability curve.
  d Assuming that the maintenance department's claim is true, find the probability that the time between successive breakdowns is at most five hours.
  e Assuming that the maintenance department's claim is true, find the probability that the time between successive breakdowns is between 100 and 300 hours.
  f Suppose that the machine breaks down five hours after its most recent breakdown. Based on your answer to part d, do you believe the maintenance department's claim? Explain.

6.59 Suppose that the number of accidents occurring in an industrial plant is described by a Poisson distribution with an average of one accident per month. Let x denote the time (in months) between successive accidents.
  a Find the probability that the time between successive accidents is
    (1) More than two months.
    (2) Between one and two months.
    (3) Less than one week (1/4 of a month).

b Suppose that an accident occurs less than one week after the plant's most recent accident. Would you consider this event unusual enough to warrant special investigation? Explain.

6.6 The Normal Probability Plot (Optional) ● ● ●

LO8 Use a normal probability plot to help decide whether data come from a normal distribution (Optional).

The **normal probability plot** is a graphic that is used to check visually whether sample data come from a normal distribution. In order to illustrate the construction and interpretation of a normal probability plot, consider the payment time case and suppose that the trucking company operates in three regions of the country—the north, central, and south regions. In each region, 24 invoices are randomly selected and the payment time for each sampled invoice is found. The payment times obtained in each region are given in Table 6.3, along with MINITAB side-by-side box plots of the data. Examination of the data and box plots indicates that the payment times for the central region are skewed to the left, while the payment times for the south region are skewed to the right. The box plot of the payment times for the north region, along with the dot plot of these payment times in Figure 6.28, indicate that the payment times for the north region are approximately normally distributed.

We will begin by constructing a normal probability plot for the payment times from the north region. We first arrange the payment times in order from smallest to largest. The ordered payment times are shown in column (1) of Table 6.4 on the next page. Next, for each ordered payment time we compute the quantity $i/(n + 1)$, where i denotes the observation's position in the ordered list of data and n denotes the sample size. For instance, for the first and second ordered payment times, we compute $1/(24 + 1) = 1/25 = .04$ and $2/(24 + 1) = 2/25 = .08$. Similarly, for the last (24th) ordered payment time, we compute $24/(24 + 1) = 24/25 = .96$. The positions ($i$ values) of all 24 payment times are given in column (2) of Table 6.4, and the corresponding values of $i/(n + 1)$ are given in column (3) of this table. We continue by computing what is called the **standardized normal quantile value** for each ordered payment time. This value (denoted O_i) is the z value that

---

TABLE 6.3   **Twenty-four Randomly Selected Payment Times for Each of Three Geographical Regions in the United States**   ⊃⊃ RegPayTime

North Region	Central Region	South Region
26	26	28
27	28	31
21	21	21
22	22	23
22	23	23
23	24	24
27	27	29
20	19	20
22	22	22
29	29	36
18	15	19
24	25	25
28	28	33
26	26	27
21	20	21
32	29	44
23	24	24
24	25	26
25	25	27
15	7	19
17	12	19
19	18	20
34	29	50
30	29	39

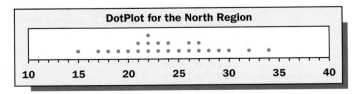

FIGURE 6.28   **Dot Plot of the Payment Times for the North Region**

TABLE 6.4   **Calculations for Normal Probability Plots in the Payment Time Example**

Ordered North Region Payment Times Column (1)	Observation Number (i) Column (2)	Area $i/(n+1)$ Column (3)	z value O_i Column (4)	Ordered Central Region Payment Times Column (5)	Ordered South Region Payment Times Column (6)
15	1	0.04	−1.75	7	19
17	2	0.08	−1.41	12	19
18	3	0.12	−1.18	15	19
19	4	0.16	−0.99	18	20
20	5	0.2	−0.84	19	20
21	6	0.24	−0.71	20	21
21	7	0.28	−0.58	21	21
22	8	0.32	−0.47	22	22
22	9	0.36	−0.36	22	23
22	10	0.4	−0.25	23	23
23	11	0.44	−0.15	24	24
23	12	0.48	−0.05	24	24
24	13	0.52	0.05	25	25
24	14	0.56	0.15	25	26
25	15	0.6	0.25	25	27
26	16	0.64	0.36	26	27
26	17	0.68	0.47	26	28
27	18	0.72	0.58	27	29
27	19	0.76	0.71	28	31
28	20	0.8	0.84	28	33
29	21	0.84	0.99	29	36
30	22	0.88	1.18	29	39
32	23	0.92	1.41	29	44
34	24	0.96	1.75	29	50

FIGURE 6.29   **Calculating Standardized Normal Quantile Values**

(a) Calculating O_1 (b) Calculating O_2 (c) Calculating O_{24}

gives an area of $i/(n+1)$ to its left under the standard normal curve. Figure 6.29 illustrates finding O_1, O_2, and O_{24}. For instance, O_1—the standardized normal quantile value corresponding to the first ordered residual—is the z value that gives an area of $1/(24+1) = .04$ to its left under the standard normal curve. As shown in Figure 6.29(a), the z value (to two decimal places) that gives a left-hand tail area closest to .04 is $O_1 = -1.75$. Similarly, O_2 is the z value that gives an area of $2/(24+1) = .08$ to its left under the standard normal curve. As shown in Figure 6.29(b), the z value (to two decimal places) that gives a left-hand tail area closest to .08 is $O_2 = -1.41$. As a final example, Figure 6.29(c) shows that O_{24}, the z value that gives an area of $24/(24+1) = .96$ to its left under the standard normal curve, is 1.75. The standardized normal quantile values corresponding to the 24 ordered payment times are given in column (4) of Table 6.4. Finally, we obtain the **normal probability plot** by plotting the 24 ordered payment times on the vertical axis versus the corresponding standardized normal quantile values (O_i values) on the horizontal axis. Figure 6.30 gives an Excel add-in (MegaStat) output of this normal probability plot.

In order to interpret the normal plot, notice that, although the areas in column (3) of Table 6.4 (that is, the $i/(n+1)$ values: .04, .08, .12, etc.) are equally spaced, the z values corresponding to

FIGURE 6.30   Excel Add-in (MegaStat) Normal Probability Plot for the North Region: Approximate Normality

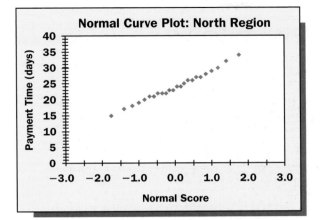

FIGURE 6.31   Excel Add-in (MegaStat) Normal Probability Plot for the Central Region: Data Skewed to the Left

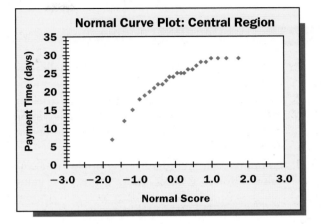

FIGURE 6.32   Excel Add-in (MegaStat) Normal Probability Plot for the South Region: Data Skewed to the Right

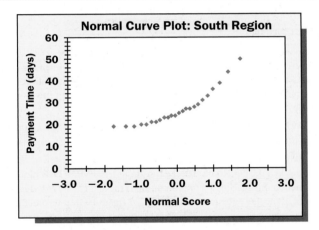

these areas are not equally spaced. Because of the mound-shaped nature of the standard normal curve, the negative z values get closer together as they get closer to the mean ($z = 0$) and the positive z values get farther apart as they get farther from the mean (more positive). If the distances between the payment times behave the same way as the distances between the z values—that is, if the distances between the payment times are proportional to the distances between the z values—then the normal probability plot will be a straight line. This would suggest that the payment times are normally distributed. Examining Figure 6.30, the normal probability plot for the payment times from the north region is approximately a straight line and, therefore, it is reasonable to assume that these payment times are approximately normally distributed.

Column (5) of Table 6.4 gives the ordered payment times for the central region, and Figure 6.31 plots these values versus the standardized normal quantile values in column (4). The resulting normal probability plot for the central region has a nonlinear appearance. The plot points rise more steeply at first and then continue to increase at a decreasing rate. This pattern indicates that the payment times for the central region are skewed to the left. Here the rapidly rising points at the beginning of the plot are due to the payment times being farther apart in the left tail of the distribution. Column (6) of Table 6.4 gives the ordered payment times for the south region, and Figure 6.32 gives the normal probability plot for this region. This plot also has a nonlinear appearance. The points rise slowly at first and then increase at an increasing rate. This pattern indicates that the payment times for the south region are skewed to the right. Here the rapidly rising points on the right side of the plot are due to the payment times being farther apart in the right tail of the distribution.

In the following box, we summarize how to construct and interpret a normal probability plot.

Normal Probability Plots

1 Order the values in the data from smallest to largest.

2 For each observation compute the area $i/(n + 1)$, where i denotes the position of the observation in the ordered listing and n is the number of observations.

3 Compute the standardized normal quantile value O_i for each observation. This is the z value

that gives an area of $i/(n + 1)$ to its left under the standard normal curve.

4 Plot the ordered data values versus the standardized normal quantile values.

5 If the resulting normal probability plot has a straight line appearance, it is reasonable to assume that the data come from a normal distribution.

Exercises for Section 6.6

CONCEPTS

connect

6.60 Discuss how a normal probability plot is constructed.

6.61 If a normal probability plot has the appearance of a straight line, what should we conclude?

METHODS AND APPLICATIONS

6.62 Consider the sample of 12 incomes given in Example 3.2 (page 105).
  a Sort the income data from smallest to largest, and compute $i/(n + 1)$ for each observation.
  b Compute the standardized normal quantile value O_i for each observation.
  c Graph the normal probability plot for the salary data and interpret this plot. Does the plot indicate that the data are skewed? Explain.   DS Incomes

6.63 Consider the 20 DVD satisfaction ratings given on page 123. Construct a normal probability plot for these data and interpret the plot.   DS DVDSat

6.64 A normal probability plot can be constructed using MINITAB. Use the selections Stat : Basic Statistics : Normality test, and select the data to be analyzed. Although the MINITAB plot is slightly different from the plot outlined in this section, its interpretation is the same. Use MINITAB to construct a normal probability plot of the gas mileage data in Table 3.1 (page 103). Interpret the plot.   DS GasMiles

Chapter Summary

In this chapter we have discussed **continuous probability distributions.** We began by learning that **a continuous probability distribution is described by a continuous probability curve** and that in this context **probabilities are areas under the probability curve.** We next studied several important continuous probability distributions—**the uniform distribution, the normal distribution,** and **the exponential distribution.** In particular, we concentrated on the normal distribution, which is the most

important continuous probability distribution. We learned about the properties of the normal curve, and we saw how to use a **normal table** to find various areas under a normal curve. We also saw that the normal curve can be employed to approximate binomial probabilities, and we demonstrated how we can use a normal curve probability to make a statistical inference. We concluded this chapter with an optional section that covers the **normal probability plot.**

Glossary of Terms

continuous probability distribution (or **probability curve**): A curve that is defined so that the probability that a random variable will be in a specified interval of numbers is the area under the curve corresponding to the interval. (page 229)

cumulative normal table: A table in which we can look up areas under the standard normal curve. (pages 236–238)

exponential distribution: A probability distribution that describes the time or space between successive occurrences of an event when the number of times the event occurs over an interval of time or space is described by a Poisson distribution. (page 256)

normal probability distribution: The most important continuous probability distribution. Its probability curve is the *bell-shaped* normal curve. (page 234)

normal probability plot: A graphic used to visually check whether sample data come from a normal distribution. (page 259)

queueing theory: A methodology that attempts to determine the number of servers that strikes an optimal balance between the time customers wait for service and the cost of providing service. (page 257)

standard normal distribution (or curve): A normal distribution (or curve) having mean 0 and standard deviation 1. (page 236)

uniform distribution: A continuous probability distribution having a rectangular shape that says the probability is distributed evenly (or uniformly) over an interval of numbers. (page 231)

z_α **point:** The point on the horizontal axis under the standard normal curve that gives a right-hand tail area equal to α. (page 245)

$-z_\alpha$ **point:** The point on the horizontal axis under the standard normal curve that gives a left-hand tail area equal to α. (page 246)

z **value:** A value that tells us the number of standard deviations that a value x is from the mean of a normal curve. If the z value is positive, then x is above the mean. If the z value is negative, then x is below the mean. (page 236)

Important Formulas

The uniform probability curve: page 231

Mean and standard deviation of a uniform distribution: page 231

The normal probability curve: page 234

z values: page 236

Finding normal probabilities: page 242

Normal approximation to the binomial distribution: page 252

The exponential probability curve: page 256

Mean and standard deviation of an exponential distribution: page 256

Constructing a normal probability plot: page 262

Supplementary Exercises

connect

6.65 In a bottle-filling process, the amount of drink injected into 16 oz bottles is normally distributed with a mean of 16 oz and a standard deviation of .02 oz. Bottles containing less than 15.95 oz do not meet the bottler's quality standard. What percentage of filled bottles do not meet the standard?

6.66 In a murder trial in Los Angeles, a shoe expert stated that the range of heights of men with a size 12 shoe is 71 inches to 76 inches. Suppose the heights of all men wearing size 12 shoes are normally distributed with a mean of 73.5 inches and a standard deviation of 1 inch. What is the probability that a randomly selected man who wears a size 12 shoe

   a Has a height outside the range 71 inches to 76 inches?

   b Is 74 inches or taller?

   c Is shorter than 70.5 inches?

6.67 In the movie *Forrest Gump,* the public school required an IQ of at least 80 for admittance.

   a If IQ test scores are normally distributed with mean 100 and standard deviation 16, what percentage of people would qualify for admittance to the school?

   b If the public school wishes 95 percent of all children to qualify for admittance, what minimum IQ test score should be required for admittance?

6.68 The amount of sales tax paid on a purchase is rounded to the nearest cent. Assume that the round-off error is uniformly distributed in the interval $-.5$ to $.5$ cent.

   a Write the formula for the probability curve describing the round-off error.

   b Graph the probability curve describing the round-off error.

   c What is the probability that the round-off error exceeds .3 cent or is less than $-.3$ cent?

   d What is the probability that the round-off error exceeds .1 cent or is less than $-.1$ cent?

   e Find the mean and the standard deviation of the round-off error.

   f Find the probability that the round-off error will be within one standard deviation of the mean.

6.69 A *consensus forecast* is the average of a large number of individual analysts' forecasts. Suppose the individual forecasts for a particular interest rate are normally distributed with a mean of 5.0 percent and a standard deviation of 1.2 percent. A single analyst is randomly selected. Find the probability that his/her forecast is

   a At least 3.5 percent.

   b At most 6 percent.

   c Between 3.5 percent and 6 percent.

6.70 Recall from Exercise 6.69 that individual forecasts of a particular interest rate are normally distributed with a mean of 5 percent and a standard deviation of 1.2 percent.
  a What percentage of individual forecasts are at or below the 10th percentile of the distribution of forecasts? What percentage are at or above the 10th percentile? Find the 10th percentile of the distribution of individual forecasts.
  b Find the first quartile, Q_1, and the third quartile, Q_3, of the distribution of individual forecasts.

6.71 The scores on the entrance exam at a well-known, exclusive law school are normally distributed with a mean score of 200 and a standard deviation equal to 50. At what value should the lowest passing score be set if the school wishes only 2.5 percent of those taking the test to pass?

6.72 A machine is used to cut a metal automobile part to its desired length. The machine can be set so that the mean length of the part will be any value that is desired. The standard deviation of the lengths always runs at .02 inch. Where should the mean be set if we want only .4 percent of the parts cut by the machine to be shorter than 15 inches long?

6.73 A motel accepts 325 reservations for 300 rooms on July 1, expecting 10 percent no-shows on average from past records. Use the normal approximation to the binomial to find the probability that all guests who arrive on July 1 will receive a room.

6.74 Suppose a software company finds that the number of errors in its software per 1,000 lines of code is described by a Poisson distribution. Furthermore, it is found that there is an average of four errors per 1,000 lines of code. Letting x denote the number of lines of code between successive errors:
  a Find the probability that there will be at least 400 lines of code between successive errors in the company's software.
  b Find the probability that there will be no more than 100 lines of code between successive errors in the company's software.

6.75 **THE INVESTMENT CASE** 🔵 InvestRet

  For each investment class in Table 3.11 (page 143), assume that future returns are normally distributed with the population mean and standard deviation given in Table 3.11. Based on this assumption:
  a For each investment class, find the probability of a return that is less than zero (that is, find the probability of a loss). Is your answer reasonable for all investment classes? Explain.
  b For each investment class, find the probability of a return that is
  (1) Greater than 5 percent.
  (2) Greater than 10 percent.
  (3) Greater than 20 percent.
  (4) Greater than 50 percent.
  c For which investment classes is the probability of a return greater than 50 percent essentially zero? For which investment classes is the probability of such a return greater than 1 percent? Greater than 5 percent?
  d For which investment classes is the probability of a loss essentially zero? For which investment classes is the probability of a loss greater than 1 percent? Greater than 10 percent? Greater than 20 percent?

6.76 The daily water consumption for an Ohio community is normally distributed with a mean consumption of 800,000 gallons and a standard deviation of 80,000 gallons. The community water system will experience a noticeable drop in water pressure when the daily water consumption exceeds 984,000 gallons. What is the probability of experiencing such a drop in water pressure?

6.77 Suppose the times required for a cable company to fix cable problems in its customers' homes are uniformly distributed between 10 minutes and 25 minutes. What is the probability that a randomly selected cable repair visit will take at least 15 minutes?

6.78 Suppose the waiting time to get food after placing an order at a fast-food restaurant is exponentially distributed with a mean of 60 seconds. If a randomly selected customer orders food at the restaurant, what is the probability that the customer will wait at least
  a 90 seconds?
  b Two minutes?

6.79 Net interest margin—often referred to as *spread*—is the difference between the rate banks pay on deposits and the rate they charge for loans. Suppose that the net interest margins for all U.S. banks are normally distributed with a mean of 4.15 percent and a standard deviation of .5 percent.
  a Find the probability that a randomly selected U.S. bank will have a net interest margin that exceeds 5.40 percent.
  b Find the probability that a randomly selected U.S. bank will have a net interest margin less than 4.40 percent.

c A bank wants its net interest margin to be less than the net interest margins of 95 percent of all U.S. banks. Where should the bank's net interest margin be set?

6.80 In an article in the November 11, 1991, issue of *Advertising Age,* Nancy Giges studies global spending patterns. Giges presents data concerning the percentage of adults in various countries who have purchased various consumer items (such as soft drinks, athletic footware, blue jeans, beer, and so on) in the past three months.

a Suppose we wish to justify the claim that fewer than 50 percent of adults in Germany have purchased blue jeans in the past three months. The survey reported by Giges found that 45 percent of the respondents in Germany had purchased blue jeans in the past three months.[2]

Assume that a random sample of 400 German adults was employed, and let p be the proportion of all German adults who have purchased blue jeans in the past three months. If, for the sake of argument, we assume that $p = .5$, use the normal approximation to the binomial distribution to calculate the probability that 45 percent or fewer of 400 randomly selected German adults would have purchased blue jeans in the past three months. Note: Because 45 percent of 400 is 180, you should calculate the probability that 180 or fewer of 400 randomly selected German adults would have purchased blue jeans in the past three months.

b Based on the probability you computed in part *a*, would you conclude that p is really less than .5? That is, would you conclude that fewer than 50 percent of adults in Germany have purchased blue jeans in the past three months? Explain.

6.81 Assume that the ages for first marriages are normally distributed with a mean of 26 years and a standard deviation of 4 years. What is the probability that a person getting married for the first time is in his or her twenties?

---

[2]Source: N. Giges, "Global Spending Patterns Emerge," *Advertising Age* (November 11, 1991), p. 64.

Appendix 6.1 ■ Normal Distribution Using Excel

Normal probability $P(X \le 31.2)$ in Example 6.3 (page 243):

- Click in the cell where you wish to place the answer. Here we have clicked in cell A15. Then select the Insert Function button f_x from the Excel toolbar.

- In the Insert Function dialog box, select Statistical from the "Or select a category:" menu, select NORMDIST from the "Select a function:" menu, and click OK.

- In the NORMDIST Function Arguments dialog box, enter the value 31.2 in the X window.

- Enter the value 33 in the Mean window.

- Enter the value 0.7 in the Standard_dev window.

- Enter the value 1 in the Cumulative window.

- Click OK in the NORMDIST Function Arguments dialog box.

- When you click OK in this dialog box, the answer will be placed in cell A15.

Normal probability $P(X < 153 \text{ or } X > 167)$ in Example 6.4 (page 244):

- Enter the headings—x, P(X < x), P(X > x)—in the spreadsheet where you wish the results to be placed. Here we will enter these headings in cells A16, B16, and C16. The calculated results will be placed below the headings.

- In cells A17 and A18, enter the values 153 and 167.

- Click in cell B17 and select the Insert Function button f_x from the Excel toolbar.

- In the Insert Function dialog box, select Statistical from the "Or select a category:" menu, select NORMDIST from the "Select a function:" menu, and click OK.

- In the NORMDIST Function Arguments dialog box, enter the cell location A17 in the X window.

- Enter the value 160.0833 in the Mean window.

- Enter the value 5.3724 in the Standard_dev window.

- Enter the value 1 in the Cumulative window.

- Click OK in the NORMDIST Function Arguments dialog box.

- When you click OK, the result for $P(X < 153)$ will be placed in cell B17. Double-click the drag-handle (in the lower right corner) of cell B17 to automatically extend the cell formula of B17 through cell B18.

- In cells C17 and C18, enter the formulas =1−B17 and =1−B18. The results for $P(X > 153)$ and $P(X > 167)$ will be placed in cells C17 and C18.

- In cell D19, enter the formula =B17+C18.

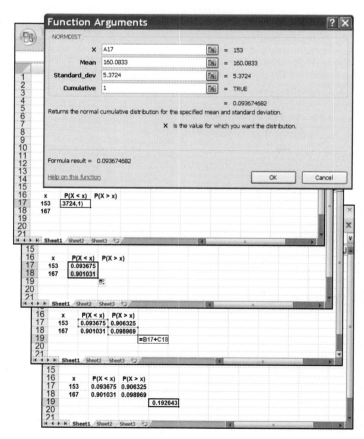

The desired probability is in cell D19, the sum of the lower tail probability for 153 and the upper tail probability for 167. This value differs slightly from the value in Example 6.4 since Excel carries out probability calculations to higher precision than can be achieved using normal probability tables.

Inverse normal probability *st* such that $P(X > st) = 0.05$ in Example 6.5 (pages 245–246):

- Click in the cell where you wish the answer to be placed. Here we will click in cell A19. Select the Insert Function button f_x from the Excel toolbar.

- In the Insert Function dialog box, select Statistical from the "Or select a category:" menu, select NORMINV from the "Select a function:" menu, and click OK.

- In the NORMINV Function Arguments dialog box, enter the value 0.95 in the Probability window; that is,

    $P(X \leq st) = 0.95$ when $P(X > st) = 0.05$.

- Enter the value 100 in the Mean window.

- Enter the value 10 in the Standard_dev window.

- Click OK in the NORMINV Function Arguments dialog window.

- When you click OK, the answer is placed in cell A19.

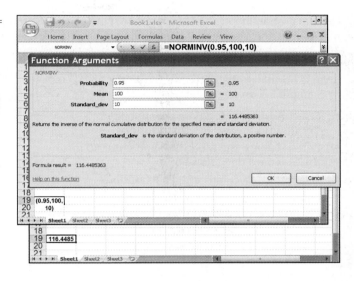

Appendix 6.2 ■ Normal Distribution Using MegaStat

Normal probability $P(X < 31.2)$ in Example 6.3 (page 243):

- Select **Add-ins : MegaStat : Probability : Continuous Probability Distributions**

- In the "Continuous Probability Distributions" dialog box, select the normal distribution tab.

- Enter the distribution mean (here equal to 33) and the distribution standard deviation (here equal to 0.7) in the appropriate boxes.

- Enter the value of *x* (here equal to 31.2) into the "Calculate p given x" window.

- Click OK in the "Continuous Probability Distributions" dialog box.

- The output includes **P(lower),** which is the area under the specified normal curve below the given value of *x*, and **P(upper),** which is the area under the specified normal curve above the given value of *x*. The value of *z* corresponding to the specified value of *x* is also included. In this case, $P(X < 31.2)$ equals $P(\text{lower}) = .0051$.

- (Optional) Click on the preview button to see the values of P(lower) and P(upper) before obtaining results in the Output worksheet.

Note that if a **standard normal distribution** is specified, 0 is entered in the mean box and 1 is entered in the standard deviation box—the "calculate P given X" box will read "Calculate P given z." In this case, when we enter a value of z in the "Calculate P given z" box, P(lower) and P(upper) are, respectively, the areas below and above the specified value of z under the standard normal curve.

Normal probability $P(X < 153 \text{ or } X > 167)$ in Example 6.4 on page 244. Enter 160.0833 into the Mean box and enter 5.3724 into the Standard Deviation box. Find P(lower) corresponding to 153 and find P(upper) corresponding to 167. When these values are placed in the output worksheet, use a simple Excel cell formula to add them together.

Inverse normal probability *st* such that $P(X > st) = 0.05$ in Example 6.5 on pages 245–246:

- Select **Add-ins : MegaStat : Probability : Continuous Probability Distributions**

- Enter 100 into the Mean box and enter 10 into the Standard deviation box.

- Select the "Calculate x given P" option.

- Enter 0.05 into the P box. This is the area under the normal curve we want to have above *st* (that is, above the desired value of *x*).

- Click OK in the "Continuous Probability Distributions" dialog box.

- The output includes P(lower) and P(upper)—as defined above—as well as the desired value of *x* (in this case *x* equals 116.4485).

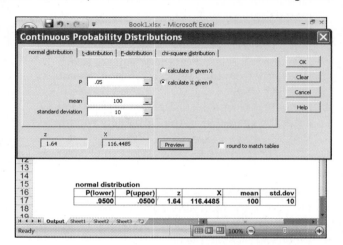

Appendix 6.3 ■ Normal Distribution Using MINITAB

Normal probability $P(X \le 31.2)$ in Example 6.3 (page 243):

- Select **Calc : Probability Distributions : Normal.**

- In the Normal Distribution dialog box, select the Cumulative probability option.

- In the Mean window, enter 33.

- In the Standard deviation window, enter 0.7.

- Click on the "Input constant" option and enter 31.2 in the "Input constant" window.

- Click OK in Normal Distribution dialog box to see the desired probability in the Session window.

Normal probability $P(X < 153$ or $X > 167)$ in Example 6.4 (page 244):

- In columns C1, C2, and C3, enter the variable names—x, P(X < x), and P(X > x).
- In column C1, enter the values 153 and 167.
- Select **Calc : Probability Distributions : Normal.**
- In the Normal Distribution dialog box, select the Cumulative probability option.
- In the Mean window, enter 160.0833.
- In the Standard deviation window, enter 5.3724.
- Click the "Input column" option, enter x in the "Input column" window, and enter 'P(X < x)' in the "Optional storage" window.
- Click OK in Normal Distribution dialog box.

- Select **Calc : Calculator.**
- In the Calculator dialog box, enter 'P(X > x)' in the "Store result in variable" window.
- Enter 1 − 'P(X < x)' in the Expression window.
- Click OK in the Calculator dialog box.

The desired probability is the sum of the lower tail probability for 153 and the upper tail probability for 167 or 0.093675 + 0.098969 = 0.192644. This value differs slightly from the value in Example 6.4 because Minitab carries out probability calculations to higher precision than can be achieved using normal probability tables.

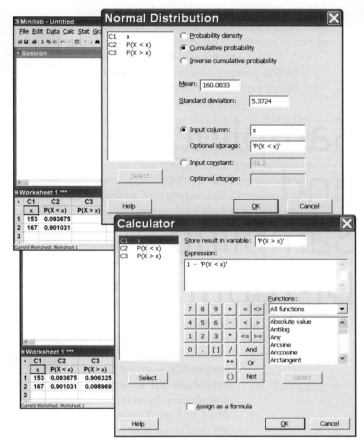

Inverse normal probability to find the number of units stocked, *st*, such that $P(X > st) = 0.05$ in Example 6.5 (pages 245–246):

- Select **Calc : Probability Distributions : Normal.**
- In the Normal Distribution dialog box, select the Inverse cumulative probability option.
- In the Mean window, enter 100.
- In the Standard deviation window, enter 10.
- Click the "Input constant" option and enter 0.95 in the "Input constant" window. That is,

    $P(X \le st) = 0.95$ when $P(X > st) = 0.05.$

- Click OK in the Normal Distribution dialog box to see the desired value of *st* in the Session window.

choosing the sample without replacement guarantees that all of the elements in the sample will be different, and thus we will have the fullest possible look at the population.

The first step in selecting a random sample is to obtain or make a numbered list of the population elements. Then, as illustrated in the following example, we can use a *random number table* or *computer-generated random numbers* to make random selections from the numbered list.

EXAMPLE 7.1 The Cell Phone Case

In order to select a random sample of 100 employees from the population of 2,136 employees on 500-minute-per-month cell phone plans, the bank will make a numbered list of the 2,136 employees on 500-minute plans. The bank can then use a **random number table,** such as Table 7.1(a), to select the random sample. To see how this is done, note that any single-digit number in the table has been chosen in such a way that any of the single-digit numbers between 0 and 9 had the same chance of being chosen. For this reason, we say that any single-digit number in the table is a **random number** between 0 and 9. Similarly, any two-digit number in the table is a random number between 00 and 99, any three digit number in the table is a random number between 000 and 999, and so forth. Note that the table entries are segmented into groups of five to make the table easier to read. Because the total number of cell phone users on the 500-minute plans (2,136) is a four-digit number, we arbitrarily select any set of four digits in the table (we have circled these digits). This number, which is 0511, identifies the first randomly selected user. Then, moving in any direction from the 0511 (up, down, right, or left—it does not matter which), we select additional sets of four digits. These succeeding sets of digits identify additional randomly selected users. Here we arbitrarily move down from 0511 in the table. The first seven sets of four digits we obtain are

0511   7156   0285   4461   3990   4919   1915

(See Table 7.1(a)—these numbers are enclosed in a rectangle.) Since there are no users numbered 7156, 4461, 3990, or 4919 (remember only 2,136 users are on 500-minute plans), we ignore these numbers. This implies that the first three randomly selected users are those numbered 0511, 0285, and 1915. Continuing this procedure, we can obtain the entire random sample of 100 users. Notice that, because we are sampling without replacement, we should ignore any set of four digits previously selected from the random number table.

While using a random number table is one way to select a random sample, this approach has a disadvantage that is illustrated by the current situation. Specifically, since most four-digit random numbers are not between 0001 and 2136, obtaining 100 different, four-digit random numbers between 0001 and 2136 will require ignoring a large number of random numbers in the random number table, and we will in fact need to use a random number table that is larger than

---

TABLE 7.1   Random Numbers

(a) A portion of a random number table

33276	85590	79936	56865	05859	90106	78188
03427	90511	69445	18663	72695	52180	90322
92737	27156	33488	36320	17617	30015	74952
85689	20285	52267	67689	93394	01511	89868
08178	74461	13916	47564	81056	97735	90707
51259	63990	16308	60756	92144	49442	40719
60268	44919	19885	55322	44819	01188	55157
94904	01915	04146	18594	29852	71585	64951
58586	17752	14513	83149	98736	23495	35749
09998	19509	06691	76988	13602	51851	58104
14346	61666	30168	90229	04734	59193	32812
74103	15227	25306	76468	26384	58151	44592
24200	64161	38005	94342	28728	35806	22851
87308	07684	00256	45834	15398	46557	18510
07351	86679	92420	60952	61280	50001	94953

(b) MINITAB output of 100 different, four-digit random numbers between 1 and 2136

705	1131	169	1703	1709	609
1990	766	1286	1977	222	43
1007	1902	1209	2091	1742	1152
111	69	2049	1448	659	338
1732	1650	7	388	613	1477
838	272	1227	154	18	320
1053	1466	2087	265	2107	1992
582	1787	2098	1581	397	1099
757	1699	567	1255	1959	407
354	1567	1533	1097	1299	277
663	40	585	1486	1021	532
1629	182	372	1144	1569	1981
1332	1500	743	1262	1759	955
1832	378	728	1102	667	1885
514	1128	1046	116	1160	1333
831	2036	918	1535	660	
928	1257	1468	503	468	

Table 7.1(a). Although larger random number tables are readily available in books of mathematical and statistical tables, a good alternative is to use a computer software package, which can generate random numbers that are between whatever values we specify. For example, Table 7.1(b) gives the MINITAB output of 100 different, four-digit random numbers that are between 0001 and 2136 (note that the "leading 0's" are not included in these four-digit numbers). If used, the random numbers in Table 7.1(b) would identify the 100 employees that form the random sample. For example, the first three randomly selected employees would be employees 705, 1990, and 1007. When the number of cellular minutes used by each randomly selected employee is found and recorded, we obtain the sample of cellular usages that has been given in Table 1.4 (see page 9).

To conclude this example, note that computer software packages sometimes generate the same random number twice and thus are sampling with replacement. Because we wished to randomly select 100 employees without replacement, we had MINITAB generate more than 100 (actually, 110) random numbers. We then ignored the repeated random numbers to obtain the 100 different random numbers in Table 7.1(b).

Next, consider the *marketing research case,* and recall that we wish to select a sample of 60 shoppers at a large metropolitan shopping mall on a particular Saturday. Because it is not possible to list and number all of the shoppers who will be at the mall on this Saturday, we cannot select a random sample of these shoppers. However, we can select an *approximately* random sample of these shoppers. To see one way to do this, note that there are 6 ten-minute intervals during each hour, and thus there are 60 ten-minute intervals during the 10-hour period from 10 A.M. to 8 P.M.—the time when the shopping mall is open. Therefore, one way to select an approximately random sample is to choose a particular location at the mall that most shoppers will walk by and then randomly select—at the beginning of each ten-minute period—one of the first shoppers that walks by the location. Here, although we could randomly select one person from any reasonable number of shoppers that walk by, we will (arbitrarily) randomly select one of the first five shoppers that walk by. For example, starting in the upper left-hand corner of Table 7.1(a) and proceeding down the first column, note that the first three random numbers between 1 and 5 are 3, 5, and 1. This implies that (1) at 10 A.M. we would select the 3rd customer that walks by; (2) at 10:10 A.M. we would select the 5th shopper that walks by; (3) at 10:20 A.M. we would select the 1st customer that walks by, and so forth. Furthermore, assume that the composite score ratings of the new bottle design that would be given by all shoppers at the mall on the Saturday are representative of the composite score ratings that would be given by all possible consumers. It then follows that the composite score ratings given by the 60 sampled shoppers can be regarded as an approximately random sample that can be used to make statistical inferences about the population of all possible consumer composite score ratings.

As another example, consider the *car mileage case,* and recall that the automaker has decided to select a sample of 50 cars by randomly selecting one car from the 100 cars produced on each of 50 consecutive production shifts. If we number the 100 cars produced on a particular production shift from 00 to 99, we can randomly select a car from the shift by using a random number table or a computer software package to obtain a random number between 00 and 99. For example, starting in the upper left-hand corner of Table 7.1(a) and proceeding down the first column, we see that the first three random numbers between 00 and 99 are 33, 3, and 92. This implies that we would select car 33 from the first production shift, car 3 from the second production shift, car 92 from the third production shift, and so forth. Moreover, because a new group of 100 cars is produced on each production shift, repeated random numbers would not be discarded. For example, if the 15th and 29th random numbers are both 7, we would select the 7th car from the 15th production shift and the 7th car from the 29th production shift. When the 50 cars are selected and tested as prescribed by the EPA, the sample of 50 mileages that has been given in Table 1.6 (see page 12) is obtained. Furthermore, recall that we waited to randomly select the 50 cars from the 50 production shifts until the midsize car manufacturing process was operating consistently over time and recall that the runs plot in Figure 1.3 (page 12) intuitively verifies that the manufacturing process is producing consistent car mileages over time. It follows that we can regard the 50 mileages in Table 1.6 as an approximately random sample that can be used to make statistical inferences about the population of all possible midsize car mileages. (In Chapter 15—on the book's website—we will discuss more precisely how to assess whether a process is operating consistently over time.)

Random (or approximately random) sampling—as well as the more advanced kinds of sampling discussed in optional Section 7.4—are types of *probability sampling*. In general, **probability sampling** is sampling where we know the chance (or probability) that each element in the population will be included in the sample. If we employ probability sampling, the sample obtained can be used to make valid statistical inferences about the sampled population. However, if we do not employ probability sampling, we cannot make valid statistical inferences.

One type of sampling that is not probability sampling is **convenience sampling,** where we select elements because they are easy or convenient to sample. For example, if we select people to interview because they look "nice" or "pleasant," we are using convenience sampling. Another example of convenience sampling is the use of **voluntary response samples,** which are frequently employed by television and radio stations and newspaper columnists. In such samples, participants self-select—that is, whoever wishes to participate does so (usually expressing some opinion). These samples overrepresent people with strong (usually negative) opinions. For example, the advice columnist Ann Landers once asked her readers, "If you had it to do over again, would you have children?" Of the nearly 10,000 parents who *voluntarily* responded, 70 percent said that they would not. A probability sample taken a few months later found that 91 percent of parents would have children again.

Another type of sampling that is not probability sampling is **judgment sampling,** where a person who is extremely knowledgeable about the population under consideration selects population elements that he or she feels are most representative of the population. Because the quality of the sample depends upon the judgment of the person selecting the sample, it is dangerous to use the sample to make statistical inferences about the population.

To conclude this section, we consider a classic example where two types of sampling errors doomed a sample's ability to make valid statistical inferences. This example occurred prior to the presidential election of 1936, when the *Literary Digest* predicted that Alf Landon would defeat Franklin D. Roosevelt by a margin of 57 percent to 43 percent. Instead, Roosevelt won the election in a landslide. *Literary Digest*'s first error was to send out sample ballots (actually, 10 million ballots) to people who were mainly selected from the *Digest*'s subscription list and from telephone directories. In 1936 the country had not yet recovered from the Great Depression, and many unemployed and low-income people did not have phones or subscribe to the *Digest*. The *Digest*'s sampling procedure excluded these people, who overwhelmingly voted for Roosevelt. Second, only 2.3 million ballots were returned, resulting in the sample being a voluntary response survey. At the same time, George Gallup, founder of the Gallup Poll, was beginning to establish his survey business. He used a probability sample to correctly predict Roosevelt's victory. In optional Section 7.5 we discuss various issues related to designing surveys and more about the errors that can occur in survey samples. Optional Sections 7.4 and 7.5 can now be read at any time and in any order.

Exercises for Section 7.1

CONCEPTS

7.1 Discuss how we select a random sample.

7.2 Explain why sampling without replacement is preferred to sampling with replacement.

METHODS AND APPLICATIONS

7.3 On the page margin, we list 15 companies that have historically performed well in the food, drink, and tobacco industries. Consider the random numbers given in the random number table of Table 7.1(a) on page 272. Starting in the upper left corner of Table 7.1(a) and moving down the two leftmost columns, we see that the first three two-digit numbers obtained are: 33, 03, and 92. Starting with these three random numbers, and moving down the two leftmost columns of Table 7.1(a) to find more two-digit random numbers, use Table 7.1 to randomly select five of these companies to be interviewed in detail about their business strategies. Hint: Note that we have numbered the companies from 1 to 15.

7.4 **THE VIDEO GAME SATISFACTION RATING CASE**   DS VideoGame

A company that produces and markets video game systems wishes to assess its customer's level of satisfaction with a relatively new model, the XYZ-Box. In the six months since the introduction of the model, the company has received 73,219 warranty registrations from purchasers. The company will randomly select 65 of these registrations and will conduct telephone interviews with the purchasers. Assume that the warranty registrations are numbered from 1 to 73,219 in a computer.

connect

Companies:
1 Altria Group
2 PepsiCo
3 Coca-Cola
4 Archer Daniels
5 Anheuser-Bush
6 General Mills
7 Sara Lee
8 Coca-Cola Enterprises
9 Reynolds American
10 Kellogg
11 ConAgra Foods
12 HJ Heinz
13 Campbell Soup
14 Pepsi Bottling Group
15 Tyson Foods

Starting in the upper left corner of Table 7.1(a) and moving down the five leftmost columns, we see that the first three five-digit numbers obtained are: 33276, 03427, and 92737. Starting with these three random numbers and moving down the five leftmost columns of Table 7.1(a) to find more five-digit random numbers, use Table 7.1 to randomly select the numbers of the first 10 warranty registrations to be included in the sample of 65 registrations.

7.5   THE BANK CUSTOMER WAITING TIME CASE   WaitTime

Recall that when the bank manager's new teller system is operating consistently over time, the manager decides to record the waiting times of a sample of 100 customers that need teller service during peak business hours. For each of 100 peak business hours, the first customer that starts waiting for service at or after a randomly selected time during the hour will be chosen. Consider the peak business hours from 2:00 P.M. to 2:59 P.M., from 3:00 P.M. to 3:59 P.M., from 4:00 P.M. to 4:59 P.M., and from 5:00 P.M. to 5:59 P.M. on a particular day. Also, assume that a computer software system generates the following four random numbers between 00 and 59: 32, 00, 18, and 47. This implies that the randomly selected times during the first three of the above peak business hours are 2:32 P.M., 3:00 P.M., and 4:18 P.M. What is the randomly selected time during the fourth of the above peak business hours?

7.6   In an article entitled "Turned Off" in the June 2–4, 1995, issue of *USA Weekend,* Don Olmsted and Gigi Anders reported results of a survey where readers were invited to write in and express their opinions about sex and violence on television. The results showed that 96 percent of respondents were very or somewhat concerned about sex on TV, and 97 percent of respondents were very or somewhat concerned about violence on TV. Do you think that these results could be generalized to all television viewers in 1995? Why or why not?

7.2 The Sampling Distribution of the Sample Mean ●●●

LO2 Describe and use the sampling distribution of the sample mean.

Introductory ideas and basic properties   Suppose that we are about to randomly select a sample of n elements (for example, cars) from a population of elements. Also, suppose that for each sampled element we will measure the value of a characteristic of interest. (For example, we might measure the mileage of each sampled car.) Before we actually select the sample, there are many different samples of n elements and corresponding measurements that we might potentially obtain. Because different samples of measurements generally have different sample means, there are many different sample means that we might potentially obtain. It follows that, *before we draw the sample, the sample mean $\bar{x}$ is a random variable.*

> The **sampling distribution of the sample mean** $\bar{x}$ is the probability distribution of the population of all possible sample means that could be obtained from all possible samples of the same size.

In order to illustrate the sampling distribution of the sample mean, we begin with an example that is based on the authors' conversations with University Chrysler/Jeep of Oxford, Ohio. In order to keep the example simple, we have used simplified car mileages to help explain the concepts.

EXAMPLE 7.2 The Car Mileage Case

This is the first year that the automaker has offered its new midsize model for sale to the public. However, last year the automaker made six preproduction cars of this new model. Two of these six cars were randomly selected for testing, and the other four were sent to auto shows at which the new model was introduced to the news media and the public. As is standard industry practice, the automaker did not test the four auto show cars before or during the five months these auto shows were held because testing can potentially harm the appearance of the cars.

In order to obtain a preliminary estimate—to be reported at the auto shows—of the midsize model's combined city and highway driving mileage, the automaker subjected the two cars selected for testing to the EPA mileage test. When this was done, the cars obtained mileages of 30 mpg and 32 mpg. The mean of this sample of mileages is

$$\bar{x} = \frac{30 + 32}{2} = 31 \text{ mpg}$$

This sample mean is the point estimate of the mean mileage μ for the population of six preproduction cars and is the preliminary mileage estimate for the new midsize model that was reported at the auto shows.

TABLE 7.2   A Probability Distribution Describing the Population of Six Individual Car Mileages

Individual Car Mileage	29	30	31	32	33	34
Probability	1/6	1/6	1/6	1/6	1/6	1/6

FIGURE 7.1   A Comparison of Individual Car Mileages and Sample Means

(a) A graph of the probability distribution describing the population of six individual car mileages

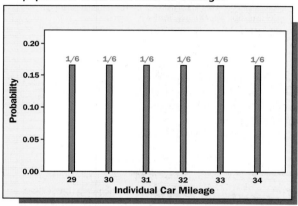

(b) A graph of the probability distribution describing the population of 15 sample means

TABLE 7.3   The Population of Sample Means

(a) The population of the 15 samples of $n = 2$ car mileages and corresponding sample means

Sample	Car Mileages	Sample Mean
1	29, 30	29.5
2	29, 31	30
3	29, 32	30.5
4	29, 33	31
5	29, 34	31.5
6	30, 31	30.5
7	30, 32	31
8	30, 33	31.5
9	30, 34	32
10	31, 32	31.5
11	31, 33	32
12	31, 34	32.5
13	32, 33	32.5
14	32, 34	33
15	33, 34	33.5

(b) A probability distribution describing the population of 15 sample means: the sampling distribution of the sample mean

Sample Mean	Frequency	Probability
29.5	1	1/15
30	1	1/15
30.5	2	2/15
31	2	2/15
31.5	3	3/15
32	2	2/15
32.5	2	2/15
33	1	1/15
33.5	1	1/15

When the auto shows were over, the automaker decided to further study the new midsize model by subjecting the four auto show cars to various tests. When the EPA mileage test was performed, the four cars obtained mileages of 29 mpg, 31 mpg, 33 mpg, and 34 mpg. Thus, the mileages obtained by the six preproduction cars were 29 mpg, 30 mpg, 31 mpg, 32 mpg, 33 mpg, and 34 mpg. The probability distribution of this population of six individual car mileages is given in Table 7.2 and graphed in Figure 7.1(a). The mean of the population of car mileages is

$$\mu = \frac{29 + 30 + 31 + 32 + 33 + 34}{6} = 31.5 \text{ mpg}$$

Note that the point estimate $\bar{x} = 31$ mpg that was reported at the auto shows is .5 mpg less than the true population mean μ of 31.5 mpg. Of course, different samples of two cars and corresponding mileages would have given different sample means. There are, in total, 15 samples of two mileages that could have been obtained by randomly selecting two cars from the population of six cars and subjecting the cars to the EPA mileage test. These samples correspond to the 15 combinations of two mileages that can be selected from the six mileages: 29, 30, 31, 32, 33, and 34. The samples are given, along with their means, in Table 7.3(a).

In order to find the probability distribution of the population of sample means, note that different sample means correspond to different numbers of samples. For example, since the sample mean of 31 mpg corresponds to 2 out of 15 samples—the sample (29, 33) and the sample (30, 32)—the probability of obtaining a sample mean of 31 mpg is 2/15. If we analyze all of the sample means in a similar fashion, we find that the probability distribution of the population of sample means is as given in Table 7.3(b). This distribution is the *sampling distribution of the sample mean*. A graph of this distribution is shown in Figure 7.1(b) and illustrates the accuracies of the different possible sample means as point estimates of the population mean. For example, whereas 3 out of 15 sample means exactly equal the population mean of 31.5 mpg, other sample means differ from the population mean by amounts varying from .5 mpg to 2 mpg.

As illustrated in Example 7.2, one of the purposes of the sampling distribution of the sample mean is to tell us how accurate the sample mean is likely to be as a point estimate of the population mean. Because the population of six individual car mileages in Example 7.2 is small, we were able (after the auto shows were over) to test all six cars, determine the values of the six car mileages, and calculate the population mean mileage. Often, however, the population of individual measurements under consideration is very large—either a large finite population or an infinite population. In this case, it would be impractical or impossible to determine the values of all of the population measurements and calculate the population mean. Instead, we randomly select a sample of individual measurements from the population and use the mean of this sample as the point estimate of the population mean. Moreover, although it would be impractical or impossible to list all of the many (perhaps trillions of) different possible sample means that could be obtained if the sampled population is very large, statisticians know various theoretical properties about the sampling distribution of these sample means. Some of these theoretical properties are intuitively illustrated by the sampling distribution of the 15 sample means in Example 7.2. Specifically, suppose that we will randomly select a sample of n individual measurements from a population of individual measurements having mean μ and standard deviation σ. Then, it can be shown that:

- **In many situations, the distribution of the population of all possible sample means looks, at least roughly, like a normal curve.** For example, consider Figure 7.1. This figure shows that, while the distribution of the population of six individual car mileages is a uniform distribution, the distribution of the population of 15 sample means has a somewhat bell-shaped appearance. Noting, however, that this rough bell-shaped appearance is not extremely close to the appearance of a normal curve, we wish to know when the distribution of all possible sample means is exactly or approximately normally distributed. Answers to this question are given in the following result.

- **If the population from which we will select the sample is normally distributed, then for any sample size n the population of all possible sample means is also normally distributed.** For example, consider the population of the mileages of all of the new midsize cars that could potentially be produced by this year's manufacturing process. As discussed in Chapter 1, we consider this population to be an infinite population because the automaker could always make "one more car." Moreover, assume that (as will be verified in a later example) this infinite population of all individual car mileages is normally distributed (see Figure 7.2), and assume that the automaker will randomly select a sample of $n = 5$ cars, test them as prescribed by the EPA, and calculate the mean of the resulting sample mileages. It then follows that the population of all possible sample means that the automaker might obtain is also normally distributed (again, see Figure 7.2). Note that there is nothing special about the sample size $n = 5$. The above boldfaced result holds—as it states—for any sample size n. Moreover, in the next subsection we will see that, even if the population from which we will select the sample is not normally distributed, the population of all possible sample means is *approximately normally distributed* if the sample size n is large (say, at least 30). Finally, note that to make Figure 7.2 easier to understand, we have hypothetically assumed that the true value of the population mean mileage μ of all of the new midsize cars is 31.6 mpg. Of course, no human being would know the true value of μ. **Our objective is to estimate μ.**

- **The mean, $\mu_{\bar{x}}$, of the population of all possible sample means is equal to μ, the mean of the population from which we will select the sample.** For example, the mean, $\mu_{\bar{x}}$, of the population of 15 sample means in Table 7.3(a) can be calculated by adding up the 15 sample

F I G U R E 7 . 2   **The Normally Distributed Population of All Individual Car Mileages and the Normally Distributed Population of All Possible Sample Means**

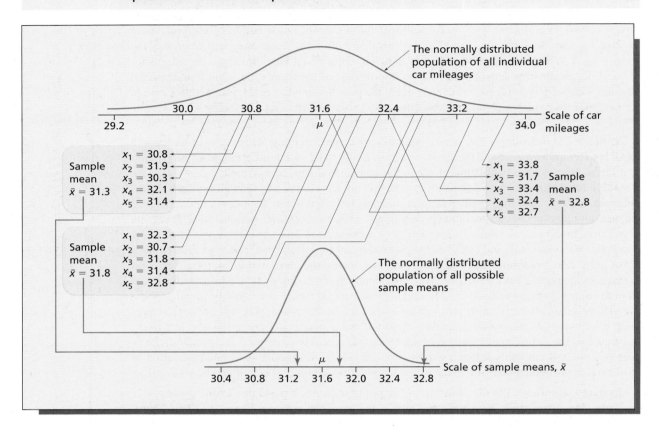

means, which gives 472.5, and dividing by 15. That is, $\mu_{\bar{x}} = 472.5/15 = 31.5$, which is the same as μ, the mean of the population of six individual car mileages in Table 7.2. The fact that $\mu_{\bar{x}}$ equals μ is graphically illustrated in Figure 7.1, which shows that the distribution of the six individual car mileages and the distribution of the 15 sample means are centered over the same mean of 31.5 mpg. The fact that $\mu_{\bar{x}}$ equals μ is also graphically illustrated in Figure 7.2, which shows that the normal distribution describing the mileages of all individual cars that could be produced this year and the normal distribution describing all possible sample means are centered over the same mean of 31.6 mpg. Furthermore, because $\mu_{\bar{x}}$ equals μ, we call the sample mean an **unbiased point estimate** of the population mean. This unbiasedness property says that, although most of the possible sample means that we might obtain are either above or below the population mean, there is no systematic tendency for the sample mean to overestimate or underestimate the population mean. That is, although we will randomly select only one sample, the unbiased sample mean is "correct on the average" in all possible samples.

- **The standard deviation, $\sigma_{\bar{x}}$, of the population of all posssible sample means is less than σ, the standard deviation of the population from which we will select the sample.** This is illustrated in both Figures 7.1 and 7.2. That is, in each figure the distribution of all possible sample means is less spread out than the distribution of all individual car mileages. Intuitively, we see that $\sigma_{\bar{x}}$ is smaller than σ because each possible sample mean is an average of n measurements. Thus, **each sample mean *averages out* high and low sample measurements and can be expected to be closer to the population mean μ than many of the individual population measurements would be.** It follows that the different possible sample means are more closely clustered around μ than are the individual population measurements. (Note that we will see that $\sigma_{\bar{x}}$ is smaller than σ only if the sample size n is greater than 1.)

The following summary box gives a formula for $\sigma_{\bar{x}}$ and also summarizes other previously discussed facts about the probability distribution of the population of all possible sample means.

The Sampling Distribution of $\bar{x}$

Assume that the population from which we will randomly select a sample of n measurements has mean μ and standard deviation σ. Then, the population of all possible sample means

1   Has a normal distribution, if the sampled population has a normal distribution.

2   Has mean $\mu_{\bar{x}} = \mu$.

3   Has standard deviation $\sigma_{\bar{x}} = \dfrac{\sigma}{\sqrt{n}}$.

The formula for $\sigma_{\bar{x}}$ in (3) holds exactly if the sampled population is infinite. If the sampled population is finite, this formula holds approximately under conditions to be discussed at the end of this section.

     Stated equivalently, the sampling distribution of $\bar{x}$ has mean $\mu_{\bar{x}} = \mu$, has standard deviation $\sigma_{\bar{x}} = \sigma/\sqrt{n}$ (if the sampled population is infinite), and is a normal distribution (if the sampled population has a normal distribution).[2]

The third result in the summary box says that, if the sampled population is infinite, then

$$\sigma_{\bar{x}} = \frac{\sigma}{\sqrt{n}}$$

In words, $\sigma_{\bar{x}}$, the standard deviation of the population of all possible sample means, equals σ, the standard deviation of the sampled population, divided by the square root of the sample size n. Furthermore, in addition to showing that $\sigma_{\bar{x}}$ is smaller than σ (assuming that the sample size n is larger than one), this formula for $\sigma_{\bar{x}}$ also says that $\sigma_{\bar{x}}$ decreases as n increases. That is, intuitively, when the sample size is larger, each possible sample averages more observations. Therefore, the resulting different possible sample means will differ from each other by less and thus will become more closely clustered around the population mean. It follows that, if we take a larger sample, we are more likely to obtain a sample mean that is near the population mean.

     We next use the car mileage case to illustrate the formula for $\sigma_{\bar{x}}$. In this and several other examples we will assume that, although we do not know the true value of the population mean μ, we do know the true value of the population standard deviation σ. Here, knowledge of σ might be based on theory or history related to the population under consideration. For example, because the automaker has been working to improve gas mileages, we cannot assume that we know the true value of the population mean mileage μ for the new midsize model. However, engineering data might indicate that the spread of individual car mileages for the automaker's midsize cars is the same from model to model and year to year. Therefore, if the mileages for previous models had a standard deviation equal to .8 mpg, it might be reasonable to assume that the standard deviation of the mileages for the new model will also equal .8 mpg. Such an assumption would, of course, be questionable, and in most real-world situations there would probably not be an actual basis for knowing σ. However, assuming that σ is known will help us to illustrate sampling distributions, and in later chapters we will see what to do when σ is unknown.

EXAMPLE 7.3 The Car Mileage Case

Part 1: Basic concepts   Consider the infinite population of the mileages of all of the new midsize cars that could potentially be produced by this year's manufacturing process. If we assume that this population is normally distributed with mean μ and standard deviation $\sigma = .8$ (see Figure 7.3(a)), and if the automaker will randomly select a sample of n cars and test them as prescribed by the EPA, it follows that the population of all possible sample means is normally distributed with mean $\mu_{\bar{x}} = \mu$ and standard deviation $\sigma_{\bar{x}} = \sigma/\sqrt{n} = .8/\sqrt{n}$. In order to show

---

[2]In Appendix C—on the book's website—we derive the formulas $\mu_{\bar{x}} = \mu$ and $\sigma_{\bar{x}} = \sigma/\sqrt{n}$.

F I G U R E 7 . 3   **A Comparison of (1) the Population of All Individual Car Mileages, (2) the Sampling Distribution of the Sample Mean $\bar{x}$ When $n = 5$, and (3) the Sampling Distribution of the Sample Mean $\bar{x}$ When $n = 50$**

(a) The population of individual mileages

The normal distribution describing the population of all individual car mileages, which has mean μ and standard deviation $\sigma = .8$

Scale of gas mileages

μ

(b) The sampling distribution of the sample mean $\bar{x}$ when $n = 5$

The normal distribution describing the population of all possible sample means when the sample size is 5, where $\mu_{\bar{x}} = \mu$ and $\sigma_{\bar{x}} = \dfrac{\sigma}{\sqrt{n}} = \dfrac{.8}{\sqrt{5}} = .358$

Scale of sample means, $\bar{x}$

μ

(c) The sampling distribution of the sample mean $\bar{x}$ when $n = 50$

The normal distribution describing the population of all possible sample means when the sample size is 50, where $\mu_{\bar{x}} = \mu$ and $\sigma_{\bar{x}} = \dfrac{\sigma}{\sqrt{n}} = \dfrac{.8}{\sqrt{50}} = .113$

Scale of sample means, $\bar{x}$

μ

that a larger sample is more likely to give a more accurate point estimate $\bar{x}$ of μ, compare taking a sample of size $n = 5$ with taking a sample of size $n = 50$. If $n = 5$, then

$$\sigma_{\bar{x}} = \frac{\sigma}{\sqrt{n}} = \frac{.8}{\sqrt{5}} = .358$$

and it follows (by the empirical rule) that 95.44 percent of all possible sample means are within plus or minus $2\sigma_{\bar{x}} = 2(.358) = .716$ mpg of the population mean μ. If $n = 50$, then

$$\sigma_{\bar{x}} = \frac{\sigma}{\sqrt{n}} = \frac{.8}{\sqrt{50}} = .113$$

and it follows that 95.44 percent of all possible sample means are within plus or minus $2\sigma_{\bar{x}} = 2(.113) = .226$ mpg of the population mean μ. Therefore, if $n = 50$, the different possible sample means that the automaker might obtain will be more closely clustered around μ than they will be if $n = 5$ (see Figures 7.3(b) and (c)). This implies that the larger sample of size $n = 50$ is more likely to give a sample mean $\bar{x}$ that is near μ.

FIGURE 7.4   The Probability That $\bar{x} \geq 31.56$ When $\mu = 31$ in the Car Mileage Case

Part 2: Statistical inference   Recall from Chapter 3 that the automaker has randomly selected a sample of $n = 50$ mileages, which has mean $\bar{x} = 31.56$. We now ask the following question: If the population mean mileage μ exactly equals 31 mpg (the minimum standard for the tax credit), what is the probability of observing a sample mean mileage that is greater than or equal to 31.56 mpg? To find this probability, recall from Chapter 2 that a histogram of the 50 mileages indicates that the population of all individual mileages is normally distributed. Assuming that the population standard deviation σ is known to equal .8 mpg, it follows that the sampling distribution of the sample mean $\bar{x}$ is a normal distribution, with mean $\mu_{\bar{x}} = \mu$ and standard deviation $\sigma_{\bar{x}} = \sigma/\sqrt{n} = .8/\sqrt{50} = .113$. Therefore,

$$P(\bar{x} \geq 31.56 \quad \text{if} \quad \mu = 31) = P\left(z \geq \frac{31.56 - \mu_{\bar{x}}}{\sigma_{\bar{x}}}\right) = P\left(z \geq \frac{31.56 - 31}{.113}\right)$$

$$= P(z \geq 4.96)$$

To find $P(z \geq 4.96)$, notice that the largest z value given in Table A.3 (page 638) is 3.99, which gives a right-hand tail area of .00003. Therefore, since $P(z \geq 3.99) = .00003$, it follows that $P(z \geq 4.96)$ is less than .00003 (see Figure 7.4). The fact that this probability is less than .00003 says that, if μ equals 31, then fewer than 3 in 100,000 of all possible sample means are at least as large as the sample mean $\bar{x} = 31.56$ that we have actually observed. Therefore, if we are to believe that μ equals 31, then we must believe that we have observed a sample mean that can be described as a smaller than 3 in 100,000 chance. Since it is extremely difficult to believe that such a small chance would occur, we have extremely strong evidence that μ does not equal 31 and that μ is, in fact, larger than 31. This evidence would probably convince the federal government that the midsize model's mean mileage μ exceeds 31 mpg and thus that the midsize model deserves the tax credit.

    To conclude this subsection, it is important to make two comments. First, the formula $\sigma_{\bar{x}} = \sigma/\sqrt{n}$ follows, in theory, from the formula for $\sigma_{\bar{x}}^2$, the variance of the population of all possible sample means. The formula for $\sigma_{\bar{x}}^2$ is $\sigma_{\bar{x}}^2 = \sigma^2/n$. Second, in addition to holding exactly if the sampled population is infinite, **the formula $\sigma_{\bar{x}} = \sigma/\sqrt{n}$ holds approximately if the sampled population is finite and much larger than (say, at least 20 times) the size of the sample.** For example, if we define the population of the mileages of all new midsize cars to be the population of the mileages of all cars that will actually be produced this year, then the population is finite. However, the population would be very large—certainly at least as large as 20 times any reasonable sample size. For example, if the automaker produces 100,000 new midsize cars this year, and if we randomly select a sample of $n = 50$ of these cars, then the population size of 100,000 is larger than 20 times the sample size of 50 (which is 1,000). It follows that, even though the population is finite and thus the formula $\sigma_{\bar{x}} = \sigma/\sqrt{n}$ would not hold exactly, this formula would hold approximately. The exact formula for $\sigma_{\bar{x}}$ when the sampled population is finite is given in a technical note at the end of this section. It is important to use this exact formula if the sampled population is finite and less than 20 times the size of the sample. **However, with the exception of the populations considered in the technical note and in Appendix D on the book's website, we will assume that all of the remaining populations to be discussed in this book are either infinite or finite and at least 20 times the size of the sample. Therefore, it will be appropriate to use the formula $\sigma_{\bar{x}} = \sigma/\sqrt{n}$.**

LO3 Explain and use the Central Limit Theorem.

Sampling a nonnormally distributed population: The Central Limit Theorem   We now consider what can be said about the sampling distribution of $\bar{x}$ when the sampled population is not normally distributed. First, as previously stated, the fact that $\mu_{\bar{x}} = \mu$ is still true. Second, as also previously stated, the formula $\sigma_{\bar{x}} = \sigma/\sqrt{n}$ is exactly correct if the sampled population is infinite and is approximately correct if the sampled population is finite and much larger than (say, at least 20 times as large as) the sample size. Third, an extremely important result called the **Central Limit Theorem** tells us that, **if the sample size n is large, then the sampling distribution of $\bar{x}$ is approximately normal, even if the sampled population is not normally distributed.**

The Central Limit Theorem

If the sample size n is sufficiently large, then the population of all possible sample means is approximately normally distributed (with mean $\mu_{\bar{x}} = \mu$ and standard deviation $\sigma_{\bar{x}} = \sigma/\sqrt{n}$), no matter what probability distribution describes the sampled population. Furthermore, the larger the sample size n is, the more nearly normally distributed is the population of all possible sample means.

The Central Limit Theorem is illustrated in Figure 7.5 for several population shapes. Notice that as the sample size increases (from 2 to 6 to 30), the populations of all possible sample means become more nearly normally distributed. This figure also illustrates that, as the sample size increases, the spread of the distribution of all possible sample means decreases (remember that this spread is measured by $\sigma_{\bar{x}}$, which decreases as the sample size increases).

How large must the sample size be for the sampling distribution of $\bar{x}$ to be approximately normal? In general, the more skewed the probability distribution of the sampled population, the larger the sample size must be for the population of all possible sample means to be approximately normally distributed. For some sampled populations, particularly those described by symmetric distributions, the population of all possible sample means is approximately normally distributed for a fairly small sample size. In addition, studies indicate that, **if the sample size is at least 30, then for most sampled populations the population of all possible sample means is approximately normally distributed.** In this book, whenever the sample size n is at least 30, we will assume that the sampling distribution of $\bar{x}$ is approximately a normal distribution. Of course, if the sampled population is exactly normally distributed, the sampling distribution of $\bar{x}$ is exactly normal for any sample size.

We can see the shapes of sampling distributions such as those illustrated in Figure 7.5 by using computer simulation. Specifically, for a population having a particular probability distribution, we can have the computer draw a given number of samples of n observations, compute the mean of each sample, and arrange the sample means into a histogram. To illustrate this, consider the upper portion of Figure 7.6, which shows the exponential distribution describing the hospital emergency room interarrival times discussed in Example 6.11 (page 257). Figure 7.6(a) gives the results of a simulation in which MINITAB randomly selected 1,000 samples of $n = 5$ interarrival times from this exponential distribution, calculated the mean of each sample, and arranged the 1,000 sample means into a histogram. Figure 7.6(b) gives the results of a simulation in which

FIGURE 7.5   **The Central Limit Theorem Says That the Larger the Sample Size Is, the More Nearly Normally Distributed Is the Population of All Possible Sample Means**

(a) Several sampled populations

$n = 2$ $n = 2$ $n = 2$ $n = 2$

$n = 6$ $n = 6$ $n = 6$ $n = 6$

$n = 30$ $n = 30$ $n = 30$ $n = 30$

(b) Corresponding populations of all possible sample means for different sample sizes

FIGURE 7.6   **Simulating the Sampling Distribution of the Sample Mean When Sampling from an Exponential Distribution**

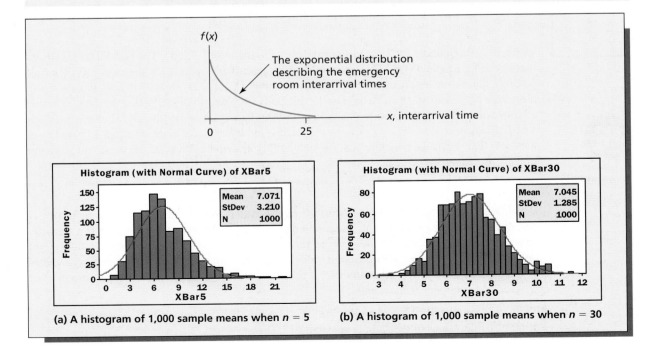

$f(x)$

The exponential distribution describing the emergency room interarrival times

x, interarrival time

Histogram (with Normal Curve) of XBar5

Mean	7.071
StDev	3.210
N	1000

Histogram (with Normal Curve) of XBar30

Mean	7.045
StDev	1.285
N	1000

(a) A histogram of 1,000 sample means when $n = 5$ (b) A histogram of 1,000 sample means when $n = 30$

MINITAB randomly selected 1,000 samples of $n = 30$ interarrival times from the exponential distribution, calculated the mean of each sample, and arranged the 1,000 sample means into a histogram. Note that, whereas the histogram in Figure 7.6(a) is somewhat skewed to the right, the histogram in Figure 7.6(b) appears approximately bell-shaped. Therefore, we might conclude that when we randomly select a sample of n observations from an exponential distribution, the sampling distribution of the sample mean is somewhat skewed to the right when $n = 5$ and is approximately normal when $n = 30$.

EXAMPLE 7.4 The Payment Time Case

Recall that a management consulting firm has installed a new computer-based, electronic billing system in a Hamilton, Ohio, trucking company. Because of the previously discussed advantages of the new billing system, and because the trucking company's clients are receptive to using this system, the management consulting firm believes that the new system will reduce the mean bill payment time by more than 50 percent. The mean payment time using the old billing system was approximately equal to, but no less than, 39 days. Therefore, if μ denotes the new mean payment time, the consulting firm believes that μ will be less than 19.5 days. To assess whether μ is less than 19.5 days, the consulting firm has randomly selected a sample of $n = 65$ invoices processed using the new billing system and has determined the payment times for these invoices. The mean of the 65 payment times is $\bar{x} = 18.1077$ days, which is less than 19.5 days. Therefore, we ask the following question: If the population mean payment time is 19.5 days, what is the probability of observing a sample mean payment time that is less than or equal to 18.1077 days? To find this probability, recall from Chapter 2 that a histogram of the 65 payment times indicates that the population of all payment times is skewed with a tail to the right. However, the Central Limit Theorem tells us that, because the sample size $n = 65$ is large, the sampling distribution of $\bar{x}$ is approximately a normal distribution with mean $\mu_{\bar{x}} = \mu$ and standard deviation $\sigma_{\bar{x}} = \sigma/\sqrt{n}$. Moreover, whereas this is the first time that the consulting company has installed an electronic billing system in a trucking company, the firm has installed electronic billing systems in other types of companies. Analysis of results from these other companies shows that, although the population mean payment time μ varies from company to company, the population standard deviation σ of payment times is the same for different companies and equals 4.2 days. Assuming that σ also equals 4.2 days for the trucking company, it follows that $\sigma_{\bar{x}}$ equals $4.2/\sqrt{65} = .5209$ and that

$$P(\bar{x} \leq 18.1077 \text{ if } \mu = 19.5) = P\left(z \leq \frac{18.1077 - 19.5}{.5209}\right) = P(z \leq -2.67)$$

which is the area under the standard normal curve to the left of -2.67. The normal table tells us that this area equals .0038. This probability says that, if μ equals 19.5, then only .0038 of all possible sample means are at least as small as the sample mean $\bar{x} = 18.1077$ that we have actually observed. Therefore, if we are to believe that μ equals 19.5, we must believe that we have observed a sample mean that can be described as a 38 in 10,000 chance. It is very difficult to believe that such a small chance would occur, so we have very strong evidence that μ does not equal 19.5 and is, in fact, less than 19.5. We conclude that the new billing system has reduced the mean bill payment time by more than 50 percent.

Unbiasedness and minimum-variance estimates   Recall that a sample statistic is any descriptive measure of the sample measurements. For instance, the sample mean $\bar{x}$ is a statistic, and so are the sample median, the sample variance s^2, and the sample standard deviation s. Not only do different samples give different values of $\bar{x}$, different samples also give different values of the median, s^2, s, or any other statistic. It follows that, *before we draw the sample, any sample statistic is a random variable,* and

The **sampling distribution of a sample statistic** is the probability distribution of the population of all possible values of the sample statistic.

In general, we wish to estimate a population parameter by using a sample statistic that is what we call an *unbiased point estimate* of the parameter.

A sample statistic is an **unbiased point estimate** of a population parameter if the mean of the population of all possible values of the sample statistic equals the population parameter.

For example, we use the sample mean $\bar{x}$ as the point estimate of the population mean μ because $\bar{x}$ **is an unbiased point estimate of μ.** That is, $\mu_{\bar{x}} = \mu$. In words, the average of all the different possible sample means (that we could obtain from all the different possible samples) equals μ.

Although we want a sample statistic to be an unbiased point estimate of the population parameter of interest, we also want the statistic to have a small standard deviation (and variance). That is, we wish the different possible values of the sample statistic to be closely clustered around the population parameter. If this is the case, when we actually randomly select one sample and compute the sample statistic, its value is likely to be close to the value of the population parameter. Furthermore, some general results apply to estimating the mean μ of a normally distributed population. In this situation, it can be shown that both the sample mean and the sample median are unbiased point estimates of μ. In fact, there are many unbiased point estimates of μ. However, it can be shown that the variance of the population of all possible sample means is smaller than the variance of the population of all possible values of any other unbiased point estimate of μ. For this reason, **we call the sample mean a minimum-variance unbiased point estimate of μ.** When we use the sample mean as the point estimate of μ, we are more likely to obtain a point estimate close to μ than if we used any other unbiased sample statistic as the point estimate of μ. This is one reason why we use the sample mean as the point estimate of the population mean.

We next consider estimating the population variance σ^2. It can be shown that if the sampled population is infinite, then s^2 **is an unbiased point estimate of σ^2.** That is, the average of all the different possible sample variances that we could obtain (from all the different possible samples) is equal to σ^2. This is why we use a divisor equal to $n - 1$ rather than n when we estimate σ^2. It can be shown that, if we used n as the divisor when estimating σ^2, we would not obtain an unbiased point estimate of σ^2. When the population is finite, s^2 may be regarded as an approximately unbiased estimate of σ^2 as long as the population is fairly large (which is usually the case).

It would seem logical to think that, because s^2 is an unbiased point estimate of σ^2, s should be an unbiased point estimate of σ. This seems plausible, but it is not the case. There is no easy way to calculate an unbiased point estimate of σ. Because of this, the usual practice is to use s as the point estimate of σ (even though it is not an unbiased estimate).

This ends our discussion of the theory of point estimation. It suffices to say that in this book we estimate population parameters by using sample statistics that statisticians generally agree are best. Whenever possible, these sample statistics are unbiased point estimates and have small variances.

Technical Note: If we randomly select a sample of size n without replacement from a finite population of size N, then it can be shown that $\sigma_{\bar{x}} = (\sigma/\sqrt{n})\sqrt{(N - n)/(N - 1)}$, where the quantity $\sqrt{(N - n)/(N - 1)}$ is called the **finite population multiplier.** If the size of the sampled population is at least 20 times the size of the sample (that is, **if $N \geq 20n$), then the finite population multiplier is approximately equal to one, and $\sigma_{\bar{x}}$ approximately equals $\sigma/\sqrt{n}$.** However, if the population size N is smaller than 20 times the size of the sample, then the finite population multiplier is substantially less than one, and we must include this multiplier in the calculation of $\sigma_{\bar{x}}$. For instance, in Example 7.2, where the standard deviation σ of the population of $N = 6$ car mileages can be calculated to be 1.7078, and where $N = 6$ is only three times the sample size $n = 2$, it follows that

$$\sigma_{\bar{x}} = \frac{\sigma}{\sqrt{n}}\sqrt{\frac{N - n}{N - 1}} = \left(\frac{1.7078}{\sqrt{2}}\right)\sqrt{\frac{6 - 2}{6 - 1}} = 1.2076(.8944) = 1.08$$

We will see how this formula can be used to make statistical inferences in Appendix D on the book's website.

Exercises for Section 7.2

CONCEPTS

connect

7.7 Suppose that we will randomly select a sample of four measurements from a larger population of measurements. The sampling distribution of the sample mean $\bar{x}$ is the probability distribution of a population. In your own words, describe the elements in this population.

7.8 What does the Central Limit Theorem tell us about the sampling distribution of the sample mean?

METHODS AND APPLICATIONS

7.9 Suppose that we will take a random sample of size n from a population having mean μ and standard deviation σ. For each of the following situations, find the mean, variance, and standard deviation of the sampling distribution of the sample mean $\bar{x}$:

    a $\mu = 10$, $\sigma = 2$, $n = 25$ **c** $\mu = 3$, $\sigma = .1$, $n = 4$
    b $\mu = 500$, $\sigma = .5$, $n = 100$ **d** $\mu = 100$, $\sigma = 1$, $n = 1,600$

7.10 For each situation in Exercise 7.9, find an interval that contains (approximately or exactly) 99.73 percent of all the possible sample means. In which cases must we assume that the population is normally distributed? Why?

7.11 Suppose that we will randomly select a sample of 64 measurements from a population having a mean equal to 20 and a standard deviation equal to 4.

    a Describe the shape of the sampling distribution of the sample mean $\bar{x}$. Do we need to make any assumptions about the shape of the population? Why or why not?

    b Find the mean and the standard deviation of the sampling distribution of the sample mean $\bar{x}$.

    c Calculate the probability that we will obtain a sample mean greater than 21; that is, calculate $P(\bar{x} > 21)$. Hint: Find the z value corresponding to 21 by using $\mu_{\bar{x}}$ and $\sigma_{\bar{x}}$ because we wish to calculate a probability about $\bar{x}$. Then sketch the sampling distribution and the probability.

    d Calculate the probability that we will obtain a sample mean less than 19.385; that is, calculate $P(\bar{x} < 19.385)$.

THE GAME SHOW CASE

Exercises 7.12 through 7.16 are based on the following situation.

Congratulations! You have just won the question-and-answer portion of a popular game show and will now be given an opportunity to select a grand prize. The game show host shows you a large revolving drum containing four identical white envelopes that have been thoroughly mixed in the drum. Each of the envelopes contains one of four checks made out for grand prizes of 20, 40, 60, and 80 thousand dollars. Usually, a contestant reaches into the drum, selects an envelope, and receives the grand prize in the envelope. Tonight, however, is a special night. You will be given the choice of either selecting one envelope or selecting two envelopes and receiving the average of the grand prizes in the two envelopes. If you select one envelope, the probability is 1/4 that you will receive any one of the individual grand prizes 20, 40, 60, and 80 thousand dollars. To see what could happen if you select two envelopes, do Exercises 7.12 through 7.16.

7.12 There are six combinations, or samples, of two grand prizes that can be randomly selected from the four grand prizes 20, 40, 60, and 80 thousand dollars. Four of these samples are (20, 40), (20, 60), (20, 80), and (40, 60). Find the other two samples.

7.13 Find the mean of each sample in Exercise 7.12.

7.14 Find the probability distribution of the population of six sample mean grand prizes.

7.15 If you select two envelopes, what is the probability that you will receive a sample mean grand prize of at least 50 thousand dollars?

7.16 Compare the probability distribution of the four individual grand prizes with the probability distribution of the six sample mean grand prizes. Would you select one or two envelopes? Why? Note: There is no one correct answer. It is a matter of opinion.

7.17 **THE BANK CUSTOMER WAITING TIME CASE**   **DS** WaitTime

Recall that the bank manager wants to show that the new system reduces typical customer waiting times to less than six minutes. One way to do this is to demonstrate that the mean of the population of all customer waiting times is less than 6. Letting this mean be μ, in this exercise we wish to investigate whether the sample of 100 waiting times provides evidence to support the claim that μ is less than 6.

For the sake of argument, we will begin by assuming that μ equals 6, and we will then attempt to use the sample to contradict this assumption in favor of the conclusion that μ is less than 6.

Recall that the mean of the sample of 100 waiting times is $\bar{x} = 5.46$ and assume that σ, the standard deviation of the population of all customer waiting times, is known to be 2.47.

a   Consider the population of all possible sample means obtained from random samples of 100 waiting times. What is the shape of this population of sample means? That is, what is the shape of the sampling distribution of $\bar{x}$? Why is this true?

b   Find the mean and standard deviation of the population of all possible sample means when we assume that μ equals 6.

c   The sample mean that we have actually observed is $\bar{x} = 5.46$. Assuming that μ equals 6, find the probability of observing a sample mean that is less than or equal to $\bar{x} = 5.46$.

d   If μ equals 6, what percentage of all possible sample means are less than or equal to 5.46? Since we have actually observed a sample mean of $\bar{x} = 5.46$, is it more reasonable to believe that (1) μ equals 6 and we have observed one of the sample means that is less than or equal to 5.46 when μ equals 6, or (2) that we have observed a sample mean less than or equal to 5.46 because μ is less than 6? Explain. What do you conclude about whether the new system has reduced the typical customer waiting time to less than six minutes?

7.18   THE VIDEO GAME SATISFACTION RATING CASE   🎮 VideoGame

Recall that a customer is considered to be very satisfied with his or her XYZ Box video game system if the customer's composite score on the survey instrument is at least 42. One way to show that customers are typically very satisfied is to show that the mean of the population of all satisfaction ratings is at least 42. Letting this mean be μ, in this exercise we wish to investigate whether the sample of 65 satisfaction ratings provides evidence to support the claim that μ exceeds 42 (and, therefore, is at least 42).

For the sake of argument, we begin by assuming that μ equals 42, and we then attempt to use the sample to contradict this assumption in favor of the conclusion that μ exceeds 42. Recall that the mean of the sample of 65 satisfaction ratings is $\bar{x} = 42.95$, and assume that σ, the standard deviation of the population of all satisfaction ratings, is known to be 2.64.

a   Consider the sampling distribution of $\bar{x}$ for random samples of 65 customer satisfaction ratings. Use the properties of this sampling distribution to find the probability of observing a sample mean greater than or equal to 42.95 when we assume that μ equals 42.

b   If μ equals 42, what percentage of all possible sample means are greater than or equal to 42.95? Since we have actually observed a sample mean of $\bar{x} = 42.95$, is it more reasonable to believe that (1) μ equals 42 and we have observed a sample mean that is greater than or equal to 42.95 when μ equals 42, or (2) that we have observed a sample mean that is greater than or equal to 42.95 because μ is greater than 42? Explain. What do you conclude about whether customers are typically very satisfied with the XYZ Box video game system?

7.19   In an article in the *Journal of Management,* Joseph Martocchio studied and estimated the costs of employee absences. Based on a sample of 176 blue-collar workers, Martocchio estimated that the mean amount of paid time lost during a three-month period was 1.4 days per employee with a standard deviation of 1.3 days. Martocchio also estimated that the mean amount of unpaid time lost during a three-month period was 1.0 day per employee with a standard deviation of 1.8 days. Suppose we randomly select a sample of 100 blue-collar workers. Based on Martocchio's estimates:

a   What is the probability that the average amount of paid time lost during a three-month period for the 100 blue-collar workers will exceed 1.5 days? Assume σ equals 1.3 days.

b   What is the probability that the average amount of unpaid time lost during a three-month period for the 100 blue-collar workers will exceed 1.5 days? Assume σ equals 1.8 days.

c   Suppose we randomly select a sample of 100 blue-collar workers, and suppose the sample mean amount of unpaid time lost during a three-month period actually exceeds 1.5 days. Would it be reasonable to conclude that the mean amount of unpaid time lost has increased above the previously estimated 1.0 day? Explain. Assume σ still equals 1.8 days.

7.20   When a pizza restaurant's delivery process is operating effectively, pizzas are delivered in an average of 45 minutes with a standard deviation of 6 minutes. To monitor its delivery process, the restaurant randomly selects five pizzas each night and records their delivery times.

a   For the sake of argument, assume that the population of all delivery times on a given evening is normally distributed with a mean of $\mu = 45$ minutes and a standard deviation of $\sigma = 6$ minutes. (That is, we assume that the delivery process is operating effectively.) Find the mean and the standard deviation of the population of all possible sample means, and calculate an interval containing 99.73 percent of all possible sample means.

b   Suppose that the mean of the five sampled delivery times on a particular evening is $\bar{x} = 55$ minutes. Using the interval that you calculated in *a*, what would you conclude about whether the restaurant's delivery process is operating effectively? Why?

METHODS AND APPLICATIONS

7.24 In each of the following cases, determine whether the sample size n is large enough to say that the sampling distribution of $\hat{p}$ is a normal distribution.

    a $p = .4$, $n = 100$ **d** $p = .8$, $n = 400$

    b $p = .1$, $n = 10$ **e** $p = .98$, $n = 1{,}000$

    c $p = .1$, $n = 50$ **f** $p = .99$, $n = 400$

7.25 In each of the following cases, find the mean, variance, and standard deviation of the sampling distribution of the sample proportion $\hat{p}$.

    a $p = .5$, $n = 250$ **c** $p = .8$, $n = 400$

    b $p = .1$, $n = 100$ **d** $p = .98$, $n = 1{,}000$

7.26 For each situation in Exercise 7.25, find an interval that contains approximately 95.44 percent of all the possible sample proportions.

7.27 Suppose that we will randomly select a sample of $n = 100$ elements from a population and that we will compute the sample proportion $\hat{p}$ of these elements that fall into a category of interest. If the true population proportion p equals .9:

    a Describe the shape of the sampling distribution of $\hat{p}$. Why can we validly describe the shape?

    b Find the mean and the standard deviation of the sampling distribution of $\hat{p}$.

7.28 For the situation in Exercise 7.27, calculate the following probabilities. In each case sketch the sampling distribution and the probability.

    a $P(\hat{p} \geq .96)$

    b $P(.855 \leq \hat{p} \leq .945)$

    c $P(\hat{p} \leq .915)$

7.29 In the July 29, 2001, issue of *The Journal News* (Hamilton, Ohio) Lynn Elber of the Associated Press reported on a study conducted by the Kaiser Family Foundation regarding parents' use of television set V-chips for controlling their childrens' TV viewing. The study asked parents who own TVs equipped with V-chips whether they use the devices to block programs with objectionable content.

    a Suppose that we wish to use the study results to justify the claim that fewer than 20 percent of parents who own TV sets with V-chips use the devices. The study actually found that 17 percent of the parents polled used their V-chips.[5] If the poll surveyed 1,000 parents, and if for the sake of argument we assume that 20 percent of parents who own V-chips actually use the devices (that is, $p = .2$), calculate the probability of observing a sample proportion of .17 or less. That is, calculate $P(\hat{p} \leq .17)$.

    b Based on the probability you computed in part a, would you conclude that fewer than 20 percent of parents who own TV sets equipped with V-chips actually use the devices? Explain.

7.30 On February 8, 2002, the Gallup Organization released the results of a poll concerning American attitudes toward the 19th Winter Olympic Games in Salt Lake City, Utah. The poll results were based on telephone interviews with a randomly selected national sample of 1,011 adults, 18 years and older, conducted February 4–6, 2002.

    a Suppose we wish to use the poll's results to justify the claim that more than 30 percent of Americans (18 years or older) say that figure skating is their favorite Winter Olympic event. The poll actually found that 32 percent of respondents reported that figure skating was their favorite event.[6] If, for the sake of argument, we assume that 30 percent of Americans (18 years or older) say figure skating is their favorite event (that is, $p = .3$), calculate the probability of observing a sample proportion of .32 or more; that is, calculate $P(\hat{p} \geq .32)$.

    b Based on the probability you computed in part a, would you conclude that more than 30 percent of Americans (18 years or older) say that figure skating is their favorite Winter Olympic event?

7.31 *Quality Progress,* February 2005, reports on improvements in customer satisfaction and loyalty made by Bank of America. A key measure of customer satisfaction is the response (on a scale from 1 to 10) to the question: "Considering all the business you do with Bank of America, what is your overall satisfaction with Bank of America?" Here, a response of 9 or 10 represents "customer delight."

    a Historically, the percentage of Bank of America customers expressing customer delight has been 48%. Suppose that we wish to use the results of a survey of 350 Bank of America customers to justify the claim that more than 48% of all current Bank of America customers would express customer delight. The survey finds that 189 of 350 randomly selected Bank of America customers express customer delight. If, for the sake of argument, we assume that the proportion of customer delight is $p = .48$, calculate the probability of observing a sample proportion greater than or equal to $189/350 = .54$. That is, calculate $P(\hat{p} \geq .54)$.

---

[5]Source: L. Elber, "Study: Parents Make Scant Use of TV V-Chip," *The Journal News* (Hamilton, Ohio), July 29, 2001, p. c5.
[6]Source: The Gallup Organization, www.gallup.com/poll/releases/, February 13, 2002.

b Based on the probability you computed in part *a*, would you conclude that more than 48 percent of current Bank of America customers express customer delight? Explain.

7.32 Again consider the survey of 350 Bank of America customers discussed in Exercise 7.31, and assume that 48% of Bank of America customers would currently express customer delight. That is, assume $p = .48$. Find:

a The probability that the sample proportion obtained from the sample of 350 Bank of America customers would be within three percentage points of the population proportion. That is, find $P(.45 \leq \hat{p} \leq .51)$.

b The probability that the sample proportion obtained from the sample of 350 Bank of America customers would be within six percentage points of the population proportion. That is, find $P(.42 \leq \hat{p} \leq .54)$.

7.33 Based on your results in Exercise 7.32, would it be reasonable to state that the survey's "margin of error" is ± 3 percentage points? ± 6 percentage points? Explain.

7.34 A special advertising section in the July 20, 1998, issue of *Fortune* magazine discusses "outsourcing." According to the article, outsourcing is "the assignment of critical, but noncore, business functions to outside specialists." This allows a company to immediately bring operations up to best-in-world standards while avoiding huge capital investments. The article includes the results of a poll of business executives addressing the benefits of outsourcing.

a Suppose we wish to use the poll's results to justify the claim that fewer than 20 percent of business executives feel that the benefits of outsourcing are either "less or much less than expected." The poll actually found that 15 percent of the respondents felt that the benefits of outsourcing were either "less or much less than expected."[7] If 1,000 randomly selected business executives were polled, and if for the sake of argument, we assume that 20 percent of all business executives feel that the benefits of outsourcing are either less or much less than expected (that is, $p = .20$), calculate the probability of observing a sample proportion of .15 or less. That is, calculate $P(\hat{p} \leq .15)$.

b Based on the probability you computed in part *a*, would you conclude that fewer than 20 percent of business executives feel that the benefits of outsourcing are either "less or much less than expected"? Explain.

7.35 The July 20, 1998, issue of *Fortune* magazine reported the results of a survey on executive training that was conducted by the Association of Executive Search Consultants. The survey showed that 75 percent of 300 polled CEOs believe that companies should have "fast-track training programs" for developing managerial talent.[8]

a Suppose we wish to use the results of this survey to justify the claim that more than 70 percent of CEOs believe that companies should have fast-track training programs. Assuming that the 300 surveyed CEOs were randomly selected, and assuming, for the sake of argument, that 70 percent of CEOs believe that companies should have fast-track training programs (that is, $p = .70$), calculate the probability of observing a sample proportion of .75 or more. That is, calculate $P(\hat{p} \geq .75)$.

b Based on the probability you computed in part *a*, would you conclude that more than 70 percent of CEOs believe that companies should have fast-track training programs? Explain.

7.4 Stratified Random, Cluster, and Systematic Sampling (Optional) ● ● ●

LO5 Describe the basic ideas of stratified random, cluster, and systematic sampling (Optional).

Random sampling is not the only kind of sampling. Methods for obtaining a sample are called **sampling designs,** and the sample we take is sometimes called a **sample survey.** In this section we explain three sampling designs that are alternatives to random sampling—**stratified random sampling, cluster sampling,** and **systematic sampling.**

One common sampling design involves separately sampling important groups within a population. Then, the samples are combined to form the entire sample. This approach is the idea behind **stratified random sampling.**

In order to select a **stratified random sample,** we divide the population into nonoverlapping groups of similar elements (people, objects, etc.). These groups are called **strata.** Then a random sample is selected from each stratum, and these samples are combined to form the full sample.

[7]Source: M. R. Ozanne and M. F. Corbette, "Outsourcing 98," *Fortune* (July 20, 1998), p. 510.
[8]Source: E. P. Gunn, "The Fast Track Is Where to Be, If You Can Find It," *Fortune* (July 20, 1998), p. 152.

It is wise to stratify when the population consists of two or more groups that differ with respect to the variable of interest. For instance, consumers could be divided into strata based on gender, age, ethnic group, or income.

As an example, suppose that a department store chain proposes to open a new store in a location that would serve customers who live in a geographical region that consists of (1) an industrial city, (2) a suburban community, and (3) a rural area. In order to assess the potential profitability of the proposed store, the chain wishes to study the incomes of all households in the region. In addition, the chain wishes to estimate the proportion and the total number of households whose members would be likely to shop at the store. The department store chain feels that the industrial city, the suburban community, and the rural area differ with respect to income and the store's potential desirability. Therefore, it uses these subpopulations as strata and takes a stratified random sample.

Taking a stratified sample can be advantageous because such a sample takes advantage of the fact that elements in the same stratum are similar to each other. It follows that a stratified sample can provide more accurate information than a random sample of the same size. As a simple example, if all of the elements in each stratum were exactly the same, then examining only one element in each stratum would allow us to describe the entire population. Furthermore, stratification can make a sample easier (or possible) to select. Recall that, in order to take a random sample, we must have a list, or **frame** of all of the population elements. Although a frame might not exist for the overall population, a frame might exist for each stratum. For example, suppose nearly all the households in the department store's geographical region have telephones. Although there might not be a telephone directory for the overall geographical region, there might be separate telephone directories for the industrial city, the suburb, and the rural area. For a more complete discussion of stratified random sampling, see Mendenhall, Schaeffer, and Ott (1986).

Sometimes it is advantageous to select a sample in stages. This is a common practice when selecting a sample from a very large geographical region. In such a case, a frame often does not exist. For instance, there is no single list of all registered voters in the United States. There is also no single list of all households in the United States. In this kind of situation, we can use **multistage cluster sampling.** To illustrate this procedure, suppose we wish to take a sample of registered voters from all registered voters in the United States. We might proceed as follows:

Stage 1: Randomly select a sample of counties from all of the counties in the United States.

Stage 2: Randomly select a sample of townships from each county selected in Stage 1.

Stage 3: Randomly select a sample of voting precincts from each township selected in Stage 2.

Stage 4: Randomly select a sample of registered voters from each voting precinct selected in Stage 3.

We use the term *cluster sampling* to describe this type of sampling because at each stage we "cluster" the voters into subpopulations. For instance, in Stage 1 we cluster the voters into counties, and in Stage 2 we cluster the voters in each selected county into townships. Also, notice that the random sampling at each stage can be carried out because there are lists of (1) all counties in the United States, (2) all townships in each county, (3) all voting precincts in each township, and (4) all registered voters in each voting precinct.

As another example, consider sampling the households in the United States. We might use Stages 1 and 2 above to select counties and townships within the selected counties. Then, if there is a telephone directory of the households in each township, we can randomly sample households from each selected township by using its telephone directory. Because *most* households today have telephones, and telephone directories are readily available, most national polls are now conducted by telephone. Further, polling organizations have recognized that many households are giving up landline phones, and have developed ways to sample households that only have cell phones.

It is sometimes a good idea to combine stratification with multistage cluster sampling. For example, suppose a national polling organization wants to estimate the proportion of all registered voters who favor a particular presidential candidate. Because the presidential preferences of voters might tend to vary by geographical region, the polling organization might divide the United States into regions (say, Eastern, Midwestern, Southern, and Western regions). The polling organization might then use these regions as strata, and might take a multistage cluster sample from each stratum (region).

The analysis of data produced by multistage cluster sampling can be quite complicated. For a more detailed discussion of cluster sampling, see Mendenhall, Schaeffer, and Ott (1986).

In order to select a random sample, we must number the elements in a frame of all the population elements. Then we use a random number table (or a random number generator on a computer) to make the selections. However, numbering all the population elements can be quite time-consuming. Moreover, random sampling is used in the various stages of many complex sampling designs (requiring the numbering of numerous populations). Therefore, it is useful to have an alternative to random sampling. One such alternative is called **systematic sampling.** In order to systematically select a sample of n elements without replacement from a frame of N elements, we divide N by n and round the result down to the nearest whole number. Calling the rounded result ℓ, we then randomly select one element from the first ℓ elements in the frame— this is the first element in the systematic sample. The remaining elements in the sample are obtained by selecting every ℓth element following the first (randomly selected) element. For example, suppose we wish to sample a population of $N = 14,327$ allergists to investigate how often they have prescribed a particular drug during the last year. A medical society has a directory listing the 14,327 allergists, and we wish to draw a systematic sample of 500 allergists from this frame. Here we compute $14,327/500 = 28.654$, which is 28 when rounded down. Therefore, we number the first 28 allergists in the directory from 1 to 28, and we use a random number table to randomly select one of the first 28 allergists. Suppose we select allergist number 19. We interview allergist 19 and every 28th allergist in the frame thereafter, so we choose allergists 19, 47, 75, and so forth until we obtain our sample of 500 allergists. In this scheme, we must number the first 28 allergists, but we do not have to number the rest because we can "count off" every 28th allergist in the directory. Alternatively, we can measure the approximate amount of space in the directory that it takes to list 28 allergists. This measurement can then be used to select every 28th allergist.

Exercises for Section 7.4

CONCEPTS

connect

7.36 When is it appropriate to use stratified random sampling? What are strata, and how should strata be selected?

7.37 When is cluster sampling used? Why do we describe this type of sampling by using the term *cluster?*

7.38 Explain how to take a systematic sample of 100 companies from the 1,853 companies that are members of an industry trade association.

7.39 Explain how a stratified random sample is selected. Discuss how you might define the strata to survey student opinion on a proposal to charge all students a $100 fee for a new university-run bus system that will provide transportation between off-campus apartments and campus locations.

7.40 Marketing researchers often use city blocks as clusters in cluster sampling. Using this fact, explain how a market researcher might use multistage cluster sampling to select a sample of consumers from all cities having a population of more than 10,000 in a large state having many such cities.

7.5 More about Surveys and Errors in Survey Sampling (Optional) ● ● ●

We have seen in Section 1.2 that people in surveys are asked questions about their behaviors, opinions, beliefs, and other characteristics. In this section we discuss various issues related to designing surveys and the errors that can occur in survey sampling.

(LO6) Describe basic types of survey questions, survey procedures, and sources of error (Optional).

Types of survey questions   Survey instruments can use **dichotomous** ("yes or no"), **multiple-choice,** or **open-ended** questions. Each type of question has its benefits and drawbacks. Dichotomous questions are usually clearly stated, can be answered quickly, and yield data that are easily analyzed. However, the information gathered may be limited by this two option format. If we limit voters to expressing support or disapproval for stem-cell research, we may not learn the nuanced reasoning that voters use in weighing the merits and moral issues involved. Similarly, in today's heterogeneous world, it would be unusual to use a dichotomous question to categorize a person's religious preferences. Asking whether respondents are Christian or non-Christian (or to use any other two categories like Jewish or non-Jewish; Muslim or non-Muslim) is certain to make some people feel their religion is being slighted. In addition, this is a crude way and unenlightening way to learn about religious preferences.

Multiple-choice questions can assume several different forms. Sometimes respondents are asked to choose a response from a list (for example, possible answers to the religion question could be Jewish; Christian; Muslim; Hindu; Agnostic; or Other). Other times, respondents are asked to choose an answer from a numerical range. We could ask the question:

"In your opinion, how important are SAT scores to a college student's success?"

Not important at all   1   2   3   4   5   Extremely important

These numerical responses are usually summarized and reported in terms of the average response, whose size tells us something about the perceived importance. The Zagat restaurant survey (www.zagat.com) asks diners to rate restaurants' food, décor, and service, each on a scale of 1 to 30 points, with a 30 representing an incredible level of satisfaction. Although the Zagat scale has an unusually wide range of possible ratings, the concept is the same as in the more common 5-point scale.

Open-ended questions typically provide the most honest and complete information because there are no suggested answers to divert or bias a person's response. This kind of question is often found on instructor evaluation forms distributed at the end of a college course. College students at Georgetown University are asked the open-ended question, "What comments would you give to the instructor?" The responses provide the instructor feedback that may be missing from the initial part of the teaching evaluation survey, which consists of numerical multiple-choice ratings of various aspects of the course. While these numerical ratings can be used to compare instructors and courses, there are no easy comparisons of the diverse responses instructors receive to the open-ended question. In fact, these responses are often seen only by the instructor and are useful, constructive tools for the teacher despite the fact they cannot be readily summarized.

Survey questionnaires must be carefully constructed so they do not inadvertently bias the results. Because survey design is such a difficult and sensitive process, it is not uncommon for a pilot survey to be taken before a lot of time, effort, and financing go into collecting a large amount of data. Pilot surveys are similar to the beta version of a new electronic product; they are tested out with a smaller group of people to work out the "kinks" before being used on a larger scale. Determination of the sample size for the final survey is an important process for many reasons. If the sample size is too large, resources may be wasted during the data collection. On the other hand, not collecting enough data for a meaningful analysis will obviously be detrimental to the study. Fortunately, there are several formulas that will help decide how large a sample should be, depending on the goal of the study and various other factors.

Types of surveys   There are several different survey types, and we will explore just a few of them. The **phone survey** is particularly well-known (and often despised). A phone survey is inexpensive and usually conducted by callers who have very little training. Because of this and the impersonal nature of the medium, the respondent may misunderstand some of the questions. A further drawback is that some people cannot be reached and that others may refuse to answer some or all of the questions. Phone surveys are thus particularly prone to have a low **response rate.**

The **response rate** is the proportion of all people whom we attempt to contact that actually respond to a survey. A low response rate can destroy the validity of a survey's results.

The popular television sit-com *Seinfeld* parodied the difficulties of collecting data through a phone survey. After receiving several calls from telemarketers, Jerry replied in exasperation:

"I'm sorry; I'm a little tied up now. Give me your home number and I'll call you back later. Oh! You don't like being called at home? Well, now you know how I feel."

Numerous complaints have been filed with the Federal Trade Commission (FTC) about the glut of marketing and survey telephone calls to private residences. The National Do Not Call Registry was created as the culmination of a comprehensive, three-year review of the Telemarketing Sales Rule (TSR) (www.ftc.gov/donotcall/). This legislation allows people to enroll their phone numbers on a website so as to prevent most marketers from calling them.

Self-administered surveys, or **mail surveys,** are also very inexpensive to conduct. However, these also have their drawbacks. Often, recipients will choose not to reply unless they receive some kind of financial incentive or other reward. Generally, after an initial mailing, the response rate will fall between 20 and 30 percent (www.pra.ca/resources/rates.pdf). Response rates can be raised with successive follow-up reminders, and after three contacts, they might reach between 65 and 75 percent. Unfortunately, the entire process can take significantly longer than a phone survey would.

Web-based surveys have become increasingly popular, but they suffer from the same problems as mail surveys. In addition, as with phone surveys, respondents may record their true reactions incorrectly because they have misunderstood some of the questions posed.

A personal interview provides more control over the survey process. People selected for interviews are more likely to respond because the questions are being asked by someone face-to-face. Questions are less likely to be misunderstood because the people conducting the interviews are typically trained employees who can clear up any confusion arising during the process. On the other hand, interviewers can potentially "lead" a respondent by body language which signals approval or disapproval of certain sorts of answers. They can also prompt certain replies by providing too much information. **Mall surveys** are examples of personal interviews. Interviewers approach shoppers as they pass by and ask them to answer the survey questions. Response rates around 50 percent are typical (http://en.wikipedia.org/wiki/Statistical_survey#Survey_methods). Personal interviews are more costly than mail or phone surveys. Obviously, the objective of the study will be important in deciding upon the survey type employed.

Errors occurring in surveys   In general, the goal of a survey is to obtain accurate information from a group, or sample, that is representative of the entire population of interest. We are trying to estimate some aspect (numerical descriptor) of the entire population from a subset of the population. This is not an easy task, and there are many pitfalls. First and foremost, the *target population* must be well defined and a *sample frame* must be chosen.

The **target population** is the entire population of interest to us in a particular study.

Are we intending to estimate the average starting salary of students graduating from any college? Or from four year colleges? Or from business schools? Or from a particular business school?

The **sample frame** is a list of sampling elements (people or things) from which the sample will be selected. It should closely agree with the target population.

Consider a study to estimate the average starting salary of students who have graduated from the business school at Miami University of Ohio over the last five years; the target population is obviously that particular group of graduates. A sample frame could be the Miami University Alumni Association's roster of business school graduates for the past five years. Although it will not be a perfect replication of the target population, it is a reasonable frame.

We now discuss two general classes of survey errors: **errors of non-observation** and **errors of observation.** From the sample frame, units are randomly chosen to be part of the sample. Simply by virtue of the fact that we are taking a sample instead of a census, we are susceptible to *sampling error.*

Sampling error is the difference between a numerical descriptor of the population and the corresponding descriptor of the sample.

Sampling error occurs because our information is incomplete. We observe only the portion of the population included in the sample while the remainder is obscured. Suppose, for example, we wanted to know about the heights of 13-year-old boys. There is extreme variation in boys' heights at this age. Even if we could overcome the logistical problems of choosing a random sample of 20 boys, there is nothing to guarantee the sample will accurately reflect heights at this age. By sheer luck of the draw, our sample could include a higher proportion of tall boys than appears in the population. We would then overestimate average height at this age (to the chagrin of the shorter boys). Although samples tend to look more similar to their parent populations as the sample sizes increase, we should always keep in mind that sample characteristics and population characteristics are not the same.

If a sample frame is not identical to the target population, we will suffer from an *error of coverage*.

> **Undercoverage** occurs when some population elements are excluded from the process of selecting the sample.

Undercoverage was part of the problem dooming the *Literary Digest* Poll of 1936. Although millions of Americans were included in the poll, the large sample size could not rescue the poll results. The sample represented those who could afford phone service and magazine subscriptions in the lean Depression years, but in excluding everyone else, it failed to yield an honest picture of the entire American populace. Undercoverage often occurs when we do not have a complete, accurate list of all the population units. If we select our sample from an incomplete list, like a telephone directory or a list of all Internet subscribers in a region, we automatically eliminate those who cannot afford phone or Internet service. Even today, 7 to 8 percent of the people in the United States do not own telephones. Low income people are often underrepresented in surveys. If underrepresented groups differ from the rest of the population with respect to the characteristic under study, the survey results will be biased.

Often, pollsters cannot find all the people they intend to survey, and sometimes people who are found will refuse to answer the questions posed. Both of these are examples of the **nonresponse** problem. Unfortunately, there may be an association between how difficult it is to find and elicit responses from people and the type of answers they give.

> **Nonresponse** occurs whenever some of the individuals who were supposed to be included in the sample are not.

For example, universities often conduct surveys to learn how graduates have fared in the workplace. The alumnus who has risen through the corporate ranks is more likely to have a current address on file with his alumni office and to be willing to share career information than a classmate who has foundered professionally. We should be politely skeptical about reports touting the average salaries of graduates of various university programs. In some surveys, 35 percent or more of the selected individuals cannot be contacted—even when several callbacks are made. In such cases, other participants are often substituted for those who cannot be contacted. If the substitutes and the originally selected participants differ with respect to the characteristic under study, the survey will be biased. Furthermore, people who will answer highly sensitive, personal, or embarrassing questions might be very different from those who will not.

As discussed in Section 1.2, the opinions of those who bother to complete a voluntary response survey may be dramatically different from those who do not. (Recall the Ann Landers question about having children.) The viewer voting on the popular television show *American Idol* is another illustration of **selection bias,** since only those who are interested in the outcome of the show will bother to phone in or text message their votes. The results of the voting are not representative of the performance ratings the country would give as a whole.

Errors of observation occur when data values are recorded incorrectly. Such errors can be caused by the data collector (the interviewer), the survey instrument, the respondent, or the data collection process. For instance, the manner in which a question is asked can influence the response. Or, the order in which questions appear on a questionnaire can influence the survey results. Or, the data collection method (telephone interview, questionnaire, personal interview, or direct observation) can influence the results. A **recording error** occurs when either the respondent or interviewer incorrectly marks an answer. Once data are collected from a survey, the results are often entered into a computer for statistical analysis. When transferring data from a survey form to a spreadsheet program like Excel, MINITAB, or MegaStat, there is potential for entering them incorrectly. Before the survey is administered, the questions need to be very carefully worded so that there is little chance of misinterpretation. A poorly framed question might yield results that lead to unwarranted decisions. Scaled questions are particularly susceptible to this type of error. Consider the question "How would you rate this course?" Without a proper explanation, the respondent may not know whether "1" or "5" is the best.

If the survey instrument contains highly sensitive questions and respondents feel compelled to answer, they may not tell the truth. This is especially true in personal interviews. We then have what is called **response bias.** A surprising number of people are reluctant to be candid about what they like to read or watch on television. People tend to over-report "good" activities like reading respected newspapers and underreport their "bad" activities like delighting in the *National Inquirer*'s stories of alien abductions and celebrity meltdowns. Imagine, then, the difficulty in getting honest answers about people's gambling habits, drug use, or sexual histories. Response bias can also occur when respondents are asked slanted questions whose wording influences the answer received. For example, consider the following question:

Which of the following best describes your views on gun control?

1 The government should take away our guns, leaving us defenseless against heavily armed criminals.

2 We have the right to keep and bear arms.

This question is biased toward eliciting a response against gun control.

Exercises for Section 7.5

CONCEPTS

7.41 Explain:
  a Three types of surveys and discuss their advantages and disadvantages.
  b Three types of survey questions and discuss their advantages and disadvantages.

7.42 Explain each of the following terms:
  a Undercoverage   **b** Nonresponse   **c** Response bias

7.43 A market research firm sends out a web-based survey to assess the impact of advertisements placed on a search engine's results page. About 65% of the surveys were answered and sent back. What types of errors are possible in this scenario?

Chapter Summary

We began this chapter by discussing what a random sample is and how to use a **random number table** or **computer-generated random numbers** to select a **random sample.** We then discussed **sampling distributions.** A **sampling distribution** is the probability distribution that describes the population of all possible values of a sample statistic. In this chapter we studied the properties of two important sampling distributions—the sampling distribution of the sample mean, $\bar{x}$, and the sampling distribution of the sample proportion, $\hat{p}$.

Because different samples that can be randomly selected from a population give different sample means, there is a population of sample means corresponding to a particular sample size. The probability distribution describing the population of all possible sample means is called the **sampling distribution of the sample mean, $\bar{x}$.** We studied the properties of this sampling distribution when the sampled population is and is not normally distributed. We found that, when the sampled population has a normal distribution, then the sampling distribution of the sample mean is a normal distribution. Furthermore, the **Central Limit Theorem** tells us that, if the sampled population is not normally distributed, then the sampling distribution of the sample mean is approximately a normal distribution when the sample size is large (at least 30). We also saw that the mean of the sampling distribution of $\bar{x}$ always equals the mean of the sampled population, and we presented formulas for the variance and the standard deviation of this sampling distribution. Finally, we explained that the sample

mean is a **minimum-variance unbiased point estimate** of the mean of a normally distributed population.

We also studied the properties of the **sampling distribution of the sample proportion $\hat{p}$.** We found that, if the sample size is large, then this sampling distribution is approximately a normal distribution, and we gave a rule for determining whether the sample size is large. We found that the mean of the sampling distribution of $\hat{p}$ is the population proportion p, and we gave formulas for the variance and the standard deviation of this sampling distribution.

Throughout our discussions of sampling distributions, we demonstrated that knowing the properties of sampling distributions can help us make statistical inferences about population parameters. In fact, we will see that the properties of various sampling distributions provide the foundation for most of the techniques to be discussed in future chapters.

We concluded this chapter with two optional sections. In the first optional section, we discussed some advanced sampling designs. Specifically, we introduced **stratified random sampling,** in which we divide a population into groups (**strata**) and then select a random sample from each group. We also introduced **multistage cluster sampling,** which involves selecting a sample in stages, and we explained how to select a **systematic sample.** In the second optional section, we discussed more about surveys, as well as some potential problems that can occur when conducting a sample survey—**undercoverage, nonresponse, response bias, and slanted questions.**

Glossary of Terms

Central Limit Theorem: A theorem telling us that when the sample size n is sufficiently large, then the population of all possible sample means is approximately normally distributed no matter what probability distribution describes the sampled population. (page 282)

cluster sampling (multistage cluster sampling): A sampling design in which we sequentially cluster population elements into subpopulations. (page 292)

convenience sampling: Sampling where we select elements because they are easy or convenient to sample. (page 274)

errors of non-observation: Sampling error related to population elements that are not observed. (page 295)

errors of observation: Sampling error that occurs when the data collected in a survey differs from the truth. (page 296)

judgment sampling: Sampling where an expert selects population elements that he/she feels are representative of the population. (page 274)

minimum-variance unbiased point estimate: An unbiased point estimate of a population parameter having a variance that is smaller than the variance of any other unbiased point estimate of the parameter. (page 285)

nonresponse: A situation in which population elements selected to participate in a survey do not respond to the survey instrument. (page 296)

probability sampling: Sampling where we know the chance (probability) that each population element will be included in the sample. (page 274)

random number table: A table containing random digits that is often used to select a random sample. (page 272)

random sample: A sample selected in such a way that every set of n elements in the population has the same chance of being selected. (page 271)

response bias: Bias in the results obtained when carrying out a statistical study that is related to how survey participants answer the survey questions. (page 296)

response rate: The proportion of all people whom we attempt to contact that actually respond to a survey. (page 294)

sample frame: A list of sampling elements from which a sample will be selected. It should closely agree with the target population. (page 295)

sampling distribution of a sample statistic: The probability distribution of the population of all possible values of the sample statistic. (page 284)

sampling distribution of the sample mean $\bar{x}$: The probability distribution of the population of all possible sample means obtained from samples of a particular size n. (page 275)

sampling distribution of the sample proportion $\hat{p}$: The probability distribution of the population of all possible sample proportions obtained from samples of a particular size n. (page 288)

sampling error: The difference between the value of a sample statistic and the population parameter; it occurs because not all of the elements in the population have been measured. (page 295)

sampling without replacement: A sampling procedure in which we do not place previously selected elements back into the population and, therefore, do not give these elements a chance to be chosen on succeeding selections. (page 271)

sampling with replacement: A sampling procedure in which we place any element that has been chosen back into the population to give the element a chance to be chosen on succeeding selections. (page 271)

selection bias: Bias in the results obtained when carrying out a statistical study that is related to how survey participants are selected. (page 296)

strata: The subpopulations in a stratified sampling design. (page 291)

stratified random sampling: A sampling design in which we divide a population into nonoverlapping subpopulations and then select a random sample from each subpopulation (stratum). (page 291)

systematic sample: A sample taken by moving systematically through the population. For instance, we might randomly select one of the first 200 population elements and then systematically sample every 200th population element thereafter. (page 293)

target population: The entire population of interest in a statistical study. (page 295)

unbiased point estimate: A sample statistic is an unbiased point estimate of a population parameter if the mean of the population of all possible values of the sample statistic equals the population parameter. (page 285)

undercoverage: A situation in sampling in which some groups of population elements are underrepresented. (page 296)

voluntary response sample: Sampling in which the sample participants self-select. (page 274)

Important Formulas

The sampling distribution of the sample mean: pages 275 and 279.
  when a population is normally distributed (page 279)
    Central Limit Theorem (page 282)

The sampling distribution of the sample proportion: page 288.

Supplementary Exercises

connect

7.44 A company that sells and installs custom designed home theatre systems claims to have sold 977 such systems last year. In order to assess whether these claimed sales are valid, an accountant numbers the company's sales invoices from 1 to 977 and plans to select a random sample of 50 sales invoices. The accountant will then contact the purchasers listed on the 50 sampled sales invoices and determine whether the sales amounts on the invoices are correct. Starting in the upper left-hand corner of Table 7.1(a) (see page 272), determine which 50 of the 977 sales invoices should be included in the random sample. Note: There are many possible answers to this exercise.

7.45 In early 1995, *The Milwaukee Sentinel,* a morning newspaper in Milwaukee, Wisconsin, and *The Milwaukee Journal,* an afternoon newspaper, merged to form *The Milwaukee Journal Sentinel.* Several weeks after the merger, a Milwaukee television station, WITI-TV, conducted a telephone call-in survey asking whether viewers liked the new *Journal Sentinel.* The survey was "not scientific" because any viewer wishing to call in could do so.

On April 26, 1995, Tim Cuprisin, in his "Inside TV & Radio" column in the *Journal Sentinel,* wrote the following comment:

> **WE DIDN'T CALL:** WITI-TV (Channel 6) did one of those polls—which they admit are unscientific—last week and found that 388 viewers like the new *Journal Sentinel* and 2,629 don't like it.
>
> We did our own unscientific poll on whether those Channel 6 surveys accurately reflect public opinion. The results: a full 100 percent of the respondents say absolutely, positively not.

Is Cuprisin's comment justified? Write a short paragraph explaining your answer.

7.46 Each day a manufacturing plant receives a large shipment of drums of Chemical ZX-900. These drums are supposed to have a mean fill of 50 gallons, while the fills have a standard deviation known to be .6 gallon.

a Suppose that the mean fill for the shipment is actually 50 gallons. If we draw a random sample of 100 drums from the shipment, what is the probability that the average fill for the 100 drums is between 49.88 gallons and 50.12 gallons?

b The plant manager is worried that the drums of Chemical ZX-900 are underfilled. Because of this, she decides to draw a sample of 100 drums from each daily shipment and will reject the shipment (send it back to the supplier) if the average fill for the 100 drums is less than 49.85 gallons. Suppose that a shipment that actually has a mean fill of 50 gallons is received. What is the probability that this shipment will be rejected and sent back to the supplier?

7.47 In its October 12, 1992, issue, *The Milwaukee Journal* published the results of an Ogilvy, Adams, and Rinehart poll of 1,250 American investors that was conducted in early October 1992. The poll investigated the stock market's appeal to investors five years after the market suffered its biggest one-day decline (in 1987).

Assume that 50 percent of all American investors in 1992 found the stock market less attractive than it was in 1987 (that is, $p = .5$). Find the probability that the sample proportion obtained from the sample of 1,250 investors would be

a Within 4 percentage points of the population proportion—that is, find $P(.46 \le \hat{p} \le .54)$.

b Within 2 percentage points of the population proportion.

c Within 1 percentage point of the population proportion.

d Based on these probabilities, would it be reasonable to claim a ± 2 percentage point margin of error? A ± 1 percentage point margin of error? Explain.

7.48 Again consider the stock market poll discussed in Exercise 7.47.

a Suppose we wish to use the poll's results to justify the claim that fewer than 50 percent of American investors in 1992 found the stock market less attractive than in 1987. The poll actually found that 41 percent of the respondents said the stock market was less attractive than in 1987. If, for the sake of argument, we assume that $p = .5$, calculate the probability of observing a sample proportion of .41 or less. That is, calculate $P(\hat{p} \le .41)$.

b Based on the probability you computed in part *a,* would you conclude that fewer than 50 percent of American investors in 1992 found the stock market to be less attractive than in 1987? Explain.

7.49 Aamco Heating and Cooling, Inc., advertises that any customer buying an air conditioner during the first 16 days of July will receive a 25 percent discount if the average high temperature for this 16-day period is more than five degrees above normal.

a If daily high temperatures in July are normally distributed with a mean of 84 degrees and a standard deviation of 8 degrees, what is the probability that Aamco Heating and Cooling will have to give its customers the 25 percent discount?

b Based on the probability you computed in part *a,* do you think that Aamco's promotion is ethical? Write a paragraph justifying your opinion.

7.50 THE TRASH BAG CASE 🄳🅂 TrashBag

Recall that the trash bag manufacturer has concluded that its new 30-gallon bag will be the strongest such bag on the market if its mean breaking strength is at least 50 pounds. In order to provide statistical evidence that the mean breaking strength of the new bag is at least 50 pounds, the manufacturer randomly selects a sample of *n* bags and calculates the mean $\bar{x}$ of the breaking

FIGURE 8.5 **The Point $z_{\alpha/2}$**

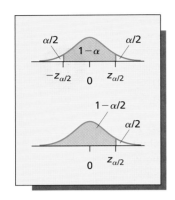

TABLE 8.2 **The Normal Point $z_{\alpha/2}$ for Various Levels of Confidence**

$100(1-\alpha)\%$	$1-\alpha$	α	$\alpha/2$	$1-\alpha/2$	$z_{\alpha/2}$
90%	.90	.10	.05	.95	$z_{.05}=1.645$
95%	.95	.05	.025	.975	$z_{.025}=1.96$
98%	.98	.02	.01	.99	$z_{.01}=2.33$
99%	.99	.01	.005	.995	$z_{.005}=2.575$

To compare the 95 percent confidence interval $[\bar{x} \pm 1.96(\sigma/\sqrt{n})]$ with the 99 percent confidence interval $[\bar{x} \pm 2.575(\sigma/\sqrt{n})]$, note that each of these confidence intervals can be expressed in the form $[\bar{x} \pm$ margin of error]. Here, for a given level of confidence, the **margin of error** expresses the furthest that the sample mean $\bar{x}$ might be from the population mean μ. Moreover, the margin of error $2.575(\sigma/\sqrt{n})$ used to compute the 99 percent interval is larger than the margin of error $1.96(\sigma/\sqrt{n})$ used to compute the 95 percent interval. Therefore, the 99 percent interval is the longer of these intervals. **In general, increasing the confidence level (1) has the advantage of making us more confident that μ is contained in the confidence interval, but (2) has the disadvantage of increasing the margin of error and thus providing a less precise estimate of the true value of μ.** Frequently, 95 percent confidence intervals are used to make conclusions. If conclusions based on stronger evidence are desired, 99 percent intervals are sometimes used. In the car mileage case, the fairly large sample size of $n = 50$ produces a 99 percent margin of error $[2.575(.8/\sqrt{50}) = .29]$ that is not much larger than the 95 percent margin of error $[1.96(.8/\sqrt{50}) = .22]$. Therefore, the 99 percent confidence interval for μ, $[31.56 \pm .29] = [31.27, 31.85]$, is not much longer than the 95 percent confidence interval for μ, $[31.56 \pm .22] = [31.34, 31.78]$.

In general, we let α denote the probability that a confidence interval for a population mean will *not* contain the population mean. This implies that $1 - \alpha$ is the probability that the confidence interval will contain the population mean. In order to find a confidence interval for a population mean that is based on a confidence coefficient of $1 - \alpha$ (that is, a **$100(1 - \alpha)$ percent confidence interval** for the population mean), we do the following:

Step 1: As illustrated in Figure 8.5, place a symmetrical area of $1 - \alpha$ under the standard normal curve, and find the area in the normal curve tails beyond the $1 - \alpha$ area. Because the entire area under the standard normal curve is 1, the combined areas in the normal curve tails are α, and the area in each tail is $\alpha/2$.

Step 2: Find the normal point $z_{\alpha/2}$ that gives a right-hand tail area under the standard normal curve equal to $\alpha/2$, and find the normal point $-z_{\alpha/2}$ that gives a left-hand tail area under this curve equal to $\alpha/2$. As shown in Figure 8.5, the area under the standard normal curve between $-z_{\alpha/2}$ and $z_{\alpha/2}$ is $(1-\alpha)$, and the area under this curve to the left of $z_{\alpha/2}$ is $1-\alpha/2$. **This implies that we can find $z_{\alpha/2}$ by looking up a cumulative area of $1-\alpha/2$ in Table A.3** (page 638).

Step 3: Form the following $100(1 - \alpha)$ percent confidence interval for the population mean.

$$[\bar{x} \pm z_{\alpha/2}\sigma_{\bar{x}}] = \left[\bar{x} \pm z_{\alpha/2}\frac{\sigma}{\sqrt{n}}\right]$$

If all possible samples were used to calculate this interval, then $100(1 - \alpha)$ percent of the resulting intervals would contain the population mean. Moreover, we call **$100(1 - \alpha)$ percent** the **confidence level** associated with the confidence interval.

The general formula that we just obtained for a $100(1 - \alpha)$ percent confidence interval for a population mean implies that we now have a formal way to find the normal point corresponding to a particular level of confidence. Specifically, we can set $100(1 - \alpha)$ percent equal to the particular level of confidence, solve for α, and use a cumulative normal table to find the normal point $z_{\alpha/2}$ corresponding to the cumulative area $1 - \alpha/2$. For example, suppose that we wish to find a 99 percent confidence interval for the population mean. Then, because $100(1 - \alpha)$ percent equals 99 percent, it follows that $1-\alpha = .99$, $\alpha = .01$, $\alpha/2 = .005$, and $1 - \alpha/2 = .995$. Looking up .995 in a cumulative normal table, we find that $z_{\alpha/2} = z_{.005} = 2.575$. This normal point is the same normal point that we previously found using the three-step procedure and the normal curves illustrated in Figure 8.4. Table 8.2 summarizes finding the values of $z_{\alpha/2}$ for different values of the confidence level $100(1 - \alpha)$ percent.

The following box summarizes the formula used in calculating a $100(1 - \alpha)$ percent confidence interval for a population mean μ. This interval is based on the normal distribution and assumes that the true value of σ is known. If (as is usually the case) σ is not known, we can use a confidence interval for μ discussed in the next section.

A Confidence Interval for a Population Mean μ: σ Known

Suppose that the sampled population is normally distributed with mean μ and standard deviation σ. Then a $100(1 - \alpha)$ percent confidence interval for μ is

$$\left[\bar{x} \pm z_{\alpha/2}\frac{\sigma}{\sqrt{n}} \right] = \left[\bar{x} - z_{\alpha/2}\frac{\sigma}{\sqrt{n}}, \bar{x} + z_{\alpha/2}\frac{\sigma}{\sqrt{n}} \right]$$

Here, $z_{\alpha/2}$ is the normal point that gives a right-hand tail area under the standard normal curve of $\alpha/2$. The normal point $z_{\alpha/2}$ can be found by looking up a cumulative area of $1 - \alpha/2$ in Table A.3 (page 638). This confidence interval is also approximately valid for non-normal populations if the sample size is large (at least 30).

EXAMPLE 8.1 The Payment Time Case

Recall that a management consulting firm has installed a new computer-based, electronic billing system in a Hamilton, Ohio, trucking company. The population mean payment time using the trucking company's old billing system was approximately equal to, but no less than, 39 days. In order to assess whether the population mean payment time, μ, using the new billing system is substantially less than 39 days, the consulting firm will use the sample of $n = 65$ payment times in Table 2.4 to find a 99 percent confidence interval for μ. The mean of the 65 payment times is $\bar{x} = 18.1077$ days, and we will assume that the true value of the population standard deviation σ for the new billing system is 4.2 days (as discussed on page 284 of Chapter 7). Then, because we previously showed that the normal point corresponding to 99 percent confidence is $z_{\alpha/2} = z_{.005} = 2.575$, a 99 percent confidence interval for μ is

$$\left[\bar{x} \pm z_{.005}\frac{\sigma}{\sqrt{n}} \right] = \left[18.1077 \pm 2.575\frac{4.2}{\sqrt{65}} \right]$$
$$= [18.1077 \pm 1.3414]$$
$$= [16.8, 19.4]$$

Recalling that the mean payment time using the old billing system is 39 days, this interval says that we are 99 percent confident that the population mean payment time using the new billing system is between 16.8 days and 19.4 days. Therefore, we are 99 percent confident that the new billing system reduces the mean payment time by at most $39 - 16.8 = 22.2$ days and by at least $39 - 19.4 = 19.6$ days.

Exercises for Section 8.1

CONCEPTS

connect

8.1 Explain why it is important to calculate a confidence interval.

8.2 Explain the meaning of the term "95 percent confidence."

8.3 Under what conditions is the confidence interval $[\bar{x} \pm z_{\alpha/2}(\sigma/\sqrt{n})]$ for μ valid?

8.4 For a fixed sample size, what happens to a confidence interval for μ when we increase the level of confidence?

8.5 For a fixed level of confidence, what happens to a confidence interval for μ when we increase the sample size?

METHODS AND APPLICATIONS

8.6 Suppose that, for a sample of size $n = 100$ measurements, we find that $\bar{x} = 50$. Assuming that σ equals 2, calculate confidence intervals for the population mean μ with the following confidence levels:

    a 95%   **b** 99%   **c** 97%   **d** 80%   **e** 99.73%   **f** 92%

8.7 **THE TRASH BAG CASE**   **DS** TrashBag

Consider the trash bag problem. Suppose that an independent laboratory has tested trash bags and has found that no 30-gallon bags that are currently on the market have a mean breaking strength of 50 pounds or more. On the basis of these results, the producer of the new, improved trash bag feels sure that its 30-gallon bag will be the strongest such bag on the market if the new trash bag's mean breaking strength can be shown to be at least 50 pounds. The mean of the sample of 40 trash bag breaking strengths in Table 1.9 is $\bar{x} = 50.575$. If we let μ denote the mean of the breaking strengths of all possible trash bags of the new type and assume that σ equals 1.65:

    a Calculate 95 percent and 99 percent confidence intervals for μ.

    b Using the 95 percent confidence interval, can we be 95 percent confident that μ is at least 50 pounds? Explain.

    c Using the 99 percent confidence interval, can we be 99 percent confident that μ is at least 50 pounds? Explain.

    d Based on your answers to parts *b* and *c*, how convinced are you that the new 30-gallon trash bag is the strongest such bag on the market?

8.8 **THE BANK CUSTOMER WAITING TIME CASE**   **DS** WaitTime

Recall that a bank manager has developed a new system to reduce the time customers spend waiting to be served by tellers during peak business hours. The mean waiting time during peak business hours under the current system is roughly 9 to 10 minutes. The bank manager hopes that the new system will have a mean waiting time that is less than six minutes. The mean of the sample of 100 bank customer waiting times in Table 1.8 is $\bar{x} = 5.46$. If we let μ denote the mean of all possible bank customer waiting times using the new system and assume that σ equals 2.47:

    a Calculate 95 percent and 99 percent confidence intervals for μ.

    b Using the 95 percent confidence interval, can the bank manager be 95 percent confident that μ is less than six minutes? Explain.

    c Using the 99 percent confidence interval, can the bank manager be 99 percent confident that μ is less than six minutes? Explain.

    d Based on your answers to parts *b* and *c*, how convinced are you that the new mean waiting time is less than six minutes?

8.9 **THE VIDEO GAME SATISFACTION RATING CASE**   **DS** VideoGame

The mean of the sample of 65 customer satisfaction ratings in Table 1.7 is $\bar{x} = 42.95$. If we let μ denote the mean of all possible customer satisfaction ratings for the XYZ Box video game system, and assume that σ equals 2.64:

    a Calculate 95 percent and 99 percent confidence intervals for μ.

    b Using the 95 percent confidence interval, can we be 95 percent confident that μ is at least 42 (recall that a very satisfied customer gives a rating of at least 42)? Explain.

    c Using the 99 percent confidence interval, can we be 99 percent confident that μ is at least 42? Explain.

    d Based on your answers to parts *b* and *c*, how convinced are you that the mean satisfaction rating is at least 42?

8.10 In an article in *Marketing Science,* Silk and Berndt investigate the output of advertising agencies. They describe ad agency output by finding the shares of dollar billing volume coming from various media categories such as network television, spot television, newspapers, radio, and so forth.

    a Suppose that a random sample of 400 U.S. advertising agencies gives an average percentage share of billing volume from network television equal to 7.46 percent, and assume that σ equals 1.42 percent. Calculate a 95 percent confidence interval for the mean percentage share of billing volume from network television for the population of all U.S. advertising agencies.

    b Suppose that a random sample of 400 U.S. advertising agencies gives an average percentage share of billing volume from spot television commercials equal to 12.44 percent, and assume that σ equals 1.55 percent. Calculate a 95 percent confidence interval for the mean percentage share of billing volume from spot television commercials for the population of all U.S. advertising agencies.

    c Compare the confidence intervals in parts *a* and *b*. Does it appear that the mean percentage share of billing volume from spot television commercials for U.S. advertising agencies is greater than the mean percentage share of billing volume from network television? Explain.

8.11 In an article in *Accounting and Business Research,* Carslaw and Kaplan investigate factors that influence "audit delay" for firms in New Zealand. Audit delay, which is defined to be the length of time (in days) from a company's financial year-end to the date of the auditor's report, has been found to affect the market reaction to the report. This is because late reports often seem to be associated with lower returns and early reports often seem to be associated with higher returns.

    Carslaw and Kaplan investigated audit delay for two kinds of public companies—owner-controlled and manager-controlled companies. Here a company is considered to be owner controlled if 30 percent or more of the common stock is controlled by a single outside investor (an investor not part of the management group or board of directors). Otherwise, a company is considered manager controlled. It was felt that the type of control influences audit delay. To quote Carslaw and Kaplan:

        Large external investors, having an acute need for timely information, may be expected to pressure the company and auditor to start and to complete the audit as rapidly as practicable.

    a Suppose that a random sample of 100 public owner-controlled companies in New Zealand is found to give a mean audit delay of $\bar{x} = 82.6$ days, and assume that σ equals 33 days. Calculate a 95 percent confidence interval for the population mean audit delay for all public owner-controlled companies in New Zealand.

    b Suppose that a random sample of 100 public manager-controlled companies in New Zealand is found to give a mean audit delay of $\bar{x} = 93$ days, and assume that σ equals 37 days. Calculate a 95 percent confidence interval for the population mean audit delay for all public manager-controlled companies in New Zealand.

    c Use the confidence intervals you computed in parts *a* and *b* to compare the mean audit delay for all public owner-controlled companies versus that of all public manager-controlled companies. How do the means compare? Explain.

8.12 In an article in the *Journal of Marketing,* Bayus studied the differences between "early replacement buyers" and "late replacement buyers" in making consumer durable good replacement purchases. Early replacement buyers are consumers who replace a product during the early part of its lifetime, while late replacement buyers make replacement purchases late in the product's lifetime. In particular, Bayus studied automobile replacement purchases. Consumers who traded in cars with ages of zero to three years and mileages of no more than 35,000 miles were classified as early replacement buyers. Consumers who traded in cars with ages of seven or more years and mileages of more than 73,000 miles were classified as late replacement buyers. Bayus compared the two groups of buyers with respect to demographic variables such as income, education, age, and so forth. He also compared the two groups with respect to the amount of search activity in the replacement purchase process. Variables compared included the number of dealers visited, the time spent gathering information, and the time spent visiting dealers.

    a Suppose that a random sample of 800 early replacement buyers yields a mean number of dealers visited of $\bar{x} = 3.3$, and assume that σ equals .71. Calculate a 99 percent confidence interval for the population mean number of dealers visited by early replacement buyers.

    b Suppose that a random sample of 500 late replacement buyers yields a mean number of dealers visited of $\bar{x} = 4.3$, and assume that σ equals .66. Calculate a 99 percent confidence interval for the population mean number of dealers visited by late replacement buyers.

    c Use the confidence intervals you computed in parts *a* and *b* to compare the mean number of dealers visited by early replacement buyers with the mean number of dealers visited by late replacement buyers. How do the means compare? Explain.

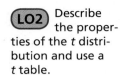

Describe the proper-ties of the *t* distri-bution and use a *t* table.

8.2 *t*-Based Confidence Intervals for a Population Mean: σ Unknown ◐ ● ●

If we do not know σ (which is usually the case), we can use the sample standard deviation s to help construct a confidence interval for μ. The interval is based on the sampling distribution of

$$t = \frac{\bar{x} - \mu}{s/\sqrt{n}}$$

If the sampled population is normally distributed, then for any sample size n this sampling distribution is what is called a *t* **distribution.**

The curve of the *t* distribution has a shape similar to that of the standard normal curve. Two *t* curves and a standard normal curve are illustrated in Figure 8.6. A *t* curve is symmetrical about zero, which is the mean of any *t* distribution. However, the *t* distribution is more spread out, or variable, than the standard normal distribution. Since the above *t* statistic is a function of two random variables, $\bar{x}$ and s, it is logical that the sampling distribution of this statistic is more vari-able than the sampling distribution of the z statistic, which is a function of only one random variable, $\bar{x}$. The exact spread, or standard deviation, of the *t* distribution depends on a parameter that is called the **number of degrees of freedom (denoted** *df***).** The number of degrees of free-dom *df* varies depending on the problem. In the present situation the sampling distribution of *t* has a number of degrees of freedom that equals the sample size minus 1. We say that this sam-pling distribution is a *t* **distribution with** $n - 1$ **degrees of freedom.** As the sample size n (and thus the number of degrees of freedom) increases, the spread of the *t* distribution decreases (see Figure 8.6). Furthermore, as the number of degrees of freedom approaches infinity, the curve of the *t* distribution approaches (that is, becomes shaped more and more like) the curve of the stan-dard normal distribution.

In order to use the *t* distribution, we employ a *t* **point that is denoted** t_α**.** As illustrated in Figure 8.7, t_α **is the point on the horizontal axis under the curve of the *t* distribution that gives a right-hand tail area equal to α.** The value of t_α in a particular situation depends upon the right-hand tail area α and the number of degrees of freedom of the *t* distribution. Values of t_α are tabulated in a *t* **table.** Such a table is given in Table A.4 of Appendix A (pages 640 and 641) and a portion of Table A.4 is reproduced in this chapter as Table 8.3. In this *t* table, the rows cor-respond to the different numbers of degrees of freedom (which are denoted as *df*). The values of *df* are listed down the left side of the table, while the columns designate the right-hand tail area α. For example, suppose we wish to find the *t* point that gives a right-hand tail area of .025 under a *t* curve having $df = 14$ degrees of freedom. To do this, we look in Table 8.3 at the row labeled 14 and the column labeled $t_{.025}$. We find that this $t_{.025}$ point is 2.145 (also see Figure 8.8). Similarly, when there are $df = 14$ degrees of freedom, we find that $t_{.005} = 2.977$ (see Table 8.3 and Figure 8.9).

FIGURE 8.6   **As the Number of Degrees of Freedom Increases, the Spread of the *t* Distribution Decreases and the *t* Curve Approaches the Standard Normal Curve**

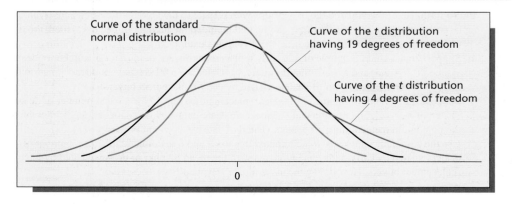

FIGURE 8.7   **An Example of a *t* Point Giving a Specified Right-Hand Tail Area (This *t* Point Gives a Right-Hand Tail Area Equal to α).**

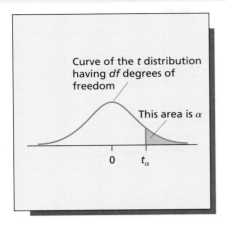

FIGURE 8.8   **The *t* Point Giving a Right-Hand Tail Area of .025 under the *t* Curve Having 14 Degrees of Freedom: $t_{.025} = 2.145$**

TABLE 8.3   **A *t* Table**

df	$t_{.100}$	$t_{.050}$	$t_{.025}$	$t_{.01}$	$t_{.005}$	$t_{.001}$	$t_{.0005}$
1	3.078	6.314	12.706	31.821	63.657	318.31	636.62
2	1.886	2.920	4.303	6.965	9.925	22.326	31.598
3	1.638	2.353	3.182	4.541	5.841	10.213	12.924
4	1.533	2.132	2.776	3.747	4.604	7.173	8.610
5	1.476	2.015	2.571	3.365	4.032	5.893	6.869
6	1.440	1.943	2.447	3.143	3.707	5.208	5.959
7	1.415	1.895	2.365	2.998	3.499	4.785	5.408
8	1.397	1.860	2.306	2.896	3.355	4.501	5.041
9	1.383	1.833	2.262	2.821	3.250	4.297	4.781
10	1.372	1.812	2.228	2.764	3.169	4.144	4.587
11	1.363	1.796	2.201	2.718	3.106	4.025	4.437
12	1.356	1.782	2.179	2.681	3.055	3.930	4.318
13	1.350	1.771	2.160	2.650	3.012	3.852	4.221
14	1.345	1.761	2.145	2.624	2.977	3.787	4.140
15	1.341	1.753	2.131	2.602	2.947	3.733	4.073
16	1.337	1.746	2.120	2.583	2.921	3.686	4.015
17	1.333	1.740	2.110	2.567	2.898	3.646	3.965
18	1.330	1.734	2.101	2.552	2.878	3.610	3.922
19	1.328	1.729	2.093	2.539	2.861	3.579	3.883
20	1.325	1.725	2.086	2.528	2.845	3.552	3.850
21	1.323	1.721	2.080	2.518	2.831	3.527	3.819
22	1.321	1.717	2.074	2.508	2.819	3.505	3.792
23	1.319	1.714	2.069	2.500	2.807	3.485	3.767
24	1.318	1.711	2.064	2.492	2.797	3.467	3.745
25	1.316	1.708	2.060	2.485	2.787	3.450	3.725
26	1.315	1.706	2.056	2.479	2.779	3.435	3.707
27	1.314	1.703	2.052	2.473	2.771	3.421	3.690
28	1.313	1.701	2.048	2.467	2.763	3.408	3.674
29	1.311	1.699	2.045	2.462	2.756	3.396	3.659
30	1.310	1.697	2.042	2.457	2.750	3.385	3.646
40	1.303	1.684	2.021	2.423	2.704	3.307	3.551
60	1.296	1.671	2.000	2.390	2.660	3.232	3.460
120	1.289	1.658	1.980	2.358	2.617	3.160	3.373
∞	1.282	1.645	1.960	2.326	2.576	3.090	3.291

FIGURE 8.9   The *t* Point Giving a
             Right-Hand Tail Area of
             .005 under the *t* Curve
             Having 14 Degrees of
             Freedom: $t_{.005} = 2.977$

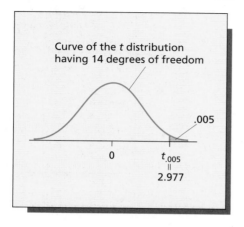

FIGURE 8.10   The Point $t_{\alpha/2}$ with
              n − 1 Degrees of
              Freedom

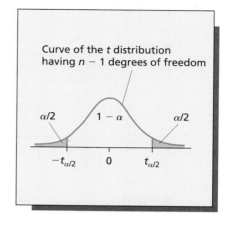

Table 8.3 gives *t* points for degrees of freedom *df* from 1 to 30. The table also gives *t* points for 40, 60, 120, and an infinite number of degrees of freedom. Looking at this table, it is useful to realize that the normal points giving the various right-hand tail areas are listed in the row of the *t* table corresponding to an infinite (∞) number of degrees of freedom. Looking at the row corresponding to ∞, we see that, for example, $z_{.025} = 1.96$. Therefore, we can use this row in the *t* table as an alternative to using the normal table when we need to find normal points (such as $z_{\alpha/2}$ in Section 8.1).

LO3 Calculate and interpret a *t*-based confidence interval for a population mean when *σ* is unknown.

Table A.4 of Appendix A (pages 640 and 641) gives *t* points for values of *df* from 1 to 100. We can use a computer to find *t* points based on values of *df* greater than 100. Alternatively, because a *t* curve based on more than 100 degrees of freedom is approximately the shape of the standard normal curve, *t* points based on values of *df* greater than 100 can be approximated by their corresponding *z* points. That is, when performing hand calculations, it is reasonable to approximate values of t_α by z_α when *df* is greater than 100.

We now present the formula for a $100(1 - \alpha)$ percent confidence interval for a population mean *μ* based on the *t* distribution.

A *t*-Based Confidence Interval for a Population Mean *μ*: *σ* Unknown

If the sampled population is normally distributed with mean *μ*, then a **$100(1 - \alpha)$ percent confidence interval for *μ*** is

$$\left[\bar{x} \pm t_{\alpha/2} \frac{s}{\sqrt{n}} \right]$$

Here *s* is the sample standard deviation, $t_{\alpha/2}$ is the *t* point giving a right-hand tail area of $\alpha/2$ under the *t* curve having *n* − 1 degrees of freedom, and *n* is the sample size. This confidence interval is also approximately valid for non-normal populations if the sample size is large (at least 30).

Before presenting an example, we need to make a few comments. First, it has been shown that, even if the sample size is not large, this confidence interval is approximately valid for many populations that are not exactly normally distributed. In particular, this interval is approximately valid for a mound-shaped, or single-peaked, population, even if the population is somewhat skewed to the right or left. Second, this interval employs the point $t_{\alpha/2}$, which as shown in Figure 8.10, gives a right-hand tail area equal to $\alpha/2$ under the *t* curve having *n* − 1 degrees of freedom. Here $\alpha/2$ is determined from the desired confidence level $100(1 - \alpha)$ percent.

EXAMPLE 8.2 The Debt-to-Equity Ratio Case

One measure of a company's financial health is its *debt-to-equity ratio*. This quantity is defined to be the ratio of the company's corporate debt to the company's equity. If this ratio is too high, it is one indication of financial instability. For obvious reasons, banks often monitor the financial health of companies to which they have extended commercial loans. Suppose that, in order to reduce risk, a large bank has decided to initiate a policy limiting the mean debt-to-equity ratio for its portfolio of commercial loans to being less than 1.5. In order to estimate the mean debt-to-equity ratio of its (current) commercial loan portfolio, the bank randomly selects a sample of 15 of its commercial loan accounts. Audits of these companies result in the following debt-to-equity ratios:

1.31	1.05	1.45	1.21	1.19
1.78	1.37	1.41	1.22	1.11
1.46	1.33	1.29	1.32	1.65

DS DebtEq

A stem-and-leaf display of these ratios is given on the page margin, and a box plot of the ratios is given below. The stem-and-leaf display looks reasonably mound-shaped, and both the stem-and-leaf display and the box plot look reasonably symmetrical. Furthermore, the sample mean and standard deviation of the ratios can be calculated to be $\bar{x} = 1.3433$ and $s = .1921$.

```
1.0 | 5
1.1 | 1 9
1.2 | 1 2 9
1.3 | 1 2 3 7
1.4 | 1 5 6
1.5 |
1.6 | 5
1.7 | 8
```

Suppose the bank wishes to calculate a 95 percent confidence interval for the loan portfolio's mean debt-to-equity ratio, μ. Because the bank has taken a sample of size $n = 15$, we have $n - 1 = 15 - 1 = 14$ degrees of freedom, and the level of confidence $100(1 - \alpha)\% = 95\%$ implies that $1 - \alpha = .95$ and $\alpha = .05$. Therefore, we use the *t* point $t_{\alpha/2} = t_{.05/2} = t_{.025}$, which—as illustrated below—is the *t* point giving a right-hand tail area of .025 under the *t* curve having 14 degrees of freedom.

Using Table 8.3 (page 315), we find that $t_{.025}$ with 14 degrees of freedom is 2.145. It follows that the 95 percent confidence interval for μ is

$$\left[\bar{x} \pm t_{.025} \frac{s}{\sqrt{n}} \right] = \left[1.3433 \pm 2.145 \frac{.1921}{\sqrt{15}} \right]$$

$$= [1.3433 \pm 0.1064]$$

$$= [1.2369, 1.4497]$$

This interval says the bank is 95 percent confident that the mean debt-to-equity ratio for its portfolio of commercial loan accounts is between 1.2369 and 1.4497. Based on this interval, the bank has strong evidence that the portfolio's mean ratio is less than 1.5 (or that the bank is in compliance with its new policy).

Recall that in the two cases discussed in Section 8.1 we calculated *z*-based confidence intervals for μ by assuming that the population standard deviation σ is known. If σ is actually not known (which would probably be true), we should compute *t*-based confidence intervals. Furthermore, recall that in each of these cases the sample size is large (at least 30). As stated in the summary box, **if the sample size is large, the *t*-based confidence interval for μ is approximately valid even if the sampled population is not normally distributed.** Therefore, consider the car mileage case and the sample of 50 mileages in Table 1.6, which has mean $\bar{x} = 31.56$ and standard deviation $s = .7977$. The 95 percent *t*-based confidence interval for the population mean mileage μ of the new midsize model is

$$\left[\bar{x} \pm t_{.025} \frac{s}{\sqrt{n}} \right] = \left[31.56 \pm 2.010 \frac{.7977}{\sqrt{50}} \right] = [31.33, 31.79]$$

where $t_{.025} = 2.010$ is based on $n - 1 = 50 - 1 = 49$ degrees of freedom—see Table A.4 (page 640). This interval says we are 95 percent confident that the model's population mean mileage μ is between 31.33 mpg and 31.79 mpg. Based on this interval, the model's EPA mileage estimate is 31 mpg, and the automaker will receive the tax credit.

As another example, the sample of 65 payment times in Table 2.4 has mean $\bar{x} = 18.1077$ and standard deviation $s = 3.9612$. The 99 percent *t*-based confidence interval for the population mean payment time using the new electronic billing system is

$$\left[\bar{x} \pm t_{.005} \frac{s}{\sqrt{n}} \right] = \left[18.1077 \pm 2.655 \frac{3.9612}{\sqrt{65}} \right] = [16.8, 19.4]$$

where $t_{.005} = 2.655$ is based on $n - 1 = 65 - 1 = 64$ degrees of freedom—see Table A.4 (page 640). Recalling that the mean payment time using the old billing system is 39 days, the interval says that we are 99 percent confident that the population mean payment time using the new billing system is between 16.8 days and 19.4 days. Therefore, we are 99 percent confident that the new billing system reduces the mean payment time by at most 22.2 days and by at least 19.6 days.

EXAMPLE 8.3 The Marketing Research Case   C

Recall that a brand group is considering a new bottle design for a popular soft drink and that Table 1.5 (page 10) gives a random sample of $n = 60$ consumer ratings of this new bottle design. Let μ denote the mean rating of the new bottle design that would be given by all consumers. In order to assess whether μ exceeds the minimum standard composite score of 25 for a successful bottle design, the brand group will calculate a 95 percent confidence interval for μ. The mean and the standard deviation of the 60 bottle design ratings are $\bar{x} = 30.35$ and $s = 3.1073$. It follows that a 95 percent confidence interval for μ is

$$\left[\bar{x} \pm t_{.025} \frac{s}{\sqrt{n}} \right] = \left[30.35 \pm 2.001 \frac{3.1073}{\sqrt{60}} \right] = [29.5, 31.2]$$

where $t_{.025} = 2.001$ is based on $n - 1 = 60 - 1 = 59$ degrees of freedom—see Table A.4 (page 640). Since the interval says we are 95 percent confident that the population mean rating of the new bottle design is between 29.5 and 31.2, we are 95 percent confident that this mean rating exceeds the minimum standard of 25 by at least 4.5 points and by at most 6.2 points.

Confidence intervals for μ can be computed using Excel and MINITAB. Figure 8.11 gives the Excel output of the information needed to calculate the *t*-based 95 percent confidence interval for the mean debt-to-equity ratio. If we consider the Excel output, we see that $\bar{x} = 1.3433$ (see "Mean"), $s = .1921$ (see "Standard Deviation"), $s/\sqrt{n} = .0496$ (see "Standard Error"), and $t_{.025}(s/\sqrt{n}) = .1064$ [see "Confidence Level (95.0%)"]. The interval, which must be hand calculated, is $[1.3433 \pm .1064] = [1.2369, 1.4497]$. The MINITAB output in Figure 8.12 tells us that the *t*-based 95 percent confidence interval for the mean debt-to-equity ratio is $[1.2370, 1.4497]$. This result is, within rounding, the same interval calculated in Example 8.2 and using the information given by Excel. The MINITAB output also gives the sample mean $\bar{x} = 1.3433$, as well as the sample standard deviation $s = .1921$ and the quantity $s/\sqrt{n} = .0496$, which is called the **standard error of the estimate** $\bar{x}$ and denoted "SE Mean" on the MINITAB output. Finally, the MINITAB output gives a box plot of the sample of 15 debt-to-equity ratios

FIGURE 8.11   The Excel Output for the Debt-to-Equity Ratio Example

STATISTICS	
Mean	1.343333
Standard Error	0.049595
Median	1.32
Mode	#N/A
Standard Deviation	0.192081
Sample Variance	0.036895
Kurtosis	0.833414
Skewness	0.805013
Range	0.73
Minimum	1.05
Maximum	1.78
Sum	20.15
Count	15
Confidence Level(95.0%)	0.106371

FIGURE 8.12   MINITAB Output of a t-Based 95 Percent Confidence Interval for the Population Mean Debt-to-Equity Ratio

```
Variable   N     Mean    StDev    SE Mean        95% CI
Ratio     15    1.3433   0.1921    0.0496    (1.2370, 1.4497)
```

and graphically illustrates under the box plot the 95 percent confidence interval for the population mean debt-to-equity ratio.

To conclude this section, we note that if the sample size n is small and the sampled population is not mound-shaped or is highly skewed, then the t-based confidence interval for the population mean might not be valid. In this case we can use a **nonparametric method**—a method that makes no assumption about the shape of the sampled population and is valid for any sample size. Nonparametric methods are discussed in Bowerman, O'Connell, and Murphree (2011).

Exercises for Section 8.2

CONCEPTS

8.13 Explain how each of the following changes as *the number of degrees of freedom* describing a *t* curve *increases:*
   a The standard deviation of the *t* curve.   **b** The points t_α and $t_{\alpha/2}$.

8.14 Discuss when it is appropriate to use the *t*-based confidence interval for μ.

METHODS AND APPLICATIONS

8.15 Using Table A.4 (page 640), find $t_{.100}$, $t_{.025}$, and $t_{.001}$ based on 11 degrees of freedom. Also, find these *t* points based on 6 degrees of freedom.

8.16 Suppose that for a sample of $n = 11$ measurements, we find that $\bar{x} = 72$ and $s = 5$. Assuming normality, compute confidence intervals for the population mean μ with the following levels of confidence:
   a 95%   **b** 99%   **c** 80%   **d** 90%   **e** 98%   **f** 99.8%

8.17 The *bad debt ratio* for a financial institution is defined to be the dollar value of loans defaulted divided by the total dollar value of all loans made. Suppose a random sample of seven Ohio banks is selected and that the bad debt ratios (written as percentages) for these banks are 7 percent, 4 percent, 6 percent, 7 percent, 5 percent, 4 percent, and 9 percent. Assuming the bad debt ratios are approximately normally distributed, the MINITAB output of a 95 percent confidence interval for the mean bad debt ratio of all Ohio banks is as follows: ⏴ BadDebt

```
Variable   N      Mean     StDev    SE Mean        95% CI
D-Ratio    7    6.00000   1.82574   0.69007   (4.31147, 7.68853)
```

connect

    a Using the $\bar{x}$ and s on the MINITAB output, verify the calculation of the 95 percent confidence interval, and calculate a 99 percent confidence interval for the mean debt-to-equity ratio.

    b Banking officials claim the mean bad debt ratio for all banks in the Midwest region is 3.5 percent and that the mean bad debt ratio for Ohio banks is higher. Using the 95 percent confidence interval, can we be 95 percent confident that this claim is true? Using the 99 percent confidence interval, can we be 99 percent confident that this claim is true?

8.18 In an article in *Quality Progress*, Blauw and During study how long it takes Dutch companies to complete five stages in the adoption of total quality control (TQC). According to Blauw and During, the adoption of TQC can be divided into five stages as follows: ⊙S TQC

   1   Knowledge: the organization has heard of TQC.
   2   Attitude formation: the organization seeks information and compares advantages and disadvantages.
   3   Decision making: the organization decides to implement TQC.
   4   Implementation: the organization implements TQC.
   5   Confirmation: the organization decides to apply TQC as a normal business activity.

    Suppose a random sample of five Dutch firms that have adopted TQC is selected. Each firm is asked to report how long it took to complete the implementation stage. The firms report the following durations (in years) for this stage: 2.5, 1.5, 1.25, 3.5, and 1.25. Assuming that the durations are approximately normally distributed, calculate a 95 percent confidence interval for the population mean duration of the implementation stage for Dutch firms. Based on the 95 percent confidence interval, is there conclusive evidence that the mean duration of the implementation stage exceeds one year? Explain. What is one possible reason for the lack of conclusive evidence?

8.19 **THE AIR TRAFFIC CONTROL CASE** ⊙S AlertTimes

    Air traffic controllers have the crucial task of ensuring that aircraft don't collide. To do this, they must quickly discern when two planes are about to enter the same air space at the same time. They are aided by video display panels that track the aircraft in their sector and alert the controller when two flight paths are about to converge. The display panel currently in use has a mean "alert time" of 15 seconds. (The alert time is the time elapsing between the instant when two aircraft enter into a collision course and when a controller initiates a call to reroute the planes.) According to Ralph Rudd, a supervisor of air traffic controllers at the Greater Cincinnati International Airport, a new display panel has been developed that uses artificial intelligence to project a plane's current flight path into the future. This new panel provides air traffic controllers with an earlier warning that a collision is likely. It is hoped that the mean "alert time," μ, for the new panel is less than 8 seconds. In order to test the new panel, 15 randomly selected air traffic controllers are trained to use the panel and their alert times for a simulated collision course are recorded. The sample alert times (in seconds) are: 7.2, 7.5, 8.0, 6.8, 7.2, 8.4, 5.3, 7.3, 7.6, 7.1, 9.4, 6.4, 7.9, 6.2, 8.7.

    a Using the fact that $\bar{x} = 7.4$ and $s = 1.026$, find a 95 percent confidence interval for the population mean alert time, μ, for the new panel.

    b Can we be 95 percent confident that μ is less than 8 seconds?

8.20 Whole Foods is an all-natural grocery chain that has 50,000 square foot stores, up from the industry average of 34,000 square feet. Sales per square foot of supermarkets average just under $400 per square foot, as reported by *USA Today* in an article on "A whole new ballgame in grocery shopping." Suppose that sales per square foot in the most recent fiscal year are recorded for a random sample of 10 Whole Foods supermarkets. The data (sales dollars per square foot) are as follows: 854, 858, 801, 892, 849, 807, 894, 863, 829, 815. Using the fact that $\bar{x} = 846.2$ and $s = 32.866$, find a 95 percent confidence interval for the population mean sales dollars per square foot for all Whole Foods supermarkets during the most recent fiscal year. Are we 95 percent confident that this mean is greater than $800, the historical average for Whole Foods? ⊙S WholeFoods

8.21 A production supervisor at a major chemical company wishes to determine whether a new catalyst, catalyst XA-100, increases the mean hourly yield of a chemical process beyond the current mean hourly yield, which is known to be roughly equal to, but no more than, 750 pounds per hour. To test the new catalyst, five trial runs using catalyst XA-100 are made. The resulting yields for the trial runs (in pounds per hour) are 801, 814, 784, 836, and 820. Assuming that all factors affecting yields of the process have been held as constant as possible during the test runs, it is reasonable to regard the five yields obtained using the new catalyst as a random sample from the population of all possible yields that would be obtained by using the new catalyst. Furthermore, we will assume that this population is approximately normally distributed. ⊙S ChemYield

    a Using the Excel output in Figure 8.13, find a 95 percent confidence interval for the mean of all possible yields obtained using catalyst XA-100.

    b Based on the confidence interval, can we be 95 percent confident that the mean yield using catalyst XA-100 exceeds 750 pounds per hour? Explain.

FIGURE 8.13   **Excel Output for Exercise 8.21**

STATISTICS	
Mean	811
Standard Error	8.786353
Median	814
Mode	#N/A
Standard Deviation	19.64688
Sample Variance	386
Kurtosis	−0.12472
Skewness	−0.23636
Range	52
Minimum	784
Maximum	836
Sum	4055
Count	5
Confidence Level(95.0%)	24.39488

FIGURE 8.14   **Excel Output for Exercise 8.22**

STATISTICS	
Mean	50.575
Standard Error	0.2599
Median	50.65
Mode	50.9
Standard Deviation	1.643753
Sample Variance	2.701923
Kurtosis	−0.2151
Skewness	−0.05493
Range	7.2
Minimum	46.8
Maximum	54
Sum	2023
Count	40
Confidence Level(95.0%)	0.525697

8.22 THE TRASH BAG CASE   📀 TrashBag

The mean and the standard deviation of the sample of 40 trash bag breaking strengths in Table 1.9 are $\bar{x} = 50.575$ and $s = 1.6438$. Calculate a t-based 95 percent confidence interval for μ, the mean of the breaking strengths of all possible trash bags of the new type. Also, find this interval using the Excel output in Figure 8.14. Are we 95 percent confident that μ is at least 50 pounds?

8.23 THE BANK CUSTOMER WAITING TIME CASE   📀 WaitTime

The mean and the standard deviation of the sample of 100 bank customer waiting times in Table 1.8 are $\bar{x} = 5.46$ and $s = 2.475$. Calculate a t-based 95 percent confidence interval for μ, the mean of all possible bank customer waiting times using the new system. Are we 95 percent confident that μ is less than six minutes?

8.24 THE VIDEO GAME SATISFACTION RATING CASE   📀 VideoGame

The mean and the standard deviation of the sample of $n = 65$ customer satisfaction ratings in Table 1.7 are $\bar{x} = 42.95$ and $s = 2.6424$. Calculate a t-based 95 percent confidence interval for μ, the mean of all possible customer satisfaction ratings for the XYZ Box video game system. Are we 95 percent confident that μ is at least 42, the minimal rating given by a very satisfied customer?

8.3 Sample Size Determination ● ● ●

LO4 Determine the appropriate sample size when estimating a population mean.

In Section 8.1 we used a sample of 50 mileages to construct a 95 percent confidence interval for the midsize model's mean mileage μ. The size of this sample was not arbitrary—it was planned. To understand this, suppose that before the automaker selected the random sample of 50 mileages, it randomly selected the following sample of five mileages:

$$30.7 \quad 31.9 \quad 30.3 \quad 32.0 \quad 31.6$$

This sample has mean $\bar{x} = 31.3$. Assuming that the population of all mileages is normally distributed and that the population standard deviation σ is known to equal .8, it follows that a 95 percent confidence interval for μ is

$$\left[\bar{x} \pm z_{.025} \frac{\sigma}{\sqrt{n}} \right] = \left[31.3 \pm 1.96 \frac{.8}{\sqrt{5}} \right]$$
$$= [31.3 \pm .701]$$
$$= [30.6, 32.0]$$

Although the sample mean $\bar{x} = 31.3$ is at least 31, the lower limit of the 95 percent confidence interval for μ is less than 31. Therefore, the midsize model's EPA mileage estimate would be 30 mpg, and the automaker would not receive its tax credit. One reason that the lower limit of this 95 percent interval is less than 31 is that the sample size of 5 is not large enough to make the interval's margin of error

$$z_{.025}\frac{\sigma}{\sqrt{n}} = 1.96\frac{.8}{\sqrt{5}} = .701$$

small enough. We can attempt to make the margin of error in the interval smaller by increasing the sample size. If we feel that the mean $\bar{x}$ of the larger sample will be at least 31.3 mpg (the mean of the small sample we have already taken), then the lower limit of a $100(1-\alpha)$ percent confidence interval for μ will be at least 31 if the margin of error is .3 or less.

We will now explain how to find the size of the sample that will be needed to make the margin of error in a confidence interval for μ as small as we wish. In order to develop a formula for the needed sample size, we will initially assume that we know σ. Then, if the population is normally distributed or the sample size is large, the z-based $100(1-\alpha)$ percent confidence interval for μ is

$$\left[\bar{x} \pm z_{\alpha/2}\frac{\sigma}{\sqrt{n}}\right]$$

To find the needed sample size, we set $z_{\alpha/2}(\sigma/\sqrt{n})$ equal to the desired margin of error and solve for n. Letting E denote the desired margin of error, we obtain

$$z_{\alpha/2}\frac{\sigma}{\sqrt{n}} = E$$

Multiplying both sides of this equation by $\sqrt{n}$ and dividing both sides by E, we obtain

$$\sqrt{n} = \frac{z_{\alpha/2}\sigma}{E}$$

Squaring both sides of this result gives us the formula for n.

Determining the Sample Size for a Confidence Interval for μ: σ Known

A sample of size

$$n = \left(\frac{z_{\alpha/2}\sigma}{E}\right)^2$$

makes the margin of error in a $100(1-\alpha)$ percent confidence interval for μ equal to E. That is, this sample size makes us $100(1-\alpha)$ percent confident that $\bar{x}$ is within E units of μ. If the calculated value of n is not a whole number, round this value up to the next whole number (so that the margin of error is at least as small as desired).

If we consider the formula for the sample size n, it intuitively follows that the value E is the farthest that the user is willing to allow $\bar{x}$ to be from μ at a given level of confidence, and the normal point $z_{\alpha/2}$ follows directly from the given level of confidence. Furthermore, because the population standard deviation σ is in the numerator of the formula for n, it follows that the more variable that the individual population measurements are, the larger is the sample size needed to estimate μ with a specified accuracy.

In order to use this formula for n, we must either know σ (which is unlikely) or we must compute an estimate of σ. We first consider the case where we know σ. For example, suppose in the car mileage situation we wish to find the sample size that is needed to make the margin of error in a 95 percent confidence interval for μ equal to .3. Assuming that σ is known to equal .8, and using $z_{.025} = 1.96$, the appropriate sample size is

$$n = \left(\frac{z_{.025}\,\sigma}{E}\right)^2 = \left(\frac{1.96(.8)}{.3}\right)^2 = 27.32$$

Rounding up, we would employ a sample of size 28.

In most real situations, of course, we do not know the true value of σ. If σ is not known, we often estimate σ by using a preliminary sample. In this case we modify the above formula for n by replacing σ by the standard deviation s of the preliminary sample and by replacing $z_{\alpha/2}$ by $t_{\alpha/2}$. Thus we obtain

$$n = \left(\frac{t_{\alpha/2}\,s}{E}\right)^2$$

where the number of degrees of freedom for the $t_{\alpha/2}$ point is the size of the preliminary sample minus 1. Intuitively, using $t_{\alpha/2}$ compensates for the fact that the preliminary sample's value of s might underestimate σ, and, therefore, give a sample size that is too small.

EXAMPLE 8.4 The Car Mileage Case

Suppose that in the car mileage situation we wish to find the sample size that is needed to make the margin of error in a 95 percent confidence interval for μ equal to .3. Assuming we do not know σ, we regard the previously discussed sample of five mileages (see page 321) as a preliminary sample. Therefore, we replace σ by the standard deviation of the preliminary sample, which can be calculated to be $s = .7583$, and we replace $z_{\alpha/2} = z_{.025} = 1.96$ by $t_{.025} = 2.776$, which is based on $n - 1 = 4$ degrees of freedom. We find that the appropriate sample size is

$$n = \left(\frac{t_{.025}\,s}{E}\right)^2 = \left(\frac{2.776(.7583)}{.3}\right)^2 = 49.24$$

Rounding up, we employ a sample of size 50.

When we make the margin of error in our 95 percent confidence interval for μ equal to .3, we can say we are 95 percent confident that the sample mean $\bar{x}$ is within .3 of μ. To understand this, suppose the true value of μ is 31.6. Recalling that the mean of the sample of 50 mileages is $\bar{x} = 31.56$, we see that this sample mean is within .3 of μ. Other samples of 50 mileages would give different sample means that would be different distances from μ. When we say that our sample of 50 mileages makes us 95 percent confident that $\bar{x}$ is within .3 of μ, we mean that **95 percent of all possible sample means based on 50 mileages are within .3 of μ** and 5 percent of such sample means are not. Therefore, when we randomly select one sample of size 50 and compute its sample mean $\bar{x} = 31.56$, we can be 95 percent confident that this sample mean is within .3 of μ.

In general, the purpose behind replacing $z_{\alpha/2}$ by $t_{\alpha/2}$ (when we are using a preliminary sample to obtain an estimate of σ) is to be **conservative,** so that we compute a sample size that is **at least as large as needed.** Because of this, as we illustrate in the next example, we often obtain a margin of error that is even smaller than we have requested.

EXAMPLE 8.5 The Car Mileage Case

To see that the sample of 50 mileages has actually produced a 95 percent confidence interval with a margin of error that is as small as we requested, recall that the 50 mileages have mean $\bar{x} = 31.56$ and standard deviation $s = .7977$. Therefore, the t-based 95 percent confidence interval for μ is

$$\left[\bar{x} \pm t_{.025}\frac{s}{\sqrt{n}}\right] = \left[31.56 \pm 2.010\frac{.7977}{\sqrt{50}}\right]$$

$$= [31.56 \pm .227]$$

$$= [31.33, 31.79]$$

where $t_{.025} = 2.010$ is based on $n - 1 = 50 - 1 = 49$ degrees of freedom—see Table A.4 (page 640). We see that the margin of error in this interval is .227, which is smaller than the .3 we asked for. Furthermore, as the automaker had hoped, the sample mean $\bar{x} = 31.56$ of the sample of 50 mileages turned out to be at least 31.3. Therefore, since the margin of error is less than .3, the lower limit of the 95 percent confidence interval is higher than 31 mpg, and the midsize model's EPA mileage estimate is 31 mpg. Because of this, the automaker will receive its tax credit.

Finally, sometimes we do not know σ and we do not have a preliminary sample that can be used to estimate σ. In this case it can be shown that, if we can make a reasonable guess of the range of the population being studied, then a conservatively large estimate of σ is this estimated range divided by 4. For example, if the automaker's design engineers feel that almost all of its midsize cars should get mileages within a range of 5 mpg, then a conservatively large estimate of σ is $5/4 = 1.25$ mpg. When employing such an estimate of σ, it is sufficient to use the z-based sample size formula $n = (z_{\alpha/2}\sigma/E)^2$, because a conservatively large estimate of σ will give us a conservatively large sample size.

Exercises for Section 8.3

CONCEPTS

connect™

8.25 Explain what is meant by the margin of error for a confidence interval. What error are we talking about in the context of an interval for μ?

8.26 Explain exactly what we mean when we say that a sample of size n makes us 99 percent confident that $\bar{x}$ is within E units of μ.

8.27 Why do we often need to take a preliminary sample when determining the size of the sample needed to make the margin of error of a confidence interval equal to E?

METHODS AND APPLICATIONS

8.28 Consider a population having a standard deviation equal to 10. We wish to estimate the mean of this population.
  a How large a random sample is needed to construct a 95 percent confidence interval for the mean of this population with a margin of error equal to 1?
  b Suppose that we now take a random sample of the size we have determined in part a. If we obtain a sample mean equal to 295, calculate the 95 percent confidence interval for the population mean. What is the interval's margin of error?

8.29 Referring to Exercise 8.11a (page 313), assume that σ equals 33. How large a random sample of public owner-controlled companies is needed to make us
  a 95 percent confident that $\bar{x}$, the sample mean audit delay, is within a margin of error of four days of μ, the population mean audit delay?
  b 99 percent confident that $\bar{x}$ is within a margin of error of four days of μ?

8.30 Referring to Exercise 8.12b, assume that σ equals .66. How large a sample of late replacement buyers is needed to make us
  a 99 percent confident that $\bar{x}$, the sample mean number of dealers visited, is within a margin of error of .04 of μ, the population mean number of dealers visited?
  b 99.73 percent confident that $\bar{x}$ is within a margin of error of .05 of μ?

8.31 Referring to Exercise 8.21 (page 320), regard the sample of five trial runs for which $s = 19.65$ as a preliminary sample. Determine the number of trial runs of the chemical process needed to make us
  a 95 percent confident that $\bar{x}$, the sample mean hourly yield, is within a margin of error of eight pounds of the population mean hourly yield μ when catalyst XA-100 is used.
  b 99 percent confident that $\bar{x}$ is within a margin of error of five pounds of μ. **DS** ChemYield

8.32 Referring to Exercise 8.20, regard the sample of 10 sales figures for which $s = 32.866$ as a preliminary sample. How large a sample of sales figures is needed to make us 95 percent confident that $\bar{x}$, the sample mean sales dollars per square foot, is within a margin of error of $10 of μ, the population mean sales dollars per square foot for all Whole Foods supermarkets. **DS** WholeFoods

8.33 **THE AIR TRAFFIC CONTROL CASE** **DS** AlertTimes

Referring to Exercise 8.19, regard the sample of 15 alert times for which $s = 1.026$ as a preliminary sample. Determine the sample size needed to make us 95 percent confident that $\bar{x}$, the sample mean alert time, is within a margin of error of .3 second of μ, the population mean alert time using the new display panel.

8.4 Confidence Intervals for a Population Proportion ● ● ●

LO5 Calculate and interpret a large sample confidence interval for a population proportion.

In Chapter 7, the soft cheese spread producer decided to replace its current spout with the new spout if p, the true proportion of all current purchasers who would stop buying the cheese spread if the new spout were used, is less than .10. Suppose that when 1,000 current purchasers are randomly selected and are asked to try the new spout, 63 say they would stop buying the spread if the new spout were used. The point estimate of the population proportion p is the sample proportion $\hat{p} = 63/1{,}000 = .063$. This sample proportion says we estimate that 6.3 percent of all current purchasers would stop buying the cheese spread if the new spout were used. Since $\hat{p}$ equals .063, we have some evidence that p is less than .10.

In order to see if there is strong evidence that p is less than .10, we can calculate a confidence interval for p. As explained in Chapter 7, if the sample size n is large, then the sampling distribution of the sample proportion $\hat{p}$ is approximately a normal distribution with mean $\mu_{\hat{p}} = p$ and standard deviation $\sigma_{\hat{p}} = \sqrt{p(1-p)/n}$. By using the same logic we used in developing confidence intervals for μ, it follows that a $100(1-\alpha)$ percent confidence interval for p is

$$\left[\hat{p} \pm z_{a/2}\sqrt{\frac{p(1-p)}{n}}\right]$$

Estimating $p(1-p)$ by $\hat{p}(1-\hat{p})$, it follows that a $100(1-\alpha)$ percent confidence interval for p can be calculated as summarized below.

A Large Sample Confidence Interval for a Population Proportion p

If the sample size n is large, a $100(1-\alpha)$ percent confidence interval for the population proportion p is

$$\left[\hat{p} \pm z_{\alpha/2}\sqrt{\frac{\hat{p}(1-\hat{p})}{n}}\right]$$

Here n should be considered large if both $n\hat{p}$ and $n(1-\hat{p})$ are at least 5.[2]

EXAMPLE 8.6 The Cheese Spread Case   C

Suppose that the cheese spread producer wishes to calculate a 99 percent confidence interval for p, the population proportion of purchasers who would stop buying the cheese spread if the new spout were used. To determine whether the sample size $n = 1{,}000$ is large enough to enable us to use the confidence interval formula just given, recall that the point estimate of p is $\hat{p} = 63/1{,}000 = .063$. Therefore, because $n\hat{p} = 1{,}000(.063) = 63$ and $n(1-\hat{p}) = 1{,}000(.937) = 937$ are both greater than 5, we can use the confidence interval formula. It follows that the 99 percent confidence interval for p is

$$\left[\hat{p} \pm z_{.005}\sqrt{\frac{\hat{p}(1-\hat{p})}{n}}\right] = \left[.063 \pm 2.575\sqrt{\frac{(.063)(.937)}{1000}}\right]$$

$$= [.063 \pm .0198]$$

$$= [.0432, .0828]$$

This interval says that we are 99 percent confident that between 4.32 percent and 8.28 percent of all current purchasers would stop buying the cheese spread if the new spout were used. Moreover, because the upper limit of the 99 percent confidence interval is less than .10, we have very strong evidence that the true proportion p of all current purchasers who would stop buying the cheese spread is less than .10. Based on this result, it seems reasonable to use the new spout.

BI

---

[2]Some statisticians suggest using the more conservative rule that both $n\hat{p}$ and $n(1-\hat{p})$ must be at least 10. Furthermore, because $\hat{p}(1-\hat{p})/(n-1)$ is an unbiased point estimate of $p(1-p)/n$, a more correct $100(1-\alpha)$ percent confidence interval for p is $[\hat{p} \pm z_{\alpha/2}\sqrt{\hat{p}(1-\hat{p})/(n-1)}]$. However, because n is large, there is little difference between intervals obtained by using this formula and those obtained by using the formula in the above box.

In order to compare the 99 percent confidence interval for p with a 95 percent confidence interval, we compute the 95 percent confidence interval as follows:

$$\left[\hat{p} \pm z_{.025} \sqrt{\frac{\hat{p}(1 - \hat{p})}{n}} \right] = \left[.063 \pm 1.96 \sqrt{\frac{(.063)(.937)}{1000}} \right]$$

$$= [.063 \pm .0151]$$

$$= [.0479, .0781]$$

Although the 99 percent confidence interval is somewhat longer than the 95 percent confidence interval, the fairly large sample size of $n = 1,000$ produces intervals that differ only slightly.

In the cheese spread example, a sample of 1,000 purchasers gives us a 99 percent confidence interval for p that has a margin of error of .0198 and a 95 percent confidence interval for p that has a margin of error of .0151. Both of these margins of errors are reasonably small. Generally, however, quite a large sample is needed in order to make the margin of error in a confidence interval for p reasonably small. The next two examples demonstrate that a sample size of 200, which most people would consider quite large, does not necessarily give a 95 percent confidence interval for p with a small margin of error.

EXAMPLE 8.7

Antibiotics occasionally cause nausea as a side effect. Scientists working for a major drug company have developed a new antibiotic called Phe-Mycin. The company wishes to estimate p, the proportion of all patients who would experience nausea as a side effect when being treated with Phe-Mycin. Suppose that a sample of 200 patients is randomly selected. When these patients are treated with Phe-Mycin, 35 patients experience nausea. The point estimate of the population proportion p is the sample proportion $\hat{p} = 35/200 = .175$. This sample proportion says that we estimate that 17.5 percent of all patients would experience nausea as a side effect of taking Phe-Mycin. Furthermore, because $n\hat{p} = 200(.175) = 35$ and $n(1 - \hat{p}) = 200(.825) = 165$ are both at least 5, we can use the previously given formula to calculate a confidence interval for p. Doing this, we find that a 95 percent confidence interval for p is

$$\left[\hat{p} \pm z_{.025} \sqrt{\frac{\hat{p}(1 - \hat{p})}{n}} \right] = \left[.175 \pm 1.96 \sqrt{\frac{(.175)(.825)}{200}} \right]$$

$$= [.175 \pm .053]$$

$$= [.122, .228]$$

This interval says we are 95 percent confident that between 12.2 percent and 22.8 percent of all patients would experience nausea as a side effect of taking Phe-Mycin. Notice that the margin of error (.053) in this interval is rather large. Therefore, this interval is fairly long, and it does not provide a very precise estimate of p.

EXAMPLE 8.8 The Marketing Ethics Case: Estimating Marketing Researchers' Disapproval Rates

In the book *Essentials of Marketing Research,* William R. Dillon, Thomas J. Madden, and Neil H. Firtle discuss a survey of marketing professionals, the results of which were originally published by Ishmael P. Akoah and Edward A. Riordan in the *Journal of Marketing Research.* In the study, randomly selected marketing researchers were presented with various scenarios involving ethical issues such as confidentiality, conflict of interest, and social acceptability. The marketing researchers were asked to indicate whether they approved or disapproved of the actions described in each scenario. For instance, one scenario that involved the issue of confidentiality was described as follows:

Use of ultraviolet ink   A project director went to the marketing research director's office and requested permission to use an ultraviolet ink to precode a questionnaire for a mail survey. The project director pointed out that although the cover letter promised confidentiality, respondent identification was needed to permit adequate cross-tabulations of the data. The marketing research director gave approval.

Of the 205 marketing researchers who participated in the survey, 117 said they disapproved of the actions taken in the scenario. It follows that a point estimate of p, the proportion of all marketing researchers who disapprove of the actions taken in the scenario, is $\hat{p} = 117/205 = .5707$. Furthermore, because $n\hat{p} = 205(.5707) = 117$ and $n(1 - \hat{p}) = 205(.4293) = 88$ are both at least 5, a 95 percent confidence interval for p is

$$\left[\hat{p} \pm z_{.025}\sqrt{\frac{\hat{p}(1 - \hat{p})}{n}}\right] = \left[.5707 \pm 1.96\sqrt{\frac{(.5707)(.4293)}{205}}\right]$$

$$= [.5707 \pm .0678]$$

$$= [.5029, .6385]$$

This interval says we are 95 percent confident that between 50.29 percent and 63.85 percent of all marketing researchers disapprove of the actions taken in the ultraviolet ink scenario. Notice that since the margin of error (.0678) in this interval is rather large, this interval does not provide a very precise estimate of p. Below we show the MINITAB output of this interval.

```
CI for One Proportion
    X      N    Sample p              95% CI
   117    205   0.570732    (0.502975, 0.638488)
```

In order to find the size of the sample needed to estimate a population proportion, we consider the theoretically correct interval

LO6 Determine the appropriate sample size when estimating a population proportion.

$$\left[\hat{p} \pm z_{\alpha/2}\sqrt{\frac{p(1 - p)}{n}}\right]$$

To obtain the sample size needed to make the margin of error in this interval equal to E, we set

$$z_{\alpha/2}\sqrt{\frac{p(1 - p)}{n}} = E$$

and solve for n. When we do this, we get the following result:

Determining the Sample Size for a Confidence Interval for p

A sample of size

$$n = p(1 - p)\left(\frac{z_{\alpha/2}}{E}\right)^2$$

makes the margin of error in a $100(1 - \alpha)$ percent confidence interval for p equal to E. That is, this sample size makes us $100(1 - \alpha)$ percent confident that $\hat{p}$ is within E units of p. If the calculated value of n is not a whole number, round this value up to the next whole number.

Looking at this formula, we see that the larger $p(1 - p)$ is, the larger n will be. To make sure n is large enough, consider Figure 8.15 on the next page, which is a graph of $p(1 - p)$ versus p. This figure shows that $p(1 - p)$ equals .25 when p equals .5. Furthermore, $p(1 - p)$ is never larger than .25. Therefore, if the true value of p could be near .5, we should set $p(1 - p)$ equal to .25. This will ensure that n is as large as needed to make the margin of error as small as desired. For

FIGURE 8.15   The Graph of $p(1 - p)$ versus p

example, suppose we wish to estimate the proportion p of all registered voters who currently favor a particular candidate for president of the United States. If this candidate is the nominee of a major political party, or if the candidate enjoys broad popularity for some other reason, then p could be near .5. Furthermore, suppose we wish to make the margin of error in a 95 percent confidence interval for p equal to .02. If the sample to be taken is random, it should consist of

$$n = p(1 - p)\left(\frac{z_{\alpha/2}}{E}\right)^2 = .25\left(\frac{1.96}{.02}\right)^2 = 2{,}401$$

registered voters. In reality, a list of all registered voters in the United States is not available to polling organizations. Therefore, it is not feasible to take a (technically correct) random sample of registered voters. For this reason, polling organizations actually employ other (more complicated) kinds of samples. We have explained some of the basic ideas behind these more complex samples in optional Section 7.4. For now, we consider the samples taken by polling organizations to be approximately random. Suppose, then, that when the sample of voters is actually taken, the proportion $\hat{p}$ of sampled voters who favor the candidate turns out to be greater than .52. It follows, because the sample is large enough to make the margin of error in a 95 percent confidence interval for p equal to .02, that the lower limit of such an interval is greater than .50. This says we have strong evidence that a majority of all registered voters favor the candidate. For instance, if the sample proportion $\hat{p}$ equals .53, we are 95 percent confident that the proportion of all registered voters who favor the candidate is between .51 and .55.

Major polling organizations conduct public opinion polls concerning many kinds of issues. Whereas making the margin of error in a 95 percent confidence interval for p equal to .02 requires a sample size of 2,401, making the margin of error in such an interval equal to .03 requires a sample size of only

$$n = p(1 - p)\left(\frac{z_{\alpha/2}}{E}\right)^2 = .25\left(\frac{1.96}{.03}\right)^2 = 1{,}067.1$$

or 1,068 (rounding up). Of course, these calculations assume that the proportion p being estimated could be near .5. However, for any value of p, increasing the margin of error from .02 to .03 substantially decreases the needed sample size and thus saves considerable time and money. For this reason, although the most accurate public opinion polls use a margin of error of .02, the vast majority of public opinion polls use a margin of error of .03 or larger.

When the news media report the results of a public opinion poll, they express the margin of error in a 95 percent confidence interval for p *in percentage points*. For instance, if the margin of error is .03, the media would say the poll's margin of error is 3 percentage points. The media seldom report the level of confidence, but almost all polling results are based on 95 percent confidence. Sometimes the media make a vague reference to the level of confidence. For instance, if the margin of error is 3 percentage points, the media might say that "the sample result will be within 3 percentage points of the population value in 19 out of 20 samples." Here

FIGURE 8.16　As p Gets Closer to .5, $p(1 - p)$ Increases

the "19 out of 20 samples" is a reference to the level of confidence, which is $100(19/20) = 100(.95) = 95$ percent.

As an example, suppose a news report says a recent poll finds that 34 percent of the public favors military intervention in an international crisis, and suppose the poll's margin of error is reported to be 3 percentage points. This means the sample taken is large enough to make us 95 percent confident that the sample proportion $\hat{p} = .34$ is within .03 (that is, 3 percentage points) of the true proportion p of the entire public that favors military intervention. That is, we are 95 percent confident that p is between .31 and .37.

If the population proportion we are estimating is substantially different from .5, setting p equal to .5 will give a sample size that is much larger than is needed. In this case, we should use our intuition or previous sample information (along with Figure 8.16) to determine the largest reasonable value for $p(1 - p)$. Figure 8.16 implies that as p gets closer to .5, $p(1 - p)$ increases. It follows that $p(1 - p)$ is maximized by the reasonable value of p that is closest to .5. Therefore, **when we are estimating a proportion that is substantially different from .5, we use the reasonable value of p that is closest to .5 to calculate the sample size needed to obtain a specified margin of error.**

EXAMPLE 8.9

Again consider estimating the proportion of all patients who would experience nausea as a side effect of taking the new antibiotic Phe-Mycin. Suppose the drug company wishes to find the size of the random sample that is needed in order to obtain a 2 percent margin of error with 95 percent confidence. In Example 8.7 we employed a sample of 200 patients to compute a 95 percent confidence interval for p. This interval, which is $[.122, .228]$, makes us very confident that p is between .122 and .228. Because .228 is the reasonable value of p that is closest to .5, the largest reasonable value of $p(1 - p)$ is $.228(1 - .228) = .1760$, and thus the drug company should take a sample of

$$n = p(1 - p)\left(\frac{z_{\alpha/2}}{E}\right)^2 = .1760\left(\frac{1.96}{.02}\right)^2 = 1{,}691 \text{ (rounded up)}$$

patients.

Finally, as a last example of choosing p for sample size calculations, suppose that experience indicates that a population proportion p is at least .75. Then, .75 is the reasonable value of p that is closest to .5, and we would use the largest reasonable value of $p(1 - p)$, which is $.75(1 - .75) = .1875$.

Exercises for Section 8.4

CONCEPTS

8.34 **a** What does a population proportion tell us about the population?
b Explain the difference between p and $\hat{p}$.
c What is meant when a public opinion poll's *margin of error* is 3 percent?

8.35 Suppose we are using the sample size formula in the box on page 327 to find the sample size needed to make the margin of error in a confidence interval for p equal to E. In each of the following situations, explain what value of p would be used in the formula for finding n:
a We have no idea what value p is—it could be any value between 0 and 1.
b Past experience tells us that p is no more than .3.
c Past experience tells us that p is at least .8.

METHODS AND APPLICATIONS

8.36 In each of the following cases, determine whether the sample size n is large enough to use the large sample formula presented in the box on page 325 to compute a confidence interval for p.
a $\hat{p} = .1$, $n = 30$ **d** $\hat{p} = .8$, $n = 400$
b $\hat{p} = .1$, $n = 100$ **e** $\hat{p} = .9$, $n = 30$
c $\hat{p} = .5$, $n = 50$ **f** $\hat{p} = .99$, $n = 200$

8.37 In each of the following cases, compute 95 percent, 98 percent, and 99 percent confidence intervals for the population proportion p.
a $\hat{p} = .4$ and $n = 100$ **c** $\hat{p} = .9$ and $n = 100$
b $\hat{p} = .1$ and $n = 300$ **d** $\hat{p} = .6$ and $n = 50$

8.38 *Quality Progress,* February 2005, reports on the results achieved by Bank of America in improving customer satisfaction and customer loyalty by listening to the 'voice of the customer.' A key measure of customer satisfaction is the response on a scale from 1 to 10 to the question: "Considering all the business you do with Bank of America, what is your overall satisfaction with Bank of America?"[3] Suppose that a random sample of 350 current customers results in 195 customers with a response of 9 or 10 representing "customer delight." Find a 95 percent confidence interval for the true proportion of all current Bank of America customers who would respond with a 9 or 10. Are we 95 percent confident that this proportion exceeds .48, the historical proportion of customer delight for Bank of America?

8.39 **THE MARKETING ETHICS CASE: CONFLICT OF INTEREST**

Consider the marketing ethics case described in Example 8.8. One of the scenarios presented to the 205 marketing researchers is as follows:

> A marketing testing firm to which X company gives most of its business recently went public. The marketing research director of X company had been looking for a good investment and proceeded to buy some $20,000 of their stock. The firm continues as X company's leading supplier for testing.

Of the 205 marketing researchers who participated in the ethics survey, 111 said that they disapproved of the actions taken in the scenario. Use this sample result to show that the 95 percent confidence interval for the proportion of all marketing researchers who disapprove of the actions taken in the conflict of interest scenario is as given in the MINITAB output below. Interpret this interval.

CI for One Proportion

```
   X     N      Sample p           95% CI
 111    205     0.541463    (0.473254, 0.609673)
```

b On the basis of this interval, is there convincing evidence that a majority of all marketing researchers disapprove of the actions taken in the conflict of interest scenario? Explain.

8.40 In a news story distributed by the *Washington Post,* Lew Sichelman reports that a substantial fraction of mortgage loans that go into default within the first year of the mortgage were approved on the basis of falsified applications. For instance, loan applicants often exaggerate their income or fail to declare debts. Suppose that a random sample of 1,000 mortgage loans that were defaulted within the first year reveals that 410 of these loans were approved on the basis of falsified applications.
a Find a point estimate of and a 95 percent confidence interval for p, the proportion of all first-year defaults that are approved on the basis of falsified applications.

---

[3]Source: "Driving Organic Growth at Bank of America," *Quality Progress* (February 2005), pp. 23–27.

b Based on your interval, what is a reasonable estimate of the minimum percentage of all first-year defaults that are approved on the basis of falsified applications?

8.41 On January 7, 2000, the Gallup Organization released the results of a poll comparing the lifestyles of today with yesteryear. The survey results were based on telephone interviews with a randomly selected national sample of 1,031 adults, 18 years and older, conducted December 20–21, 1999.[4]

a The Gallup poll found that 42 percent of the respondents said that they spend less than three hours watching TV on an average weekday. Based on this finding, calculate a 99 percent confidence interval for the proportion of all U.S. adults who say that they spend less than three hours watching TV on an average weekday. Based on this interval, is it reasonable to conclude that more than 40 percent of all U.S. adults say they spend less than three hours watching TV on an average weekday?

b The Gallup poll found that 60 percent of the respondents said they took part in some form of daily activity (outside of work, including housework) to keep physically fit. Based on this finding, find a 95 percent confidence interval for the proportion of all U.S. adults who say they take part in some form of daily activity to keep physically fit. Based on this interval, is it reasonable to conclude that more than 50 percent of all U.S. adults say they take part in some form of daily activity to keep physically fit?

c In explaining its survey methods, Gallup states the following: "For results based on this sample, one can say with 95 percent confidence that the maximum error attributable to sampling and other random effects is plus or minus 3 percentage points." Explain how your calculations for part *b* verify that this statement is true.

8.42 In an article in the *Journal of Advertising,* Weinberger and Spotts compare the use of humor in television ads in the United States and the United Kingdom. They found that a substantially greater percentage of U.K. ads use humor.

a Suppose that a random sample of 400 television ads in the United Kingdom reveals that 142 of these ads use humor. Find a point estimate of and a 95 percent confidence interval for the proportion of all U.K. television ads that use humor.

b Suppose a random sample of 500 television ads in the United States reveals that 122 of these ads use humor. Find a point estimate of and a 95 percent confidence interval for the proportion of all U.S. television ads that use humor.

c Do the confidence intervals you computed in parts *a* and *b* suggest that a greater percentage of U.K. ads use humor? Explain. How might an ad agency use this information?

8.43 In an article in *CA Magazine,* Neil Fitzgerald surveyed Scottish business customers concerning their satisfaction with aspects of their banking relationships. Fitzgerald reports that, in 418 telephone interviews conducted by George Street Research, 67 percent of the respondents gave their banks a high rating for overall satisfaction.

a Assuming that the sample is randomly selected, calculate a 99 percent confidence interval for the proportion of all Scottish business customers who give their banks a high rating for overall satisfaction.

b Based on this interval, can we be 99 percent confident that more than 60 percent of all Scottish business customers give their banks a high rating for overall satisfaction?

8.44 In the March 16, 1998, issue of *Fortune* magazine, the results of a survey of 2,221 MBA students from across the United States conducted by the Stockholm-based academic consulting firm Universum showed that only 20 percent of MBA students expect to stay at their first job five years or more.[5] Assuming that a random sample was employed, find a 95 percent confidence interval for the proportion of all U.S. MBA students who expect to stay at their first job five years or more. Based on this interval, is there strong evidence that fewer than one-fourth of all U.S. MBA students expect to stay?

8.45 *Consumer Reports* (January 2005) indicates that profit margins on extended warranties are much greater than on the purchase of most products.[6] In this exercise we consider a major electronics retailer that wishes to increase the proportion of customers who buy extended warranties on digital cameras. Historically, 20 percent of digital camera customers have purchased the retailer's extended warranty. To increase this percentage, the retailer has decided to offer a new warranty that is less expensive and more comprehensive. Suppose

[4]Source: The Gallup Organization, www.gallup.com/poll/releases/, January 7, 2000.

[5]Source: Shelly Branch, "MBAs: What Do They Really Want," *Fortune,* March 16, 1998, p. 167.

[6]*Consumer Reports,* January 2005, page 51.

that three months after starting to offer the new warranty, a random sample of 500 customer sales invoices shows that 152 out of 500 digital camera customers purchased the new warranty. Find a 95 percent confidence interval for the proportion of all digital camera customers who have purchased the new warranty. Are we 95 percent confident that this proportion exceeds .20?

8.46 The manufacturer of the ColorSmart-5000 television set claims 95 percent of its sets last at least five years without needing a single repair. In order to test this claim, a consumer group randomly selects 400 consumers who have owned a ColorSmart-5000 television set for five years. Of these 400 consumers, 316 say their ColorSmart-5000 television sets did not need a repair, whereas 84 say their ColorSmart-5000 television sets did need at least one repair.

    a Find a 99 percent confidence interval for the proportion of all ColorSmart-5000 television sets that have lasted at least five years without needing a single repair.

    b Does this confidence interval provide strong evidence that the percentage of all ColorSmart-5000 television sets that last at least five years without a single repair is less than the 95 percent claimed by the manufacturer? Explain.

8.47 In the book *Cases in Finance,* Nunnally and Plath present a case in which the estimated percentage of uncollectible accounts varies with the age of the account. Here the age of an unpaid account is the number of days elapsed since the invoice date.

    Suppose an accountant believes the percentage of accounts that will be uncollectible increases as the ages of the accounts increase. To test this theory, the accountant randomly selects 500 accounts with ages between 31 and 60 days from the accounts receivable ledger dated one year ago. The accountant also randomly selects 500 accounts with ages between 61 and 90 days from the accounts receivable ledger dated one year ago.

    a If 10 of the 500 accounts with ages between 31 and 60 days were eventually classified as uncollectible, find a point estimate of and a 95 percent confidence interval for the proportion of all accounts with ages between 31 and 60 days that will be uncollectible.

    b If 27 of the 500 accounts with ages between 61 and 90 days were eventually classified as uncollectible, find a point estimate of and a 95 percent confidence interval for the proportion of all accounts with ages between 61 and 90 days that will be uncollectible.

    c Based on these intervals, is there strong evidence that the percentage of all accounts aged between 61 and 90 days that will be uncollectible is higher than the percentage of all accounts aged between 31 and 60 days that will be uncollectible? Explain.

8.48 Consider Exercise 8.41*b* and suppose we wish to find the sample size *n* needed in order to be 95 percent confident that $\hat{p}$, the sample proportion of respondents who said they took part in some sort of daily activity to keep physically fit, is within a margin of error of .02 of *p*, the population proportion of all U.S. adults who say that they take part in such activity. In order to find an appropriate value for $p(1 - p)$, note that the 95 percent confidence interval for *p* that you calculated in Exercise 8.41*b* was [.57, .63]. This indicates that the reasonable value for *p* that is closest to .5 is .57, and thus the largest reasonable value for $p(1 - p)$ is $.57(1 - .57) = .2451$. Calculate the required sample size *n*.

8.49 Referring to Exercise 8.46, determine the sample size needed in order to be 99 percent confident that $\hat{p}$, the sample proportion of ColorSmart-5000 television sets that last at least five years without a single repair, is within a margin of error of .03 of *p*, the population proportion of sets that last at least five years without a single repair.

8.50 Suppose we conduct a poll to estimate the proportion of voters who favor a major presidential candidate. Assuming that 50 percent of the electorate could be in favor of the candidate, determine the sample size needed so that we are 95 percent confident that $\hat{p}$, the sample proportion of voters who favor the candidate, is within a margin of error of .01 of *p*, the population proportion of all voters who are in favor of the candidate.

Distinguish between confidence intervals and tolerance intervals (Optional).

8.5 A Comparison of Confidence Intervals and Tolerance Intervals (Optional) ● ● ●

In this section we compare confidence intervals with tolerance intervals. We saw in Chapter 3 that a tolerance interval is an interval that is meant to contain a specified percentage (often 68.26 percent, 95.44 percent, or 99.73 percent) of the **individual** population measurements. By contrast, a confidence interval for the population mean μ is an interval that is meant to contain one thing—the population mean μ—and the confidence level associated with the confidence interval expresses how sure we are that this interval contains μ. Often we choose the confidence level to be 95 percent or 99 percent because such a confidence level is usually considered high enough to provide convincing evidence about the true value of μ.

EXAMPLE 8.10 The Car Mileage Case

Recall in the car mileage case that the mean and the standard deviation of the sample of 50 mileages are $\bar{x} = 31.56$ and $s = .7977$. Also, recall that we have concluded in Example 3.8 (page 114) that the estimated tolerance intervals $[\bar{x} \pm s] = [30.8, 32.4]$, $[\bar{x} \pm 2s] = [30.0, 33.2]$, and $[\bar{x} \pm 3s] = [29.2, 34.0]$ imply that approximately (1) 68.26 percent of all individual cars will obtain mileages between 30.8 mpg and 32.4 mpg; (2) 95.44 percent of all individual cars will obtain mileages between 30.0 mpg and 33.2 mpg; and (3) 99.73 percent of all individual cars will obtain mileages between 29.2 mpg and 34.0 mpg. By contrast, we have seen in Section 8.2 (page 318) that a 95 percent t-based confidence interval for the mean, μ, of the mileages of all individual cars is $[\bar{x} \pm 2.010 \, (s/\sqrt{50})] = [31.33, 31.79]$. This interval says that we are 95 percent confident that μ is between 31.33 mpg and 31.79 mpg. Figure 8.17 graphically depicts the three estimated tolerance intervals and the 95 percent confidence interval, which are shown below a histogram of the 50 mileages. Note that the estimated tolerance intervals, which are meant to contain the *many* mileages that comprise specified percentages of all individual cars, are longer than the 95 percent confidence interval, which is meant to contain the *single* population mean μ.

FIGURE 8.17   A Comparison of Confidence Intervals and Tolerance Intervals

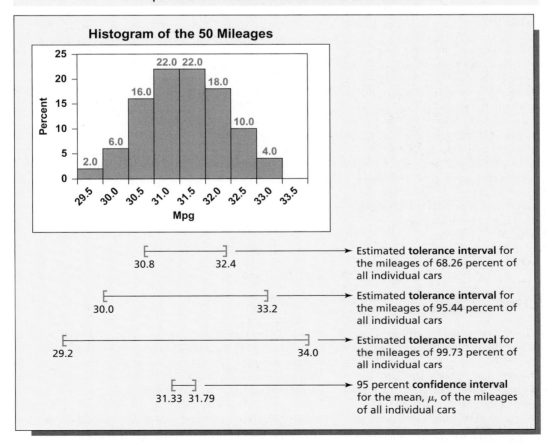

Exercises for Section 8.5

CONCEPTS

connect

8.51 What is a tolerance interval meant to contain?

8.52 What is a confidence interval for the population mean meant to contain?

8.53 Intuitively, why is a tolerance interval longer than a corresponding confidence interval?

METHODS AND APPLICATIONS

In Exercises 8.54 through 8.56 we give the mean and the standard deviation of a sample that has been randomly selected from a population. For each exercise, find estimated tolerance intervals that contain approximately 68.26 percent, 95.44 percent, and 99.73 percent of the individual population measurements. Also, find a 95 percent confidence interval for the population mean. Interpret the estimated tolerance intervals and the confidence interval in the context of the situation related to the exercise.

8.54 THE TRASH BAG CASE DS TrashBag

The mean and the standard deviation of the sample of 40 trash bag breaking strengths are $\bar{x} = 50.575$ and $s = 1.6438$.

8.55 THE BANK CUSTOMER WAITING TIME CASE DS WaitTime

The mean and the standard deviation of the sample of 100 bank customer waiting times are $\bar{x} = 5.46$ and $s = 2.475$.

8.56 THE VIDEO GAME SATISFACTION RATING CASE DS VideoGame

The mean and the standard deviation of the sample of 65 customer satisfaction ratings are $\bar{x} = 42.95$ and $s = 2.6424$.

Chapter Summary

In this chapter we discussed **confidence intervals** for population **means** and **proportions.** First, we studied how to compute a confidence interval for a **population mean.** We saw that when the population standard deviation σ is known, we can use the **normal distribution** to compute a confidence interval for a population mean. When σ is not known, if the population is normally distributed (or at least mound-shaped) or if the sample size n is large, we use the t **distribution** to compute this interval. We also studied how to find the size of the sample needed if we wish to compute a confidence interval for a mean with a prespecified *confidence level* and with a prespecified *margin of error.* Figure 8.18 is a flowchart summarizing our discussions concerning how to compute an appropriate confidence interval for a population mean.

Next we saw that we are often interested in estimating the proportion of population units falling into a category of interest. We showed how to compute a large sample confidence interval for a **population proportion,** and we saw how to find the sample size needed to estimate a population proportion with a prespecified *confidence level* and with a prespecified *margin of error.*

In optional Section 8.5 we concluded this chapter by comparing confidence intervals for μ with tolerance intervals. We emphasized that a tolerance interval is meant to contain a specified percentage of the individual population measurements, while the confidence interval is meant to contain only one number—the population mean.

Glossary of Terms

confidence coefficient: The (before sampling) probability that a confidence interval for a population parameter will contain the population parameter. (page 308)

confidence interval: An interval of numbers computed so that we can be very confident (say, 95 percent confident) that a population parameter is contained in the interval. (page 305)

confidence level: The percentage of time that a confidence interval would contain a population parameter if all possible samples were used to calculate the interval. (pages 307 and 310)

degrees of freedom (for a t curve): A parameter that describes the exact spread of the curve of a t distribution. (page 314)

margin of error: The quantity that is added to and subtracted from a point estimate of a population parameter to obtain a confidence interval for the parameter. It gives the maximum distance between the population parameter of interest and its point estimate when we assume the parameter is inside the confidence interval. (page 310)

FIGURE 8.18 Computing an Appropriate Confidence Interval for a Population Mean

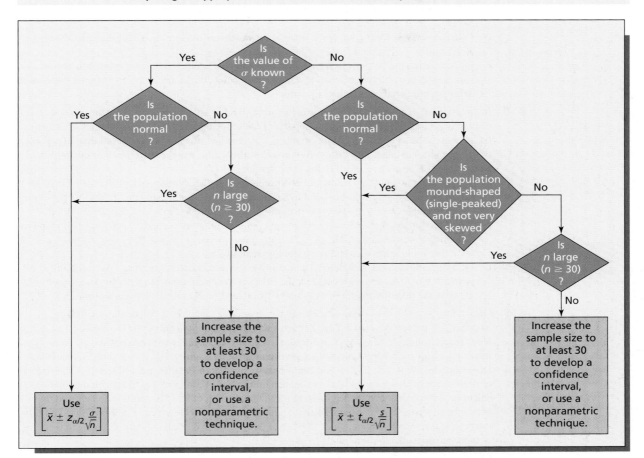

standard error of the estimate $\bar{x}$: The point estimate of $\sigma_{\bar{x}}$. (page 318)

t distribution: A commonly used continuous probability distribution that is described by a distribution curve similar to a normal curve. The t curve is symmetrical about zero and is more spread out than a standard normal curve. (page 314 and 315)

t point, t_α: The point on the horizontal axis under a t curve that gives a right-hand tail area equal to α. (page 314)

t table: A table of t point values listed according to the area in the tail of the t curve and according to values of the degrees of freedom. (pages 315–316)

Important Formulas

A z-based confidence interval for a population mean μ with σ known: page 311

A t-based confidence interval for a population mean μ with σ unknown: page 316

Sample size when estimating μ: page 322

A large sample confidence interval for a population proportion p: page 325

Sample size when estimating p: page 327

Supplementary Exercises

8.57 In an article in the *Journal of Accounting Research,* Ashton, Willingham, and Elliott studied audit delay (the length of time from a company's fiscal year-end to the date of the auditor's report) for industrial and financial companies. In the study, a random sample of 250 industrial companies yielded a mean audit delay of 68.04 days with a standard deviation of 35.72 days, while a random sample of 238 financial companies yielded a mean audit delay of 56.74 days with a standard deviation of 34.87 days. Use these sample results to do the following:

a   Calculate a 95 percent confidence interval for the mean audit delay for all industrial companies. Note: $t_{.025} = 1.97$ when $df = 249$.

b   Calculate a 95 percent confidence interval for the mean audit delay for all financial companies. Note: $t_{.025} = 1.97$ when $df = 237$.

c   By comparing the 95 percent confidence intervals you calculated in parts *a* and *b*, is there strong evidence that the mean audit delay for financial companies is shorter than the mean audit delay for industrial companies? Explain.

8.58   In an article in *Accounting and Business Research,* Beattie and Jones investigate the use and abuse of graphic presentations in the annual reports of United Kingdom firms. The authors found that 65 percent of the sampled companies graph at least one key financial variable, but that 30 percent of the graphics are materially distorted (nonzero vertical axis, exaggerated trend, or the like). Results for U.S. firms have been found to be similar.

a   Suppose that in a random sample of 465 graphics from the annual reports of United Kingdom firms, 142 of the graphics are found to be distorted. Find a point estimate of and a 95 percent confidence interval for the proportion of all U.K. annual report graphics that are distorted.

b   Based on this interval, can we be 95 percent confident that more than 25 percent of all graphics appearing in the annual reports of U.K. firms are distorted? Explain. Does this suggest that auditors should understand proper graphing methods?

c   Determine the sample size needed in order to be 95 percent confident that $\hat{p}$, the sample proportion of U.K. annual report graphics that are distorted, is within a margin of error of .03 of p, the population proportion of all U.K. annual report graphics that are distorted.

8.59   On January 4, 2000, the Gallup Organization released the results of a poll dealing with the likelihood of computer-related Y2K problems and the possibility of terrorist attacks during the New Year's holiday at the turn of the century.[7] The survey results were based on telephone interviews with a randomly selected national sample of 622 adults, 18 years and older, conducted December 28, 1999. The Gallup poll found that 61 percent of the respondents believed that one or more terrorist attacks were likely to happen on the New Year's holiday. Based on this finding, calculate a 95 percent confidence interval for the proportion of all U.S. adults who believed that one or more terrorist attacks were likely to happen on the 2000 New Year's holiday. Based on this interval, is it reasonable to conclude that fewer than two-thirds of all U.S. adults believed that one or more terrorist attacks were likely?

8.60   Refer to Exercise 8.59. In explaining its survey methods, Gallup states the following: "For results based on this sample, one can say with 95 percent confidence that the maximum error attributable to sampling and other random effects is plus or minus 4 percentage points." Explain how your calculations for Exercise 8.59 verify that this statement is true.

8.61   **THE DISK BRAKE CASE**

National Motors has equipped the ZX-900 with a new disk brake system. We define the stopping distance for a ZX-900 to be the distance (in feet) required to bring the automobile to a complete stop from a speed of 35 mph under normal driving conditions using this new brake system. In addition, we define μ to be the mean stopping distance of all ZX-900s. One of the ZX-900's major competitors is advertised to achieve a mean stopping distance of 60 feet. National Motors would like to claim in a new advertising campaign that the ZX-900 achieves a shorter mean stopping distance.

Suppose that National Motors randomly selects a sample of $n = 81$ ZX-900s. The company records the stopping distance of each automobile and calculates the mean and standard deviation of the sample of $n = 81$ stopping distances to be $\bar{x} = 57.8$ ft and $s = 6.02$ ft.

a   Calculate a 95 percent confidence interval for μ. Can National Motors be 95 percent confident that μ is less than 60 ft? Explain.

b   Using the sample of $n = 81$ stopping distances as a preliminary sample, find the sample size necessary to make National Motors 95 percent confident that $\bar{x}$ is within a margin of error of one foot of μ.

[7]Source: **The Gallup Organization,** www.gallup.com/poll/releases/, January 4, 2000.

8.62 In an article in the *Journal of Retailing,* J. G. Blodgett, D. H. Granbois, and R. G. Walters investigated negative word-of-mouth consumer behavior. In a random sample of 201 consumers, 150 reported that they engaged in negative word-of-mouth behavior (for instance, they vowed never to patronize a retailer again). In addition, the 150 respondents who engaged in such behavior, on average, told 4.88 people about their dissatisfying experience (with a standard deviation equal to 6.11).

   a Use these sample results to compute a 95 percent confidence interval for the proportion of all consumers who engage in negative word-of-mouth behavior. On the basis of this interval, would it be reasonable to claim that more than 70 percent of all consumers engage in such behavior? Explain.

   b Use the sample results to compute a 95 percent confidence interval for the population mean number of people who are told about a dissatisfying experience by consumers who engage in negative word-of-mouth behavior. On the basis of this interval, would it be reasonable to claim that these dissatisfied consumers tell, on average, at least three people about their bad experience? Explain. Note: $t_{.025} = 1.98$ when $df = 149$.

8.63 **THE CIGARETTE ADVERTISEMENT CASE**   **DS** ModelAge

   A random sample of 50 perceived age estimates for a model in a cigarette advertisement showed that $\bar{x} = 26.22$ years and that $s = 3.7432$ years.

   a Use this sample to calculate a 95 percent confidence interval for the population mean age estimate for all viewers of the ad.

   b Remembering that the cigarette industry requires that models must appear at least 25 years old, does the confidence interval make us 95 percent confident that the population mean perceived age estimate is at least 25? Is the mean perceived age estimate much more than 25? Explain.

8.64 In an article in the *Journal of Management Information Systems,* Mahmood and Mann investigate how information technology (IT) investment relates to company performance. In particular, Mahmood and Mann obtain sample data concerning IT investment for companies that use information systems effectively. Among the variables studied are the company's IT budget as a percentage of company revenue, percentages of the IT budget spent on staff and training, and number of PCs and terminals as a percentage of total employees.

   a Suppose a random sample of 15 companies considered to use information systems effectively yields a sample mean IT budget as a percentage of company revenue of $\bar{x} = 2.73$ with a standard deviation of $s = 1.64$. Assuming that IT budget percentages are approximately normally distributed, calculate a 99 percent confidence interval for the mean IT budget as a percentage of company revenue for all firms that use information systems effectively. Does this interval provide evidence that a firm can successfully use information systems with an IT budget that is less than 5 percent of company revenue? Explain.

   b Suppose a random sample of 15 companies considered to use information systems effectively yields a sample mean number of PCs and terminals as a percentage of total employees of $\bar{x} = 34.76$ with a standard deviation of $s = 25.37$. Assuming approximate normality, calculate a 99 percent confidence interval for the mean number of PCs and terminals as a percentage of total employees for all firms that use information systems effectively. Why is this interval so wide? What can we do to obtain a narrower (more useful) confidence interval?

8.65 **THE INVESTMENT CASE**   **DS** InvestRet

   Suppose that random samples of 50 returns for each of the following investment classes give the indicated sample mean and sample standard deviation:

   > Fixed annuities: $\bar{x} = 7.83\%$, $s = .51\%$
   > Domestic large cap stocks: $\bar{x} = 13.42\%$, $s = 15.17\%$
   > Domestic midcap stocks: $\bar{x} = 15.03\%$, $s = 18.44\%$
   > Domestic small cap stocks: $\bar{x} = 22.51\%$, $s = 21.75\%$

   a For each investment class, compute a 95 percent confidence interval for the population mean return.

   b Do these intervals suggest that the current population mean return for each investment class differs from the historical (1970 to 1994) mean return given in Table 3.11 (page 143)? Explain.

8.66 **THE INTERNATIONAL BUSINESS TRAVEL EXPENSE CASE**

   Recall that the mean and the standard deviation of a random sample of 35 one-day travel expenses in Moscow are $\bar{x} = \$538$ and $s = \$41$. Find a 95 percent confidence interval for the mean, μ, of all one-day travel expenses in Moscow.

8.67   THE UNITED KINGDOM INSURANCE CASE

Assume that the U.K. insurance survey is based on 1,000 randomly selected U.K. households and that 640 of these households spent money for life insurance in 1993. Find a 95 percent confidence interval for the proportion, p, of all U.K. households that spent money for life insurance in 1993.

8.68   How safe are child car seats? *Consumer Reports* (May 2005) tested the safety of child car seats in 30 mph crashes. They found "slim safety margins" for some child car seats. Suppose that *Consumer Reports* simulates the safety of the market-leading child car seat. Their test consists of placing the maximum claimed weight in the car seat and simulating crashes at higher and higher miles per hour until a problem occurs. The following data identify the speed at which a problem with the car seat (such as the strap breaking, seat shell cracked, strap adjuster broke, detached from base, etc.) first appeared: 31.0, 29.4, 30.4, 28.9, 29.7, 30.1, 32.3, 31.7, 35.4, 29.1, 31.2, 30.2. Using the fact that $\bar{x} = 30.7833$ and $s = 1.7862$, find a 95 percent confidence interval for the population mean speed at which a problem with the car seat first appears. Are we 95 percent confident that this mean is at least 30 mph?   **DS** CarSeat

8.69   In Exercise 2.85 (page 77), we briefly described a series of international quality standards called ISO 9000. In the results of a Quality Systems Update/Deloitte & Touche survey of ISO 9000 registered companies published by CEEM Information Systems, 515 of 620 companies surveyed reported that they are encouraging their suppliers to pursue ISO 9000 registration.[8]

a   Using these survey results, compute a 95.44 percent confidence interval for the proportion of all ISO 9000 registered companies that encourage their suppliers to pursue ISO 9000 registration. Assume here that the survey participants have been randomly selected.

b   Based on this interval, is there conclusive evidence that more than 75 percent of all ISO 9000 registered companies encourage their suppliers to pursue ISO 9000 registration?

8.70   Internet Exercise

What is the average selling price of a home? The Data and Story Library (DASL) contains data, including the sale price, for a random sample of 117 homes sold in Albuquerque, New Mexico. Go to the DASL website (http://lib.stat.cmu.edu/DASL/) and retrieve the home price data set (http://lib.stat.cmu.edu/DASL/Datafiles/homedat.html.) Use MINITAB, Excel, or MegaStat to produce appropriate graphical (histogram, stem-and-leaf, box plot) and numerical summaries of the price data. Identify, from your numerical summaries, the sample mean and standard deviation. Use these summaries to construct a 99% confidence interval for μ, the population mean sale price. Use statistical software (MINITAB, Excel, or MegaStat) to compute a 99% confidence interval for μ. Do the results of your hand calculations agree with those from your statistical software?

Technical note: There are many ways to capture the home price data from the DASL site. One simple way is to select just the rows containing the data values (and not the labels), copy, paste directly into an Excel or MINITAB worksheet, add your own variable labels, and save the resulting worksheet. It is possible to copy the variable labels from DASL as well, but the differences in alignment and the intervening blank line add to the difficulty.   **DS** AlbHome

Appendix 8.1 ■ Confidence Intervals Using Excel

The instruction block in this section begins by describing the entry of data into an Excel spreadsheet. Alternatively, the data may be downloaded from this book's website. The appropriate data file name is given at the top of the instruction block. Please refer to Appendix 1.1 for further information about entering data, saving data, and printing results when using Excel.

Confidence interval for a population mean in Figure 8.11 on page 319 (data file: DebtEq.xlsx):

- Enter the debt-to-equity ratio data from Example 8.2 (page 317) into cells A2 to A16 with the label Ratio in cell A1.
- Select **Data : Data Analysis : Descriptive Statistics.**
- Click OK in the Data Analysis dialog box.

---

[8]Source: *Is ISO 9000 for You?* (Fairfax, VA: CEEM Information Services).

- In the Descriptive Statistics dialog box, enter A1 : A16 into the Input Range window.

- Place a checkmark in the "Labels in first row" checkbox.

- Under output options, select "New Worksheet Ply" to have the output placed in a new worksheet and enter the name Output for the new worksheet.

- Place checkmarks in the Summary Statistics and "Confidence Level for Mean" checkboxes. This produces a *t*-based margin of error for a confidence interval.

- Type 95 in the "Confidence Level for Mean" box.

- Click OK in the Descriptive Statistics dialog box.

- A descriptive statistics summary will be displayed in cells A3 through B16 in the Output worksheet. Drag the column borders to reveal complete labels for all of the descriptive statistics.

- Type the heading "95% Confidence Interval" into cells D13 to E13.

- Compute the lower bound of the interval by typing the formula = B3 − B16 into cell D15. This subtracts the margin of error of the interval (labeled "Confidence Level (95%)") from the sample mean.

- Compute the upper bound of the interval by typing the formula = B3 + B16 into cell E15.

Appendix 8.2 ■ Confidence Intervals Using MegaStat

Confidence interval for the population mean debt-to-equity ratio in Example 8.2 on page 317:

- Select **Add-Ins : MegaStat : Confidence Intervals / Sample Size**

- In the "Confidence Intervals / Sample Size" dialog box, click on the "Confidence Interval—mean" tab.

- Enter the sample mean (here equal to 1.3433) into the Mean window.

- Enter the sample standard deviation (here equal to .1921) into the "Std Dev" window.

- Enter the sample size (here equal to 15) into the "n" window.

- Select a level of confidence from the pull-down menu or type a desired percentage.

- Select a *t*-based or *z*-based interval by clicking on "t" or "z." Here we request a *t*-based interval.

- Click OK in the "Confidence Intervals / Sample Size" dialog box.

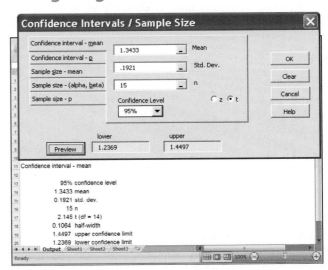

Confidence interval for a population proportion in the cheese spread situation of Example 8.6 on page 325:

- In the "Confidence Intervals / Sample Size" dialog box, click on the "Confidence interval—p" tab.

- Enter the sample proportion (here equal to .063) into the "p" window.

- Enter the sample size (here equal to 1000) into the "n" window.

- Select a level of confidence from the pull-down menu or type a desired percentage.

- Click OK in the "Confidence Intervals / Sample Size" dialog box.

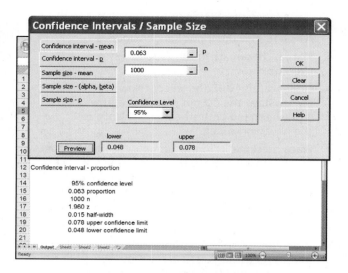

Sample size determination for a proportion problem on page 328:

- In the "Confidence Intervals / Sample Size" dialog box, click on the "Sample size—p" tab.

- Enter the desired margin of error (here equal to 0.02) into the "E" window and enter an estimate of the population proportion into the "p" window.

- Select a level of confidence from the pull-down menu or type a desired percentage.

- Click OK in the "Confidence Intervals / Sample Size" dialog box.

Sample size determination for a population mean problem is done by clicking on the "Sample Size—mean" tab. Then enter a desired margin of error, an estimate of the population standard deviation, and the desired level of confidence. Click OK.

Appendix 8.3 ■ Confidence Intervals Using MINITAB

The instruction blocks in this section each begins by describing the entry of data into the MINITAB data window. Alternatively, the data may be downloaded from this book's website. The appropriate data file name is given at the top of each instruction block. Please refer to Appendix 1.3 for further information about entering data, saving data, and printing results when using MINITAB.

Confidence interval for a population mean in Figure 8.12 on page 319 (data file: Ratio.MTW):

- In the Data window, enter the debt-to-equity ratio data from Example 8.2 (page 317) into a single column with variable name Ratio.
- Select **Stat : Basic Statistics : 1-Sample t.**
- In the "1-Sample t (Test and Confidence Interval)" dialog box, select "Samples in columns."
- Select the variable name Ratio into the "Samples in columns" window.
- Click the Options... button.
- In the "1-Sample t—Options" dialog box, enter the desired level of confidence (here 95.0) into the "Confidence level" window.
- Select "not equal" from the Alternative drop-down menu, and click OK in the "1-Sample t—Options" dialog box.
- To produce a boxplot of the data with a graphical representation of the confidence interval, click the Graphs... button, check the "Boxplot of data" checkbox, and click OK in the "1-Sample t—Graphs" dialog box.
- Click OK in "1-Sample t (Test and Confidence Interval)" dialog box.
- The confidence interval is given in the Session window, and the boxplot appears in a graphics window.

A "1-Sample Z" interval is also available in MINITAB under Basic Statistics. It requires a user-specified value of the population standard deviation, which is rarely known.

Confidence interval for a population proportion in the marketing ethics situation of Example 8.8 on pages 326 and 327:

- Select **Stat : Basic Statistics : 1 Proportion**
- In the "1 Proportion (Test and Confidence Interval)" dialog box, select "Summarized data."
- Enter the number of trials (here equal to 205) and the number of successes (or events) (here equal to 117) into the appropriate windows.
- Click on the Options... button.
- In the "1 Proportion—Options" dialog box, enter the desired level of confidence (here 95.0) into the "Confidence level" window.
- Select "not equal" from the Alternative drop-down menu.
- Check the "Use test and interval based on normal distribution" checkbox.
- Click OK in the "1 Proportion—Options" dialog box.
- Click OK in the "1 Proportion (Test and Confidence Interval)" dialog box.
- The confidence interval will be displayed in the Session window.

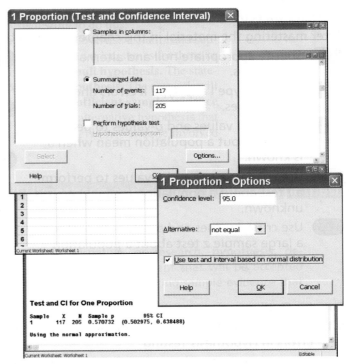

"greater than" a particular number, or if the statement says that the parameter is "less than" a particular number, then (for reasons to be discussed later) we make the statement the *alternative hypothesis, H_a*, and we make the opposite of the statement the *null hypothesis, H_0*. We illustrate these ideas in the following two cases.

EXAMPLE 9.1 The Trash Bag Case[1]

A leading manufacturer of trash bags produces the strongest trash bags on the market. The company has developed a new 30-gallon bag using a specially formulated plastic that is stronger and more biodegradable than other plastics. This plastic's increased strength allows the bag's thickness to be reduced, and the resulting cost savings will enable the company to lower its bag price by 25 percent. The company also believes the new bag is stronger than its current 30-gallon bag.

The manufacturer wants to advertise the new bag on a major television network. In addition to promoting its price reduction, the company also wants to claim the new bag is better for the environment and stronger than its current bag. The network is convinced of the bag's environmental advantages on scientific grounds. However, the network questions the company's claim of increased strength and requires statistical evidence to justify this claim. Although there are various measures of bag strength, the manufacturer and the network agree to employ "breaking strength." A bag's breaking strength is the amount of a representative trash mix (in pounds) that, when loaded into a bag suspended in the air, will cause the bag to rip or tear. Tests show that the current bag has a mean breaking strength that is very close to (but does not exceed) 50 pounds. The new bag's mean breaking strength μ is unknown and in question. Because the trash bag manufacturer wishes to show that *μ is greater than 50 pounds,* we make the statement that *μ is greater than 50 pounds* the alternative hypothesis, H_a, and we make the statement that *μ is less than or equal to 50 pounds* the null hypothesis, H_0. (Note that the *null hypothesis* says that the new trash bag is *not stronger* than the former bag.) We summarize the null and alternative hypotheses by saying that we are testing

$$H_0: \mu \leq 50 \quad \text{versus} \quad H_a: \mu > 50$$

The network will run the manufacturer's commercial if a random sample of n new bags provides sufficient evidence to reject $H_0: \mu \leq 50$ in favor of $H_a: \mu > 50$.

EXAMPLE 9.2 The Payment Time Case

Recall that a management consulting firm has installed a new computer-based, electronic billing system for a Hamilton, Ohio, trucking company. Because of the system's advantages, and because the trucking company's clients are receptive to using this system, the management consulting firm believes that the new system will reduce the mean bill payment time by more than 50 percent. The mean payment time using the old billing system was approximately equal to, but no less than, 39 days. Therefore, if μ denotes the mean payment time using the new system, the consulting firm believes and wishes to show that *μ is less than 19.5 days.* It follows that we make the statement that *μ is less than 19.5 days* the alternative hypothesis, H_a, and we make the statement that *μ is greater than or equal to 19.5 days* the null hypothesis, H_0. The consulting firm will randomly select a sample of n invoices and determine if their payment times provide sufficient evidence to reject $H_0: \mu \geq 19.5$ in favor of $H_a: \mu < 19.5$. If such evidence exists, the consulting firm will conclude that the new electronic billing system has reduced the Hamilton trucking company's mean bill payment time by more than 50 percent. This conclusion will be used to help demonstrate the benefits of the new billing system both to the Hamilton company and to other trucking companies that are considering using such a system.

---

[1]This case is based on conversations by the authors with several employees working for a leading producer of trash bags. For purposes of confidentiality, we have agreed to withhold the company's name.

In some situations we need to evaluate a statement that says that a population parameter exactly equals a particular number. It then follows that we make the statement that the population parameter *equals* the particular number the *null hypothesis, H_0,* and we make the statement that the population parameter *does not equal* the particular number the *alternative hypothesis, H_a.* We demonstrate this in the following case.

EXAMPLE 9.3 The Valentine's Day Chocolate Case[2]

A candy company annually markets a special 18 ounce box of assorted chocolates to large retail stores for Valentine's Day. This year the candy company has designed an extremely attractive new valentine box and will fill the box with an especially appealing assortment of chocolates. For this reason, the candy company subjectively projects—based on past experience and knowledge of the candy market—that sales of its valentine box will be 10 percent higher than last year. However, since the candy company must decide how many valentine boxes to produce, the company needs to assess whether it is reasonable to plan for a 10 percent increase in sales.

Before the beginning of each Valentine's Day sales season, the candy company sends large retail stores information about its newest valentine box of assorted chocolates. This information includes a description of the box of chocolates, as well as a preview of advertising displays that the candy company will provide to help retail stores sell the chocolates. Each retail store then places a single (nonreturnable) order of valentine boxes to satisfy its anticipated customer demand for the Valentine's Day sales season. Last year the mean order quantity of large retail stores was 300 boxes per store. If the projected 10 percent sales increase will occur, the mean order quantity, μ, of large retail stores this year will *equal* 330 boxes per store. Therefore, the candy company will test the *null hypothesis H_0: $\mu = 330$* versus the *alternative hypothesis H_a: $\mu \neq 330$.* Here, the alternative hypothesis, H_a says that μ might be greater than or less than 330 boxes. If μ turns out to be greater than 330 boxes and the candy company bases its production on a projected mean order quantity of 330 boxes, the company will fail to satisfy demand for its valentine box. If μ turns out to be less than 330 boxes and the candy company bases its production on a projected mean order quantity of 330 boxes, the company will produce more valentine boxes than it can sell.

To perform the hypothesis test, the candy company will randomly select a sample of n large retail stores and will make an early mailing to these stores promoting this year's valentine box. The candy company will then ask each retail store to report how many valentine boxes it anticipates ordering. If the sample data do not provide sufficient evidence to reject H_0: $\mu = 330$ in favor of H_a: $\mu \neq 330$, the candy company will base its production on the projected 10 percent sales increase. On the other hand, if there is sufficient evidence to reject H_0: $\mu = 330$, the candy company will change its production plans.

We next summarize the sets of null and alternative hypotheses that we have thus far considered.

$$H_0: \mu \leq 50 \qquad H_0: \mu \geq 19.5 \qquad H_0: \mu = 330$$
$$\text{versus} \qquad \text{versus} \qquad \text{versus}$$
$$H_a: \mu > 50 \qquad H_a: \mu < 19.5 \qquad H_a: \mu \neq 330$$

The alternative hypothesis H_a: $\mu > 50$ is called a **one-sided, greater than alternative** hypothesis, whereas H_a: $\mu < 19.5$ is called a **one-sided, less than alternative** hypothesis, and H_a: $\mu \neq 330$ is called a **two-sided, not equal to alternative** hypothesis. Many of the alternative hypotheses we consider in this book are one of these three types. Also, note that each null hypothesis we have considered involves an **equality**. For example, the null hypothesis H_0: $\mu \leq 50$ says that μ is either less than or **equal to** 50. We will see that, in general, the approach we use to test a null hypothesis versus an alternative hypothesis requires that the null hypothesis involve an equality. For this reason, **we always formulate the null and alternative hypotheses so that the null hypothesis involves an equality.**

[2]Thanks to Krogers of Oxford, Ohio, for helpful discussions concerning this case.

The idea of a test statistic Suppose that in the trash bag case the manufacturer randomly selects a sample of $n = 40$ new trash bags. Each of these bags is tested for breaking strength, and the sample mean $\bar{x}$ of the 40 breaking strengths is calculated. In order to test $H_0: \mu \leq 50$ versus $H_a: \mu > 50$, we utilize the **test statistic**

$$z = \frac{\bar{x} - 50}{\sigma_{\bar{x}}} = \frac{\bar{x} - 50}{\sigma/\sqrt{n}}$$

The test statistic z measures the distance between $\bar{x}$ and 50. The division by $\sigma_{\bar{x}}$ says that this distance is measured in units of the standard deviation of all possible sample means. For example, a value of z equal to, say, 2.4 would tell us that $\bar{x}$ is 2.4 such standard deviations above 50. In general, a value of the test statistic that is less than or equal to zero results when $\bar{x}$ is less than or equal to 50. This provides no evidence to support rejecting H_0 in favor of H_a because the point estimate $\bar{x}$ indicates that μ is probably less than or equal to 50. However, a value of the test statistic that is greater than zero results when $\bar{x}$ is greater than 50. This provides evidence to support rejecting H_0 in favor of H_a because the point estimate $\bar{x}$ indicates that μ might be greater than 50. Furthermore, the farther the value of the test statistic is above 0 (the farther $\bar{x}$ is above 50), the stronger is the evidence to support rejecting H_0 in favor of H_a.

Hypothesis testing and the legal system If the value of the test statistic z is far enough above zero, we reject H_0 in favor of H_a. To see how large z must be in order to reject H_0, we must understand that **a hypothesis test rejects a null hypothesis H_0 only if there is strong statistical evidence against H_0.** This is similar to our legal system, which rejects the innocence of the accused only if evidence of guilt is beyond a reasonable doubt. For instance, the network will reject $H_0: \mu \leq 50$ and run the trash bag commercial only if the test statistic z is far enough above zero to show beyond a reasonable doubt that $H_0: \mu \leq 50$ is false and $H_a: \mu > 50$ is true. A test statistic that is only slightly greater than zero might not be convincing enough. However, because such a test statistic would result from a sample mean $\bar{x}$ that is slightly greater than 50, it would provide some evidence to support rejecting $H_0: \mu \leq 50$, and it certainly would not provide strong evidence supporting $H_0: \mu \leq 50$. Therefore, if the value of the test statistic is not large enough to convince us to reject H_0, **we do not say that we accept H_0. Rather we say that we do not reject H_0** because the evidence against H_0 is not strong enough. Again, this is similar to our legal system, where the lack of evidence of guilt beyond a reasonable doubt results in a verdict of **not guilty,** but does not prove that the accused is innocent.

LO2 Describe Type I and Type II errors and their probabilities.

Type I and Type II errors and their probabilities To determine exactly how much statistical evidence is required to reject H_0, we consider the errors and the correct decisions that can be made in hypothesis testing. These errors and correct decisions, as well as their implications in the trash bag advertising example, are summarized in Tables 9.1 and 9.2. Across the top of each table are listed the two possible "states of nature." Either $H_0: \mu \leq 50$ is true, which says the manufacturer's claim that μ is greater than 50 is false, or H_0 is false, which says the claim is true. Down the left side of each table are listed the two possible decisions we can make in the hypothesis test. Using the sample data, we will either reject $H_0: \mu \leq 50$, which implies that the claim will be advertised, or we will not reject H_0, which implies that the claim will not be advertised.

In general, the two types of errors that can be made in hypothesis testing are defined as follows:

Type I and Type II Errors

If we reject H_0 when it is true, this is a **Type I error.**
If we do not reject H_0 when it is false, this is a **Type II error.**

As can be seen by comparing Tables 9.1 and 9.2, if we commit a Type I error, we will advertise a false claim. If we commit a Type II error, we will fail to advertise a true claim.

We now let the symbol α (pronounced **alpha**) **denote the probability of a Type I error,** and we let β (pronounced **beta**) **denote the probability of a Type II error.** Obviously, we would like both α and β to be small. A common (but not the only) procedure is to base a hypothesis test on taking a sample of a fixed size (for example, $n = 40$ trash bags) and on setting

TABLE 9.1   Type I and Type II Errors

Decision	State of Nature	
	$H_0: \mu \leq 50$ True	$H_0: \mu \leq 50$ False
Reject $H_0: \mu \leq 50$	Type I error	Correct decision
Do not reject $H_0: \mu \leq 50$	Correct decision	Type II error

TABLE 9.2   The Implications of Type I and Type II Errors in the Trash Bag Example

Decision	State of Nature	
	Claim False	Claim True
Advertise the claim	Advertise a false claim	Advertise a true claim
Do not advertise the claim	Do not advertise a false claim	Do not advertise a true claim

α equal to a small prespecified value. Setting α low means there is only a small chance of rejecting H_0 when it is true. This implies that we are requiring strong evidence against H_0 before we reject it.

We sometimes choose α as high as .10, but we usually choose α between .05 and .01. A frequent choice for α is .05. In fact, our former student tells us that the network often tests advertising claims by setting the probability of a Type I error equal to .05. That is, the network will run a commercial making a claim if the sample evidence allows it to reject a null hypothesis that says the claim is not valid in favor of an alternative hypothesis that says the claim is valid with α set equal to .05. Since a Type I error is deciding that the claim is valid when it is not, the policy of setting α equal to .05 says that, in the long run, the network will advertise only 5 percent of all invalid claims made by advertisers.

One might wonder why the network does not set α lower—say at .01. One reason is that **it can be shown that, for a fixed sample size, the lower we set α, the higher is β, and the higher we set α, the lower is β.** Setting α at .05 means that β, the probability of failing to advertise a true claim (a Type II error), will be smaller than it would be if α were set at .01. As long as (1) the claim to be advertised is plausible and (2) the consequences of advertising the claim even if it is false are not terribly serious, then it is reasonable to set α equal to .05. However, if either (1) or (2) is not true, then we might set α lower than .05. For example, suppose a pharmaceutical company wishes to advertise that it has developed an effective treatment for a disease that has formerly been very resistant to treatment. Such a claim is (perhaps) difficult to believe. Moreover, if the claim is false, patients suffering from the disease would be subjected to false hope and needless expense. In such a case, it might be reasonable for the network to set α at .01 because this would lower the chance of advertising the claim if it is false. We usually do not set α lower than .01 because doing so often leads to an unacceptably large value of β. We explain some methods for computing the probability of a Type II error in optional Section 9.5. However, β can be difficult or impossible to calculate in many situations, and we often must rely on our intuition when deciding how to set α.

Exercises for Section 9.1

CONCEPTS

9.1   Define each of the following: Type I error, α, Type II error, β.

9.2   When testing a hypothesis, why don't we set the probability of a Type I error to be extremely small? Explain.

METHODS AND APPLICATIONS

9.3   THE VIDEO GAME SATISFACTION RATING CASE   ⚉ VideoGame

Recall that "very satisfied" customers give the XYZ-Box video game system a rating that is at least 42. Suppose that the manufacturer of the XYZ-Box wishes to use the 65 satisfaction ratings to provide evidence supporting the claim that the mean composite satisfaction rating for the XYZ-Box exceeds 42.

a Letting μ represent the mean composite satisfaction rating for the XYZ-Box, set up the null and alternative hypotheses needed if we wish to attempt to provide evidence supporting the claim that μ exceeds 42.

b In the context of this situation, interpret making a Type I error; interpret making a Type II error.

9.4   **THE BANK CUSTOMER WAITING TIME CASE** 🎬 WaitTime

Recall that a bank manager has developed a new system to reduce the time customers spend waiting for teller service during peak hours. The manager hopes the new system will reduce waiting times from the current 9 to 10 minutes to less than 6 minutes.

Suppose the manager wishes to use the 100 waiting times to support the claim that the mean waiting time under the new system is shorter than six minutes.

a Letting μ represent the mean waiting time under the new system, set up the null and alternative hypotheses needed if we wish to attempt to provide evidence supporting the claim that μ is shorter than six minutes.

b In the context of this situation, interpret making a Type I error; interpret making a Type II error.

9.5   An automobile parts supplier owns a machine that produces a cylindrical engine part. This part is supposed to have an outside diameter of three inches. Parts with diameters that are too small or too large do not meet customer requirements and must be rejected. Lately, the company has experienced problems meeting customer requirements. The technical staff feels that the mean diameter produced by the machine is off target. In order to verify this, a special study will randomly sample 100 parts produced by the machine. The 100 sampled parts will be measured, and if the results obtained cast a substantial amount of doubt on the hypothesis that the mean diameter equals the target value of three inches, the company will assign a problem-solving team to intensively search for the causes of the problem.

a The parts supplier wishes to set up a hypothesis test so that the problem-solving team will be assigned when the null hypothesis is rejected. Set up the null and alternative hypotheses for this situation.

b In the context of this situation, interpret making a Type I error; interpret making a Type II error.

9.6   The Crown Bottling Company has just installed a new bottling process that will fill 16-ounce bottles of the popular Crown Classic Cola soft drink. Both overfilling and underfilling bottles are undesirable: Underfilling leads to customer complaints and overfilling costs the company considerable money. In order to verify that the filler is set up correctly, the company wishes to see whether the mean bottle fill, μ, is close to the target fill of 16 ounces. To this end, a random sample of 36 filled bottles is selected from the output of a test filler run. If the sample results cast a substantial amount of doubt on the hypothesis that the mean bottle fill is the desired 16 ounces, then the filler's initial setup will be readjusted.

a The bottling company wants to set up a hypothesis test so that the filler will be readjusted if the null hypothesis is rejected. Set up the null and alternative hypotheses for this hypothesis test.

b In the context of this situation, interpret making a Type I error; interpret making a Type II error.

9.7   Consolidated Power, a large electric power utility, has just built a modern nuclear power plant. This plant discharges waste water that is allowed to flow into the Atlantic Ocean. The Environmental Protection Agency (EPA) has ordered that the waste water may not be excessively warm so that thermal pollution of the marine environment near the plant can be avoided. Because of this order, the waste water is allowed to cool in specially constructed ponds and is then released into the ocean. This cooling system works properly if the mean temperature of waste water discharged is 60°F or cooler. Consolidated Power is required to monitor the temperature of the waste water. A sample of 100 temperature readings will be obtained each day, and if the sample results cast a substantial amount of doubt on the hypothesis that the cooling system is working properly (the mean temperature of waste water discharged is 60°F or cooler), then the plant must be shut down and appropriate actions must be taken to correct the problem.

a Consolidated Power wishes to set up a hypothesis test so that the power plant will be shut down when the null hypothesis is rejected. Set up the null and alternative hypotheses that should be used.

b In the context of this situation, interpret making a Type I error; interpret making a Type II error.

c The EPA periodically conducts spot checks to determine whether the waste water being discharged is too warm. Suppose the EPA has the power to impose very severe penalties (for example, very heavy fines) when the waste water is excessively warm. Other things being equal, should Consolidated Power set the probability of a Type I error equal to $\alpha = .01$ or $\alpha = .05$? Explain.

9.2 z Tests about a Population Mean: σ Known ● ● ●

LO3   Use critical values and p-values to perform a z test about a population mean when σ is known.

In this section we discuss hypothesis tests about a population mean that are *based on the normal distribution*. These tests are called z **tests,** and they require that the *true value of the population standard deviation σ is known*. Of course, in most real-world situations the true value of σ is not known. However, the concepts and calculations of hypothesis testing are most easily illustrated using the normal distribution. Therefore, in this section we will assume that—through theory or history related to the population under consideration—we know σ. When σ is unknown, we test hypotheses about a population mean by using the *t distribution*. In Section 9.3 we study *t* **tests,** and we will revisit the examples of this section assuming that σ is unknown.

Testing a "greater than" alternative hypothesis by using a critical value rule   In Section 9.1 we explained how to set up appropriate null and alternative hypotheses. We also discussed how to specify a value for α, the probability of a Type I error (also called the **level of significance**) of the hypothesis test, and we introduced the idea of a test statistic. We can use these concepts to begin developing a five-step hypothesis-testing procedure. We will introduce these steps in the context of the trash bag case and testing a "greater than" alternative hypothesis.

Step 1: State the null hypothesis H_0 and the alternative hypothesis H_a. In the trash bag case, we will test H_0: $\mu \le 50$ versus H_a: $\mu > 50$. Here, μ is the mean breaking strength of the new trash bag.

Step 2: Specify the level of significance α. The television network will run the commercial stating that the new trash bag is stronger than the former bag if we can reject H_0: $\mu \le 50$ in favor of H_a: $\mu > 50$ by setting α equal to .05.

Step 3: Select the test statistic. In order to test H_0: $\mu \le 50$ versus H_a: $\mu > 50$, we will test the modified null hypothesis H_0: $\mu = 50$ versus H_a: $\mu > 50$. The idea here is that if there is sufficient evidence to reject the hypothesis that μ equals 50 in favor of $\mu > 50$, then there is certainly also sufficient evidence to reject the hypothesis that μ is less than or equal to 50. In order to test H_0: $\mu = 50$ versus H_a: $\mu > 50$, we will randomly select a sample of $n = 40$ new trash bags and calculate the mean $\bar{x}$ of the breaking strengths of these bags. We will then utilize the **test statistic**

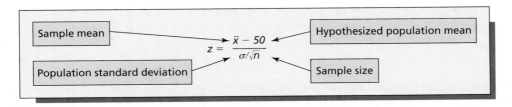

A positive value of this test statistic results from an $\bar{x}$ that is greater than 50 and thus provides evidence against H_0: $\mu = 50$ and in favor of H_a: $\mu > 50$. Moreover, the manufacturer has improved its trash bags multiple times in the past. Studies show that the population standard deviation σ of individual trash bag breaking strengths has remained constant for each of these updates and equals 1.65 pounds.

Step 4: Determine the critical value rule for deciding whether to reject H_0. To decide how large the test statistic z must be to reject H_0 in favor of H_a by setting the probability of a Type I error equal to α, we note that different samples would give different sample means and thus different values of z. **Because the sample size $n = 40$ is large, the Central Limit Theorem tells us that the sampling distribution of z is (approximately) a standard normal distribution if the null hypothesis H_0: $\mu = 50$ is true.** Therefore, we do the following:

- Place the probability of a Type I error, α, in the right-hand tail of the standard normal curve and use the normal table (see Table A.3, page 638) to find the normal point z_α. Here z_α, which we call a **critical value,** is the point on the horizontal axis under the standard normal curve that gives a right-hand tail area equal to α.

- **Reject H_0: $\mu = 50$ in favor of H_a: $\mu > 50$ if and only if the test statistic z is greater than the critical value z_α.** (This is called a **right tailed critical value rule.**)

FIGURE 9.1   A Right Tailed Critical Value Rule for Testing H_0: $\mu = 50$ versus H_a: $\mu > 50$ by Setting $\alpha = .05$

Figure 9.1 illustrates that since we have set α equal to .05, we should use the critical value $z_\alpha = z_{.05} = 1.645$ (see Table A.3). This says that we should reject H_0 if $z > 1.645$ and we should not reject H_0 if $z \leq 1.645$. Moreover, the α of .05 says that there is only a 5 percent chance of z being greater than 1.645 if H_0: $\mu = 50$ is true. Therefore, if the sample that we will actually select gives a value of z that is greater than 1.645 and thus causes us to reject H_0: $\mu = 50$, we can be intuitively confident that we have made the right decision. This is because we will have rejected H_0 by using a test that allows only a 5 percent chance of wrongly rejecting H_0. In general, if we can reject a null hypothesis in favor of an alternative hypothesis by setting the probability of a Type I error equal to α, we say that we have **statistical significance at the α level.**

Step 5: **Collect the sample data, compute the value of the test statistic, and decide whether to reject H_0. Interpret the statistical results.** When the sample of $n = 40$ new trash bags is randomly selected, the mean of the breaking strengths is calculated to be $\bar{x} = 50.575$ pounds. Assuming that σ is 1.65 pounds, the value of the test statistic is

$$z = \frac{\bar{x} - 50}{\sigma/\sqrt{n}} = \frac{50.575 - 50}{1.65/\sqrt{40}} = 2.20$$

Because $z = 2.20$ is greater than the critical value $z_{.05} = 1.645$, we can reject H_0: $\mu = 50$ in favor of H_a: $\mu > 50$ by setting α equal to .05. Therefore, we conclude (at an α of .05) that the population mean breaking strength of the new trash bag exceeds 50 pounds. Furthermore, this conclusion has **practical importance** to the trash bag manufacturer because it means that the television network will approve running commercials claiming that the new trash bag is stronger than the former bag. Note, however, that the point estimate of μ, $\bar{x} = 50.575$, indicates that μ is not much larger than 50. Therefore, the trash bag manufacturer can claim only that its new bag is slightly stronger than its former bag. Of course, this might be practically important to consumers who feel that, because the new bag is 25 percent less expensive and is more environmentally sound, it is definitely worth purchasing if it has any strength advantage. However, to customers who are looking only for a substantial increase in bag strength, the statistical results would not be practically important. Notice that the point estimate of the parameter involved in a hypothesis test can help us to assess practical importance.

A *p*-value for testing a "greater than" alternative hypothesis   To decide whether to reject the null hypothesis H_0 at level of significance α, steps 4 and 5 of the five-step critical value procedure compare the test statistic value to a critical value. Another way to make this decision is to calculate a ***p*-value,** which measures the likelihood of the sample results if the null hypothesis H_0 is true. **Sample results that are not likely if H_0 is true are evidence that H_0 is not true.** To test H_0 by using a *p*-value procedure, we use the same first three steps used by the critical value procedure and the new steps 4 and 5:

FIGURE 9.2   The *p*-Value for Testing H_0: $\mu = 50$ versus H_a: $\mu > 50$.

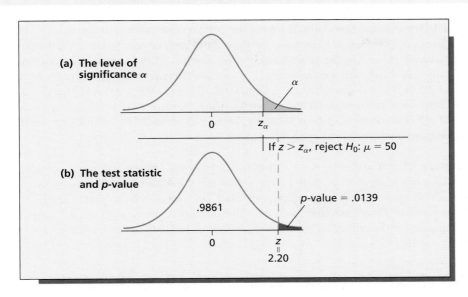

Step 4: Collect the sample data, compute the value of the test statistic, and compute the *p*-value. The *p*-value for testing a null hypothesis H_0 versus an alternative hypothesis H_a is defined as follows:

The ***p*-value** is the probability, computed assuming that the null hypothesis H_0 is true, of observing a value of the test statistic that is at least as contradictory to H_0 and supportive of H_a as the value actually computed from the sample data.

In the trash bag case, the value of the test statistic computed from the sample data is $z = 2.20$. Because we are testing H_0: $\mu = 50$ versus the **greater than** alternative hypothesis H_a: $\mu > 50$, this positive test statistic value contradicts H_0 and supports H_a. A value of the test statistic that is at least as contradictory to H_0 and supportive of H_a as $z = 2.20$ is a value of the test statistic that is **greater than or equal to** $z = 2.20$. Therefore, the *p*-value is the probability, computed assuming that H_0: $\mu = 50$ is true, of observing a value of the test statistic that is greater than or equal to $z = 2.20$. As illustrated in Figure 9.2(b), this ***p*-value is the area under the standard normal curve to the right of $z = 2.20$** and equals $1 - .9861 = .0139$ (see Table A.3, page 638). The *p*-value of .0139 says that, if H_0: $\mu = 50$ is true, then only 139 in 10,000 of all possible test statistic values are at least as large, or contradictory to H_0, as the value $z = 2.20$. That is, if we are to believe that H_0 is true, we must believe that we have observed a test statistic value that can be described as having a 139 in 10,000 chance. It is difficult to believe that we have observed such a small chance, but is this evidence strong enough to reject H_0: $\mu = 50$ and run the trash bag commercial? As discussed in step 5, this depends on the level of significance α used by the television network.

Step 5: Reject H_0 if the *p*-value is less than α. Interpret the statistical results. Consider the two normal curves in Figures 9.2(a) and (b). These normal curves show that if the *p*-value of .0139 is less than a particular level of significance α, the test statistic value $z = 2.20$ is greater than the critical value z_α, and thus we can reject H_0: $\mu = 50$ at level of significance α. For example, recall that the television network has set α equal to .05. Then, **because the *p*-value of .0139 is less than the α of .05, we would reject H_0: $\mu = 50$ at level of significance .05** and thus run the trash bag commercial on the network.

Comparing the critical value and *p*-value methods   Thus far we have seen that we can reject H_0: $\mu = 50$ in favor of H_a: $\mu > 50$ at level of significance α if **the test statistic z is greater than the critical value z_α,** or equivalently, **the *p*-value is less than α.** Because different television networks sometimes have different policies for evaluating an advertising claim, different television networks sometimes use different values of α when evaluating the same advertising claim. For example, whereas the network of the previous example used an α value of .05 to evaluate the trash bag claim, three other networks might use three different α values (say, .04, .025, and .01) to evaluate this claim. If we use the critical value method to test H_0: $\mu = 50$ versus H_a: $\mu > 50$ at each of these α values, we would have to look up a different critical value z_α for each different α value. On the other hand, the p-value of .0139 is **more efficient** because it immediately tells us whether we can reject H_0 at each different α value. Specifically, because the p-value of .0139 is less than each of the α values .05, .04, and .025, we would reject H_0 and thus run the trash bag commercial on the networks using these α values. However, because the p-value of .0139 is greater than the α value .01, we would not reject H_0 and thus not run the trash bag commercial on the network using this α value.

A summary of the five steps of hypothesis testing   In the real world, in spite of the greater efficiency of the p-value, both critical values and p-values are used to test hypotheses. For example, NBC uses critical value rules, whereas CBS uses p-values, to statistically evaluate advertising claims. Throughout this book we will (formally or informally) use the following five steps to implement the critical value and p-value approaches to hypothesis testing.

The Five Steps of Hypothesis Testing

1   State the null hypothesis H_0 and the alternative hypothesis H_a.

2   Specify the level of significance α.

3   Select the test statistic.

Using a critical value rule:

4   Determine the critical value rule for deciding whether to reject H_0.

5   Collect the sample data, compute the value of the test statistic, and decide whether to reject H_0. Interpret the statistical results.

Using a *p*-value:

4   Collect the sample data, compute the value of the test statistic, and compute the p-value.

5   Reject H_0 at level of significance α if the p-value is less than α. Interpret the statistical results.

Testing a "less than" alternative hypothesis by using a critical value rule   Consider the payment time case. In order to study whether the new electronic billing system reduces the mean bill payment time by more than 50 percent, the management consulting firm will test H_0: $\mu \geq 19.5$ versus H_a: $\mu < 19.5$ (step 1). A Type I error (concluding that H_a: $\mu < 19.5$ is true when H_0: $\mu \geq 19.5$ is true) would result in the consulting firm overstating the benefits of the new billing system, both to the company in which it has been installed and to other companies that are considering installing such a system. Because the consulting firm desires to have only a 1 percent chance of doing this, the firm will set α **equal to .01** (step 2).

To perform the hypothesis test, we will test the modified null hypothesis H_0: $\mu = 19.5$ versus H_a: $\mu < 19.5$. We will randomly select a sample of $n = 65$ invoices paid using the new billing system and calculate the mean $\bar{x}$ of the payment times of these invoices. Then, because the sample size is large, the Central Limit Theorem applies, and we will utilize the **test statistic (step 3)**

$$z = \frac{\bar{x} - 19.5}{\sigma/\sqrt{n}}$$

A value of the test statistic z that is less than zero results when $\bar{x}$ is less than 19.5. This provides evidence to support rejecting H_0 in favor of H_a because the point estimate $\bar{x}$ indicates that μ might be less than 19.5. To decide how much less than zero the test statistic must be to reject H_0 in favor

FIGURE 9.3   Testing H_0: $\mu = 19.5$ versus H_a: $\mu < 19.5$ by Using a Critical Value and a *p*-Value

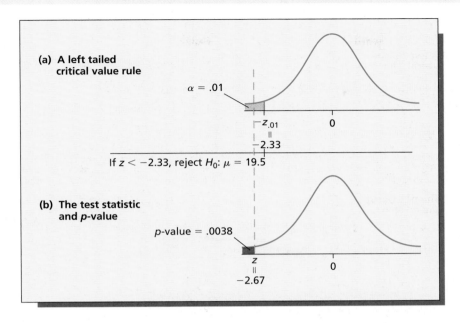

of H_a at significance level α, we will use the **left tailed critical value rule** illustrated in Figure 9.3(a). Specifically, we will place α in the left-hand tail of the standard normal curve and **reject H_0: $\mu = 19.5$ in favor of H_a: $\mu < 19.5$ if and only if the test statistic z is less than the critical value $-z_\alpha$ (step 4).** Here, $-z_\alpha$ is the point on the horizontal axis under the standard normal curve that gives a left-hand tail area equal to α. Because α equals .01, the critical value $-z_\alpha$ is $-z_{.01} = -2.33$ [see Figure 9.3(a)].

When the sample of $n = 65$ invoices is randomly selected, the mean of the payment times of these invoices is calculated to be $\bar{x} = 18.1077$ days. Assuming that the population standard deviation σ of payment times for the new electronic billing system is 4.2 days (as discussed on page 284 of Chapter 7), the **value of the test statistic** is

$$z = \frac{\bar{x} - 19.5}{\sigma/\sqrt{n}} = \frac{18.1077 - 19.5}{4.2/\sqrt{65}} = -2.67$$

Because $z = -2.67$ is less than the critical value $-z_{.01} = -2.33$, we can reject H_0: $\mu = 19.5$ in favor of H_a: $\mu < 19.5$ by setting α equal to .01 (step 5). Therefore, we conclude (at an α of .01) that the population mean payment time for the new electronic billing system is less than 19.5 days. This, along with the fact that the sample mean $\bar{x} = 18.1077$ is slightly less than 19.5, implies that it is reasonable for the management consulting firm to conclude (and claim) that the new electronic billing system has reduced the population mean payment time by slightly more than 50 percent.

A *p*-value for testing a "less than" alternative hypothesis   The value of the test statistic computed from the sample data is $z = -2.67$. Because we are testing H_0: $\mu = 19.5$ versus the **less than** alternative hypothesis H_a: $\mu < 19.5$, a value of the test statistic that is at least as contradictory to H_0 and supportive of H_a as $z = -2.67$ is a value of the test statistic that is **less than or equal to $z = -2.67$.** Therefore, the *p*-value is the probability, computed assuming that H_0: $\mu = 19.5$ is true, of observing a value of the test statistic that is less than or equal to $z = -2.67$. As illustrated in Figure 9.3(b), this ***p*-value is the area under the standard normal curve to the left of $z = -2.67$ (step 4)** and equals .0038 (see Table A.3, page 638). The *p*-value of .0038 says that, if H_0: $\mu = 19.5$ is true, then only 38 in 10,000 of all possible test statistic values are at least as negative, or contradictory to H_0, as the value $z = -2.67$. Moreover, recall that the management consulting firm has set α equal to .01. **Because the *p*-value of .0038 is less than the α of .01, we can reject H_0: $\mu = 19.5$ in favor of H_a: $\mu < 19.5$ by setting α equal to .01** (step 5).

FIGURE 9.4   Testing $H_0: \mu = 330$ versus $H_a: \mu \neq 330$ by Using Critical Values and the p-Value

Testing a "not equal to" alternative hypothesis by using a critical value rule   Consider the Valentine's Day chocolate case. To assess whether this year's sales of its valentine box of assorted chocolates will be 10 percent higher than last year's, the candy company will test $H_0: \mu = 330$ versus $H_a: \mu \neq 330$ (step 1). Here, μ is the mean order quantity of this year's valentine box by large retail stores. If the candy company does not reject $H_0: \mu = 330$ and $H_0: \mu = 330$ is false (a Type II error) the candy company will base its production of valentine boxes on a 10 percent projected sales increase that is not correct. Since the candy company wishes to have a reasonably small probability of making this Type II error, the company will set α **equal to .05** (step 2). Setting α equal to .05 rather than .01 makes the probability of a Type II error smaller than it would be if α were set at .01. (See Section 9.5 for more on Type II errors.)

    To perform the hypothesis test, the candy company will randomly select $n = 100$ large retail stores and will make an early mailing to these stores promoting this year's valentine box of assorted chocolates. The candy company will then ask each sampled retail store to report its anticipated order quantity of valentine boxes and will calculate the mean $\bar{x}$ of the reported order quantities. Since the sample size is large, the Central Limit Theorem applies, and we will utilize the **test statistic** (step 3)

$$z = \frac{\bar{x} - 330}{\sigma / \sqrt{n}}$$

A value of the test statistic that is greater than 0 results when $\bar{x}$ is greater than 330. This provides evidence to support rejecting H_0 in favor of H_a because the point estimate $\bar{x}$ indicates that μ might be greater than 330. Similarly, a value of the test statistic that is less than 0 results when $\bar{x}$ is less than 330. This also provides evidence to support rejecting H_0 in favor of H_a because the point estimate $\bar{x}$ indicates that μ might be less than 330. To decide how different from zero (positive or negative) the test statistic must be in order to reject H_0 in favor of H_a at significance level α, we will use the **two tailed critical value rule** illustrated in Figure 9.4(a). Specifically, we will divide α into two equal parts and **reject $H_0: \mu = 330$ in favor of $H_a: \mu \neq 330$ if and only if the test statistic z is greater than the critical value $z_{\alpha/2}$ or less than the critical value $-z_{\alpha/2}$ (step 4).** Note that this is equivalent to saying that we should **reject H_0 if and only if the absolute value of the test statistic, $|z|$, is greater than the critical value $z_{\alpha/2}$.** Because $\alpha/2 = .05/2 = .025$, it follows that the critical values $z_{\alpha/2}$ and $-z_{\alpha/2}$ are $z_{.025} = 1.96$ and $-z_{.025} = -1.96$ [see Figure 9.4(a)].

When the sample of $n = 100$ large retail stores is randomly selected, the mean of their reported order quantities is calculated to be $\bar{x} = 326$ boxes. Assuming that the population standard deviation σ of large retail store order quantities for this year's valentine box will be 40 boxes (the same as it was for previous years' valentine boxes), the value of the test statistic is

$$z = \frac{\bar{x} - 330}{\sigma/\sqrt{n}} = \frac{326 - 330}{40/\sqrt{100}} = -1$$

Because $z = -1$ is between the critical values $-z_{.025} = -1.96$ and $z_{.025} = 1.96$ (or, equivalently, because $|z| = 1$ is less than $z_{.025} = 1.96$), we cannot reject $H_0: \mu = 330$ in favor of $H_a: \mu \neq 330$ by setting α equal to .05 (step 5). Therefore, we cannot conclude (at an α of .05) that the population mean order quantity of this year's valentine box by large retail stores will differ from 330 boxes. It follows that the candy company will base its production of valentine boxes on the ten percent projected sales increase.

A p-value for testing a "not equal to" alternative hypothesis   The value of the test statistic computed from the sample data is $z = -1$. Because the alternative hypothesis $H_a: \mu \neq 330$ says that μ might be greater or less than 330, both positive and negative test statistic values contradict $H_0: \mu = 330$ and support $H_a: \mu \neq 330$. It follows that a value of the test statistic that is at least as contradictory to H_0 and supportive of H_a as $z = -1$ is a value of the test statistic that is greater than or equal to 1 or less than or equal to -1. Therefore, the p-value is the probability, computed assuming that $H_0: \mu = 330$ is true, of observing a value of the test statistic that is greater than or equal to 1 or less than or equal to -1. As illustrated in Figure 9.4 (b), this p-value equals the area under the standard normal curve to the right of 1, plus the area under this curve to the left of -1. But, by the symmetry of the normal curve, the sum of these two areas, and thus the **p-value, is twice the area under the standard normal curve to the right of $|z| = 1$, the absolute value of the test statistic (step 4).** Because the area under the standard normal curve to the right of $|z| = 1$ is $1 - .8413 = .1587$ (see Table A.3, page 638), the p-value is $2(.1587) = .3174$. The p-value of .3174 says that, if $H_0: \mu = 330$ is true, then 31.74 percent of all possible test statistic values are at least as contradictory to H_0 as $z = -1$. Moreover, recall that the candy company has set α equal to .05. **Because the p-value of .3174 is greater than the α of .05, we cannot reject $H_0: \mu = 330$ in favor of $H_a: \mu \neq 330$ by setting α equal to .05 (step 5).**

A general procedure for testing a hypothesis about a population mean   In general, let μ_0 be the value for μ specified in the null hypothesis. Then, the following summary box gives the critical value and p-value procedures for performing (1) a right tailed test of $H_0: \mu = \mu_0$ versus $H_a: \mu > \mu_0$ (for example, $H_0: \mu = 50$ versus $H_a: \mu > 50$); (2) a left tailed test of $H_0: \mu = \mu_0$ versus $H_a: \mu < \mu_0$ (for example, $H_0: \mu = 19.5$ versus $H_a: \mu < 19.5$); and (3) a two tailed test of $H_0: \mu = \mu_0$ versus $H_a: \mu \neq \mu_0$ (for example, $H_0: \mu = 330$ versus $H_a: \mu \neq 330$).

Testing a Hypothesis about a Population Mean When σ Is Known

Using confidence intervals to test hypotheses   Confidence intervals can be used to test hypotheses. Specifically, it can be proven that we can reject $H_0: \mu = \mu_0$ in favor of $H_a: \mu \neq \mu_0$ by setting the probability of a Type I error equal to α if and only if the $100(1 - \alpha)$ percent confidence interval for μ does not contain μ_0. For example, consider the Valentine's Day chocolate case and testing $H_0: \mu = 330$ versus $H_a: \mu \neq 330$ by setting α equal to .05. To do this, we use the mean $\bar{x} = 326$ of the sample of $n = 100$ reported order quantities to calculate the 95 percent confidence interval for μ to be

$$\left[\bar{x} \pm z_{\alpha/2} \frac{\sigma}{\sqrt{n}} \right] = \left[326 \pm 1.96 \frac{40}{\sqrt{100}} \right] = [318.2, 333.8]$$

Because this interval does contain 330, we cannot reject $H_0: \mu = 330$ in favor of $H_a: \mu \neq 330$ by setting α equal to .05.

Whereas we can use **two-sided confidence intervals** to test "not equal to" alternative hypotheses, we must use **one-sided confidence intervals** to test "greater than" or "less than" alternative hypotheses. We will not study one-sided confidence intervals in this book. However, it should be emphasized that we do not need to use confidence intervals (one-sided or two-sided) to test hypotheses. We can test hypotheses by using test statistics and critical values or p-values, and these are the approaches that we will feature throughout this book.

Measuring the weight of evidence against the null hypothesis   As originally defined, the p-value is a probability that measures the likelihood of the sample results if the null hypothesis H_0 is true. **The smaller the p-value is, the less likely are the sample results if the null hypothesis H_0 is true. Therefore, the stronger is the evidence that H_0 is false and that the alternative hypothesis H_a is true.** Interpreted in this way, the p-value can be regarded as a measure of the **weight of evidence** against the null hypothesis and in favor of the alternative hypothesis. Through statistical practice, statisticians have concluded (somewhat subjectively) that:

Interpreting the Weight of Evidence against the Null Hypothesis

If the p-value for testing H_0 is less than

- .10, we have **some evidence** that H_0 is false.
- .05, we have **strong evidence** that H_0 is false.

- .01, we have **very strong evidence** that H_0 is false.
- .001, we have **extremely strong evidence** that H_0 is false.

We will frequently use these conclusions in future examples. Understand, however, that there are really no sharp borders between different weights of evidence. Rather, there is really only increasingly strong evidence against the null hypothesis as the p-value decreases. For example, the trash bag manufacturer, in addition to deciding whether $H_0: \mu = 50$ can be rejected in favor of $H_a: \mu > 50$ at each television network's chosen value of α, would almost certainly wish to know how much evidence there is that its new trash bag is stronger than its former trash bag. The p-value for testing $H_0: \mu = 50$ is .0139, which is less than .05 but not less than .01. Therefore, we have strong evidence, but not very strong evidence, that $H_0: \mu = 50$ is false and $H_a: \mu > 50$ is true. As another example, the p-value in the payment time case is .0038. This provides very strong evidence, but not extremely strong evidence, that $H_0: \mu = 19.5$ is false and $H_a: \mu < 19.5$ is true. Finally, the p-value in the Valentine's Day chocolate case is .3174. This provides little evidence that $H_0: \mu = 330$ is false and $H_a: \mu \neq 330$ is true.

Exercises for Section 9.2

CONCEPTS

connect

9.8   Explain what a critical value is, and explain how it is used to test a hypothesis.

9.9   Explain what a p-value is, and explain how it is used to test a hypothesis.

METHODS AND APPLICATIONS

9.10 Suppose that we wish to test H_0: $\mu = 80$ versus H_a: $\mu > 80$, where σ is known to equal 20. Also, suppose that a sample of $n = 100$ measurements randomly selected from the population has a mean of $\bar{x} = 85$.
   a Calculate the value of the test statistic z.
   b By comparing z with a critical value, test H_0 versus H_a at $\alpha = .05$.
   c Calculate the *p*-value for testing H_0 versus H_a.
   d Use the *p*-value to test H_0 versus H_a at each of $\alpha = .10, .05, .01,$ and $.001$.
   e How much evidence is there that H_0: $\mu = 80$ is false and H_a: $\mu > 80$ is true?

9.11 Suppose that we wish to test H_0: $\mu = 20$ versus H_a: $\mu < 20$, where σ is known to equal 7. Also, suppose that a sample of $n = 49$ measurements randomly selected from the population has a mean of $\bar{x} = 18$.
   a Calculate the value of the test statistic z.
   b By comparing z with a critical value, test H_0 versus H_a at $\alpha = .01$.
   c Calculate the *p*-value for testing H_0 versus H_a.
   d Use the *p*-value to test H_0 versus H_a at each of $\alpha = .10, .05, .01,$ and $.001$.
   e How much evidence is there that H_0: $\mu = 20$ is false and H_a: $\mu < 20$ is true?

9.12 Suppose that we wish to test H_0: $\mu = 40$ versus H_a: $\mu \neq 40$, where σ is known to equal 18. Also, suppose that a sample of $n = 81$ measurements randomly selected from the population has a mean of $\bar{x} = 35$.
   a Calculate the value of the test statistic z.
   b By comparing z with critical values, test H_0 versus H_a at $\alpha = .05$.
   c Calculate the *p*-value for testing H_0 versus H_a.
   d Use the *p*-value to test H_0 versus H_a at each of $\alpha = .10, .05, .01,$ and $.001$.
   e How much evidence is there that H_0: $\mu = 40$ is false and H_a: $\mu \neq 40$ is true?

9.13 **THE VIDEO GAME SATISFACTION RATING CASE**   DS VideoGame

Recall that "very satisfied" customers give the XYZ-Box video game system a rating that is at least 42. Suppose that the manufacturer of the XYZ-Box wishes to use the random sample of 65 satisfaction ratings to provide evidence supporting the claim that the mean composite satisfaction rating for the XYZ-Box exceeds 42.
   a Letting μ represent the mean composite satisfaction rating for the XYZ-Box, set up the null hypothesis H_0 and the alternative hypothesis H_a needed if we wish to attempt to provide evidence supporting the claim that μ exceeds 42.
   b The random sample of 65 satisfaction ratings yields a sample mean of $\bar{x} = 42.954$. Assuming that σ equals 2.64, use critical values to test H_0 versus H_a at each of $\alpha = .10, .05, .01,$ and $.001$.
   c Using the information in part *b*, calculate the *p*-value and use it to test H_0 versus H_a at each of $\alpha = .10, .05, .01,$ and $.001$.
   d How much evidence is there that the mean composite satisfaction rating exceeds 42?

9.14 **THE BANK CUSTOMER WAITING TIME CASE**   DS WaitTime

Recall that a bank manager has developed a new system to reduce the time customers spend waiting for teller service during peak hours. The manager hopes the new system will reduce waiting times from the current 9 to 10 minutes to less than 6 minutes.
   Suppose the manager wishes to use the random sample of 100 waiting times to support the claim that the mean waiting time under the new system is shorter than six minutes.
   a Letting μ represent the mean waiting time under the new system, set up the null and alternative hypotheses needed if we wish to attempt to provide evidence supporting the claim that μ is shorter than six minutes.
   b The random sample of 100 waiting times yields a sample mean of $\bar{x} = 5.46$ minutes. Assuming that $\sigma = 2.47$ minutes, use critical values to test H_0 versus H_a at each of $\alpha = .10, .05, .01,$ and $.001$.
   c Using the information in part *b*, calculate the *p*-value and use it to test H_0 versus H_a at each of $\alpha = .10, .05, .01,$ and $.001$.
   d How much evidence is there that the new system has reduced the mean waiting time to below six minutes?

9.15 Consolidated Power, a large electric power utility, has just built a modern nuclear power plant. This plant discharges waste water that is allowed to flow into the Atlantic Ocean. The Environmental Protection Agency (EPA) has ordered that the waste water may not be excessively warm so that thermal pollution of the marine environment near the plant can be avoided. Because of this order, the waste water is allowed to cool in specially constructed ponds and is then released into the ocean. This cooling system works properly if the mean temperature of waste water discharged is 60°F or cooler. Consolidated Power is required to monitor the temperature of the waste water. A sample of 100 temperature readings will be obtained each day, and if the sample results cast a substantial amount of doubt on the hypothesis that the cooling system is working properly (the mean temperature of waste water discharged is 60°F or cooler), then the plant must be shut down and appropriate actions must be taken to correct the problem.

a Consolidated Power wishes to set up a hypothesis test so that the power plant will be shut down when the null hypothesis is rejected. Set up the null hypothesis H_0 and the alternative hypothesis H_a that should be used.

b Suppose that Consolidated Power decides to use a level of significance of $\alpha = .05$, and suppose a random sample of 100 temperature readings is obtained. If the sample mean of the 100 temperature readings is $\bar{x} = 60.482$, test H_0 versus H_a and determine whether the power plant should be shut down and the cooling system repaired. Perform the hypothesis test by using a critical value and a p-value. Assume $\sigma = 2$.

9.16 Do part b of Exercise 9.15 if $\bar{x} = 60.262$.

9.17 Do part b of Exercise 9.15 if $\bar{x} = 60.618$.

9.18 An automobile parts supplier owns a machine that produces a cylindrical engine part. This part is supposed to have an outside diameter of three inches. Parts with diameters that are too small or too large do not meet customer requirements and must be rejected. Lately, the company has experienced problems meeting customer requirements. The technical staff feels that the mean diameter produced by the machine is off target. In order to verify this, a special study will randomly sample 100 parts produced by the machine. The 100 sampled parts will be measured, and if the results obtained cast a substantial amount of doubt on the hypothesis that the mean diameter equals the target value of three inches, the company will assign a problem-solving team to intensively search for the causes of the problem.

a The parts supplier wishes to set up a hypothesis test so that the problem-solving team will be assigned when the null hypothesis is rejected. Set up the null and alternative hypotheses for this situation.

b A sample of 40 parts yields a sample mean diameter of $\bar{x} = 3.006$ inches. Assuming σ equals .016, use a critical value and a p-value to test H_0 versus H_a by setting α equal to .05. Should the problem-solving team be assigned?

9.19 The Crown Bottling Company has just installed a new bottling process that will fill 16-ounce bottles of the popular Crown Classic Cola soft drink. Both overfilling and underfilling bottles are undesirable: Underfilling leads to customer complaints and overfilling costs the company considerable money. In order to verify that the filler is set up correctly, the company wishes to see whether the mean bottle fill, μ, is close to the target fill of 16 ounces. To this end, a random sample of 36 filled bottles is selected from the output of a test filler run. If the sample results cast a substantial amount of doubt on the hypothesis that the mean bottle fill is the desired 16 ounces, then the filler's initial setup will be readjusted.

a The bottling company wants to set up a hypothesis test so that the filler will be readjusted if the null hypothesis is rejected. Set up the null and alternative hypotheses for this hypothesis test.

b Suppose that Crown Bottling Company decides to use a level of significance of $\alpha = .01$, and suppose a random sample of 36 bottle fills is obtained from a test run of the filler. For each of the following four sample means—$\bar{x} = 16.05$, $\bar{x} = 15.96$, $\bar{x} = 16.02$, and $\bar{x} = 15.94$—determine whether the filler's initial setup should be readjusted. In each case, use a critical value, a p-value, and a confidence interval. Assume that σ equals .1.

9.20 THE DISK BRAKE CASE

National Motors has equipped the ZX-900 with a new disk brake system. We define μ to be the mean stopping distance (from a speed of 35 mph) of all ZX-900s. National Motors would like to claim that the ZX-900 achieves a shorter mean stopping distance than the 60 ft claimed by a competitor.

a Set up the null and alternative hypotheses needed to support National Motors' claim.

b A television network will allow National Motors to advertise its claim if the appropriate null hypothesis can be rejected at $\alpha = .05$. If a random sample of 81 ZX-900s have a mean stopping distance of $\bar{x} = 57.8$ ft, will National Motors be allowed to advertise the claim? Assume that $\sigma = 6.02$ ft and justify your answer using both a critical value and a p-value.

9.3 *t* Tests about a Population Mean: *σ* Unknown ● ● ●

LO4 Use critical values and *p*-values to perform a *t* test about a population mean when *σ* is unknown.

If we do not know *σ* (which is usually the case), we can base a hypothesis test about *μ* on the sampling distribution of

$$\frac{\bar{x} - \mu}{s/\sqrt{n}}$$

If the sampled population is normally distributed (or if the sample size is large—at least 30), then this sampling distribution is exactly (or approximately) a **t distribution having *n* − 1 degrees of freedom.** This leads to the following results:

A *t* Test about a Population Mean: *σ* Unknown

| **Null Hypothesis** | $H_0\colon \mu = \mu_0$ | **Test Statistic** | $t = \dfrac{\bar{x} - \mu_0}{s/\sqrt{n}}$ $df = n - 1$ | **Assumptions** | Normal population or Large sample size |

EXAMPLE 9.4 The Debt-to-Equity Ratio Case   **C**

One measure of a company's financial health is its *debt-to-equity ratio.* This quantity is defined to be the ratio of the company's corporate debt to the company's equity. If this ratio is too high, it is one indication of financial instability. For obvious reasons, banks often monitor the financial health of companies to which they have extended commercial loans. Suppose that, in order to reduce risk, a large bank has decided to initiate a policy limiting the mean debt-to-equity ratio for its portfolio of commercial loans to being less than 1.5. In order to assess whether the mean debt-to-equity ratio *μ* of its (current) commercial loan portfolio is less than 1.5, the bank will test the **null hypothesis $H_0\colon \mu = 1.5$ versus the alternative hypothesis $H_a\colon \mu < 1.5$.** In this situation, a Type I error (rejecting $H_0\colon \mu = 1.5$ when $H_0\colon \mu = 1.5$ is true) would result in the bank concluding that the mean debt-to-equity ratio of its commercial loan portfolio is less than 1.5 when it is not. Because the bank wishes to be very sure that it does not commit this Type I error, it will test H_0 versus H_a by using a **.01 level of significance.** To perform the hypothesis test, the bank randomly selects a sample of 15 of its commercial loan accounts. Audits of these companies result in the following debt-to-equity ratios (arranged in increasing order): 1.05, 1.11, 1.19, 1.21, 1.22, 1.29, 1.31, 1.32, 1.33, 1.37, 1.41, 1.45, 1.46, 1.65, and 1.78. The mound-shaped stem-and-leaf display of these ratios is given on the page margin and indicates that the population of all debt-to-equity ratios is (approximately) normally distributed. It follows that it is appropriate to calculate the value of the **test statistic *t* in the summary box.** Furthermore, since $H_a\colon \mu < 1.5$ implies a left tailed test, we should **reject $H_0\colon \mu = 1.5$ if the value of *t* is less than the critical value** $-t_\alpha = -t_{.01} = -2.624$. Here, $-t_{.01} = -2.624$ is based on $n - 1 = 15 - 1 = 14$ degrees of freedom (see Table A.4, on page 640), and this critical value is illustrated in Figure 9.5(a). The mean and the standard deviation of the random sample of $n = 15$ debt-to-equity ratios are $\bar{x} = 1.3433$ and $s = .1921$. This implies that the **value of the test statistic is**

$$t = \frac{\bar{x} - 1.5}{s/\sqrt{n}} = \frac{1.3433 - 1.5}{.1921/\sqrt{15}} = -3.1589$$

1.0	5
1.1	1 9
1.2	1 2 9
1.3	1 2 3 7
1.4	1 5 6
1.5	
1.6	5
1.7	8

DS DebtEq

FIGURE 9.5   Testing H_0: $\mu = 1.5$ versus H_a: $\mu < 1.5$ by Using a Critical Value and the p-Value

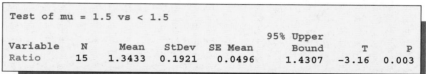

Since $t = -3.1589$ is less than $-t_{.01} = -2.624$, we reject H_0: $\mu = 1.5$ in favor of H_a: $\mu < 1.5$. That is, we conclude (at an α of .01) that the population mean debt-to-equity ratio of the bank's commercial loan portfolio is less than 1.5. This, along with the fact that the sample mean $\bar{x} = 1.3433$ is slightly less than 1.5, implies that it is reasonable for the bank to conclude that the population mean debt-to-equity ratio of its commercial loan portfolio is slightly less than 1.5.

The p-value for testing H_0: $\mu = 1.5$ versus H_a: $\mu < 1.5$ is the area under the curve of the t distribution having 14 degrees of freedom to the left of $t = -3.1589$. Tables of t points (such as Table A.4) are not complete enough to give such areas for most t statistic values, so we use computer software packages to calculate p-values that are based on the t distribution. For example, Excel tells us that the p-value for testing H_0: $\mu = 1.5$ versus H_a: $\mu < 1.5$ is .00348, which is given in the rounded form .003 on the MINITAB output at the bottom of Figure 9.5. The p-value of .00348 says that if we are to believe that H_0 is true, we must believe that we have observed a test statistic value that can be described as having a 348 in 100,000 chance. Moreover, because the p-value of .00348 is between .01 and .001, we have very strong evidence, but not extremely strong evidence, that H_0: $\mu = 1.5$ is false and H_a: $\mu < 1.5$ is true. That is, we have very strong evidence that the mean debt-to-equity ratio of the bank's commercial loan portfolio is less than 1.5.

Recall that in three cases discussed in Section 9.2 we tested hypotheses by assuming that the population standard deviation σ is known and by using z tests. If σ is actually not known in these cases (which would probably be true), we should test the hypotheses under consideration by using t tests. Furthermore, recall that in each case the sample size is large (at least 30). **In general, it can be shown that if the sample size is large, the t test is approximately valid even if the sampled population is not normally distributed (or mound shaped).** Therefore, consider the Valentine's Day chocolate case and testing H_0: $\mu = 330$ versus H_a: $\mu \neq 330$ at the **.05 level of significance.** To perform the hypothesis test, assume that we will randomly select $n = 100$ large

FIGURE 9.6 Testing H_0: $\mu = 330$ versus H_a: $\mu \neq 330$ by Using Critical Values and the p-Value

```
Test of mu = 330 vs not = 330

Variable    N     Mean    StDev  SE Mean      95% CI            T       P
Boxes      100   326.00   39.10    3.91   (318.24, 333.76)   -1.02   0.309
```

retail stores and use their anticipated order quantities to calculate the value of the **test statistic t in the summary box.** Then, since the alternative hypothesis H_a: $\mu \neq 330$ implies a two tailed test, we will **reject H_0: $\mu = 330$ if the absolute value of t is greater than $t_{\alpha/2} = t_{.025} = 1.984$ (based on $n - 1 = 99$ degrees of freedom)**—see Figure 9.6(a). Suppose that when the sample is randomly selected, the mean and the standard deviation of the $n = 100$ reported order quantities are calculated to be $\bar{x} = 326$ and $s = 39.1$. The **value of the test statistic** is

$$t = \frac{\bar{x} - 330}{s/\sqrt{n}} = \frac{326 - 330}{39.1/\sqrt{100}} = -1.023$$

Since $|t| = 1.023$ is less than $t_{.025} = 1.984$, we cannot reject H_0: $\mu = 330$ by setting α equal to .05. It follows that we cannot conclude (at an α of .05) that this year's population mean order quantity of the valentine box by large retail stores will differ from 330 boxes. Therefore, the candy company will base its production of valentine boxes on the 10 percent projected sales increase. The p-value for the hypothesis test is twice the area under the t distribution curve having 99 degrees of freedom to the right of $|t| = 1.023$. Using a computer, we find that this p-value is .3088 (see Figure 9.6(b)), which provides little evidence against H_0: $\mu = 330$ and in favor of H_a: $\mu \neq 330$. In Exercises 9.24 and 9.25, the reader will assume that σ is unknown in the payment time and trash bag cases and will perform appropriate t tests in these cases.

To conclude this section, note that if the sampled population is not approximately normally distributed and the sample size is not large, it might be appropriate to use a **nonparametric test about the population median** [see Bowerman, O'Connell, and Murphree (2011)].

Exercises for Section 9.3

CONCEPTS

9.21 What assumptions must be met in order to carry out a t test about a population mean?

9.22 How do we decide whether to use a z test or a t test when testing a hypothesis about a population mean?

connect

METHODS AND APPLICATIONS

9.23   Suppose that a random sample of nine measurements from a normally distributed population gives a sample mean of $\bar{x} = 2.57$ and a sample standard deviation of $s = .3$. Use critical values to test H_0: $\mu = 3$ versus H_a: $\mu \neq 3$ using levels of significance $\alpha = .10$, $\alpha = .05$, $\alpha = .01$, and $\alpha = .001$.

9.24   Consider the payment time case. The mean and the standard deviation of the sample of $n = 65$ payment times are $\bar{x} = 18.1077$ and $s = 3.9612$. Test H_0: $\mu = 19.5$ versus H_a: $\mu < 19.5$ by setting α equal to .01 and using a critical value rule. Also, interpret the (computer calculated) p-value of .0031 for the test.   **DS** PayTime

9.25   Consider the trash bag case. The mean and the standard deviation of the sample of $n = 40$ trash bag breaking strengths are $\bar{x} = 50.575$ and $s = 1.6438$. Test H_0: $\mu = 50$ versus H_a: $\mu > 50$ by setting α equal to .05 and using a critical value rule. Also, interpret the (computer calculated) p-value of .0164 for the test.   **DS** TrashBag

9.26   THE AIR TRAFFIC CONTROL CASE   **DS** AlertTimes

Recall that it is hoped that the mean alert time, μ, using the new display panel is less than eight seconds. Formulate the null hypothesis H_0 and the alternative hypothesis H_a that would be used to attempt to provide evidence that μ is less than eight seconds. Discuss the meanings of a Type I error and a Type II error in this situation. The mean and the standard deviation of the sample of $n = 15$ alert times are $\bar{x} = 7.4$ and $s = 1.0261$. Test H_0 versus H_a by setting α equal to .05 and using a critical value. Also, interpret the p-value of .0200 for the test. Assume that the population of all alert times using the new display panel is approximately normally distributed.

9.27   The *bad debt ratio* for a financial institution is defined to be the dollar value of loans defaulted divided by the total dollar value of all loans made. Suppose that a random sample of seven Ohio banks is selected and that the bad debt ratios (written as percentages) for these banks are 7%, 4%, 6%, 7%, 5%, 4%, and 9%.   **DS** BadDebt

a   Banking officials claim that the mean bad debt ratio for all Midwestern banks is 3.5 percent and that the mean bad debt ratio for Ohio banks is higher. Set up the null and alternative hypotheses needed to attempt to provide evidence supporting the claim that the mean bad debt ratio for Ohio banks exceeds 3.5 percent. Discuss the meanings of a Type I error and a Type II error in this situation.

b   Assuming that bad debt ratios for Ohio banks are approximately normally distributed, use a critical value and the given sample information to test the hypotheses you set up in part *a* by setting α equal to .01. Also, interpret the p-value of .006 for the test.

9.28   How might practical importance be defined for the situation in Exercise 9.27?

9.29   THE VIDEO GAME SATISFACTION RATING CASE   **DS** VideoGame

Recall that "very satisfied" customers give the XYZ-Box video game system a composite satisfaction rating that is at least 42.

a   Letting μ represent the mean composite satisfaction rating for the XYZ-Box, set up the null and alternative hypotheses needed if we wish to attempt to provide evidence supporting the claim that μ exceeds 42.

b   The mean and the standard deviation of a sample of $n = 65$ customer satisfaction ratings are $\bar{x} = 42.95$ and $s = 2.6424$. Use a critical value to test the hypotheses you set up in part *a* by setting α equal to .01. Also, interpret the p-value of .0025 for the test.

9.30   THE BANK CUSTOMER WAITING TIME CASE   **DS** WaitTime

Recall that a bank manager has developed a new system to reduce the time customers spend waiting for teller service during peak hours. The manager hopes the new system will reduce waiting times from the current 9 to 10 minutes to less than 6 minutes.

a   Letting μ represent the mean waiting time under the new system, set up the null and alternative hypotheses needed if we wish to attempt to provide evidence supporting the claim that μ is shorter than six minutes.

b   The mean and the standard deviation of a sample of 100 bank customer waiting times are $\bar{x} = 5.46$ and $s = 2.475$. Use a critical value to test the hypotheses you set up in part *a* by setting α equal to .05. Also, interpret the p-value of .0158 for the test.

9.31   Consider a chemical company that wishes to determine whether a new catalyst, catalyst XA-100, changes the mean hourly yield of its chemical process from the historical process mean of 750 pounds per hour. When five trial runs are made using the new catalyst, the following yields (in pounds per hour) are recorded: 801, 814, 784, 836, and 820.   **DS** ChemYield

a Letting μ be the mean of all possible yields using the new catalyst, set up the null and alternative hypotheses needed if we wish to attempt to provide evidence that μ differs from 750 pounds.

b The mean and the standard deviation of the sample of 5 catalyst yields are $\bar{x} = 811$ and $s = 19.647$. Using a critical value and assuming approximate normality, test the hypotheses you set up in part *a* by setting α equal to .01. The *p*-value for the hypothesis test is given in the Excel output on the page margin. Interpret this *p*-value.

t-statistic
6.942585
p-value
0.002261

9.32 Recall from Exercise 8.12 that Bayus (1991) studied the mean numbers of auto dealers visited by early and late replacement buyers. Letting μ be the mean number of dealers visited by all late replacement buyers, set up the null and alternative hypotheses needed if we wish to attempt to provide evidence that μ differs from 4 dealers. A random sample of 100 late replacement buyers yields a mean and a standard deviation of the number of dealers visited of $\bar{x} = 4.32$ and $s = .67$. Use critical values to test the hypotheses you set up by setting α equal to .10, .05, .01, and .001. Do we estimate that μ is less than 4 or greater than 4?

9.33 In 1991 the average interest rate charged by U.S. credit card issuers was 18.8 percent. Since that time, there has been a proliferation of new credit cards affiliated with retail stores, oil companies, alumni associations, professional sports teams, and so on. A financial officer wishes to study whether the increased competition in the credit card business has reduced interest rates. To do this, the officer will test a hypothesis about the current mean interest rate, μ, charged by all U.S. credit card issuers. To perform the hypothesis test, the officer randomly selects $n = 15$ credit cards and obtains the following interest rates (arranged in increasing order): 14.0, 14.6, 15.3, 15.6, 15.8, 16.4, 16.6, 17.0, 17.3, 17.6, 17.8, 18.1, 18.4, 18.7, and 19.2. A stem-and-leaf display of the interest rates is given on the page margin, and the MINITAB and Excel outputs for testing $H_0: \mu = 18.8$ versus $H_a: \mu < 18.8$ follow. Interpret these outputs. **DS** CreditCd

14	06
15	368
16	46
17	0368
18	147
19	2

```
Test of mu = 18.8 vs < 18.8                              t-statistic
                                                           -4.97
Variable     N      Mean    StDev    SE Mean      T        P      p-value
Rate        15    16.8267  1.5378    0.3971     -4.97    0.000    0.000103
```

9.4 z Tests about a Population Proportion ● ● ●

In this section we study a large sample hypothesis test about a population proportion (that is, about the fraction of population elements that possess some characteristic). We begin with an example.

LO5 Use critical values and *p*-values to perform a large sample *z* test about a population proportion.

EXAMPLE 9.5 The Cheese Spread Case   C

Recall that the soft cheese spread producer has decided that replacing the current spout with the new spout is profitable only if p, the true proportion of all current purchasers who would stop buying the cheese spread if the new spout were used, is less than .10. The producer feels that it is unwise to change the spout unless it has very strong evidence that p is less than .10. Therefore, the spout will be changed if and only if the null hypothesis $H_0: p = .10$ can be rejected in favor of the alternative hypothesis $H_a: p < .10$ at the .01 level of significance.

In order to see how to test this kind of hypothesis, remember that when n is large, the sampling distribution of

$$\frac{\hat{p} - p}{\sqrt{\dfrac{p(1 - p)}{n}}}$$

is approximately a standard normal distribution. Let p_0 denote a specified value between 0 and 1 (its exact value will depend on the problem), and consider testing the null hypothesis $H_0: p = p_0$. We then have the following result:

A Large Sample Test about a Population Proportion

Null Hypothesis	Test Statistic	Assumptions[3]
$H_0: p = p_0$	$z = \dfrac{\hat{p} - p_0}{\sqrt{\dfrac{p_0(1 - p_0)}{n}}}$	$np_0 \geq 5$ and $n(1 - p_0) \geq 5$

Critical Value Rule			p-Value (Reject H_0 if p-Value < α)		
$H_a: p > p_0$	$H_a: p < p_0$	$H_a: p \neq p_0$	$H_a: p > p_0$	$H_a: p < p_0$	$H_a: p \neq p_0$
Do not reject H_0 | Reject H_0	Reject H_0 | Do not reject H_0	Reject H_0 | Do not reject H_0 | Reject H_0			
Reject H_0 if $z > z_\alpha$	Reject H_0 if $z < -z_\alpha$	Reject H_0 if $\|z\| > z_{\alpha/2}$—that is, $z > z_{\alpha/2}$ or $z < -z_{\alpha/2}$	p-value = area to the right of z	p-value = area to the left of z	p-value = twice the area to the right of |z|

EXAMPLE 9.6 The Cheese Spread Case   C

We have seen that the cheese spread producer wishes to test $H_0: p = .10$ versus $H_a: p < .10$, where p is the proportion of all current purchasers who would stop buying the cheese spread if the new spout were used. The producer will use the new spout if H_0 can be rejected in favor of H_a at the **.01 level of significance.** To perform the hypothesis test, we will randomly select $n = 1,000$ current purchasers of the cheese spread, find the proportion ($\hat{p}$) of these purchasers who would stop buying the cheese spread if the new spout were used, and calculate the value of the **test statistic z in the summary box.** Then, since the alternative hypothesis $H_a: p < .10$ implies a left tailed test, we will **reject $H_0: p = .10$ if the value of z is less than** $-z_\alpha = -z_{.01} = -2.33$. (Note that using this procedure is valid because $np_0 = 1,000(.10) = 100$ and $n(1 - p_0) = 1,000(1 - .10) = 900$ are both at least 5.) Suppose that when the sample is randomly selected, we find that 63 of the 1,000 current purchasers say they would stop buying the cheese spread if the new spout were used. Since $\hat{p} = 63/1,000 = .063$, the **value of the test statistic** is

$$z = \frac{\hat{p} - p_0}{\sqrt{\dfrac{p_0(1 - p_0)}{n}}} = \frac{.063 - .10}{\sqrt{\dfrac{.10(1 - .10)}{1,000}}} = -3.90$$

Because $z = -3.90$ is less than $-z_{.01} = -2.33$, we reject $H_0: p = .10$ in favor of $H_a: p < .10$. That is, we conclude (at an α of .01) that the proportion of all current purchasers who would stop buying the cheese spread if the new spout were used is less than .10. It follows that the company will use the new spout. Furthermore, the point estimate $\hat{p} = .063$ says we estimate that 6.3 percent of all current customers would stop buying the cheese spread if the new spout were used.

Although the cheese spread producer has made its decision by setting α equal to a single, pre-chosen value (.01), it would probably also wish to know the weight of evidence against H_0 and in favor of H_a. The p-value is the area under the standard normal curve to the left of $z = -3.90$. Table A.3 (page 638) tells us that this area is .00005. Because this p-value is less than .001, we

---

[3]Some statisticians suggest using the more conservative rule that both np_0 and $n(1 - p_0)$ must be at least 10.

have extremely strong evidence that H_a: $p < .10$ is true. That is, we have extremely strong evidence that fewer than 10 percent of all current purchasers would stop buying the cheese spread if the new spout were used.

EXAMPLE 9.7

Recent medical research has sought to develop drugs that lessen the severity and duration of viral infections. Virol, a relatively new drug, has been shown to provide relief for 70 percent of all patients suffering from viral upper respiratory infections. A major drug company is developing a competing drug called Phantol. The drug company wishes to investigate whether Phantol is more effective than Virol. To do this, the drug company will test a hypothesis about the true proportion, p, of all patients whose symptoms would be relieved by Phantol. **The null hypothesis to be tested is H_0: $p = .70$, and the alternative hypothesis is H_a: $p > .70$.** If H_0 can be rejected in favor of H_a at the **.05 level of significance,** the drug company will conclude that Phantol helps more than the 70 percent of patients helped by Virol. To perform the hypothesis test, we will randomly select $n = 300$ patients having viral upper respiratory infections, find the proportion ($\hat{p}$) of these patients whose symptoms are relieved by Phantol and calculate the value of the **test statistic z in the summary box.** Then, since the alternative hypothesis H_a: $p > .70$ implies a right tailed test, we will **reject H_0: $p = .70$ if the value of z is greater than $z_\alpha = z_{.05} = 1.645$.** (Note that using this procedure is valid because $np_0 = 300(.70) = 210$ and $n(1 - p_0) = 300(1 - .70) = 90$ are both at least 5.) Suppose that when the sample is randomly selected, we find that Phantol provides relief for 231 of the 300 patients. Since $\hat{p} = 231/300 = .77$, the **value of the test statistic** is

$$z = \frac{\hat{p} - p_0}{\sqrt{\dfrac{p_0(1 - p_0)}{n}}} = \frac{.77 - .70}{\sqrt{\dfrac{(.70)(1 - .70)}{300}}} = 2.65$$

Because $z = 2.65$ is greater than $z_{.05} = 1.645$, we reject H_0: $p = .70$ in favor of H_a: $p > .70$. That is, we conclude (at an α of .05) that Phantol will provide relief for more than 70 percent of all patients suffering from viral upper respiratory infections. More specifically, the point estimate $\hat{p} = .77$ of p says that we estimate that Phantol will provide relief for 77 percent of all such patients. Comparing this estimate to the 70 percent of all patients whose symptoms are relieved by Virol, we conclude that Phantol is somewhat more effective.

The *p*-value for testing H_0: $p = .70$ versus H_a: $p > .70$ is the area under the standard normal curve to the right of $z = 2.65$. This *p*-value is $(1.0 - .9960) = .004$ (see Table A.3, page 638), and it provides very strong evidence against H_0: $p = .70$ and in favor of H_a: $p > .70$. That is, we have very strong evidence that Phantol will provide relief for more than 70 percent of all patients suffering from viral upper respiratory infections.

EXAMPLE 9.8 The Electronic Article Surveillance Case

A sports equipment discount store is considering installing an electronic article surveillance device and is concerned about the proportion, p, of all consumers who would never shop in the store again if the store subjected them to a false alarm. Suppose that industry data for general discount stores says that 15 percent of all consumers say that they would never shop in a store again if the store subjected them to a false alarm. To determine whether this percentage is different for the sports equipment discount store, the store will test the **null hypothesis H_0: $p = .15$ versus the alternative hypothesis H_a: $p \neq .15$** at the **.05 level of significance.** To perform the hypothesis test, the store will randomly select $n = 500$ consumers, find the proportion $\hat{p}$ of these consumers who say that they would never shop in the store again if the store subjected them to a false alarm, and calculate the value of the **test statistic z in the summary box.** Then, since the alternative hypothesis H_a: $p \neq .15$ implies a two tailed test, we will **reject H_0: $p = .15$ if $|z|$, the absolute value of the test statistic z, is greater than $z_{\alpha/2} = z_{.025} = 1.96$.** (Note that using this procedure is valid because $np_0 = (500)(.15) = 75$ and $n(1 - p_0) = (500)(1 - .15) = 425$ are both at least 5.)

Suppose that when the sample is randomly selected, we find that 70 out of 500 consumers say that they would never shop in the store again if the store subjected them to a false alarm. Since $\hat{p} = 70/500 = .14$, the **value of the test statistic** is

$$z = \frac{\hat{p} - p_0}{\sqrt{\dfrac{p_0(1 - p_0)}{n}}} = \frac{.14 - .15}{\sqrt{\dfrac{.15(1 - .15)}{500}}} = -.63$$

BI

Because $|z| = .63$ is less than $z_{.025} = 1.96$, we cannot reject $H_0: p = .15$ in favor of $H_a: p \neq .15$. That is, we cannot conclude (at an α of .05) that the percentage of all people who would never shop in the sports discount store again if the store subjected them to a false alarm differs from the general discount store percentage of 15 percent.

The p-value for testing $H_0: p = .15$ versus $H_a: p \neq .15$ is twice the area under the standard normal curve to the right of $|z| = .63$. Because the area under the standard normal curve to the right of $|z| = .63$ is $(1 - .7357) = .2643$ (see Table A.3, page 638), the p-value is $2(.2643) = .5286$. This p-value is large and provides little evidence against $H_0: p = .15$ and in favor of $H_a: p \neq .15$. That is, we have little evidence that the percentage of people who would never shop in the sports discount store again if the store subjected them to a false alarm differs from the general discount store percentage of 15 percent.

Technical note   Excel often expresses a p-value in scientific notation. For example, suppose that the test statistic z for testing a "greater than" alternative hypothesis about a population proportion equaled 7.98. If Excel calculated the p-value for the hypothesis test—the area under the standard normal curve to the right of $z = 7.98$—Excel would express the p-value as 7.77 E−16. To get the decimal point equivalent, the "E−16" says that we must move the decimal point 16 places to the left. Therefore, the p-value is .000000000000000777.

Exercises for Section 9.4

CONCEPTS

connect

9.34   If we wish to test a hypothesis to provide evidence supporting the claim that fewer than 5 percent of the units produced by a process are defective, formulate the null and alternative hypotheses.

9.35   What condition must be satisfied in order to appropriately use the methods of this section?

METHODS AND APPLICATIONS

9.36   Suppose we test $H_0: p = .3$ versus $H_a: p \neq .3$ and that a random sample of $n = 100$ gives a sample proportion $\hat{p} = .20$.
   a Test H_0 versus H_a at the .01 level of significance by using critical values. What do you conclude?
   b Find the p-value for this test.
   c Use the p-value to test H_0 versus H_a by setting α equal to .10, .05, .01, and .001. What do you conclude at each value of α?

9.37   **THE MARKETING ETHICS CASE: CONFLICT OF INTEREST**

Recall that a conflict of interest scenario was presented to a sample of 205 marketing researchers and that 111 of these researchers disapproved of the actions taken.
   a Let p be the proportion of all marketing researchers who disapprove of the actions taken in the conflict of interest scenario. Set up the null and alternative hypotheses needed to attempt to provide evidence supporting the claim that a majority (more than 50 percent) of all marketing researchers disapprove of the actions taken.
   b Assuming that the sample of 205 marketing researchers has been randomly selected, use critical values and the previously given sample information to test the hypotheses you set up in part a at the .10, .05, .01, and .001 levels of significance. How much evidence is there that a majority of all marketing researchers disapprove of the actions taken?
   c Suppose a random sample of 1,000 marketing researchers reveals that 540 of the researchers disapprove of the actions taken in the conflict of interest scenario. Use critical values to determine how much evidence there is that a majority of all marketing researchers disapprove of the actions taken.

d Note that in parts b and c the sample proportion $\hat{p}$ is (essentially) the same. Explain why the results of the hypothesis tests in parts b and c differ.

9.38 Last year, television station WXYZ's share of the 11 P.M. news audience was approximately equal to, but no greater than, 25 percent. The station's management believes that the current audience share is higher than last year's 25 percent share. In an attempt to substantiate this belief, the station surveyed a random sample of 400 11 P.M. news viewers and found that 146 watched WXYZ.

a Let p be the current proportion of all 11 P.M. news viewers who watch WXYZ. Set up the null and alternative hypotheses needed to attempt to provide evidence supporting the claim that the current audience share for WXYZ is higher than last year's 25 percent share.

b Use critical values and the following MINITAB output to test the hypotheses you set up in part a at the .10, .05, .01, and .001 levels of significance. How much evidence is there that the current audience share is higher than last year's 25 percent share?

```
Test of p = 0.25 vs p > 0.25

Sample     X      N     Sample p     Z-Value     P-Value
1         146    400    0.365000        5.31       0.000
```

c Find the p-value for the hypothesis test in part b. Use the p-value to carry out the test by setting α equal to .10, .05, .01, and .001. Interpret your results.

d Do you think that the result of the station's survey has practical importance? Why or why not?

9.39 In the book *Essentials of Marketing Research,* William R. Dillon, Thomas J. Madden, and Neil H. Firtle discuss a marketing research proposal to study day-after recall for a brand of mouthwash. To quote the authors:

The ad agency has developed a TV ad for the introduction of the mouthwash. The objective of the ad is to create awareness of the brand. The objective of this research is to evaluate the awareness generated by the ad measured by aided- and unaided-recall scores.

A minimum of 200 respondents who claim to have watched the TV show in which the ad was aired the night before will be contacted by telephone in 20 cities.

The study will provide information on the incidence of unaided and aided recall.

Suppose a random sample of 200 respondents shows that 46 of the people interviewed were able to recall the commercial without any prompting (unaided recall).

a In order for the ad to be considered successful, the percentage of unaided recall must be above the category norm for a TV commercial for the product class. If this norm is 18 percent, set up the null and alternative hypotheses needed to attempt to provide evidence that the ad is successful.

b Use the previously given sample information to compute the p-value for the hypothesis test you set up in part a. Use the p-value to carry out the test by setting α equal to .10, .05, .01, and .001. How much evidence is there that the TV commercial is successful?

c Do you think the result of the ad agency's survey has practical importance? Explain your opinion.

9.40 An airline's data indicate that 50 percent of people who begin the online process of booking a flight never complete the process and pay for the flight. To reduce this percentage, the airline is considering changing its website so that the entire booking process, including flight and seat selection and payment, can be done on two simple pages rather than the current four pages. A random sample of 300 customers who begin the booking process are provided with the new system, and 117 of them do not complete the process. Formulate the null and alternative hypotheses needed to attempt to provide evidence that the new system has reduced the noncompletion percentage. Use critical values and a p-value to perform the hypothesis test by setting α equal to .10, .05, .01, and .001.

9.41 Suppose that a national survey finds that 73 percent of restaurant employees say that work stress has a negative impact on their personal lives. A random sample of 200 employees of a large restaurant chain finds that 141 employees say that work stress has a negative impact on their personal lives. Formulate the null and alternative hypotheses needed to attempt to provide evidence that the percentage of work-stressed employees for the restaurant chain differs from the national percentage. Use critical values and a p-value to perform the hypothesis test by setting α equal to .10, .05, .01, and .001.

9.42 The manufacturer of the ColorSmart-5000 television set claims that 95 percent of its sets last at least five years without needing a single repair. In order to test this claim, a consumer group randomly selects 400 consumers who have owned a ColorSmart-5000 television set for five years. Of these 400 consumers, 316 say that their ColorSmart-5000 television sets did not need repair, while 84 say that their ColorSmart-5000 television sets did need at least one repair.

   a Letting p be the proportion of ColorSmart-5000 television sets that last five years without a single repair, set up the null and alternative hypotheses that the consumer group should use to attempt to show that the manufacturer's claim is false.

   b Use critical values and the previously given sample information to test the hypotheses you set up in part *a* by setting α equal to .10, .05, .01, and .001. How much evidence is there that the manufacturer's claim is false?

   c Do you think the results of the consumer group's survey have practical importance? Explain your opinion.

LO6 Calculate Type II error probabilities and the power of a test, and determine sample size (Optional).

9.5 Type II Error Probabilities and Sample Size Determination (Optional) ● ● ●

As we have seen, we often take action (for example, advertise a claim) on the basis of having rejected the null hypothesis. In this case, we know the chances that the action has been taken erroneously because we have prespecified α, the probability of rejecting a true null hypothesis. However, sometimes we must act (for example, decide how many Valentine's Day boxes of chocolates to produce) on the basis of *not* rejecting the null hypothesis. If we must do this, it is best to know the probability of not rejecting a false null hypothesis (a Type II error). If this probability is not small enough, we may change the hypothesis testing procedure. In order to discuss this further, we must first see how to compute the probability of a Type II error.

As an example, the Federal Trade Commission (FTC) often tests claims that companies make about their products. Suppose coffee is being sold in cans that are labeled as containing three pounds, and also suppose that the FTC wishes to determine if the mean amount of coffee μ in all such cans is at least three pounds. To do this, the FTC tests $H_0: \mu \geq 3$ (or $\mu = 3$) versus $H_a: \mu < 3$ by setting $\alpha = .05$. Suppose that a sample of 35 coffee cans yields $\bar{x} = 2.9973$. Assuming that σ is known to equal .0147, we see that because

$$z = \frac{2.9973 - 3}{.0147/\sqrt{35}} = -1.08$$

is not less than $-z_{.05} = -1.645$, we cannot reject $H_0: \mu \geq 3$ by setting $\alpha = .05$. Since we cannot reject H_0, we cannot have committed a Type I error, which is the error of rejecting a true H_0. However, we might have committed a Type II error, which is the error of not rejecting a false H_0. Therefore, before we make a final conclusion about μ, we should calculate the probability of a Type II error.

A Type II error is not rejecting $H_0: \mu \geq 3$ when H_0 is false. Because any value of μ that is less than 3 makes H_0 false, there is a different Type II error (and, therefore, a different Type II error probability) associated with each value of μ that is less than 3. In order to demonstrate how to calculate these probabilities, we will calculate the probability of not rejecting $H_0: \mu \geq 3$ when in fact μ equals 2.995. This is the probability of failing to detect an average underfill of .005 pound. For a fixed sample size (for example, $n = 35$ coffee can fills), the value of β, the probability of a Type II error, depends upon how we set α, the probability of a Type I error. Since we have set $\alpha = .05$, we reject H_0 if

$$\frac{\bar{x} - 3}{\sigma/\sqrt{n}} < -z_{.05}$$

or, equivalently, if

$$\bar{x} < 3 - z_{.05}\frac{\sigma}{\sqrt{n}} = 3 - 1.645\frac{.0147}{\sqrt{35}} = 2.9959126$$

Therefore, we do not reject H_0 if $\bar{x} \geq 2.9959126$. It follows that β, the probability of not rejecting $H_0: \mu \geq 3$ when μ equals 2.995, is

$$\beta = P(\bar{x} \geq 2.9959126 \text{ when } \mu = 2.995)$$

$$= P\left(z \geq \frac{2.9959126 - 2.995}{.0147/\sqrt{35}}\right)$$

$$= P(z \geq .37) = 1 - .6443 = .3557$$

FIGURE 9.7   Calculating β When μ Equals 2.995

This calculation is illustrated in Figure 9.7. Similarly, it follows that β, the probability of not rejecting H_0: $\mu \geq 3$ when μ equals 2.99, is

$$\beta = P(\overline{x} \geq 2.9959126 \text{ when } \mu = 2.99)$$

$$= P\left(z \geq \frac{2.9959126 - 2.99}{.0147/\sqrt{35}}\right)$$

$$= P(z \geq 2.38) = 1 - .9913 = .0087$$

It also follows that β, the probability of not rejecting H_0: $\mu \geq 3$ when μ equals 2.985, is

$$\beta = P(\overline{x} \geq 2.9959126 \text{ when } \mu = 2.985)$$

$$= P\left(z \geq \frac{2.9959126 - 2.985}{.0147/\sqrt{35}}\right)$$

$$= P(z \geq 4.39)$$

This probability is less than .00003 (because z is greater than 3.99).

In Figure 9.8 we illustrate the values of β that we have calculated. Notice that the closer an alternative value of μ is to 3 (the value specified by H_0: $\mu = 3$), the larger is the associated value of β. Although alternative values of μ that are closer to 3 have larger associated probabilities of Type II errors, these values of μ have associated Type II errors with less serious consequences. For example, we are more likely not to reject H_0: $\mu = 3$ when $\mu = 2.995$ ($\beta = .3557$) than we are not to reject H_0: $\mu = 3$ when $\mu = 2.99$ ($\beta = .0087$). However, not rejecting H_0: $\mu = 3$ when $\mu = 2.995$, which means that we are failing to detect an average underfill of .005 pound, is less serious than not rejecting H_0: $\mu = 3$ when $\mu = 2.99$, which means that we are failing to detect a larger average underfill of .01 pound. In order to decide whether a particular hypothesis test adequately controls the probability of a Type II error, we must determine which Type II errors are serious, and then we must decide whether the probabilities of these errors are small enough. For

FIGURE 9.8   How β Changes as the Alternative Value of μ Changes

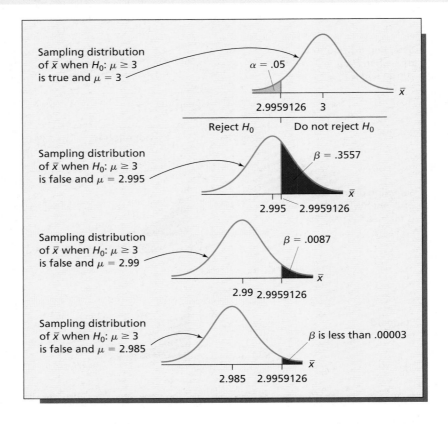

example, suppose that the FTC and the coffee producer agree that failing to reject H_0: $\mu = 3$ when μ equals 2.99 is a serious error, but that failing to reject H_0: $\mu = 3$ when μ equals 2.995 is not a particularly serious error. Then, since the probability of not rejecting H_0: $\mu = 3$ when μ equals 2.99 is .0087, which is quite small, we might decide that the hypothesis test adequately controls the probability of a Type II error. To understand the implication of this, recall that the sample of 35 coffee cans, which has $\bar{x} = 2.9973$, does not provide enough evidence to reject H_0: $\mu \geq 3$ by setting $\alpha = .05$. We have just shown that the probability that we have failed to detect a serious underfill is quite small (.0087), so the FTC might decide that no action should be taken against the coffee producer. Of course, this decision should also be based on the variability of the fills of the individual cans. Because $\bar{x} = 2.9973$ and $\sigma = .0147$, we estimate that 99.73 percent of all individual coffee can fills are contained in the interval $[\bar{x} \pm 3\sigma] = [2.9973 \pm 3(.0147)] = [2.9532, 3.0414]$. If the FTC believes it is reasonable to accept fills as low as (but no lower than) 2.9532 pounds, this evidence also suggests that no action against the coffee producer is needed.

Suppose, instead, that the FTC and the coffee producer had agreed that failing to reject H_0: $\mu \geq 3$ when μ equals 2.995 is a serious mistake. The probability of this Type II error is .3557, which is large. Therefore, we might conclude that the hypothesis test is not adequately controlling the probability of a serious Type II error. In this case, we have two possible courses of action. First, we have previously said that, for a fixed sample size, the lower we set α, the higher is β, and the higher we set α, the lower is β. Therefore, if we keep the sample size fixed at $n = 35$ coffee cans, we can reduce β by increasing α. To demonstrate this, suppose we increase α to .10. In this case we reject H_0 if

$$\frac{\bar{x} - 3}{\sigma / \sqrt{n}} < -z_{.10}$$

or, equivalently, if

$$\bar{x} < 3 - z_{.10}\frac{\sigma}{\sqrt{n}} = 3 - 1.282\frac{.0147}{\sqrt{35}} = 2.9968145$$

Therefore, we do not reject H_0 if $\bar{x} \geq 2.9968145$. It follows that β, the probability of not rejecting $H_0: \mu \geq 3$ when μ equals 2.995, is

$$\beta = P(\bar{x} \geq 2.9968145 \text{ when } \mu = 2.995)$$

$$= P\left(z \geq \frac{2.9968145 - 2.995}{.0147/\sqrt{35}}\right)$$

$$= P(z \geq .73) = 1 - .7673 = .2327$$

We thus see that increasing α from .05 to .10 reduces β from .3557 to .2327. However, β is still too large, and, besides, we might not be comfortable making α larger than .05. Therefore, if we wish to decrease β and maintain α at .05, we must increase the sample size. We will soon present a formula we can use to find the sample size needed to make both α and β as small as we wish.

Once we have computed β, we can calculate what we call the *power* of the test.

> The **power** of a statistical test is the probability of rejecting the null hypothesis when it is false.

Just as β depends upon the alternative value of μ, so does the power of a test. In general, **the power associated with a particular alternative value of μ equals $1 - \beta$,** where β is the probability of a Type II error associated with the same alternative value of μ. For example, we have seen that, when we set $\alpha = .05$, the probability of not rejecting $H_0: \mu \geq 3$ when μ equals 2.99 is .0087. Therefore, the power of the test associated with the alternative value 2.99 (that is, the probability of rejecting $H_0: \mu \geq 3$ when μ equals 2.99) is $1 - .0087 = .9913$.

Thus far we have demonstrated how to calculate β when testing a *less than* alternative hypothesis. In the following box we present (without proof) a method for calculating the probability of a Type II error when testing a *less than*, a *greater than*, or a *not equal to* alternative hypothesis:

Calculating the Probability of a Type II Error

Assume that the sampled population is normally distributed, or that a large sample will be taken. Consider testing $H_0: \mu = \mu_0$ versus one of $H_a: \mu > \mu_0$, $H_a: \mu < \mu_0$, or $H_a: \mu \neq \mu_0$. Then, if we set the probability of a Type I error equal to α and randomly select a sample of size n, the probability, β, of a Type II error corresponding to the alternative value μ_a of μ is (exactly or approximately) equal to the area under the standard normal curve to the left of

$$z^* - \frac{|\mu_0 - \mu_a|}{\sigma/\sqrt{n}}$$

Here z^* equals z_α if the alternative hypothesis is one-sided ($\mu > \mu_0$ or $\mu < \mu_0$), in which case the method for calculating β is exact. Furthermore, z^* equals $z_{\alpha/2}$ if the alternative hypothesis is two-sided ($\mu \neq \mu_0$), in which case the method for calculating β is approximate.

EXAMPLE 9.9 The Valentine's Day Chocolate Case

In the Valentine's Day chocolate case we are testing $H_0: \mu = 330$ versus $H_a: \mu \neq 330$ by setting $\alpha = .05$. We have seen that the mean of the reported order quantities of a random sample of $n = 100$ large retail stores is $\bar{x} = 326$. Assuming that σ equals 40, it follows that because

$$z = \frac{326 - 330}{40/\sqrt{100}} = -1$$

is between $-z_{.025} = -1.96$ and $z_{.025} = 1.96$, we cannot reject $H_0: \mu = 330$ by setting $\alpha = .05$. Since we cannot reject H_0, we might have committed a Type II error. Suppose that the candy company decides that failing to reject $H_0: \mu = 330$ when μ differs from 330 by as many as 15 valentine boxes (that is, when μ is 315 or 345) is a serious Type II error. Because we have set α

equal to .05, β for the alternative value $\mu_a = 315$ (that is, the probability of not rejecting H_0: $\mu = 330$ when μ equals 315) is the area under the standard normal curve to the left of

$$z^* - \frac{|\mu_0 - \mu_a|}{\sigma/\sqrt{n}} = z_{.025} - \frac{|\mu_0 - \mu_a|}{\sigma/\sqrt{n}}$$

$$= 1.96 - \frac{|330 - 315|}{40/\sqrt{100}}$$

$$= -1.79$$

Here $z^* = z_{\alpha/2} = z_{.05/2} = z_{.025}$ since the alternative hypothesis ($\mu \neq 330$) is two-sided. The area under the standard normal curve to the left of -1.79 is .0367. Therefore, β for the alternative value $\mu_a = 315$ is .0367. Similarly, it can be verified that β for the alternative value $\mu_a = 345$ is .0367. It follows, because we cannot reject H_0: $\mu = 330$ by setting $\alpha = .05$, and because we have just shown that there is a reasonably small (.0367) probability that we have failed to detect a serious (that is, a 15 valentine box) deviation of μ from 330, that it is reasonable for the candy company to base this year's production of valentine boxes on the projected mean order quantity of 330 boxes per large retail store.

In the following box we present (without proof) a formula that tells us the sample size needed to make both the probability of a Type I error and the probability of a Type II error as small as we wish:

Calculating the Sample Size Needed to Achieve Specified Values of α and β

Assume that the sampled population is normally distributed, or that a large sample will be taken. Consider testing H_0: $\mu = \mu_0$ versus one of H_a: $\mu > \mu_0$, H_a: $\mu < \mu_0$, or H_a: $\mu \neq \mu_0$. Then, in order to make the probability of a Type I error equal to α and the probability of a Type II error corresponding to the alternative value μ_a of μ equal to β, we should take a sample of size

$$n = \frac{(z^* + z_\beta)^2 \sigma^2}{(\mu_0 - \mu_a)^2}$$

Here z^* equals z_α if the alternative hypothesis is one-sided ($\mu > \mu_0$ or $\mu < \mu_0$), and z^* equals $z_{\alpha/2}$ if the alternative hypothesis is two-sided ($\mu \neq \mu_0$). Also, z_β is the point on the scale of the standard normal curve that gives a right-hand tail area equal to β.

EXAMPLE 9.10

Again consider the coffee fill example and suppose we wish to test H_0: $\mu \geq 3$ (or $\mu = 3$) versus H_a: $\mu < 3$. If we wish α to be .05 and β for the alternative value $\mu_a = 2.995$ of μ to be .05, we should take a sample of size

$$n = \frac{(z^* + z_\beta)^2 \sigma^2}{(\mu_0 - \mu_a)^2} = \frac{(z_\alpha + z_\beta)^2 \sigma^2}{(\mu_0 - \mu_a)^2}$$

$$= \frac{(z_{.05} + z_{.05})^2 \sigma^2}{(\mu_0 - \mu_a)^2}$$

$$= \frac{(1.645 + 1.645)^2 (.0147)^2}{(3 - 2.995)^2}$$

$$= 93.5592 = 94 \text{ (rounding up)}$$

Here, $z^* = z_\alpha = z_{.05} = 1.645$ because the alternative hypothesis ($\mu < 3$) is one-sided, and $z_\beta = z_{.05} = 1.645$.

Although we have set both α and β equal to the same value in the coffee fill situation, it is not necessary for α and β to be equal. As an example, again consider the Valentine's Day chocolate case, in which we are testing H_0: $\mu = 330$ versus H_a: $\mu \neq 330$. Suppose that the candy company decides that failing to reject H_0: $\mu = 330$ when μ differs from 330 by as many as 15 valentine boxes (that is, when μ is 315 or 345) is a serious Type II error. Furthermore, suppose that it is also decided that this Type II error is more serious than a Type I error. Therefore, α will be set equal to .05 and β for the alternative value $\mu_a = 315$ (or $\mu_a = 345$) of μ will be set equal to .01. It follows that the candy company should take a sample of size

$$n = \frac{(z^* + z_\beta)^2 \sigma^2}{(\mu_0 - \mu_a)^2} = \frac{(z_{\alpha/2} + z_\beta)^2 \sigma^2}{(\mu_0 - \mu_a)^2}$$

$$= \frac{(z_{.025} + z_{.01})^2 \sigma^2}{(\mu_0 - \mu_a)^2}$$

$$= \frac{(1.96 + 2.326)^2 (40)^2}{(330 - 315)^2}$$

$$= 130.62 = 131 \text{ (rounding up)}$$

Here, $z^* = z_{\alpha/2} = z_{.05/2} = z_{.025} = 1.96$ because the alternative hypothesis ($\mu \neq 330$) is two-sided, and $z_\beta = z_{.01} = 2.326$ (see the bottom row of the t table on page 315).

To conclude this section, we point out that the methods we have presented for calculating the probability of a Type II error and determining sample size can be extended to other hypothesis tests that utilize the normal distribution. We will not, however, present the extensions in this book.

Exercises for Section 9.5

CONCEPTS

9.43 We usually take action on the basis of having rejected the null hypothesis. When we do this, we know the chances that the action has been taken erroneously because we have prespecified α, the probability of rejecting a true null hypothesis. Here, it is obviously important to know (prespecify) α, the probability of a Type I error. When is it important to know the probability of a Type II error? Explain why.

9.44 Explain why we are able to compute many different values of β, the probability of a Type II error, for a single hypothesis test.

9.45 Explain what is meant by
   a A serious Type II error.
   b The power of a statistical test.

9.46 In general, do we want the power corresponding to a serious Type II error to be near 0 or near 1? Explain.

METHODS AND APPLICATIONS

9.47 Again consider the Consolidated Power waste water situation. Remember that the power plant will be shut down and corrective action will be taken on the cooling system if the null hypothesis H_0: $\mu \leq 60$ is rejected in favor of H_a: $\mu > 60$. In this exercise we calculate probabilities of various Type II errors in the context of this situation.
   a Recall that Consolidated Power's hypothesis test is based on a sample of $n = 100$ temperature readings and assume that σ equals 2. If the power company sets $\alpha = .025$, calculate the probability of a Type II error for each of the following alternative values of μ: 60.1, 60.2, 60.3, 60.4, 60.5, 60.6, 60.7, 60.8, 60.9, 61.
   b If we want the probability of making a Type II error when μ equals 60.5 to be very small, is Consolidated Power's hypothesis test adequate? Explain why or why not. If not, and if we wish to maintain the value of α at .025, what must be done?
   c The **power curve** for a statistical test is a plot of the power $= 1 - \beta$ on the vertical axis versus values of μ that make the null hypothesis false on the horizontal axis. Plot the power curve for Consolidated Power's test of H_0: $\mu \leq 60$ versus H_a: $\mu > 60$ by plotting power $= 1 - \beta$ for each of the alternative values of μ in part a. What happens to the power of the test as the alternative value of μ moves away from 60?

9.48 Again consider the automobile parts supplier situation. Remember that a problem-solving team will be assigned to rectify the process producing the cylindrical engine parts if the null hypothesis $H_0: \mu = 3$ is rejected in favor of $H_a: \mu \neq 3$. In this exercise we calculate probabilities of various Type II errors in the context of this situation.

   a Suppose that the parts supplier's hypothesis test is based on a sample of $n = 100$ diameters and that σ equals .023. If the parts supplier sets $\alpha = .05$, calculate the probability of a Type II error for each of the following alternative values of μ: 2.990, 2.995, 3.005, 3.010.

   b If we want both the probabilities of making a Type II error when μ equals 2.995 and when μ equals 3.005 to be very small, is the parts supplier's hypothesis test adequate? Explain why or why not. If not, and if we wish to maintain the value of α at .05, what must be done?

   c Plot the power of the test versus the alternative values of μ in part *a*. What happens to the power of the test as the alternative value of μ moves away from 3?

9.49 In the Consolidated Power hypothesis test of $H_0: \mu \leq 60$ versus $H_a: \mu > 60$ (as discussed in Exercise 9.47) find the sample size needed to make the probability of a Type I error equal to .025 and the probability of a Type II error corresponding to the alternative value $\mu_a = 60.5$ equal to .025. Here, assume σ equals 2.

9.50 In the automobile parts supplier's hypothesis test of $H_0: \mu = 3$ versus $H_a: \mu \neq 3$ (as discussed in Exercise 9.48) find the sample size needed to make the probability of a Type I error equal to .05 and the probability of a Type II error corresponding to the alternative value $\mu_a = 3.005$ equal to .05. Here, assume σ equals .023.

LO7 Describe the properties of the chi-square distribution and use a chi-square table (Optional).

9.6 The Chi-Square Distribution (Optional) ● ● ●

Sometimes we can make statistical inferences by using the **chi-square distribution.** The probability curve of the χ^2 (pronounced *chi-square*) distribution is skewed to the right. Moreover, the exact shape of this probability curve depends on a parameter that is called the **number of degrees of freedom** (denoted *df*). Figure 9.9 illustrates chi-square distributions having 2, 5, and 10 degrees of freedom.

In order to use the chi-square distribution, we employ a **chi-square point,** which is denoted χ^2_α. As illustrated in the upper portion of Figure 9.10, χ^2_α is the point on the horizontal axis under the curve of the chi-square distribution that gives a right-hand tail area equal to α. The value of χ^2_α in a particular situation depends on the right-hand tail area α and the number of degrees of freedom (*df*) of the chi-square distribution. Values of χ^2_α are tabulated in a **chi-square table.** Such a table is given in Table A.10 of Appendix A (page 648); a portion of this table is reproduced as Table 9.3. Looking at the chi-square table, the rows correspond to the appropriate number of degrees of freedom (values of which are listed down the left side of the table), while the columns designate the right-hand tail area α. For example, suppose we wish to find the chi-square point that gives a right-hand tail area of .05 under a chi-square curve having 5 degrees of freedom. To do this, we look in Table 9.3 at the row labeled 5 and the column labeled $\chi^2_{.05}$. We find that this $\chi^2_{.05}$ point is 11.0705 (see the shaded area in Table 9.3 and lower portion of Figure 9.10).

| FIGURE 9.9 | Chi-Square Distributions with 2, 5, and 10 Degrees of Freedom | FIGURE 9.10 Chi-Square Points |

TABLE 9.3   **A Portion of the Chi-Square Table**

Degrees of Freedom (df)	$\chi^2_{.10}$	$\chi^2_{.05}$	$\chi^2_{.025}$	$\chi^2_{.01}$	$\chi^2_{.005}$
1	2.70554	3.84146	5.02389	6.63490	7.87944
2	4.60517	5.99147	7.37776	9.21034	10.5966
3	6.25139	7.81473	9.34840	11.3449	12.8381
4	7.77944	9.48773	11.1433	13.2767	14.8602
5	9.23635	11.0705	12.8325	15.0863	16.7496
6	10.6446	12.5916	14.4494	16.8119	18.5476

9.7 Statistical Inference for a Population Variance (Optional) ● ● ●

LO8 Use the chi-square distribution to make statistical inferences about population variances (Optional).

A jelly and jam producer has a filling process that is supposed to fill jars with 16 ounces of grape jelly. Through long experience with the filling process, the jelly and jam producer knows that the population of all fills produced by the process is normally distributed with a mean of 16 ounces, a variance of .000625, and a standard deviation of .025 ounce. Using the Empirical Rule, it follows that 99.73 percent of all jar fills produced by the process are in the tolerance interval $[16 \pm 3(.025)] = [15.925, 16.075]$. In order to be competitive with the tightest specifications in the jelly and jam industry, the producer has decided that at least 99.73 percent of all jar fills must be between 15.95 ounces and 16.05 ounces. Because the tolerance limits [15.925, 16.075] of the current filling process are not inside the specification limits [15.95, 16.05], the jelly and jam producer designs a new filling process that will hopefully reduce the variance of the jar fills. A random sample of $n = 30$ jars filled by the new process is selected, and the mean and the variance of the corresponding jar fills are found to be $\bar{x} = 16$ ounces and $s^2 = .000121$. In order to attempt to show that the variance, σ^2, of the population of all jar fills that would be produced by the new process is less than .000625, we can use the following result:

Statistical Inference for a Population Variance

Suppose that s^2 is the variance of a sample of n measurements randomly selected from a normally distributed population having variance σ^2. The sampling distribution of the statistic $(n-1)s^2/\sigma^2$ is a chi-square distribution having $n-1$ degrees of freedom. This implies that

1 A 100$(1 - \alpha)$ percent confidence interval for σ^2 is

$$\left[\frac{(n-1)s^2}{\chi^2_{\alpha/2}}, \frac{(n-1)s^2}{\chi^2_{1-(\alpha/2)}} \right]$$

Here $\chi^2_{\alpha/2}$ and $\chi^2_{1-(\alpha/2)}$ are the points under the curve of the chi-square distribution having $n-1$ degrees of freedom that give right-hand tail areas of, respectively, $\alpha/2$ and $1 - (\alpha/2)$.

2 We can test $H_0: \sigma^2 = \sigma_0^2$ at level of significance α by using the test statistic

$$\chi^2 = \frac{(n-1)s^2}{\sigma_0^2}$$

and by using the critical value rule or p-value that is positioned under the appropriate alternative hypothesis. **We reject H_0 if the p-value is less than α.**

$H_a: \sigma^2 > \sigma_0^2$

Do not reject H_0 | Reject H_0

α

χ^2_α

Reject H_0 if $\chi^2 > \chi^2_\alpha$

$H_a: \sigma^2 < \sigma_0^2$

Reject H_0 | Do not reject H_0

α

$\chi^2_{1-\alpha}$

Reject H_0 if $\chi^2 < \chi^2_{1-\alpha}$

$H_a: \sigma^2 \neq \sigma_0^2$

Reject H_0 | Do not reject H_0 | Reject H_0

$\alpha/2$ $\alpha/2$

$\chi^2_{1-\alpha/2}$ $\chi^2_{\alpha/2}$

Reject H_0 if $\chi^2 > \chi^2_{\alpha/2}$ or $\chi^2 < \chi^2_{1-(\alpha/2)}$

p-value

χ^2

p-value = area to the right of χ^2

χ^2

p-value = area to the left of χ^2

χ^2

p-value = 2A See note for A.

Note: A is the area to the right of χ^2, or the area to the left of χ^2, whichever is smaller.

FIGURE 9.11 Testing H_0: $\sigma^2 = .000625$ versus H_a: $\sigma^2 < .000625$ by Setting $\alpha = .05$

FIGURE 9.12 The Chi-Square Points $\chi^2_{.025}$ and $\chi^2_{.975}$

The assumption that the sampled population is normally distributed must hold fairly closely for the statistical inferences just given about σ^2 to be valid. When we check this assumption in the jar fill situation, we find that a histogram (not given here) of the sample of $n = 30$ jar fills is bell-shaped and symmetrical. In order to assess whether the jar fill variance σ^2 for the new filling process is less than .000625, we test **the null hypothesis H_0: $\sigma^2 = .000625$ versus the alternative hypothesis H_a: $\sigma^2 < .000625$.** If H_0 can be rejected in favor of H_a at the **.05 level of significance,** we will conclude that the new process has reduced the variance of the jar fills. Since the histogram of the sample of $n = 30$ jar fills is bell-shaped and symmetrical, **the appropriate test statistic is given in the summary box.** Furthermore, since H_a: $\sigma^2 < .000625$ implies a left tailed test, we should **reject H_0: $\sigma^2 = .000625$ if the value of χ^2 is less than the critical value $\chi^2_{1-\alpha} = \chi^2_{.95} = 17.7083$.** Here $\chi^2_{.95} = 17.7083$ is based on $n - 1 = 30 - 1 = 29$ degrees of freedom, and this critical value is illustrated in Figure 9.11. Since the sample variance is $s^2 = .000121$, the **value of the test statistic** is

$$\chi^2 = \frac{(n-1)s^2}{\sigma_0^2} = \frac{(29)(.000121)}{.000625} = 5.6144$$

Since $\chi^2 = 5.6144$ is less than $\chi^2_{.95} = 17.7083$, we reject H_0: $\sigma^2 = .000625$ in favor of H_a: $\sigma^2 < .000625$. That is, we conclude (at an α of .05) that the new process has reduced the population variance of the jar fills. Moreover, the p-value for the test is less than .001 (see the figure on the page margin). Therefore, we have extremely strong evidence that the population jar fill variance has been reduced.

In order to compute a 95 percent confidence interval for σ^2, we note that $\alpha = .05$. Therefore, $\chi^2_{\alpha/2}$ is $\chi^2_{.025}$ and $\chi^2_{1-(\alpha/2)}$ is $\chi^2_{.975}$. Table A.10 (page 648) tells us that these points (based on $n - 1 = 29$ degrees of freedom) are $\chi^2_{.025} = 45.7222$ and $\chi^2_{.975} = 16.0471$ (see Figure 9.12). It follows that a 95 percent confidence interval for σ^2 is (see Figure 9.12)

$$\left[\frac{(n-1)s^2}{\chi^2_{\alpha/2}}, \frac{(n-1)s^2}{\chi^2_{1-(\alpha/2)}}\right] = \left[\frac{(29)(.000121)}{45.7222}, \frac{(29)(.000121)}{16.0471}\right]$$
$$= [.000076746, .00021867]$$

Moreover, taking square roots of both ends of this interval, we find that a 95 percent confidence interval for σ is [.008760, .01479]. The upper end of this interval, .01479, is an estimate of the largest that σ for the new process might reasonably be. Recalling that the estimate of the population mean jar fill μ for the new process is $\bar{x} = 16$, and using .01479 as the estimate of σ, we estimate that (at the worst) 99.73 percent of all jar fills that would be produced with the new process are in the tolerance interval $[16 \pm 3(.01479)] = [15.956, 16.044]$. This tolerance interval is narrower than the tolerance interval of [15.925, 16.075] for the old jar filling process and is within the specification limits of [15.95, 16.05].

Exercises for Sections 9.6 and 9.7

CONCEPTS

connect

9.51 What assumption must hold to make statistical inferences about a population variance?

9.52 Define the meaning of the chi-square points $\chi^2_{\alpha/2}$ and $\chi^2_{1-(\alpha/2)}$. Hint: Draw a picture.

METHODS AND APPLICATIONS

9.53 A random sample of $n = 30$ metal hardness depths has an s^2 of .0885 and a bell-shaped and symmetrical histogram. If σ^2 denotes the corresponding population variance, test $H_0: \sigma^2 = .2209$ versus $H_a: \sigma^2 < .2209$ by setting α equal to .05.

Exercises 9.54 and 9.55 relate to the following situation: Consider an engine parts supplier and suppose the supplier has determined that the mean and the variance of the population of all cylindrical engine part outside diameters produced by the current machine are, respectively, 3 inches and .0005. To reduce this variance, a new machine is designed, and a random sample of $n = 25$ outside diameters produced by this new machine has a mean of $\bar{x} = 3$ inches, a variance of $s^2 = .00014$, and a bell-shaped and symmetrical histogram.

9.54 In order for a cylindrical engine part to give an engine long life, the outside diameter of the part must be between the specification limits of 2.95 inches and 3.05 inches. Assuming normality, determine whether 99.73 percent of the outside diameters produced by the current machine are within the specification limits.

9.55 If σ^2 denotes the variance of the population of all outside diameters that would be produced by the new machine, test $H_0: \sigma^2 = .0005$ versus $H_a: \sigma^2 < .0005$ by setting α equal to .05. Also, find 95 percent confidence intervals for σ^2 and σ. Using the upper end of the 95 percent confidence interval for σ, and assuming $\mu = 3$, determine whether 99.73 percent of the outside diameters produced by the new machine are within the specification limits.

9.56 A manufacturer of coffee vending machines has designed a new, less expensive machine. The current machine is known to dispense an average of 6 fl. oz., with a standard deviation of .2 fl. oz., into cups. When the new machine is tested using 15 cups, the mean and the standard deviation of the fills are found to be 6 fl. oz. and .214 fl. oz. Test $H_0: \sigma = .2$ versus $H_a: \sigma \neq .2$ at levels of significance .05 and .01. Assume normality.

9.57 In Exercise 9.56, test $H_0: \sigma = .2$ versus $H_a: \sigma > .2$ at levels of significance .05 and .01.

Chapter Summary

We began this chapter by learning about the two hypotheses that make up the structure of a hypothesis test. The **null hypothesis** is the statement being tested. The null hypothesis is often a statement of "no difference" or "no effect," and it is not rejected unless there is convincing sample evidence that it is false. The **alternative,** or, **research, hypothesis** is a statement that is accepted only if there is convincing sample evidence that it is true and that the null hypothesis is false. In some situations, the alternative hypothesis is a statement for which we need to attempt to find supportive evidence. We also learned that two types of errors can be made in a hypothesis test. A **Type I error** occurs when we reject a true null hypothesis, and a **Type II error** occurs when we do not reject a false null hypothesis.

We studied two commonly used ways to conduct a hypothesis test. The first involves comparing the value of a test statistic with what is called a **critical value,** and the second employs what is called a **p-value.** The p-value measures the weight of evidence against the null hypothesis. The smaller the p-value, the more we doubt the null hypothesis.

The specific hypothesis tests we covered in this chapter all dealt with a hypothesis about one population parameter. First, we studied a test about a **population mean** that is based on the assumption that the population standard deviation σ **is known.** This test employs the **normal distribution.** Second, we studied a test about a population mean that assumes that σ **is unknown.** We learned that this test is based on the t **distribution.** Figure 9.13 presents a flowchart summarizing how to select an appropriate test statistic to test a hypothesis about a population mean. Then we presented a test about a **population proportion** that is based on the **normal distribution.** Next (in optional Section 9.5) we studied Type II error probabilities, and we showed how we can find the sample size needed to make both the probability of a Type I error and the probability of a serious Type II error as small as we wish. We concluded this chapter by discussing (in optional Sections 9.6 and 9.7) the **chi-square distribution** and its use in making statistical inferences about a **population variance.**

Glossary of Terms

alternative (research) hypothesis: A statement that will be accepted only if there is convincing sample evidence that it is true. Sometimes it is a statement for which we need to attempt to find supportive evidence. (page 343)

FIGURE 9.13   Selecting an Appropriate Test Statistic to Test a Hypothesis about a Population Mean

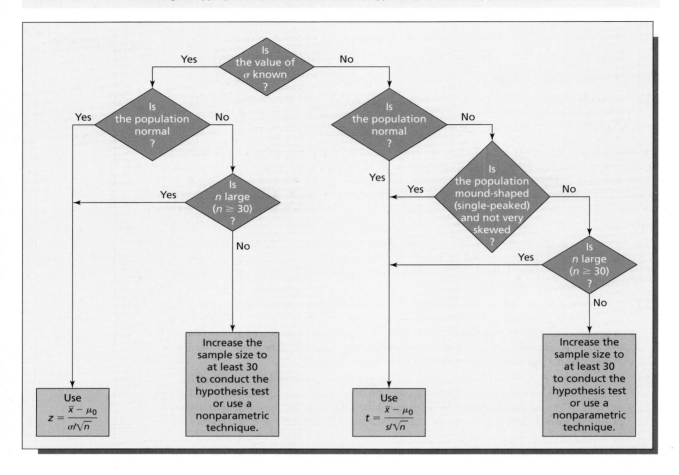

chi-square distribution: A useful continuous probability distribution. Its probability curve is skewed to the right, and the exact shape of the probability curve depends on the number of degrees of freedom associated with the curve. (page 374)

critical value: The value of the test statistic is compared with a critical value in order to decide whether the null hypothesis can be rejected. (pages 349, 353, 354)

greater than alternative: An alternative hypothesis that is stated as a *greater than* ($>$) inequality. (page 345)

less than alternative: An alternative hypothesis that is stated as a *less than* ($<$) inequality. (page 345)

not equal to alternative: An alternative hypothesis that is stated as a *not equal to* ($\neq$) inequality. (page 345)

null hypothesis: The statement being tested in a hypothesis test. It is often a statement of "no difference" or "no effect." (page 343)

p-value (probability value): The probability, computed assuming that the null hypothesis H_0 is true, of observing a value of the test statistic that is at least as contradictory to H_0 and supportive of H_a as the value actually computed from the sample data. The p-value measures how much doubt is cast on the null hypothesis by the sample data. The smaller the p-value, the more we doubt the null hypothesis. (pages 351, 353, 355)

test statistic: A statistic computed from sample data in a hypothesis test. It is either compared with a critical value or used to compute a p-value. (page 349)

two-sided alternative hypothesis: An alternative hypothesis that is stated as a *not equal to* ($\neq$) inequality. (page 345)

Type I error: Rejecting a true null hypothesis. (page 346)

Type II error: Failing to reject a false null hypothesis. (page 346)

Important Formulas and Tests

Hypothesis Testing steps: page 352

A hypothesis test about a population mean (σ known): page 355

A t test about a population mean (σ unknown): page 359

A hypothesis test about a population proportion: page 364

Calculating the probability of a Type II error: page 371

Sample size determination to achieve specified values of α and β: page 372

Statistical inference about a population variance: page 375

Supplementary Exercises

9.58 The auditor for a large corporation routinely monitors cash disbursements. As part of this process, the auditor examines check request forms to determine whether they have been properly approved. Improper approval can occur in several ways. For instance, the check may have no approval, the check request might be missing, the approval might be written by an unauthorized person, or the dollar limit of the authorizing person might be exceeded.

connect

  a Last year the corporation experienced a 5 percent improper check request approval rate. Since this was considered unacceptable, efforts were made to reduce the rate of improper approvals. Letting p be the proportion of all checks that are now improperly approved, set up the null and alternative hypotheses needed to attempt to demonstrate that the current rate of improper approvals is lower than last year's rate of 5 percent.

  b Suppose that the auditor selects a random sample of 625 checks that have been approved in the last month. The auditor finds that 18 of these 625 checks have been improperly approved. Use critical values and this sample information to test the hypotheses you set up in part a at the .10, .05, .01, and .001 levels of significance. How much evidence is there that the rate of improper approvals has been reduced below last year's 5 percent rate?

  c Find the p-value for the test of part b. Use the p-value to carry out the test by setting α equal to .10, .05, .01, and .001. Interpret your results.

  d Suppose the corporation incurs a $10 cost to detect and correct an improperly approved check. If the corporation disburses at least 2 million checks per year, does the observed reduction of the rate of improper approvals seem to have practical importance? Explain your opinion.

9.59 **THE CIGARETTE ADVERTISEMENT CASE** **DS** ModelAge

Recall that the cigarette industry requires that models in cigarette ads must appear to be at least 25 years old. Also recall that a sample of 50 people is randomly selected at a shopping mall. Each person in the sample is shown a "typical cigarette ad" and is asked to estimate the age of the model in the ad.

  a Let μ be the mean perceived age estimate for all viewers of the ad, and suppose we consider the industry requirement to be met if μ is at least 25. Set up the null and alternative hypotheses needed to attempt to show that the industry requirement is not being met.

  b Suppose that a random sample of 50 perceived age estimates gives a mean of $\bar{x} = 23.663$ years and a standard deviation of $s = 3.596$ years. Use these sample data and critical values to test the hypotheses of part a at the .10, .05, .01, and .001 levels of significance.

  c How much evidence do we have that the industry requirement is not being met?

  d Do you think that this result has practical importance? Explain your opinion.

9.60 **THE CIGARETTE ADVERTISEMENT CASE** **DS** ModelAge

Consider the cigarette ad situation discussed in Exercise 9.59. Using the sample information given in that exercise, the p-value for testing H_0 versus H_a can be calculated to be .0057.

  a Determine whether H_0 would be rejected at each of $\alpha = .10$, $\alpha = .05$, $\alpha = .01$, and $\alpha = .001$.

  b Describe how much evidence we have that the industry requirement is not being met.

9.61 In an article in the *Journal of Retailing,* Kumar, Kerwin, and Pereira study factors affecting merger and acquisition activity in retailing. As part of the study, the authors compare the characteristics of "target firms" (firms targeted for acquisition) and "bidder firms" (firms attempting to make acquisitions). Among the variables studied in the comparison were earnings per share, debt-to-equity ratio, growth rate of sales, market share, and extent of diversification.

  a Let μ be the mean growth rate of sales for all target firms (firms that have been targeted for acquisition in the last five years and that have not bid on other firms), and assume growth rates are approximately normally distributed. Furthermore, suppose a random sample of 25 target firms yields a sample mean sales growth rate of $\bar{x} = 0.16$ with a standard deviation of $s = 0.12$. Use critical values and this sample information to test $H_0: \mu \leq .10$ versus $H_a: \mu > .10$ by setting α equal to .10, .05, .01, and .001. How much evidence is there that the mean growth rate of sales for target firms exceeds .10 (that is, exceeds 10 percent)?

  b Now let μ be the mean growth rate of sales for all firms that are bidders (firms that have bid to acquire at least one other firm in the last five years), and again assume growth rates are approximately normally distributed. Furthermore, suppose a random sample of 25 bidders yields a sample mean sales growth rate of $\bar{x} = 0.12$ with a standard deviation of $s = 0.09$. Use critical values and this sample information to test $H_0: \mu \leq .10$ versus $H_a: \mu > .10$ by setting α equal to .10, .05, .01, and .001. How much evidence is there that the mean growth rate of sales for bidders exceeds .10 (that is, exceeds 10 percent)?

9.62   A consumer electronics firm has developed a new type of remote control button that is designed to operate longer before becoming intermittent. A random sample of 35 of the new buttons is selected and each is tested in continuous operation until becoming intermittent. The resulting lifetimes are found to have a sample mean of $\bar{x} = 1{,}241.2$ hours and a sample standard deviation of $s = 110.8$.

   a   Independent tests reveal that the mean lifetime (in continuous operation) of the best remote control button on the market is 1,200 hours. Letting μ be the mean lifetime of the population of all new remote control buttons that will or could potentially be produced, set up the null and alternative hypotheses needed to attempt to provide evidence that the new button's mean lifetime exceeds the mean lifetime of the best remote button currently on the market.

   b   Using the previously given sample results, use critical values to test the hypotheses you set up in part *a* by setting α equal to .10, .05, .01, and .001. What do you conclude for each value of α?

   c   Suppose that $\bar{x} = 1{,}241.2$ and $s = 110.8$ had been obtained by testing a sample of 100 buttons. Use critical values to test the hypotheses you set up in part *a* by setting α equal to .10, .05, .01, and .001. Which sample (the sample of 35 or the sample of 100) gives a more statistically significant result? That is, which sample provides stronger evidence that H_a is true?

   d   If we define practical importance to mean that μ exceeds 1,200 by an amount that would be clearly noticeable to most consumers, do you think that the result has practical importance? Explain why the samples of 35 and 100 both indicate the same degree of practical importance.

   e   Suppose that further research and development effort improves the new remote control button and that a random sample of 35 buttons gives $\bar{x} = 1{,}524.6$ hours and $s = 102.8$ hours. Test your hypotheses of part *a* by setting α equal to .10, .05, .01, and .001.
   (1)   Do we have a highly statistically significant result? Explain.
   (2)   Do you think we have a practically important result? Explain.

9.63   Again consider the remote control button lifetime situation discussed in Exercise 9.62. Using the sample information given in the introduction to Exercise 9.62, the *p*-value for testing H_0 versus H_a can be calculated to be .0174.

   a   Determine whether H_0 would be rejected at each of $\alpha = .10$, $\alpha = .05$, $\alpha = .01$, and $\alpha = .001$.

   b   Describe how much evidence we have that the new button's mean lifetime exceeds the mean lifetime of the best remote button currently on the market.

9.64   Several industries located along the Ohio River discharge a toxic substance called carbon tetrachloride into the river. The state Environmental Protection Agency monitors the amount of carbon tetrachloride pollution in the river. Specifically, the agency requires that the carbon tetrachloride contamination must average no more than 10 parts per million. In order to monitor the carbon tetrachloride contamination in the river, the agency takes a daily sample of 100 pollution readings at a specified location. If the mean carbon tetrachloride reading for this sample casts substantial doubt on the hypothesis that the average amount of carbon tetrachloride contamination in the river is at most 10 parts per million, the agency must issue a shutdown order. In the event of such a shutdown order, industrial plants along the river must be closed until the carbon tetrachloride contamination is reduced to a more acceptable level. Assume that the state Environmental Protection Agency decides to issue a shutdown order if a sample of 100 pollution readings implies that H_0: $\mu \leq 10$ can be rejected in favor of H_a: $\mu > 10$ by setting $\alpha = .01$. If σ equals 2, calculate the probability of a Type II error for each of the following alternative values of μ: 10.1, 10.2, 10.3, 10.4, 10.5, 10.6, 10.7, 10.8, 10.9, and 11.0.

9.65   **THE INVESTMENT CASE** 📀 InvestRet

Suppose that random samples of 50 returns for each of the following investment classes give the indicated sample mean and sample standard deviation:

Fixed annuities: $\bar{x} = 7.83\%$, $s = .51\%$
Domestic large-cap stocks: $\bar{x} = 13.42\%$, $s = 15.17\%$
Domestic midcap stocks: $\bar{x} = 15.03\%$, $s = 18.44\%$
Domestic small-cap stocks: $\bar{x} = 22.51\%$, $s = 21.75\%$

   a   For each investment class, set up the null and alternative hypotheses needed to test whether the current mean return differs from the historical (1970 to 1994) mean return given in Table 3.11 (page 143).

   b   Test each hypothesis you set up in part *a* at the .05 level of significance. What do you conclude? For which investment classes does the current mean return differ from the historical mean?

9.66   **THE UNITED KINGDOM INSURANCE CASE**

Assume that the U.K. insurance survey is based on 1,000 randomly selected United Kingdom households and that 640 of these households spent money to buy life insurance in 1993.

a If p denotes the proportion of all U.K. households that spent money to buy life insurance in 1993, set up the null and alternative hypotheses needed to attempt to justify the claim that more than 60 percent of U.K. households spent money to buy life insurance in 1993.

b Test the hypotheses you set up in part a by setting $\alpha = .10, .05, .01,$ and $.001$. How much evidence is there that more than 60 percent of U.K. households spent money to buy life insurance in 1993?

9.67 How safe are child car seats? *Consumer Reports* (May 2005) tested the safety of child car seats in 30 mph crashes. They found "slim safety margins" for some child car seats. Suppose that *Consumer Reports* simulates the safety of the market-leading child car seat. Their test consists of placing the maximum claimed weight in the car seat and simulating crashes at higher and higher miles per hour until a problem occurs. The following data identify the speed at which a problem with the car seat (such as the strap breaking, seat shell cracked, strap adjuster broke, detached from base, etc.) first appeared: 31.0, 29.4, 30.4, 28.9, 29.7, 30.1, 32.3, 31.7, 35.4, 29.1, 31.2, 30.2. Let μ denote the true mean speed at which a problem with the car seat first appears. The following MINITAB output gives the results of using the sample data to test $H_0: \mu = 30$ versus $H_a: \mu > 30$.   DS CarSeat

```
Test of mu = 30 vs > 30

Variable   N     Mean    StDev   SE Mean    T      P
mph       12   30.7833   1.7862   0.5156   1.52   0.078
```

How much evidence is there that μ exceeds 30 mph?

9.68 *Consumer Reports* (January 2005) indicates that profit margins on extended warranties are much greater than on the purchase of most products.[4] In this exercise we consider a major electronics retailer that wishes to increase the proportion of customers who buy extended warranties on digital cameras. Historically, 20 percent of digital camera customers have purchased the retailer's extended warranty. To increase this percentage, the retailer has decided to offer a new warranty that is less expensive and more comprehensive. Suppose that three months after starting to offer the new warranty, a random sample of 500 customer sales invoices shows that 152 out of 500 digital camera customers purchased the new warranty. Letting p denote the proportion of all digital camera customers who have purchased the new warranty, calculate the p-value for testing $H_0: p = .20$ versus $H_a: p > .20$. How much evidence is there that p exceeds .20? Does the difference between $\hat{p}$ and .2 seem to be practically important? Explain your opinion.

9.69 *Fortune* magazine has periodically reported on the rise of fees and expenses charged by stock funds.

a Suppose that 10 years ago the average annual expense for stock funds was 1.19 percent. Let μ be the current mean annual expense for all stock funds, and assume that stock fund annual expenses are approximately normally distributed. If a random sample of 12 stock funds gives a sample mean annual expense of $\bar{x} = 1.63\%$ with a standard deviation of $s = .31\%$, use critical values and this sample information to test $H_0: \mu \leq 1.19\%$ versus $H_a: \mu > 1.19\%$ by setting α equal to .10, .05, .01, and .001. How much evidence is there that the current mean annual expense for stock funds exceeds the average of 10 years ago?

b Do you think that the result in part a has practical importance? Explain your opinion.

9.70 Internet Exercise

Are American consumers comfortable using their credit cards to make purchases over the Internet? Suppose that a noted authority suggests that credit cards will be firmly established on the Internet once the "80 percent barrier" is broken; that is, as soon as more than 80 percent of those who make purchases over the Internet are willing to use a credit card to pay for their transactions. A recent Gallup Poll (story, survey results, and analysis can be found at http://www.gallup.com/poll/releases/ pr000223.asp) found that, out of $n = 302$ Internet purchasers surveyed, 267 have paid for Internet purchases using a credit card. Based on the results of the Gallup survey, is there sufficient evidence to conclude that the proportion of Internet purchasers willing to use a credit card now exceeds 0.80? Set up the appropriate null and alternative hypotheses, test at the 0.05 and 0.01 levels of significance, and calculate a p-value for your test.

Go to the Gallup Organization website (http://www. gallup.com). Select an interesting current poll and prepare a brief written summary of the poll or some aspect thereof. Include a statistical test for the significance of a proportion (you may have to make up your own value for the hypothesized proportion p_0) as part of your report. For example, you might select a political poll and test whether a particular candidate is preferred by a majority of voters ($p > 0.50$).

---

[4]*Consumer Reports,* January 2005, page 51.

Appendix 9.1 ■ One-Sample Hypothesis Testing Using Excel

The instruction block in this section begins by describing the entry of data into an Excel spreadsheet. Alternatively, the data may be downloaded from this book's website. The appropriate data file name is given at the top of the instruction block. Please refer to Appendix 1.1 for further information about entering data, saving data, and printing results.

Hypothesis test for a population mean in Exercise 9.33 on page 363 (data file: CreditCd.xlsx):

The Data Analysis ToolPak in Excel does not explicitly provide for one-sample tests of hypotheses. A one-sample test can be conducted using the Descriptive Statistics component of the Analysis ToolPak and a few additional computations using Excel.

Descriptive statistics:

- Enter the interest rate data from Exercise 9.33 (page 363) into cells A2:A16 with the label Rate in cell A1.
- Select **Data : Data Analysis : Descriptive Statistics.**
- Click OK in the Data Analysis dialog box.
- In the Descriptive Statistics dialog box, enter A1:A16 into the Input Range box.
- Place a checkmark in the "Labels in first row" check box.
- Under output options, select "New Worksheet Ply" to have the output placed in a new worksheet and enter the name Output for the new worksheet.
- Place a checkmark in the Summary Statistics checkbox.
- Click OK in the Descriptive Statistics dialog box.

The resulting block of descriptive statistics is displayed in the Output worksheet and the entries needed to carry out the test computations have been entered into the range D3:E6.

Computation of the test statistic and p-value:

- In cell E7, use the formula

  = (E3 − E4)/(E5/SQRT(E6))

  to compute the test statistic t ($= -4.970$).
- Click on cell E8 and then select the Insert Function button f_x on the Excel toolbar.
- In the Insert Function dialog box, select Statistical from the "Or select a category:" menu, select TDIST from the "Select a function:" menu, and click OK in the Insert Function dialog box.
- In the TDIST Function Arguments dialog box, enter abs(E7) in the X window.
- Enter 14 in the Deg_freedom window.
- Enter 1 in the Tails window to select a one-tailed test.
- Click OK in the TDIST Function Arguments dialog box.
- The p-value related to the test will be placed in cell E8.

Appendix 9.2 ■ One-Sample Hypothesis Testing Using MegaStat

The instructions in this section begin by describing the entry of data into an Excel worksheet. Alternatively, the data may be downloaded from this book's website. The appropriate data file name is given at the top of each instruction block. Please refer to Appendix 1.1 for further information about entering data and saving and printing results in Excel. Please refer to Appendix 1.2 for more information about using MegaStat.

Hypothesis test for a population mean in Exercise 9.33 on page 363 (data file: CreditCd.xlsx):

- Enter the interest rate data from Exercise 9.33 (page 363) into cells A2:A16 with the label Rate in cell A1.

- Select **Add-Ins : MegaStat : Hypothesis Tests : Mean vs. Hypothesized Value**

- In the "Hypothesis Test: Mean vs. Hypothesized Value" dialog box, click on "data input" and use the autoexpand feature to enter the range A1: A16 into the Input Range window.

- Enter the hypothesized value (here equal to 18.8) into the Hypothesized Mean window.

- Select the desired alternative (here "less than") from the drop-down menu in the Alternative box.

- Click on t-test and click OK in the "Hypothesis Test: Mean vs. Hypothesized Value" dialog box.

- A hypothesis test employing summary data can be carried out by clicking on "summary data," and by entering a range into the Input Range window that contains the following— label; sample mean; sample standard deviation; sample size n.

A z test can be carried out (in the unlikely event that the population standard deviation is known) by clicking on "z-test."

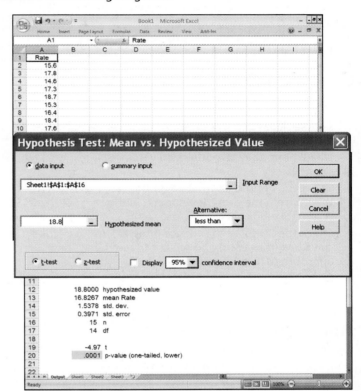

Hypothesis test for a population proportion. Consider testing H_0: $p = .05$ versus H_a: $p > .05$, where $n = 250$ and $\hat{p} = .16$.

- Select **Add-Ins : MegaStat : Hypothesis Tests : Proportion vs. Hypothesized Value**

- In the "Hypothesis Test: Proportion vs. Hypothesized Value" dialog box, enter the hypothesized value (here equal to 0.05) into the "Hypothesized p" window.

- Enter the observed sample proportion (here equal to 0.16) into the "Observed p" window.

- Enter the sample size (here equal to 250) into the "n" window.

- Select the desired alternative (here "greater than") from the drop-down menu in the Alternative box.

- Check the "Display confidence interval" checkbox (if desired), and select or type the appropriate level of confidence.

- Click OK in the "Hypothesis Test: Proportion vs. Hypothesized Value" dialog box.

Hypothesis test for a population variance Consider testing H_0: $\sigma^2 = .2209$ versus H_a: $\sigma^2 < .2209$, where $n = 30$ and $s^2 = .0885$ (see Exercise 9.53 on page 377).

- Enter a label (in this case Depth) into cell A1, the sample variance (here equal to .0885) into cell A2, and the sample size (here equal to 30) into cell A3.

- Select **Add-Ins : MegaStat : Hypothesis Tests : Chi-square Variance Test**

- Click on "summary input."

- Enter the range A1:A3 into the Input Range window—that is, enter the range containing the data label, the sample variance, and the sample size.

- Enter the hypothesized value (here equal to 0.2209) into the "Hypothesized variance" window.

- Select the desired alternative (in this case "less than") from the drop-down menu in the Alternative box.

- Check the "Display confidence interval" checkbox (if desired) and select or type the appropriate level of confidence.

- Click OK.

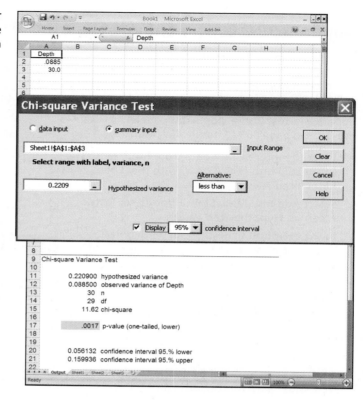

Appendix 9.3 ■ One-Sample Hypothesis Testing Using MINITAB

Hypothesis test for a population mean in Exercise 9.33 on page 363 (data file: CreditCd.MTW):

- In the Data window, enter the interest rate data from Exercise 9.33 (page 363) into a single column with variable name Rate.

- Select **Stat : Basic Statistics : 1-Sample t.**

- In the "1-Sample t (Test and Confidence Interval)" dialog box, select the "Samples in columns" option.

- Select the variable name Rate into the "Samples in columns" window.

- Place a checkmark in the "Perform hypothesis test" checkbox.

- Enter the hypothesized mean (here 18.8) into the "Hypothesized mean" window.

- Click the Options... button, select the desired alternative (in this case "less than") from the Alternative drop-down menu, and click OK in the "1-Sample t-Options" dialog box.

- To produce a boxplot of the data with a graphical representation of the hypothesis test, click the Graphs... button in the "1-Sample t (Test and Confidence Interval)" dialog box, check the "Boxplot of data" checkbox, and click OK in the "1-Sample t—Graphs" dialog box.

- Click OK in the "1-Sample t (Test and Confidence Interval)" dialog box.

- The t test results are given in the Session window, and the boxplot is displayed in a graphics window.

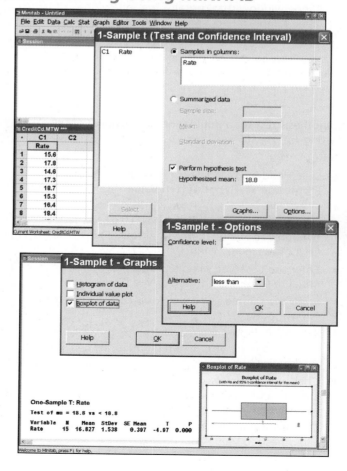

A "1-Sample Z" test is also available in MINITAB under Basic Statistics. It requires a user-specified value of the population standard deviation, which is rarely known.

Hypothesis test for a population proportion in Exercise 9.38 on page 367:

- Select **Stat : Basic Statistics : 1 Proportion**
- In the "1 Proportion (Test and Confidence Interval)" dialog box, select the "Summarized data" option.
- Enter the sample number of successes (here equal to 146) into the "Number of events" window.
- Enter the sample size (here equal to 400) into the "Number of trials" window.
- Place a checkmark in the "Perform hypothesis test" checkbox.
- Enter the hypothesized proportion (here equal to 0.25) into the "Hypothesized proportion" window.
- Click on the Options... button.
- In the "1 Proportion—Options" dialog box, select the desired alternative (in this case "greater than") from the Alternative drop-down menu.
- Place a checkmark in the "Use test and interval based on normal distribution" checkbox.
- Click OK in the "1 Proportion—Options" dialog box and click OK in the "1 Proportion (Test and Confidence Interval)" dialog box.
- The hypothesis test results are given in the Session window.

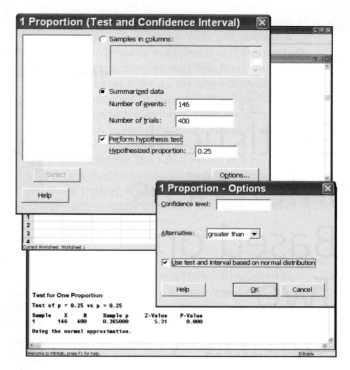

Hypothesis test and confidence intervals for a population variance in the example on pages 375 and 376 where the hypothesized variance is .000625 and the hypothesized standard deviation is .025.

- Select **Stat : Basic Statistics : 1 Variance**
- In the "1 Variance" dialog box, click on "Summarized data."
- Place a check mark in the "Perform hypothesis test" checkbox.
- Enter the sample size (here 30), the sample standard deviation (here .011— that is, $(.011)^2 = .000121$), and the hypothesized standard deviation (here .025—that is, $(.025)^2 = .000625$) in the appropriate windows.
- Click the Options... button, enter the desired level of confidence (here, 95.0), select the desired alternative (in this case "less than"), and click OK.
- Click OK in the "1 Variance" dialog box.
- The results are given in the Session window.
- Because we have chosen a one sided alternative (less than), we get a one sided confidence interval (not discussed in this book). To obtain a two sided confidence interval, repeat the steps above and change the alternative to "not equal".

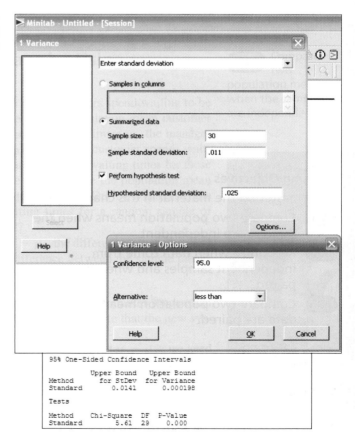

F I G U R E   1 0 . 1   **The Sampling Distribution of $\bar{x}_1 - \bar{x}_2$ Has Mean $\mu_1 - \mu_2$ and Standard Deviation $\sigma_{\bar{x}_1 - \bar{x}_2}$**

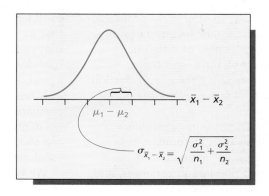

sample of n_2 measurements from another population having mean μ_2 and variance σ_2^2. Let $\bar{x}_2$ be the mean of this sample. Different samples from the first population would give different values of $\bar{x}_1$, and different samples from the second population would give different values of $\bar{x}_2$—so different pairs of samples from the two populations would give different values of $\bar{x}_1 - \bar{x}_2$. In the following box we describe the **sampling distribution of $\bar{x}_1 - \bar{x}_2$,** which is the probability distribution of all possible values of $\bar{x}_1 - \bar{x}_2$:

The Sampling Distribution of $\bar{x}_1 - \bar{x}_2$

I f the randomly selected samples are **independent** of each other,[2] then the population of all possible values of $\bar{x}_1 - \bar{x}_2$

1 Has a normal distribution if each sampled population has a normal distribution, or has approximately a normal distribution if the sampled populations are not normally distributed and each of the sample sizes n_1 and n_2 is large.

2 Has mean $\mu_{\bar{x}_1 - \bar{x}_2} = \mu_1 - \mu_2$

3 Has standard deviation $\sigma_{\bar{x}_1 - \bar{x}_2} = \sqrt{\dfrac{\sigma_1^2}{n_1} + \dfrac{\sigma_2^2}{n_2}}$

Figure 10.1 illustrates the sampling distribution of $\bar{x}_1 - \bar{x}_2$. Using this sampling distribution, we can find a confidence interval for and test a hypothesis about $\mu_1 - \mu_2$ by using the normal distribution. However, the interval and test assume that the true values of the population variances σ_1^2 and σ_2^2 are known, which is very unlikely. Therefore, we will estimate σ_1^2 and σ_2^2 by using s_1^2 and s_2^2, the variances of the samples randomly selected from the populations being compared, and base a confidence interval and a hypothesis test on the t distribution. There are two approaches to doing this. The first approach gives theoretically correct confidence intervals and hypothesis tests but assumes that the population variances σ_1^2 and σ_2^2 are equal. The second approach does not require that σ_1^2 and σ_2^2 are equal but gives only approximately correct confidence intervals and hypothesis tests. In the bank customer waiting time situation, the sample variances are $s_1^2 = 4.8237$ and $s_2^2 = 1.7927$. The difference in these sample variances makes it questionable to assume that the population variances are equal. More will be said later about deciding whether it can be assumed that two population variances are equal and about choosing

---

[2]This means that there is no relationship between the measurements in one sample and the measurements in the other sample.

between the two t-distribution approaches in a particular situation. For now, we will first consider the case where the population variances σ_1^2 and σ_2^2 can be assumed to be equal. Denoting the common value of these variances as σ^2, it follows that

$$\sigma_{\bar{x}_1 - \bar{x}_2} = \sqrt{\frac{\sigma_1^2}{n_1} + \frac{\sigma_2^2}{n_2}} = \sqrt{\frac{\sigma^2}{n_1} + \frac{\sigma^2}{n_2}} = \sqrt{\sigma^2 \left(\frac{1}{n_1} + \frac{1}{n_2} \right)}$$

Because we are assuming that $\sigma_1^2 = \sigma_2^2 = \sigma^2$, we do not need separate estimates of σ_1^2 and σ_2^2. Instead, we combine the results of the two independent random samples to compute a single estimate of σ^2. This estimate is called the **pooled estimate** of σ^2, and it is a weighted average of the two sample variances s_1^2 and s_2^2. Denoting the pooled estimate as s_p^2, it is computed using the formula

$$s_p^2 = \frac{(n_1 - 1)s_1^2 + (n_2 - 1)s_2^2}{n_1 + n_2 - 2}$$

Using s_p^2, the estimate of $\sigma_{\bar{x}_1 - \bar{x}_2}$ is

$$\sqrt{s_p^2 \left(\frac{1}{n_1} + \frac{1}{n_2} \right)}$$

and we form the statistic

$$\frac{(\bar{x}_1 - \bar{x}_2) - (\mu_1 - \mu_2)}{\sqrt{s_p^2 \left(\frac{1}{n_1} + \frac{1}{n_2} \right)}}$$

It can be shown that, if we have randomly selected independent samples from two normally distributed populations having equal variances, then the sampling distribution of this statistic is a t distribution having $(n_1 + n_2 - 2)$ degrees of freedom. Therefore, we can obtain the following confidence interval for $\mu_1 - \mu_2$:

A t-Based Confidence Interval for the Difference between Two Population Means: Equal Variances

Suppose we have randomly selected independent samples from two normally distributed populations having equal variances. Then, a **100(1 − α) percent confidence interval for $\mu_1 - \mu_2$** is

$$\left[(\bar{x}_1 - \bar{x}_2) \pm t_{\alpha/2} \sqrt{s_p^2 \left(\frac{1}{n_1} + \frac{1}{n_2} \right)} \right] \quad \text{where} \quad s_p^2 = \frac{(n_1 - 1)s_1^2 + (n_2 - 1)s_2^2}{n_1 + n_2 - 2}$$

and $t_{\alpha/2}$ is based on $(n_1 + n_2 - 2)$ degrees of freedom.

EXAMPLE 10.1 The Catalyst Comparison Case

A production supervisor at a major chemical company must determine which of two catalysts, catalyst XA-100 or catalyst ZB-200, maximizes the hourly yield of a chemical process. In order to compare the mean hourly yields obtained by using the two catalysts, the supervisor runs the process using each catalyst for five one-hour periods. The resulting yields (in pounds per hour)

| TABLE 10.1 | Yields of a Chemical Process Obtained Using Two Catalysts | Catalyst |

Catalyst XA-100	Catalyst ZB-200	
801	752	
814	718	
784	776	
836	742	
820	763	
$\bar{x}_1 = 811$	$\bar{x}_2 = 750.2$	
$s_1^2 = 386$	$s_2^2 = 484.2$	

for each catalyst, along with the means, variances, and box plots[3] of the yields, are given in Table 10.1. Assuming that all other factors affecting yields of the process have been held as constant as possible during the test runs, it seems reasonable to regard the five observed yields for each catalyst as a random sample from the population of all possible hourly yields for the catalyst. Furthermore, since the sample variances $s_1^2 = 386$ and $s_2^2 = 484.2$ do not differ substantially (notice that $s_1 = 19.65$ and $s_2 = 22.00$ differ by even less), it might be reasonable to conclude that the population variances are approximately equal.[4] It follows that the pooled estimate

$$s_p^2 = \frac{(n_1 - 1)s_1^2 + (n_2 - 1)s_2^2}{n_1 + n_2 - 2}$$

$$= \frac{(5 - 1)(386) + (5 - 1)(484.2)}{5 + 5 - 2} = 435.1$$

is a point estimate of the common variance σ^2.

We define μ_1 as the mean hourly yield obtained by using catalyst XA-100, and we define μ_2 as the mean hourly yield obtained by using catalyst ZB-200. If the populations of all possible hourly yields for the catalysts are normally distributed, then a 95 percent confidence interval for $\mu_1 - \mu_2$ is

$$\left[(\bar{x}_1 - \bar{x}_2) \pm t_{.025}\sqrt{s_p^2\left(\frac{1}{n_1} + \frac{1}{n_2}\right)} \right]$$

$$= \left[(811 - 750.2) \pm 2.306\sqrt{435.1\left(\frac{1}{5} + \frac{1}{5}\right)} \right]$$

$$= [60.8 \pm 30.4217]$$

$$= [30.38, \ 91.22]$$

Here $t_{.025} = 2.306$ is based on $n_1 + n_2 - 2 = 5 + 5 - 2 = 8$ degrees of freedom. This interval tells us that we are 95 percent confident that the mean hourly yield obtained by using catalyst XA-100 is between 30.38 and 91.22 pounds higher than the mean hourly yield obtained by using catalyst ZB-200.

Suppose we wish to test a hypothesis about $\mu_1 - \mu_2$. In the following box we describe how this can be done. Here we test the null hypothesis $H_0: \mu_1 - \mu_2 = D_0$, where D_0 is a number whose value varies depending on the situation. Often D_0 will be the number 0. In such a case, the null hypothesis $H_0: \mu_1 - \mu_2 = 0$ says there is **no difference** between the population means μ_1 and μ_2. In this case, each alternative hypothesis in the box implies that the population means μ_1 and μ_2 differ in a particular way.

---

[3]All of the box plots presented in this chapter and in Chapter 11 have been obtained using MINITAB.
[4]We describe how to test the equality of two variances in Section 10.5 (although, as we will explain, this test has drawbacks).

A *t* Test about the Difference between Two Population Means: Equal Variances

Null Hypothesis $H_0: \mu_1 - \mu_2 = D_0$

Test Statistic $t = \dfrac{(\bar{x}_1 - \bar{x}_2) - D_0}{\sqrt{s_p^2\left(\dfrac{1}{n_1} + \dfrac{1}{n_2}\right)}}$

Assumptions   Independent samples and Equal variances and either Normal populations or Large sample sizes

| Critical Value Rule | | | p-Value (Reject H_0 if p-Value $< \alpha$) | | |

Here t_α, $t_{\alpha/2}$, and the p-values are based on $n_1 + n_2 - 2$ degrees of freedom.

EXAMPLE 10.2 The Catalyst Comparison Case

In order to compare the mean hourly yields obtained by using catalysts XA-100 and ZB-200, we will test $H_0: \mu_1 - \mu_2 = 0$ versus $H_a: \mu_1 - \mu_2 \neq 0$ at the **.05 level of significance**. To perform the hypothesis test, we will use the sample information in Table 10.1 to calculate the value of the **test statistic *t* in the summary box**. Then, because $H_a: \mu_1 - \mu_2 \neq 0$ implies a two tailed test, we will **reject $H_0: \mu_1 - \mu_2 = 0$ if the absolute value of *t* is greater than $t_{\alpha/2} = t_{.025} = 2.306$**. Here the $t_{\alpha/2}$ point is based on $n_1 + n_2 - 2 = 5 + 5 - 2 = 8$ degrees of freedom. Using the data in Table 10.1, the **value of the test statistic** is

$$t = \frac{(\bar{x}_1 - \bar{x}_2) - D_0}{\sqrt{s_p^2\left(\dfrac{1}{n_1} + \dfrac{1}{n_2}\right)}} = \frac{(811 - 750.2) - 0}{\sqrt{435.1\left(\dfrac{1}{5} + \dfrac{1}{5}\right)}} = 4.6087$$

Because $|t| = 4.6087$ is greater than $t_{.025} = 2.306$, we can reject $H_0: \mu_1 - \mu_2 = 0$ in favor of $H_a: \mu_1 - \mu_2 \neq 0$. We conclude (at an α of .05) that the mean hourly yields obtained by using the two catalysts differ. Furthermore, the point estimate $\bar{x}_1 - \bar{x}_2 = 811 - 750.2 = 60.8$ says we estimate that the mean hourly yield obtained by using catalyst XA-100 is 60.8 pounds higher than the mean hourly yield obtained by using catalyst ZB-200.

Figure 10.2(a) gives the Excel output for using the equal variance *t* statistic to test H_0 versus H_a. The outputs tell us that $t = 4.6087$ and that the associated *p*-value is .001736. This very small *p*-value tells us that we have very strong evidence against $H_0: \mu_1 - \mu_2 = 0$ and in favor of $H_a: \mu_1 - \mu_2 \neq 0$. In other words, we have very strong evidence that the mean hourly yields obtained by using the two catalysts differ. (Note that in Figure 10.2(b) we give the Excel output for using an *unequal variances t statistic,* which is discussed on the following pages, to perform the hypothesis test.)

FIGURE 10.2   **Excel Outputs for Testing the Equality of Means in the Catalyst Comparison Case**

(a) The Excel Output Assuming Equal Variances

t-Test: Two-Sample Assuming Equal Variances

	XA-100	ZB-200
Mean	811	750.2
Variance	386	484.2
Observations	5	5
Pooled Variance	435.1	
Hypothesized Mean Diff	0	
df	8	
t Stat	4.608706	
P(T<=t) one-tail	0.000868	
t Critical one-tail	1.859548	
P(T<=t) two-tail	0.001736	
t Critical two-tail	2.306004	

(b) The Excel Output Assuming Unequal Variances

t-Test: Two-Sample Assuming Unequal Variances

	XA-100	ZB-200
Mean	811	750.2
Variance	386	484.2
Observations	5	5
Hypothesized Mean Diff	0	
df	8	
t Stat	4.608706	
P(T<=t) one-tail	0.000868	
t Critical one-tail	1.859548	
P(T<=t) two-tail	0.001736	
t Critical two-tail	2.306004	

When the sampled populations are normally distributed and the population variances σ_1^2 and σ_2^2 differ, the following can be shown.

t-Based Confidence Intervals for $\mu_1 - \mu_2$, and t Tests about $\mu_1 - \mu_2$: Unequal Variances

1 When the sample sizes n_1 and n_2 are equal, the "equal variances" t-based confidence interval and hypothesis test given in the preceding two boxes are approximately valid even if the population variances σ_1^2 and σ_2^2 differ substantially. As a rough rule of thumb, if the larger sample variance is not more than three times the smaller sample variance when the sample sizes are equal, we can use the equal variances interval and test.

2 Suppose that the larger sample variance is more than three times the smaller sample variance when the sample sizes are equal or suppose that both the sample sizes and the sample variances differ substantially. Then, we can use an approximate procedure that is sometimes called an "unequal variances" procedure. This procedure says that an **approximate 100(1 − α) percent confidence interval for $\mu_1 - \mu_2$ is**

$$\left[(\bar{x}_1 - \bar{x}_2) \pm t_{\alpha/2} \sqrt{\frac{s_1^2}{n_1} + \frac{s_2^2}{n_2}} \right]$$

Furthermore, we can test H_0: $\mu_1 - \mu_2 = D_0$ by using the test statistic

$$t = \frac{(\bar{x}_1 - \bar{x}_2) - D_0}{\sqrt{\frac{s_1^2}{n_1} + \frac{s_2^2}{n_2}}}$$

and by using the previously given critical value and p-value conditions.

For both the interval and the test, the degrees of freedom are equal to

$$df = \frac{(s_1^2/n_1 + s_2^2/n_2)^2}{\frac{(s_1^2/n_1)^2}{n_1 - 1} + \frac{(s_2^2/n_2)^2}{n_2 - 1}}$$

Here, if df is not a whole number, we can round df down to the next smallest whole number.

In general, both the "equal variances" and the "unequal variances" procedures have been shown to be approximately valid when the sampled populations are only approximately normally distributed (say, if they are mound-shaped). Furthermore, although the above summary box might seem to imply that we should use the unequal variances procedure only if we cannot use the equal variances procedure, this is not necessarily true. In fact, since the unequal variances procedure can be shown to be a very accurate approximation whether or not the population variances are equal and for most sample sizes (here, both n_1 and n_2 should be at least 5), **many statisticians believe that it is best to use the unequal variances procedure in almost every situation.** If each of n_1 and n_2 is large (at least 30), both the equal variances procedure and the unequal variances procedure are approximately valid, no matter what probability distributions describe the sampled populations.

To illustrate the unequal variances procedure, consider the bank customer waiting time situation, and recall that $\mu_1 - \mu_2$ is the difference between the mean customer waiting time under the current system and the mean customer waiting time under the new system. Because of cost considerations, the bank manager wants to implement the new system only if it reduces the mean waiting time by more than three minutes. Therefore, the manager will test the **null hypothesis H_0: $\mu_1 - \mu_2 = 3$ versus the alternative hypothesis H_a: $\mu_1 - \mu_2 > 3$.** If H_0 can be rejected in favor of H_a at the **.05 level of significance,** the manager will implement the new system. Recall that a random sample of $n_1 = 100$ waiting times observed under the current system gives a sample mean $\bar{x}_1 = 8.79$ and a sample variance $s_1^2 = 4.8237$. Also, recall that a random sample of $n_2 = 100$ waiting times observed during the trial run of the new system yields a sample mean $\bar{x}_2 = 5.14$ and a sample variance $s_2^2 = 1.7927$. Since each sample is large, we can use the **unequal variances test statistic t in the summary box.** The degrees of freedom for this statistic are

$$df = \frac{(s_1^2/n_1 + s_2^2/n_2)^2}{\dfrac{(s_1^2/n_1)^2}{n_1 - 1} + \dfrac{(s_2^2/n_2)^2}{n_2 - 1}}$$

$$= \frac{[(4.8237/100) + (1.7927/100)]^2}{\dfrac{(4.8237/100)^2}{99} + \dfrac{(1.7927/100)^2}{99}}$$

$$= 163.657$$

which we will round down to 163. Therefore, because H_a: $\mu_1 - \mu_2 > 3$ implies a right tailed test, we will **reject H_0: $\mu_1 - \mu_2 = 3$ if the value of the test statistic t is greater than $t_\alpha = t_{.05} = 1.65$** (which is based on 163 degrees of freedom and has been found using a computer). Using the sample data, the **value of the test statistic** is

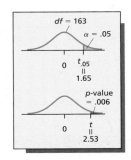

$$t = \frac{(\bar{x}_1 - \bar{x}_2) - 3}{\sqrt{\dfrac{s_1^2}{n_1} + \dfrac{s_2^2}{n_2}}} = \frac{(8.79 - 5.14) - 3}{\sqrt{\dfrac{4.8237}{100} + \dfrac{1.7927}{100}}} = \frac{.65}{.25722} = 2.53$$

Because $t = 2.53$ is greater than $t_{.05} = 1.65$, we reject H_0: $\mu_1 - \mu_2 = 3$ in favor of H_a: $\mu_1 - \mu_2 > 3$. We conclude (at an α of .05) that $\mu_1 - \mu_2$ is greater than 3 and, therefore, that the new system reduces the population mean customer waiting time by more than 3 minutes. Therefore, the bank manager will implement the new system. Furthermore, the point estimate $\bar{x}_1 - \bar{x}_2 = 3.65$ says that we estimate that the new system reduces mean waiting time by 3.65 minutes.

Figure 10.3 gives the MINITAB output of using the unequal variances procedure to test H_0: $\mu_1 - \mu_2 = 3$ versus H_a: $\mu_1 - \mu_2 > 3$. The output tells us that $t = 2.53$ and that the associated p-value is .006. The very small p-value tells us that we have very strong evidence against H_0: $\mu_1 - \mu_2 = 3$ and in favor of H_a: $\mu_1 - \mu_2 > 3$. That is, we have very strong evidence that $\mu_1 - \mu_2$ is greater than 3 and, therefore, that the new system reduces the mean customer waiting time by more than 3 minutes. To find a 95 percent confidence interval for $\mu_1 - \mu_2$, note that we can use a computer to find that $t_{.025}$ based on 163 degrees of freedom is 1.97. It follows that the 95 percent confidence interval for $\mu_1 - \mu_2$ is

$$\left[(\bar{x}_1 - \bar{x}_2) \pm t_{.025}\sqrt{\frac{s_1^2}{n_1} + \frac{s_2^2}{n_2}} \right] = \left[(8.79 - 5.14) \pm 1.97\sqrt{\frac{4.8237}{100} + \frac{1.7927}{100}} \right]$$

$$= [3.65 \pm .50792]$$

$$= [3.14, 4.16]$$

This interval says that we are 95 percent confident that the new system reduces the mean of all customer waiting times by between 3.14 minutes and 4.16 minutes.

FIGURE 10.3   **MINITAB Output of the Unequal Variances Procedure for the Bank Customer Waiting Time Situation**

Two-Sample T-Test and CI

```
Sample      N    Mean    StDev   SE Mean
Current   100    8.79     2.20      0.22
New       100    5.14     1.34      0.13

Difference = mu(1) - mu(2)
Estimate for difference:  3.650
95% lower bound for difference:  3.224
T-Test of difference = 3 (vs >):
T-Value = 2.53     P-Value = 0.006  DF = 163
```

FIGURE 10.4   **MINITAB Output of the Unequal Variances Procedure for the Catalyst Comparison Case**

Two-Sample T-Test and CI: XA-100, ZB-200

```
             N    Mean    StDev   SE Mean
XA-100       5   811.0     19.6       8.8
ZB-200       5   750.2     22.0       9.8

Difference = mu (XA-100) - mu (ZB-200)
Estimate for difference:  60.8000
95% CI for difference:  (29.6049, 91.9951)
T-Test of difference = 0 (vs not =):
  T-Value = 4.61     P-Value = 0.002  DF = 7
```

In general, the degrees of freedom for the unequal variances procedure will always be less than or equal to $n_1 + n_2 - 2$, the degrees of freedom for the equal variances procedure. For example, if we use the unequal variances procedure to analyze the catalyst comparison data in Table 10.1, we can calculate df to be 7.9. This is slightly less than $n_1 + n_2 - 2 = 5 + 5 - 2 = 8$, the degrees of freedom for the equal variances procedure. Figure 10.2(b) gives the Excel output, and Figure 10.4 gives the MINITAB output, of the unequal variances analysis of the catalyst comparison data. Note that the Excel unequal variances procedure rounds $df = 7.9$ up to 8 and obtains the same results as did the equal variances procedure (see Figure 10.2(a)). On the other hand, MINITAB rounds $df = 7.9$ down to 7 and finds that a 95 percent confidence interval for $\mu_1 - \mu_2$ is [29.6049, 91.9951]. MINITAB also finds that the test statistic for testing $H_0: \mu_1 - \mu_2 = 0$ versus $H_a: \mu_1 - \mu_2 \neq 0$ is $t = 4.61$ and that the associated p-value is .002. These results do not differ by much from the results given by the equal variances procedure.

To conclude this section, it is important to point out that if the sample sizes n_1 and n_2 are not large (at least 30), and if we fear that the sampled populations might be far from normally distributed, we can use a **nonparametric method.** One nonparametric method for comparing populations when using independent samples is the **Wilcoxon rank sum test.** This test is discussed in Bowerman, O'Connell, and Murphree (2011).

Exercises for Section 10.1

CONCEPTS

connect

For each of the formulas described below, list all of the assumptions that must be satisfied in order to validly use the formula.

10.1   The confidence interval in the formula box on page 389.

10.2   The hypothesis test described in the formula box on page 391.

10.3   The confidence interval and hypothesis test described in the formula box on page 392.

METHODS AND APPLICATIONS

Suppose we have taken independent, random samples of sizes $n_1 = 7$ and $n_2 = 7$ from two normally distributed populations having means μ_1 and μ_2, and suppose we obtain $\bar{x}_1 = 240$, $\bar{x}_2 = 210$, $s_1 = 5$, and $s_2 = 6$. Using the equal variances procedure do Exercises 10.4, 10.5, and 10.6.

10.4   Calculate a 95 percent confidence interval for $\mu_1 - \mu_2$. Can we be 95 percent confident that $\mu_1 - \mu_2$ is greater than 20? Explain why we can use the equal variances procedure here.

10.5   Use critical values to test the null hypothesis $H_0: \mu_1 - \mu_2 \leq 20$ versus the alternative hypothesis $H_a: \mu_1 - \mu_2 > 20$ by setting α equal to .10, .05, .01, and .001. How much evidence is there that the difference between μ_1 and μ_2 exceeds 20?

10.6   Use critical values to test the null hypothesis $H_0: \mu_1 - \mu_2 = 20$ versus the alternative hypothesis $H_a: \mu_1 - \mu_2 \neq 20$ by setting α equal to .10, .05, .01, and .001. How much evidence is there that the difference between μ_1 and μ_2 is not equal to 20?

10.7   Repeat Exercises 10.4 through 10.6 using the unequal variances procedure. Compare your results to those obtained using the equal variances procedure.

10.8 The October 7, 1991, issue of *Fortune* magazine reported on the rapid rise of fees and expenses charged by mutual funds. Assuming that stock fund expenses and municipal bond fund expenses are each approximately normally distributed, suppose a random sample of 12 stock funds gives a mean annual expense of 1.63 percent with a standard deviation of .31 percent, and an independent random sample of 12 municipal bond funds gives a mean annual expense of 0.89 percent with a standard deviation of .23 percent. Let μ_1 be the mean annual expense for stock funds, and let μ_2 be the mean annual expense for municipal bond funds. Do parts *a*, *b*, and *c* by using the equal variances procedure. Then repeat *a*, *b*, and *c* using the unequal variances procedure. Compare your results.

  a Set up the null and alternative hypotheses needed to attempt to establish that the mean annual expense for stock funds is larger than the mean annual expense for municipal bond funds. Test these hypotheses at the .05 level of significance. What do you conclude?

  b Set up the null and alternative hypotheses needed to attempt to establish that the mean annual expense for stock funds exceeds the mean annual expense for municipal bond funds by more than .5 percent. Test these hypotheses at the .05 level of significance. What do you conclude?

  c Calculate a 95 percent confidence interval for the difference between the mean annual expenses for stock funds and municipal bond funds. Can we be 95 percent confident that the mean annual expense for stock funds exceeds that for municipal bond funds by more than .5 percent? Explain.

10.9 In the book *Business Research Methods,* Donald R. Cooper and C. William Emory (1995) discuss a manager who wishes to compare the effectiveness of two methods for training new salespeople. The authors describe the situation as follows:

> The company selects 22 sales trainees who are randomly divided into two experimental groups—one receives type *A* and the other type *B* training. The salespeople are then assigned and managed without regard to the training they have received. At the year's end, the manager reviews the performances of salespeople in these groups and finds the following results:

	A Group	*B* Group
Average Weekly Sales	$\bar{x}_1 = \$1{,}500$	$\bar{x}_2 = \$1{,}300$
Standard Deviation	$s_1 = 225$	$s_2 = 251$

  a Set up the null and alternative hypotheses needed to attempt to establish that type *A* training results in higher mean weekly sales than does type *B* training.

  b Because different sales trainees are assigned to the two experimental groups, it is reasonable to believe that the two samples are independent. Assuming that the normality assumption holds, and using the equal variances procedure, test the hypotheses you set up in part *a* at levels of significance .10, .05, .01, and .001. How much evidence is there that type *A* training produces results that are superior to those of type *B*?

  c Use the equal variances procedure to calculate a 95 percent confidence interval for the difference between the mean weekly sales obtained when type *A* training is used and the mean weekly sales obtained when type *B* training is used. Interpret this interval.

10.10 A marketing research firm wishes to compare the prices charged by two supermarket chains— Miller's and Albert's. The research firm, using a standardized one-week shopping plan (grocery list), makes identical purchases at 10 of each chain's stores. The stores for each chain are randomly selected, and all purchases are made during a single week.

  The shopping expenses obtained at the two chains, along with box plots of the expenses, are as follows: **DS** ShopExp

Miller's

$119.25	$121.32	$122.34	$120.14	$122.19
$123.71	$121.72	$122.42	$123.63	$122.44

Albert's

$111.99	$114.88	$115.11	$117.02	$116.89
$116.62	$115.38	$114.40	$113.91	$111.87

Because the stores in each sample are different stores in different chains, it is reasonable to assume that the samples are independent, and we assume that weekly expenses at each chain are normally distributed.

  a Letting μ_M be the mean weekly expense for the shopping plan at Miller's, and letting μ_A be the mean weekly expense for the shopping plan at Albert's, Figure 10.5 gives the MINITAB output of the test of $H_0: \mu_M - \mu_A = 0$ (that is, there is no difference between μ_M and μ_A) versus $H_a: \mu_M - \mu_A \neq 0$ (that is, μ_M and μ_A differ). Note that MINITAB has employed the

FIGURE 10.5 **MINITAB Output of Testing the Equality of Mean Weekly Expenses at Miller's and Albert's Supermarket Chains (for Exercise 10.10)**

```
Two-sample T for Millers vs Alberts

               N      Mean     StDev    SE Mean
Millers       10     121.92    1.40      0.44
Alberts       10     114.81    1.84      0.58

Difference = mu(Millers)- mu(Alberts)    Estimate for difference: 7.10900
95% CI for difference:  (5.57350, 8.64450)
T-Test of diff = 0 (vs not =): T-Value = 9.73   P-Value = 0.000   DF = 18
Both use Pooled StDev = 1.6343
```

equal variances procedure. Use the sample data to show that $\bar{x}_M = 121.92$, $s_M = 1.40$, $\bar{x}_A = 114.81$, $s_A = 1.84$, and $t = 9.73$.

b Using the t statistic given on the output and critical values, test H_0 versus H_a by setting α equal to .10, .05, .01, and .001. How much evidence is there that the mean weekly expenses at Miller's and Albert's differ?

c Figure 10.5 gives the p-value for testing H_0: $\mu_M - \mu_A = 0$ versus H_a: $\mu_M - \mu_A \neq 0$. Use the p-value to test H_0 versus H_a by setting α equal to .10, .05, .01, and .001. How much evidence is there that the mean weekly expenses at Miller's and Albert's differ?

d Figure 10.5 gives a 95 percent confidence interval for $\mu_M - \mu_A$. Use this confidence interval to describe the size of the difference between the mean weekly expenses at Miller's and Albert's. Do you think that these means differ in a practically important way?

e Set up the null and alternative hypotheses needed to attempt to establish that the mean weekly expense for the shopping plan at Miller's exceeds the mean weekly expense at Albert's by more than $5. Test the hypotheses at the .10, .05, .01, and .001 levels of significance. How much evidence is there that the mean weekly expense at Miller's exceeds that at Albert's by more than $5?

10.11 A large discount chain compares the performance of its credit managers in Ohio and Illinois by comparing the mean dollar amounts owed by customers with delinquent charge accounts in these two states. Here a small mean dollar amount owed is desirable because it indicates that bad credit risks are not being extended large amounts of credit. Two independent, random samples of delinquent accounts are selected from the populations of delinquent accounts in Ohio and Illinois, respectively. The first sample, which consists of 10 randomly selected delinquent accounts in Ohio, gives a mean dollar amount of $524 with a standard deviation of $68. The second sample, which consists of 20 randomly selected delinquent accounts in Illinois, gives a mean dollar amount of $473 with a standard deviation of $22.

a Set up the null and alternative hypotheses needed to test whether there is a difference between the population mean dollar amounts owed by customers with delinquent charge accounts in Ohio and Illinois.

b Figure 10.6 gives the MINITAB output of using the unequal variances procedure to test the equality of mean dollar amounts owed by customers with delinquent charge accounts in Ohio and Illinois. Assuming that the normality assumption holds, test the hypotheses you set up in part a by setting α equal to .10, .05, .01, and .001. How much evidence is there that the mean dollar amounts owed in Ohio and Illinois differ?

c Assuming that the normality assumption holds, calculate a 95 percent confidence interval for the difference between the mean dollar amounts owed in Ohio and Illinois. Based on this interval, do you think that these mean dollar amounts differ in a practically important way?

10.12 A loan officer compares the interest rates for 48-month fixed-rate auto loans and 48-month variable-rate auto loans. Two independent, random samples of auto loan rates are selected. A sample of eight 48-month fixed-rate auto loans had the following loan rates: 🅳🆂 AutoLoan

8.29%   7.75%   7.50%   7.99%   7.75%   7.99%   9.40%   8.00%

while a sample of five 48-month variable-rate auto loans had loan rates as follows:

7.59%   6.75%   6.99%   6.50%   7.00%

a Set up the null and alternative hypotheses needed to determine whether the mean rates for 48-month fixed-rate and variable-rate auto loans differ.

b Figure 10.7 gives the Excel output of using the equal variances procedure to test the hypotheses you set up in part a. Assuming that the normality and equal variances assumptions hold, use the Excel output and critical values to test these hypotheses by setting α equal to

---

FIGURE 10.6   MINITAB Output of Testing the Equality of Mean Dollar Amounts Owed for Ohio and Illinois (for Exercise 10.11)

Two-Sample T-Test and CI

```
Sample      N     Mean    StDev   SE Mean
Ohio       10    524.0     68.0        22
Illinois   20    473.0     22.0       4.9

Difference = mu(1) - mu(2)
Estimate for difference:  51.0
95% CI for difference:  (1.1, 100.9)
T-Test of difference = 0 (vs not =):
   T-Value = 2.31     P-Value = 0.046  DF = 9
```

FIGURE 10.7   Excel Output of Testing the Equality of Mean Loan Rates for Fixed and Variable 48-Month Auto Loans (for Exercise 10.12)

t-Test: Two-Sample Assuming Equal Variances

	Fixed-Rate (%)	Variable-Rate (%)
Mean	10.0838	8.966
Variance	0.3376	0.1637
Observations	8	5
Pooled Variance	0.2744	
Hypothesized Mean Difference	0	
df	11	
t Stat	3.7431	
P(T<=t) one-tail	0.0016	
t Critical one-tail	1.7959	
P(T<=t) two-tail	0.0032	
t Critical two-tail	2.2010	

.10, .05, .01, and .001. How much evidence is there that the mean rates for 48-month fixed- and variable-rate auto loans differ?

c   Figure 10.7 gives the *p*-value for testing the hypotheses you set up in part *a*. Use the *p*-value to test these hypotheses by setting α equal to .10, .05, .01, and .001. How much evidence is there that the mean rates for 48-month fixed- and variable-rate auto loans differ?

d   Calculate a 95 percent confidence interval for the difference between the mean rates for fixed- and variable-rate 48-month auto loans. Can we be 95 percent confident that the difference between these means exceeds .4 percent? Explain.

e   Use a hypothesis test to establish that the difference between the mean rates for fixed- and variable-rate 48-month auto loans exceeds .4 percent. Use α equal to .05.

10.2 Paired Difference Experiments ● ● ●

EXAMPLE 10.3 The Repair Cost Comparison Case   C

Home State Casualty, specializing in automobile insurance, wishes to compare the repair costs of moderately damaged cars (repair costs between $700 and $1,400) at two garages. One way to study these costs would be to take two independent samples (here we arbitrarily assume that each sample is of size $n = 7$). First we would randomly select seven moderately damaged cars that have recently been in accidents. Each of these cars would be taken to the first garage (garage 1), and repair cost estimates would be obtained. Then we would randomly select seven *different* moderately damaged cars, and repair cost estimates for these cars would be obtained at the second garage (garage 2). This sampling procedure would give us independent samples because the cars taken to garage 1 differ from those taken to garage 2. However, because the repair costs for moderately damaged cars can range from $700 to $1,400, there can be substantial differences in damages to moderately damaged cars. These differences might tend to conceal any real differences between repair costs at the two garages. For example, suppose the repair cost estimates for the cars taken to garage 1 are higher than those for the cars taken to garage 2. This difference might exist because garage 1 charges customers more for repair work than does garage 2. However, the difference could also arise because the cars taken to garage 1 are more severely damaged than the cars taken to garage 2.

LO2   Recognize when data come from independent samples and when they are paired.

    To overcome this difficulty, we can perform a **paired difference experiment.** Here we could randomly select one sample of $n = 7$ moderately damaged cars. The cars in this sample would be taken to both garages, and a repair cost estimate for each car would be obtained at each garage. The advantage of the paired difference experiment is that the repair cost estimates at the two garages are obtained for the same cars. Thus, any true differences in the repair cost estimates would not be concealed by possible differences in the severity of damages to the cars.

    Suppose that when we perform the paired difference experiment, we obtain the repair cost estimates in Table 10.2 (these estimates are given in units of $100). To analyze these data, we

TABLE 10.2   **A Sample of $n = 7$ Paired Differences of the Repair Cost Estimates at Garages 1 and 2 (Cost Estimates in Hundreds of Dollars)**   Ⓓ Repair

Sample of $n = 7$ Damaged Cars	Repair Cost Estimates at Garage 1	Repair Cost Estimates at Garage 2	Sample of $n = 7$ Paired Differences
Car 1	$ 7.1	$ 7.9	$d_1 = -.8$
Car 2	9.0	10.1	$d_2 = -1.1$
Car 3	11.0	12.2	$d_3 = -1.2$
Car 4	8.9	8.8	$d_4 = .1$
Car 5	9.9	10.4	$d_5 = -.5$
Car 6	9.1	9.8	$d_6 = -.7$
Car 7	10.3	11.7	$d_7 = -1.4$
	$\bar{x}_1 = 9.329$	$\bar{x}_2 = 10.129$	$\bar{d} = -.8 = \bar{x}_1 - \bar{x}_2$
			$s_d^2 = .2533$
			$s_d = .5033$

calculate the difference between the repair cost estimates at the two garages for each car. The resulting **paired differences** are given in the last column of Table 10.2. The mean of the sample of $n = 7$ paired differences is

$$\bar{d} = \frac{-.8 + (-1.1) + (-1.2) + \cdots + (-1.4)}{7} = -.8$$

which equals the difference between the sample means of the repair cost estimates at the two garages

$$\bar{x}_1 - \bar{x}_2 = 9.329 - 10.129 = -.8$$

Furthermore, $\bar{d} = -.8$ (that is, $-\$80$) is the point estimate of

$$\mu_d = \mu_1 - \mu_2$$

the mean of the population of all possible paired differences of the repair cost estimates (for all possible moderately damaged cars) at garages 1 and 2 (which is equivalent to μ_1, the mean of all possible repair cost estimates at garage 1, minus μ_2, the mean of all possible repair cost estimates at garage 2). This says we estimate that the mean of all possible repair cost estimates at garage 1 is $80 less than the mean of all possible repair cost estimates at garage 2.

In addition, the variance and standard deviation of the sample of $n = 7$ paired differences

$$s_d^2 = \frac{\sum_{i=1}^{7}(d_i - \bar{d})^2}{7 - 1} = .2533$$

and

$$s_d = \sqrt{.2533} = .5033$$

are the point estimates of σ_d^2 and σ_d, the variance and standard deviation of the population of all possible paired differences.

LO3 Compare two population means when the data are paired.

In general, suppose we wish to compare two population means, μ_1 and μ_2. Also suppose that we have obtained two different measurements (for example, repair cost estimates) on the same n units (for example, cars), and suppose we have calculated the n paired differences between these measurements. Let $\bar{d}$ and s_d be the mean and the standard deviation of these n paired differences. If it is reasonable to assume that the paired differences have been randomly selected from a normally distributed (or at least mound-shaped) population of paired differences with mean μ_d and standard deviation σ_d, then the sampling distribution of

$$\frac{\bar{d} - \mu_d}{s_d/\sqrt{n}}$$

is a t distribution having $n - 1$ degrees of freedom. This implies that we have the following confidence interval for μ_d:

A Confidence Interval for the Mean, μ_d, of a Population of Paired Differences

Let μ_d be the mean of a **normally distributed population of paired differences**, and let $\bar{d}$ and s_d be the mean and standard deviation of a sample of n paired differences that have been randomly selected from the population. Then, a **100(1 − α) percent**

confidence interval for $\mu_d = \mu_1 - \mu_2$ is

$$\left[\bar{d} \pm t_{\alpha/2} \frac{s_d}{\sqrt{n}} \right]$$

Here $t_{\alpha/2}$ is based on $(n-1)$ degrees of freedom.

EXAMPLE 10.4 The Repair Cost Comparison Case

Using the data in Table 10.2, and assuming that the population of paired repair cost differences is normally distributed, a 95 percent confidence interval for $\mu_d = \mu_1 - \mu_2$ is

$$\left[\bar{d} \pm t_{.025} \frac{s_d}{\sqrt{n}} \right] = \left[-.8 \pm 2.447 \frac{.5033}{\sqrt{7}} \right]$$
$$= [-.8 \pm .4654]$$
$$= [-1.2654, -.3346]$$

Here $t_{.025} = 2.447$ is based on $n - 1 = 7 - 1 = 6$ degrees of freedom. This interval says that Home State Casualty can be 95 percent confident that μ_d, the mean of all possible paired differences of the repair cost estimates at garages 1 and 2, is between $-\$126.54$ and $-\$33.46$. That is, we are 95 percent confident that μ_1, the mean of all possible repair cost estimates at garage 1, is between \$126.54 and \$33.46 less than μ_2, the mean of all possible repair cost estimates at garage 2.

We can also test a hypothesis about μ_d, the mean of a population of paired differences. We show how to test the null hypothesis

$$H_0: \mu_d = D_0$$

in the following box. Here the value of the constant D_0 depends on the particular problem. Often D_0 equals 0, and the null hypothesis $H_0: \mu_d = 0$ says that μ_1 and μ_2 do not differ.

Testing a Hypothesis about the Mean, μ_d, of a Population of Paired Differences

| Null Hypothesis $H_0: \mu_d = D_0$ | Test Statistic $t = \dfrac{\bar{d} - D_0}{s_d/\sqrt{n}}$ $df = n - 1$ | Assumptions | Normal population of paired differences or Large sample size. |

EXAMPLE 10.5 The Repair Cost Comparison Case

Home State Casualty currently contracts to have moderately damaged cars repaired at garage 2. However, a local insurance agent suggests that garage 1 provides less expensive repair service that is of equal quality. Because it has done business with garage 2 for years, Home State has decided to give some of its repair business to garage 1 only if it has very strong evidence that μ_1, the mean repair cost estimate at garage 1, is smaller than μ_2, the mean repair cost estimate at garage 2—that is, if $\mu_d = \mu_1 - \mu_2$ is less than zero. Therefore, we will test $H_0: \mu_d = 0$ or, equivalently, $H_0: \mu_1 - \mu_2 = 0$, versus $H_a: \mu_d < 0$ or, equivalently, $H_a: \mu_1 - \mu_2 < 0$, at the .01 level of significance. To perform the hypothesis test, we will use the sample data in Table 10.2 to calculate the value of the **test statistic t in the summary box.** Because $H_a: \mu_d < 0$ implies a left tailed test, we will **reject $H_0: \mu_d = 0$ if the value of t is less than $-t_\alpha = -t_{.01} = -3.143$.** Here the t_α point is based on $n - 1 = 7 - 1 = 6$ degrees of freedom. Using the data in Table 10.2, the **value of the test statistic** is

$$t = \frac{\bar{d} - D_0}{s_d/\sqrt{n}} = \frac{-.8 - 0}{.5033/\sqrt{7}} = -4.2053$$

Because $t = -4.2053$ is less than $-t_{.01} = -3.143$, we can reject $H_0: \mu_d = 0$ in favor of H_a: $\mu_d < 0$. We conclude (at an α of .01) that μ_1, the mean repair cost estimate at garage 1, is less than μ_2, the mean repair cost estimate at garage 2. As a result, Home State will give some of its repair business to garage 1. Furthermore, Figure 10.8 gives the MINITAB output of this hypothesis test and shows us that the p-value for the test is .003. Since this p-value is very small, we have very strong evidence that H_0 should be rejected and that μ_1 is less than μ_2.

Figure 10.9 shows the Excel output for testing $H_0: \mu_d = 0$ versus $H_a: \mu_d < 0$ (the "one-tail" test) and for testing $H_0: \mu_d = 0$ versus $H_a: \mu_d \neq 0$ (the "two-tail" test). The Excel p-value for testing $H_0: \mu_d = 0$ versus $H_a: \mu_d < 0$ is .002826, which in the rounded form .003 is the same as

---

FIGURE 10.8   MINITAB Output of Testing $H_0: \mu_d = 0$ versus $H_a: \mu_d < 0$

```
Paired T for Garage1 - Garage2

            N      Mean      StDev     SE Mean
Garage1     7     9.3286     1.2500     0.4724
Garage2     7    10.1286     1.5097     0.5706
Difference  7    -0.800000   0.503322   0.190238

T-Test of mean difference = 0 (vs < 0):
            T-Value = -4.21       P-Value = 0.003
```

Boxplot of Differences
(with Ho and 95% t based CI for the mean)

FIGURE 10.9   Excel Output of Testing $H_0: \mu_d = 0$

t-Test: Paired Two Sample for Means

	Garage1	Garage2
Mean	9.328571	10.12857
Variance	1.562381	2.279048
Observations	7	7
Pearson Correlation	0.950744	
Hypothesized Mean	0	
df	6	
t Stat	-4.20526	
P(T<=t) one-tail	0.002826	
t Critical one-tail	1.943181	
P(T<=t) two-tail	0.005653	
t Critical two-tail	2.446914	

the MINITAB p-value. This very small p-value tells us that Home State has very strong evidence that the mean repair cost at garage 1 is less than the mean repair cost at garage 2. The Excel p-value for testing H_0: $\mu_d = 0$ versus H_a: $\mu_d \neq 0$ is .005653.

In general, an experiment in which we have obtained two different measurements on the same n units is called a **paired difference experiment.** The idea of this type of experiment is to remove the variability due to the variable (for example, the amount of damage to a car) on which the observations are paired. In many situations, a paired difference experiment will provide more information than an independent samples experiment. As another example, suppose that we wish to assess which of two different machines produces a higher hourly output. If we randomly select 10 machine operators and randomly assign 5 of these operators to test machine 1 and the others to test machine 2, we would be performing an independent samples experiment. This is because different machine operators test machines 1 and 2. However, any difference in machine outputs could be obscured by differences in the abilities of the machine operators. For instance, if the observed hourly outputs are higher for machine 1 than for machine 2, we might not be able to tell whether this is due to (1) the superiority of machine 1 or (2) the possible higher skill level of the operators who tested machine 1. Because of this, it might be better to randomly select five machine operators, thoroughly train each operator to use both machines, and have each operator test both machines. We would then be **pairing on the machine operator,** and this would remove the variability due to the differing abilities of the operators.

The formulas we have given for analyzing a paired difference experiment are based on the t distribution. These formulas assume that the population of all possible paired differences is normally distributed (or at least mound-shaped). If the sample size is large (say, at least 30), the t based interval and tests of this section are approximately valid no matter what the shape of the population of all possible paired differences. If the sample size is small, and if we fear that the population of all paired differences might be far from normally distributed, we can use a nonparametric method. One nonparametric method for comparing two populations when using a paired difference experiment is the **Wilcoxon signed ranks test,** which is discussed in Bowerman, O'Connell, and Murphree (2011).

Exercises for Section 10.2

CONCEPTS

connect

10.13 Explain how a paired difference experiment differs from an independent samples experiment in terms of how the data for these experiments are collected.

10.14 Why is a paired difference experiment sometimes more informative than an independent samples experiment? Give an example of a situation in which a paired difference experiment might be advantageous.

10.15 What assumptions must be satisfied to appropriately carry out a paired difference experiment? When can we carry out a paired difference experiment no matter what the shape of the population of all paired differences might be?

10.16 Suppose a company wishes to compare the hourly output of its employees before and after vacations. Explain how you would collect data for a paired difference experiment to make this comparison.

METHODS AND APPLICATIONS

10.17 Suppose a sample of 11 paired differences that has been randomly selected from a normally distributed population of paired differences yields a sample mean of $\bar{d} = 103.5$ and a sample standard deviation of $s_d = 5$.
   a Calculate 95 percent and 99 percent confidence intervals for $\mu_d = \mu_1 - \mu_2$. Can we be 95 percent confident that the difference between μ_1 and μ_2 exceeds 100? Can we be 99 percent confident?
   b Test the null hypothesis H_0: $\mu_d \leq 100$ versus H_a: $\mu_d > 100$ by setting α equal to .05 and .01. How much evidence is there that $\mu_d = \mu_1 - \mu_2$ exceeds 100?
   c Test the null hypothesis H_0: $\mu_d \geq 110$ versus H_a: $\mu_d < 110$ by setting α equal to .05 and .01. How much evidence is there that $\mu_d = \mu_1 - \mu_2$ is less than 110?

10.18 Suppose a sample of 49 paired differences that have been randomly selected from a normally distributed population of paired differences yields a sample mean of $\bar{d} = 5$ and a sample standard deviation of $s_d = 7$.

  a Calculate a 95 percent confidence interval for $\mu_d = \mu_1 - \mu_2$. Can we be 95 percent confident that the difference between μ_1 and μ_2 is greater than 0?

  b Test the null hypothesis $H_0: \mu_d = 0$ versus the alternative hypothesis $H_a: \mu_d \neq 0$ by setting α equal to .10, .05, .01, and .001. How much evidence is there that μ_d differs from 0? What does this say about how μ_1 and μ_2 compare?

  c The p-value for testing $H_0: \mu_d \leq 3$ versus $H_a: \mu_d > 3$ equals .0256. Use the p-value to test these hypotheses with α equal to .10, .05, .01, and .001. How much evidence is there that μ_d exceeds 3? What does this say about the size of the difference between μ_1 and μ_2?

10.19 On its website, the *Statesman Journal* newspaper (Salem, Oregon, 1999) reports mortgage loan interest rates for 30-year and 15-year fixed-rate mortgage loans for a number of Willamette Valley lending institutions. Of interest is whether there is any systematic difference between 30-year rates and 15-year rates (expressed as annual percentage rate or APR) and, if there is, the size of that difference. Table 10.3 displays mortgage loan rates and the difference between 30-year and 15-year rates for nine randomly selected lending institutions. Assuming that the population of paired differences is normally distributed: **DS** Mortgage99

  a Set up the null and alternative hypotheses needed to determine whether there is a difference between mean 30-year rates and mean 15-year rates.

  b Figure 10.10 gives the MINITAB output for testing the hypotheses that you set up in part *a*. Use the output and critical values to test these hypotheses by setting α equal to .10, .05, .01, and .001. How much evidence is there that mean mortgage loan rates for 30-year and 15-year terms differ?

TABLE 10.3   **1999 Mortgage Loan Interest Rates for Nine Randomly Selected Willamette Valley Lending Institutions** **DS** Mortgage99

Lending Institution	30-Year	15-Year	Difference
American Mortgage N.W. Inc.	6.715	6.599	0.116
City and Country Mortgage	6.648	6.367	0.281
Commercial Bank	6.740	6.550	0.190
Landmark Mortgage Co.	6.597	6.362	0.235
Liberty Mortgage, Inc.	6.425	6.162	0.263
MaPS Credit Union	6.880	6.583	0.297
Mortgage Brokers, Inc.	6.900	6.800	0.100
Mortgage First Corp.	6.675	6.394	0.281
Silver Eagle Mortgage	6.790	6.540	0.250

(Column header spanning 30-Year and 15-Year: **Annual Percentage Rate**)

Source: Salem Homeplace Mortgage Rates Directory, www.salemhomeplace.com/pages/finance/, *Statesman Journal Newspaper*, Salem, Oregon, January 4, 1999.

FIGURE 10.10   **MINITAB Paired Difference t Test of the Mortgage Loan Rate Data (for Exercise 10.19)**

```
Paired T for 30-Year - 15-Year

             N        Mean        StDev      SE Mean
30-Year      9     6.70778      0.14635      0.04878
15-Year      9     6.48411      0.18396      0.06132
Difference   9     0.223667     0.072750     0.024250

95% CI for mean difference: (0.167746, 0.279587)
T-Test of mean difference = 0 (vs not = 0):
                             T-Value = 9.22   P-Value = 0.000
```

c Figure 10.10 gives the *p*-value for testing the hypotheses that you set up in part *a*. Use the *p*-value to test these hypotheses by setting α equal to .10, .05, .01, and .001. How much evidence is there that mean mortgage loan rates for 30-year and 15-year terms differ?

d Calculate a 95 percent confidence interval for the difference between mean mortgage loan rates for 30-year rates versus 15-year rates. Interpret this interval.

10.20 In the book *Essentials of Marketing Research,* William R. Dillon, Thomas J. Madden, and Neil H. Firtle (1993) present preexposure and postexposure attitude scores from an advertising study involving 10 respondents. The data for the experiment are given in Table 10.4. Assuming that the differences between pairs of postexposure and preexposure scores are normally distributed: **DS** AdStudy

a Set up the null and alternative hypotheses needed to attempt to establish that the advertisement increases the mean attitude score (that is, that the mean postexposure attitude score is higher than the mean preexposure attitude score).

b Test the hypotheses you set up in part *a* at the .10, .05, .01, and .001 levels of significance. How much evidence is there that the advertisement increases the mean attitude score?

c Estimate the minimum difference between the mean postexposure attitude score and the mean preexposure attitude score. Justify your answer.

10.21 National Paper Company must purchase a new machine for producing cardboard boxes. The company must choose between two machines. The machines produce boxes of equal quality, so the company will choose the machine that produces (on average) the most boxes. It is known that there are substantial differences in the abilities of the company's machine operators. Therefore National Paper has decided to compare the machines using a paired difference experiment. Suppose that eight randomly selected machine operators produce boxes for one hour using machine 1 and for one hour using machine 2, with the following results: **DS** BoxYield

Machine Operator

	1	2	3	4	5	6	7	8
Machine 1	53	60	58	48	46	54	62	49
Machine 2	50	55	56	44	45	50	57	47

a Assuming normality, perform a hypothesis test to determine whether there is a difference between the mean hourly outputs of the two machines. Use $\alpha = .05$.

b Estimate the minimum and maximum differences between the mean outputs of the two machines. Justify your answer.

10.22 During 2004 a company implemented a number of policies aimed at reducing the ages of its customers' accounts. In order to assess the effectiveness of these measures, the company randomly selects 10 customer accounts. The average age of each account is determined for the years 2003 and 2004. These data are given in Table 10.5. Assuming that the population of paired differences between the average ages in 2004 and 2003 is normally distributed: **DS** AcctAge

a Set up the null and alternative hypotheses needed to establish that the mean average account age has been reduced by the company's new policies.

TABLE 10.4 Preexposure and Postexposure Attitude Scores (for Exercise 10.20) **DS** AdStudy

Subject	Preexposure Attitudes (A_1)	Postexposure Attitudes (A_2)	Attitude Change (d_i)
1	50	53	3
2	25	27	2
3	30	38	8
4	50	55	5
5	60	61	1
6	80	85	5
7	45	45	0
8	30	31	1
9	65	72	7
10	70	78	8

Source: W. R. Dillon, T. J. Madden, and N. H. Firtle, *Essentials of Marketing Research* (Burr Ridge, IL: Richard D. Irwin, 1993), p. 435. Copyright © 1993. Reprinted by permission of McGraw-Hill Companies, Inc.

TABLE 10.5 Average Account Ages in 2003 and 2004 for 10 Randomly Selected Accounts (for Exercise 10.22) **DS** AcctAge

Account	Average Age of Account in 2004 (Days)	Average Age of Account in 2003 (Days)
1	27	35
2	19	24
3	40	47
4	30	28
5	33	41
6	25	33
7	31	35
8	29	51
9	15	18
10	21	28

FIGURE 10.11   **Excel Output of a Paired Difference Analysis of the Account Age Data (for Exercise 10.22)**

t-Test: Paired Two Sample for Means

	04 Age	03 Age
Mean	27	34
Variance	53.55556	104.2222
Observations	10	10
Pearson Correlation	0.804586	
Hypothesized Mean	0	
df	9	
t Stat	−3.61211	
P(T<=t) one-tail	0.00282	
t Critical one-tail	1.833114	
P(T<=t) Two-tail	0.005641	
t Critical two-tail	2.262159	

TABLE 10.6   **Weekly Study Time Data for Students Who Perform Well on the MidTerm**   ⊙S StudyTime

Students	1	2	3	4	5	6	7	8
Before	15	14	17	17	19	14	13	16
After	9	9	11	10	19	10	14	10

b Figure 10.11 gives the Excel output needed to test the hypotheses of part *a*. Use critical values to test these hypotheses by setting α equal to .10, .05, .01, and .001. How much evidence is there that the mean average account age has been reduced?

c Figure 10.11 gives the *p*-value for testing the hypotheses of part *a*. Use the *p*-value to test these hypotheses by setting α equal to .10, .05, .01, and .001. How much evidence is there that the mean average account age has been reduced?

d Calculate a 95 percent confidence interval for the mean difference in the average account ages between 2004 and 2003. Estimate the minimum reduction in the mean average account ages from 2003 to 2004.

10.23 Do students reduce study time in classes where they achieve a higher midterm score? In a *Journal of Economic Education* article (Winter 2005), Gregory Krohn and Catherine O'Connor studied student effort and performance in a class over a semester. In an intermediate macroeconomics course, they found that "students respond to higher midterm scores by reducing the number of hours they subsequently allocate to studying for the course."[5] Suppose that a random sample of $n = 8$ students who performed well on the midterm exam was taken and weekly study times before and after the exam were compared. The resulting data are given in Table 10.6. Assume that the population of all possible paired differences is normally distributed.

a Set up the null and alternative hypotheses to test whether there is a difference in the population mean study time before and after the midterm exam.

b Below we present the MINITAB output for the paired differences test. Use the output and critical values to test the hypotheses at the .10, .05, and .01 levels of significance. Has the population mean study time changed?

Paired T-Test and CI: StudyBefore, StudyAfter

```
Paired T for StudyBefore - StudyAfter
              N    Mean     StDev   SE Mean
StudyBefore   8   15.6250   1.9955   0.7055
StudyAfter    8   11.5000   3.4226   1.2101
Difference    8    4.12500  2.99702  1.05961

95% CI for mean difference: (1.61943, 6.63057)
T-Test of mean difference = 0 (vs not = 0): T-Value = 3.89  P-Value = 0.006
```

c Use the *p*-value to test the hypotheses at the .10, .05, and .01 levels of significance. How much evidence is there against the null hypothesis?

[5]Source: "Student Effort and Performance over the Semester," *Journal of Economic Education,* Winter 2005, pages 3–28.

10.3 Comparing Two Population Proportions by Using Large, Independent Samples ● ● ●

EXAMPLE 10.6 The Advertising Media Case

LO4 Compare two population proportions using large independent samples.

Suppose a new product was test marketed in the Des Moines, Iowa, and Toledo, Ohio, metropolitan areas. Equal amounts of money were spent on advertising in the two areas. However, different advertising media were employed in the two areas. Advertising in the Des Moines area was done entirely on television, while advertising in the Toledo area consisted of a mixture of television, radio, newspaper, and magazine ads. Two months after the advertising campaigns commenced, surveys are taken to estimate consumer awareness of the product. In the Des Moines area, 631 out of 1,000 randomly selected consumers are aware of the product, whereas in the Toledo area 798 out of 1,000 randomly selected consumers are aware of the product. We define p_1 to be the true proportion of all consumers in the Des Moines area who are aware of the product and p_2 to be the true proportion of all consumers in the Toledo area who are aware of the product. It follows that, since the sample proportions of consumers who are aware of the product in the Des Moines and Toledo areas are

$$\hat{p}_1 = \frac{631}{1,000} = .631$$

and

$$\hat{p}_2 = \frac{798}{1,000} = .798$$

then a point estimate of $p_1 - p_2$ is

$$\hat{p}_1 - \hat{p}_2 = .631 - .798 = -.167$$

This says we estimate that p_1 is .167 less than p_2. That is, we estimate that the percentage of all consumers who are aware of the product in the Toledo area is 16.7 percentage points higher than the percentage in the Des Moines area.

In order to find a confidence interval for and to carry out a hypothesis test about $p_1 - p_2$, we need to know the properties of the sampling distribution of $\hat{p}_1 - \hat{p}_2$. In general, therefore, consider randomly selecting n_1 elements from a population, and assume that a proportion p_1 of all the elements in the population fall into a particular category. Let $\hat{p}_1$ denote the proportion of elements in the sample that fall into the category. Also, consider randomly selecting a sample of n_2 elements from a second population, and assume that a proportion p_2 of all the elements in this population fall into the particular category. Let $\hat{p}_2$ denote the proportion of elements in the second sample that fall into the category.

The Sampling Distribution of $\hat{p}_1 - \hat{p}_2$

If the randomly selected samples are independent of each other, then the population of all possible values of $\hat{p}_1 - \hat{p}_2$:

1 Approximately has a normal distribution if each of the sample sizes n_1 and n_2 is large. Here n_1 and n_2 are large enough if n_1p_1, $n_1(1 - p_1)$, n_2p_2, and $n_2(1 - p_2)$ are all at least 5.

2 Has mean $\mu_{\hat{p}_1 - \hat{p}_2} = p_1 - p_2$

3 Has standard deviation $\sigma_{\hat{p}_1 - \hat{p}_2} = \sqrt{\dfrac{p_1(1 - p_1)}{n_1} + \dfrac{p_2(1 - p_2)}{n_2}}$

If we estimate p_1 by $\hat{p}_1$ and p_2 by $\hat{p}_2$ in the expression for $\sigma_{\hat{p}_1 - \hat{p}_2}$, then the sampling distribution of $\hat{p}_1 - \hat{p}_2$ implies the following $100(1 - \alpha)$ percent confidence interval for $p_1 - p_2$.

A Large Sample Confidence Interval for the Difference between Two Population Proportions[6]

Suppose we randomly select a sample of size n_1 from a population, and let $\hat{p}_1$ denote the proportion of elements in this sample that fall into a category of interest. Also suppose we randomly select a sample of size n_2 from another population, and let $\hat{p}_2$ denote the proportion of elements in this second sample that fall into the category of interest. Then, if each of the sample sizes n_1 and n_2 is large

($n_1\hat{p}_1$, $n_1(1 - \hat{p}_1)$, $n_2\hat{p}_2$, and $n_2(1 - \hat{p}_2)$ must all be at least 5), and if the random samples are independent of each other, a **100(1 − α) percent confidence interval for $p_1 - p_2$** is

$$\left[(\hat{p}_1 - \hat{p}_2) \pm z_{\alpha/2}\sqrt{\frac{\hat{p}_1(1 - \hat{p}_1)}{n_1} + \frac{\hat{p}_2(1 - \hat{p}_2)}{n_2}} \right]$$

EXAMPLE 10.7 The Advertising Media Case

Recall that in the advertising media situation described at the beginning of this section, 631 of 1,000 randomly selected consumers in Des Moines are aware of the new product, while 798 of 1,000 randomly selected consumers in Toledo are aware of the new product. Also recall that

$$\hat{p}_1 = \frac{631}{1,000} = .631$$

and

$$\hat{p}_2 = \frac{798}{1,000} = .798$$

Because $n_1\hat{p}_1 = 1,000(.631) = 631$, $n_1(1 - \hat{p}_1) = 1,000(1 - .631) = 369$, $n_2\hat{p}_2 = 1,000(.798) = 798$, and $n_2(1 - \hat{p}_2) = 1,000(1 - .798) = 202$ are all at least 5, both n_1 and n_2 can be considered large. It follows that a 95 percent confidence interval for $p_1 - p_2$ is

$$\left[(\hat{p}_1 - \hat{p}_2) \pm z_{.025}\sqrt{\frac{\hat{p}_1(1 - \hat{p}_1)}{n_1} + \frac{\hat{p}_2(1 - \hat{p}_2)}{n_2}} \right]$$

$$= \left[(.631 - .798) \pm 1.96\sqrt{\frac{(.631)(.369)}{1,000} + \frac{(.798)(.202)}{1,000}} \right]$$

$$= [-.167 \pm .0389]$$

$$= [-.2059, \ -.1281]$$

This interval says we are 95 percent confident that p_1, the proportion of all consumers in the Des Moines area who are aware of the product, is between .2059 and .1281 less than p_2, the proportion of all consumers in the Toledo area who are aware of the product. Thus, we have substantial evidence that advertising the new product by using a mixture of television, radio, newspaper, and magazine ads (as in Toledo) is more effective than spending an equal amount of money on television commercials only.

---

[6]More correctly, because $\hat{p}_1(1 - \hat{p}_1)/(n_1 - 1)$ and $\hat{p}_2(1 - \hat{p}_2)/(n_2 - 1)$ are unbiased point estimates of $p_1(1 - p_1)/n_1$ and $p_2(1 - p_2)/n_2$, a point estimate of $\sigma_{\hat{p}_1 - \hat{p}_2}$ is

$$s_{\hat{p}_1 - \hat{p}_2} = \sqrt{\frac{\hat{p}_1(1 - \hat{p}_1)}{n_1 - 1} + \frac{\hat{p}_2(1 - \hat{p}_2)}{n_2 - 1}}$$

and a 100(1 − α) percent confidence interval for $p_1 - p_2$ is $[(\hat{p}_1 - \hat{p}_2) \pm z_{\alpha/2} s_{\hat{p}_1 - \hat{p}_2}]$. Because both n_1 and n_2 are large, there is little difference between the interval obtained by using this formula and those obtained by using the formula in the box above.

To test the null hypothesis $H_0: p_1 - p_2 = D_0$, we use the test statistic

$$z = \frac{(\hat{p}_1 - \hat{p}_2) - D_0}{\sigma_{\hat{p}_1 - \hat{p}_2}}$$

A commonly employed special case of this hypothesis test is obtained by setting D_0 equal to 0. In this case, the null hypothesis $H_0: p_1 - p_2 = 0$ says there is **no difference** between the population proportions p_1 and p_2. When $D_0 = 0$, the best estimate of the common population proportion $p = p_1 = p_2$ is obtained by computing

$$\hat{p} = \frac{\text{the total number of elements in the two samples that fall into the category of interest}}{\text{the total number of elements in the two samples}}$$

Therefore, the point estimate of $\sigma_{\hat{p}_1 - \hat{p}_2}$ is

$$s_{\hat{p}_1 - \hat{p}_2} = \sqrt{\frac{\hat{p}(1 - \hat{p})}{n_1} + \frac{\hat{p}(1 - \hat{p})}{n_2}}$$

$$= \sqrt{\hat{p}(1 - \hat{p})\left(\frac{1}{n_1} + \frac{1}{n_2}\right)}$$

For the case where $D_0 \neq 0$, the point estimate of $\sigma_{\hat{p}_1 - \hat{p}_2}$ is obtained by estimating p_1 by $\hat{p}_1$ and p_2 by $\hat{p}_2$. With these facts in mind, we present the following procedure for testing $H_0: p_1 - p_2 = D_0$:

A Hypothesis Test about the Difference between Two Population Proportions

Null Hypothesis $H_0: p_1 - p_2 = D_0$ **Test Statistic** $z = \dfrac{(\hat{p}_1 - \hat{p}_2) - D_0}{\sigma_{\hat{p}_1 - \hat{p}_2}}$ **Assumptions**   Independent samples and Large sample sizes

Critical Value Rule			p-Value (Reject H_0 if p-Value $< \alpha$)		
$H_a: p_1 - p_2 > D_0$	$H_a: p_1 - p_2 < D_0$	$H_a: p_1 - p_2 \neq D_0$	$H_a: p_1 - p_2 > D_0$	$H_a: p_1 - p_2 < D_0$	$H_a: p_1 - p_2 \neq D_0$
Reject H_0 if $z > z_\alpha$	Reject H_0 if $z < -z_\alpha$	Reject H_0 if $|z| > z_{\alpha/2}$—that is, $z > z_{\alpha/2}$ or $z < -z_{\alpha/2}$	p-value = area to the right of z	p-value = area to the left of z	p-value = twice the area to the right of $|z|$

Note:

1 If $D_0 = 0$, we estimate $\sigma_{\hat{p}_1 - \hat{p}_2}$ by

$$s_{\hat{p}_1 - \hat{p}_2} = \sqrt{\hat{p}(1 - \hat{p})\left(\frac{1}{n_1} + \frac{1}{n_2}\right)}$$

2 If $D_0 \neq 0$, we estimate $\sigma_{\hat{p}_1 - \hat{p}_2}$ by

$$s_{\hat{p}_1 - \hat{p}_2} = \sqrt{\frac{\hat{p}_1(1 - \hat{p}_1)}{n_1} + \frac{\hat{p}_2(1 - \hat{p}_2)}{n_2}}$$

EXAMPLE 10.8 The Advertising Media Case

Recall that p_1 is the proportion of all consumers in the Des Moines area who are aware of the new product and that p_2 is the proportion of all consumers in the Toledo area who are aware of the new product. To test for the equality of these proportions, we will test $H_0: p_1 - p_2 = 0$ versus $H_a: p_1 - p_2 \neq 0$ at the **.05 level of significance.** Because both of the Des Moines and Toledo samples are large (see Example 10.7), we will calculate the value of the **test statistic z in the summary box** (where $D_0 = 0$). Since $H_a: p_1 - p_2 \neq 0$ implies a two tailed test, we will **reject $H_0: p_1 - p_2 = 0$ if the absolute value of z is greater than** $z_{\alpha/2} = z_{.05/2} = z_{.025} = 1.96$. Because 631 out of 1,000 randomly selected Des Moines residents were aware of the product and 798 out of 1,000 randomly selected Toledo residents were aware of the product, the estimate of $p = p_1 = p_2$ is

$$\hat{p} = \frac{631 + 798}{1,000 + 1,000} = \frac{1,429}{2,000} = .7145$$

and the **value of the test statistic is**

$$z = \frac{(\hat{p}_1 - \hat{p}_2) - D_0}{\sqrt{\hat{p}(1 - \hat{p})(\frac{1}{n_1} + \frac{1}{n_2})}} = \frac{(.631 - .798) - 0}{\sqrt{(.7145)(.2855)(\frac{1}{1,000} + \frac{1}{1,000})}} = \frac{-.167}{.0202} = -8.2673$$

Because $|z| = 8.2673$ is greater than 1.96, we can reject $H_0: p_1 - p_2 = 0$ in favor of $H_a: p_1 - p_2 \neq 0$. We conclude (at an α of .05) that the proportions of all consumers who are aware of the product in Des Moines and Toledo differ. Furthermore, the point estimate $\hat{p}_1 - \hat{p}_2 = .631 - .798 = -.167$ says we estimate that the percentage of all consumers who are aware of the product in Toledo is 16.7 percentage points higher than the percentage of all consumers who are aware of the product in Des Moines. The p-value for this test is twice the area under the standard normal curve to the right of $|z| = 8.2673$. Since the area under the standard normal curve to the right of 3.99 is .00003, the p-value for testing H_0 is less than $2(.00003) = .00006$. It follows that we have extremely strong evidence that $H_0: p_1 - p_2 = 0$ should be rejected in favor of $H_a: p_1 - p_2 \neq 0$. That is, this small p-value provides extremely strong evidence that p_1 and p_2 differ. Figure 10.12 presents the MINITAB output of the hypothesis test of $H_0: p_1 - p_2 = 0$ versus $H_a: p_1 - p_2 \neq 0$ and of a 95 percent confidence interval for $p_1 - p_2$. Note that the MINITAB output gives a value of the test statistic z (that is, the value -8.41) that is slightly different from the value -8.2673 calculated above. The reason is that, even though we are testing $H_0: p_1 - p_2 = 0$, MINITAB uses the second formula in the summary box (rather than the first formula) to calculate $s_{\hat{p}_1 - \hat{p}_2}$.

FIGURE 10.12   **MINITAB Output of Statistical Inference in the Advertising Media Case**

```
Test and CI for Two Proportions

Sample    X      N    Sample p
1        631   1000   0.631000
2        798   1000   0.798000

Difference = p(1) - p(2)
Estimate for difference: -0.167
95% CI for difference: (-0.205906, -0.128094)
Test of difference = 0 (vs not = 0): Z = -8.41, P-value = 0.000
```

Exercises for Section 10.3

CONCEPTS

10.24   Explain what population is described by the sampling distribution of $\hat{p}_1 - \hat{p}_2$.

10.25   What assumptions must be satisfied in order to use the methods presented in this section?

METHODS AND APPLICATIONS

In Exercises 10.26 through 10.28 we assume that we have selected two independent random samples from populations having proportions p_1 and p_2 and that $\hat{p}_1 = 800/1,000 = .8$ and $\hat{p}_2 = 950/1,000 = .95$.

10.26 Calculate a 95 percent confidence interval for $p_1 - p_2$. Interpret this interval. Can we be 95 percent confident that $p_1 - p_2$ is less than 0? That is, can we be 95 percent confident that p_1 is less than p_2? Explain.

10.27 Test H_0: $p_1 - p_2 = 0$ versus H_a: $p_1 - p_2 \neq 0$ by using critical values and by setting α equal to .10, .05, .01, and .001. How much evidence is there that p_1 and p_2 differ? Explain.

10.28 Test H_0: $p_1 - p_2 \geq -.12$ versus H_a: $p_1 - p_2 < -.12$ by using a p-value and by setting α equal to .10, .05, .01, and .001. How much evidence is there that p_2 exceeds p_1 by more than .12? Explain.

10.29 In an article in the *Journal of Advertising*, Weinberger and Spotts compare the use of humor in television ads in the United States and in the United Kingdom. Suppose that independent random samples of television ads are taken in the two countries. A random sample of 400 television ads in the United Kingdom reveals that 142 use humor, while a random sample of 500 television ads in the United States reveals that 122 use humor.

   a Set up the null and alternative hypotheses needed to determine whether the proportion of ads using humor in the United Kingdom differs from the proportion of ads using humor in the United States.

   b Test the hypotheses you set up in part *a* by using critical values and by setting α equal to .10, .05, .01, and .001. How much evidence is there that the proportions of U.K. and U.S. ads using humor are different?

   c Set up the hypotheses needed to attempt to establish that the difference between the proportions of U.K. and U.S. ads using humor is more than .05 (five percentage points). Test these hypotheses by using a p-value and by setting α equal to .10, .05, .01, and .001. How much evidence is there that the difference between the proportions exceeds .05?

   d Calculate a 95 percent confidence interval for the difference between the proportion of U.K. ads using humor and the proportion of U.S. ads using humor. Interpret this interval. Can we be 95 percent confident that the proportion of U.K. ads using humor is greater than the proportion of U.S. ads using humor?

10.30 In the book *Essentials of Marketing Research*, William R. Dillon, Thomas J. Madden, and Neil H. Firtle discuss a research proposal in which a telephone company wants to determine whether the appeal of a new security system varies between homeowners and renters. Independent samples of 140 homeowners and 60 renters are randomly selected. Each respondent views a TV pilot in which a test ad for the new security system is embedded twice. Afterward, each respondent is interviewed to find out whether he or she would purchase the security system.

    Results show that 25 out of the 140 homeowners definitely would buy the security system, while 9 out of the 60 renters definitely would buy the system.

   a Letting p_1 be the proportion of homeowners who would buy the security system, and letting p_2 be the proportion of renters who would buy the security system, set up the null and alternative hypotheses needed to determine whether the proportion of homeowners who would buy the security system differs from the proportion of renters who would buy the security system.

   b Find the test statistic z and the p-value for testing the hypotheses of part *a*. Use the p-value to test the hypotheses with α equal to .10, .05, .01, and .001. How much evidence is there that the proportions of homeowners and renters differ?

   c Calculate a 95 percent confidence interval for the difference between the proportions of homeowners and renters who would buy the security system. On the basis of this interval, can we be 95 percent confident that these proportions differ? Explain.

    Note: An Excel add-in (MegaStat) output of the hypothesis test and confidence interval in parts *b* and *c* is given in Appendix 10.2 on page 428.

10.31 In the book *Cases in Finance*, Nunnally and Plath (1995) present a case in which the estimated percentage of uncollectible accounts varies with the age of the account. Here the age of an unpaid account is the number of days elapsed since the invoice date.

    An accountant believes that the percentage of accounts that will be uncollectible increases as the ages of the accounts increase. To test this theory, the accountant randomly selects independent samples of 500 accounts with ages between 31 and 60 days and 500 accounts with ages between 61 and 90 days from the accounts receivable ledger dated one year ago. When the sampled accounts are examined, it is found that 10 of the 500 accounts with ages between 31 and 60 days were eventually classified as uncollectible, while 27 of the 500 accounts with ages between 61 and 90 days were eventually classified as uncollectible. Let p_1 be the proportion of accounts with ages between 31 and 60 days that will be uncollectible, and let p_2 be the proportion of accounts with ages between 61 and 90 days that will be uncollectible. Use the MINITAB output below to determine how much evidence there is that we should reject $H_0: p_1 - p_2 = 0$ in favor of $H_a: p_1 - p_2 \neq 0$. Also, identify a 95 percent confidence interval for $p_1 - p_2$, and estimate the smallest that the difference between p_1 and p_2 might be.

Test and CI for Two Proportions

```
Sample             X    N    Sample p
1 (31 to 60 days)  10   500  0.020000    Difference = p(1) - p(2)
2 (61 to 90 days   27   500  0.054000    Estimate for difference:  -0.034

95% CI for difference:  (-0.0573036, -0.0106964)
Test for difference = 0 (vs not = 0):  Z = -2.85    P-Value = 0.004
```

10.32   On January 7, 2000, the Gallup Organization released the results of a poll comparing the lifestyles of today with yesteryear. The survey results were based on telephone interviews with a randomly selected national sample of 1,031 adults, 18 years and older, conducted December 20–21, 1999. The poll asked several questions and compared the 1999 responses with the responses given in polls taken in previous years. Below we summarize some of the poll's results.[7]

Percentage of respondents who

1	Had taken a vacation lasting six days or more within the last 12 months:	December 1999 42%	December 1968 62%
2	Took part in some sort of daily activity to keep physically fit:	December 1999 60%	September 1977 48%
3	Watched TV more than four hours on an average weekday:	December 1999 28%	April 1981 25%
4	Drove a car or truck to work:	December 1999 87%	April 1971 81%

Assuming that each poll was based on a randomly selected national sample of 1,031 adults and that the samples in different years are independent:

a   Let p_1 be the December 1999 population proportion of U.S. adults who had taken a vacation lasting six days or more within the last 12 months, and let p_2 be the December 1968 population proportion who had taken such a vacation. Calculate a 99 percent confidence interval for the difference between p_1 and p_2. Interpret what this interval says about how these population proportions differ.

b   Let p_1 be the December 1999 population proportion of U.S. adults who took part in some sort of daily activity to keep physically fit, and let p_2 be the September 1977 population proportion who did the same. Carry out a hypothesis test to attempt to justify that the proportion who took part in such daily activity increased from September 1977 to December 1999. Use $\alpha = .05$ and explain your result.

c   Let p_1 be the December 1999 population proportion of U.S. adults who watched TV more than four hours on an average weekday, and let p_2 be the April 1981 population proportion who did the same. Carry out a hypothesis test to determine whether these population proportions differ. Use $\alpha = .05$ and interpret the result of your test.

d   Let p_1 be the December 1999 population proportion of U.S. adults who drove a car or truck to work, and let p_2 be the April 1971 population proportion who did the same. Calculate a 95 percent confidence interval for the difference between p_1 and p_2. On the basis of this interval, can it be concluded that the 1999 and 1971 population proportions differ?

10.33   In the book *International Marketing*, Philip R. Cateora reports the results of an MTV-commissioned study of the lifestyles and spending habits of the 14–34 age group in six countries. The survey results are given in Table 10.7.   ⓓⓢ PurchPct

a   As shown in Table 10.7, 96 percent of the 14- to 34-year-olds surveyed in the United States had purchased soft drinks in the last three months, while 90 percent of the 14- to 34-year-olds surveyed in Australia had done the same. Assuming that these results were obtained from

TABLE 10.7   Results of an MTV-Commissioned Survey of the Lifestyles and Spending Habits of the 14–34 Age Group in Six Countries   DS PurchPct

Which of the Following Have You Purchased in the Past Three Months?

Product	Percentage in United States	Percentage in Australia	Percentage in Brazil	Percentage in Germany	Percentage in Japan	Percentage in United Kingdom
Soft drinks	96%	90%	93%	83%	91%	94%
Fast food	94	94	91	70	86	85
Athletic footwear	59	40	54	33	30	49
Blue jeans	56	39	62	45	42	44
Beer*	46	50	60	46	57	57
Cigarettes*	24	33	30	38	39	40

*Among adults 18+. Source: Yankelovich Clancy Shulman.

Source: Philip R. Cateora, *International Marketing,* 9th ed. (Burr Ridge, IL: Richard D. Irwin, 1993), p. 262. Copyright © 1993. Reprinted by permission of McGraw-Hill Companies, Inc.

independent random samples of 500 respondents in each country, carry out a hypothesis test that tests the equality of the population proportions of 14- to 34-year-olds in the United States and in Australia who have purchased soft drinks in the last three months. Also, calculate a 95 percent confidence interval for the difference between these two population proportions, and use this interval to estimate the largest and smallest values that the difference between these proportions might be. Based on your confidence interval, do you feel that this result has practical importance?

b   Again as shown in Table 10.7, 40 percent of the 14- to 34-year-olds surveyed in Australia had purchased athletic footwear in the last three months, while 54 percent of the 14- to 34-year-olds surveyed in Brazil had done the same. Assuming that these results were obtained from independent random samples of 500 respondents in each country, carry out a hypothesis test that tests the equality of the population proportions of 14- to 34-year-olds in Australia and in Brazil who have purchased athletic footwear in the last three months. Also, calculate a 95 percent confidence interval for the difference between these two population proportions, and use this interval to estimate the largest and smallest values that the difference between these proportions might be. Based on your confidence interval, do you feel that this result has practical importance?

10.4 Comparing Two Population Variances by Using Independent Samples ● ● ●

We have seen that we often wish to compare two population means. In addition, it is often useful to compare two population variances. For example, we might compare the variances of the fills that would be produced by two processes that are supposed to fill jars with 16 ounces of strawberry preserves. Or, as another example, we might wish to compare the variance of the chemical yields obtained when using Catalyst XA-100 with that obtained when using Catalyst ZB-200. Here the catalyst that produces yields with the smaller variance is giving more consistent (or predictable) results.

If σ_1^2 and σ_2^2 are the population variances that we wish to compare, one approach is to test the null hypothesis

$$H_0: \sigma_1^2 = \sigma_2^2$$

We might test H_0 versus an alternative hypothesis of, for instance,

$$H_a: \sigma_1^2 > \sigma_2^2$$

Dividing by σ_2^2, we see that testing these hypotheses is equivalent to testing

$$H_0: \frac{\sigma_1^2}{\sigma_2^2} = 1 \qquad \text{versus} \qquad H_a: \frac{\sigma_1^2}{\sigma_2^2} > 1$$

FIGURE 10.13   *F* **Distribution Curves and F Points**

(a) The point F_α corresponding to df_1 and df_2 degrees of freedom

(b) The point $F_{.05}$ corresponding to 4 and 7 degrees of freedom

Intuitively, we would reject H_0 in favor of H_a if s_1^2/s_2^2 is significantly larger than 1. Here s_1^2 is the variance of a random sample of n_1 observations from the population with variance σ_1^2, and s_2^2 is the variance of a random sample of n_2 observations from the population with variance σ_2^2. To decide exactly how large s_1^2/s_2^2 must be in order to reject H_0, we need to consider the sampling distribution of s_1^2/s_2^2.[8]

> **LO5** Describe the properties of the *F* distribution and use an *F* table.

It can be shown that, if the null hypothesis H_0: $\sigma_1^2/\sigma_2^2 = 1$ is true, then the population of all possible values of s_1^2/s_2^2 is described by what is called an **F distribution.** In general, as illustrated in Figure 10.13, the curve of the *F* distribution is skewed to the right. Moreover, the exact shape of this curve depends on two parameters that are called the **numerator degrees of freedom (denoted df_1)** and the **denominator degrees of freedom (denoted df_2).** The values of df_1 and df_2 that describe the sampling distribution of s_1^2/s_2^2 are given in the following result:

The Sampling Distribution of s_1^2/s_2^2

Suppose we randomly select independent samples from two normally distributed populations having variances σ_1^2 and σ_2^2. Then, if the null hypothesis H_0: $\sigma_1^2/\sigma_2^2 = 1$ is true, the population of all possible values of s_1^2/s_2^2 has an **F distribution** with $df_1 = (n_1 - 1)$ **numerator degrees of freedom** and with $df_2 = (n_2 - 1)$ **denominator degrees of freedom.**

In order to use the *F* distribution, we employ an **F point,** which is denoted F_α. As illustrated in Figure 10.13(a), F_α **is the point on the horizontal axis under the curve of the *F* distribution that gives a right-hand tail area equal to α.** The value of F_α in a particular situation depends on the size of the right-hand tail area (the size of α) and on the numerator degrees of freedom (df_1) and the denominator degrees of freedom (df_2). Values of F_α are given in an **F table.** Tables A.5, A.6, A.7, and A.8 (pages 642–645) give values of $F_{.10}$, $F_{.05}$, $F_{.025}$, and $F_{.01}$, respectively. Each table tabulates values of F_α according to the appropriate numerator degrees of freedom (values listed across the top of the table) and the appropriate denominator degrees of freedom (values listed down the left side of the table). A portion of Table A.6, which gives values of $F_{.05}$, is reproduced in this chapter as Table 10.8. For instance, suppose we wish to find the *F* point that gives a right-hand tail area of .05 under the curve of the *F* distribution having 4 numerator and

---

[8]Note that we divide by σ_2^2 to form a null hypothesis of the form H_0: $\dfrac{\sigma_1^2}{\sigma_2^2} = 1$ rather than subtracting σ_2^2 to form a null hypothesis of the form H_0: $\sigma_1^2 - \sigma_2^2 = 0$. This is because the population of all possible values of $s_1^2 - s_2^2$ has no known sampling distribution.

TABLE 10.8 A Portion of an *F* Table: Values of $F_{.05}$

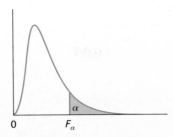

df_1	Numerator Degrees of Freedom (df_1)													
df_2	1	2	3	4	5	6	7	8	9	10	12	15	20	24
1	161.4	199.5	215.7	224.6	230.2	234.0	236.8	238.9	240.5	241.9	243.9	245.9	248.0	249.1
2	18.51	19.00	19.16	19.25	19.30	19.33	19.35	19.37	19.38	19.40	19.41	19.43	19.45	19.45
3	10.13	9.55	9.28	9.12	9.01	8.94	8.89	8.85	8.81	8.79	8.74	8.70	8.66	8.64
4	7.71	6.94	6.59	6.39	6.26	6.16	6.09	6.04	6.00	5.96	5.91	5.86	5.80	5.77
5	6.61	5.79	5.41	5.19	5.05	4.95	4.88	4.82	4.77	4.74	4.68	4.62	4.56	4.53
6	5.99	5.14	4.76	4.53	4.39	4.28	4.21	4.15	4.10	4.06	4.00	3.94	3.87	3.84
7	5.59	4.71	4.25	4.12	3.97	3.87	3.79	3.73	3.68	3.64	3.57	3.51	3.44	3.41
8	5.32	4.46	4.07	3.84	3.69	3.58	3.50	3.44	3.39	3.35	3.28	3.22	3.15	3.12
9	5.12	4.26	3.86	3.63	3.48	3.37	3.29	3.23	3.18	3.14	3.07	3.01	2.94	2.90
10	4.96	4.10	3.71	3.48	3.33	3.22	3.14	3.07	3.02	2.98	2.91	2.85	2.77	2.74
11	4.84	3.98	3.59	3.36	3.20	3.09	3.01	2.95	2.90	2.85	2.79	2.72	2.65	2.61
12	4.75	3.89	3.49	3.26	3.11	3.00	2.91	2.85	2.80	2.75	2.69	2.62	2.54	2.51
13	4.67	3.81	3.41	3.18	3.03	2.92	2.83	2.77	2.71	2.67	2.60	2.53	2.46	2.42
14	4.60	3.74	3.34	3.11	2.96	2.85	2.76	2.70	2.65	2.60	2.53	2.46	2.39	2.35
15	4.54	3.68	3.29	3.06	2.90	2.79	2.71	2.64	2.59	2.54	2.48	2.40	2.33	2.29
16	4.49	3.63	3.24	3.01	2.85	2.74	2.66	2.59	2.54	2.49	2.42	2.35	2.28	2.24
17	4.45	3.59	3.20	2.96	2.81	2.70	2.61	2.55	2.49	2.45	2.38	2.31	2.23	2.19
18	4.41	3.55	3.16	2.93	2.77	2.66	2.58	2.51	2.46	2.41	2.34	2.27	2.19	2.15
19	4.38	3.52	3.13	2.90	2.74	2.63	2.54	2.48	2.42	2.38	2.31	2.23	2.16	2.11
20	4.35	3.49	3.10	2.87	2.71	2.60	2.51	2.45	2.39	2.35	2.28	2.20	2.12	2.08
21	4.32	3.47	3.07	2.84	2.68	2.57	2.49	2.42	2.37	2.32	2.25	2.18	2.10	2.05
22	4.30	3.44	3.05	2.82	2.66	2.55	2.46	2.40	2.34	2.30	2.23	2.15	2.07	2.03
23	4.28	3.42	3.03	2.80	2.64	2.53	2.44	2.37	2.32	2.27	2.20	2.13	2.05	2.01
24	4.26	3.40	3.01	2.78	2.62	2.51	2.42	2.36	2.30	2.25	2.18	2.11	2.03	1.98
25	4.24	3.39	2.99	2.76	2.60	2.49	2.40	2.34	2.28	2.24	2.16	2.09	2.01	1.96
26	4.23	3.37	2.98	2.74	2.59	2.47	2.39	2.32	2.27	2.22	2.15	2.07	1.99	1.95
27	4.21	3.35	2.96	2.73	2.57	2.46	2.37	2.31	2.25	2.20	2.13	2.06	1.97	1.93
28	4.20	3.34	2.95	2.71	2.56	2.45	2.36	2.29	2.24	2.19	2.12	2.04	1.96	1.91
29	4.18	3.33	2.93	2.70	2.55	2.43	2.35	2.28	2.22	2.18	2.10	2.03	1.94	1.90
30	4.17	3.32	2.92	2.69	2.53	2.42	2.33	2.27	2.21	2.16	2.09	2.01	1.93	1.89
40	4.08	3.23	2.84	2.61	2.45	2.34	2.25	2.18	2.12	2.08	2.00	1.92	1.84	1.79
60	4.00	3.15	2.76	2.53	2.37	2.25	2.17	2.10	2.04	1.99	1.92	1.84	1.75	1.70
120	3.92	3.07	2.68	2.45	2.29	2.17	2.09	2.02	1.96	1.91	1.83	1.75	1.66	1.61
∞	3.84	3.00	2.60	2.37	2.21	2.10	2.01	1.94	1.88	1.83	1.75	1.67	1.57	1.52

Denominator Degrees of Freedom (df_2)

7 denominator degrees of freedom. To do this, we scan across the top of Table 10.8 until we find the column corresponding to 4 numerator degrees of freedom, and we scan down the left side of the table until we find the row corresponding to 7 denominator degrees of freedom. The table entry in this column and row is the desired *F* point. We find that the $F_{.05}$ point is 4.12 [see Figure 10.13(b) and Table 10.8].

We now present the procedure for testing the equality of two population variances when the alternative hypothesis is one-tailed.

LO6 Compare two population variances when the samples are independent.

Testing the Equality of Population Variances versus a One-Tailed Alternative Hypothesis

Suppose we randomly select independent samples from two normally distributed populations—populations 1 and 2. Let s_1^2 be the variance of the random sample of n_1 observations from population 1, and let s_2^2 be the variance of the random sample of n_2 observations from population 2.

1 In order to test $H_0\colon \sigma_1^2 = \sigma_2^2$ versus $H_a\colon \sigma_1^2 > \sigma_2^2$, define the test statistic

$$F = \frac{s_1^2}{s_2^2}$$

and define the corresponding p-value to be the area to the right of F under the curve of the F distribution having $df_1 = n_1 - 1$ numerator degrees of freedom and $df_2 = n_2 - 1$ denominator degrees of freedom. We can reject H_0 at level of significance α if and only if

a $F > F_\alpha$ or, equivalently,

b p-value $< \alpha$.

Here F_α is based on $df_1 = n_1 - 1$ and $df_2 = n_2 - 1$ degrees of freedom.

2 In order to test $H_0\colon \sigma_1^2 = \sigma_2^2$ versus $H_a\colon \sigma_1^2 < \sigma_2^2$, define the test statistic

$$F = \frac{s_2^2}{s_1^2}$$

and define the corresponding p-value to be the area to the right of F under the curve of the F distribution having $df_1 = n_2 - 1$ numerator degrees of freedom and $df_2 = n_1 - 1$ denominator degrees of freedom. We can reject H_0 at level of significance α if and only if

a $F > F_\alpha$ or, equivalently,

b p-value $< \alpha$.

Here F_α is based on $df_1 = n_2 - 1$ and $df_2 = n_1 - 1$ degrees of freedom.

Reject H_0 if $F > F_\alpha$

EXAMPLE 10.9

Process 1	Process 2
15.9841	15.9622
16.0150	15.9736
15.9964	15.9753
15.9916	15.9802
15.9949	15.9802
16.0003	15.9860
15.9884	15.9885
16.0016	15.9897
16.0260	15.9903
16.0216	15.9920
16.0065	15.9928
15.9997	15.9934
15.9909	15.9973
16.0043	16.0014
15.9881	16.0016
16.0078	16.0053
15.9934	16.0053
16.0150	16.0098
16.0057	16.0102
15.9928	16.0252
15.9987	16.0316
16.0131	16.0331
15.9981	16.0384
16.0025	16.0386
15.9898	16.0401

DS Preserves

A jelly and jam producer has decided to purchase one of two jar-filling processes—process 1 or process 2—to fill 16-ounce jars with strawberry preserves. Process 1 is slightly more expensive than process 2, but the maker of process 1 claims that σ_1^2, the variance of all fills that would be produced by process 1, is less than σ_2^2, the variance of all fills that would be produced by process 2. To test $H_0\colon \sigma_1^2 = \sigma_2^2$ versus $H_a\colon \sigma_1^2 < \sigma_2^2$ (or, equivalently, $H_a\colon \sigma_2^2 > \sigma_1^2$) the jelly and jam producer measures the fills of 25 randomly selected jars produced by each process. The jar fill measurements for each process are given in the page margin. A histogram (not shown here) for each sample is bell-shaped and symmetrical, the sample sizes are $n_1 = 25$ and $n_2 = 25$, and the sample variances are $s_1^2 = .000118$ and $s_2^2 = .0004847$. Therefore, we compute the test statistic

$$F = \frac{s_2^2}{s_1^2} = \frac{.0004847}{.000118} = 4.1168$$

and we compare this value with F_α based on $df_1 = n_2 - 1 = 25 - 1 = 24$ numerator degrees of freedom and $df_2 = n_1 - 1 = 25 - 1 = 24$ denominator degrees of freedom. If we test H_0 versus H_a at the .05 level of significance, then Table 10.8 tells us that when $df_1 = 24$ and $df_2 = 24$, we have $F_{.05} = 1.98$. Because $F = 4.1168$ is greater than $F_{.05} = 1.98$, we can reject $H_0\colon \sigma_1^2 = \sigma_2^2$ in favor of $H_a\colon \sigma_1^2 < \sigma_2^2$. That is, we conclude (at on α of .05) that the variance of all fills that would be produced by process 1 is less than the variance of all fills that would be produced by process 2. That is, process 1 produces more consistent fills.

.05

$F_{.05} = 1.98$

FIGURE 10.14   Excel Output for Testing $H_0: \sigma_1^2 = \sigma_2^2$ versus $H_a: \sigma_1^2 < \sigma_2^2$

F-Test Two-Sample for Variances

	Process 2	Process 1
Mean	16.001756	16.00105
Variance	0.0004847	0.000118
Observations	25	25
df	24	24
F	4.1167856	
P(F<=f) one-tail	0.0004787	
F Critical one-tail	1.9837596	

The p-value for testing H_0 versus H_a is the area to the right of $F = 4.1168$ under the curve of the F distribution having 24 numerator degrees of freedom and 24 denominator degrees of freedom. The Excel output in Figure 10.14 tells us that this p-value equals 0.0004787. Since this p-value is less than .001, we have extremely strong evidence to support rejecting H_0 in favor of H_a. That is, there is extremely strong evidence that process 1 produces jar fills that are more consistent (less variable) than the jar fills produced by process 2.

Next consider the catalyst comparison situation of Example 10.1, and suppose the production supervisor wishes to use the sample data in Table 10.1 to determine whether σ_1^2, the variance of the chemical yields obtained by using Catalyst XA-100, differs from σ_2^2, the variance of the chemical yields obtained by using Catalyst ZB-200. To do this, the supervisor will test the null hypothesis $H_0: \sigma_1^2 = \sigma_2^2$ versus the alternative hypothesis $H_a: \sigma_1^2 \neq \sigma_2^2$. Because $n_1 = 5$, $n_2 = 5$, $s_1^2 = 386$, and $s_2^2 = 484.2$ (see Table 10.1), we can compute (assuming normality):

$$F = \frac{s_1^2}{s_2^2} = \frac{386}{484.2} = .797$$

As illustrated in Figure 10.15, if we set $\alpha = .05$, we compare F with the critical values $F_{.975}$ and $F_{.025}$ under the curve of the F distribution having $n_1 - 1 = 4$ numerator and $n_2 - 1 = 4$ denominator degrees of freedom. We see that we can easily find the appropriate upper-tail critical value to be $F_{.025} = 9.60$. In order to find the lower-tail critical value, $F_{.975}$, we use the following relationship:

$F_{(1-\alpha)}$ with df_1 numerator and df_2 denominator degrees of freedom

$$= \frac{1}{F_\alpha \text{ with } df_2 \text{ numerator and } df_1 \text{ denominator degrees of freedom}}$$

FIGURE 10.15   Critical Values for Testing $H_0: \sigma_1^2 = \sigma_2^2$ versus $H_a: \sigma_1^2 \neq \sigma_2^2$ with $\alpha = .05$

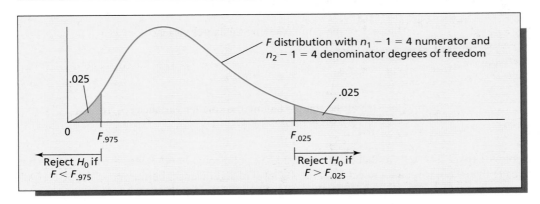

This says that for the F curve with 4 numerator and 4 denominator degrees of freedom, $F_{(1-.025)} = F_{.975} = 1/F_{.025} = 1/9.60 = .104$. Therefore, because $F = .797$ is not greater than $F_{.025} = 9.60$ and since $F = .797$ is not less than $F_{.975} = .104$, we cannot reject H_0 in favor of H_a at the .05 level of significance.

Although we can calculate the lower-tail critical value for this hypothesis test as just illustrated, it is common practice to compute the test statistic F so that its value is always greater than 1. This means that we will always compare F with the upper-tail critical value when carrying out the test. This can be done by always calculating F to be the larger of s_1^2 and s_2^2 divided by the smaller of s_1^2 and s_2^2. We obtain the following result:

Testing the Equality of Population Variances (Two Tailed Alternative)

Suppose we randomly select independent samples from two normally distributed populations and define all notation as in the previous box. Then, in order to test H_0: $\sigma_1^2 = \sigma_2^2$ versus H_a: $\sigma_1^2 \neq \sigma_2^2$, define the test statistic

$$F = \frac{\text{the larger of } s_1^2 \text{ and } s_2^2}{\text{the smaller of } s_1^2 \text{ and } s_2^2}$$

and let

$df_1 = \{$the size of the sample having the larger variance$\} - 1$

$df_2 = \{$the size of the sample having the smaller variance$\} - 1$

Also, define the corresponding p-value to be twice the area to the right of F under the curve of the F distribution having df_1 numerator degrees of

freedom and df_2 denominator degrees of freedom. We can reject H_0 at level of significance α if and only if

1 $F > F_{\alpha/2}$ or, equivalently,

2 p-value $< \alpha$.

Here $F_{\alpha/2}$ is based on df_1 and df_2 degrees of freedom.

EXAMPLE 10.10 The Catalyst Comparison Case

In the catalyst comparison situation, we can reject H_0: $\sigma_1^2 = \sigma_2^2$ in favor of H_a: $\sigma_1^2 \neq \sigma_2^2$ at the .05 level of significance if

$$F = \frac{\text{the larger of } s_1^2 \text{ and } s_2^2}{\text{the smaller of } s_1^2 \text{ and } s_2^2} = \frac{484.2}{386} = 1.2544$$

is greater than $F_{\alpha/2} = F_{.05/2} = F_{.025}$. Here the degrees of freedom are

$$df_1 = \{\text{the size of the sample having the larger variance}\} - 1$$
$$= n_2 - 1 = 5 - 1 = 4$$

and

$$df_2 = \{\text{the size of the sample having the smaller variance}\} - 1$$
$$= n_1 - 1 = 5 - 1 = 4$$

Table A.7 (page 644) tells us that the appropriate $F_{.025}$ point equals 9.60. Because $F = 1.2544$ is not greater than 9.60, we cannot reject H_0 at the .05 level of significance. Furthermore, the MINITAB output at the top of the next page tells us that the p-value for this hypothesis test is 0.831.

Test for Equal Variances: ZB-200, XA-100

```
F-Test (Normal Distribution)
Test Statistic = 1.25,
p-value = 0.831
```

Since the p-value is large, we have little evidence that the variabilities of the yields produced by Catalysts XA-100 and ZB-200 differ.

It has been suggested that the F test of H_0: $\sigma_1^2 = \sigma_2^2$ be used to choose between the equal variances and unequal variances t based procedures when comparing two means (as described in Section 10.1). Certainly the F test is one approach to making this choice. However, studies have shown that the validity of the F test is very sensitive to violations of the normality assumption—much more sensitive, in fact, than the equal variances procedure is to violations of the equal variances assumption. While opinions vary, some statisticians believe that this is a serious problem and that the F test should never be used to choose between the equal variances and unequal variances procedures. Others feel that performing the test for this purpose is reasonable if the test's limitations are kept in mind.

As an example for those who believe that using the F test is reasonable, we found in Example 10.10 that we do not reject H_0: $\sigma_1^2 = \sigma_2^2$ at the .05 level of significance in the context of the catalyst comparison situation. Further, the p-value related to the F test, which equals 0.831, tells us that there is little evidence to suggest that the population variances differ. It follows that it might be reasonable to compare the mean yields of the catalysts by using the equal variances procedures (as we have done in Examples 10.1 and 10.2).

Exercises for Section 10.4

CONCEPTS

10.34 Explain what population is described by the sampling distribution of s_1^2/s_2^2.

10.35 Intuitively explain why a value of s_1^2/s_2^2 that is substantially greater than 1 provides evidence that σ_1^2 is not equal to σ_2^2.

connect

METHODS AND APPLICATIONS

10.36 Use Table 10.8 to find the $F_{.05}$ point for each of the following:
 a $df_1 = 3$ numerator degrees of freedom and $df_2 = 14$ denominator degrees of freedom.
 b $df_1 = 6$ and $df_2 = 10$.
 c $df_1 = 2$ and $df_2 = 22$.
 d $df_1 = 7$ and $df_2 = 5$.
 Use Tables A.5, A.6, A.7, and A.8 (pages 642–645) to find the following F_α points:
 e $F_{.10}$ with $df_1 = 4$ numerator degrees of freedom and $df_2 = 7$ denominator degrees of freedom.
 f $F_{.01}$ with $df_1 = 3$ and $df_2 = 25$.
 g $F_{.025}$ with $df_1 = 7$ and $df_2 = 17$.
 h $F_{.05}$ with $df_1 = 9$ and $df_2 = 3$.

10.37 Suppose two independent random samples of sizes $n_1 = 9$ and $n_2 = 7$ that have been taken from two normally distributed populations having variances σ_1^2 and σ_2^2 give sample variances of $s_1^2 = 100$ and $s_2^2 = 20$.
 a Test H_0: $\sigma_1^2 = \sigma_2^2$ versus H_a: $\sigma_1^2 \neq \sigma_2^2$ with $\alpha = .05$. What do you conclude?
 b Test H_0: $\sigma_1^2 \leq \sigma_2^2$ versus H_a: $\sigma_1^2 > \sigma_2^2$ with $\alpha = .05$. What do you conclude?

10.38 Suppose two independent random samples of sizes $n_1 = 5$ and $n_2 = 16$ that have been taken from two normally distributed populations having variances σ_1^2 and σ_2^2 give sample standard deviations of $s_1 = 5$ and $s_2 = 9$.
 a Test H_0: $\sigma_1^2 = \sigma_2^2$ versus H_a: $\sigma_1^2 \neq \sigma_2^2$ with $\alpha = .05$. What do you conclude?
 b Test H_0: $\sigma_1^2 \geq \sigma_2^2$ versus H_a: $\sigma_1^2 < \sigma_2^2$ with $\alpha = .01$. What do you conclude?

10.39 Consider the situation of Exercise 10.11 (page 396). Use the sample information to test H_0: $\sigma_1^2 = \sigma_2^2$ versus H_a: $\sigma_1^2 \neq \sigma_2^2$ with $\alpha = .05$. Based on this test, does it make sense to believe that the unequal variances procedure is appropriate? Explain.

10.40 Consider the situation of Exercise 10.12 (page 396). ◯§ AutoLoan
a Use the Excel output in Figure 10.7 (page 397) and a critical value to test H_0: $\sigma_1^2 = \sigma_2^2$ versus H_a: $\sigma_1^2 \neq \sigma_2^2$ with $\alpha = .05$. What do you conclude?
b Does it make sense to use the equal variances procedure in this situation?

10.41 The stopping distances of a random sample of $n_1 = 16$ Fire-Hawk compact cars have a mean of $\bar{x}_1 = 57.2$ feet and a standard deviation of $s_1 = 4.81$ feet. The stopping distances of a random sample of $n_2 = 16$ Lance compact cars have a mean of $\bar{x}_2 = 62.7$ feet and a standard deviation of $s_2 = 7.56$ feet. Here, each stopping distance is measured from a speed of 35 mph. If σ_1^2 and σ_2^2 denote the corresponding population variances, test H_0: $\sigma_1^2 = \sigma_2^2$ versus H_a: $\sigma_1^2 < \sigma_2^2$ by setting α equal to .05 and using a critical value (assume normality).

Chapter Summary

This chapter has explained **how to compare two populations** by using confidence intervals and hypothesis tests. First we discussed how to compare **two population means** by using **independent samples.** Here the measurements in one sample are not related to the measurements in the other sample. When the population variances are unknown, **t-based** inferences are appropriate if the populations are normally distributed or the sample sizes are large. Both **equal variances and unequal variances t-based procedures** exist. We learned that, because it can be difficult to compare the population variances, many statisticians believe that it is almost always best to use the unequal variances procedure.

Sometimes samples are not independent. We learned that one such case is what is called a **paired difference experiment.** Here we obtain two different measurements on the same sample units, and we can compare two population means by using a confidence interval or by conducting a hypothesis test that employs the differences between the pairs of measurements. We next explained how to compare **two population proportions** by using **large, independent samples.** Finally, we concluded this chapter by discussing how to compare **two population variances** by using independent samples, and we learned that this comparison is done by using a test based on the **F distribution.**

Glossary of Terms

F distribution: A continuous probability curve having a shape that depends on two parameters—the numerator degrees of freedom, df_1, and the denominator degrees of freedom, df_2. (pages 412–413)

independent samples experiment: An experiment in which there is no relationship between the measurements in the different samples. (page 388)

paired difference experiment: An experiment in which two different measurements are taken on the same units and inferences are made using the differences between the pairs of measurements. (page 401)

sampling distribution of $\hat{p}_1 - \hat{p}_2$: The probability distribution that describes the population of all possible values of $\hat{p}_1 - \hat{p}_2$, where $\hat{p}_1$ is the sample proportion for a random sample taken from one population and $\hat{p}_2$ is the sample proportion for a random sample taken from a second population. (page 405)

sampling distribution of s_1^2/s_2^2: The probability distribution that describes the population of all possible values of s_1^2/s_2^2, where s_1^2 is the sample variance of a random sample taken from one population and s_2^2 is the sample variance of a random sample taken from a second population. (page 412)

sampling distribution of $\bar{x}_1 - \bar{x}_2$: The probability distribution that describes the population of all possible values of $\bar{x}_1 - \bar{x}_2$, where $\bar{x}_1$ is the sample mean of a random sample taken from one population and $\bar{x}_2$ is the sample mean of a random sample taken from a second population. (page 388)

Important Formulas and Tests

Sampling distribution of $\bar{x}_1 - \bar{x}_2$ (independent random samples): page 388

t-based confidence interval for $\mu_1 - \mu_2$ when $\sigma_1^2 = \sigma_2^2$: page 389

t-based confidence interval for $\mu_1 - \mu_2$ when $\sigma_1^2 \neq \sigma_2^2$: page 392

t test about $\mu_1 - \mu_2$ when $\sigma_1^2 = \sigma_2^2$: page 391

t test about $\mu_1 - \mu_2$ when $\sigma_1^2 \neq \sigma_2^2$: page 392

Confidence interval for μ_d: page 399

A hypothesis test about μ_d: page 399

Sampling distribution of $\hat{p}_1 - \hat{p}_2$ (independent random samples): page 405

Large sample confidence interval for $p_1 - p_2$: page 406

Large sample hypothesis test about $p_1 - p_2$: page 407

Sampling distribution of s_1^2/s_2^2 (independent random samples): page 412

A hypothesis test about the equality of σ_1^2 and σ_2^2: pages 414 and 416

Supplementary Exercises

10.42 In its February 2, 1998, issue, *Fortune* magazine published the results of a Yankelovich Partners survey of 600 adults that investigated their ideas about marriage, divorce, and the contributions of the corporate wife. The survey results are shown in Figure 10.16. For each statement in the figure, the proportions of men and women who agreed with the statement are given. Assuming that the survey results were obtained from independent random samples of 300 men and 300 women:

    a For each statement, carry out a hypothesis test that tests the equality of the population proportions of men and women who agree with the statement. Use α equal to .10, .05, .01, and .001. How much evidence is there that the population proportions of men and women who agree with each statement differ?

    b For each statement, calculate a 95 percent confidence interval for the difference between the population proportion of men who agree with the statement and the population proportion of women who agree with the statement. Use the interval to help assess whether you feel that the difference between population proportions has practical significance.

Exercises 10.43 and 10.44 deal with the following situation:

    In an article in the *Journal of Retailing,* Kumar, Kerwin, and Pereira study factors affecting merger and acquisition activity in retailing by comparing "target firms" and "bidder firms" with respect to several financial and marketing-related variables. If we consider two of the financial variables included in the study, suppose a random sample of 36 "target firms" gives a mean earnings per share of \$1.52 with a standard deviation of \$0.92, and that this sample gives a mean debt-to-equity ratio of 1.66 with a standard deviation of 0.82. Furthermore, an independent random sample of 36 "bidder firms" gives a mean earnings per share of \$1.20 with a standard deviation of \$0.84, and this sample gives a mean debt-to-equity ratio of 1.58 with a standard deviation of 0.81.

10.43   **a** Set up the null and alternative hypotheses needed to test whether the mean earnings per share for all "target firms" differs from the mean earnings per share for all "bidder firms." Test these hypotheses at the .10, .05, .01, and .001 levels of significance. How much evidence is there that these means differ? Explain.

    b Calculate a 95 percent confidence interval for the difference between the mean earnings per share for "target firms" and "bidder firms." Interpret the interval.

F I G U R E 10.16 **The Results of a Yankelovich Partners Survey of 600 Adults on Marriage, Divorce, and the Contributions of the Corporate Wife (All Respondents with Income \$50,000 or More)**

People were magnanimous on the general proposition:
- In a divorce in a long-term marriage where the husband works outside the home and the wife is not employed for pay, the wife should be entitled to half the assets accumulated during the marriage.
  - 93% of women agree
  - 85% of men agree

But when we got to the goodies, a gender gap began to appear . . .
- The pension accumulated during the marriage should be split evenly.
  - 80% of women agree
  - 68% of men agree
- Stock options granted during the marriage should be split evenly.
  - 77% of women agree
  - 62% of men agree

. . . and turned into a chasm over the issue of how important a stay-at-home wife is to a husband's success.
- Managing the household and child rearing are extremely important to a husband's success.
  - 57% of women agree
  - 41% of men agree
- A corporate wife who also must travel, entertain, and act as a sounding board is extremely important to the success of a high-level business executive.
  - 51% of women agree
  - 28% of men agree
- The lifestyle of a corporate wife is more of a job than a luxury.
  - 73% of women agree
  - 57% of men agree

Source: Reprinted from the February 2, 1998, issue of *Fortune.* Copyright 1998 Time, Inc. Reprinted by permission.

10.44   **a** Set up the null and alternative hypotheses needed to test whether the mean debt-to-equity ratio for all "target firms" differs from the mean debt-to-equity ratio for all "bidder firms." Test these hypotheses at the .10, .05, .01, and .001 levels of significance. How much evidence is there that these means differ? Explain.

   b Calculate a 95 percent confidence interval for the difference between the mean debt-to-equity ratios for "target firms" and "bidder firms." Interpret the interval.

   c Based on the results of this exercise and Exercise 10.43, does a firm's earnings per share or the firm's debt-to-equity ratio seem to have the most influence on whether a firm will be a "target" or a "bidder"? Explain.

10.45   What impact did the September 11 terrorist attack have on U.S. airline demand? An analysis was conducted by Ito and Lee, "Assessing the impact of the September 11 terrorist attacks on U.S. airline demand," in the *Journal of Economics and Business* (January–February 2005). They found a negative short-term effect of over 30% and an ongoing negative impact of over 7%. Suppose that we wish to test the impact by taking a random sample of 12 airline routes before and after 9/11. Passenger miles (millions of passenger miles) for the same routes were tracked for the 12 months prior to and the 12 months immediately following 9/11. Assume that the population of all possible paired differences is normally distributed.

   a Set up the null and alternative hypotheses needed to determine whether there was a reduction in mean airline passenger demand.

   b Below we present the MINITAB output for the paired differences test. Use the output and critical values to test the hypotheses at the .10, .05, and .01 levels of significance. Has the population mean airline demand been reduced?

Paired T-Test and CI: Before911, After911

Paired T for Before911 - After911

	N	Mean	StDev	SE Mean
Before911	12	117.333	26.976	7.787
After911	12	87.583	25.518	7.366
Difference	12	29.7500	10.3056	2.9750

T-Test of mean difference = 0 (vs > 0): T-Value = 10.00   P-Value = 0.000

   c Use the *p*-value to test the hypotheses at the .10, .05, and .01 levels of significance. How much evidence is there against the null hypothesis?

10.46   In the book *Essentials of Marketing Research*, William R. Dillon, Thomas J. Madden, and Neil H. Firtle discuss evaluating the effectiveness of a test coupon. Samples of 500 test coupons and 500 control coupons were randomly delivered to shoppers. The results indicated that 35 of the 500 control coupons were redeemed, while 50 of the 500 test coupons were redeemed.

   a In order to consider the test coupon for use, the marketing research organization required that the proportion of all shoppers who would redeem the test coupon be statistically shown to be greater than the proportion of all shoppers who would redeem the control coupon. Assuming that the two samples of shoppers are independent, carry out a hypothesis test at the .01 level of significance that will show whether this requirement is met by the test coupon. Explain your conclusion.

   b Use the sample data to find a point estimate and a 95 percent interval estimate of the difference between the proportions of all shoppers who would redeem the test coupon and the control coupon. What does this interval say about whether the test coupon should be considered for use? Explain.

   c Carry out the test of part *a* at the .10 level of significance. What do you conclude? Is your result statistically significant? Compute a 90 percent interval estimate instead of the 95 percent interval estimate of part *b*. Based on the interval estimate, do you feel that this result is practically important? Explain.

10.47   A marketing manager wishes to compare the mean prices charged for two brands of CD players. The manager conducts a random survey of retail outlets and obtains independent random samples of prices with the following results:

	Onkyo	JVC
Sample mean, $\bar{x}$	$189	$145
Sample standard deviation, s	$ 12	$ 10
Sample size	6	12

Assuming normality and equal variances:

a Use an appropriate hypothesis test to determine whether the mean prices for the two brands differ. How much evidence is there that the mean prices differ?

b Use an appropriate 95 percent confidence interval to estimate the difference between the mean prices of the two brands of CD players. Do you think that the difference has practical importance?

c Use an appropriate hypothesis test to provide evidence supporting the claim that the mean price of the Onkyo CD player is more than $30 higher than the mean price for the JVC CD player. Set α equal to .05.

10.48 Consider the situation of Exercise 10.47. Use the sample information to test H_0: $\sigma_1^2 = \sigma_2^2$ versus H_a: $\sigma_1^2 \neq \sigma_2^2$ with $\alpha = .05$. Based on this test, does it make sense to use the equal variances procedure? Explain.

10.49 Internet Exercise

a A prominent issue of the 2000 U.S. presidential campaign was campaign finance reform. A *Washington Post*/ABC News poll (reported April 4, 2000) found that 63 percent of 1,083 American adults surveyed believed that stricter campaign finance laws would be effective (a lot or somewhat) in reducing the influence of money in politics. Was this view uniformly held or did it vary by gender, race, or political party affiliation? A summary of survey responses, broken down by gender, is given in the table below.

Summary of Responses	Male	Female	All
Believe reduce influence, *p*	59%	66%	63%
Number surveyed, *n*	520	563	1,083

[Source: *Washington Post* website: www.washington-post.com/wp-srv/politics/polls/vault/vault.htm.

Is there sufficient evidence in this survey to conclude that the proportion of individuals who believed that campaign finance laws can reduce the influence of money in politics differs between females and males? Set up the appropriate null and alternative hypotheses. Conduct your test at the .05 and .01 levels of significance and calculate the *p*-value for your test. Make sure your conclusion is clearly stated.

b Search the World Wide Web for an interesting recent political poll dealing with an issue or political candidates, where responses are broken down by gender or some other two-category classification. (A list of high-potential websites is given below.) Use a difference in proportions test to determine whether political preference differs by gender or other two-level grouping.

Political polls on the World Wide Web:

ABC News:	www.abcnews.go.com/pollingunit
Washington Post:	www.washingtonpost.com/wp-dyn/content/politics/polls/?nid=roll_polls
Gallup:	www.gallup.com/Home.aspx
Polling Report:	www.pollingreport.com
Rasmussen Reports:	www.rasmussenreports.com/public_content/politics
Zogby International:	www.zogby.com/features/zogbytables3.cfm
CBS News Poll Database:	www.cbsnews.com/stories/2007/10/12/politics/main3362530.shtml?tag=cbsnewsMainColumnArea;cbsnewsMainColumnArea.0

Appendix 10.1 ■ Two-Sample Hypothesis Testing Using Excel

The instruction blocks in this section each begins by describing the entry of data into an Excel spreadsheet. Alternatively, the data may be downloaded from this book's website. The appropriate data file name is given at the top of each instruction block. Please refer to Appendix 1.1 for further information about entering data, saving data, and printing results when using Excel.

Test for the difference between means, equal variances, in Figure 10.2(b) on page 392 (data file: Catalyst.xlsx):

- Enter the data from Table 10.1 (page 390) into two columns: yields for catalyst XA-100 in column A and yields for catalyst ZB-200 in column B, with labels XA-100 and ZB-200.

- Select **Data : Data Analysis : t-Test: Two-Sample Assuming Equal Variances** and click OK in the Data Analysis dialog box.

- In the t-Test dialog box, enter A1: A6 in the "Variable 1 Range" window.

- Enter B1:B6 in the "Variable 2 Range" window.

- Enter 0 (zero) in the "Hypothesized Mean Difference" box.

- Place a checkmark in the Labels checkbox.

- Enter 0.05 into the Alpha box.

- Under output options, select "New Worksheet Ply" to have the output placed in a new worksheet and enter the name Output for the new worksheet.

- Click OK in the t-Test dialog box.

- The output will be displayed in a new worksheet.

Note: The *t* test assuming unequal variances can be done by selecting **Data : Data Analysis : t-Test : Two-Sample Assuming Unequal Variances.**

Hypothesis test for the equality of two variances in Figure 10.14 on page 415 (data file: Preserves.xlsx):

- Enter the Preserves data (on page 414) into columns A and B with the label "Process 1" in cell A1 and the label "Process 2" in cell B1.

- Select **Data : Data Analysis : F-Test Two-Sample for Variances**.

- In the F-Test dialog box, enter B1:B26 in the "Variable 1 Range" window. (since Process 2 has the higher sample standard deviation).

- Enter A1:A26 in the "Variable 2 Range" window.

- Place a checkmark in the Labels checkbox.

- Enter .05 in the Alpha box.

- Under output options, select "New Worksheet Ply" and enter the name Output to have the output placed in a new worksheet named Output.

- Click OK in the F-test dialog box.

- The output will be displayed in the new worksheet.

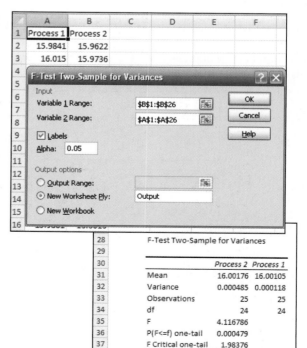

Test for paired differences in Figure 10.9 on page 400 (data file: Repair.xlsx):

- Enter the data from Table 10.2 (page 398) into two columns: costs for Garage 1 in column A and costs for Garage 2 in column B, with labels Garage1 and Garage2.

- Select **Data : Data Analysis : t-Test: Paired Two Sample for Means** and click OK in the Data Analysis dialog box.

- In the t-Test dialog box, enter A1:A8 into the "Variable 1 Range" window.

- Enter B1:B8 into the "Variable 2 Range" window.

- Enter 0 (zero) in the "Hypothesized Mean Difference" box.

- Place a checkmark in the Labels checkbox.

- Enter 0.05 into the Alpha box.

- Under output options, select "New Worksheet Ply" to have the output placed in a new worksheet and enter the name Output for the new worksheet.

- Click OK in the t-Test dialog box.

- The output will be displayed in a new worksheet.

Appendix 10.2 ■ Two-Sample Hypothesis Testing Using MegaStat

The instructions in this section begin by describing the entry of data into an Excel worksheet. Alternatively, the data may be downloaded from this book's website. The appropriate data file name is given at the top of each instruction block. Please refer to Appendix 1.1 for further information about entering data and saving and printing results in Excel. Please refer to Appendix 1.2 for more information about using MegaStat.

Test for the difference between means, equal variances, similar to Figure 10.2(a) on page 392 (data file: Catalyst.xlsx):

- Enter the data from Table 10.1 (page 390) into two columns: yields for catalyst XA-100 in column A and yields for catalyst ZB-200 in column B, with labels XA-100 and ZB-200.

- Select **MegaStat : Hypothesis Tests : Compare Two Independent Groups**

- In the "Hypothesis Test: Compare Two Independent Groups" dialog box, click on "data input."

- Click in the Group 1 window and use the autoexpand feature to enter the range A1:A6.

- Click in the Group 2 window and use the autoexpand feature to enter the range B1:B6.

- Enter the Hypothesized Difference (here equal to 0) into the so labeled window.

- Select an Alternative (here "not equal") from the drop-down menu in the Alternative box.

- Click on "t-test (pooled variance)" to request the equal variances test described on page 391.

- Check the "Display confidence interval" checkbox, and select or type a desired level of confidence.

- Check the "Test for equality of variances" checkbox to request the *F* test described on pages 414 and 416.

- Click OK in the "Hypothesis Test: Compare Two Independent Groups" dialog box.

- The *t* test assuming unequal variances described on page 392 can be done by clicking "t-test (unequal variances)".

Test for paired differences similar to Figure 10.9 on page 400 (data file: Repair.xlsx):

- Enter the data from Table 10.2 (page 398) into two columns: costs for Garage 1 in column A and costs for Garage 2 in column B, with labels Garage1 and Garage2.

- Select **Add-Ins : MegaStat : Hypothesis Tests : Paired Observations.**

- In the "Hypothesis Test: Paired Observations" dialog box, click on "data input."

- Click in the Group 1 window, and use the autoexpand feature to enter the range A1:A8.

- Click in the Group 2 window, and use the autoexpand feature to enter the range B1:B8.

- Enter the Hypothesized difference (here equal to 0) into the so labeled window.

- Select an Alternative (here "not equal") from the drop-down menu in the Alternative box.

- Click on "t-test."

- Click OK in the "Hypothesis Test: Paired Observations" dialog box.

- If the sample sizes are large, a test based on the normal distribution can be done by clicking on "z-test."

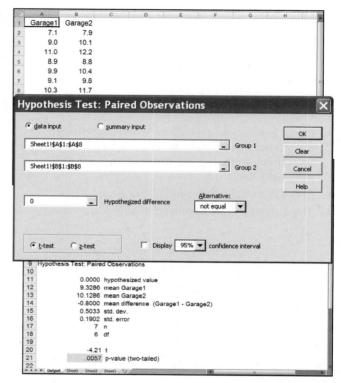

Hypothesis Test and Confidence Interval for Two Independent Proportions in Exercise 10.30 on page 409:

- Select **Add-Ins : MegaStat : Hypothesis Tests: Compare Two Independent Proportions.**

- In the "Hypothesis Test: Compare Two Proportions" dialog box, enter the number of successes *x* (here equal to 25) and the sample size *n* (here equal to 140) for homeowners in the "x" and "n" Group 1 windows.

- Enter the number of successes *x* (here equal to 9) and the sample size *n* (here equal to 60) for renters in the "x" and "n" Group 2 windows.

- Enter the Hypothesized difference (here equal to 0) into the so labeled window.

- Select an Alternative (here "not equal") from the drop-down menu in the Alternative box.

- Check the "Display confidence interval" checkbox, and select or type a desired level of confidence (here equal to 95%).

- Click OK in the "Hypothesis Test: Compare Two Proportions" dialog box.

Appendix 10.3 ■ Two-Sample Hypothesis Testing Using MINITAB

The instruction blocks in this section each begins by describing the entry of data into the MINITAB data window. Alternatively, the data may be downloaded from this book's website. The appropriate data file name is given at the top of each instruction block. Please refer to Appendix 1.3 for further information about entering data, saving data, and printing results when using MINITAB.

Test for the difference between means, unequal variances, in Figure 10.4 on page 394 (data file: Catalyst.MTW):

- In the data window, enter the data from Table 10.1 (page 390) into two columns with variable names XA-100 and ZB-200.

- Select **Stat : Basic Statistics : 2-Sample t**.

- In the "2-Sample t (Test and Confidence Interval)" dialog box, select the "Samples in different columns" option.

- Select the XA-100 variable into the First window.

- Select the ZB-200 variable into the Second window.

- Click on the Options… button, enter the desired level of confidence (here, 95.0) in the "Confidence level" window, enter 0.0 in the "Test difference" window, and select "not equal" from the Alternative pull-down menu. Click OK in the "2-Sample t—Options" dialog box.

- To produce yield by catalyst type boxplots, click the Graphs… button, check the "Boxplots of data" checkbox, and click OK in the "2 Sample t—Graphs" dialog box.

- Click OK in the "2-Sample t (Test and Confidence Interval)" dialog box.

- The results of the two-sample *t* test (including the *t* statistic and *p*-value) and the confidence interval for the difference between means appear in the Session window, while the boxplots will be displayed in a graphics window.

- A test for the difference between two means when the **variances are equal** can be performed by placing a checkmark in the "Assume Equal Variances" checkbox in the "2-Sample t (Test and Confidence Interval)" dialog box.

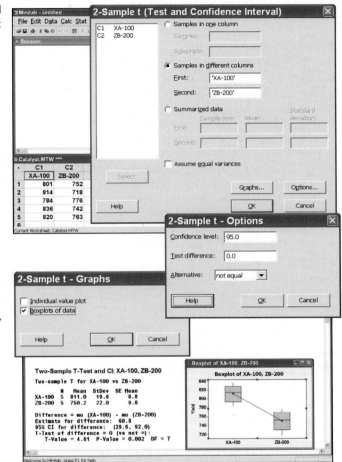

Test for paired differences in Figure 10.8 on page 400 (data file: Repair.MTW):

- In the Data window, enter the data from Table 10.2 (page 398) into two columns with variable names Garage1 and Garage2.
- Select **Stat : Basic Statistics : Paired t.**
- In the "Paired t (Test and Confidence Interval)" dialog box, select the "Samples in columns" option.
- Select Garage1 into the "First sample" window and Garage2 into the "Second sample" window.
- Click the Options... button.
- In the "Paired t—Options" dialog box, enter the desired level of confidence (here, 95.0) in the "Confidence level" window, enter 0.0 in the "Test mean" window, select "less than" from the Alternative pull-down menu, and click OK.
- To produce a boxplot of differences with a graphical summary of the test, click the Graphs... button, check the "Boxplot of differences" checkbox, and click OK in the "Paired t—Graphs" dialog box.
- Click OK in the "Paired t (Test and Confidence Interval)" dialog box.

The results of the paired t-test are given in the Session window, and graphical output is displayed in a graphics window.

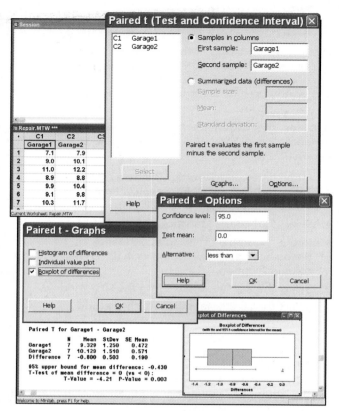

Hypothesis test and confidence interval for two Independent proportions in Figure 10.12 on page 408:

- Select **Stat : Basic Statistics : 2 Proportions.**
- In the "2 Proportions (Test and Confidence Interval)" dialog box, select the "Summarized data" option.
- Enter the sample size for Des Moines (equal to 1000) into the "First—Trials" window, and enter the number of successes for Des Moines (equal to 631) into the "First—Events" window.
- Enter the sample size for Toledo (equal to 1000) into the "Second—Trials" window, and enter the number of successes for Toledo (equal to 798) into the "Second—Events" window.
- Click on the Options... button.
- In the "2 Proportions—Options" dialog box, enter the desired level of confidence (here 95.0) into the "Confidence level" window.
- Enter 0.0 into the "Test difference" window because we are testing that the difference between the two proportions equals zero.

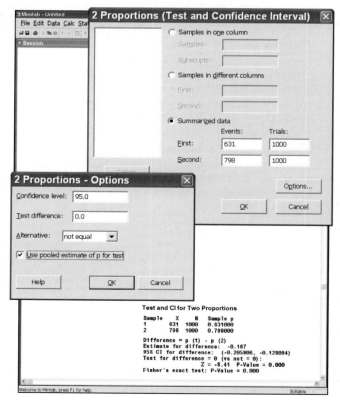

- Select the desired alternative hypothesis (here "not equal") from the Alternative drop-down menu.
- Check the "Use pooled estimate of p for test" checkbox because "Test difference" equals zero. Do not check this box in cases where "Test difference" does not equal zero.
- Click OK in the "2 Proportions—Options" dialog box.
- Click OK in the "2 Proportions (Test and Confidence Interval)" dialog box to obtain results for the test in the Session window.

Test for equality of variances at the top of page 417 (data file: Catalyst.MTW):

- Select **Stat : Basic Statistics : 2 Variances.**
- Enter the labels XA-100 and ZB-200 into columns C1 and C2. Then enter the catalyst comparison data into columns C1 and C2—yields for catalyst XA-100 in column C1 and yields for catalyst ZB-200 in column C2.
- In the "2 Variances" dialog box, select the "Samples in different columns" option.
- In the "2 Variances" dialog box, enter 'ZB-200' into the "First" window (because the ZB-200 yields have the larger sample variance) and enter 'XA-100' into the "Second" window (because the XA-100 yields have the smaller sample variance).
- Click OK in the "2 Variances" dialog box.
- The F statistic and the p-value for the two-sided test will be displayed in the session window (along with additional output that we do not describe in this book). A graphical summary of the test is shown in a graphics window like the one to the right titled "Test for Equal Variances for ZB-200, XA-100."

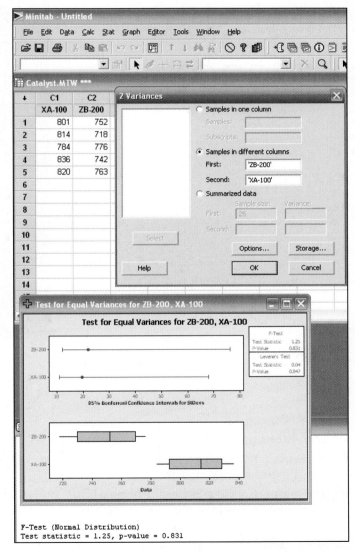

CHAPTER 11

Experimental Design and Analysis of Variance

Learning Objectives

After mastering the material in this chapter, you will be able to:

(LO1) Explain the basic terminology and concepts of experimental design.

(LO2) Compare several different population means by using a one-way analysis of variance.

(LO3) Compare treatment effects and block effects by using a randomized block design.

(LO4) Assess the effects of two factors on a response variable by using a two-way analysis of variance.

(LO5) Describe what happens when two factors interact.

Chapter Outline

11.1 Basic Concepts of Experimental Design

11.2 One-Way Analysis of Variance

11.3 The Randomized Block Design

11.4 Two-Way Analysis of Variance

n Chapter 10 we learned that business improvement often involves making **comparisons.** In that chapter we presented several confidence intervals and several hypothesis testing procedures for comparing two population means. However, business improvement often requires that we compare more than two population means. For instance, we might compare the mean sales obtained by using three different advertising campaigns in order to improve a company's marketing process. Or, we might compare the mean production output obtained by using four different manufacturing process designs to improve productivity.

In this chapter we extend the methods presented in Chapter 10 by considering statistical procedures for **comparing two or more population means.** Each of the methods we discuss is called an **analysis of variance (ANOVA)** procedure. We also present some basic concepts of **experimental design,** which involves deciding how to collect data in a way that allows us to most effectively compare population means.

We explain the methods of this chapter in the context of four cases:

The Gasoline Mileage Case: An oil company wishes to develop a reasonably priced gasoline that will deliver improved mileages. The company uses **one-way analysis of variance** to compare the effects of three types of gasoline on mileage in order to find the gasoline type that delivers the highest mean mileage.

The Defective Cardboard Box Case: A paper company performs an experiment to investigate the effects of four production methods on the number of defective cardboard boxes produced in an hour. The company uses a **randomized block** ANOVA to determine which production method yields the smallest mean number of defective boxes.

The Shelf Display Case: A commercial bakery supplies many supermarkets. In order to improve the effectiveness of its supermarket shelf displays the company wishes to compare the effects of shelf display height (bottom, middle, or top) and width (regular or wide) on monthly demand. The bakery employs **two-way analysis of variance** to find the display height and width combination that produces the highest monthly demand.

11.1 Basic Concepts of Experimental Design ● ● ●

LO1 Explain the basic terminology and concepts of experimental design.

In many statistical studies a variable of interest, called the **response variable** (or **dependent variable**), is identified. Then data are collected that tell us about how one or more **factors** (or **independent variables**) influence the variable of interest. If we cannot control the factor(s) being studied, we say that the data obtained are **observational.** For example, suppose that in order to study how the size of a home relates to the sales price of the home, a real estate agent randomly selects 50 recently sold homes and records the square footages and sales prices of these homes. Because the real estate agent cannot control the sizes of the randomly selected homes, we say that the data are observational.

If we can control the factors being studied, we say that the data are **experimental.** Furthermore, in this case the values, or **levels,** of the factor (or combination of factors) are called **treatments.** The purpose of most experiments is **to compare and estimate the effects of the different treatments on the response variable.** For example, suppose that an oil company wishes to study how three different gasoline types (A, B, and C) affect the mileage obtained by a popular midsized automobile model. Here the response variable is gasoline mileage, and the company will study a single factor—gasoline type. Since the oil company can control which gasoline type is used in the midsized automobile, the data that the oil company will collect are experimental. Furthermore, the treatments—the levels of the factor gasoline type—are gasoline types A, B, and C.

In order to collect data in an experiment, the different treatments are assigned to objects (people, cars, animals, or the like) that are called **experimental units.** For example, in the gasoline mileage situation, gasoline types A, B, and C will be compared by conducting mileage tests using a midsized automobile. The automobiles used in the tests are the experimental units.

In general, when a treatment is applied to more than one experimental unit, it is said to be **replicated.** Furthermore, when the analyst controls the treatments employed and how they are applied to the experimental units, a **designed experiment** is being carried out. A commonly used, simple experimental design is called the **completely randomized experimental design.**

> In a **completely randomized experimental design,** independent random samples of experimental units are assigned to the treatments.

As illustrated in the following examples we can sometimes assign *independent* random samples of experimental units to the treatments by assigning *different* random samples of experimental units to different treatments.

EXAMPLE 11.1 The Gasoline Mileage Case

North American Oil Company is attempting to develop a reasonably priced gasoline that will deliver improved gasoline mileages. As part of its development process, the company would like to compare the effects of three types of gasoline (*A*, *B*, and *C*) on gasoline mileage. For testing purposes, North American Oil will compare the effects of gasoline types *A*, *B*, and *C* on the gasoline mileage obtained by a popular midsized model called the Fire-Hawk. Suppose the company has access to 1,000 Fire-Hawks that are representative of the population of all Fire-Hawks, and suppose the company will utilize a completely randomized experimental design that employs samples of size five. In order to accomplish this, five Fire-Hawks will be randomly selected from the 1,000 available Fire-Hawks. These autos will be assigned to gasoline type *A*. Next, five *different* Fire-Hawks will be randomly selected from the remaining 995 available Fire-Hawks. These autos will be assigned to gasoline type *B*. Finally, five *different* Fire-Hawks will be randomly selected from the remaining 990 available Fire-Hawks. These autos will be assigned to gasoline type *C*.

Each randomly selected Fire-Hawk is test driven using the appropriate gasoline type (treatment) under normal conditions for a specified distance, and the gasoline mileage for each test drive is measured. We let x_{ij} denote the jth mileage obtained when using gasoline type *i*. The mileage data obtained are given in Table 11.1. Here we assume that the set of gasoline mileage observations obtained by using a particular gasoline type is a sample randomly selected from the infinite population of all Fire-Hawk mileages that could be obtained using that gasoline type. Examining the box plots shown next to the mileage data, we see some evidence that gasoline type *B* yields the highest gasoline mileages.

TABLE 11.1   **The Gasoline Mileage Data**   GasMile2

Gasoline Type *A*	Gasoline Type *B*	Gasoline Type *C*
$x_{A1} = 34.0$	$x_{B1} = 35.3$	$x_{C1} = 33.3$
$x_{A2} = 35.0$	$x_{B2} = 36.5$	$x_{C2} = 34.0$
$x_{A3} = 34.3$	$x_{B3} = 36.4$	$x_{C3} = 34.7$
$x_{A4} = 35.5$	$x_{B4} = 37.0$	$x_{C4} = 33.0$
$x_{A5} = 35.8$	$x_{B5} = 37.6$	$x_{C5} = 34.9$

EXAMPLE 11.2 The Shelf Display Case

The Tastee Bakery Company supplies a bakery product to many supermarkets in a metropolitan area. The company wishes to study the effect of the shelf display height employed by the supermarkets on monthly sales (measured in cases of 10 units each) for this product. Shelf display height, the factor to be studied, has three levels—bottom (*B*), middle (*M*), and top (*T*)—which are the treatments. To compare these treatments, the bakery uses a completely randomized experimental design. For each shelf height, six supermarkets (the experimental units) of equal sales potential are randomly selected, and each supermarket displays the product using its assigned shelf height for a month. At the end of the month, sales of the bakery product (the response variable) at the 18 participating stores are recorded, giving the data in Table 11.2. Here we assume that the set of sales amounts for each display height is a sample randomly selected from the population of all sales amounts that could be obtained (at supermarkets of the given sales potential) at that display height. Examining the box plots that are shown next to the sales data, we seem to have evidence that a middle display height gives the highest bakery product sales.

TABLE 11.2 The Bakery Product Sales Data ⑤ BakeSale

Bottom (B)	Shelf Display Height Middle (M)	Top (T)
58.2	73.0	52.4
53.7	78.1	49.7
55.8	75.4	50.9
55.7	76.2	54.0
52.5	78.4	52.1
58.9	82.1	49.9

11.2 One-Way Analysis of Variance ● ● ●

LO2 Compare several different population means by using a one-way analysis of variance.

Suppose we wish to study the effects of p **treatments** (treatments $1, 2, \ldots, p$) on a **response variable.** For any particular treatment, say treatment i, we define μ_i and σ_i to be the mean and standard deviation of the population of all possible values of the response variable that could potentially be observed when using treatment i. Here we refer to μ_i as **treatment mean i.** The goal of **one-way analysis of variance** (often called **one-way ANOVA**) is to estimate and compare the effects of the different treatments on the response variable. We do this by **estimating and comparing the treatment means** $\mu_1, \mu_2, \ldots, \mu_p$. Here we assume that a sample has been randomly selected for each of the p treatments by employing a completely randomized experimental design. We let n_i denote the size of the sample that has been randomly selected for treatment i, and we let x_{ij} denote the jth value of the response variable that is observed when using treatment i. It then follows that the point estimate of μ_i is $\bar{x}_i$, the average of the sample of n_i values of the response variable observed when using treatment i. It further follows that the point estimate of σ_i is s_i, the standard deviation of the sample of n_i values of the response variable observed when using treatment i.

For example, consider the gasoline mileage situation. We let μ_A, μ_B, and μ_C denote the means and σ_A, σ_B, and σ_C denote the standard deviations of the populations of all possible gasoline mileages using gasoline types A, B, and C. To estimate these means and standard deviations, North American Oil has employed a completely randomized experimental design and has obtained the samples of mileages in Table 11.1. The means of these samples— $\bar{x}_A = 34.92$, $\bar{x}_B = 36.56$, and $\bar{x}_C = 33.98$—are the point estimates of μ_A, μ_B, and μ_C. The standard deviations of these samples—$s_A = .7662$, $s_B = .8503$, and $s_C = .8349$—are the point estimates of σ_A, σ_B, and σ_C. Using these point estimates, we will (later in this section) test to see whether there are any statistically significant differences between the treatment means μ_A, μ_B, and μ_C. If such differences exist, we will estimate the magnitudes of these differences. This will allow North American Oil to judge whether these differences have practical importance.

The one-way ANOVA formulas allow us to test for significant differences between treatment means and allow us to estimate differences between treatment means. The validity of these formulas requires that the following assumptions hold:

Assumptions for One-Way Analysis of Variance

1 Constant variance—the p populations of values of the response variable associated with the treatments have equal variances.

2 Normality—the p populations of values of the response variable associated with the treatments all have normal distributions.

3 Independence—the samples of experimental units associated with the treatments are randomly selected, independent samples.

The one-way ANOVA results are not very sensitive to violations of the equal variances assumption. Studies have shown that this is particularly true when the sample sizes employed are equal (or nearly equal). Therefore, a good way to make sure that unequal variances will not be a problem is to take samples that are the same size. In addition, it is useful to compare the sample standard deviations $s_1, s_2, \ldots, s_p$ to see if they are reasonably equal. As a general rule, *the one-way ANOVA results will be approximately correct if the largest sample standard deviation is no more than twice the smallest sample standard deviation.* The variations of the samples can also be compared by constructing a box plot for each sample (as we have done for the gasoline mileage data in Table 11.1). Several statistical texts also employ the sample variances to test the equality of the population variances [see Bowerman and O'Connell (1990) for two of these tests]. However, these tests have some drawbacks—in particular, their results are very sensitive to violations of the normality assumption. Because of this, there is controversy as to whether these tests should be performed.

The normality assumption says that each of the p populations is normally distributed. This assumption is not crucial. It has been shown that the one-way ANOVA results are approximately valid for mound-shaped distributions. It is useful to construct a box plot and/or a stem-and-leaf display for each sample. If the distributions are reasonably symmetric, and if there are no outliers, the ANOVA results can be trusted for sample sizes as small as 4 or 5. As an example, consider the gasoline mileage study of Example 11.1. The box plots of Table 11.1 suggest that the variability of the mileages in each of the three samples is roughly the same. Furthermore, the sample standard deviations $s_A = .7662$, $s_B = .8503$, and $s_C = .8349$ are reasonably equal (the largest is not even close to twice the smallest). Therefore, it is reasonable to believe that the constant variance assumption is satisfied. Moreover, because the sample sizes are the same, unequal variances would probably not be a serious problem anyway. Many small, independent factors influence gasoline mileage, so the distributions of mileages for gasoline types A, B, and C are probably mound-shaped. In addition, the box plots of Table 11.1 indicate that each distribution is roughly symmetric with no outliers. Thus, the normality assumption probably approximately holds. Finally, because North American Oil has employed a completely randomized design, the independence assumption probably holds. This is because the gasoline mileages in the different samples were obtained for *different* Fire-Hawks.

Testing for significant differences between treatment means　As a preliminary step in one-way ANOVA, we wish to determine whether there are any statistically significant differences between the treatment means $\mu_1, \mu_2, \ldots, \mu_p$. To do this, we test the null hypothesis

$$H_0\colon \mu_1 = \mu_2 = \cdots = \mu_p$$

This hypothesis says that all the treatments have the same effect on the mean response. We test H_0 versus the alternative hypothesis

$$H_a\colon \text{At least two of } \mu_1, \mu_2, \ldots, \mu_p \text{ differ}$$

This alternative says that at least two treatments have different effects on the mean response.

To carry out such a test, we compare what we call the **between-treatment variability** to the **within-treatment variability.** For instance, suppose we wish to study the effects of three gasoline types (X, Y, and Z) on mean gasoline mileage, and consider Figure 11.1(a). This figure depicts three independent random samples of gasoline mileages obtained using gasoline types X, Y, and Z. Observations obtained using gasoline type X are plotted as blue dots (●), observations obtained using gasoline type Y are plotted as red dots (●), and observations obtained using gasoline type Z are plotted as green dots (●). Furthermore, the sample treatment means are labeled as "type X mean," "type Y mean," and "type Z mean." We see that the variability of the sample treatment means—that is, the **between-treatment variability**—is not large compared to the variability within each sample (the **within-treatment variability**). In this case, the differences between the sample treatment means could quite easily be the result of sampling variation. Thus we would not have sufficient evidence to reject

$$H_0\colon \mu_X = \mu_Y = \mu_Z$$

Next look at Figure 11.1(b), which depicts a different set of three independent random samples of gasoline mileages. Here the variability of the sample treatment means (the between-treatment variability) is large compared to the variability within each sample. This would probably provide

FIGURE 11.1   **Comparing Between-Treatment Variability and Within-Treatment Variability**

(a) Between-treatment variability is not large compared to within-treatment variability. Do not reject H_0: $\mu_X = \mu_Y = \mu_Z$

(b) Between-treatment variability is large compared to within-treatment variability. Reject H_0: $\mu_X = \mu_Y = \mu_Z$

enough evidence to tell us to reject H_0: $\mu_X = \mu_Y = \mu_Z$ in favor of H_a: At least two of $\mu_X, \mu_Y,$ and μ_Z differ. We would conclude that at least two of gasoline types X, Y, and Z have different effects on mean mileage.

In order to numerically compare the between-treatment and within-treatment variability, we can define several **sums of squares** and **mean squares.** To begin, we define n to be the total number of experimental units employed in the one-way ANOVA, and we define $\bar{x}$ to be the overall mean of all observed values of the response variable. Then we define the following:

The **treatment sum of squares** is

$$SST = \sum_{i=1}^{p} n_i(\bar{x}_i - \bar{x})^2$$

In order to compute SST, we calculate the difference between each sample treatment mean $\bar{x}_i$ and the overall mean $\bar{x}$, we square each of these differences, we multiply each squared difference by the number of observations for that treatment, and we sum over all treatments. The SST measures the variability of the sample treatment means. For instance, if all the sample treatment means ($\bar{x}_i$ values) were equal, then the treatment sum of squares would be equal to 0. The more the $\bar{x}_i$ values vary, the larger will be SST. In other words, the **treatment sum of squares** measures the amount of **between-treatment variability.**

As an example, consider the gasoline mileage data in Table 11.1. In this experiment we employ a total of

$$n = n_A + n_B + n_C = 5 + 5 + 5 = 15$$

experimental units. Furthermore, the overall mean of the 15 observed gasoline mileages is

$$\bar{x} = \frac{34.0 + 35.0 + \cdots + 34.9}{15} = \frac{527.3}{15} = 35.153$$

Then

$$\begin{aligned} SST &= \sum_{i=A,B,C} n_i(\bar{x}_i - \bar{x})^2 \\ &= n_A(\bar{x}_A - \bar{x})^2 + n_B(\bar{x}_B - \bar{x})^2 + n_C(\bar{x}_C - \bar{x})^2 \\ &= 5(34.92 - 35.153)^2 + 5(36.56 - 35.153)^2 + 5(33.98 - 35.153)^2 \\ &= 17.0493 \end{aligned}$$

In order to measure the within-treatment variability, we define the following quantity:

The **error sum of squares** is

$$SSE = \sum_{j=1}^{n_1}(x_{1j} - \bar{x}_1)^2 + \sum_{j=1}^{n_2}(x_{2j} - \bar{x}_2)^2 + \cdots + \sum_{j=1}^{n_p}(x_{pj} - \bar{x}_p)^2$$

Here x_{1j} is the jth observed value of the response in the first sample, x_{2j} is the jth observed value of the response in the second sample, and so forth. The formula above says that we compute SSE by calculating the squared difference between each observed value of the response and its corresponding treatment mean and by summing these squared differences over all the observations in the experiment.

The SSE measures the variability of the observed values of the response variable around their respective treatment means. For example, if there were no variability within each sample, the error sum of squares would be equal to 0. The more the values within the samples vary, the larger will be SSE.

As an example, in the gasoline mileage study, the sample treatment means are $\bar{x}_A = 34.92$, $\bar{x}_B = 36.56$, and $\bar{x}_C = 33.98$. It follows that

$$SSE = \sum_{j=1}^{n_A}(x_{Aj} - \bar{x}_A)^2 + \sum_{j=1}^{n_B}(x_{Bj} - \bar{x}_B)^2 + \sum_{j=1}^{n_C}(x_{Cj} - \bar{x}_C)^2$$

$$= [(34.0 - 34.92)^2 + (35.0 - 34.92)^2 + (34.3 - 34.92)^2 + (35.5 - 34.92)^2 + (35.8 - 34.92)^2]$$

$$+ [(35.3 - 36.56)^2 + (36.5 - 36.56)^2 + (36.4 - 36.56)^2 + (37.0 - 36.56)^2 + (37.6 - 36.56)^2]$$

$$+ [(33.3 - 33.98)^2 + (34.0 - 33.98)^2 + (34.7 - 33.98)^2 + (33.0 - 33.98)^2 + (34.9 - 33.98)^2]$$

$$= 8.028$$

Finally, we define a sum of squares that measures the total amount of variability in the observed values of the response:

The **total sum of squares** is

$$SSTO = SST + SSE$$

The variability in the observed values of the response must come from one of two sources—the between-treatment variability or the within-treatment variability. It follows that the total sum of squares equals the sum of the treatment sum of squares and the error sum of squares. Therefore, the **SST and SSE are said to partition the total sum of squares.** For the gasoline mileage study

$$SSTO = SST + SSE = 17.0493 + 8.028 = 25.0773$$

In order to decide whether there are any statistically significant differences between the treatment means, it makes sense to compare the amount of between-treatment variability to the amount of within-treatment variability. This comparison suggests the following F test:

An *F* Test for Differences between Treatment Means

Suppose that we wish to compare p treatment means $\mu_1, \mu_2, \ldots, \mu_p$ and consider testing

H_0: $\mu_1 = \mu_2 = \cdots = \mu_p$ versus H_a: At least two of $\mu_1, \mu_2, \ldots, \mu_p$ differ
     (all treatment means are equal)   (at least two treatment means differ)

To perform the hypothesis test, define the **treatment mean square** to be $MST = SST/(p - 1)$ and define the **error mean square** to be $MSE = SSE/(n - p)$. Also, define the F statistic

$$F = \frac{MST}{MSE} = \frac{SST/(p - 1)}{SSE/(n - p)}$$

and its p-value to be the area under the F curve with $p - 1$ and $n - p$ degrees of freedom to the right of F. We can reject H_0 in favor of H_a at level of significance α if either of the following equivalent conditions holds:

1 $F > F_\alpha$ **2** p-value $< \alpha$

Here the F_α point is based on $p - 1$ numerator and $n - p$ denominator degrees of freedom.

A large value of F results when SST, which measures the between-treatment variability, is large compared to SSE, which measures the within-treatment variability. If F is large enough, this implies that H_0 should be rejected. The rejection point F_α tells us when F is large enough to allow us to reject H_0 at level of significance α. When F is large, the associated p-value is small. If this p-value is less than α, we can reject H_0 at level of significance α.

EXAMPLE 11.3 The Gasoline Mileage Case   C

Consider the North American Oil Company data in Table 11.1. The company wishes to determine whether any of gasoline types A, B, and C have different effects on mean Fire-Hawk gasoline mileage. That is, we wish to see whether there are any statistically significant differences between μ_A, μ_B, and μ_C. To do this, we test the null hypothesis $H_0: \mu_A = \mu_B = \mu_C$, which says that gasoline types A, B, and C have the same effects on mean gasoline mileage. We test H_0 versus the alternative H_a: At least two of μ_A, μ_B, and μ_C differ, which says that at least two of gasoline types A, B, and C have different effects on mean gasoline mileage.

Since we have previously computed SST to be 17.0493 and SSE to be 8.028, and because we are comparing $p = 3$ treatment means, we have

$$MST = \frac{SST}{p-1} = \frac{17.0493}{3-1} = 8.525$$

and

$$MSE = \frac{SSE}{n-p} = \frac{8.028}{15-3} = 0.669$$

It follows that

$$F = \frac{MST}{MSE} = \frac{8.525}{0.669} = 12.74$$

In order to test H_0 at the .05 level of significance, we use $F_{.05}$ with $p - 1 = 3 - 1 = 2$ numerator and $n - p = 15 - 3 = 12$ denominator degrees of freedom. Table A.6 (page 643) tells us that this F point equals 3.89, so we have

$$F = 12.74 > F_{.05} = 3.89$$

Therefore, we reject H_0 at the .05 level of significance. This says we have strong evidence that at least two of the treatment means μ_A, μ_B, and μ_C differ. In other words, we conclude that at least two of gasoline types A, B, and C have different effects on mean gasoline mileage.

The results of an analysis of variance are often summarized in what is called an **analysis of variance table.** This table gives the sums of squares (SST, SSE, $SSTO$), the mean squares (MST and MSE), and the F statistic and its related p-value for the ANOVA. The table also gives the degrees of freedom associated with each source of variation—treatments, error, and total. Table 11.3 gives the ANOVA table for the gasoline mileage problem. Notice that in the column labeled "Sums of Squares," the values of SST and SSE sum to $SSTO$.

Figure 11.2 gives the MINITAB and Excel output of an analysis of variance of the gasoline mileage data. Note that the upper portion of the MINITAB output and the lower portion of the Excel output give the ANOVA table of Table 11.3. Also, note that each output gives the value $F = 12.74$ and the related p-value, which equals .001 (rounded). Since this p-value is less than .05, we reject H_0 at the .05 level of significance.

Pairwise comparisons   If the one-way ANOVA F test says that at least two treatment means differ, then we investigate which treatment means differ and we estimate how large the differences are. We do this by making what we call **pairwise comparisons** (that is, we compare treatment means *two at a time*). One way to make these comparisons is to compute point estimates of and confidence intervals for **pairwise differences.** For example, in the gasoline mileage case we might estimate the pairwise differences $\mu_A - \mu_B$, $\mu_A - \mu_C$, and $\mu_B - \mu_C$. Here, for instance, the pairwise difference $\mu_A - \mu_B$ can be interpreted as the change in mean mileage achieved by changing from using gasoline type B to using gasoline type A.

TABLE 11.3   Analysis of Variance Table for Testing $H_0: \mu_A = \mu_B = \mu_C$ in the Gasoline Mileage Problem ($p = 3$ Gasoline Types, $n = 15$ Observations)

Source	Degrees of Freedom	Sums of Squares	Mean Squares	F Statistic	p-Value
Treatments	$p - 1 = 3 - 1$ $= 2$	$SST = 17.0493$	$MST = \dfrac{SST}{p-1}$ $= \dfrac{17.0493}{3-1}$ $= 8.525$	$F = \dfrac{MST}{MSE}$ $= \dfrac{8.525}{0.669}$ $= 12.74$	0.001
Error	$n - p = 15 - 3$ $= 12$	$SSE = 8.028$	$MSE = \dfrac{SSE}{n-p}$ $= \dfrac{8.028}{15-3}$ $= 0.669$		
Total	$n - 1 = 15 - 1$ $= 14$	$SSTO = 25.0773$			

FIGURE 11.2   MINITAB and Excel Output of an Analysis of Variance of the Gasoline Mileage Data in Table 11.1

(a) The MINITAB output

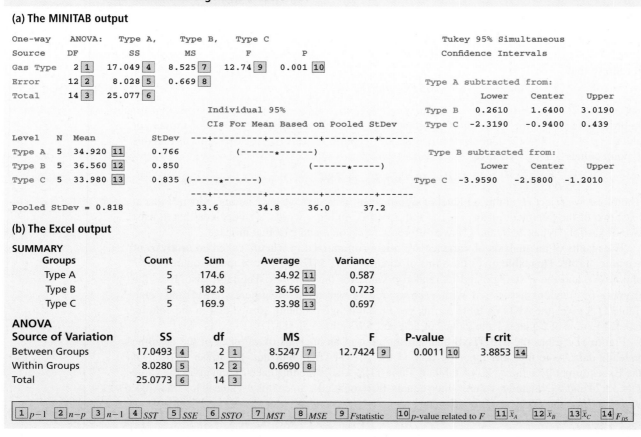

```
One-way  ANOVA:  Type A,   Type B,   Type C                    Tukey 95% Simultaneous
Source   DF      SS        MS        F        P                Confidence Intervals
Gas Type  2[1]   17.049[4]  8.525[7]  12.74[9]  0.001[10]
Error    12[2]    8.028[5]  0.669[8]                           Type A subtracted from:
Total    14[3]   25.077[6]                                                Lower    Center    Upper
                            Individual 95%                      Type B    0.2610   1.6400    3.0190
                            CIs For Mean Based on Pooled StDev  Type C   -2.3190  -0.9400    0.439

Level   N   Mean      StDev  ---+---------+---------+---------+------
Type A  5   34.920[11] 0.766          (------*------)            Type B subtracted from:
Type B  5   36.560[12] 0.850                   (------*-----)              Lower    Center    Upper
Type C  5   33.980[13] 0.835  (-----*------)                    Type C   -3.9590  -2.5800  -1.2010
                            ---+---------+---------+---------+------
Pooled StDev = 0.818          33.6      34.8      36.0      37.2
```

(b) The Excel output

SUMMARY

Groups	Count	Sum	Average	Variance
Type A	5	174.6	34.92 [11]	0.587
Type B	5	182.8	36.56 [12]	0.723
Type C	5	169.9	33.98 [13]	0.697

ANOVA

Source of Variation	SS	df	MS	F	P-value	F crit
Between Groups	17.0493 [4]	2 [1]	8.5247 [7]	12.7424 [9]	0.0011 [10]	3.8853 [14]
Within Groups	8.0280 [5]	12 [2]	0.6690 [8]			
Total	25.0773 [6]	14 [3]				

[1] $p-1$ [2] $n-p$ [3] $n-1$ [4] SST [5] SSE [6] $SSTO$ [7] MST [8] MSE [9] Fstatistic   [10] p-value related to F [11] $\bar{x}_A$ [12] $\bar{x}_B$ [13] $\bar{x}_C$ [14] $F_{.05}$

There are two approaches to calculating confidence intervals for pairwise differences. The first involves computing the usual, or **individual, confidence interval** for each pairwise difference. Here, if we are computing $100(1 - \alpha)$ percent confidence intervals, we are $100(1 - \alpha)$ percent confident that each individual pairwise difference is contained in its respective interval. That is, the confidence level associated with each (individual) comparison is $100(1 - \alpha)$ percent, and we refer to α as the **comparisonwise error rate.** However, we are less than $100(1 - \alpha)$ percent confident that all of the pairwise differences are simultaneously contained in their respective intervals. A more conservative approach is to compute **simultaneous confidence intervals**. Such intervals make us $100(1 - \alpha)$ percent confident that all of the pairwise differences are simulta-neously contained in their respective intervals. That is, when we compute simultaneous intervals, the overall confidence level associated with all the comparisons being made in the experiment is $100(1 - \alpha)$ percent, and we refer to α as the **experimentwise error rate.**

Several kinds of simultaneous confidence intervals can be computed. In this book we present what is called the **Tukey formula** for simultaneous intervals. We do this because, *if we are in-terested in studying all pairwise differences between treatment means, the Tukey formula yields the most precise (shortest) simultaneous confidence intervals.* In general, a Tukey simultaneous $100(1 - \alpha)$ percent confidence interval is longer than the corresponding individual $100(1 - \alpha)$ percent confidence interval. Thus, intuitively, we are paying a penalty for simultaneous confi-dence by obtaining longer intervals. In the following box, we present the formula for Tukey simultaneous confidence intervals for pairwise differences. We also present the formula for a confidence interval for a single treatment mean, which we might use after we have used pairwise comparisons to determine the "best" treatment.

Estimation in One-Way ANOVA

1 Consider the **pairwise difference** $\mu_i - \mu_h$, which can be interpreted to be the change in the mean value of the response variable associated with changing from using treatment h to using treat-ment i. Then, a **point estimate of the difference** $\mu_i - \mu_h$ is $\bar{x}_i - \bar{x}_h$ where $\bar{x}_i$ and $\bar{x}_h$ are the sample treatment means associated with treatments i and h.

2 A **Tukey simultaneous $100(1 - \alpha)$ percent confi-dence interval for $\mu_i - \mu_h$ is**

$$\left[(\bar{x}_i - \bar{x}_h) \pm q_\alpha \sqrt{\frac{MSE}{m}} \right]$$

Here, the value q_α is obtained from Table A.9 (pages 646–647), which is a **table of percentage**

points of the studentized range. In this table q_α is listed corresponding to values of p and $n - p$. Fur-thermore, we assume that the sample sizes n_i and n_h are equal to the same value, which we denote as m. If n_i and n_h are not equal, we replace $q_\alpha \sqrt{MSE/m}$ by $(q_\alpha / \sqrt{2})\sqrt{MSE[(1/n_i) + (1/n_h)]}$.

3 A **point estimate of the treatment mean μ_i is $\bar{x}_i$** and an **individual $100(1 - \alpha)$ percent confidence interval for μ_i is**

$$\left[\bar{x}_i \pm t_{\alpha/2} \sqrt{\frac{MSE}{n_i}} \right]$$

Here, the $t_{\alpha/2}$ point is based on $n - p$ degrees of freedom.

EXAMPLE 11.4 The Gasoline Mileage Case

In the gasoline mileage study, we are comparing $p = 3$ treatment means (μ_A, μ_B, and μ_C). Fur-thermore, each sample is of size $m = 5$, there are a total of $n = 15$ observed gas mileages, and the *MSE* found in Table 11.3 is .669. Because $q_{.05} = 3.77$ is the entry found in Table A.9 (page 646) corresponding to $p = 3$ and $n - p = 12$, a Tukey simultaneous 95 percent confidence interval for $\mu_B - \mu_A$ is

$$\left[(\bar{x}_B - \bar{x}_A) \pm q_{.05} \sqrt{\frac{MSE}{m}} \right] = \left[(36.56 - 34.92) \pm 3.77 \sqrt{\frac{.669}{5}} \right]$$

$$= [1.64 \pm 1.379]$$

$$= [.261, 3.019]$$

Similarly, Tukey simultaneous 95 percent confidence intervals for $\mu_A - \mu_C$ and $\mu_B - \mu_C$ are, respectively,

$$[(\bar{x}_A - \bar{x}_C) \pm 1.379] \qquad \text{and} \qquad [(\bar{x}_B - \bar{x}_C) \pm 1.379]$$

$$= [(34.92 - 33.98) \pm 1.379] \qquad\qquad = [(36.56 - 33.98) \pm 1.379]$$

$$= [-0.439, 2.319] \qquad\qquad\qquad = [1.201, 3.959]$$

These intervals make us simultaneously 95 percent confident that (1) changing from gasoline type A to gasoline type B increases mean mileage by between .261 and 3.019 mpg, (2) changing from gasoline type C to gasoline type A might decrease mean mileage by as much as .439 mpg or might increase mean mileage by as much as 2.319 mpg, *and* (3) changing from gasoline type C to gasoline type B increases mean mileage by between 1.201 and 3.959 mpg. The first and third of these intervals make us 95 percent confident that μ_B is at least .261 mpg greater than μ_A and at least 1.201 mpg greater than μ_C. Therefore, we have strong evidence that gasoline type B yields the highest mean mileage of the gasoline types tested. Furthermore, noting that $t_{.025}$ based on $n - p = 12$ degrees of freedom is 2.179, it follows that an individual 95 percent confidence interval for μ_B is

$$\left[\bar{x}_B \pm t_{.025} \sqrt{\frac{MSE}{n_B}} \right] = \left[36.56 \pm 2.179 \sqrt{\frac{.669}{5}} \right]$$
$$= [35.763, 37.357]$$

This interval says we can be 95 percent confident that the mean mileage obtained by using gasoline type B is between 35.763 and 37.357 mpg. Notice that this confidence interval is graphed on the MINITAB output of Figure 11.2. This output also shows the 95 percent confidence intervals for μ_A and μ_C and gives Tukey simultaneous 95 percent intervals for $\mu_B - \mu_A$, $\mu_C - \mu_A$, and $\mu_C - \mu_B$. Note that the last two Tukey intervals on the output are the "negatives" of the Tukey intervals that we hand calculated for $\mu_A - \mu_C$ and $\mu_B - \mu_C$.

In general, when we use a completely randomized experimental design, it is important to compare the treatments by using experimental units that are essentially the same with respect to the characteristic under study. For example, in the gasoline mileage case we have used cars of the same type (Fire-Hawks) to compare the different gasoline types, and in the shelf display case we have used grocery stores of the same sales potential for the bakery product to compare the shelf display heights (the reader will analyze the data for this case in the exercises). Sometimes, however, it is not possible to use experimental units that are essentially the same with respect to the characteristic under study. One approach to dealing with this situation is to employ **a randomized block design.** This experimental design is discussed in Section 11.3.

To conclude this section, we note that if we fear that the normality and/or equal variances assumptions for one-way analysis of variance do not hold, we can use a nonparametric approach to compare several populations. One such approach is the Kruskal–Wallis H test, which is discussed in Bowerman, O'Connell, and Murphree (2011).

Exercises for Section 11.2

connect

CONCEPTS

11.1   Define the meaning of the terms *response variable, factor, treatments,* and *experimental units.*

11.2   Explain the assumptions that must be satisfied in order to validly use the one-way ANOVA formulas.

11.3   Explain the difference between the between-treatment variability and the within-treatment variability when performing a one-way ANOVA.

11.4   Explain why we conduct pairwise comparisons of treatment means.

METHODS AND APPLICATIONS

11.5   **THE SHELF DISPLAY CASE**   DS BakeSale

Consider Example 11.2, and let μ_B, μ_M, and μ_T represent the mean monthly sales when using the bottom, middle, and top shelf display heights, respectively. Figure 11.3 gives the MINITAB output of a one-way ANOVA of the bakery sales study data in Table 11.2 (page 431).

a   Test the null hypothesis that μ_B, μ_M, and μ_T are equal by setting $\alpha = .05$. On the basis of this test, can we conclude that the bottom, middle, and top shelf display heights have different effects on mean monthly sales?

b   Consider the pairwise differences $\mu_M - \mu_B$, $\mu_T - \mu_B$, and $\mu_T - \mu_M$. Find a point estimate of and a Tukey simultaneous 95 percent confidence interval for each pairwise difference. Interpret the meaning of each interval in practical terms. Which display height maximizes mean sales?

c   Find 95 percent confidence intervals for μ_B, μ_M, and μ_T. Interpret each interval.

FIGURE 11.3   MINITAB Output of a One-Way ANOVA of the Bakery Sales Study Data in Table 11.2

```
One-way ANOVA: Bakery Sales versus Display Height
                                                        Tukey 95% Simultaneous
Source           DF      SS      MS      F      P        Confidence Intervals
Display Height    2  2273.88 1136.94 184.57  0.000
Error            15    92.40    6.16                     Bottom subtracted from:
Total            17  2366.28                                     Lower   Center   Upper
                              Individual 95%            Middle  17.681   21.400  25.119
                              CIs For Mean Based on Pooled StDev  Top    -8.019   -4.300  -0.581
Level    N    Mean   StDev  --------+---------+---------+---------+-
Bottom   6  55.800   2.477          (--*-)                Middle subtracted from:
Middle   6  77.200   3.103                      (--*-)           Lower   Center   Upper
Top      6  51.500   1.648  (-*--)                        Top   -29.419  -25.700 -21.981

                            --------+---------+---------+---------+-
  Pooled StDev = 2.482         56.0      64.0      72.0      80.0
```

FIGURE 11.4   MINITAB Output of a One-Way ANOVA of the Display Panel Study Data in Table 11.4

```
One-way ANOVA: Time versus Display
                                                        Tukey 95% Simultaneous
Source    DF     SS     MS     F      P                  Confidence Intervals
Display    2  500.17 250.08 30.11  0.000
Error      9   74.75   8.31                             A subtracted from:
Total     11  574.92                                            Lower   Center   Upper
                        Individual 95%                  B      -9.692   -4.000   1.692
                        CIs For Mean Based on Pooled StDev  C   5.558   11.250  16.942
Level   N   Mean   StDev  -+---------+---------+---------+--------
A       4  24.500  2.646             (-----*----)
B       4  20.500  2.646    (----*-----)                B subtracted from:
C       4  35.750  3.304                      (-----*----)        Lower   Center   Upper
                          -+---------+---------+---------+--------  C   9.558   15.250  20.942
  Pooled StDev = 2.882    18.0      24.0      30.0      36.0
```

11.6 A study compared three different display panels for use by air traffic controllers. Each display panel was tested in a simulated emergency condition; 12 highly trained air traffic controllers took part in the study. Four controllers were randomly assigned to each display panel. The time (in seconds) needed to stabilize the emergency condition was recorded. The results of the study are given in Table 11.4. Let μ_A, μ_B, and μ_C represent the mean times to stabilize the emergency condition when using display panels A, B, and C, respectively. Figure 11.4 gives the MINITAB output of a one-way ANOVA of the display panel data   DS Display

   a Test the null hypothesis that μ_A, μ_B, and μ_C are equal by setting $\alpha = .05$. On the basis of this test, can we conclude that display panels A, B, and C have different effects on the mean time to stabilize the emergency condition?

   b Consider the pairwise differences $\mu_B - \mu_A$, $\mu_C - \mu_A$, and $\mu_C - \mu_B$. Find a point estimate of and a Tukey simultaneous 95 percent confidence interval for each pairwise difference. Interpret the results by describing the effects of changing from using each display panel to using each of the other panels. Which display panel minimizes the time required to stabilize the emergency condition?

11.7 A consumer preference study compares the effects of three different bottle designs (A, B, and C) on sales of a popular fabric softener. A completely randomized design is employed. Specifically, 15 supermarkets of equal sales potential are selected, and 5 of these supermarkets are randomly assigned to each bottle design. The number of bottles sold in 24 hours at each supermarket is recorded. The data obtained are displayed in Table 11.5. Let μ_A, μ_B, and μ_C represent mean daily sales using bottle designs A, B, and C, respectively. Figure 11.5 gives the Excel output of a one-way ANOVA of the bottle design study data.   DS BottleDes

   a Test the null hypothesis that μ_A, μ_B, and μ_C are equal by setting $\alpha = .05$. That is, test for statistically significant differences between these treatment means at the .05 level of significance. Based on this test, can we conclude that bottle designs A, B, and C have different effects on mean daily sales?

   b Consider the pairwise differences $\mu_B - \mu_A$, $\mu_C - \mu_A$, and $\mu_C - \mu_B$. Find a point estimate of and a Tukey simultaneous 95 percent confidence interval for each pairwise difference. Interpret the results in practical terms. Which bottle design maximizes mean daily sales?

TABLE 11.4
Display Panel Study Data
DS Display

Display Panel		
A	B	C
21	24	40
27	21	36
24	18	35
26	19	32

TABLE 11.5
Bottle Design Study Data
DS BottleDes

Bottle Design		
A	B	C
16	33	23
18	31	27
19	37	21
17	29	28
13	34	25

FIGURE 11.5   Excel Output of a One-Way ANOVA of the Bottle Design Study Data in Table 11.5

SUMMARY

Groups	Count	Sum	Average	Variance
DESIGN A	5	83	16.6	5.3
DESIGN B	5	164	32.8	9.2
DESIGN C	5	124	24.8	8.2

ANOVA

Source of Variation	SS	df	MS	F	P-Value	F crit
Between Groups	656.1333	2	328.0667	43.35683	3.23E-06	3.88529
Within Groups	90.8	12	7.566667			
Total	746.9333	14				

TABLE 11.6   Golf Ball Durability Test Results and a Plot of the Results   Ⓓ GolfBall

		Brand		
Alpha	Best	Century	Divot	
281	270	218	364	
220	334	244	302	
274	307	225	325	
242	290	273	337	
251	331	249	355	

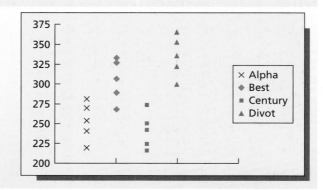

FIGURE 11.6   Excel Output of a One-Way ANOVA of the Golf Ball Durability Data

SUMMARY

Groups	Count	Sum	Average	Variance
Alpha	5	1268	253.6	609.3
Best	5	1532	306.4	740.3
Century	5	1209	241.8	469.7
Divot	5	1683	336.6	605.3

ANOVA

Source of Variation	SS	df	MS	F	P-Value	F crit
Between Groups	29860.4	3	9953.4667	16.420798	3.853E-05	3.2388715
Within Groups	9698.4	16	606.15			
Total	39558.8	19				

    c   Find a 95 percent confidence interval for each of the treatment means μ_A, μ_B, and μ_C. Interpret these intervals.

11.8   In order to compare the durability of four different brands of golf balls (ALPHA, BEST, CENTURY, and DIVOT), the National Golf Association randomly selects five balls of each brand and places each ball into a machine that exerts the force produced by a 250-yard drive. The number of simulated drives needed to crack or chip each ball is recorded. The results are given in Table 11.6. The Excel output of a one-way ANOVA of these data is shown in Figure 11.6. Test for statistically significant differences between the treatment means μ_{ALPHA}, μ_{BEST}, μ_{CENTURY}, and μ_{DIVOT}. Set $\alpha = .05$.   Ⓓ GolfBall

11.9   Perform pairwise comparisons of the treatment means in Exercise 11.8 by using Tukey simultaneous 95 percent confidence intervals. Which brand(s) are most durable? Find a 95 percent confidence interval for each of the treatment means.

11.3 The Randomized Block Design ● ● ●

Not all experiments employ a completely randomized design. For instance, suppose that when we employ a completely randomized design, we fail to reject the null hypothesis of equality of treatment means because the within-treatment variability (which is measured by the *SSE*) is large. This could happen because differences between the experimental units are concealing true differences between the treatments. We can often remedy this by using what is called a **randomized block design.**

EXAMPLE 11.5 The Defective Cardboard Box Case

The Universal Paper Company manufactures cardboard boxes. The company wishes to investigate the effects of four production methods (methods 1, 2, 3, and 4) on the number of defective boxes produced in an hour. To compare the methods, the company could utilize a completely randomized design. For each of the four production methods, the company would select several (say, as an example, three) machine operators, train each operator to use the production method to which he or she has been assigned, have each operator produce boxes for one hour, and record the number of defective boxes produced. The three operators using any one production method would be *different* from those using any other production method. That is, the completely randomized design would utilize a total of 12 machine operators. However, the abilities of the machine operators could differ substantially. These differences might tend to conceal any real differences between the production methods. To overcome this disadvantage, the company will employ a **randomized block experimental design.** This involves randomly selecting three machine operators and training each operator thoroughly to use all four production methods. Then each operator will produce boxes for one hour using each of the four production methods. The order in which each operator uses the four methods should be random. We record the number of defective boxes produced by each operator using each method. The advantage of the randomized block design is that the defective rates obtained by using the four methods result from employing the *same* three operators. Thus any true differences in the effectiveness of the methods would not be concealed by differences in the operators' abilities.

When Universal Paper employs the randomized block design, it obtains the 12 defective box counts in Table 11.7. We let x_{ij} denote the number of defective boxes produced by machine operator j using production method i. For example, $x_{32} = 5$ says that 5 defective boxes were produced by machine operator 2 using production method 3 (see Table 11.7). In addition to the 12 defective box counts, Table 11.7 gives the sample mean of these 12 observations, which is $\bar{x} = 7.5833$, and also gives **sample treatment means** and **sample block means.** The sample treatment means are the average defective box counts obtained when using production methods 1, 2, 3, and 4. Denoting these sample treatment means as $\bar{x}_{1\bullet}, \bar{x}_{2\bullet}, \bar{x}_{3\bullet}$, and $\bar{x}_{4\bullet}$, we see from Table 11.7 that $\bar{x}_{1\bullet} = 10.3333, \bar{x}_{2\bullet} = 10.3333, \bar{x}_{3\bullet} = 5.0$, and $\bar{x}_{4\bullet} = 4.6667$. Because $\bar{x}_{3\bullet}$ and $\bar{x}_{4\bullet}$ are less than $\bar{x}_{1\bullet}$ and $\bar{x}_{2\bullet}$, we estimate that the mean number of defective boxes produced per hour by production method 3 or 4 is less than the mean number of defective boxes produced per hour by production method 1 or 2. The sample block means are the average defective box counts obtained by machine operators 1, 2, and 3. Denoting these sample block means as $\bar{x}_{\bullet 1}, \bar{x}_{\bullet 2}$, and $\bar{x}_{\bullet 3}$, we see from Table 11.7 that $\bar{x}_{\bullet 1} = 6.0, \bar{x}_{\bullet 2} = 7.75$, and $\bar{x}_{\bullet 3} = 9.0$. Because $\bar{x}_{\bullet 1}, \bar{x}_{\bullet 2}$, and $\bar{x}_{\bullet 3}$ differ, we have evidence that the abilities of the machine operators differ and thus that using the machine operators as blocks is reasonable.

TABLE 11.7 Numbers of Defective Cardboard Boxes Obtained by Production Methods 1, 2, 3, and 4 and Machine Operators 1, 2, and 3   ◍ CardBox

Treatment (Production Method)	Block (Machine Operator) 1	2	3	Sample Treatment Mean
1	9	10	12	10.3333
2	8	11	12	10.3333
3	3	5	7	5.0
4	4	5	5	4.6667
Sample Block Mean	6.0	7.75	9.0	$\bar{x} = 7.5833$

In general, a **randomized block design** compares p treatments (for example, production methods) by using b blocks (for example, machine operators). Each block is used exactly once to measure the effect of each and every treatment. The advantage of the randomized block design over the completely randomized design is that we are comparing the treatments by using the *same* experimental units. Thus any true differences in the treatments will not be concealed by differences in the experimental units.

In order to analyze the data obtained in a randomized block design, we define

x_{ij} = the value of the response variable observed when block j uses treatment i

$\bar{x}_{i\bullet}$ = the mean of the b values of the response variable observed when using treatment i

$\bar{x}_{\bullet j}$ = the mean of the p values of the response variable observed when using block j

$\bar{x}$ = the mean of the total of the bp values of the response variable that we have observed in the experiment

The ANOVA procedure for a randomized block design partitions the **total sum of squares (SSTO)** into three components: the **treatment sum of squares (SST)**, the **block sum of squares (SSB)**, and the **error sum of squares (SSE)**. The formula for this partitioning is

$$SSTO = SST + SSB + SSE$$

We define each of these sums of squares and show how they are calculated for the defective cardboard box data as follows (note that $p = 4$ and $b = 3$):

Step 1: Calculate SST, which measures the amount of between-treatment variability:

$$
\begin{aligned}
SST &= b \sum_{i=1}^{p} (\bar{x}_{i\bullet} - \bar{x})^2 \\
&= 3[(\bar{x}_{1\bullet} - \bar{x})^2 + (\bar{x}_{2\bullet} - \bar{x})^2 + (\bar{x}_{3\bullet} - \bar{x})^2 + (\bar{x}_{4\bullet} - \bar{x})^2] \\
&= 3[(10.3333 - 7.5833)^2 + (10.3333 - 7.5833)^2 \\
&\quad + (5.0 - 7.5833)^2 + (4.6667 - 7.5833)^2] \\
&= 90.9167
\end{aligned}
$$

Step 2: Calculate SSB, which measures the amount of variability due to the blocks:

$$
\begin{aligned}
SSB &= p \sum_{j=1}^{b} (\bar{x}_{\bullet j} - \bar{x})^2 \\
&= 4[(\bar{x}_{\bullet 1} - \bar{x})^2 + (\bar{x}_{\bullet 2} - \bar{x})^2 + (\bar{x}_{\bullet 3} - \bar{x})^2] \\
&= 4[(6.0 - 7.5833)^2 + (7.75 - 7.5833)^2 + (9.0 - 7.5833)^2] \\
&= 18.1667
\end{aligned}
$$

Step 3: Calculate $SSTO$, which measures the total amount of variability:

$$
\begin{aligned}
SSTO &= \sum_{i=1}^{p} \sum_{j=1}^{b} (x_{ij} - \bar{x})^2 \\
&= (9 - 7.5833)^2 + (10 - 7.5833)^2 + (12 - 7.5833)^2 \\
&\quad + (8 - 7.5833)^2 + (11 - 7.5833)^2 + (12 - 7.5833)^2 \\
&\quad + (3 - 7.5833)^2 + (5 - 7.5833)^2 + (7 - 7.5833)^2 \\
&\quad + (4 - 7.5833)^2 + (5 - 7.5833)^2 + (5 - 7.5833)^2 \\
&= 112.9167
\end{aligned}
$$

Step 4: Calculate SSE, which measures the amount of variability due to the error:

$$
\begin{aligned}
SSE &= SSTO - SST - SSB \\
&= 112.9167 - 90.9167 - 18.1667 \\
&= 3.8333
\end{aligned}
$$

These sums of squares are shown in Table 11.8, which is the ANOVA table for a randomized block design. This table also gives the degrees of freedom, mean squares, and F statistics used to

TABLE 11.8 ANOVA Table for the Randomized Block Design with p Treatments and b Blocks

Source of Variation	Degrees of Freedom	Sum of Squares	Mean Square	F
Treatments	$p - 1 = 3$	$SST = 90.9167$	$MST = \dfrac{SST}{p - 1} = 30.3056$	$F(\text{treatments}) = \dfrac{MST}{MSE} = 47.4348$
Blocks	$b - 1 = 2$	$SSB = 18.1667$	$MSB = \dfrac{SSB}{b - 1} = 9.0833$	$F(\text{blocks}) = \dfrac{MSB}{MSE} = 14.2174$
Error	$(p - 1)(b - 1) = 6$	$SSE = 3.8333$	$MSE = \dfrac{SSE}{(p - 1)(b - 1)} = .6389$	
Total	$pb - 1 = 11$	$SSTO = 112.9167$		

test the hypotheses of interest in a randomized block experiment, as well as the values of these quantities for the defective cardboard box data.

Of main interest is the test of the null hypothesis H_0 that **no differences exist between the treatment effects** on the mean value of the response variable versus the alternative hypothesis H_a that **at least two treatment effects differ.** We can reject H_0 in favor of H_a at level of significance α if $F(\text{treatments})$ is greater than the F_α point based on $p - 1$ numerator and $(p - 1)(b - 1)$ denominator degrees of freedom. In the defective cardboard box case, $F_{.05}$ based on $p - 1 = 3$ numerator and $(p - 1)(b - 1) = 6$ denominator degrees of freedom is 4.76 (see Table A.6, page 643). Because $F(\text{treatments}) = 47.4348$ (see Table 11.8) is greater than $F_{.05} = 4.76$, we reject H_0 at the .05 level of significance. Therefore, we have strong evidence that at least two production methods have different effects on the mean number of defective boxes produced per hour.

It is also of interest to test the null hypothesis H_0 that **no differences exist between the block effects** on the mean value of the response variable versus the alternative hypothesis H_a that **at least two block effects differ.** We can reject H_0 in favor of H_a at level of significance α if $F(\text{blocks})$ is greater than the F_α point based on $b - 1$ numerator and $(p - 1)(b - 1)$ denominator degrees of freedom. In the defective cardboard box case, $F_{.05}$ based on $b - 1 = 2$ numerator and $(p - 1)(b - 1) = 6$ denominator degrees of freedom is 5.14 (see Table A.6, page 643). Because $F(\text{blocks}) = 14.2174$ (see Table 11.8) is greater than $F_{.05} = 5.14$, we reject H_0 at the .05 level of significance. Therefore, we have strong evidence that at least two machine operators have different effects on the mean number of defective boxes produced per hour.

Figure 11.7 gives the MINITAB and Excel outputs of a randomized block ANOVA of the defective cardboard box data. The p-value of .000 ($<.001$) related to $F(\text{treatments})$ provides extremely strong evidence of differences in production method effects. The p-value of .0053 related to $F(\text{blocks})$ provides very strong evidence of differences in machine operator effects.

If, in a randomized block design, we conclude that at least two treatment effects differ, we can perform pairwise comparisons to determine how they differ.

Point Estimates and Confidence Intervals in a Randomized Block ANOVA

Consider the **difference between the effects of treatments i and h on the mean value of the response variable.** Then:

1 A **point estimate** of this difference is $\bar{x}_{i\cdot} - \bar{x}_{h\cdot}$.

2 A **Tukey simultaneous $100(1 - \alpha)$ percent confidence interval** for this difference is

$$\left[(\bar{x}_{i\cdot} - \bar{x}_{h\cdot}) \pm q_\alpha \frac{s}{\sqrt{b}} \right]$$

Here the value q_α is obtained from Table A.9 (pages 646–647), which is a table of percentage points of the studentized range. In this table q_α is listed corresponding to values of p and $(p - 1)(b - 1)$.

FIGURE 11.7   MINITAB and Excel Outputs of a Randomized Block ANOVA of the Defective Box Data

(a) The MINITAB Output

```
Rows: Method    Columns: Operator
            1          2          3        All     Method     Mean            Operator     Mean
  1       9.000     10.000     12.000     10.333      1      10.3333  12         1         6.00   16
  2       8.000     11.000     12.000     10.333      2      10.3333  13         2         7.75   17
  3       3.000      5.000      7.000      5.000      3       5.0000  14         3         9.00   18
  4       4.000      5.000      5.000      4.667      4       4.6667  15
 All      6.000      7.750      9.000      7.583
```

Two-way ANOVA: Rejects versus Method, Operator

Source	DF	SS	MS	F	P
Method	3	90.917 [1]	30.3056 [5]	47.43 [8]	0.000 [9]
Operator	2	18.167 [2]	9.0833 [6]	14.22 [10]	0.005 [11]
Error	6	3.833 [3]	0.6389 [7]		
Total	11	112.917 [4]			

(b) The Excel output

ANOVA: Two-Factor Without Replication

Summary	Count	Sum	Average	Variance
Method1	3	31	10.3333 [12]	2.3333
Method2	3	31	10.3333 [13]	4.3333
Method3	3	5	5 [14]	4
Method4	3	14	4.6667 [15]	0.3333
Operator1	4	24	6 [16]	8.6667
Operator2	4	31	7.75 [17]	10.25
Operator3	4	36	9 [18]	12.6667

ANOVA

Source of Variation	SS	df	MS	F	P-value	F crit
Method	90.9167 [1]	3	30.3056 [5]	47.4348 [8]	0.0001 [9]	4.7571
Operator	18.1667 [2]	2	9.0833 [6]	14.2174 [10]	0.0053 [11]	5.1433
Error	3.8333 [3]	6	0.6389 [7]			
Total	112.9167 [4]	11				

[1] SST	[2] SSB	[3] SSE	[4] SSTO	[5] MST	[6] MSB	[7] MSE	[8] F(treatments)	[9] p-value for F(treatments)
[10] F(blocks)	[11] p-value for F(blocks)	[12] $\bar{x}_{1\cdot}$	[13] $\bar{x}_{2\cdot}$	[14] $\bar{x}_{3\cdot}$	[15] $\bar{x}_{4\cdot}$	[16] $\bar{x}_{\cdot1}$	[17] $\bar{x}_{\cdot2}$	[18] $\bar{x}_{\cdot3}$

EXAMPLE 11.6 The Defective Cardboard Box Case

We have previously concluded that we have extremely strong evidence that at least two production methods have different effects on the mean number of defective boxes produced per hour. We have also seen that the sample treatment means are $\bar{x}_{1\cdot} = 10.3333$, $\bar{x}_{2\cdot} = 10.3333$, $\bar{x}_{3\cdot} = 5.0$, and $\bar{x}_{4\cdot} = 4.6667$. Since $\bar{x}_{4\cdot}$ is the smallest sample treatment mean, we will use Tukey simultaneous 95 percent confidence intervals to compare the effect of production method 4 with the effects of production methods 1, 2, and 3. To compute these intervals, we first note that $q_{.05} = 4.90$ is the entry in Table A.9 (page 646) corresponding to $p = 4$ and $(p - 1)(b - 1) = 6$. Also, note that the *MSE* found in the randomized block ANOVA table is .639 (see Figure 11.7), which implies that $s = \sqrt{.639} = .7994$. It follows that a Tukey simultaneous 95 percent confidence interval for the difference between the effects of production methods 4 and 1 on the mean number of defective boxes produced per hour is

$$\left[(\bar{x}_{4\cdot} - \bar{x}_{1\cdot}) \pm q_{.05} \frac{s}{\sqrt{b}} \right] = \left[(4.6667 - 10.3333) \pm 4.90 \left(\frac{.7994}{\sqrt{3}} \right) \right]$$

$$= [-5.6666 \pm 2.2615]$$

$$= [-7.9281, -3.4051]$$

Furthermore, it can be verified that a Tukey simultaneous 95 percent confidence interval for the difference between the effects of production methods 4 and 2 on the mean number of defective boxes produced per hour is also $[-7.9281, -3.4051]$. Therefore, we can be 95 percent confident that changing from production method 1 or 2 to production method 4 decreases the mean number of defective boxes produced per hour by a machine operator by between 3.4051 and 7.9281 boxes. A Tukey simultaneous 95 percent confidence interval for the difference between the effects of production methods 4 and 3 on the mean number of defective boxes produced per hour is

$$[(\bar{x}_{4\cdot} - \bar{x}_{3\cdot}) \pm 2.2615] = [(4.6667 - 5) \pm 2.2615]$$
$$= [-2.5948, \ 1.9282]$$

This interval tells us (with 95 percent confidence) that changing from production method 3 to production method 4 might decrease the mean number of defective boxes produced per hour by as many as 2.5948 boxes or might increase this mean by as many as 1.9282 boxes. In other words, because this interval contains 0, we cannot conclude that the effects of production methods 4 and 3 differ.

Exercises for Section 11.3

CONCEPTS

11.10 In your own words, explain why we sometimes employ the randomized block design.

11.11 Describe what *SSTO*, *SST*, *SSB*, and *SSE* measure.

11.12 How can we test to determine if the blocks we have chosen are reasonable?

METHODS AND APPLICATIONS

11.13 A marketing organization wishes to study the effects of four sales methods on weekly sales of a product. The organization employs a randomized block design in which three salesman use each sales method. The results obtained are given in Figure 11.8, along with the Excel output of a randomized block ANOVA of these data.   **DS** SaleMeth

    a Test the null hypothesis H_0 that no differences exist between the effects of the sales methods (treatments) on mean weekly sales. Set $\alpha = .05$. Can we conclude that the different sales methods have different effects on mean weekly sales?

    b Test the null hypothesis H_0 that no differences exist between the effects of the salesmen (blocks) on mean weekly sales. Set $\alpha = .05$. Can we conclude that the different salesmen have different effects on mean weekly sales?

    c Use Tukey simultaneous 95 percent confidence intervals to make pairwise comparisons of the sales method effects on mean weekly sales. Which sales method(s) maximize mean weekly sales?

FIGURE 11.8   **The Sales Method Data and the Excel Output of a Randomized Block ANOVA**   **DS** SaleMeth

ANOVA: Two-Factor without Replication

Sales Method, i	Salesman, j A	B	C	SUMMARY	Count	Sum	Average	Variance
1	32	29	30	Method 1	3	91	30.3333	2.3333
2	32	30	28	Method 2	3	90	30	4
3	28	25	23	Method 3	3	76	25.3333	6.3333
4	25	24	23	Method 4	3	72	24	1
				Salesman A	4	117	29.25	11.5833
				Salesman B	4	108	27	8.6667
				Salesman C	4	104	26	12.6667

ANOVA

Source of Variation	SS	df	MS	F	P-value	F crit
Rows	93.5833	3	31.1944	36.2258	0.0003	4.7571
Columns	22.1667	2	11.0833	12.8710	0.0068	5.1433
Error	5.1667	6	0.8611			
Total	120.9167	11				

TABLE 11.9	Results of a Bottle Design Experiment
	DS BottleDes2

	Supermarket, j			
Bottle Design, i	1	2	3	4
A	16	14	1	6
B	33	30	19	23
C	23	21	8	12

TABLE 11.10	Results of a Keyboard Experiment
	DS Keyboard

	Keyboard Brand		
Data Entry Specialist	A	B	C
1	77	67	63
2	71	62	59
3	74	63	59
4	67	57	54

11.14 A consumer preference study involving three different bottle designs (A, B, and C) for the jumbo size of a new liquid laundry detergent was carried out using a randomized block experimental design, with supermarkets as blocks. Specifically, four supermarkets were supplied with all three bottle designs, which were priced the same. Table 11.9 gives the number of bottles of each design sold in a 24-hour period at each supermarket. If we use these data, SST, SSB, and SSE can be calculated to be 586.1667, 421.6667, and 1.8333, respectively.   DS BottleDes2

    a Test the null hypothesis H_0 that no differences exist between the effects of the bottle designs on mean daily sales. Set $\alpha = .05$. Can we conclude that the different bottle designs have different effects on mean sales?

    b Test the null hypothesis H_0 that no differences exist between the effects of the supermarkets on mean daily sales. Set $\alpha = .05$. Can we conclude that the different supermarkets have different effects on mean sales?

    c Use Tukey simultaneous 95 percent confidence intervals to make pairwise comparisons of the bottle design effects on mean daily sales. Which bottle design(s) maximize mean sales?

11.15 To compare three brands of computer keyboards, four data entry specialists were randomly selected. Each specialist used all three keyboards to enter the same kind of text material for 10 minutes, and the number of words entered per minute was recorded. The data obtained are given in Table 11.10. If we use these data, SST, SSB, and SSE can be calculated to be 392.6667, 143.5833, and 2.6667, respectively.   DS Keyboard

    a Test the null hypothesis H_0 that no differences exist between the effects of the keyboard brands on the mean number of words entered per minute. Set $\alpha = .05$.

    b Test the null hypothesis H_0 that no differences exist between the effects of the data entry specialists on the mean number of words entered per minute. Set $\alpha = .05$.

    c Use Tukey simultaneous 95 percent confidence intervals to make pairwise comparisons of the keyboard brand effects on the mean number of words entered per minute. Which keyboard brand maximizes the mean number of words entered per minute?

11.16 The Coca-Cola Company introduced new Coke in 1985. Within three months of this introduction, negative consumer reaction forced Coca-Cola to reintroduce the original formula of Coke as Coca-Cola classic. Suppose that two years later, in 1987, a marketing research firm in Chicago compared the sales of Coca-Cola classic, new Coke, and Pepsi in public building vending machines. To do this, the marketing research firm randomly selected 10 public buildings in Chicago having both a Coke machine (selling Coke classic and new Coke) and a Pepsi machine.

FIGURE 11.9   The Coca-Cola Data and a MINITAB Output of a Randomized Block ANOVA of the Data

	Building									
	1	2	3	4	5	6	7	8	9	10
Coke Classic	45	136	134	41	146	33	71	224	111	87
New Coke	6	114	56	14	39	20	42	156	61	140
Pepsi	24	90	100	43	51	42	68	131	74	107

Two-way ANOVA: Cans versus Drink, Building

Source	DF	SS	MS	F	P
Drink	2	7997.6	3998.80	5.78	0.011
Building	9	55573.5	6174.83	8.93	0.000
Error	18	12443.7	691.32		
Total	29	76014.8			

Descriptive Statistics: Cans

Variable	Drink	Mean
Cans	Coke Classic	102.8
	New Coke	64.8
	Pepsi	73.0

The data—in number of cans sold over a given period of time—and a MINITAB randomized block ANOVA of the data are given in Figure 11.9.   **DS** Coke

a   Test the null hypothesis H_0 that no differences exist between the mean sales of Coca-Cola classic, new Coke, and Pepsi in Chicago public building vending machines. Set $\alpha = .05$.

b   Make pairwise comparisons of the mean sales of Coca-Cola classic, new Coke, and Pepsi in Chicago public building vending machines by using Tukey simultaneous 95 percent confidence intervals.

c   By the mid-1990s the Coca-Cola Company had discontinued making new Coke and had returned to making only its original product. Is there evidence in the 1987 study that this might happen? Explain your answer.

11.4 Two-Way Analysis of Variance ● ● ●

LO4 Assess the effects of two factors on a response variable by using a two-way analysis of variance.

Many response variables are affected by more than one factor. Because of this we must often conduct experiments in which we study the effects of several factors on the response. In this section we consider studying the effects of **two factors** on a response variable. To begin, recall that in Example 11.2 we discussed an experiment in which the Tastee Bakery Company investigated the effect of shelf display height on monthly demand for one of its bakery products. This one-factor experiment is actually a simplification of a two-factor experiment carried out by the Tastee Bakery Company. We discuss this two-factor experiment in the following example.

EXAMPLE 11.7 The Shelf Display Case

The Tastee Bakery Company supplies a bakery product to many metropolitan supermarkets. The company wishes to study the effects of two factors—**shelf display height** and **shelf display width**—on **monthly demand** (measured in cases of 10 units each) for this product. The factor "display height" is defined to have three levels: B (bottom), M (middle), and T (top). The factor "display width" is defined to have two levels: R (regular) and W (wide). The **treatments** in this experiment are **display height and display width combinations.** These treatments are

$$BR \quad BW \quad MR \quad MW \quad TR \quad TW$$

Here, for example, the notation BR denotes the treatment "bottom display height and regular display width." For each display height and width combination the company randomly selects a sample of $m = 3$ metropolitan area supermarkets (all supermarkets used in the study will be of equal sales potential). Each supermarket sells the product for one month using its assigned display height and width combination, and the month's demand for the product is recorded. The six samples obtained in this experiment are given in Table 11.11 on the next page. We let $x_{ij,k}$ denote the monthly demand obtained at the kth supermarket that used display height i and display width j. For example, $x_{MW,2} = 78.4$ is the monthly demand obtained at the second supermarket that used a middle display height and a wide display.

In addition to giving the six samples, Table 11.11 gives the **sample treatment mean** for each display height and display width combination. For example, $\bar{x}_{BR} = 55.9$ is the mean of the sample of three demands observed at supermarkets using a bottom display height and a regular display width. The table also gives the sample mean demand for each level of display height (B, M, and T) and for each level of display width (R and W). Specifically,

$\bar{x}_{B\bullet} = 55.8 =$ the mean of the six demands observed when using a bottom display height

$\bar{x}_{M\bullet} = 77.2 =$ the mean of the six demands observed when using a middle display height

$\bar{x}_{T\bullet} = 51.5 =$ the mean of the six demands observed when using a top display height

$\bar{x}_{\bullet R} = 60.8 =$ the mean of the nine demands observed when using a regular display width

$\bar{x}_{\bullet W} = 62.2 =$ the mean of the nine demands observed when using a wide display

Finally, Table 11.11 gives $\bar{x} = 61.5$, which is the overall mean of the total of 18 demands observed in the experiment. Because $\bar{x}_{M\bullet} = 77.2$ is considerably larger than $\bar{x}_{B\bullet} = 55.8$ and $\bar{x}_{T\bullet} = 51.5$, we estimate that mean monthly demand is highest when using a middle display height. Since $\bar{x}_{\bullet R} = 60.8$ and $\bar{x}_{\bullet W} = 62.2$ do not differ by very much, we estimate there is little difference between the effects of a regular display width and a wide display on mean monthly demand.

TABLE 11.11   Six Samples of Monthly Demands for a Bakery Product   DS BakeSale2

Display Height	Display Width		
	R	W	
B	58.2	55.7	
	53.7	52.5	
	55.8	58.9	
	$\bar{x}_{BR} = 55.9$	$\bar{x}_{BW} = 55.7$	$\bar{x}_{B\cdot} = 55.8$
M	73.0	76.2	
	78.1	78.4	
	75.4	82.1	
	$\bar{x}_{MR} = 75.5$	$\bar{x}_{MW} = 78.9$	$\bar{x}_{M\cdot} = 77.2$
T	52.4	54.0	
	49.7	52.1	
	50.9	49.9	
	$\bar{x}_{TR} = 51.0$	$\bar{x}_{TW} = 52.0$	$\bar{x}_{T\cdot} = 51.5$
	$\bar{x}_{\cdot R} = 60.8$	$\bar{x}_{\cdot W} = 62.2$	$\bar{x} = 61.5$

FIGURE 11.10   Graphical Analysis of the Bakery Demand Data

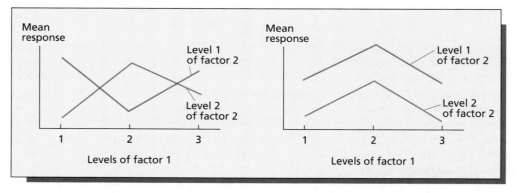

Figure 11.10 presents a graphical analysis of the bakery demand data. In this figure we plot, for each display width (*R* and *W*), the change in the sample treatment mean demand associated with changing the display height from bottom (*B*) to middle (*M*) to top (*T*). Note that, for either a regular display width (*R*) or a wide display (*W*), the middle display height (*M*) gives the highest mean monthly demand. Also, note that, for either a bottom, middle, or top display height, there is little difference between the effects of a regular display width and a wide display on mean monthly demand. This sort of graphical analysis is useful in determining whether a condition called **interaction** exists. In general, for two factors that might affect a response variable, we say that **interaction exists if the relationship between the mean response and one factor depends on the other factor.** This is clearly true in the leftmost figure below:

LO5   Describe what happens when two factors interact.

Specifically, this figure shows that at levels 1 and 3 of factor 1, level 1 of factor 2 gives the highest mean response, whereas at level 2 of factor 1, level 2 of factor 2 gives the highest mean response. On the other hand, the **parallel** line plots in the rightmost figure indicate a lack of interaction between factors 1 and 2. Because the sample mean plots in Figure 11.10 look essentially parallel, we might intuitively conclude that there is little or no interaction between display height and display width.

Suppose we wish to study the effects of two factors on a response variable. We assume that the first factor, which we refer to as **factor 1,** has *a* **levels** (levels 1, 2, . . . , *a*). Further, we assume that the second factor, which we will refer to as **factor 2,** has *b* **levels** (levels 1, 2, . . . , *b*). Here a **treatment** is considered to be a **combination of a level of factor 1 and a level of factor 2.** It follows that there are a total of *ab* treatments, and we assume that we will employ a *completely randomized experimental design* in which we will assign *m* randomly selected experimental units to each treatment. This procedure results in our observing *m* values of the response variable for each of the *ab* treatments, and in this case we say that we are performing a **two-factor factorial experiment.**

In addition to graphical analysis, analysis of variance is a useful tool for analyzing the data from a two-factor factorial experiment. To explain the ANOVA approach for analyzing such an experiment, we define

$x_{ij,k}$ = the kth value of the response variable observed when using level i of factor 1 and level j of factor 2

$\bar{x}_{ij}$ = the mean of the m values observed when using the ith level of factor 1 and the jth level of factor 2

$\bar{x}_{i\bullet}$ = the mean of the bm values observed when using the ith level of factor 1

$\bar{x}_{\bullet j}$ = the mean of the am values observed when using the jth level of factor 2

$\bar{x}$ = the mean of the total of abm values that we have observed in the experiment

The ANOVA procedure for a two-factor factorial experiment partitions the **total sum of squares (SSTO)** into four components: the **factor 1 sum of squares-SS(1)**, the **factor 2 sum of squares-SS(2)**, the **interaction sum of squares-SS(int)**, and the **error sum of squares-SSE**. The formula for this partitioning is as follows:

$$SSTO = SS(1) + SS(2) + SS(\text{int}) + SSE$$

We define each of these sums of squares and show how they are calculated for the shelf display data as follows (note that $a = 3$, $b = 2$, and $m = 3$):

Step 1: Calculate $SSTO$, which measures the total amount of variability:

$$SSTO = \sum_{i=1}^{a} \sum_{j=1}^{b} \sum_{k=1}^{m} (x_{ij,k} - \bar{x})^2$$

$$= (58.2 - 61.5)^2 + (53.7 - 61.5)^2 + \cdots + (49.9 - 61.5)^2 = 2{,}366.28$$

Step 2: Calculate $SS(1)$, which measures the amount of variability due to the different levels of factor 1:

$$SS(1) = bm \sum_{i=1}^{a} (\bar{x}_{i\bullet} - \bar{x})^2$$

$$= 2 \cdot 3[(\bar{x}_{B\bullet} - \bar{x})^2 + (\bar{x}_{M\bullet} - \bar{x})^2 + (\bar{x}_{T\bullet} - \bar{x})^2]$$

$$= 6[(55.8 - 61.5)^2 + (77.2 - 61.5)^2 + (51.5 - 61.5)^2] = 2{,}273.88$$

Step 3: Calculate $SS(2)$, which measures the amount of variability due to the different levels of factor 2:

$$SS(2) = am \sum_{j=1}^{b} (\bar{x}_{\bullet j} - \bar{x})^2$$

$$= 3 \cdot 3[(\bar{x}_{\bullet R} - \bar{x})^2 + (\bar{x}_{\bullet W} - \bar{x})^2]$$

$$= 9[(60.8 - 61.5)^2 + (62.2 - 61.5)^2] = 8.82$$

Step 4: Calculate $SS(\text{int})$, which measures the amount of variability due to the interaction between factors 1 and 2:

$$SS(\text{int}) = m \sum_{i=1}^{a} \sum_{j=1}^{b} (\bar{x}_{ij} - \bar{x}_{i\bullet} - \bar{x}_{\bullet j} + \bar{x})^2$$

$$= 3[(\bar{x}_{BR} - \bar{x}_{B\bullet} - \bar{x}_{\bullet R} + \bar{x})^2 + (\bar{x}_{BW} - \bar{x}_{B\bullet} - \bar{x}_{\bullet W} + \bar{x})^2$$
$$+ (\bar{x}_{MR} - \bar{x}_{M\bullet} - \bar{x}_{\bullet R} + \bar{x})^2 + (\bar{x}_{MW} - \bar{x}_{M\bullet} - \bar{x}_{\bullet W} + \bar{x})^2$$
$$+ (\bar{x}_{TR} - \bar{x}_{T\bullet} - \bar{x}_{\bullet R} + \bar{x})^2 + (\bar{x}_{TW} - \bar{x}_{T\bullet} - \bar{x}_{\bullet W} + \bar{x})^2]$$

$$= 3[(55.9 - 55.8 - 60.8 + 61.5)^2 + (55.7 - 55.8 - 62.2 + 61.5)^2$$
$$+ (75.5 - 77.2 - 60.8 + 61.5)^2 + (78.9 - 77.2 - 62.2 + 61.5)^2$$
$$+ (51.0 - 51.5 - 60.8 + 61.5)^2 + (52.0 - 51.5 - 62.2 + 61.5)^2] = 10.08$$

TABLE 11.12   Two-Way ANOVA Table

Source of Variation	Degrees of Freedom	Sum of Squares	Mean Square	F
Factor 1	$a - 1 = 2$	$SS(1) = 2{,}273.88$	$MS(1) = \dfrac{SS(1)}{a-1} = 1136.94$	$F(1) = \dfrac{MS(1)}{MSE} = 185.6229$
Factor 2	$b - 1 = 1$	$SS(2) = 8.82$	$MS(2) = \dfrac{SS(2)}{b-1} = 8.82$	$F(2) = \dfrac{MS(2)}{MSE} = 1.44$
Interaction	$(a-1)(b-1) = 2$	$SS(\text{int}) = 10.08$	$MS(\text{int}) = \dfrac{SS(\text{int})}{(a-1)(b-1)} = 5.04$	$F(\text{int}) = \dfrac{MS(\text{int})}{MSE} = .8229$
Error	$ab(m-1) = 12$	$SSE = 73.50$	$MSE = \dfrac{SSE}{ab(m-1)} = 6.125$	
Total	$abm - 1 = 17$	$SSTO = 2{,}366.28$		

Step 5: Calculate SSE, which measures the amount of variability due to the error:

$$SSE = SSTO - SS(1) - SS(2) - SS(\text{int})$$
$$= 2{,}366.28 - 2{,}273.88 - 8.82 - 10.08 = 73.50$$

These sums of squares are shown in Table 11.12, which is called a **two-way analysis of variance (ANOVA) table.** This table also gives the degrees of freedom, mean squares, and F statistics used to test the hypotheses of interest in a two-factor factorial experiment, as well as the values of these quantities for the shelf display data.

We first test the null hypothesis H_0 that **no interaction exists between factors 1 and 2** versus the alternative hypothesis H_a that **interaction does exist.** We can reject H_0 in favor of H_a at level of significance α if $F(\text{int})$ is greater than the F_α point based on $(a-1)(b-1)$ numerator and $ab(m-1)$ denominator degrees of freedom. In the shelf display case, $F_{.05}$ based on $(a-1)(b-1) = 2$ numerator and $ab(m-1) = 12$ denominator degrees of freedom is 3.89 (see Table A.6, page 643). Because $F(\text{int}) = .8229$ (see Table 11.12) is less than $F_{.05} = 3.89$, we cannot reject H_0 at the .05 level of significance. We conclude that little or no interaction exists between shelf display height and shelf display width. That is, we conclude that the relationship between mean demand for the bakery product and shelf display height depends little (or not at all) on the shelf display width. Further, we conclude that the relationship between mean demand and shelf display width depends little (or not at all) on the shelf display height. Therefore, we can test the significance of each factor separately.

To test the significance of factor 1, we test the null hypothesis H_0 that **no differences exist between the effects of the different levels of factor 1** on the mean response versus the alternative hypothesis H_a that **at least two levels of factor 1 have different effects.** We can reject H_0 in favor of H_a at level of significance α if $F(1)$ is greater than the F_α point based on $a - 1$ numerator and $ab(m-1)$ denominator degrees of freedom. In the shelf display case, $F_{.05}$ based on $a - 1 = 2$ numerator and $ab(m-1) = 12$ denominator degrees of freedom is 3.89. Because $F(1) = 185.6229$ (see Table 11.12) is greater than $F_{.05} = 3.89$, we can reject H_0 at the .05 level of significance. Therefore, we have strong evidence that at least two of the bottom, middle, and top display heights have different effects on mean monthly demand.

To test the significance of factor 2, we test the null hypothesis H_0 that **no differences exist between the effects of the different levels of factor 2** on the mean response versus the alternative hypothesis H_a that **at least two levels of factor 2 have different effects.** We can reject H_0 in favor of H_a at level of significance α if $F(2)$ is greater than the F_α point based on $b - 1$ numerator and $ab(m-1)$ denominator degrees of freedom. In the shelf display case, $F_{.05}$ based on $b - 1 = 1$ numerator and $ab(m-1) = 12$ denominator degrees of freedom is 4.75. Because $F(2) = 1.44$ (see Table 11.12) is less than $F_{.05} = 4.75$, we cannot reject H_0 at the .05 level of significance. Therefore, we do not have strong evidence that the regular display width and the wide display have different effects on mean monthly demand.

FIGURE 11.11   **MINITAB and Excel Outputs of a Two-Way ANOVA of the Shelf Display Data**

(a) The MINITAB Output

```
Rows : Height    Columns : Width
 Cell Contents : Demand  : Mean

               Regular    Wide     All      Height    Mean        Width     Mean
     Bottom    55.90     55.70    55.80     Bottom    55.8 16      Regular   60.8 19
     Middle    75.50     78.90    77.20     Middle    77.2 17      Wide      62.2 20
     Top       51.00     52.00    51.50     Top       51.5 18
     All       60.80     62.20    61.50
```

Two-way ANOVA: Demand versus Height, Width

Source	DF	SS	MS	F	P
Height	2	2273.88 [1]	1136.94 [6]	185.62 [10]	0.000 [11]
Width	1	8.82 [2]	8.82 [7]	1.44 [12]	0.253 [13]
Interaction	2	10.08 [3]	5.04 [8]	0.82 [14]	0.462 [15]
Error	12	73.50 [4]	6.12 [9]		
Total	17	2366.28 [5]			

(b) The Excel Output

ANOVA: Two-Factor With Replication

SUMMARY	Regular	Wide	Total
Bottom			
Count	3	3	6
Sum	167.7	167.1	334.8
Average	55.9	55.7	55.8 [16]
Variance	5.07	10.24	6.136
Middle			
Count	3	3	6
Sum	226.5	236.7	463.2
Average	75.5	78.9	77.2 [17]
Variance	6.51	8.89	9.628
Top			
Count	3	3	6
Sum	153.0	156.0	309.0
Average	51.0	52.0	51.5 [18]
Variance	1.8	4.2	2.7
Total			
Count	9	9	
Sum	547.2	559.8	
Average	60.8 [19]	62.2 [20]	
Variance	129.405	165.277	

ANOVA

Source of Variation	SS	df	MS	F	P-value	F crit
Height	2273.88 [1]	2	1136.94 [6]	185.6229 [10]	0.0000 [11]	3.8853
Width	8.82 [2]	1	8.82 [7]	1.4400 [12]	0.2533 [13]	4.7472
Interaction	10.08 [3]	2	5.04 [8]	0.8229 [14]	0.4625 [15]	3.8853
Within	73.5 [4]	12	6.125 [9]			
Total	2366.28 [5]	17				

[1] SS(1)	[2] SS(2)	[3] SS(int)	[4] SSE	[5] SSTO	[6] MS(1)	[7] MS(2)	[8] MS(int)	[9] MSE	[10] $F(1)$	[11] p-value for $F(1)$
[12] $F(2)$	[13] p-value for $F(2)$	[14] F(int)	[15] p-value for F(int)	[16] $\bar{x}_{B \cdot}$	[17] $\bar{x}_{M \cdot}$	[18] $\bar{x}_{T \cdot}$	[19] $\bar{x}_{\cdot R}$	[20] $\bar{x}_{\cdot W}$		

    Noting that Figure 11.11 gives MINITAB and Excel outputs of a two-way ANOVA for the shelf display data, we next discuss how to make pairwise comparisons.

FIGURE 11.12   The Display Panel Data and the MINITAB Output of a Two-Way ANOVA ⓓⓢ Display2

Display Panel	Emergency Condition			
	1	2	3	4
A	17	25	31	14
	14	24	34	13
B	15	22	28	9
	12	19	31	10
C	21	29	32	15
	24	28	37	19

Two-way ANOVA: Time versus Panel, Condition

Source	DF	SS	MS	F	P
Panel	2	218.58	109.292	26.49	0.000
Condition	3	1247.46	415.819	100.80	0.000
Interaction	6	16.42	2.736	0.66	0.681
Error	12	49.50	4.125		
Total	23	1531.96			

Tabulated statistics: Panel, Condition

```
Rows:    Panel     Columns:   Condition

              1        2        3        4       All
  A        15.50    24.50    32.50    13.50    21.50
  B        13.50    20.50    29.50     9.50    18.25
  C        22.50    28.50    34.50    17.00    25.63
  All      17.17    24.50    32.17    13.33    21.79
  Cell Contents:     Time   :   Mean
```

FIGURE 11.13   The Telemarketing Data and the Excel Output of a Two-Way ANOVA ⓓⓢ TelMktResp

Time of Day	Position of Advertisement			
	On the Hour	On the Half-Hour	Early in Program	Late in Program
10:00 morning	42	36	62	51
	37	41	68	47
	41	38	64	48
4:00 afternoon	62	57	88	67
	60	60	85	60
	58	55	81	66
9:00 evening	100	97	127	105
	96	96	120	101
	103	101	126	107

ANOVA: Two-Factor With Replication

Summary	Hour	Half-Hour	Early	Late	Total
Morning					
Count	3	3	3	3	12
Sum	120	115	194	146	575
Average	40	38.3	64.7	48.7	47.9
Variance	7	6.3	9.3	4.3	123.7
Afternoon					
Count	3	3	3	3	12
Sum	180	172	254	193	799
Average	60	57.3	84.7	64.3	66.6
Variance	4	6.3	12.3	14.3	132.4
Evening					
Count	3	3	3	3	12
Sum	299	294	373	313	1279
Average	99.67	98	124.3	104.3	106.6
Variance	12.33	7	14.3	9.3	128.3
Total					
Count	9	9	9	9	
Sum	599	581	821	652	
Average	66.56	64.56	91.22	72.44	
Variance	697.53	701.78	700.69	625.03	

ANOVA

Source of Variation	SS	df	MS	F	P-value	F crit
Sample	21560.89	2	10780.444	1209.02	8.12E-25	3.403
Columns	3989.42	3	1329.B06	149.14	1.19E-15	3.009
Interaction	25.33	6	4.222	0.47	0.8212	2.508
Within	214	24	8.917			
Total	25789.64	35				

Chapter Summary

We began this chapter by introducing some basic concepts of **experimental design.** We saw that we carry out an experiment by setting the values of one or more **factors** before the values of the **response variable** are observed. The different values (or levels) of a factor are called **treatments,** and the purpose of most experiments is to compare and estimate the effects of the various treatments on the response variable. We saw that the different treatments are assigned to **experimental units,** and we discussed the **completely randomized experimental design.** This design assigns independent, random samples of experimental units to the treatments.

We began studying how to analyze experimental data by discussing **one-way analysis of variance (one-way ANOVA).** Here we study how one factor (having p levels) affects the response variable. In particular, we learned how to use this methodology to test for differences between the **treatment means** and to estimate the size of pairwise differences between the treatment means.

Sometimes, even if we randomly select the experimental units, differences between the experimental units conceal differences between the treatments. In such a case, we learned that we can employ a **randomized block design.** Each **block** (experimental unit or set of experimental units) is used exactly once to measure the effect of each and every treatment. Because we are comparing the treatments by using the same experimental units, any true differences between the treatments will not be concealed by differences between the experimental units.

The last technique we studied in this chapter was **two-way analysis of variance (two-way ANOVA).** Here we study the effects of two factors by carrying out a **two-factor factorial experiment.** If there is little or no interaction between the two factors, then we are able to study the significance of each of the two factors separately. On the other hand, if substantial interaction exists between the two factors, we study the nature of the differences between the treatment means.

Glossary of Terms

analysis of variance table: A table that summarizes the sums of squares, mean squares, F statistic(s), and p-value(s) for an analysis of variance. (pages 436, 443, and 450)

completely randomized experimental design: An experimental design in which independent, random samples of experimental units are assigned to the treatments. (page 430)

experimental units: The entities (objects, people, and so on) to which the treatments are assigned. (page 429)

factor: A variable that might influence the response variable; an independent variable. (page 429)

interaction: When the relationship between the mean response and one factor depends on the level of the other factor. (page 448)

one-way ANOVA: A method used to estimate and compare the effects of the different levels of a single factor on a response variable. (page 431)

randomized block design: An experimental design that compares p treatments by using b blocks (experimental units or sets of

experimental units). Each block is used exactly once to measure the effect of each and every treatment. (page 441)

replication: When a treatment is applied to more than one experimental unit. (page 429)

response variable: The variable of interest in an experiment; the dependent variable. (page 429)

treatment: A value (or level) of a factor (or combination of factors). (page 429)

treatment mean: The mean value of the response variable obtained by using a particular treatment. (page 431)

two-factor factorial experiment: An experiment in which we randomly assign m experimental units to each combination of levels of two factors. (page 448)

two-way ANOVA: A method used to study the effects of two factors on a response variable. (page 449)

Important Formulas and Tests

One-way ANOVA sums of squares: pages 433–434

One-way ANOVA F test: page 434

One-way ANOVA table: page 436

Estimation in one-way ANOVA: page 437

Randomized block sums of squares: page 442

Randomized block ANOVA table: page 443

Estimation in a randomized block experiment: page 443

Two-way ANOVA sums of squares: pages 449–450

Two-way ANOVA table: page 450

Estimation in two-way ANOVA: page 452

Supplementary Exercises

11.21 An experiment is conducted to study the effects of two sales approaches—high-pressure (H) and low-pressure (L)—and to study the effects of two sales pitches (1 and 2) on the weekly sales of a product. The data in Table 11.13 on the next page are obtained by using a completely randomized

TABLE 11.13 Results of the Sales Approach Experiment ⦿ SaleMeth2

Sales Pressure	Sales Pitch 1	Sales Pitch 2
H	32	32
	29	30
	30	28
L	28	25
	25	24
	23	23

TABLE 11.14 Reduction of Cholesterol Levels ⦿ CholRed

Drug		
X	Y	Z
22	40	15
31	35	9
19	47	14
27	41	11
25	39	21
18	33	5

FIGURE 11.14 Excel Output of a Two-Way ANOVA of the Sales Approach Data

ANOVA: Two-Factor With Replication

SUMMARY	Pitch 1	Pitch 2	Total
High Pressure			
Count	3	3	6
Sum	91	90	181
Average	30.3333	30	30.1667
Variance	2.3333	4	2.5667
Low Pressure			
Count	3	3	6
Sum	76	72	148
Average	25.3333	24	24.6667
Variance	6.3333	1	3.4667
Total			
Count	6	6	
Sum	167	162	
Average	27.8333	27	
Variance	10.9667	12.8	

ANOVA

Source of Variation	SS	df	MS	F	P-value	F crit
Pressure	90.75	1	90.75	26.5610	0.0009	5.3177
Pitch	2.0833	1	2.0833	0.6098	0.4574	5.3177
Interaction	0.75	1	0.75	0.2195	0.6519	5.3177
Within	27.3333	8	3.4167			
Total	120.917	11				

TABLE 11.15 Results of the House Profitability Study ⦿ HouseProf

Foreman	House Design A		House Design B		House Design C	
1	10.2	10.65	12.2	11.95	19.4	18.80
	11.1		11.7		18.2	
2	9.7	10.25	11.6	11.80	13.6	13.15
	10.8		12.0		12.7	

FIGURE 11.15 An Interaction Plot

design, and Figure 11.14 gives the Excel output of a two-way ANOVA of the sales experiment data. ⦿ SaleMeth2

a Perform graphical analysis to check for interaction between sales pressure and sales pitch.

b Test for interaction by setting $\alpha = .05$.

c Test for differences in the effects of the levels of sales pressure by setting $\alpha = .05$.

d Test for differences in the effects of the levels of sales pitch by setting $\alpha = .05$.

11.22 A drug company wishes to compare the effects of three different drugs (X, Y, and Z) that are being developed to reduce cholesterol levels. Each drug is administered to six patients at the recommended dosage for six months. At the end of this period the reduction in cholesterol level is recorded for each patient. The results are given in Table 11.14. Using these data we obtain $SSTO = 2547.8$, $SSE = 395.7$, $\bar{x}_X = 23.67$, $\bar{x}_Y = 39.17$, and $\bar{x}_Z = 12.50$. Completely analyze these data using one-way ANOVA. ⦿ CholRed

11.23 A small builder of speculative homes builds three basic house designs and employs two foremen. The builder has used each foreman to build two houses of each design and has obtained the profits given in Table 11.15 (the profits are given in thousands of dollars, and the sample means are enclosed in blue rectangles). If we use two-way ANOVA, we find that the p-value related to $F(\text{int})$ is .001. Is this consistent with what you see in Figure 11.15? Explain your answer. Using the fact that $MSE = .39$, find an individual 95 percent confidence interval for the true mean profit when foreman 1 builds house design 3. ⦿ HouseProf

Appendix 11.1 ■ Experimental Design and Analysis of Variance Using Excel

The instruction blocks in this section each begins by describing the entry of data into an Excel spreadsheet. Alternatively, the data may be downloaded from this book's website. The appropriate data file name is given at the top of each instruction block. Please refer to Appendix 1.1 for further information about entering data, saving data, and printing results when using Excel.

One-way ANOVA in Figure 11.2(b) on page 436 (data file: GasMile2.xlsx):

- Enter the gasoline mileage data from Table 11.1 (page 430) as follows: type the label "Type A" in cell A1 with its five mileage values in cells A2 to A6; type the label "Type B" in cell B1 with its five mileage values in cells B2 to B6; type the label "Type C" in cell C1 with its five mileage values in cells C2 to C6.

- Select **Data : Data Analysis : Anova : Single Factor** and click OK in the Data Analysis dialog box.

- In the "Anova: Single Factor" dialog box, enter A1:C6 into the "Input Range" window.

- Select the "Grouped by: Columns" option.

- Place a checkmark in the "Labels in first row" checkbox.

- Enter 0.05 into the Alpha box

- Under output options, select "New Worksheet Ply" to have the output placed in a new worksheet and enter the name Output for the new worksheet.

- Click OK in the "Anova: Single Factor" dialog box.

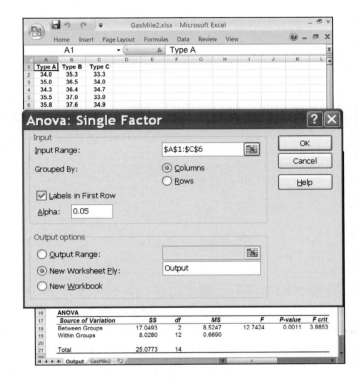

Randomized block ANOVA in Figure 11.8 on page 445 (data file: SaleMeth.xlsx):

- Enter the sales methods data from Figure 11.8 (page 445) as shown in the screen.

- Select **Data : Data Analysis : Anova: Two-Factor Without Replication** and click OK in the Data Analysis dialog box.

- In the "Anova: Two Factor Without Replication" dialog box, enter A1:D5 into the "Input Range" window.

- Place a checkmark in the "Labels" checkbox.

- Enter 0.05 in the Alpha box.

- Under output options, select "New Worksheet Ply" to have the output placed in a new worksheet and enter the name Output for the new worksheet.

- Click OK in the "Anova: Two-Factor Without Replication" dialog box.

Two-way ANOVA in Figure 11.14 on page 456 (data file: SaleMeth2.xlsx):

- Enter the sales approach experiment data from Table 11.13 (page 456) as shown in the screen.

- Select **Data : Data Analysis : Anova : Two-Factor With Replication** and click OK in the Data Analysis dialog box.

- In the "Anova: Two-Factor With Replication" dialog box, enter A1:C7 into the "Input Range" window.

- Enter the value 3 into the "Rows per Sample" box (this indicates the number of replications).

- Enter 0.05 in the Alpha box.

- Under output options, select "New Worksheet Ply" to have the output placed in a new worksheet and enter the name Output for the new worksheet.

- Click OK in the "Anova: Two-Factor With Replication" dialog box.

Appendix 11.2 ■ Experimental Design and Analysis of Variance Using MegaStat

The instructions in this section begin by describing the entry of data into an Excel worksheet. Alternatively, the data may be downloaded from this book's website. The appropriate data file name is given at the top of each instruction block. Please refer to Appendix 1.1 for further information about entering data, saving data, and printing results in Excel. Please refer to Appendix 1.2 for more information about using MegaStat.

One-way ANOVA similar to Figure 11.2(b) on page 436 (data file: GasMile2.xlsx):

- Enter the gas mileage data in Table 11.1 (page 430) into columns A, B, and C—Type A mileages in column A (with label "Type A"), Type B mileages in column B (with label "Type B"), and Type C mileages in column C (with label "Type C"). Note that the input columns for the different groups must be side by side. However, the number of observations in each group can be different.

- Select **Add-Ins : MegaStat : Analysis of Variance : One-Factor ANOVA.**

- In the One-Factor ANOVA dialog box, use the autoexpand feature to enter the range A1:C6 into the Input Range window.

- If desired, request "Post-hoc Analysis" to obtain Tukey simultaneous comparisons and pairwise t tests. Select from the options: "Never," "Always," or "When $p < .05$." The option "When $p < .05$" gives post-hoc analysis when the p-value for the F statistic is less than .05.

- Check the Plot Data checkbox to obtain a plot comparing the groups.

- Click OK in the One-Factor ANOVA dialog box.

Randomized block ANOVA similar to Figure 11.7(b) on page 444 (data file: CardBox.xlsx):

- Enter the cardboard box data in Table 11.7 (page 441) in the arrangement shown in the screen. Here each column corresponds to a **treatment** (in this case, a production method) and each row corresponds to a **block** (in this case, a machine operator). Identify the production methods using the labels Method 1, Method 2, Method 3, and Method 4 in cells B1, C1, D1, and E1. Identify the blocks using the labels Operator 1, Operator 2, and Operator 3 in cells A2, A3, and A4.

- Select **Add-Ins : MegaStat : Analysis of Variance : Randomized Blocks ANOVA.**

- In the Randomized Blocks ANOVA dialog box, click in the Input Range window and enter the range A1:E4.

- If desired, request "Post-hoc Analysis" to obtain Tukey simultaneous comparisons and pairwise *t*-tests. Select from the options: "Never," "Always," or "When $p < .05$." The option "When $p < .05$" gives post-hoc analysis when the *p*-value related to the *F* statistic for the treatments is less than .05.

- Check the Plot Data checkbox to obtain a plot comparing the treatments.

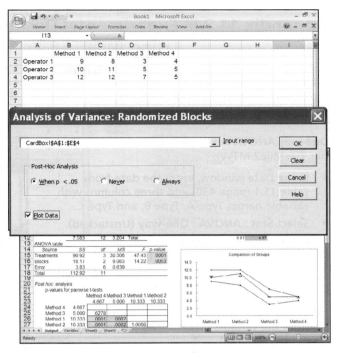

Two-way ANOVA similar to Figure 11.11(b) on page 451 (data file: BakeSale2.xlsx):

- Enter the bakery demand data in Table 11.11 (page 448) in the arrangement shown in the screen. Here the row labels Bottom, Middle, and Top are the levels of factor 1 (in this case, shelf display height) and the column labels Regular and Wide are the levels of factor 2 (in this case, shelf display width). The arrangement of the data is as laid out in Table 11.11.

- Select **Add-Ins : MegaStat : Analysis of Variance: Two-Factor ANOVA.**

- In the Two-Factor ANOVA dialog box, enter the range A1:C10 into the Input Range window.

- Type 3 into the "Replications per Cell" window.

- Check the "Interaction Plot by Factor 1" and "Interaction Plot by Factor 2" checkboxes to obtain interaction plots.

- If desired, request "Post-hoc Analysis" to obtain Tukey simultaneous comparisons and pairwise *t*-tests. Select from the options: "Never," "Always," and "When $p < .05$." The option "When $p < .05$" gives post-hoc analysis when the *p*-value related to the *F* statistic for a factor is less than .05. Here we have selected "Always."

- Click OK in the Two-Factor ANOVA dialog box.

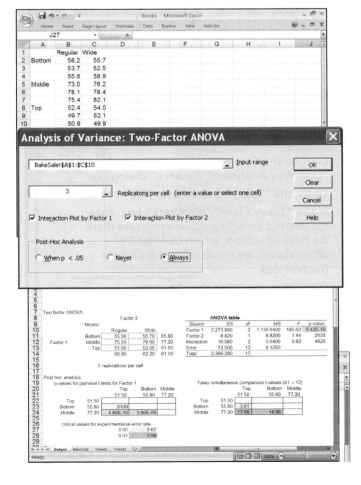

Notice that the scenario that defines a multinomial experiment is similar to that which defines a binomial experiment. In fact, a binomial experiment is simply a multinomial experiment where k equals 2 (there are two possible outcomes on each trial).

In general, the probabilities $p_1, p_2, \ldots, p_k$ are unknown, and we estimate their values. Or, we compare estimates of these probabilities with a set of specified values. We now look at such an example.

EXAMPLE 12.1 The Microwave Oven Preference Case

Suppose the microwave oven wholesaler wishes to compare consumer preferences in Milwaukee with the historical market shares in Cleveland. If the consumer preferences in Milwaukee are substantially different, the wholesaler will consider changing its policies for stocking the ovens. Here we will define

p_1 = the proportion of Milwaukee consumers who prefer brand 1

p_2 = the proportion of Milwaukee consumers who prefer brand 2

p_3 = the proportion of Milwaukee consumers who prefer brand 3

p_4 = the proportion of Milwaukee consumers who prefer brand 4

Remembering that the historical market shares for brands 1, 2, 3, and 4 in Cleveland are 20 percent, 35 percent, 30 percent, and 15 percent, we test the null hypothesis

$$H_0: p_1 = .20, \quad p_2 = .35, \quad p_3 = .30, \quad \text{and} \quad p_4 = .15$$

which says that consumer preferences in Milwaukee are consistent with the historical market shares in Cleveland. We test H_0 versus

$$H_a: \text{the previously stated null hypothesis is not true}$$

To test H_0 we must compare the "observed frequencies" given in Table 12.2 with the "expected frequencies" for the brands calculated on the assumption that H_0 is true. For instance, if H_0 is true, we would expect $400(.20) = 80$ of the 400 Milwaukee consumers surveyed to prefer brand 1. Denoting this expected frequency for brand 1 as E_1, the expected frequencies for brands 2, 3, and 4 when H_0 is true are $E_2 = 400(.35) = 140$, $E_3 = 400(.30) = 120$, and $E_4 = 400(.15) = 60$. Recalling that Table 12.2 gives the observed frequency for each brand, we have $f_1 = 102$, $f_2 = 121, f_3 = 120$, and $f_4 = 57$. We now compare the observed and expected frequencies by computing a **chi-square statistic** as follows:

$$\chi^2 = \sum_{i=1}^{k=4} \frac{(f_i - E_i)^2}{E_i}$$

$$= \frac{(102 - 80)^2}{80} + \frac{(121 - 140)^2}{140} + \frac{(120 - 120)^2}{120} + \frac{(57 - 60)^2}{60}$$

$$= \frac{484}{80} + \frac{361}{140} + \frac{0}{120} + \frac{9}{60} = 8.7786$$

Chi-square curve with $k - 1 = 3$ degrees of freedom

Clearly, the more the observed frequencies differ from the expected frequencies, the larger χ^2 will be and the more doubt will be cast on the null hypothesis. If the chi-square statistic is large enough (beyond a rejection point), then we reject H_0.

To find an appropriate rejection point, it can be shown that, when the null hypothesis is true, the sampling distribution of χ^2 is approximately a χ^2 distribution with $k - 1 = 4 - 1 = 3$ degrees of freedom. If we wish to test H_0 at the .05 level of significance, we reject H_0 if and only if

$$\chi^2 > \chi^2_{.05}$$

FIGURE 12.1 Output of a MINITAB Session That Computes the Chi-Square Statistic and Its Related *p*-Value for the Oven Wholesaler Example

Minitab - Chi Square Example.MPJ

File Edit Data Calc Stat Graph Editor Tools Window Help

Session

Sum of ChiSq   **Data Display**

Sum of ChiSq = 8.77857   PValue
                             0.0323845

Worksheet 1 ***

	C1	C2	C3	C4	C5	C6	C7	C8
	Frequency	MarketShr	Expected	ChiSq	PValue			
1	102	0.20	80	6.05000	0.0323845			
2	121	0.35	140	2.57857				
3	120	0.30	120	0.00000				
4	57	0.15	60	0.15000				
5								
6								

Current Worksheet: Worksheet 1   Editable

Since Table A.10 (page 648) tells us that the $\chi^2_{.05}$ point corresponding to $k - 1 = 3$ degrees of freedom equals 7.81473, we find that

$$\chi^2 = 8.7786 > \chi^2_{.05} = 7.81473$$

and we reject H_0 at the .05 level of significance. Alternatively, the *p*-value for this hypothesis test is the area under the curve of the chi-square distribution having 3 degrees of freedom to the right of $\chi^2 = 8.7786$. This *p*-value can be calculated to be .0323845. Since this *p*-value is less than .05, we can reject H_0 at the .05 level of significance. Although there is no single MINITAB dialog box that produces a chi-square goodness of fit test, Figure 12.1 shows the output of a MINITAB session that computes the chi-square statistic and its related *p*-value for the oven wholesaler problem.

We conclude that the preferences of all consumers in Milwaukee for the four brands of ovens are not consistent with the historical market shares in Cleveland. Based on this conclusion, the wholesaler should consider changing its stocking policies for microwave ovens when it enters the Milwaukee market. To study how to change its policies, the wholesaler might compute a 95 percent confidence interval for, say, the proportion of consumers in Milwaukee who prefer brand 2. Since $\hat{p}_2 = 121/400 = .3025$, this interval is (see Section 8.4, page 325)

$$\left[\hat{p}_2 \pm z_{.025} \sqrt{\frac{\hat{p}_2(1 - \hat{p}_2)}{n_2}} \right] = \left[.3025 \pm 1.96 \sqrt{\frac{.3025(1 - .3025)}{400}} \right]$$

$$= [.2575, .3475]$$

Since this entire interval is below .35, it suggests that (1) the market share for brand 2 ovens in Milwaukee will be smaller than the 35 percent market share that this brand commands in Cleveland, and (2) fewer brand 2 ovens (on a percentage basis) should be stocked in Milwaukee. Notice here that by restricting our attention to one particular brand (brand 2), we are essentially combining the other brands into a single group. It follows that we now have two possible outcomes—"brand 2" and "all other brands." Therefore, we have a binomial experiment, and we can employ the methods of Section 8.4, which are based on the binomial distribution.

In the following box we give a general chi-square goodness-of-fit test for multinomial probabilities:

A Goodness-of-Fit Test for Multinomial Probabilities

Consider a **multinomial experiment** in which each of n randomly selected items is classified into one of k groups. We let

f_i = the number of items classified into group i (that is, the ith observed frequency)

$E_i = np_i$

= the expected number of items that would be classified into group i if p_i is the probability of a randomly selected item being classified into group i (that is, the ith expected frequency)

If we wish to test

H_0: the values of the multinomial probabilities are $p_1, p_2, \ldots, p_k$—that is, the probability of a randomly selected item being classified into group 1 is p_1, the probability of a randomly selected item being classified into group 2 is p_2, and so forth

versus

H_a: at least one of the multinomial probabilities is not equal to the value stated in H_0

we define the **chi-square goodness-of-fit statistic** to be

$$\chi^2 = \sum_{i=1}^{k} \frac{(f_i - E_i)^2}{E_i}$$

Also, define the p-value related to χ^2 to be the area under the curve of the chi-square distribution having $k - 1$ degrees of freedom to the right of χ^2.

Then, we can reject H_0 in favor of H_a at level of significance α if either of the following equivalent conditions holds:

1 $\chi^2 > \chi_\alpha^2$

2 p-value $< \alpha$

Here the χ_α^2 point is based on $k - 1$ degrees of freedom.

This test is based on the fact that it can be shown that, when H_0 is true, the sampling distribution of χ^2 is approximately a chi-square distribution with $k - 1$ degrees of freedom, if the sample size n is large. **It is generally agreed that n should be considered large if all of the "expected cell frequencies" (E_i values) are at least 5.** Furthermore, recent research implies that this condition on the E_i values can be somewhat relaxed. For example, Moore and McCabe (1993) indicate that **it is reasonable to use the chi-square approximation if the number of groups (k) exceeds 4, the average of the E_i values is at least 5, and the smallest E_i value is at least 1.** Notice that in Example 12.1 all of the E_i values are much larger than 5. Therefore, the chi-square test is valid.

A special version of the chi-square goodness of fit test for multinomial probabilities is called a **test for homogeneity.** This involves testing the null hypothesis that all of the multinomial probabilities are equal. For instance, in the microwave oven situation we would test

$$H_0: p_1 = p_2 = p_3 = p_4 = .25$$

which would say that no single brand of microwave oven is preferred to any of the other brands (equal preferences). If this null hypothesis is rejected in favor of

$$H_a: \text{At least one of } p_1, p_2, p_3, \text{ and } p_4 \text{ exceeds } .25$$

we would conclude that there is a preference for one or more of the brands. Here each of the expected cell frequencies equals $.25(400) = 100$. Remembering that the observed cell frequencies are $f_1 = 102, f_2 = 121, f_3 = 120$, and $f_4 = 57$, the chi-square statistic is

$$\chi^2 = \sum_{i=1}^{4} \frac{(f_i - E_i)^2}{E_i}$$

$$= \frac{(102 - 100)^2}{100} + \frac{(121 - 100)^2}{100} + \frac{(120 - 100)^2}{100} + \frac{(57 - 100)^2}{100}$$

$$= .04 + 4.41 + 4 + 18.49 = 26.94$$

Since $\chi^2 = 26.94$ is greater than $\chi_{.05}^2 = 7.81473$ (see Table A.10 on page 648 with $k - 1 = 4 - 1 = 3$ degrees of freedom), we reject H_0 at level of significance .05. We conclude that preferences for the four brands are not equal and that at least one brand is preferred to the others.

Normal distributions We have seen that many statistical methods are based on the assumption that a random sample has been selected from a normally distributed population. We can check the validity of the normality assumption by using frequency distributions, stem-and-leaf displays, histograms, and normal plots. Another approach is to use a chi-square goodness-of-fit test to check the normality assumption. We show how this can be done in the following example.

LO2 Perform a goodness-of-fit test for normality.

EXAMPLE 12.2 The Car Mileage Case

Consider the sample of 50 gas mileages given in Table 1.6 (page 12). A histogram of these mileages (see Figure 2.9, page 46) is symmetrical and bell-shaped. This suggests that the sample of mileages has been randomly selected from a normally distributed population. In this example we use a chi-square goodness-of-fit test to check the normality of the mileages.

To perform this test, we first divide the number line into intervals (or categories). One way to do this is to use the class boundaries of the histogram in Figure 2.9. Table 12.3 gives these intervals and also gives observed frequencies (counts of the number of mileages in each interval), which have been obtained from the histogram of Figure 2.9. The chi-square test is done by comparing these observed frequencies with the expected frequencies in the rightmost column of Table 12.3. To explain how the expected frequencies are calculated, we first use the sample mean $\bar{x} = 31.56$ and the sample standard deviation $s = .798$ of the 50 mileages as point estimates of the population mean μ and population standard deviation σ. Then, for example, consider p_1, the probability that a randomly selected mileage will be in the first interval (less than 30.0) in Table 12.3, if the population of all mileages is normally distributed. We estimate p_1 to be

$$p_1 = P(\text{mileage} < 30.0) = P\left(z < \frac{30.0 - 31.56}{.798}\right)$$

$$= P(z < -1.95) = .0256$$

It follows that $E_1 = 50p_1 = 50(.0256) = 1.28$ is the expected frequency for the first interval under the normality assumption. Next, if we consider p_2, the probability that a randomly selected mileage will be in the second interval in Table 12.3 if the population of all mileages is normally distributed, we estimate p_2 to be

$$p_2 = P(30.0 \leq \text{mileage} < 30.5) = P\left(\frac{30.0 - 31.56}{.798} \leq z < \frac{30.5 - 31.56}{.798}\right)$$

$$= P(-1.95 \leq z < -1.33) = .0918 - .0256 = .0662$$

It follows that $E_2 = 50p_2 = 50(.0662) = 3.31$ is the expected frequency for the second interval under the normality assumption. The other expected frequencies are computed similarly. In general, p_i is the probability that a randomly selected mileage will be in interval i if the population of all possible mileages is normally distributed with mean 31.56 and standard deviation .798, and E_i is the expected number of the 50 mileages that would be in interval i if the population of all possible mileages has this normal distribution.

It seems reasonable to reject the null hypothesis

$$H_0: \text{the population of all mileages is normally distributed}$$

in favor of the alternative hypothesis

$$H_a: \text{the population of all mileages is not normally distributed}$$

TABLE 12.3 **Observed and Expected Cell Frequencies for a Chi-Square Goodness-of-Fit Test for Testing the Normality of the Population of Gasoline Mileages** 🗂 GasMiles

Interval	Observed Frequency (f_i)	p_i If the Population of Mileages Is Normally Distributed	Expected Frequency, $E_i = np_i = 50p_i$
Less than 30.0	1	$p_1 = P(\text{mileage} < 30.0) = .0256$	$E_1 = 50(.0256) = 1.28$
$30.0 < 30.5$	3	$p_2 = P(30.0 \leq \text{mileage} < 30.5) = .0662$	$E_2 = 50(.0662) = 3.31$
$30.5 < 31.0$	8	$p_3 = P(30.5 \leq \text{mileage} < 31.0) = .1502$	$E_3 = 50(.1502) = 7.51$
$31.0 < 31.5$	11	$p_4 = P(31.0 \leq \text{mileage} < 31.5) = .2261$	$E_4 = 50(.2261) = 11.305$
$31.5 < 32.0$	11	$p_5 = P(31.5 \leq \text{mileage} < 32.0) = .2407$	$E_5 = 50(.2407) = 12.035$
$32.0 < 32.5$	9	$p_6 = P(32.0 \leq \text{mileage} < 32.5) = .1722$	$E_6 = 50(.1722) = 8.61$
$32.5 < 33.0$	5	$p_7 = P(32.5 \leq \text{mileage} < 33.0) = .0831$	$E_7 = 50(.0831) = 4.155$
Greater than 33.0	2	$p_8 = P(\text{mileage} > 33.0) = .0359$	$E_8 = 50(.0359) = 1.795$

if the observed frequencies in Table 12.3 differ substantially from the corresponding expected frequencies in Table 12.3. We compare the observed frequencies with the expected frequencies under the normality assumption by computing the chi-square statistic

Chi-square curve with 5 degrees of freedom
p-value = .994
0   $x^2 = .43242$

$$\chi^2 = \sum_{i=1}^{8} \frac{(f_i - E_i)^2}{E_i}$$

$$= \frac{(1 - 1.28)^2}{1.28} + \frac{(3 - 3.31)^2}{3.31} + \frac{(8 - 7.51)^2}{7.51} + \frac{(11 - 11.305)^2}{11.305}$$

$$+ \frac{(11 - 12.035)^2}{12.035} + \frac{(9 - 8.61)^2}{8.61} + \frac{(5 - 4.155)^2}{4.155} + \frac{(2 - 1.795)^2}{1.795}$$

$$= .43242$$

Since we have estimated $m = 2$ parameters (μ and σ) in computing the expected frequencies (E_i values), it can be shown that the sampling distribution of χ^2 is approximately a chi-square distribution with $k - 1 - m = 8 - 1 - 2 = 5$ degrees of freedom. Therefore, we can reject H_0 at level of significance α if

$$\chi^2 > \chi_\alpha^2$$

where the χ_α^2 point is based on $k - 1 - m = 8 - 1 - 2 = 5$ degrees of freedom. If we wish to test H_0 at the .05 level of significance, Table A.10 tells us that $\chi_{.05}^2 = 11.0705$. Therefore, since

$$\chi^2 = .43242 < \chi_{.05}^2 = 11.0705$$

we cannot reject H_0 at the .05 level of significance, and we cannot reject the hypothesis that the population of all mileages is normally distributed. Therefore, for practical purposes it is probably reasonable to assume that the population of all mileages is approximately normally distributed and that inferences based on this assumption are valid. Finally, the *p*-value for this test, which is the area under the chi-square curve having 5 degrees of freedom to the right of $\chi^2 = .43242$, can be shown to equal .994. Since this *p*-value is large (much greater than .05), we have little evidence to support rejecting the null hypothesis (normality).

Note that although some of the expected cell frequencies in Table 12.3 are not at least 5, the number of classes (groups) is 8 (which exceeds 4), the average of the expected cell frequencies is at least 5, and the smallest expected cell frequency is at least 1. Therefore, it is probably reasonable to consider the result of this chi-square test valid. If we choose to base the chi-square test on the more restrictive assumption that all of the expected cell frequencies are at least 5, then we can combine adjacent cell frequencies as follows:

Original f_i Values	Original p_i Values	Original E_i Values	Combined E_i Values	Combined p_i Values	Combined f_i Values
1	.0256	1.28			
3	.0662	3.31	12.1	.2420	12
8	.1502	7.51			
11	.2261	11.305	11.305	.2261	11
11	.2407	12.035	12.035	.2407	11
9	.1722	8.61	8.61	.1722	9
5	.0831	4.155			
2	.0359	1.795	5.95	.1190	7

When we use these combined cell frequencies, the chi-square approximation is based on $k - 1 - m = 5 - 1 - 2 = 2$ degrees of freedom. We find that $\chi^2 = .30102$ and that the *p*-value = .860. Since this *p*-value is much greater than .05, we cannot reject the hypothesis of normality at the .05 level of significance.

In Example 12.2 we based the intervals employed in the chi-square goodness-of-fit test on the class boundaries of a histogram for the observed mileages. Another way to establish intervals for such a test is to compute the sample mean $\bar{x}$ and the sample standard deviation s and to use intervals based on the Empirical Rule as follows:

Interval 1: less than $\bar{x} - 2s$

Interval 2: $\bar{x} - 2s < \bar{x} - s$

Interval 3: $\bar{x} - s < \bar{x}$

Interval 4: $\bar{x} < \bar{x} + s$

Interval 5: $\bar{x} + s < \bar{x} + 2s$

Interval 6: greater than $\bar{x} + 2s$

However, care must be taken to ensure that each of the expected frequencies is large enough (using the previously discussed criteria).

No matter how the intervals are established, we use $\bar{x}$ as an estimate of the population mean μ and we use s as an estimate of the population standard deviation σ when we calculate the expected frequencies (E_i values). Since we are estimating $m = 2$ population parameters, the rejection point χ_α^2 is based on $k - 1 - m = k - 1 - 2 = k - 3$ degrees of freedom, where k is the number of intervals employed.

In the following box we summarize how to carry out this chi-square test:

A Goodness-of-Fit Test for a Normal Distribution

1 We will test the following null and alternative hypotheses:

    H_0: the population has a normal distribution

    H_a: the population does not have a normal distribution

2 Select a random sample of size n and compute the sample mean $\bar{x}$ and sample standard deviation s.

3 Define k intervals for the test. Two reasonable ways to do this are to use the classes of a histogram of the data or to use intervals based on the Empirical Rule.

4 Record the observed frequency (f_i) for each interval.

5 Calculate the expected frequency (E_i) for each interval under the normality assumption. Do this by computing the probability that a normal variable having mean $\bar{x}$ and standard deviation s is within the interval and by multiplying this probability by n. Make sure that each expected frequency is large enough. If necessary, combine intervals to make the expected frequencies large enough.

6 Calculate the chi-square statistic

$$\chi^2 = \sum_{i=1}^{k} \frac{(f_i - E_i)^2}{E_i}$$

and define the p-value for the test to be the area under the curve of the chi-square distribution having $k - 3$ degrees of freedom to the right of χ^2.

7 Reject H_0 in favor of H_a at level of significance α if either of the following equivalent conditions holds:

    a $\chi^2 > \chi_\alpha^2$ **b** p-value $< \alpha$

Here, the χ_α^2 point is based on $k - 3$ degrees of freedom.

While chi-square goodness-of-fit tests are often used to verify that it is reasonable to assume that a random sample has been selected from a normally distributed population, such tests can also check other distribution forms. For instance, we might verify that it is reasonable to assume that a random sample has been selected from a Poisson distribution. In general, **the number of degrees of freedom for the chi-square goodness-of-fit test will equal $k - 1 - m$,** where k is the number of intervals or categories employed in the test and m is the number of population parameters that must be estimated to calculate the needed expected frequencies.

Exercises for Section 12.1

CONCEPTS

12.1 Describe the characteristics that define a multinomial experiment.

12.2 Give the conditions that the expected cell frequencies must meet in order to validly carry out a chi-square goodness-of-fit test.

12.3 Explain the purpose of a goodness-of-fit test.

12.4 When performing a chi-square goodness-of-fit test, explain why a large value of the chi-square statistic provides evidence that H_0 should be rejected.

12.5 Explain two ways to obtain intervals for a goodness-of-fit test of normality.

connect

METHODS AND APPLICATIONS

12.6 The shares of the U.S. automobile market held in 1990 by General Motors, Japanese manufacturers, Ford, Chrysler, and other manufacturers were, respectively, 36%, 26%, 21%, 9%, and 8%. Suppose that a new survey of 1,000 new-car buyers shows the following purchase frequencies:

GM	Japanese	Ford	Chrysler	Other
391	202	275	53	79

a Show that it is appropriate to carry out a chi-square test using these data. DS AutoMkt

b Test to determine whether the current market shares differ from those of 1990. Use $\alpha = .05$.

12.7 Last rating period, the percentages of viewers watching several channels between 11 P.M. and 11:30 P.M. in a major TV market were as follows: DS TVRate

WDUX (News)	WWTY (News)	WACO (*Cheers* Reruns)	WTJW (News)	Others
15%	19%	22%	16%	28%

Suppose that in the current rating period, a survey of 2,000 viewers gives the following frequencies:

WDUX (News)	WWTY (News)	WACO (*Cheers* Reruns)	WTJW (News)	Others
182	536	354	151	777

a Show that it is appropriate to carry out a chi-square test using these data.

b Test to determine whether the viewing shares in the current rating period differ from those in the last rating period at the .10 level of significance. What do you conclude?

12.8 In the *Journal of Marketing Research* (November 1996), Gupta studied the extent to which the purchase behavior of **scanner panels** is representative of overall brand preferences. A scanner panel is a sample of households whose purchase data are recorded when a magnetic identification card is presented at a store checkout. The table below gives peanut butter purchase data collected by the A. C. Nielson Company using a panel of 2,500 households in Sioux Falls, South Dakota. The data were collected over 102 weeks. The table also gives the market shares obtained by recording all peanut butter purchases at the same stores during the same period. DS ScanPan

a Show that it is appropriate to carry out a chi-square test.

b Test to determine whether the purchase behavior of the panel of 2,500 households is consistent with the purchase behavior of the population of all peanut butter purchasers. Assume here that purchase decisions by panel members are reasonably independent, and set $\alpha = .05$.

Brand	Size	Number of Purchases by Household Panel	Market Shares
Jif	18 oz.	3,165	20.10%
Jif	28	1,892	10.10
Jif	40	726	5.42
Peter Pan	10	4,079	16.01
Skippy	18	6,206	28.56
Skippy	28	1,627	12.33
Skippy	40	1,420	7.48
Total		19,115	

Goodness-of-Fit Test

obs	expected	O − E	(O − E)²/E	% of chisq
3165	3842.115	−677.115	119.331	13.56
1892	1930.615	−38.615	0.772	0.09
726	1036.033	−310.033	92.777	10.54
4079	3060.312	1018.689	339.092	38.52
6206	5459.244	746.756	102.147	11.60
1627	2356.880	−729.880	226.029	25.68
1420	1429.802	−9.802	0.067	0.01
19115	19115.000	0.000	880.216	100.00

880.22 chisquare   6 df   0.0000 p-value

Source: Reprinted with permission from *The Journal of Marketing Research*, published by the American Marketing Association, Vol. 33, S. Gupta et al., "Do Household Scanner Data Provide Representative Inferences from Brand Choices? A Comparison with Store Data," p. 393 (Table 6).

12.9 The purchase frequencies for six different brands of videotape are observed at a video store over one month: DS VidTape

Brand	Memorex	Scotch	Kodak	TDK	BASF	Sony
Purchase Frequency	131	273	119	301	176	200

a Carry out a test of homogeneity for these data with $\alpha = .025$.

b Interpret the result of your test.

12.10 A wholesaler has recently developed a computerized sales invoicing system. Prior to implementing this system, a manual system was used. The distribution of the number of errors per invoice for the manual system is as follows: **DS** Invoice2

Errors per Invoice	0	1	2	3	More Than 3
Percentage of Invoices	87%	8%	3%	1%	1%

After implementation of the computerized system, a random sample of 500 invoices gives the following error distribution:

Errors per Invoice	0	1	2	3	More Than 3
Number of Invoices	479	10	8	2	1

a Show that it is appropriate to carry out a chi-square test using these data.
b Use the following Excel output to determine whether the error percentages for the computerized system differ from those for the manual system at the .05 level of significance. What do you conclude?

```
   pi       Ei       fi     (f-E)^2/E
 0.87      435      479       4.4506
 0.08       40       10      22.5000
 0.03       15        8       3.2667
 0.01        5        2       1.8000
 0.01        5        1       3.2000
                  Chi-      35.21724    p-value 0.0000001096
                 Square
```

12.11 **THE PAYMENT TIME CASE**

Consider the sample of 65 payment times given in Table 2.4 (page 42). Use these data to carry out a chi-square goodness-of-fit test to test whether the population of all payment times is normally distributed by doing the following: **DS** PayTime

a It can be shown that $\bar{x} = 18.1077$ and that $s = 3.9612$ for the payment time data. Use these values to compute the intervals

   (1)   Less than $\bar{x} - 2s$ (4) $\bar{x} < \bar{x} + s$
   (2) $\bar{x} - 2s < \bar{x} - s$ (5) $\bar{x} + s < \bar{x} + 2s$
   (3) $\bar{x} - s < \bar{x}$ (6)   Greater than $\bar{x} + 2s$

b Assuming that the population of all payment times is normally distributed, find the probability that a randomly selected payment time will be contained in each of the intervals found in part a. Use these probabilities to compute the expected frequency under the normality assumption for each interval.

c Verify that the average of the expected frequencies is at least 5 and that the smallest expected frequency is at least 1. What does this tell us?

d Formulate the null and alternative hypotheses for the chi-square test of normality.

e For each interval given in part a, find the observed frequency. Then calculate the chi-square statistic needed for the chi-square test of normality.

f Use the chi-square statistic to test normality at the .05 level of significance. What do you conclude?

12.12 **THE MARKETING RESEARCH CASE**

Consider the sample of 60 bottle design ratings given in Table 1.5 (page 10). Use these data to carry out a chi-square goodness-of-fit test to determine whether the population of all bottle design ratings is normally distributed. Use $\alpha = .05$, and note that $\bar{x} = 30.35$ and $s = 3.1073$ for the 60 bottle design ratings.   **DS** Design

12.13 **THE BANK CUSTOMER WAITING TIME CASE**

Consider the sample of 100 waiting times given in Table 1.8 (page 13). Use these data to carry out a chi-square goodness-of-fit test to determine whether the population of all waiting times is normally distributed. Use $\alpha = .10$, and note that $\bar{x} = 5.46$ and $s = 2.475$ for the 100 waiting times.   **DS** WaitTime

12.14 The table on the next page gives a frequency distribution describing the number of errors found in thirty 1,000-line samples of computer code. Suppose that we wish to determine whether the number of errors can be described by a Poisson distribution with mean $\mu = 4.5$. Using the Poisson probability tables, fill in the table. Then perform an appropriate chi-square goodness-of-fit test at the .05 level of significance. What do you conclude about whether the number of errors can be described by a Poisson distribution with $\mu = 4.5$? Explain. 📀 CodeErr

Number of Errors	Observed Frequency	Probability Assuming Errors Are Poisson Distributed with $\mu = 4.5$	Expected Frequency
0–1	6		
2–3	5		
4–5	7		
6–7	8		
8 or more	4		

LO3 Decide whether two qualitative variables are independent by using a chi-square test for independence.

12.2 A Chi-Square Test for Independence ● ● ●

We have spent considerable time in previous chapters studying relationships between variables. One way to study the relationship between two variables is to classify multinomial count data on two scales (or dimensions) by setting up a *contingency table*.

EXAMPLE 12.3 The Client Satisfaction Case

A financial institution sells several kinds of investment products—a stock fund, a bond fund, and a tax-deferred annuity. The company is examining whether customer satisfaction depends on the type of investment product purchased. To do this, 100 clients are randomly selected from the population of clients who have purchased shares in exactly one of the funds. The company records the fund type purchased by these clients and asks each sampled client to rate his or her level of satisfaction with the fund as high, medium, or low. Table 12.4 on page 474 gives the survey results.

We can look at the data in Table 12.4 in an organized way by constructing a **contingency table** (also called a **two-way cross-tabulation or cross-classification table**). Such a table classifies the data on two dimensions—type of fund and degree of client satisfaction. Figure 12.2 gives Excel and MINITAB outputs of a contingency table of fund type versus level of satisfaction. This table consists of a row for each fund type and a column for each level of satisfaction. Together, the rows and columns form a "cell" for each fund type–satisfaction level combination. That is, there is a cell for each "contingency" with respect to fund type and satisfaction level. Both the Excel and MINITAB outputs give a **cell frequency** for each cell. On the MINITAB output, this is the top number given in the cell. The cell frequency is a count (observed frequency) of the number of surveyed clients with the cell's fund type–satisfaction level combination. For instance, 15 of the surveyed clients invest in the bond fund and report high satisfaction, while 24 of the surveyed clients invest in the tax-deferred annuity and report medium satisfaction. In addition to the cell frequencies, each output also gives:

Row totals (at the far right of each table): These are counts of the numbers of clients who invest in each fund type. These row totals tell us that

1 30 clients invest in the bond fund.

2 30 clients invest in the stock fund.

3 40 clients invest in the tax-deferred annuity.

Column totals (at the bottom of each table): These are counts of the numbers of clients who report high, medium, and low satisfaction. These column totals tell us that

1 40 clients report high satisfaction.

2 40 clients report medium satisfaction.

3 20 clients report low satisfaction.

Overall total (the bottom-right entry in each table): This tells us that a total of 100 clients were surveyed.

Besides the row and column totals, the MINITAB output gives **row and column percentages** (below the row and column totals). For example, 30.00 percent of the surveyed clients invest in the bond fund, and 20.00 percent of the surveyed clients report low satisfaction. Furthermore, in

FIGURE 12.2 Excel and MINITAB Outputs of a Contingency Table of Fund Type versus Level of Client Satisfaction (See the Survey Results in Table 12.4) 🖸 Invest

(a) The Excel Output

	A	B	C	D	E	F	G
1							
2	Count of FundType	SatRating					
3	FundType	HIGH	MED	LOW	Grand Total		
4	BOND	15	12	3	30		
5	STOCK	24	4	2	30		
6	TAXDEF	1	24	15	40		
7	Grand Total	40	40	20	100		
8							
9			12	12	6	30	
10			12	12	6	30	
11			16	16	8	40	
12			40	40	20	100	
13							

14		0.75	0	1.5	2.25
15		12	5.3333	2.6667	20
16		14.0625	4	6.125	24.1875
17		26.8125	9.3333	10.2917	a 46.4375
18					
19				b	0.000000002

CrossTab   Invest

ᵃChi-square statistic.
ᵇp-value for chi-square.

(b) The MINITAB Output

Rows: FundType   Columns: SatRating

	High	Med	Low	All
Bond	15	12	3	30
	50.00	40.00	10.00	100.00
	37.50	30.00	15.00	30.00
	12	12	6	30
Stock	24	4	2	30
	80.00	13.33	6.67	100.00
	60.00	10.00	10.00	30.00
	12	12	6	30
TaxDef	1	24	15	40
	2.50	60.00	37.50	100.00
	2.50	60.00	75.00	40.00
	16	16	8	40
All	40	40	20	100
	40.00	40.00	20.00	100.00
	100.00	100.00	100.00	100.00
	40	40	20	100

Pearson Chi-Square = 46.438, DF = 4
P-Value = 0.000

Cell Contents: Count
                     % of Row
                     % of Column
                     Expected count

addition to a cell frequency, the MINITAB output gives a **row percentage** and a **column percentage** for each cell (these are below the cell frequency in each cell). For instance, looking at the "bond fund–high satisfaction cell," we see that the 15 clients in this cell make up 50.0 percent of the 30 clients who invest in the bond fund, and they make up 37.5 percent of the 40 clients who report high satisfaction. We will explain the last number that appears in each cell of the MINITAB output later in this section.

Looking at the contingency tables, it appears that the level of client satisfaction may be related to the fund type. We see that higher satisfaction ratings seem to be reported by stock and bond fund investors, while holders of tax-deferred annuities report lower satisfaction ratings. To carry out a formal statistical test we can test the null hypothesis

H_0: fund type and level of client satisfaction are independent

versus

H_a: fund type and level of client satisfaction are dependent

In order to perform this test, we compare the counts (or **observed cell frequencies**) in the contingency table with the counts we would expect if we assume that fund type and level of satisfaction are independent. Because these latter counts are computed by assuming independence, we call them the **expected cell frequencies under the independence assumption.** We illustrate how to calculate these expected cell frequencies by considering the cell corresponding to the bond fund and high client satisfaction. We first use the data in the contingency table to compute an estimate of the probability that a randomly selected client invests in the bond fund. Denoting this probability as p_B, we estimate p_B by dividing the row total for the bond fund by the total number of clients surveyed. That is, denoting the row total for the bond fund as r_B and letting n denote the total number of clients surveyed, the estimate of p_B is $r_B/n = 30/100 = .3$. Next we compute an estimate of the probability that a randomly selected client will report high satisfaction. Denoting this probability as p_H, we estimate p_H by dividing the column total for high

TABLE 12.4   Results of a Customer Satisfaction Survey Given to 100 Randomly Selected Clients Who Invest in One of Three Fund Types—a Bond Fund, a Stock Fund, or a Tax-Deferred Annuity   DS Invest

Client	Fund Type	Level of Satisfaction	Client	Fund Type	Level of Satisfaction	Client	Fund Type	Level of Satisfaction
1	BOND	HIGH	35	STOCK	HIGH	69	BOND	MED
2	STOCK	HIGH	36	BOND	MED	70	TAXDEF	MED
3	TAXDEF	MED	37	TAXDEF	MED	71	TAXDEF	MED
4	TAXDEF	MED	38	TAXDEF	LOW	72	BOND	HIGH
5	STOCK	LOW	39	STOCK	HIGH	73	TAXDEF	MED
6	STOCK	HIGH	40	TAXDEF	MED	74	TAXDEF	LOW
7	STOCK	HIGH	41	BOND	HIGH	75	STOCK	HIGH
8	BOND	MED	42	BOND	HIGH	76	BOND	HIGH
9	TAXDEF	LOW	43	BOND	LOW	77	TAXDEF	LOW
10	TAXDEF	LOW	44	TAXDEF	LOW	78	BOND	MED
11	STOCK	MED	45	STOCK	HIGH	79	STOCK	HIGH
12	BOND	LOW	46	BOND	HIGH	80	STOCK	HIGH
13	STOCK	HIGH	47	BOND	MED	81	BOND	MED
14	TAXDEF	MED	48	STOCK	HIGH	82	TAXDEF	MED
15	TAXDEF	MED	49	TAXDEF	MED	83	BOND	HIGH
16	TAXDEF	LOW	50	TAXDEF	MED	84	STOCK	MED
17	STOCK	HIGH	51	STOCK	HIGH	85	STOCK	HIGH
18	BOND	HIGH	52	TAXDEF	MED	86	BOND	MED
19	BOND	MED	53	STOCK	HIGH	87	TAXDEF	MED
20	TAXDEF	MED	54	TAXDEF	MED	88	TAXDEF	LOW
21	TAXDEF	MED	55	STOCK	LOW	89	STOCK	HIGH
22	BOND	HIGH	56	BOND	HIGH	90	TAXDEF	MED
23	TAXDEF	MED	57	STOCK	HIGH	91	BOND	HIGH
24	TAXDEF	LOW	58	BOND	MED	92	TAXDEF	HIGH
25	STOCK	HIGH	59	TAXDEF	LOW	93	TAXDEF	LOW
26	BOND	HIGH	60	TAXDEF	LOW	94	TAXDEF	LOW
27	TAXDEF	LOW	61	STOCK	MED	95	STOCK	HIGH
28	BOND	MED	62	BOND	LOW	96	BOND	HIGH
29	STOCK	HIGH	63	STOCK	HIGH	97	BOND	MED
30	STOCK	HIGH	64	TAXDEF	MED	98	STOCK	HIGH
31	BOND	MED	65	TAXDEF	MED	99	TAXDEF	MED
32	TAXDEF	MED	66	TAXDEF	LOW	100	TAXDEF	MED
33	BOND	HIGH	67	STOCK	HIGH			
34	STOCK	MED	68	BOND	HIGH			

satisfaction by the total number of clients surveyed. That is, denoting the column total for high satisfaction as c_H, the estimate of p_H is $c_H/n = 40/100 = .4$. Next, assuming that investing in the bond fund and reporting high satisfaction are **independent,** we compute an estimate of the probability that a randomly selected client invests in the bond fund and reports high satisfaction. Denoting this probability as p_{BH}, we can compute its estimate by recalling from Section 4.4 that if two events A and B are statistically independent, then $P(A \cap B)$ equals $P(A)P(B)$. It follows that, if we assume that investing in the bond fund and reporting high satisfaction are independent, we can compute an estimate of p_{BH} by multiplying the estimate of p_B by the estimate of p_H. That is, the estimate of p_{BH} is $(r_B/n)(c_H/n) = (.3)(.4) = .12$. Finally, we compute an estimate of the expected cell frequency under the independence assumption. Denoting the expected cell frequency as E_{BH}, the estimate of E_{BH} is

$$\hat{E}_{BH} = n \left(\frac{r_B}{n}\right)\left(\frac{c_H}{n}\right) = 100(.3)(.4) = 12$$

This estimated expected cell frequency is given in the MINITAB output of Figure 12.2(b) as the last number under the observed cell frequency for the bond fund–high satisfaction cell.

Noting that the expression for $\hat{E}_{BH}$ can be written as

$$\hat{E}_{BH} = n\left(\frac{r_B}{n}\right)\left(\frac{c_H}{n}\right) = \frac{r_B c_H}{n}$$

we can generalize to obtain a formula for the estimated expected cell frequency for any cell in the contingency table. Letting $\hat{E}_{ij}$ denote the estimated expected cell frequency corresponding to row i and column j in the contingency table, we see that

$$\hat{E}_{ij} = \frac{r_i c_j}{n}$$

where r_i is the row total for row i and c_j is the column total for column j. For example, for the fund type–satisfaction level contingency table, we obtain

$$\hat{E}_{SL} = \frac{r_S c_L}{n} = \frac{30(20)}{100} = \frac{600}{100} = 6$$

and

$$\hat{E}_{TM} = \frac{r_T c_M}{n} = \frac{40(40)}{100} = \frac{1,600}{100} = 16$$

These (and the other estimated expected cell frequencies under the independence assumption) are the last numbers below the observed cell frequencies in the MINITAB output of Figure 12.2(b). Intuitively, these estimated expected cell frequencies tell us what the contingency table looks like if fund type and level of client satisfaction are independent. A table of estimated expected cell frequencies is also given below the contingency table on the Excel output of Figure 12.2(a).

To test the null hypothesis of independence, we will compute a chi-square statistic that compares the observed cell frequencies with the estimated expected cell frequencies calculated assuming independence. Letting f_{ij} denote the observed cell frequency for cell ij, we compute

$$\chi^2 = \sum_{\text{all cells}} \frac{(f_{ij} - \hat{E}_{ij})^2}{\hat{E}_{ij}}$$

$$= \frac{(f_{BH} - \hat{E}_{BH})^2}{\hat{E}_{BH}} + \frac{(f_{BM} - \hat{E}_{BM})^2}{\hat{E}_{BM}} + \cdots + \frac{(f_{TL} - \hat{E}_{TL})^2}{\hat{E}_{TL}}$$

$$= \frac{(15 - 12)^2}{12} + \frac{(12 - 12)^2}{12} + \frac{(3 - 6)^2}{6} + \frac{(24 - 12)^2}{12} + \frac{(4 - 12)^2}{12}$$

$$+ \frac{(2 - 6)^2}{6} + \frac{(1 - 16)^2}{16} + \frac{(24 - 16)^2}{16} + \frac{(15 - 8)^2}{8}$$

$$= 46.4375$$

If the value of the chi-square statistic is large, this indicates that the observed cell frequencies differ substantially from the expected cell frequencies calculated by assuming independence. Therefore, the larger the value of chi-square, the more doubt is cast on the null hypothesis of independence.

To find an appropriate rejection point, we let r denote the number of rows in the contingency table and we let c denote the number of columns. Then, it can be shown that, when the null hypothesis of independence is true, the sampling distribution of χ^2 is approximately a χ^2 distribution with $(r - 1)(c - 1) = (3 - 1)(3 - 1) = 4$ degrees of freedom. If we test H_0 at the .05 level of significance, we reject H_0 if and only if

$$\chi^2 > \chi^2_{.05}$$

Since Table A.10 (page 648) tells us that the $\chi^2_{.05}$ point corresponding to $(r - 1)(c - 1) = 4$ degrees of freedom equals 9.48773, we have

$$\chi^2 = 46.4375 > \chi^2_{.05} = 9.48773$$

and we reject H_0 at the .05 level of significance. We conclude that fund type and level of client satisfaction are not independent.

FIGURE 12.5   MINITAB Output of a Chi-Square Test for Independence in the Coupon Redemption Study

```
Expected counts are below observed counts

           Midtown   North   South   Total
High            69       97      52     218
             72.67    72.67   72.67

Medium         101       93      76     270
             90.00    90.00   90.00

Low             30       10      72     112
             37.33    37.33   37.33

Total          200      200     200     600

Chi-Sq = 71.476, DF = 4, P-Value = 0.000
```

TABLE 12.12   A Sample of 65 Customer Satisfaction Ratings

DS VideoGame

39	46	42	40	45	44	44	44	45
45	44	46	46	46	41	46	46	
38	40	40	41	43	38	48	39	
42	39	47	43	47	43	44	41	
42	40	44	39	43	36	41	44	
41	42	43	43	41	44	45	42	
38	45	45	46	40	44	44	47	
42	44	45	45	43	45	44	43	

12.29   Internet Exercise

A report on the 1995 National Health Risk Behavior Survey, conducted by the Centers for Disease Control and Prevention, can be found at the CDC website [http://www.cdc.gov: More Data & Statistics: CDC Data & Statistics Resources, Surveys Tab: CDC Surveys, Youth Risk Behavior Surveillance System (YRBSS): Publications and Data Files, YRBSS Publications: MMWR: Youth Risk Behavior Surveillance – National College Health Risk Behavior Survey – United States, 1995, or, directly, go to www.cdc.gov/mmwr/PDF/SS/SS4504.pdf]. Among the issues addressed in the survey was whether the subjects had, in the prior 30 days, ridden with a driver who had been drinking alcohol. Does the proportion of students exhibiting this selected risk behavior vary by ethnic group? The report includes tables summarizing the "Ridden Drinking" risk behavior by ethnic group (Table 3) and the ethnic composition (Table 1) for a sample of $n = 4,609$ college students. The "Ridden Drinking" and ethnic group information is extracted from Tables 1 and 3 and is displayed as proportions or probabilities in the leftmost panel of the table below. Note that the values in the body of the leftmost panel are given as conditional prob-

abilities, the probabilities of exhibiting the "Ridden Drinking" risk behavior, given ethnic group. These conditional probabilities can be multiplied by the appropriate marginal probabilities to compute the joint probabilities for all the risk behavior by ethnic group combinations to obtain the summaries in the center panel. Finally, the joint probabilities are multiplied by the sample size to obtain projected counts for the number of students in each "Ridden Drinking" by ethnic group combination. The "Other" ethnic group was omitted from the Table 3 summaries and is thus not included in this analysis.

Is there sufficient evidence to conclude that the proportion of college students exhibiting the "Ridden Drinking" behavior varies by ethnic group? Conduct a chi-square test for independence using the projected count data provided in the rightmost panel of the summary table. (Data are available in MINITAB and Excel files, YouthRisk.mtw and YouthRisk.xls.) Test at the 0.01 level of significance and report an approximate p-value for your test. Be sure to clearly state your hypotheses and conclusion.   DS YouthRisk

	Conditional Probabilities [Table 3: P(R|E). Table 1: P(E)]			Joint Probabilities [P(ER) = P(R|E)P(E)]			Projected Counts [n = 4609] [n(ER) = P(ER) × 4609]		
	Ridden Drinking?			Ridden Drinking?			Ridden Drinking?		
Ethnic	%Y|Eth	%N|Eth	% Ethnic	Yes	No	Total	Yes	No	Total
White	0.383	0.617	0.728	0.2788	0.4492	0.7280	1,285	2,070	3,355
Black	0.275	0.725	0.103	0.0283	0.0747	0.1030	131	344	475
Hispanic	0.307	0.693	0.071	0.0218	0.0492	0.0710	100	227	327

Appendix 12.1 ■ Chi-Square Tests Using Excel

The instruction blocks in this section each begins by describing the entry of data into an Excel spreadsheet. Alternatively, the data may be downloaded from this book's website. The appropriate data file name is given at the top of each instruction block. Please refer to Appendix 1.1 for further information about entering data, saving data, and printing results when using Excel.

Chi-square goodness-of-fit test in Exercise 12.10 on page 471 (data file: Invoice2.xlsx):

- In the first row of the spreadsheet, enter the following column headings in order—Percent, Expected, Number, and ChiSqContribution.

- Beginning in cell A2, enter the "percentage of invoice figures" from Exercise 12.10 as decimal fractions into column A.

- Compute expected values. Enter the formula =500*A2 into cell B2 and press Enter. Copy this formula through cell B6 by double-clicking the drag handle (in the lower right corner) of cell B2.

- Enter the "number of invoice figures" from Exercise 12.10 into cells C2 through C6.

- Compute cell chi-square contributions. In cell D2, enter the formula =(C2 − B2)^2/B2 and press Enter. Copy this formula through cell D6 by double-clicking the drag handle (in the lower right corner) of cell D2.

- Compute the chi-square statistic in cell D8. Use the mouse to select the range of cells D2:D8 and click the Σ button on the Excel ribbon.

- Click on an empty cell, say cell A15, and select the Insert Function button f_x on the Excel ribbon.

- In the Insert Function dialog box, select Statistical from the "Or select a category:" menu, select CHIDIST from the "Select a function:" menu, and click OK.

- In the "CHIDIST Function Arguments" dialog box, enter D8 into the "X" box and 3 into the "Deg_freedom" box.

- Click OK in the "CHIDIST Function Arguments" dialog box to produce the *p*-value related to the chi-square statistic in cell A15.

Contingency table and chi-square test of independence in Figure 12.2(a) on page 473 (data file: Invest.xlsx):

- Follow the instructions given in Appendix 2.1 for using a PivotTable to construct a crosstabulation table of fund type versus level of customer satisfaction and place the table in a new worksheet.

To compute a table of expected values:

- In cell B9, type the formula =$E4*B$7/$E$7 (be very careful to include the $ in all the correct places) and press the Enter key (to obtain the expected value 12 in cell B9).

- Click on cell B9 and use the mouse to point the cursor to the drag handle (in the lower right corner) of the cell. The cursor will change to a black cross. Using the black cross, drag the handle right to cell D9 and release the mouse button to fill cells C9 : D9. With B9:D9 still selected, use the black cross to drag the handle down to cell D11. Release the mouse button to fill cells B10 : D11.

- To add marginal totals, select the range B9 : E12 and click the Σ button on the Excel ribbon.

To compute the chi-square statistic:

- In cell B15, type the formula = (B4 – B9)^2/B9 and press the Enter key to obtain the cell contribution 0.75 in cell B15.

- Click on cell B15 and (using the procedure described above) use the "black cross cursor" to drag the cell handle right to cell D15 and then down to cell D17 (obtaining the cell contributions in cells B15 : D17).

- To add marginal totals, select the range B15 : E18 and click the Σ button on the Excel ribbon.

- The chi-square statistic is in cell E18 (= 46.4375).

To compute the p-value for the chi-square test of independence:

- Click on an empty cell, say E20.
- Select the Insert Function button f_x on the Excel ribbon.
- In the Insert Function dialog box, select Statistical from the "Or select a category:" menu, select CHIDIST from the "Select a function:" menu, and click OK.
- In the "CHIDIST Function Arguments" dialog box, enter E18 (the cell location of the chi-square statistic) into the "X" window and 4 into the "Deg_freedom" window.
- Click OK in the "CHIDIST Function Arguments" dialog box to produce the p-value related to the chi-square statistic in cell E20.

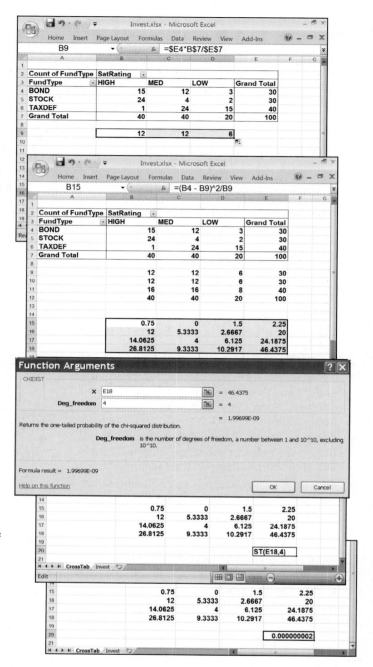

Appendix 12.2 ■ Chi-Square Tests Using MegaStat

The instructions in this section begin by describing the entry of data into an Excel worksheet. Alternatively, the data may be downloaded from this book's website. The appropriate data file name is given at the top of each instruction block. Please refer to Appendix 1.1 for further information about entering data, saving data, and printing results in Excel. Please refer to Appendix 1.2 for more information about using MegaStat.

Contingency table and chi-square test of independence similar to Figure 12.2(a) on page 473 (data file: Invest.xlsx):

- Follow the instructions given in Appendix 2.2 for using MegaStat to construct a crosstabulation table of fund type versus level of customer satisfaction.

- After having made entries to specify the row and column variables for the table, in the list of Output Options place a checkmark in the "chi-square" checkbox.

- If desired, row, column, and cell percentages can be obtained by placing checkmarks in the "% of row," "% of column," and "% of total" checkboxes in the list of Output Options. Here we have elected to not request these percentages.

- Click OK in the Crosstabulation dialog box.

- The value of the chi-square statistic (= 46.44) and its related p-value (= 0.000000002) are given below the crosstabulation table.

Crosstabulation					
			Satisfaction Rating		
		HIGH	MED	LOW	Total
Fund Type	BOND	15	12	3	30
	STOCK	24	4	2	30
	TAXDEF	1	24	15	40
	Total	40	40	20	100

46.44 chi-square
4 df
0.000000002 p-value

Chi-square goodness-of-fit test for the scanner panel data in Exercise 12.8 on page 470 (data file: ScanPan.xlsx):

- Enter the scanner panel data in Exercise 12.8 (page 470) as shown in the screen with the number of purchases for each brand in column C and with the market share for each brand (expressed as a percentage) in column D. Note that the total number of purchases for all brands equals 19,115 (which is in cell C11).

- In cell E4, type the cell formula =D4*19115 and press enter to compute the expected frequency for the Jif—18 ounce brand/size combination. Copy this cell formula (by double-clicking the drag handle in the lower right corner of cell E4) to compute the expected frequencies for each of the other brands in cells E5 through E10.

- Select **Add-Ins : MegaStat : Chi-square/ Crosstab : Goodness of Fit Test.**

- In the "Goodness of Fit Test" dialog box, click in the "Observed values Input range" window and enter the range C4:C10. Enter this range by dragging with the mouse—the autoexpand feature cannot be used in the "Goodness of Fit Test" dialog box.

- Click in the "Expected values Input range" window, and enter the range E4 : E10. Again, enter this range by dragging with the mouse.

- Click OK in the "Goodness of Fit Test" dialog box.

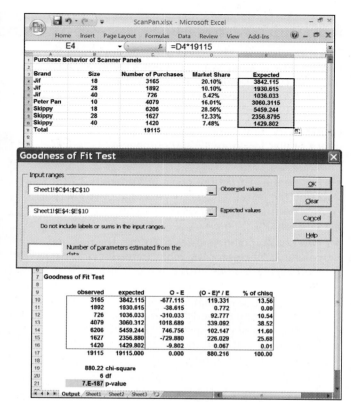

Chi-square test for independence with contingency table input data in the depreciation situation of Exercise 12.18 on page 478 (data file: DeprMeth.xlsx):

- Enter the depreciation method contingency table data in Table 12.5 on page 478 as shown in the screen—depreciation methods in rows and countries in columns.

- Select **Add-Ins : MegaStat : Chi-square/Crosstab : Contingency Table.**

- In the "Contingency Table Test for Independence" dialog box, click in the Input Range window and (by dragging the mouse) enter the range A4 : D7. Note that the entered range may contain row and column labels, but the range should not include the "total row" or "total column."

- In the list of Output Options, check the chi-square checkbox to obtain the results of the chi-square test for independence.

- If desired, row, column, and cell percentages can be obtained by placing checkmarks in the "% of row," "% of column," and "% of total" checkboxes in the list of Output Options. Here we have elected to not request these percentages.

- Click OK in the "Contingency Table Test for Independence" dialog box.

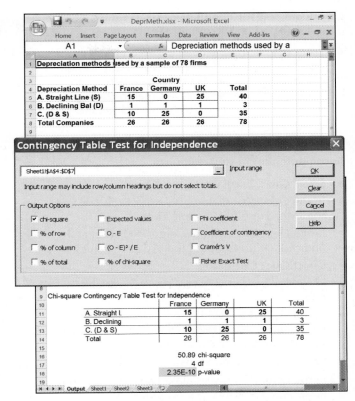

Appendix 12.3 ■ Chi-Square Tests Using MINITAB

The instruction blocks in this section each begins by describing the entry of data into the MINITAB Data window. Alternatively, the data may be downloaded from this book's website. The appropriate data file name is given at the top of each instruction block. Please refer to Appendix 1.3 for further information about entering data, saving data, and printing results when using MINITAB.

Chi-square test for goodness-of-fit in Figure 12.1 on page 465 (data file: MicroWav.MTW):

- Enter the microwave oven data from Tables 12.1 and 12.2 on page 463—observed frequencies in column C1 with variable name Frequency and market shares (entered as decimal fractions) in column C2 with variable name MarketShr.

To compute the chi-square statistic:

- Select **Calc : Calculator**.
- In the Calculator dialog box, enter Expected into the "Store result in variable" box.
- In the Expression window, enter 400*MarketShr and click OK to compute the expected values.
- Select **Calc : Calculator**.
- Enter ChiSq into the "Store result in variable" box.
- In the Expression window enter the formula (Frequency − Expected)**2/Expected and click OK to compute the cell chi-square contributions.
- Select **Calc : Column Statistics**.
- In the Column Statistics dialog box, click on Sum.
- Enter ChiSq in the "Input variable" box.
- Enter k1 in the "Store result in" box and click OK to compute the chi-square statistic and to store it as the constant k1.
- The chi-square statistic will be displayed in the session window.

To compute the *p*-value for the test:

We first compute the probability of obtaining a value of the chi-square statistic that is less than or equal to the computed value (= 8.77857):

- Select **Calc : Probability Distributions : Chi-Square**.
- In the Chi-Square Distribution dialog box, click on "Cumulative probability."
- Enter 3 in the "Degrees of freedom" box.
- Click the "Input constant" option and enter k1 into the corresponding box.
- Enter k2 into the "Optional storage" box.
- Click OK in the Chi-Square Distribution dialog box. This computes the needed probability and stores its value as a constant, k2.

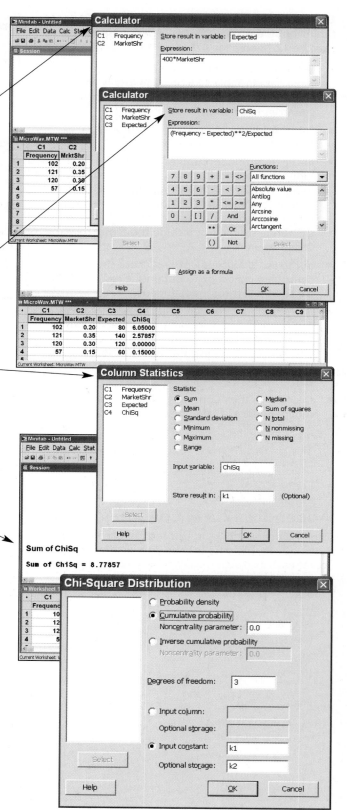

- Select **Calc : Calculator.**
- In the Calculator dialog box, enter PValue into the "Store result in variable" box.
- In the Expression window, enter the formula $1 - k2$, and click OK to compute the p-value related to the chi-square statistic.

To display the p-value:

- Select **Data : Display Data.**
- Enter PValue in the "Columns, constants, and matrices to display" window and click OK.

Sum of ChiSq (= 8.77857) is the chi-square statistic, and PValue (= 0.0323845) is the corresponding p-value.

Cross-tabulation table and chi-square test of independence for the client satisfaction data as in Figure 12.2(b) on page 473 (data file: Invest.MTW):

- Follow the instructions for constructing a cross-tabulation table of fund type versus level of client satisfaction as given in Appendix 2.3.
- After entering the categorical variables into the "Cross Tabulation and Chi-Square" dialog box, click on the Chi-Square... button.
- In the "Cross Tabulation—Chi-Square" dialog box, place checkmarks in the "Chi-Square analysis" and "Expected cell counts" check boxes and click OK.
- Click OK in the "Cross Tabulation and Chi-Square" dialog box to obtain results in the Session window.

The chi-square statistic can also be calculated from summary data by entering the cell counts from Table 12.2 and by selecting "Chi-Square Test (Table in Worksheet)" from the Stat : Tables submenu.

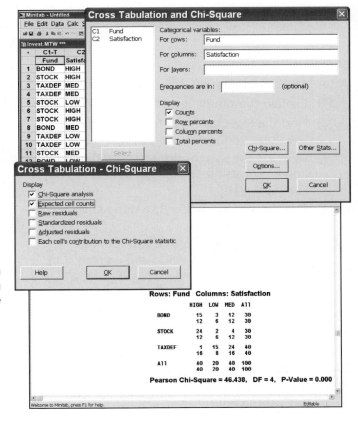

CHAPTER 13

Simple Linear Regression Analysis

Learning Objectives

After mastering the material in this chapter, you will be able to:

- **(LO1)** Explain the simple linear regression model.
- **(LO2)** Find the least squares point estimates of the slope and y-intercept.
- **(LO3)** Describe the assumptions behind simple linear regression and calculate the standard error.
- **(LO4)** Test the significance of the slope and y-intercept.
- **(LO5)** Calculate and interpret a confidence interval for a mean value and a prediction interval for an individual value.

- **(LO6)** Calculate and interpret the simple coefficients of determination and correlation.
- **(LO7)** Test hypotheses about the population correlation coefficient.
- **(LO8)** Test the significance of a simple linear regression model by using an F test.
- **(LO9)** Use residual analysis to check the assumptions of simple linear regression.

Chapter Outline

13.1 The Simple Linear Regression Model and the Least Squares Point Estimates

13.2 Model Assumptions and the Standard Error

13.3 Testing the Significance of the Slope and y-Intercept

13.4 Confidence and Prediction Intervals

13.5 Simple Coefficients of Determination and Correlation (This section may be read anytime after reading Section 13.1)

13.6 Testing the Significance of the Population Correlation Coefficient

13.7 An F Test for the Model

13.8 The QHIC Case

13.9 Residual Analysis

13.10 Some Shortcut Formulas (Optional)

anagers often make decisions by studying the relationships between variables, and process improvements can often be made by understanding how changes in one or more variables affect the process output. **Regression analysis** is a statistical technique in which we use observed data to relate a variable of interest, which is called the **dependent (or response) variable,** to one or more **independent (or predictor) variables.** The objective is to build a **regression model,** or **prediction equation,** that can be used to **describe, predict,** and **control** the dependent variable on the basis of the independent variables. For example, a company might wish to improve its marketing process. After collecting data concerning the demand for a product, the product's price, and the advertising expenditures made to promote the product, the company might use regression analysis to develop an equation to predict demand on the basis of price and advertising expenditure. Predictions of demand for various price–advertising expenditure combinations can then be used to evaluate potential changes in the company's marketing strategies.

In the next three chapters we give a thorough presentation of regression analysis. We begin in this chapter by presenting **simple linear regression** analysis. Using this technique is appropriate when we are relating a dependent variable to a single independent variable and when *a straight-line model* describes the relationship between these two variables. We explain many of the methods of this chapter in the context of two new cases:

The Tasty Sub Shop Case: A business entrepreneur uses simple linear regression analysis to predict the yearly revenue for a potential restaurant site on the basis of the number of residents living near the site. The entrepreneur then uses the prediction to assess the profitability of the potential restaurant site.

The QHIC Case: The marketing department at Quality Home Improvement Center (QHIC) uses simple linear regression analysis to predict home upkeep expenditure on the basis of home value. Predictions of home upkeep expenditures are used to help determine which homes should be sent advertising brochures promoting QHIC's products and services.

13.1 The Simple Linear Regression Model and the Least Squares Point Estimates ● ● ●

LO1 Explain the simple linear regression model.

The simple linear regression model   The **simple linear regression model** assumes that the relationship between the **dependent variable, which is denoted y,** and the **independent variable, denoted x,** can be approximated by a straight line. We can tentatively decide whether there is an approximate straight-line relationship between y and x by making a **scatter diagram,** or **scatter plot,** of y versus x. First, data concerning the two variables are observed in pairs. To construct the scatter plot, each value of y is plotted against its corresponding value of x. If the y values tend to increase or decrease in a straight-line fashion as the x values increase, and if there is a scattering of the (x, y) points around the straight line, then it is reasonable to describe the relationship between y and x by using the simple linear regression model. We illustrate this in the following case study.

EXAMPLE 13.1 The Tasty Sub Shop Case: Predicting Yearly Revenue for a Potential Restaurant Site

Part 1: Purchasing a restaurant franchise   Quiznos Sub Shops and other restaurant chains sell franchises to business entrepreneurs. Unlike McDonald's, Pizza Hut, and certain other chains, Quiznos does not construct a standard, recognizable building to house each of its restaurants. Instead, the entrepreneur wishing to purchase a Quiznos franchise finds a suitable site, which includes a suitable geographical location and suitable store space to rent. Then, when Quiznos approves the site, Quiznos hires an architect and a contractor to remodel the store rental space and thus "build" the Quiznos restaurant. Quiznos will help an entrepreneur evaluate potential sites, will help negotiate leases, and will provide national advertising and other support once a franchise is purchased. However, strict regulations prevent Quiznos (and other chains) from predicting how profitable an entrepreneur's potential restaurant might be. These regulations

TABLE 13.1	The Tasty Sub Shop Revenue Data

DS TastySub1

Restaurant	Population Size, x (Thousands of Residents)	Yearly Revenue, y (Thousands of Dollars)
1	20.8	527.1
2	27.5	548.7
3	32.3	767.2
4	37.2	722.9
5	39.6	826.3
6	45.1	810.5
7	49.9	1040.7
8	55.4	1033.6
9	61.7	1090.3
10	64.6	1235.8

FIGURE 13.1   Excel Output of a Scatter Plot of *y* versus *x*

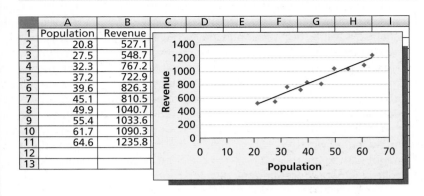

exist to prevent restaurant chains from overpredicting profit and thus misleading an entrepreneur into purchasing a franchise that might not be successful. As stated on the Quiznos website:[1]

> There are strict regulations in the franchise industry that limit our ability to estimate how successful your business could be. You need to do this yourself, but we can give some guidance. . . . Your sales primarily depend on the quality of the site, and your skill as an operator. So to estimate what your sales might be, look at other Quiznos restaurants that are in similar sites to the one you are reviewing. Find one with similar demographics (nearby employer and residence counts). . . . Ask that operator what their sales are.

Part 2: The Tasty Sub Shop Sales Data   In this case study, we suppose that there is a restaurant chain—The Tasty Sub Shop—that is similar to Quiznos in the way it sells franchises to business entrepreneurs. We will also suppose that there is an entrepreneur who has found several potential sites for a Tasty Sub Shop restaurant. Similar to most existing Tasty Sub restaurant sites, each of the entrepreneur's sites is a store rental space located in an outdoor shopping area that is close to one or more residential areas. For a Tasty Sub restaurant built on such a site, yearly revenue is known to partially depend on (1) the number of residents living near the site and (2) the amount of business and shopping near the site. Referring to the number of residents living near a site as *population size* and to the yearly revenue for a Tasty Sub restaurant built on the site as *yearly revenue*, the entrepreneur will—in this chapter—try in predict the **dependent (response) variable** yearly revenue (*y*) on the basis of the **independent (predictor) variable** population size (*x*). (In the next chapter the entrepreneur will also use the amount of business and shopping near a site to help predict yearly revenue.) To predict yearly revenue on the basis of population size, the entrepreneur randomly selects 10 existing Tasty Sub restaurants that are built on sites similar to the sites that the entrepreneur is considering. The entrepreneur then asks the owner of each existing restaurant what the restaurant's revenue *y* was last year and estimates—with the help of the owner and published demographic information—the number of residents, or population size *x*, living near the site. The values of *y* (measured in thousands of dollars) and *x* (measured in thousands of residents) that are obtained are given in Table 13.1. In Figure 13.1 we give an Excel output of a scatter plot of *y* versus *x*. This plot shows (1) a tendency for the yearly revenues to increase in a straight-line fashion as the population sizes increase and (2) a scattering of points around the straight line. A **regression model** describing the relationship between *y* and *x* must represent these two characteristics. We now develop such a model.

Part 3: The simple linear regression model   The **simple linear regression model** relating *y* to *x* can be expressed as follows:

$$y = \beta_0 + \beta_1 x + \varepsilon$$

---

[1]www.quiznosfranchises.com/top-food-franchise-faqs.

FIGURE 13.2   The Simple Linear Regression Model Relating Yearly Revenue (*y*) to Population (*x*)

This model says that the values of *y* can be represented by a *mean level* ($\mu_y = \beta_0 + \beta_1 x$) that changes in a straight line fashion as *x* changes, combined with random fluctuations (described by the error term ε) that cause the values of *y* to deviate from the mean level. Here:

1   The **mean level** $\mu_y = \beta_0 + \beta_1 x$ is the mean yearly revenue corresponding to a particular population size *x*. That is, noting that different Tasty Sub restaurants could potentially be built near different populations of the same size *x*, the mean level $\mu_y = \beta_0 + \beta_1 x$ is the mean of the yearly revenues that would be obtained by all such restaurants. In addition, because $\mu_y = \beta_0 + \beta_1 x$ is the equation of a straight line, the mean yearly revenues that correspond to increasing values of the population size *x* lie on a straight line. For example, Table 13.1 tells us that 32,300 residents live near restaurant 3 and 45,100 residents live near restaurant 6. It follows that the mean yearly revenue for all Tasty Sub restaurants that could potentially be built near populations of 32,300 residents is $\beta_0 + \beta_1 (32.3)$. Similarly, the mean yearly revenue for all Tasty Sub restaurants that could potentially be built near populations of 45,100 residents is $\beta_0 + \beta_1 (45.1)$. Figure 13.2 depicts these two mean yearly revenues as triangles that lie on the straight line $\mu_y = \beta_0 + \beta_1 x$, which we call the **line of means.** The unknown parameters β_0 and β_1 are the **y-intercept** and the **slope** of the line of means. When we estimate β_0 and β_1 in the next subsection, we will be able to estimate mean yearly revenue μ_y on the basis of the population size *x*.

2   The **y-intercept** β_0 of the line of means can be understood by considering Figure 13.2. As illustrated in this figure, the y-intercept β_0 is the mean yearly revenue for all Tasty Sub restaurants that could potentially be built near populations of zero residents. However, since it is unlikely that a Tasty Sub restaurant would be built near a population of zero residents, this interpretation of β_0 is of dubious practical value. There are many regression situations where the y-intercept β_0 lacks a practical interpretation. In spite of this, statisticians have found that β_0 is almost always an important component of the line of means and thus of the simple linear regression model.

3   The **slope** β_1 of the line of means can also be understood by considering Figure 13.2. As illustrated in this figure, the slope β_1 is the change in mean yearly revenue that is associated with a one-unit increase (that is, a 1,000 resident increase) in the population size *x*.

4   The **error term** ε of the simple linear regression model accounts for any factors affecting yearly revenue other than the population size *x*. Such factors would include the amount of

F I G U R E   1 3 . 3   **The Simple Linear Regression Model (Here the Slope β_1 Is Positive)**

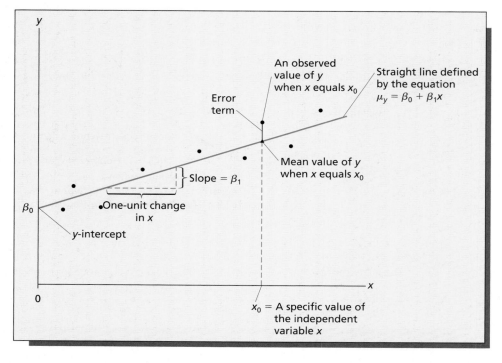

business and shopping near a restaurant and the skill of the owner as an operator of the restaurant. For example, Figure 13.2 shows that the error term for restaurant 3 is positive. Therefore, the observed yearly revenue $y = 767.2$ for restaurant 3 is above the corresponding mean yearly revenue for all restaurants that have $x = 32.3$. As another example, Figure 13.2 also shows that the error term for restaurant 6 is negative. Therefore, the observed yearly revenue $y = 810.5$ for restaurant 6 is below the corresponding mean yearly revenue for all restaurants that have $x = 45.1$. Of course, since we do not know the true values of β_0 and β_1, the relative positions of the quantities pictured in Figure 13.2 are only hypothetical.

With the Tasty Sub Shop example as background, we are ready to define the **simple linear regression model relating the dependent variable y to the independent variable x.** We suppose that we have gathered n observations—each observation consists of an observed value of x and its corresponding value of y. Then:

The Simple Linear Regression Model

The **simple linear (or straight line) regression model** is: $y = \beta_0 + \beta_1 x + \varepsilon$
Here

1 $\mu_y = \beta_0 + \beta_1 x$ is the **mean value** of the dependent variable y when the value of the independent variable is x.

2 β_0 is the **y-intercept.** β_0 is the mean value of y when x equals zero.

3 β_1 is the **slope.** β_1 is the change (amount of increase or decrease) in the mean value of y

associated with a one-unit increase in x. If β_1 is positive, the mean value of y increases as x increases. If β_1 is negative, the mean value of y decreases as x increases.

4 ε is an **error term** that describes the effects on y of all factors other than the value of the independent variable x.

This model is illustrated in Figure 13.3 (note that x_0 in this figure denotes a specific value of the independent variable x). The y-intercept β_0 and the slope β_1 are called **regression parameters.**

FIGURE 13.4 **An Estimated Regression Line Drawn through the Tasty Sub Shop Revenue Data**

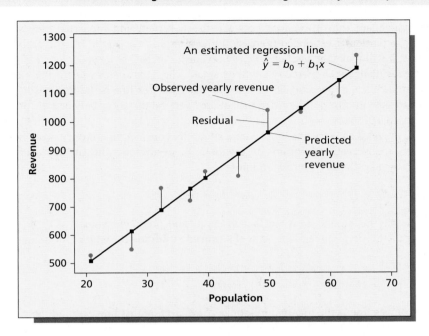

In addition, we have interpreted the slope β_1 to be the change in the mean value of y associated with a one-unit increase in x. We sometimes refer to this change as *the effect of the independent variable x on the dependent variable y*. However, we cannot prove that a *change in an independent variable causes a change in the dependent variable*. Rather, regression can be used only to establish that the two variables move together and that the independent variable contributes information for predicting the dependent variable. For instance, regression analysis might be used to establish that as liquor sales have increased over the years, college professors' salaries have also increased. However, this does not prove that increases in liquor sales cause increases in college professors' salaries. Rather, both variables are influenced by a third variable—long-run growth in the national economy.

The least squares point estimates Suppose that we have gathered n observations (x_1, y_1), (x_2, y_2), ..., (x_n, y_n), where each observation consists of a value of an independent variable x and a corresponding value of a dependent variable y. Also, suppose that a scatter plot of the n observations indicates that the simple linear regression model relates y to x. In order to estimate the y-intercept β_0 and the slope β_1 of the line of means of this model, we could visually draw a line—called an **estimated regression line**—through the scatter plot. Then, we could read the y-intercept and slope off the estimated regression line and use these values as the point estimates of β_0 and β_1. Unfortunately, if different people visually drew lines through the scatter plot, their lines would probably differ from each other. What we need is the "best line" that can be drawn through the scatter plot. Although there are various definitions of what this best line is, one of the most useful best lines is the *least squares line*.

To understand the least squares line, we let

$$\hat{y} = b_0 + b_1 x$$

LO2 Find the least squares point estimates of the slope and *y*-intercept.

denote the general equation of an estimated regression line drawn through a scatter plot. Here, since we will use this line to predict y on the basis of x, we call $\hat{y}$ *the predicted value of y* when the value of the independent variable is x. In addition, b_0 is the y-intercept and b_1 is the slope of the estimated regression line. When we determine numerical values for b_0 and b_1, these values will be the point estimates of the y-intercept β_0 and the slope β_1 of the line of means. To explain which estimated regression line is the least squares line, we begin with the Tasty Sub Shop situation. Figure 13.4 shows an estimated regression line drawn through a scatter plot of the Tasty

Sub Shop revenue data. In this figure the red dots represent the 10 observed yearly revenues and the black squares represent the 10 predicted yearly revenues given by the estimated regression line. Furthermore, the line segments drawn between the red dots and black squares represent *residuals,* which are the differences between the observed and predicted yearly revenues. Intuitively, if a particular estimated regression line provides a good "fit" to the Tasty Sub Shop revenue data, it will make the predicted yearly revenues "close" to the observed yearly revenues, and thus the residuals given by the line will be small. The *least squares line* is the line that minimizes the sum of squared residuals. That is, the least squares line is the line positioned on the scatter plot so as to minimize the sum of the squared vertical distances between the observed and predicted yearly revenues.

To define the least squares line in a general situation, consider an arbitrary observation (x_i, y_i) in a sample of n observations. For this observation, the **predicted value of the dependent variable y** given by an estimated regression line is

$$\hat{y}_i = b_0 + b_1 x_i$$

Furthermore, the difference between the observed and predicted values of y, $y_i - \hat{y}_i$, is the **residual** for the observation, and the **sum of squared residuals** for all n observations is

$$SSE = \sum_{i=1}^{n} (y_i - \hat{y}_i)^2$$

The **least squares line** is the line that minimizes SSE. To find this line, we find the values of the y-intercept b_0 and slope b_1 that give values of $\hat{y}_i = b_0 + b_1 x_i$ that minimize SSE. These values of b_0 and b_1 are called the **least squares point estimates** of β_0 and β_1. Using calculus, it can be shown that these estimates are calculated as follows:[2]

The Least Squares Point Estimates

For the simple linear regression model:

1 The **least squares point estimate of the slope β_1** is $b_1 = \dfrac{SS_{xy}}{SS_{xx}}$ where

$$SS_{xy} = \sum (x_i - \bar{x})(y_i - \bar{y}) = \sum x_i y_i - \frac{\left(\sum x_i\right)\left(\sum y_i\right)}{n} \quad \text{and} \quad SS_{xx} = \sum (x_i - \bar{x})^2 = \sum x_i^2 - \frac{\left(\sum x_i\right)^2}{n}$$

2 The **least squares point estimate of the y-intercept β_0** is $b_0 = \bar{y} - b_1 \bar{x}$ where

$$\bar{y} = \frac{\sum y_i}{n} \quad \text{and} \quad \bar{x} = \frac{\sum x_i}{n}$$

Here n is the number of observations (an observation is an observed value of x and its corresponding value of y).

The following example illustrates how to calculate these point estimates and how to use these point estimates to estimate mean values and predict individual values of the dependent variable. Note that the quantities SS_{xy} and SS_{xx} used to calculate the least squares point estimates are also used throughout this chapter to perform other important calculations.

---

[2]In order to simplify notation, we will often drop the limits on summations in this and subsequent chapters. That is, instead of using the summation $\sum_{i=1}^{n}$ we will simply write $\sum$.

EXAMPLE 13.2 The Tasty Sub Shop Case

Part 1: Calculating the least squares point estimates   Again consider the Tasty Sub Shop problem. To compute the least squares point estimates of the regression parameters β_0 and β_1 we first calculate the following preliminary summations:

y_i	x_i	x_i^2	$x_i y_i$
527.1	20.8	$(20.8)^2 = 432.64$	$(20.8)(527.1) = 10963.68$
548.7	27.5	$(27.5)^2 = 756.25$	$(27.5)(548.7) = 15089.25$
767.2	32.3	$(32.3)^2 = 1{,}043.29$	$(32.3)(767.2) = 24780.56$
722.9	37.2	$(37.2)^2 = 1{,}383.84$	$(37.2)(722.9) = 26891.88$
826.3	39.6	$(39.6)^2 = 1{,}568.16$	$(39.6)(826.3) = 32721.48$
810.5	45.1	$(45.1)^2 = 2{,}034.01$	$(45.1)(810.5) = 36553.55$
1040.7	49.9	$(49.9)^2 = 2{,}490.01$	$(49.9)(1040.7) = 51930.93$
1033.6	55.4	$(55.4)^2 = 3{,}069.16$	$(55.4)(1033.6) = 57261.44$
1090.3	61.7	$(61.7)^2 = 3{,}806.89$	$(61.7)(1090.3) = 67271.51$
1235.8	64.6	$(64.6)^2 = 4{,}173.16$	$(64.6)(1235.8) = 79832.68$
$\sum y_i = 8603.1$	$\sum x_i = 434.1$	$\sum x_i^2 = 20{,}757.41$	$\sum x_i y_i = 403{,}296.96$

Using these summations, we calculate SS_{xy} and SS_{xx} as follows.

$$SS_{xy} = \sum x_i y_i - \frac{\left(\sum x_i\right)\left(\sum y_i\right)}{n}$$

$$= 403{,}296.96 - \frac{(434.1)(8603.1)}{10}$$

$$= 29{,}836.389$$

$$SS_{xx} = \sum x_i^2 - \frac{\left(\sum x_i\right)^2}{n}$$

$$= 20{,}757.41 - \frac{(434.1)^2}{10}$$

$$= 1913.129$$

It follows that the least squares point estimate of the slope β_1 is

$$b_1 = \frac{SS_{xy}}{SS_{xx}} = \frac{29{,}836.389}{1913.129} = 15.596$$

Furthermore, because

$$\bar{y} = \frac{\sum y_i}{n} = \frac{8603.1}{10} = 860.31 \quad \text{and} \quad \bar{x} = \frac{\sum x_i}{n} = \frac{434.1}{10} = 43.41$$

the least squares point estimate of the y-intercept β_0 is

$$b_0 = \bar{y} - b_1\bar{x} = 860.31 - (15.596)(43.41) = 183.31$$

(where we have used more decimal place accuracy than shown to obtain the result 183.31).

Since $b_1 = 15.596$, we estimate that mean yearly revenue at Tasty Sub restaurants increases by 15.596 (that is by $15,596) for each one-unit (1,000 resident) increase in the population size x. Since $b_0 = 183.31$, we estimate that mean yearly revenue for all Tasty Sub restaurants that could potentially be built near populations of zero residents is $183,310. However, since it is unlikely that a Tasty Sub restaurant would be built near a population of zero residents, this interpretation is of dubious practical value.

The least squares line

$$\hat{y} = b_0 + b_1 x = 183.31 + 15.596x$$

is sometimes called the *least squares prediction equation*. In Table 13.2 (on the next page) we summarize using this prediction equation to calculate the predicted yearly revenues and the

TABLE 13.2   Calculation of *SSE* Obtained by Using the Least Squares Point Estimates

y_i	x_i	$\hat{y}_i = 183.31 + 15.596x_i$	$y_i - \hat{y}_i$
527.1	20.8	$183.31 + 15.596(20.8) = 507.69$	19.41
548.7	27.5	$183.31 + 15.596(27.5) = 612.18$	−63.48
767.2	32.3	687.04	80.16
722.9	37.2	763.46	−40.56
826.3	39.6	800.89	25.41
810.5	45.1	886.67	−76.17
1040.7	49.9	961.53	79.17
1033.6	55.4	1047.30	−13.70
1090.3	61.7	1145.55	−55.25
1235.8	64.6	1190.78	45.02

$$SSE = \sum(y_i - \hat{y}_i)^2 = (19.41)^2 + (-63.48)^2 + \cdots + (45.02)^2 = 30,460.21$$

Note: the predictions and residuals in this table are taken from MINITAB, which uses values of b_0 and b_1 that are more precise than the rounded values we have calculated by hand. If you use the formula $\hat{y}_i = 183.31 + 15.596x_i$, your figures may differ slightly from those given here.

FIGURE 13.5   The MINITAB Output of the Least Squares Line

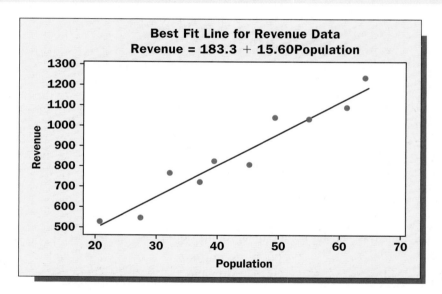

residuals for the 10 observed Tasty Sub restaurants. For example, since the population size for restaurant 1 was 20.8, the predicted yearly revenue for restaurant 1 is

$$\hat{y}_1 = 183.31 + 15.596(20.8) = 507.69$$

It follows, since the observed yearly revenue for restaurant 1 was $y_1 = 527.1$, that the residual for restaurant 1 is

$$y_1 - \hat{y}_1 = 527.1 - 507.69 = 19.41$$

If we consider all of the residuals in Table 13.2 and add their squared values, we find that *SSE*, the sum of squared residuals, is 30,460.21. This *SSE* value will be used throughout this chapter. Figure 13.5 gives the MINITAB output of the least squares line. Note that this output gives (within rounding) the least squares estimates $b_0 = 183.3$ and $b_1 = 15.60$. In general, we will rely on Excel and MINITAB to compute the least squares estimates (and to perform many other regression calculations).

Part 2: Estimating a mean yearly revenue and predicting an individual yearly revenue   We define the **experimental region** to be the range of the previously observed population sizes. Referring to Table 13.2, we see that the experimental region consists of the range

FIGURE 13.6   Point Estimation and Point Prediction, and the Danger of Extrapolation

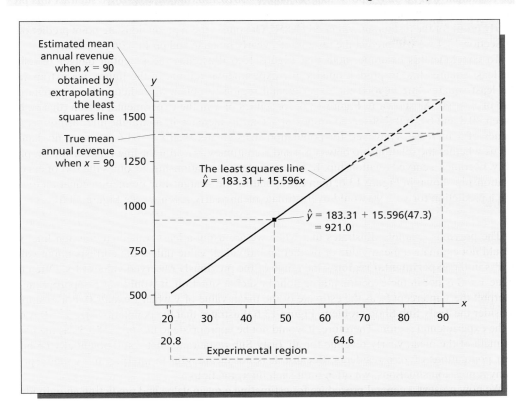

of population sizes from 20.8 to 64.6. The simple linear regression model relates yearly revenue y to population size x for values of x that are in the experimental region. For such values of x, the least squares line is the estimate of the line of means. It follows that the point on the least squares line corresponding to a population size of x

$$\hat{y} = b_0 + b_1 x$$

is the point estimate of $\beta_0 + \beta_1 x$, the mean yearly revenue for all Tasty Sub restaurants that could potentially be built near populations of size x. In addition, we predict the error term ε to be 0. Therefore, $\hat{y}$ is also the *point prediction* of an *individual value* $y = \beta_0 + \beta_1 x + \varepsilon$, which is the yearly revenue for a single (individual) Tasty Sub restaurant that is built near a population of size x. Note that the reason we predict the error term ε to be zero is that, because of several *regression assumptions* to be discussed in the next section, ε has a 50 percent chance of being positive and a 50 percent chance of being negative.

For example, suppose that one of the business entrepreneur's potential restaurant sites is near a population of 47,300 residents. Because $x = 47.3$ is in the experimental region,

$$\hat{y} = 183.31 + 15.596(47.3)$$
$$= 921.0 \text{ (that is, \$921,000)}$$

is

1   The **point estimate** of the mean yearly revenue for all Tasty Sub restaurants that could potentially be built near populations of 47,300 residents.

2   The **point prediction** of the yearly revenue for a single Tasty Sub restaurant that is built near a population of 47,300 residents.

Figure 13.6 illustrates $\hat{y} = 921.0$ as a square on the least squares line. Moreover, suppose that the yearly rent and other fixed costs for the entrepreneur's potential restaurant will be \$257,550 and that (according to Tasty Sub corporate headquarters) the yearly food and other variable costs for the restaurant will be 60 percent of the yearly revenue. Because we predict that the yearly revenue

Service Call	Number of Copiers Serviced, x	Number of Minutes Required, y
1	4	109
2	2	58
3	5	138
4	7	189
5	1	37
6	3	82
7	4	103
8	5	134
9	2	68
10	4	112
11	6	154

DS SrvcTime

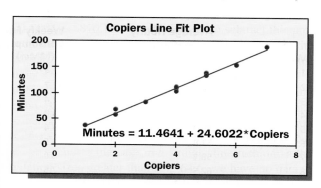

a Find the least squares point estimates b_0 and b_1 on the computer output and report their values. Interpret b_0 and b_1. Does the interpretation of b_0 make practical sense?

b Use the least squares line to compute a point estimate of the mean time to service four copiers and a point prediction of the time to service four copiers on a single call.

13.6   THE FRESH DETERGENT CASE   DS Fresh

Enterprise Industries produces Fresh, a brand of liquid laundry detergent. In order to study the relationship between price and demand for the large bottle of Fresh, the company has gathered data concerning demand for Fresh over the last 30 sales periods (each sales period is four weeks). Here, for each sales period,

   y = demand for the large bottle of Fresh (in hundreds of thousands of bottles) in the sales period, and

   x = the difference between the average industry price (in dollars) of competitors' similar detergents and the price (in dollars) of Fresh as offered by Enterprise Industries in the sales period.

The data and MINITAB output from fitting a least squares regression line to the data follow below.

Fresh Detergent Demand Data

Sales Period	y	x		Sales Period	y	x
1	7.38	−.05		24	8.50	.10
2	8.51	.25		25	8.75	.50
3	9.52	.60		26	9.21	.60
4	7.50	0		27	8.27	−.05
5	9.33	.25		28	7.67	0
6	8.28	.20		29	7.93	.05
7	8.75	.15		30	9.26	.55
8	7.87	.05				
9	7.10	−.15				
10	8.00	.15				
11	7.89	.20				
12	8.15	.10				
13	9.10	.40				
14	8.86	.45				
15	8.90	.35				
16	8.87	.30				
17	9.26	.50				
18	9.00	.50				
19	8.75	.40				
20	7.95	−.05				
21	7.65	−.05				
22	7.27	−.10				
23	8.00	.20				

DS Fresh

a Find the least squares point estimates b_0 and b_1 on the computer output and report their values. Interpret b_0 and b_1. Does the interpretation of b_0 make practical sense?

b Use the least squares line to compute a point estimate of the mean demand in all sales periods when the price difference is .10 and a point prediction of the actual demand in an individual sales period when the price difference is .10.

13.7   THE DIRECT LABOR COST CASE   Ⓓ DirLab

An accountant wishes to predict direct labor cost (y) on the basis of the batch size (x) of a product produced in a job shop. Data for 12 production runs are given in the table below, along with the Excel output from fitting a least squares regression line to the data.

Direct Labor Cost Data   Ⓓ DirLab

Direct Labor Cost, y ($100s)	Batch Size, x
71	5
663	62
381	35
138	12
861	83
145	14
493	46
548	52
251	23
1024	100
435	41
772	75

Batch Size Line Fit Plot

LaborCost = 18.488 + 10.146*BSize

a By using the formulas illustrated in Example 13.2 (see page 497) and the data provided, verify that (within rounding) $b_0 = 18.488$ and $b_1 = 10.146$, as shown on the Excel output.

b Interpret the meanings of b_0 and b_1. Does the interpretation of b_0 make practical sense?

c Write the least squares prediction equation.

d Use the least squares line to obtain a point estimate of the mean direct labor cost for all batches of size 60 and a point prediction of the direct labor cost for an individual batch of size 60.

13.8   THE REAL ESTATE SALES PRICE CASE   Ⓓ RealEst

A real estate agency collects data concerning y = the sales price of a house (in thousands of dollars), and x = the home size (in hundreds of square feet). The data are given in the table below. The MINITAB output from fitting a least squares regression line to the data is on the next page.

Real Estate Sales Price Data   Ⓓ RealEst

Sales Price (y)	Home Size (x)	Sales Price (y)	Home Size (x)
180	23	165.9	21
98.1	11	193.5	24
173.1	20	127.8	13
136.5	17	163.5	19
141	15	172.5	25

Source: Reprinted with permission from *The Real Estate Appraiser and Analyst,* Spring 1986 issue. Copyright 1986 by the Appraisal Institute, Chicago, Illinois.

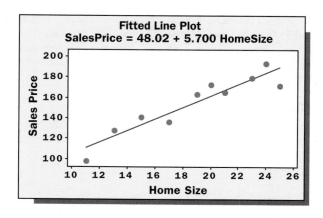

Fitted Line Plot
SalesPrice = 48.02 + 5.700 HomeSize

a By using the formulas illustrated in Example 13.2 (see page 497) and the data provided, verify that (within rounding) $b_0 = 48.02$ and $b_1 = 5.700$, as shown on the MINITAB output.
b Interpret the meanings of b_0 and b_1. Does the interpretation of b_0 make practical sense?
c Write the least squares prediction equation.
d Use the least squares line to obtain a point estimate of the mean sales price of all houses having 2,000 square feet and a point prediction of the sales price of an individual house having 2,000 square feet.

LO3 Describe the assumptions behind simple linear regression and calculate the standard error.

13.2 Model Assumptions and the Standard Error ● ● ●

Model assumptions   In order to perform hypothesis tests and set up various types of intervals when using the simple linear regression model

$$y = \beta_0 + \beta_1 x + \varepsilon$$

we need to make certain assumptions about the error term ε. At any given value of x, there is a population of error term values that could potentially occur. These error term values describe the different potential effects on y of all factors other than the value of x. Therefore, these error term values explain the variation in the y values that could be observed when the independent variable is x. Our statement of the simple linear regression model assumes that μ_y, the mean of the population of all y values that could be observed when the independent variable is x, is $\beta_0 + \beta_1 x$. This model also implies that $\varepsilon = y - (\beta_0 + \beta_1 x)$, so this is equivalent to assuming that the mean of the corresponding population of potential error term values is 0. In total, we make four assumptions (called the **regression assumptions**) about the simple linear regression model. These assumptions can be stated in terms of potential y values or, equivalently, in terms of potential error term values. Following tradition, we begin by stating these assumptions in terms of potential error term values:

The Regression Assumptions

1 At any given value of x, the population of potential error term values has a **mean equal to 0**.

2 Constant Variance Assumption
At any given value of x, the population of potential error term values has a variance that does not depend on the value of x. That is, the different populations of potential error term values corresponding to different values of x have **equal variances**. We denote the **constant variance as σ^2**.

3 Normality Assumption
At any given value of x, the population of potential error term values has a **normal distribution**.

4 Independence Assumption
Any one value of the error term ε is **statistically independent** of any other value of ε. That is, the value of the error term ε corresponding to an observed value of y is statistically independent of the value of the error term corresponding to any other observed value of y.

FIGURE 13.7　An Illustration of the Model Assumptions

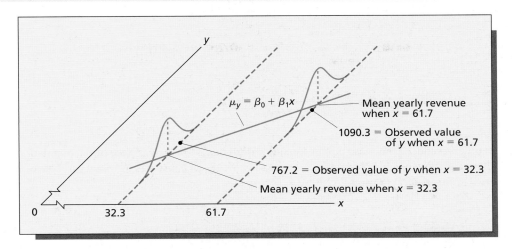

Taken together, the first three assumptions say that, at any given value of x, the population of potential error term values is **normally distributed** with **mean zero** and a **variance σ^2 that does not depend on the value of x.** Because the potential error term values cause the variation in the potential y values, these assumptions imply that the population of all y values that could be observed when the independent variable is x is **normally distributed** with **mean $\beta_0 + \beta_1 x$** and **a variance σ^2 that does not depend on x.** These three assumptions are illustrated in Figure 13.7 in the context of the Tasty Sub Shop problem. Specifically, this figure depicts the populations of yearly revenues corresponding to two values of the population size x—32.3 and 61.7. Note that these populations are shown to be normally distributed with different means (each of which is on the line of means) and with the same variance (or spread).

The independence assumption is most likely to be violated when time series data are being utilized in a regression study. For example, the fuel consumption data in Exercise 13.3 are time series data. Intuitively, the independence assumption says that there is no pattern of positive error terms being followed (in time) by other positive error terms, and there is no pattern of positive error terms being followed by negative error terms. That is, there is no pattern of higher-than-average y values being followed by other higher-than-average y values, and there is no pattern of higher-than-average y values being followed by lower-than-average y values.

It is important to point out that the regression assumptions very seldom, if ever, hold exactly in any practical regression problem. However, it has been found that regression results are not extremely sensitive to mild departures from these assumptions. In practice, only pronounced departures from these assumptions require attention. In Section 13.9 we show how to check the regression assumptions. Prior to doing this, we will suppose that the assumptions are valid in our examples.

In Section 13.1 we stated that, when we predict an individual value of the dependent variable, we predict the error term to be 0. To see why we do this, note that the regression assumptions state that, at any given value of the independent variable, the population of all error term values that can potentially occur is normally distributed with a mean equal to 0. Since we also assume that successive error terms (observed over time) are statistically independent, each error term has a 50 percent chance of being positive and a 50 percent chance of being negative. Therefore, it is reasonable to predict any particular error term value to be 0.

The mean square error and the standard error　To present statistical inference formulas in later sections, we need to be able to compute point estimates of σ^2 and σ, the constant variance and standard deviation of the error term populations. The point estimate of σ^2 is called the **mean square error** and the point estimate of σ is called the **standard error.** In the following box, we show how to compute these estimates:

The Mean Square Error and the Standard Error

I f the regression assumptions are satisfied and *SSE* is the sum of squared residuals:

1 The point estimate of σ^2 is the **mean square error**

$$s^2 = \frac{SSE}{n - 2}$$

2 The point estimate of σ is the **standard error**

$$s = \sqrt{\frac{SSE}{n - 2}}$$

In order to understand these point estimates, recall that σ^2 is the variance of the population of *y* values (for a given value of *x*) around the mean value μ_y. Because $\hat{y}$ is the point estimate of this mean, it seems natural to use

$$SSE = \sum (y_i - \hat{y}_i)^2$$

to help construct a point estimate of σ^2. We divide *SSE* by $n - 2$ because it can be proven that doing so makes the resulting s^2 an unbiased point estimate of σ^2. Here we call $n - 2$ the **number of degrees of freedom** associated with *SSE*.

EXAMPLE 13.3 The Tasty Sub Shop Case

Consider the Tasty Sub Shop situation, and recall that in Table 13.2 (page 498) we have calculated the sum of squared residuals to be $SSE = 30{,}460.21$. It follows, because we have observed $n = 10$ yearly revenues, that the point estimate of σ^2 is the mean square error

$$s^2 = \frac{SSE}{n - 2} = \frac{30{,}460.21}{10 - 2} = 3807.526$$

This implies that the point estimate of σ is the standard error

$$s = \sqrt{s^2} = \sqrt{3807.526} = 61.7052$$

To conclude this section, note that in optional Section 13.10 we present a shortcut formula for calculating *SSE*. The reader may study Section 13.10 now or at any later point.

Exercises for Section 13.2

connect

CONCEPTS

13.9   What four assumptions do we make about the simple linear regression model?

13.10 What is estimated by the mean square error, and what is estimated by the standard error?

METHODS AND APPLICATIONS

13.11 THE FUEL CONSUMPTION CASE   DS FuelCon1

When a least squares line is fit to the 8 observations in the fuel consumption data, we obtain $SSE = 2.568$. Calculate s^2 and s.

13.12 THE STARTING SALARY CASE   DS StartSal

When a least squares line is fit to the 7 observations in the starting salary data, we obtain $SSE = 1.438$. Calculate s^2 and s.

13.13 THE SERVICE TIME CASE   DS SrvcTime

When a least squares line is fit to the 11 observations in the service time data, we obtain $SSE = 191.7017$. Calculate s^2 and s.

13.14 **THE FRESH DETERGENT CASE**   DS Fresh

When a least squares line is fit to the 30 observations in the Fresh detergent data, we obtain $SSE = 2.806$. Calculate s^2 and s.

13.15 **THE DIRECT LABOR COST CASE**   DS DirLab

When a least squares line is fit to the 12 observations in the labor cost data, we obtain $SSE = 746.7624$. Calculate s^2 and s.

13.16 **THE REAL ESTATE SALES PRICE CASE**   DS RealEst

When a least squares line is fit to the 10 observations in the real estate sales price data, we obtain $SSE = 896.8$. Calculate s^2 and s.

13.17 Ten sales regions of equal sales potential for a company were randomly selected. The advertising expenditures (in units of \$10,000) in these 10 sales regions were purposely set during July of last year at, respectively, 5, 6, 7, 8, 9, 10, 11, 12, 13 and 14. The sales volumes (in units of \$10,000) were then recorded for the 10 sales regions and found to be, respectively, 89, 87, 98, 110, 103, 114, 116, 110, 126, and 130. Assuming that the simple linear regression model is appropriate, it can be shown that $b_0 = 66.2121$, $b_1 = 4.4303$, and $SSE = 222.8242$. Calculate s^2 and s.   DS SalesPlot

13.3 Testing the Significance of the Slope and *y*-Intercept ● ● ●

LO4 Test the significance of the slope and *y*-intercept.

Testing the significance of the slope A simple linear regression model is not likely to be useful unless there is a **significant relationship between *y* and *x*.** In order to judge the significance of the relationship between *y* and *x*, we test the null hypothesis

$$H_0: \beta_1 = 0$$

which says that there is no change in the mean value of *y* associated with an increase in *x*, versus the alternative hypothesis

$$H_a: \beta_1 \neq 0$$

which says that there is a (positive or negative) change in the mean value of *y* associated with an increase in *x*. It would be reasonable to conclude that *x* is significantly related to *y* if we can be quite certain that we should reject H_0 in favor of H_a.

In order to test these hypotheses, recall that we compute the least squares point estimate b_1 of the true slope β_1 by using a sample of *n* observed values of the dependent variable *y*. Different samples of *n* observed *y* values would yield different values of the least squares point estimate b_1. It can be shown that, if the regression assumptions hold, then the population of all possible values of b_1 is normally distributed with a mean of β_1 and with a standard deviation of

$$\sigma_{b_1} = \frac{\sigma}{\sqrt{SS_{xx}}}$$

The standard error *s* is the point estimate of σ, so it follows that a point estimate of σ_{b_1} is

$$s_{b_1} = \frac{s}{\sqrt{SS_{xx}}}$$

which is called the **standard error of the estimate b_1.** Furthermore, if the regression assumptions hold, then the population of all values of

$$\frac{b_1 - \beta_1}{s_{b_1}}$$

has a *t* distribution with $n - 2$ degrees of freedom. It follows that, if the null hypothesis $H_0: \beta_1 = 0$ is true, then the population of all possible values of the test statistic

$$t = \frac{b_1}{s_{b_1}}$$

has a *t* distribution with $n - 2$ degrees of freedom. Therefore, we can test the significance of the regression relationship as follows:

A Confidence Interval for the Slope

f the regression assumptions hold, a **100(1 − α) percent confidence interval for the true slope β_1 is** **[$b_1 \pm t_{\alpha/2} s_{b_1}$].** Here $t_{\alpha/2}$ is based on $n - 2$ degrees of freedom.

EXAMPLE 13.5 The Tasty Sub Shop Case

The Excel and MINITAB outputs in Figure 13.8 tell us that $b_1 = 15.596$ and $s_{b_1} = 1.411$. Thus, for instance, because $t_{.025}$ based on $n - 2 = 10 - 2 = 8$ degrees of freedom equals 2.306, a 95 percent confidence interval for β_1 is

$$[b_1 \pm t_{.025} s_{b_1}] = [15.596 \pm 2.306(1.411)]$$

$$= [12.342, 18.849]$$

(where we have used more decimal place accuracy than shown to obtain the final result). This interval says we are 95 percent confident that, if the population size increases by one thousand residents, then mean yearly revenue will increase by at least $12,342 and by at most $18,849. Also, because the 95 percent confidence interval for β_1 does not contain 0, we can reject H_0: $\beta_1 = 0$ in favor of H_a: $\beta_1 \neq 0$ at level of significance .05. Note that the 95 percent confidence interval for β_1 is given on the Excel output but not on the MINITAB output (see Figure 13.8).

Testing the significance of the y-intercept   We can also test the significance of the y-intercept β_0. We do this by testing the null hypothesis H_0: $\beta_0 = 0$ versus the alternative hypothesis H_a: $\beta_0 \neq 0$. **If we can reject H_0 in favor of H_a by setting the probability of a Type I error equal to α, we conclude that the intercept β_0 is significant at the α level.** To carry out the hypothesis test, we use the test statistic

$$t = \frac{b_0}{s_{b_0}} \quad \text{where} \quad s_{b_0} = s\sqrt{\frac{1}{n} + \frac{\bar{x}^2}{SS_{xx}}}$$

Here the critical value and p-value conditions for rejecting H_0 are the same as those given previously for testing the significance of the slope, except that t is calculated as b_0/s_{b_0}. For example, if we consider the Tasty Sub Shop problem and the Excel and MINITAB outputs in Figure 13.8, we see that $b_0 = 183.31$, $s_{b_0} = 64.27$, $t = 2.85$, and p-value = .021. Because $t = 2.85 > t_{.025} = 2.306$ and p-value < .05, we can reject H_0: $\beta_0 = 0$ in favor of H_a: $\beta_0 \neq 0$ at the .05 level of significance. This provides strong evidence that the y-intercept β_0 of the line of means does not equal 0 and thus is significant. Therefore, we should include β_0 in the Tasty Sub Shop revenue model.

In general, if we fail to conclude that the intercept is significant at a level of significance of .05, it might be reasonable to drop the y-intercept from the model. However, it is common practice to include the y-intercept whether or not H_0: $\beta_0 = 0$ is rejected. In fact, experience suggests that it is definitely safest, when in doubt, to include the intercept β_0.

Exercises for Section 13.3

CONCEPTS

connect

13.18   What do we conclude if we can reject H_0: $\beta_1 = 0$ in favor of H_a: $\beta_1 \neq 0$ by setting
   a α equal to .05?   **b** α equal to .01?

13.19   Give an example of a practical application of the confidence interval for β_1.

METHODS AND APPLICATIONS

In Exercises 13.20 through 13.25, we refer to Excel and MINITAB outputs of simple linear regression analyses of the data sets related to the six case studies introduced in the exercises for Section 13.1. Using the appropriate output for each case study,
a Find the least squares point estimates b_0 and b_1 of β_0 and β_1 on the output and report their values.
b Find SSE and s on the computer output and report their values.

c   Find s_{b_1} and the t statistic for testing the significance of the slope on the output and report their values. Show (within rounding) how t has been calculated by using b_1 and s_{b_1} from the computer output.

d   Using the t statistic and appropriate critical value, test H_0: $\beta_1 = 0$ versus H_a: $\beta_1 \neq 0$ by setting α equal to .05. Is the slope (regression relationship) significant at the .05 level?

e   Using the t statistic and appropriate critical value, test H_0: $\beta_1 = 0$ versus H_a: $\beta_1 \neq 0$ by setting α equal to .01. Is the slope (regression relationship) significant at the .01 level?

f   Find the p-value for testing H_0: $\beta_1 = 0$ versus H_a: $\beta_1 \neq 0$ on the output and report its value. Using the p-value, determine whether we can reject H_0 by setting α equal to .10, .05, .01, and .001. How much evidence is there that the slope (regression relationship) is significant?

g   Calculate the 95 percent confidence interval for β_1 using numbers on the output. Interpret the interval.

h   Calculate the 99 percent confidence interval for β_1 using numbers on the output.

i   Find s_{b_0} and the t statistic for testing the significance of the y intercept on the output and report their values. Show (within rounding) how t has been calculated by using b_0 and s_{b_0} from the computer output.

j   Find the p-value for testing H_0: $\beta_0 = 0$ versus H_a: $\beta_0 \neq 0$ on the computer output and report its value. Using the p-value, determine whether we can reject H_0 by setting α equal to .10, .05, .01, and .001. What do you conclude about the significance of the y intercept?

k   Using the data set and s from the computer output, hand calculate (within rounding) SS_{xx}, s_{b_0}, and s_{b_1}.

13.20   **THE FUEL CONSUMPTION CASE**   DS FuelCon1

The Excel and MINITAB outputs of a simple linear regression analysis of the data set for this case (see Exercise 13.3 on page 500) are given in Figures 13.9 and 13.10. Labeled Excel and MINITAB outputs are on page 509 in Figure 13.8. Use whichever package is taught in your class.

13.21   **THE STARTING SALARY CASE**   DS StartSal

The MINITAB output of a simple linear regression analysis of the data set for this case (see Exercise 13.4 on page 501) is given in Figure 13.11. Recall that a labeled MINITAB regression output is on page 509.

FIGURE 13.9   **Excel Output of a Simple Linear Regression Analysis of the Fuel Consumption Data**

Regression Statistics

Multiple R	0.9484
R Square	0.8995
Adjusted R Square	0.8827
Standard Error	0.6542
Observations	8

ANOVA	df	SS	MS	F	Significance F
Regression	1	22.9808	22.9808	53.6949	0.0003
Residual	6	2.5679	0.4280		
Total	7	25.5488			

	Coefficients	Standard Error	t Stat	P-value	Lower 95%	Upper 95%
Intercept	15.8379	0.8018	19.7535	1.09E-06	13.8760	17.7997
TEMP	−0.1279	0.0175	−7.3277	0.0003	−0.1706	−0.0852

FIGURE 13.10   **MINITAB Output of a Simple Linear Regression Analysis of the Fuel Consumption Data**

```
The regression equation is
FuelCons = 15.8 - 0.128 Temp

Predictor         Coef        SE Coef           T          P
Constant       15.8379         0.8018       19.75      0.000
Temp          -0.12792        0.01746       -7.33      0.000

S = 0.654209       R-Sq = 89.9%        R-Sq(adj) = 88.3%

Analysis of Variance
Source            DF           SS          MS          F          P
Regression         1       22.981      22.981      53.69      0.000
Residual Error     6        2.568       0.428
Total              7       25.549

Values of Predictors for New Obs      Predicted Values for New Observations
New Obs   Temp                        New Obs     Fit    SE Fit       95% CI              95% PI
     1    40.0                              1  10.721     0.241  (10.130, 11.312)   (9.015, 12.427)
```

FIGURE 13.11   **MINITAB Output of a Simple Linear Regression Analysis of the Starting Salary Data**

```
The regression equation is
StartSal = 14.8 + 5.71 GPA

Predictor     Coef   SE Coef      T      P
Constant    14.816    1.235   12.00  0.000
GPA         5.7066   0.3953   14.44  0.000

S = 0.536321   R-Sq = 97.7%   R-Sq(adj) = 97.2%

Analysis of Variance
Source          DF       SS       MS       F      P
Regression       1   59.942   59.942  208.39  0.000
Residual Error   5    1.438    0.288
Total            6   61.380

Values of Predictors for New Obs     Predicted Values for New Observations
New Obs   GPA                        New Obs      Fit   SE Fit        95% CI              95% PI
      1  3.25                              1   33.362    0.213  (32.813, 33.911)   (31.878, 34.846)
```

FIGURE 13.12   **Excel Output of a Simple Linear Regression Analysis of the Service Time Data**

Regression Statistics

Multiple R	0.9952
R Square	0.9905
Adjusted R Square	0.9894
Standard Error	4.6152
Observations	11

ANOVA	df	SS	MS	F	Significance F
Regression	1	19918.8438	19918.844	935.149	2.094E-10
Residual	9	191.7017	21.300184		
Total	10	20110.5455			

	Coefficients	Standard Error	t Stat	P-value	Lower 95%	Upper 95%
Intercept	11.4641	3.4390	3.3335	0.0087	3.6845	19.2437
Copiers	24.6022	0.8045	30.5802	2.09E-10	22.7823	26.4221

13.22   THE SERVICE TIME CASE   DS SrvcTime

The Excel output of a simple linear regression analysis of the data set for this case (see Exercise 13.5 on pages 501 and 502) is given in Figure 13.12. Recall that a labeled Excel regression output is on page 509.

13.23   THE FRESH DETERGENT CASE   DS Fresh

The MINITAB output of a simple linear regression analysis of the data set for this case (see Exercise 13.6 on page 502) is given in Figure 13.13. Recall that a labeled MINITAB regression output is on page 509.

13.24   THE DIRECT LABOR COST CASE   DS DirLab

The Excel output of a simple linear regression analysis of the data set for this case (see Exercise 13.7 on page 503) is given in Figure 13.14. Recall that a labeled Excel regression output is on page 509.

13.25   THE REAL ESTATE SALES PRICE CASE   DS RealEst

The MINITAB output of a simple linear regression analysis of the data set for this case (see Exercise 13.8 on page 503) is given in Figure 13.15. Recall that a labeled MINITAB regression output is on page 509.

13.26   Find and interpret a 95 percent confidence interval for the slope β_1 of the simple linear regression model describing the sales volume data in Exercise 13.17 (page 507).   DS SalesPlot

FIGURE 13.13   **MINITAB Output of a Simple Linear Regression Analysis of the Fresh Detergent Demand Data**

```
The regression equation is
Demand = 7.81 + 2.67 PriceDif

Predictor      Coef    SE Coef       T      P
Constant    7.81409    0.07988   97.82  0.000
PriceDif     2.6652     0.2585   10.31  0.000

S = 0.316561   R-Sq = 79.2%   R-Sq(adj) = 78.4%

Analysis of Variance
Source           DF       SS       MS        F      P
Regression        1   10.653   10.653   106.30  0.000
Residual Error   28    2.806    0.100
Total            29   13.459

Values of Predictors for New Obs    Predicted Values for New Observations
New Obs  PriceDif                   New Obs     Fit  SE Fit      95% CI            95% PI
      1     0.100                         1  8.0806  0.0648  (7.9479, 8.2133)  (7.4187, 8.7425)
      2     0.250                         2  8.4804  0.0586  (8.3604, 8.6004)  (7.8209, 9.1398)
```

FIGURE 13.14   **Excel Output of a Simple Linear Regression Analysis of the Direct Labor Cost Data**

Regression Statistics						
Multiple R	0.9996					
R Square	0.9993					
Adjusted R Square	0.9992					
Standard Error	8.6415					
Observations	12					

ANOVA	df	SS	MS	F	Significance F	
Regression	1	1024592.9043	1024592.9043	13720.4677	5.04E-17	
Residual	10	746.7624	74.6762			
Total	11	1025339.6667				

	Coefficients	Standard Error	t Stat	P-value	Lower 95%	Upper 95%
Intercept	18.4875	4.6766	3.9532	0.0027	8.0674	28.9076
BatchSize (x)	10.1463	0.0866	117.1344	5.04E-17	9.9533	10.3393

FIGURE 13.15   **MINITAB Output of a Simple Linear Regression Analysis of the Real Estate Sales Price Data**

```
The regression equation is
SPrice = 48.0 + 5.70 HomeSize

Predictor     Coef   SE Coef      T      P
Constant     48.02     14.41   3.33  0.010
HomeSize    5.7003    0.7457   7.64  0.000

S = 10.5880      R-Sq = 88.0%      R-Sq(adj) = 86.5%

Analysis of Variance
Source           DF       SS       MS       F      P
Regression        1   6550.7   6550.7   58.43  0.000
Residual Error    8    896.8    112.1
Total             9   7447.5

Values of Predictors for New Obs    Predicted Values for New Observations
New Obs  HomeSize                   New Obs     Fit  SE Fit        95% CI              95% PI
      1      20.0                         1  162.03    3.47  (154.04, 170.02)  (136.34, 187.72)
```

FIGURE 13.16   **Excel Output of a Simple Linear Regression Analysis of the Fast-Food Restaurant Rating Data**

Regression Statistics

Multiple R	0.9873
R Square	0.9747
Adjusted R Square	0.9684
Standard Error	0.1833
Observations	6

ANOVA	df	SS	MS	F	Significance F
Regression	1	5.1817	5.1817	154.2792	0.0002
Residual	4	0.1343	0.0336		
Total	5	5.3160			

	Coefficients	Standard Error	t Stat	P-value	Lower 95%	Upper 95%
Intercept	−0.1602	0.3029	−0.5289	0.6248	−1.0011	0.6807
MeanTaste (x)	1.2731	0.1025	12.4209	0.0002	0.9885	1.5577

13.27   THE FAST-FOOD RESTAURANT RATING CASE   📀 FastFood

In the early 1990s researchers at The Ohio State University studied consumer ratings of six fast-food restaurants: Borden Burger, Hardee's, Burger King, McDonald's, Wendy's, and White Castle. Each of 406 randomly selected individuals gave each restaurant a rating of 1, 2, 3, 4, 5, or 6 on the basis of taste, and then ranked the restaurants from 1 through 6 on the basis of overall preference. In each case, 1 is the best rating and 6 the worst. The mean ratings given by the 406 individuals are given in the following table:

Restaurant	Mean Taste	Mean Preference
Borden Burger	3.5659	4.2552
Hardee's	3.329	4.0911
Burger King	2.4231	3.0052
McDonald's	2.0895	2.2429
Wendy's	1.9661	2.5351
White Castle	3.8061	4.7812

Figure 13.16 gives the Excel output of a simple linear regression analysis of this data. Here, mean preference is the dependent variable and mean taste is the independent variable. Recall that a labeled Excel regression output is given on page 509.

a   Find the least squares point estimate b_1 of β_1 on the computer output. Report and interpret this estimate.

b   Find the 95 percent confidence interval for β_1 on the output. Report and interpret the interval.

LO5   Calculate and interpret a confidence interval for a mean value and a prediction interval for an individual value.

13.4 Confidence and Prediction Intervals ● ● ●

If the regression relationship between y and x is significant, then

$$\hat{y} = b_0 + b_1 x_0$$

is the **point estimate of the mean value of y** when the value of the independent variable x is x_0. We have also seen that $\hat{y}$ is the **point prediction of an individual value of y** when the value of the independent variable x is x_0. In this section we will assess the accuracy of $\hat{y}$ as both a point estimate and a point prediction. To do this, we will find a **confidence interval for the mean value of y** and a **prediction interval for an individual value of y**.

Because each possible sample of n values of the dependent variable gives values of b_0 and b_1 that differ from the values given by other samples, different samples give different values of

$\hat{y} = b_0 + b_1 x_0$. If the regression assumptions hold, a confidence interval for the mean value of y is based on the estimated standard deviation of the normally distributed population of all possible values of $\hat{y}$. This estimated standard deviation is called the **standard error of $\hat{y}$,** is denoted $s_{\hat{y}}$, and is given by the formula

$$s_{\hat{y}} = s\sqrt{\frac{1}{n} + \frac{(x_0 - \bar{x})^2}{SS_{xx}}}$$

Here, s is the standard error (see Section 13.2), $\bar{x}$ is the average of the n previously observed values of x, and $SS_{xx} = \Sigma x_i^2 - (\Sigma x_i)^2/n$.

As explained above, a confidence interval for the mean value of y is based on the standard error $s_{\hat{y}}$. A prediction interval for an individual value of y is based on a more complex standard error: the estimated standard deviation of the population of all possible values of $y - \hat{y}$, the prediction error obtained when predicting y by $\hat{y}$. We refer to this estimated standard deviation as the **standard error of $y - \hat{y}$** and denote it as $s_{(y-\hat{y})}$. If the regression assumptions hold, the formula for $s_{(y-\hat{y})}$ is

$$s_{(y-\hat{y})} = s\sqrt{1 + \frac{1}{n} + \frac{(x_0 - \bar{x})^2}{SS_{xx}}}$$

Intuitively, the "extra 1" under the radical in the formula for $s_{(y-\hat{y})}$ accounts for the fact that there is *more uncertainty* in predicting an individual value $y = \beta_0 + \beta_1 x_0 + \varepsilon$ than in estimating the mean value $\beta_0 + \beta_1 x_0$ (because we must predict the error term ε when predicting an individual value). Therefore, as shown in the following summary box, the prediction interval for an individual value of y is longer than the confidence interval for the mean value of y.

A Confidence Interval and a Prediction Interval

I f the regression assumptions hold,

1 A 100$(1 - \alpha)$ percent confidence interval for the mean value of y when x equals x_0 is

$$\left[\hat{y} \pm t_{\alpha/2}s\sqrt{\frac{1}{n} + \frac{(x_0 - \bar{x})^2}{SS_{xx}}}\right]$$

2 A 100$(1 - \alpha)$ percent prediction interval for an individual value of y when x equals x_0 is

$$\left[\hat{y} \pm t_{\alpha/2}s\sqrt{1 + \frac{1}{n} + \frac{(x_0 - \bar{x})^2}{SS_{xx}}}\right]$$

Here, $t_{\alpha/2}$ is based on $(n - 2)$ degrees of freedom.

The summary box tells us that both the formula for the confidence interval and the formula for the prediction interval use the quantity $1/n + (x_0 - \bar{x})^2/SS_{xx}$. We will call this quantity the **distance value,** because it is a measure of the distance between x_0, the value of x for which we will make a point estimate or a point prediction, and $\bar{x}$, the average of the previously observed values of x. The farther that x_0 is from $\bar{x}$, which represents the center of the experimental region, the larger is the distance value, and thus the longer are both the confidence interval $[\hat{y} \pm t_{\alpha/2}s\sqrt{\text{distance value}}]$ and the prediction interval $[\hat{y} \pm t_{\alpha/2}s\sqrt{1 + \text{distance value}}]$. Said another way, when x_0 is farther from the center of the data, $\hat{y} = b_0 + b_1 x_0$ is likely to be less accurate as both a point estimate and a point prediction.

EXAMPLE 13.6 The Tasty Sub Shop Case

In the Tasty Sub Shop problem, recall that one of the business entrepreneur's potential sites is near a population of 47,300 residents. Also, recall that

$$\hat{y} = b_0 + b_1 x_0$$
$$= 183.31 + 15.596(47.3)$$
$$= 921.0 \text{ (that is, \$921,000)}$$

is the point estimate of the mean yearly revenue for all Tasty Sub restaurants that could potentially be built near populations of 47,300 residents and is the point prediction of the yearly revenue for a single Tasty Sub restaurant that is built near a population of 47,300 residents. Using the information in Example 13.2 (page 497), we compute

$$\text{distance value} = \frac{1}{n} + \frac{(x_0 - \bar{x})^2}{SS_{xx}}$$
$$= \frac{1}{10} + \frac{(47.3 - 43.41)^2}{1913.129}$$
$$= .1079$$

Since $s = 61.7052$ (see Example 13.3 on page 506) and since $t_{\alpha/2} = t_{.025}$ based on $n - 2 = 10 - 2 = 8$ degrees of freedom equals 2.306, it follows that a 95 percent confidence interval for the mean yearly revenue when $x = 47.3$ is

$$[\hat{y} \pm t_{\alpha/2} s \sqrt{\text{distance value}}]$$
$$= [921.0 \pm 2.306(61.7052)\sqrt{.1079}]$$
$$= [921.0 \pm 46.74]$$
$$= [874.3, 967.7]$$

This interval says we are 95 percent confident that the mean yearly revenue for all Tasty Sub restaurants that could potentially be built near populations of 47,300 residents is between $874,300 and $967,700.

Because the entrepreneur would be operating a single Tasty Sub restaurant that is built near a population of 47,300 residents, the entrepreneur is interested in obtaining a prediction interval for the yearly revenue of such a restaurant. A 95 percent prediction interval for this revenue is

$$[\hat{y} \pm t_{\alpha/2} s \sqrt{1 + \text{distance value}}]$$
$$= [921.0 \pm 2.306(61.7052)\sqrt{1.1079}]$$
$$= [921.0 \pm 149.77]$$
$$= [771.2, 1070.8]$$

This interval says that we are 95 percent confident that the yearly revenue for a single Tasty Sub restaurant that is built near a population of 47,300 residents will be between $771,200 and $1,070,800. Moreover, recall that the yearly rent and other fixed costs for the entrepreneur's potential restaurant will be $257,550 and that (according to Tasty Sub corporate headquarters) the yearly food and other variable costs for the restaurant will be 60 percent of the yearly revenue. Using the lower end of the 95 percent prediction interval [771.2, 1070.8], we predict that (1) the restaurant's yearly operating cost will be $257,550 + .6($771,200) = $720,270 and (2) the restaurant's yearly profit will be $771,200 − $720,270 = $50,930. Using the upper end of the 95 percent prediction interval [771.2, 1070.8], we predict that (1) the restaurant's yearly

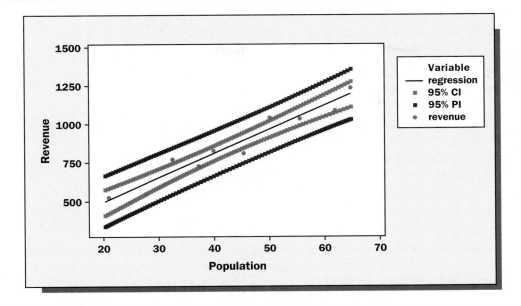

operating cost will be $257,550 + .6($1,070,800) = $900,030 and (2) the restaurant's yearly profit will be $1,070,800 − $900,030 = $170,770. Combining the two predicted profits, it follows that we are 95 percent confident that the potential restaurant's yearly profit will be between $50,930 and $170,770. If the entrepreneur decides that this is an acceptable range of potential yearly profits, then the entrepreneur might decide to purchase a Tasty Sub franchise for the potential restaurant site. In Chapter 14 we will use a *multiple regression model* to reduce the range of the predicted yearly profits for the potential Tasty Sub restaurant.

Below we repeat the bottom of the MINITAB output in Figure 13.8(b) on page 509. This output gives (within rounding) the point estimate and prediction $\hat{y} = 921.0$, the 95 percent confidence interval for the mean value of y when x equals 47.3, and the 95 percent prediction interval for an individual value of y when x equals 47.3.

```
Predicted Values for New Observations
New Obs    Fit    SE Fit       95% CI              95% PI
      1  921.0     20.3   (874.2, 967.7)    (771.2, 1070.7)
```

Although the MINITAB output does not directly give the distance value, it does give $s_{\hat{y}} = s\sqrt{\text{distance value}}$ under the heading "SE Fit." A little algebra shows that this implies that the distance value equals $(s_{\hat{y}}/s)^2$. Specifically, because $s_{\hat{y}} = 20.3$ and $s = 61.7052$, the distance value equals $(20.3/61.7052)^2 = .1082$. Note that, because MINITAB rounds $s_{\hat{y}}$, this calculation of the distance value is slightly less accurate than the previous hand calculation that obtained a distance value of .1079.

To conclude this example, note that Figure 13.17 illustrates the MINITAB output of the 95 percent confidence and prediction intervals corresponding to all values of x in the experimental region. Here $\bar{x} = 43.41$ can be regarded as the center of the experimental region. Notice that the farther x_0 is from $\bar{x} = 43.41$, the larger is the distance value and, therefore, the longer are the 95 percent confidence and prediction intervals. These longer intervals are undesirable because they give us less information about mean and individual values of y.

Exercises for Section 13.4

CONCEPTS

13.28 What is the difference between a confidence interval and a prediction interval?

13.29 What does the distance value measure? How does the distance value affect a confidence or prediction interval?

METHODS AND APPLICATIONS

13.30 **THE FUEL CONSUMPTION CASE** ⒟Ⓢ FuelCon1

The following partial MINITAB regression output for the fuel consumption data relates to predicting the city's fuel consumption (in MMcf of natural gas) in a week that has an average hourly temperature of 40°F.

```
Predicted Values for New Observations
New Obs      Fit    SE Fit        95% CI              95% PI
     1    10.721     0.241   (10.130, 11.312)    (9.015, 12.427)
```

a Report (as shown on the computer output) a point estimate of and a 95 percent confidence interval for the mean fuel consumption for all weeks having an average hourly temperature of 40°F.

b Report (as shown on the computer output) a point prediction of and a 95 percent prediction interval for the fuel consumption in a single week that has an average hourly temperature of 40°F.

c Remembering that $s = .6542$; $SS_{xx} = 1{,}404.355$; $\bar{x} = 43.98$; and $n = 8$, hand calculate the distance value when $x_0 = 40$. Remembering that the distance value equals $(s_{\hat{y}}/s)^2$, use s and $s_{\hat{y}}$ from the computer output to calculate (within rounding) the distance value using this formula. Note that, because MINITAB rounds $s_{\hat{y}}$, the first hand calculation is the more accurate calculation of the distance value.

d Remembering that for the fuel consumption data $b_0 = 15.84$ and $b_1 = -.1279$, calculate (within rounding) the confidence interval of part *a* and the prediction interval of part *b*.

e Suppose that next week the city's average hourly temperature will be 40°F. Also, suppose that the city's natural gas company will use the point prediction $\hat{y} = 10.721$ and order 10.721 MMcf of natural gas to be shipped to the city by a pipeline transmission system. The company will have to pay a fine to the transmission system if the city's actual gas useage y differs from the order of 10.721 MMcf by more than 10.5 percent—that is, is outside of the range $[10.721 \pm .105(10.721)] = [9.595, 11.847]$. Discuss why the 95 percent prediction interval for y, [9.015, 12.427], says that y might be outside of the allowable range and thus does not make the company 95 percent confident that it will avoid paying a fine.
Note: In the exercises of Chapter 14 we will use multiple regression analysis to predict y accurately enough that the company is likely to avoid paying a fine.

13.31 **THE STARTING SALARY CASE** ⒟Ⓢ StartSal

The following partial MINITAB regression output for the starting salary data relates to predicting the starting salary of a marketing graduate having a grade point average of 3.25.

```
Predicted Values for New Observations
New Obs     Fit    SE Fit        95% CI              95% PI
     1   33.362     0.213   (32.813, 33.911)    (31.878, 34.846)
```

a Report (as shown on the computer output) a point estimate of and a 95 percent confidence interval for the mean starting salary of all marketing graduates having a grade point average of 3.25.

b Report (as shown on the computer output) a point prediction of and a 95 percent prediction interval for the starting salary of an individual marketing graduate having a grade point average of 3.25.

c Remembering that $s = .536321$ and that the distance value equals $(s_{\hat{y}}/s)^2$, use $s_{\hat{y}}$ from the computer output to hand calculate the distance value when $x = 3.25$.

d Remembering that for the starting salary data $n = 7$, $b_0 = 14.816$, and $b_1 = 5.7066$, hand calculate (within rounding) the confidence interval of part *a* and the prediction interval of part *b*.

13.32 **THE SERVICE TIME CASE** ⓓⓢ SrvcTime

The following partial Excel add-in (MegaStat) regression output for the service time data relates to predicting service times for 1, 2, 3, 4, 5, 6, and 7 copiers.

Predicted values for: Minutes (y)

Copiers (x)	Predicted	95% Confidence Intervals		95% Prediction Intervals		Leverage
		lower	upper	lower	upper	
1	36.066	29.907	42.226	23.944	48.188	0.348
2	60.669	55.980	65.357	49.224	72.113	0.202
3	85.271	81.715	88.827	74.241	96.300	0.116
4	109.873	106.721	113.025	98.967	120.779	0.091
5	134.475	130.753	138.197	123.391	145.559	0.127
6	159.077	154.139	164.016	147.528	170.627	0.224
7	183.680	177.233	190.126	171.410	195.950	0.381

a Report (as shown on the computer output) a point estimate of and a 95 percent confidence interval for the mean time to service four copiers.

b Report (as shown on the computer output) a point prediction of and a 95 percent prediction interval for the time to service four copiers on a single call.

c For this case: $n = 11$, $b_0 = 11.4641$, $b_1 = 24.6022$, and $s = 4.615$. Using this information and a distance value (called **Leverage** on the add-in output), hand calculate (within rounding) the confidence interval of part a and the prediction interval of part b.

d If we examine the service time data, we see that there was at least one call on which Accu-Copiers serviced each of 1, 2, 3, 4, 5, 6, and 7 copiers. The 95 percent confidence intervals for the mean service times on these calls might be used to schedule future service calls. To understand this, note that a person making service calls will (in, say, a year or more) make a very large number of service calls. Some of the person's individual service times will be below, and some will be above, the corresponding mean service times. However, since the very large number of individual service times will average out to the mean service times, it seems fair to both the efficiency of the company and to the person making service calls to schedule service calls by using estimates of the mean service times. Therefore, suppose we wish to schedule a call to service five copiers. Examining the computer output, we see that a 95 percent confidence interval for the mean time to service five copiers is [130.753, 138.197]. Since the mean time might be 138.197 minutes, it would seem fair to allow 138 minutes to make the service call. Now suppose we wish to schedule a call to service four copiers. Determine how many minutes to allow for the service call.

13.33 **THE FRESH DETERGENT CASE** ⓓⓢ Fresh

The following partial MINITAB regression output for the Fresh detergent data relates to predicting demand for future sales periods in which the price difference will be .10 (see New Obs 1) and .25 (see New Obs2).

```
Predicted Values for New Observations
New Obs    Fit   SE Fit       95% CI              95% PI
      1  8.0806  0.0648  (7.9479, 8.2133)  (7.4187, 8.7425)
      2  8.4804  0.0586  (8.3604, 8.6004)  (7.8209, 9.1398)
```

a Report (as shown on the computer output) a point estimate of and a 95 percent confidence interval for the mean demand for Fresh in all sales periods when the price difference is .10.

b Report (as shown on the computer output) a point prediction of and a 95 percent prediction interval for the actual demand for Fresh in an individual sales period when the price difference is .10.

c Remembering that $s = .316561$ and that the distance value equals $(s_{\hat{y}}/s)^2$, use $s_{\hat{y}}$ from the computer output to hand calculate the distance value when $x = .10$.

d For this case: $n = 30$, $b_0 = 7.81409$, $b_1 = 2.6652$, and $s = .316561$. Using this information, and your result from part c, find 99 percent confidence and prediction intervals for mean and individual demands when $x = .10$.

e Repeat parts a, b, c, and d when $x = .25$.

Intuitively, this equation implies that the explained variation represents the amount of the total variation in the observed values of y that is explained by the predictor variable x (and the simple linear regression model).

We now define the **simple coefficient of determination** to be

$$r^2 = \frac{\text{Explained variation}}{\text{Total variation}}$$

That is, r^2 is the proportion of the total variation in the n observed values of y that is explained by the simple linear regression model. Neither the explained variation nor the total variation can be negative (both quantities are sums of squares). Therefore, r^2 is greater than or equal to 0. Because the explained variation must be less than or equal to the total variation, r^2 cannot be greater than 1. The nearer r^2 is to 1, the larger is the proportion of the total variation that is explained by the model, and the greater is the utility of the model in predicting y. If the value of r^2 is not reasonably close to 1, the independent variable in the model does not provide accurate predictions of y. In such a case, a different predictor variable must be found in order to accurately predict y. It is also possible that no regression model employing a single predictor variable will accurately predict y. In this case the model must be improved by including more than one independent variable. We show how to do this in Chapter 14.

The Simple Coefficient of Determination, r^2

For the simple linear regression model

1 Total variation $= \sum (y_i - \bar{y})^2$

2 Explained variation $= \sum (\hat{y}_i - \bar{y})^2$

3 Unexplained variation $= \sum (y_i - \hat{y}_i)^2$

4 Total variation = Explained variation
　　 + Unexplained variation

5 The simple coefficient of determination is

$$r^2 = \frac{\text{Explained variation}}{\text{Total variation}}$$

6 r^2 is the proportion of the total variation in the n observed values of the dependent variable that is explained by the simple linear regression model.

EXAMPLE 13.7 The Tasty Sub Shop Case

For the Tasty Sub data (see Table 13.1 on page 492) we have seen that $\bar{y} = (527.1 + 548.7 + \cdots + 1235.8)/10 = 8603.1/10 = 860.31$. It follows that the total variation is

$$\sum (y_i - \bar{y})^2 = (527.1 - 860.31)^2 + (548.7 - 860.31)^2 + \cdots + (1235.8 - 860.31)^2$$

$$= 495{,}776.51$$

Furthermore, we found in Table 13.2 (page 498) that the unexplained variation is $SSE = 30{,}460.21$. Therefore, we can compute the explained variation and r^2 as follows:

$$\text{Explained variation} = \text{Total variation} - \text{Unexplained variation}$$

$$= 495{,}776.51 - 30{,}460.21 = 465{,}316.30$$

$$r^2 = \frac{\text{Explained variation}}{\text{Total variation}} = \frac{465{,}316.30}{495{,}776.51} = .939$$

This value of r^2 says that the regression model explains 93.9 percent of the total variation in the 10 observed yearly revenues.

FIGURE 13.19　An Illustration of Different Values of the Simple Correlation Coefficient

(a) $r = 1$: perfect positive correlation

(b) Positive correlation (positive r): y increases as x increases in a straight-line fashion

(c) Little correlation (r near 0): little linear relationship between y and x

(d) Negative correlation (negative r): y decreases as x increases in a straight-line fashion

(e) $r = -1$: perfect negative correlation

The simple correlation coefficient, r　People often claim that two variables are correlated. For example, a college admissions officer might feel that the academic performance of college students (measured by grade point average) is correlated with the students' scores on a standardized college entrance examination. This means that college students' grade point averages are related to their college entrance exam scores. One measure of the relationship between two variables y and x is the **simple correlation coefficient.** We define this quantity as follows:

The Simple Correlation Coefficient

The **simple correlation coefficient between y and x,** denoted by r, is

$$r = +\sqrt{r^2} \quad \text{if } b_1 \text{ is positive} \qquad \text{and} \qquad r = -\sqrt{r^2} \quad \text{if } b_1 \text{ is negative}$$

where b_1 is the slope of the least squares line relating y to x. This correlation coefficient **measures the strength of the linear relationship between y and x.**

Because r^2 is always between 0 and 1, the correlation coefficient r is between -1 and 1. A value of r near 0 implies little linear relationship between y and x. A value of r close to 1 says that y and x have a strong tendency to move together in a straight-line fashion with a positive slope and, therefore, that y and x are highly related and **positively correlated.** A value of r close to -1 says that y and x have a strong tendency to move together in a straight-line fashion with a negative slope and, therefore, that y and x are highly related and **negatively correlated.** Figure 13.19 illustrates these relationships. Notice that when $r = 1$, y and x have a perfect linear relationship with a positive slope, whereas when $r = -1$, y and x have a perfect linear relationship with a negative slope.

EXAMPLE 13.8 The Tasty Sub Shop Case

In the Tasty Sub Shop problem, we found that $b_1 = 15.596$ and $r^2 = .939$. It follows that the simple correlation coefficient between y (yearly revenue) and x (population size) is

$$r = +\sqrt{r^2} = +\sqrt{.939} = .969$$

This simple correlation coefficient says that x and y have a strong tendency to move together in a linear fashion with a positive slope. We have seen this tendency in Figure 13.1 (page 492), which indicates that y and x are positively correlated.

If we have computed the least squares slope b_1 and r^2, the method given in the previous box provides the easiest way to calculate r. The simple correlation coefficient can also be calculated using the formula

$$r = \frac{SS_{xy}}{\sqrt{SS_{xx}\,SS_{yy}}}$$

Here SS_{xy} and SS_{xx} have been defined in Section 13.1 on page 496, and SS_{yy} denotes the total variation, which has been defined in this section. Furthermore, this formula for r automatically gives r the correct ($+$ or $-$) sign. For instance, in the Tasty Sub Shop problem, $SS_{xy} = 29{,}836.389$, $SS_{xx} = 1913.129$, and $SS_{yy} = 495{,}776.51$ (see Examples 13.2 on page 497 and 13.7 on page 522). Therefore

$$r = \frac{SS_{xy}}{\sqrt{SS_{xx}\,SS_{yy}}}$$

$$= \frac{29{,}836.389}{\sqrt{(1{,}913.129)(495{,}776.51))}} = .969$$

It is important to make two points. First, **the value of the simple correlation coefficient is not the slope of the least squares line.** If we wish to find this slope, we should use the previously given formula for b_1.[3] Second, **high correlation does not imply that a cause-and-effect relationship exists.** When r indicates that y and x are highly correlated, this says that y and x have a strong tendency to move together in a straight-line fashion. The correlation does not mean that changes in x cause changes in y. Instead, some other variable (or variables) could be causing the apparent relationship between y and x. For example, suppose that college students' grade point averages and college entrance exam scores are highly positively correlated. This does not mean that earning a high score on a college entrance exam causes students to receive a high grade point average. Rather, other factors such as intellectual ability, study habits, and attitude probably determine both a student's score on a college entrance exam and a student's college grade point average. In general, while the simple correlation coefficient can show that variables tend to move together in a straight-line fashion, scientific theory must be used to establish cause-and-effect relationships.

A technical note In optional Section 13.10 we present some shortcut formulas for calculating the total, explained, and unexplained variations. Also, for those who have already read Section 13.3, r^2, the explained variation, the unexplained variation, and the total variation are calculated by Excel and MINITAB. These quantities are identified on the Excel and MINITAB outputs of Figure 13.8 (page 509) by, respectively, the labels 9, 10, 11, and 12. These outputs also give an "adjusted r^2." We will explain the meaning of this quantity in Chapter 14.

---

[3]Essentially, the difference between r and b_1 is a change of scale. It can be shown that b_1 and r are related by the equation $b_1 = (SS_{yy}/SS_{xx})^{1/2}\, r$.

Exercises for Section 13.5

CONCEPTS

13.36 Discuss the meanings of the total variation, the unexplained variation, and the explained variation.

13.37 What does the simple coefficient of determination measure?

METHODS AND APPLICATIONS

In Exercises 13.38 through 13.43, we give the total variation, the unexplained variation (*SSE*), and the least squares point estimate b_1 that are obtained when simple linear regression is used to analyze the data set related to each of six previously discussed case studies. Using the information given in each exercise, find the explained variation, the simple coefficient of determination (r^2), and the simple correlation coefficient (r). Interpret r^2.

13.38 THE FUEL CONSUMPTION CASE ⒟Ⓢ FuelCon1

Total variation = 25.549; *SSE* = 2.568; $b_1 = -.12792$

13.39 THE STARTING SALARY CASE ⒟Ⓢ StartSal

Total variation = 61.380; *SSE* = 1.438; $b_1 = 5.7066$

13.40 THE SERVICE TIME CASE ⒟Ⓢ SrvcTime

Total variation = 20,110.5455; *SSE* = 191.7017; $b_1 = 24.6022$

13.41 THE FRESH DETERGENT CASE ⒟Ⓢ Fresh

Total variation = 13.459; *SSE* = 2.806; $b_1 = 2.6652$

13.42 THE DIRECT LABOR COST CASE ⒟Ⓢ DirLab

Total variation = 1,025,339.6667; *SSE* = 746.7624; $b_1 = 10.1463$

13.43 THE REAL ESTATE SALES PRICE CASE ⒟Ⓢ RealEst

Total variation = 7447.5; *SSE* = 896.8; $b_1 = 5.7003$

13.6 Testing the Significance of the Population Correlation Coefficient ● ● ●

LO7 Test hypotheses about the population correlation coefficient.

We have seen that the simple correlation coefficient measures the linear relationship between the observed values of *x* and the observed values of *y* that make up the sample. A similar coefficient of linear correlation can be defined for the population of *all possible combinations of observed values of x and y*. We call this coefficient the **population correlation coefficient** and denote it by the symbol **ρ** (pronounced **rho**). We use *r* as the point estimate of ρ. In addition, we can carry out a hypothesis test. Here we test the null hypothesis H_0: **$\rho = 0$, which says there is no linear relationship between *x* and *y*,** against the alternative H_a: **$\rho \neq 0$, which says there is a positive or negative linear relationship between *x* and *y*.** This test employs the test statistic

$$t = \frac{r\sqrt{n - 2}}{\sqrt{1 - r^2}}$$

and is based on the assumption that the population of all possible observed combinations of values of *x* and *y* has a **bivariate normal probability distribution.** See Wonnacott and Wonnacott (1981) for a discussion of this distribution. It can be shown that the preceding test statistic *t* and the *p*-value used to test H_0: $\rho = 0$ versus H_a: $\rho \neq 0$ are equal to, respectively, the test statistic $t = b_1/s_{b_1}$ and the *p*-value used to test H_0: $\beta_1 = 0$ versus H_a: $\beta_1 \neq 0$, where β_1 is the slope in the simple linear regression model. Keep in mind, however, that although the mechanics involved in these hypothesis tests are the same, these tests are based on different assumptions (remember that the test for significance of the slope is based on the regression assumptions). If the bivariate normal distribution assumption for the test concerning ρ is badly violated, we can use a non-parametric approach to correlation. One such approach is **Spearman's rank correlation coefficient.** This approach is discussed in Bowerman, O'Connell, and Murphree (2011).

EXAMPLE 13.9 The Tasty Sub Shop Case

Again consider testing the significance of the slope in the Tasty Sub Shop problem. Recall that in Example 13.4 (page 508) we found that $t = 11.05$ and that the p-value related to this t statistic is less than .001. We therefore (if the regression assumptions hold) can reject $H_0: \beta_1 = 0$ at level of significance .05, .01, or .001, and we have extremely strong evidence that x is significantly related to y. This also implies (if the population of all possible observed combinations of x and y has a bivariate normal probability distribution) that we can reject $H_0: \rho = 0$ in favor of $H_a: \rho \neq 0$ at level of significance .05, .01, or .001. It follows that we have extremely strong evidence of a linear relationship, or correlation, between x and y. Furthermore, because we have previously calculated r to be .969, we estimate that x and y are positively correlated.

Exercises for Section 13.6

CONCEPTS

13.44 Explain what is meant by the population correlation coefficient ρ.

13.45 Explain how we test $H_0: \rho = 0$ versus $H_a: \rho \neq 0$. What do we conclude if we reject $H_0: \rho = 0$?

METHODS AND APPLICATIONS

13.46 THE STARTING SALARY CASE ⑤ StartSal

Consider testing $H_0: \beta_1 = 0$ versus $H_a: \beta_1 \neq 0$. Figure 13.11 (page 512) tells us that $t = 14.44$ and that the related p-value is less than .001. Assuming that the bivariate normal probability distribution assumption holds, test $H_0: \rho = 0$ versus $H_a: \rho \neq 0$ by setting α equal to .05, .01, and .001. What do you conclude about how x and y are related?

13.47 THE SERVICE TIME CASE ⑤ SrvcTime

Consider testing $H_0: \beta_1 = 0$ versus $H_a: \beta_1 \neq 0$. Figure 13.12 (page 512) tells us that $t = 30.5802$ and that the related p-value is less than .001. Assuming that the bivariate normal probability distribution assumption holds, test $H_0: \rho = 0$ versus $H_a: \rho \neq 0$ by setting α equal to .05, .01, and .001. What do you conclude about how x and y are related?

LO8 Test the significance of a simple linear regression model by using an F test.

13.7 An F Test for the Model ● ● ●

In this section we discuss an F test that can be used to test the significance of the regression relationship between x and y. Sometimes people refer to this as testing the significance of the simple linear regression model. For simple linear regression, this test is another way to test the null hypothesis $H_0: \beta_1 = 0$ (the relationship between x and y is not significant) versus $H_a: \beta_1 \neq 0$ (the relationship between x and y is significant). If we can reject H_0 at level of significance α, we often say that **the simple linear regression model is significant at level of significance α.**

An F Test for the Simple Linear Regression Model

Suppose that the regression assumptions hold, and define the **overall F statistic** to be

$$F(model) = \frac{\text{Explained variation}}{(\text{Unexplained variation})/(n - 2)}$$

Also define the p-value related to F(model) to be the area under the curve of the F distribution (having 1 numerator and $n - 2$ denominator degrees of freedom) to the right of F(model)—see Figure 13.20(b).

We can reject $H_0: \beta_1 = 0$ in favor of $H_a: \beta_1 \neq 0$ at level of significance α if either of the following equivalent conditions holds:

1 $F(model) > F_\alpha$
2 p-value $< \alpha$

Here the point F_α is based on 1 numerator and $n - 2$ denominator degrees of freedom.

FIGURE 13.20(a)   The F Test Critical Value

FIGURE 13.20(a)   The F Test Critical Value

FIGURE 13.20(b)   The F Test p-Value

The first condition in the box says we should reject H_0: $\beta_1 = 0$ (and conclude that the relationship between x and y is significant) when $F(\text{model})$ is large. This is intuitive because a large overall F statistic would be obtained when the explained variation is large compared to the unexplained variation. This would occur if x is significantly related to y, which would imply that the slope β_1 is not equal to 0. Figure 13.20(a) illustrates that we reject H_0 when $F(\text{model})$ is greater than F_α. As can be seen in Figure 13.20(b), when $F(\text{model})$ is large, the related p-value is small. When the p-value is small enough [resulting from an $F(\text{model})$ statistic that is large enough], we reject H_0. Figure 13.20(b) illustrates that the second condition in the box (p-value $< \alpha$) is an equivalent way to carry out this test.

EXAMPLE 13.10 The Tasty Sub Shop Case

Consider the Tasty Sub Shop problem and the following partial MINITAB output of the simple linear regression analysis relating yearly revenue y to population size x:

```
Analysis of Variance
Source            DF          SS           MS           F        P-value
Regression         1       465316       465316       122.21       0.000
Residual Error     8        30460         3808
Total              9       495777
```

Looking at this output, we see that the explained variation is 465,316 and the unexplained variation is 30,460. It follows that

$$F(\text{model}) = \frac{\text{Explained variation}}{(\text{Unexplained variation})/(n-2)}$$

$$= \frac{465{,}316}{30{,}460/(10-2)} = \frac{465{,}316}{3808}$$

$$= 122.21$$

Note that this overall F statistic is given on the MINITAB output and is also given on the following partial Excel output:

ANOVA	df	SS	MS	F	Significance F
Regression	1	465316.3004	465316.3004	122.2096	0.0000
Residual	8	30460.2086	3807.5261		
Total	9	495776.5090			

The p-value related to F(model) is the area to the right of 122.21 under the curve of the F distribution having 1 numerator and 8 denominator degrees of freedom. This p-value is given on both the MINITAB output (labeled "p") and the Excel output (labeled "Significance F") and is less than .001. If we wish to test the significance of the regression relationship with level of significance $\alpha = .05$, we use the critical value $F_{.05}$ based on 1 numerator and 8 denominator degrees of freedom. Using Table A.6 (page 643), we find that $F_{.05} = 5.32$. Since F(model) = 122.21 $> F_{.05} = 5.32$, we can reject H_0: $\beta_1 = 0$ in favor of H_a: $\beta_1 \neq 0$ at level of significance .05. Alternatively, since the p-value is smaller than .05, .01, and .001, we can reject H_0 at level of significance .05, .01, or .001. Therefore, we have extremely strong evidence that H_0: $\beta_1 = 0$ should be rejected and that the regression relationship between x and y is significant. That is, we might say that we have extremely strong evidence that the simple linear model relating y to x is significant.

Testing the significance of the regression relationship between y and x by using the overall F statistic and its related p-value is equivalent to doing this test by using the t statistic and its related p-value. Specifically, it can be shown that $(t)^2 = F$(model) and that $(t_{\alpha/2})^2$ based on $n - 2$ degrees of freedom equals F_α based on 1 numerator and $n - 2$ denominator degrees of freedom. It follows that the critical value conditions

$$|t| > t_{\alpha/2} \quad \text{and} \quad F(\text{model}) > F_\alpha$$

are equivalent. Furthermore, the p-values related to t and F(model) can be shown to be equal. Because these tests are equivalent, it would be logical to ask why we have presented the F test. There are two reasons. First, most standard regression computer packages include the results of the F test as a part of the regression output. Second, the F test has a useful generalization in multiple regression analysis (where we employ more than one predictor variable). The F test in multiple regression is not equivalent to a t test. This is further explained in Chapter 14.

Exercises for Section 13.7

CONCEPTS

connect

13.48 What are the null and alternative hypotheses for the F test in simple linear regression?

13.49 The F test in simple linear regression is equivalent to what other test?

METHODS AND APPLICATIONS

In Exercises 13.50 through 13.55, we give MINITAB and Excel outputs of simple linear regression analyses of the data sets related to six previously discussed case studies. Using the appropriate computer output,
a Use the explained variation and the unexplained variation as given on the computer output to calculate (within rounding) the F(model) statistic.
b Utilize the F(model) statistic and the appropriate critical value to test H_0: $\beta_1 = 0$ versus H_a: $\beta_1 \neq 0$ by setting α equal to .05. What do you conclude about the regression relationship between y and x?
c Utilize the F(model) statistic and the appropriate critical value to test H_0: $\beta_1 = 0$ versus H_a: $\beta_1 \neq 0$ by setting α equal to .01. What do you conclude about the regression relationship between y and x?
d Find the p-value related to F(model) on the computer output and report its value. Using the p-value, test the significance of the regression model at the .10, .05, .01, and .001 levels of significance. What do you conclude?
e Show that the F(model) statistic is (within rounding) the square of the t statistic for testing H_0: $\beta_1 = 0$ versus H_a: $\beta_1 \neq 0$. Also, show that the $F_{.05}$ critical value is the square of the $t_{.025}$ critical value.

Note that in the lower right hand corner of each output we give (in parentheses) the number of observations, n, used to perform the regression analysis and the t statistic for testing H_0: $\beta_1 = 0$ versus H_a: $\beta_1 \neq 0$.

13.50   THE FUEL CONSUMPTION CASE   DS FuelCon1

ANOVA	df	SS	MS	F	Significance F
Regression	1	22.9808	22.9808	53.6949	0.0003
Residual	6	2.5679	0.4280		
Total	7	25.5488			(n=8; t=-7.33)

13.51 THE STARTING SALARY CASE DS StartSal

```
Analysis of Variance
Source              DF      SS       MS        F        P
Regression           1   59.942   59.942   208.39   0.000
Residual Error       5    1.438    0.288
Total                6   61.380           (n=7; t=14.44)
```

13.52 THE SERVICE TIME CASE DS SrvcTime

ANOVA	SS	df	MS	F	p-value
Regression	19,918.8438	1	19,918.8438	935.15	2.09E-10
Residual	191.7017	9	21.3002		
Total	20,110.5455	10		(n=11; t=30.580)	

13.53 THE FRESH DETERGENT CASE DS Fresh

```
Analysis of Variance
Source              DF      SS       MS        F        P
Regression           1   10.653   10.653   106.30   0.000
Residual Error      28    2.806    0.100
Total               29   13.459           (n=30; t=10.31)
```

13.54 THE DIRECT LABOR COST CASE DS DirLab

ANOVA	df	SS	MS	F	Significance F
Regression	1	1024592.9043	1024592.9043	13720.4677	5.04E-17
Residual	10	746.7624	74.6762		
Total	11	1025339.6667		(n=12; t=117.1344)	

13.55 THE REAL ESTATE SALES PRICE CASE DS RealEst

```
Analysis of Variance
Source              DF      SS       MS        F        P
Regression           1   6550.7   6550.7   58.43   0.000
Residual Error       8    896.8    112.1
Total                9   7447.5           (n=10; t=7.64)
```

13.8 The QHIC Case ● ● ●

Quality Home Improvement Center (QHIC) operates five stores in a large metropolitan area. The marketing department at QHIC wishes to study the relationship between x, home value (in thousands of dollars), and y, yearly expenditure on home upkeep (in dollars). A random sample of 40 homeowners is taken and asked to estimate their expenditures during the previous year on the types of home upkeep products and services offered by QHIC. Public records of the county auditor are used to obtain the previous year's assessed values of the homeowner's homes. The resulting x and y values, as well as a scatter plot of these values, are given in Figure 13.21. The Excel output included in this figure tells us that the least squares point estimates of the y-intercept β_0 and the slope β_1 are $b_0 = -348.3921$ and $b_1 = 7.2583$. The p-value associated with b_1 implies there is a significant linear relationship between x and y. In addition, because $b_1 = 7.2583$, we estimate that mean yearly upkeep expenditure increases by \$7.26 for each additional \$1,000 increase in home value. Consider a home worth \$220,000, and note that $x_0 = 220$ is in the range of previously observed values of x: 48.9 to 286.18. It follows that

$$\hat{y} = b_0 + b_1 x_0$$

$$= -348.3921 + 7.2583(220)$$

$$= 1,248.43 \text{ (or } \$1,248.43\text{)}$$

FIGURE 13.21   The QHIC Upkeep Expenditure Data, Scatterplot, and Excel Output   QHIC

Home	Value of Home, x (Thousands of Dollars)	Upkeep Expenditure, y (Dollars)	Home	Value of Home, x (Thousands of Dollars)	Upkeep Expenditure, y (Dollars)
1	237.00	1,412.08	21	153.04	849.14
2	153.08	797.20	22	232.18	1,313.84
3	184.86	872.48	23	125.44	602.06
4	222.06	1,003.42	24	169.82	642.14
5	160.68	852.90	25	177.28	1,038.80
6	99.68	288.48	26	162.82	697.00
7	229.04	1,288.46	27	120.44	324.34
8	101.78	423.08	28	191.10	965.10
9	257.86	1,351.74	29	158.78	920.14
10	96.28	378.04	30	178.50	950.90
11	171.00	918.08	31	272.20	1,670.32
12	231.02	1,627.24	32	48.90	125.40
13	228.32	1,204.76	33	104.56	479.78
14	205.90	857.04	34	286.18	2,010.64
15	185.72	775.00	35	83.72	368.36
16	168.78	869.26	36	86.20	425.60
17	247.06	1,396.00	37	133.58	626.90
18	155.54	711.50	38	212.86	1,316.94
19	224.20	1,475.18	39	122.02	390.16
20	202.04	1,413.32	40	198.02	1,090.84

Regression Statistics

Multiple R	0.9430
R Square	0.8892
Adjusted R Square	0.8863
Standard Error	146.8973
Observations	40

ANOVA	df	SS	MS	F	Significance F
Regression	1	6582759.6972	6582759.6972	305.0564	0.0000
Residual	38	819995.5427	21578.8301		
Total	39	7402755.2399			

	Coefficients	Standard Error	t Stat	P-value	Lower 95%	Upper 95%
Intercept	−348.3921	76.1410	−4.5756	0.0000	−502.5314	−194.2527
Value	7.2583	0.4156	17.4659	0.0000	6.4170	8.0995

is the point estimate of the mean yearly upkeep expenditure for all homes worth $220,000 and is the point prediction of a yearly upkeep expenditure for an individual home worth $220,000.

    The marketing department at QHIC wishes to determine which homes should be sent advertising brochures promoting QHIC's products and services. If the marketing department has decided to send an advertising brochure to any home that has a predicted yearly upkeep expenditure of at least $500, then a home worth $220,000 would be sent an advertising brochure. This is because the predicted yearly upkeep expenditure for such a home is (as calculated above) $1,248.43. Other homes can be evaluated in a similar fashion.

13.9 Residual Analysis ● ● ●

LO9 Use residual analysis to check the assumptions of simple linear regression.

In this section we explain how to check the validity of the regression assumptions. The required checks are carried out by analyzing the **regression residuals.** The residuals are defined as follows:

For any particular observed value of y, the corresponding **residual** is

$$e = y - \hat{y} = (\text{observed value of } y - \text{predicted value of } y)$$

where the predicted value of y is calculated using the **least squares prediction equation**

$$\hat{y} = b_0 + b_1 x$$

    The linear regression model $y = \beta_0 + \beta_1 x + \varepsilon$ implies that the error term ε is given by the equation $\varepsilon = y - (\beta_0 + \beta_1 x)$. Since $\hat{y}$ in the previous box is clearly the point estimate of $\beta_0 + \beta_1 x$, we see that the residual $e = y - \hat{y}$ is the point estimate of the error term ε. If the regression assumptions are valid, then, for any given value of the independent variable, the population of potential error term values will be normally distributed with mean 0 and variance σ^2 (see the regression assumptions in Section 13.2 on page 504). Furthermore, the different error terms will be statistically independent. Because the residuals provide point estimates of the error terms, it follows that

If the regression assumptions hold, the residuals should look like they have been randomly and independently selected from normally distributed populations having mean 0 and variance σ^2.

    In any real regression problem, the regression assumptions will not hold exactly. In fact, it is important to point out that mild departures from the regression assumptions do not seriously hinder our ability to use a regression model to make statistical inferences. Therefore, we are looking for pronounced, rather than subtle, departures from the regression assumptions. Because of this, we will require that the residuals only approximately fit the description just given.

Residual plots   One useful way to analyze residuals is to plot them versus various criteria. The resulting plots are called **residual plots.** To construct a residual plot, we compute the residual for each observed y value. The calculated residuals are then plotted versus some criterion. To validate the regression assumptions, we make residual plots against (1) values of the independent variable x; (2) values of $\hat{y}$, the predicted value of the dependent variable; and (3) the time order in which the data have been observed (if the regression data are time series data).

    We next look at an example of constructing residual plots. Then we explain how to use these plots to check the regression assumptions.

EXAMPLE 13.11 The QHIC Case

Figure 13.21 gives the QHIC upkeep expenditure data and a scatterplot of the data. If we use a simple linear regression model to describe the QHIC data, we find that the least squares point estimates of β_0 and β_1 are $b_0 = -348.3921$ and $b_1 = 7.2583$. The Excel add-in (MegaStat) output in

The assumption of correct functional form   If the functional form of a regression model is incorrect, the residual plots constructed by using the model often display a pattern suggesting the form of a more appropriate model. For instance, if we use a simple linear regression model when the true relationship between y and x is curved, the residual plot will have a curved appearance. For example, the scatter plot of upkeep expenditure, y, versus home value, x, in Figure 13.21 (page 530) has either a straight-line or slightly curved appearance. We used a simple linear regression model to describe the relationship between y and x, but note that there is a "dip," or slightly curved appearance, in the upper left portion of each residual plot in Figure 13.22. Therefore, both the scatter plot and residual plots indicate that there might be a slightly curved relationship between y and x. Later in this section we discuss one way to model curved relationships.

The normality assumption   If the normality assumption holds, a histogram and/or stem-and-leaf display of the residuals should look reasonably bell-shaped and reasonably symmetric about 0. Figure 13.24(a) gives the MINITAB output of a stem-and-leaf display of the residuals from the simple linear regression model describing the QHIC data. The stem-and-leaf display looks fairly bell-shaped and symmetric about 0. However, the tails of the display look somewhat long and "heavy" or "thick," indicating a possible violation of the normality assumption.

Another way to check the normality assumption is to construct a **normal plot** of the residuals. To make a normal plot, we first arrange the residuals in order from smallest to largest. Letting the ordered residuals be denoted as $e_{(1)}, e_{(2)}, \ldots, e_{(n)}$ we denote the ith residual in the ordered listing as $e_{(i)}$. We plot $e_{(i)}$ on the vertical axis against a point called $z_{(i)}$ on the horizontal axis. Here $z_{(i)}$ is defined to be the point on the horizontal axis under the standard normal curve so that the area under this curve to the left of $z_{(i)}$ is $(3i - 1)/(3n + 1)$. For example, recall in the QHIC case that there are $n = 40$ residuals given in Figure 13.22(a). It follows that, when $i = 1$, then

$$\frac{3i - 1}{3n + 1} = \frac{3(1) - 1}{3(40) + 1} = \frac{2}{121} = .0165$$

Therefore, $z_{(1)}$ is the normal point having an area of .0165 under the standard normal curve to its left. Thus, as illustrated in Figure 13.24(b), $z_{(1)}$ equals -2.13. Because the smallest residual in Figure 13.22(a) is -289.044, the first point plotted is $e_{(1)} = -289.044$ on the vertical scale versus $z_{(1)} = -2.13$ on the horizontal scale. When $i = 2$, it can be verified that $(3i - 1)/(3n + 1)$ equals .0413 and thus that $z_{(2)} = -1.74$. Therefore, because the second-smallest residual in Figure 13.24(a) is -259.958, the second point plotted is $e_{(2)} = -259.958$ on the vertical scale versus $z_{(2)} = -1.74$ on the horizontal scale. This process is continued until the entire normal plot is constructed. The Excel add-in (MegaStat) output of this plot is given in Figure 13.24(c).

An equivalent plot is shown in Figure 13.24(d), which is a MINITAB output. In this figure, we plot the percentage $p_{(i)}$ of the area under the standard normal curve to the left of $z_{(i)}$ on the vertical axis. Thus, the first point plotted in this normal plot is $e_{(1)} = -289.044$ on the horizontal scale versus $p_{(1)} = (.0165)(100) = 1.65$ on the vertical scale, and the second point plotted is $e_{(2)} = -259.958$ on the horizontal scale versus $p_{(2)} = (.0413)(100) = 4.13$ on the vertical scale. It is important to note that the scale on the vertical axis does not have the usual spacing between the percentages. The spacing reflects the distance between the z-scores that correspond to the percentages in the standard normal distribution. Hence, if we wished to create the plot in Figure 13.24(d) by hand, we would need special graphing paper with this vertical scale.

It can be proven that, if the normality assumption holds, then the expected value of the ith ordered residual $e_{(i)}$ is proportional to $z_{(i)}$. Therefore, a plot of the $e_{(i)}$ values on the horizontal scale versus the $z_{(i)}$ values on the vertical scale (or equivalently, the $e_{(i)}$ values on the horizontal scale versus the $p_{(i)}$ values on the vertical scale) should have a straight-line appearance. That is, if the normality assumption holds, then the normal plot should have a straight-line appearance. A normal plot that does not look like a straight line (admittedly, a subjective decision) indicates that the normality assumption is violated. Since the normal plots in Figure 13.24 have some curvature (particularly in the upper right portion), there is a possible violation of the normality assumption.

FIGURE 13.24   **Stem-and-Leaf Display and Normal Plots of the Residuals from the Simple Linear Regression Model Describing the QHIC Data**

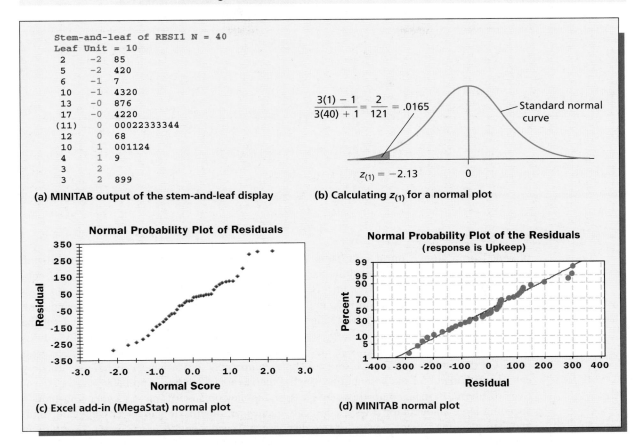

(a) MINITAB output of the stem-and-leaf display

(b) Calculating $z_{(1)}$ for a normal plot

(c) Excel add-in (MegaStat) normal plot

(d) MINITAB normal plot

It is important to realize that violations of the constant variance and correct functional form assumptions can often cause a histogram and/or stem-and-leaf display of the residuals to look nonnormal and can cause the normal plot to have a curved appearance. Because of this, it is usually a good idea to use residual plots to check for nonconstant variance and incorrect functional form before making any final conclusions about the normality assumption. Later in this section we discuss a procedure that sometimes remedies simultaneous violations of the constant variance, correct functional form, and normality assumptions.

The independence assumption   The independence assumption is most likely to be violated when the regression data are **time series data**—that is, data that have been collected in a time sequence. For such data the time-ordered error terms can be **autocorrelated.** Intuitively, we say that error terms occurring over time have **positive autocorrelation** if a positive error term in time period i tends to produce, or be followed by, another positive error term in time period $i + k$ (some later time period) and if a negative error term in time period i tends to produce, or be followed by, another negative error term in time period $i + k$. In other words, positive autocorrelation exists when positive error terms tend to be followed over time by positive error terms and when negative error terms tend to be followed over time by negative error terms. Positive autocorrelation in the error terms is depicted in Figure 13.25(a), which illustrates that **positive autocorrelation can produce a cyclical error term pattern over time.** The simple linear regression model implies that a positive error term produces a greater-than-average value of y and a negative error term produces a smaller-than-average value of y. It follows that positive autocorrelation in the error terms means that greater-than-average values of y tend to be followed by greater-than-average values of y, and smaller-than-average values of y tend to be followed by smaller-than-average values of y. An example of positive autocorrelation could hypothetically be

FIGURE 13.25   **Positive and Negative Autocorrelation**

(a) Positive Autocorrelation in the Error Terms: Cyclical Pattern

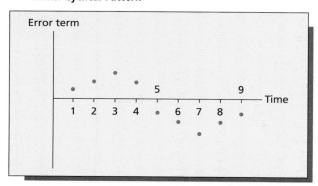

(b) Negative Autocorrelation in the Error Terms: Alternating Pattern

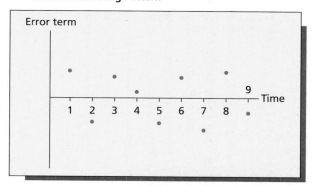

provided by a simple linear regression model relating demand for a product to advertising expenditure. Here we assume that the data are time series data observed over a number of consecutive sales periods. One of the factors included in the error term of the simple linear regression model is competitors' advertising expenditure for their similar products. If, for the moment, we assume that competitors' advertising expenditure significantly affects the demand for the product, then a higher-than-average competitors' advertising expenditure probably causes demand for the product to be lower than average and hence probably causes a negative error term. On the other hand, a lower-than-average competitors' advertising expenditure probably causes the demand for the product to be higher than average and hence probably causes a positive error term. If, then, competitors tend to spend money on advertising in a cyclical fashion—spending large amounts for several consecutive sales periods (during an advertising campaign) and then spending lesser amounts for several consecutive sales periods—a negative error term in one sales period will tend to be followed by a negative error term in the next sales period, and a positive error term in one sales period will tend to be followed by a positive error term in the next sales period. In this case the error terms would display positive autocorrelation, and thus these error terms would not be statistically independent.

Intuitively, error terms occurring over time have **negative autocorrelation** if a positive error term in time period i tends to produce, or be followed by, a negative error term in time period $i + k$ and if a negative error term in time period i tends to produce, or be followed by, a positive error term in time period $i + k$. In other words, negative autocorrelation exists when positive error terms tend to be followed over time by negative error terms and negative error terms tend to be followed over time by positive error terms. An example of negative autocorrelation in the error terms is depicted in Figure 13.25(b), which illustrates that **negative autocorrelation in the error terms can produce an alternating pattern over time.** It follows that negative autocorrelation in the error terms means that greater-than-average values of y tend to be followed by smaller-than-average values of y and smaller-than-average values of y tend to be followed by greater-than-average values of y. An example of negative autocorrelation might be provided by a retailer's weekly stock orders. Here a larger-than-average stock order one week might result in an oversupply and hence a smaller-than-average order the next week.

The **independence assumption** basically says that the time-ordered error terms display no positive or negative autocorrelation. This says that **the error terms occur in a random pattern over time.** Such a random pattern would imply that the error terms (and their corresponding y values) are statistically independent.

Because the residuals are point estimates of the error terms, a residual plot versus time is used to check the independence assumption. If a residual plot versus the data's time sequence has a cyclical appearance, the error terms are positively autocorrelated, and the independence assumption is violated. If a plot of the time-ordered residuals has an alternating pattern, the error terms are negatively autocorrelated, and again the independence assumption is violated.

However, if a plot of the time-ordered residuals displays a random pattern, the error terms have little or no autocorrelation. In such a case, it is reasonable to conclude that the independence assumption holds.

EXAMPLE 13.12

Figure 13.26(a) presents data concerning weekly sales at Pages Bookstore (Sales), Pages weekly advertising expenditure (Adver), and the weekly advertising expenditure of Pages main competitor (Compadv). Here the sales values are expressed in thousands of dollars, and the advertising expenditure values are expressed in hundreds of dollars. Figure 13.26(a) also gives the MINITAB output of the residuals that are obtained when a simple linear regression analysis is performed relating Pages sales to Pages advertising expenditure. These residuals are plotted versus time in Figure 13.26(b). We see that the residual plot has a cyclical pattern. This tells us that the error terms for the model are positively autocorrelated and the independence assumption is violated. Furthermore, there tend to be positive residuals when the competitor's advertising expenditure is lower (in weeks 1 through 8 and weeks 14, 15, and 16) and negative residuals when the competitor's advertising expenditure is higher (in weeks 9 through 13). Therefore, the competitor's advertising expenditure seems to be causing the positive autocorrelation.

FIGURE 13.26   **Pages Bookstore Sales and Advertising Data, and Residual Analysis**

(a) **The data and the MINITAB output of the residuals from a simple linear regression relating Pages sales to Pages advertising expenditure**   DS BookSales

Observation	Adver	Compadv	Sales	Predicted	Residual
1	18	10	22	18.7	3.3
2	20	10	27	23.0	4.0
3	20	15	23	23.0	−0.0
4	25	15	31	33.9	−2.9
5	28	15	45	40.4	4.6
6	29	20	47	42.6	4.4
7	29	20	45	42.6	2.4
8	28	25	42	40.4	1.6
9	30	35	37	44.7	−7.7
10	31	35	39	46.9	−7.9
11	34	35	45	53.4	−8.4
12	35	30	52	55.6	−3.6
13	36	30	57	57.8	−0.8
14	38	25	62	62.1	−0.1
15	41	20	73	68.6	4.4
16	45	20	84	77.3	6.7

Durbin-Watson = 0.65

(b) **A plot of the residuals in Figure 13.26(a) versus time**

To conclude this example, note that the simple linear regression model relating Pages sales to Pages advertising expenditure has a standard error, s, of 5.038. The residual plot in Figure 13.26(b) includes grid lines that are placed one and two standard errors above and below the residual mean of 0. Such grid lines help us to better diagnose potential violations of the regression assumptions.

When the independence assumption is violated, various remedies can be employed. One approach is to identify which independent variable left in the error term (for example, competitors' advertising expenditure) is causing the error terms to be autocorrelated. We can then remove this independent variable from the error term and insert it directly into the regression model, forming a **multiple regression model.** (Multiple regression models are discussed in Chapter 14.)

The Durbin–Watson test   One type of positive or negative autocorrelation is called **first-order autocorrelation.** It says that ε_t, the error term in time period t, is related to ε_{t-1}, the error term in time period $t - 1$. To check for first-order autocorrelation, we can use the **Durbin–Watson statistic**

$$d = \frac{\sum_{t=2}^{n}(e_t - e_{t-1})^2}{\sum_{t=1}^{n}e_t^2}$$

where $e_1, e_2, \ldots, e_n$ are the time-ordered residuals.

Intuitively, small values of d lead us to conclude that there is positive autocorrelation. This is because, if d is small, the differences $(e_t - e_{t-1})$ are small. This indicates that the adjacent residuals e_t and e_{t-1} are of the same magnitude, which in turn says that the adjacent error terms ε_t and ε_{t-1} are positively correlated. Consider testing the null hypothesis H_0 **that the error terms are not autocorrelated** versus the alternative hypothesis H_a **that the error terms are positively autocorrelated.** Durbin and Watson have shown that there are points (denoted $d_{L,\alpha}$ and $d_{U,\alpha}$) such that, if α is the probability of a Type I error, then

1 If $d < d_{L,\alpha}$, we reject H_0.

2 If $d > d_{U,\alpha}$, we do not reject H_0.

3 If $d_{L,\alpha} \leq d \leq d_{U,\alpha}$, the test is inconclusive.

Reject H_0 $d_{L,\alpha}$ Test inconclusive $d_{U,\alpha}$ Do not reject H_0

So that the Durbin–Watson test may be easily done, tables containing the points $d_{L,\alpha}$ and $d_{U,\alpha}$ have been constructed. These tables give the appropriate $d_{L,\alpha}$ and $d_{U,\alpha}$ points for various values of α; k, the number of independent variables used by the regression model; and n, the number of observations. Tables A.11, A.12, and A.13 (pages 649–650) give these points for $\alpha = .05$, $\alpha = .025$, and $\alpha = .01$. A portion of Table A.11 is given in Table 13.3. Note that when we are considering a simple linear regression model, which uses *one* independent variable, we look up the points $d_{L,\alpha}$ and $d_{U,\alpha}$ under the heading "$k = 1$." Other values of k are used when we study multiple regression models in Chapter 14. Using the residuals in Figure 13.26(a), the Durbin–Watson statistic for the simple linear regression model relating Pages sales to Pages advertising expenditure is calculated to be

$$d = \frac{\sum_{t=2}^{16}(e_t - e_{t-1})^2}{\sum_{t=1}^{16}e_t^2}$$

$$= \frac{(4.0 - 3.3)^2 + (0.0 - 4.0)^2 + \cdots + (6.7 - 4.4)^2}{(3.3)^2 + (4.0)^2 + \cdots + (6.7)^2}$$

$$= .65$$

A MINITAB output of the Durbin–Watson statistic is given at the bottom of Figure 13.26(a). To test for positive autocorrelation, we note that there are $n = 16$ observations and the regression

TABLE 13.3   Critical Values for the Durbin–Watson d Statistic ($\alpha = .05$)

| | $k = 1$ | | $k = 2$ | | $k = 3$ | | $k = 4$ | |
n	$d_{L,.05}$	$d_{U,.05}$	$d_{L,.05}$	$d_{U,.05}$	$d_{L,.05}$	$d_{U,.05}$	$d_{L,.05}$	$d_{U,.05}$
15	1.08	1.36	0.95	1.54	0.82	1.75	0.69	1.97
16	1.10	1.37	0.98	1.54	0.86	1.73	0.74	1.93
17	1.13	1.38	1.02	1.54	0.90	1.71	0.78	1.90
18	1.16	1.39	1.05	1.53	0.93	1.69	0.82	1.87
19	1.18	1.40	1.08	1.53	0.97	1.68	0.86	1.85
20	1.20	1.41	1.10	1.54	1.00	1.68	0.90	1.83

model uses $k = 1$ independent variable. Therefore, if we set $\alpha = .05$, Table 13.3 tells us that $d_{L,.05} = 1.10$ and $d_{U,.05} = 1.37$. Since $d = .65$ is less than $d_{L,.05} = 1.10$, we reject the null hypothesis of no autocorrelation. That is, we conclude (at an α of .05) that there is positive (first-order) autocorrelation.

It can be shown that the Durbin–Watson statistic d is always between 0 and 4. Large values of d (and hence small values of $4 - d$) lead us to conclude that there is negative autocorrelation because if d is large, this indicates that the differences $(e_t - e_{t-1})$ are large. This says that the adjacent error terms ε_t and ε_{t-1} are negatively autocorrelated. Consider testing the null hypothesis H_0 **that the error terms are not autocorrelated** versus the alternative hypothesis H_a **that the error terms are negatively autocorrelated.** Durbin and Watson have shown that based on setting the probability of a Type I error equal to α, the points $d_{L,\alpha}$ and $d_{U,\alpha}$ are such that

1 If $(4 - d) < d_{L,\alpha}$, we reject H_0.

2 If $(4 - d) > d_{U,\alpha}$, we do not reject H_0.

3 If $d_{L,\alpha} \leq (4 - d) \leq d_{U,\alpha}$, the test is inconclusive.

Reject H_0 $d_{L,\alpha}$ Test inconclusive $d_{U,\alpha}$ Do not reject H_0

As an example, for the Pages sales simple linear regression model, we see that

$$(4 - d) = (4 - .65) = 3.35 > d_{U,.05} = 1.37$$

Therefore, on the basis of setting α equal to .05, we do not reject the null hypothesis of no autocorrelation. That is, there is no evidence of negative (first-order) autocorrelation.

We can also use the Durbin–Watson statistic to test for positive or negative autocorrelation. Specifically, consider testing the null hypothesis H_0 **that the error terms are not autocorrelated** versus the alternative hypothesis H_a **that the error terms are positively or negatively autocorrelated.** Durbin and Watson have shown that, based on setting the probability of a Type I error equal to α, we perform both the above described test for positive autocorrelation and the above described test for negative autocorrelation by using the critical values $d_{L,\alpha/2}$ and $d_{U,\alpha/2}$ for each test. If **either test** says to reject H_0, then we reject H_0. If **both tests** say to not reject H_0, then we do not reject H_0. Finally, if **either test** is inconclusive, then the overall test is inconclusive. For example, consider testing for positive or negative autocorrelation in the Pages sales model. If we set α equal to .05, then $\alpha/2 = .025$, and we need to find the points $d_{L,.025}$ and $d_{U,.025}$ when $n = 16$ and $k = 1$. Looking up these points in Table A.12 (page 649), we find that $d_{L,.025} = .98$ and $d_{U,.025} = 1.24$. Since $d = .65$ is less than $d_{L,.025} = .98$, we reject the null hypothesis of no autocorrelation. That is, we conclude (at an α of .05) that there is first-order autocorrelation.

Although we have used the Pages sales model in these examples to demonstrate the Durbin–Watson tests for (1) positive autocorrelation, (2) negative autocorrelation, and (3) positive or negative autocorrelation, we must in practice choose one of these Durbin–Watson tests in a particular situation. Since positive autocorrelation is more common in real time series data than negative autocorrelation, the Durbin–Watson test for positive autocorrelation is used more often than the other two tests. Also, note that each Durbin–Watson test assumes that the population of all possible residuals at any time t has a normal distribution.

Transforming the dependent variable: A possible remedy for violations of the constant variance, correct functional form, and normality assumptions In general, if a data or residual plot indicates that the error variance of a regression model increases as an

FIGURE 13.37   Data Plots for Exercise 13.65   ⊙ WestStk

(a) Time Series Plot of y versus t

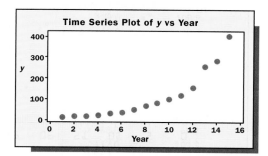

(b) Time Series Plot of Natural Logarithm of y versus t

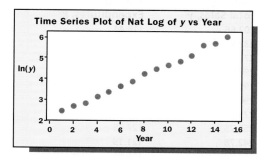

FIGURE 13.38   MINITAB Output of a Regression Analysis of the Steakhouse Data Using the Model $y^* = \beta_0 + \beta_1 x + \varepsilon$, where $y^* = \ln y$ (for Exercise 13.65)

```
The regression equation is
ln(y) = 2.07 + 0.257 Year

Predictor         Coef      SE Coef         T         P
Constant       2.07012      0.04103     50.45     0.000
Year          0.256880     0.004513     56.92     0.000

S = 0.0755161   R-Sq = 99.6%   R-Sq(adj) = 99.6%    Durbin-Watson statistic = 1.87643

Analysis of Variance
Source           DF          SS        MS         F          P
Regression        1      18.477    18.477   3239.97      0.000
Residual Error   13       0.074     0.006
Total            14      18.551

Values of Predictors for New Obs      Predicted Values for New Observations
New Obs   Year                        Obs     Fit   SE Fit        95% CI              95% PI
    1       16                          1  6.1802   0.0410   (6.0916, 6.2689)   (5.9945, 6.3659)
```

13.10 Some Shortcut Formulas (Optional) ● ● ●

Calculating the sum of squared residuals A shortcut formula for the sum of squared residuals is

$$SSE = SS_{yy} - \frac{SS_{xy}^2}{SS_{xx}}$$

where

$$SS_{yy} = \sum (y_i - \bar{y})^2 = \sum y_i^2 - \frac{\left(\sum y_i\right)^2}{n}$$

For example, consider the Tasty Sub Shop case. If we square each of the ten observed yearly revenues in Table 13.1 (page 492) and add up the resulting squared values, we find that $\sum y_i^2 = 7{,}897{,}109.47$. We have also found in Example 13.2 (page 497) that $\sum y_i = 8603.1$, $SS_{xy} = 29{,}836.389$ and $SS_{xx} = 1{,}913.129$. It follows that

$$SS_{yy} = \sum y_i^2 - \frac{\left(\sum y_i\right)^2}{n} = 7{,}897{,}109.47 - \frac{(8603.1)^2}{10} = 495{,}776.51$$

and

$$SSE = SS_{yy} - \frac{SS_{xy}^2}{SS_{xx}} = 495{,}776.51 - \frac{(29{,}836.389)^2}{1913.129}$$

$$= 495{,}776.51 - 465{,}316.30 = 30{,}460.21$$

Finally, note that SS_{xy}^2/SS_{xx} equals b_1SS_{xy}. However, we recommend using the first of these expressions, because doing so usually gives less round-off error.

Calculating the total, explained, and unexplained variations   The **unexplained variation** is SSE, and thus the shortcut formula for SSE is a shortcut formula for the unexplained variation. The quantity SS_{yy} defined on page 546 is the **total variation,** and thus the shortcut formula for SS_{yy} is a shortcut formula for the total variation. Lastly, it can be shown that the expression SS_{xy}^2/SS_{xx} equals the **explained variation** and thus is a shortcut formula for this quantity.

Chapter Summary

This chapter has discussed **simple linear regression analysis,** which relates a **dependent variable** to a single **independent (predictor) variable.** We began by considering the **simple linear regression model,** which employs two parameters: the **slope** and **y intercept.** We next discussed how to compute the **least squares point estimates** of these parameters and how to use these estimates to calculate a **point estimate of the mean value of the dependent variable** and a **point prediction of an individual value** of the dependent variable. Then, after considering the assumptions behind the simple linear regression model, we discussed **testing the significance of the regression relationship** (slope), calculating a **confidence interval** for the mean value of the dependent variable, and calculating a **prediction interval** for an individual value of the dependent variable. We next explained several measures of the utility of the simple linear regression model. These include the **simple coefficient of determination** and an **F test for the simple linear model.** We concluded this chapter by giving a discussion of using **residual analysis** to detect violations of the regression assumptions. We learned that we can sometimes remedy violations of these assumptions by **transforming** the dependent variable.

Glossary of Terms

dependent variable: The variable that is being described, predicted, or controlled. (page 491)

distance value: A measure of the distance between a particular value x_0 of the independent variable x and $\bar{x}$, the average of the previously observed values of x (the center of the experimental region). (page 515)

error term: The difference between an individual value of the dependent variable and the corresponding mean value of the dependent variable. (page 494)

experimental region: The range of the previously observed values of the independent variable. (page 498)

independent variable: A variable used to describe, predict, and control the dependent variable. (page 491)

least squares point estimates: The point estimates of the slope and y intercept of the simple linear regression model that minimize the sum of squared residuals. (pages 496–497)

negative autocorrelation: The situation in which positive error terms tend to be followed over time by negative error terms and negative error terms tend to be followed over time by positive error terms. (page 536)

normal plot: A residual plot that is used to check the normality assumption. (page 534)

positive autocorrelation: The situation in which positive error terms tend to be followed over time by positive error terms and

negative error terms tend to be followed over time by negative error terms. (page 535)

residual: The difference between the observed value of the dependent variable and the corresponding predicted value of the dependent variable. (pages 496, 531)

residual plot: A plot of the residuals against some criterion. The plot is used to check the validity of one or more regression assumptions. (page 531)

simple coefficient of determination: The proportion of the total variation in the observed values of the dependent variable that is explained by the simple linear regression model. (page 522)

simple correlation coefficient: A measure of the linear association between two variables. (page 523)

simple linear regression model: An equation that describes the straight-line relationship between a dependent variable and an independent variable. (page 494)

slope (of the simple linear regression model): The change in the mean value of the dependent variable that is associated with a one-unit increase in the value of the independent variable. (page 494)

y-intercept (of the simple linear regression model): The mean value of the dependent variable when the value of the independent variable is 0. (page 494)

Appendix 13.2 ■ Simple Linear Regression Analysis Using MegaStat

The instructions in this section begin by describing the entry of data into an Excel worksheet. Alternatively, the data may be downloaded from this book's website. The appropriate data file name is given at the top of each instruction block. Please refer to Appendix 1.1 for further information about entering data, saving data, and printing results in Excel. Please refer to Appendix 1.2 for more information about using MegaStat.

Simple linear regression for the service time data in Exercise 13.5 on page 501 (data file: SrvcTime.xlsx):

- Enter the service time data (page 502) with the numbers of copiers serviced in column A with label Copiers and with the service times in column B with label Minutes.

- Select **Add-Ins : MegaStat : Correlation/ Regression : Regression Analysis.**

- In the Regression Analysis dialog box, click in the Independent Variables window and use the autoexpand feature to enter the range A1 : A12.

- Click in the Dependent Variable window and use the autoexpand feature to enter the range B1 : B12.

- Check the appropriate Options and Residuals checkboxes as follows:

  1 Check "Test Intercept" to include a y-intercept and to test its significance.

  2 Check "Output Residuals" to obtain a list of the model residuals.

  3 Check "Plot Residuals by Observation," and "Plot Residuals by Predicted Y and X" to obtain residual plots versus time, versus the predicted values of y, and versus the values of the independent variable.

  4 Check "Normal Probability Plot of Residuals" to obtain a normal plot.

  5 Check "Durbin-Watson" for the Durbin–Watson statistic.

To obtain a **point prediction** of y when four computers will be serviced (as well as a confidence interval and prediction interval):

- Click on the drop-down menu above the Predictor Values window and select "Type in predictor values."

- Type the value of the independent variable for which a prediction is desired (here equal to 4) into the Predictor Values window.

- Select a desired level of confidence (here 95%) from the Confidence Level drop-down menu or type in a value.

- Click OK in the Regression Analysis dialog box.

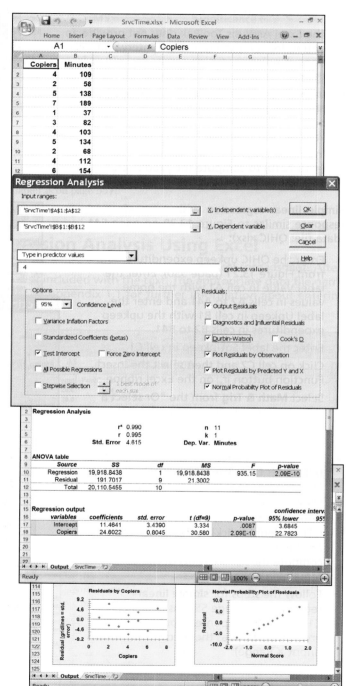

To compute several point predictions of *y*—say, when 1, 2, 3, and 4 computers will be serviced—(and to compute corresponding confidence and prediction intervals):

- Enter the values of *x* for which predictions are desired into a column in the spreadsheet—these values can be in any column. Here we have entered the values 1, 2, 3, and 4 into cells E1 through E4.

- Click on the drop-down menu above the predictor values box and select "Predictor values from spreadsheet cells."

- Enter the range E1 : E4 into the predictor values box.

- Click OK in the Regression Analysis dialog box.

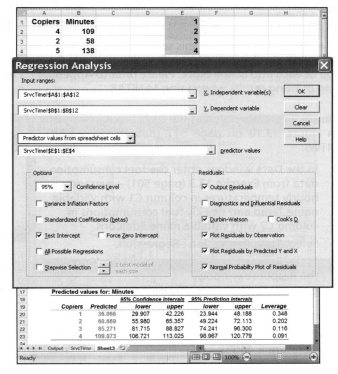

Simple linear regression with a transformed response similar to Figure 13.30 on page 541 (data file: QHIC.xlsx):

- Enter the QHIC data from Figure 13.21 (page 530)—the home values in column A (with label Value) and the upkeep expenditures in column B (with label Upkeep).

- Follow the instructions on page 553 in Appendix 13.1 to calculate the square roots of the upkeep expenditures in column C (with label SRUpkeep).

- Select **Add-Ins : MegaStat : Correlation/ Regression : Regression Analysis.**

- In the Regression Analysis dialog box, click in the Independent variables window, and use the AutoExpand feature to enter the range A1 : A41.

- Click in the Dependent variable window and use the AutoExpand feature to enter the range C1 : C41.

- Check the "Test Intercept" checkbox to include a *y*-intercept and test its significance.

To compute a **point prediction of the square root of *y*** (as well as a confidence interval and prediction interval) for a house having a value of $220,000:

- Select "Type in predictor values" from the drop-down menu above the predictor values window.

- Type 220 into the predictor values window.

- Select a desired level of confidence (here 95%) from the drop-down menu in the Confidence Level box or type in a value.

- Click OK in the Regression Analysis dialog box.

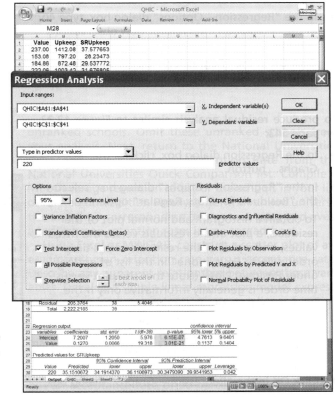

restaurants in Table 14.1. If any particular values of b_0, b_1, and b_2 are good point estimates, they will make the predicted yearly revenue for each restaurant fairly close to the observed yearly revenue for the restaurant. This will make the restaurant's *residual*—the difference between the restaurant's observed and predicted yearly revenues—fairly small (in magnitude). We define the **least squares point estimates** to be the values of b_0, b_1, and b_2 that minimize *SSE*, the sum of squared residuals for the 10 restaurants.

Appendix 13.3 ■ Simple Linear Regression Analysis Using MINITAB

FIGURE 14.1	Plot of y (Yearly Revenue) versus x_1 (Population Size)

FIGURE 14.2	Plot of y (Yearly Revenue) versus x_2 (Business Rating)

FIGURE 14.4   Excel and MINITAB Outputs of a Regression Analysis of the Tasty Sub Shop Revenue Data in Table 14.1 Using the Model $y_i = \beta_0 + \beta_1 x_1 + \beta_2 x_2 + \varepsilon$

(a) The Excel output

Regression Statistics

Multiple R	0.9905
R Square	0.9810 [8]
Adjusted R Square	0.9756 [9]
Standard Error	36.6856 [7]
Observations	10

ANOVA	df	SS	MS	F	Significance F
Regression	2	486355.7 [10]	243177.8	180.689 [13]	9.46E-07 [14]
Residual	7	9420.8 [11]	1345.835		
Total	9	495776.5 [12]			

	Coefficients	Standard Error [4]	t Stat [5]	P-value [6]	Lower 95% [19]	Upper 95% [19]
Intercept	125.289 [1]	40.9333	3.06	0.0183	28.4969	222.0807
population	14.1996 [2]	0.9100	15.60	1.07E-06	12.0478	16.3517
bus_rating	22.8107 [3]	5.7692	3.95	0.0055	9.1686	36.4527

(b) The MINITAB output

```
The regression equation is
revenue = 125 + 14.2 population + 22.8 bus_rating

Predictor          Coef       SE Coef[4]              T[5]           P[6]
Constant         125.29[1]     40.93                 3.06          0.018
population        14.1996[2]    0.91                 15.6          0.000
bus_rating        22.811[3]     5.769                3.95          0.006

S = 36.6856[7]              R-Sq = 98.10%[8]         R-Sq(adj) = 97.6%[9]

Analysis of Variance
Source             DF         SS                  MS              F              P
Regression          2      486356[10]           243178        180.69[13]     0.000[14]
Residual Error      7        9421[11]             1346
Total               9      495777[12]

Predicted Values for New Observations
     New Obs     Fit[15]         SE Fit[16]          95% CI[17]            95% PI[18]
        1        956.6             15            (921.0, 992.2)      (862.8, 1050.4)

Values of Predictors for New Observations
     New Obs      population        bus_rating
        1           47.3                7
```

[1] b_0	[2] b_1	[3] b_2	[4] s_{b_j} = standard error of the estimate b_j	[5] t statistics	[6] p-values for t statistics	[7] s = standard error

[8] R^2	[9] Adjusted R^2	[10] Explained variation	[11] SSE = Unexplained variation	[12] Total variation	[13] F(model) statistic

[14] p-value for F(model)   [15] $\hat{y}$ = point prediction when x_1 = 47.3 and x_2 = 7   [16] $s_{\hat{y}}$ = standard error of the estimate $\hat{y}$

[17] 95% confidence interval when x_1 = 47.3 and x_2 = 7   [18] 95% prediction interval when x_1 = 47.3 and x_2 = 7   [19] 95% confidence interval for β_j

The formula for the least squares point estimates of the parameters in a multiple regression model is expressed using a branch of mathematics called **matrix algebra.** This formula is presented in Bowerman and O'Connell (1990). In the main body of the book, we will rely on Excel and MINITAB to compute the needed estimates. For example, consider the Excel and MINITAB outputs in Figure 14.4. These outputs tell us that the least squares point estimates of β_0, β_1, and β_2 in the Tasty Sub Shop revenue model are $b_0 = 125.29$, $b_1 = 14.1996$, and $b_2 = 22.811$ (see [1], [2], and [3]). The point estimate $b_1 = 14.1996$ of β_1 says we estimate that mean yearly revenue increases by \$14,199.60 when the population size increases by 1,000 residents and the business rating does not change. The point estimate $b_2 = 22.811$ of β_2 says we estimate that mean yearly revenue increases by \$22,811 when there is a one-unit increase in the business rating and the population size does not change.

TABLE 14.2 The Point Predictions and Residuals Using the Least Squares Point Estimates, $b_0 = 125.29$, $b_1 = 14.1996$, and $b_2 = 22.811$

Restaurant	Population Size, x_1 (Thousands of Residents)	Business Rating, x_2	Yearly Revenue, y (Thousands of Dollars)	Predicted Yearly Revenue $\hat{y} = 125.29 + 14.1996x_1 + 22.811x_2$	Residual, $y - \hat{y}$
1	20.8	3	527.1	489.07	38.03
2	27.5	2	548.7	561.40	−12.70
3	32.3	6	767.2	720.80	46.40
4	37.2	5	722.9	767.57	−44.67
5	39.6	8	826.3	870.08	−43.78
6	45.1	3	810.5	834.12	−23.62
7	49.9	9	1040.7	1039.15	1.55
8	55.4	5	1033.6	1026.00	7.60
9	61.7	4	1090.3	1092.65	−2.35
10	64.6	7	1235.8	1202.26	33.54

$$SSE = (38.03)^2 + (-12.70)^2 + \cdots + (33.54)^2 = 9420.8$$

The equation

$$\hat{y} = b_0 + b_1x_1 + b_2x_2$$
$$= 125.29 + 14.1996x_1 + 22.811x_2$$

is called the **least squares prediction equation.** In Table 14.2 we summarize using this prediction equation to calculate the predicted yearly revenues and the residuals for the 10 observed Tasty Sub restaurants. For example, since the population size and business rating for restaurant 1 were 20.8 and 3, the predicted yearly revenue for restaurant 1 is

$$\hat{y} = 125.29 + 14.1996(20.8) + 22.811(3)$$
$$= 489.07$$

It follows, since the observed yearly revenue for restaurant 1 was $y = 527.1$, that the residual for restaurant 1 is

$$y - \hat{y} = 527.1 - 489.07 = 38.03$$

If we consider all of the residuals in Table 14.2 and add their squared values, we find that **SSE, the sum of squared residuals,** is 9420.8. This *SSE* value is given on the Excel and MINITAB outputs in Figure 14.4 (see [11]) and will be used throughout this chapter.

Part 3: Estimating means and predicting individual values　　The least squares prediction equation is the equation of a plane—called the **least squares plane**—in three-dimensional space. The least squares plane is the estimate of the plane of means. It follows that the point on the least squares plane corresponding to the population size x_1 and the business rating x_2

$$\hat{y} = b_0 + b_1x_1 + b_2x_2$$
$$= 125.29 + 14.1996x_1 + 22.811x_2$$

is the point estimate of $\beta_0 + \beta_1x_1 + \beta_2x_2$, the mean yearly revenue for all Tasty Sub restaurants that could potentially be built near populations of size x_1 and business/shopping areas having a rating of x_2. In addition, since we predict the error term to be 0, $\hat{y}$ is also the point prediction of $y = \beta_0 + \beta_1x_1 + \beta_2x_2 + \varepsilon$, the yearly revenue for a single Tasty Sub restaurant that is built near a population of size x_1 and a business/shopping area having a rating of x_2.

　　For example, suppose that one of the business entrepreneur's potential restaurant sites is near a population of 47,300 residents and a business/shopping area having a rating of 7. It follows that

$$\hat{y} = 125.29 + 14.1996(47.3) + 22.811(7)$$
$$= 956.6 \text{ (that is, \$956.600)}$$

FIGURE 14.5   Excel and MINITAB Outputs of a Regression Analysis of the Fuel Consumption Data
               Using the Model $y = \beta_0 + \beta_1 x_1 + \beta_2 x_2 + \varepsilon$

(a) The Excel output

Regression Statistics

Multiple R	0.9867
R Square	0.9736
Adjusted R Square	0.9631
Standard Error	0.3671
Observations	8

ANOVA	df	SS	MS	F	Significance F
Regression	2	24.8750	12.4375	92.3031	0.0001
Residual	5	0.6737	0.1347		
Total	7	25.5488			

	Coefficients	Standard Error	t Stat	P-value	Lower 95%	Upper 95%
Intercept	13.1087	0.8557	15.3193	2.15E-05	10.9091	15.3084
TEMP	-0.0900	0.0141	-6.3942	0.0014	-0.1262	-0.0538
CHILL	0.0825	0.0220	3.7493	0.0133	0.0259	0.1391

(b) The MINITAB output

```
The regression equation is
FuelCons = 13.1 - 0.0900 Temp + 0.0825 Chill

Predictor        Coef       SE Coef           T          P
Constant      13.1087        0.8557       15.32      0.000
Temp         -0.09001       0.01408       -6.39      0.001
Chill         0.08249       0.02200        3.75      0.013

s = 0.367078      R-Sq = 97.4%       R-Sq(adj) = 96.3%

Analysis of Variance
Source           DF          SS          MS          F          P
Regression        2      24.875      12.438      92.30      0.000
Residual Error    5       0.674       0.135
Total             7      25.549

Values of Predictors for New Obs     Predicted Values for New Observations
New Obs Temp Chill                   New Obs     Fit     SE Fit      95% CI            95% PI
    1   40.0  10.0                       1    10.333      0.170  (9.895, 10.771)  (9.293, 11.374)
```

FIGURE 14.6   MINITAB Output of a Regression Analysis of the Real Estate Sales Price Data Using
               the Model $y = \beta_0 + \beta_1 x_1 + \beta_2 x_2 + \varepsilon$

```
The regression equation is
SalesPrice = 29.3 + 5.61 HomeSize + 3.83 Rating

Predictor     Coef   SE Coef       T        P
Constant    29.347     4.891    6.00    0.001
HomeSize    5.6128    0.2285   24.56    0.000
Rating      3.8344    0.4332    8.85    0.000

S = 3.24164   R-Sq = 99.0%   R-Sq(adj) = 98.7%

Analysis of Variance
Source          DF       SS       MS       F        P
Regression       2   7374.0   3687.0  350.87    0.000
Residual Error   7     73.6     10.5
Total            9   7447.5

Values of Predictors for New Obs     Predicted Values for New Observations
New Obs  HomeSize  Rating            New Obs    Fit   SE Fit       95% CI              95% PI
    1      20.0     8.00                 1   172.28     1.57  (168.56, 175.99)  (163.76, 180.80)
```

The agency wishes to develop a regression model that can be used to predict the sales prices of future houses it will list. Figure 14.6 gives the MINITAB output of a regression analysis of the real estate sales price data in Table 14.4 using the model

$$y = \beta_0 + \beta_1 x_1 + \beta_2 x_2 + \varepsilon$$

a Using the MINITAB output, identify and interpret b_1 and b_2, the least squares point estimates of β_1 and β_2.

b Calculate a point estimate of the mean sales price of all houses having 2,000 square feet and a rating of 8, and a point prediction of the sales price of a single house having 2,000 square feet and a rating of 8. Find this point estimate (prediction), which is given at the bottom of the MINITAB output, and verify that it equals (within rounding) your calculated value.

14.5   THE FRESH DETERGENT CASE   DS Fresh2

Enterprise Industries produces Fresh, a brand of liquid laundry detergent. In order to manage its inventory more effectively and make revenue projections, the company would like to better predict demand for Fresh. To develop a prediction model, the company has gathered data concerning demand for Fresh over the last 30 sales periods (each sales period is defined to be a four-week period). The demand data are presented in Table 14.5. Here, for each sales period,

y = the demand for the large size bottle of Fresh (in hundreds of thousands of bottles) in the sales period

x_1 = the price (in dollars) of Fresh as offered by Enterprise Industries in the sales period

x_2 = the average industry price (in dollars) of competitors' similar detergents in the sales period

x_3 = Enterprise Industries' advertising expenditure (in hundreds of thousands of dollars) to promote Fresh in the sales period

Figure 14.7 gives the Excel output of a regression analysis of the Fresh Detergent demand data in Table 14.5 using the model

$$y = \beta_0 + \beta_1 x_1 + \beta_2 x_2 + \beta_3 x_3 + \varepsilon$$

a Find (on the output) and report the values of b_1, b_2, and b_3, the least squares point estimates of β_1, β_2, and β_3. Interpret b_1, b_2, and b_3.

TABLE 14.5   Historical Data Concerning Demand for Fresh Detergent   DS Fresh2

Sales Period	Price for Fresh, x_1	Average Industry Price, x_2	Advertising Expenditure for Fresh, x_3	Demand for Fresh, y	Sales Period	Price for Fresh, x_1	Average Industry Price, x_2	Advertising Expenditure for Fresh, x_3	Demand for Fresh, y
1	3.85	3.80	5.50	7.38	16	3.80	4.10	6.80	8.87
2	3.75	4.00	6.75	8.51	17	3.70	4.20	7.10	9.26
3	3.70	4.30	7.25	9.52	18	3.80	4.30	7.00	9.00
4	3.70	3.70	5.50	7.50	19	3.70	4.10	6.80	8.75
5	3.60	3.85	7.00	9.33	20	3.80	3.75	6.50	7.95
6	3.60	3.80	6.50	8.28	21	3.80	3.75	6.25	7.65
7	3.60	3.75	6.75	8.75	22	3.75	3.65	6.00	7.27
8	3.80	3.85	5.25	7.87	23	3.70	3.90	6.50	8.00
9	3.80	3.65	5.25	7.10	24	3.55	3.65	7.00	8.50
10	3.85	4.00	6.00	8.00	25	3.60	4.10	6.80	8.75
11	3.90	4.10	6.50	7.89	26	3.65	4.25	6.80	9.21
12	3.90	4.00	6.25	8.15	27	3.70	3.65	6.50	8.27
13	3.70	4.10	7.00	9.10	28	3.75	3.75	5.75	7.67
14	3.75	4.20	6.90	8.86	29	3.80	3.85	5.80	7.93
15	3.75	4.10	6.80	8.90	30	3.70	4.25	6.80	9.26

FIGURE 14.7   **Excel Output of a Regression Analysis of the Fresh Detergent Demand Data Using the Model** $y = \beta_0 + \beta_1 x_1 + \beta_2 x_2 + \beta_3 x_3 + \varepsilon$

(a) The Excel output

Regression Statistics

Multiple R	0.9453
R Square	0.8936
Adjusted R Square	0.8813
Standard Error	0.2347
Observations	30

ANOVA	df	SS	MS	F	Significance F
Regression	3	12.0268	4.0089	72.797	8.883E-13
Residual	26	1.4318	0.0551		
Total	29	13.4586			

	Coefficients	Standard Error	t Stat	P-value	Lower 95%	Upper 95%
Intercept	7.5891	2.4450	3.1039	0.0046	2.5633	12.6149
Price (X1)	-2.3577	0.6379	-3.6958	0.0010	-3.6690	-1.0464
IndPrice (X2)	1.6122	0.2954	5.4586	0.0000	1.0051	2.2193
AdvExp (X3)	0.5012	0.1259	3.9814	0.0005	0.2424	0.7599

(b) Prediction using an Excel add-in (MegaStat)

Predicted values for: Demand (y)

Price (x1)	IndPrice (x2)	AdvExp (x3)	Predicted	95% Confidence Interval lower	95% Confidence Interval upper	95% Prediction Interval lower	95% Prediction Interval upper	Leverage
3.7	3.9	6.5	8.4107	8.3143	8.5070	7.9188	8.9025	0.040

TABLE 14.6   **Hospital Labor Needs Data**   ⅅⓈ HospLab

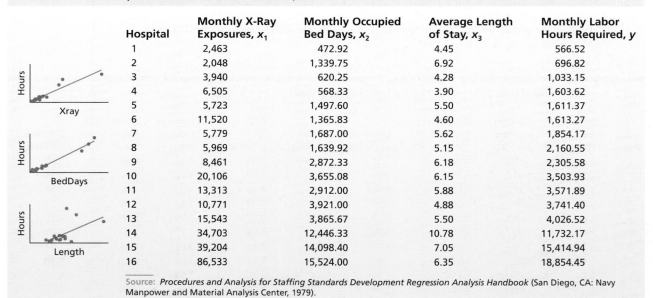

Hospital	Monthly X-Ray Exposures, x_1	Monthly Occupied Bed Days, x_2	Average Length of Stay, x_3	Monthly Labor Hours Required, y
1	2,463	472.92	4.45	566.52
2	2,048	1,339.75	6.92	696.82
3	3,940	620.25	4.28	1,033.15
4	6,505	568.33	3.90	1,603.62
5	5,723	1,497.60	5.50	1,611.37
6	11,520	1,365.83	4.60	1,613.27
7	5,779	1,687.00	5.62	1,854.17
8	5,969	1,639.92	5.15	2,160.55
9	8,461	2,872.33	6.18	2,305.58
10	20,106	3,655.08	6.15	3,503.93
11	13,313	2,912.00	5.88	3,571.89
12	10,771	3,921.00	4.88	3,741.40
13	15,543	3,865.67	5.50	4,026.52
14	34,703	12,446.33	10.78	11,732.17
15	39,204	14,098.40	7.05	15,414.94
16	86,533	15,524.00	6.35	18,854.45

Source: *Procedures and Analysis for Staffing Standards Development Regression Analysis Handbook* (San Diego, CA: Navy Manpower and Material Analysis Center, 1979).

b Consider the demand for Fresh Detergent in a future sales period when Enterprise Industries' price for Fresh will be $x_1 = 3.70$, the average price of competitors' similar detergents will be $x_2 = 3.90$ and Enterprise Industries' advertising expenditure for Fresh will be $x_3 = 6.50$. The point prediction of this demand is given at the bottom of the Excel add-in output. Report this point prediction and show (within rounding) how it has been calculated.

14.6 THE HOSPITAL LABOR NEEDS CASE   ⅅⓈ HospLab

Table 14.6 presents data concerning the need for labor in 16 U.S. Navy hospitals. Here, y = monthly labor hours required; x_1 = monthly X-ray exposures; x_2 = monthly occupied bed

FIGURE 14.8   **Excel Output of a Regression Analysis of the Hospital Labor Needs Data Using the Model** $y = \beta_0 + \beta_1 x_1 + \beta_2 x_2 + \beta_3 x_3 + \varepsilon$

(a) The Excel output

Regression Statistics

Multiple R	0.9981
R Square	0.9961
Adjusted R Square	0.9952
Standard Error	387.1598
Observations	16

ANOVA	df	SS	MS	F	Significance F
Regression	3	462327889.4	154109296.5	1028.1309	9.92E-15
Residual	12	1798712.2	149892.7		
Total	15	464126601.6			

	Coefficients	Standard Error	t Stat	P-value	Lower 95%	Upper 95%
Intercept	1946.8020	504.1819	3.8613	0.0023	848.2840	3045.3201
XRay (x1)	0.0386	0.0130	2.9579	0.0120	0.0102	0.0670
BedDays (x2)	1.0394	0.0676	15.3857	2.91E-09	0.8922	1.1866
LengthStay (x3)	-413.7578	98.5983	-4.1964	0.0012	-628.5850	-198.9306

(b) Prediction Using an Excel add-in (MegaStat)

Predicted values for: LaborHours

XRay (x1)	BedDays (x2)	LengthStay (x3)	Predicted	95% Confidence Interval lower	95% Confidence Interval upper	95% Prediction Interval lower	95% Prediction Interval upper	Leverage
56194	14077.88	6.89	15,896.2473	15,378.0313	16,414.4632	14,906.2361	16,886.2584	0.3774

days (a hospital has one occupied bed day if one bed is occupied for an entire day); and $x_3 =$ average length of patients' stay (in days). Figure 14.8 gives the Excel output of a regression analysis of the data using the model

$$y = \beta_0 + \beta_1 x_1 + \beta_2 x_2 + \beta_3 x_3 + \varepsilon$$

Note that the variables x_1, x_2, and x_3 are denoted as XRay, BedDays, and LengthStay on the output.

a Find (on the output) and report the values of b_1, b_2, and b_3, the least squares point estimates of β_1, β_2, and β_3. Interpret b_1, b_2, and b_3.

b Consider a questionable hospital for which XRay = 56,194, BedDays = 14,077.88, and LengthStay = 6.89. A point prediction of the labor hours corresponding to this combination of values of the independent variables is given on the Excel add-in output. Report this point prediction and show (within rounding) how it has been calculated.

c If the actual number of labor hours used by the questionable hospital was $y = 17,207.31$, how does this y value compare with the point prediction?

14.2 Model Assumptions and the Standard Error ● ● ●

Model assumptions   In order to perform hypothesis tests and set up various types of intervals when using the multiple regression model

$$y = \beta_0 + \beta_1 x_1 + \beta_2 x_2 + \cdots + \beta_k x_k + \varepsilon$$

we need to make certain assumptions about the error term ε. At any given combination of values of $x_1, x_2, \ldots, x_k$, there is a population of error term values that could potentially occur. These error term values describe the different potential effects on y of all factors other than the combination of values of $x_1, x_2, \ldots, x_k$. Therefore, these error term values explain the variation in the y values that could be observed at the combination of values of $x_1, x_2, \ldots, x_k$. We make the following four assumptions about the potential error term values.

LO2 Explain the assumptions behind multiple regression and calculate the standard error.

Assumptions for the Multiple Regression Model

1 At any given combination of values of x_1, x_2, ..., x_k, the population of potential error term values has a mean equal to 0.

2 **Constant variance assumption:** At any given combination of values of x_1, x_2, ..., x_k, the population of potential error term values has a variance that does not depend on the combination of values of x_1, x_2, ..., x_k. That is, the different populations of potential error term values corresponding to different combinations of values of x_1, x_2, ..., x_k have equal variances. We denote the constant variance as σ^2.

3 **Normality assumption:** At any given combination of values of x_1, x_2, ..., x_k, the population of potential error term values has a **normal distribution**.

4 **Independence assumption:** Any one value of the error term ε is **statistically independent** of any other value of ε. That is, the value of the error term ε corresponding to an observed value of y is statistically independent of the error term corresponding to any other observed value of y.

Taken together, the first three assumptions say that, at any given combination of values of x_1, x_2, ..., x_k, the population of potential error term values is normally distributed with mean 0 and a variance σ^2 that does not depend on the combination of values of x_1, x_2, ..., x_k. Because the potential error term values cause the variation in the potential y values, the first three assumptions imply that, at any given combination of values of x_1, x_2, ..., x_k, the population of y values that could be observed is normally distributed with mean $\beta_0 + \beta_1 x_1 + \beta_2 x_2 + \cdots + \beta_k x_k$ and a variance σ^2 that does not depend on the combination of values of x_1, x_2, ..., x_k. Furthermore, the independence assumption says that, when time series data are utilized in a regression study, there are no patterns in the error term values. In Section 14.11 we show how to check the validity of the regression assumptions. That section can be read at any time after Section 14.7. As in simple linear regression, only pronounced departures from the assumptions must be remedied.

The mean square error and the standard error   To present statistical inference formulas in later sections, we need to be able to compute point estimates of σ^2 and σ (the constant variance and standard deviation of the different error term populations). We show how to do this in the following box:

The Mean Square Error and the Standard Error

Suppose that the multiple regression model

$$y = \beta_0 + \beta_1 x_1 + \beta_2 x_2 + \cdots + \beta_k x_k + \varepsilon$$

utilizes k independent variables and thus has $(k + 1)$ parameters β_0, β_1, β_2, ..., β_k. Then, if the regression assumptions are satisfied, and if SSE denotes the sum of squared residuals for the model:

1 A point estimate of σ^2 is the **mean square error**

$$s^2 = \frac{SSE}{n - (k + 1)}$$

2 A point estimate of σ is the **standard error**

$$s = \sqrt{\frac{SSE}{n - (k + 1)}}$$

In order to explain these point estimates, recall that σ^2 is the variance of the population of y values (for given values of x_1, x_2, ..., x_k) around the mean value μ_y. Since $\hat{y}$ is the point estimate of this mean, it seems natural to use $SSE = \Sigma(y_i - \hat{y}_i)^2$ to help construct a point estimate of σ^2. We divide SSE by $n - (k + 1)$ because it can be proven that doing so makes the resulting s^2 an unbiased point estimate of σ^2. We call $n - (k + 1)$ the **number of degrees of freedom** associated with SSE.

We will see in Section 14.6 that if a particular regression model gives a small standard error, then the model will give short prediction intervals and thus accurate predictions of individual y values. For example, Table 14.2 (page 563) shows that SSE for the Tasty Sub Shop revenue model

$$y = \beta_0 + \beta_1 x_1 + \beta_2 x_2 + \varepsilon$$

is 9420.8. Since this model utilizes $k = 2$ independent variables and thus has $k + 1 = 3$ parameters (β_0, β_1, and β_2), a point estimate of σ^2 is the mean square error

$$s^2 = \frac{SSE}{n - (k + 1)} = \frac{9420.8}{10 - 3} = \frac{9420.8}{7} = 1345.835$$

and a point estimate of σ is the standard error $s = \sqrt{1345.835} = 36.6856$. Note that $SSE = 9420.8$, $s^2 = 1345.835$, and $s = 36.6856$ are given on the Excel and MINITAB outputs in Figure 14.4 (page 562). Also note that the s of 36.6856 for the two independent variable model is less than the s of 61.7052 for the simple linear regression model that uses only the population size to predict yearly revenue (see Example 13.3, page 506).

14.3 R^2 and Adjusted R^2 ● ● ●

The multiple coefficient of determination, R^2   In this section we discuss several ways to assess the utility of a multiple regression model. We first discuss a quantity called the **multiple coefficient of determination,** which is denoted R^2. The formulas for R^2 and several other related quantities are given in the following box:

LO3 Calculate and interpret the multiple and adjusted multiple coefficients of determination.

The Multiple Coefficient of Determination, R^2

For the multiple regression model:

1 **Total variation** $= \sum (y_i - \bar{y})^2$
2 **Explained variation** $= \sum (\hat{y}_i - \bar{y})^2$
3 **Unexplained variation** $= \sum (y_i - \hat{y}_i)^2$
4 **Total variation = Explained variation + Unexplained variation**

5 The **multiple coefficient of determination** is

$$R^2 = \frac{\text{Explained variation}}{\text{Total variation}}$$

6 R^2 is the proportion of the total variation in the n observed values of the dependent variable that is explained by the overall regression model.
7 **Multiple correlation coefficient** $= R = \sqrt{R^2}$

As an example, consider the Tasty Sub Shop revenue model

$$y = \beta_0 + \beta_1 x_1 + \beta_2 x_2 + \varepsilon$$

and the following MINITAB output:

```
S = 36.6856    R-Sq = 98.10%   R-Sq(adj) = 97.6%


Analysis of Variance
Source            DF        SS        MS        F        P
Regression         2    486356    243178    180.69    0.000
Residual Error     7      9421      1346
Total              9    495777
```

This output tells us that the total variation (SS Total), explained variation (SS Regression), and unexplained variation (SS Residual Error) for the model are, respectively, 495,777, 486,356, and 9,421. The output also tells us that the multiple coefficient of determination is

$$R^2 = \frac{\text{Explained variation}}{\text{Total variation}} = \frac{486,356}{495,777} = .981 \quad (98.1\% \text{ on the output})$$

which implies that the multiple correlation coefficient is $R = \sqrt{.981} = .9905$. The value of $R^2 = .981$ says that the two independent variable Tasty Sub Shop revenue model explains 98.1 percent of the total variation in the 10 observed yearly revenues. Note this R^2 value is larger than the r^2 of .939 for the simple linear regression model that uses only the population size to predict yearly revenue. Also note that the quantities given on the MINITAB output are given on the following Excel output.

Regression Statistics

Multiple R	0.9905
R Square	0.9810
Adjusted R Square	0.9756
Standard Error	36.6856
Observations	10

ANOVA	df	SS	MS	F	Significance F
Regression	2	486355.7	243177.8	180.689	9.46E-07
Residual	7	9420.8	1345.835		
Total	9	495776.5			

Adjusted R^2 Even if the independent variables in a regression model are unrelated to the dependent variable, they will make R^2 somewhat greater than 0. To avoid overestimating the importance of the independent variables, many analysts recommend calculating an *adjusted* multiple coefficient of determination.

Adjusted R^2

The **adjusted multiple coefficient of determination (adjusted R^2)** is

$$\bar{R}^2 = \left(R^2 - \frac{k}{n-1}\right)\left(\frac{n-1}{n-(k+1)}\right)$$

where R^2 is the multiple coefficient of determination, n is the number of observations, and k is the number of independent variables in the model under consideration.

To briefly explain this formula, note that it can be shown that subtracting $k/(n-1)$ from R^2 helps avoid overestimating the importance of the k independent variables. Furthermore, multiplying $[R^2 - (k/(n-1))]$ by $(n-1)/(n-(k+1))$ makes $\bar{R}^2$ equal to 1 when R^2 equals 1.

As an example, consider the Tasty Sub Shop revenue model

$$y = \beta_0 + \beta_1 x_1 + \beta_2 x_2 + \varepsilon$$

Since we have seen that $R^2 = .981$, it follows that

$$\bar{R}^2 = \left(R^2 - \frac{k}{n-1}\right)\left(\frac{n-1}{n-(k+1)}\right)$$

$$= \left(.981 - \frac{2}{10-1}\right)\left(\frac{10-1}{10-(2+1)}\right)$$

$$= .9756$$

which is given on the MINITAB and Excel outputs.

If R^2 is less than $k/(n-1)$ (which can happen), then $\bar{R}^2$ will be negative. In this case, statistical software systems set $\bar{R}^2$ equal to 0. Historically, R^2 and $\bar{R}^2$ have been popular measures of model utility—possibly because they are unitless and between 0 and 1. In general, we desire R^2 and $\bar{R}^2$ to be near 1. However, sometimes even if a regression model has an R^2 and an $\bar{R}^2$ that are near 1, the model is still not able to predict accurately. We will discuss assessing a model's ability to predict accurately, as well as using R^2 and $\bar{R}^2$ to help choose a regression model, as we proceed through the rest of this chapter.

14.4 The Overall *F* Test ● ● ●

LO4 Test the significance of a multiple regression model by using an *F* test.

Another way to assess the utility of a regression model is to test the significance of the regression relationship between y and $x_1, x_2, \ldots, x_k$. For the multiple regression model, we test the null hypothesis $H_0: \beta_1 = \beta_2 = \cdots = \beta_k = 0$, which says that **none of the independent variables** $x_1,$ $x_2, \ldots, x_k$ **is significantly related to** y **(the regression relationship is not significant)**, versus the alternative hypothesis H_a: At least one of $\beta_1, \beta_2, \ldots, \beta_k$ does not equal 0, which says that **at least one of the independent variables is significantly related to** y **(the regression relationship is significant)**. If we can reject H_0 at level of significance α, we say that **the multiple regression model is significant at level of significance** α. We carry out the test as follows:

An *F* Test for the Multiple Regression Model

Suppose that the regression assumptions hold and that the multiple regression model has $(k + 1)$ parameters, and consider testing

$$H_0: \beta_1 = \beta_2 = \cdots = \beta_k = 0$$

versus

H_a: At least one of $\beta_1, \beta_2, \ldots, \beta_k$ does not equal 0.

We define the **overall *F* statistic** to be

$$F(\text{model}) = \frac{(\text{Explained variation})/k}{(\text{Unexplained variation})/[n - (k + 1)]}$$

Also define the *p*-value related to *F*(model) to be the area under the curve of the *F* distribution (having k and $[n - (k + 1)]$ degrees of freedom) to the right of *F*(model). Then, we can reject H_0 in favor of H_a at level of significance α if either of the following equivalent conditions holds:

1 $F(\text{model}) > F_\alpha$

2 *p*-value $< \alpha$

Here the point F_α is based on k numerator and $n - (k + 1)$ denominator degrees of freedom.

Condition 1 is intuitively reasonable because a large value of *F*(model) would be caused by an explained variation that is large relative to the unexplained variation. This would occur if at least one independent variable in the regression model significantly affects y, which would imply that H_0 is false and H_a is true.

EXAMPLE 14.2 The Tasty Sub Shop Case

Consider the Tasty Sub Shop revenue model

$$y = \beta_0 + \beta_1 x_1 + \beta_2 x_2 + \varepsilon$$

and the following MINITAB output

```
Analysis of Variance
Source          DF      SS       MS       F       P
Regression       2   486356   243178   180.69   0.000
Residual Error   7     9421     1346
Total            9   495777
```

This output tells us that the explained and unexplained variations for this model are, respectively, 486,356 and 9,421. It follows, since there are $k = 2$ independent variables, that

$$F(\text{model}) = \frac{(\text{Explained variation})/k}{(\text{Unexplained variation})/[n - (k + 1)]}$$

$$= \frac{486{,}356/2}{9421/[10 - (2 + 1)]} = \frac{243{,}178}{1345.8}$$

$$= 180.69$$

Note that this overall F statistic is given on the MINITAB output and is also given on the following Excel output:

ANOVA	df	SS	MS	F	Significance F
Regression	2	486355.7	243177.8	180.689	9.46E-07
Residual	7	9420.8	1345.835		
Total	9	495776.5			

The p-value related to $F(model)$ is the area to the right of 180.69 under the curve of the F distribution having $k = 2$ numerator and $n - (k + 1) = 10 - 3 = 7$ denominator degrees of freedom. Both the MINITAB and Excel outputs say this p-value is less than .001.

If we wish to test the significance of the regression model at level of significance $\alpha = .05$, we use the critical value $F_{.05}$ based on 2 numerator and 7 denominator degrees of freedom. Using Table A.6 (page 643), we find that $F_{.05} = 4.74$. Since $F(model) = 180.69 > F_{.05} = 4.74$, we can reject H_0 in favor of H_a at level of significance .05. Alternatively, since the p-value is smaller than .05, .01, and .001, we can reject H_0 at level of significance .05, .01, and .001. Therefore, we have extremely strong evidence that the Tasty Sub Shop revenue model is significant. That is, we have extremely strong evidence that at least one of the independent variables x_1 and x_2 in the model is significantly related to y.

If the overall F test tells us that at least one independent variable in a regression model is significant, we next attempt to decide which independent variables are significant. In the next section we discuss one way to do this.

Exercises for Sections 14.2, 14.3, and 14.4

CONCEPTS

connect™

14.7 What is estimated by the mean square error, and what is estimated by the standard error?

14.8 **a** What do R^2 and $\overline{R}^2$ measure? **b** How do R^2 and $\overline{R}^2$ differ?

14.9 What is the purpose of the overall F test?

METHODS AND APPLICATIONS

In Exercises 14.10 to 14.13 we give Excel and MINITAB outputs of regression analyses of the data sets related to four case studies introduced in Section 14.1. Above each output we give the regression model and the number of observations, n, used to perform the regression analysis under consideration. Using the appropriate model, sample size n, and output:

1 Report SSE, s^2, and s as shown on the output. Calculate s^2 from SSE and other numbers.

2 Report the total variation, unexplained variation, and explained variation as shown on the output.

3 Report R^2 and $\overline{R}^2$ as shown on the output. Interpret R^2 and $\overline{R}^2$. Show how $\overline{R}^2$ has been calculated from R^2 and other numbers.

4 Calculate the $F(model)$ statistic by using the explained variation, the unexplained variation, and other relevant quantities. Find $F(model)$ on the output to check your answer (within rounding).

5 Use the $F(model)$ statistic and the appropriate critical value to test the significance of the linear regression model under consideration by setting α equal to .05.

6 Use the $F(model)$ statistic and the appropriate critical value to test the significance of the linear regression model under consideration by setting α equal to .01.

7 Find the p-value related to $F(model)$ on the output. Using the p-value, test the significance of the linear regression model by setting $\alpha = .10, .05, .01,$ and .001. What do you conclude?

14.10 **THE FUEL CONSUMPTION CASE** ⒹⓈ FuelCon2

Model: $y = \beta_0 + \beta_1 x_1 + \beta_2 x_2 + \varepsilon$ Sample size: $n = 8$

The output follows on the next page:

```
S = 0.367078    R-Sq = 97.4%    R-Sq(adj) = 96.3%

Analysis of Variance
Source            DF      SS      MS      F       P
Regression         2  24.875  12.438  92.30   0.000
Residual Error     5   0.674   0.135
Total              7  25.549
```

14.11   THE REAL ESTATE SALES PRICE CASE   ⒹⓈ RealEst2

Model: $y = \beta_0 + \beta_1 x_1 + \beta_2 x_2 + \varepsilon$ Sample size: $n = 10$

```
S = 3.24164    R-Sq = 99.0%    R-Sq(adj) = 98.7%

Analysis of Variance
Source            DF      SS       MS       F        P
Regression         2  7374.0  3687.0  350.87   0.000
Residual Error     7    73.6    10.5
Total              9  7447.5
```

14.12   THE FRESH DETERGENT CASE   ⒹⓈ Fresh2

Model: $y = \beta_0 + \beta_1 x_1 + \beta_2 x_2 + \beta_3 x_3 + \varepsilon$ Sample size: $n = 30$

Regression Statistics

Multiple R	0.9453
R Square	0.8936
Adjusted R Square	0.8813
Standard Error	0.2347
Observations	30

ANOVA	df	SS	MS	F	Significance F
Regression	3	12.0268	4.0089	72.7973	0.0000
Residual	26	1.4318	0.0551		
Total	29	13.4586			

14.13   THE HOSPITAL LABOR NEEDS CASE   ⒹⓈ HospLab

Model: $y = \beta_0 + \beta_1 x_1 + \beta_2 x_2 + \beta_3 x_3 + \varepsilon$ Sample size: $n = 16$

Regression Statistics

Multiple R	0.9981
R Square	0.9961
Adjusted R Square	0.9952
Standard Error	387.1598
Observations	16

ANOVA	df	SS	MS	F	Significance F
Regression	3	462327889.4	154109296.5	1028.1309	9.92E-15
Residual	12	1798712.2	149892.7		
Total	15	464126601.6			

14.5 Testing the Significance of an Independent Variable ◦ ● ●

LO5 Test the significance of a single independent variable.

Consider the multiple regression model

$$y = \beta_0 + \beta_1 x_1 + \beta_2 x_2 + \cdots + \beta_k x_k + \varepsilon$$

In order to gain information about which independent variables significantly affect y, we can test the significance of a single independent variable. We arbitrarily refer to this variable as x_j and assume that it is multiplied by the parameter β_j. For example, if $j = 1$, we are testing the significance of x_1, which is multiplied by β_1; if $j = 2$, we are testing the significance of x_2, which is

a Report (as shown on the output) a point estimate of and a 95 percent confidence interval for the mean sales price of all houses having 2,000 square feet and a rating of 8.

b Report (as shown on the output) a point prediction of and a 95 percent prediction interval for the actual sales price of an individual house having 2,000 square feet and a rating of 8.

c Find 99 percent confidence and prediction intervals for the mean and actual sales prices referred to in parts *a* and *b*. Hint: $n = 10$ and $s = 3.24164$. Optional technical note needed.

14.24 THE FRESH DETERGENT CASE Fresh2

Consider the demand for Fresh Detergent in a future sales period when Enterprise Industries' price for Fresh will be $x_1 = 3.70$, the average price of competitors' similar detergents will be $x_2 = 3.90$, and Enterprise Industries' advertising expenditure for Fresh will be $x_3 = 6.50$. A 95 percent prediction interval for this demand is given on the following Excel add-in (MegaStat) output:

	95% Confidence Interval		95% Prediction Interval		
Predicted	**lower**	**upper**	**lower**	**upper**	**Leverage**
8.4107	8.3143	8.5070	7.9188	8.9025	0.040

a Find and report the 95 percent prediction interval on the output. If Enterprise Industries plans to have in inventory the number of bottles implied by the upper limit of this interval, it can be very confident that it will have enough bottles to meet demand for Fresh in the future sales period. How many bottles is this? If we multiply the number of bottles implied by the lower limit of the prediction interval by the price of Fresh ($3.70), we can be very confident that the resulting dollar amount will be the minimal revenue from Fresh in the future sales period. What is this dollar amount?

b Calculate a 99 percent prediction interval for the demand for Fresh in the future sales period. Hint: $n = 30$ and $s = .235$. Optional technical note needed. The distance value equals **Leverage**.

14.25 THE HOSPITAL LABOR NEEDS CASE HospLab

Consider a questionable hospital for which XRay = 56,194, BedDays = 14,077.88, and LengthStay = 6.89. A 95 percent prediction interval for the labor hours corresponding to this combination of values of the independent variables is given on the following Excel add-in (MegaStat) output:

	95% Confidence Interval		95% Prediction Interval		
Predicted	**lower**	**upper**	**lower**	**upper**	**Leverage**
15,896.2473	15,378.0313	16,414.4632	14,906.2361	16,886.2584	0.3774

Find and report the prediction interval on the output. Then, use this interval to determine if the actual number of labor hours used by the questionable hospital ($y = 17,207.31$) is unusually low or high.

14.7 The Sales Territory Performance Case ● ● ●

Suppose the sales manager of a company wishes to evaluate the performance of the company's sales representatives. Each sales representative is solely responsible for one sales territory, and the manager decides that it is reasonable to measure the performance, *y*, of a sales representative by using the yearly sales of the company's product in the representative's sales territory. The manager feels that sales performance *y* substantially depends on five independent variables:

x_1 = number of months the representative has been employed by the company

x_2 = sales of the company's product and competing products in the sales territory (a measure of sales potential)

x_3 = dollar advertising expenditure in the territory

x_4 = weighted average of the company's market share in the territory for the previous four years

x_5 = change in the company's market share in the territory over the previous four years

In Figure 14.10 we present values of *y* and x_1 through x_5 for 25 randomly selected sales representatives. To understand the values of *y* and x_2 in the table, note that sales of the company's

FIGURE 14.10 Sales Territory Performance Study Data ⓓⓢ SalePerf

	Sales, y	Time with Company, x_1	Market Potential, x_2	Advertising, x_3	Market Share, x_4	Market Share Change, x_5
	3,669.88	43.10	74,065.11	4,582.88	2.51	0.34
	3,473.95	108.13	58,117.30	5,539.78	5.51	0.15
	2,295.10	13.82	21,118.49	2,950.38	10.91	−0.72
	4,675.56	186.18	68,521.27	2,243.07	8.27	0.17
	6,125.96	161.79	57,805.11	7,747.08	9.15	0.50
	2,134.94	8.94	37,806.94	402.44	5.51	0.15
	5,031.66	365.04	50,935.26	3,140.62	8.54	0.55
	3,367.45	220.32	35,602.08	2,086.16	7.07	−0.49
	6,519.45	127.64	46,176.77	8,846.25	12.54	1.24
	4,876.37	105.69	42,053.24	5,673.11	8.85	0.31
	2,468.27	57.72	36,829.71	2,761.76	5.38	0.37
	2,533.31	23.58	33,612.67	1,991.85	5.43	−0.65
	2,408.11	13.82	21,412.79	1,971.52	8.48	0.64
	2,337.38	13.82	20,416.87	1,737.38	7.80	1.01
	4,586.95	86.99	36,272.00	10,694.20	10.34	0.11
	2,729.24	165.85	23,093.26	8,618.61	5.15	0.04
	3,289.40	116.26	26,878.59	7,747.89	6.64	0.68
	2,800.78	42.28	39,571.96	4,565.81	5.45	0.66
	3,264.20	52.84	51,866.15	6,022.70	6.31	−0.10
	3,453.62	165.04	58,749.82	3,721.10	6.35	−0.03
	1,741.45	10.57	23,990.82	860.97	7.37	−1.63
	2,035.75	13.82	25,694.86	3,571.51	8.39	−0.43
	1,578.00	8.13	23,736.35	2,845.50	5.15	0.04
	4,167.44	58.54	34,314.29	5,060.11	12.88	0.22
	2,799.97	21.14	22,809.53	3,552.00	9.14	−0.74

Source: This data set is from a research study published in "An Analytical Approach for Evaluation of Sales Territory Performance," *Journal of Marketing,* January 1972, 31–37 (authors are David W. Cravens, Robert B. Woodruff, and Joseph C. Stamper). We have updated the situation in our case study to be more modern.

product or any competing product are measured in hundreds of units of the product sold. Therefore, for example, the first sales figure of 3,669.88 in Figure 14.10 means that the first randomly selected sales representative sold 366,988 units of the company's product during the year.

Plots of y versus x_1 through x_5 are given in Figure 14.10. Since each plot has an approximate straight-line appearance, it is reasonable to relate y to x_1 through x_5 by using the regression model

$$y = \beta_0 + \beta_1 x_1 + \beta_2 x_2 + \beta_3 x_3 + \beta_4 x_4 + \beta_5 x_5 + \varepsilon$$

The main objective of the regression analysis is to help the sales manager evaluate sales performance by comparing actual performance to predicted performance. The manager has randomly selected the 25 representatives from all the representatives the company considers to be effective and wishes to use a regression model based on effective representatives to evaluate questionable representatives.

Figure 14.11 on the next page gives the Excel output of a regression analysis of the sales territory performance data using the five independent variable model. This output tells us that the least squares point estimates of the model parameters are $b_0 = -1{,}113.7879$, $b_1 = 3.6121$, $b_2 = .0421$, $b_3 = .1289$, $b_4 = 256.9555$, and $b_5 = 324.5334$. In addition, because the output tells us that the p-values associated with Time, MktPoten, Adver, and MktShare are all less than .01, we have very strong evidence that these variables are significantly related to y and, thus, are important in this model. Since the p-value associated with Change is .0530, we have close to strong evidence that this variable is also important.

FIGURE 14.11   **Excel Output of a Regression Analysis of the Sales Territory Performance Data Using the Model $y = \beta_0 + \beta_1 x_1 + \beta_2 x_2 + \beta_3 x_3 + \beta_4 x_4 + \beta_5 x_5 + \varepsilon$**

(a) The Excel output

Regression Statistics

Multiple R	0.9566
R Square	0.9150
Adjusted R Square	0.8926
Standard Error	430.2319
Observations	25

ANOVA	df	SS	MS	F	Significance F
Regression	5	37862658.9002	7572531.7800	40.9106	0.0000
Residual	19	3516890.0266	185099.4751		
Total	24	41379548.9269			

	Coefficients	Standard Error	t Stat	P-value	Lower 95%	Upper 95%
Intercept	-1113.7879	419.8869	-2.6526	0.0157	-1992.6213	-234.9545
Time	3.6121	1.1817	3.0567	0.0065	1.1388	6.0854
MktPoten	0.0421	0.0067	6.2527	0.0000	0.0280	0.0562
Adver	0.1289	0.0370	3.4792	0.0025	0.0513	0.2064
MktShare	256.9555	39.1361	6.5657	0.0000	175.0428	338.8683
Change	324.5334	157.2831	2.0634	0.0530	-4.6638	653.7307

(b) Prediction using an Excel add-in (MegaStat)

Predicted values for: Sales

Predicted	95% Confidence Interval		95% Prediction Interval		Leverage
	lower	upper	lower	upper	
4,181.74333	3,884.90651	4,478.58015	3,233.59431	5,129.89235	0.109

Consider a questionable sales representative for whom Time = 85.42, MktPoten = 35,182.73, Adver = 7,281.65, MktShare = 9.64, and Change = .28. The point prediction of the sales, y, corresponding to this combination of values of the independent variables is

$$\hat{y} = -1,113.7879 + 3.6121(85.42) + .0421(35,182.73)$$
$$+ .1289(7,281.65) + 256.9555(9.64) + 324.5334(.28)$$
$$= 4,181.74 \text{ (that is, 418,174 units)}$$

In addition to giving this point prediction, the Excel output tells us that a 95 percent prediction interval for y is [3233.59, 5129.89]. Furthermore, suppose that the actual sales y for the questionable representative were 3,087.52. This actual sales figure is less than the point prediction $\hat{y} = 4,181.74$ and is less than the lower bound of the 95 percent prediction interval for y, [3233.59, 5129.89]. Therefore, we conclude that there is strong evidence that the actual performance of the questionable representative is less than predicted performance. We should investigate the reason for this. Perhaps the questionable representative needs special training.

 Use dummy variables to model qualitative independent variables.

14.8 Using Dummy Variables to Model Qualitative Independent Variables ● ● ●

While the levels (or values) of a quantitative independent variable are numerical, the levels of a **qualitative** independent variable are defined by describing them. For instance, the type of sales technique used by a door-to-door salesperson is a qualitative independent variable. Here we might define three different levels—high pressure, medium pressure, and low pressure.

TABLE 14.8	The Electronics World Sales Volume Data		
	DS Electronics1		
Store	Number of Households, x	Location	Sales Volume, y
1	161	Street	157.27
2	99	Street	93.28
3	135	Street	136.81
4	120	Street	123.79
5	164	Street	153.51
6	221	Mall	241.74
7	179	Mall	201.54
8	204	Mall	206.71
9	214	Mall	229.78
10	101	Mall	135.22

FIGURE 14.12   Plot of the Sales Volume Data and a Geometrical Interpretation of the Model $y = \beta_0 + \beta_1 x + \beta_2 D_M + \varepsilon$

We can model the effects of the different levels of a qualitative independent variable by using what we call **dummy variables** (also called **indicator variables**). Such variables are usually defined so that they take on two values—either 0 or 1. To see how we use dummy variables, we begin with an example.

EXAMPLE 14.6

Part 1: The data and data plots   Suppose that Electronics World, a chain of stores that sells audio and video equipment, has gathered the data in Table 14.8. These data concern store sales volume in July of last year (y, measured in thousands of dollars), the number of households in the store's area (x, measured in thousands), and the location of the store (on a suburban street or in a suburban shopping mall—a qualitative independent variable). Figure 14.12 gives a data plot of y versus x. Stores having a street location are plotted as solid dots, while stores having a mall location are plotted as asterisks. Notice that the line relating y to x for mall locations has a higher y-intercept than does the line relating y to x for street locations.

Part 2: A dummy variable model   In order to model the effects of the street and shopping mall locations, we define a dummy variable denoted D_M as follows:

$$D_M = \begin{cases} 1 & \text{if a store is in a mall location} \\ 0 & \text{otherwise} \end{cases}$$

Using this dummy variable, we consider the regression model

$$y = \beta_0 + \beta_1 x + \beta_2 D_M + \varepsilon$$

This model and the definition of D_M imply that

1   For a street location, mean sales volume equals

$$\beta_0 + \beta_1 x + \beta_2 D_M = \beta_0 + \beta_1 x + \beta_2(0)$$
$$= \beta_0 + \beta_1 x$$

2   For a mall location, mean sales volume equals

$$\beta_0 + \beta_1 x + \beta_2 D_M = \beta_0 + \beta_1 x + \beta_2(1)$$
$$= (\beta_0 + \beta_2) + \beta_1 x$$

FIGURE 14.13   **Excel Output of a Regression Analysis of the Sales Volume Data Using the Model**
$y = \beta_0 + \beta_1 x + \beta_2 D_M + \varepsilon$

Regression Statistics

Multiple R	0.9913
R Square	0.9827
Adjusted R Square	0.9778
Standard Error	7.3288
Observations	10

ANOVA	df	SS	MS	F	Significance F
Regression	2	21411.7977	10705.8989	199.3216	6.75E-07
Residual	7	375.9817	53.7117		
Total	9	21787.7795			

	Coefficients	Standard Error	t Stat	P-value	Lower 95%	Upper 95%
Intercept	17.3598	9.4470	1.8376	0.1087	-4.9788	39.6985
Households (x)	0.8510	0.0652	13.0439	3.63E-06	0.6968	1.0053
DummyMall	29.2157	5.5940	5.2227	0.0012	15.9881	42.4434

Thus, the dummy variable allows us to model the situation illustrated in Figure 14.12. Here, the lines relating mean sales volume to x for street and mall locations have different y intercepts, β_0 and $(\beta_0 + \beta_2)$, and the same slope β_1. Note that β_2 is the difference between the mean monthly sales volume for stores in mall locations and the mean monthly sales volume for stores in street locations, when all these stores have the same number of households in their areas. That is, we can say that β_2 represents the effect on mean sales of a mall location compared to a street location. The Excel output in Figure 14.13 tells us that the least squares point estimate of β_2 is $b_2 = 29.2157$. This says that for any given number of households in a store's area, we estimate that the mean monthly sales volume in a mall location is \$29,215.70 greater than the mean monthly sales volume in a street location.

Part 3: A dummy variable model for comparing three locations   In addition to the data concerning street and mall locations in Table 14.8, Electronics World has also collected data concerning downtown locations. The complete data set is given in Table 14.9 and plotted in Figure 14.14. Here stores having a downtown location are plotted as open circles. A model describing these data is

$$y = \beta_0 + \beta_1 x + \beta_2 D_M + \beta_3 D_D + \varepsilon$$

Here the dummy variable D_M is as previously defined and the dummy variable D_D is defined as follows

$$D_D = \begin{cases} 1 & \text{if a store is in a downtown location} \\ 0 & \text{otherwise} \end{cases}$$

It follows that

1   For a street location, mean sales volume equals

$$\beta_0 + \beta_1 x + \beta_2 D_M + \beta_3 D_D = \beta_0 + \beta_1 x + \beta_2 (0) + \beta_3 (0)$$
$$= \beta_0 + \beta_1 x$$

2   For a mall location, mean sales volume equals

$$\beta_0 + \beta_1 x + \beta_2 D_M + \beta_3 D_D = \beta_0 + \beta_1 x + \beta_2 (1) + \beta_3 (0)$$
$$= (\beta_0 + \beta_2) + \beta_1 x$$

TABLE 14.9   **The Complete Electronics World Sales Volume Data**
⊙ Electronics2

Store	Number of Households, x	Location	Sales Volume, y
1	161	Street	157.27
2	99	Street	93.28
3	135	Street	136.81
4	120	Street	123.79
5	164	Street	153.51
6	221	Mall	241.74
7	179	Mall	201.54
8	204	Mall	206.71
9	214	Mall	229.78
10	101	Mall	135.22
11	231	Downtown	224.71
12	206	Downtown	195.29
13	248	Downtown	242.16
14	107	Downtown	115.21
15	205	Downtown	197.82

FIGURE 14.14   **Plot of the Complete Electronics World Sales Volume Data and a Geometrical Interpretation of the Model**
$$y = \beta_0 + \beta_1 x + \beta_2 D_M + \beta_3 D_D + \varepsilon$$

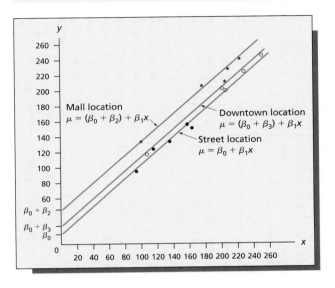

3   For a downtown location, mean sales volume equals

$$\beta_0 + \beta_1 x + \beta_2 D_M + \beta_3 D_D = \beta_0 + \beta_1 x + \beta_2(0) + \beta_3(1)$$
$$= (\beta_0 + \beta_3) + \beta_1 x$$

Thus the dummy variables allow us to model the situation illustrated in Figure 14.14. Here the lines relating mean sales volume to x for street, mall, and downtown locations have different y-intercepts, β_0, $(\beta_0 + \beta_2)$, and $(\beta_0 + \beta_3)$, and the same slope β_1. Note that β_2 represents the effect on mean sales of a mall location compared to a street location, and β_3 represents the effect on mean sales of a downtown location compared to a street location. Furthermore, the difference between β_2 and β_3, $\beta_2 - \beta_3$, represents the effect on mean sales of a mall location compared to a downtown location.

Part 4: Comparing the three locations   Figure 14.15 gives the MINITAB and Excel outputs of a regression analysis of the sales volume data using the dummy variable model. These outputs tell us that the least squares point estimate of β_2 is $b_2 = 28.374$. This says that for any given number of households in a store's area, we estimate that the mean monthly sales volume in a mall location is \$28,374 greater than the mean monthly sales volume in a street location. Furthermore, since the Excel output tells us that a 95 percent confidence interval for β_2 is [18.5545, 38.193], we are 95 percent confident that for any given number of households in a store's area, the mean monthly sales volume in a mall location is between \$18,554.50 and \$38,193 greater than the mean monthly sales volume in a street location. The MINITAB and Excel outputs also show that the t statistic for testing $H_0: \beta_2 = 0$ versus $H_a: \beta_2 \neq 0$ equals 6.36 and that the related p-value is less than .001. Therefore, we have very strong evidence that there is a difference between the mean monthly sales volumes in mall and street locations.

We next note that the outputs in Figure 14.15 show that the least squares point estimate of β_3 is $b_3 = 6.864$. Therefore, we estimate that for any given number of households in a store's area, the mean monthly sales volume in a downtown location is \$6,864 greater than the mean monthly sales volume in a street location. Furthermore, the Excel output shows that a 95 percent confidence interval for β_3 is $[-3.636, 17.3635]$. This says we are 95 percent confident that for any given number of households in a store's area, the mean monthly sales volume in a downtown

FIGURE 14.15 **MINITAB and Excel Outputs of a Regression Analysis of the Sales Volume Data Using the Model** $y = \beta_0 + \beta_1 x + \beta_2 D_M + \beta_3 D_D + \varepsilon$

(a) The MINITAB output

```
The regression equation is
Sales = 15.0 + 0.869 Households + 28.4 DMall + 6.86 DDowntown

Predictor      Coef   SE Coef      T      P
Constant     14.978     6.188   2.42  0.034
Households  0.86859   0.04049  21.45  0.000
DMall        28.374     4.461   6.36  0.000
DDowntown     6.864     4.770   1.44  0.178

S = 6.34941   R-Sq = 98.7%   R-Sq(adj) = 98.3%

Analysis of Variance
Source           DF     SS      MS       F      P
Regression        3  33269   11090  275.07  0.000
Residual Error   11    443      40
Total            14  33712

Values of Predictors for New Obs         Predicted Values for New Observations
New Obs  Households  DMall DDowntown   New Obs     Fit  SE Fit        95% CI              95% PI
      1         200      1         0         1  217.07    2.91  (210.65, 223.48)  (201.69, 232.45)
```

(b) The Excel output

Regression Statistics

Multiple R	0.9934
R Square	0.9868
Adjusted R Square	0.9833
Standard Error	6.3494
Observations	15

ANOVA

	df	SS	MS	F	Significance F
Regression	3	33268.6953	11089.5651	275.0729	1.27E-10
Residual	11	443.4650	40.3150		
Total	14	33712.1603			

	Coefficients	Standard Error	t Stat	P-value	Lower 95%	Upper 95%
Intercept	14.9777	6.1884	2.4203	0.0340	1.3570	28.5984
Households (x)	0.8686	0.0405	21.4520	2.52E-10	0.7795	0.9577
DummyMall	28.3738	4.4613	6.3600	5.37E-05	18.5545	38.1930
DummyDtown	6.8638	4.7705	1.4388	0.1780	-3.6360	17.3635

location is between $3,636 less than and $17,363.50 greater than the mean monthly sales volume in a street location. The MINITAB and Excel outputs also show that the t statistic and p-value for testing H_0: $\beta_3 = 0$ versus H_a: $\beta_3 \neq 0$ are $t = 1.44$ and p-value $= .178$. Therefore, we do not have strong evidence that there is a difference between the mean monthly sales volumes in downtown and street locations.

Finally, note that, since $b_2 = 28.374$ and $b_3 = 6.864$, the point estimate of $\beta_2 - \beta_3$ is $b_2 - b_3 = 28.374 - 6.864 = 21.51$. Therefore, we estimate that mean monthly sales volume in a mall location is $21,510 higher than mean monthly sales volume in a downtown location. Near the end of this section we show how to compare the mall and downtown locations by using a confidence interval and a hypothesis test. We will find that there is very strong evidence that the mean monthly sales volume in a mall location is higher than the mean monthly sales volume in a downtown location. In summary, the mall location seems to give a higher mean monthly sales volume than either the street or downtown location.

Part 5: Predicting a future sales volume Suppose that Electronics World wishes to predict the sales volume in a future month for an individual store that has 200,000 households in its area and is located in a shopping mall. The point prediction of this sales volume is (since $D_M = 1$

FIGURE 14.16   **Geometrical Interpretation of the Sales Volume Model**
$$y = \beta_0 + \beta_1 x + \beta_2 D_M + \beta_3 x D_M + \varepsilon$$

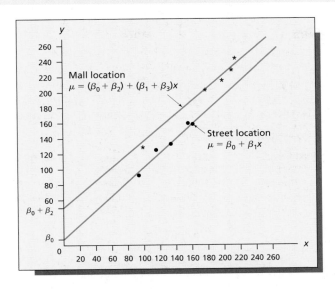

and $D_D = 0$ when a store is in a shopping mall)

$$\hat{y} = b_0 + b_1(200) + b_2(1) + b_3(0)$$
$$= 14.978 + .8686(200) + 28.374(1)$$
$$= 217.07$$

This point prediction is given at the bottom of the MINITAB output in Figure 14.15(a). The corresponding 95 percent prediction interval, which is [201.69, 232.45], says we are 95 percent confident that the sales volume in a future sales period for an individual mall store that has 200,000 households in its area will be between \$201,690 and \$232,450.

Part 6: Interaction models   Consider the Electronics World data for street and mall locations given in Table 14.8 (page 585) and the model

$$y = \beta_0 + \beta_1 x + \beta_2 D_M + \beta_3 x D_M + \varepsilon$$

This model uses the *cross-product,* or *interaction, term* $x D_M$ and implies that

1   For a street location, mean sales volume equals (since $D_M = 0$)

$$\beta_0 + \beta_1 x + \beta_2(0) + \beta_3 x(0) = \beta_0 + \beta_1 x$$

2   For a mall location, mean sales volume equals (since $D_M = 1$)

$$\beta_0 + \beta_1 x + \beta_2(1) + \beta_3 x(1) = (\beta_0 + \beta_2) + (\beta_1 + \beta_3)x$$

As illustrated in Figure 14.16, if we use this model, then the straight lines relating mean sales volume to x for street and mall locations have *different y-intercepts* and *different slopes*. The *different slopes* imply that this model assumes *interaction* between x and store location. Such a model is appropriate if the relationship between mean sales volume and x depends on (that is, is different for) the street and mall store locations. In general, **interaction** exists between two independent variables if the relationship between (for example, the slope of the line relating) the mean value of the dependent variable and one of the independent variables depends upon the value (or level) of the other independent variable. Figure 14.17 gives the Excel output of a regression analysis of the sales volume data using the interaction model. Here D_M and $x D_M$ are labeled as DM and XDM, respectively, on the output. The Excel output tells us that the p-value related to the significance of $x D_M$ is .5886. This large p-value tells us that the interaction term is not significant. It follows that the no-interaction model on page 585 seems best.

FIGURE 14.17   **Excel Output Using the Interaction Model**
$$y = \beta_0 + \beta_1 x + \beta_2 D_M + \beta_3 x D_M + \varepsilon$$

Regression Statistics

Multiple R	0.9918
R Square	0.9836
Adjusted R Square	0.9755
Standard Error	7.7092
Observations	10

ANOVA

	df	SS	MS	F	Significance F
Regression	3	21431.1861	7143.7287	120.1995988	9.531E-06
Residual	6	356.5933	59.4322		
Total	9	21787.7795			

	Coefficients	Standard Error	t Stat	P-value	Lower 95%	Upper 95%
Intercept	7.9004	19.3142	0.4090	0.6967	-39.3598	55.1606
Households	0.9207	0.1399	6.5792	0.0006	0.5783	1.2631
DM	42.7297	24.3812	1.7526	0.1302	-16.9289	102.3884
XDM	-0.0917	0.1606	-0.5712	0.5886	-0.4846	0.3012

Next, consider the Electronics World data for street, mall, and downtown locations given in Table 14.9 (page 587). In modeling these data, if we believe that interaction exists between the number of households in a store's area and store location, we might consider using the model

$$y = \beta_0 + \beta_1 x + \beta_2 D_M + \beta_3 D_D + \beta_4 x D_M + \beta_5 x D_D + \varepsilon$$

Similar to Figure 14.16, this model implies that the straight lines relating mean sales volume to x for the street, mall, and downtown locations have *different y-intercepts* and *different slopes*. If we perform a regression analysis of the sales volume data using this interaction model, we find that the p-values related to the significance of $x D_M$ and $x D_D$ are large (.5334 and .8132, respectively). Since these interaction terms are not significant, it seems best to employ the no-interaction model on page 586.

In general, if we wish to model the effect of a qualitative independent variable having a levels, we use $a - 1$ dummy variables. Consider the kth such dummy variable D_k ($k = 1, 2, \ldots$ or $a - 1$). The parameter β_k multiplying D_k represents the mean difference between the level of y when the qualitative variable assumes level k and when it assumes the level a. For example, if we wish to compare the effects on sales, y, of four different types of advertising campaigns—television (T), radio (R), magazine (M), and mailed coupons (C)—we might employ the model

$$y = \beta_0 + \beta_1 D_T + \beta_2 D_R + \beta_3 D_M + \varepsilon$$

Since this model does not use a dummy variable to represent the mailed coupon advertising campaign, the parameter β_1 is the difference between mean sales when a television advertising campaign is used and mean sales when a mailed coupon advertising campaign is used. The interpretations of β_2 and β_3 follow similarly. As another example, if we wish to employ a confidence interval and a hypothesis test to compare the mall and downtown locations in the Electronics World example, we can use the model

$$y = \beta_0 + \beta_1 x + \beta_2 D_S + \beta_3 D_M + \varepsilon$$

Here the dummy variable D_M is as previously defined, and

$$D_S = \begin{cases} 1 & \text{if a store is in a street location} \\ 0 & \text{otherwise} \end{cases}$$

Since this model does not use a dummy variable to represent the downtown location, the parameter β_2 expresses the effect on mean sales of a street location compared to a downtown location, and the parameter β_3 expresses the effect on mean sales of a mall location compared to a downtown location.

The Excel output of the least squares point estimates of the parameters of this model is as follows:

	Coefficients	Standard Error	t Stat	P-value	Lower 95%	Upper 95%
Intercept	21.8415	8.5585	2.5520	0.0269	3.0044	40.6785
Households (x)	0.8686	0.0405	21.4520	2.52E-10	0.7795	0.9577
DummyStreet	-6.8638	4.7705	-1.4388	0.1780	-17.3635	3.6360
DummyMall	21.5100	4.0651	5.2914	0.0003	12.5628	30.4572

Since the least squares point estimate of β_3 is $b_3 = 21.51$, we estimate that for any given number of households in a store's area, the mean monthly sales volume in a mall location is \$21,510 higher than the mean monthly sales volume in a downtown location. The Excel output tells us that a 95 percent confidence interval for β_3 is [12.5628, 30.4572]. Therefore, we are 95 percent confident that for any given number of households in a store's area, the mean monthly sales volume in a mall location is between \$12,562.80 and \$30,457.20 greater than the mean monthly sales volume in a downtown location. The Excel output also shows that the t statistic and p-value for testing $H_0: \beta_3 = 0$ versus $H_a: \beta_3 \neq 0$ in this model are, respectively, 5.2914 and .0003. Therefore, we have very strong evidence that there is a difference between the mean monthly sales volumes in mall and downtown locations.

In some situations dummy variables represent the effects of unusual events or occurrences that may have an important impact on the dependent variable. For instance, suppose we wish to build a regression model relating quarterly sales of automobiles (y) to automobile prices (x_1), fuel prices (x_2), and personal income (x_3). If an autoworkers' strike occurred in a particular quarter that had a major impact on automobile sales, then we might define a dummy variable D_S to be equal to 1 if an autoworkers' strike occurs and to be equal to 0 otherwise. The least squares point estimate of the regression parameter multiplied by D_S would estimate the effect of the strike on mean auto sales. Finally, dummy variables can be used to model the impact of regularly occuring *seasonal* influences on time series data—for example, the impact of the hot summer months on soft drink sales. This is discussed in Supplementary Exercises 14.51 and 14.52 at the end of this chapter.

Exercises for Section 14.8

CONCEPTS

14.26   What is a qualitative independent variable?

14.27   How do we use dummy variables to model the effects of a qualitative independent variable?

14.28   What does the parameter multiplied by a dummy variable express?

connect

METHODS AND APPLICATIONS

14.29   Neter, Kutner, Nachtsheim, and Wasserman (1996) relate the speed, y, with which a particular insurance innovation is adopted to the size of the insurance firm, x, and the type of firm. The dependent variable y is measured by the number of months elapsed between the time the first firm adopted the innovation and the time the firm being considered adopted the innovation. The size of the firm, x, is measured by the total assets of the firm, and the type of firm—a qualitative independent variable—is either a mutual company or a stock company. The data in Table 14.10 on the next page are observed.   **DS** InsInnov

     a   Discuss why the data plot in the page margin indicates that the model

$$y = \beta_0 + \beta_1 x + \beta_2 D_S + \varepsilon$$

     might appropriately describe the observed data. Here D_S equals 1 if the firm is a stock company and 0 if the firm is a mutual company.

     b   The model of part *a* implies that the mean adoption time of an insurance innovation by mutual companies having an asset size x equals

$$\beta_0 + \beta_1 x + \beta_2(0) = \beta_0 + \beta_1 x$$

Plot of the Insurance Innovation Data

Months

Size

- Mutual
- × Stock
- —— Linear (Mutual)
- —— Linear (Stock)

TABLE 14.10   The Insurance Innovation Data   DS InsInnov

Firm	Number of Months Elapsed, y	Size of Firm (Millions of Dollars), x	Type of Firm	Firm	Number of Months Elapsed, y	Size of Firm (Millions of Dollars), x	Type of Firm
1	17	151	Mutual	11	28	164	Stock
2	26	92	Mutual	12	15	272	Stock
3	21	175	Mutual	13	11	295	Stock
4	30	31	Mutual	14	38	68	Stock
5	22	104	Mutual	15	31	85	Stock
6	0	277	Mutual	16	21	224	Stock
7	12	210	Mutual	17	20	166	Stock
8	19	120	Mutual	18	13	305	Stock
9	4	290	Mutual	19	30	124	Stock
10	16	238	Mutual	20	14	246	Stock

FIGURE 14.18   Excel Output of a Regression Analysis of the Insurance Innovation Data Using the Model $y = \beta_0 + \beta_1 x + \beta_2 D_S + \varepsilon$

Regression Statistics

Multiple R	0.9461
R Square	0.8951
Adjusted R Square	0.8827
Standard Error	3.2211
Observations	20

ANOVA	df	SS	MS	F	Significance F
Regression	2	1,504.4133	752.2067	72.4971	4.77E-09
Residual	17	176.3867	10.3757		
Total	19	1,680.8			

	Coefficients	Standard Error	t Stat	P-value	Lower 95%	Upper 95%
Intercept	33.8741	1.8139	18.6751	9.15E-13	30.0472	37.7010
Size of Firm (x)	-0.1017	0.0089	-11.4430	2.07E-09	-0.1205	-0.0830
DummyStock	8.0555	1.4591	5.5208	3.74E-05	4.9770	11.1339

and that the mean adoption time by stock companies having an asset size x equals

$$\beta_0 + \beta_1 x + \beta_2(1) = \beta_0 + \beta_1 x + \beta_2$$

The difference between these two means equals the model parameter β_2. In your own words, interpret the practical meaning of β_2.

c   Figure 14.18 presents the Excel output of a regression analysis of the insurance innovation data using the model of part a. Using the output, test $H_0: \beta_2 = 0$ versus $H_a: \beta_2 \neq 0$ by setting $\alpha = .05$ and .01. Interpret the practical meaning of the result of this test. Also, use the computer output to find, report, and interpret a 95 percent confidence interval for β_2.

d   If we add the interaction term xD_S to the model of part a, we find that the p-value related to this term is .9821. What does this imply?

14.30   THE FLORIDA POOL HOME CASE   DS PoolHome

Table 3.12 (page 145) gives the selling price (Price, expressed in thousands of dollars), the square footage (SqrFt), the number of bathrooms (Bathrms), and the niceness rating (Niceness, expressed as an integer from 1 to 7) of 80 homes randomly selected from all homes sold in a Florida city during the last six months. (The random selections were made from homes having between 2,000 and 3,500 square feet.) Table 3.12 also gives values of the dummy variable Pool?, which equals 1 if a home has a pool and 0 otherwise. Figure 14.19 presents the MINITAB output of a regression analysis of these data using the model

$$\text{Price} = \beta_0 + \beta_1 \times \text{SqrFt} + \beta_2 \times \text{Bathrms} + \beta_3 \times \text{Niceness} + \beta_4 \times \text{Pool?} + \varepsilon$$

a   Noting that β_4 is the effect on mean sales price of a home having a pool, find (on the output) a point estimate of this effect. If the average current purchase price of the pools in the sample is

FIGURE 14.19   MINITAB Output of a Regression Analysis of the Florida Pool Home Data Using the Model Price $= \beta_0 + \beta_1 \cdot$ SqrFt $+ \beta_2 \cdot$ Bathrms $+ \beta_3 \cdot$ Niceness $+ \beta_4 \cdot$ Pool? $+ \varepsilon$

```
The regression equation is
Price = 25.0 + 0.0526 SqrFt + 10.0 Bathrms + 10.0 Niceness + 25.9 Pool?


Predictor     Coef   SE Coef       T       P
Constant     24.98     16.63    1.50   0.137
SqrFt      0.05264   0.00659    7.98   0.000
Bathrms     10.043     3.729    2.69   0.009
Niceness    10.042    0.7915   12.69   0.000
Pool?       25.862     3.575    7.23   0.000


S = 13.532     R-Sq = 87.40%   R-Sq(adj) = 86.80%


Analysis of Variance
Source          DF       SS      MS       F       P
Regression       4    95665   23916  130.61   0.000
Residual Error  75    13734     183
Total           79   109399
```

$32,500, find a point estimate of the percentage of a pool's cost that a customer buying a pool can expect to recoup when selling his (or her) home.

b   If we add various combinations of the interaction terms SqrFt · Pool?, Bathrooms · Pool?, and Niceness · Pool? to the above model, we find that the p-values related to these terms are greater than .05. What does this imply?

14.31 THE SHELF DISPLAY CASE   DS BakeSale

The Tastee Bakery Company supplies a bakery product to many supermarkets in a metropolitan area. The company wishes to study the effect of the height of the shelf display employed by the supermarkets on monthly sales, y (measured in cases of 10 units each), for this product. Shelf display height has three levels—bottom (B), middle (M), and top (T). For each shelf display height, six supermarkets of equal sales potential will be randomly selected, and each supermarket will display the product using its assigned shelf height for a month. At the end of the month, sales of the bakery product at the 18 participating stores will be recorded. When the experiment is carried out, the data in Table 14.11 are obtained. Here we assume that the set of sales amounts for each display height is a sample that has been randomly selected from the population of all sales amounts that could be obtained (at supermarkets of the given sales potential) when using that display height. To compare the population mean sales amounts μ_B, μ_M, and μ_T that would be obtained by using the bottom, middle, and top display heights, we use the following dummy variable regression model:

$$y = \beta_B + \beta_M D_M + \beta_T D_T + \varepsilon$$

Here D_M equals 1 if a middle display height is used and 0 otherwise; D_T equals 1 if a top display height is used and 0 otherwise. Figure 14.20 on the next page presents the MINITAB output of a regression analysis of the bakery sales study data using this model.[1]

a   By using the definitions of the dummy variables, show that

$$\mu_B = \beta_B \qquad \mu_M = \beta_B + \beta_M \qquad \mu_T = \beta_B + \beta_T$$

b   Use the overall F statistic to test H_0: $\beta_M = \beta_T = 0$, or, equivalently, H_0: $\mu_B = \mu_M = \mu_T$. Interpret the practical meaning of the result of this test.

c   Show that your results in part a, imply that

$$\mu_M - \mu_B = \beta_M \qquad \mu_T - \mu_B = \beta_T \qquad \mu_M - \mu_T = \beta_M - \beta_T$$

TABLE 14.11
Bakery Sales Study Data (Sales in Cases)
DS BakeSale

Shelf Display Height		
Bottom (B)	Middle (M)	Top (T)
58.2	73.0	52.4
53.7	78.1	49.7
55.8	75.4	50.9
55.7	76.2	54.0
52.5	78.4	52.1
58.9	82.1	49.9

---

[1]In general, the regression approach of this exercise produces the same comparisons of several population means that are produced by **one-way analysis of variance** (see Section 11.2).

FIGURE 14.20 MINITAB Output of a Dummy Variable Regression Analysis of the Bakery Sales Data in Table 14.11

```
The regression equation is
Bakery Sales = 55.8 + 21.4 DMiddle - 4.30 DTop

Predictor    Coef   SE Coef      T       P
Constant   55.800    1.013   55.07   0.000
DMiddle    21.400    1.433   14.93   0.000
DTop       -4.300    1.433   -3.00   0.009

S = 2.48193   R-Sq = 96.1%   R-Sq(adj) = 95.6%

Analysis of Variance
Source            DF      SS      MS       F       P
Regression         2  2273.9  1136.9  184.57   0.000
Residual Error    15    92.4     6.2
Total             17  2366.3

Values of Predictors for New Obs    Predicted Values for New Observations
New Obs  DMiddle   DTop             New Obs    Fit  SE Fit      95% CI              95% PI
      1        1      0                   1  77.200   1.013  (75.040, 79.360)  (71.486, 82.914)
```

TABLE 14.12

Advertising Campaigns Used by Enterprise Industries

DS Fresh3

Sales Period	Advertising Campaign
1	B
2	B
3	B
4	A
5	C
6	A
7	C
8	C
9	B
10	C
11	A
12	C
13	C
14	A
15	B
16	B
17	B
18	A
19	B
20	B
21	C
22	A
23	A
24	A
25	A
26	B
27	C
28	B
29	C
30	C

Then use the least squares point estimates of the model parameters to find a point estimate of each of the three differences in means. Also, find a 95 percent confidence interval for and test the significance of each of the first two differences in means. Interpret your results.

d Find a point estimate of mean sales when using a middle display height, a 95 percent confidence interval for mean sales when using a middle display height, and a 95 percent prediction interval for sales at an individual supermarket that employs a middle display height (see the bottom of the MINITAB output in Figure 14.20).

e Consider the following alternative model

$$y = \beta_T + \beta_B D_B + \beta_M D_M + \varepsilon$$

Here D_B equals 1 if a bottom display height is used and 0 otherwise. The MINITAB output of the least squares point estimates of the parameters of this model is as follows:

```
Predictor      Coef    SE Coef       T        P
Constant     51.500     1.013    50.83    0.000
DBottom       4.300     1.433     3.00    0.009
DMiddle      25.700     1.433    17.94    0.000
```

Since β_M expresses the effect of the middle display height with respect to the effect of the top display height, β_M equals $\mu_M - \mu_T$. Use the MINITAB output to calculate a 95 percent confidence interval for and test the significance of $\mu_M - \mu_T$. Interpret your results.

14.32 THE FRESH DETERGENT CASE DS Fresh3

Recall from Exercise 14.5 that Enterprise Industries has observed the historical data in Table 14.5 (page 567) concerning y (demand for Fresh liquid laundry detergent), x_1 (the price of Fresh), x_2 (the average industry price of competitors' similar detergents), and x_3 (Enterprise Industries' advertising expenditure for Fresh). To ultimately increase the demand for Fresh, Enterprise Industries' marketing department is comparing the effectiveness of three different advertising campaigns. These campaigns are denoted as campaigns A, B, and C. Campaign A consists entirely of television commercials, campaign B consists of a balanced mixture of television and radio commercials, and campaign C consists of a balanced mixture of television, radio, newspaper, and magazine ads. To conduct the study, Enterprise Industries has randomly selected one advertising campaign to be used in each of the 30 sales periods in Table 14.5. Although logic would indicate that each of campaigns A, B, and C should be used in 10 of the 30 sales periods, Enterprise Industries has made previous commitments to the advertising media involved in the study. As a result, campaigns A, B, and C were randomly assigned to, respectively, 9, 11, and 10 sales periods. Furthermore, advertising was done in only the first three weeks of each sales period, so that the carryover effect of the campaign used in a sales period to the next sales period would be minimized. Table 14.12 lists the campaigns used in the sales periods.

To compare the effectiveness of advertising campaigns A, B, and C, we define two dummy variables. Specifically, we define the dummy variable D_B to equal 1 if campaign B is used in a

FIGURE 14.21   **Excel Output of a Dummy Variable Regression Model Analysis of the Fresh Demand Data**

Regression Statistics

Multiple R	0.9797
R Square	0.9597
Adjusted R Square	0.9513
Standard Error	0.1503
Observations	30

ANOVA	df	SS	MS	F	Significance F
Regression	5	12.9166	2.5833	114.3862	6.237E-16
Residual	24	0.5420	0.0226		
Total	29	13.4586			

	Coefficients	Standard Error	t Stat	P-value	Lower 95%	Upper 95%
Intercept	8.7154	1.5849	5.4989	1.1821E-05	5.4443	11.9866
Price (X1)	-2.7680	0.4144	-6.6790	6.5789E-07	-3.6234	-1.9127
Ind Price (X2)	1.6667	0.1913	8.7110	6.7695E-09	1.2718	2.0616
AdvExp (X3)	0.4927	0.0806	6.1100	2.6016E-06	0.3263	0.6592
DB	0.2695	0.0695	3.8804	0.0007	0.1262	0.4128
DC	0.4396	0.0703	6.2496	1.8506E-06	0.2944	0.5847

Predicted values for: Demand using an Excel add-in (MegaStat)

	95% Confidence Interval		95% Prediction Interval		
Predicted	lower	upper	lower	upper	Leverage
8.61621	8.51380	8.71862	8.28958	8.94285	0.109

sales period and 0 otherwise. Furthermore, we define the dummy variable D_C to equal 1 if campaign C is used in a sales period and 0 otherwise. Figure 14.21 presents the Excel and Excel add-in (MegaStat) output of a regression analysis of the Fresh demand data by using the model

$$y = \beta_0 + \beta_1 x_1 + \beta_2 x_2 + \beta_3 x_3 + \beta_4 D_B + \beta_5 D_C + \varepsilon$$

a   In this model the parameter β_4 represents the effect on mean demand of advertising campaign B compared to advertising campaign A, and the parameter β_5 represents the effect on mean demand of advertising campaign C compared to advertising campaign A. Use the regression output to find and report a point estimate of each of the above effects and to test the significance of each of the above effects. Also, find and report a 95 percent confidence interval for each of the above effects. Interpret your results.

b   The prediction results at the bottom of the output correspond to a future period when Fresh's price will be $x_1 = 3.70$, the average price of similar detergents will be $x_2 = 3.90$, Fresh's advertising expenditure will be $x_3 = 6.50$, and advertising campaign C will be used. Show (within rounding) how $\hat{y} = 8.61621$ is calculated. Then find, report, and interpret a 95 percent confidence interval for mean demand and a 95 percent prediction interval for an individual demand when $x_1 = 3.70$, $x_2 = 3.90$, $x_3 = 6.50$, and campaign C is used.

c   Consider the alternative model

$$y = \beta_0 + \beta_1 x_1 + \beta_2 x_2 + \beta_3 x_3 + \beta_4 D_A + \beta_5 D_C + \varepsilon$$

Here D_A equals 1 if advertising campaign A is used and equals 0 otherwise. Describe the effect represented by the regression parameter β_5.

d   The Excel output of the least squares point estimates of the parameters of the model of part c is as follows.

	Coefficients	Standard Error	t Stat	P-value	Lower 95%	Upper 95%
Intercept	8.9849	1.5971	5.6259	8.61E-06	5.6888	12.2811
Price (X1)	-2.7680	0.4144	-6.6790	6.58E-07	-3.6234	-1.9127
Ind Price (X2)	1.6667	0.1913	8.7110	6.77E-09	1.2718	2.0616
AdvExp (X3)	0.4927	0.0806	6.1100	2.60E-06	0.3263	0.6592
DA	-0.2695	0.0695	-3.8804	0.0007	-0.4128	-0.1262
DC	0.1701	0.0669	2.5429	0.0179	0.0320	0.3081

based on the sizes of the orders by the accounts and other workload-related criteria (WKLOAD); and $x_8 =$ an aggregate rating on eight dimensions of the representative's performance, made by a sales manager and expressed on a 1–7 scale (RATING).

Table 14.14 gives the observed values of x_6, x_7, and x_8, and Figure 14.26(a) presents the MINITAB output of a **correlation matrix** for the sales territory performance data. Examining the first column of this matrix, we see that the simple correlation coefficient between SALES and WKLOAD is $-.117$ and that the p-value for testing the significance of the relationship between SALES and WKLOAD is .577. This indicates that there is little or no relationship between SALES and WKLOAD. However, the simple correlation coefficients between SALES and the other seven independent variables range from .402 to .754, with associated p-values ranging from .046 to .000. This indicates the existence of potentially useful relationships between SALES and these seven independent variables.

While simple correlation coefficients (and scatter plots) give us a preliminary understanding of the data, they cannot be relied upon alone to tell us which independent variables are significantly related to the dependent variable. One reason for this is a condition called *multicollinearity*. **Multicollinearity** is said to exist among the independent variables in a regression situation if these independent variables are related to or dependent upon each other. One way to investigate multicollinearity is to examine the correlation matrix. To understand this, note that all of the simple correlation coefficients not located in the first column of this matrix measure the **simple correlations between the independent variables.** For example, the simple correlation coefficient between ACCTS and TIME is .758, which says that the ACCTS values increase as the TIME values increase. Such a relationship makes sense because it is logical that the longer a sales representative has been with the company, the more accounts he or she handles. Statisticians often regard multicollinearity in a data set to be severe if at least one simple correlation coefficient between the independent variables is at least .9. Since the largest such simple correlation coefficient in Figure 14.26(a) is .758, this is not true for the sales territory performance data. Note, however, that even moderate multicollinearity can be a potential problem. This will be demonstrated later using the sales territory performance data.

Another way to measure multicollinearity is to use **variance inflation factors.** Consider a regression model relating a dependent variable y to a set of independent variables $x_1, \ldots, x_{j-1}, x_j, x_{j+1}, \ldots, x_k$. The **variance inflation factor VIF_j** for the independent variable x_j in this set is denoted VIF_j and is defined by the equation

$$VIF_j = \frac{1}{1 - R_j^2}$$

where R_j^2 is the multiple coefficient of determination for the regression model that relates x_j to all the other independent variables $x_1, \ldots, x_{j-1}, x_{j+1}, \ldots, x_k$ in the set. For example, Figure 14.26(b) gives the MINITAB output of the t statistics, p-values, and variance inflation factors

TABLE 14.14

Values of ACCTS, WKLOAD, and RATING

DS SalePerf2

Accounts, x_6	Work-load, x_7	Rating, x_8
74.86	15.05	4.9
107.32	19.97	5.1
96.75	17.34	2.9
195.12	13.40	3.4
180.44	17.64	4.6
104.88	16.22	4.5
256.10	18.80	4.6
126.83	19.86	2.3
203.25	17.42	4.9
119.51	21.41	2.8
116.26	16.32	3.1
142.28	14.51	4.2
89.43	19.35	4.3
84.55	20.02	4.2
119.51	15.26	5.5
80.49	15.87	3.6
136.58	7.81	3.4
78.86	16.00	4.2
136.58	17.44	3.6
138.21	17.98	3.1
75.61	20.99	1.6
102.44	21.66	3.4
76.42	21.46	2.7
136.58	24.78	2.8
88.62	24.96	3.9

FIGURE 14.26 **MINITAB Output of the Correlation Matrix and a Regression Analysis for the Sales Territory Performance Situation**

(a) The correlation matrix

	Sales	Time	MktPoten	Adver	MktShare	Change	Accts	WkLoad
Time	0.623 0.001							
MktPoten	0.598 0.002	0.454 0.023						
Adver	0.596 0.002	0.249 0.230	0.174 0.405					
MktShare	0.484 0.014	0.106 0.613	-0.211 0.312	0.264 0.201				
Change	0.489 0.013	0.251 0.225	0.268 0.195	0.377 0.064	0.085 0.685			
Accts	0.754 0.000	0.758 0.000	0.479 0.016	0.200 0.338	0.403 0.046	0.327 0.110		
WkLoad	-0.117 0.577	-0.179 0.391	-0.259 0.212	-0.272 0.188	0.349 0.087	-0.288 0.163	-0.199 0.341	
Rating	0.402 0.046	0.101 0.631	0.359 0.078	0.411 0.041	-0.024 0.911	0.549 0.004	0.229 0.272	-0.277 0.180

Cell contents: Pearson correlation
P-Value

(b) The t statistics, p-values, and variance inflation factors for the eight-independent-variables model.

Predictor	Coef	SE Coef	T	P	VIF
Constant	-1507.8	778.6	-1.94	0.071	
Time	2.010	1.931	1.04	0.313	3.343
MktPoten	0.037205	0.008202	4.54	0.000	1.978
Adver	0.15099	0.04711	3.21	0.006	1.910
MktShare	199.02	67.03	2.97	0.009	3.236
Change	290.9	186.8	1.56	0.139	1.602
Accts	5.551	4.776	1.16	0.262	5.639
WkLoad	19.79	33.68	0.59	0.565	1.818
Rating	8.2	128.5	0.06	0.950	1.809

for the sales territory performance model that relates y to all eight independent variables. The largest variance inflation factor is $VIF_6 = 5.639$. To calculate VIF_6, MINITAB first calculates the multiple coefficient of determination for the regression model that relates x_6 to x_1, x_2, x_3, x_4, x_5, x_7, and x_8 to be $R_6^2 = .822673$. It then follows that

$$VIF_6 = \frac{1}{1 - R_6^2} = \frac{1}{1 - .822673} = 5.639$$

In general, if $R_j^2 = 0$, which says that x_j is not related to the other independent variables, then the variance inflation factor VIF_j equals 1. On the other hand, if $R_j^2 > 0$, which says that x_j is related to the other independent variables, then $(1 - R_j^2)$ is less than 1, making VIF_j greater than 1. Generally, the multicollinearity between independent variables is considered (1) severe if the largest variance inflation factor is greater than 10 and (2) moderately strong if the largest variance inflation factor is greater than 5. Moreover, if the mean of the variance inflation factors is substantially greater than 1 (sometimes a difficult criterion to assess), multicollinearity might be problematic. In the sales territory performance model, the largest variance inflation factor, $VIF_6 = 5.639$, is greater than 5. Therefore, we might classify the multicollinearity as being moderately strong.

The reason that VIF_j is called the variance inflation factor is that it can be shown that, when VIF_j is greater than 1, then the standard deviation σ_{b_j} of the population of all possible values of the least squares point estimate b_j is likely to be inflated beyond its value when $R_j^2 = 0$. If σ_{b_j} is greatly inflated, two slightly different samples of values of the dependent variable can yield two substantially different values of b_j. It follows that, when strong multicollinearity exists, sampling variation can result in least squares point estimates that differ substantially from the true values of the regression parameters. In fact, some of the least squares point estimates may have a sign (positive or negative) that differs from the sign of the true value of the parameter (we will see an example of this in the exercises). Therefore, when strong multicollinearity exists, it is dangerous to interpret the individual least squares point estimates.

The most important problem caused by multicollinearity is that, even when multicollinearity is not severe, it can hinder our ability to use the t statistics and related p-values to assess the importance of the independent variables. Recall that we can reject $H_0: \beta_j = 0$ in favor of $H_a: \beta_j \neq 0$ at level of significance α if and only if the absolute value of the corresponding t statistic is greater than $t_{\alpha/2}$ based on $n - (k + 1)$ degrees of freedom, or, equivalently, if and only if the related p-value is less than α. Thus the larger (in absolute value) the t statistic is and the smaller the p-value is, the stronger is the evidence that we should reject $H_0: \beta_j = 0$ and the stronger is the evidence that the independent variable x_j is significant. When multicollinearity exists, the sizes of the t statistic and of the related p-value **measure the additional importance of the independent variable x_j over the combined importance of the other independent variables in the regression model.** Since two or more correlated independent variables contribute redundant information, multicollinearity often causes the t statistics obtained by relating a dependent variable to a set of correlated independent variables to be smaller (in absolute value) than the t statistics that would be obtained if separate regression analyses were run, where each separate regression analysis relates the dependent variable to a smaller set (for example, only one) of the correlated independent variables. Thus multicollinearity can cause some of the correlated independent variables to appear less important—in terms of having small absolute t statistics and large p-values—than they really are. Another way to understand this is to note that since multicollinearity inflates σ_{b_j}, it inflates the point estimate s_{b_j} of σ_{b_j}. Since $t = b_j/s_{b_j}$, an inflated value of s_{b_j} can (depending on the size of b_j) cause t to be small (and the related p-value to be large). This would suggest that x_j is not significant even though x_j may really be important.

For example, Figure 14.26(b) tells us that when we perform a regression analysis of the sales territory performance data using a model that relates y to all eight independent variables, the p-values related to TIME, MKTPOTEN, ADVER, MKTSHARE, CHANGE, ACCTS, WKLOAD, and RATING are, respectively, .313, .000, .006, .009, .139, .262, .565, and .950. By contrast, recall from Figure 14.11 (page 584) that when we perform a regression analysis of the sales territory performance data using a model that relates y to the first five independent variables, the p-values related to TIME, MKTPOTEN, ADVER, MKTSHARE, and CHANGE are, respectively, .0065, .0001, .0025, .0001, and .0530. Note that TIME (p-value = .0065) is significant at the

.01 level and CHANGE (p-value $= .0530$) is significant at the .06 level in the five independent variable model. However, when we consider the model that uses all eight independent variables, neither TIME (p-value $= .313$) nor CHANGE (p-value $= .139$) is significant at the .10 level. The reason that TIME and CHANGE seem more significant in the five independent variable model is that, since this model uses fewer variables, TIME and CHANGE contribute less overlapping information and thus have more additional importance in this model.

Comparing regression models on the basis of R^2, s, adjusted R^2, prediction interval length, and the C statistic   We have seen that when multicollinearity exists in a model, the p-value associated with an independent variable in the model measures the additional importance of the variable over the combined importance of the other variables in the model. Therefore, it can be difficult to use the p-values to determine which variables to retain and which variables to remove from a model. The implication of this is that we need to evaluate more than the *additional importance* of each independent variable in a regression model. We also need to evaluate how well the independent variables *work together* to accurately describe, predict, and control the dependent variable. One way to do this is to determine if the *overall* model gives a high R^2 and $\overline{R}^2$, a small s, and short prediction intervals.

It can be proved that **adding any independent variable to a regression model, even an unimportant independent variable, will decrease the unexplained variation and will increase the explained variation.** Therefore, since the total variation $\Sigma(y_i - \overline{y})^2$ depends only on the observed y values and thus remains unchanged when we add an independent variable to a regression model, it follows that **adding any independent variable to a regression model will increase**

$$R^2 = \frac{\textbf{Explained variation}}{\textbf{Total variation}}$$

This implies that R^2 cannot tell us (by decreasing) that adding an independent variable is undesirable. That is, although we wish to obtain a model with a large R^2, there are better criteria than R^2 that can be used to *compare* regression models.

One better criterion is the standard error

$$s = \sqrt{\frac{SSE}{n - (k + 1)}}$$

When we add an independent variable to a regression model, the number of model parameters $(k + 1)$ increases by one, and thus the number of degrees of freedom $n - (k + 1)$ decreases by one. If the decrease in $n - (k + 1)$, which is used in the denominator to calculate s, is proportionally more than the decrease in SSE (the unexplained variation) that is caused by adding the independent variable to the model, then s will increase. **If s increases, this tells us that we should not add the independent variable to the model,** because the new model would give longer prediction intervals and thus less accurate predictions. If s decreases, the new model is likely to give shorter prediction intervals but (as we will see) is not guaranteed to do so. Thus, it can be useful to compare the lengths of prediction intervals for different models. Also, it can be shown that the standard error s decreases if and only if $\overline{R}^2$ (adjusted R^2) increases. It follows that, if we are comparing regression models, the model that gives the smallest s gives the largest $\overline{R}^2$.

EXAMPLE 14.9 The Sales Territory Performance Case

Figure 14.27 gives MINITAB output resulting from calculating R^2, $\overline{R}^2$, and s for **all possible regression models** based on all possible combinations of the eight independent variables in the sales territory performance situation (the values of C_p on the output will be explained after we complete this example). The MINITAB output gives the two best models of each size in terms of s and $\overline{R}^2$—the two best one-variable models, the two best two-variable models, the two best

FIGURE 14.27   **MINITAB Output of the Best Two Sales Territory Performance Regression Models of Each Size**

Vars	R-Sq	R-Sq(adj)	Mallows C-p	S	Time	MktPoten	Adver	Mktshare	Change	Accts	WkLoad	Rating
1	56.8	55.0	67.6	881.09						X		
1	38.8	36.1	104.6	1049.3	X							
2	77.5	75.5	27.2	650.39		X				X		
2	74.6	72.3	33.1	691.10		X		X				
3	84.9	82.7	14.0	545.51		X	X	X				
3	82.8	80.3	18.4	582.64		X	X			X		
4	90.0	88.1	5.4	453.84		X	X	X		X		
4	89.6	87.5	6.4	463.95	X	X	X	X				
5	91.5	89.3	4.4	430.23	X	X	X	X	X			
5	91.2	88.9	5.0	436.75		X	X	X	X	X		
6	92.0	89.4	5.4	428.00	X	X	X	X	X	X		
6	91.6	88.9	6.1	438.20		X	X	X	X	X	X	
7	92.2	89.0	7.0	435.67	X	X	X	X	X	X	X	
7	92.0	88.8	7.3	440.30	X	X	X	X	X	X		X
8	92.2	88.3	9.0	449.03	X	X	X	X	X	X	X	X

three-variable models, and so on. Examining the output, we see that the three models having the smallest values of s and largest values of $\overline{R}^2$ are

1   The six-variable model that contains

TIME, MKTPOTEN, ADVER, MKTSHARE, CHANGE, ACCTS

and has $s = 428.00$ and $\overline{R}^2 = 89.4$; we refer to this model as Model 1.

2   The five-variable model that contains

TIME, MKTPOTEN, ADVER, MKTSHARE, CHANGE

and has $s = 430.23$ and $\overline{R}^2 = 89.3$; we refer to this model as Model 2.

3   The seven-variable model that contains

TIME, MKTPOTEN, ADVER, MKTSHARE, CHANGE, ACCTS, WKLOAD

and has $s = 435.67$ and $\overline{R}^2 = 89.0$; we refer to this model as Model 3.

To see that s can increase when we add an independent variable to a regression model, note that s increases from 428.00 to 435.67 when we add WKLOAD to Model 1 to form Model 3. In this case, although it can be verified that adding WKLOAD decreases the unexplained variation from 3,297,279.3342 to 3,226,756.2751, this decrease has not been enough to offset the change in the denominator of

$$s^2 = \frac{SSE}{n - (k + 1)}$$

which decreases from $25 - 7 = 18$ to $25 - 8 = 17$. To see that prediction interval lengths might increase even though s decreases, consider adding ACCTS to Model 2 to form Model 1. This decreases s from 430.23 to 428.00. However, consider a questionable sales representative for whom TIME = 85.42, MKTPOTEN = 35,182.73, ADVER = 7,281.65, MKTSHARE = 9.64, CHANGE = .28, and ACCTS = 120.61. The 95 percent prediction interval given by Model 2 for sales corresponding to this combination of values of the independent variables is [3,233.59, 5,129.89] and has length $5,129.89 - 3,233.59 = 1896.3$. The 95 percent prediction interval given by Model 1 for such sales is [3,193.86, 5,093.14] and has length $5,093.14 - 3,193.86 = 1,899.28$. In other words, even though Model 2 has a slightly larger s, it gives a slightly shorter prediction interval. (For those who have studied the formula for a prediction interval, $[\hat{y} \pm t_{\alpha/2} s \sqrt{1 + \text{distance value}}]$, Model 2 gives a slightly shorter 95 percent prediction interval because it uses one less variable and thus can be verified to give slightly smaller values of $t_{.025}$ and the distance value.) In addition, the extra independent variable ACCTS in Model 1 can be verified to have a p-value of .2881. Therefore, we conclude that Model 2 is better than Model 1 and is, in fact, the "best" sales territory performance model (using only linear independent variables).

Another quantity that can be used for comparing regression models is called the **C statistic** (also often called the C_p **statistic**). To show how to calculate the C statistic, suppose that we wish to choose an appropriate set of independent variables from p potential independent variables. We first calculate the mean square error, which we denote as s_p^2, for the model using all p potential independent variables. Then, if SSE denotes the unexplained variation for another particular model that has k independent variables, it follows that the C statistic for this model is

$$C = \frac{SSE}{s_p^2} - [n - 2(k + 1)]$$

For example, consider the sales territory performance case. It can be verified that the mean square error for the model using all $p = 8$ independent variables is 201,621.21 and that the SSE for the model using the first $k = 5$ independent variables (Model 2 in the previous example) is 3,516,812.7933. It follows that the C statistic for this latter model is

$$C = \frac{3,516,812.7933}{201,621.21} - [25 - 2(5 + 1)] = 4.4$$

Since the C statistic for a given model is a function of the model's SSE, and since we want SSE to be small, **we want C to be small**. Although adding an unimportant independent variable to a regression model will decrease SSE, adding such a variable can increase C. This can happen when the decrease in SSE caused by the addition of the extra independent variable is not enough to offset the decrease in $n - 2(k + 1)$ caused by the addition of the extra independent variable (which increases k by 1). It should be noted that although adding an unimportant independent variable to a regression model can increase both s^2 and C, there is no exact relationship between s^2 and C.

While we want C to be small, it can be shown from the theory behind the C statistic that **we also wish to find a model for which the C statistic roughly equals $k + 1$**, the number of parameters in the model. **If a model has a C statistic substantially greater than $k + 1$, it can be shown that this model has substantial *bias* and is undesirable.** Thus, although we want to find a model for which C is as small as possible, if C for such a model is substantially greater than $k + 1$, we may prefer to choose a different model for which C is slightly larger and more nearly equal to the number of parameters in that (different) model. **If a particular model has a small value of C and C for this model is less than $k + 1$, then the model should be considered desirable.** Finally, it should be noted that for the model that includes all p potential independent variables (and thus utilizes $p + 1$ parameters), it can be shown that $C = p + 1$.

If we examine Figure 14.27, we see that Model 2 of the previous example has the smallest C statistic. The C statistic for this model equals 4.4. Since $C = 4.4$ is less than $k + 1 = 6$, the model is not biased. Therefore, this model should be considered best with respect to the C statistic.

Stepwise regression   In some situations it is useful to employ an **iterative model selection procedure,** where at each step a single independent variable is added to or deleted from a regression model, and a new regression model is evaluated. We now discuss one such procedure— **stepwise regression.**

Stepwise regression begins by considering all of the one-independent-variable models and choosing the model for which the p-value related to the independent variable in the model is the smallest. If this p-value is less than α_{entry}, an α value for "entering" a variable, the independent variable is the first variable entered into the stepwise regression model and stepwise regression continues. Stepwise regression then considers the remaining independent variables not in the stepwise model and chooses the independent variable which, when paired with the first independent variable entered, has the smallest p-value. If this p-value is less than α_{entry}, the new variable is entered into the stepwise model. Moreover, the stepwise procedure checks to see if the p-value

FIGURE 14.28   The MINITAB Output of Sales Territory Performance Stepwise Regression

$(\alpha_{\text{entry}} = \alpha_{\text{stay}} = .10)$

Step	1	2	3	4
Constant	709.32	50.30	-327.23	-1441.94
Accts	21.7	19.0	15.6	9.2
T-Value	5.50	6.41	5.19	3.22
P-Value	0.000	0.000	0.000	0.004
Adver		0.227	0.216	0.175
T-Value		4.50	4.77	4.74
P-Value		0.000	0.000	0.000
MktPoten			0.0219	0.0382
T-Value			2.53	4.79
P-Value			0.019	0.000
MktShare				190
T-Value				3.82
P-Value				0.001
S	881	650	583	454
R-Sq	56.85	77.51	82.77	90.04
R-Sq(adj)	54.97	75.47	80.31	88.05
Mallows C-p	67.6	27.2	18.4	5.4

TABLE 14.15   Squared Variables and Interaction Variables in the Sales Territory Performance Situation

SQT	=	TIME*TIME
SQMP	=	MKTPOTEN*MKTPOTEN
SQA	=	ADVER*ADVER
SQMS	=	MKTSHARE*MKTSHARE
SQC	=	CHANGE*CHANGE
TMP	=	TIME*MKTPOTEN
TA	=	TIME*ADVER
TMS	=	TIME*MKTSHARE
TC	=	TIME*CHANGE
MPA	=	MKTPOTEN*ADVER
MPMS	=	MKTPOTEN*MKTSHARE
MPC	=	MKTPOTEN*CHANGE
AMS	=	ADVER*MKTSHARE
AC	=	ADVER*CHANGE
MSC	=	MKTSHARE*CHANGE

related to the first variable entered into the stepwise model is less then α_{stay}, an α value for allowing a variable to stay in the stepwise model. This is done because multicollinearity could have changed the p-value of the first variable entered into the stepwise model. The stepwise procedure continues this process and concludes when no new independent variable can be entered into the stepwise model. It is common practice to set both α_{entry} and α_{stay} equal to .05 or .10.

For example, again consider the sales territory performance data. We let $x_1, x_2, x_3, x_4, x_5, x_6, x_7,$ and x_8 be the eight potential independent variables employed in the stepwise procedure. Figure 14.28 gives the MINITAB output of the stepwise regression employing these independent variables where both α_{entry} and α_{stay} have been set equal to .10. The stepwise procedure (1) adds ACCTS (x_6) on the first step; (2) adds ADVER (x_3) and retains ACCTS on the second step; (3) adds MKTPOTEN (x_2) and retains ACCTS and ADVER on the third step; and (4) adds MKTSHARE (x_4) and retains ACCTS, ADVER, and MKTPOTEN on the fourth step. The procedure terminates after step 4 when no more independent variables can be added. Therefore, the stepwise procedure arrives at the model that utilizes $x_2, x_3, x_4,$ and x_6. Note that this model is not the model using $x_1, x_2, x_3, x_4,$ and x_5 that was obtained by evaluating all possible regression models and that has the smallest C statistic of 4.4. In general, stepwise regression can miss finding the best regression model but is useful in **data mining,** where there is a massive number of independent variables and all possible regression models cannot be evaluated.

Some advanced model building methods: Using squared and interaction variables and the partial F test   We have concluded that perhaps the best sales territory performance model using only linear independent variables is the model using TIME, MKTPOTEN, ADVER, MKTSHARE, and CHANGE. We have also seen in Section 14.9 that using squared variables (which model quadratic curvature) and interaction variables can improve a regression model. In Table 14.15 we present the five squared variables and the ten (pairwise) interaction variables that can be formed using TIME, MKTPOTEN, ADVER, MKTSHARE, and CHANGE. Consider having MINITAB evaluate all possible models involving these squared and interaction variables, where the five linear variables are included in each possible model. If we have MINITAB do this and find the best model of each size in terms of s, we obtain the output in Figure 14.29. (Note that we do not include values of the C statistic on the output because it can be shown that this statistic can give misleading results when using squared and interaction variables.) Examining the output, we see that the model that uses 12 squared and interaction variables (or a total

FIGURE 14.29   **MINITAB Comparisons Using Squared and Interaction Variables**

```
                                    S     S
                         S  Q  S  Q  S  T     T           M
                         Q  M  Q  M  Q  M  T  M  T  P  M  P  M  A     M
Vars  R-Sq  R-Sq(adj)      S   T  P  A  S  C  P  A  S  C  A  S  C  S  C  C
  1   94.2     92.2    365.87                            X
  2   95.8     94.1    318.19   X                         X
  3   96.5     94.7    301.61   X                         X  X
  4   97.0     95.3    285.54   X                 X  X       X
  5   97.5     95.7    272.05   X                 X  X       X  X
  6   98.1     96.5    244.00   X     X           X  X       X           X
  7   98.7     97.4    210.70   X  X              X  X       X     X  X
  8   99.0     97.8    193.95   X  X        X     X  X       X     X  X
  9   99.2     98.0    185.45   X  X     X        X  X       X     X  X  X
 10   99.3     98.2    175.70   X  X     X        X  X       X  X  X  X  X
 11   99.4     98.2    177.09   X  X     X     X  X  X  X    X  X  X  X  X
 12   99.5     98.2    174.60   X  X     X     X  X  X  X  X X  X  X  X  X
 13   99.5     98.1    183.22   X  X  X     X  X  X  X  X  X X  X  X  X  X
 14   99.6     97.9    189.77   X  X        X  X  X  X  X  X X  X  X  X  X  X
 15   99.6     97.4    210.78   X  X  X  X  X  X  X  X  X  X X  X  X  X  X  X
```

of 17 variables, including the 5 linear variables) has the smallest s ($= 174.6$) of any model. Unfortunately, although we would like to test the significance of the independent variables in this model, extreme multicollinearity (relationships between the independent variables) exists when using squared and interaction variables. Thus, the usual t tests for assessing the significance of individual independent variables might not be reliable. As an alternative, we will use a *partial F test*. Specifically, considering the model with the smallest s of 174.6 and a total of 17 variables to be a *complete model*, we will use this test to assess whether at least one variable in the *subset* of 12 squared and interaction variables in this model is significant.

The Partial F Test: An F Test for a Portion of a Regression Model

Suppose that the regression assumptions hold, and consider a **complete model** that uses k independent variables. To assess whether at least one of the independent variables in a subset of k^* independent variables in this model is significant, we test the null hypothesis

H_0: All of the β_j coefficients corresponding to the independent variables in the subset are zero

which says that none of the independent variables in the subset are significant. We test H_0 versus

H_a: At least one of the β_j coefficients corresponding to the independent variables in the subset is not equal to zero

which says that at least one of the independent variables in the subset is significant. Let SSE_C denote the unexplained variation for the complete model, and let SSE_R denote the unexplained variation for the

reduced model that uses all k independent variables **except** for the k^* independent variables in the subset. Also, define

$$F(\text{partial}) = \frac{(SSE_R - SSE_C)/k^*}{SSE_C/[n - (k + 1)]}$$

and define the p-value related to $F(\text{partial})$ to be the area under the curve of the F distribution (having k^* and $[n - (k + 1)]$ degrees of freedom) to the right of $F(\text{partial})$. Then, we can reject H_0 in favor of H_a at level of significance α if either of the following equivalent conditions holds:

1 $F(\text{partial}) > F_\alpha$

2 $p\text{-value} < \alpha$

Here the point F_α is based on k^* numerator and $n - (k + 1)$ denominator degrees of freedom.

Using Excel or MINITAB, we find that the unexplained variation for the *complete model* that uses all $k = 17$ variables is $SSE_C = 213{,}396.12$ and the unexplained variation for the *reduced model* that does not use the $k^* = 12$ squared and interaction variables (and thus uses only the 5 linear variables) is $SSE_R = 3{,}516{,}859.2$. It follows that

$$F(\text{partial}) = \frac{(SSE_R - SSE_C)/k^*}{SSE_C/[n - (k + 1)]}$$

$$= \frac{(3,516,859.2 - 213,396.12)/12}{213,396.12/[25 - (17 + 1)]}$$

$$= \frac{3,303,463.1/12}{213,396.12/7} = 9.03$$

Because $F_{.05}$ based on $k^* = 12$ numerator and $n - (k + 1) = 7$ denominator degrees of freedom is 3.57 (see Table A.6 on page 643), and because $F(\text{partial}) = 9.03$ is greater than $F_{.05} = 3.57$, we conclude (at an α of .05) that at least one of the 12 squared and interaction variables in the 17-variable model is significant. In the exercises, the reader will do further analysis and use another partial F test to pick a model that is perhaps better than the 17-variable model.

Exercises for Section 14.10

CONCEPTS

14.38 What is multicollinearity? What problems can be caused by multicollinearity?

14.39 Discuss how we compare regression models.

METHODS AND APPLICATIONS

14.40 **THE HOSPITAL LABOR NEEDS CASE** ⑤ HospLab2

Recall that Table 14.6 (page 568) presents data concerning the need for labor in 16 U.S. Navy hospitals. This table gives values of the dependent variable Hours (monthly labor hours) and of the independent variables Xray (monthly X-ray exposures), BedDays (monthly occupied bed days—a hospital has one occupied bed day if one bed is occupied for an entire day), and Length (average length of patients' stay, in days). The data in Table 14.6 are part of a larger data set analyzed by the Navy. The complete data set consists of two additional independent variables— Load (average daily patient load) and Pop (eligible population in the area, in thousands)—values of which are given on the page margin. Figures 14.30 and 14.31 give Excel and MINITAB outputs of multicollinearity analysis and model building for the complete hospital labor needs data set.

a Find the three largest simple correlation coefficients among the independent variables and the three largest variance inflation factors in Figure 14.30.

b Which of the independent variables are most strongly involved in multicollinearity?

c Do any least squares point estimates have a sign (positive or negative) that is different from what we would intuitively expect—another indication of multicollinearity?

Load	Pop
15.57	18.0
44.02	9.5
20.42	12.8
18.74	36.7
49.20	35.7
44.92	24.0
55.48	43.3
59.28	46.7
94.39	78.7
128.02	180.5
96.00	60.9
131.42	103.7
127.21	126.8
409.20	169.4
463.70	331.4
510.22	371.6

FIGURE 14.30   **Multicollinearity and a Regression Analysis in the Hospital Labor Needs Situation**

(a) Excel output of the correlation matrix

	Hours(y)	Xray(x1)	BedDays(x2)	Length(x3)	Load(x4)	Pop(x5)
Hours(y)	1					
Xray(x1)	0.9425	1				
BedDays(x2)	0.9889	0.9048	1			
Length(x3)	0.5603	0.4243	0.6609	1		
Load(x4)	0.9886	0.9051	0.9999	0.6610	1	
Pop(x5)	0.9465	0.9124	0.9328	0.4515	0.9353	1

(b) A MINITAB regression analysis

```
Predictor      Coef    SE Coef      T       P      VIF
Constant      2270.4     670.8    3.38   0.007
Xray(x1)     0.04112   0.01368    3.01   0.013     8.1
BedDays(x2)    1.413     1.925    0.73   0.48    8684.2
Length(x3)    -467.9     131.6   -3.55   0.005     4.2
Load(x4)       -9.30     60.81   -0.15   0.882   9334.5
Pop(x5)       -3.223     4.474   -0.72   0.488    23.0
```

FIGURE 14.31 **The MINITAB Output of Model Building for the Hospital Labor Needs Data**

(a) The two best models of each size

Vars	R-Sq	R-Sq(adj)	Mallows Cp	S	X r a y s 1	D a y s 2	L g t h 3	L o a d 4	P o p 5
1	97.8	97.6	52.3	856.71	X				
1	97.7	97.6	54	867.67				X	
2	99.3	99.2	9.5	489.13	X	X			
2	99.3	99.2	11.1	509.82			X	X	
3	99.6	99.5	3.3	387.16	X	X	X		
3	99.6	99.4	5	415.47	X		X	X	
4	99.7	99.5	4	381.56	X	X	X		X
4	99.6	99.5	4.5	390.88	X	X	X	X	
5	99.7	99.5	6	399.71	X	X	X	X	X

(b) Stepwise regression ($\alpha_{entry} = \alpha_{stay} = .10$)

Step	1	2	3
Constant	-70.23	2741.24	1946.80
BedDays	1.101	1.223	1.039
T-Value	24.87	36.30	15.39
P-Value	0.000	0.000	0.000
Length		-572	-414
T-Value		-5.47	-4.20
P-Value		0.000	0.001
XRay			0.039
T-Value			2.96
P-Value			0.012
S	857	489	387
R-Sq	97.79	99.33	99.61

d Figure 14.31(a) indicates that the two best hospital labor needs models are the model using Xray, BedDays, Pop, and Length, which we will call Model 1, and the model using Xray, BedDays, and Length, which we will call Model 2. Which model gives the smallest value of s and the largest value of $\bar{R}^2$? Which model gives the smallest value of C? Consider a questionable hospital for which Xray = 56,194, BedDays = 14,077.88, Pop = 329.7, and Length = 6.89. The 95 percent prediction intervals given by Models 1 and 2 for labor hours corresponding to this combination of values of the independent variables are, respectively, [14,888.43, 16,861.30] and [14,906.24, 16,886.26]. Which model gives the shortest prediction interval?

e Which model is chosen by stepwise regression in Figure 14.31(b)? Overall, which model seems best?

14.41 THE SALES TERRITORY PERFORMANCE CASE

Consider Figure 14.29 on page 608. The model using 12 squared and interaction variables has the smallest s. However, if we desire a somewhat simpler model, note that s does not increase substantially until we move from a model having seven squared and interaction variables to a model having six such variables. Moreover, we might subjectively conclude that the s of 210.70 for the model using 7 squared and interaction variables is not that much larger than the s of 174.6 for the model using 12 squared and interaction variables. Using the fact that the unexplained variations for these respective models are 532,733.88 and 213,396.12, perform a partial F test to assess whether at least one of the extra five squared and interaction variables is significant. If none of the five extra variables are significant, we might consider the simpler model to be best. **DS** SalePerf

LO10 Use residual analysis to check the assumptions of multiple regression.

14.11 Residual Analysis in Multiple Regression ● ● ●

Basic residual analysis　For a multiple regression model we plot the residuals given by the model against (1) values of each independent variable, (2) values of the predicted value of the dependent variable, and (3) the time order in which the data have been observed (if the regression data are time series data). A fanning-out pattern on a residual plot indicates an increasing error variance; a funneling-in pattern indicates a decreasing error variance. Both violate the constant variance assumption. A curved pattern on a residual plot indicates that the functional form of the regression model is incorrect. If the regression data are time series data, a cyclical pattern on the residual plot versus time suggests positive autocorrelation, while an alternating pattern suggests negative autocorrelation. Both violate the independence assumption. On the other hand, if all residual plots have (at least approximately) a horizontal band appearance, then it is reasonable to believe that the constant variance, correct functional form, and independence assumptions approximately hold. To check the normality assumption, we can construct a histogram, stem-and-leaf display, and normal plot of the residuals. The histogram and stem-and-leaf display should look bell-shaped and symmetric about 0; the normal plot should have a straight-line appearance.

FIGURE 14.32   Residual Plots for the Sales Territory Performance Model

(a) Normal plot of the residuals   (b) Plot of the residuals versus predicted sales

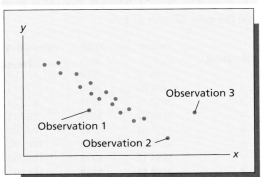

FIGURE 14.33   Outlying Observations

To illustrate these ideas, consider the sales territory performance data in Figure 14.10 (page 583). Figure 14.11 (page 584) gives the Excel output of a regression analysis of these data using the model that relates y to $x_1, x_2, x_3, x_4,$ and x_5. The least squares point estimates on the output give the prediction equation

$$\hat{y} = -1,113.7879 + 3.6121x_1 + .0421x_2 + .1289x_3 + 256.9555x_4 + 324.5334x_5$$

Using this prediction equation, we can calculate the predicted sales values and residuals given on the page margin. For example, observation 10 corresponds to a sales representative for whom $x_1 = 105.69$, $x_2 = 42,053.24$, $x_3 = 5,673.11$, $x_4 = 8.85$, and $x_5 = .31$. If we insert these values into the prediction equation, we obtain a predicted sales value of $\hat{y}_{10} = 4,143.597$. Since the actual sales for the sales representative are $y_{10} = 4,876.370$, the residual e_{10} equals the difference between $y_{10} = 4,876.370$ and $\hat{y}_{10} = 4,143.597$, which is 732.773. The normal plot of the residuals in Figure 14.32(a) has an approximate straight-line appearance. The plot of the residuals versus predicted sales in Figure 14.32(b) has a horizontal band appearance, as do the plots of the residuals versus the independent variables (these plots are not given here). We conclude that the regression assumptions approximately hold for the sales territory performance model.

Outliers   An observation that is well separated from the rest of the data is called an **outlier,** and an observation may be an outlier with respect to its y value and/or its x values. We illustrate these ideas by considering Figure 14.33, which is a hypothetical plot of the values of a dependent variable y against an independent variable x. Observation 1 in this figure is outlying with respect to its y value, but not with respect to its x value. Observation 2 is outlying with respect to its x value, but since its y value is consistent with the regression relationship displayed by the nonoutlying observations, it is not outlying with respect to its y value. Observation 3 is an outlier with respect to its x value and its y value.

It is important to identify outliers because (as we will see) outliers can have adverse effects on a regression analysis and thus are candidates for removal from a data set. Moreover, in addition to using data plots, we can use more sophisticated procedures to detect outliers. These procedures are particularly important when we are performing a multiple regression analysis and thus simple data plots are unlikely to tell us what we need to know. To illustrate, we consider the data in Figure 14.34(a), which concerns the need for labor in 17 U.S. Navy hospitals. Specifically, this table gives values of the dependent variable Hours (y, monthly labor hours required) and of the independent variables Xray (x_1, monthly X-ray exposures), BedDays (x_2, monthly occupied bed days—a hospital has one occupied bed day if one bed is occupied for an entire day), and Length (x_3, average length of patients' stay, in days). When we perform a regression analysis of these data using the model relating y to $x_1, x_2,$ and x_3, we obtain the Excel add-in (MegaStat) output of residuals and outlier diagnostics shown in Figure 14.34(b), as well as the residual plot shown in Figure 14.34(c). (MINITAB gives the same diagnostics, and at the end of this section we will give formulas for most of these diagnostics). We now explain the meanings of the diagnostics.

Obs	Predicted	Residual
1	3,504.990	164.890
2	3,901.180	−427.230
3	2,774.866	−479.766
4	4,911.872	−236.312
5	5,415.196	710.764
6	2,026.090	108.850
7	5,126.127	−94.467
8	3,106.925	260.525
9	6,055.297	464.153
10	4,143.597	732.773
11	2,503.165	−34.895
12	1,827.065	706.245
13	2,478.083	−69.973
14	2,351.344	−13.964
15	4,797.688	−210.738
16	2,904.099	−174.859
17	3,362.660	−73.260
18	2,907.376	−106.596
19	3,625.026	−360.826
20	4,056.443	−602.823
21	1,409.835	331.615
22	2,494.101	−458.351
23	1,617.561	−39.561
24	4,574.903	−407.463
25	2,488.700	311.270

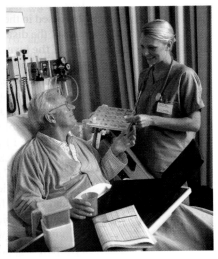

TABLE 14.16   **Measurements Taken on 63 Single-Family Residences**   OxHome

Residence	Sales Price, y ($\times$ $1,000)	Square Feet, x_1	Rooms, x_2	Bedrooms, x_3	Age, x_4	Residence	Sales Price, y ($\times$ $1,000)	Square Feet, x_1	Rooms, x_2	Bedrooms, x_3	Age, x_4
1	53.5	1,008	5	2	35	33	63.0	1,053	5	2	24
2	49.0	1,290	6	3	36	34	60.0	1,728	6	3	26
3	50.5	860	8	2	36	35	34.0	416	3	1	42
4	49.9	912	5	3	41	36	52.0	1,040	5	2	9
5	52.0	1,204	6	3	40	37	75.0	1,496	6	3	30
6	55.0	1,204	5	3	10	38	93.0	1,936	8	4	39
7	80.5	1,764	8	4	64	39	60.0	1,904	7	4	32
8	86.0	1,600	7	3	19	40	73.0	1,080	5	2	24
9	69.0	1,255	5	3	16	41	71.0	1,768	8	4	74
10	149.0	3,600	10	5	17	42	83.0	1,503	6	3	14
11	46.0	864	5	3	37	43	90.0	1,736	7	3	16
12	38.0	720	4	2	41	44	83.0	1,695	6	3	12
13	49.5	1,008	6	3	35	45	115.0	2,186	8	4	12
14	105.0	1,950	8	3	52	46	50.0	888	5	2	34
15	152.5	2,086	7	3	12	47	55.2	1,120	6	3	29
16	85.0	2,011	9	4	76	48	61.0	1,400	5	3	33
17	60.0	1,465	6	3	102	49	147.0	2,165	7	3	2
18	58.5	1,232	5	2	69	50	210.0	2,353	8	4	15
19	101.0	1,736	7	3	67	51	60.0	1,536	6	3	36
20	79.4	1,296	6	3	11	52	100.0	1,972	8	3	37
21	125.0	1,996	7	3	9	53	44.5	1,120	5	3	27
22	87.9	1,874	5	2	14	54	55.0	1,664	7	3	79
23	80.0	1,580	5	3	11	55	53.4	925	5	3	20
24	94.0	1,920	5	3	14	56	65.0	1,288	5	3	2
25	74.0	1,430	9	3	16	57	73.0	1,400	5	3	2
26	69.0	1,486	6	3	27	58	40.0	1,376	6	3	103
27	63.0	1,008	5	2	35	59	141.0	2,038	12	4	62
28	67.5	1,282	5	3	20	60	68.0	1,572	6	3	29
29	35.0	1,134	5	2	74	61	139.0	1,545	6	3	9
30	142.5	2,400	9	4	15	62	140.0	1,993	6	3	4
31	92.2	1,701	5	3	15	63	55.0	1,130	5	2	21
32	56.0	1,020	6	3	16						

TABLE 14.17

The Least Squares Point Estimates for Exercise 14.47

$b_0 = 10.3676$
   (.3710)
$b_1 = .0500$
   (<.001)
$b_2 = 6.3218$
   (.0152)
$b_3 = -11.1032$
   (.0635)
$b_4 = -.4319$
   (.0002)

of bedrooms x_3, and age x_4 for each of 63 single-family residences recently sold in the OxHome community. When we perform a regression analysis of these data using the model

$$y = \beta_0 + \beta_1 x_1 + \beta_2 x_2 + \beta_3 x_3 + \beta_4 x_4 + \varepsilon$$

we find that the least squares point estimates of the model parameters and their associated p-values (given in parentheses) are as shown in Table 14.17. Discuss why the estimates $b_2 = 6.3218$ and $b_3 = -11.1032$ suggest that it might be more profitable when building a house of a specified square footage (1) to include both a (smaller) living room and family room rather than a (larger) great room and (2) to not increase the number of bedrooms (at the cost of another type of room) that would normally be included in a house of the specified square footage. Note: Based on the statistical results, the builder realized that there are many families with children in a college town and that the parents in such families would rather have one living area for the children (the family room) and a separate living area for themselves (the living room). The builder started modifying his open-space homes accordingly and greatly increased his profits.

14.48 **THE FRESH DETERGENT CASE** Fresh3

Recall from Exercise 14.32 (page 594) that Enterprise Industries has advertised Fresh liquid laundry detergent by using three different advertising campaigns—advertising campaign A (television commercials), advertising campaign B (a balanced mixture of television and radio commercials) and advertising campaign C (a balanced mixture of television, radio, newspaper, and magazine ads). To compare the effectiveness of these advertising campaigns, consider using two models, Model 1 and Model 2, that are shown with corresponding partial Excel outputs in Figure 14.35. In these models y is demand for Fresh; x_4 is the price difference; x_3 is Enterprise

FIGURE 14.35   Excel Output for the Fresh Detergent Case

(a) Partial Excel output for the model $y = \beta_0 + \beta_1 x_4 + \beta_2 x_3 + \beta_3 x_3^2 + \beta_4 x_4 x_3 + \beta_5 D_B + \beta_6 D_C + \varepsilon$

	Coefficients	Standard Error	t Stat	P-value	Lower 95%	Upper 95%
Intercept	25.612696	4.7938	5.3429	2.00E-05	15.6960	35.5294
X4	9.0587	3.0317	2.9880	0.0066	2.7871	15.3302
X3	−6.5377	1.5814	−4.1342	0.0004	−9.8090	−3.2664
X3SQ	0.5844	0.1299	4.5001	0.0002	0.3158	0.8531
X4X3	−1.1565	0.4557	−2.5376	0.0184	−2.0992	−0.2137
DB	0.2137	0.0622	3.4380	0.0022	0.0851	0.3423
DC	0.3818	0.0613	6.2328	2.33E-06	0.2551	0.5085

(b) Partial Excel output for the model $y = \beta_0 + \beta_1 x_4 + \beta_2 x_3 + \beta_3 x_3^2 + \beta_4 x_4 x_3 + \beta_5 D_A + \beta_6 D_C + \varepsilon$

	Coefficients	Standard Error	t Stat	P-value	Lower 95%	Upper 95%
Intercept	25.8264	4.7946	5.3866	1.80E-05	15.9081	35.7447
X4	9.05868	3.0317	2.9880	0.0066	2.7871	15.3302
X3	−6.5377	1.5814	−4.1342	0.0004	−9.8090	−3.2664
X3SQ	0.58444	0.1299	4.5001	0.0002	0.3158	0.8531
X4X3	−1.1565	0.4557	−2.5376	0.0184	−2.0992	−0.2137
DA	−0.2137	0.0622	−3.4380	0.0022	−0.3423	−0.0851
DC	0.16809	0.0637	2.6385	0.0147	0.0363	0.2999

Industries' advertising expenditure for Fresh; D_A equals 1 if advertising campaign A is used in a sales period and 0 otherwise; D_B equals 1 if advertising campaign B is used in a sales period and 0 otherwise; and D_C equals 1 if advertising campaign C is used in a sales period and 0 otherwise. Moreover, in Model 1 the parameter β_5 represents the effect on mean demand of advertising campaign B compared to advertising campaign A, and the parameter β_6 represents the effect on mean demand of advertising campaign C compared to advertising campaign A. In Model 2 the parameter β_6 represents the effect on mean demand of advertising campaign C compared to advertising campaign B.

a   Compare advertising compaigns A, B, and C by finding 95 percent confidence intervals for
    (1) β_5 and β_6 in Model 1 and (2) β_6 in Model 2. Interpret the intervals.
b   A point prediction of and a 95 percent prediction interval for Fresh demand when $x_4 = .20$, $x_3 = 6.50$, and campaign C will be used are 8.50068 (that is, 850,068 bottles) and [8.21322, 8.78813]. Show that Model 1 and Model 2 give the same point prediction.

14.49   In the article "The Effect of Promotion Timing on Major League Baseball Attendance" (*Sport Marketing Quarterly,* December 1999), T. C. Boyd and T. C. Krehbiel use data from six major league baseball teams having outdoor stadiums to study the effect of promotion timing on major league baseball attendance. One of their regression models describes game attendance in 1996 as follows (*p*-values less than .10 are shown in parentheses under the appropriate independent variables):

Attendance = 2,521 + 106.5 *Temperature* + 12.33 *Winning %* + .2248 *OpWin %*
            (<.001)   (<.001)   (<.001)

      − 424.2 *DayGame* + 4,845 *Weekend* + 1,192 *Rival* + 4,745 *Promotion*
            (<.001)   (<.10)   (<.001)

      + 5,059 *Promo*DayGame* − 4,690 *Promo*Weekend* + 696.5 *Promo*Rival*
            (<.001)   (<.001)

In this model, *Temperature* is the high temperature recorded in the city on game day; *Winning %* is the home team's winning percentage at the start of the game; *OpWin %* is a dummy variable that equals 1 if the opponent's winning percentage was .500 or higher and 0 otherwise; *DayGame* is a dummy variable that equals 1 if the game was a day game and 0 otherwise; *Weekend* is a dummy variable that equals 1 if the game was on a Friday, Saturday, or Sunday and 0 otherwise; *Rival* is a dummy variable that equals 1 if the opponent was a rival and 0 otherwise; *Promotion* is a dummy variable that equals 1 if the home team ran a promotion during the game and 0 otherwise. Using

TABLE 14.18

Number of Bathrooms OxHome2

Bath	Bath
1.0	2.0
1.0	1.5
1.0	1.0
1.0	1.5
1.0	2.0
1.5	1.5
1.5	1.0
2.0	1.5
2.0	1.5
2.5	2.0
1.0	2.5
1.0	2.0
2.0	2.5
1.5	1.0
2.0	1.0
1.5	1.0
1.0	2.0
1.5	2.5
1.0	2.0
1.5	2.0
2.5	1.0
2.0	2.0
1.0	1.0
2.5	1.5
2.0	1.5
2.0	1.0
1.0	2.0
2.0	1.0
1.0	2.0
2.5	2.0
2.0	2.0
1.0	

the model, Boyd and Krehbiel conclude that "promotions run during day games and on weekdays are likely to result in greater attendance increases." Carefully explain why the following part of their model justifies this conclusion: $+ 5{,}059$ *Promo*DayGame* $- 4{,}690$ *Promo*Weekend*

14.50 Table 14.18 on the page margin gives the number of bathrooms for each of the 63 homes in Table 14.16. Using the following MINITAB output of the best single model of each size in terms of $\overline{R}^2$, s, and C, determine which overall model seems best: OxHome2

```
                                                R
                                        S  O  B     B
                                        Q  O  E  A  A
                           Mallows      F  M  D  G  T
Vars  R-Sq  R-Sq(adj)        Cp      S  T  S  S  E  H
  1   63.3    62.7         18.9  21.382  X
  2   69.1    68.1          8.6  19.782  X        X
  3   70.9    69.4          6.9  19.372  X  X     X
  4   72.6    70.7          5.3  18.962  X  X  X  X
  5   73.2    70.8          6.0  18.971  X  X  X  X  X
```

14.51   TREND AND SEASONAL PATTERNS: PART 1

Table 14.19 presents quarterly sales of the TRK-50 mountain bike for the previous four years at a bicycle shop in Switzerland. The MINITAB plot in Figure 14.36 shows that the bike sales exhibit an upward *linear trend* (that is, an upward straight line movement over time) and a strong *seasonal pattern*, with bike sales being higher in the spring and summer quarters than in the winter and fall quarters. If we let y_t denote the number of TRK-50 mountain bikes sold in time period t at the Swiss bike shop, then a regression model describing y_t is

$$y_t = \beta_0 + \beta_1 t + \beta_{Q2}Q_2 + \beta_{Q3}Q_3 + \beta_{Q4}Q_4 + \varepsilon_t$$

Here the expression $(\beta_0 + \beta_1 t)$ models the linear trend evident in Figure 14.36 and Q_2, Q_3, and Q_4 are dummy variables defined for quarters 2, 3, and 4. Specifically, Q_2 equals 1 if quarterly bike sales were observed in quarter 2 (spring) and 0 otherwise; Q_3 equals 1 if quarterly bike sales were observed in quarter 3 (summer) and 0 otherwise; Q_4 equals 1 if quarterly bike sales were observed in quarter 4 (fall) and 0 otherwise. Note that we have not defined a dummy variable for quarter 1 (winter). It follows that the regression parameters β_{Q2}, β_{Q3}, and β_{Q4} compare quarters 2, 3, and 4 with quarter 1. Intuitively, for example, β_{Q4} is the difference, excluding trend, between

TABLE 14.19   Quarterly Sales of the TRK-50 Mountain Bike BikeSales

Year	Quarter	t	Sales, y_t
1	1 (Winter)	1	10
	2 (Spring)	2	31
	3 (Summer)	3	43
	4 (Fall)	4	16
2	1	5	11
	2	6	33
	3	7	45
	4	8	17
3	1	9	13
	2	10	34
	3	11	48
	4	12	19
4	1	13	15
	2	14	37
	3	15	51
	4	16	21

FIGURE 14.36   MINITAB Plot of TRK-50 Bike Sales

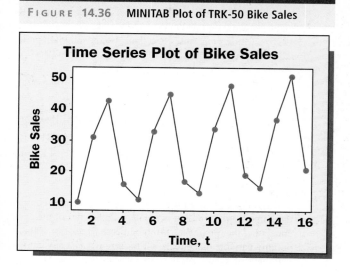

FIGURE 14.37   MINITAB Output of an Analysis of the Quarterly Bike Sales by Using
                Dummy Variable Regression

```
The regression equation is
BikeSales = 8.75 + 0.500 Time + 21.0 Q2 + 33.5 Q3 + 4.50 Q4

Predictor       Coef   SE Coef       T      P
Constant      8.7500    0.4281   20.44  0.000
Time          0.50000  0.03769   13.27  0.000
Q2           21.0000    0.4782   43.91  0.000
Q3           33.5000    0.4827   69.41  0.000
Q4            4.5000    0.4900    9.18  0.000

S = 0.674200    R-Sq = 99.8%    R-Sq(adj) = 99.8%

Values of Predictors for New Obs    Predicted Values for New Observations
New Obs  Time    Q2   Q3   Q4     New Obs    Fit   SE Fit      95% CI                95% PI
      1  17.0     0    0    0           1  17.250   0.506   (16.137, 18.363)   (15.395, 19.105)
      2  18.0     1    0    0           2  38.750   0.506   (37.637, 39.863)   (36.895, 40.605)
      3  19.0     0    1    0           3  51.750   0.506   (50.637, 52.863)   (49.895, 53.605)
      4  20.0     0    0    1           4  23.250   0.506   (22.137, 24.363)   (21.395, 25.105)
```

the level of the time series (y_t) in quarter 4 (fall) and the level of the time series in quarter 1 (winter). A positive β_{Q4} would imply that, excluding trend, bike sales in the fall can be expected to be higher than bike sales in the winter. A negative β_{Q4} would imply that, excluding trend, bike sales in the fall can be expected to be lower than bike sales in the winter.

Figure 14.37 gives the MINITAB output of a regression analysis of the quarterly bike sales by using the dummy variable model. Interpret the least squares point estimates $b_{Q2} = 21$, $b_{Q3} = 33.5$, and $b_{Q4} = 4.5$ of β_{Q2}, β_{Q3}, and β_{Q4}. Also note that near the bottom of the MINITAB output there are point predictions of and 95 percent prediction intervals for y_{17}, y_{18}, y_{19}, and y_{20}, bike sales in periods 17, 18, 19, and 20 (quarters 1, 2, 3 and 4 of next year). Show how the point predictions have been calculated.

14.52 **TREND AND SEASONAL PATTERNS: PART 2**

Table 14.20 gives the monthly international passenger totals over the last 11 years for an airline company. A plot of these passenger totals reveals an upward trend with increasing variation, and the natural logarithmic transformation is found to best equalize the variation (see Figure 14.38(a) and (b)). Figure 14.38(c) gives the MINITAB output of a regression analysis of the monthly international passenger totals by using the model   DS AirPass

$$\ln y_t = \beta_0 + \beta_1 t + \beta_{M1}M_1 + \beta_{M2}M_2 + \cdots + \beta_{M11}M_{11} + \varepsilon_t$$

Here $M_1, M_2, \ldots, M_{11}$ are appropriately defined dummy variables for January (month 1) through November (month 11). Let y_{133} denote the international passenger totals in month 133 (January of next year). The MINITAB output tells us that a point prediction of and a 95 percent prediction interval for $\ln y_{133}$ are, respectively, 6.08610 and [5.96593, 6.20627]. Using the least squares

TABLE 14.20   **Monthly International Passenger Totals (Thousands of Passengers)**   DS AirPass

Year	Jan.	Feb.	Mar.	Apr.	May	June	July	Aug.	Sept.	Oct.	Nov.	Dec.
1	112	118	132	129	121	135	148	148	136	119	104	118
2	115	126	141	135	125	149	170	170	158	133	114	140
3	145	150	178	163	172	178	199	199	184	162	146	166
4	171	180	193	181	183	218	230	242	209	191	172	194
5	196	196	236	235	229	243	264	272	237	211	180	201
6	204	188	235	227	234	264	302	293	259	229	203	229
7	242	233	267	269	270	315	364	347	312	274	237	278
8	284	277	317	313	318	374	413	405	355	306	271	306
9	315	301	356	348	355	422	465	467	404	347	305	336
10	340	318	362	348	363	435	491	505	404	359	310	337
11	360	342	406	396	420	472	548	559	463	407	362	405

Source: *FAA Statistical Handbook of Civil Aviation* (several annual issues). These data were originally presented by Box and Jenkins (1976). We have updated the situation in this exercise to be more modern.

Multiple linear regression with a quadratic term similar to Figure 14.23 on page 597 (data file: GasAdd.xlsx):

- Enter the gas mileage data from Table 14.13 (page 597)—mileages (with label Mileage) in column A and units of additive (with label Units) in column B. (Units are listed second in order to be adjacent to the squared units predictor.)

- Enter UnitsSq into cell C1.

- Click on cell C2, and enter the formula =B2*B2. Press "Enter" to compute the squared value of Units for the first observation.

- Copy the cell formula of C2 through cell C16 (by double-clicking the drag handle in the lower right corner of cell C2) to compute the squared units for the remaining observations.

- Select **Data : Data Analysis : Regression** and click OK in the Data Analysis dialog box.

- In the Regression dialog box:
  Enter A1 : A16 into the "Input Y Range" window.
  Enter B1 : C16 into the "Input X Range" window.

- Place a checkmark in the Labels checkbox.

- Select the "New Worksheet Ply" Output option.

- Click OK in the Regression dialog box to obtain the regression output in a new worksheet.

Appendix 14.2 ■ Multiple Regression Analysis Using MegaStat

The instructions in this section begin by describing the entry of data into an Excel worksheet. Alternatively, the data may be downloaded from this book's website. The appropriate data file name is given at the top of each instruction block. Please refer to Appendix 1.1 for further information about entering data, saving data, and printing results in Excel. Please refer to Appendix 1.2 for more information about using MegaStat.

Multiple regression similar to Figure 14.5 on page 566 (data file: FuelCon2.xlsx):

- Enter the fuel consumption data in Table 14.3 (page 565) as shown—temperature (with label Temp) in column A, chill index (with label Chill) in column B, and fuel consumption (with label FuelCons) in column C. Note that Temp and Chill are contiguous columns (that is, they are next to each other). This is not necessary, but it makes selection of the independent variables (as described below) easiest.

- Select **Add-Ins : MegaStat : Correlation/ Regression : Regression Analysis**

- In the Regression Analysis dialog box, click in the Independent Variables window and use the autoexpand feature to enter the range A1 : B9. Note that if the independent variables are not next to each other, hold the CTRL key down while making selections and then autoexpand.

- Click in the Dependent Variable window and enter the range C1 : C9.

- Check the appropriate Options and Residuals checkboxes as follows:

  1 Check "Test Intercept" to include a y-intercept and to test its significance.

  2 Check "Output Residuals" to obtain a list of the model residuals.

  3 Check "Plot Residuals by Observation" and "Plot Residuals by Predicted Y and X" to obtain residual plots versus time, versus the predicted values of y, and versus the values of each independent variable (see Section 14.11).

  4 Check "Normal Probability Plot of Residuals" to obtain a normal plot (see Section 14.11).

  5 Check "Diagnostics and Influential Residuals" to obtain diagnostics (see Section 14.11).

  6 Check "Durbin-Watson" to obtain the Durbin–Watson statistic (see Section 13.9) and check "Variance Inflation Factors" (see Section 14.10).

To obtain a **point prediction** of y when temperature equals 40 and chill index equals 10 (as well as a confidence interval and prediction interval):

- Click on the drop-down menu above the Predictor Values window and select "Type in predictor values."

- Type 40 and 10 (separated by at least one blank space) into the Predictor Values window.

(Continues across page)

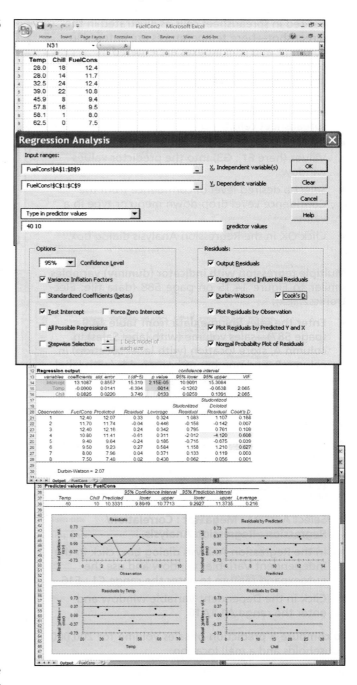

- Select a desired level of confidence (here 95%) from the Confidence Level drop-down menu or type in a value.

- Click OK in the Regression Analysis dialog box.

Appendix **A**

Statistical Tables

Table A.1 A Binomial Probability Table

Table A.2 A Poisson Probability Table

Table A.3 Cumulative Areas under the Standard Normal Curve

Table A.4 A t Table: Values of t_α

Table A.5 An F Table: Values of $F_{.10}$

Table A.6 An F Table: Values of $F_{.05}$

Table A.7 An F Table: Values of $F_{.025}$

Table A.8 An F Table: Values of $F_{.01}$

Table A.9 Percentage Points of the Studentized Range

Table A.10 A Chi-Square Table: Values of χ^2_α

Table A.11 Critical Values for the Durbin–Watson d Statistic ($\alpha = .05$)

Table A.12 Critical Values for the Durbin–Watson d Statistic ($\alpha = .025$)

Table A.13 Critical Values for the Durbin–Watson d Statistic ($\alpha = .01$)

Table A.14 A Table of Areas under the Standard Normal Curve

TABLE A.1   A Binomial Probability Table:
             Binomial Probabilities (*n* between 2 and 6)

n = 2   **p**

x↓	.05	.10	.15	.20	.25	.30	.35	.40	.45	.50	
0	.9025	.8100	.7225	.6400	.5625	.4900	.4225	.3600	.3025	.2500	2
1	.0950	.1800	.2550	.3200	.3750	.4200	.4550	.4800	.4950	.5000	1
2	.0025	.0100	.0225	.0400	.0625	.0900	.1225	.1600	.2025	.2500	0
	.95	.90	.85	.80	.75	.70	.65	.60	.55	.50	x↑

n = 3   **p**

x↓	.05	.10	.15	.20	.25	.30	.35	.40	.45	.50	
0	.8574	.7290	.6141	.5120	.4219	.3430	.2746	.2160	.1664	.1250	3
1	.1354	.2430	.3251	.3840	.4219	.4410	.4436	.4320	.4084	.3750	2
2	.0071	.0270	.0574	.0960	.1406	.1890	.2389	.2880	.3341	.3750	1
3	.0001	.0010	.0034	.0080	.0156	.0270	.0429	.0640	.0911	.1250	0
	.95	.90	.85	.80	.75	.70	.65	.60	.55	.50	x↑

n = 4   **p**

x↓	.05	.10	.15	.20	.25	.30	.35	.40	.45	.50	
0	.8145	.6561	.5220	.4096	.3164	.2401	.1785	.1296	.0915	.0625	4
1	.1715	.2916	.3685	.4096	.4219	.4116	.3845	.3456	.2995	.2500	3
2	.0135	.0486	.0975	.1536	.2109	.2646	.3105	.3456	.3675	.3750	2
3	.0005	.0036	.0115	.0256	.0469	.0756	.1115	.1536	.2005	.2500	1
4	.0000	.0001	.0005	.0016	.0039	.0081	.0150	.0256	.0410	.0625	0
	.95	.90	.85	.80	.75	.70	.65	.60	.55	.50	x↑

n = 5   **p**

x↓	.05	.10	.15	.20	.25	.30	.35	.40	.45	.50	
0	.7738	.5905	.4437	.3277	.2373	.1681	.1160	.0778	.0503	.0313	5
1	.2036	.3281	.3915	.4096	.3955	.3602	.3124	.2592	.2059	.1563	4
2	.0214	.0729	.1382	.2048	.2637	.3087	.3364	.3456	.3369	.3125	3
3	.0011	.0081	.0244	.0512	.0879	.1323	.1811	.2304	.2757	.3125	2
4	.0000	.0005	.0022	.0064	.0146	.0284	.0488	.0768	.1128	.1563	1
5	.0000	.0000	.0001	.0003	.0010	.0024	.0053	.0102	.0185	.0313	0
	.95	.90	.85	.80	.75	.70	.65	.60	.55	.50	x↑

n = 6   **p**

x↓	.05	.10	.15	.20	.25	.30	.35	.40	.45	.50	
0	.7351	.5314	.3771	.2621	.1780	.1176	.0754	.0467	.0277	.0156	6
1	.2321	.3543	.3993	.3932	.3560	.3025	.2437	.1866	.1359	.0938	5
2	.0305	.0984	.1762	.2458	.2966	.3241	.3280	.3110	.2780	.2344	4
3	.0021	.0146	.0415	.0819	.1318	.1852	.2355	.2765	.3032	.3125	3
4	.0001	.0012	.0055	.0154	.0330	.0595	.0951	.1382	.1861	.2344	2
5	.0000	.0001	.0004	.0015	.0044	.0102	.0205	.0369	.0609	.0938	1
6	.0000	.0000	.0000	.0001	.0002	.0007	.0018	.0041	.0083	.0156	0
	.95	.90	.85	.80	.75	.70	.65	.60	.55	.50	x↑

(table continued)

TABLE A.1 *(continued)*
Binomial Probabilities (*n* equal to 16 and 18)

n = 16   p

x↓	.05	.10	.15	.20	.25	.30	.35	.40	.45	.50	
0	.4401	.1853	.0743	.0281	.0100	.0033	.0010	.0003	.0001	.0000	16
1	.3706	.3294	.2097	.1126	.0535	.0228	.0087	.0030	.0009	.0002	15
2	.1463	.2745	.2775	.2111	.1336	.0732	.0353	.0150	.0056	.0018	14
3	.0359	.1423	.2285	.2463	.2079	.1465	.0888	.0468	.0215	.0085	13
4	.0061	.0514	.1311	.2001	.2252	.2040	.1553	.1014	.0572	.0278	12
5	.0008	.0137	.0555	.1201	.1802	.2099	.2008	.1623	.1123	.0667	11
6	.0001	.0028	.0180	.0550	.1101	.1649	.1982	.1983	.1684	.1222	10
7	.0000	.0004	.0045	.0197	.0524	.1010	.1524	.1889	.1969	.1746	9
8	.0000	.0001	.0009	.0055	.0197	.0487	.0923	.1417	.1812	.1964	8
9	.0000	.0000	.0001	.0012	.0058	.0185	.0442	.0840	.1318	.1746	7
10	.0000	.0000	.0000	.0002	.0014	.0056	.0167	.0392	.0755	.1222	6
11	.0000	.0000	.0000	.0000	.0002	.0013	.0049	.0142	.0337	.0667	5
12	.0000	.0000	.0000	.0000	.0000	.0002	.0011	.0040	.0115	.0278	4
13	.0000	.0000	.0000	.0000	.0000	.0000	.0002	.0008	.0029	.0085	3
14	.0000	.0000	.0000	.0000	.0000	.0000	.0000	.0001	.0005	.0018	2
15	.0000	.0000	.0000	.0000	.0000	.0000	.0000	.0000	.0001	.0002	1
	.95	.90	.85	.80	.75	.70	.65	.60	.55	.50	x↑

n = 18   p

x↓	.05	.10	.15	.20	.25	.30	.35	.40	.45	.50	
0	.3972	.1501	.0536	.0180	.0056	.0016	.0004	.0001	.0000	.0000	18
1	.3763	.3002	.1704	.0811	.0338	.0126	.0042	.0012	.0003	.0001	17
2	.1683	.2835	.2556	.1723	.0958	.0458	.0190	.0069	.0022	.0006	16
3	.0473	.1680	.2406	.2297	.1704	.1046	.0547	.0246	.0095	.0031	15
4	.0093	.0700	.1592	.2153	.2130	.1681	.1104	.0614	.0291	.0117	14
5	.0014	.0218	.0787	.1507	.1988	.2017	.1664	.1146	.0666	.0327	13
6	.0002	.0052	.0301	.0816	.1436	.1873	.1941	.1655	.1181	.0708	12
7	.0000	.0010	.0091	.0350	.0820	.1376	.1792	.1892	.1657	.1214	11
8	.0000	.0002	.0022	.0120	.0376	.0811	.1327	.1734	.1864	.1669	10
9	.0000	.0000	.0004	.0033	.0139	.0386	.0794	.1284	.1694	.1855	9
10	.0000	.0000	.0001	.0008	.0042	.0149	.0385	.0771	.1248	.1669	8
11	.0000	.0000	.0000	.0001	.0010	.0046	.0151	.0374	.0742	.1214	7
12	.0000	.0000	.0000	.0000	.0002	.0012	.0047	.0145	.0354	.0708	6
13	.0000	.0000	.0000	.0000	.0000	.0002	.0012	.0045	.0134	.0327	5
14	.0000	.0000	.0000	.0000	.0000	.0000	.0002	.0011	.0039	.0117	4
15	.0000	.0000	.0000	.0000	.0000	.0000	.0000	.0002	.0009	.0031	3
16	.0000	.0000	.0000	.0000	.0000	.0000	.0000	.0000	.0001	.0006	2
17	.0000	.0000	.0000	.0000	.0000	.0000	.0000	.0000	.0000	.0001	1
	.95	.90	.85	.80	.75	.70	.65	.60	.55	.50	x↑

TABLE A.1 *(concluded)*
Binomial Probabilities (*n* equal to 20)

n = 20   **p**

x↓	.05	.10	.15	.20	.25	.30	.35	.40	.45	.50	
0	.3585	.1216	.0388	.0115	.0032	.0008	.0002	.0000	.0000	.0000	20
1	.3774	.2702	.1368	.0576	.0211	.0068	.0020	.0005	.0001	.0000	19
2	.1887	.2852	.2293	.1369	.0669	.0278	.0100	.0031	.0008	.0002	18
3	.0596	.1901	.2428	.2054	.1339	.0716	.0323	.0123	.0040	.0011	17
4	.0133	.0898	.1821	.2182	.1897	.1304	.0738	.0350	.0139	.0046	16
5	.0022	.0319	.1028	.1746	.2023	.1789	.1272	.0746	.0365	.0148	15
6	.0003	.0089	.0454	.1091	.1686	.1916	.1712	.1244	.0746	.0370	14
7	.0000	.0020	.0160	.0545	.1124	.1643	.1844	.1659	.1221	.0739	13
8	.0000	.0004	.0046	.0222	.0609	.1144	.1614	.1797	.1623	.1201	12
9	.0000	.0001	.0011	.0074	.0271	.0654	.1158	.1597	.1771	.1602	11
10	.0000	.0000	.0002	.0020	.0099	.0308	.0686	.1171	.1593	.1762	10
11	.0000	.0000	.0000	.0005	.0030	.0120	.0336	.0710	.1185	.1602	9
12	.0000	.0000	.0000	.0001	.0008	.0039	.0136	.0355	.0727	.1201	8
13	.0000	.0000	.0000	.0000	.0002	.0010	.0045	.0146	.0366	.0739	7
14	.0000	.0000	.0000	.0000	.0000	.0002	.0012	.0049	.0150	.0370	6
15	.0000	.0000	.0000	.0000	.0000	.0000	.0003	.0013	.0049	.0148	5
16	.0000	.0000	.0000	.0000	.0000	.0000	.0000	.0003	.0013	.0046	4
17	.0000	.0000	.0000	.0000	.0000	.0000	.0000	.0000	.0002	.0011	3
18	.0000	.0000	.0000	.0000	.0000	.0000	.0000	.0000	.0000	.0002	2
	.95	.90	.85	.80	.75	.70	.65	.60	.55	.50	x↑

Source: Binomial Probability Table from STATISTICAL THINKING FOR MANAGERS, 3rd Edition by D. K. Hildebrand & L. Ott, © 1991. Reprinted with permission of South-Western, a division of Thomson Learning, www.thomsonrights.com. Fax 800 730-2215.

TABLE A.2 **A Poisson Probability Table**
Poisson Probabilities (*μ* between .1 and 2.0)

μ

x	.1	.2	.3	.4	.5	.6	.7	.8	.9	1.0
0	.9048	.8187	.7408	.6703	.6065	.5488	.4966	.4493	.4066	.3679
1	.0905	.1637	.2222	.2681	.3033	.3293	.3476	.3595	.3659	.3679
2	.0045	.0164	.0333	.0536	.0758	.0988	.1217	.1438	.1647	.1839
3	.0002	.0011	.0033	.0072	.0126	.0198	.0284	.0383	.0494	.0613
4	.0000	.0001	.0003	.0007	.0016	.0030	.0050	.0077	.0111	.0153
5	.0000	.0000	.0000	.0001	.0002	.0004	.0007	.0012	.0020	.0031
6	.0000	.0000	.0000	.0000	.0000	.0000	.0001	.0002	.0003	.0005

μ

x	1.1	1.2	1.3	1.4	1.5	1.6	1.7	1.8	1.9	2.0
0	.3329	.3012	.2725	.2466	.2231	.2019	.1827	.1653	.1496	.1353
1	.3662	.3614	.3543	.3452	.3347	.3230	.3106	.2975	.2842	.2707
2	.2014	.2169	.2303	.2417	.2510	.2584	.2640	.2678	.2700	.2707
3	.0738	.0867	.0998	.1128	.1255	.1378	.1496	.1607	.1710	.1804
4	.0203	.0260	.0324	.0395	.0471	.0551	.0636	.0723	.0812	.0902
5	.0045	.0062	.0084	.0111	.0141	.0176	.0216	.0260	.0309	.0361
6	.0008	.0012	.0018	.0026	.0035	.0047	.0061	.0078	.0098	.0120
7	.0001	.0002	.0003	.0005	.0008	.0011	.0015	.0020	.0027	.0034
8	.0000	.0000	.0001	.0001	.0001	.0002	.0003	.0005	.0006	.0009

(table continued)

TABLE A.3　Cumulative Areas under the Standard Normal Curve

z	0.00	0.01	0.02	0.03	0.04	0.05	0.06	0.07	0.08	0.09
−3.9	0.00005	0.00005	0.00004	0.00004	0.00004	0.00004	0.00004	0.00004	0.00003	0.00003
−3.8	0.00007	0.00007	0.00007	0.00006	0.00006	0.00006	0.00006	0.00005	0.00005	0.00005
−3.7	0.00011	0.00010	0.00010	0.00010	0.00009	0.00009	0.00008	0.00008	0.00008	0.00008
−3.6	0.00016	0.00015	0.00015	0.00014	0.00014	0.00013	0.00013	0.00012	0.00012	0.00011
−3.5	0.00023	0.00022	0.00022	0.00021	0.00020	0.00019	0.00019	0.00018	0.00017	0.00017
−3.4	0.00034	0.00032	0.00031	0.00030	0.00029	0.00028	0.00027	0.00026	0.00025	0.00024
−3.3	0.00048	0.00047	0.00045	0.00043	0.00042	0.00040	0.00039	0.00038	0.00036	0.00035
−3.2	0.00069	0.00066	0.00064	0.00062	0.00060	0.00058	0.00056	0.00054	0.00052	0.00050
−3.1	0.00097	0.00094	0.00090	0.00087	0.00084	0.00082	0.00079	0.00076	0.00074	0.00071
−3.0	0.00135	0.00131	0.00126	0.00122	0.00118	0.00114	0.00111	0.00107	0.00103	0.00100
−2.9	0.0019	0.0018	0.0018	0.0017	0.0016	0.0016	0.0015	0.0015	0.0014	0.0014
−2.8	0.0026	0.0025	0.0024	0.0023	0.0023	0.0022	0.0021	0.0021	0.0020	0.0019
−2.7	0.0035	0.0034	0.0033	0.0032	0.0031	0.0030	0.0029	0.0028	0.0027	0.0026
−2.6	0.0047	0.0045	0.0044	0.0043	0.0041	0.0040	0.0039	0.0038	0.0037	0.0036
−2.5	0.0062	0.0060	0.0059	0.0057	0.0055	0.0054	0.0052	0.0051	0.0049	0.0048
−2.4	0.0082	0.0080	0.0078	0.0075	0.0073	0.0071	0.0069	0.0068	0.0066	0.0064
−2.3	0.0107	0.0104	0.0102	0.0099	0.0096	0.0094	0.0091	0.0089	0.0087	0.0084
−2.2	0.0139	0.0136	0.0132	0.0129	0.0125	0.0122	0.0119	0.0116	0.0113	0.0110
−2.1	0.0179	0.0174	0.0170	0.0166	0.0162	0.0158	0.0154	0.0150	0.0146	0.0143
−2.0	0.0228	0.0222	0.0217	0.0212	0.0207	0.0202	0.0197	0.0192	0.0188	0.0183
−1.9	0.0287	0.0281	0.0274	0.0268	0.0262	0.0256	0.0250	0.0244	0.0239	0.0233
−1.8	0.0359	0.0351	0.0344	0.0336	0.0329	0.0322	0.0314	0.0307	0.0301	0.0294
−1.7	0.0446	0.0436	0.0427	0.0418	0.0409	0.0401	0.0392	0.0384	0.0375	0.0367
−1.6	0.0548	0.0537	0.0526	0.0516	0.0505	0.0495	0.0485	0.0475	0.0465	0.0455
−1.5	0.0668	0.0655	0.0643	0.0630	0.0618	0.0606	0.0594	0.0582	0.0571	0.0559
−1.4	0.0808	0.0793	0.0778	0.0764	0.0749	0.0735	0.0721	0.0708	0.0694	0.0681
−1.3	0.0968	0.0951	0.0934	0.0918	0.0901	0.0885	0.0869	0.0853	0.0838	0.0823
−1.2	0.1151	0.1131	0.1112	0.1093	0.1075	0.1056	0.1038	0.1020	0.1003	0.0985
−1.1	0.1357	0.1335	0.1314	0.1292	0.1271	0.1251	0.1230	0.1210	0.1190	0.1170
−1.0	0.1587	0.1562	0.1539	0.1515	0.1492	0.1469	0.1446	0.1423	0.1401	0.1379
−0.9	0.1841	0.1814	0.1788	0.1762	0.1736	0.1711	0.1685	0.1660	0.1635	0.1611
−0.8	0.2119	0.2090	0.2061	0.2033	0.2005	0.1977	0.1949	0.1922	0.1894	0.1867
−0.7	0.2420	0.2389	0.2358	0.2327	0.2296	0.2266	0.2236	0.2206	0.2177	0.2148
−0.6	0.2743	0.2709	0.2676	0.2643	0.2611	0.2578	0.2546	0.2514	0.2482	0.2451
−0.5	0.3085	0.3050	0.3015	0.2981	0.2946	0.2912	0.2877	0.2843	0.2810	0.2776
−0.4	0.3446	0.3409	0.3372	0.3336	0.3300	0.3264	0.3228	0.3192	0.3156	0.3121
−0.3	0.3821	0.3783	0.3745	0.3707	0.3669	0.3632	0.3594	0.3557	0.3520	0.3483
−0.2	0.4207	0.4168	0.4129	0.4090	0.4052	0.4013	0.3974	0.3936	0.3897	0.3859
−0.1	0.4602	0.4562	0.4522	0.4483	0.4443	0.4404	0.4364	0.4325	0.4286	0.4247
−0.0	0.5000	0.4960	0.4920	0.4880	0.4840	0.4801	0.4761	0.4721	0.4681	0.4641

TABLE A.3   Cumulative Areas under the Standard Normal Curve (*concluded*)

z	0.00	0.01	0.02	0.03	0.04	0.05	0.06	0.07	0.08	0.09
0.0	0.5000	0.5040	0.5080	0.5120	0.5160	0.5199	0.5239	0.5279	0.5319	0.5359
0.1	0.5398	0.5438	0.5478	0.5517	0.5557	0.5596	0.5636	0.5675	0.5714	0.5753
0.2	0.5793	0.5832	0.5871	0.5910	0.5948	0.5987	0.6026	0.6064	0.6103	0.6141
0.3	0.6179	0.6217	0.6255	0.6293	0.6331	0.6368	0.6406	0.6443	0.6480	0.6517
0.4	0.6554	0.6591	0.6628	0.6664	0.6700	0.6736	0.6772	0.6808	0.6844	0.6879
0.5	0.6915	0.6950	0.6985	0.7019	0.7054	0.7088	0.7123	0.7157	0.7190	0.7224
0.6	0.7257	0.7291	0.7324	0.7357	0.7389	0.7422	0.7454	0.7486	0.7518	0.7549
0.7	0.7580	0.7611	0.7642	0.7673	0.7704	0.7734	0.7764	0.7794	0.7823	0.7852
0.8	0.7881	0.7910	0.7939	0.7967	0.7995	0.8023	0.8051	0.8078	0.8106	0.8133
0.9	0.8159	0.8186	0.8212	0.8238	0.8264	0.8289	0.8315	0.8340	0.8365	0.8389
1.0	0.8413	0.8438	0.8461	0.8485	0.8508	0.8531	0.8554	0.8577	0.8599	0.8621
1.1	0.8643	0.8665	0.8686	0.8708	0.8729	0.8749	0.8770	0.8790	0.8810	0.8830
1.2	0.8849	0.8869	0.8888	0.8907	0.8925	0.8944	0.8962	0.8980	0.8997	0.9015
1.3	0.9032	0.9049	0.9066	0.9082	0.9099	0.9115	0.9131	0.9147	0.9162	0.9177
1.4	0.9192	0.9207	0.9222	0.9236	0.9251	0.9265	0.9279	0.9292	0.9306	0.9319
1.5	0.9332	0.9345	0.9357	0.9370	0.9382	0.9394	0.9406	0.9418	0.9429	0.9441
1.6	0.9452	0.9463	0.9474	0.9484	0.9495	0.9505	0.9515	0.9525	0.9535	0.9545
1.7	0.9554	0.9564	0.9573	0.9582	0.9591	0.9599	0.9608	0.9616	0.9625	0.9633
1.8	0.9641	0.9649	0.9656	0.9664	0.9671	0.9678	0.9686	0.9693	0.9699	0.9706
1.9	0.9713	0.9719	0.9726	0.9732	0.9738	0.9744	0.9750	0.9756	0.9761	0.9767
2.0	0.9772	0.9778	0.9783	0.9788	0.9793	0.9798	0.9803	0.9808	0.9812	0.9817
2.1	0.9821	0.9826	0.9830	0.9834	0.9838	0.9842	0.9846	0.9850	0.9854	0.9857
2.2	0.9861	0.9864	0.9868	0.9871	0.9875	0.9878	0.9881	0.9884	0.9887	0.9890
2.3	0.9893	0.9896	0.9898	0.9901	0.9904	0.9906	0.9909	0.9911	0.9913	0.9916
2.4	0.9918	0.9920	0.9922	0.9925	0.9927	0.9929	0.9931	0.9932	0.9934	0.9936
2.5	0.9938	0.9940	0.9941	0.9943	0.9945	0.9946	0.9948	0.9949	0.9951	0.9952
2.6	0.9953	0.9955	0.9956	0.9957	0.9959	0.9960	0.9961	0.9962	0.9963	0.9964
2.7	0.9965	0.9966	0.9967	0.9968	0.9969	0.9970	0.9971	0.9972	0.9973	0.9974
2.8	0.9974	0.9975	0.9976	0.9977	0.9977	0.9978	0.9979	0.9979	0.9980	0.9981
2.9	0.9981	0.9982	0.9982	0.9983	0.9984	0.9984	0.9985	0.9985	0.9986	0.9986
3.0	0.99865	0.99869	0.99874	0.99878	0.99882	0.99886	0.99889	0.99893	0.99897	0.99900
3.1	0.99903	0.99906	0.99910	0.99913	0.99916	0.99918	0.99921	0.99924	0.99926	0.99929
3.2	0.99931	0.99934	0.99936	0.99938	0.99940	0.99942	0.99944	0.99946	0.99948	0.99950
3.3	0.99952	0.99953	0.99955	0.99957	0.99958	0.99960	0.99961	0.99962	0.99964	0.99965
3.4	0.99966	0.99968	0.99969	0.99970	0.99971	0.99972	0.99973	0.99974	0.99975	0.99976
3.5	0.99977	0.99978	0.99978	0.99979	0.99980	0.99981	0.99981	0.99982	0.99983	0.99983
3.6	0.99984	0.99985	0.99985	0.99986	0.99986	0.99987	0.99987	0.99988	0.99988	0.99989
3.7	0.99989	0.99990	0.99990	0.99990	0.99991	0.99991	0.99992	0.99992	0.99992	0.99992
3.8	0.99993	0.99993	0.99993	0.99994	0.99994	0.99994	0.99994	0.99995	0.99995	0.99995
3.9	0.99995	0.99995	0.99996	0.99996	0.99996	0.99996	0.99996	0.99996	0.99997	0.99997

TABLE A.4   **A _t_ Table: Values of _t_$_\alpha$ for _df_ = 1 through 48**

df	$t_{.100}$	$t_{.05}$	$t_{.025}$	$t_{.01}$	$t_{.005}$	$t_{.001}$	$t_{.0005}$
1	3.078	6.314	12.706	31.821	63.657	318.309	636.619
2	1.886	2.920	4.303	6.965	9.925	22.327	31.599
3	1.638	2.353	3.182	4.541	5.841	10.215	12.924
4	1.533	2.132	2.776	3.747	4.604	7.173	8.610
5	1.476	2.015	2.571	3.365	4.032	5.893	6.869
6	1.440	1.943	2.447	3.143	3.707	5.208	5.959
7	1.415	1.895	2.365	2.998	3.499	4.785	5.408
8	1.397	1.860	2.306	2.896	3.355	4.501	5.041
9	1.383	1.833	2.262	2.821	3.250	4.297	4.781
10	1.372	1.812	2.228	2.764	3.169	4.144	4.587
11	1.363	1.796	2.201	2.718	3.106	4.025	4.437
12	1.356	1.782	2.179	2.681	3.055	3.930	4.318
13	1.350	1.771	2.160	2.650	3.012	3.852	4.221
14	1.345	1.761	2.145	2.624	2.977	3.787	4.140
15	1.341	1.753	2.131	2.602	2.947	3.733	4.073
16	1.337	1.746	2.120	2.583	2.921	3.686	4.015
17	1.333	1.740	2.110	2.567	2.898	3.646	3.965
18	1.330	1.734	2.101	2.552	2.878	3.610	3.922
19	1.328	1.729	2.093	2.539	2.861	3.579	3.883
20	1.325	1.725	2.086	2.528	2.845	3.552	3.850
21	1.323	1.721	2.080	2.518	2.831	3.527	3.819
22	1.321	1.717	2.074	2.508	2.819	3.505	3.792
23	1.319	1.714	2.069	2.500	2.807	3.485	3.768
24	1.318	1.711	2.064	2.492	2.797	3.467	3.745
25	1.316	1.708	2.060	2.485	2.787	3.450	3.725
26	1.315	1.706	2.056	2.479	2.779	3.435	3.707
27	1.314	1.703	2.052	2.473	2.771	3.421	3.690
28	1.313	1.701	2.048	2.467	2.763	3.408	3.674
29	1.311	1.699	2.045	2.462	2.756	3.396	3.659
30	1.310	1.697	2.042	2.457	2.750	3.385	3.646
31	1.309	1.696	2.040	2.453	2.744	3.375	3.633
32	1.309	1.694	2.037	2.449	2.738	3.365	3.622
33	1.308	1.692	2.035	2.445	2.733	3.356	3.611
34	1.307	1.691	2.032	2.441	2.728	3.348	3.601
35	1.306	1.690	2.030	2.438	2.724	3.340	3.591
36	1.306	1.688	2.028	2.434	2.719	3.333	3.582
37	1.305	1.687	2.026	2.431	2.715	3.326	3.574
38	1.304	1.686	2.024	2.429	2.712	3.319	3.566
39	1.304	1.685	2.023	2.426	2.708	3.313	3.558
40	1.303	1.684	2.021	2.423	2.704	3.307	3.551
41	1.303	1.683	2.020	2.421	2.701	3.301	3.544
42	1.302	1.682	2.018	2.418	2.698	3.296	3.538
43	1.302	1.681	2.017	2.416	2.695	3.291	3.532
44	1.301	1.680	2.015	2.414	2.692	3.286	3.526
45	1.301	1.679	2.014	2.412	2.690	3.281	3.520
46	1.300	1.679	2.013	2.410	2.687	3.277	3.515
47	1.300	1.678	2.012	2.408	2.685	3.273	3.510
48	1.299	1.677	2.011	2.407	2.682	3.269	3.505

TABLE A.4   *(concluded)*
A *t* Table: Values of t_α for *df* = 49 through 100, 120, and ∞

df	$t_{.100}$	$t_{.05}$	$t_{.025}$	$t_{.01}$	$t_{.005}$	$t_{.001}$	$t_{.0005}$
49	1.299	1.677	2.010	2.405	2.680	3.265	3.500
50	1.299	1.676	2.009	2.403	2.678	3.261	3.496
51	1.298	1.675	2.008	2.402	2.676	3.258	3.492
52	1.298	1.675	2.007	2.400	2.674	3.255	3.488
53	1.298	1.674	2.006	2.399	2.672	3.251	3.484
54	1.297	1.674	2.005	2.397	2.670	3.248	3.480
55	1.297	1.673	2.004	2.396	2.668	3.245	3.476
56	1.297	1.673	2.003	2.395	2.667	3.242	3.473
57	1.297	1.672	2.002	2.394	2.665	3.239	3.470
58	1.296	1.672	2.002	2.392	2.663	3.237	3.466
59	1.296	1.671	2.001	2.391	2.662	3.234	3.463
60	1.296	1.671	2.000	2.390	2.660	3.232	3.460
61	1.296	1.670	2.000	2.389	2.659	3.229	3.457
62	1.295	1.670	1.999	2.388	2.657	3.227	3.454
63	1.295	1.669	1.998	2.387	2.656	3.225	3.452
64	1.295	1.669	1.998	2.386	2.655	3.223	3.449
65	1.295	1.669	1.997	2.385	2.654	3.220	3.447
66	1.295	1.668	1.997	2.384	2.652	3.218	3.444
67	1.294	1.668	1.996	2.383	2.651	3.216	3.442
68	1.294	1.668	1.995	2.382	2.650	3.214	3.439
69	1.294	1.667	1.995	2.382	2.649	3.213	3.437
70	1.294	1.667	1.994	2.381	2.648	3.211	3.435
71	1.294	1.667	1.994	2.380	2.647	3.209	3.433
72	1.293	1.666	1.993	2.379	2.646	3.207	3.431
73	1.293	1.666	1.993	2.379	2.645	3.206	3.429
74	1.293	1.666	1.993	2.378	2.644	3.204	3.427
75	1.293	1.665	1.992	2.377	2.643	3.202	3.425
76	1.293	1.665	1.992	2.376	2.642	3.201	3.423
77	1.293	1.665	1.991	2.376	2.641	3.199	3.421
78	1.292	1.665	1.991	2.375	2.640	3.198	3.420
79	1.292	1.664	1.990	2.374	2.640	3.197	3.418
80	1.292	1.664	1.990	2.374	2.639	3.195	3.416
81	1.292	1.664	1.990	2.373	2.638	3.194	3.415
82	1.292	1.664	1.989	2.373	2.637	3.193	3.413
83	1.292	1.663	1.989	2.372	2.636	3.191	3.412
84	1.292	1.663	1.989	2.372	2.636	3.190	3.410
85	1.292	1.663	1.988	2.371	2.635	3.189	3.409
86	1.291	1.663	1.988	2.370	2.634	3.188	3.407
87	1.291	1.663	1.988	2.370	2.634	3.187	3.406
88	1.291	1.662	1.987	2.369	2.633	3.185	3.405
89	1.291	1.662	1.987	2.369	2.632	3.184	3.403
90	1.291	1.662	1.987	2.368	2.632	3.183	3.402
91	1.291	1.662	1.986	2.368	2.631	3.182	3.401
92	1.291	1.662	1.986	2.368	2.630	3.181	3.399
93	1.291	1.661	1.986	2.367	2.630	3.180	3.398
94	1.291	1.661	1.986	2.367	2.629	3.179	3.397
95	1.291	1.661	1.985	2.366	2.629	3.178	3.396
96	1.290	1.661	1.985	2.366	2.628	3.177	3.395
97	1.290	1.661	1.985	2.365	2.627	3.176	3.394
98	1.290	1.661	1.984	2.365	2.627	3.175	3.393
99	1.290	1.660	1.984	2.365	2.626	3.175	3.392
100	1.290	1.660	1.984	2.364	2.626	3.174	3.390
120	1.289	1.658	1.980	2.358	2.617	3.160	3.373
∞	1.282	1.645	1.960	2.326	2.576	3.090	3.291

Source: Provided by J. B. Orris using Excel.

TABLE A.5   An F Table: Values of $F_{.10}$

df_2 \ df_1	1	2	3	4	5	6	7	8	9	10	12	15	20	24	30	40	60	120	∞
1	39.86	49.50	53.59	55.83	57.24	58.20	58.91	59.44	59.86	60.19	60.71	61.22	61.74	62.00	62.26	62.53	62.79	63.06	63.33
2	8.53	9.00	9.16	9.24	9.29	9.33	9.35	9.37	9.38	9.39	9.41	9.42	9.44	9.45	9.46	9.47	9.47	9.48	9.49
3	5.54	5.46	5.39	5.34	5.31	5.28	5.27	5.25	5.24	5.23	5.22	5.20	5.18	5.18	5.17	5.16	5.15	5.14	5.13
4	4.54	4.32	4.19	4.11	4.05	4.01	3.98	3.95	3.94	3.92	3.90	3.87	3.84	3.83	3.82	3.80	3.79	3.78	3.76
5	4.06	3.78	3.62	3.52	3.45	3.40	3.37	3.34	3.32	3.30	3.27	3.24	3.21	3.19	3.17	3.16	3.14	3.12	3.10
6	3.78	3.46	3.29	3.18	3.11	3.05	3.01	2.98	2.96	2.94	2.90	2.87	2.84	2.82	2.80	2.78	2.76	2.74	2.72
7	3.59	3.26	3.07	2.96	2.88	2.83	2.78	2.75	2.72	2.70	2.67	2.63	2.59	2.58	2.56	2.54	2.51	2.49	2.47
8	3.46	3.11	2.92	2.81	2.73	2.67	2.62	2.59	2.56	2.54	2.50	2.46	2.42	2.40	2.38	2.36	2.34	2.32	2.29
9	3.36	3.01	2.81	2.69	2.61	2.55	2.51	2.47	2.44	2.42	2.38	2.34	2.30	2.28	2.25	2.23	2.21	2.18	2.16
10	3.29	2.92	2.73	2.61	2.52	2.46	2.41	2.38	2.35	2.32	2.28	2.24	2.20	2.18	2.16	2.13	2.11	2.08	2.06
11	3.23	2.86	2.66	2.54	2.45	2.39	2.34	2.30	2.27	2.25	2.21	2.17	2.12	2.10	2.08	2.05	2.03	2.00	1.97
12	3.18	2.81	2.61	2.48	2.39	2.33	2.28	2.24	2.21	2.19	2.15	2.10	2.06	2.04	2.01	1.99	1.96	1.93	1.90
13	3.14	2.76	2.56	2.43	2.35	2.28	2.23	2.20	2.16	2.14	2.10	2.05	2.01	1.98	1.96	1.93	1.90	1.88	1.85
14	3.10	2.73	2.52	2.39	2.31	2.24	2.19	2.15	2.12	2.10	2.05	2.01	1.96	1.94	1.91	1.89	1.86	1.83	1.80
15	3.07	2.70	2.49	2.36	2.27	2.21	2.16	2.12	2.09	2.06	2.02	1.97	1.92	1.90	1.87	1.85	1.82	1.79	1.76
16	3.05	2.67	2.46	2.33	2.24	2.18	2.13	2.09	2.06	2.03	1.99	1.94	1.89	1.87	1.84	1.81	1.78	1.75	1.72
17	3.03	2.64	2.44	2.31	2.22	2.15	2.10	2.06	2.03	2.00	1.96	1.91	1.86	1.84	1.81	1.78	1.75	1.72	1.69
18	3.01	2.62	2.42	2.29	2.20	2.13	2.08	2.04	2.00	1.98	1.93	1.89	1.84	1.81	1.78	1.75	1.72	1.69	1.66
19	2.99	2.61	2.40	2.27	2.18	2.11	2.06	2.02	1.98	1.96	1.91	1.86	1.81	1.79	1.76	1.73	1.70	1.67	1.63
20	2.97	2.59	2.38	2.25	2.16	2.09	2.04	2.00	1.96	1.94	1.89	1.84	1.79	1.77	1.74	1.71	1.68	1.64	1.61
21	2.96	2.57	2.36	2.23	2.14	2.08	2.02	1.98	1.95	1.92	1.87	1.83	1.78	1.75	1.72	1.69	1.66	1.62	1.59
22	2.95	2.56	2.35	2.22	2.13	2.06	2.01	1.97	1.93	1.90	1.86	1.81	1.76	1.73	1.70	1.67	1.64	1.60	1.57
23	2.94	2.55	2.34	2.21	2.11	2.05	1.99	1.95	1.92	1.89	1.84	1.80	1.74	1.72	1.69	1.66	1.62	1.59	1.55
24	2.93	2.54	2.33	2.19	2.10	2.04	1.98	1.94	1.91	1.88	1.83	1.78	1.73	1.70	1.67	1.64	1.61	1.57	1.53
25	2.92	2.53	2.32	2.18	2.09	2.02	1.97	1.93	1.89	1.87	1.82	1.77	1.72	1.69	1.66	1.63	1.59	1.56	1.52
26	2.91	2.52	2.31	2.17	2.08	2.01	1.96	1.92	1.88	1.86	1.81	1.76	1.71	1.68	1.65	1.61	1.58	1.54	1.50
27	2.90	2.51	2.30	2.17	2.07	2.00	1.95	1.91	1.87	1.85	1.80	1.75	1.70	1.67	1.64	1.60	1.57	1.53	1.49
28	2.89	2.50	2.29	2.16	2.06	2.00	1.94	1.90	1.87	1.84	1.79	1.74	1.69	1.66	1.63	1.59	1.56	1.52	1.48
29	2.89	2.50	2.28	2.15	2.06	1.99	1.93	1.89	1.86	1.83	1.78	1.73	1.68	1.65	1.62	1.58	1.55	1.51	1.47
30	2.88	2.49	2.28	2.14	2.05	1.98	1.93	1.88	1.85	1.82	1.77	1.72	1.67	1.64	1.61	1.57	1.54	1.50	1.46
40	2.84	2.44	2.23	2.09	2.00	1.93	1.87	1.83	1.79	1.76	1.71	1.66	1.61	1.57	1.54	1.51	1.47	1.42	1.38
60	2.79	2.39	2.18	2.04	1.95	1.87	1.82	1.77	1.74	1.71	1.66	1.60	1.54	1.51	1.48	1.44	1.40	1.35	1.29
120	2.75	2.35	2.13	1.99	1.90	1.82	1.77	1.72	1.68	1.65	1.60	1.55	1.48	1.45	1.41	1.37	1.32	1.26	1.19
∞	2.71	2.30	2.08	1.94	1.85	1.77	1.72	1.67	1.63	1.60	1.55	1.49	1.42	1.38	1.34	1.30	1.24	1.17	1.00

Numerator Degrees of Freedom (df_1)

Denominator Degrees of Freedom (df_2)

Source: M. Merrington and C. M. Thompson, "Tables of Percentage Points of the Inverted Beta (F)-Distribution," Biometrika 33 (1943), pp. 73–88. Reproduced by permission of the Biometrika Trustees.

TABLE A.6 An F Table: Values of $F_{.05}$

df_2 \ df_1	1	2	3	4	5	6	7	8	9	10	12	15	20	24	30	40	60	120	∞
1	161.4	199.5	215.7	224.6	230.2	234.0	236.8	238.9	240.5	241.9	243.9	245.9	248.0	249.1	250.1	251.1	252.2	253.3	254.3
2	18.51	19.00	19.16	19.25	19.30	19.33	19.35	19.37	19.38	19.40	19.41	19.43	19.45	19.45	19.46	19.47	19.48	19.49	19.50
3	10.13	9.55	9.28	9.12	9.01	8.94	8.89	8.85	8.81	8.79	8.74	8.70	8.66	8.64	8.62	8.59	8.57	8.55	8.53
4	7.71	6.94	6.59	6.39	6.26	6.16	6.09	6.04	6.00	5.96	5.91	5.86	5.80	5.77	5.75	5.72	5.69	5.66	5.63
5	6.61	5.79	5.41	5.19	5.05	4.95	4.88	4.82	4.77	4.74	4.68	4.62	4.56	4.53	4.50	4.46	4.43	4.40	4.36
6	5.99	5.14	4.76	4.53	4.39	4.28	4.21	4.15	4.10	4.06	4.00	3.94	3.87	3.84	3.81	3.77	3.74	3.70	3.67
7	5.59	4.74	4.35	4.12	3.97	3.87	3.79	3.73	3.68	3.64	3.57	3.51	3.44	3.41	3.38	3.34	3.30	3.27	3.23
8	5.32	4.46	4.07	3.84	3.69	3.58	3.50	3.44	3.39	3.35	3.28	3.22	3.15	3.12	3.08	3.04	3.01	2.97	2.93
9	5.12	4.26	3.86	3.63	3.48	3.37	3.29	3.23	3.18	3.14	3.07	3.01	2.94	2.90	2.86	2.83	2.79	2.75	2.71
10	4.96	4.10	3.71	3.48	3.33	3.22	3.14	3.07	3.02	2.98	2.91	2.85	2.77	2.74	2.70	2.66	2.62	2.58	2.54
11	4.84	3.98	3.59	3.36	3.20	3.09	3.01	2.95	2.90	2.85	2.79	2.72	2.65	2.61	2.57	2.53	2.49	2.45	2.40
12	4.75	3.89	3.49	3.26	3.11	3.00	2.91	2.85	2.80	2.75	2.69	2.62	2.54	2.51	2.47	2.43	2.38	2.34	2.30
13	4.67	3.81	3.41	3.18	3.03	2.92	2.83	2.77	2.71	2.67	2.60	2.53	2.46	2.42	2.38	2.34	2.30	2.25	2.21
14	4.60	3.74	3.34	3.11	2.96	2.85	2.76	2.70	2.65	2.60	2.53	2.46	2.39	2.35	2.31	2.27	2.22	2.18	2.13
15	4.54	3.68	3.29	3.06	2.90	2.79	2.71	2.64	2.59	2.54	2.48	2.40	2.33	2.29	2.25	2.20	2.16	2.11	2.07
16	4.49	3.63	3.24	3.01	2.85	2.74	2.66	2.59	2.54	2.49	2.42	2.35	2.28	2.24	2.19	2.15	2.11	2.06	2.01
17	4.45	3.59	3.20	2.96	2.81	2.70	2.61	2.55	2.49	2.45	2.38	2.31	2.23	2.19	2.15	2.10	2.06	2.01	1.96
18	4.41	3.55	3.16	2.93	2.77	2.66	2.58	2.51	2.46	2.41	2.34	2.27	2.19	2.15	2.11	2.06	2.02	1.97	1.92
19	4.38	3.52	3.13	2.90	2.74	2.63	2.54	2.48	2.42	2.38	2.31	2.23	2.16	2.11	2.07	2.03	1.98	1.93	1.88
20	4.35	3.49	3.10	2.87	2.71	2.60	2.51	2.45	2.39	2.35	2.28	2.20	2.12	2.08	2.04	1.99	1.95	1.90	1.84
21	4.32	3.47	3.07	2.84	2.68	2.57	2.49	2.42	2.37	2.32	2.25	2.18	2.10	2.05	2.01	1.96	1.92	1.87	1.81
22	4.30	3.44	3.05	2.82	2.66	2.55	2.46	2.40	2.34	2.30	2.23	2.15	2.07	2.03	1.98	1.94	1.89	1.84	1.78
23	4.28	3.42	3.03	2.80	2.64	2.53	2.44	2.37	2.32	2.27	2.20	2.13	2.05	2.01	1.96	1.91	1.86	1.81	1.76
24	4.26	3.40	3.01	2.78	2.62	2.51	2.42	2.36	2.30	2.25	2.18	2.11	2.03	1.98	1.94	1.89	1.84	1.79	1.73
25	4.24	3.39	2.99	2.76	2.60	2.49	2.40	2.34	2.28	2.24	2.16	2.09	2.01	1.96	1.92	1.87	1.82	1.77	1.71
26	4.23	3.37	2.98	2.74	2.59	2.47	2.39	2.32	2.27	2.22	2.15	2.07	1.99	1.95	1.90	1.85	1.80	1.75	1.69
27	4.21	3.35	2.96	2.73	2.57	2.46	2.37	2.31	2.25	2.20	2.13	2.06	1.97	1.93	1.88	1.84	1.79	1.73	1.67
28	4.20	3.34	2.95	2.71	2.56	2.45	2.36	2.29	2.24	2.19	2.12	2.04	1.96	1.91	1.87	1.82	1.77	1.71	1.65
29	4.18	3.33	2.93	2.70	2.55	2.43	2.35	2.28	2.22	2.18	2.10	2.03	1.94	1.90	1.85	1.81	1.75	1.70	1.64
30	4.17	3.32	2.92	2.69	2.53	2.42	2.33	2.27	2.21	2.16	2.09	2.01	1.93	1.89	1.84	1.79	1.74	1.68	1.62
40	4.08	3.23	2.84	2.61	2.45	2.34	2.25	2.18	2.12	2.08	2.00	1.92	1.84	1.79	1.74	1.69	1.64	1.58	1.51
60	4.00	3.15	2.76	2.53	2.37	2.25	2.17	2.10	2.04	1.99	1.92	1.84	1.75	1.70	1.65	1.59	1.53	1.47	1.39
120	3.92	3.07	2.68	2.45	2.29	2.17	2.09	2.02	1.96	1.91	1.83	1.75	1.66	1.61	1.55	1.50	1.43	1.35	1.25
∞	3.84	3.00	2.60	2.37	2.21	2.10	2.01	1.94	1.88	1.83	1.75	1.67	1.57	1.52	1.46	1.39	1.32	1.22	1.00

Numerator Degrees of Freedom (df_1)

Denominator Degrees of Freedom (df_2)

Source: M. Merrington and C. M. Thompson, "Tables of Percentage Points of the Inverted Beta (F)-Distribution," *Biometrika* 33 (1943), pp. 73–88. Reproduced by permission of the Biometrika Trustees.

TABLE A.7　An F Table: Values of $F_{.025}$

Numerator Degrees of Freedom (df_1)

df_2 \ df_1	1	2	3	4	5	6	7	8	9	10	12	15	20	24	30	40	60	120	∞
1	647.8	799.5	864.2	899.6	921.8	937.1	948.2	956.7	963.3	968.6	976.7	984.9	993.1	997.2	1,001	1,006	1,010	1,014	1,018
2	38.51	39.00	39.17	39.25	39.30	39.33	39.36	39.37	39.39	39.40	39.41	39.43	39.45	39.46	39.46	39.47	39.48	39.49	39.50
3	17.44	16.04	15.44	15.10	14.88	14.73	14.62	14.54	14.47	14.42	14.34	14.25	14.17	14.12	14.08	14.04	13.99	13.95	13.90
4	12.22	10.65	9.98	9.60	9.36	9.20	9.07	8.98	8.90	8.84	8.75	8.66	8.56	8.51	8.46	8.41	8.36	8.31	8.26
5	10.01	8.43	7.76	7.39	7.15	6.98	6.85	6.76	6.68	6.62	6.52	6.43	6.33	6.28	6.23	6.18	6.12	6.07	6.02
6	8.81	7.26	6.60	6.23	5.99	5.82	5.70	5.60	5.52	5.46	5.37	5.27	5.17	5.12	5.07	5.01	4.96	4.90	4.85
7	8.07	6.54	5.89	5.52	5.29	5.12	4.99	4.90	4.82	4.76	4.67	4.57	4.47	4.42	4.36	4.31	4.25	4.20	4.14
8	7.57	6.06	5.42	5.05	4.82	4.65	4.53	4.43	4.36	4.30	4.20	4.10	4.00	3.95	3.89	3.84	3.78	3.73	3.67
9	7.21	5.71	5.08	4.72	4.48	4.32	4.20	4.10	4.03	3.96	3.87	3.77	3.67	3.61	3.56	3.51	3.45	3.39	3.33
10	6.94	5.46	4.83	4.47	4.24	4.07	3.95	3.85	3.78	3.72	3.62	3.52	3.42	3.37	3.31	3.26	3.20	3.14	3.08
11	6.72	5.26	4.63	4.28	4.04	3.88	3.76	3.66	3.59	3.53	3.43	3.33	3.23	3.17	3.12	3.06	3.00	2.94	2.88
12	6.55	5.10	4.47	4.12	3.89	3.73	3.61	3.51	3.44	3.37	3.28	3.18	3.07	3.02	2.96	2.91	2.85	2.79	2.72
13	6.41	4.97	4.35	4.00	3.77	3.60	3.48	3.39	3.31	3.25	3.15	3.05	2.95	2.89	2.84	2.78	2.72	2.66	2.60
14	6.30	4.86	4.24	3.89	3.66	3.50	3.38	3.29	3.21	3.15	3.05	2.95	2.84	2.79	2.73	2.67	2.61	2.55	2.49
15	6.20	4.77	4.15	3.80	3.58	3.41	3.29	3.20	3.12	3.06	2.96	2.86	2.76	2.70	2.64	2.59	2.52	2.46	2.40
16	6.12	4.69	4.08	3.73	3.50	3.34	3.22	3.12	3.05	2.99	2.89	2.79	2.68	2.63	2.57	2.51	2.45	2.38	2.32
17	6.04	4.62	4.01	3.66	3.44	3.28	3.16	3.06	2.98	2.92	2.82	2.72	2.62	2.56	2.50	2.44	2.38	2.32	2.25
18	5.98	4.56	3.95	3.61	3.38	3.22	3.10	3.01	2.93	2.87	2.77	2.67	2.56	2.50	2.44	2.38	2.32	2.26	2.19
19	5.92	4.51	3.90	3.56	3.33	3.17	3.05	2.96	2.88	2.82	2.72	2.62	2.51	2.45	2.39	2.33	2.27	2.20	2.13
20	5.87	4.46	3.86	3.51	3.29	3.13	3.01	2.91	2.84	2.77	2.68	2.57	2.46	2.41	2.35	2.29	2.22	2.16	2.09
21	5.83	4.42	3.82	3.48	3.25	3.09	2.97	2.87	2.80	2.73	2.64	2.53	2.42	2.37	2.31	2.25	2.18	2.11	2.04
22	5.79	4.38	3.78	3.44	3.22	3.05	2.93	2.84	2.76	2.70	2.60	2.50	2.39	2.33	2.27	2.21	2.14	2.08	2.00
23	5.75	4.35	3.75	3.41	3.18	3.02	2.90	2.81	2.73	2.67	2.57	2.47	2.36	2.30	2.24	2.18	2.11	2.04	1.97
24	5.72	4.32	3.72	3.38	3.15	2.99	2.87	2.78	2.70	2.64	2.54	2.44	2.33	2.27	2.21	2.15	2.08	2.01	1.94
25	5.69	4.29	3.69	3.35	3.13	2.97	2.85	2.75	2.68	2.61	2.51	2.41	2.30	2.24	2.18	2.12	2.05	1.98	1.91
26	5.66	4.27	3.67	3.33	3.10	2.94	2.82	2.73	2.65	2.59	2.49	2.39	2.28	2.22	2.16	2.09	2.03	1.95	1.88
27	5.63	4.24	3.65	3.31	3.08	2.92	2.80	2.71	2.63	2.57	2.47	2.36	2.25	2.19	2.13	2.07	2.00	1.93	1.85
28	5.61	4.22	3.63	3.29	3.06	2.90	2.78	2.69	2.61	2.55	2.45	2.34	2.23	2.17	2.11	2.05	1.98	1.91	1.83
29	5.59	4.20	3.61	3.27	3.04	2.88	2.76	2.67	2.59	2.53	2.43	2.32	2.21	2.15	2.09	2.03	1.96	1.89	1.81
30	5.57	4.18	3.59	3.25	3.03	2.87	2.75	2.65	2.57	2.51	2.41	2.31	2.20	2.14	2.07	2.01	1.94	1.87	1.79
40	5.42	4.05	3.46	3.13	2.90	2.74	2.62	2.53	2.45	2.39	2.29	2.18	2.07	2.01	1.94	1.88	1.80	1.72	1.64
60	5.29	3.93	3.34	3.01	2.79	2.63	2.51	2.41	2.33	2.27	2.17	2.06	1.94	1.88	1.82	1.74	1.67	1.58	1.48
120	5.15	3.80	3.23	2.89	2.67	2.52	2.39	2.30	2.22	2.16	2.05	1.94	1.82	1.76	1.69	1.61	1.53	1.43	1.31
∞	5.02	3.69	3.12	2.79	2.57	2.41	2.29	2.19	2.11	2.05	1.94	1.83	1.71	1.64	1.57	1.48	1.39	1.27	1.00

Denominator Degrees of Freedom (df_2)

Source: M. Merrington and C. M. Thompson, "Tables of Percentage Points of the Inverted Beta (F)-Distribution," Biometrika 33 (1943), pp. 73–88. Reproduced by permission of the Biometrika Trustees.

TABLE A.8   An F Table: Values of $F_{.01}$

Numerator Degrees of Freedom (df_1)

df_2 \\ df_1	1	2	3	4	5	6	7	8	9	10	12	15	20	24	30	40	60	120	∞
1	4,052	4,999.5	5,403	5,625	5,764	5,859	5,928	5,982	6,022	6,056	6,106	6,157	6,209	6,235	6,261	6,287	6,313	6,339	6,366
2	98.50	99.00	99.17	99.25	99.30	99.33	99.36	99.37	99.39	99.40	99.42	99.43	99.45	99.46	99.47	99.47	99.48	99.49	99.50
3	34.12	30.82	29.46	28.71	28.24	27.91	27.67	27.49	27.35	27.23	27.05	26.87	26.69	26.60	26.50	26.41	26.32	26.22	26.13
4	21.20	18.00	16.69	15.98	15.52	15.21	14.98	14.80	14.66	14.55	14.37	14.20	14.02	13.93	13.84	13.75	13.65	13.56	13.46
5	16.26	13.27	12.06	11.39	10.97	10.67	10.46	10.29	10.16	10.05	9.89	9.72	9.55	9.47	9.38	9.29	9.20	9.11	9.02
6	13.75	10.92	9.78	9.15	8.75	8.47	8.26	8.10	7.98	7.87	7.72	7.56	7.40	7.31	7.23	7.14	7.06	6.97	6.88
7	12.25	9.55	8.45	7.85	7.46	7.19	6.99	6.84	6.72	6.62	6.47	6.31	6.16	6.07	5.99	5.91	5.82	5.74	5.65
8	11.26	8.65	7.59	7.01	6.63	6.37	6.18	6.03	5.91	5.81	5.67	5.52	5.36	5.28	5.20	5.12	5.03	4.95	4.86
9	10.56	8.02	6.99	6.42	6.06	5.80	5.61	5.47	5.35	5.26	5.11	4.96	4.81	4.73	4.65	4.57	4.48	4.40	4.31
10	10.04	7.56	6.55	5.99	5.64	5.39	5.20	5.06	4.94	4.85	4.71	4.56	4.41	4.33	4.25	4.17	4.08	4.00	3.91
11	9.65	7.21	6.22	5.67	5.32	5.07	4.89	4.74	4.63	4.54	4.40	4.25	4.10	4.02	3.94	3.86	3.78	3.69	3.60
12	9.33	6.93	5.95	5.41	5.06	4.82	4.64	4.50	4.39	4.30	4.16	4.01	3.86	3.78	3.70	3.62	3.54	3.45	3.36
13	9.07	6.70	5.74	5.21	4.86	4.62	4.44	4.30	4.19	4.10	3.96	3.82	3.66	3.59	3.51	3.43	3.34	3.25	3.17
14	8.86	6.51	5.56	5.04	4.69	4.46	4.28	4.14	4.03	3.94	3.80	3.66	3.51	3.43	3.35	3.27	3.18	3.09	3.00
15	8.68	6.36	5.42	4.89	4.56	4.32	4.14	4.00	3.89	3.80	3.67	3.52	3.37	3.29	3.21	3.13	3.05	2.96	2.87
16	8.53	6.23	5.29	4.77	4.44	4.20	4.03	3.89	3.78	3.69	3.55	3.41	3.26	3.18	3.10	3.02	2.93	2.84	2.75
17	8.40	6.11	5.18	4.67	4.34	4.10	3.93	3.79	3.68	3.59	3.46	3.31	3.16	3.08	3.00	2.92	2.83	2.75	2.65
18	8.29	6.01	5.09	4.58	4.25	4.01	3.84	3.71	3.60	3.51	3.37	3.23	3.08	3.00	2.92	2.84	2.75	2.66	2.57
19	8.18	5.93	5.01	4.50	4.17	3.94	3.77	3.63	3.52	3.43	3.30	3.15	3.00	2.92	2.84	2.76	2.67	2.58	2.49
20	8.10	5.85	4.94	4.43	4.10	3.87	3.70	3.56	3.46	3.37	3.23	3.09	2.94	2.86	2.78	2.69	2.61	2.52	2.42
21	8.02	5.78	4.87	4.37	4.04	3.81	3.64	3.51	3.40	3.31	3.17	3.03	2.88	2.80	2.72	2.64	2.55	2.46	2.36
22	7.95	5.72	4.82	4.31	3.99	3.76	3.59	3.45	3.35	3.26	3.12	2.98	2.83	2.75	2.67	2.58	2.50	2.40	2.31
23	7.88	5.66	4.76	4.26	3.94	3.71	3.54	3.41	3.30	3.21	3.07	2.93	2.78	2.70	2.62	2.54	2.45	2.35	2.26
24	7.82	5.61	4.72	4.22	3.90	3.67	3.50	3.36	3.26	3.17	3.03	2.89	2.74	2.66	2.58	2.49	2.40	2.31	2.21
25	7.77	5.57	4.68	4.18	3.85	3.63	3.46	3.32	3.22	3.13	2.99	2.85	2.70	2.62	2.54	2.45	2.36	2.27	2.17
26	7.72	5.53	4.64	4.14	3.82	3.59	3.42	3.29	3.18	3.09	2.96	2.81	2.66	2.58	2.50	2.42	2.33	2.23	2.13
27	7.68	5.49	4.60	4.11	3.78	3.56	3.39	3.26	3.15	3.06	2.93	2.78	2.63	2.55	2.47	2.38	2.29	2.20	2.10
28	7.64	5.45	4.57	4.07	3.75	3.53	3.36	3.23	3.12	3.03	2.90	2.75	2.60	2.52	2.44	2.35	2.26	2.17	2.06
29	7.60	5.42	4.54	4.04	3.73	3.50	3.33	3.20	3.09	3.00	2.87	2.73	2.57	2.49	2.41	2.33	2.23	2.14	2.03
30	7.56	5.39	4.51	4.02	3.70	3.47	3.30	3.17	3.07	2.98	2.84	2.70	2.55	2.47	2.39	2.30	2.21	2.11	2.01
40	7.31	5.18	4.31	3.83	3.51	3.29	3.12	2.99	2.89	2.80	2.66	2.52	2.37	2.29	2.20	2.11	2.02	1.92	1.80
60	7.08	4.98	4.13	3.65	3.34	3.12	2.95	2.82	2.72	2.63	2.50	2.35	2.20	2.12	2.03	1.94	1.84	1.73	1.60
120	6.85	4.79	3.95	3.48	3.17	2.96	2.79	2.66	2.56	2.47	2.34	2.19	2.03	1.95	1.86	1.76	1.66	1.53	1.38
∞	6.63	4.61	3.78	3.32	3.02	2.80	2.64	2.51	2.41	2.32	2.18	2.04	1.88	1.79	1.70	1.59	1.47	1.32	1.00

Denominator Degrees of Freedom (df_2)

Source: M. Merrington and C. M. Thompson, "Tables of Percentage Points of the Inverted Beta (F)-Distribution," *Biometrika* 33 (1943), pp. 73–88. Reproduced by permission of the Biometrika Trustees.

TABLE A.9   Percentage Points of the Studentized Range
(Note: r is the "first value" and v is the "second value" referred to in Chapter 11.)

Entry is $q_{.05}$

r

v	2	3	4	5	6	7	8	9	10	11	12	13	14	15	16	17	18	19	20
1	18.0	27.0	32.8	37.1	40.4	43.1	45.4	47.4	49.1	50.6	52.0	53.2	54.3	55.4	56.3	57.2	58.0	58.8	59.6
2	6.08	8.33	9.80	10.9	11.7	12.4	13.0	13.5	14.0	14.4	14.7	15.1	15.4	15.7	15.9	16.1	16.4	16.6	16.8
3	4.50	5.91	6.82	7.50	8.04	8.48	8.85	9.18	9.46	9.72	9.95	10.2	10.3	10.5	10.7	10.8	11.0	11.1	11.2
4	3.93	5.04	5.76	6.29	6.71	7.05	7.35	7.60	7.83	8.03	8.21	8.37	8.52	8.66	8.79	8.91	9.03	9.13	9.23
5	3.64	4.60	5.22	5.67	6.03	6.33	6.58	6.80	6.99	7.17	7.32	7.47	7.60	7.72	7.83	7.93	8.03	8.12	8.21
6	3.46	4.34	4.90	5.30	5.63	5.90	6.12	6.32	6.49	6.65	6.79	6.92	7.03	7.14	7.24	7.34	7.43	7.51	7.59
7	3.34	4.16	4.68	5.06	5.36	5.61	5.82	6.00	6.16	6.30	6.43	6.55	6.66	6.76	6.85	6.94	7.02	7.10	7.17
8	3.26	4.04	4.53	4.89	5.17	5.40	5.60	5.77	5.92	6.05	6.18	6.29	6.39	6.48	6.57	6.65	6.73	6.80	6.87
9	3.20	3.95	4.41	4.76	5.02	5.24	5.43	5.59	5.74	5.87	5.98	6.09	6.19	6.28	6.36	6.44	6.51	6.58	6.64
10	3.15	3.88	4.33	4.65	4.91	5.12	5.30	5.46	5.60	5.72	5.83	5.93	6.03	6.11	6.19	6.27	6.34	6.40	6.47
11	3.11	3.82	4.26	4.57	4.82	5.03	5.20	5.35	5.49	5.61	5.71	5.81	5.90	5.98	6.06	6.13	6.20	6.27	6.33
12	3.08	3.77	4.20	4.51	4.75	4.95	5.12	5.27	5.39	5.51	5.61	5.71	5.80	5.88	5.95	6.02	6.09	6.15	6.21
13	3.06	3.73	4.15	4.45	4.69	4.88	5.05	5.19	5.32	5.43	5.53	5.63	5.71	5.79	5.86	5.93	5.99	6.05	6.11
14	3.03	3.70	4.11	4.41	4.64	4.83	4.99	5.13	5.25	5.36	5.46	5.55	5.64	5.71	5.79	5.85	5.91	5.97	6.03
15	3.01	3.67	4.08	4.37	4.59	4.78	4.94	5.08	5.20	5.31	5.40	5.49	5.57	5.65	5.72	5.78	5.85	5.90	5.96
16	3.00	3.65	4.05	4.33	4.56	4.74	4.90	5.03	5.15	5.26	5.35	5.44	5.52	5.59	5.66	5.73	5.79	5.84	5.90
17	2.98	3.63	4.02	4.30	4.52	4.70	4.86	4.99	5.11	5.21	5.31	5.39	5.47	5.54	5.61	5.67	5.73	5.79	5.84
18	2.97	3.61	4.00	4.28	4.49	4.67	4.82	4.96	5.07	5.17	5.27	5.35	5.43	5.50	5.57	5.63	5.69	5.74	5.79
19	2.96	3.59	3.98	4.25	4.47	4.65	4.79	4.92	5.04	5.14	5.23	5.31	5.39	5.46	5.53	5.59	5.65	5.70	5.75
20	2.95	3.58	3.96	4.23	4.45	4.62	4.77	4.90	5.01	5.11	5.20	5.28	5.36	5.43	5.49	5.55	5.61	5.66	5.71
24	2.92	3.53	3.90	4.17	4.37	4.54	4.68	4.81	4.92	5.01	5.10	5.18	5.25	5.32	5.38	5.44	5.49	5.55	5.59
30	2.89	3.49	3.85	4.10	4.30	4.46	4.60	4.72	4.82	4.92	5.00	5.08	5.15	5.21	5.27	5.33	5.38	5.43	5.47
40	2.86	3.44	3.79	4.04	4.23	4.39	4.52	4.63	4.73	4.82	4.90	4.98	5.04	5.11	5.16	5.22	5.27	5.31	5.36
60	2.83	3.40	3.74	3.98	4.16	4.31	4.44	4.55	4.65	4.73	4.81	4.88	4.94	5.00	5.06	5.11	5.15	5.20	5.24
120	2.80	3.36	3.68	3.92	4.10	4.24	4.36	4.47	4.56	4.64	4.71	4.78	4.84	4.90	4.95	5.00	5.04	5.09	5.13
∞	2.77	3.31	3.63	3.86	4.03	4.17	4.29	4.39	4.47	4.55	4.62	4.68	4.74	4.80	4.85	4.89	4.93	4.97	5.01

TABLE A.9 (concluded)

Entry is $q_{.01}$

r

v	2	3	4	5	6	7	8	9	10	11	12	13	14	15	16	17	18	19	20
1	90.0	135	164	186	202	216	227	237	246	253	260	266	272	277	282	286	290	294	298
2	14.0	19.0	22.3	24.7	26.6	28.2	29.5	30.7	31.7	32.6	33.4	34.1	34.8	35.4	36.0	36.5	37.0	37.5	37.9
3	8.26	10.6	12.2	13.3	14.2	15.0	15.6	16.2	16.7	17.1	17.5	17.9	18.2	18.5	18.8	19.1	19.3	19.5	19.8
4	6.51	8.12	9.17	9.96	10.6	11.1	11.5	11.9	12.3	12.6	12.8	13.1	13.3	13.5	13.7	13.9	14.1	14.2	14.4
5	5.70	6.97	7.80	8.42	8.91	9.32	9.67	9.97	10.2	10.5	10.7	10.9	11.1	11.2	11.4	11.6	11.7	11.8	11.9
6	5.24	6.33	7.03	7.56	7.97	8.32	8.61	8.87	9.10	9.30	9.49	9.65	9.81	9.95	10.1	10.2	10.3	10.4	10.5
7	4.95	5.92	6.54	7.01	7.37	7.68	7.94	8.17	8.37	8.55	8.71	8.86	9.00	9.12	9.24	9.35	9.46	9.55	9.65
8	4.74	5.63	6.20	6.63	6.96	7.24	7.47	7.68	7.87	8.03	8.18	8.31	8.44	8.55	8.66	8.76	8.85	8.94	9.03
9	4.60	5.43	5.96	6.35	6.66	6.91	7.13	7.32	7.49	7.65	7.78	7.91	8.03	8.13	8.23	8.32	8.41	8.49	8.57
10	4.48	5.27	5.77	6.14	6.43	6.67	6.87	7.05	7.21	7.36	7.48	7.60	7.71	7.81	7.91	7.99	8.07	8.15	8.22
11	4.39	5.14	5.62	5.97	6.25	6.48	6.67	6.84	6.99	7.13	7.25	7.36	7.46	7.56	7.65	7.73	7.81	7.88	7.95
12	4.32	5.04	5.50	5.84	6.10	6.32	6.51	6.67	6.81	6.94	7.06	7.17	7.26	7.36	7.44	7.52	7.59	7.66	7.73
13	4.26	4.96	5.40	5.73	5.98	6.19	6.37	6.53	6.67	6.79	6.90	7.01	7.10	7.19	7.27	7.34	7.42	7.48	7.55
14	4.21	4.89	5.32	5.63	5.88	6.08	6.26	6.41	6.54	6.66	6.77	6.87	6.96	7.05	7.12	7.20	7.27	7.33	7.39
15	4.17	4.83	5.25	5.56	5.80	5.99	6.16	6.31	6.44	6.55	6.66	6.76	6.84	6.93	7.00	7.07	7.14	7.20	7.26
16	4.13	4.78	5.19	5.49	5.72	5.92	6.08	6.22	6.35	6.46	6.56	6.66	6.74	6.82	6.90	6.97	7.03	7.09	7.15
17	4.10	4.74	5.14	5.43	5.66	5.85	6.01	6.15	6.27	6.38	6.48	6.57	6.66	6.73	6.80	6.87	6.94	7.00	7.05
18	4.07	4.70	5.09	5.38	5.60	5.79	5.94	6.08	6.20	6.31	6.41	6.50	6.58	6.65	6.72	6.79	6.85	6.91	6.96
19	4.05	4.67	5.05	5.33	5.55	5.73	5.89	6.02	6.14	6.25	6.34	6.43	6.51	6.58	6.65	6.72	6.78	6.84	6.89
20	4.02	4.64	5.02	5.29	5.51	5.69	5.84	5.97	6.09	6.19	6.29	6.37	6.45	6.52	6.59	6.65	6.71	6.76	6.82
24	3.96	4.54	4.91	5.17	5.37	5.54	5.69	5.81	5.92	6.02	6.11	6.19	6.26	6.33	6.39	6.45	6.51	6.56	6.61
30	3.89	4.45	4.80	5.05	5.24	5.40	5.54	5.65	5.76	5.85	5.93	6.01	6.08	6.14	6.20	6.26	6.31	6.36	6.41
40	3.82	4.37	4.70	4.93	5.11	5.27	5.39	5.50	5.60	5.69	5.77	5.84	5.90	5.96	6.02	6.07	6.12	6.17	6.21
60	3.76	4.28	4.60	4.82	4.99	5.13	5.25	5.36	5.45	5.53	5.60	5.67	5.73	5.79	5.84	5.89	5.93	5.98	6.02
120	3.70	4.20	4.50	4.71	4.87	5.01	5.12	5.21	5.30	5.38	5.44	5.51	5.56	5.61	5.66	5.71	5.75	5.79	5.83
∞	3.64	4.12	4.40	4.60	4.76	4.88	4.99	5.08	5.16	5.23	5.29	5.35	5.40	5.45	5.49	5.54	5.57	5.61	5.65

Source: Henry Scheffé, The Analysis of Variance, pp. 414–16, ©1959 by John Wiley & Sons, Inc. Reprinted by permission of John Wiley & Sons, Inc.

T A B L E A . 10   A Chi-Square Table: Values of χ^2_α

df	$\chi^2_{.995}$	$\chi^2_{.99}$	$\chi^2_{.975}$	$\chi^2_{.95}$	$\chi^2_{.90}$	$\chi^2_{.10}$	$\chi^2_{.05}$	$\chi^2_{.025}$	$\chi^2_{.01}$	$\chi^2_{.005}$
1	.0000393	.0001571	.0009821	.0039321	.0157908	2.70554	3.84146	5.02389	6.63490	7.87944
2	.0100251	.0201007	.0506356	.102587	.210720	4.60517	5.99147	7.37776	9.21034	10.5966
3	.0717212	.114832	.215795	.341846	.584375	6.25139	7.81473	9.34840	11.3449	12.8381
4	.206990	.297110	.484419	.710721	1.063623	7.77944	9.48773	11.1433	13.2767	14.8602
5	.411740	.554300	.831211	1.145476	1.61031	9.23635	11.0705	12.8325	15.0863	16.7496
6	.675727	.872085	1.237347	1.63539	2.20413	10.6446	12.5916	14.4494	16.8119	18.5476
7	.989265	1.239043	1.68987	2.16735	2.83311	12.0170	14.0671	16.0128	18.4753	20.2777
8	1.344419	1.646482	2.17973	2.73264	3.48954	13.3616	15.5073	17.5346	20.0902	21.9550
9	1.734926	2.087912	2.70039	3.32511	4.16816	14.6837	16.9190	19.0228	21.6660	23.5893
10	2.15585	2.55821	3.24697	3.94030	4.86518	15.9871	18.3070	20.4831	23.2093	25.1882
11	2.60321	3.05347	3.81575	4.57481	5.57779	17.2750	19.6751	21.9200	24.7250	26.7569
12	3.07382	3.57056	4.40379	5.22603	6.30380	18.5494	21.0261	23.3367	26.2170	28.2995
13	3.56503	4.10691	5.00874	5.89186	7.04150	19.8119	22.3621	24.7356	27.6883	29.8194
14	4.07468	4.66043	5.62872	6.57063	7.78953	21.0642	23.6848	26.1190	29.1413	31.3193
15	4.60094	5.22935	6.26214	7.26094	8.54675	22.3072	24.9958	27.4884	30.5779	32.8013
16	5.14224	5.81221	6.90766	7.96164	9.31223	23.5418	26.2962	28.8454	31.9999	34.2672
17	5.69724	6.40776	7.56418	8.67176	10.0852	24.7690	27.5871	30.1910	33.4087	35.7185
18	6.26481	7.01491	8.23075	9.39046	10.8649	25.9894	28.8693	31.5264	34.8053	37.1564
19	6.84398	7.63273	8.90655	10.1170	11.6509	27.2036	30.1435	32.8523	36.1908	38.5822
20	7.43386	8.26040	9.59083	10.8508	12.4426	28.4120	31.4104	34.1696	37.5662	39.9968
21	8.03366	8.89720	10.28293	11.5913	13.2396	29.6151	32.6705	35.4789	38.9321	41.4010
22	8.64272	9.54249	10.9823	12.3380	14.0415	30.8133	33.9244	36.7807	40.2894	42.7956
23	9.26042	10.19567	11.6885	13.0905	14.8479	32.0069	35.1725	38.0757	41.6384	44.1813
24	9.88623	10.8564	12.4011	13.8484	15.6587	33.1963	36.4151	39.3641	42.9798	45.5585
25	10.5197	11.5240	13.1197	14.6114	16.4734	34.3816	37.6525	40.6465	44.3141	46.9278
26	11.1603	12.1981	13.8439	15.3791	17.2919	35.5631	38.8852	41.9232	45.6417	48.2899
27	11.8076	12.8786	14.5733	16.1513	18.1138	36.7412	40.1133	43.1944	46.9630	49.6449
28	12.4613	13.5648	15.3079	16.9279	18.9392	37.9159	41.3372	44.4607	48.2782	50.9933
29	13.1211	14.2565	16.0471	17.7083	19.7677	39.0875	42.5569	45.7222	49.5879	52.3356
30	13.7867	14.9535	16.7908	18.4926	20.5992	40.2560	43.7729	46.9792	50.8922	53.6720
40	20.7065	22.1643	24.4331	26.5093	29.0505	51.8050	55.7585	59.3417	63.6907	66.7659
50	27.9907	29.7067	32.3574	34.7642	37.6886	63.1671	67.5048	71.4202	76.1539	79.4900
60	35.5346	37.4848	40.4817	43.1879	46.4589	74.3970	79.0819	83.2976	88.3794	91.9517
70	43.2752	45.4418	48.7576	51.7393	55.3290	85.5271	90.5312	95.0231	100.425	104.215
80	51.1720	53.5400	57.1532	60.3915	64.2778	96.5782	101.879	106.629	112.329	116.321
90	59.1963	61.7541	65.6466	69.1260	73.2912	107.565	113.145	118.136	124.116	128.299
100	67.3276	70.0648	74.2219	77.9295	82.3581	118.498	124.342	129.561	135.807	140.169

Source: C. M. Thompson, "Tables of the Percentage Points of the χ^2 Distribution," *Biometrika* 32 (1941), pp. 188–89. Reproduced by permission of the Biometrika Trustees.

TABLE A.12   Critical Values for the Durbin–Watson d Statistic ($\alpha = .025$)

	k = 1		k = 2		k = 3		k = 4		k = 5	
n	$d_{L,.025}$	$d_{U,.025}$	$d_{L,.025}$	$d_{U,.025}$	$d_{L,.025}$	$d_{U,.025}$	$d_{L,.025}$	$d_{U,.025}$	$d_{L,.025}$	$d_{U,.025}$
15	0.95	1.23	0.83	1.40	0.71	1.61	0.59	1.84	0.48	2.09
16	0.98	1.24	0.86	1.40	0.75	1.59	0.64	1.80	0.53	2.03
17	1.01	1.25	0.90	1.40	0.79	1.58	0.68	1.77	0.57	1.98
18	1.03	1.26	0.93	1.40	0.82	1.56	0.72	1.74	0.62	1.93
19	1.06	1.28	0.96	1.41	0.86	1.55	0.76	1.72	0.66	1.90
20	1.08	1.28	0.99	1.41	0.89	1.55	0.79	1.70	0.70	1.87
21	1.10	1.30	1.01	1.41	0.92	1.54	0.83	1.69	0.73	1.84
22	1.12	1.31	1.04	1.42	0.95	1.54	0.86	1.68	0.77	1.82
23	1.14	1.32	1.06	1.42	0.97	1.54	0.89	1.67	0.80	1.80
24	1.16	1.33	1.08	1.43	1.00	1.54	0.91	1.66	0.83	1.79
25	1.18	1.34	1.10	1.43	1.02	1.54	0.94	1.65	0.86	1.77
26	1.19	1.35	1.12	1.44	1.04	1.54	0.96	1.65	0.88	1.76
27	1.21	1.36	1.13	1.44	1.06	1.54	0.99	1.64	0.91	1.75
28	1.22	1.37	1.15	1.45	1.08	1.54	1.01	1.64	0.93	1.74
29	1.24	1.38	1.17	1.45	1.10	1.54	1.03	1.63	0.96	1.73
30	1.25	1.38	1.18	1.46	1.12	1.54	1.05	1.63	0.98	1.73
31	1.26	1.39	1.20	1.47	1.13	1.55	1.07	1.63	1.00	1.72
32	1.27	1.40	1.21	1.47	1.15	1.55	1.08	1.63	1.02	1.71
33	1.28	1.41	1.22	1.48	1.16	1.55	1.10	1.63	1.04	1.71
34	1.29	1.41	1.24	1.48	1.17	1.55	1.12	1.63	1.06	1.70
35	1.30	1.42	1.25	1.48	1.19	1.55	1.13	1.63	1.07	1.70
36	1.31	1.43	1.26	1.49	1.20	1.56	1.15	1.63	1.09	1.70
37	1.32	1.43	1.27	1.49	1.21	1.56	1.16	1.62	1.10	1.70
38	1.33	1.44	1.28	1.50	1.23	1.56	1.17	1.62	1.12	1.70
39	1.34	1.44	1.29	1.50	1.24	1.56	1.19	1.63	1.13	1.69
40	1.35	1.45	1.30	1.51	1.25	1.57	1.20	1.63	1.15	1.69
45	1.39	1.48	1.34	1.53	1.30	1.58	1.25	1.63	1.21	1.69
50	1.42	1.50	1.38	1.54	1.34	1.59	1.30	1.64	1.26	1.69
55	1.45	1.52	1.41	1.56	1.37	1.60	1.33	1.64	1.30	1.69
60	1.47	1.54	1.44	1.57	1.40	1.61	1.37	1.65	1.33	1.69
65	1.49	1.55	1.46	1.59	1.43	1.62	1.40	1.66	1.36	1.69
70	1.51	1.57	1.48	1.60	1.45	1.63	1.42	1.66	1.39	1.70
75	1.53	1.58	1.50	1.61	1.47	1.64	1.45	1.67	1.42	1.70
80	1.54	1.59	1.52	1.62	1.49	1.65	1.47	1.67	1.44	1.70
85	1.56	1.60	1.53	1.63	1.51	1.65	1.49	1.68	1.46	1.71
90	1.57	1.61	1.55	1.64	1.53	1.66	1.50	1.69	1.48	1.71
95	1.58	1.62	1.56	1.65	1.54	1.67	1.52	1.69	1.50	1.71
100	1.59	1.63	1.57	1.65	1.55	1.67	1.53	1.70	1.51	1.72

TABLE A.11   Critical Values for the Durbin–Watson d Statistic ($\alpha = .05$)

	k = 1		k = 2		k = 3		k = 4		k = 5	
n	$d_{L,.05}$	$d_{U,.05}$	$d_{L,.05}$	$d_{U,.05}$	$d_{L,.05}$	$d_{U,.05}$	$d_{L,.05}$	$d_{U,.05}$	$d_{L,.05}$	$d_{U,.05}$
15	1.08	1.36	0.95	1.54	0.82	1.75	0.69	1.97	0.56	2.21
16	1.10	1.37	0.98	1.54	0.86	1.73	0.74	1.93	0.62	2.15
17	1.13	1.38	1.02	1.54	0.90	1.71	0.78	1.90	0.67	2.10
18	1.16	1.39	1.05	1.53	0.93	1.69	0.82	1.87	0.71	2.06
19	1.18	1.40	1.08	1.53	0.97	1.68	0.86	1.85	0.75	2.02
20	1.20	1.41	1.10	1.54	1.00	1.68	0.90	1.83	0.79	1.99
21	1.22	1.42	1.13	1.54	1.03	1.67	0.93	1.81	0.83	1.96
22	1.24	1.43	1.15	1.54	1.05	1.66	0.96	1.80	0.86	1.94
23	1.26	1.44	1.17	1.54	1.08	1.66	0.99	1.79	0.90	1.92
24	1.27	1.45	1.19	1.55	1.10	1.66	1.01	1.78	0.93	1.90
25	1.29	1.45	1.21	1.55	1.12	1.66	1.04	1.77	0.95	1.89
26	1.30	1.46	1.22	1.55	1.14	1.65	1.06	1.76	0.98	1.88
27	1.32	1.47	1.24	1.56	1.16	1.65	1.08	1.76	1.01	1.86
28	1.33	1.48	1.26	1.56	1.18	1.65	1.10	1.75	1.03	1.85
29	1.34	1.48	1.27	1.56	1.20	1.65	1.12	1.74	1.05	1.84
30	1.35	1.49	1.28	1.57	1.21	1.65	1.14	1.74	1.07	1.83
31	1.36	1.50	1.30	1.57	1.23	1.65	1.16	1.74	1.09	1.83
32	1.37	1.50	1.31	1.57	1.24	1.65	1.18	1.73	1.11	1.82
33	1.38	1.51	1.32	1.58	1.26	1.65	1.19	1.73	1.13	1.81
34	1.39	1.51	1.33	1.58	1.27	1.65	1.21	1.73	1.15	1.81
35	1.39	1.52	1.34	1.58	1.28	1.65	1.22	1.73	1.16	1.80
36	1.40	1.52	1.35	1.59	1.29	1.65	1.24	1.73	1.18	1.80
37	1.42	1.53	1.36	1.59	1.31	1.66	1.25	1.72	1.19	1.80
38	1.43	1.54	1.37	1.59	1.32	1.66	1.26	1.72	1.21	1.79
39	1.43	1.54	1.38	1.60	1.33	1.66	1.27	1.72	1.22	1.79
40	1.44	1.54	1.39	1.60	1.34	1.66	1.29	1.72	1.23	1.79
45	1.48	1.57	1.43	1.62	1.38	1.67	1.34	1.72	1.29	1.78
50	1.50	1.59	1.46	1.63	1.42	1.67	1.38	1.72	1.34	1.77
55	1.53	1.60	1.49	1.64	1.45	1.68	1.41	1.72	1.38	1.77
60	1.55	1.62	1.51	1.65	1.48	1.69	1.44	1.73	1.41	1.77
65	1.57	1.63	1.54	1.66	1.50	1.70	1.47	1.73	1.44	1.77
70	1.58	1.64	1.55	1.67	1.52	1.70	1.49	1.74	1.46	1.77
75	1.60	1.65	1.57	1.68	1.54	1.71	1.51	1.74	1.49	1.77
80	1.61	1.66	1.59	1.69	1.56	1.72	1.53	1.74	1.51	1.77
85	1.62	1.67	1.60	1.70	1.57	1.72	1.55	1.75	1.52	1.77
90	1.63	1.68	1.61	1.70	1.59	1.73	1.57	1.75	1.54	1.78
95	1.64	1.69	1.62	1.71	1.60	1.73	1.58	1.75	1.56	1.78
100	1.65	1.69	1.63	1.72	1.61	1.74	1.59	1.76	1.57	1.78

TABLE A.14 A Table of Areas under the Standard Normal Curve

z	.00	.01	.02	.03	.04	.05	.06	.07	.08	.09
0.0	.0000	.0040	.0080	.0120	.0160	.0199	.0239	.0279	.0319	.0359
0.1	.0398	.0438	.0478	.0517	.0557	.0596	.0636	.0675	.0714	.0753
0.2	.0793	.0832	.0871	.0910	.0948	.0987	.1026	.1064	.1103	.1141
0.3	.1179	.1217	.1255	.1293	.1331	.1368	.1406	.1443	.1480	.1517
0.4	.1554	.1591	.1628	.1664	.1700	.1736	.1772	.1808	.1844	.1879
0.5	.1915	.1950	.1985	.2019	.2054	.2088	.2123	.2157	.2190	.2224
0.6	.2257	.2291	.2324	.2357	.2389	.2422	.2454	.2486	.2517	.2549
0.7	.2580	.2611	.2642	.2673	.2704	.2734	.2764	.2794	.2823	.2852
0.8	.2881	.2910	.2939	.2967	.2995	.3023	.3051	.3078	.3106	.3133
0.9	.3159	.3186	.3212	.3238	.3264	.3289	.3315	.3340	.3365	.3389
1.0	.3413	.3438	.3461	.3485	.3508	.3531	.3554	.3577	.3599	.3621
1.1	.3643	.3665	.3686	.3708	.3729	.3749	.3770	.3790	.3810	.3830
1.2	.3849	.3869	.3888	.3907	.3925	.3944	.3962	.3980	.3997	.4015
1.3	.4032	.4049	.4066	.4082	.4099	.4115	.4131	.4147	.4162	.4177
1.4	.4192	.4207	.4222	.4236	.4251	.4265	.4279	.4292	.4306	.4319
1.5	.4332	.4345	.4357	.4370	.4382	.4394	.4406	.4418	.4429	.4441
1.6	.4452	.4463	.4474	.4484	.4495	.4505	.4515	.4525	.4535	.4545
1.7	.4554	.4564	.4573	.4582	.4591	.4599	.4608	.4616	.4625	.4633
1.8	.4641	.4649	.4656	.4664	.4671	.4678	.4686	.4693	.4699	.4706
1.9	.4713	.4719	.4726	.4732	.4738	.4744	.4750	.4756	.4761	.4767
2.0	.4772	.4778	.4783	.4788	.4793	.4798	.4803	.4808	.4812	.4817
2.1	.4821	.4826	.4830	.4834	.4838	.4842	.4846	.4850	.4854	.4857
2.2	.4861	.4864	.4868	.4871	.4875	.4878	.4881	.4884	.4887	.4890
2.3	.4893	.4896	.4898	.4901	.4904	.4906	.4909	.4911	.4913	.4916
2.4	.4918	.4920	.4922	.4925	.4927	.4929	.4931	.4932	.4934	.4936
2.5	.4938	.4940	.4941	.4943	.4945	.4946	.4948	.4949	.4951	.4952
2.6	.4953	.4955	.4956	.4957	.4959	.4960	.4961	.4962	.4963	.4964
2.7	.4965	.4966	.4967	.4968	.4969	.4970	.4971	.4972	.4973	.4974
2.8	.4974	.4975	.4976	.4977	.4977	.4978	.4979	.4979	.4980	.4981
2.9	.4981	.4982	.4982	.4983	.4984	.4984	.4985	.4985	.4986	.4986
3.0	.4987	.4987	.4987	.4988	.4988	.4989	.4989	.4989	.4990	.4990

Source: A. Hald, *Statistical Tables and Formulas* (New York: Wiley, 1952), abridged from Table 1. Reproduced by permission of the publisher.

TABLE A.13 Critical Values for the Durbin–Watson d Statistic ($\alpha = .01$)

n	k = 1 $d_{L,01}$	k = 1 $d_{U,01}$	k = 2 $d_{L,01}$	k = 2 $d_{U,01}$	k = 3 $d_{L,01}$	k = 3 $d_{U,01}$	k = 4 $d_{L,01}$	k = 4 $d_{U,01}$	k = 5 $d_{L,01}$	k = 5 $d_{U,01}$
15	0.81	1.07	0.70	1.25	0.59	1.46	0.49	1.70	0.39	1.96
16	0.84	1.09	0.74	1.25	0.63	1.44	0.53	1.66	0.44	1.90
17	0.87	1.10	0.77	1.25	0.67	1.43	0.57	1.63	0.48	1.85
18	0.90	1.12	0.80	1.26	0.71	1.42	0.61	1.60	0.52	1.80
19	0.93	1.13	0.83	1.26	0.74	1.41	0.65	1.58	0.56	1.77
20	0.95	1.15	0.86	1.27	0.77	1.41	0.68	1.57	0.60	1.74
21	0.97	1.16	0.89	1.27	0.80	1.41	0.72	1.55	0.63	1.71
22	1.00	1.17	0.91	1.28	0.83	1.40	0.75	1.54	0.66	1.69
23	1.02	1.19	0.94	1.29	0.86	1.40	0.77	1.53	0.70	1.67
24	1.04	1.20	0.96	1.30	0.88	1.41	0.80	1.53	0.72	1.66
25	1.05	1.21	0.98	1.30	0.90	1.41	0.83	1.52	0.75	1.65
26	1.07	1.22	1.00	1.31	0.93	1.41	0.85	1.52	0.78	1.64
27	1.09	1.23	1.02	1.32	0.95	1.41	0.88	1.51	0.81	1.63
28	1.10	1.24	1.04	1.32	0.97	1.41	0.90	1.51	0.83	1.62
29	1.12	1.25	1.05	1.33	0.99	1.42	0.92	1.51	0.85	1.61
30	1.13	1.26	1.07	1.34	1.01	1.42	0.94	1.51	0.88	1.61
31	1.15	1.27	1.08	1.34	1.02	1.42	0.96	1.51	0.90	1.60
32	1.16	1.28	1.10	1.35	1.04	1.43	0.98	1.51	0.92	1.60
33	1.17	1.29	1.11	1.36	1.05	1.43	1.00	1.51	0.94	1.59
34	1.18	1.30	1.13	1.36	1.07	1.43	1.01	1.51	0.95	1.59
35	1.19	1.31	1.14	1.37	1.08	1.44	1.03	1.51	0.97	1.59
36	1.21	1.32	1.15	1.38	1.10	1.44	1.04	1.51	0.99	1.59
37	1.22	1.32	1.16	1.38	1.11	1.45	1.06	1.51	1.00	1.59
38	1.23	1.33	1.18	1.39	1.12	1.45	1.07	1.52	1.02	1.58
39	1.24	1.34	1.19	1.39	1.14	1.45	1.09	1.52	1.03	1.58
40	1.25	1.34	1.20	1.40	1.15	1.46	1.10	1.52	1.05	1.58
45	1.29	1.38	1.24	1.42	1.20	1.48	1.16	1.53	1.11	1.58
50	1.32	1.40	1.28	1.45	1.24	1.49	1.20	1.54	1.16	1.59
55	1.36	1.43	1.32	1.47	1.28	1.51	1.25	1.55	1.21	1.59
60	1.38	1.45	1.35	1.48	1.32	1.52	1.28	1.56	1.25	1.60
65	1.41	1.47	1.38	1.50	1.35	1.53	1.31	1.57	1.28	1.61
70	1.43	1.49	1.40	1.52	1.37	1.55	1.34	1.58	1.31	1.61
75	1.45	1.50	1.42	1.53	1.39	1.56	1.37	1.59	1.34	1.62
80	1.47	1.52	1.44	1.54	1.42	1.57	1.39	1.60	1.36	1.62
85	1.48	1.53	1.46	1.55	1.43	1.58	1.41	1.60	1.39	1.63
90	1.50	1.54	1.47	1.56	1.45	1.59	1.43	1.61	1.41	1.64
95	1.51	1.55	1.49	1.57	1.47	1.60	1.45	1.62	1.42	1.64
100	1.52	1.56	1.50	1.58	1.48	1.60	1.46	1.63	1.44	1.65

Source: J. Durbin and G. S. Watson, "Testing for Serial Correlation in Least Squares Regression, II," *Biometrika* 30 (1951), pp. 159–78. Reproduced by permission of the Biometrika Trustees.

Answers to Most Odd-Numbered Exercises

Chapter 1

1.3 Cross-sectional; time series
1.5 $398,000
1.7 Calculator sales tend to increase over time
1.13 Between .4 and 11.6 minutes; 60%
1.17 Ordinal; nominative; ordinal; nominative; ordinal; nominative
1.19 Between 152° and 170°

Chapter 2

2.5 a. 144
b. 36

2.7 a.

Pizza Chain	Frequency	Relative Frequency
Domino's	5	.20
Godfather's	3	.12
Little Caesar's	2	.08
Papa John's	9	.36
Pizza Hut	6	.24
	25	1.00

2.21 a. Between 40 and 46.
b. Slightly skewed with a tail to the left.
2.23 a. Between 48 and 53.
b. Symmetrical
2.29 Although most growth rates are ≤61%, 7 of the companies have growth rates of 70% or higher.
2.37 The distribution has a tail to the right.
2.39 That was a highly unusual year for Maris.
2.41 b. Slightly skewed with tail to left.
c. No. 19 of 65 customers (29.2%) had scores below 42.
2.45 a. 17
b. 14
c. Those who prefer Rola seem to have purchased it while those who prefer Koka have not tended to purchase Rola.
2.47 a. 22
b. 4
c. Those who prefer Rola appear to consume more Cola.
2.49 b. 1st row: 79.7%, 20.3%, 100%
2nd row: 65.8%, 34.2%, 100%
c. 1st column: 50.2%, 49.8%, 100%
2nd column: 33.0%, 67.0%, 100%
d. Viewers concerned with violence are more likely to say quality has declined.
2.51 The more generous a person is, the less likely they are to leave without tipping.
2.57 There is a positive linear relationship between home size and price.
2.59 To respond to competition from satellite TV, cable rates dropped substantially. As satellite rates increased, cable rates could increase and still remain competitive.
2.61 Consumers tend to give better taste ratings to the restaurants they prefer.
2.65 a. No.
b. Yes, strong trend.
c. The line graph is better because it makes the growth apparent, but it exaggerates the trend.
d. No.
2.67 The most frequent manufacturing quality rating is average (20 out of 37). Only Lexus received best rating.
2.69 All three regions have about 20% of their automobiles receiving ratings of better than most or higher. About average is the most frequent rating for all three regions. The US has the lowest percentage in the worst category.
2.71 See answer to 2.69.
2.73 Although the Pacific Rim and European regions have higher percentages of cars receiving better or best design ratings, they also have higher percentages of cars receiving the worst ratings. US cars consistently receive average ratings.
2.75 a. $k = 6$.
d. Skewed with a tail to the left.
2.77 26%. Probably.
2.79 The distribution is skewed with a tail to the right.
2.81 The distribution is skewed with a tail to the right.
2.83 The distribution has a tail to the right with one outlying value.
2.85 a. Heights: 12, 4.8, 3.8, 4.4, .84
2.87 The vertical scale has been broken, exaggerating the Chevy advantage.

Chapter 3

3.3 a. 9.6, 10, 10
b. 103.33, 100, 90
3.5 a. Yes, $\bar{x} = 42.954 > 42$
b. $\bar{x} <$ median $= 43$. There is a slight skewness to the left.
3.7 a. Yes, $\bar{x} = 50.575 > 50$.
b. median $= 50.650$. They are close because the distribution is nearly symmetric.
3.9 Slight skewness to left; US is lowest.
3.11 Skewed to right; US is highest.
3.13 Skewed to right. US is above mean and median.
3.15 a. Skewed right.
b. About 33%; about 50%.
3.19 range $= 10$; $\sigma^2 = 11.6$; $\sigma = 3.4059$
3.21 a. Revenue: 20.2; 44.6641; 6.6831
Profit: 29,079; 54692275.3; 7395.42
b. z-scores: $-.176$; 2.886; -1.046; $-.161$; $-.590$; $-.166$; $-.140$; $-.214$; $-.187$; $-.207$

3.23 a. The rule is appropriate.
b. [48.9312, 52.2188];
[47.2875, 53.8626];
[45.6436, 55.5064]
c. Yes
d. 67.5%, 95%, 100%
Yes
3.25 a. Somewhat reasonable
b. [40.3076, 45.5924];
[37.6652, 48.2348];
[35.0228, 50.8772]
c. Yes
d. 63%, 98.46%, 100%; Yes
3.27 a. $[-72.99, 94.85]$, $[-5.72, 31.72]$, $[-47.87, 116.77]$
c. 383.9, 72, 119.4
RS Internet Age is most risky;
Franklin Income A is least risky
3.31 a. 192   c. 141   e. 132
b. 152   d. 171   f. 30
3.33 30 year rates higher; variability similar; Average of differences is .444
3.35 a. All categories
b. Most: strategic quality planning; quality and operational results. Least: Info. and analysis; human
3.39 a. Strong positive linear association between x and y.
b. $\hat{y} = 134.4751$
3.43 a. Weighted mean $= 13.56\%$
b. Unweighted mean $= 10.72\%$
3.45 a. 4.6 lb.
b. 3.8289
3.47 a. 51.5; 81.61; 9.0338
3.51 .4142
3.53 a. 0.39436
b. $2139
3.57 a. about 65%
b. about 425 UKL.
3.59 a. 151.25%
b. Pools might be installed in homes that are larger and nicer than ordinary.

Chapter 4

4.3 b1. *AA*
b2. *AA*, *BB*, *CC*
b3. *AB*, *AC*, *BA*, *BC*, *CA*, *CB*
b4. *AA*, *AB*, *AC*, *BA*, *CA*
b5. *AA*, *AB*, *BA*, *BB*
c. 1/9, 1/3, 2/3, 5/9, 4/9
4.5 b1. *PPPN*, *PPNP*, *PNPP*, *NPPP*
b2. Outcomes with ≤2 *P*'s (11)
b3. Outcomes with ≥1 *P* (15)
b4. *PPPP*, *NNNN*
c. 1/4, 11/16, 15/16, 1/8
4.7 .15
4.11 a1. .25
a2. .40
a3. .10
c1. .55
c2. .45
c3. .45

4.13   a. 5/8
      b. 21/40
      c. 19/40
      d. 3/8
      e. 31/40
4.15   103/300
4.19   a. .6
      b. .4
      c. Dependent
4.21   .55
4.23   .1692
4.25   .31
4.27   b. .40
      c. Yes, $P(FRAUD|FIRE) = P(FRAUD)$
4.29   a. .874
      b. .996
      c. .004
4.31   .999946
4.33   a. .0295
      b. .9705
      c. Probably not
4.37   .0976; .6098; .2927
4.39   a. .0892
      b. No. Too many paying customers
        would lose credit.
4.41   .1549; .8319; .0133
4.43   .2466; .6164; .1370
4.51   .001
4.53   1/56
4.55   1/9; 1/9; 4/9
4.57   .04; .56; .26; .32
4.59   .9029
4.61   .9436
4.63   .721
4.65   .362
4.67   .502
4.69   Slight dependence
4.71   a. .2075
      b. .25
      c. .105
      d. .42
      e. Yes since $P(bonus) <$
        $P(bonus|training)$
4.73   .3077
4.75   a. .1860
      b. Yes since $P(schizophrenia) <$
        $P(schizophrenia|atrophy)$
      c. .625
      d. Yes
      e. .833

Chapter 5

5.3   a. Discrete
      b. Discrete
      c. Continuous
      d. Discrete
      e. Discrete
      f. Continuous
      g. Continuous
5.5 $p(x) \geq 0$, each x
      $\sum_{all\ x} p(x) = 1$
5.9   a. .8, .4
      b. 1.15, .90967
      c. 1.6, 2.1071
5.11   a. .667, .444, .667, [−.667, 2.001],
       [−1.334, 2.668]
      b. 1.5, .75, .866, [−.232, 3.232],
       [−1.098, 4.098]
      c. 2, 1, 1, [0, 4], [−1, 5]

5.13   b. $500
5.15   a.

x	$p(x)$
$400	.995
−$49,600	.005

      b. $150
      c. $1,250
5.17   −$4.20
5.19   a. $p(x) = $ .1099, .0879, .3077,
       .2967, .1978
      b. 3.38
5.23   a. $p(x) = $
      $\dfrac{5!}{x!\,(5-x)!}(.3)^x(.7)^{5-x}$
      $x = 0, 1, 2, 3, 4, 5$
      c. .1323
      d. .9692
      e. .8369
      f. .0308
      g. .1631
      h. $\mu_x = 1.5,\ \sigma_x^2 = 1.05,$
       $\sigma_x = 1.024695$
      i. [−.54939, 3.54939], .9692
5.25   a. $p(x) = $
      $\dfrac{15!}{x!\,(15-x)!}(.9)^x(.1)^{15-x}$
      b1. .4509
      b2. .9873
      b3. .5491
      b4. .1837
      b5. .0022
      c. No, $P(x \leq 9)$ is very small
5.27   a1. .0625
      a2. .3125
      b1. .4119
      b2. .2517
      b3. .0059
      c. No, $P(x < 5)$ is very small
5.29   a. .9996, .0004
      b. .4845, .5155
      c. $p = 1/35$
      d. .000040019
5.33   a. $\mu_x = 2, \sigma_x^2 = 2, \sigma_x = 1.414$
      b. [−.828, 4.828], .9473
       [−2.242, 6.242], .9955
5.35   a. .7852
      b. .2148
      c. .1912
      d. .0087
5.37   a. Approximately zero
      b. Rate of comas unusually high.
5.41   a. 0
      b. .0714
      c. .4286
      d. .4286
      e. .0714
      f. .9286
      g. .5
      h. .9286
5.43   a. .1273
      b. .8727
5.45 $\dfrac{\binom{450}{14}\binom{50}{1}}{\binom{500}{15}} + \dfrac{\binom{450}{15}\binom{50}{0}}{\binom{500}{15}} \approx .5490$
5.47   a.

x	$p(x)$
0	4/9
1	4/9
2	1/9

      b. $p(x) = $ .49; .42; .09
      c. $p(x) = $ .54; .42; .04

5.49   a.

x	$p(x)$
−2	25/55
−1	16/55
0	9/55
1	4/55
2	1/55

      c. −1.091
      d. 1.064; 1.032
5.51   b. 87,000
      c. 75%
      d. [46,454, 127,546]; 95%
5.53   a. .7373
      b1. .01733
      b2. .42067
      b3. .61291
      b4. .02361
      c. No. The probability is very small.
5.55   a. .2231
      b. .9344
      c. .9913
      d. .0025
5.57   .0025. Claim is probably not true.
5.59   .0037. Business failures are probably
      increasing.
5.61   .3328. The claim seems reasonable.

Chapter 6

6.7 $h = 1/125$
6.9   a. 3, 3, 1.73205
      b. [1.268, 4.732], .5774
6.11   a. $f(x) = 1/20$ for $120 \leq x \leq 140$
      c. .5
      d. .25
6.13 $c = 1/6$
6.15   a. 4.5   b. 1.0, .5774
6.23   a. −1, one σ below μ
      b. −3, three σ below μ
      c. 0, equals μ
      d. 2, two σ above μ
      e. 4, four σ above μ
6.25   a. 2.33   d. −2.33
      b. 1.645   e. −1.645
      c. 2.05   f. −1.28
6.27   a. 696   f. 335.5
      b. 664.5   g. 696
      c. 304   h. 700
      d. 283   i. 300
      e. 717
6.29   a1. .9830
      a2. .0033
      a3. .0456
      b. 947
6.31   a. .0013
      b. Claim probably not true
6.33   .0424
6.35   a. 10%, 90%, −13.968
      b. −1.402, 26.202
6.37   a. $[\mu \pm 2.33\sigma]$
      b. [46.745, 54.405]
6.39   a. A: .3085
       B: .4013
       B is investigated more often
      b. A: .8413
       B: .6915
       A is investigated more often
      c. B
      d. Investigate if cost variance
       exceeds $5,000
       .5987
6.41 $\mu = 700, \sigma = 100$
6.43   Both np and $n(1-p) \geq 5$

6.45 a. $np = 80$ and $n(1 - p) = 120$
      both ≥ 5
    b1. .0558
    b2. .9875
    b3. .0125
    b4. .0025
    b5. .0015

6.47 a1. $np = 200$ and $n(1 - p) = 800$
      both ≥ 5
    a2. 200, 12.6491
    a3. Less than .001
    b. No

6.49 a. Less than .001
    b. No

6.55 a. $3e^{-3x}$ for $x \geq 0$
    c. .9502
    d. .4226
    e. .0025
    f. 1/3, 1/9, 1/3
    g. .9502

6.57 a. $(2/3)e^{-(2/3)x}$ for $x \geq 0$
    c1. .8647
    c2. .2498
    c3. .0695
    c4. .2835

6.59 a1. .1353
    a2. .2325
    a3. .2212
    b. Probably not, probability is .2212

6.61 That the data come from a normal population.

6.65 .0062

6.67 a. .8944
    b. 73

6.69 a. .8944
    b. .7967
    c. .6911

6.71 298

6.73 .9306

6.77 2/3

6.79 a. .0062
    b. .6915
    c. 3.3275%

6.81 .7745

Chapter 7

7.3 Coca-Cola; Coca-Cola Enterprises; Reynolds American; Pepsi Bottling Group; Sara Lee

7.5 5:47

7.9 a. 10, .16, .4
    b. 500, .0025, .05
    c. 3, .0025, .05
    d. 100, .000625, .025

7.11 a. Normally distributed
      No, sample size is large (≥ 30)
    b. $\mu_{\bar{x}} = 20$, $\sigma_{\bar{x}} = .5$
    c. .0228
    d. .1093

7.13 30, 40, 50, 50, 60, 70

7.15 2/3

7.17 a. Normal distribution because $n \geq 30$
    b. 6, .247
    c. .0143
    d. 1.43%, conclude $\mu < 6$

7.19 a. .2206
    b. .0027
    c. Yes

7.25 a. .5, .001, .0316
    b. .1, .0009, .03
    c. .8, .0004, .02
    d. .98, .0000196, .004427

7.27 a. Approximately normal
    b. .9, .03

7.29 a. .0089
    b. Yes

7.31 a. .0122
    b. Yes.

7.33 No; yes.

7.35 a. .0294
    b. Yes.

7.41 a. Phone, mail, and mall surveys
    b. Dichotomous, multiple choice, and open-ended

7.43 selection bias, errors of observation, recording error (among others).

7.47 a. .9953
    b. .8414
    c. .5222
    d. No; no.

7.49 a. .0062

7.51 11.63; $[-26.76, 19.76]$

7.53 a. $\mu = .55$; $\sigma = .86458$
    b. Normally distributed;
      $\mu_{\bar{x}} = .55$; $\sigma_{\bar{x}} = .086458$
    d. .0104

Chapter 8

8.5 It becomes shorter.

8.7 a. [50.064, 51.086]; [49.967, 51.183].
    b. Yes. All values in the interval exceed 50.
    c. No. Some values in the interval are below 50.

8.9 a. [42.31, 43.59]; [42.19, 43.71]
    b. Yes. All values in the interval exceed 42.
    c. Yes. All values exceed 42.

8.11 a. [76.132, 89.068]
    b. [85.748, 100.252]
    c. Intervals overlap; not clear which is shorter.

8.15 1.363, 2.201, 4.025
    1.440, 2.447, 5.208

8.17 a. [3.442, 8.558]
    b. Can be 95% confident, cannot be 99% confident

8.19 a. [6.832, 7.968]
    b. Yes, 95% interval is below 8.

8.21 a. [786.609, 835.391]
    b. Yes, 95% interval is above 750

8.23 [4.969, 5.951]; Yes

8.29 a. $n = 262$
    b. $n = 452$

8.31 a. $n = 47$
    b. $n = 328$

8.33 $n = 54$

8.35 a. $p = .5$
    b. $p = .3$
    c. $p = .8$

8.37 Part a. [.304, .496],
            [.286, .514],
            [.274, .526]
    Part b. [.066, .134],
            [.060, .140],
            [.055, .145]
    Part c. [.841, .959],
            [.830, .970],
            [.823, .977]
    Part d. [.464, .736],
            [.439, .761],
            [.422, .778]

8.39 a. [.473, .610]
    b. No, the interval extends below .5.

8.41 a. [.3804, .4596], no
    b. [.5701, .6299], yes
    c. 95% margin of error is .03

8.43 a. [.611, .729]
    b. Yes, interval above .6

8.45 [.264, .344]
    Yes, 95% interval exceeds .20.

8.47 a. $\hat{p} = .02$, [.0077, .0323]
    b. $\hat{p} = .054$, [.034, .074]
    c. Yes

8.49 Using $p = .73754$ and $z_{.005} = 2.576$,
    $n = 1429.13$ (or $n = 1430$)

8.55 68.26%: [2.985, 7.935]
    95.44%: [0.510, 10.410]
    99.73%: [0, 12.885]
    95% CI: [4.9690, 5.9510]

8.57 a. [63.590, 72.490]
    b. [52.287, 61.193]
    c. Yes. The entire interval is below the interval for industrial companies.

8.59 a. [.5717, .6483]; Yes.

8.61 a. [56.469, 59.131]. Yes, the interval is below 60.
    b. 144

8.63 a. [25.1560, 27.2840]
    b. Yes, not much more than 25

8.65 fa: [7.685%, 7.975%];
      differs from 8.31%
    dlcs: [9.108%, 17.732%]; does not
      differ from 11.71%
    dms: [9.788%, 20.272%]; does not
      differ from 13.64%
    dscs: [16.327%, 28.693%]; differs from 14.93%

8.67 [.61025, .66975]

8.69 a. [.8005, .8608]
    b. Yes, interval is above .75

Chapter 9

9.3 a. $H_0: \mu \leq 42$ versus $H_a: \mu > 42$
    b. Type I: decide $\mu > 42$ when it isn't.
      Type II: decide $\mu \leq 42$ when it isn't.

9.5 a. $H_0: \mu = 3''$ versus $H_a: \mu \neq 3''$
    b. Type I: assign the team when it is not needed
      Type II: do not assign the team when it is needed

9.7 a. $H_0: \mu \leq 60°$ versus $H_a: \mu > 60°$
    b. Type I: shut down unnecessarily
      Type II: fail to shut down when water is too warm.
    c. .05 to reduce β and avoid severe penalties occurring with Type II errors.

9.11 a. -2.0
    b. Fail to reject H_0
    c. .0228
    d. Can reject H_0 at $\alpha = .10$ and .05; fail to reject H_0 at $\alpha = .01$ and .001.
    e. Strong

9.13 a. $H_0: \mu \leq 42$ versus $H_a: \mu > 42$
    b. $z = 2.91$. Since this exceeds the critical values 1.28, 1.645, and 2.33, can reject H_0 at $\alpha = .1, .05$, and .01. Fail to reject H_0 at $\alpha = .001$
    c. p-value = .0018. Same conclusion as part (b)
    d. Very strong

9.15 a. $H_0: \mu \leq 60$ versus $H_a: \mu > 60$
    b. $z = 2.41$; p-value = .0080. Since $z > 1.645$ and p-value $< .05$, reject H_0 and shut down

9.17 $z = 3.09$ and p-value $= .001$. Since $z > 1.645$ and p-value $< .05$, shut down the plant.

9.19 a. $H_0: \mu = 16$ versus $H_a: \mu \neq 16$
b. $z = 3.00$, p-value $= .0027$, critical values ± 2.575, [16.007, 16.093], reject H_0 and decide to readjust; $z = -2.40$, p-value $= .0164$, ± 2.575, [15.917, 16.003], fail to reject H_0 so don't readjust, $z = 1.20$, p-value $= .2302$, ± 2.575, [15.977, 16.063], fail to reject H_0 so don't readjust; $z = -3.60$, p-value $= .00032$, ± 2.575, [15.897, 15.983], reject H_0 and decide to readjust

9.23 $t = -4.30$; reject H_0 at .10, .05, and .01, but not at .001.

9.25 $t = 2.21 > 1.685$. Reject H_0 and decide $\mu > 50$. Since $p = .0164$, we have strong evidence that $\mu > 50$.

9.27 a. $H_0: \mu \leq 3.5$ versus $H_a: \mu > 3.5$
b. $t = 3.62$; reject H_0 at $\alpha = .10$, .05, and .01 but not .001. There is very strong evidence.
d. Since the p-value is very low, we can be very confident $\mu > 3.5$.

9.29 a. $H_0: \mu \leq 42$ versus $H_a > 42$
b. $t = 2.90 > 2.386$, so reject H_0 and decide $\mu > 42$. Since the p-value $= .0026$, we have very strong evidence that $\mu > 42$.

9.31 a. $H_0: \mu = 750$ versus $H_a: \mu \neq 750$
b. $t = 6.94 > 4.604$; reject H_0. Since the p-value $< .01$, we have very strong evidence that $\mu \neq 750$.

9.33 Since $t = -4.97$ and p-value $= .000$, there is extremely strong evidence that $\mu < 18.8$

9.37 a. $H_0: p \leq .5$ versus $H_a: p > .5$
b. $z = 1.19$. Do not reject H_0 at any α. There is little evidence.
c. $z = 2.53$. Reject H_0 at .10, .05, and .01, but not at .001.

9.39 a. $H_0: p \leq .18$ versus $H_a: p > .18$
b. $z = 1.84$; p-value $= .0329$. Reject H_0 at $\alpha = .10$ and .05; do not reject H_0 at $\alpha = .01$, .001. There is strong evidence.
c. Possibly.

9.41 $H_0: p = .73$ versus $H_a: p \neq .73$
$z = -.80$ and p-value $= .4238$ provide insufficient evidence to reject H_0 at any α.

9.47 a. .9279; .8315; .6772; .4840; .2946; .1492; .0618; .0207; .0055; .00118
b. No. Must increase n.
c. The power increases.

9.49 246

9.53 $\chi^2 = 11.618 < 17.7083$. Reject H_0.

9.55 $\chi^2 = 6.72 < 13.8484$. Reject H_0.
CI for σ^2: [.0000854, .0002709]
CI for σ: [.00924, .01646]
Yes, 99.73% are within the specification limits

9.57 $\chi^2 = 16.029$. Do not reject H_0 at either α.

9.59 a. $H_0: \mu \geq 25$ versus $H_a: \mu < 25$
b. $t = -2.63$. Reject H_0 at all α's except .001.
c. Since p-value $= .0057$, reject H_0 at all α's except .001; very strong evidence.
d. Possibly, because $\bar{x}$ is more than 1.3 years under 25

9.61 a. $t = 2.50$. Reject H_0 at $\alpha = .10$, .05, .01 but not .001; very strong.
b. $t = 1.11$. Do not reject H_0 at any α.

9.63 a. Reject H_0 at $\alpha = .10$ and .05 but not at .01 or .001.
b. Strong evidence

9.65 a. FA: $H_0: \mu = 8.31\%$ vs $H_a: \mu \neq 8.31\%$; DLC: $H_0: \mu = 11.71\%$ vs $H_a: \mu \neq 11.71\%$; DMC: $H_0: \mu = 13.64\%$ vs $H_a: \mu \neq 13.64\%$; DSC: $H_0: \mu = 14.93\%$ vs $H_a: \mu \neq 14.93\%$
b. FA: $t = -6.66$. Reject H_0. DLC: $t = .80$. Do not reject H_0. DMC: $t = .53$. Do not reject H_0. DSC: $t = 2.46$. Reject H_0. Conclude current means differ for FA and DSC.

9.67 There is some evidence.

9.69 a. $t = 4.92$. Reject H_0 at every α. There is extremely strong evidence the current mean is higher.
b. Yes. Extra expenses erode fundholders' account values.

Chapter 10

10.5 $t = 3.39$; reject H_0 at $\alpha = .10$, .05, .01 but not .001; very strong evidence.

10.7 Assuming unequal variances in all three problems: for 10.4 the interval is [23.503, 36.497] and we can be 95% confident. For 10.5, $t = 3.39$ with 11 $d.f.$; reject H_0 at $\alpha = .10$, .05, .01 but not .001; very strong. For 10.6, $t = 3.39$ with 11 $d.f.$; reject H_0 at $\alpha = .10$, .05, .01 but not .001; very strong

10.9 a. $H_0: \mu_1 - \mu_2 \leq 0$ versus $H_a: \mu_1 - \mu_2 > 0$
b. $t = 1.97$; reject H_0 at .10 and .05 but not .01 or .001; strong evidence.
c. [-12.01, 412.01]. A's mean could be anywhere from $12.01 lower to $412.01 higher than B's.

10.11 a. $H_0: \mu_1 - \mu_2 = 0$ versus $H_a: \mu_1 - \mu_2 \neq 0$
b. Reject H_0 at $\alpha = .10$, .05 but not .01 or .001; strong evidence
c. [$1.10, $100.90]

10.17 a. [100.141, 106.859]; yes. [98.723, 108.277]; no
b. $t = 2.32$; reject H_0 at $\alpha = .05$ but not .01; strong
c. $t = -4.31$; reject H_0 at $\alpha = .05$, .01; extremely strong.

10.19 a. $H_0: \mu_d = 0$ versus $H_a: \mu_d \neq 0$
b. $t = 9.22$; reject H_0 at each level of α; extremely strong.
c. p-value $= .000$; reject H_0 at each α; extremely strong.
d. [.1677, .2796]; 30 year loan rates are between .1677% and .2796% higher

10.21 a. $t = 6.18$; decide there is a difference.
b. A 95% confidence interval is [2.01, 4.49], so we can estimate the minimum to be 2.01 and the maximum to be 4.49.

10.23 a. $H_0: \mu_d = 0$ versus $H_a: \mu_d \neq 0$
b. $t = 3.89$; reject H_0 at all α except .001; yes
c. p-value $= .006$; reject H_0 at all α except .001; very strong evidence

10.27 $z = -10.14$; reject H_0 at each value of α; extremely strong evidence

10.29 a. $H_0: p_1 - p_2 = 0$ versus $H_a: p_1 - p_2 \neq 0$
b. $z = 3.63$; reject H_0 at each value of α
c. $H_0: p_1 - p_2 \leq .05$ versus $H_a: p_1 - p_2 > .05$
$z = 1.99$ and p-value $= .0233$; strong evidence
d. [.0509, .1711]; yes

10.31 p-value $= .004$; very strong evidence [$-.057$, $-.011$]; $-.057$

10.33 a. $z = 3.72$; reject $H_0: p_1 - p_2 = 0$ at $\alpha = .001$; [.029, .091]; largest: .091; smallest: .029
b. $z = -4.435$; reject $H_0: p_1 - p_2 = 0$ at $\alpha = .001$; [$-.079$, $-.201$]; largest: .079; smallest: .201

10.37 a. $F = 5 < F_{.025} = 5.60$. Do not reject H_0.
b. $F = 5 > F_{.05} = 4.15$. Reject H_0.

10.39 $F = 9.554 > F_{.025} = 2.88$ Unequal variances approach is appropriate.

10.41 $F = 2.470 > F_{.05} = 2.40$. Reject H_0.

10.43 a. $H_0: \mu_T - \mu_B = 0$ versus $H_a: \mu_T - \mu_B \neq 0$
$t = 1.54$; cannot reject H_0 at any values of α; little or no evidence
b. [$-.09$, .73]

10.45 a. $H_0: \mu_d = 0$ versus $H_a: \mu_d > 0$
b. $t = 10.00$; reject H_0 at all levels of α
c. p-value $= .000$; reject H_0 at all levels of α; extremely strong evidence

10.47 a. $t = 8.251$; reject $H_0: \mu_O - \mu_{JVC} = 0$ at $\alpha = .001$
b. [$32.69, $55.31]; probably
c. $t = 2.625$; reject $H_0: \mu_O - \mu_{JVC} \leq 30$ at $\alpha = .05$

Chapter 11 (Answers to several Even-Numbered Exercises also given)

11.1 Factor = independent variables in a designed experiment
treatments = values of a factor (or combination of factors)
experimental units = entities to which treatments are assigned
response variable = the dependent variable (or variable of interest)

11.5 a. $F = 184.57$, p-value $= .000$; reject H_0 and decide shelf height affects sales.
b. Point estimate of $\mu_M - \mu_B$ is 21.4; [17.681, 25.119], $\mu_T - \mu_B$: -4.3; [-8.019, $-.581$], $\mu_T - \mu_M$: -25.7; [-29.419, -21.981].
c. μ_B: [53.65, 57.96]
μ_M: [75.04, 79.36]
μ_T: [49.34, 53.66]

11.7 a. $F = 43.36$, p-value $= .000$; reject H_0; designs affect sales
b. B $-$ A: [11.56, 20.84]
C $-$ A: [3.56, 12.84]
C $-$ B: [-12.64, -3.36]
c. μ_A: [13.92, 19.28]
μ_B: [30.12, 35.48]
μ_C: [22.12, 27.48]

11.8 $F = 16.42$; p-value $< .001$; reject H_0; brands differ

11.9 Divot $-$ Alpha: [38.41, 127.59]
Divot $-$ Century: [50.21, 139.39]

Divot − Best: [−14.39, 74.79]
Century − Alpha: [−56.39, 32.79]
Century − Best: [−109.19, −20.01]
Best − Alpha: [8.21, 97.39]
Best and Divot appear to be most durable
Divot: [313.26, 359.94]
Best: [283.06, 329.74]
Alpha: [230.26, 276.94]
Century: [218.46, 265.14]

11.13 a. $F = 36.23$; p-value = .000; reject H_0; sales methods differ
b. $F = 12.87$; p-value = .007; reject H_0; salesman effects differ
c. Method 1 − Method 2: [−2.30, 2.96]
Method 1 − Method 3: [2.38, 7.62]
Method 1 − Method 4: [3.70, 8.96]
Method 2 − Method 3: [2.04, 7.29]
Method 2 − Method 4: [3.37, 8.63]
Method 3 − Method 4: [−1.29, 3.96]
Methods 1 and 2

11.15 a. $F = 441.75$ and p-value = .000; reject H_0; keyboard brand effects differ.
b. $F = 107.69$ and p-value = .000; reject H_0; specialist effects differ.
c. A − B: [8.55, 11.45]
A − C: [12.05, 14.95]
B − C: [2.05, 4.95]
Keyboard A

11.16 a. $F = 5.78$ and p-value = .0115; reject H_0; soft drink brands affect sales.
b. Coke Classic − New Coke: [7.982, 68.018]
Coke Classic − Pepsi: [−.218, 59.818]
New Coke − Pepsi: [−38.218, 21.818]
c. Yes, mean sales of Coke Classic were significantly higher than those for New Coke.

11.17 A combination of a level of factor 1 and a level of factor 2.

11.19 a. Plot suggests little interaction. $F = .66$ and p-value = .681; do not reject H_0. Conclude no interaction.
b. $F = 26.49$ and p-value = .000; reject H_0; display panel effects differ.
c. $F = 100.80$ and p-value = .000; reject H_0; emergency condition effects differ.
d. A − B: [.49, 5.91]
A − C: [−6.81, −1.39]
B − C: [−10.01, −4.59]
e. 1 − 2: [−10.43, −4.17]
1 − 3: [−18.13, −11.87]
1 − 4: [.77, 7.03]

11.21 a. Plot suggests little or no interaction.
b. $F(\text{int}) = .2195$ and p-value = .2195; do not reject H_0; conclude no interaction.
c. $F(1) = 26.5610$ and p-value = .0009; reject H_0; sales pressure effects differ.

d. $F(2) = .6098$ and p-value = .4574; do not reject H_0; sales pitch effects do not differ.

11.23 p-value of .001 for $F(\text{int})$ says reject H_0; conclude interaction exists. House design C and foreman 1: [17.72, 19.88]

Chapter 12

12.7 a. Each $E_i \geq 5$
b. $\chi^2 = 300.605$; reject H_0

12.9 a. $\chi^2 = 137.14$; reject H_0
b. Differences between brand preferences

12.11 a1. $[-\infty, 10.185]$
a2. [10.185, 14.147]
a3. [14.147, 18.108]
a4. [18.108, 22.069]
a5. [22.069, 26.030]
a6. [26.030, ∞]
b. 1.5, 9, 22, 22, 9, 1.5
c. Can use χ^2 test
e. 1, 9, 30, 15, 8, 2
$\chi^2 = 5.50$
f. Fail to reject; normal

12.13 Fail to reject H_0; normal

12.17 a.
	40%
	60%
20%	80%
b. 16%	24%
40%	60%
80%	30%
4%	56%
6.67%	93.33%
20%	70%
c. $\chi^2 = 16.667$; reject H_0
d. Yes

12.19 a.
		24.24%
		22.73%
		53.03%
51.515%	48.485%	
b. For Heavy/Yes cell: cell: 18.18%; row: 75%; column: 35.29%
c. $\chi^2 = 6.86$; fail to reject H_0
d. Possibly; can reject H_0 at $\alpha = .05$

12.21 a. $\chi^2 = 16.385$; reject H_0
b. [−.216, −.072]

12.23 $\chi^2 = 65.90$; reject H_0: [.270, .376]

12.25 b. $\chi^2 = 20.940$; reject H_0
c. Dependent

12.27 $\chi^2 = 71.48$; reject H_0

Chapter 13

13.3 a. $b_0 = 15.84$; $b_1 = -.1279$
b_0 is the estimated mean fuel consumption when the temperature is $0°$ F. b_1 is the estimated change in mean fuel consumption corresponding to a $1°$ increase in temperature.
c. 10.724 MMcF in each case.

13.5 a. $b_0 = 11.4641$; $b_1 = 24.6022$
b_0 is the estimated mean length of a service call when 0 copiers are serviced (not practical!) while b_1 is the estimated change in mean length of a call when 1 more copier must be serviced.
b. 109.87 minutes in each case

13.7 b. b_0 is the estimated mean direct labor cost when the batch size is 0 (not practical!) while b_1 is the estimated mean change in labor cost when the batch size increases by one unit.
c. $\hat{y} = 18.488 + 10.146x$
d. 627.248 or $62,724.80 in each case.

13.11 $s^2 = .428$; $s = .654$
13.13 21.3002; 4.6152
13.15 74.6762; 8.6415
13.17 27.8530; 5.2776
13.21 a. $b_0 = 14.816$; $b_1 = 5.7066$
b. SSE = 1.438; $s = .5363$
c. $s_{b_1} = .3953$; $t = 14.44$
d. $t > 2.571$; reject H_0. Yes, there is strong evidence that $\beta_1 \neq 0$.
e. $t > 4.032$; reject H_0. Yes, there is very strong evidence that $\beta_1 \neq 0$.
f. p-value = .000. Can reject H_0 at all α's. Extremely strong evidence.
g. [4.6903, 6.7229]
h. [4.1128, 7.3004]
i. $s_{b_0} = 1.235$; $t = 12.00$
j. p-value = .000. Can reject H_0 at all α's. There is extremely strong evidence that $\beta_0 \neq 0$.
k. $SS_{xx} = 1.84069$; $s_{b_0} = 1.235$; $s_{b_1} = .3953$

13.23 a. $b_0 = 7.81409$; $b_1 = 2.6652$
b. SSE = 2.806; $s = .316561$
c. $s_{b_1} = .2585$; $t = 10.31$
d. $t > 2.048$; reject H_0. Yes, there is strong evidence that $\beta_1 \neq 0$.
e. $t > 2.763$; reject H_0. Yes, there is very strong evidence that $\beta_1 \neq 0$
f. p-value = .000. Can reject H_0 at all α's. There is extremely strong evidence that $\beta_1 \neq 0$.
g. [2.1358, 3.1946]
h. [1.9510, 3.3794]
i. $s_{b_0} = .07988$; $t = 97.82$
j. p-value = .000. Can reject H_0 at all α's. There is extremely strong evidence that $\beta_0 \neq 0$.
k. $SS_{xx} = 1.49967$; $s_{b_0} = .07988$; $s_{b_1} = .2585$

13.25 a. $b_0 = 48.02$; $b_1 = 5.7003$
b. SSE = 896.8; $s = 10.5880$
c. $s_{b_1} = .7457$; $t = 7.64$
d. $t > 2.306$; reject H_0. Yes, there is strong evidence that $\beta_1 \neq 0$.
e. $t > 3.355$; reject H_0. Yes, there is very strong evidence that $\beta_1 \neq 0$.
f. p-value = .000. Can reject H_0 at all α's. There is extremely strong evidence that $\beta_1 \neq 0$.
g. [3.9807, 7.4199]
h. [3.1985, 8.2021]
i. $s_{b_0} = 14.41$; $t = 3.33$
j. p-value = .010. Can reject H_0 at $\alpha = .10$, .05 but not at .01 or .001. There is strong evidence that $\beta_0 \neq 0$
k. $SS_{xx} = 201.6$; $s_{b_0} = 14.41$; $s_{b_1} = .7457$

13.27 a. $b_1 = 1.2731$. We estimate that for every increase of one unit in mean taste, mean preference will increase by 1.2731
b. [.9885, 1.5577]. We are 95% confident β_1 is in this interval.

13.31 a. 33.362; [32.813, 33.911]
    b. 33.362; [31.878, 34.846]
    c. .15773
13.33 a. 8.0806; [7.9479, 8.2133]
    b. 8.0806; [7.4187, 8.7425]
    c. .041902
    d. [7.9016, 8.2597]; [7.1877, 8.9735]
    e. (i) 8.4804; [8.3604, 8.6004]
        (ii) 8.4804; [7.8209, 9.1398]
        (iii) .034267
        (iv) [8.3185, 8.6423]; [7.5909, 9.3699]
13.35 a. 162.03; [154.04, 170.02]
    b. 162.03; [136.34, 187.72]
    c. The second.
13.39 Explained variation $= 59.942$; $r^2 = .977$; $r = .988$
13.41 Explained variation $= 10.653$; $r^2 = .792$; $r = .890$
13.43 Explained variation $= 6550.7$, $r^2 = .880$; $r = .938$
13.47 Reject H_0: $\rho = 0$ at all four values of α
13.49 t-test for significance of β_1
13.51 a. $F = 208.39$
    b. $F > 6.61$. Reject H_0 and conclude there is a significant relationship at $\alpha = .05$
    c. $F > 16.26$. Reject H_0 and conclude significant relationship at $\alpha = .01$
    d. p-value $= .000$. Can reject H_0 at all levels of α. There is extremely strong evidence of a regression relationship.
13.53 a. $F = 106.30$
    b. $F > 4.20$. Reject H_0; significant relationship at $\alpha = .05$
    c. $F > 7.64$. Reject H_0; significant relationship at $\alpha = .01$
    d. p-value $= .000$. Can reject H_0 at all levels of α. There is extremely strong evidence of a regression relationship.
13.55 a. $F = 58.43$
    b. $F > 5.32$. Reject H_0; significant relationship at $\alpha = .05$.
    c. $F > 11.26$. Reject H_0; significant relationship at $\alpha = .01$
    d. p-value $= .000$. Can reject H_0 at all levels of α. There is extremely strong evidence of a regression relationship.
13.59 Approximate horizontal band appearance. No violations indicated.
13.61 No violations indicated.
13.63 Cyclical plot
13.65 b. Point prediction: 483.089; PI: [401.216, 581.668]
    c. 1.293 Growth of about 29% per year.
13.67 a. $b_1 = -6.4424$. For each unit increase in width difference, we estimate the mean accident rate will fall by 6.44.
    b. p-value $= .000$. There is extremely strong evidence that $\beta_1 \neq 0$.
    c. $r^2 = .984$. 98.4% of the variability in the accident rate is explained by width difference.
13.69 For aggressive, $b_1^* = .0163$; [.0075, .0251]. For defensive, $b_1^* = -.0046$; [$-.0066, -.0026$]. For neutral, $b_1^* = .0087$; [.0051, .0123].

13.71 a. $F = 21.1299 > 8.18$; significant relationship at $\alpha = .01$
    b. $b_1 = 2082.0153$; 95% CI: [1749.0005, 2415.0301] There is very strong evidence that as minority population increases, the number of customers per branch increases.

Chapter 14
14.3 a. $b_1 = -.0900$; $b_2 = .0825$
    b. 10.334 in each case.
14.5 a. $b_1 = -2.3577$; $b_2 = 1.6122$; $b_3 = .5012$
    b. $\hat{y} = 8.4111$
14.7 σ^2, σ
14.11 1. SSE $= 73.6$; $s^2 = 10.5$; $s = 3.24164$
    2. Total variation $= 7447.5$; SSE $= 73.6$; Explained variation $= 7374.0$
    3. $R^2 = 99.0\%$; $\bar{R}^2 = 98.7\%$
    4. F(model) $= 350.87$
    5. $350.87 > F_{.05} = 4.74$. Decide at least one of β_1, β_2 is not 0.
    6. $350.87 > F_{.01} = 9.55$
    7. p-value $= .000$. The model is significant at each level of α.
14.13 1. SSE $= 1,798,712.2$; $s^2 = 149,892.7$; $s = 387.1598$
    2. Total variation $= 464,126,601.6$; SSE $= 1,798,712.2$; Explained variation $= 462,327,889.4$
    3. $R^2 = 99.61\%$; $\bar{R}^2 = 99.52\%$
    4. F(model) $= 1028.1309$
    5. $1028.1309 > F_{.05} = 3.49$. Decide at least one of β_1, β_2, β_3 is not 0.
    6. $1028.1309 > F_{.01} = 5.95$
    7. p-value $= .000$. The model is significant at each level of α.
14.17 1. $b_0 = 29.347$, $s_{b_0} = 4.891$, $t = 6.00$; $b_1 = 5.6128$, $s_{b_1} = .2285$, $t = 24.56$; $b_2 = 3.8344$, $s_{b_2} = .4332$, $t = 8.85$
    2. β_0: $t = 6.00 > 2.365$. Reject H_0 and conclude $\beta_0 \neq 0$ at $\alpha = .05$
    β_1: $t = 24.56 > 2.365$; Reject H_0 and conclude $\beta_1 \neq 0$ at $\alpha = .05$
    β_2: $t = 8.85 > 2.365$. Reject H_0 and conclude $\beta_2 \neq 0$ at $\alpha = .05$
    Both x_1 and x_2 are significantly related to y at $\alpha = .05$.
    3. As in part 2, all 3 t statistics exceed the critical value 3.499, so conclude β_0, β_1, and β_2 all differ from 0 at $\alpha = .01$. Both x_1 and x_2 are significantly related to y.
    4. β_0: p-value $= .001$. Can reject H_0 at every α except .001.
    β_1: p-value $= .000$. Can reject H_0 at every α.
    β_2: p-value $= .000$. Can reject H_0 at every α.
    There is extremely strong evidence that x_1 and x_2 are related to y.
    5. β_0: [17.780, 40.914]
    β_1: [5.072, 6.153]
    β_2: [2.810, 4.860]
    6. β_0: [12.233, 46.461]
    β_1: [4.813, 6.412]
    β_2: [2.319, 5.350]
14.19 1. $b_0 = 1946.8020$, $s_{b_0} = 504.1819$, $t = 3.8613$;
    $b_1 = .0386$, $s_{b_1} = .0130$, $t = 2.9579$;
    $b_2 = 1.0394$, $s_{b_2} = .0676$, $t = 15.3857$;

$b_3 = -413.7578$, $s_{b_3} = 98.5983$, $t = -4.1964$
    2. β_0: $t = 3.8613 > 2.179$. Reject H_0 at $\alpha = .05$
    β_1: $t = 2.9579 > 2.179$. Reject H_0 at $\alpha = .05$
    β_2: $t = 15.3857 > 2.179$. Reject H_0 at $\alpha = .05$
    β_3: $t = -4.1964 < -2.179$. Reject H_0 at $\alpha = .05$
    x_1, x_2, and x_3 are significantly related to y at $\alpha = .05$.
    3. β_0: $t = 3.8613 > 3.055$. Reject H_0 at $\alpha = .01$.
    β_1: $t = 2.9579 < 3.055$. Cannot reject H_0 at $\alpha = .01$
    β_2: $t = 15.3857 > 3.055$. Reject H_0 at $\alpha = .01$
    β_3: $t = -4.1964 < -3.055$. Reject H_0 at $\alpha = .01$
    x_2 and x_3 are significantly related to y at $\alpha = .01$.
    4. β_0: p-value $= .0023$. Can reject H_0 at every α except .001
    β_1: p-value $= .0120$. Can reject H_0 at $\alpha = .10$ and .05 but not at .01 or .001.
    β_2: p-value $= .000$. Can reject H_0 at every α.
    β_3: p-value $= .0012$. Can reject H_0 at every α except .001.
    Evidence is extremely strong for x_2, very strong for x_3 and strong for x_1.
    5. β_0: [848.1896, 3045.4144]
    β_1: [.0103, .0669]
    β_2: [.8921, 1.1867]
    β_3: [$-628.6035, -198.9121$]
    6. β_0: [406.5263, 3487.0777]
    β_1: [$-.0011, .0783$]
    β_2: [.8329, 1.2459]
    β_3: [$-714.9756, -112.5400$]
14.23 a. 172.28; [168.56, 175.99]
    b. 172.28; [163.76, 180.80]
    c. [166.79, 177.77]; [159.68, 184.88]
14.25 [14,906.24, 16,886.26] Unusually high
14.29 a. Parallel linear plots with different intercepts.
    b. β_2 = mean difference between adoption times of stock and mutual companies of the same size.
    c. $|t_2| = 5.5208$; p-value $< .001$. Reject H_0 at both α values. Significant difference between company types. [4.9770, 11.1339]
    d. Slopes equal; no interaction.
14.31 b. $F = 184.57$; p-value $< .001$; reject H_0. Display heights affect sales.
    c. 21.4; [18.35, 24.45]; $|t_M| = 14.93$. Reject H_0: $\beta_M = 0$. Middle and bottom heights yield different mean sales. -4.3; [$-7.35, -1.25$]; $|t_T| = 3.00$. Reject H_0: $\beta_T = 0$. Top and bottom heights yield different mean sales. Estimate of $\beta_M - \beta_T$ is 25.7.
    d. 77.2; [75.04, 79.36]; [71.486, 82.914]
    e. [22.65, 28.75]; $|t| = 17.94$, p-value $< .001$. Reject H_0: $\beta_M = 0$. Middle and top heights yield different mean sales.
14.33 a. No interaction between expenditure and campaign type.
    b. 8.61178; [8.27089, 8.95266]; slightly longer.

14.37 b. Predicted price rises faster when $x_2 = 8$.

14.41 F(partial) $= 2.095$; $F_{.05} = 3.97$ (based on 5 numerator and 7 denominator degrees of freedom); F(partial) is less than $F_{.05}$, so conclude that none of the extra five squared and interaction terms is significant.

14.45 Option 1: Normal plot fairly straight; No outliers.
Option 2: No outliers.
Both options reasonable, but using

dummy variable for large hospitals gave slightly smaller s and a residual plot versus predicted that has more of a horizontal band appearance. It seems hospital 17 is not an outlier, given large hospital inefficiency.

14.47 The positive coefficient on x_2 (rooms) and the negative coefficient on x_3 (bedrooms) indicate that houses of a fixed size sell for higher prices when the open space is carved into more rooms that aren't bedrooms.

14.49 For example, increased attendance on weekday day games against rivals is estimated to be $4{,}745 + 5{,}059 + 696.5 = 10{,}500.5$. Promotions yield much larger increases when offered at weekday day games.

14.51 We estimate that average bike sales in spring, summer, and fall will be 21, 33.5, and 4.5 units higher than in winter.
$\hat{y}_{17} = 8.75 + .5(17) = 17.25$

References

Abraham, B., and J. Ledolter. *Statistical Methods for Forecasting.* New York, NY: John Wiley & Sons, 1983.

Akaah, Ishmael P., and Edward A. Riordan. "Judgments of Marketing Professionals about Ethical Issues in Marketing Research: A Replication and Extension." *Journal of Marketing Research,* February 1989, pp. 112–20.

Ashton, Robert H., John J. Willingham, and Robert K. Elliott. "An Empirical Analysis of Audit Delay." *Journal of Accounting Research* 25, no. 2 (Autumn 1987), pp. 275–92.

Axcel, Amir. *Complete Business Statistics.* 3rd ed. Burr Ridge, IL: Irwin/McGraw-Hill, 1996.

Bayus, Barry L. "The Consumer and Durable Replacement Buyer." *Journal of Marketing* 55 (January 1991), pp. 42–51.

Beattie, Vivien, and Michael John Jones. "The Use and Abuse of Graphs in Annual Reports: Theoretical Framework and Empirical Study." *Accounting and Business Research* 22, no. 88 (Autumn 1992), pp. 291–303.

Blauw, Jan Nico, and Willem E. During. "Total Quality Control in Dutch Industry." *Quality Progress* (February 1990), pp. 50–51.

Blodgett, Jeffrey G., Donald H. Granbois, and Rockney G. Walters. "The Effects of Perceived Justice on Complainants' Negative Word-of-Mouth Behavior and Repatronage Intentions." *Journal of Retailing* 69, no. 4 (Winter 1993), pp. 399–428.

Bowerman, Bruce L., and Richard T. O'Connell. *Forecasting and Time Series: An Applied Approach.* 3rd ed. Belmont, CA: Duxbury Press, 1993.

Bowerman, Bruce L., and Richard T. O'Connell. *Linear Statistical Models: An Applied Approach.* 2nd ed. Boston, MA: PWS-KENT Publishing Company, 1990, pp. 457, 460–64, 729–974.

Bowerman, Bruce L., Richard T. O'Connell, and Emily S. Murphree. *Business Statistics in Practice.* 6th ed. Burr Ridge, IL: McGraw-Hill, Irwin, 2011.

Box, G. E. P., and G. M. Jenkins. *Time Series Analysis: Forecasting and Control.* 2nd ed. San Francisco, CA: Holden-Day, 1976.

Boyd, Thomas C., and Timothy C. Krehbiel. "The Effect of Promotion Timing on Major League Baseball Attendance." *Sport Marketing Quarterly* 8, no. 4 (1999), pp. 23–34.

Brown, R. G. *Smoothing, Forecasting and Prediction of Discrete Time Series.* Englewood Cliffs, NJ: Prentice Hall, 1962.

Carey, John, Robert Neff, and Lois Therrien. "The Prize and the Passion." *Business Week* (Special 1991 bonus issue: The Quality Imperative), January 15, 1991, pp. 58–59.

Carslaw, Charles A. P. N., and Steven E. Kaplan. "An Examination of Audit Delay: Further Evidence from New Zealand." *Accounting and Business Research* 22, no. 85 (1991), pp. 21–32.

Cateora, Philip R. *International Marketing.* 9th ed. Homewood, IL: Irwin/McGraw-Hill, 1993, p. 262.

Clemen, Robert T. *Making Hard Decisions: An Introduction to Decision Analysis.* 2nd ed. Belmont, CA: Duxbury Press, 1996, p. 443.

Conlon, Edward J., and Thomas H. Stone. "Absence Schema and Managerial Judgment." *Journal of Management* 18, no. 3 (1992), pp. 435–54.

Cooper, Donald R., and C. William Emory. *Business Research Methods.* 5th ed. Homewood, IL: Richard D. Irwin, 1995, pp. 434–38, 450–51, 458–68.

Cuprisin, Tim. "Inside TV & Radio." *The Milwaukee Journal Sentinel,* April 26, 1995.

Dawson, Scott. "Consumer Responses to Electronic Article Surveillance Alarms." *Journal of Retailing* 69, no. 3 (Fall 1993), pp. 353–62.

Deming, W. Edwards. *Out of the Crisis.* Cambridge, MA: Massachusetts Institute of Technology Center for Advanced Engineering Study, 1986, pp. 18–96, 312–14.

Dielman, Terry. *Applied Regression Analysis for Business and Economics.* Belmont, CA: Duxbury Press, 1996.

Dillon, William R., Thomas J. Madden, and Neil H. Firtle. *Essentials of Marketing Research.* Homewood, IL: Richard D. Irwin Inc., 1993, pp. 382–84, 416–17, 419–20, 432–33, 445, 462–64, 524–27.

Dondero, Cort. "SPC Hits the Road." *Quality Progress,* January 1991, pp. 43–44.

Draper, N., and H. Smith. *Applied Regression Analysis.* 2nd ed. New York, NY: John Wiley & Sons, 1981.

Farnum, Nicholas R. *Modern Statistical Quality Control and Improvement.* Belmont, CA: Duxbury Press, 1994, p. 55.

Fitzgerald, Neil. "Relations Overcast by Cloudy Conditions." *CA Magazine,* April 1993, pp. 28–35.

Garvin, David A. *Managing Quality.* New York, NY: Free Press/ Macmillan, 1988.

Gibbons, J. D. *Nonparametric Statistical Inference.* 2nd ed. New York, NY: McGraw-Hill, 1985.

Gitlow, Howard, Shelly Gitlow, Alan Oppenheim, and Rosa Oppenheim. *Tools and Methods for the Improvement of Quality.* Homewood, IL: Richard D. Irwin, 1989, pp. 14–25, 533–53.

Guthrie, James P., Curtis M. Grimm, and Ken G. Smith. "Environmental Change and Management Staffing: A Reply." *Journal of Management* 19, no. 4 (1993), pp. 889–96.

Kuhn, Susan E. "A Closer Look at Mutual Funds: Which Ones Really Deliver?" *Fortune,* October 7, 1991, pp. 29–30.

Kumar, V., Roger A. Kerin, and Arun Pereira. "An Empirical Assessment of Merger and Acquisition Activity in Retailing." *Journal of Retailing* 67, no. 3 (Fall 1991), pp. 321–38.

Magee, Robert P. *Advanced Managerial Accounting.* New York, NY: Harper & Row, 1986, p. 223.

Mahmood, Mo Adam, and Gary J. Mann. "Measuring the Organizational Impact of Information Technology Investment: An Exploratory Study." *Journal of Management Information Systems* 10, no. 1 (Summer 1993), pp. 97–122.

Martocchio, Joseph J. "The Financial Cost of Absence Decisions." *Journal of Management* 18, no. 1 (1992), pp. 133–52.

Mendenhall, W., and J. Reinmuth. *Statistics for Management Economics.* 4th ed. Boston, MA: PWS-KENT Publishing Company, 1982.

The Miami University Report. Miami University, Oxford, OH, vol. 8, no. 26, 1989.

Moore, David S. *The Basic Practice of Statistics.* 2nd ed. New York: W. H. Freeman and Company, 2000.

Moore, David S., and George P. McCabe. *Introduction to the Practice of Statistics.* 2nd ed. New York: W. H. Freeman, 1993.

Morris, Michael H., Ramon A. Avila, and Jeffrey Allen. "Individualism and the Modern Corporation: Implications for Innovation and Entrepreneurship." *Journal of Management* 19, no. 3 (1993), pp. 595–612.

Neter, J., M. Kutner, C. Nachtsheim, and W. Wasserman. *Applied Linear Statistical Models.* 4th ed. Homewood, IL: Irwin/ McGraw-Hill, 1996.

Neter, J., W. Wasserman, and M. H. Kutner. *Applied Linear Statistical Models.* 2nd ed. Homewood, IL: Richard D. Irwin, 1985.

Nunnally, Bennie H., Jr., and D. Anthony Plath. *Cases in Finance.* Burr Ridge, IL: Richard D. Irwin, 1995, pp. 12-1–12-7.

Olmsted, Dan, and Gigi Anders. "Turned Off." *USA Weekend,* June 2–4, 1995.

Ott, Lyman. *An Introduction to Statistical Methods and Data Analysis.* 2nd ed. Boston, MA: PWS-Kent, 1987.

Schaeffer, R. L., William Mendenhall, and Lyman Ott. *Elementary Survey Sampling.* 3rd ed. Boston, MA: Duxbury Press, 1986.

Scherkenbach, William. *The Deming Route to Quality and Productivity: Road Maps and Roadblocks.* Washington, D.C.: Ceepress Books, 1986.

Seigel, James C. "Managing with Statistical Models." SAE Technical Paper 820520. Warrendale, PA: Society for Automotive Engineers, Inc., 1982.

Sichelman, Lew. "Random Checks Find Loan Application Fibs." *The Journal-News* (Hamilton, Ohio), Sept. 26, 1992 (originally published in *The Washington Post*).

Siegel, Andrew F. *Practical Business Statistics.* 2nd ed. Homewood, IL: Richard D. Irwin, 1990, p. 588.

Silk, Alvin J., and Ernst R. Berndt. "Scale and Scope Effects on Advertising Agency Costs." *Marketing Science* 12, no. 1 (Winter 1993), pp. 53–72.

Stevenson, William J. *Production/Operations Management.* 6th ed. Homewood, IL: Irwin/McGraw-Hill, 1999, p. 228.

Thomas, Anisya S., and Kannan Ramaswamy. "Environmental Change and Management Staffing: A Comment." *Journal of Management* 19, no. 4 (1993), pp. 877–87.

Von Neumann, J., and O. Morgenstern. *Theory of Games and Economic Behavior.* 2nd ed. Princeton, NJ: Princeton University Press, 1947.

Walton, Mary. *The Deming Management Method.* New York, NY: Dodd, Mead & Company, 1986.

Weinberger, Marc G., and Harlan E. Spotts. "Humor in U.S. versus U.K. TV Commercials: A Comparison." *Journal of Advertising* 18, no. 2 (1989), pp. 39–44.

Wright, Thomas A., and Douglas G. Bonett. "Role of Employee Coping and Performance in Voluntary Employee Withdrawal: A Research Refinement and Elaboration." *Journal of Management* 19, no. 1 (1993) pp. 147–61.

Photo Credits

Chapter 1
Page 2: © ML Harris/Getty Images
Page 6: © Brand X Pictures/PunchStock
Page 9: © John Foxx Images/Imagestate
Page 10: © AFP/Getty Images
Page 16: © Dave Robertson/Masterfile

Chapter 2
Page 34: © Janis Christie/Getty Images
Page 35: © Stan Honda/AFP/Getty Images
Page 56: © Stockbyte/Getty Images
Page 61: © Digital Vision/Getty Images
Page 70: © Comstock/JupiterImages

Chapter 3
Page 100: © Javier Larrea/age footstock
Page 102: © Stockbyte/Getty Images
Page 116: © Andy Ridder/VISUM/The Image Works

Chapter 4
Page 154: © Colorblind/Getty Images
Page 172: © Royalty Free/Corbis

Chapter 5
Page 190: © AFP/Getty Images
Page 197: © Don Smetzer/Getty Images
Page 204: © John Gress/Reuters/Corbis

Chapter 6
Page 228: © Chris P Batson/Alamy
Page 241: © Blend Images/Getty Images
Page 244: © Rick Bowmer/AP Images

Chapter 7
Page 270: © Royalty-Free/Corbis
Page 276: © David McNew/Getty Images

Page 284: © Royalty Free/Corbis
Page 294: © Michael N. Paras/age footstock

Chapter 8
Page 304: © Steve Cole/Getty Images
Page 320: © Brian Pieters/Masterfile

Chapter 9
Page 342: © David Katzenstein
Page 344: © Yellow Dog Productions/Getty Images
Page 345: © Steve Cole/Getty Images

Chapter 10
Page 386: © Comstock Images/Getty Images
Page 387: © Digital Vision/Getty Images
Page 397: © Spencer Grant/PhotoEdit

Chapter 11
Page 428: Special Thank You to Savemart, Oakdale, CA.
© Jill Braaten

Chapter 12
Page 462: © Jill Braaten

Chapter 13
Page 490: © blue jean images/Getty Images
Page 529: © Royalty Free/Corbis

Chapter 14
Page 558: © Royalty Free/Corbis
Page 582: © Ryan McVay/Getty Images
Page 587: © Justin Sullivan/Getty Images.

Index

Page numbers followed by n refer to notes.

A

Accenture, 42
ACNielsen, 6
Addition rule, 166, 167, 168
Adjusted multiple coefficient of
    determination, 572
Akaah, Ishmael P., 326
Alam, Pervaiz, 480, 481
Alson, Jeff, 11n
Alternative (research) hypothesis, 343–345;
    see also Hypothesis testing
  definition, 377
  greater than, 349–351
  less than, 352–353
  not equal to, 354–355
  one-sided, 345, 349–356
  two-sided, 345, 371–373
Analysis of variance (ANOVA), 429
  one-way, 431–438
  randomized block design, 441–445
  two-way, 447–453
Analysis of variance table, 435, 442–443, 455
Andrews, R. L., 565
ANOVA; *see* Analysis of variance
Ashton, Robert H., 335
Autocorrelation
  first-order, 538–539
  negative, 536
  positive, 535–536

B

Back-to-back stem-and-leaf displays,
    58–59
Bar charts, 36–37, 73; *see also* Pareto charts
Barnett, A., 188
Bayes' theorem, 178–181, 185
Bayesian statistics, 181, 185
Bayus, Barry L., 313, 363
Beattie, Vivien, 336
Bell-shaped curve, 113–114; *see also*
    Normal curve
Berndt, Ernst R., 313
Between-treatment variability, 432–433
Binomial distribution, 203–211
  definition, 221
  mean, variance, and standard deviation, 211
  normal approximation of, 252–255
Binomial experiments, 205, 221
Binomial formula, 205–206
Binomial random variables, 205, 221
Binomial tables, 207–208, 221, 631–635
Bissell, H. H., 548
Bivariate normal probability distribution, 525
Blauw, Jan Nico, 320
Block, Stanley B., 72, 201, 202
Blodgett, Jeffrey G., 337
Bloomberg, 6
Boundaries, class, 43
Bowerman, Bruce L., 181, 319, 361, 394, 401,
    438, 525, 562, 580

Box-and-whiskers displays (box plots),
    123–125, 141
Boyd, Thomas C., 617–618
Branch, Shelly, 331n

C

C statistic, 606
Carslaw, Charles A. P. N., 313
Categorical (qualitative) variables, 4, 14–15, 16
Categories, 463
Cateora, Philip R., 410, 411
CBS, 352
Cell frequencies, 472, 473, 476
Cell percentages, 472–473
Cells, 463
Censuses, 7, 16
Central Limit Theorem, 282–285, 298
Central tendency, 101–107
  definition, 141
  mean, 101–103, 105–107
  measures of, 101
  median, 103–104, 105–107
  mode, 104, 105–107
Chambers, S., 551
Charts; *see* Graphs
Chebyshev's Theorem, 116–117, 141
Chi-square distribution, 374, 378
Chi-square goodness-of-fit tests, 463
  for multinomial probabilities, 463–466
  for normality, 467–469
Chi-square point, 374
Chi-square statistic, 464, 466
Chi-square table, 374–375, 648
Chi-square test for independence, 463,
    472–477, 480
Class boundaries, 43
Class lengths, 42–43, 45, 46
Class midpoints, 45, 73
Cleary, Barbara A., 41
Cluster sampling, 292–293, 298
Coates, R., 16
Coefficient of variation, 117–118, 141
Column percentages, 63, 472–473
Comparisonwise error rate, 436
Complement, of event, 163–165, 185
Complete models, 608
Completely randomized experimental design,
    429–430, 438, 455
Conditional probability, 169–171, 185
Confidence coefficient, 308, 334
Confidence intervals, 305
  compared to tolerance intervals, 332–333
  definition, 334
  general formula, 308–311
  multiple regression model, 578, 579–581
  one-sided, 356
  for population mean, known standard deviation,
    305–311
  for population mean, unknown standard
    deviation, 314–319
  for population proportion, 325–329

randomized block design, 443
sample sizes, 321–324
simple linear regression, 510, 514–517
simultaneous, 436–437
testing hypotheses with, 356
two-sided, 356
two-way ANOVA, 452
Confidence level, 305, 307, 310, 334
Constant variance assumption
  multiple linear regression, 570
  residual analysis, 533, 535
  simple linear regression model, 504
Contingency tables, 165, 463, 472–473, 480
Continuity correction, 253
Continuous probability distribution, 229–230, 262
Continuous random variables, 191–192, 221
Convenience sampling, 274, 298
Cook's distance measure, 613–614
Cooper, Donald R., 126, 127, 395, 478, 481
Corbette, M. F., 291n
Correlation
  auto-, 535–536
  causation and, 524
  negative, 131–132, 523
  positive, 131, 523
Correlation coefficient
  definition, 141
  multiple, 571–572
  population, 132, 525
  sample, 131–132
  simple, 523–524
Correlation matrix, 602
Counting rules, 161, 182–184
Covariance
  definition, 129, 141
  population, 132
  sample, 129–131
  of two random variables, 200
Cravens, David W., 583
Critical value rule, 349–350, 352, 359
Critical values, 351–352, 378
Cross-sectional data, 4, 16
Cross-tabulation tables, 61–64, 73
Cumulative frequency distributions, 49–50, 73
Cumulative normal table, 236–239, 262
Cumulative percent frequencies, 50
Cumulative percent frequency distribution, 73
Cumulative percentage point, 39
Cumulative relative frequencies, 50
Cumulative relative frequency distribution, 73
Cuprisin, Tim, 299
Curvature rates, 596

D

D'Ambrosio, P., 551
Data; *see also* Observations; Variables
  definition, 3, 16
  sources, 5–6
Data sets, 3, 16
Decision theory, 181, 185; *see also*
    Bayes' theorem

Degrees of freedom (*df*), 314, 334, 374
Deleted residuals, 613
Deloitte & Touche Consulting, 42
Denman, D. W., 76
Dependent events, 173, 185
Dependent variables; *see also* Regression
  analysis; Response variables
    definition, 547
    predicted values, 496
    in simple linear regression, 491
    transformation, 539–542
Descriptive statistics, 8, 16, 35; *see also* Central
    tendency; Variance
    grouped data, 135–137
    variation measures, 110–118
Designed experiments, 429; *see also* Experiments
df; *see* Degrees of freedom
Dichotomous questions, 293–294
Dillon, William R., 9n, 69, 169, 326, 367, 403,
    409, 420, 479
Discrete random variables, 191
    definition, 221
    mean (expected value), 195–198
    probability distributions, 192–200
    standard deviation, 198–200
    variance, 198–199
Distance values, 515, 547, 580–581, 612
Distributions; *see* Frequency distributions
Dot plots, 54–55, 73
Dow Jones & Company, 6
Dummy variables, 584–591, 615
Dun & Bradstreet, 6
Durbin, J., 649, 650
Durbin–Watson statistic, 538–539
    critical values, 649–650
During, Willem E., 320

E

Educational Testing Service, 6
Elber, Lynn, 177, 290
Elements, 3, 4, 7, 16
Elliott, Robert K., 335
Emenyonu, Emmanuel N., 478
Emory, C. William, 126, 127, 395, 478, 481
Empirical Rule
    areas under normal curve and, 235, 240–241
    definition, 141
    for normally distributed population, 113–114
    skewness and, 116
Environmental Protection Agency (EPA),
    11, 12, 116
Equality, 345
Ernst & Young Consulting, 42
Error mean square (MSE), 434
Error sum of squares (SSE), 434, 442,
    449, 450
Error term, 493–494, 547
Errors
    of non-observation, 295–296, 298
    of observation, 295, 296–297, 298
    sampling, 295–297
    in surveys, 295–297
Estimated regression line, 495–496
Events, 158–159
    complement, 163–165
    definition, 158, 185
    dependent, 173
    independent, 172–174
    intersection of, 166
    mutually exclusive, 166–168
    probability, 159–161
    union of, 166
Excel applications
    analysis of variance, 435, 436, 457–458
    Analysis ToolPak, 82

bar charts, 36–37, 81
binomial probabilities, 207, 224
chi-square tests, 483–484
confidence intervals, 318, 319, 338–339
contingency tables, 473
crosstabulation tables, 86–87
experimental design, 457–458
frequency histograms, 47, 82–85
frequency polygons, 85
getting started, 18–23
hypergeometric probabilities, 224
hypothesis testing, 382
interaction model, 599
least squares line, 147
least squares point estimates, 562
multiple linear regression, 620–622
multiple regression analysis, 583–584
normal distribution, 266–267
numerical descriptive statistics, 146–149
ogives, 86
Pareto charts, 38–39
pie charts, 37, 38, 82
Poisson probabilities, 225
p-values, 366
random numbers, 301
randomized block ANOVA, 443, 444
runs plot, 21
sample correlation coefficient, 149
sample covariance, 148
scatter plots, 87
simple linear regression analysis, 509, 552–553
tabular and graphical methods, 80–87
two-sample hypothesis testing, 422–423
two-way ANOVA, 451
Expected value of random variable, 195–198, 221
Experimental outcomes, 155–156, 182–184
Experimental region, 498–499, 500, 547
Experimental studies, 6, 16
Experimental units, 429, 455
Experiments
    basic design concepts, 429–431
    binomial, 205
    definition, 155, 185
    independent samples, 418
    paired differences, 397–401
    randomized, 429–430, 438
    randomized block design, 441–445
    sample spaces, 157
    two-factor factorial, 448–449
Experimentwise error rate, 437
Explained variation, 521, 524, 547, 604
Exponential distribution, 256–257, 262–263
Extreme outliers, 123–124, 141

F

F distribution, 412–413, 418
F point, 412–413
F table, 412–413, 642–645
F test, 417
    differences between treatment means, 434–435
    overall, 573–574
    partial, 608–609
    simple linear regression model, 526–528
Factors, 6, 16, 429, 448, 455
Farnum, Nicholas R., 142, 216
Federal Trade Commission (FTC), 294–295, 368
Ferguson, J. T., 565
Finite population multiplier, 285
Finite populations, 11, 16
First-order autocorrelation, 538–539
First quartile, 121–122, 141
Firtle, Neil H., 9n, 69, 169, 326, 367, 403, 409,
    420, 479
Fitzgerald, Neil, 331
Five-number summary, 122–123

Ford, John K., 300
Frames, 292, 295–296
Freeman, L., 16
Frequencies; *see also* Relative frequencies
    cumulative, 49–50
    definition, 35
    finding, 44
Frequency bar charts, 36–37
Frequency distributions, 35–36, 44
    constructing, 45
    cumulative, 49–50
    definition, 73
    mound-shaped, 47, 116
    shapes, 47–48, 105
    skewness, 47, 105, 116
Frequency histograms; *see* Histograms
Frequency polygons, 48–49, 73
Frommer, F. J., 214n

G

Gallup, George, 274
Gallup Organization, 79
Gaudard, M., 16
General multiplication rule, 171
Geometric mean, 139, 141
Giges, Nancy, 265
Goodness-of-fit tests
    for multinomial probabilities, 463–466, 480
    for normality, 467–469, 480
Graduate Management Admission Council, 6
Granbois, Donald H., 337
Graphs
    bar charts, 36–37
    box-and-whiskers displays, 123–125
    dot plots, 54–55
    frequency polygons, 48–49
    histograms, 42–47
    misleading, 70–71
    normal probability plots, 259–262
    ogives, 50
    Pareto charts, 38–39
    pie charts, 37, 38
    residual plots, 531–532
    scatter plots, 67–68, 491
    stem-and-leaf displays, 56–59, 534–535
Gray, Sidney J., 478
Greater than alternative hypothesis, 345,
    349–351, 378
Grouped data, 135–137, 141
Gunn, E. P., 291n
Gupta, S., 470

H

Hald, A., 650
Hartley, H. O., 315
Heller, Jeffrey, 128
Hildebrand, D. K., 635, 637
Hirt, Geoffrey A., 72, 201, 202
Histograms, 42
    constructing, 42–47
    definition, 73
    percent frequency, 45
    relative frequency, 45
Homogeneity, test for, 466, 480
Horizontal bar charts, 37
Howard, Theresa, 9n
Hypergeometric distribution, 212, 219–220, 221
Hypothesis testing, 343
    about population mean, 349–356
    about population proportion, 363–366
    alternative hypothesis, 343–345
    confidence intervals, 356
    critical value rule, 349–350, 351–352
    legal system and, 346

Hypothesis testing—*Cont.*
    null hypothesis, 343–345, 356
    one-sided alternative hypothesis, 345, 349–356
    p-values, 350–352, 355
    steps, 352
    t tests, 359–361
    two-sided alternative hypothesis, 371–373
    Type I and Type II errors, 346–347, 349, 368–373
    weight of evidence, 356
    z tests, 349–356, 363–366

I

Independence assumption
    chi-square test, 463, 472–477
    multiple linear regression, 570
    residual analysis, 535–537
    simple linear regression model, 504
Independent events, 172–174, 185
Independent samples
    comparing population means, 387–394
    comparing population proportions, 405–408
    comparing population variances, 411–417
Independent samples experiment, 418
Independent variables; *see also* Regression analysis
    adding to models, 604
    definition, 547
    interaction, 589, 598–600
    multicollinearity, 601–604
    significance, 575–578
    in simple linear regression, 491
Indicator variables; *see* Dummy variables
Infinite populations, 11, 16
Information Resources, Inc., 6
Inner fences, 123, 124, 141
Interaction, 450, 455, 589, 615
Interaction sum of squares, 449
Interaction variables, 598–600, 607–608
Interquartile range (IQR), 123, 141
Intersection, of events, 166
Interval variables, 14, 16
Intervals of values, 229
IQR; *see* Interquartile range

J

Jones, Michael John, 336
Judgment sampling, 274, 298

K

Kaplan, Steven E., 313
Kerrich, John, 156n
Kerwin, Roger A., 379, 419
Krehbiel, Timothy C., 617–618
Krohn, Gregory, 404
Kruskal-Wallis *H* test, 438
Kumar, V., 379, 419
Kutner, M., 591

L

Landon, Alf, 274
Least squares line, 132–133, 141, 496
Least squares plane, 563
Least squares point estimates
    definition, 547
    means, 563–564
    multiple regression model, 561–563
    simple linear regression model, 495–500
Least squares prediction equation, 497–498, 563
Leaves, 56–57
Left-hand tail area, 239, 246

Less than alternative hypothesis, 345, 352–353, 378
Level of significance, 349
Leverage values, 612; *see also* Distance values
Levy, Haim, 550
Liebeck, Stella, 16
Line charts; *see* Runs plots
Line of means, 493
Linear regression models; *see* Multiple regression model; Simple linear regression model
Linear relationships, 67, 129
Literary Digest poll (1936), 274, 296
Logarithmic transformation, 540
Long-run relative frequencies, 156

M

Ma, Lan, 5
Madden, Thomas J., 9n, 69, 169, 326, 367, 403, 409, 420, 479
Magee, Robert P., 251
Mahmood, Mo Adam, 337
Mail surveys, 295
Makridakis, S., 545
Mann, Gary J., 337
Mann-Whitney test; *see* Wilcoxon rank sum test
Margin of error, 310, 328–329, 334
Martocchio, Joseph J., 287
Mason, J. M., 548
Matrix algebra, 562
Mazis, M. B., 76
McCabe, George P., 466, 476
McGee, V. E., 545
Mean; *see also* Population mean
    binomial random variable, 211
    compared to median and mode, 105–107
    discrete random variable, 195–198
    geometric, 139
    least squares point estimates, 563–564
    normal distribution, 234–235
    Poisson random variable, 217
    sample, 102–103, 136
    weighted, 134–135
Mean level, 493, 560
Mean square error, 505–506, 570–571
Mean squares, 433, 434
Measurements, 4, 7, 14, 16
Measures of variation, 110, 141
Median, 103–104, 105–107, 141
MegaStat applications
    analysis of variance, 458–459
    bar charts, 88
    binomial probabilities, 226
    box-and-whiskers display, 150
    chi-square tests, 485–487
    confidence intervals, 339–340
    crosstabulation tables, 90–91
    dot plots, 90
    experimental design, 458–459
    frequency polygons, 89
    getting started, 23–27
    histograms, 88–89
    hypergeometric probabilities, 226
    hypothesis testing, 383–384
    least squares line, 150
    multiple linear regression, 623–625
    normal distribution, 267–268
    normal plot, 534
    numerical descriptive statistics, 149–151
    ogives, 89
    Poisson probabilities, 226
    random numbers, 302
    runs plot, 26–27
    sample correlation coefficient, 151
    scatter plots, 91
    simple linear regression analysis, 554–555

stem-and-leaf display, 90
    tabular and graphical methods, 88–91
    two-sample hypothesis testing, 423–424
Meier, Heidi Hylton, 480, 481
Mendenhall, William, 292, 293
Merrington, M., 413, 642, 643, 644, 645
Mild outliers, 123–124, 141
Minimum-variance unbiased point estimate, 284–285, 298
MINITAB applications
    analysis of variance, 435, 436, 460–461
    bar charts, 37, 92–93
    binomial probabilities, 210, 227
    box-and-whiskers display, 124, 152
    chi-square tests, 487–489
    confidence intervals, 318–319, 340–341
    contingency tables, 472–473
    correlation matrices, 602
    crosstabulation tables, 98
    distance values, 581
    dot plots, 97
    Durbin–Watson statistic, 538–539
    experimental design, 460–461
    five-number summary, 122–123
    frequency histograms, 46, 95–96
    frequency polygons, 96
    getting started, 27–33
    hypergeometric probabilities, 227
    hypothesis testing, 360, 384–385
    least squares line, 152, 498
    least squares point estimates, 562
    multiple linear regression, 626–629
    normal distribution, 268–269
    normal plot, 534
    numerical descriptive statistics, 151–153
    ogives, 97
    pie charts, 94
    Poisson distribution, 216, 227
    quadratic regression, 597, 598
    random numbers, 272, 273, 302
    randomized block ANOVA, 443, 444
    residual plots, 532, 537
    runs plot, 29–30
    sample correlation coefficient, 153
    sample covariance, 153
    sampling distribution of sample mean, 282–284
    sampling distributions, 303
    scatter plots, 99
    simple linear regression analysis, 509, 556–557
    stem-and-leaf display, 57–58, 98
    stepwise regression, 607
    tabular and graphical methods, 92–99
    transformation of dependent variable, 541–542
    two-sample hypothesis testing, 425–427
    two-way ANOVA, 451
    unequal variances procedure, 393–394
    variance inflation factors, 602–603
Mode, 104, 105–107, 141
Model building
    adding independent variables, 604
    comparing models, 604–606
    multicollinearity, 601–604
Moore, David S., 466, 476
Mound-shaped distributions, 47, 116, 141
MSE; *see* Error mean square
MST; *see* Treatment mean square
Multicollinearity, 601–604, 615
Multinomial experiments, 463–464, 480
Multiple choice questions, 293–294
Multiple coefficient of determination, 571–572
Multiple correlation coefficient, 571–572
Multiple regression model, 538, 559–565, 615
    assumptions, 569–570
    confidence intervals, 578, 579–581
    dummy variables, 584–591

least squares point estimates, 561–563
mean square error, 570–571
multicollinearity, 601–604
multiple coefficient of determination, 571–572
multiple correlation coefficient, 571–572
overall F test, 573–574
point estimation, 563–564
point prediction, 564
prediction intervals, 579–581
quadratic, 596, 607
regression parameters, 560–561, 564
residual analysis, 610–614
significance of independent variable, 575–578
standard error, 570–571
stepwise regression, 606–607
Multiplication rule
general, 171
for independent events, 174
Multistage cluster sampling, 292–293
Murphree, Emily S., 319, 361, 394, 401, 438, 525
Mutually exclusive events, 166–168, 185
Myers, Dale H., 128

N

Nachtsheim, C., 591
NBC, 352
Negative autocorrelation, 536, 547
Negative correlation, 131–132
Neter, J., 591
Nominative variables, 14, 15, 16
Nonparametric methods, 319, 361
    Kruskal-Wallis H test, 438
    Spearman's rank correlation coefficient, 525
    Wilcoxon rank sum test, 394
    Wilcoxon signed ranks test, 401
Nonresponse, 296, 298
Normal curve, 113–114
    areas under, 235–241
    cumulative areas under, 236–240
    definition, 141
    left-hand tail area, 239, 246
    points on horizontal axis, 244–245, 246
    properties, 234–235
    right-hand tail area, 238, 239–240, 244–246
Normal distribution
    approximation of binomial distribution, 252–255
    bivariate, 525
    Empirical Rule, 113–114
    goodness-of-fit test, 467–469
Normal probability distribution, 234, 242, 263
Normal probability plot, 259, 534
    constructing, 259–260, 262
    definition, 263, 547
    interpreting, 260–262
Normal table, 235, 650
    cumulative, 236–239, 638–639
Normality assumption
    chi-square goodness-of-fit test, 467–469
    multiple linear regression, 570
    residual analysis, 534
    simple linear regression model, 504
Not equal to alternative hypothesis, 345, 354–355, 378
Null hypothesis, 343–345, 356, 378; *see also* Hypothesis testing
Nunnally, Bennie H., Jr., 332, 409

O

Observational studies, 6, 16
Observations, 7, 155, 429
O'Connell, Richard T., 181, 319, 361, 394, 401, 438, 525, 562, 580
O'Connor, Catherine, 404

Ogives, 50, 73
One-sample hypothesis testing; *see* Hypothesis testing
One-sided alternative hypothesis, 345, 349–356
One-sided confidence intervals, 356
One-way ANOVA, 431–438
    assumptions, 431–432
    between-treatment variability, 432–433
    definition, 455
    estimation, 437
    pairwise comparisons, 435–438
    testing for significant differences between treatment means, 432–435
    within-treatment variability, 432–434
Open-ended questions, 293–294
Ordinal variables, 14–15, 16
Orris, J. B., 23, 641
Ott, L., 292, 293, 635, 637
Outer fences, 123, 124, 141
Outliers, 611–613
    definition, 73, 123
    detecting, 55, 59, 123–124
    mild and extreme, 123–124
Overall F test, 573–574
Ozanne, M. R., 291n

P

Paired differences experiment, 397–401, 418
Pairwise comparisons, 435–438
Parabolas, 596
Parameters, binomial distribution, 211
Pareto, Vilfredo, 38
Pareto charts, 38–39, 73
Pareto principle, 38
Partial F test, 608–609
Pearson, E. S., 315
Pearson, Michael A., 480, 481
Percent bar charts, 37
Percent frequencies, 36
    cumulative, 50
Percent frequency distributions, 36, 44, 73
Percent frequency histograms, 45
Percentage points, 328–329
Percentiles, 120–121, 141; *see also* Quartiles
Pereira, Arun, 379, 419
Perry, E. S., 76
Phone surveys, 294–295
Pie charts, 37, 38, 73
Pilkington, G. B., II, 548
Plane of means, 560, 563
Plath, D. Anthony, 332, 409
Point estimates, 101, 564; *see also* Least squares point estimates
    definition, 141
    minimum-variance unbiased, 284–285
    randomized block design, 443
    two-way ANOVA, 452
    unbiased, 278, 284–285
Point prediction, 564
Poisson distribution, 213–217, 221
Poisson probability table, 635–637
Poisson random variable, 214, 217, 221
Polls; *see* Surveys
Pooled estimates, 389
Population correlation coefficient, 132, 525
Population covariance, 132
Population mean, 101, 102–103
    comparing using independent samples, 387–394
    confidence intervals, known standard deviation, 305–311
    confidence intervals, unknown standard deviation, 314–319
    definition, 141
    grouped data, 137

paired differences experiment, 397–401
    t tests, 359–361
    z tests, 349–356
Population parameter, 101, 141
Population proportion
    comparing using large, independent samples, 405–408
    confidence intervals, 325–329
    z tests, 363–366
Population standard deviation, 111–112, 141
Population variance, 111–112
    comparing with independent samples, 411–417
    definition, 141
    grouped data, 137
    statistical inference, 375–376
Populations, 7–8, 16
    comparing, 387
    finite, 11, 16, 285
    infinite, 11, 16
Positive autocorrelation, 535–536, 547
Positive correlation, 131
Posterior probability, 178, 179, 185
Power, of statistical test, 371
Power curve, 373
Prediction intervals, 514–517, 579–581
Preliminary samples, 323–324
Prior probability, 178, 185
Probability, 155–156
    classical, 156
    conditional, 169–171
    of event, 159–161, 185
    subjective, 156
Probability curves, 229
Probability density function, 229
Probability distributions; *see also* Binomial distribution; Normal distribution
    continuous, 229–230
    of discrete random variable, 192–200, 221
    uniform, 231–233
Probability rules, 163
    addition rule, 166, 167, 168
    multiplication rule, 171, 174
    rule of complements, 163
Probability sampling, 274, 298
Processes, 11–12, 16
Proportion; *see* Population proportion; Sample proportion
pth percentile, 120–121
p-value (probability value)
    compared to critical value method, 351–352
    definition, 378
    greater than alternative hypothesis testing, 350–352
    less than alternative hypothesis testing, 352–353
    not equal to alternative hypothesis testing, 355
    t tests, 359
    testing null hypothesis, 356

Q

Quadratic regression model, 596, 607
Qualitative data, graphical summaries; *see* Bar charts; Pie charts
Qualitative variables, 4, 16
    dummy variables, 584–591
    measurement scales, 14–15
Quality, Pareto principle, 38
Quantitative data, graphical summaries; *see* Frequency distributions; Histograms
Quantitative variables, 4, 14, 16
Quartic root transformation, 540
Quartiles, 121–123
Queueing theory, 257, 263
Queues, 257

R

Random number table, 8, 272, 298
Random samples
    completely randomized experimental design,
        429–430, 438
    definition, 271, 298
    frames, 292
    importance, 274
    sampling with replacement, 271
    sampling without replacement, 271–272
    selecting, 8
    stratified, 291–292
Random selection, 271
Random variables; *see also* Discrete
        random variables
    binomial, 205
    continuous, 191–192
    definition, 191, 221
Randomized block design, 438, 441–445
    confidence intervals, 443
    definition, 455
    point estimates, 443
Ranges, 110–111
    definition, 141
    interquartile, 123
Ranking, 14
Rare event approach, 209
Ratio variables, 14, 16
Rebalancing, 78–79
Recording errors, 296
Reduced models, 608
Regression analysis, 491, 604–606; *see also*
        Multiple regression model; Simple linear
        regression model
Regression assumptions, 504–505
Regression model, 492
Regression parameters, 494, 560–561, 564
Regression residuals, 531; *see also* Residuals
Rejection point; *see* Critical value rule
Relative frequencies
    cumulative, 50
    definition, 36, 44
    long-run, 156
Relative frequency distributions, 36, 73
Relative frequency histograms, 45
Replication, 429, 455
Research hypothesis; *see* Alternative
        (research) hypothesis
Residual analysis
    assumption of correct functional form,
        534, 535
    constant variance assumption, 533, 535
    independence assumption, 535–537
    multiple regression, 610–614
    normality assumption, 534
    simple linear regression model, 531–537
    transformation of dependent variable, 539–542
Residual plots, 531–532, 547
Residuals
    definition, 547
    deleted, 613
    in multiple regression, 563
    in simple linear regression, 496, 531
    studentized, 613, 614
    sum of squared, 496, 546–547, 563
Response bias, 296–297, 298
Response rates, 294, 295, 298
Response variables, 6, 16, 429, 455
Right-hand tail area, 238, 239–240, 244–246
Ringold, D. J., 76
Riordan, Edward A., 326
Roosevelt, Franklin D., 274
Row percentages, 63, 472–473
Rule of complements, 163
Runs plots, 5, 68

S

Sample block means, 441
Sample correlation coefficient, 131–132
Sample covariance, 129–131
Sample frames, 292, 295–296, 298
Sample mean, 102–103, 136, 141; *see also*
        Sampling distribution of sample mean
Sample proportion, sampling distribution of,
        288–289
Sample sizes, 102
    for confidence interval for population
        proportion, 327–329
    definition, 141
    determination, 294, 321–324
    sampling distribution and, 282–284
    Type I and Type II error probabilities, 372
Sample space outcomes, 157–158, 161, 185
Sample spaces, 157, 185
Sample standard deviation, 112–113, 141
Sample statistic
    definition, 101–102, 141
    sampling distribution of, 284–285
Sample treatment means, 441
Sample variance, 112–113, 136–137, 141
Samples; *see also* Independent samples;
        Random samples
    cluster, 292–293
    definition, 7, 16
    of measurements, 7
    preliminary, 323–324
    systematic, 293
    voluntary response, 274, 296
Sampling
    convenience, 274
    judgment, 274
    probability, 274
    with replacement, 271, 298
    without replacement, 271–272, 298
    for surveys, 291–293
    undercoverage, 296
Sampling distribution comparing population
        means, 388, 418
Sampling distribution comparing population
        proportions, 405–408, 418
Sampling distribution comparing population
        variances, 412, 418
Sampling distribution of sample mean,
        275–282, 298
    Central Limit Theorem, 282–285
    unbiasedness and minimum-variance estimates,
        284–285
Sampling distribution of sample proportion,
        288–289, 298
Sampling distribution of sample statistic,
        284–285, 298
Sampling error, 295–297, 298
Scatter plots, 67–68, 73–74, 491, 531–532
Schaeffer, R. L., 292, 293
Scheffe, Henry, 647
Second quartile, 121–122
Selection bias, 296, 298
Shift parameters, 596
Sichelman, Lew, 330
Silk, Alvin J., 313
Sills, Jonathan, 110
Simonoff, Jeffrey S., 5
Simple coefficient of determination, 520–522, 547
Simple correlation coefficient, 523–524, 547
Simple linear regression model, 491–495
    assumptions, 504–505
    confidence intervals, 510, 514–517
    definition, 547
    distance values, 515
    Durbin–Watson statistic, 538–539
    F test, 526–528
    least squares point estimates, 495–500
    mean square error, 505–506
    point estimation, 500
    point prediction, 500
    prediction intervals, 514–517
    residual analysis, 531–537
    significance of slope, 507–509
    significance of *y*-intercept, 510
    simple coefficient of determination, 520–522
    simple correlation coefficient, 523–524
    standard error, 505–506
Simpson, O. J., 181
Simultaneous confidence intervals, 436–437
Skewed to left, 47, 74, 105–106
Skewed to right, 47, 74, 105
Skewness, Empirical Rule and, 116
Slope, 132
Slope, of simple linear regression model, 493, 494
    confidence interval, 510
    definition, 547
    least squares point estimates, 496
    significance, 507–509
Spearman's rank correlation coefficient, 525
Spotts, Harlan E., 331, 409
Square root transformation, 539–540
Squared variables, 596–598, 607–608
SSE; *see* Error sum of squares
SST; *see* Treatment sum of squares
SSTO; *see* Total sum of squares
Stamper, Joseph C., 583
Standard deviation
    binomial random variable, 211
    normal distribution, 234–235
    Poisson random variable, 217
    population, 111–112
    of random variable, 198–200, 221
    sample, 112–113
Standard error, 505–506, 515, 570–571
Standard error of the estimate, 318, 335, 507, 576
Standard normal curve, areas under, 244–246,
        638–639, 650
Standard normal distribution, 236, 263
Standardized normal quantile value, 259–260
Standardized value; *see z*-scores
States of nature, 179
Statistical inference
    definition, 8, 16
    generalizing, 155
    for population variance, 375–376
    rare event approach, 209
Statistical significance, 350
Statistics, 3
Stem-and-leaf displays, 56, 74
    back-to-back, 58–59
    constructing, 56–58
    of residuals, 534–535
    symmetrical, 57
Stems, 56
Stepwise regression, 606–607, 615
Stevens, Doug L., 8
Straight-line relationships; *see*
        Linear relationships
Strata, 291, 298
Stratified random samples, 291–292, 298
Studentized deleted residuals, 613, 614
Studentized range, percentage points of, 646–647
Studentized residuals, 613, 614
Subjective probability, 156, 185
Sum of squared residuals (errors), 496,
        546–547, 563
Sums of squares, 433
Surveys
    definition, 16
    errors, 295–297
    Literary Digest poll (1936), 274, 296
    mail, 295

margins of error, 328–329
nonresponse, 296
phone, 294–295
pilot, 294
questions, 6, 293–294
response rates, 294, 295
sample sizes, 294
sampling designs, 291–293
Symmetrical distributions, 47, 74, 105, 106
Systematic samples, 293, 298

T

t distribution, 314, 335, 359
t points, 314–316, 335
t table, 314–316, 335, 640–641
t tests, 359–361
Target population, 295, 298
Test statistic, 346
    definition, 378
    unequal variance, 393–394
    z tests, 349–350
Third quartile, 121–122, 141
Thompson, C. M., 413, 642, 643, 644, 645, 648
Time series data, 4, 16, 505
    autocorrelation, 535–536, 539
    residual plots, 531
Time series plots, 5, 6, 16, 68; *see also* Runs plots
Tolerance intervals, 114–115, 248
    compared to confidence intervals, 332–333
    definition, 141
Total sum of squares (SSTO), 434, 442, 449
Total variation, 521, 524, 547, 604
Transformation of dependent variable, 539–542
Travel Industry of America, 6
Treatment mean square (MST), 434
Treatment means, 431, 441, 455
Treatment sum of squares (SST), 433–434, 442
Treatments, 429, 431, 448, 455
Tukey formula, 437
Two-factor factorial experiments, 448–449, 455
Two-sided alternative hypothesis, 345, 371–373, 378
Two-sided confidence intervals, 356
Two-way ANOVA, 447–453
    confidence intervals, 452

definition, 455
    point estimates, 452
Two-way ANOVA table, 450
Two-way cross-classification tables; *see*
    Contingency tables
Type I errors, 346–347, 349, 378
Type II errors, 346–347, 368–373, 378

U

Unbiased point estimate, 278, 284–285, 298
Undercoverage, 296, 298
Unequal variance test statistic, 393–394
Unexplained variation, 521, 524, 547, 604
Unger, L., 9n
Uniform distribution, 231–233, 263
Union, of events, 166
U.S. Bureau of the Census, 5, 17
U.S. Department of Energy, 11

V

Values of variables, 4
Variables, 3, 16; *see also* Dependent variables;
    Discrete random variables; Independent
    variables; Qualitative variables
    quantitative, 4, 14
    random, 191–192, 205, 221
    response, 6
Variables, relationships between
    crosstabulation tables, 61–64
    linear, 67, 129
    scatter plots, 67–68
Variance; *see also* Analysis of variance;
    Population variance
    binomial random variable, 211
    minimum-variance unbiased point estimate,
        284–285
    normal distribution, 234
    Poisson random variable, 217
    of random variable, 198–199, 221
    sample, 112–113, 136–137
Variance inflation factors (VIF), 602–603
Variation
    coefficient of, 117–118
    explained, 521, 524, 547, 604

measures of, 110–118
    total, 521, 524, 547, 604
    unexplained, 521, 524, 547, 604
Venn diagrams, 163
Vertical bar charts, 37
VIF; *see* Variance inflation factors
Voluntary response samples, 274
Voluntary response surveys, 296, 298

W

Wainer, Howard, 71
Walsh, Bryan, 11n
Walters, Rockney G., 337
Wasserman, W., 591
Watson, G. S., 649, 650
Weight of evidence, 356
Weighted mean, 134–135, 141
Weinberger, Marc G., 331, 409
Wheelwright, S. C., 545
Whiskers, 123, 124
Wilcoxon rank sum test, 394
Wilcoxon signed ranks test, 401
Willingham, John J., 335
Within-treatment variability, 432–434
Woodruff, Robert B., 583
Woods, D. L., 548

Y

y intercept, 132, 596
y intercept, of simple linear regression model,
    493, 494
    definition, 547
    least squares point estimates, 496
    significance, 510

Z

z_α point, 244–245, 263
$-z_\alpha$ point, 246, 263
z tests
    about population mean, 349–356
    about population proportion, 363–366
z values, 236, 248, 263; *see also* Normal table
z-scores, 117, 141

Case Index

A

Advertising Media Case, 387, 405, 406, 408
Air Traffic Control Case, 320, 324, 362

B

Bank Customer Waiting Time Case, 13–14, 52,
    108, 119, 275, 286–287, 312, 321,
    334, 348, 357, 362, 471

C

Car Mileage Case, 3, 11–12, 56–58, 102–103,
    112–113, 114–116, 191–192, 229,
    241–242, 243, 273, 275–277, 279–281,
    305–307, 323–324, 333, 467–468
Catalyst Comparison Case, 387, 389–390,
    391–392, 416–417
Cell Phone Case, 3, 8–9, 107, 272–273
Cheese Spread Case, 229, 254–255, 289, 305,
    325–326, 343, 363, 364–365
Cigarette Advertisement Case, 76, 337, 379
Client Satisfaction Case, 35, 472–475, 476–477
Coffee Temperature Case, 16, 229, 244

D

Debt-to-Equity Ratio Case, 317, 343, 359–360
Defective Cardboard Box Case, 429, 441,
    444–445
Direct Labor Cost Case, 503, 507, 512, 520,
    525, 529
Disk Brake Case, 336, 358

E

Electronic Article Surveillance Case, 365–366

F

Fast-Food Restaurant Rating Case, 69, 514
Florida Pool Home Case, 144–145, 592–593
Fresh Detergent Case, 502, 507, 512, 519, 525,
    529, 543, 567–568, 575, 579, 582,
    594–596, 598–600, 616–617

Fuel Consumption Case, 68, 133–134,
    500–501, 506, 511, 518, 525, 528,
    543, 565, 574–575, 578–579,
    581, 614

G

Game Show Case, 286
Gasoline Additive Case, 597–598
Gasoline Mileage Case, 429, 430, 431, 435,
    437–438

H

Hospital Labor Needs Case, 568–569, 575,
    579, 582, 609–610, 614–615
Household Income Case, 105–106

I

International Business Travel Expense Case,
    144, 337
Investment Case, 142–144, 264, 337, 380
Investor Satisfaction Case, 61–64

M

Marketing Ethics Case, 326–327, 330, 366–367
Marketing Research Case, 3, 9–10, 51, 106,
    273, 318, 471
Microwave Oven Preference Case, 464–465

O

Oil Drilling Case, 180–182

P

Payment Time Case, 35, 42–45, 106–107, 113,
    284, 305, 311, 343, 344, 471

Q

QHIC Case, 491, 529–532, 540–542

R

Real Estate Sales Price Case, 68, 503–504,
    507, 512, 520, 525, 529, 565–567,
    575, 579, 581–582
Repair Cost Comparison Case, 387, 397–398,
    399, 400–401

S

Sales Territory Performance Case, 559,
    582–584, 604–606, 610
Service Time Case, 134, 501–502, 506, 512,
    519, 525, 526, 543
Shelf Display Case, 429, 430–431, 438–439,
    447–448, 452–453, 593–594
Song Rating Case, 155, 175–176, 178,
    196–197, 203
Starting Salary Case, 501, 506, 511, 518, 525,
    526, 529
Stock Return Case, 300

T

Tasty Sub Shop Case, 491–494, 497–500, 506,
    508–509, 510, 516–517, 522, 524,
    526, 527–528, 544, 559–564,
    573–574, 577, 578, 579–580, 614
Trash Bag Case, 14, 53, 60, 108–109, 119,
    250–251, 299–300, 312, 321, 334,
    343, 344

U

United Kingdom Insurance Case, 144, 300,
    338, 380–381

V

Valentine's Day Chocolate Case, 343, 345,
    371–372
VALIC Case, 125–126
Video Game Satisfaction Rating Case, 13, 52,
    61, 108, 119, 274–275, 297, 312, 321,
    334, 347–348, 357, 362, 481

A *t* Table

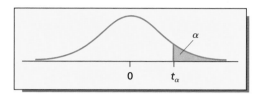

df	$t_{.100}$	$t_{.050}$	$t_{.025}$	$t_{.01}$	$t_{.005}$	$t_{.001}$	$t_{.0005}$
1	3.078	6.314	12.706	31.821	63.657	318.31	636.62
2	1.886	2.920	4.303	6.965	9.925	22.326	31.598
3	1.638	2.353	3.182	4.541	5.841	10.213	12.924
4	1.533	2.132	2.776	3.747	4.604	7.173	8.610
5	1.476	2.015	2.571	3.365	4.032	5.893	6.869
6	1.440	1.943	2.447	3.143	3.707	5.208	5.959
7	1.415	1.895	2.365	2.998	3.499	4.785	5.408
8	1.397	1.860	2.306	2.896	3.355	4.501	5.041
9	1.383	1.833	2.262	2.821	3.250	4.297	4.781
10	1.372	1.812	2.228	2.764	3.169	4.144	4.587
11	1.363	1.796	2.201	2.718	3.106	4.025	4.437
12	1.356	1.782	2.179	2.681	3.055	3.930	4.318
13	1.350	1.771	2.160	2.650	3.012	3.852	4.221
14	1.345	1.761	2.145	2.624	2.977	3.787	4.140
15	1.341	1.753	2.131	2.602	2.947	3.733	4.073
16	1.337	1.746	2.120	2.583	2.921	3.686	4.015
17	1.333	1.740	2.110	2.567	2.898	3.646	3.965
18	1.330	1.734	2.101	2.552	2.878	3.610	3.922
19	1.328	1.729	2.093	2.539	2.861	3.579	3.883
20	1.325	1.725	2.086	2.528	2.845	3.552	3.850
21	1.323	1.721	2.080	2.518	2.831	3.527	3.819
22	1.321	1.717	2.074	2.508	2.819	3.505	3.792
23	1.319	1.714	2.069	2.500	2.807	3.485	3.767
24	1.318	1.711	2.064	2.492	2.797	3.467	3.745
25	1.316	1.708	2.060	2.485	2.787	3.450	3.725
26	1.315	1.706	2.056	2.479	2.779	3.435	3.707
27	1.314	1.703	2.052	2.473	2.771	3.421	3.690
28	1.313	1.701	2.048	2.467	2.763	3.408	3.674
29	1.311	1.699	2.045	2.462	2.756	3.396	3.659
30	1.310	1.697	2.042	2.457	2.750	3.385	3.646
40	1.303	1.684	2.021	2.423	2.704	3.307	3.551
60	1.296	1.671	2.000	2.390	2.660	3.232	3.460
120	1.289	1.658	1.980	2.358	2.617	3.160	3.373
∞	1.282	1.645	1.960	2.326	2.576	3.090	3.291

Cumulative Areas under the Standard Normal Curve

z	0.00	0.01	0.02	0.03	0.04	0.05	0.06	0.07	0.08	0.09
−3.9	0.00005	0.00005	0.00004	0.00004	0.00004	0.00004	0.00004	0.00004	0.00003	0.00003
−3.8	0.00007	0.00007	0.00007	0.00006	0.00006	0.00006	0.00006	0.00005	0.00005	0.00005
−3.7	0.00011	0.00010	0.00010	0.00010	0.00009	0.00009	0.00008	0.00008	0.00008	0.00008
−3.6	0.00016	0.00015	0.00015	0.00014	0.00014	0.00013	0.00013	0.00012	0.00012	0.00011
−3.5	0.00023	0.00022	0.00022	0.00021	0.00020	0.00019	0.00019	0.00018	0.00017	0.00017
−3.4	0.00034	0.00032	0.00031	0.00030	0.00029	0.00028	0.00027	0.00026	0.00025	0.00024
−3.3	0.00048	0.00047	0.00045	0.00043	0.00042	0.00040	0.00039	0.00038	0.00036	0.00035
−3.2	0.00069	0.00066	0.00064	0.00062	0.00060	0.00058	0.00056	0.00054	0.00052	0.00050
−3.1	0.00097	0.00094	0.00090	0.00087	0.00084	0.00082	0.00079	0.00076	0.00074	0.00071
−3.0	0.00135	0.00131	0.00126	0.00122	0.00118	0.00114	0.00111	0.00107	0.00103	0.00100
−2.9	0.0019	0.0018	0.0018	0.0017	0.0016	0.0016	0.0015	0.0015	0.0014	0.0014
−2.8	0.0026	0.0025	0.0024	0.0023	0.0023	0.0022	0.0021	0.0021	0.0020	0.0019
−2.7	0.0035	0.0034	0.0033	0.0032	0.0031	0.0030	0.0029	0.0028	0.0027	0.0026
−2.6	0.0047	0.0045	0.0044	0.0043	0.0041	0.0040	0.0039	0.0038	0.0037	0.0036
−2.5	0.0062	0.0060	0.0059	0.0057	0.0055	0.0054	0.0052	0.0051	0.0049	0.0048
−2.4	0.0082	0.0080	0.0078	0.0075	0.0073	0.0071	0.0069	0.0068	0.0066	0.0064
−2.3	0.0107	0.0104	0.0102	0.0099	0.0096	0.0094	0.0091	0.0089	0.0087	0.0084
−2.2	0.0139	0.0136	0.0132	0.0129	0.0125	0.0122	0.0119	0.0116	0.0113	0.0110
−2.1	0.0179	0.0174	0.0170	0.0166	0.0162	0.0158	0.0154	0.0150	0.0146	0.0143
−2.0	0.0228	0.0222	0.0217	0.0212	0.0207	0.0202	0.0197	0.0192	0.0188	0.0183
−1.9	0.0287	0.0281	0.0274	0.0268	0.0262	0.0256	0.0250	0.0244	0.0239	0.0233
−1.8	0.0359	0.0351	0.0344	0.0336	0.0329	0.0322	0.0314	0.0307	0.0301	0.0294
−1.7	0.0446	0.0436	0.0427	0.0418	0.0409	0.0401	0.0392	0.0384	0.0375	0.0367
−1.6	0.0548	0.0537	0.0526	0.0516	0.0505	0.0495	0.0485	0.0475	0.0465	0.0455
−1.5	0.0668	0.0655	0.0643	0.0630	0.0618	0.0606	0.0594	0.0582	0.0571	0.0559
−1.4	0.0808	0.0793	0.0778	0.0764	0.0749	0.0735	0.0721	0.0708	0.0694	0.0681
−1.3	0.0968	0.0951	0.0934	0.0918	0.0901	0.0885	0.0869	0.0853	0.0838	0.0823
−1.2	0.1151	0.1131	0.1112	0.1093	0.1075	0.1056	0.1038	0.1020	0.1003	0.0985
−1.1	0.1357	0.1335	0.1314	0.1292	0.1271	0.1251	0.1230	0.1210	0.1190	0.1170
−1.0	0.1587	0.1562	0.1539	0.1515	0.1492	0.1469	0.1446	0.1423	0.1401	0.1379
−0.9	0.1841	0.1814	0.1788	0.1762	0.1736	0.1711	0.1685	0.1660	0.1635	0.1611
−0.8	0.2119	0.2090	0.2061	0.2033	0.2005	0.1977	0.1949	0.1922	0.1894	0.1867
−0.7	0.2420	0.2389	0.2358	0.2327	0.2296	0.2266	0.2236	0.2206	0.2177	0.2148
−0.6	0.2743	0.2709	0.2676	0.2643	0.2611	0.2578	0.2546	0.2514	0.2482	0.2451
−0.5	0.3085	0.3050	0.3015	0.2981	0.2946	0.2912	0.2877	0.2843	0.2810	0.2776
−0.4	0.3446	0.3409	0.3372	0.3336	0.3300	0.3264	0.3228	0.3192	0.3156	0.3121
−0.3	0.3821	0.3783	0.3745	0.3707	0.3669	0.3632	0.3594	0.3557	0.3520	0.3483
−0.2	0.4207	0.4168	0.4129	0.4090	0.4052	0.4013	0.3974	0.3936	0.3897	0.3859
−0.1	0.4602	0.4562	0.4522	0.4483	0.4443	0.4404	0.4364	0.4325	0.4286	0.4247
−0.0	0.5000	0.4960	0.4920	0.4880	0.4840	0.4801	0.4761	0.4721	0.4681	0.4641